Church History
Volume One

THE NEW WESTMINSTER DICTIONARY OF

Church History

Volume One

EDITOR

Robert Benedetto

Director of the Flora Lamson Hewlett Library
Graduate Theological Union, Berkeley, California

ASSOCIATE EDITORS

James O. Duke

Professor of History of Christianity and History of Christian Thought
Brite Divinity School, Fort Worth, Texas

Carter Lindberg

Professor Emeritus of Church History
Boston University School of Theology, Boston, Massachusetts

Christopher Ocker

Professor of Church History
San Francisco Theological Seminary, San Anselmo,
and the Graduate Theological Union, Berkeley, California

Rebecca H. Weaver

Professor of Church History
Union Theological Seminary and Presbyterian School
of Christian Education
Richmond, Virginia

Westminster John Knox Press
LOUISVILLE • LONDON

Scripture quotations, unless otherwise indicated, are from the New Revised Standard Version of the Bible, copyright © 1989 by the Division of Christian Education of the National Council of the Churches of Christ in the U.S.A., and used by permission.

Cover design by designpointinc.com

First edition
Published by Westminster John Knox Press
Louisville, Kentucky

This book is printed on acid-free paper that meets the American National Standards Institute Z39.48 standard. ♾

PRINTED IN THE UNITED STATES OF AMERICA

08 09 10 11 12 13 14 15 16—10 9 8 7 6 5 4 3 2 1

Library of Congress Cataloging-in-Publication Data

The new Westminster dictionary of church history / Robert Benedetto, editor.—1st ed.
    p. cm.
  Rev. ed. of: The Westminster dictionary of church history. 1971.
  ISBN 978-0-664-22416-5 (alk. paper)
  1. Church history—Dictionaries.   I. Benedetto, Robert.   II. Title: Westminster dictionary of church history.
  BR95.W496 2008
  270.03—dc22

                                                                                    2007045708

Contents

Publisher's Note

The New Westminster Dictionary of Church History is an authoritative guide to the major persons, events, and movements in the history of Christianity. A number of scholars have contributed their expertise on the subjects in this book, providing accurate, clear, and accessible coverage for each entry. Their work provides users with the key elements for understanding the various topics and opens the way to further study with a short bibliography.

This work could not have been published without the fine cooperation of these scholars and the dedicated editors who have labored long and hard on this project. Westminster John Knox Press would like to express deep thanks to editor Robert Benedetto, who has expertly overseen the entire project and been involved in the countless details, which has enabled this reference work to come to fruition. He has been ably assisted by associate editors James O. Duke, Carter Lindberg, Christopher Ocker, and Rebecca H. Weaver. All members of this editorial team have worked with great competence in a collegial way to make this an outstanding reference volume. For all their efforts, we are grateful.

As the Christian church continues to develop, its understandings are enriched and deepened when it looks to its past to gain insight for the future. This reference work is offered as a resource for all who wish to learn from and contemplate the church's history as an expression of Christian faith.

Donald K. McKim
Westminster John Knox Press

Preface

The Westminster Dictionary of Church History, under the editorship of Jerald Brauer of the University of Chicago, ably served a generation of pastors, students, and scholars during the last decades of the twentieth century. Although the book was published in 1971 and reflects the scholarship of the mid-1960s, many of its articles can still be read with profit. The book was planned by a team of scholars that included Robert M. Grant, Jaroslav J. Pelikan, James H. Nichols, Richard Luman, Jules Moreau, and Brian A. Gerrish. Grant served as editor for the early church (to 600), Luman and Moreau were editors of the medieval period (600–1300), Gerrish was editor for the Reformation era (1300–1700), and Brauer served as editor for the modern period (post-1700). The volume had 140 contributors, was ecumenical in scope, and gave the most coverage to the modern period, more particularly to American religious history.

However, over the past forty years the book gradually began to show its age. It no longer represented the latest scholarship in patristics and in other fields of study. Its focus on Europe and on the American churches provided able coverage for the Western tradition, but the book lacked coverage of the Eastern tradition, particularly Eastern Orthodoxy, and wider coverage of the global spread of Christianity. And while the book was ecumenical in its viewpoint, it drew few international contributors and lacked articles by and about women and people of color, so that it no longer represented the modern church in its diverse makeup and multiplicity of cultural forms.

For these reasons, Westminster John Knox Press commissioned a new dictionary that would both continue the tradition of the WDCH as well as replace it. The present work continues the tradition by providing "an immediate, accurate, introductory definition and explanation" concerning the major personalities, events, facts, and movements in the history of Christianity. Like its predecessor, it "does not intend to be definitive, nor do the entries pretend to be exhaustive." *The New Westminster Dictionary of Church History* relies on other dictionaries published by Westminster John Knox Press, such as *The New Westminster Dictionary of Christian Spirituality*, and therefore does not intend to supplant more specialized dictionaries or larger encyclopedias. The NWDCH also follows its predecessor by adopting its general editorial framework consisting of four periods and having, in this case, an associate editor responsible for each period: early (Rebecca H. Weaver), medieval (Christopher Ocker), Reformation (Carter Lindberg), and modern (James O. Duke). The dictionary continues to have an ecumenical orientation and continues to devote substantial coverage to the modern period; in fact, all of volume 2 covers the post-1700 period.

While the NWDCH follows the tradition of its predecessor, it also departs from the work in several important ways: it has more contributors and its contributors are more diverse; its coverage is broader in scope, especially for the post-1700 period; all of the articles are signed; and each article includes a brief bibliography, leading the reader to more detailed information.

Such a large work as this (volume 1 contains 1,419 articles written by 203 contributors) would have been impossible to produce without the expertise of the associate editors and the knowledge and cooperation of its many contributors. We owe them our deep appreciation for a job well done.

At the same time the editors are saddened by the loss of three of our historians—Ian Gillman, Michael Goodich, and Stanley R. Hall—who died before this volume was completed. We are pleased to have these last articles as part of their many contributions to church history.

In addition to the editors and contributors, other scholars, proofreaders, and assistants have also helped in various capacities, including Jennifer Kile, Kirk J. Nolan, Carolyn D. Nicholson, and Caryl J. Woulfe. Finally, Westminster John Knox Press should be acknowledged for its support in bringing volume 1 to a successful conclusion. *Soli Deo gloria.*

Robert Benedetto
Editor

Contributors

Marvin L. Anderson
Lecturer in History, University of Toronto, Toronto, Ontario, Canada
Andreas Karlstadt; Thomas Müntzer; Toleration in the Reformation

Mary Elizabeth Anderson
Assistant Professor of Religion, Saint Olaf College, Northfield, Minnesota
John Agricola; Sebastian Franck

Kenneth G. Appold
Associate Professor of Reformation History, Princeton Theological Seminary, Princeton, New Jersey
Robert Barclay; Belgic Confession; Guy de Brès; Marie Dentière; Guillaume Farel; Albert Hardenberg; Caspar Olevianus; Caritas Pirckheimer; Willibald Pirckheimer; Walter Travers; Peter Martyr Vermigli; Westminster Assembly; Westminster Confession

Harold W. Attridge
Professor of New Testament and Dean of the Yale Divinity School, New Haven, Connecticut
Ebionites; Elchasaites; Gnosticism; Jewish Christianity, Early; Josephus; Nag Hammadi

Oliver Auge
Professor of the History of the Middle Ages, Ernst Moritz Arndt University, Greifswald, Germany.
Canons and Canonesses; Collegiate Church; Prebends

Lewis Ayres
Professor of Historical Theology, Candler School of Theology, Emory University, Atlanta, Georgia
Arius and Arianism; Athanasius of Alexandria; Basil of Caesarea; Constantinople, First Council of; Eusebius of Nicomedia; Hellenization; Pneumatomachians

William S. Babcock
Professor of Church History Emeritus, Perkins School of Theology, Southern Methodist University, Dallas, Texas
Augustine of Hippo; Monica; Simplicianus of Milan; Tyconius

Irena Backus
Professor Titulaire, Institut d'Histoire de la Réformation, University of Geneva, Switzerland
Patristics, Reformation

J. Wayne Baker
Professor of History, University of Akron, Ohio
Heinrich Bullinger; Helvetic Confessions; Leo Jud; Johannes Oecolampadius; Huldrych Zwingli

Michel Rene Barnes
Associate Professor of Theology, Marquette University, Milwaukee, Wisconsin
Eugenius of Carthage; Eunomius of Cyzicus; Gregory of Nyssa; Homoians; Neoplatonism; Phoebadius; Caius Marius Victorinus

Sébastien Barret
Member of the Sonderforschungsbereich 537 "Institutionalität und Geschichtlichkeit," Technische Universität, Dresden, Germany
Cluny; Mendicant Orders

Priscilla Baumann
Independent Scholar, formerly Distinguished Instructor of Art History, Radcliffe Institute for Advanced Study, Harvard University, Cambridge, Massachusetts
Art, Reformation; Hans Baldung; Baroque; Pieter Bruegel (the Elder); Albrecht Dürer El Greco; Matthias Grünewald; Hans Holbein (the Younger); Leonardo da Vinci; Buonarroti Michelangelo; Petrarch (Francesco Petrarca); Plague; Raphael; Rilman Riemenschneider

John Behr
Dean and Professor of Patristics, St.
Vladimir's Orthodox Theological Semi-
nary, Crestwood, New York
Apologists, Early Christian; Docetism;
Irenaeus

Robert M. Berchman
Professor of Philosophy and Religious Stud-
ies, Dowling College, Oakdale, New York,
and Senior Fellow, Institute of Advanced
Theology, Bard College, Annandale-on-
Hudson, New York
Iamblichus; Marcus Aurelius; Mithraism;
Mystery Religions; Neopythagoreanism;
Porphyry; Proclus; Socrates; Stoicism

David Berger
Professor of Jewish History, Yeshiva Univer-
sity, New York, New York
Maimonides; *Nizzahon Vetus*

Mary Catherine Berglund
Minister of Children's Formation and Worship, St. Paul's Catholic Church, Richmond, Virginia
Doxology; Feasts of the Church; Hymns,
Early Christian; Litany; Liturgical Calendar, Significance of; Lord's Prayer; *Phos
hilaron*; *Te Deum*

Rainer Berndt
Professor and Director, Hugh of St. Victor
Institute, St. Georgen Gradaute School of
Philosophy and Theology, Frankfurt, Ger-
many
Andrew of St. Victor; Anselm of Canterbury;
Berengar of Tours; Hugh of St. Victor;
Johannes Trithemius; Lanfranc; Richard of
St. Victor; Rupert of Deutz

D. Jeffrey Bingham
Chair of the Department of Theological Stud-
ies, Dallas Theological Seminary, Dallas,
Texas
Aristides; Aristo of Pella; Arnobius of Sicca;
Athenagoras; Justin Martyr; Minucius
Felix; Tatian; Theophilus of Antioch

Raymond A. Blacketer
Pastor at Neerlandia Christian Reformed
Church, Neerlandia, Alberta
Jacobus Arminius; Dirck Coornhert; Jean De
Labadie; Dort, Canons of; Dort, Synod of;
Golden Bull; Franciscus Gomarus;
Jansenism; Jean à Lasco; Marten Micron;
Nadere Reformatie; Netherlands, Reforma-
tion in the; Remonstrance of 1610

Monica J. Blanchard
Curator of the Semitics/Institute of Christian
Oriental Research (ICOR) Collections at
the Catholic University of America, Wash-
ington, DC
Eznik of Kolb; Gregory the Illuminator;
Moses Khorenac'i

Paul M. Blowers
Professor of Church History, Emmanuel
School of Religion, Johnson City,
Tennessee
Apokatastasis; Celsus; Conversion; Diviniza-
tion; Dualism; Fathers of the Eastern
Church; Pasch and the Paschal Contro-
versy; Perfectionism; Quartodecimans

Charles A. Bobertz
Professor of Theology, St. John's School of
Theology and Seminary in Collegeville,
Minnesota
Cornelius; Cyprian of Carthage; Novatian;
Stephen I

Curtis Bostick
Professor of History, Southern Utah University, Cedar City, Utah. John Wyclif

James Brashler
Professor of Bible, Union Theological Semi-
nary and Presbyterian School of Christian
Education, Richmond, Virginia
Apocryphal Writings; Dead Sea Scrolls; Early
Christian Apocalyptic Literature; Pseude-
pigraphy; Simon Magus

Mirko Breitenstein
Member of the Sonderforschungsbereich 537
"Institutionalität und Geschichtlichkeit,"
Technische Universität, Dresden, Germany
Mendicant Schools; Monastic Schools

Christopher B. Brown
Assistant Professor of Church History at
Boston University School of Theology in
Boston, Massachusetts
Edward VI; Elizabeth I; Great Western
Schism; Jane Grey; Martin Luther; Refor-
mation Social Welfare

Stephen Brown
Professor, Department of Theology, Boston
College, Boston, Massachusetts
Henry of Ghent

Charles Burnett
Lecturer in the History of Islamic Influences
in Europe, Warburg Institute, University of
London, England

Adelard of Bath; Abu Nasr Al-Farabi; Ya'qub ibn Ishaq Al-Kindi; Averroes; Avicebron; Avicenna

Ronald P. Byars
Professor Emeritus of Preaching and Worship, Union Theological Seminary and Presbyterian School of Christian Education, Richmond, Virginia
Eucharist; Laity; Lectionary

Amy R. Caldwell
Doctoral Candidate at the University of California, Santa Barbara, in Reformation Political History, and Instructor at California State University, Channel Islands
Conrad Grebel; Mennonites; Menno Simons

J. Laurel Carrington
Professor of History at St. Olaf College in Northfield, Minnesota
Sebastian Brant; George Buchanan; Guillaume Budé; Rubianus Crotus; John Donne; Desiderius Erasmus; Pietro Pomponazzi; Renaissance Platonism; Lorenzo Valla

J. David Cassel
Professor of Theological Studies at Hanover College in Hanover, Indiana
Jerusalem, Destruction of; Philo; *Sophia*

Robert Chazan
Professor of Hebrew and Judaic Studies, New York University, New York, New York
Jewish Martyrdom; Jewish Polemic against Christianity; Moses ben Nachman

Angela Russell Christman
Professor, Department of Theology, Loyola College, Maryland
Bible in the Early Church; Septuagint

Linda J. Clark
Professor of Sacred Music, School of Theology, Boston University, Boston, Massachusetts
John Blow; Paul Gerhardt; Michael Praetorius; Reformation Liturgies; Reformation Music; Thomas Tallis

Peter D. Clarke
Lecturer in Medieval History, University of Southampton, England
Interdict; Papal Dispensations

Michael Compton
Department of World Languages, Mills E. Godwin High School, Richmond, Virginia; Adjunct Assistant Professor, Department of

Religion, University of Richmond, Richmond, Virginia
Addai; Agrapha; John Chrysostom; Lucian of Samosata

Susanne Conrad
Member of the Sonderforschungsbereich 537 "Institutionalität und Geschichtlichkeit," Technische Universität, Dresden, Germany
Observant Movements

John J. Contreni
Justin S. Morrill Dean of the College of Liberal Arts, Purdue University, West Lafayette, Indiana
Aachen; Alcuin; Carolingian Church; Carolingian Renaissance; Carolingian Schools; Charlemagne; Charles Martel; Coronation Rites; Donation of Constantine; Haimo of Auxerre; *Heliand*; Investiture; John Scottus; Medieval Kingship; *Opus Caroli Regis Contra Synodum (Libri Carolini)*; Truce of God

S. Peter Cowe
Professor of Armenian Studies, University of California, Los Angeles
Armenian Christianity; Grigor Tat'ewac'i; Latin Envoys to Medieval Armenia; Sebeos

Paul Crawford
Assistant Professor of History, California University of Pennsylvania, California, Pennsylvania
Children's Crusade; Crusades; Hospitallers; Military (or Military-Religious) Orders; Templars (Poor Knights of the Temple of Solomon)

Brian E. Daley, SJ
Professor of Theology, University of Notre Dame, Notre Dame, Indiana
Christology in the Early Church; Eschatology; *Henoticon*; Leontius of Byzantium; Proclus of Constantinople

Thomas Dandelet
Associate Professor, Department of History, University of California, Berkeley
Papal States

David P. Daniel
Head of the Department of Church History and History of Dogma at the Evangelical Theological Faculty at Comenius University in Bratislava, Slovakia
Bohemian Brethren (Unitas Fratrum); Hungary, Reformation in; Jan Hus; Hussites; Mary of Hungary; Taborites; Utraquists

Lars-Arne Dannenberg
Member of the Sonderforschungsbereich 537
"Institutionalität und Geschichtlichkeit,"
Technische Universität, Dresden, Germany
Abbots and Abbesses; Monasteries, Dual-Sex

Marianne M. Delaporte
Assistant Professor of Religious Studies,
Notre Dame de Namur, Belmont,
California
Anglo-Saxon Christianity; Augustine of Can-
terbury; Celtic Christianity; Columba; Con-
version of Europe; Cuthbert; Merovingian
Church; Sigibert I and Brunichilde; Wear-
mouth and Jarrow; Whitby, Synod of

Mark Damien Delp
Associate Professor of Philosophy, Graduate
Theological Union, Berkeley, California
Christian Platonism; Pseudo-Dionysius; Siger
of Brabant; William of Moerbeke

Nancy van Deusen
Professor of Musicology, Claremont Graduate
University, Claremont, California
Chant; Divine Office; Gregorian Chant; Litur-
gical Calendar; Liturgical Music; Liturgy
of the Mass

Marianne Djuth
Professor of Philosophy, Canisius College,
Buffalo, New York
Arnobius the Younger; Boniface I; Julian of
Eclanum; Mani; Orosius, Paulus; Pelagius;
Traducianism; Zosimus

John Patrick Donnelly, SJ
Professor, Department of History, Marquette
University, Milwaukee, Wisconsin
Edmund Campion; Peter Canisius; Diego
Laínez; Luis de Molina; Matteo Ricci;
Thomas Stapleton; Francisco Suárez

Lisa D. Maugans Driver
Assistant Professor of Theology, Valparaiso
University, Valparaiso, Indiana
Amphilochius of Iconium; Diodore of Tarsus;
Early Christian Rhetoric; Ephesus, Coun-
cils of; Eudoxia; Messalianism; Preaching
in the Early Church; Theodore of Mopsues-
tia; Theodoret of Cyrrhus; Theotokos;
Three Chapters

Steven D. Driver
Director of Formation, Immanuel Lutheran
Church, Valparaiso, Indiana
Tall Brothers; Theophilus of Alexandria

Gisela Drossbach
Privatdozent, Stephan Kuttner Institute of
Medieval Canon Law, Munich, Germany
Hospitals; Konrad of Megenberg

Peter A. Dykema
Associate Professor of History, Arkansas Tech
University, Russellville, Arkansas
Anticlericalism, Medieval and Reformation

O. C. Edwards Jr.
President and Professor Emeritus of Preaching, Seabury-Western Theological Seminary, Evanston, Illinois
Preaching, Medieval

Joris van Eijnatten
Professor, Faculty of Arts, Free University,
Amsterdam, Netherlands
Michel Baius; Jean Bolland; Johannes Coc-
ceius; Johannes Wessel Gansfort; Daniel
Papebroch; William of Orange; Won-
deryear

Carlos M. N. Eire
Professor in the Department of History, Yale
University, New Haven, Connecticut
Melchior Cano; Iconoclasm; Bartolomé de
Las Casas; Philip II of Spain; Domingo de
Soto; Spain, Reformation in; Alfonso de
Valdés; Juan de Valdés; Francisco de Vito-
ria; Juan Luis Vives

David B. Eller
Former Director, Young Center for Anabaptist
and Pietist Studies, and Professor of His-
tory and Religion, Elizabethtown College,
Elizabethtown, Pennsylvania
Gottfried Arnold; Georg Blaurock (Cajacob);
Hans Bünderlin; Hans Denck; August Her-
mann Francke; Pilgram Marpeck; Radical
Reformation; Melchior Rinck; Bernard
Rothmann; Michael Sattler; Schleitheim
Confession; Caspar von Ossig Schwenck-
feld; Swiss Brethren

Donna Spivey Ellington
Professor of History, Gardner Webb Univer-
sity, Boiling Springs, North Carolina
Marian Devotion; Pilgrimage; Relics

Susanna Elm
Professor of History at the University of Cali-
fornia, Berkeley
Deacon and Deaconess; Firmilian; Gregory of
Nazianzus; Macrina the Younger;
Pachomius; Subintroductae; Synesius of
Cyrene

Christopher Elwood
Professor of Historical Theology at Louisville Presbyterian Theological Seminary, Louisville, Kentucky
Jerome Bolsec; Catholic League; Chambre Ardente; Classis; Company of Pastors; Libertines; Marguerite d'Angoulême; Clément Marot; Meaux Circle; Montbéliard, Colloquy of; Nicodemism; Pierre Robert Olivetan; Presbyterianism; Rochelle, Synod of; Solemn League and Covenant; John Spottiswoode; Edward Stillingfleet; John Tillotson; Toleration Act

Daniel Eppley
Assistant Professor of the History of Christianity, Department of Religion and Philosophy, McMurry University, Abilene, Texas
Wiliam Chillingworth; John Fisher; Richard Hooker; John Hooper; John Jewel; Andrew Melville; Thomas More; Nonconformity; John Owen; John Ponet; Praemunire; Scots Confession

Everett Ferguson
Distinguished Scholar in Residence at Abilene Christian University, Abilene, Texas
Acts of the Martyrs; Architecture in Early Christianity; Holy Sepulcher, Church of the; Nativity, Church of the; Ravenna, Churches of; Sabina; St. Catherine's, Monastery of; St, Peter's, Church of

Alberto Ferreiro
Professor of History, Seattle Pacific University, Seattle, Washington
Adoptionism; Isidore of Seville; Martin of Braga; Mozarab Rite; Priscillian; Reconquest; Visigothic Hispano-Roman Councils

Deborah Fleetham
Adjunct Professor, Purdue University Indiana
Germany (HRE, Austria, Prussia), Reformation in (with Charles D. Gunnoe Jr.)

Karlfried Froehlich
Professor of Church History Emeritus, Princeton Theological Seminary, Princeton, New Jersey
Bible in the Early Medieval Church; Peter Comestor; Hugh of St. Cher; Stephen Langton; Ordinary Gloss

Elizabeth Gerhardt
Assistant Professor, Religion and Sociology, Roberts Wesleyan College, Rochester, New York
Acts of Supremacy; Acts of Uniformity; Admonition Controversy; Advertisements,

Book of; Girolamo Aleandro; William Allen; Caesar Borgia; Brethren of the Common Life; Index of Prohibited Books; Giovanni Pico della Mirandola; Pius II; Pius IV; Johannes Reuchlin; Michael Servetus; Fausto Sozzini; Lelio Sozzini

Ian Gillman†
Former Head of Department, Studies in Religion, University of Queensland, Australia
Al-o-pen; Christianity in T'ang and Yuan China; Franciscan Envoys to Medieval China; Giovanni de Pian del Carpini; Nestorian Missionary Enterprise

Michael Goodich†
Professor of General History, University of Haifa, Israel
Brigitte of Sweden; Dorothy (Schwartze) of Montau; Medieval Saints' Lives; Miracles in the Middle Ages; Sainthood

Bruce Gordon
Lecturer in History and Associate Director of the Reformation Studies Institute, University of St. Andrews, St. Andrews, Scotland
Eucharistic Controversies in the Reformation; Geneva Catechism; Switzerland, Reformation in; Johannes Zwick

Andrew Gow
Professor of History, University of Alberta, Edmonton, Alberta
Apocalypticism, Medieval; Medieval Satire

D. Jonathan Grieser
Assistant Professor of Religion, Furman University, Greenville, South Carolina
Ludwig Hätzer; Melchior Hoffman; Hans Hut; John of Leiden; David Joris; Felix Mantz; Jan Matthijs; Dirk Philips; Obbe Philips; Peter Riedemann

John E. Griswold
United Methodist Pastor, Hollywood, Florida
Anglicanism; Anne Askew; Miles Coverdale; Oliver Cromwell; Fifth Monarchy Men; John Foxe; Edmund Grindal; Reginald Pole; Cuthbert Tunstall; William Tyndale; John Whitgift

Theresa Gross-Diaz
Professor of European Medieval History, Loyola University, Chicago, Illinois
Four Books of Sentences; Gilbert of Poitiers; Peter Lombard

Charles D. Gunnoe Jr.
Professor of History, Aquinas College, Grand Rapids, Michigan
Charles V; Defenestration of Prague; Germany (HRE, Austria, Prussia), Reformation in (with Deborah Fleetham); Interims; Reformation, Second; Ursinus

Mary Jane Haemig
Professor of Church History, Luther Seminary, St. Paul, Minnesota
Johann Eberlin von Günzburg; Berchtold Haller; Karl von Miltitz; Preaching, Reformation; Protestation of Speyer; Valentin Weigel; Joachim Westphal; Zwickau Prophets

Stanley R. Hall†
Associate Professor of Liturgics, Austin Presbyterian Theological Seminary, Austin, Texas
Liturgical Books; Sacraments

William Harmless, SJ
Professor of Theology, Creighton University, Omaha, Nebraska
Antony; John Cassian; Catechumenate; Evagrius of Pontus; Monasticism, Early Egyptian and Palestinian; Palladius; Serapion of Thmuis

Joel F. Harrington
Professor of History, Vanderbilt University, Nashville, Tennessee
Capuchins; Disputations; Worms, Edict of

Zachary Hayes, OFM
Professor of Spirituality, Catholic Theological Union, Chicago, Illinois
Alexander of Hales; Bonaventure, St.

Johannes Heil
Ignatz-Bubis Foundation Professor of the Religion, History, and Culture of European Judaism, Institute of Jewish Studies, Heidelberg, Germany
Agobard of Lyon; Gottschalk of Orbais; Hincmar of Reims; Hrabanus Maurus; Sedulius Scottus; Theodulf of Orléans

Yitzhak Hen
Professor of Medieval History, Ben Gurion University of the Negev, Israel
Chrodegang; Columbanus; Gregory of Tours; Willibrord

Kurt K. Hendel
Distinguished Professor of Reformation History, Lutheran School of Theology, Chicago, Illinois
Johannes Brenz; Johannes Bugenhagen; Lefèvre d'Étaples; Moritz of Saxony; Thomas Murner; Pack Affair; Urbanus Rhegius; Hans Sachs; Franz von Sickingen

Suzanne S. Hequet
PhD student, Luther Seminary, St. Paul, Minnesota
Otto Brunfels; Martin Bucer; Wolfgang Capito; Regensburg Colloquy; Jakob Sturm; Johann Sturm; Swabian League; Tetrapolitan Confession; Visitations

Arthur G. Holder
Professor of Christian Spirituality, Graduate Theological Union, Berkeley, California
Bede; Benedict of Nursia; Gregory I

David R. Holeton
Professor of Liturgical History, Charles University, Prague, Czech Republic
Jerome of Prague; Matthias of Janov

Joshua Holo
Associate Professor of Jewish History, Hebrew Union College—Jewish Institute of Religion, Los Angeles, California
Byzantine Church and the Jews

Vittorio Hösle
Paul Kimball Professor of Arts and Letters, University of Notre Dame, Notre Dame, Indiana
Ramon Llull

David G. Hunter
Professor of Catholic Studies, University of Kentucky, Lexington, Kentucky
Ambrosiaster; Celibacy of Clergy; Helvidius; Jovinian; Marriage, Early Christian; Sexuality, Early Christian; Siricius

Clayton N. Jefford
Professor of Scripture at St. Meinrad School of Theology in St. Meinrad, Indiana
Barnabas, Epistle of; Clement of Rome and Pseudo-Clementine Literature; *Didache*; *Diognetus, Epistle to*; Hermas; Ignatius of Antioch; Papias; Polycarp

Robin M. Jensen
Professor of the History of Christian Worship and Art, Vanderbilt University, Nashville, Tennessee
Art in Early Christianity; Catacombs; Dura Europos; Good Shepherd; Labarum; Orant

Phyllis G. Jestice
Associate Professor of Medieval/Early Modern European Church History, University of Southern Mississippi, Hattiesburg, Mississippi
Thomas Becket; Bernard of Chartres; Bernard of Clairvaux; Bruno the Carthusian; Cathedral Schools; Chartres, School of; Courtly Love; Gerhoch of Reichersberg; Gorzian Reform; Historiography, Medieval; Historiography of Medieval Christianity (Contemporary); John Gualbert; Guibert of Nogent; Matilda of Tuscany; Odo of Cluny; Otto I; Otto of Freising; Ottonian-Salian Imperial Church System; Papal Election Decree; Peter Damian; Peter the Venerable

Allen E. Jones
Associate Professor in the Department of History at Troy University, Alabama
Avitus of Vienne; Clotilda; Clovis; Constantius II; Denis; Diocletian; Evagrius Scholasticus; Gennadius of Marseilles; Germanus of Auxerre; Hagiography; Hypatia; Orange, Councils of; Procopius of Caesarea; Pulcheria; Semi-Pelagianism; Theodosius I; Theodosius II; Valerian; Zeno

Ken Sundet Jones
Doctoral Candidate, Luther Seminary, St. Paul, Minnesota
Michael Gaismaier; Jakob Strauss

Annette Kehnel
Professor of Medieval History, Institut für Geschichte, Universität Mannheim, Germany
Dominican Order; Irish Monasticism; Kilian

Joseph F. Kelly
Professor of Christian History and Chairperson of the Department of Religious Studies at John Carroll University, University Heights, Ohio
Alexandrian Christianity; Antiochian Christianity; Apostles' Creed; Astrology and Numerology in Early Christianity; Augustinianism; Cappadocians; David of Wales; Ecclesiastical Centers of Early Christianity; Ethiopian Christianity; *Filioque*; Finnian of Clonard; Heresy in Early and Medieval Christianity; Honoratus of Lérins; Niceta of Remesiana; Ninian; Patrick; Reccared; Rufinus of Aquileia; *Rule of the Master*; Toledo, Councils of

Robert A. Kitchen
Minister of Knox-Metropolitan United Church in Regina, Saskatchewan
Abgar V; Aphrahat; Jacob Baradaeus; Dadisho Qatraya; Dyophysitism; Ibas; Jacob of Edessa; Jacob of Serug; John of Antioch; John of Ephesus; Joseph Hazzaya; Mar Thoma (St. Thomas) Church; Maronite Church (Antiochian Syrian Maronite Church); Narsai; Nestorius; Philoxenus of Mabbug; Romanos the Melodist; Thomas of Marga

William E. Klingshirn
Professor of Greek and Latin, The Catholic University of America, Washington, DC
Caesaria the Elder; Caesaria the Younger; Caesarius of Arles; Divination and Magic; Gaul; Julianus Pomerius; Radegund; Symmachus

Robert Kolb
Professor in the Institute for Mission Studies, Concordia Theological Seminary, St. Louis, Missouri
Jacobus Acontius; Jacob Amman; Nikolaus von Amsdorf; Jacob Andreae; Johann Arndt; Augsburg Confession; Book of Concord; Georg Calixt; Abraham Calov; Camisards; Martin Chemnitz; Jean Crespin; Bible Translations, Early Modern; Matthias Flacius; Marburg Colloquy; Maulbronn Colloquy; Paris Foreign Mission Society; Philip, Landgrave of Hesse; Philosophy of Christ; Johannes Sleidan; Terminism

Judith L. Kovacs
Associate Professor of Religious Studies, University of Virginia, Charlottesville, Virginia
Clement of Alexandria

Rebecca Krawiec
Assistant Professor of Religious Studies, Canisius College, Buffalo, New York
Abba and Amma; Encratites; Macarius the Great; Mary of Egypt; Meletian Schisms; John Moschus; Sabas; Shenoute of Atripe; Symeon Stylites (Symeon the Elder)

Philip D. W. Krey
President, Lutheran Theological Seminary, Philadelphia, Pennsylvania
Peter Auriol; Matthias Döring; Nicholas of Lyra; Paul of Burgos

Malcolm D. Lambert
Former Reader in Medieval History, University of Bristol, England
Cathars; Valdes; Waldensianism

Niklaus Largier

Professor of German Literature, University of
California, Berkeley, California

Meister Eckhart; Johannes Tauler; *Theologia
Germanica*

Richard A. Layton

Associate Professor, Program for the Study of
Religion, University of Illinois, Urbana-
Champaign

Apostolic Fathers; Ecumenical Council; Rule
of Faith

Fred van Lieburg

Assistant Professor of Church History, Vrije
Universiteit, Amsterdam, Netherlands

Willem Teellinck

Joseph T. Lienhard

Professor of Theology, Fordham University,
Bronx, New York

Acacius of Caesarea; Asterius the Sophist;
Authority in the Early Church; Basil of
Ancyra; Epiphanius of Salamis; Eusebius
of Vercelli; Jerome; Lucian of Antioch;
Lucifer of Cagliari; Marcellus of Ancyra;
Pamphilus of Caesarea; Vulgate

Carter Lindberg

Professor Emeritus of Church History, Boston
University School of Theology, Boston,
Massachusetts

Anabaptists; Historiography of the Reformation (Contemporary); Martyrology; Melchiorites; George Wishart

David A. Lopez

Lecturer in Humanities, University of Houston, Clear Lake, Texas

John Ball; *De Haeretico Comburendo*; Guy
Fawkes; Ferrara-Florence, Council of;
Forty-two Articles; Gunpowder Plot; Hugh
Latimer; Latitudinarianism; Marprelate
Tracts; Pilgrimage of Grace; John Purvey;
Thirty-nine Articles; Vestiarian Contro-
versy; Vienne, Council of

Alden R. Ludlow

Independent Scholar, Brookline, Massachusetts

Richard Bancroft; Robert Barnes; Catherine
of Aragon; William Cecil; Clarendon Code;
John Colet; Thomas Cranmer; Thomas
Cromwell; Elizabethan Settlement; Stephen
Gardiner; Patrick Hamilton; Hampton
Court Conference; James I of England;
Lambeth Articles; William Laud; Lollardy;
Mary Tudor (Mary I); Katherine Parr;

Simon Patrick; John Pym; Restoration
Acts; Nicholas Ridley; John Rogers; Root
and Branch Petition; John Udall; Uniformity Acts; Thomas Cardinal Wolsey

Eugene M. Ludwig, OFM, Cap.

Professor of History and Patristic Theology,
Graduate Theological Union, Berkeley,
California

Abbasid Caliphate; Bar Hebraeus; John
Bessarion of Nicaea; Christians under
Islam; Church of the East in the Middle
Ages; Demetrios Cydones; Dorotheus of
Gaza; Evergetinos; Hunain ibn Ishaq; Isaac
of Ninevah; Ishu-Yab II; Ishu-Yab III;
Jacobite Church; John the Grammarian of
Caesarea; Mar Aba I; Maximus the Confes-
sor; Michael VIII Paleologus; Monothe-
lites; Mount Athos; Nicephorus I;
Orthodoxy; Patriarchs; John Philoponus of
Alexandria; George Gemistus Plethon;
Constantine Psellus; Sacraments, Ortho-
dox; Scythian Monks; Sophronius; Stephen
Bar Sudayli; Theophylact; Umayyad
Caliphate; Uniate Churches

Eric Lund

Professor, Department of Religion, St. Olaf
College, Northfield, Minnesota

Pierre Bayle; Gabriel Biel; Jacob Böhme;
John Capreolus; Deism; René Descartes;
Gottfried Wilhelm Leibniz; John Locke;
John Mill; Isaac Newton; Blaise Pascal;
Johann Andreas Quenstedt; Armand Jean
du Plessis, Duke of Richelieu; Richard
Simon; John Spencer; Baruch Spinoza

Barbara J. MacHaffie

Professor Emerita of History and Religion,
Marietta College, Marietta, Ohio

Agnes; Egeria; Helena; Proba; Thecla

Scott M. Marr

Doctoral Candidate, History Department,
Boston University, Boston,
Massachusetts

Affair of the Placards; Amboise, Conspiracy
of; Louis de Berquin; Bologna, Concordat
of; Calendar, Reform of; Cateau-
Cambrésis, Treaty of; Catherine de
Médici; Philippe Duplessis-Mornay;
Francis I; Francis II; Huguenots; Nantes,
Edict of; Pragmatic Sanction of Bourges

Roderick Martin

Doctoral Candidate, History Department,
University of Virginia, Charlottesville,
Virginia

Francis Bacon; Jacques-Bénigne Bossuet; Giordono Bruno; Nicholas Copernicus; Family of Love; François Fénelon; Galileo Galilei; Gallican Articles; Johann Geiler of Kaisersberg; Johann Gutenberg; Madame Guyon; Cornelius Hoen; King's Book; Niccolo Machiavelli; Michel Montaigne; Henry Nicholas; Nonjurors; Paracelsus; Johann Weyer; Witchcraft

Timothy Maschke
Professor of Pre-Seminary Studies, Concordia University Wisconsin, Mequon, Wisconsin
Gravamina; Hagenau Conference; Historiography, Reformation; Sebastian Münster; Bernardino Ochino; Oratory of Divine Love; Reformation Colloquies; Paolo Sarpi; Theatines; Pier Paolo Vergerio

Ralph W. Mathisen
Professor of History, Classics, and Medieval Studies, University of Illinois at Urbana-Champaign, Champaign-Urbana, Illinois
Alaric; Attila; Barbarian Invasions; Constantine the Great; Decius; Marcian; Milan, Edict of; Roman Empire; Theoderic I

Mickey L. Mattox
Professor in the Department of Theology, Marquette University, Milwaukee, Wisconsin
Judaizers; Papacy, Renaissance and Reformation; Albertus Pighius; Poland, Reformation in; Polish Brethren; Sabbatarianism; Socinianism

Brian Patrick McGuire
Professor of Medieval History, Institute of History and Social Theory, Roskilde University, Denmark
Avignon Papacy; Pierre D'Ailly; Jean Gerson; Papacy, Medieval

Elsie Anne McKee
Professor of Reformation Studies and the History of Worship, Princeton Theological Seminary, Princeton, New Jersey
Katharina Schütz Zell; Matthew Zell

Donald K. McKim
Executive Editor for Theology and Reference, Westminster John Knox Press, Louisville, Kentucky
Calvinism; Dissenters; Peter Ramus

Steven A. McKinion
Professor of Historical Theology and Patristics at Southeastern Baptist Theological Seminary, Wake Forest, North Carolina
Acacius of Constantinople; Apollinarius; Chalcedon, Definition of; Cyril of Alexandria; Dioscorus of Alexandria; Eutyches; Flavian of Constantinople; Leontius of Jerusalem; Monophysitism; Neochalcedonians; Peter the Fuller; Severus of Antioch; Theopaschite Formula; Trisagion; Vigilius

Jane E. Merdinger
Professor of Church History, Catholic University of America, Washington, DC
Carthage, Councils of; Church and State in Early Christianity; Innocent I of Rome; Optatus of Milevis; Parmenian; Quodvultdeus; Victor of Vita

Gesine Mierke
Assistant to the Chair of Medieval Literature and Language, Technische Universität, Chemnitz, Germany
Chapels

Gregory J. Miller
Associate Professor of History and Chair of the History, Philosophy, and Social Sciences Department at Malone College, Canton, Ohio
Theodor Bibliander; Dositheus; Hermann of Wied; Islam, Reformation Understanding of; Jeremiah II; Casper Megander; Mohács, Battle of; Old Believers (Raskolniki); Ottoman Empire; Konrad Pellikan; Prophesyings; Sacramentarianism; James Ussher; Girolamo Zanchi

J. Travis Moger
Regents Special Fellow, University of California, Santa Barbara
Balthasar Hubmaier; Jacob Hutter; Hutterites

Ingun Montgomery
Professor in the Department of Church History, Faculty of Theology, University of Oslo, Norway
Laurentius Andreae; Gustavus Adolphus; Laurentius Norvegus; Axel Oxenstierna; David Waengler Pareus; Laurentius Petri; Olaus Petri; Scandinavia, Reformation in; Gustavus Vasa

Victoria M. Morse
Associate Professor of History, Carleton College, Ottawa, Ontario, Canada
Angela of Foligno; Catherine of Siena; Pastoral Care; Regular Clergy; Secular Clergy

Joseph G. Mueller, SJ
Assistant Professor of Theology at Marquette
University, Milwaukee, Wisconsin
Church Order, Early; Cyril of Jerusalem; *Disciplina Arcani*; Excommunication

Anne Müller
Research Fellow, Research Center for Comparative History of Religious Orders,
Catholic University, Eichstätt, Germany
Franciscan Order; Lindisfarne

Paul V. Murphy
Associate Professor in the Department of History at John Carroll University, University
Heights, Ohio
Claudio Aquaviva; Robert Bellarmine;
Charles Borromeo; Gian Matteo Giberti;
Giles of Viterbo; Francis Xavier

James Arne Nestingen
Professor of Church History, Luther Seminary, St. Paul, Minnesota
Confutation of the Augsburg Confession;
Andreas Osiander; Peace of Augsburg;
Wittenberg Concord; Worms, Diet of

Adrienne Nock Ambrose
Assistant Professor, Religious Studies, University of the Incarnate Word, San Antonio,
Texas
Devotional Images; Elisabeth of Schönau;
Gertrude of Helfta; Hadewijch of Brabant;
Hildegard of Bingen; Julian of Norwich;
Margery Kempe; Mechthild of Magdeburg;
Pietà; Rosary; Virgin Mary in Medieval Art

William North
Assistant Professor of Medieval History, Carleton College, Northfield, Minnesota
Boethius; Cassiodorus; Dionysius Exiguus;
Fulgentius of Ruspe; Martin of Tours

Jörg Oberste
Professor of Medieval History, University of
Regensburg, Germany
Benedict of Aniane; Boniface; Cistercian
Order; Dominic

Christopher Ocker
Professor of Church History, San Francisco
Theological Seminary, San Anselmo, and
the Graduate Theological Union, Berkeley,
California
Altars; Benedict XII; Na Prous Boneta;
Carthusian Order; Angelo Clareno; Eugenius IV; Richard FitzRalph; Franciscan
Spirituals; Inquisition, Medieval; Joachim

of Fiora; Joan of Arc; John XXII; Masses
for the Dead; Monasticism, Medieval Western; Nicholas of Cusa; Olivi, Peter John;
Patron and Patronage Right; Premonstratensian Order; Proprietary Churches
and Monasteries; Ubertino da Casale;
William of St. Amour; Windesheim Congregation

Varda Koch Ocker
Assistant Professor of Hebrew, Defense Language Institute, Monterey, California
Islam and the Western Church; Marriage,
Medieval Church; Western Church and
the Jews

Jeannine E. Olson
Professor of History, Rhode Island College,
Providence, Rhode Island
Guillaume Briçonnet; Church Offices; Gallican Confession; Henry IV of France;
Jeanne of Navarre; Pacification of Ghent;
Poissy, Colloquy of; Renée of France;
Pierre Viret

Erhard "Erik" P. Opsahl
Teacher of History, Spanish, and Journalism
at Luther Preparatory School in Watertown,
Wisconsin
Baltic Crusade; First Crusade; Fourth Crusade; Latin Kingdom of Jerusalem; Teutonic Order

Charles H. Parker
Associate Professor of History at Saint Louis
University, St. Louis, Missouri
Wealth and Charity

Ota Pavlíček
Assistant at the Charles University, Prague
Jerome of Prague

Mark Gregory Pegg
Associate Professor of European History,
Washington University, St. Louis, Missouri
Dualism, Medieval

Michael D. Peterson
Librarian at San Francisco Theological Seminary, Graduate Theological Union Library,
Berkeley, California
Byzantine Rite; John Climacus; Crucifixion
in Art in the Orthodox Church; Great
Schism; Gregory Palamas; Hagia Sophia;
Hesychasm; Icon; Iconography; Irene;
John of Damascus; Joseph of Volokolamsk;
Justinian I; Nil Sorsky; Photian Schism;
Sergius of Radonezh; Theodora I;
Theodore the Studite; Vladimir

Paul B. Pixton
Professor of History, Brigham Young University, Provo, Utah
Basel, Council of; Councils, Later Middle Ages; Gregory VII; Lateran Councils; Metropolitan Bishops; Reform Papacy; Sacred College; Worms, Concordat of

Ute Possekel
Resident Research Fellow, Pappas Patristic Institute, Holy Cross Greek Orthodox School of Theology, Brookline, Massachusetts
Bardaisan; Ephrem the Syrian; Rabbula

Franz Posset
Independent Scholar
Thomas de Vio Cajetan; Lorenzo Campeggio; Johannes Cochlaeus; Gasparo Contarini; Johannes Eck; Hieronymus Emser; Sylvester Prierias

Darleen Pryds
Associate Professor of Christian Spirituality, Franciscan School of Theology, Berkeley, California
Beguines; Clare of Assisi; Francis of Assisi; Preaching, Medieval Women's

Nathan Baruch Rein
Associate Professor of Philosophy and Religion, Ursinus College, Collegeville, Pennsylvania
Babylonian Captivity of the Church; Confessionalization; *Magdeburg Centuries*; Magdeburg Confession; Pamphlets; Printing; Reformation Confessions

Todd M. Richardson
Post-Doctoral Fellow, Department of Art History, University of Leiden, Netherlands
Beatrice of Nazareth; Geert Groote; Marguerite Porete; Mysticism, Medieval Women's; Florentius Radewijns; Jan van Ruusbroec; Thomas à Kempis

Donavon L. Riley
Doctoral Student, Luther Seminary, St. Ial, Minnesota
Philipp Nicolai; Neils Palladius; Peder Palladius; Lazarus Spengler; Stockholm Bloodbath; *Swabian Syngramma*; Hans Tausen

David Rohrbacher
Assistant Professor of Classics, New College of Florida, Sarasota, Florida
Ammianus Marcellinus; Eusebius of Caesarea; Historiography, Early Christian; His-

toriography of Early Christianity (Contemporary); Philostorgius; Socrates of Constantinople; Sozomen

Rady Roldán-Figueroa
Assistant Professor of Historical Studies, Department of Religion, Baylor University, Waco, Texas
Joseph Acosta; Pedro de Alcántara; Alumbrados; Juan de Ávila; Domingo Báñez; Bible in the Reformation; Antonio del Corro; Juan de la Cruz; Juan Díaz; Francisco Jiménez de Cisneros; Juan de Torquemada; Marranos; Juan Pérez de Pineda; Constantino Ponce de la Fuente; Francisco de los Ángeles Quiñones; Casiodoro de Reina; Alfonso Salmerón; Juan Ginés de Sepúlveda; Tomás de Torquemada

Miri Rubin
Professor of European History, Queen Mary, University of London, United Kingdom
Blood Libel; Corpus Christi; Passion Plays; Ritual Murder; Sacrament, Medieval Definition; Transubstantiation

William R. Russell
Visiting Lecturer at Candler School of Theology at Emory University, Atlanta, Georgia
Anti-Semitism, Reformation; Beneficio di Christo; Cabbala; Carmelites, Discalced; Consilium de Emendanda Ecclesia; Italy, Reformation in; Joselmann of Rosheim; Giovanni Morone; Paola Antonia Negri; Filippo Neri; Reformation Contributions to Education; Camillo Renato; Ursulines.

Rodney S. Sadler Jr.
Associate Professor of Bible at Union Theological Seminary and Presbyterian School of Christian Education, Charlotte, North Carolina
Basilides; Cainites; Carpocratians; Cerdo; Cerinthus; Lost Books of the Bible; Mandeism; Saturninus; Sethians; Valentinus

David P. Scaer
Professor of Systematic Theology, Concordia Theological Seminary, Fort Wayne, Indiana
Johann Gerhard; Gnesio-Lutherans; Heidelberg Catechism; Edward Herbert; Tileman Hesshus; Thomas Hobbes; Ulrich von Hutten; Justus Jonas; Georg Major; Justus Menius; Casper Peucer; Julius Pflug; Racovian Catechism; Reformation Catechisms

Peter J. Scagnelli
Lecturer, School of Theology, Boston University, Boston, Massachusetts
Adrian VI; Alexander VI; Angela Merici; Barnabites; Caesar Baronius; Black Rubric; Book of Common Prayer; Clement VII; Controversial Theologians; Douai, College of; Francis de Sales; Julius II; Lateran Council, Fifth; Leo X; Marie de l'Incarnation; Paul III; Paul IV; Recusancy; Sacred Heart of Jesus, Devotion to the; Sixtus IV; Somaschi; Vincent de Paul

Richard Schenk, OP
Professor of Philosophy and Theology, Graduate Theological Union, Berkeley, California
Albert the Great; Richard Fishacre; Robert Kilwardby; Thomas Aquinas; Thomism; William of Auvergne

David M. Scholer
Professor of New Testament, Fuller Theological Seminary, Pasadena, California
Aetius of Antioch; Cecilia; Lawrence; Pionius

John N. Schumacher, SJ
Professor Emeritus of Church History, Loyola School of Theology, Philippines
Domingo de Salazar

Markus Schürer
Technische Universität, Dresden, Germany
Benedictine Rule; Carmelite Order

Douglas H. Shantz
Chair of Christian Thought, University of Calgary, Alberta
Collegium Philobiblicum; John Amos Comenius; *Ecclesiola in Ecclesia*; Christian Hoburg; Heinrich Müller; Philadelphianism; Pietism; Philipp Jakob Spener

Teresa M. Shaw
Research Associate Professor of Religion, Claremont Graduate University, Claremont, California
Ethics and Social Teaching, Early Christian; Eustochium; Fasting and Fast Days; Galen; Julian; Marcella; Melania the Elder; Melania the Younger; Olympias; Paula

Lorna Shoemaker
Assistant Professor of Church History, Christian Theological Seminary, Indianapolis, Indiana
Annates; Benefices; Boniface VIII; Conciliarism; Denys van Rijkel; Giles of Rome;

Gregory IX; Innocent III; Innocent IV; Shroud of Turin

Horace Six-Means
Assistant Professor, Hood Theological Seminary, Salisbury, North Carolina
Bishops, Early and Medieval

Stanley H. Skreslet
Professor of Christian Mission, Union Theological Seminary and Presbyterian School of Christian Education, Richmond, Virginia
Copts and Coptic Church

Thomas A. Smith
Assistant Vice President for Undergraduate Studies, The University of Northern Colorado in Greeley, Colorado
Athanasian Creed; *Decretum Gelasianum*; Magnus Felix Ennodius; Faustus; Gelasius I; Hilary, Bishop of Arles; Prosper of Aquitaine; Salvian of Marseilles; Valerian; Vincent of Lérins

Nancy Katherine Spatz Lucid
Independent Scholar, San Jose, California
Cloister Gardens; Paradise (in Churches)

Ralf M. W. Stammberger
Research Associate, Hugh of St. Victor Institute, St. Georgen Graduate School of Philosophy and Theology, Frankfurt am Main, Germany
Peter Abelard; Anselm of Laon; Heloise; Liberal Arts

Kenneth B. Steinhauser
Professor of Theological Studies, Saint Louis University, St. Louis, Missouri
Alexandria, Library of; Marcus Tullius Cicero; Epictetus; Epicurus and Epicureanism; Fathers of the Western Church; Lactantius; Leo I; Seneca the Younger

Andrea Sterk
Associate Professor of Church History, University of Florida, Gainesville, Florida
Cyril and Methodius; Ludmila; Monasticism, Byzantine; Old Church Slavonic; Sava of Serbia; Wenceslas

Kirsi Stjerna
Professor of Reformation Church History, Lutheran Theological Seminary, Gettysburg, Pennsylvania
Mikael Agricola; Anne of Cleves; Argula von Stauff von Grumbach; Augustinus Triumphus of Ancona; Anne Boleyn; Catherine of Genoa; Christian III; Vittoria Colonna;

Elisabeth of Brandenburg; Elisabeth of Braunschweig; Niels Hemmingsen; Reformation, Women and the; Heinrich Seuse; Teresa of Avila

William B. Sweetser Jr.
Pastor of First Presbyterian Church, Spruce Pine, North Carolina, and Adjunct Assistant Professor of Church History, Union-PSCE in Charlotte, North Carolina
Acoemetae; Bordeaux Pilgrim; Catherine of Alexandria; Genevieve; George; *Laus Perennis*; St. Nicholas; Sebaste, Forty Martyrs of; Severinus; Theban Legion; Ursula; St. Valentine; Zeno of Verona

Charles M. Swezey
Professor Emeritus of Theology and Ethics, Union Theological Seminary and Presbyterian School of Christian Education, Richmond, Virginia
Peace and War in Christian Thought

William Tabbernee
President and Distinguished Professor of the History of Christianity, Phillips Theological Seminary, Tulsa, Oklahoma
Montanus, Montanism; Perpetua and Felicitas; Scillitan Martyrs

Johannes M. M. H. Thijssen
Professor of Ancient and Medieval Philosophy, Radboud University of Nijmegen, Netherlands
Aristotle and Medieval Theology; Thomas Bradwardine; Gregory of Rimini; Robert Holcot; Nicholas of Autrecourt; Nominalism; John Pecham; Scholasticism; John Duns Scotus; Étienne Tempier; Universals; William of Ockham; Adam Wodeham

Maureen A. Tilley
Visiting Professor of Theology, Fordham University, New York, New York
Blandina; Caecilian; Confessor; Donatism and Donatus; Lucilla; Persecution and Martyrdom in the Early Church

John Tonkin
Professor of History, University of Western Australia, Nedlands, Western Australia
Pierre Charron; Erastianism; Florimond de Raemond; George Fox; Friends, Society of; Inquisition, Early Modern; Kappel, Peace of; Observantism; Precisionism; Quietism;

François Rabelais; Girolamo Savonarola; Seekers; Vadian; Georg Witzel

Tarmo Toom
Associate Professor of Divinity, John Leland Center for Theological Studies, Arlington, Virginia
Anomoeans; Callistus I; Gaius; Gregory of Elvira; Hippolytus; Monarchianism; Noetus of Smyrna; Paul of Samosata; Peter of Alexandria; Sabellius; Sixtus II; Synods of Sirmium; Trinity in Early Christian Controversy; Ulfila

John L. Treloar, SJ
Associate Professor of the History of Late Medieval Philosophy, Jesuit School of Theology, Berkeley, California
Marsilio Ficino

Martin Treu
Director of the Lutherhaus, Wittenberg, Germany
Albert of Brandenburg; Albert of Prussia; Lucas Cranach (the Elder); Lucas Cranach (the Younger); Frederick III; Katharina von Bora; Schmalkald League; Schmalkald War; Georg Spalatin; Johann von Staupitz; Johann Tetzel

Joseph W. Trigg
Rector of Christ Church, LaPlata, Maryland
Apelles; Gregory Thaumaturgus; Marcion; Melito; Methodius; Origen; Procopius of Gaza; Victorinus of Poetovio

Dennis E. Trout
Associate Professor of Classics, University of Missouri, Columbia
Decimus Magnus Ausonius; Damasus I; Firmicus Maternus; Galla Placidia; Gildas; Hadrian; Gaius Vettius Aquilinus Juvencus; Latin Poetry, Early Christian; Macarius Magnes; Nero; Paganism and Early Christianity; Paulinus of Nola; Pliny the Younger; Prudentius, Aurelius Clemens; Sedulius; Sidonius Apollinaris; Gaius Tranquillus Suetonius; Sulpicius Severus; Cornelius Tacitus; Venantius Fortunatus; Virgil

Carl Trueman
Professor of Church History and Historical Theology, Westminster Theological Seminary, Philadelphia, Pennsylvania
William Ames; Richard Baxter; Robert Browne; Thomas Cartwright; England,

Reformation in; William Perkins;
Puritanism; Refugee and Stranger
Churches

J. Jeffery Tyler
Professor of Religion, Hope College, Holland, Michigan
Archbishops, Medieval; Archdeacon; Bishops, Late Middle Ages and Reformation; Cathedral Chapter; Provinces, Ecclesiastical

Richard Paul Vaggione, OHC
Faculty of Divinity, Trinity College, Toronto, Ontario
Alexander of Alexandria; Didymus the Blind; Eustathius of Antioch; Hosius of Cordova; Logos; Nicaea, First Council of; *Oikonomia*

Daniel G. Van Slyke
Associate Professor of Church History, Kenrick-Glennon Seminary, St. Louis, Missouri
Baptism; Confirmation; Healing, Religious; Latin Rite

Dewey D. Wallace Jr.
Professor of Religion, George Washington University, Washington, DC
Bay Psalm Book; Half-Way Covenant; Anne Hutchinson; Cotton Mather; Increase Mather; Puritanism in New England; Salem Witch Trials

Rebecca H. Weaver
Professor of Church History, Union Theological Seminary and Presbyterian School of Christian Education, Richmond, Virginia
Jesus in Early Christianity; Nicene Creed; Paul in Early Christianity

James Michael Weiss
Episcopal Priest, Associate Professor of Church History and Director of the Senior Capstone Program at Boston College, Boston, Massachusetts
Beatus Rhenanus (Rhinower); Stanislaus Hosius; Humanism; Renaissance

Timothy J. Wengert
Professor of the History of Christianity, Lutheran Theological Seminary, Philadelphia, Pennsylvania
Adiaphora and Adiaphorist Controversies; Antinomianism; Formula of Concord; Lutheranism; Philip Melanchthon; Philippists

Achim Wesjohann
Member of the Sonderforschungsbereich 537 "Institutionalität und Geschichtlichkeit," Technische Universität, Dresden, Germany
Anthony of Padua; Benedictine Order

Benjamin W. Westervelt
Associate Professor of History, Lewis and Clark College, Portland, Oregon
Early Modern Catholicism; Ignatius Loyola; Society of Jesus; *Spiritual Exercises*; Trent, Council of; Tridentine Profession of Faith

David Whitford
Associate Professor of the History of Christianity, United Theological Seminary, Trotwood, Ohio
Francogallia; François Hotman; Knights' Revolt; Juan de Mariana; Münster Revolt; Peasants' War; Resistance Theory; Rome, Sack of; Thirty Years' War; Twelve Articles of the Peasants; Westphalia, Peace of

D. H. Williams
Professor of Religion in Patristics and Historical Theology, Baylor University, Waco, Texas
Ambrose; Ariminum, Council of; Hilary, Bishop of Poitiers; Julius I; Liberius; Photinus; Praxeas; Serdica, Council of; Tertullian of Carthage

Steven J. Williams
Associate Professor of History, New Mexico Highlands University, Las Vegas, New Mexico
Aristotle, Translations of; Roger Bacon; Robert Grosseteste; Quodlibetal Disputations; Universities, Rise of; William of Auxerre

Anders Winroth
Professor of Medieval History, Yale University, New Haven, Connecticut
Canon Law; *Corpus Iuris Canonici*; *Corpus Iuris Civilis*; Decretals; Gratian

John Witte Jr.
Professor of Law and Ethics, Emory University, Atlanta, Georgia
Jean Bodin; Church Orders, Reformation; Hugo Grotius; Protestant Law; Samuel

von Pufendorf; Reformation Marriage
Courts

Michael Wolfe
Professor, Department of History, St. John's
University, New York, New York
Carnival; Gaspard de Coligny; France,
Reformation in; Nîmes, Synod of; Poli-
tiques; Gérard Roussel; St. Bartholo-
mew's Day Massacre; Wars of Religion
in France

Markus Wriedt
Professor of Church History/Historical Theol-
ogy, Marquette University, Milwaukee,
Wisconsin, and Goethe University, Frank-
furt am Main, Germany
Hermits of St. Augustine; Indulgences;
Penance

Harry Yeide Jr.
Professor of Ethics and the Sociology of Reli-
gion, George Washington University,
Washington, DC
Moravians

Randall C. Zachman
Professor of Theology, University of Notre
Dame, Notre Dame, Indiana
John Calvin; Sebastian Castellion;
Consistory of Geneva; John Craig; John
Knox; John Major; Reformed Church;
Jacopo Sadoleto

Jonathan Zophy
Professor, Department of History, University
of Houston, Clear Lake, Texas
Henry VIII; Mary Stuart

List of Articles

Abbreviations

General

BCE	before the common era
c.	circa, about
CE	common era
cent.	century, centuries
d.	died
ET	English translation
f., ff.	following
fl.	flourished
Ger.	German
Gk.	Greek
Heb.	Hebrew
HRE	Holy Roman Empire
Lat.	Latin
LXX	Septuagint
MS	manuscript
n.	note; footnote
n.d.	no date
NS	new series
NT	New Testament
OT	Old Testament
r.	ruled
repr.	reprint
trans.	translated
Univ.	university
v.	alternate reading
vol.	volume

Publications

ACCS	Ancient Christian Commentary on Scripture
ACO	*Acta conciliorum oecumenicorum*
ACW	Ancient Christian Writers
AFH	*Archivum Franciscanum historicum*
AHDLMA	Les Archives d'histoire doctrinale et littéraire du Moyen Age
AnBoll	Analecta Bollandiana
ANF	*Ante-Nicene Fathers*
ANRW	*Aufstieg und Niedergang der römischen Welt*
ARG	*Archiv für Reformationsgeschichte*

ARTS	*The Arts in Religious and Theological Studies*
Aug	*Augustinianum*
AugStud	*Augustinian Studies*
BA	*Biblical Archaeologist*
BASOR	*Bulletin of the American Schools of Oriental Research*
BGPTMA	Beitrage zur Geschichte der Philosophie und Theologie des Mittelalters
BHS	*Biblia Hebraica Stuttgartensia*
BJRL	*Bulletin of the John Rylands University Library of Manchester*
BRRP	*Bohemian Reformation and Religious Practice*
BLE	*Bulletin de littérature ecclésiastique*
CCCM	Corpus Christianorum: Continuatio mediaevalis
CCSG	Corpus Christianorum: Series graeca
CCSL	Corpus Christianorum: Series latina
CH	*Church History*
CHR	*Catholic Historical Review*
CNS	*Cristianesimo nella storia*
CPG	*Clavis patrum graecorum*
CPL	*Clavis patrum latinorum*
CSCO	Corpus scriptorum christianorum orientalium
CSEL	Corpus scriptorum ecclesiasticorum latinorum
CTM	*Concordia Theological Monthly*
CTQ	*Concordia Theological Quarterly*
DACL	*Dictionnaire d'archéologie chrétienne et de liturgie*
DHGE	*Dictionnaire d'histoire et de géographie ecclésiastiques*
DOP	*Dumbarton Oaks Papers*
DRev	*Downside Review*
EgT	*Eglise et théologie*
FC	Fathers of the Church
FZPT	*Freiburger Zeitschrift für Philosophie und Theologie*
GCS	Die griechischen christlichen Schriftsteller der ersten [drei] Jahrhunderte
GNO	Gregorii Nysseni Opera
GOTR	*Greek Orthodox Theological Review*
HTR	*Harvard Theological Review*
IBMR	*International Bulletin of Missionary Research*
ITQ	*Irish Theological Quarterly*
JECS	*Journal of Early Christian Studies*
JEH	*Journal of Ecclesiastical History*
JFSR	*Journal of Feminist Studies in Religion*
JHI	*Journal of the History of Ideas*
JPH	*Journal of Presbyterian History*
JR	*Journal of Religion*
JRAS	*Journal of the Royal Asiatic Society*
JRH	*Journal of Religious History*
JRS	*Journal of Roman Studies*
JTS	*Journal of Theological Studies*
LCL	Loeb Classical Library
LMS	London Missionary Society

LQ	*Lutheran Quarterly*
LTK	*Lexicon für Theologie und Kirche*
MGH	Monumenta Germaniae Historica
MS	*Mediaeval Studies*
MScRel	*Mélanges de science religieuse*
NCE	New Catholic Encyclopedia
NPNF	Nicene and Post-Nicene Fathers
NTApocr	New Testament Apocrypha
OCuT	Oxford Editions of Cuneiform Texts
OrChrAn	Orientalia christiana analecta
ParOr	*Parole de l'orient*
PBA	Proceedings of the British Academy
PBSR	Papers of the British School at Rome
PG	Patrologia graeca
PL	Patrologia latina
PMLA	Proceedings of the Modern Language Association
PO	Patrologia orientalis
PTS	Patristische Texte und Studien
RBén	*Revue bénédictine*
RBPH	*Revue belge de philologie et d'histoire*
REAug	*Revue des études augustiniennes*
RelSRev	*Religious Studies Review*
RGG	*Religion in Geschichte und Gegenwart*
RHE	*Revue d'histoire ecclésiastique*
RQ	*Römische Quartalschrift für christliche Altertumskunde und Kirchengeschichte*
RSC	*Rivista di studi classici*
RSPT	*Revue des sciences philosophiques et théologiques*
RSR	*Recherches de science religieuse*
RTAM	*Recherches de théologie ancienne et médiévale*
SBET	*Scottish Bulletin of Evangelical Theology*
SC	Sources chrétiennes
SCH	Studies in Church History
SCJ	*The Sixteenth Century Journal*
SecCent	*Second Century*
SJT	Scottish Journal of Theology
SOPMA	Scriptores ordinis praedicatorum medii aevi
StPatr	Studia patristica
StudMon	Studia monastica
SVTQ	*St. Vladimir's Theological Quarterly*
TJT	*Toronto Journal of Theology*
TRE	*Theologische Realenzyklopädie*
TS	*Theological Studies*
VC	*Vigiliae christianae*
VL	*Vetus Latina: Die Reste der altlateinischen Bibel*
VTSup	Supplements to Vetus Testamentum
ZAC	*Zeitschrift für Antikes Christentum/Journal of Ancient Christianity*
ZDMG	*Zeitschrift der deutschen morgenländischen Gesellschaft*

| ZKG | *Zeitschrift für Kirchengeschichte* |
| ZRGG | *Zeitschrift für Religions- und Geistesgeschichte* |

Greek and Latin Works

Abbr.	*Author*	*Work*
1 Apol.	Euomius	*Apologia I*
1 Apol.	Justin Martyr	*Apologia I*
Adv. omn. haer	Pseudo-Tertullian	*Adversus omnium haeresium*
Apol.	Tertullian	*Apologeticus*
Apol. sec.	Athanasius	*Apologia secunda*
B.J.	Josephus	*Bellum judaicum*
Bab.	John Chrysostom	*De sancto hieromartyre Babyla*
C. Ar.	Athanasius	*Orationes contra Arianos*
Carn. Chr.	Tertullian	*De carne Christi*
Chron.	Sulpicius Severus	*Chronicorum Libri duo*
Comm. Jo.	Origen	*Commentarii in evangelium Joannis*
Conf.	Augustine	*Confessionum libri XIII (Confessions)*
Cont. Cels.	Origen	*Contra Celsum*
Dial.	Justin Martyr	*Dialogus cum Tryphone*
Did.	—	*Didache*
Dom. or.	Cyprian	*De dominica oratione*
Enarrat. Ps.	Augustine	*Enarrationes in Psalmos*
Ep.	Ambrose	*Epistulae*
Ep.	Basil of Caesaria	*Epistulae*
Ep. cler. Alex	Athanasius	*Epistula ad clerum Alexandriae*
Fr. Jo.	Origen	*Fragmenta in evangelium Joannis*
Fr. Prov.	Hippolytus	*Fragmenta in Proverbia*
Gorg.	Plato	*Gorgias*
Grat. Chr.	Augustine	*De gratia Christi, et de peccato originali*
Hist. eccl.	Eusebius	*Historia ecclesiastica*
Haer.	Iranaeus	*Adversus haereses*
Haer.	Hippolytus	*Refutatio omnium haeresium*
Hist. eccl.	Socrates	*Historia ecclesiastica*
Hist. eccl.	Sozomen	*Historia ecclesiastica*
Hist. eccl.	Theodoret	*Historia ecclesiastica*
Hom. Eph.	John Chrysostom	*Homiliae in epistulam ad Ephesios*
Hom. Gen.	John Chrysostom	*Homiliae in Genesim*
Leg.	Athenagoras	*Legatio pro Christianis*
Leg.	Philo	*Legum allegoriae*
Mort.	Lactantius	*De mortibus persecutorum*
Off.	Ambrose	*De officiis ministrorum*
Or. Bas.	Gregory of Nazianzus	*Oratio in laudem Basilii*
Paed.	Clement	*Paedagogus*
Pan.	Epiphanius	*Panarion*
Perist.	Prudentius	*Peristefanon*
Praescr.	Tertullian	*De praescriptione haereticorum*

Abbr.	*Author*	*Work*
Prax.	Tertullian	*Adversus Praxean*
Princ.	Origen	*De principiis*
Protr.	Clement	*Protrepticus*
Rom.	Ignatius of Antioch	*Pros Romaious*
Spect.	Tertullian	*De spectaculis*
Strom.	Clement	*Stromata*
Syn.	Athanasius	*De synodis*
Trad. ap.	Hippolytus	*Traditio apostolica*
Trin.	Novation	*De Trinitate*
Vir. ill.	Gennaduis	*De viris illustribus*
Vir. ill.	Jerome	*De viris illustribus*
Vit. Const.	Eusebius of Caesarea	*Vita Constantini*

Aachen Romans called this site in modern western Germany *Aquisgranum* for its principal feature, thermal baths. King Pepin III (r. 751–768) of the Franks built a small villa there to accommodate his visits. Charlemagne (r. 768–814), his son, built an elaborate palace complex on the site in the 790s and adopted Aachen as his principal residence and de facto capital of the Carolingian Empire. The palace complex, including the surviving octagonal chapel, was inspired by Italian models and incorporated marble columns brought from Rome and Ravenna.

Charlemagne and Louis the Pious (r. 814–840), his son, administered their far-flung empire from the halls and baths of Aachen. Byzantine Greeks, Slavs, Bulgars, Scandinavians, Iberian Muslims, Anglo-Saxons, Italian dukes, and papal representatives trouped to Aachen on diplomatic missions. Frankish nobles, monks, priests, merchants, and prostitutes also contributed to the cosmopolitan mix of the Carolingian capital. The court attracted scholars who celebrated in verse and prose the sense of energy and purpose that radiated from the policymakers at Aachen, the "second Rome."

Aachen's political importance waned after the breakup of the Carolingian Empire into competing kingdoms in the 840s, but its symbolic importance grew. German kings and Holy Roman Emperors in succeeding centuries arranged their coronations at Aachen in an effort to legitimate their rule and capitalize on the near mythical luster of Charlemagne.

R. E. Sullivan, *Aix-la-Chapelle in the Age of Charlemagne* (1963).

JOHN J. CONTRENI

Abba and Amma These terms refer to ascetic men and women in leadership positions. According to the New Testament, both Jesus (Mark 14:36) and Paul (Rom. 8:15; Gal. 4:6) used the Aramaic word for father, *abba*, from which "abbot" is derived. The idea of spiritual fathership that these biblical passages suggest became a dominant theme among early Egyp-

tian solitary monks who adopted the term *abba* to indicate a holy man who had achieved a degree of spiritual perfection through his ascetic feats. The literature of the anchorites reflects this spiritual status: the *Sayings* of the abbas are their means of teaching their students. In communal monasticism, *abba* became a more specific term, meaning "head of the monastery," both a spiritual and a legislative position. The term spread to the West (and was adopted in Latin) through the writings of John Cassian. However, the abbot became central to medieval monasticism through the Rule of Benedict, which made the abbot "Christ's representative" since, in a reference to Romans, they share the same name: *abba. Amma* is a Greek word which in the East became a female equivalent to the male ascetics' *abba*. In its pre-Christian usage, the term meant "foster mother" or "nurse." By the fourth century, according to Palladius (*Lausiac History* 24), it identified women who were "spiritual mothers" in their communities. Ammas also led the more anchoritic life, as the *Sayings* of Sarah, Theodora, and Syncletica attest.

S. Elm, *"Virgins of God": Making of Asceticism in Late Antiquity* (1994); G. Gould, *The Desert Fathers on Monastic Community* (1993); A. de Vogüé, *Community and Abbot in the Rule of St. Benedict*, 2 vols. (1979–1993); C. H. Lawrence, "Sisters or Handmaids," in *Medieval Monasticism*, 3rd ed. (2000); B. Ward, trans., "Sayings of the Desert Mothers Sarah, Syncletica, and Theodora," in *Maenads, Martyrs, Matrons, Monastics*, ed. R. S. Kraemer (1988), 117–24; B. Ward, trans., *The Sayings of the Desert Fathers: The Alphabetical Collection* (1980).

REBECCA KRAWIEC

Abbasid Caliphate The Abbasid dynasty traces its origin to Abbas, the uncle of Muhammad. It is the successor to the Umayyad dynasty and lasted from 750 until its extinction by the Mongols in 1258. Although the Abbasids never controlled the entire empire, they were an important force in Islamic history. The first Abbasid caliph, Abu-l Abbas, known also as

Saffah the Spiller (of the Umayyads' blood), inaugurated a line of 37 caliphs in Baghdad. There were two factors contributing to the success of the Abbasids against the Umayyads. The first was the family connection to the Prophet that initially attracted the support of the nascent Shi'ite movement. Later the Shi'ites would find Abbasid support for them lukewarm, and they ended by supporting Fatimid claims to the caliphate. The other factor was the willingness of the Abbasids to incorporate non-Arabs into the religious and cultural structure in ways that the Umayyads would not. It is no accident that they located their capital in Baghdad.

The Abbasid court took on the trappings of its Persian predecessor and was renowned for its splendor and ritual. The Abbasid caliphs of the eighth century were promoters of learning and culture. Under the patronage of al-Ma'mun (r. 813–833), a center of learning known as the *Bayt al-Hikma*, or House of Wisdom, was established where many classical Greek works were translated into Arabic, frequently through the medium of Syriac and greatly aided by Christian scholars. The numeric system of India, including the zero, contributed to Arab mathematical sciences, including the development of algebra. Later ninth-century caliphs were less receptive to the influence of non-Islamic peoples.

Under al-Mutasim (r. 833–842) the experiences of revolution and social division induced the caliphate to recruit a military force of mamluks, or slaves, conquered peoples, and converted non-Arabs. Many of them were Turkish horsemen, but Mamluk armies might include Slavs and African Berbers as well. Other Muslim rulers also adopted this very un-Arab practice that would have major repercussions. These private armies displaced the native Arab and Persian forces, and in the tenth century they became a political power in their own right.

By the mid-tenth century, the authority of the caliphate had declined and the real power in Baghdad was not the Abbasid caliphs but the Buyid dynasty amirs, who were Shi'ite. The Abbasids retained the title of caliph, even after the coming of the Sunni Seljuk Turks, until the end of the dynasty in 1258, when the Mongols brought Abbasid culture to an end and threw its libraries into the Tigris River.

A Mamluk soldier was able to bring an uncle of the last Abbasid caliph to Cairo, and a series of nominal Abbasid rulers contributed a color of legitimacy to the Egyptian Mamluk regime until its conquest by the Ottoman Turks in 1517.

F. Robinson, ed., *The Cambridge Illustrated History of the Islamic World* (1998); N. Shaban, *Islamic History: A New Interpretation*, vol. 2 (1976); T. Sonn, *A Brief History of Islam* (2004).

EUGENE M. LUDWIG, OFM CAP.

Abbots and Abbesses Abbot or abbess denotes the superior of a monastic community. The term developed from the biblical-Aramaean *aba* and the Greek-Latin *abbas* (Father). It first appeared in late antiquity in the East and referred to the honored recognition shown by most ascetic groups to their charismatic leader. The ambivalence inherent in the concept of fatherhood clearly shaped the position of the abbot. On the one hand, he was the loving and caring protector and guardian; on the other hand, he had unlimited leadership both in spiritual and jurisdictional concerns as well as administrative and disciplinary duties. Minimal institutionalization is still apparent in the *Apophthegmata*, where the abbot is admonished, "Be a model to your brothers, not a lawgiver" (Saying 174). The gradually evolving concern for institutional permanence of the religious communities led to the drawing up of rules, which also included instructions for the abbot. In the East, from the days of Pachomius and Basil onward, cenobitic monasticism advanced the legalization of the *Hegumenos*. In the West, the monastic conceptions of the Benedictine rule became decisive, whereby the method of electing the abbot ensured a relative autonomy. Yet the bishop also claimed authority over the communities, which opened up the possibilities for external influence. The "lordship of the abbot" was then gradually restricted by the hierarchy of the nonmonastic church, which subjected the figure of the abbot to rigid, normative restraints and also limited the political dimensions of the abbatial office. Nevertheless, abbots took over more and more important positions in the imperial organization, but through these positions they also became the pawn of political interests (lay abbots). The successive exemptions of monasteries and, finally, ecclesiastical reform restricted episcopal claims as well as external influence on monasteries. The formation of monastic orders from the twelfth century onward brought about a modified conception of the abbatial-office form of constitutionalization. A new *ius particulare* bound the abbot within strict organizational patterns and limited abbatial autonomy for the benefit of the power of the order superior and the general chapter. A clearly defined understanding of the abbatial office and indoctrination led finally to provisions concerning personal suitability, such as minimum age or the necessity of clerical ordination. The latter, never mentioned in the Benedictine rule, had been advanced alongside the gradual clericalization of the monasteries. Ways of verifying competence and qualifications replaced the once stable and almost insulated monastic microcosm.

Today the abbot still holds power over his community. The abbess is fundamentally to be regarded as the female counterpart to the abbot in a convent. Although occasional attempts were made to place her also as the superior over a male monastery (based on the biblical concept of Mary's lordship), there proved to be significant differences concerning the power granted to her, particularly in the areas of pastoral duties and the care of souls.

G. Constable, *Monastic Tithes* (1964); W. Horn, *On the Origins of the Medieval Cloister* (1973).
LARS-A. DANNENBERG

Abelard, Peter (1079–1142), theologian and philosopher. Abelard was the pupil of Roscelin of Compiègne, William of Champeaux, and Anselm of Laon, with all of whom he had serious disputes. He taught dialectic in Melun and Corbeil (1102–1105) and later at Ste. Geneviève outside of Paris. In 1114 he became master at the cathedral school of Paris, where he fell in love with Heloise, the niece of canon Fulbert. When she became pregnant, he abducted her. He subsequently married her after the birth of their son Astrolabe. Because Abelard wanted to keep the marriage secret, Fulbert felt betrayed and had him castrated (1117). Heloise then entered the monastery of Argenteuil; Abelard became a monk at St. Denis. Soon afterward he retreated to a cell, where he wrote the *Theologia summi boni* (*Theology of the Highest Good*), which was directed against the tritheistic teachings of Roscelin and was itself condemned at a council in Soissons (1121). He founded a hermitage dedicated to the Paraclete in 1122, which developed into a school. He was elected abbot of St. Gildas de Rhuys in Brittany (1125) but encountered strong opposition when he tried to introduce reforms of the monastic life there. In 1133 he returned to Ste. Geneviève in Paris, where he taught and wrote his major theological works. On the initiative of William of St. Thierry, Bernard of Clairvaux accused him of heresy. He was condemned again at a council in Sens (1141) on the basis of *capitula*, "chapters," that paraphrased his teachings. Peter the Venerable received him into the community of Cluny. He died at St. Marcel and was buried at the Paraclete.

Peter Abelard's insistence on the accessibility of things through language led him to deny an independent existence of universals without becoming an ontological nominalist. He introduced this awareness of the role of language into theological debate. He assigned the terms "power," "wisdom," and "benignity" to the three persons of the Trinity and showed that knowledge of these was accessible to Jews and Gentiles alike. Whereas the *Theologia summi boni* and the *Theologia Christiana* (*Christian Theology*, 1121–1126) are organized by these terms, the *Theologia scholarium* (*Theology of Scholars*) treats faith, charity, and sacrament as necessary elements of salvation. In his *Commentary on Romans* Abelard deals with the concept of law and ethical questions. In his *Ethica* he further underlines the importance of intention for establishing guilt. We have an autobiographical report of his life in the *Historia Calamitatum* (*History of Calamities*, c. 1131) and a number of other letters, poems, and liturgical texts from his hand.

B. Boyer and R. McKeon, eds., *Sic et Non* (1977); CCCM 11–13, 190; M. T. Clanchy, *Abelard* (1997); B. Geyer, ed., *Logica* BGPTMA 21 (1919–33); D. Luscombe, *The School of Peter Abelard* (1969); J. Marenbon, *The Philosophy of Peter Abelard* (1999); Marenbon, ed., *Collationes* (2001); C. Mews, *Abelard and Heloise* (2004); Mews, *Peter Abelard* (1995); C. Mews and N. Chiavaroli, eds., *Love Letters* (2001); J. Monfrin, ed., *Historia calamitatum* (1959); J. T. Muckle, ed., *Letters* in *MS* 12, 15, and 17 (1950, 1953, 1955); PL 178; L. M. de Rijk, ed., *Dialectica* (1972); M. F. Romig, ed., *Hexaemeron* (1981); P. de Santis, ed., *Sermones* (2002); J. Szövérffy, ed., *Hymnarius* (1975).
RALF M. W. STAMMBERGER

Abgar V (4 BCE–50 CE), one of a succession of kings of Edessa (Urfa) by the same name. According to the anonymous third- or fourth-century Syriac *Teaching of Addai*, Abgar, who was ill, heard of the miracles of Christ and wrote a letter to Jesus asking him to come to Edessa. Jesus wrote back that he could not come then but promised to send one of his disciples after his ascension. The *Teaching of Addai* includes Christ's letter, as does Eusebius of Caesarea (*Hist. eccl.* 1.13). Jesus also granted a blessing to the city of Edessa that it should never be conquered, a concept the Eddessenes cherished for centuries. In some versions, a portrait of Christ was also brought back to Edessa.

Judas Thomas later sent Addai (Thaddeus), who healed the king and evangelized the city. Some believe the historical setting of this story occurred during the reign of Abgar VIII (177–212), who converted to Christianity. The *Chronicle of Edessa* reports that the flood of 201 destroyed the Christian church building, the first evidence of a Christian community.

J. B. Segal, *The Blessed City* (1970), 62–73; G. Howard, trans., *The Teaching of Addai* (1981); W. Bauer, *Orthodoxy and Heresy in Earliest Christianity* (1971), 1–43.

ROBERT A. KITCHEN

Abu al-Faraj   *see* Bar Hebraeus

Acacius of Caesarea (c. 300–365/366),

Arianizing bishop. Acacius succeeded Eusebius as bishop of Caesarea in 340. He attended the Dedication Council of Antioch in 341 and sided with the Greek bishops at Sardica/ Philippopolis in 343, after which the Western bishops tried to depose him. He ordained Cyril bishop of Jerusalem c. 350 but later turned against him for reasons of jurisdiction. From 357 on, Acacius was active in doctrinal disputes. At the Synod of Seleucia in 359 he produced a creed that rejected *homoousios* (same in essence), *homoiousios* (like in essence), and *anomoios* (unlike) and proposed the homoian phrase "like the Father," by which he meant "in will only." Acacius had the reputation of being an opportunist and theologically fickle (see Socrates, *Ecclesiastical History* 2.40; Sozomen, *Ecclesiastical History* 4.22). In 360 at Constantinople, Acacius championed a homoian creed. He engineered the election of Melitius at Antioch in 360/361 but soon turned on him. In 363, under Jovian, Acacius was reconciled with Melitius and signed the Creed of Nicaea, but the following year, under Valens, he returned to the neo-Arian position. Acacius wrote a work against Marcellus of Ancyra of which Epiphanius of Salamis preserved some extensive fragments.

Epiphanius, *Pan.* 72 (fragments of Acacius's writing against Marcellus); J. T. Lienhard,

"Acacius of Caesarea: *Contra Marcellum*, Historical and Theological Considerations," *CNS* 10 (1989): 1–22.

JOSEPH T. LIENHARD

Acacius of Constantinople (d. 491),

bishop of Constantinople (471–491). Acacius's importance relates to two developments concerning the Council of Chalcedon. He expanded the council's statement regarding Constantinople's honor into jurisdiction over the church in the East. He facilitated the reception of the *Definition* of Chalcedon in opposition to those who claimed it was a doctrinal innovation in violation of the canons of Nicaea. In 482, Acacius authored the *Henoticon* of Emperor Zeno, which was intended as a compromise with moderate Monophysites. The formula of the *Henoticon* avoided "nature" language and any mention of Chalcedon. Monophysites such as Peter the Fuller in Antioch and Peter Mongus in Egypt supported the doctrinal statement in the *Henoticon*. Felix III of Rome rejected the language of the *Henoticon* and excommunicated Acacius in 484 due to his perceived Monophysitism. The Acacian schism ensued between Rome and Constantinople and lasted until Emperor Justin rescinded the *Henoticon* in 518. Acacius's name was removed from the diptychs of the church after the reunion. The *Henoticon* can be found in Evagrius's *Ecclesiastical History* 3.14.

P. T. Camelot, *Ephesus und Chalkedon* (1976); W. H. C. Frend, *The Rise of the Monophysite Movement* (1972).

STEVEN A. MCKINION

Acoemetae ("sleepless ones")   An order of

monks founded c. 390 near Zeugma (southeast Turkey). Arising from the chaotic milieu of Syrian monasticism, the Acoemetae were known for their strict asceticism, literal biblical interpretation, and unique form of prayer. Alexander the Acoemete (c. 350–c. 430), their founder, rejected the set hours of prayer then developing a consensus throughout the monastic world. In contrast, he divided his monks into alternating choirs so the Psalms would be chanted without interruption; hence "sleepless" monks.

The Acoemetae moved to Constantinople (c. 425) and came to symbolize unwavering orthodoxy. Public acclaim, Empress Pulcheria's patronage, and monastic allies enabled them to withstand condemnation by the Synod of Constantinople (426) while establishing two new monasteries. They became known as implacable opponents of the Monophysites under their third abbot, Marcellus (400–484). He testified at the fourth session of the Council of Chalcedon (451) concerning the orthodoxy of other abbots and established a monastery in Constantinople whose holdings became the source for the *Patrologia Graeca*. They sided with Rome in the Acacian schism (484–534), but Pope John II excommunicated the Acoemetae as Nestorians in 534.

———

J. Baguenard, trans., *Les Moines Acémètes: Vie des saints Alexandre, Marcel et Jean Calybite* (1988); J. Garrigues and J. Legrez, *Moines dans l'assemblée des fidèles: A l'epoque des pères IVe–VIIe Siècle* (1992).

WILLIAM B. SWEETSER JR.

Acontius, Jacobus (c. 1514–1566/1567),

advocate of religious toleration. Italian-born and educated, Acontius fled from his position as a notary for Cardinal Christoforo Madruzzo in Trent to Basel in 1557 fearing arrest because of his Protestant convictions. He became acquainted with other exiles in Zurich (B. Ochino, C. S. Curione) before settling in England as a fortifications engineer. Under the impact of the persecution of the French Huguenots, he developed his argument for toleration, constructing a core of fundamental dogmas necessary for salvation (excluding the Trinity and the real presence) and advocating toleration for those who accepted them (*Stratagemata Satanae,* Basel 1565). Execution of heretics by secular or ecclesiastical authorities earned his condemnation. Though placed under church discipline for his defense of Baptists, he continued to write historical, philosophical, and theological works.

———

D. Cantimori, *Italian Heretics of the Sixteenth Century* (1979); W. K. Jordan, *The Development of Religious Toleration in England*, vol. 1 (1932).

ROBERT KOLB

Acosta, Joseph (c. 1540–1600), Spanish

Catholic missionary, geographer, and historian. Acosta joined the Society of Jesus (1552) and then studied at the Univ. of Alcalá, during which period (1559–1567) he was ordained to the priesthood. In 1571, after short teaching engagements at Ocaña and Plasencia, Acosta left for Lima, Peru. He traveled widely throughout Peru while performing other duties, first as professor of theology and later as provincial (1576–1581). He participated in the third council of Lima (1582) and wrote the

Spanish text of three catechisms that were translated into indigenous languages. After returning to Spain (1587), he published the works that have made him a figure of interest for a wide array of modern scholars. Chief among these works is his *Historia natural y moral de las Indias* (1590).

———

J. de Acosta, *Historia natural y moral de las Indias* (1962); C. M. Burgaleta, *José de Acosta, S.J. (1540–1600): His Life and Thought* (1999).

RADY ROLDÁN-FIGUEROA

Acts of Supremacy These two parlia-

mentary acts established the monarch as head of the Church of England. The Supremacy of the Crown Act (1534) designated Henry VIII and his successors "the only supreme head of the Church of England" and established the English church independent of the papacy. Mary repealed the Act in 1554, and Elizabeth I subsequently restored the legislation in a revised form. In the first act of her reign, Elizabeth issued the Act of Supremacy (1559), in which she was designated "the only supreme governor of this realm, and all of her highness' dominions and countries, as well in all spiritual and ecclesiastical things as temporal." All clergy and public officials were required to take an oath of obedience to the church, and the act restored the election of bishops.

———

C. Haigh, *English Reformations: Religion, Politics, and Society under the Tudors* (1993); C. Lindberg, *The European Reformations* (1996).

ELIZABETH GERHARDT

Acts of the Martyrs This title is often

used broadly to refer to the accounts of martyrdom in the early centuries of the Christian church regardless of literary form. It is also used in a narrower, technical sense for the reports of the trial and condemnation of martyrs before Roman officials, the contents of which are principally the questions asked by the government authority and the answers by the accused, concluded by the official sentence. In this latter judicial sense, the Acts (*acta* or *gesta*) are distinguished from the narratives of the last days and deaths of martyrs, known as "Passions" (*passiones* in Latin or *martyria* in Greek and borrowed in Latin).

Two of the most important early accounts of martyrdom are contained in letters from the churches of which the martyrs were members. Both are important for the emerging theology of martyrdom. The letter form provides the framework for narratives of the trial, suffering, and execution of Christians. The *Martyrdom of Polycarp*, which describes events that probably occurred about 155/156, is a letter from the church at Smyrna, where Polycarp was bishop, to the church at Philomelium in Phrygia. It is the earliest postcanonical account of martyrdom and the first certain use of "martyr" in the Christian sense of a witness who died for the faith. Its theme is "martyrdom according to the gospel," commending the example of Polycarp, who did not volunteer for martyrdom but, when arrested and tried, maintained his faithfulness according to the pattern set by Jesus.

The *Letter of the Churches of Vienne and Lyons*, preserved by Eusebius in his *Ecclesiastical History*, describes the persecution in 177 against Christians in the Rhone valley. The letter is marked by its christological content (Christ suffers in and with his servants) and its incorporation of biblical texts and allusions into its narrative. The centerpiece of the story is the heroism of the slave girl Blandina, at whose courage and endurance through brutal tortures even pagans marveled. The work makes the distinction between confessors, who confessed their faith but were not put to death, and martyrs, whose testimony to Christ resulted in their death.

Among the important *Acta* are the *Acts of Justin and His Companions*, which survives in three recensions that show expansion in content and theological expression. Others include the *Acts of the Martyrs of Scilli* (in North Africa), the earliest surviving work of Christian Latin (c. 180), the *Acts of SS. Carpus, Papylus, and Agathonice* (in Pergamum), and the *Acts of Cyprian* of Carthage. A papyrus from Egypt preserved the text of the *Acts of Phileas*, bishop of Thmuis, martyred in 306.

A passion account in Latin, the *Passion of Perpetua and Felicitas* (Carthage, 203), is remarkable for its inclusion of the diaries of Perpetua, making her one of the few female writers in early Christianity, and of Saturus. Felicitas was a slave girl who gave birth a month early and so was able to join in the desired martyrdom at the same time with her associates. In this work and other North African accounts of martyrdom, visions are prominent.

Eusebius left an account of the *Martyrs of Palestine*, a valuable source for the persecution launched under Diocletian in the early fourth century. Martyrdom was not limited to the Roman Empire, and the *Acts of the Persian Martyrs* recounts the extensive martyrdoms under the Persian empire in the fourth and fifth centuries.

Christians wrote exhortations to martyrdom (Tertullian, *To the Martyrs*; Origen, *Exhortation to Martyrdom*; Cyprian, *To Fortunatus*), and in the fourth century preachers gave panegyrics on the martyrs. These latter stressed moral exhortation more than historical accuracy and so prepared for an increase in legendary accounts of martyrdom and the rise of hagiography.

Many of the martyr accounts were read at annual liturgical services on the anniversary of the martyr's death, celebrated as the birthday to immortality. The martyr literature expresses early Christianity's break with the pagan world but also its witness to that world. Although the Christians' willingness to die for their faith evoked scorn from some pagan observers, in others it provoked inquiry into the nature of Christianity that resulted in conversions. The acts and passions contain apologetic features but were written especially to strengthen the faithful spiritually.

T. D. Barnes, "Pre-Decian *ACTA MARTYRUM*," *JTS*, NS 19 (1968): 509–31; D. Boyarin, *Dying for God: Martyrdom and the Making of Christianity and Judaism* (1999); W. H. C. Frend, *Martyrdom and Persecution in the Early Church* (1965); H. Musurillo, *The Acts of the Christian Martyrs* (1972); R. D. Young, *In Procession before the World: Martyrdom as Public Liturgy in Early Christianity* (2001).

EVERETT FERGUSON

Acts of Uniformity These four Parliamentary acts mandated attendance at Anglican services and use of the Book of Common Prayer. The first act (1549), under Edward VI, required use of the Prayer Book and established penalties for nonconformity. The second act (1552) replaced use of the first Prayer Book with a more "reformed" edition and enforced church attendance. The third act (1559), under Elizabeth, was issued as a result of Mary's repealing of the second act. The third act required the use of a revised form of the Edwardian Book of Common Prayer, retained clerical vestments, church music, and ornaments, and imposed fines on the laity for church absences. This act was part of the Elizabethan compromise that established the Anglican Church in England. The fourth act (1662), under Charles II, occurred after the Puritan revolt. It reestablished Anglicanism and adherence to the Prayer Book.

A. G. Dickens, *The English Reformation* (2nd ed., 1989); N. L. Jones, *Faith by Statute: Par-*

liament and the Settlement of Religion 1559 (1982).

ELIZABETH GERHARDT

Addai (Addaeus), first-century missionary, probably legendary. The name is perhaps a corruption of Thaddaeus, who according to Mark 3:18 was one of the Twelve, and according to tradition was apostle to Edessa. The *Doctrine of Addai*, a Syriac work composed in the late fourth century, relates Addai's work in Edessa and his conversion of King Abgar "the Black." Eusebius (*Hist. eccl.* 1.13) relates the same story, although he calls Addai "Thaddaeus" and understands him to be one of the 70, not the 12. Eusebius also relates that Abgar and Jesus had exchanged letters. Abgar had written to request Jesus to come heal him; Jesus replied that he would send someone after his ascension. Eusebius goes on to say that, after the ascension, Addai was sent to Edessa, where he healed many, including Abgar, and proclaimed the gospel. Eusebius claims that he received this story from the archives of Edessa and that he translated them from the Syriac.

G. Phillips, *The Doctrine of Addai* (1876).
MICHAEL COMPTON

Adelard of Bath (c. 1080–c. 1150), a humanist and pioneer in the translation of Arabic mathematical works into Latin. After a seven-year study tour of Sicily, southern Italy, and the Middle East, Adelard spent his life in Bath and in the households of the Duke of Normandy and of his bishops. Adelard wrote original texts in a fine Latin style on the advantages of studying the seven liberal arts (*On the Same and the Different*) and on natural phenomena (*Questions on Nature*), demonstrating in the latter work the superiority of rational arguments over unthinking acceptance of authorities. At the same time, he translated a corpus of mathematical works from Arabic to provide the necessary training and information for astrologers and doctors. This corpus included the first translation of the full text of Euclid's *Elements* and a more easily digestible redaction of the same text that proved enormously popular and provided a paradigm for writing theological works on the same pattern (e.g., Nicolas of Amiens, *On the Art of the Catholic Faith*). He also translated the first full set of astronomical tables and a text on how to make talismans for purposes such as driving vermin out of Bath.

C. Burnett, ed., *Adelard of Bath: An English Scientist of the Early Twelfth Century* (1987); Burnett, ed., *Adelard of Bath: Conversations with His Nephew* (1998).
CHARLES BURNETT

Adiaphora and Adiaphorist Controversies   This Greek Stoic term denotes conditions that are neither virtues nor vices. Seneca and Cicero used the concept (Lat., *indifferentia*, "indifferent matters"), which medieval theologians borrowed to designate works that Christians were not bound to perform (works of supererogation). In the *Summa theologiae* (I-II, q.18, a.8 and 9), Thomas Aquinas argued that such indifferent actions are only theoretically possible.

Martin Luther's approach to the law and faith renewed discussion of this topic. For him, works neither commanded nor forbidden by God merit nothing in God's sight and are indifferent (Ger., *mitteldinge*). Christians are to serve God and neighbor in love. Questions first arose during the Wittenberg Unrest of 1521–1522 with Luther at the Wartburg Castle. Upon his return in March 1522, Luther preached against changes in liturgical practice instituted during his absence and even allowed Communion of the laity using only bread for the sake of weak consciences and good order. Philip Melanchthon argued similarly in the *Loci communes* of 1521. As late as 1528 Melanchthon's *Instruction by the Visitors* allowed Communion in one kind.

In the wake of the 1525 Peasants' War, Melanchthon excluded civil order from adiaphora and later complained about using the term to excuse lawlessness. He employed the Greek term in the 1531 Apology of the Augsburg Confession (XV, 52; cf. XXVII, 27), stating that out of love for the weak, evangelicals should obey any human regulations that could be followed without sin.

The defeat of the evangelical princes in Germany during the Schmalkald War led to the "adiaphoristic controversy" among Lutheran theologians. At the Diet of Augsburg in 1548, the victorious emperor Charles V imposed a provisional solution to the religious divisions in the empire, pending the final decision of a church council. Called the Augsburg Interim, it allowed evangelicals little more than married priests and Communion in both kinds (bread and wine) and demanded a return to pre-Reformation ceremonies.

The theologians of Electoral Saxony, led by Melanchthon, rejected this but also worked on an alternative that maintained Lutheran theology while allowing great latitude in reestablishing ceremonies considered adiaphora. This compromise, never approved by a provincial diet meeting in Leipzig but nicknamed the "Leipzig Interim" by opponents, came under harsh attack from Matthias Flacius of Croatia and other Lutheran theologians, whom Melanchthon called "Gnesio-Lutherans" (genuine Lutherans). They argued that during persecution, when compromise with anti-Christian forces was demanded, even adiaphora was no longer adiaphora. Pastoral concerns motivated all parties. Defenders of Melanchthon's position, called Philippists, wanted to avoid harsher measures by the emperor. Gnesio-Lutherans wanted to protect believers from the offense resulting from a rollback of external reforms tied to confession of faith. Although the political causes of this dispute effectively ended with the 1555 Peace of Augsburg, theologians continued debating the question of adiaphora and related topics. Not until 1580, with the publication of *The Book of Concord*, did Lutherans agree (in the Formula of Concord, X) that in times of persecution even adiaphora become uncompromising matters of confession.

Controversies also arose in England between 1550 and 1573. Already under Edward VI, John Hooper, nominated to be bishop of Gloucester, at first balked at having to wear a surplice. With the Elizabethan settlement of 1559, the "Vestiarian controversy" again flared up in which some clergy, returning from exile after the Marian persecutions and influenced by John Knox, refused to wear what they termed "popish" garments. Under pressure from both Queen Elizabeth and Matthew Parker, archbishop of Canterbury, most clergy conformed. Exceptions included Miles Coverdale and John Foxe. During similar dissent a year later in London, portions of a tract by Flacius were published. One of the first "Puritan" tracts also appeared. The controversy focused more on obedience to civil authorities in religious matters than on adiaphora. An opinion from Heinrich Bullinger rejecting the radicals' arguments helped quiet matters down. In 1572 after attempts to reform the Book of Common Prayer had failed, the "Admonition controversy" erupted, sparked by the publication of a pamphlet attacking a variety of practices (including episcopal polity) in the Church of England, *Admonition to Parliament*. A second *Admonition*, perhaps written by Thomas Cartwright, followed. As a result, Richard Hooker included a defense of episcopal polity in his well-known *Ecclesiastical Polity*.

D. J. McGinn, *The Admonition Controversy* (1949); W. Rosin and R. D. Preus, eds., *A Contemporary Look at the Formula of Concord* (1978); B. J. Verkamp, *The Indifferent Mean: Adiaphorism in the English Reformation to 1554* (1977).

TIMOTHY J. WENGERT

Admonition Controversy (1572–1573)

Originated with Puritan manifestos appealing to Parliament to eradicate the episcopal structure of the English church. Written by John Field and Thomas Wilcox, the First Admonition called for a radical reorganization of the church after a Reformed model and the enforcement of stricter church discipline. As a result of the first manifesto, its reformist authors were banished to Newgate Prison on July 7, 1572. The controversy continued, fueled by the letters of continental reformers. Dubiously attributed to Thomas Cartwright, the Second Admonition to Parliament appeared in 1573. The treatise set forth a Presbyterian form of church government and sought to weaken Elizabeth's hold on ecclesiastical matters. Elizabeth suppressed the Second Admonition and its supporting letters by a royal proclamation issued June 11, 1573.

P. Lake, *Anglicans and Puritans: Presbyterianism and English Conformist Thought from Whitgift to Hooker* (1988); D. J. McGinn, *Admonition Controversy* (1949).

ELIZABETH GERHARDT

Adoptionism

A heresy that surfaced in the eighth century in central Spain. Its advocates taught the double sonship of Christ, that is, as divine he was the Son of God, but as human he was adopted by God as his Son. The teaching was a rehashing of the Christology taught in the patristic era by Theodore of Mopsuestia and Nestorius, whose views were condemned as heresy in the early church. The main apologist for adoptionism in Spain was Elipandus, archbishop of Toledo, who attempted to correct the Christology of his detractors regarding the incarnation. The explanation of the archbishop proved to be so unsatisfactory that the matter was referred to Pope Adrian I, who condemned the terminology of "adopted son" because it was deemed to be too Nestorian. Elipandus responded by rejecting the opinion of the pope and instead aligned himself with a sympathizer, Felix, the bishop of Urgel. Since Felix's diocese was in the Carolingian Empire it provoked the intervention of Charlemagne, who was loyal to the papacy. A provincial council was convened by Charlemagne in Frankfurt in 794 with the full approval of the pope to settle the dispute once and for all. The orthodox position (Chalcedonian) was defended by the renowned theologian Alcuin of York, personal teacher of the emperor, while the adoptionists were given the opportunity to present their position. Adoptionism was condemned as heretical, the adoptionists were allowed to return to Spain, but the teaching did not spread any further. Elipandus, however, remained true to his own position while at the same time not breaking with the pope or openly defying the decision of the council.

J. C. Cavadini, *The Last Christology of the West: Adoptionism in Spain and Gaul, 785–820* (1993); J. F. Rivera, *El Adopcionismo en España (s. VIII): Historia y Doctrina* (1980).
                                    ALBERTO FERREIRO

Adrian VI (1459–1523), Dutch cardinal and theologian, elected pope in 1522, last non-Italian pontiff until 1978. Adrian succeeded Leo X. The scholarly and ascetic antithesis of his immediate predecessors, Adrian strove valiantly, though unsuccessfully, to overcome a legacy of spiritual and financial bankruptcy. Educated by the reform-minded Brethren of the Common Life, Adrian was tutor to the future Charles V as well as a popular professor of theology at Louvain, friend of Erasmus yet grand inquisitor for Spain. As pope, Adrian candidly acknowledged curial responsibility for ecclesiastical corruption but rejected Luther's reform. He rallied Europe against Islam but barely kept Christian princes from warring on each other. His attempts to reform the papal court's extravagance were thwarted by recalcitrant clerics and caricatured by humanists as a barbaric contempt for the arts.

E. Duffy, *Saints and Sinners: A History of the Popes* (1997); R. P. McBrien, *Lives of the Popes* (1997).
                                    PETER J. SCAGNELLI

Advertisements, Book of (1566) A list of thirty-nine regulations on liturgical conduct issued by Archbishop Parker of Canterbury. The Advertisements establish minimal standards for clergy, including use of the surplice in place of the traditional vestments. Elizabeth did not adopt the provisions and thereby weakened their authority.

P. Hughes, *The Reformation in England* (1952).
                                    ELIZABETH GERHARDT

Advowson *see* Patron and Patronage Right

Aetius of Antioch (c. 313–c. 365/367), bishop and a leader in the neo-Arian Anomoean party. Born perhaps in Cilicia, Aetius lived mostly in Antioch. He was ordained a deacon by the Arian Leontius of Antioch (c. 345) and later consecrated a bishop in the rule of Julian the Apostate. Aetius was educated by Arian leaders and became a leader himself of the neo-Arian "radical" Anomoean party (*anomoios* = dissimilar; the Father and the Son are dissimilar in essence). His *Syntagmation*, a short work of a preface and 36 articles, is preserved by Epiphanius (*Pan.* 76.11; see also 76.14–54). He argued that God did not generate the Son and was distinct from the Son, with the Son subordinate to God. He and his views were condemned at the Councils of Ancyra (358) and Constantinople (360).

M. R. Barnes and D. H. Williams, *Arianism after Arius* (1993); R. P. C. Hanson, *The Search for the Christian Doctrine of God* (1988), 598–611; T. A. Kopecek, *A History of Neo-Arianism*, vol. 1 (1979); J. T. Lienhard, "The Epistle of the Synod of Ancyra, 358: A Reconsideration," in *Arianism: Historical and Theological Reassessments*, ed. R. C. Gregg (1985), 313–19; L. R. Wickham, "Aetius and the Doctrine of Divine Ingeneracy," StPatr 11, no. 2 (1972): 259–63; L. R. Wickham, "The *Syntagmation* of Aetius the Anomoean," *JTS* 19 (1968): 532–69.
                                    DAVID M. SCHOLER

Affair of the Placards In the early morning of October 17, 1534, proponents of religious reform hung placards (broadsheets) in Paris and other cities in northern France. Written by Antoine Marcourt, a French refugee pastor, printed in Switzerland, and smuggled into France, these broadsheets denounced in violent language the "horrible, gross, and insupportable abuse of the popish mass." This assault on Catholicism infuriated Parisians, and Francis I, fearful of the threat that reform enthusiasts posed to the civic order, immediately stepped up arrests and executions of suspected Protestants. In the wake of persecution, many of those hoping for religious reform fled France for safety abroad, including John Calvin. Although Francis later offered pardon for exiles provided they abjured their "error," the government's policy had passed from tolerating moderate religious reform to prosecuting religious heterodoxy.

G. Berthoud, *Antoine Marcourt* (1973); D. R. Kelley, *The Beginning of Ideology: Consciousness and Society in the French Reformation* (1981).

SCOTT M. MARR

Agnes (third or fourth cent.), virgin and martyr. The daughter of a noble Roman family, she was executed at the age of twelve or thirteen, possibly during the persecution of Decius or of Diocletian. References to Agnes by Ambrose, Pope Damasus, Prudentius, and in the hymn *Agnes beatae virginis* are contradictory. The fifth-century *Acts of Martyrdom of St. Agnes* attempts to harmonize the details of her life. Agnes is presented in later writing as a beautiful and wealthy young woman whose vow of virginity leads her frustrated suitors to denounce her to the local governor as a Christian. Sent to a brothel where she is miraculously protected, the steadfast Agnes is finally beheaded.

The story of Agnes embodies the popular theme of a woman incurring the wrath of secular authorities because of her rejection of marriage, but it develops the idea further. Agnes is presented as rejecting her suitors so she can be faithful to her marriage promises to Christ, who miraculously ensures that her virginity remains intact until the moment of consummation at the time of her martyrdom.

G. Márkus, ed., *The Radical Tradition: Revolutionary Saints in the Battle for Justice and Human Rights* (1993); J. Schroeder, "Virgin and Martyr: Divine Protection from Sexual Assault in the *Peristephanon* of Prudentius," in *Miracles in Jewish and Christian Antiquity: Imagining Truth* (1999).

BARBARA J. MACHAFFIE

Agobard of Lyon (c. 769–840), theologian and bishop, probably of Spanish origin. Agobard was educated at the court of Charlemagne's son Louis ("the Pious") in Aquitania. In 814, when Louis became emperor, Agobard was appointed chorepiscopus at the side of Archbishop Leidrade at Lyon and in 816 became the latter's successor. Already his early activities there showed him to be an ardent advocate of orthodoxy. Against the adoptionist bishop Felix of Urgel, who was then imprisoned at Lyon, he was engaged in defending the Trinitarian dogma. Through his lifelong struggle against what he considered to be misbelief and super-

stition, he aimed at creating a true Christian identity. Agobard was a veritable acolyte of the "Reform" program, yet he lacked the necessary political influence and intellectual flexibility. The former intimate of Louis soon became one of his harshest critics. The quarrels that mark Agobard's episcopate started at the latest in 821 (Attigny) when Agobard claimed in vain for the restitution of ecclesiastical property. He supported the revolt of Louis's sons in 833 and was therefore deposed in 835. In 839 he was restored as archbishop and remained, though rather isolated, in duty at Lyon until his death. Agobard is known for his attempt to use anti-Jewish arguments in his conflict with the court, but his impact on the regulation of Jewish matters in the Carolingian society remained, all in all, rather weak. Since only one complete manuscript of his works has survived, one should conclude that his influence remained generally limited, but it is more his modern awareness of issues such as rationality versus mythology or his anti-Jewish agitation that made him one of the most quoted names among ninth-century theologians.

L. van Acker, ed., *Agobardi Lugdunensis opera omnia*, in CCCM 52 (1981); E. Boshof, *Erzbischof Agobard von Lyon: Leben und Werk* (1969); J. Cohen, *Living Letters of the Law: Ideas of the Jew in Medieval Christianity* (1999), 123–45; J. Heil, "Agobard, Amulo, das Kirchengut und die Juden von Lyon," *Francia* 25, no. 1 (1998): 39–76.

JOHANNES HEIL

Agrapha The term refers to "unwritten" sayings of Jesus, that is, sayings (*logia*) not recorded in the canonical Gospels. This term is also used to describe variant sayings in the manuscripts of the canonical Gospels: the longer ending of Mark contains an *agraphon*, as does the Freer Logion after Mark 16:14. There are thus *agrapha* in the New Testament (e.g., Acts 20:35), but usually the term denotes extracanonical sayings by Jesus as well as stories about him.

Outside the New Testament, *agrapha* appear in various early Christian writings, especially in citations of works no longer extant (*Gospel of the Nazoreans*, *Gospel of the Ebionites*, *Gospel of the Hebrews*, *Gospel of the Egyptians*). The most famous collection now is the Coptic *Gospel of Thomas*, which contains many otherwise unknown sayings of Jesus, along with many that are similar if not identical to canonical sayings.

While the authenticity of *agrapha* must be decided on a case-by-case basis, the *agrapha* themselves are especially valuable for understanding the historical situation of the documents in which they appear.

A. Resch, *Agrapha: Aussercanonische Schriftfragmente* (1906); W. Stroker, *Extracanonical Sayings of Jesus* (1989).

MICHAEL COMPTON

Agricola, John (1492?–1566), German Lutheran reformer. A native of Eisleben, Agricola studied medicine in Leipzig before going to Wittenberg, where he became the student and friend of Martin Luther. In Wittenberg he served as a catechist, preacher, and biblical lecturer until 1525. He spent the next decade in Eisleben as a preacher and the rector of the new Latin school. Here he wrote catechetical and exegetical works as well as a collection of German proverbs.

Agricola is perhaps known best for his role in the antinomian controversy. His first "war of words" over the place of the law in repentance was with Philip Melanchthon. Some ten years later, after returning to Wittenberg, Agricola opposed Luther himself. Agricola argued for a complete antithesis between law and gospel and eventually regarded any preaching of the law as unevangelical. In 1540 the Brandenburg elector appointed him court preacher and superintendent in Berlin. Agricola collaborated on the Augsburg Interim (1548) but later attacked it, siding with the Gnesio-Lutherans over the Philippists.

G. Olms, *Johann Agricola von Eisleben: Ein Beitrag zur Reformationsgeschichte* (1881); T. J. Wengert, *Law and Gospel: Philip Melanchthon's Debate with John Agricola of Eisleben over Potenitentia* (1997).

MARY ELIZABETH ANDERSON

Agricola, Mikael (1507–1557), reformer and father of Finnish literature. Agricola led the implementation of the Reformation in and the cultivation of the national identity of the not yet independent Finland. From a peasant family, the humanist reformer and educator was schooled in Viipuri and ordained in 1531 before his studies in Wittenberg with Luther and Melanchthon (1536–39). With a master's degree in theology and humanist studies, he laid the foundation for the written Finnish language and for elementary education with his ABC book (containing two catechisms). He provided the first written religious sources in Finnish with his catechism (1543), translation of the New Testament (1548), and his original prayer book (1544, containing sections on the calendar, astronomy, theology, and hygiene). He translated parts of the Old Testament and wrote the first handbook for the Finnish Mass (1549), drawing on the work of the Swedish Reformer Olaus Petri. Before becoming the bishop of Turku in 1554, he served as Bishop Martin Skytte's secretary, as the Swedish king's peace negotiator with Russia, and as the principal of the cathedral school of Turku (1539–1548).

T. Clark, *Mikael Agricola and His ABC-kiria* (1992); J. Gummerus, *Michael Agricola, der Reformator Finnlands: Sein Leben und sein Werk* (1941); S. Heininen, *Mikael Agricola raamatunsuomentajana* (1999).

KIRSI STJERNA

Aix-la-Chappelle   *see* Aachen

Alaric (c. 370–410), Visigothic chieftain. In 394 Alaric revolted against the Eastern emperor Theodosius (379–395), and his Goths devastated Thrace and Greece. He invaded Italy in 401, but after being defeated by the general Stilicho, he withdrew to Greece. After the Western emperor Honorius (395–423) refused to pay him for past services, Alaric invaded Italy again in 408 and besieged Rome. The siege was alternately lifted and renewed as Honorius, safely lodged in Ravenna, dithered and refused to name Alaric "Master of Soldiers." In 409, Alaric allowed the Senate to name a new emperor, Priscus Attalus, who converted to Arianism (the Gothic form of Christianity) and granted Alaric his desired rank. On August 24, 410, Alaric seized Rome. The ensuing sack lasted only three days, and the churches were generally left untouched. The damage was more psychological than material. After eight hundred years, Rome had fallen; it was no longer *Roma Invicta* ("Unconquered Rome"). Subsequently, Alaric traveled south, hoping to cross to Sicily. After the Gothic fleet was wrecked, Alaric turned back north. On this journey he became ill and died. He reportedly was buried in the bed of the Busento River after the stream had been diverted. His sack of Rome went down in history as the beginning of the end of the western Roman Empire.

M. Brion, *Alaric the Goth* (1932).

RALPH W. MATHISEN

Albert of Brandenburg (1490–1545), cardinal and archbishop of Mainz and Magdeburg. Albert, brother of Joachim I, the Elector of Brandenburg, received a humanist education. In 1515 Pope Leo X granted Albert permission to market an indulgence in his territories in order to discharge his debt to the Vatican for the papal dispensation for his ecclesiastical promotion. Johann Tetzel handled the sale of the indulgence. Martin Luther reacted with a letter to Albert dated October 31, 1517, that included ninety-five theses against the abuse of indulgences. Albert did not allow a discussion of the theses but sent them to Rome, where a heresy trial against Luther was initiated. A typical representative of the Renaissance church, Albert sought to develop in Halle a monastic foundation, a large relic collection, and a new university. He took a mediating position in the church politics of the 1520s and 1530s. In spite of this he saw in Luther, who repeatedly attacked him, a particular enemy. In 1540, under the pressure of the Reformation movement, Albert relinquished the archbishopric of Magdeburg. He withdrew to Mainz, where he later died.

F. Schrader, "Kardinal Albrecht von Brandenburg im Spannungsfeld zwischen Alter und Neuer Kirche," in *Von Konstanz nach Trient*, ed. R. Bäumer (1972).

MARTIN TREU

Albert of Prussia (1490–1568), reformer of Prussia. Albert, cousin of Cardinal Albert of Brandenburg, was from an early age designated for the clerical estate. From 1511 Albert, as Grand Master of the Teutonic Order, introduced the Reformation into Prussia on Luther's advice. In 1525 in Krakow, Albert renounced his title and as a duke received the Order's territory as a fiefdom from the Polish king. Albert directed the subsequent secularization with a firm hand, but his success was due largely to the fact that the Order's territory was not a part of the German Empire. In 1526, Albert married a daughter of the king of Denmark, a move that fostered the development of the Reformation in both areas. In 1540 the first church order for Prussia appeared, showing signs of Albert's strong influence. A pious Lutheran, Albert authored prayers and hymns. He founded the Univ. of Königsberg (today, Kaliningrad) in 1545, the second Protestant educational institution, after the Univ. of Marburg. It developed into a strong Lutheran center of education and faith in Eastern Europe. Albert was a personal friend of Luther and the other Wittenberg Reformers.

W. Hubatsch, "Albert of Brandenburg-Ansbach, Grand Master of the Order of the Teutonic Knights and Duke in Prussia, 1490–1568," *Studies in Medieval and Modern German History* (1985); P. Tschackert, *Herzog Albrecht als reformatorische Persönlichkeit* (1894).

MARTIN TREU

Albert the Great (c. 1201–1280), German theologian, philosopher, scientist, and churchman. Born to the knightly family "de Lauingen," plausibly in Lauingen (Bavarian-Swabian Danube), Albert studied at Padua, where he joined the Dominicans in the 1220s. After his initial theological formation at Cologne, he served as conventual lector from the 1230s at Hildesheim, Freiberg (Saxony), Regensburg, and Strasbourg. In the early 1240s he was sent to Paris, becoming master of theology in 1245. Soon after his Parisian regency (1245–1248), Albert began his extracurricular project of paraphrases (at points corrective and complementary) for the works of Aristotle. His goal was a comprehensive account of natural knowledge utilizing Neoplatonic and Arabic sources and his own deliberate observations of the natural and cultural worlds.

In its scope, critical methodology, and detail, his learning was legendary but not without critics, including Dominicans, of its secularity. In May 1248 Albert joined in the condemnation of the Talmud at Paris before returning to Cologne (1248–1254) as founding lector of the Dominican *studium generale* there. Albert's role (in at least twenty cases) as mediator between conflicting parties, notably between ruling prelates and citizenry, began during this period.

Also notable was Albert's influence on Thomas Aquinas, who was among Albert's students in Cologne (alongside Ulrich of Strasbourg). Thomas began his Dominican formation at Paris c. 1245. As academic assistant (*baccalaureus*) to Albert, Thomas transcribed Albert's courses on the *Corpus Dionysiacum* and the *Nicomachean Ethics* of Aristotle.

Even as provincial of the German Dominicans (1254–1257), Albert continued his project of using his own words to make the full range of natural learning intelligible to the West. At the General Chapter of Valenciennes in 1259, Albert helped shape the Dominican statutes for a form of religious observance marked by academic study. He kept at academic and field work while acting as bishop of Regensburg (1260–1262), as a familiar guest of the papal curia at Viterbo and Orvieto (1261–1263), and as general preacher for the Crusades (1263–1264). Despite episcopal status, "dominus Albertus" returned to Dominican community and teaching in the prioral schools, first at Würzburg, briefly at Strasbourg, and, for the final ten years of his life, in Cologne, where he also served as chief author of a theological *summa*. Albert lectured on all four Gospels and at least nine books of the Old Testament.

While providing inspiration for the even more Neoplatonic (Proclus) "German Albert School" of the thirteenth and fourteenth centuries and the "Albertinism" of the fifteenth, Albert's theological legacy is his methodological insistence upon a form of academic theology that provides for the relative autonomy and importance of nontheological disciplines and non-Christian sources. Known to near contemporaries as *Albertus magnus, doctor universalis*, and *doctor expertus*, Albert was beatified in 1622 and declared a saint and doctor of the church in 1931.

_____

Opera omnia, B. Geyer et al. (1951 sqq.); Albertus-Magnus-Institut, ed., *Lectio Albertina* (1999); R. Imbach and C. Flüeler, eds., *Albert der Grosse und die deutsche Dominikanerschule— philosophische Perspektiven* (1985); G. Meyer and A. Zimmermann, eds., *Albertus Magnus, Doctor universalis: 1280/1980* (1980); W. Senner, ed., *Albertus Magnus* (2001); S. Tugwell, ed., *Albert and Thomas: Selected Writings* (1988); J. A. Weisheipl, ed., *Albertus Magnus and the Sciences* (1980); A. Zimmermann and G. Vuillemin-Diem, eds., *Albert der Grosse. Seine Zeit, sein Werk, seine Wirkung* (1981).

RICHARD SCHENK, OP

Albigensies *see* Cathars

Alcántara, Pedro de (1499–1562), Spanish Franciscan reformer, mystic, and saint of the Roman Catholic Church. He studied philosophy and canon law at the Univ. of Salamanca and joined the Friars Minor Conventual in 1515. After 1517, he joined the Observant Friars Minor. He was ordained a priest in 1524. From 1538 to 1541 he was provincial of the San Gabriel chapter of the observants of Santiago. He took an important role in religious reforms within the Observant Friars Minor in Portugal during his stay there beginning in 1541. By 1554, however, tensions had developed within the Observant Friars Minor around his reforms,

leading to his eventual return to the conventuals. After his election in 1559 as commissary general of the reformed conventuals of Spain, he proceeded to organize the new province of San José. Alcántara's spiritual testament was his *Tratado de la oración y meditación* (1556–1557). He was beatified by Gregory XV on April 18, 1622, and canonized by Clement IX on April 28, 1669.

_____

A. B. Manzano, *San Pedro de Alcántara (1499–1562): Estudio documentado y crítico de su vida*, 2nd ed. (1995); E. R. Romero, *Un extremeño universal: San Pedro de Alcántara* (1999).

RADY ROLDÁN-FIGUEROA

Alcuin (c. 735–804), Anglo-Saxon cleric and master of the cathedral school at York. In the 780s he joined an international team of intellectuals and reformers drawn to the court of Charlemagne, king of the Franks (768–814). Alcuin advised the king and tutored several of his children. In 796, he left the court to serve as abbot of the prestigious monastery of St. Martin in Tours. Alcuin's impact on European culture was wide ranging. Many of his pupils became reformers and political and religious leaders. He wrote or adapted widely used pedagogical works on the liberal arts, corrected the text of the Vulgate, and commented on several biblical books. He helped fashion Carolingian religious policy on Christology, conversion, and baptism. His hundreds of letters to friends, disciples, and members of the royal family are an invaluable source for the history of his times. His many poems, including the important metrical epitaph of Pope Hadrian (772–795), a long celebration of the bishops, kings, and saints of York, his lament on the sacking of Lindisfarne by Vikings, and numerous commemorative pieces are historically important and testify to the public utility of written culture in the Carolingian world.

_____

S. Allott, trans., *Alcuin of York, c. A.D. 732 to 804: His Life and Letters* (1974); D. A. Bullough, *Alcuin: Achievement and Reputation* (2004).

JOHN J. CONTRENI

Aleandro, Girolamo (1480–1542), Italian humanist, papal envoy and cardinal, and opponent of Luther. Erasmus encouraged Aleandro to teach in Paris, where he became rector of the university. Aleandro was one of two papal envoys commissioned by Pope Leo X to publish and enforce *Exsurge Domine* against Luther. At the Diet of Worms he denounced Luther and wanted him condemned without trial. He ordered Luther's books burned throughout Europe. In 1524 he was appointed archbishop of Brindisi, and in 1538 he was made a cardinal; he died shortly thereafter.

C. Lindberg, *The European Reformations* (1996); H. Oberman, *Luther: Man between God and the Devil* (1989).

ELIZABETH GERHARDT

Alexander VI (1431–1503), elected pope in 1492. Created cardinal at twenty-five by his uncle, Pope Callistus III, father of Cesare and Lucretia Borgia and at least six other children by several mistresses, ruthless and vindictive in the pursuit of personal power and family fortune, Alexander VI is universally considered the most deplorable pope in history. Alexander drew the line of demarcation between Spain and Portugal for the exploration of the New World, but his true program lay closer to home. Shifting alliances with Naples, France, and the Turkish sultan, he generated a labyrinth of political intrigue, often violent, whose ultimate goal was the Borgia family's supremacy throughout Italy. The Dominican Savanarola challenged Alexander to personal and ecclesial reform but was excommunicated and, eventually, executed. In ironic contrast to the spiritual decay of his pontificate, Alexander patronized great artists, whose legacy of beauty adorns Rome still. Though his death was blamed on malaria, Alexander, alleged to have poisoned several enemies, may have mistakenly ingested at a dinner a poison intended, perhaps by himself, for his cardinal host.

E. Duffy, *Saints and Sinners: A History of the Popes* (1997); R. P. McBrien, *Lives of the Popes* (1997).

PETER J. SCAGNELLI

Alexander of Alexandria (d. 328), bishop of Alexandria, early opponent of Arius. Alexander became bishop of Alexandria in 313, succeeding the martyr Peter and his short-lived successor Achillas. He governed the church in Egypt during the Roman Empire's transition from pagan to Christian, and he supervised the construction of several new churches. He is remembered today chiefly for his opposition to the rigorist bishop Melitius and the Alexandrian presbyter Arius. Athana-

sius, Alexander's secretary and successor, may have helped write his two surviving official letters. Athanasius portrays Alexander's theology as identical with his own, but prior to the breach with Arius in 318 the irenic Alexander was not so easily classified. After the breach he excommunicated Arius and denounced his theology bitterly. As earlier in the case of Melitius, what was at issue was partly a matter of theology and partly a power struggle within the Alexandrian church. Once beyond the borders of Egypt, however, theology came to the fore, and this controversy was a major factor in Constantine's decision to call the first ecumenical council at Nicaea in 325. Alexander and Athanasius were prominent at the council, which condemned both Arius and Melitius. Thereafter Alexander resisted all efforts at reconciliation.

CPG (1974–) 2.2000–2021; *ANF* (1868–73) 6.291–302; J. Quasten, *Patrology*, vol. 3 (1963), 13–19; R. P. C. Hanson, *The Search for the Christian Doctrine of God* (1988), 129–78.

RICHARD PAUL VAGGIONE, OHC

Alexander of Hales (c. 1185–1245), English friar minor, the first Franciscan professor of theology at the Univ. of Paris, known by the title Irrefutable Doctor. Alexander was born in Hales, Shropshire, in England and studied at the Univ. of Paris, completing his arts education sometime before 1210. He then took up the study of theology and became a regent master around the year 1220. He was one of the first to offer lectures on the *Sentences* of Peter Lombard, for which he was criticized by Roger Bacon. In 1236 he entered the Franciscan order, a move which secured a university chair for the Franciscans. Alexander was active in the internal affairs of the Franciscan order and coauthored an exposition of the Rule of St. Francis. In the political sphere, he was involved in peace negotiations between England and France. He played an important role in the affairs of the church, helping to draft *Parens scientiarum*, a document issued by Pope Gregory IX which helped to reorganize the Univ. of Paris. He also took part in the first Council of Lyon (1244–1245).

Alexander was an influential teacher, and his scholarship may well be seen as a major factor in opening the golden age of scholasticism. While Alexander did not hesitate to quote freely from the writings of Aristotle, his work belongs to a period when Aristotelian philosophy had not yet become a serious dialogue partner in the development of theology. Yet his work helped the movement to a more systematic use of Aristotelian philosophy in theology. Alexander's own theology was Neoplatonic in tone, drawing upon the works of Augustine, Pseudo-Dionysius, and Boethius. His influence on younger Franciscan theologians also helps to explain the Neoplatonic strain in later Franciscan theology. His works include a *Gloss on the Four Books of the Sentences, Disputed Questions "Before He Was a Friar," Quodlibetal Questions, Disputed Questions "After He Became a Friar,"* and a massive *Summa of Theology.* The authorship of the *Summa* has been particularly problematic. It is best seen as a collaborative work of the early Franciscans under the guidance of Alexander.

P. Boehner, "The System of Metaphysics of Alexander of Hales," *Franciscan Studies* 5 (1945): 366–414; V. Doucet, "The History of the Problem of the Authenticity of the Summa," *Franciscan Studies* 7 (1947): 26–41, 274–312; I. Herscher, "A Bibliography of Alexander of Hales," *Franciscan Studies* 5 (1945): 434–54; K. Osborne, ed., *The History of Franciscan Theology* (1994), 1–38; W. Principe, *Alexander of Hales' Theology of the Hypostatic Union* (1967).
                                ZACHARY HAYES, OFM

Alexandria, Library of   Ptolemy I Soter (323–283 BCE), founder of the dynasty that ruled Egypt from the death of Alexander the Great in 323 BCE until the Roman conquest in 28 BCE, gathered a collection of books on the Platonic ideal of the philosopher-king and so began the library at Alexandria. The first literary evidence of a library at Alexandria is found in the *Letter of Aristeas,* which records the legendary account of the Septuagint translation of the Hebrew Old Testament by seventy-two Jewish scholars brought to Alexandria by Ptolemy II.

The library was probably located near the Museum, a place of culture and learning dedicated to the Muses. It housed professional copyists, and professional librarians managed and catalogued the collection, which has been estimated at 700,000 volumes. Supposedly Ptolemy II purchased the library that had belonged to Aristotle. Ptolemy III Euergetes is said to have borrowed copies of Aeschylus, Sophocles, and Euripides from Athens and never returned them, forfeiting a substantial deposit.

The library's destruction is shrouded in mystery. Plutarch records that it was burned as Julius Caesar attacked Pompey in the harbor of Alexandria. Another legend attributes its extinction to Theophilus of Alexandria, who destroyed the Serapeum and the neighboring library out of antipagan fervor. Yet another legend places its destruction during the Muslim period at the order of Caliph Omar of Damascus, since the Qur'an had rendered its existence superfluous. Indeed, there may have been several libraries in Alexandria, destroyed at different times. In the Christian era the extensive personal library of Origen found its way from Alexandria to Caesarea, where Eusebius used the collection in writing his *Ecclesiastical History.*

L. Canfora, *The Vanished Library* (1989); E. D. Johnson and M. H. Harris, *History of Libraries in the Western World* (1976).
                         KENNETH B. STEINHAUSER

Alexandrian Christianity   When Alexander the Great conquered Egypt in 332 BCE, he founded the Mediterranean city he named after himself. A Greek dynasty, the Ptolemies, ruled Egypt until the Roman conquest, and they shaped Alexandria into a commercial and cultural powerhouse that had ties to the Mediterranean, the Near East, and Africa on the Nile. In the third century BCE came Palestinian Jews, fleeing the poverty of their homeland. Eventually Jews made up almost a third of the city's population.

The earliest Christian missionaries often followed the path of the Jewish Diaspora, and in the first century now unknown ones went to Alexandria. The apostle Paul's fellow missionary Apollos was an Alexandrian Jew.

Tradition claims that the evangelist Mark founded the Alexandrian community, but scholars have no real knowledge of the city's Christians until the late second century when a Sicilian named Pantaenus founded the catechetical school there. Reflecting the cosmopolitan nature of their city, Christian scholars accepted the learned traditions of both Greeks and Jews, especially the Jewish scholar Philo (d. c. 50 CE), who accepted Greek learning in his often allegorical exposition of the Scriptures. When it came to Greek culture, the Alexandrian Christians were generally more open-minded than their coreligionists, who often feared it.

From Alexandria came a succession of great scholars: Clement of Alexandria (c. 150–c. 220) demonstrated the value of learning from Greek culture; Origen (c. 185–254) created Christian biblical scholarship in many forms (textual criticism, exegesis); Athanasius (c. 296–373) played a decisive role in establishing the Christian doctrine of the Trinity; Cyril of Alexandria (c. 378–444) greatly influenced ancient Christology. From Alexandria also came thinkers who fell outside the Christian mainstream, such as several prominent Gnostics who could not reconcile themselves to the Christians' acceptance of the Hebrew Bible but who still promoted some important theological concepts.

The patriarch (bishop) of Alexandria dominated Egyptian Christianity and played a role in both ecclesiastical and secular politics. Fifth-century patriarchs ruled like tyrants, and three successive patriarchs (Theophilus, Cyril, Dioscorus) engineered the deposition of three bishops of the rival see of Constantinople (John Chrysostom in 403, Nestorius in 431, Flavian in 449). After the ecumenical council of Chalcedon (451), a combination of opponents drove Dioscorus from office in a dispute over the divine and human natures of Christ. His followers, called Monophysites (after their belief in Christ's one nature), established their own church, survived Byzantine persecution, and still exist in Egypt today as the Oriental Orthodox.

The Arab conquest of 642 put an end to the greatness of Alexandrian Christianity.

C. W. Griggs, *Early Egyptian Christianity from Its Origins to 451 C.E.* (1990); C. Haas, *Alexandria in Late Antiquity* (1997); B. Pearson and J. Goehring, eds., *The Roots of Egyptian Christianity* (1986).

JOSEPH F. KELLY

Al-Farabi, Abu Nasr (c. 870–950), known as the "Second Philosopher" among the Arabs, since he followed so faithfully the teaching of the "First Philosopher," Aristotle. Of Turkish origin, he established the Arabic tradition of writing detailed commentaries on the works of Aristotle, which culminated in the work of Averroes. His *Classification of the Sciences* was important for establishing the curriculum of studies in Arabic and (through its Latin translations) Western schools and universities. His *Book on Music* is the most wide-ranging text on musical theory and practice in medieval Arabic. He was particularly interested in ethics. His greatest work is his *On the Perfect State*, which sets out the structure of the human society that he believes is realizable in an Islamic state. He takes into account Plato's *Republic* but does not advocate a perfect state under a philosopher king. He rather envisages an elite of men who have "true vision," and believes in human freedom and responsibility, matched by divine justice. He led an ascetic life in Baghdad before joining, in his old age, the court of Sayf al-Dawla in Aleppo, where he died.

Abu Nasr al-Farabi, *On the Perfect State,* ed. R. Walzer (1985); F. W. Zimmerman, trans. and comm., *Al-Farabi's Commentary and Short Treatise on Aristotle's De Interpretatione* (1981).

CHARLES BURNETT

Al-Kindi, Ya'qub ibn Ishaq (c. 800–870), known as the "Philosopher of the Arabs," was the first Muslim philosopher to attempt to integrate Greek philosophy into Islam. The caliph of Baghdad, al-Ma'mun (813–833), put him in charge of the translation activity in the *Bayt al-Hikma* ("House of Wisdom") that he had founded. Under al-Kindi's direction several Christian philosophers translated works of Aristotle and certain texts by the neo-Platonists Plotinus and Proclus that eventually became known as the *Theology of Aristotle* and the *Book of the Pure Good*, respectively. This mixture of Peripatetic and Neoplatonic philosophy became a hallmark of Arabic *falsafa* and was passed on to the West via translations made from Arabic into Latin in Toledo in the later twelfth century. Al-Kindi himself used this material (and a wide range of other texts, including the Qur'an) to write two kinds of texts: the *risala* (literally, "letter"), or short treatise addressing particular philosophical or scientific questions; and more systematic treatises, of which the surviving ones deal with metaphysics ("On First Philosophy"), astrology, and medicine. Over 250 titles are listed in medieval bibliographies, but only a handful of works survive, most of them in a single manuscript in Istanbul (Aya Sofya 4832).

R. Rashed, J. Jolivet et al., eds., *Oeuvres philosophiques et scientifiques d'al-Kindi,* 5 vols. (1996–); P. Travaglia, *Magic, Causality, and Intentionality: The Doctrine of Rays in al-Kindi* (1999); P. Adamson, "Before Essence and Existence: Al-Kindi's Conception of Being," *Journal of the History of Philosophy* 40 (2002): 297–312.

CHARLES BURNETT

Allen, William (1532–1594), English theologian and cardinal. Allen defended Roman Catholicism in England during the reign of Elizabeth I. After being forced into exile in 1565, he established a training college for missionaries to England in Douai (1568), in the Spanish Netherlands. The Douai version of the Bible was produced there, in addition to a plethora of Roman Catholic propaganda by the

Douai press. Commissioned by Pope Gregory XIII, he set up a similar college, the English College at Rome, where he later died. The politically naive theologian encouraged his countrymen to side with Spain against England in 1588, thereby incurring the wrath of many English Roman Catholics. He became a cardinal in 1587 and archbishop of Malines in 1589.

S. Doran, *Elizabeth I and Religion, 1558–1603* (1994); C. Haigh, *English Reformations: Religion, Politics, and Society under the Tudors* (1993).

ELIZABETH GERHARDT

Al-o-pen, the Chinese name of the seventh-century Syrian monk credited as the pioneer leader of the Christian church in China. His Syriac name was probably Yahb-allaha, and his work is documented both in a 638 CE decree of the T'ang emperor T'ai-tsung and on the Sian-fu stele of 781 CE (see *Christianity in T'ang and Yuan China*). Welcomed on his arrival at Chang-an (Sian) in 635, the scriptures he carried were examined by the emperor himself. The 638 decree authorized the dissemination of their teachings, seen as "mysterious, wonderful, calm" and "the salvation of living beings." It also sanctioned the building, in the capital, of a monastery for twenty-one monks. The emperor Kao-tsu in 649 hailed Al-o-pen as a "great patron and spiritual leader of the empire," which confirmed his leadership status in church and community. He is further regarded as the author of the "Jesus Messiah Sutra" (635–638) and "A Discourse on Monotheism" (641–642), documents found at Tunhuang in 1908. They provide outlines of Christian doctrine, despite problems with the use of accurate and relevant Chinese terminology. Theologically orthodox, they also show groundbreaking efforts to relate Christian ethics to those of a Confucian culture.

I. Gillman and H. J. Klimkeit, *Christians in Asia before 1500* (1999); A. C. Moule, *Christians in China before AD 1550* (1930); P. Y. Saeki, ed., *The Nestorian Documents and Relics in China* (2nd ed., 1951).

IAN GILLMAN†

Altars (θυσιαστήριον, τράπεζα, βωμός, *ara, mensa,* and *altare,* the last term becoming the most common designation in the Latin West.) A structure upon which religious offerings are made, including the blood sacrifices of the ancient Jewish temple. The table used for the Christian sacrament of the Eucharist was early associated with the temple altar (for example, in Heb. 13:10 and by Ignatius of Antioch). Sermons and commentaries since late antiquity frequently associated the sacrament of the Eucharist with the crucifixion and its prefiguration in the temple cult of ancient Israel. Altars assumed a variety of shapes before the conversion of Constantine (semicircle, round, rectangle, square). They ordinarily consisted of a top set on one to five or more legs; they were made of wood, stone, or even metal. Since the fourth century they became largely permanent structures, usually stone, often in block or chest form. The latter shape was the most common in medieval Europe since Carolingian times. It was superseded in the sixteenth century by the sarcophagus altar, which became very popular in the eighteenth century. Altars were placed over, or contained the relics of, a martyr or other saint, and they could be located at any of several places in a church: near the entrance to the presbyterium (chancel), at the front wall of the apse, or even within the nave. Before the sixth century each church contained only one altar, as remains the case in Eastern churches today, but multiple altars became increasingly common in the West after the sixth century. The use of side altars in churches for private devotion and memorialization of the dead began to proliferate in Europe in the ninth and tenth centuries. In the eleventh and twelfth centuries, the deposition of relics in the altar became a formal prerequisite to its consecration. Since the thirteenth century, side altars were often endowed by guilds and confraternities, as well as by prominent families. The retable, originally a modest structure above or behind the altar, grew both in size and pictorial programs, providing the setting for painted panels and carvings to display the passion and deeds of Christ or themes and stories about Mary or the patron saints of donating guilds, confraternities, and families. A consecrated host kept in a pyx was stored upon the altar or in a tabernacle, a locked structure upon the altar or in a nearby wall, and displayed for adoration in an ornate monstrance. Altar cloths were used since the third century. By the eleventh century in Europe, crosses or crucifixes, candles, and an osculatorium (a holy object or, commonly by the thirteenth century, a board used for the liturgical kiss of peace) were commonly placed upon altars. The priest performing the eucharistic sacrifice faced east, following the ancient Christian practice of turning in that direction for prayer. If the apse was in the east of the church, he stood before the altar with his back to onlookers. If the apse was in the west, he stood behind the altar facing onlookers.

J. Braun, *Der christliche Altar*, 2 vols. (1924); K. Gamber, *Sancta sanctorum: Studien zur liturgischen Ausstattung der Kirche vor allem des Altarraums* (1981); H. Leclercq, "Autel," *Dictionnaire d'archeologie chretienne et de liturgie*, vol. 1 (1907–1953), 3155–89; Roger Reynolds, "Altar-Altar Apparatus," *Dictionary of the Middle Ages*, vol. 1 (1982), 221–25; A. Stuiber, P. Poscharsky, "Altar II, III, IV, V," in *TRE* (1976–) 2:308–327.

CHRISTOPHER OCKER

Alumbrados Religious movement centered between Toledo and Guadalajara, in the kingdom of Castile, between 1519 and 1529. Several theories explain the origins of the alumbrados as a movement in continuity with German or Italian mysticism; a *converso* (converts from Judaism and Islam accused of continuing or reverting to their previous practices) movement; or a movement influenced by Sufism. The alumbrados are also seen in continuity with the religious reforms of Cardinal Francisco Jiménez de Cisneros. Three distinct tendencies were labeled as "alumbrados" by the Spanish authorities, namely, "recogidos," "visionaries," and "dexados." The main figures of the dexados, or "alumbrados of Toledo," were Isabel de la Cruz and Pedro Ruiz de Alacaraz. Isabel de la Cruz was a Franciscan tertiary. Pedro Ruiz de Alcaraz, on the other hand, was an accountant and secretary at the service of the noble Mendoza family in their bastion at Guadalajara. Eventually, Pedro Ruiz de Alcaraz joined the court of the marquis of Villena in Escalona, Toledo, where he served as a lay preacher and catechist. Some scholars have stressed that the main characteristic of the dexados was their belief in the possibility of an unmediated experience of the divine by the believer engaged in silent prayer. The alumbrados of Toledo were condemned by the 1525 edict of Toledo, and the leading figures were both arrested and condemned by the Inquisition.

A. Marquez, *Los alumbrados: Orígenes y filosofía (1525–1559)* (2nd ed., 1980); J. C. Nieto, *El Renacimiento y la otra España* (1997).

RADY ROLDÁN-FIGUEROA

Amboise, Conspiracy of After the inexperienced Francis II ascended the French throne in July 1559, effective control of the government passed to Francis, duke of Guise, and his brother Charles, cardinal of Lorraine. The Guises's policy of religious persecution aroused resentment, and a conspiracy developed, principally among provincial nobles, to topple the Guises. Calvinism had already made great advances in France, most importantly among the nobility, whose patronage was vital to the movement's success. The Conspiracy of Amboise involved political rivalries with the campaign to spread Calvinism in France.

Jean du Barry, a Protestant nobleman, organized the conspiracy, which sought to surround the royal court at Amboise, arrest the Guise brothers, and give control of the royal council to another noble family, preferably the Bourbons. John Calvin, informed of the conspirators' intentions, distanced himself from the conspiracy, objecting that it lacked legal legitimacy and was not based on the word of God. Instead, he counseled the faithful to endure their struggle patiently. Without Calvin's endorsement, few French Protestant congregations backed the conspiracy.

In March 1560, the conspirators assembled around Amboise. The Guises learned of the plot, and royal troops captured the conspirators, executing hundreds on the spot. The conspiracy's failure proved disastrous for the French Calvinist movement, as Catholics saw in the conspiracy proof that Protestantism only invited sedition and civil disorder.

R. M. Kingdon, *Geneva and the Coming of the Wars of Religion in France, 1555–1563* (1956); N. M. Sutherland, *The Huguenot Struggle for Recognition* (1980).

SCOTT M. MARR

Ambrose (c. 338–397), bishop of Milan. Born into Roman high society, Ambrose had no intentions as a young man of pursuing an episcopal office. Like his brother Satyrus, he was trained in law and had already begun a career in imperial service. As a promising protégé of the praetorian prefect, Petronius Probus, Ambrose was appointed provincial governor (*consularis*) of northern Italy. When the "Arian" bishop of Milan, Auxentius, died in 374, Ambrose entered the city basilica in order to quell the disturbances that threatened to escalate over the choosing of a successor. His success in doing so incited popular enthusiasm to elect him as bishop.

It was, nevertheless, a problematic appointment. Ambrose hailed from a Christian family, but, typical of those who wielded civic or military authority, he had not been baptized. He himself observed that he had not been "brought up nor trained from childhood in the bosom of the church." Indeed, his lack of ecclesiastical qualification and theological training was exactly what made him so amenable to a crowd sharply divided over the details of doctrinal issues. Both the emperor Valentinian I and Probus encouraged Ambrose to accept the position for the sake of civil order. Within a week's time, Ambrose was baptized and hurried through the lower ranks of clergy to bishop, barely satisfying conciliar prohibitions that forbade the ordination of novices.

Once installed as bishop, Ambrose continued to follow ostensibly the neutral religious policies of Valentinian I, which preserved an uneasy peace in Milan. In the meantime, the new bishop discharged his pastoral obligations by addressing himself to the study of Scripture and Latin and Greek theology. His works on major themes and characters in Genesis and the Song of Songs reveal an influence of Philonic exegesis as well as familiarity with Origen and Basil of Casearea. It would therefore become automatic for Ambrose to interpret biblical passages as possessing more than one meaning. Analogous to God as Trinity, Scripture could yield "a threefold wisdom": the natural (literal), the moral, and the rational (allegorical) (*Exposition of Luke's Gospel,* Prologue 2). Allegory and typology were especially fruitful when understanding the Old Testament in relation to the events and truths of the gospel (e.g., *The Mysteries* 1.7, 35–38, 44). It is from Ambrose's sermons that Augustine would discover how allegorizing the Old Testament could lead him out of the exegetical constraints with which Manicheanism had chained him. Indeed, sermons were the original form for expressing much of the bishop's theology. Evidence from most of Ambrose's writings indicates that they were the composite product of a collection of sermons edited as a single whole.

Ambrose also wrote several small treatises on virginity defending the divine calling of the virgin as a living martyr to the elite households of Milan, many of whom were not happy to lose their filial guarantees of family succession to the church. The pre- and postpartum virginity of Mary is asserted as a model for young women to follow.

The bishop's entry into doctrinal controversy began as a written response on his part to accusations of heresy made against him by anti-Nicenes in Milan. He now took up an unambiguous defense of the Nicene Creed as the only standard of orthodox Christianity. In *On the Faith* (books 1–2 and later, 3–5) Ambrose attacked his homoian opponents as Arians using the same kinds of polemical arguments employed against Arius a half century before, namely, that the Son is created and unlike the Father in substance. In opposition to this view, Ambrose declared that the divine nature is declared to be common to the Father, Son, and Holy Spirit: "We confess Father and Son and Holy Spirit with the result that the fullness of divinity and unity of power exist in perfect Trinity." In fact, there are no attributes of the Father that the divine nature of Christ does not share. The unity (*unum*) of the Father and Son is affirmed to the extent that there is no multiplicity (*multiplex*) because they are *indifferens* (not different) (*On the Faith* 1.2, 17).

Ambrose's attempts to secure the emperor Gratian's political support for the pro-Nicene cause did not succeed until just before the Council of Aquileia (381), where he managed the deposition of two homoian prelates and other lesser clergy on the grounds of heresy. Even so, Ambrose's two other major theological treatises, *On the Holy Spirit* and *On the Incarnation of the Lord,* reveal that the struggle with anti-Nicene theology was not fully over. The latter treatise demonstrates a marked progression in the bishop's understanding of his opponents. Ambrose argued for the complete separation of the divine and human natures in Christ in order to avoid any tendency to diminish the fully divine status of the incarnate Son.

It may be said that Ambrose was not as much an original thinker as a passionate pleader and organizer. Whether opposing anti-Nicenes or aristocratic pagans, such as Q. Aurelius Symmachus, against whom he effectively stifled all attempts to restore the Altar of Victory to the Roman senate, Ambrose was a master at orchestrating social and political resources to his benefit. His active building program in Milan and promotion of martyr cults established an undisputed hegemony for pro-Nicene orthodoxy and his memory. At the same time, a deep piety is exhibited in his letters and sermons, as well as in his identification with the poor, embrace of hardship, and willingness to endure martyrdom.

N. McLynn, *Ambrose of Milan: Church and Court in a Christian Capital* (1994); A. Paredi, *Saint Ambrose: His Life and Times* (1964); D. H. Williams, *Ambrose of Milan and the End of the Nicene-Arian Conflicts* (1995); Williams, "Polemics and Politics in Ambrose of Milan's

De fide," JTS 46 (1995): 519–31; B. Ramsey, *Ambrose* (1997).

D. H. WILLIAMS

Ambrosiaster ("Pseudo-Ambrose"), fourth-century biblical commentator. "Ambrosiaster" is the name given to the author of the first complete Latin commentary on the Pauline epistles, ascribed in most manuscripts to Ambrose. The Romans commentary exists in three versions, the Corinthians commentary in two, and the rest in one version. The same author is responsible for a series of *Questions on the Old and New Testaments*, attributed in the Middle Ages to Augustine. The precise identity of the Ambrosiaster has remained a mystery to scholars, though some information about him can be gleaned from the commentaries. He wrote at Rome during the reign of Pope Damasus (366–384) and was, almost certainly, a member of the Roman clergy. Ambrosiaster was knowledgeable about Jewish customs and often used Roman legal terminology. The commentaries and questions are based on the Old Latin versions of the Bible and are therefore a valuable witness to the pre-Vulgate text.

CSEL 50 (1908); CSEL 81/1–3 (1966–1969); O. Heggelbacher, *Vom römischen zum christlichen Recht* (1959); Heggelbacher, "Beziehungen zwischen Ambrosiaster und Maximus von Turin?" in *FZPT* 41 (1994): 5–44; D. G. Hunter, "The Paradise of Patriarchy: Ambrosiaster on Woman as (Not) God's Image," *JTS* 43 (1992): 447–69; S.-L. Rockliffe, *Ambrosiaster's Political Theology* (2007); A. Souter, *A Study of Ambrosiaster* (1905); L. Speller, "Ambrosiaster and the Jews," StPatr 17 (1982): 72–78.

DAVID G. HUNTER

Ames, William (1576–1633), leading Puritan theologian not only in England but also in the Netherlands and North America. Born in Ipswich, Suffolk, and educated at Christ's College, Cambridge, Ames came under the influence of William Perkins, who became both his tutor and his close friend. In 1610 the increasingly vigorous anti-Puritan policies of the crown forced Ames to the Netherlands, where he did pastoral work on behalf of the English Merchant Adventurers. In 1619 he was offered a professorship at the Univ. of Franeker, which post he assumed in 1622. He spent the next decade engaged in formulating Reformed theology against the background of the Remonstrant–Counter-Remonstrant controversy that followed the Synod of Dordt. In the late 1620s he considered a move to the New World and even engaged in correspondence to that effect with John Winthrop, but the plans never came to fruition. Ames subsequently accepted a call to an Independent church in Rotterdam in 1632, where he died in October 1633.

Ames's work is significant in two major areas: his *Medulla Theologica* (1622) and his *Conscience with the Power and Cases Thereof* (1632) both represent significant contributions to the development of post-Reformation Reformed practical and casuistical theology; and his *Bellarmine Disarmed* (1628) is one of the most significant Reformed responses to the great Jesuit thinker and a major example of seventeenth-century Reformed polemic.

K. L. Sprunger, *The Learned Doctor William Ames* (1972); W. J. van Asselt and E. Dekker, eds., *Reformation and Scholasticism: An Ecumenical Enterprise* (2001).

CARL TRUEMAN

Amman, Jacob (c. 1644–1730), founder, with his brother Ulrich, of the Amish Anabaptists. Born in Erlenbach, Simmental (canton Bern), he converted to Anabaptism before 1680 and became a teacher and congregational leader in Emmental. He led a schism among the Swiss Anabaptists over issues of the social shunning of the excommunicated, the frequency of the Lord's Supper, and appropriate clothing (he opposed all jewelry and insisted on traditional plain garb). He required foot washing and subscription to the Dordrecht Confession of Faith of 1632, with its simple, clear statements on baptism, excommunication, the Lord's Supper, oaths, and opposition to all use of violence. Persecution drove him to Alsace, where he organized and led the groups until his death. Many of his followers immigrated to North America in the eighteenth and nineteenth centuries.

J. A. Hostetler, *Amish Society* (4th ed., 1993); L. Hege and C. Wiebe, eds., *The Amish* (1996).

ROBERT KOLB

Ammianus Marcellinus (c. 330–after 391), Roman historian. He wrote a history in Latin in thirty-one books covering the period from 96 to 378, of which the last eighteen books survive. His richly detailed narrative is our major source for the history of the empire from 351 to the battle of Adrianople (378). He wrote particularly to extol the virtues of the emperor Julian, "the Apostate," whom he served as an officer during the emperor's military success in Gaul and failed invasion of Persia. Ammianus is generally considered a relatively fair historian in the context of the highly contentious later fourth century, despite his paganism and partisanship on behalf of Julian, although the extent of his fairness remains the subject of sharp critical debate. In addition to his praise of Julian, he also treats critically the reigns of the emperors Constantius II, Jovian, Valentinian, and Valens. His history is written in emulation of the classical histories of Livy, Sallust, and Tacitus, and is marked by elevated prose, frequent use of Greek and Roman republican examples, and extensive digressions on geographical, ethnographical, religious, and scientific topics.

T. D. Barnes, *Ammianus Marcellinus and the Representation of Historical Reality* (1998); J. F. Matthews, *The Roman Empire of Ammianus* (1989); D. Rohrbacher, *The Historians of Late Antiquity* (2002).

DAVID ROHRBACHER

Amphilochius of Iconium (340/345–398/404), bishop of Iconium (Konya). Amphilochius was a cousin of Gregory of Nazianzus through his maternal uncle, Amphilochius the Elder. In 373 after an early career in government, Amphilochius joined the many family and friends whom Basil of Caesarea coerced into the episcopacy in his defense of orthodoxy and his personal honor. Consecrated to the province of Lycaonia, Amphilochius was briefly driven from his see under the Arian emperor Valens, only to return once Theodosius became emperor in 379. He sought advice from Basil, which prompted the latter to compose letters on disciplinary and theological issues, as well as the treatise *On the Holy Spirit*. As a neo-Nicene he participated in the Council of Constantinople (381). He helped condemn Messalians both at the Synod of Side (383) and through his *Against the Heretics*, which is a blistering attack against various irregular ascetics. Amphilochius stood against the Macedonians at the Synod of Iconium (376). In addition to the forenamed treatise, six homilies, one statement of faith, a didactic poem, and some fragments are extant.

C. Bonis, "What Are the Heresies Combated in the Work of Amphilochius, Metropolitan of Iconium 'Regarding False Asceticism'?" *GOTR* 9, no. 1 (1963): 79–96; C. Datema, *Amphilochii Iconiensis opera* (1978); K. Holl,

Amphilochius von Ikonium in seinem Verhältnis zu den grossen Kappadoziern (1904).

LISA D. MAUGANS DRIVER

Amsdorf, Nikolaus von (1483–1565), Lutheran reformer. Amsdorf studied in Wittenberg, becoming arts professor and one of Luther's earliest and most ardent supporters. Sent by Luther to introduce reform in Magdeburg (1524), he served there until appointed Lutheran bishop of Naumburg-Zeitz (1542). Driven into exile during the Schmalkald War (1546), he returned to Magdeburg and led opposition to the religious policies of the new Saxon elector, Moritz, over compromise with Roman Catholic policy. This provoked public disputes with Melanchthon (foreshadowed by earlier disagreements between them) and his Wittenberg colleagues. Although Amsdorf was not the author of the Magdeburg Confession of 1550, as is sometimes alleged, its justification of armed resistance to tyrannous oppressors of the Christian faith reflects views he expressed as early as 1523. Amsdorf participated in forming the Gnesio-Lutheran movement in the 1550s, contributing to the pamphlet literature of the controversies over the proper formulation of Luther's teaching. In the adiaphoristic controversy, he insisted on clear confession of the faith, rejecting compromise based on so-called neutral matters of church practice (adiaphora). He taught that good works are necessary for Christian living but opposed Georg Major's proposition that "good works are necessary for salvation," reviving Luther's argument that "good works are detrimental for salvation" if they are regarded as meritorious for forgiveness. He also rejected any active positive role of the human will apart from the action of the Holy Spirit in conversion.

P. Brunner, *Nikolaus von Amsdorf als Bischof von Naumburg* (1961); R. Kolb, *Nikolaus von Amsdorf* (1978).

ROBERT KOLB

Anabaptists Pejorative label applied to Reformation-era dissident communities because of their distinctive views on baptism. These communities understood baptism to be contingent upon a mature confession of faith rather than a sacrament administered to infants who neither understood nor evidenced a Christian life. Anabaptists themselves strenuously rejected the label "Anabaptists." Recent classification of these various dissident communities tends to put them under the general rubric of

"Radical Reformation." Historically, Anabaptist communities have identified themselves by places of origin or significant leaders, for example, Swiss Brethren, Hutterites (after Jacob Hutter, c. 1500–1536), and Mennonites (after Menno Simons, 1496–1561). The heterogeneous origins and leaders of Anabaptism have complicated historical and theological efforts to achieve a consensus on its definition. The three main expressions of Anabaptism were the Moravian-Hutterites of Austrian origin, the Swiss Brethren of southern Germany and Switzerland, and the Mennonites of the Low Countries and northern Germany.

Anabaptists envisioned the church as a voluntary community whose truth was manifest in its members' conduct and belief, frequently expressed as opposition to and separation from the world. Those not meeting the standards for church membership were to be expelled. The major Anabaptist confession of faith, the Schleitheim Confession (1527), rejected what most of their contemporaries assumed were normal obligations of citizenship: judicial oaths, tithes, and military service. Hence, establishment authorities perceived Anabaptists as seditionists subversive of the social order. In general, Anabaptists were socially radical and anticlerical in that they desired to restore contemporary society to their perception of the New Testament community, especially as portrayed in the Christian communism of the book of Acts and the radical discipleship of the Sermon on the Mount. The ideal of restoring the early church, however, spawned radically different expressions that ranged from absolute pacifism to an apocalyptic crusade to usher in the kingdom of God.

The first criticisms of infant baptism arose among some of Martin Luther's initial followers and then opponents such as Andreas Bodenstein von Karlstadt, Thomas Müntzer, and Nicholas Storch. Although they did not create communities based on believer's baptism, their ideas spread to Zurich and informed the evangelical opponents of Ulrich Zwingli. Conrad Grebel (1498–1526), the reputed founder of Swiss Anabaptism, initially an active supporter of Zwingli, called for a voluntary church consisting only of true believers, independent of the state. The Grebel circle argued that what is not biblically commanded should be prohibited, that the Lord's Supper is not a sacrament but a symbol of the covenant with God, that baptism is a sign of faith and therefore should not be administered to infants, and that the church is identified by the righteous lives of its members and lives under the cross of persecution.

When these concerns were pressed, a public disputation was held in which Zwingli's views dominated. The town council then ordered all unbaptized children to be baptized within the next eight days under penalty of expulsion from Zurich. Grebel and a few others gathered in response on January 21, 1524. Grebel baptized George Blaurock, a married former priest, and then others; other acts defying both Zwingli and the Zurich council followed. In response, the town council mandated the death penalty with the precedent of the Justinian Code (533) that viewed rebaptism as both heretical and rebellious and thus a capital offense.

Later the imperial Diet of Speyer (1529) also imposed the death penalty upon Anabaptists. The association of some Anabaptists with the violence of the Peasants' War (1525) and the militant effort to create the New Jerusalem in the city of Münster (1534–1535) further stimulated persecution against Anabaptists. An unintended consequence of persecution was to validate Anabaptist apocalypticism and their conviction they were the true church because the true church lives under the cross. Consequently, Anabaptist martyrologies such as the *Martyrs' Mirror* became important sources for their piety.

Anabaptist faithfulness and perseverance under persecution and oppression contributed to the gradual development of the idea of religious toleration and liberty. The Anabaptists' insistence upon a voluntary separate church contributed to the modern idea of pluralism and constitutional separation of church and state.

H.-J. Goertz, *The Anabaptists* (1996); H. J. Hillerbrand, ed., *Anabaptist Bibliography, 1520–1630* (1991); W. Klaassen, *Anabaptism: Neither Catholic nor Protestant* (2001); C. A. Snyder and L. A. H. Hecht, eds., *Profiles of Anabaptist Women* (1998); J. Stayer, *Anabaptists and the Sword*, 2nd ed. (1976); Stayer, *The German Peasants' War and Anabaptist Community of Goods* (1991); Stayer, "The Significance of Anabaptism and Anabaptist Research," in *Radicalism and Dissent in the Sixteenth Century*, ed. H.-J. Goertz and J. Stayer (2002), 77–88; G. H. Williams, *The Radical Reformation* (2nd ed., 1992).

CARTER LINDBERG

Andreae, Jacob (1528–1590), Lutheran church leader, coauthor of the Formula of Concord. After studying in Tübingen, Andreae became a deacon in Stuttgart (1546) but was dismissed at the introduction of the Augsburg

Interim in Württemberg. He became pastor and ecclesiastical superintendent in Göppingen (1553) and dean, chancellor, and professor in Tübingen (1560). Having dedicated his life to searching for church unity, Andreae sought agreement on the Lord's Supper with Theodore Beza (1556). His duke, Christoph, sent him on several missions to help organize churches according to Lutheran principles and to reconcile disputes, such as on justification in Prussia (1554) and on free will in Saxony (1563). In 1568–1570, while assisting in the reformation of Brauschweig-Wolfenbüttel, Andreae sought to end disputes among Lutherans with five brief articles of agreement. When that effort failed, he wrote *Six Christian Sermons* on the divisions among theologians of the Augsburg Confession (1573), refining its ideas into the Swabian Concord (1574), efforts that concluded in the Formula of Concord (1577). Polemic against Calvinist and Roman Catholic opponents dominated Andreae's later career.

J. Ebel, "Jacob Andreae als Verfasser der Konkordienformel," *ZKG* 89 (1978): 78–119; R. Kolb, *Andreae and the Formula of Concord* (1977).

ROBERT KOLB

Andreae, Laurentius (c. 1470–1552),
Swedish reformer and statesman. After obtaining his master's degree at the Univ. of Rostock in 1498, he returned home and became archdeacon in Strängnäs. After the execution of Bishop Mattias by the Danish king Christian II in 1520, he took the charge of the diocese.

Laurentius became the coadjutor of Gustavus Vasa, who liberated Sweden from Danish hegemony, and proclaimed him the elected king of Sweden in 1523. Appointed the king's secretary, he became a member of the council of the state and archdeacon of the archdiocese of Uppsala and inspired the king's ecclesiastical policy. He cooperated with Olaus Petri in the development of an independent Reformation church in Sweden.

In the early 1530s Andreae lost the king's favor when he opposed the king's effort to gain full power over the church. In the Diet of Örebro (1539–1540) he was sentenced to death for high treason but was reprieved with a heavy fine. He spent his last years in retirement in Strängnäs. Along with Olaus Petri he was engaged in the Swedish translation of the New Testament (1526), and he wrote "A Short Introduction to the Creed and Good Deeds" (1528).

N. Lindqvist, *Översättaren av Nya Testamentet 1526* (1929–1930).

INGUN MONTGOMERY

Andrew of St. Victor (d. 1175), canon of
the abbey of St. Victor in Paris, abbot of Wigmore, Bible scholar. Born in England, Andrew must have been a pupil of Hugh of Saint-Victor at the abbey after which they are both named. In his own writings Andrew, to a certain extent, distanced himself from his master Hugh's exegetical methods and theological interests. But Andrew continued, in his way, Hugh's literal exegesis of the Bible by restricting himself to commentaries on the Old Testament. That is to say, Andrew wrote commentaries to the historical books, all the prophets, Proverbs, and Ecclesiastes.

Between 1148/1149 and 1153 Andrew was called for the first time to become abbot of the newly founded Victorine community at Wigmore (Herefordshire). In 1153 he returned to Paris and dedicated himself again to intellectual activities. In 1161, the canon regulars of Wigmore called him back as their abbot. This second time he held this office until his death in 1175.

As to his exegetical work, Andrew practiced an interpretation of the Old Testament that mainly followed the well-known late antique-medieval program of studying *littera-sensus-sententia*. The broad spectrum of sources of which Andrew could make use (classical authors, church fathers, Jewish exegetes) reflects a humanist culture and his deep knowledge of history. He used both humanist culture and a deep knowledge of history to develop a method of Christian theology as exegesis.

R. Berndt, *André de Saint-Victor (d. 1175): Exégète et théologien*, in *Bibliotheca Victorina*, vol. 2 (1991).

RAINER BERNDT

Angela Merici (c. 1474–1540), Franciscan
tertiary, educator, founder of the Ursuline teaching Sisters, canonized in 1807. Angela Merici faced a society in which education was largely the privilege of rich young men and confined primarily to monastic schools. Women's roles and rights were defined by their fathers, husbands, and prelates. These realities shaped Angela's perception of society and its transformation by the education of women. Leading a small group of unmarried women, Angela set out to educate poor girls, free of

charge, in their homes. These "companions," the first such reform movement specifically for women, lived a new form of noncloistered religious life without formal vows or religious habit. Angela insisted that she and her band of teachers were the "Company" (*compagnia*) of Saint Ursula, not an order. Angela's vision did not long survive her death. Though still permitted to teach, the Ursulines were reorganized as a more traditional cloistered community.

M. Buser, *Also in Your Midst: Reflections on the Spirituality of Saint Angela Merici* (1990); P. Caraman, *Saint Angela: The Life of Angela Merici, Foundress of the Ursulines (1474–1540)* (1963); M. Reidy, *The First Ursuline: The Story of Saint Angela Merici* (1961).

PETER J. SCAGNELLI

Angela of Foligno (d. 1309), Italian mystic and Franciscan tertiary. Apart from the date of Angela's death, there are few certainties in her biography. According to the standard account, she was born around 1248 and became a Franciscan tertiary after the deaths of her husband and sons. During a pilgrimage to Assisi, a visionary experience led her to disclose to her confessor the mystical path that she had begun following. The *Memorial* produced by her confessor reflects, according to this view, her own account of her mystical experiences, focused on Christ's passion and on the transfiguration of human love and sexuality. The *Instructions* are records, written by her followers, of her teaching to a mixed group of men and women. The works (collectively, the *Liber de vera fidelium experientia*, the *Book of the True Experience of the Faithful*) strongly emphasize poverty, and it has been suggested provocatively that her works reflect not Angela's experiences but the views of a group of male spiritual Franciscans.

Although Angela was never canonized, she was recognized locally as "blessed" immediately after her death. This title was officially confirmed by Pope Clement XI in 1701. The writings associated with her name influenced later thinkers as diverse as Teresa of Avila and Georges Bataille; she is often referred to as Saint Angela, especially in France.

Angela of Foligno, *Complete Works*, ed. P. Lachance (1993); G. Barone and J. Dalarun, eds., *Angèle de Foligno: Le dossier* (1999); B. McGinn, *The Flowering of Mysticism: Men and Women in the New Mysticism (1200–1350)* (1998).

VICTORIA MORSE

Anglicanism The term refers to the range of theological reflection and religious and political life and practice characteristic of, but no longer limited to, the distinctly English Church as it emerged through the reformation and reforms of the sixteenth century. Most Anglican scholars understand the term more broadly, however, tracing its origins neither to the sixteenth-century reformation, nor to John Henry Newman's formal use of the term in 1864, but to its theological or ecclesial roots in Athanasius and Augustine.

In the centuries since the reign of Henry VIII, Anglicanism has developed as a truly global community. Even in its broader sense, however, Anglicanism has flourished almost exclusively where the English crown or the British Empire enjoyed at least some political predominance. The Elizabethan Settlement, in 1559, brought relative calm to a previously contentious Church of England in which the political and theological struggles under Protestant and Catholic monarchs found a working resolution. Anglicanism offered a middle way between Catholic and Protestant, particularly Calvinist, alternatives. In the seventeenth century the English Church assumed an increasingly Puritan character. This direction may be seen especially during the years of the English Civil War, which saw the promulgation of the Westminster Confession in 1646 and the deposition and execution of Charles I in 1649. The restoration of the monarchy (1660) saw a steady and comprehensive return to the Anglican *via media*. The Book of Common Prayer, initially developed and published in the reign of Edward VI, was reissued in revised form in 1662 and gradually provided a single, shared liturgical form, used in varied practice, for the Church of England and for Anglicanism worldwide.

In the midst of its emergence within and separation from the history of English political and cultural fortunes, Anglicanism displays several distinctive theological and practical features. It rests not on the formidable theology of a central figure or a set of doctrinal confessional documents but on patristic theological sources and conciliar theological patterns. Theological development in Anglicanism might be traced best not through the work of a particular pastor or systematic theologian but through a study of the Book of Common Prayer and related commentaries, or, better still, through an appreciation of changes in liturgy and worship. The dynamic interaction between the life of the church on the one hand, and Scripture, reason, and tradition (especially the fruit of patristic councils) on the other, shape Anglican theology as practiced theology. *Lex orandi, lex credendi*—"the law of praying is the law of belief"—has proved a helpful, comprehensive notion in discussions of Anglican theology and practice. The movement from *lex orandi* to *lex credendi* involves a vigorous reliance on the traditions that undergird Christian faith, most especially on the liturgical expressions of those traditions. Anglican theology depends on and finds critical pragmatic expression within liturgy, which shapes and revises the life and practices of the church. While Anglicanism continually presents the benefits of practiced theology, it also presents the complex struggle of an ongoing search for livable consensus. From its earliest days, Anglicanism has been both challenged and blessed by an insistence on a practical "middle way."

P. Avis, *Anglicanism and the Christian Church: Theological Resources in Historical Perspective* (1989); G. R. Evans and J. R. Wright, eds., *The Anglican Tradition: A Handbook of Sources* (1991); S. Sykes, *The Integrity of Anglicanism* (1978); S. Sykes, J. Booty, and J. Knight, eds., *The Study of Anglicanism* (1999).
JOHN E. GRISWOLD

Anglo-Saxon Christianity

Prior to the arrival of the Angles and Saxons, Britain was the home of a Celtic people, the Britons. Christianity probably entered Britain along with the Romans. As the Romans retreated, it is uncertain how much Christianity remained in Britain under Anglo-Saxon rule. The British monk Gildas, in *The Ruin of Britain*, describes the pagan takeover as occurring between 450 and 550.

Anglo-Saxon Christianity was a mixture of Roman, Celtic, and Germanic influences, supporting strong church-state relations while maintaining the Celtic importance of monasteries. It is known for its fusion of Christian and heroic warrior Germanic literature, which spread an eschatological spirituality typical of the age. It evolved as the religion of the nobility, integrating the elite's worldly customs and values, much to the dismay of such theologians as Bede and Alcuin.

The conversion of the Anglo-Saxons came from two sides. Augustine of Canterbury (d. 604), sent by Gregory the Great, arrived in Kent in 597 and proceeded to convert King Aethelberht and over ten thousand Englishmen. After the death of Augustine, the expansion of the church experienced setbacks as Mellitus, bishop

of London, was driven out, and he and Justus, bishop of Rochester, fled to Gaul for a time.

From the north came conversion led by Aidan of Iona, who established himself at Lindisfarne (c. 635) at the request of King Oswald of Northumbria. Oswald's predecessor, Edwin, had converted to Christianity upon marrying a Christian princess, Ethelberga, who arrived with her chaplain, Paulinus from Kent. The Synod of Whitby (664), which decided in favor of the Roman date for Easter, gave the Roman missionaries sway over Northumbria, sending those who insisted upon the Celtic usages back to Iona and later Ireland. The man who followed Augustine, Theodore of Tarsus (d. c. 690), was sent to Canterbury by the pope along with Hadrian, an African monk, and Benedict Biscop. Together these men set about reforming the English church and establishing centers of learning. Biscop founded the monasteries of Wearmouth and Jarrow. Jarrow is best known for its monk Bede (d. c. 734); his *Ecclesiastical History* contains much of what is known about the Anglo-Saxon church. Hadrian and Theodore set up schools throughout England and strove to bring the Anglo-Saxon church into unity with Rome, imposing the Roman custom upon all of England in 669. Theodore also organized the diocesan system. In order to accomplish this reorganization, Theodore held many synods of bishops. While he sponsored all things Roman, Theodore chose the Celtic penitential system, writing his own penitential, which foreshadowed the role of the parish priest.

Monasteries remained essential, the centers of learning, and monks did the missionary work. Anglo-Saxon missions to the Continent were at their height in the eighth century. Wilfrid went to the Frisians in 678 on his way to Rome, followed by Willilbrord, who was to become the first bishop of Utrecht (d. 739). The most influential missionary was Boniface, bishop of Germany, who helped organize the Frankish and German churches before being martyred at Dokkhum in 754. Alcuin (d. 804), the great liturgical scholar, made a trip of a different sort, as he became a chief advisor to Charlemagne and spread Anglo-Saxon learned Latinity throughout the Carolingian realm.

In 793, however, the Danes landed at Lindisfarne, causing the monks to flee with the body of St. Cuthbert and other relics. The Danes continued their conquests over the Anglo-Saxons until 878 when Alfred, king of Wessex, won a decisive battle. In an effort to replace the books that the Vikings had destroyed, Alfred began a program promoting learning in English, translating

Bede and others. Alfred also opened a school in Winchester modeled on Charlemagne's.

The monastic revival of the late tenth century was lead by Dunstan (d. 988), archbishop of Canterbury, Ethelwold, abbot of Abingdon, and Oswald, a monk of Fleury. While these men promoted ties with the Continent and founded many monasteries and convents, enforcing the Rule of St. Benedict, their reform was cut short by Viking attacks beginning in 980. In 1016, Cnut, king of Denmark and Norway, became king of England, marrying Emma, the widow of Ethelred the Unready, his Anglo-Saxon predecessor. His reign was peaceful, and he promoted clerks to his service, notably Wulfstan, archbishop of York, who helped him codify English law. The end of his reign was to be the end of Anglo-Saxon Christianity as such. Emma's son by Ethelred, Edward the Confessor, arrived from Normandy, bringing Normans into positions of power. In 1066 the Norman Conquest under William the Conqueror brought an end to Anglo-Saxon Christianity.

R. Boenig, *Anglo-Saxon Spirituality: Selected Writings* (2000); H. Mayr-Harting, *The Coming of Christianity to Anglo-Saxon England* (3rd ed., 1991).

MARIANNE M. DELAPORTE

Annates Taxes imposed upon newly acquired church benefices, annates equaled one year's revenue from the benefice after expenses for management and maintenance (also "first-fruits"). Although annates were originally assessed by local bishops, they were rapidly transformed to a source of papal income. Theoretically, papal annates affected only benefices granted by the pope; in practice, by the time of Pope Clement V (1305–1314), they affected almost all benefices. It often took decades for endowed clerics to render amounts due, and being transferred did not obviate the necessity of completing payment for a prior benefice. Abuse of the system led to antipapal sentiment throughout Europe, especially since the fourteenth century; polemicists during the Great Schism and subsequent reformers in the fifteenth century questioned the principle but, although annates were banned by the Council of Basel, papal agents continued to demand and have varied success collecting them.

King Henry VIII of England (r. 1509–1547) withheld annates to force a papal divorce decree (an unsuccessful strategy). By letters patent on July 9, 1533, and the Appointment of Bishops Act of 1533–1534, he annexed annates and tithes to the English crown, confirmed in the First Fruits and Tenths Act of 1534. And, responding to heightened resistance, the Council of Trent severely limited papal annates; in the twenty-first century only a very few Italian benefices still pay them.

W. E. Lunt, *Papal Revenues in the Middle Ages*, 2 vols. (1965).

LORNA SHOEMAKER

Anne of Cleves (1515–1557), the fourth wife of Henry VIII of England. Anne was a political choice at a time when England would benefit from Lutheran alliances, should the emperor and the king of France ally against the Protestant countries. However, as the foreign-born daughter of the Catholic Maria of Jülich-Berg and the Lutheran Duke John III of Cleves, Anne proved ill-pleasing to the king, who soon proceeded to marry another young woman, Katherine Howard. Queen only from January to July 1540, Anne agreed to the annulment on the grounds of childhood engagement to the Duke of Lorraine and a not-consummated marriage with Henry. "The King's sister" remained in England, with upkeep, and outlived Henry and his last two wives.

A. Fraser, *The Wives of Henry VIII* (1992); R. MacEntegart, "Fatal Matrimony: Henry VIII and the Marriage to Anne of Cleves," in *Henry VIII: A European Court in England*, ed. D. Starkey (1991).

KIRSI STJERNA

Anomoeans Fourth-century subordinationist, second-generation Arian theologians. They were refuted by almost every major contemporary pro-Nicene author, including Basil of Caesarea and Gregory of Nazianzus. "Anomoeans" comes from the Greek *anomoios*, meaning "unlike or dissimilar." The Anomoeans, who created a separate church, were said to teach that the Son was "dissimilar" to God. The main representatives of the Anomoeans, Aetius and Eunomius, did not deny all likeness between the Father and the Son, yet they insisted that like entities must be unlike in some respects. They argued that although the Son was similar to the Father, the Son was said to be "unlike" God as far as the divine essence was concerned. To clarify this central point, Anomoeans preferred to employ the designations "other" (*heteros*) or "incomparable" (*asugkritos*), as they spoke about the natures of the Son and God. Anomoeans identified God's unique nature with "unbegottenness" (*agennesia*). The term "unbegotten" or "ingenerate" expresses two distinct attributes: (1) not to be dependent on any other being but to be uncaused and (2) not to have a beginning but to exist eternally. Since begetting is a process and since process implies mutability, the immutable God cannot be the begetter of the Son. Because God is essentially "unbegotten" and the Son is "begotten," they have to be ontologically different; the Son has to be subordinated to God. "My glory I will not give to another" (Isa. 42:8). If God and the Offspring were the same, then the divine essence must be both ingenerated and generated, which is absurd.

Because the Anomoeans denied the consubstantiality of the three divine persons, the Nicene literature has called them "radical Arians" or "neo-Arians," but such labels ignore the differences between Arian and Anomoean theology. Unlike Arians, Anomoeans claimed that both God's essence and energies could be known, because words such as "unbegotten" and "father" match exactly with reality observed, that is, with God's essence and energy. The Son is the product of God's activity and not of God's essence, for God's essence and activity are not the same thing (Eunomius, *I Apol.* 22). On the basis of Rom. 1:20 ("the divine nature . . . [has] been understood and seen through the things he has made") and John 17:3 ("that they may know you, the only true God, and Jesus"), the Anomoeans argued that the created Son made the uncreated God known.

The formal and ecumenical condemnation of Anomoeans took place at the Council of Constantinople in 381, which established the reaffirmed Nicene faith as Trinitarian orthodoxy. Despite the edict of Theodosius II to burn the writings of Anomoeans in 398, several of their texts—mostly extracts selected for polemical purposes—are still extant.

J. Behr, *The Nicene Faith*, part 2 (2004); M. E. Butler, "Neo-Arianism: Its Antecedents and Tenets," *SVTQ* 36, no. 4 (1992): 355–71; R. P. Vaggione, *Eunomius of Cyzicus and the Nicene Revolution* (2000); M. Wiles, "Eunomius: Hair-Splitting Dialectician or Defender of the Accessibility of Salvation?" in *The Making of Orthodoxy*, ed. R. Williams (1989), 157–72.

TARMO TOOM

Anselm of Canterbury (1033/1034–1109), Benedictine monk, prior, abbot, archbishop, theologian. Anselm was born in Aosta (Piedmont) and died as archbishop of Canterbury. Before entering the Benedictine monastery

of Bec (Normandy) in 1060, he received a broad intellectual formation in the schools of Burgundy (Cluny) and Normandy. He continued his education under the guidance of Lanfranc, the prior of the monastery at Bec. He succeeded Lanfranc in 1063 as master of the school and as prior of the abbey. He became abbot of Bec in 1078. After Lanfranc's death in 1093, Anselm was elected archbishop of Canterbury, primate of the Church of England. Because of King William II's resistance to papal confirmation of Anselm's election, the bestowal of the *pallium* was delayed until 1095. The continuing quarrel with William II caused Anselm to look for help in Rome and to stay away from England (1098–1100). He spent these years in Lyon and Rome. It is true that Henry I invited him to come back to his diocese, but during a conflict over investiture, Anselm left England again until Pope Paschal II concluded a compromise with Henry I (1103–1106). He assumed his episcopal responsibilities and tried to reorganize the English clergy along the lines of the Gregorian reform and his Benedictine ideals. His life and activities have been described by his pupil and secretary Eadmer, a monk of Canterbury.

Writings. Anselm left 3 meditations and 19 prayers, as well as 472 letters, the first group of which (Ep. 1–147) were written at Bec, and the second group (Ep. 148–472) when Anselm was archbishop of Canterbury. Probably his first work was the philosophical treatise *De grammatico* (*On Grammar*, perhaps composed as early as 1070), which discusses the question whether "the white" (*albedo*) is still an adjective, and therefore only a quality (*accidens*), or whether it is a substance. In the *Monologion* (1075–1076) he explains the doctrine of God as supreme Good in terms very close to Augustine's. There followed his *Proslogion*, which concentrates on the so-called ontological proof of God's existence (chaps. 2–4: *quo nihil maius cogitari possit*, "than which nothing greater can be thought"). In his *De veritate* (*On the Truth*), *De libertate arbitrii* (*On Freedom of Choice*) and *De casu diaboli* (*On the Fall of the Devil*), written between 1080 and 1086, Anselm explains one or two biblical texts. With his *Epistola de incarnatione verbi* (*Letter on the Incarnation of the Word*, 1092–1094), he tries to answer Roscelin of Compiegne, who accused him of heresy. Perhaps Anselm had been provoked to write the *Cur Deus homo* (*Why the God-Man*, 1094–1098) following discussions with his former pupil Gilbert Crispin, whose *Disputatio Iudei et Christiani* (*Disputation of a Jew and a Christian*) demonstrates the necessity of the incarnation. In *Cur Deus homo* Anselm tries to show Boso that God's incarnation in Christ has to be postulated even without any knowledge about Christ and divine revelation, in order to permit the possibility of conceiving mankind's salvation. The related problem, whether the Virgin herself has been without any sin, is the topic of Anselm's *De conceptu virginali et peccato mortali* (*On the Virginal Conception and Mortal Sin*, 1100–1101). According to the wish of Pope Urban II, Anselm took part in the Synod of Bari in 1089, where he discussed with the Greeks the *filioque*. In his late treatise *De processione Spiritus sancti* (*On the Procession of the Holy Spirit*, 1102), he shows that the procession of the Spirit from the Father and the Son can be understood according to the equity of inner-Trinitarian relations. Anselm dedicates the *Epistola de sacrificio azymi et fermentati* (*Letter on the Unleavened and Leavened Sacrifice*, 1106–1107), a work of ecumenical importance within the context of the debate with the Greek church, to the question of whether the eucharistic bread continues to be substantially the same after consecration. In his last work, *De concordia praescientiae, praedestinationis et gratiae Dei cum libero arbitrio* (*On the Harmony of the Prescience, Predestination, and Grace of God*, 1107–1108), Anselm tries to complete his doctrine of predestination and divine foreknowledge and to harmonize it with the work of divine grace and human collaboration by means of free will. The collection of notes *Liber de humanis moribus per similitudines* (*Book on Human Manners by Similitudes*), which is not to be ascribed directly to Anselm, reflects the monastic conferences he held on his travels.

Most of Anselm's works are composed in the form of dialogue. Following mainly Augustine, he advanced the philosophical thinking of his age, in order to strengthen faith by the help of reason (*rationes necessariae*). Anselm intended to penetrate the *sense* of faith on the principle of *Credo ut intelligam*, "I believe that I may understand." Another center of theological interest to him was the interaction between divine and human liberty in the course of history. These interests made him one of the most important and famous writers of early medieval scholasticism. In general he adopted moderate philosophical positions, for instance, in the debate about "universals."

Influence. His views, philosophical as well as theological, enjoyed wide reception in the following centuries. Abelard believed that Anselm's explanation of divine incarnation should be taken seriously. The Victorines, particularly Achard and Richard, were influenced by him with respect to their understanding of God. His doctrine of rectitude and free will impressed deeply the Cistercians Bernard of Clairvaux and Isaac of Stella. Thomas Aquinas was not convinced by Anselm's ontological argument, but he recounted it in his *Summa theologiae*. Descartes, Leibniz, and Christian Wolff resumed Anselm's philosophical apologetics for the Christian faith. Immanuel Kant integrated the ontological argument into his *Critique of Pure Reason*. Recently this argument has raised a lot of sympathetic philosophical interest. Also, in the fields of soteriology and Christology Anselm continues to stimulate theologians.

J. Hopkins and H. Richardson, trans., *Anselm of Canterbury: Complete Philosophical and Theological Treatises* (2000); F. S. Schmitt, ed., *Anselmi Opera omnia*, 8 vols. (1938, 1946–1961); E. Bencivenga, *Logic and Other Nonsense: The Case of Anselm and His God* (1993); M. Corbin, *La Pâque de Dieu: Quatre études sur Anselme de Cantorbéry* (1997); B. Davies and G. R. Evans, ed. and trans., *Anselm of Canterbury: The Major Works* (1998); M. Enders, *Wahrheit und Notwendigkeit: Die Theorie der Wahrheit bei Anselm von Canterbury* (1999); R. Majeran and E. I. Zielinski, eds., *Saint Anselm Bishop and Thinker: Papers Read at a Conference Held in the Catholic Univ. of Lublin on 24–26 September 1996* (1999); RGG⁴ 1 (1998): 515–16; J. L. Scherb, *Anselms philosophische Theologie: Programm-Durchführung-Grundlagen* (2000); TRE 2 (1978): 759–78.

RAINER BERNDT

Anselm of Laon

Anselm of Laon (1050–1117), canon and dean at Laon cathedral, and from 1080 head of the school at Laon together with his brother Radulf (d. 1131/1133). His works are based on scriptural exegesis and can be divided into three groups. (1) *Commentaries*: Anselm's authorship of the commentary on the Psalms (in PL 116, attributed to Haimo of Halberstadt) and the Song of Songs is now generally accepted. That of the commentary on the Pauline letters (PL 153) is less certain. (2) *Glosses*: Anselm and the school at Laon developed what was later to become the *Glossa ordinaria*, a collection of authoritative interpretative material accompanying the books of the Bible (in PL 113 and 114, attributed to Walafrid Strabo). The glosses on the Psalms, the Pauline letters, and

John probably go back to Anselm himself. (3) *Sentences*: Whereas the first two categories are organized according to the sequence of the biblical text, the *sententiae* are organized in a systematic fashion, following the order of creation and redemption and unveiling a deeper understanding of Scripture. This scheme was imposed on them subsequent to their composition in a teaching context. Which sentences go back directly to Anselm is still under discussion, as they were continuously added to and rearranged by his followers. A strong pastoral concern can be read from the sentences.

O. Lottin, *Psychologie et morale* 5 (1959); H. Weisweiler, *Das Schrifttum der Schule*, BGPTMA 33 (1936); M. Colish, AHDLMA 61 (1986), 7–22; V. Flint, *RTAM* 43 (1976), 89–110; J. Leclercq, *RTAM* 16 (1949), 29–39; B. Smalley, *The Bible in the Middle Ages* (3rd ed., 1983).

RALF M. W. STAMMBERGER

Anthony of Padua (c. 1195–1231), saint,

Franciscan theologian and preacher, born in Lisbon, died in Arcella (near Padua, Italy). His original name was Fernando. As an Augustinian canon, he witnessed the translation of the relics of the first five Franciscan martyrs from Morocco to Coimbra. It prompted him in 1220 to transfer to the Friars Minor in St. Anthony at Olivares, where he adopted the name of the monastery's patron saint. Longing for martyrdom, he traveled to Africa. After falling severely ill he tried to return but was driven to Sicily by a sea storm. In Sicily fellow Italian friars received him. At the Franciscan general chapter of 1221 at Assisi he was transferred to the province of Romagna, then lived as a hermit in Montepaolo near Forlì, and finally was sent to preach against heretics. From 1222 onward he preached in northern Italy; from 1224 in France. Later he became provincial minister of the Romagna province. Anthony was not only a very successful preacher but also the first teacher of theology in the Franciscan order. However, many of the theological works that have been ascribed to him in the past are unauthentic. He was canonized very soon after his death by Pope Gregory IX (May 30, 1232). In 1946 Pope Pius XII declared him "doctor of the church" (*doctor evangelicus*). Today he is venerated especially in Padua, Portugal, and Brazil.

B. Costa et al., eds., *Sancti Antonii Patavini: Sermones Dominicales et Festivi*, 3 vols.

(1979); R. M. Huber, *Anthony of Padua, Doctor of the Church Universal* (1948).

ACHIM WESJOHANN

Anticlericalism, Medieval and Reformation

Anticlericalism may be understood as a cluster of attitudes and actions that criticized the behavior of clergy, attacked abuses of clerical power, or even rejected the fundamental legitimacy of clerical claims to power and privilege. Because the term originated in the nineteenth century to describe lay resistance to the political power of the clergy, its application to medieval and Reformation polemic can obscure the fact that many of the participants in the earlier debates were themselves priests, bishops, pastors, and monks. Likewise, it is crucial to note that during the Middle Ages and Reformation, the goal of such critique, no matter the source, was usually the reform rather than the abolition of the clerical estate.

One common form of anticlericalism in the Middle Ages was the satirical tradition, which railed against stereotypical sins of the clergy: sloth, stupidity, greed, lust, and gluttony. This type of critique, famous from Chaucer's *Canterbury Tales* and Dante's *Inferno,* poked fun at the clergy's foibles and sought to reform behavior and end the abuse of power, rather than overthrow clerical privilege. That the church was fully willing to tolerate such attacks is evident in surviving ecclesiastical artwork depicting clerics as fools, agents of scandal, or even being led off by demons to eternal punishment. More extreme were the anticlerical and apocalyptic assaults of heretical groups such as the Cathars, the spiritual Franciscans, or the Lollards, all of which defied the teachings of the institutional church and portrayed it as having gone astray.

Conflicts between the church hierarchy and the secular powers of Europe also gave rise to distinctive forms of medieval anticlericalism. Beginning in the eleventh century, the Gregorian reform sought to free the church from secular influence. Later still, Popes Innocent III and Boniface VIII articulated visions of Christian society that gave the pope ultimate power over spiritual as well as temporal affairs. As struggles unfolded over the lay investiture of bishops and taxation of clergy, royal apologists attacked papal power and clerical immunities, often resorting to vicious personal attacks, even as their royal and imperial patrons tried to depose independently minded popes and bishops. Conflicts between church and state continued in the late Middle Ages as cities, territories, and kingdoms established more control over priests and monks by limiting clerical privileges—in essence, turning clergy into citizens and subjects. In part due to the Avignon Papacy (1305–1377) and the Great Schism (1378–1417), late medieval popes struggled to maintain control over the ecclesiastical hierarchy throughout Europe. In their place, city councils, princes, and kings used rights of patronage, jurisdiction, and lordship to curtail clerical legal and economic immunities, to push through their own models of monastic and episcopal reform, and to mobilize church resources for secular purposes. Resistance on the part of the clergy was often met by lists of complaints—*gravamina*—produced by civil and princely authorities, which hammered away at clerical abuses and excessive privileges. Medieval forms of anticlericalism continued in Catholic lands throughout the early modern era.

Ever since the sixteenth century, it has been common to explain the causes of the Protestant Reformation by pointing to the "corruption" of the late medieval church. Today many historians deny the notion of widespread clerical laxity in the late Middle Ages, stressing that early Protestant sources absorbed the medieval satirical tradition and exaggerated the moral failings of the clergy. Treatises and eyewitness accounts that were once considered reliable are now viewed as propaganda. This is not, however, to deny the dynamic impact of anticlerical sentiments during the Reformation.

Protestant leaders offered a more radical critique of clerical status than did their medieval predecessors. Writing in the early 1520s, Martin Luther rejected the priests' claim to stand as mediators between humanity and God and quickly expanded his attack to reject clerical claims to sacramental, legal, economic, and political powers. While the Reformers' argument had at its core a theological concern, the social ramifications were obvious. Anticlerical attitudes clearly fueled the urban strife, pamphlet wars, iconoclastic riots, and peasant uprisings that characterized the 1520s in Germany and later decades elsewhere in Europe. Apocalyptic beliefs only intensified such attitudes. Princes and city councils sought to preserve harmony and "right religion" by establishing full control over ecclesiastical affairs, completing the efforts of their medieval counterparts. These new state churches turned their efforts toward forging Protestant cultures and educating the populace to become obedient Protestant subjects. A similar process

occurred in Catholic lands. As state officials, pastors and priests were often viewed as interlopers in local affairs, meddling in people's lives. With new state sponsorship, the powers and privileges of the clergy, both Catholic and Protestant, survived the Reformation. Anticlericalism survived the Reformation as well.

———

P. A. Dykema and H. A. Oberman, *Anticlericalism in Late Medieval and Early Modern Europe* (1993); C. Haigh, "Anticlericalism in the English Reformation," *History* 68 (1983): 391–407. S. C. Karant-Nunn, "Neoclericalism and Anticlericalism in Saxony, 1555–1675," *Journal of Interdisciplinary History* 24 (1994): 615–37.

PETER A. DYKEMA

Antinomianism   A term used to designate disputes among Protestant theologians, especially in the sixteenth century, over the role of law in the Christian life. Broadly conceived, the word is equivalent to "licentiousness." Thus, in the *Institutes* (II.vii.13) John Calvin attacks "libertines" for wanting to do away with the law. In the early seventeenth century, disputes among Puritans, notably between John Cotton and Anne Hutchinson, also included similar charges of antinomianism against the latter.

More narrowly, the term refers to a series of disputes among Lutheran theologians in the sixteenth century over the degree to which the law played in Christian living. A clash in 1527 involved Philip Melanchthon and John Agricola over whether faith and true repentance were a response to the threat of condemnation under the law or to the hope offered by the gospel. Martin Luther intervened and proposed compromise language, granting that general faith in God preceded repentance but that justifying faith arose only from condemnation of the law.

In 1536, John Agricola left his teaching post in Eisleben for the Univ. of Wittenberg. Clashes over the role of the law in the Christian life erupted between him and Luther in the first antinomian controversies. Several in Luther's inner circle accused Agricola of antinomianism, while anonymous theses accused Luther and Melanchthon of abandoning the gospel for the law. Agricola argued that not violation of the law but of the gospel formed the heart of preaching repentance. By contrast, Melanchthon in 1534 first defined a "third use" of the law (beyond a civil use restraining evil and a theological use condemning sin), guiding the forgiven sinner to perform good works. He also held that good works were necessary.

In his own attack on antinomianism, Luther argued that attempts to eliminate the law from the Christian life turned gospel into law. The law still restrained and condemned sin. After a brief reconciliation between him and Agricola, trouble again broke out when Luther banned Agricola's summary of the Gospels. Circulation of anonymous theses restricting the law to its civil use caused Luther to hold a series of disputations at the Univ. of Wittenberg. In the 1539 tract *Against the Antinomians*, he portrayed antinomianism as an attempt, apart from Christ's forgiveness, to avoid God's wrath. Eliminating the word "law" from theology did not lessen the effects of the law in condemning sinners and driving them to repentance. Agricola appealed to the university rector and then to the Elector of Saxony, but the filing of countercharges by Luther and his colleagues precipitated his flight to Berlin and a formal cease-fire.

A second set of antinomian controversies erupted in conjunction with debates over adiaphora begun in 1548. Melanchthon defined the gospel as "the entire teaching of Christ," whereas Matthias Flacius (1520–1575) and other Gnesio-Lutherans ("true Lutherans") defined it more narrowly as consolation. After Melanchthon's death, Paul Crell (1531–1579), a Philippist who argued that only the gospel could reveal the sin of unbelief, caused Johann Wigand (1523–1587) to insist this was an antinomian confusion of law and gospel. The Formula of Concord of 1577, article V, allowed both a broad and narrow definition of the term "gospel."

Another dispute arose directly from the adiaphoristic controversy, but among Gnesio-Lutherans. To combat the proposition of Georg Major (1502–1574) that good works are necessary for salvation, theses from a synod in Eisenach in 1556 proposed that such works were only necessary hypothetically. Although defended by some Gnesio-Lutherans, including Flacius and Wigand, others, such as Andreas Poach (1516–1585) of Erfurt and Anton Otto (b. 1505?) objected and attacked the notion of a third use of the law. The Holy Spirit, not the law, caused good works. The Altenburg Colloquy of 1568–1569 discussed these "antinomian" views, as did article VI of the Formula of Concord.

A third dispute arose between a student of Melanchthon's and John Agricola's brother-in-law Andreas Musculus (1514–1581). Musculus insisted that good works arise from faith spontaneously, while his opponent insisted that a third use of the law implied no coercion. As Electoral Brandenburg's official representative in talks leading to the Formula of Concord, Musculus saw to it that compromise language favoring his position became a part of article VI.

———

E. Battis, *Saints and Sectaries: Anne Hutchinson and the Antinomian Controversy in the Massachusetts Bay Colony* (1962); M. U. Edwards, *Luther and the False Brethren* (1975); W. Rosin and R. D. Preus, eds., *A Contemporary Look at the Formula of Concord* (1978); T. Wengert, *Law and Gospel: Philip Melanchthon's Debate with John Agricola of Eisleben over Poenitentia* (1997).

                                    TIMOTHY J. WENGERT

Antiochian Christianity

Seleucus I, a general under Alexander the Great, later ruled Syria and in 300 BCE founded Antioch, which sits beside the river Orontes near the Mediterranean coast and was the cultural and commercial capital of ancient Syria. Via migrants from Palestine, Antioch formed part of the Jewish Diaspora.

Christianity appeared early in Antioch via missionaries who preached to the Jews of the city. There Jesus' disciples were first called "Christians" (Acts 11:26), followers of the *Christos*, or "anointed one." The apostle Paul launched his first missionary journey from Antioch, and there, in defense of his mission to Gentiles, Paul stood up to Peter, head of the Twelve, and representatives from James, brother of Jesus (Gal. 2).

In the early second century, Ignatius, bishop of Antioch, was sent to Rome for execution. He wrote several letters on his journey, describing a tumultuous church divided by those who wished to keep Jewish customs, those wishing to adopt gnostic ideas, and a middle party which he headed. Ignatius thought order could be kept only by an authoritarian bishop, the first instance in church history of a monarchical prelacy.

Another Antiochian bishop, Theophilus, wrote a defense of the faith against pagan criticisms (c. 160); his work shows a budding Trinitarian theology. Another bishop, Paul of Samosata (260–268), scandalized the community by his high living and his low theology, until his deposition. In these same centuries, the Antiochian church also evangelized much of the Syrian countryside and beyond.

Antioch suffered much in early fourth-century persecutions but emerged to play an important role in the Christian empire. Antioch produced a school famous for its interpretation of Scripture, which emphasized a more literal and historical interpretation than the allegorical method widely used in Alexandria and elsewhere. Its scholars included Diodore of Tarsus (d. c. 392) and Theodore of Mopsuestia (c. 350–428). Deservedly best known was John "Chrysostom," or "Golden-tongued," the greatest preacher of the ancient church (c. 350–407). John and Nestorius (d. 451) both left Antioch to become bishops of Constantinople, the eastern Roman capital, but neither could survive the snake pit of imperial politics. Both fell victim to bishops of Alexandria who always strove to weaken Constantinople.

The last great Antiochian name is Severus, who established the Monophysite church in Syria—hitherto an anti-Monophysite bastion—and evangelized heavily until deposed by the emperor in 518. Persian conquests of the city in 540 and 611 preceded its final fall to the Arabs in 637.

D. S. Wallace-Hadrill, *Christian Antioch* (1982); M. Zetterhold, *The Formation of Christianity in Antioch* (2003).

JOSEPH F. KELLY

Anti-Semitism, Medieval *see* Blood Libel; Byzantine Church and the Jews; Jewish Martyrdom; Ritual Murder; Western Church and the Jews

Anti-Semitism, Reformation Anti-Semitism is an ethnically focused, racially based hatred of Jews as a people, coupled with the conviction that Jews are by nature corrupt and threaten society at large. This hatred has expressed itself politically and culturally most severely in the violent persecution of Jews at various points throughout history. Scholars distinguish between "anti-Semitism," a term coined by Wilhelm Maar in the late nineteenth century, and "anti-Judaism" as a religiously focused, theologically based opposition to Jewish scriptural interpretations, ideas, traditions, and practices. Anti-Semitism in Reformation Europe was one of a long-standing set of cultural assumptions exacerbated by the centuries-long role of the Christian church as a dominating social force in Western culture.

Anti-Semitic assumptions were inherited and, in notable ways, were passed on and intensified by the Reformation. For generations, Jews had often been blamed for the various disasters and discontents that confronted late medieval and early modern society (e.g., plagues, famines, emerging urban squalor, inflation). It even became common to blame Jews for local situations, such as poor weather, untimely deaths, and lackluster harvests. Particularly gruesome was the "blood libel" that charged Jews with the ritual killing of Christian children so the blood might be used for various Jewish rites (e.g., the baking of Passover bread). Jews were also accused of stealing consecrated Communion bread in order to violate it ritually. Faced with these kinds of accusations, the Jews of late medieval Europe endured personal humiliation and vandalism directed at their homes, businesses, and synagogues (particularly as such violence became connected with popular church observances such as passion plays and Easter). Such persecution, particularly in times of cultural upheaval, could also become much more extreme, resulting in expulsion and pogroms.

During the Reformation, Jews also suffered from the notion that they were at least partially responsible for the social and religious turmoil that rocked early modern Europe. Even prior to the sixteenth century, Jews were blamed for their supposed encouragement of reform movements, such as the one led by the Bohemian Jan Hus (1372–1415). Similarly, various Roman Catholic quarters charged Jews with supporting Luther, as well as aiding the threatening Ottoman invasion of Eastern Europe.

Some Protestants feared "Judaizing" tendencies among their contemporaries, even accusing one another of being "secret Jews." Strasbourg's normally conciliatory Martin Bucer advocated limits on civil rights for Jews. In addition, leaders of the "left-wing" of the Reformation (e.g., Münzer, Hoffman, Hubmaier) blamed Jews for social ills, sometimes even making anti-Semitism an important aspect of their programs.

Notable in this regard is the work of Martin Luther, who wrote a number of treatises referring to relations between Jews and Christians. In particular, his infamous 1543 anti-Jewish tract, *On the Jews and Their Lies*, placed inherited theological condemnations of Judaism in the context of popular religious, social, and economic rumors and stereotypes, as he recommended to his readers the violent suppression of Judaism. For Luther, the presence of the Jewish religion undermined the stability of the emerging German nation. Given his stature as a leading Protestant voice, Luther's anti-Jewish writings have had an inordinately large influence.

At the same time, however, the Protestant Andreas Osiander criticized anti-Semitic assertions, and John Calvin left no written or reported opinion on Jewish-Christian relations. Calvin's silence on the matter is puzzling, although it could be related to the fact that Jews had been expelled from Switzerland some forty years prior to his arrival in Geneva.

By 1570 Jews had virtually disappeared from Western Europe. Their exodus can be seen as the continuation of a process begun centuries earlier of separating Jews from Christians in the West: sociologically by ghettos, geographically by expulsion and emigration, religiously by conversion. Out of these developments arose the establishment of significant Jewish populations in Lithuania, Poland, Russia, and Turkey. This pattern continued until the twentieth century, when the Holocaust further decimated European Jewry.

E. Carlebach, et al., eds., *Jewish History and Jewish Memory* (1998); R. P.-C. Hsia, *The Myth of Ritual Murder: Jews and Magic in Reformation Germany*; D. Cohn-Shebok, *The Crucified Jew: Twenty Centuries of Christian Anti-Semitism* (1992); W. Nicholls, *Christian Antisemitism: A History of Hate* (1993); W. Nijenhuis, *Bucer and the Jews* (1972); H. Oberman, *The Roots of Antisemitism in the Age of Renaissance and Reformation* (1981); J. Parks, *The Jew in the Medieval Community* (1976); L. Poliakov, *The History of Anti-semitism* (1974); K. Stow, *Catholic Thought and Papal Jewish Policy, 1555–1593*; J. Trachtenberg, *The Devil and the Jews* (1993).

WILLIAM R. RUSSELL

Antony (c. 254–356), hermit, monastic pioneer. His fame is due largely to the *Life of Antony*, written soon after his death by Athanasius, bishop of Alexandria. While the *Life* has a historical core, Athanasius's political and theological biases profoundly color the final portrait. Antony was reportedly an uneducated Egyptian peasant, orphaned in his late teens. Hearing at church the story of Jesus and the rich young man (Matt. 19), he sold what he had and gave the proceeds to the poor. He apprenticed himself to a local holy man and adopted a life of stern asceticism. He later enclosed himself in a tomb, where he endured fierce demonic temptations—an episode that became a favorite subject of late medieval art. He continued his *anachōresis* (withdrawal), moving to an abandoned desert fortress where he lived as a hermit for twenty years. His disciples, in Athanasius's famous phrase, "made the desert a city." Later he withdrew to "Inner Mountain," perhaps Mount Qulzum near the Red Sea, where today one finds

the Monastery of St. Antony. Athanasius portrays Antony as a fearless hero who charmed crocodiles and learned philosophers, whose wisdom was sought by emperors, judges, and peasants alike, and whose preternatural powers enabled him to peer into the future and fend off the fiercest demons. Antony appears as a solemn guardian of orthodoxy, warning followers against schismatic Melitians and heretical Arians. Athanasius's *Life* became one of the most influential biographies in the history of Christianity, setting standards for medieval hagiography. Augustine records in the *Confessions* how, in 386, Antony's story helped catalyze his own dramatic conversion in the garden in Milan.

Stories of and sayings by Antony appear in other classics of desert spirituality, especially the *Apophthegmata Patrum*. Recent research has focused on seven *Letters* attributed to Antony, now preserved in a Georgian translation. The Antony of the *Letters* is not the illiterate Antony of the *Life*. He uses sophisticated Origenist terminology, stresses "knowledge" (*gnosis*), and advocates asceticism to restore one's original nature.

D. Brakke, *Demons and the Making of the Monk* (2006); Brakke, *Athanasius and Asceticism* (1998); W. Harmless, *Desert Christians* (2004); S. Rubenson, *The Letters of St. Antony* (1995).

WILLIAM HARMLESS, SJ

Apelles (second cent.), teacher, follower of Marcion. We know about Apelles only from his opponents. They say that he was a disciple of Marcion who modified the latter's teachings. He postulated only one first principle of existence instead of Marcion's two and criticized the Jewish Scriptures as false, not just the product of an inferior god. He wrote *Syllogisms* and *Manifestations*. In *Syllogisms* Apelles applied logic to demonstrate the falsity of the early chapters of Genesis. He asked, for example, how Adam and Eve could be held morally responsible for eating from the tree of the knowledge of good and evil. How could they know that disobedience was wrong without the very knowledge of good and evil that they did not yet have? He also asked how an ark constructed according to the dimensions given could possibly hold all the animals it was said to hold. *Manifestations* gave the sayings of Philoumene, a woman who, according to the account of Rhodo in Eusebius (*Hist. eccl.* 5.13), persuaded him to modify his previous Marcionite positions.

R. M. Grant, "The Syllogistic Exegesis of Apelles," in *Heresy and Criticism: The Search for Authenticity in Early Christian Literature* (1993): 75–88; K. Greschat, *Apelles und Hermogenes: Zwei theologische Lehrer des zweiten Jahrhunderts* (2000); A. von Harnack, *Marcion: The Gospel of the Alien God* (1990): 113–21.

JOSEPH W. TRIGG

Aphrahat (mid-fourth cent.), "the Persian Sage," spiritual writer, ascetic. Nothing is known of his life except that he lived through the persecution of Shapur II in Sassanian Persia. He wrote a series of twenty-three "demonstrations" on various aspects of the spiritual and ascetic life and in defense of the Christian church against Judaizing tendencies (338–345). The first twenty-two demonstrations are an acrostic, each demonstration beginning with the successive letters of the Syriac alphabet. The twenty-third demonstration is the longest, a discourse on "the grape/cluster" (Isa. 65:8). Topics include traditional themes: faith, love, fasting, prayer, humility, Sabbath, resurrection of the dead. The most significant demonstrations for the setting of the early Persian church are Demonstration Six, "On the *Bnay Qyāmā*," and Demonstration Seven, "On the Penitent." The *bnay/bnat qyāmā* (sons/daughters of the covenant), forerunners to the monastic movement, were a consecrated group of men and women living and ministering in the community. Aphrahat denounced the practice of "spiritual marriage," in which sons and daughters lived together for mutual support.

ET of Demonstrations 1, 5, 6, 8, 17, 21, 22, *NPNF*, 2nd series, vol. 13, 115–433; Demonstrations 11–19, 21, and parts of 23 in J. Neusner, *Aphrahat and Judaism* (1971); Demonstration 4 in S. Brock, *The Syriac Fathers on Prayer and the Spiritual Life* (1987), 1–28.

ROBERT A. KITCHEN

Apocalypticism, Medieval Latin (European) Christendom developed an elaborate eschatology quite different from that of the Eastern and ancient churches, beginning in late antiquity. The various streams of Western apocalyptic thought, centered on divergent interpretations of the book of Revelation (read intertextually with Ezekiel and Daniel), have not been given equal attention. Christian scholars, especially historians of the church and of theology (e.g., Bernard McGinn, Daniel Verhelst, Beryl Smalley), have tended to focus on the more recognizable, orthodox, and respectable varieties of apocalyptic thought that were current among theologians and other educated clerics. Roughly speaking, these ideas were based on a conventional set of readings from the Hebrew prophets, including Ezekiel and Daniel, read through the lens of Revelation and various epistles of Paul, and on the momentous events cryptically described or foreseen in Revelation itself. Although a great variety of opinion arose regarding the precise sequence of events foretold in Scripture for the end of time, and regarding the stage in that sequence in which humanity currently found itself—before or after the unchaining of Satan, before, during, or after the expected "thousand-year reign of peace"—it was generally agreed that at the end of time, apocalyptic destroyers, usually known by the Christian term "Gog and Magog," would arise in the east, attack Christendom, and lay waste to it, as part of the "tribulation" or persecution of the true church. A great struggle between the forces of good, sometimes led by Enoch and Elijah, sometimes by the archangel Michael, sometimes by Christ himself, against the forces of evil, led by Satan (or by a shadowy figure known as the antichrist), would culminate in the defeat of evil and the conversion of the (remaining) Jews to Christianity, ushering in either a thousand years of peace and prosperity or the Last Judgment itself. Even if the precise chronology was not agreed upon—Augustine, citing the Gospel of Matthew, specifically warned that it was not possible to know the hour or the day of the end but that one should be ever vigilant and prepare oneself—learned Christians agreed in a very broad and general way about the events that could be expected at the end.

Richard Landes, Johannes Fried, and others have argued that the years 800 and 1000 (among others) were moments of apocalyptic expectation and fear. Citing the famous tenth-century letter of Adso, abbot of Montier-en-Der, in response to a query from Queen Gerberga, as well as a host of other contemporary texts, Landes demonstrates how even the upper echelons of late Carolingian society were gripped at the approach of this millennial event by apprehension and doubt. Fried has proven the extent to which the court of Otto III, the Holy Roman Emperor, was also caught up in millennial excitement and anticipation. Heavy criticism has been brought to bear, especially in France, against Landes's corollary argument that the Peace of God was part of a large-scale lay millennial movement, but no one has yet managed to explain away the many texts that document apocalyptic angst at the turn of the millennium.

In the high Middle Ages, a number of rather novel learned opinions regarding the end arose, chief among them the seven-part division of the ages of the world by the Calabrian abbot Gioacchino da Fiore (Joachim of Fiore). Arguing that humanity found itself in the sixth age of the world—a scheme based on the concept of the Sabbath and the sabbatical millennium—Joachim foresaw the beginning of a new and final age of humankind in 1260. Joachimism gained ground throughout the thirteenth century among Franciscans and other Christian groups with a utopian bent.

Below or beyond the level of learned apocalyptic exegesis and thought was a bewildering multiplicity of apocalyptic beliefs, based in part on literary and legendary sources. One of the most influential yet least known sources of apocalyptic beliefs in the high and later Middle Ages was the *Historia scholastica* (c. 1169) by the Parisian master Peter Comestor. James H. Morey discusses its popularity, sources, and reception, noting that the *Historia*, "one of the most popular books in the late Middle Ages," has received no critical edition or major study and has been neglected in the standard works on scholastic study of the Bible. Beryl Smalley's *The Study of the Bible in the Middle Ages* concentrates on Stephen Langton and Peter the Chanter, but Smalley notes that Comestor's "influence on medieval vernacular religious literature was more significant than either Langton's or Peter the Chanter's" (8). The many early translations into the European vernaculars prove the point: a Saxon version was made c. 1248, the Dutch *Rijmbijbel* in c. 1271, the French *Bible historiale* dates to c. 1295, and Portuguese and Czech translations were made in the fourteenth century. A number of German versions of the *Historia* appeared in hundreds of manuscripts in the later fourteenth and fifteenth centuries and made their way into print in the form of the so-called Antichrist Block-Books by the 1450s, an indication of their contemporary importance and popularity.

In the tradition of the *Historia* and therefore in many other cases, the "destroyers" from the north ("Gog from the land of Magog" in Ezekiel, "Gog and Magog" in Revelation) were reconfigured as various peoples ("real" and "imaginary," from our perspective) inhabiting the east and/or northeast. They were identified as or called, variously, the Tatars, the ten lost tribes of Israel, the Red Jews, the "unclean peoples," and later were considered to be the Turks. These peoples would become the followers of the antichrist at the end of days and attack Christendom (the "true church"). Such ideas, long since disavowed and buried by Reformation biblicism and Enlightenment rationalism, gained new adherents in Protestant millennial sects in the nineteenth century and form the bedrock of current-day fundamentalists' millennial expectations regarding Israel, the tribulation, and the antichrist.

A. Gow, *The Red Jews: Antisemitism in an Apocalyptic Age* (1995); R. Landes, A. Gow, D. C. Van Meeter, *The Apocalyptic Year 1000: Religious Expectation and Social Change, 950–1050* (2003); J. H. Morey, "Peter Comestor, Biblical Paraphrase, and the Medieval Popular Bible," *Speculum* 68, no. 1 (1993): 6–35; B. McGinn, *Apocalypticism in the Western Tradition* (1994); W. Verbeke, D. Verhelst, A. Welkenhuysen, eds., *The Use and Abuse of Eschatology in the Middle Ages* (1988); B. Smalley, *The Study of the Bible in the Middle Ages* (3rd ed., 1983).

ANDREW GOW

Apocryphal Writings

Apocryphal Writings Between approximately 250 BCE and 400 CE, Jewish and Christian authors produced a variety of writings that testify to the vitality and diversity of Second Temple Judaism and emerging early Christianity. *Apocrypha* is a Greek word that means "hidden things," and it was initially applied to certain documents whose content was thought to be secret or mysterious.

Within the large corpus of apocryphal documents there is a collection of Jewish writings from the last two centuries BCE that are referred to as a part of intertestamental literature, since most of them were originally written or narrate events that occurred in the period between the time of the later prophets of the Hebrew Bible and the writing of the NT documents. Roman Catholic and Orthodox Christians have accepted some of these documents as Scripture and designate them as deuterocanonical ("second canon") writings, while Protestant Christians refer to this body of literature as the Apocrypha and do not accord it canonical status.

The Apocrypha includes historical writings (e.g., 1 Esdras, 1 and 2 Maccabees), wisdom literature (e.g., Ecclesiasticus, Wisdom of Solomon), prophecy (e.g., Baruch), apocalyptic writing (e.g., 2 Esdras), short stories (e.g.,

Tobit and Judith), and liturgical writings (e.g., Prayer of Azariah and Song of the Three Young Jews, Prayer of Manasseh). Protestant Christians, following the Reformation practice of relying upon the Masoretic Text of the Hebrew Bible and wishing to deny canonical support for certain Roman Catholic practices, consider these writings instructive but not canonical. Roman Catholics, who find in these writings support for beliefs regarding prayers for the dead and the salvific value of good deeds, affirmed their canonical status at the Council of Trent in 1546.

In addition to the writings included in the Apocrypha, many other Jewish documents related to the Hebrew Bible or Second Temple Judaism are extant. In some scholarly circles this corpus of literature is referred to as the Pseudepigrapha ("false writings"), since in many instances authorship is falsely attributed to a revered or well-known figure from the biblical tradition. Some of these works have come to light in recent manuscript discoveries such as the Dead Sea Scrolls and the Nag Hammadi codices. Many of these writings are apocalyptic (e.g., *1 Enoch, Jubilees, War Scroll, Apocalypse of Adam*), while others are commentaries or expansions of works now included in the Hebrew Bible (e.g., *Genesis Apocryphon, Commentary on Habakkuk*), or writings that supplement biblical traditions (e.g., *Testaments of the Twelve Patriarchs, Odes of Solomon*, and *Ascension of Isaiah*).

Current scholarship stresses the value of the apocryphal writings for understanding the broad range of theological perspectives and religious practices that characterized the formative period from which classical Judaism and early Christianity arose. These writings attest to the vitality of Jewish faith communities in the Diaspora as they responded to their Greco-Roman or Persian cultural environment. Especially illuminating are the creative ways earlier traditions from the Torah and the prophetic writings have been reinterpreted in documents that reflect new cultural realities facing the Jewish people. These documents also enable a deeper appreciation and better understanding of the Jewish origins of Christianity.

Christian writers produced a large corpus of apocryphal literature relating to the New Testament during the first three centuries of the Christian church. Much of this material supplements NT traditions and often prominently features NT figures. Other writings are hagiographic in nature and focus on the piety of the apostles and other early Christian saints. Most of these documents were originally written in Greek or Latin, and they were translated into many other languages including Syriac, Coptic, Ethiopic, and Slavonic. They frequently survive only in translations that are fragmentary or edited versions of the original. Recovery of the original text is often the result of scholarly investigation, and the results are therefore sometimes hypothetical.

The NT apocryphal writings include several different genres: Gospels (e.g., *Gospel of Thomas, Gospel of Philip, Gospel of Mary*), narratives describing the acts of the apostles (e.g., *Acts of John, Acts of Peter, Acts of Andrew*), apocalypses (e.g., *Apocalypse of James, Apocalypse of Peter*), epistles (e.g., *Third Epistle to the Corinthians, Epistle to the Laodiceans, Letter of Peter to Phillip*), and narratives about the infancy of Jesus (e.g., *Protevangelium of James, Infancy Gospel of Thomas*). These documents were written anonymously or pseudonymously and circulated widely throughout early Christian communities. They reflect a wide variety of theological perspectives ranging from Jewish Christianity to encratism and Gnosticism in addition to works that reflect the theological perspective of emerging orthodox Christianity.

The discovery of the Nag Hammadi codices in upper Egypt in 1945 considerably increased the number of extant apocryphal writings related to early Christianity. Included in this collection of mostly gnostic documents were Coptic versions of the *Gospel of Thomas, Gospel of Philip, Apocryphon of John, Apocalypse of Peter, First* and *Second Apocalypses of James, Treatise on the Resurrection*, and many other apocryphal early Christian writings. Some of the documents in this collection appear to be related to Jewish tradition (e.g., *Apocalypse of Adam*), while others have been linked with Sethian Gnosticism (*Three Steles of Seth, Allogenes*, and *Zostrianos*).

J. H. Charlesworth, ed., *The Old Testament Pseudepigrapha*, 2 vols. (1983, 1985); L. Di-Tommaso, *A Bibliography of Pseudepigrapha Research 1850–1999* (2001); D. J. Harrington, SJ, *Invitation to the Apocrypha* (1999); E. Hennecke and W. Schneemelcher, *New Testament Apocrypha*, 2 vols. (1992); J. M. Robinson, ed., *The Nag Hammadi Library in English* (3rd ed., 1990).

JAMES BRASHLER

Apokatastasis The term refers to the prospect of the final universal restoration of creatures to God. Two biblical texts proved especially pivotal to its conceptualization: Paul's projection that God through Christ will be "all in all" (1 Cor. 15:24–28) and Peter's declaration that Christ must remain in heaven until the "restoration of all things" (*apokatastasis pantôn*) by God (Acts 3:21).

Though often equated with universalism (the salvation of all beings), early exponents couched the *apokatastasis* in God's eschatological victory over evil, which would still entail a purgatorial state. Clement of Alexandria (c. 150–215) interpreted the final judgment precisely as a refiner's fire leading the wicked to salvation. Origen (186–254) theorized the *apokatastasis* as a recovery of the prehistoric *stasis*, or rest, enjoyed by spiritual creatures before their fall and embodiment. The history of embodied spiritual creatures was a long rehabilitative process in which the free will of each creature (possibly even Satan himself) was being trained against evil—a process that could in principle repeat itself until all creatures were finally persuaded to embrace good and resume their original union with God.

Later admirers of Origen reasserted his teaching on the *apokatastasis* sometimes with important adjustments. Gregory of Nyssa (335–395) shared Origen's hope of all creatures being saved but argued that the final restoration would be a return not to a prehistorical unity but to that ultimate perfection that God originally projected for humanity in the fullness (*plērōma*) of its creaturely potential. The ascetical theologian Evagrius of Pontus (346–399) and other monastic disciples of Origen, however, radicalized his teaching on the *apokatastasis*, which fueled criticism from opponents (Jerome, Augustine, et al.) and the formal condemnation of Origenism by the Fifth Ecumenical Council (Constantinople, 553).

To the extent that Gregory of Nyssa heavily modified the notion of *apokatastasis*, while Maximus the Confessor (580–662) later outlined the divine plan for universal salvation alongside warnings of everlasting punishment for the wicked, the principle of a universal restoration was subsumed in Eastern Orthodox eschatology as a Christian *hope*, not a fixed dogma. Within a decidedly different philosophical context, the *apokatastasis* theme resurfaced in Russian Christianity in the early twentieth century in the ex-Marxist theologians Nicolas Berdyaev (1874–1948) and Sergius Bulgakov (1871–1944), who projected their own visions of the ultimate restoration and transfiguration of all creation.

B. Daley, *The Hope of the Early Church* (1991).
PAUL M. BLOWERS

Apollinaris, Sidonius *see* Sidonius Apollinaris

Apollinarius

(c. 315–392), bishop of Laodicea. Apollinarius and his father, also Apollinarius, were both Nicenes who were excommunicated by the Arian bishop of Laodicea, George. After George was deposed at the Synod of Alexandria (360), Pelagius, a so-called homoian, replaced him. Apollinarius, a friend and supporter of Athanasius, led the Nicene party at Laodicea after his father's death.

Apollinarius was well trained in classical rhetoric. When the pagan emperor Julian barred Christians from teaching the classics, Apollinarius composed gospel dialogues in formal rhetorical style.

His repute comes from his understanding of the humanity of Christ. As a staunch opponent of the Arians, Apollinarius insisted on the complete divinity of Christ. For Christ to be fully God, there must be only one subject in Jesus, the divine subject. To admit a second, human subject in Christ would result in Christ's death being merely the death of a human being. Consequently, Apollinarius was an opponent of Antiochene Christology.

His own Christology centered around his conception of Christ as a "living union" of the Logos with human flesh. Rather than a static, jigsaw-like union, Apollinarius conceived of a dynamic union in which the Logos was in complete control of the life of Christ. All actions and sayings of Jesus were to be attributed to the Logos. Apollinarius claimed that whereas human beings comprised a human mind, a human soul, and a human body, Jesus comprised a human soul, a human body, and the Logos. Apollinarius thus called Jesus human, but not a complete human being.

Apollinarianism was rejected not only by the Antiochenes but also by Athanasius and the Cappadocians. Gregory of Nazianzus crafted a response to the heresy in his letters to Cledonius, in which he made his now famous remark, "What has not been assumed cannot be saved." Ultimately, Apollinarianism was rejected because it did not allow for an acceptable soteriology in which God assumed complete humanity in order to redeem it.

H. Lietzmann, *Apollinaris und seine Schule* (1904); R. A. Norris, *Manhood and Christ*

(1963); C. E. Raven, *Apollinarism* (1923); M. Richard, "L'introduction du mot 'hypostase,'" *MScRel* 2 (1945): 5–32, 243–70.

STEVEN A. MCKINION

Apologists, Early Christian

The title "apologist" is used to refer to writers who presented an account of the Christian faith and life for those outside their community of faith, usually in the face of pagan accusations and persecutions. Although there are some apologetic passages in the New Testament (e.g., Acts 17 and the book of Revelation) and apologetic writings after the third century, the title "apologist" is usually reserved for the writers of the second and early third centuries. In this period, confronted with persecution, prejudice, and popular slander, Christian writers had to defend to the state the right of Christianity to exist, to present a reasoned account of their beliefs to the educated classes from which they were beginning to gain converts, and to dispel common misconceptions of their rites and practices.

The first specifically apologetic work known is Quadratus's *Apology* to the emperor Hadrian (117–138), of which a short fragment is preserved by Eusebius (*Hist. eccl.* 4.3). Aristides, a Christian philosopher at Athens, addressed an *Apology* either to Hadrian or Antoninus Pius (138–161) early in his reign. Aristo of Pella (c. 140) seems to have been the first to address an apology to Judaism. In the work, now lost, entitled *A Controversy between Jason and Papiscus concerning Christ* (cf. Origen, *Contra Celsum* 4.52), Jason, a baptized Jew, converts Papiscus by demonstrating that the messianic prophecies of Scripture are fulfilled in Christ.

The most extensive apologetic works from the second century were written by Justin, a Greek philosopher from Palestine, who converted to Christianity and settled in Rome, where he cultivated disciples and eventually was martyred (c. 163–167). In the opening chapters of his *Dialogue with Trypho the Jew*, Justin presents a stylized account of his quest for truth through the various schools of philosophy, which he found inadequate, and the fulfillment of his search in Christianity. In the remainder of the treatise, he seeks to demonstrate that the texts of Scripture (i.e., the OT in the Septuagint version) testify to Christ. In addition, Justin composed two *Apologies*, the first addressed to Emperor Antoninus Pius and his adopted sons and the second a kind of "postscript." In these *Apologies* Justin defends the rationality of Christian faith and practice and argues that Christianity is the fulfillment of "seeds of rea-son" implanted in all, so that whatever glimpses of truth there are in the philosophers (who also, he claims, took their ideas from the books of Moses, not understanding fully what they read) belong properly to Christians. Other writings are also attributed to Justin, but their authenticity is doubtful; the *Oration to the Greeks* and the *Exhortation to the Greeks* are both apologetic in character but of an uncertain date.

One of Justin's students was Tatian, a native of Syria, educated in Greek philosophy and rhetoric. After Justin's death, Tatian is reported to have returned to the East as an Encratite (Irenaeus, *Against the Heresies* 1.28.1), though it is likely that his asceticism reflected his native Christianity. Tatian composed a passionate attack against Greek civilization and a defense of the venerability of Christianity, known as the *Oration to the Greeks*, as well as the *Diatessaron*, a harmony of the four Gospels.

Athenagoras, described as an Athenian philosopher, addressed a *Supplication for the Christians* to Marcus Aurelius (161–180) and his son around 177, rebutting accusations made against Christians and presenting a first philosophical account of Christian monotheism. A treatise *On the Resurrection of the Dead* is also attributed, though less certainly, to Athenagoras. A few years later, Theophilus of Antioch composed *To Autolycus*, a set of three books in which he sets out the Christian ideas of God and creation to demonstrate their superiority over pagan myths. Theophilus also developed an account of how the Word of God relates to the Father and was the first to use the word "Trinity." Of uncertain date and authorship is the *Letter to Diognetus*, which sets itself the task of explaining (1) why the gods of the Greeks and the superstitions of Judaism should not be tolerated, (2) the manner of Christian life as the soul of the world, and (3) the unique revelation of God in Christ. Also of unknown date is the *Mockery of the Pagan Philosophers*, a heavily sarcastic and condemnatory work by Hermias, about whom we know nothing. Three other apologists are known to have written most probably during the time of Marcus Aurelius: Miltiades, a rhetorician of Asia Minor, composed an *Apology for Christian Philosophy* (cf. Eusebius, *Hist. eccl.* 5.17.5); Apollinaris of Hierapolis wrote a number of apologetic works during this period (cf. Eusebius, *Hist. eccl.* 4.27); and Melito of Sardis also presented an *Apology* to the emperor, of which only fragments now remain (in Eusebius, *Hist. eccl.* 4.26).

In the Latin-speaking world, Tertullian, a trained rhetorician who probably practiced as a lawyer before converting to Christianity, wrote his *Apology* and *To the Nations* in 197, appealing for the toleration of Christianity, rebutting allegations of Christian immorality, attacking pagan superstition, and arguing that Christians were in fact exemplary citizens. Many of his other works have an apologetic character. Tertullian often sets himself against pagan culture—"What has Athens to do with Jerusalem?" (*Prescription* 7)—yet every page of his betrays his rhetorical training and his debt to philosophy, especially Stoicism. Closely related to Tertullian's *Apology*, though it is unclear whether it is dependent or is the source, is the *Octavius* by Minucis Felix, a dialogue between Octavius, a Christian, and Caecilius, a pagan, who is persuaded and converted.

Apologetic texts were written by later writers such as Origen, Cyprian, and many thereafter, but these are not usually classified as "apologists." The apologists are those who at that particular historical juncture began the task, necessary to the gospel, of addressing the world, both the state and culture. Their approaches, as indicated, vary.

H. Chadwick, *Early Christian Thought and the Classical Tradition* (1966); R. M. Grant, *Greek Apologists of the 2nd Century* (1988); E. Osborn, *Tertullian: First Theologian of the West* (1997).

JOHN BEHR

Apostles' Creed

The designation refers to a Latin creed whose final form was set in eighth-century France. The creed long predates the eight century but is not so old as its name suggests. According to the Italian writer Rufinus of Aquileia (345–411), before filling Christ's command to evangelize all nations (Matt. 28:11), the twelve apostles met to work out a summary of Christian teaching, such as the oneness of God and Christ's resurrection. They created a creed of twelve elements, with each apostle contributing one element.

While it is possible that Jesus' disciples saw the need for a summation of Christian basics, Rufinus's account is pure legend. Yet the Apostles' Creed is indeed ancient. Ambrose of Milan mentioned it by name for the first time in 390, but scholars believe it dates back to second-century Rome, the church that Rufinus claimed best preserved the creed. The Old Roman Creed grew out of the interrogation given to baptismal candidates. The presiding minister would ask, "Do you believe in God, the Father Almighty?" The candidate would reply, "I believe," and the minister would go on to the next question. As the language of second-century Rome was Greek, the earliest formulation would have been in Greek, with a change to Latin in the third century. Primitive creeds were also used for benedictions and as ways to preserve Christians from heresy, the assumption being that knowing the basics would protect them. About 340 a Greek writer named Marcellus of Ancyra reproduced a creed in Greek that matches the one cited by Rufinus. Since Marcellus's version shows no evidence of being a translation, scholars speculate that he knew the Greek version of the Old Roman Creed.

Rufinus's book helped to popularize the creed in the West. In the preface to his *Commentary* on it, he says that his home church of Aquileia used a version of its own that was similar to the Roman one. Apparently the Roman church began to regularize the wording of the creed in the fifth century, and the creed spread with Roman influence. The Gallic writer Faustus of Riez (d. c. 490) says that the creed came from "the Apostles and the Fathers of the Church." Another Gallic writer, Caesarius of Arles (470–542) attributed the creed to "the blessed Apostles."

In the early Middle Ages local churches returned to emending the creed for their own use. The now familiar wording from eighth-century France was popularized in the Latin West by the religious reforms of Charlemagne (768–814). The wide acceptance of this creed by Western Christians has made it a useful tool in contemporary ecumenism, and many modern theologians continue to write commentaries upon it.

H. de Lubac, *The Christian Faith* (1986); E. Ferguson, *The Early Christians Speak* (1999), 19–28; Rufinus, *Commentary on the Apostles' Creed* (1955); P. Smulders, "Some Riddles in the Apostles' Creed," *Studies in Early Christianity* 4 (1993): 146–72; F. Young, *The Making of Creeds* (1991).

JOSEPH F. KELLY

Apostolic Constitutions   see Church Order, Early

Apostolic Fathers

The designation refers to a small, diverse set of texts from the late first and early second centuries, regarded as representative of apostolic doctrine. The distinction originally rested on the theory, not frequently supported in modern scholarship, that the authors transmit the teachings of the apostles through having had either direct personal contact with first-generation Christian leaders or instruction from the disciples of the apostles.

The boundaries of the group are not firmly defined. Ancient ecclesiastical writers, although highly concerned with apostolic tradition, did not distinguish a specific set of writers as authoritatively representative of apostolic doctrine. The earliest modern edition of Apostolic Fathers (1672) represented five figures: a letter attributed to Barnabas, two letters attributed to Clement of Rome, the seven genuine letters of Ignatius of Antioch, writings by and about Polycarp of Smyrna, and the *Shepherd*, an apocalyptic treatise by Hermas. Subsequent editors expanded the list to include an anonymous apologetic brief addressed to Diognetus, the apology of Quadratus, fragments from an exegetical treatise by Papias of Hierapolis, and an early church manual known as the *Didache*, or "Teaching of the Twelve Apostles." A useful criterion for defining the corpus is proposed by R. M. Grant, who excludes Quadratus and the letter to Diognetus in the translation series produced under his direction. Grant reasonably judges that the term properly should designate those writings directed toward the communal formation of Christian identity rather than the explanation of Christian teaching to outside critics.

However defined, this diverse corpus presents numerous problems with respect to authenticity, dating, provenance, and textual unity. The chronological span of the writings ranges from c. 96 for *1 Clement* to the second half of the second century for the *Martyrdom of Polycarp*, a range that overlaps with the dating of the canonical NT Scriptures. Several of the writings—*1 Clement, Barnabas*, the *Shepherd*, and the *Didache*—were revered as canonical Scripture by some communities. Such overlap points to the artificiality of any rigid boundary between the creation and transmission of tradition grounded in apostolic witness. The geographic origin of the writings embraces important yet far-flung centers of second-century Christianity: Rome, Asia Minor, Syria, and Alexandria. The authenticity of the writings varies: *2 Clement* and *Barnabas* are regarded as inauthentic, the authenticity and/or integrity of Ignatius and Polycarp are contested, the unity of the *Shepherd* is questionable, and *1 Clement* and the *Didache* are widely identified as anonymous documents. Direct links between the individual writers and apostolic instruction also are difficult to sustain.

Subsequent tradition (primarily attested by the late-second-century theologian Irenaeus of Lyon) asserted that Polycarp, Papias, and Clement all enjoyed contact with the apostles or their disciples, with Irenaeus claiming that Clement "still had their preaching sounding in his ears and their tradition before his eyes" (*Against Heresies* 3.3). These connections were already questioned in antiquity regarding Papias (Eusebius, *Hist. eccl.* 3.39.5–7) and have been contested for the others in recent scholarship.

This diversity precludes distillation of a unified "apostolic" theology from the corpus. The writings do not address a uniform set of issues or display consensus on the proper authorities or subjects for theological exposition. They appropriate a diverse pool of sources: *Polycarp* bears a strong resemblance to the Pastoral Epistles, *Papias* presents an exposition of the sayings of the Lord, and *Barnabas* offers an allegorical application of NT Scriptures. More broadly, they occupy widely variant positions on the theological continuum. The *Shepherd*, *Barnabas*, and the *Didache* are deeply influenced by Jewish Christianity, while Ignatius contends against "Judaizing" elements in churches in Asia Minor. The most consistent feature of writings in this corpus is a pastoral orientation. Doctrines of God and Christ, greatly elaborated in the subsequent centuries, are invoked primarily to support the moral aims of the writer. Even for Ignatius, the most theologically developed of the Apostolic Fathers, concern with Christ is more devotional than speculative. The most repeated concern is in the maintenance of church order and unity, to which these authors give sustained consideration. A broad range of ecclesiastical issues are addressed in these texts, including penance and moral discipline, balancing claims of ordained and charismatic authority, and the conduct and significance of ritual life. The Fathers are of interest not because they apply well-defined apostolic tradition to resolve disputes on these matters but because they negotiate varying, and sometimes competing, models of Christian community. These diverse models reflect a stage in Christian ecclesiology when individual communities enjoyed a high degree of authority to direct their affairs.

As the interest in community life shows, the label "Apostolic Fathers" retains use primarily to identify an important set of witnesses to the formation of the institutions that enabled the development of Christian tradition. These texts show a burgeoning literary enterprise directed toward the care and sustenance of a network of

Christian communities. The Apostolic Fathers provide valuable insight into a critical transition in Christianity, but their significance does not derive from a unique and distinct relationship to apostolic origins.

J. A. Draper, ed., *The "Didache" in Modern Research* (1996); O. B. Knoch, *Religion: Vorkonstantinisches Christentum: Apostolische Väter und Apologeten ANRW* 2.27 (1993); R. M. Grant, *The Apostolic Fathers*, 6 vols. (1964–1968); R. Hvalvik, *The Struggle for Scripture and Covenant: The Purpose of the Epistle of Barnabas and Jewish-Christian Competition in the Second Century* (1996); C. M. Jefford et al., *Reading the Apostolic Fathers* (1996); H. Lohmann, *Drohung und Verheissung: Exegetische Untersuchungen zur Eschatologie bei den Apostolischen Vätern* (1989); C. Osiek, *Shepherd of Hermas: A Commentary* (1999); J. C. Paget, *The Epistle of Barnabas: Outlook and Background* (1994); W. R. Schoedel, *Ignatius of Antioch: A Commentary on the Letters of Ignatius of Antioch* (1985).
RICHARD A. LAYTON

Aquaviva, Claudio (1543–1615), superior general of the Society of Jesus (Jesuits) from 1581 until his death. Neapolitan by birth, Aquaviva entered the Jesuits in 1567. He served as rector of the Jesuit college at Naples and superior of the Provinces of Naples and Rome prior to his election as Jesuit general. Aquaviva's generalate witnessed the number of Jesuits rise from approximately 5,000 to 13,000. He turned aside an effort by a group of Spanish Jesuits to reduce the authority of the Jesuit general and decentralize the Society of Jesus. His efforts to maintain the internal structure of the Jesuits, however, contributed to a greater rigidity in Jesuit life than envisioned by Ignatius Loyola. This is seen in his exact regulations concerning the spiritual formation of Jesuits. In 1599 Aquaviva promulgated the final edition of the *Ratio studiorum*, or *Plan of Studies*, that served as the fundamental document for Jesuit schools worldwide, a system that oversaw 372 schools in operation at the time of Aquaviva's death.

W. V. Bangert, *A History of the Society of Jesus* (1972); J. de Guibert, *The Jesuits: Their Spiritual Doctrine and Practice* (1964); C. Sommervogel et al., *Bibliothèque de la Compagnie de Jésus*, vol. 1 (1890–1931), 480–91.
PAUL V. MURPHY

Aquinas, Thomas   *see* Thomas Aquinas

Archbishops, Medieval Originally bishops of higher dignity, but not necessarily possessing the jurisdiction of metropolitans. By the ninth century the submission of bishops to their metropolitan archbishop, the definition of an archiepiscopal province, and the intermediary position of the archbishop between pope and bishop had become established.

In the West, the juridical and political roles of the archbishop became increasingly concrete. In 1215 Pope Innocent III (1198–1216) mandated a considerable task for his archbishops: through their archiepiscopal administrations, provincial synods, and bishops, they were to proclaim and enact the reforms of the Fourth Lateran Council. Innocent's charge illustrates the mediating position of the archiepiscopacy between papacy and church as well as the ecclesiastical oversight expected of archbishops. The authority of the medieval archiepiscopate is rooted in the development of early medieval metropolitans and their rights to convoke provincial synods, preside over legal cases involving bishops, and assist in filling vacant episcopal sees.

During the twelfth and thirteenth centuries, canon law further clarified the responsibilities of archbishops in their provinces as follows: to confirm episcopal elections; consecrate new bishops; convoke and preside over synods; make visitation to churches, foundations, cities, and dioceses; censure and discipline wayward clergy and laity; receive appeals from episcopal tribunals; appoint clergy to unfilled offices (right of devolution); and grant indulgences. Moreover, an archbishop exercised episcopal oversight of his own particular archdiocese (in contrast to his province).

Beyond their ecclesiastical and sacramental responsibilities, archbishops often had princely status and wielded considerable secular power. They raised armies, undertook diplomatic missions, ruled temporal territories as feudal lords, and convened with other magnates in political assemblies. The archbishops of Mainz, Trier, and Cologne served as archchancellors and electors of the HRE. A new German king received his crown and anointing from the archbishop of Cologne. The archbishop of Canterbury summoned his bishops to convocations held in conjunction with sessions of Parliament. Archiepiscopal prominence in matters ecclesiastical and political led to predictable difficulties for churchmen maneuvering between papal and royal demands. In addition to the direct confrontations between temporal and sacred powers characteristic of the investiture controversy and the Great Western Schism (1378–1417), disgruntled clergy defied archiepiscopal jurisdiction and appealed their cases directly to the papacy or sought the intercession of royal courts. Within the province, visitations could prove particularly contentious. Clergy were regularly hostile to archiepiscopal scrutiny and in some cases denied an archbishop access to episcopal cities, monasteries, and churches. Such resistance compromised the efforts of archbishops to reform their provinces as the Fourth Lateran Council had decreed.

B. Arnold, *Princes and Territories in Medieval Germany* (1991); J. Dahmus, *William Courtenay: Archbishop of Canterbury 1381–1396* (1966); R. M. Haines, *Archbishop John Stratford: Political Revolutionary and Champion of the Liberties of the English Church c. 1275/80–1348* (1986); P. S. Lewis, *Later Medieval France: The Polity* (1968); P. B. Pixton, *The German Episcopacy and the Implementation of the Decrees of the Fourth Lateran Council 1216–1245: Watchmen on the Tower* (1995); A. S. Popek, *The Rights and Obligations of Metropolitans: A Historical Synopsis and Commentary* (1947).

J. JEFFERY TYLER

Archdeacon Described by Pope Clement III (1187–1191) as the "eye of the bishop," the archdeacon brought the state of the diocese to the bishop's attention while serving as chief administrative and legal representative of the bishop on the local level. The archidiaconate appears as a fixed structure of diocesan government as early as the tenth century, as increasing ecclesiastical and political demands made it virtually impossible for the bishop to attend to all matters in person. Although in smaller dioceses, especially in Italy, one archdeacon sufficed, in England, France, and Germany larger dioceses were usually divided into multiple archdeaconries. At the high point of their influence during the thirteenth century, archdeacons came to rival episcopal rule in local, ecclesiastical, and moral matters. Archdeacons made visitations to monasteries and parish churches, installed and organized the clergy, and enforced disciplinary canons among clergy and laity. Their tribunals held jurisdiction over minor infractions of church law such as deviant sexual conduct, marital conflict, drunkenness, and violation of Sunday and feast day prohibitions. During the later Middle Ages, bishops often countered and diminished the authority of archdeacons

through the creation and appointment of new officers such as the official and vicar general.

J. A. Brundage, *Medieval Canon Law* (1995); H. E. Feine, *Kirchliche Rechtsgeschichte: Die katholische Kirche* (1964); *Probate Records of the Courts of the Bishop and Archdeacon of Oxford 1516–1732*, 2 vols. (1981, 1985); A. H. Thompson, "Diocesan Organization in the Middle Ages: Archdeacons and Rural Deans," PBA 29 (1943), 153–94.

J. JEFFERY TYLER

Architecture in Early Christianity Christians initially met in houses or in available public spaces. Literary evidence indicates that by the end of the second century and certainly during the third century Christians had their own meeting places. In some cases, parts of a house were reserved for church use, such as the fourth-century Lullingstone villa in Kent, England. In others, a house was acquired by a church and remodeled, such as the church at Dura Europos (240s). The latter were called *domus ecclesiae*, or "church's house." Sometimes commercial property containing a hall was adapted for church use. The double church begun by Bishop Theodore at Aquileia in the early fourth century represents the simple halls built for Christian use (*aula ecclesiae*, "church's hall").

Unlike pagan temples, which were houses for the cult statue of the deity, Christian buildings were assembly places for worshipers. The closest analogies were Jewish synagogues and meeting places for clubs and mystery religions. By the third century the word for "church" *ekklēsia* (assembly), was being used for the place of meeting. Another term used was "Lord's house." Slower in acceptance were words from non-Christian religions such as "temple" or "holy place." The use in Rome of a *titulus* (the marble slab that bore the name of the owner) derives from the practice of meeting in the home of a person whose name was then given to a church building on the site. The term "basilica," derived from the Greek for "royal," was used broadly for any "royal house" but is now a technical architectural term.

A distinctively Christian architectural style emerged with the emperor Constantine, who showed his favor for Christianity by extending the practice of imperial construction of public buildings to include monumental churches. The first of the Constantinian basilicas was the five-aisled Lateran basilica, built for the bishop of Rome. Also in Rome was the Church of St.

Peter, copied later in the fourth century at St. Paul's Outside the Walls. The sites of salvation history were commemorated by the Church of the Nativity in Bethlehem, the Church of the Holy Sepulcher in Jerusalem, and the Eleona on the site of the ascension on the Mount of Olives. Major cities of the empire also received new church buildings. The Constantinian churches often had their entrance on the eastern end, as was true of pagan temples, but the normal Christian orientation became a western entrance with the apse on the east.

Antecedents were the basilicas for judicial, commercial, and reception purposes. These were single-aisled rectangular halls with a raised tribunal (platform) and an apse on one short end. The Christian basilicas added other features: a courtyard, narthex, and other rooms. Although there were many variations, typically there were two or sometimes four side aisles, separated by colonnades from the taller nave (so providing a clerestory). The apse was normally semicircular but could be rectangular. It protruded from the side wall but could be inscribed. The roof was often timber trusses covered with tiles. Cemetery basilicas followed the general plan but included an ambulatory from the side aisles around the apse.

The principal furnishings were an altar, initially wood but soon normally of stone, located either in the apse or immediately in front of it; a chair (*cathedra*) in the apse or behind the altar for the celebrant, with benches for the presbyters, often in a semicircle around the apse (known as a *synthronon*); and in the nave an ambo (pulpit or reading desk) ascended by steps from which the Scriptures were read. The congregation usually stood. Floors and walls often were in mosaic, the content of which was for the most part decorative and not specifically Christian. Windows might be wood gratings or in more expensive buildings glass or alabaster.

A central plan was used for baptisteries and martyria (monuments to martyrs). The baptistery might be a room or rooms attached to the church or a separate building (sometimes divided into space for preliminaries, the baptism itself, and the anointing), and might be a rectangle, a square, a circle, or an octagon. The octagonal baptisteries spread from Rome and Milan to become common in Provence, Ravenna, Istria, and Dalmatia. Fonts were usually centered in the baptismal room and came in various shapes: rectangle, circle, cross, quatrefoil, hexagon, octagon.

Martyria followed the central plan common in Roman mausolea and focused on the tomb or shrine of the martyr. Among the martyria from the fifth century with significant remains are the octagonal Martyrion of Philip near Hierapolis, Turkey, Abu Mena near Alexandria, Egypt, and Qal'at Si'man near Antioch, Syria, which has four basilicas extending as a cross from the central octagon. Intact is San Vitale, Ravenna (sixth century).

Efforts to combine the basilical hall with the stone vaulted roof of martyria resulted in the domed basilica, the most outstanding representative of which is Hagia Sophia in Istanbul. The Orthodox Church developed a distinctive architecture (which flowered in the eleventh century) combining the basilica and a central plan to form a building in the shape of a Greek cross with four equal arms from a central crossing that was covered by a dome. In the West the basilica developed into Romanesque churches (with the best representatives from the twelfth century) with thick walls, large columns with rounded arches to support vaulted stone roofs, and bell towers. These were followed by the Gothic churches (twelfth to fourteenth centuries) in the shape of the Latin cross, formed by the transept crossing the nave near the east end, with tall spires, pointed arches, thin walls with flying buttresses, and much window space filled with stained glass.

J. G. Davies, *The Origin and Development of Early Christian Church Architecture* (1953); W. E. Kleinbauer, *Early Christian and Byzantine Architecture: An Annotated Bibliography* (1992); R. Krautheimer, *Early Christian and Byzantine Architecture* (4th ed., 1986); W. L. MacDonald, *Early Christian and Byzantine Architecture* (1962, 1977); L. M. White, *The Social Origins of Christian Architecture*, 2 vols. (1990, 1997).

EVERETT FERGUSON

Argula von Stauff von Grumbach

(1492–1554?), pioneering Protestant woman writer. A member of the independent von Stauff family, Argula served as a maid-in-waiting to Kunigunde, daughter of the emperor Frederick III. In 1516 she married Friedrich von Grumbach, a Catholic landowner in Bavaria. Their children George, Hans Georg, Gottfried, and Apollonia were raised Protestant. Argula was respected by many of the Reformers, including Luther, whom she met in Coburg in 1530, and was well versed in the Scriptures and the Reformers' works. She rose to defend a young student at the Univ. of Ingolstadt, Arsacius Seehofer, who was accused of espousing Lutheran theology. Seehofer's arrest and forced renouncement of his faith in 1522 outraged Argula who, after consulting Andreas Osiander, wrote a letter filled with biblical quotations challenging the university to give proof of Seehofer's guilt.

Many of her letters and poems were published until 1524, when censorship increased and her husband was removed from his position as an administrator at Dietfurt. Argula continued to advocate for Protestant congregations and theological dialogues, and she attended the Diet of Augsburg. Never identifying herself as a "Lutheran," she proclaimed the supremacy of Scripture and the priesthood of all believers. Three years into widowhood, Argula married Count von Schlick and would bury him and three of her children before her own death in obscurity.

S. Halbach, *Argula von Grumbach als Verfasserin reformatorischer Flugschriften* (1992); P. Matheson, ed., *Argula von Grumbach: A Woman's Voice in the Reformation* (1995).

KIRSI STJERNA

Ariminum, Council of

As Constantius II sought to unify the empire religiously, an "ecumenical" council and the issuing of a single creed were proposed in early spring of 359. In fact, two councils were convened—one in Italy at Ariminum and the other in Asia Minor at Seleucia—with the joint purpose of ratifying a comprehensive confession of faith. Some four hundred bishops from the West gathered in May 359 and remained in session for eight months.

In the council's early deliberations, the Nicene definition of the Son as the same substance as the Father (*homoousios*) would have been ratified had not a vocal minority of bishops introduced another formula: "the Son was like [*homoios*] the Father in all things." This was rejected by the majority. The emperor, however, favored the homoian formula as less controversial, since it had been commonly accepted in the 330s and 340s and avoided using nonscriptural terminology, a problem that *homoousios* faced. As the council dragged on, the emperor demanded unanimity, and a stripped-down version of the homoian creed was finally approved: "the Son was like the Father." The bishops departed in ostensible unity, and the formula was ratified officially in Constantinople in January 360. Only later was it recognized that the new homoian creed gave latitude to an "Arian" interpretation, a realiza-

tion to which Jerome directed his famous epitaph, "The whole world groaned and was amazed to find itself Arian." Although the homoian hegemony was short-lived, the Ariminum and Nicene creeds functioned as rival confessional rallying points for the next half century.

Y.-M. Duval, "La 'manoeuvre frauduleuse' de Rimini à la recherche du *Liber adversus Vrsacium et Valentem*," *Hilaire et Son Temps* (1969); D. H. Williams, *Ambrose of Milan and the End of the Nicene-Arian Conflicts* (1995).

D. H. WILLIAMS

Aristides

(second cent.), apologist. He is commonly considered the Athenian author of the earliest intact Christian apology. Besides Eusebius's reference to him as a man devoted to the faith, very little is known about him. Eusebius (*Hist. eccl.* 4.3.3; *Chronicle* 125), Jerome (Letter 70.4; *Lives of Illustrious Men* 20), and others in the early church refer to Aristides' *Apology*. A complete Syriac version discovered in 1889 revealed that a medieval novel, *Life of Barlaam and Josaphat*, contains two chapters from the *Apology* in Greek. Armenian fragments and two Greek papyrus fragments also exist. The *Apology*, addressed either to the emperor Hadrian or Antoninus Pius, uses a philosophical argument to show that Christianity is supreme. From an argument for the existence of a transcendent God, it moves to an evaluation of four primary systems of thought (Barbarian, Greek, Jewish, Christian). It concludes that three of these systems lead to a false view of God because they do not have a means to look beyond this world. Christianity alone has an accurate view of God (and thus an ability to serve God properly) because of the divine revelation through Christ.

Aristides, *Apologie*, ed. and trans. M. Guiorgadzé et al. (2003); J. R. Harris, trans., and J. R. Robinson, ed., *The Apology of Aristides on Behalf of the Christians*, TS, vol. 1 (1891; repr. 1967); H. J. M. Milne, "A New Fragment of the Apology of Aristides," *JTS* 25 (1923–1924): 73–77.

D. JEFFREY BINGHAM

Aristo of Pella

(second cent.), apologist. He is known primarily through his work *Dialogue between Jason and Papiscus*, a polemic against Judaism in the form of a dialogue between a Judeo-Christian (Jason) and a Jew

(Papiscus). The use of allegorical exegesis and an Alexandrian character lead many to believe it was written from Alexandria. The only surviving piece of the work is the preface to a Latin translation found in the pseudo-Cyprian works. Jerome cites the *Dialogue* in his *Commentary on Galatians* (2.3) and *Questions on Genesis* (1.1). Origen, against Celsus's complaints about the work, says it is a conversation between a Christian and a Jew regarding the Jewish Scriptures in which the Christian is proving that predictions regarding the Christ fit Jesus.

"Aristo of Pella" in PG 5 (1857), 1271–86; B. P. Pratten, trans., "Remains of the Second and Third Centuries," *ANF* 8 (repr. 1986), 749–50; J. C. T. Otto, ed., *Corpus Apologetarum Christianorum*, vol. 9 (1872; repr. 1969): 349–63; J. E. Bruns, "Altercatio Jasonis et Papisci, Philo, and Anastasius the Sinaite," *TS* (1973): 287–94; A. L. Williams, *Adversus Judaeos: A Bird's-Eye View of Christian Apology until the Renaissance* (1935): 28–30.

D. JEFFREY BINGHAM

Aristotle and Medieval Theology

Medieval intellectual life in the West was thoroughly shaped by Christianity, both in its sources and its institutions. The Bible was considered to be the sacred text, which contained the truth revealed by God. Other important authoritative sources were the church fathers, whose views came to be assembled in collections of opinions (*sententiae*) by the end of the twelfth century. The most important venues of philosophy and theology were ecclesiastical institutions: the monasteries, the cathedral schools, and, from the beginning of the thirteenth century, the universities.

Around 1125, this Christian culture came into contact with the first great influx into Western Europe of Latin translations of Aristotle's philosophical works. Before that time, only a few texts of Aristotle's logic had been known to medieval thinkers, such as *On Interpretation*, *Categories*, and Porphyry's *Isagoge* (an introduction to the *Categories)*. Together these texts constituted a field that was known as dialectic. Thinkers such as Berengar of Tours (c. 1000–1088) advocated the use of Aristotle's dialectic for understanding theological issues. He claimed, for instance, that from an Aristotelian perspective, the change of bread and wine into the flesh and blood of Christ during the Eucharist was incomprehensible. After the priest had proclaimed his holy formula, the bread still had all the "accidents" (i.e., properties) of bread, so

there was no reason to believe that the "substance" of bread had changed into the substance of the body of Christ. For, according to Aristotelian dialectic, the accidents or perceptible properties inhered in the substance and indicated its nature. On the basis of his Aristotelian analysis of what was going on during the Eucharist, Berengar concluded that the claim of a change had to be taken in a symbolic way and not in a literal way, as his contemporaries believed. He was condemned for upholding this view.

In contrast to Berengar, Peter Damian (c. 1007–1072) saw the study of dialectic as a dangerous influence on Christianity. According to him, it is blasphemous to believe that God is bound by the rules of logic and the laws of nature. God is omnipotent, and hence many arguments, and even the principle of noncontradiction, lose their power, as is also apparent from many miraculous stories in the Bible. God can undo the past, and the Virgin Mary can give birth to a child. Polemics against vain curiosity (*vana curiositas*) and against the acquisition of knowledge for its own sake during this period should also be seen in this light.

During the thirteenth century, at the time of the nascent universities in Europe, resistance to Aristotle's teaching for understanding Christianity often took the form of ecclesiastical prohibitions and condemnations. By this time almost all works by Aristotle were available in a Latin translation and came to be gradually incorporated into the curriculum. In 1210 ecclesiastical authorities at Paris forbade lecturing on Aristotle's "natural books" (*libri naturales*). The prohibition was repeated in the 1215 statutes of the Univ. of Paris, but at the same time the document stipulates the teaching of Aristotle's logic and ethics. In 1231, Pope Gregory IX issued the bull *Parens scientiarum*, which somewhat modified the earlier prohibition to read Aristotle's works on natural philosophy by ordering that these works should be examined and purged of what could cause the suspicion of error. The papal letter is especially important because it identifies a group of thinkers as "philosophers" (*artistae, philosophi*), who are distinct from theologians and to whom should be left the study of Aristotle. It should be noted that these prohibitions to study certain works by Aristotle were limited to Paris.

The year 1255 is often presented as an important turning point in the assimilation of Aristotle's works. In that year the Univ. of Paris passed legislation that made almost all of Aristotle's known works, and also some pseudo-Aristotelian works, required reading. From that time on all university intellectuals were exposed to lectures and disputations that were based on Aristotle's text. Yet the appropriation of this material was a gradual process, as is clear from condemnations and censures that were issued in the 1270s. The main concern of this legislation was that masters from the arts faculty should refrain from discussing theological matters, and that when they discussed philosophical matters they should do so in accordance with faith. In addition, many specific propositions or articles (*articuli*) were condemned. The best-known condemnations are those that were issued by Bishop Tempier in 1270 (10 articles) and 1277 (219 articles) in Paris. Not all of the positions represented by these articles can be found in the works of contemporary masters of arts, such as Siger of Brabant and Boethius of Dacia. Other articles hark back to Aristotle's views or on their interpretations by Avicenna and Averroes. Many have remained unidentified. Some of the censured articles clearly challenged Christian orthodox teaching, whereas others are more difficult to place from a contemporary perspective. In those cases, Tempier's own theological views or those of his advisors may have played a role. Some of the more obvious issues, which had already been noted by the theologian Bonaventure a few years prior to Tempier's condemnation, concerned the world's eternity and the unity of the intellect. In *Physics*, Aristotle had proved that the world is eternal, that is, without a beginning. This view was in contradiction to the Christian doctrine about the world's creation, which was supposed to imply a beginning in time. The thesis of the unity of the intellect was derived from an obscure passage in Aristotle's *On the Soul* (*De anima*), interpreted in a certain way by Averroes. It stated that there is one and the same intellect for all human beings. This thesis contradicts the Christian teaching about personal immortality and individual moral responsibility.

In dealing with issues involving Aristotle and theology, some thinkers took the approach to distinguish between philosophical and theological discourse. In this way, medieval thinkers would typically claim that they were discussing a certain issue according to philosophy, or according to what Aristotle might have meant, rather than according to truth. This approach granted autonomy to philosophical inquiry, but at the same time, the doctrines of Christian revelation remained protected, because for Christians, both philosophers and theologians, they were true.

G. D. Bernard, "Aristoteles Latinus," in *The Cambridge History of Later Medieval Philosophy*, ed. N. Kretzmann, A. Kenny, and J. Pinborg (1982), 45–79; J. M. M. H. Thijssen, *Censure and Heresy at the University of Paris, 1200–1400* (1998); F. Van Steenberghen, *Aristotle in the West: The Origins of Latin Aristotelianism* (1970); J. F. Wippel, *Medieval Reactions to the Encounter between Faith and Reason* (1995).

J. M. M. H. THIJSSEN

Aristotle, Translations of

While Aristotle did not conceive it as such, the Aristotelian corpus constitutes an encyclopedia of knowledge, as the ancient commentators realized. This view of things was taken over by Christian intellectuals and helped to propel the translation of Aristotle's work into Latin.

We can distinguish three crucial phases in this large movement of translation. In the early sixth century, Boethius translated most if not all of the *Organon* (the logical writings). Used in his own theological tractates, these logical works influenced theological thinking to c. 1100 and beyond. Phase two occurred during the high Middle Ages. Four men, James of Venice, Burgundio of Pisa, Michael Scot, and William of Moerbeke, were principally responsible for making available translations of many of Aristotle's treatises, including the *libri naturales* (the books on natural philosophy). These became central to the new speculative theology called scholasticism. Finally, armed with a genuine understanding of classical antiquity, mastery of Greek, and improved critical tools, Renaissance scholars produced new, more accurate editions of Aristotle's work.

It would be difficult to overestimate the impact of these translations on our intellectual life. In philosophy and theology, science and political science, Western civilization is still to a significant degree "Aristotelian."

Aristoteles Latinus: Codices (1939–1961); *Aristoteles Latinus* (1951–).

STEVEN J. WILLIAMS

Arius and Arianism

Arius (d. 337) was a priest and teacher in Alexandria. In 318 or 320 Arius came into conflict with his bishop, Alexander, who taught that the Son, although "between created and uncreated" was always with the Father and eternally generated from the Father. If God is always Father, then the Son must always be with the Father: one cannot be a father without a child. Arius (preferring to see the language of Father and Son as secondary to other terminologies) objected that there is only one God and that the Word or Son existed by the will of God from "before the ages" but not eternally and without sharing God's being. Both Arius and Alexander drew on long-standing themes in Alexandrian theology, and both were to some extent innovators.

After some initial local meetings, a council of bishops met at the behest of Constantine at Nicaea in 325. The council issued a creed that said that the Son was generated "from the essence of the Father" and was *homoousios* (sharing the same being) with the Father. Arius was exiled. This dispute reflected and stimulated tension between different theological trajectories present at the time it erupted; Nicaea did nothing to diffuse this tension. The technical terminology used in the creed seems to have been chosen as an ad hoc tool to censure Arius and was not clearly defined even by its supporters. Arius died in 337 after having been readmitted to communion by many.

Arianism. This term may be traced back to Athanasius, bishop of Alexandria from 328, who was exiled in 336. The charges against him were of malfeasance. While some seem to have been well founded, his accusers were theological opponents. Athanasius, however, presented the opposition to him as purely theological, and in the *Orations against the Arians* developed an account of an "Arian" conspiracy since Nicaea. This terminology was accepted by many Western theologians and increasingly by some Easterners in later decades. Non-Nicene Christians were labeled as Arian, regardless of the substance of their theological positions.

Many Eastern bishops from 325 through 350 may be termed "Eusebian," being broadly in a tradition that encompassed both Eusebius of Caesarea and Eusebius of Nicomedia. Without disavowing Nicaea, they held that there is a basic ontological distinction between Father and Son but also insisted that there is an ineffable closeness between Father and Son such that the Son's being can be said to be from the Father in some indescribable sense. For some the Son is "the exact image of the Father's substance" (cf. Wis. 7:25; Heb. 1:3); for others the Son is a unique product of the Father's will.

The controversy shifted considerably during the 350s, as the emperor Constantius supported an increasingly subordinationist theology. By the last few years of the decade the adherents of this position argued that the Son is only "like" (*homoios*) the Father: clearly distinct and

ontologically inferior. The Homoians rejected any use of *ousia* terminology. The most radical wing of this movement, represented by Aetius and his disciple Eunomius, insisted that Father and Son were unlike in *ousia*. Their teaching affected the perception of the Homoian movement generally and produced a strong reaction. During the 370s and 380s, Eunomians or "Heterousians" (*heteros* = other) increasingly became a distinct ecclesial group.

In 359–360 Constantius called two councils which, under his pressure, promulgated a homoian creed intended to function as a universal marker of orthodox faith. In reaction, several groups coalesced around the Nicene Creed as the only alternative to the homoian creed. As they slowly came together, these groups agreed on the principles within which the Nicene Creed should be understood: that God's immaterial and incomprehensible being is not divided and that the persons are truly distinct from each other. Between 360 and 380 there was also an evolution of terminologies that distinguish what is one from what is three in God: God is one in nature, power, glory, or essence, while there are three persons or *hypostases*. This last development also occurred through polemic against those who doubted the full divinity of the Spirit. These theologies represent a real development over those of Nicaea's original architects and have been called neo- or proto-Nicene by many modern scholars.

After the accession of the pro-Nicene emperor Theodosius, the Council of Constantinople met in 381 and promulgated a revised version of Nicaea's creed, adding clauses on the Spirit to insist that "with the Father and the Son He is worshiped and glorified." Groups of non-Nicene Christians continued to be a real force within the Christian world through the next century, but increasingly they became distinct ecclesial groups.

L. Ayres, *Nicaea and Its Legacy* (2004); M. R. Barnes, "The Fourth Century as Trinitarian Canon," in *Christian Origins*, ed. L. Ayres and G. Jones (1998): 47–67; R. P. C. Hanson, *The Search for the Christian Doctrine of God* (1988); J. T. Lienhard, "Ousia and Hypostasis: The Cappadocian Settlement and the Theology of 'One Hypostasis,'" in *The Trinity*, ed. S. T. Davis et al. (2000): 99–121; R. D. Williams, *Arius* (1987).

LEWIS AYRES

Armenian Christianity

Christianity developed in Armenia over the second and third

centuries as a result of initiatives from Edessa and Caesarea enshrined in traditions of an apostolate of Saints Thaddeus and Bartholemew. It evolved a hierarchically structured form in the fourth century after the martyrdom of St. Hṙip'simē and her companions and with the consecration of the confessor St. Gregory the Illuminator as bishop of Greater Armenia in c. 314 (traditional date 301) and the baptism of King Trdat III and the Armenian court. Influence from pagan culture can be observed in folk practices relating to the main feasts, the maintenance of animal sacrifice as a response to answered prayer, and the activities of popular saints such as Sergius (Sargis). During the fourth century Armenia reflected regional and broader trends, including representation at the Council of Nicaea (325), the spread of Arianism in court circles, and provision of institutions for the poor and sick on the model of Sebaste. In 387 most of the country passed under Sasanian suzerainty, provoking a series of revolts against large-scale attempts to reintroduce Zoroastrianism, until the dynasty's demise in the 640s. The revolt of 451 culminated in the martyrdom of the commander Vardan Mamikonian and many of his troops, which retains symbolic significance in the present. The transfer outside Roman authority assisted in preserving various early rites such as the joint celebration of Christ's nativity and baptism on January 6 and a one-week pre-Lenten fast. Also early is the address of the Trisagion prayer to Christ rather than the Trinity. The Armenian church also forged close links with its neighbors Iberia (Eastern Georgia) and Caucasian Albania, which evinced a similar developmental pattern.

With the assistance of the hierarch Sahak, the chorepiscopus Mashtots created an alphabet in c. 406, inaugurating a process of translation from Greek and Syriac that extended through the mid-eighth century, encompassing the Bible, liturgical, hagiographical, and theological works, followed by school and philosophical texts, some of which now survive only in Armenian. Indigenous Christian Armenian literature opened with a number of hagiographical, polemical, homiletic, and historical texts. During the 420s the church was administered by Persian candidates who introduced the title of *catholicos* to signify Armenia's autocephaly from Western intervention. However, in the aftermath of the Council of Ephesus (431), the church manifested a powerful opposition to Nestorian dualism, reaffirmed by synods of Duin in c. 505 and 553. Moreover, the

form of protomonasticism that became rooted in Armenia at this time was informed by the West Syrian model of rigorist asceticism.

In contrast to the Copts and West Syrians, Armenia experienced a long engagement with Chalcedonian Christology (451–c. 690), marked by debates generally initiated by the Byzantine emperors that, however, elicited only short-term acquiescence from the Armenian side, which increasingly aligned itself with Alexandrian philosophy and theology. Armenian condemnation of Chalcedon at a synod of 608 was followed by explorations of the "compromise" positions of monothelitism and monergism during the seventh century. This period also witnessed widespread church construction in various styles (basilica, cross-in-square, rotunda, etc.), many of which are still extant. The ensuing Arab epoch (640s–c. 884) permitted doctrinal and canonical retrenchment in synods convoked by the able catholicos Yovhannes Odznets'i (r. 717–728) condemning the iconoclastic sect of Paulicians and Armenian aphthartodocetists, counteracting their extremism with the particularly Armenian doctrine of the incorruptibility of Christ's flesh articulated in a non-Eutychian manner.

The waning of the caliphate's central control facilitated renewed statehood under the Bagratid dynasty (884–1064), coinciding with Middle Byzantine expansion and reflected theologically in discussions with Patriarch Photius (mid-ninth cent.). Spirituality now focused on interiority rather than outward asceticism, practiced in new cenobitic monasteries often governed by St. Basil's rule under the oversight of the Armenian cleric with the rank of *vardapet* (doctor of theology). It found its highest expression in the *Book of Lamentation* by the mystical poet Grigor Narekats'i (d. 1003). Some monasteries also founded schools of higher learning, such as Gladzor, which attracted students from all over the Armenian lands. This period also witnessed struggles against the iconoclastic Tondrakite sect by means of *khachk'ars* ("cross-stones"), an indigenous form of liturgical art. After the destruction of the group's center at Tondrak, adherents were deported to Philippopolis (Plovdiv) in Bulgaria. Transforming their belief system in the course of their geographical migration, they influenced later sects such as the Bogomils and Albigensians. Byzantine incorporation of the various Anatolian Armenian kingdoms led to the attempt to suppress the Armenian catholicate, too, after inconclusive unity talks in 1065. Further discussions on union (1165–1180) occurred between the emperor Manuel and the catholicos Nerses Shnorhali ("the Gracious") and the latter's successor, Grigor Tghay, as well as between Alexios III and Nerses Lambronats'i in 1197. Both sets of discussions were inconclusive.

The fall of the capital of Ani to the Seljuks provoked a major exodus from the Armenian plateau and the expansion of communities on the Crimea, Kievan Rus', Poland, and the western Black Sea coast, in addition to Italy and Egypt, requiring the construction of new churches for their spiritual needs. Meanwhile, the center of gravity moved south to Cilicia, where a robust Armenian state emerged that evolved into the rank of kingdom (1198–1375) under the suzerainty of the German emperor and an ostensible church union with Rome on the basis of interchange during the Crusades. Though Armenians rejected the Latin *filioque* doctrine in 1251 and that of Petrine primacy in 1262, Mamluk pressure forced the hierarchy to adopt doctrinal and ritual adaptations in hopes of gaining Western military aid in unpopular synods of 1307 and 1316. Pope John XXII's establishment of a Dominican archdiocese at Sultaniya in 1318 introduced Latin theology to the area of Greater Armenia, instituting the first systematic translation of Latin thought into another language and founding the Armenian order of the Fratres Unitores (1356), which, despite many vicissitudes, continued into the eighteenth century. Although opposing doctrines such as purgatory, scholars such as Yovhan Orotnec'i (d. 1387) and his pupil Grigor Tat'ewac'I (d. 1409) benefited from the Western insights on sacramental theology and angelology newly in circulation. This phase of dialogue with Rome concluded with a ratification of the Council of Florence (1439) by the catholicos, though it was rejected by the majority of the hierarchy, provoking the creation of an anti-catholicate at Ejmiacin in 1441 that thereafter established itself as the church's primary see.

The absorption of most of Armenia into the Ottoman Empire in the early sixteenth century led to the community's legal identification in terms of its confession (*millet*). The growth of the Armenian patriarchate of Constantinople resulted in tensions with the other major sees of Ejmiacin, Sis, and Jerusalem, which were resolved by a synod in 1651. Subsequent patriarchs of stature included Yovhannes Kolot (r. 1715–1741) and Yakob Nalean (r. 1741–1749; 1752–1764). Theatine, Capuchin, and Jesuit missions associated with the Counter-Reformation

in the same century issued in the creation of a new Uniate Armenian monastic order named after its founder Mkhit'ar Sebastats'i (1676–1749), which has been active in the areas of publication, schooling, and religious scholarship. It has mother houses in Venice and Vienna. Similarly, an Armenian Catholic patriarchate was founded in 1740 with its seat in Lebanon, its faithful being represented by a distinct Catholic millet since 1831. American missionary activity over the first decades of the nineteenth century laid the groundwork for a parallel Protestant millet, which gained ratification in 1846.

The *polozhenie* of 1836 regulated the legal status of the Armenian church in the East on incorporation into the Russian Empire, while the Armenian Constitution of 1863 significantly democratized the operation of the original Armenian Ottoman millet, infusing much greater lay participation, certain provisions of which are still in force. In contravention of article 61 of the Congress of Berlin (1878), however, Ottoman violations of Armenian religious freedom went unchecked, leading to a series of massacres in 1895–1896 and 1909 and thereafter a concerted program of deportation and genocide of the Armenian population of eastern Anatolia. Among the one and a half million victims who perished during the years 1915–1923 were some four thousand clergy. Only in 1929 was the catholicate of Sis reestablished at Antelias, north of Beirut. These demographic changes accelerated the process by which the Armenian church now bears pastoral responsibility for a worldwide diaspora.

Meanwhile, the installation of Soviet orders in the Armenian Republic in 1920 witnessed persecution of religion and the church, which reached its height under Stalin's Years of Terror (1936–1938). The Soviet authorities were implicated in the death of the catholicos, after which the primatial see remained vacant until 1945. Despite a degree of instrumentalization during the Cold War years, the long catholicate of Vazgen Palchyan (1955–1994) provided the church with a measure of stability. In 1962 both catholicates of the Armenian church were extended membership in the World Council of Churches and were later spectators at Vatican II. The Catholicate of Sis also played a major role in the creation of the Middle East Council of Churches in 1974 and in Islam-Christian dialogue.

Since the collapse of the Soviet Union, new arenas have opened up in the Republic of Armenia for social and philanthropic diaconia and for religious instruction in school, with teachers being trained at a theological faculty at the Erevan State University, opened in 1995. The church also has a much more visible profile, with its own radio and television channels and periodical press. The constitution ratified in 1995 maintains freedom of religion, conscience, and expression and, while recognizing a special relation with the apostolic church historically, rejects the state establishment of any denomination.

———

S. P. Cowe, "The Armenians in the Era of the Crusades (1050–1350)" and "Church and Diaspora: The Case of the Armenians," in *The Cambridge History of Christianity*, vol. 5, *Eastern Christianity*, ed. M. Angold (2006), 404–29, 430–56; K. H. Maksoudian, *Chosen of God: The Election of the Catholicos of All Armenians from the Fourth Century to the Present* (1995); M. Ormanian, *The Church of Armenia* (2nd ed., 1955).

S. PETER COWE

Arminius, Jacobus (1560–1609), Dutch scholastic theologian and controversialist. Jacob Harmenszoon (Arminius) studied at Leiden, Basel, in Geneva with Theodore Beza, and in Padua and Rome. Ordained in the Dutch Reformed Church, Arminius came to reject both varieties of Reformed predestinarian doctrine, supralapsarian and infralapsarian, favoring instead a synergistic understanding of salvation in which human free will was the decisive factor. He was particularly influenced by the Jesuit theology of Luis de Molina and Francisco Suárez and incorporated their perspective on divine middle knowledge (*scientia media*) into his own conceptualization of divine grace and human freedom. With speculative subtlety Arminius hypothesized a fourfold divine decree in which divine election was based on foreseen faith in the individual. Human faith was assisted by universally available divine grace, which the human will could either resist or accept. Arminius first stirred up controversy while a pastor in Amsterdam, in a series of sermons on Romans. As a professor at Leiden, Arminius came into open conflict with the Calvinist Franciscus Gomarus over the issue of predestination. He wrote a pamphlet criticizing the predestinarian theology of William Perkins and carried on an epistolary debate with Leiden professor Franciscus Junius. After Arminius's death, his sympathizers formed the Remonstrant party in the Dutch Reformed Church. Their antipredestinarian views were rejected at the Synod of Dort. Recent scholarship has argued that Arminius's doctrine was not simply a variant of but a radical alternative to Reformed teaching on predestination.

———

C. Bangs, *Arminius: A Study in the Dutch Reformation* (2nd ed., 1985); R. A. Muller, *God, Creation, and Providence in the Thought of Jacob Arminius* (1991).

RAYMOND A. BLACKETER

Arndt, Johann (1555–1623), Lutheran pastor and devotional writer. After study in Helmstadt, Basel, Strasbourg, and perhaps Wittenberg, Arndt became a pastor, although his formal academic work had not included theology but focused on Paracelsian medicine. He was removed from his pastorate in Anhalt because he opposed the introduction of Calvinism (1590) and served as a pastor in Quedlinburg, Braunschweig, Eisleben, and as superintendent of the churches of Braunschweig-Lüneburg at Celle. Scholars debate the precise balance between the influences of Luther and other Lutheran theologians, especially Martin Chemnitz, on the one hand, and on the other, the medieval mystic tradition of Thomas à Kempis, Johann Tauler, and others upon his widely published devotional works, especially *Four Books on True Christianity* (1605, 1620) and *Little Garden of Paradise* (1612). His volumes of sermons on the Sunday Gospel pericopes, on the catechism, and on the Psalter, as well as devotional writings, were also widely used in orthodox and pietistic Lutheranism. He defined "true Christianity" as a life of repentance, the daily dying of the sinner and resurrection of the new creature, restored to the image of God through the gospel of Christ.

———

E. Axmacher, *Johann Arndt und Paul Gerhardt* (2001).

ROBERT KOLB

Arnobius of Sicca (c. third–fourth cent.), apologist and rhetorician in Africa. Jerome provides some detail regarding his life (*Chronicle* 253–327 CE; *Lives of Illustrious Men* 79, 80; *Letters* 58.10, 70.5). His sole extant work, *Adversus Nationes*, was composed to substantiate the sincerity of his conversion from opposition to adherence to Christianity. The work, which lacks any biblical citation, responds to the charge that Christianity was a novel religion manufactured by Jesus, a sorcerer and imposter, and thus was responsible for the ills of Roman society. Arnobius argues that Christianity, rooted in the will of an eternal, unchanging God and centered around Jesus, is the only hope for society. He includes a thorough and noteworthy account of ancient pagan religion's beliefs and practices. Similarity to early Christian Gnosticism is evident in Arnobius's assertions about the corporeality, and thus weakness, of the soul. Because he believed the soul to be corporeal, he argued that it must be from an intermediate source, not God, and that it is mortal by nature. Immortality is received through the knowledge of the transcendent God.

Arnobius of Sicca, *Adversus Nationes*, ed. H. Le Bonniec (1982); Arnobius, *The Case against the Pagans*, ACW 7–8 (1949); M. Edwards, "The Flowering of Latin Apologetic: Lactantius and Arnobius," in *Apologetics in the Roman Empire,* ed. M. Edwards et al. (1999); M. B. Simmons, *Arnobius of Sicca: Religious Conflict and Competition in the Age of Diocletian* (1995).

D. JEFFREY BINGHAM

Arnobius the Younger (d. after 451),

Christian exegete and polemicist. Little is known about Arnobius's personal life. It is possible that he was a monk of African origin who spent some time in Rome. Despite the scant details, care should be taken to distinguish him from Arnobius of Sicca, the fourth-century rhetorician and apologist.

An important source of information about Arnobius's theological views is his *Conflictus cum Serapione*. Written around 450, this work provides an account of a debate between an Egyptian Monophysite and Arnobius. Arnobius's support for Augustine's anti-Pelagianism surfaces in the course of the debate.

In addition to this work, Morin argues that Arnobius is the author of four other books: the *Expositiunculae in Evangelium*, brief accounts of the Gospels of Matthew, Luke, and John; the *Liber Gregoriam*, a *consolatio* (work of consolation); the *Commentarii in Psalmos*, an anti-Augustinian interpretation of the Psalms; and the *Praedestinatus*, another anti-Augustinian work that rejects Augustine's teaching on grace and predestination. Scholars continue to debate the attribution of the latter two works to Arnobius because their contents contradict the pro-Augustinian stance of the *Conflictus*.

CPL (1995), 239–43; H. A. Kayser, *Die Schriften des sogenannten Arnobius junior, dogmengeschichtlich und literarisch untersucht* (1912); G. Morin, "Étude d'ensemble sur Arnobe le Jeune," RBén 28 (1911): 154–90.

MARIANNE DJUTH

Arnold, Gottfried (1666–1714), Lutheran

church historian and devotional writer. He studied theology at the Univ. of Wittenberg. He met Philip Jacob Spener (1635–1705) in Dresden in 1689 and was converted to Pietist ideals. Following the 1697 publication of *The First Love*, an important study of the early Christians, Arnold was appointed to the faculty of the Univ. of Giessen. He resigned the following year and briefly retired to Quedlinburg, a center of radical Pietist activity. In 1701 he again took up pastoral work.

The author of more than 130 hymns and 40 books, mostly stressing an inner experience of Christianity, Arnold's landmark work was the controversial *Impartial History of the Church and Heresy* (1699–1700), based on a critical use of primary source material. His fresh interpretation of church history demonstrated that those whom the church had dismissed as heretics were often, in fact, the more faithful and true Christians. Arnold's portrayal of church history was tremendously important in the development of Pietism, including radical Pietist groups.

P. C. Erb, *Pietists, Protestants, and Mysticism: The Use of Late Medieval Spiritual Texts in the Work of Gottfried Arnold 1666–1714* (1989); F. E. Stoeffler, *German Pietism during the 18th Century* (1973).

DAVID B. ELLER

Art in Early Christianity The earliest

examples of explicitly Christian visual art are usually dated to the late second or early third century. They were discovered primarily in the area around Rome, particularly in the Christian catacombs along the ancient Via Appia. In the pre-Constantinian era, a majority of the extant monuments were created specifically for a funerary context (catacomb frescoes and sarcophagus relief sculptures), but collections of decorated lamps, engraved gems, etched glass, molded ceramic bowls and plates, and small sculptures carved in the round offer some exceptions. Three important early Christian monuments, the house church at Dura Europos in present-day Syria and two in England—the Christian "chapel" found in the Roman villa at Lullingstone in Kent and the floor mosaic at Hinton St. Mary in Dorset—provide additional exceptions to the Roman and funerary context of early Christian art.

Specific subject matter rather than formal aspects of style or details of composition is what distinguishes these earliest examples of Christian art from either Jewish or pagan works. In general, early Christian art draws its themes from certain recognizable Christian symbols and from biblical and some extra-canonical literature. The most common symbols that may be identified as having specific Christian significance include the dove with olive branch, anchor, chalice, fish, and boat. The image of a shepherd carrying a sheep over his shoulders was borrowed from contemporary pagan iconography and associated with the Christian Good Shepherd. The image of an *orant*—a veiled, standing figure with hands outstretched in prayer (usually female)—may represent the Christian soul, although in pagan imagery it referred to the virtue of piety.

Certain scenes from Old and New Testaments are represented with great frequency in painting and relief sculpture. The popularity of NT imagery indicates the continuing use of the Septuagint as a prophetic witness to Christ and the Christian gospel, since the imagery may be correlated with typological interpretations common in theological treatises, homilies, prayers, and liturgical documents. A sequential series of episodes from the Jonah story is among the most popular of early Christian visual images, showing Jonah being thrown overboard into the mouth of the waiting sea creature, being spit up onto dry land, and reclining under his gourd vine. The interpretation of this iconography, especially since it occurs in a cemeterial context, associates the story of Jonah with the death and resurrection symbolized in Christian baptism and the promise of eternal life for the baptized. Other common NT themes include the representation of Adam and Eve, Noah, Abraham and Isaac, Moses receiving the law, and Moses striking the rock in the wilderness.

New Testament images appear in Christian art of the third and early fourth centuries and most frequently portray Jesus healing and working wonders. The multiplication of loaves and changing water to wine appear juxtaposed with depictions of Jesus healing (e.g., the paralytic, the man born blind, the woman with an issue of blood) and Jesus raising the dead Lazarus or Jairus's daughter. Christ's baptism by John appears less frequently and usually shows him as a small, nude child. The nativity of Christ is most commonly represented by a depiction of the visitation of the (normally three) magi to the Christ child, who is seated on the lap of his mother. In almost every instance of this image, all the figures are shown in profile.

Jesus' giving the law to his disciples, Jesus' entrance into Jerusalem, and scenes from the passion began to appear around the mid-fourth century. Although an empty cross appeared in many of these compositions during the latter half of the fourth century, an actual crucifixion scene is almost unknown prior to the fifth century and rare until the sixth and seventh centuries in both the eastern and western parts of the Roman Empire. The transition from an early iconographic emphasis on Jesus' works to his passion and ascension may indicate that Christian visual art was being affected by the theological discussions and controversies of the late fourth and early fifth centuries.

Following the conversion of Constantine, Christian art attracted wealthy and powerful patrons who financed the development of a monumental style of art for new or renovated Christian churches, shrines, baptisteries, and mausolea in all regions of the empire. New iconographic themes began to appear in glass mosaics found on walls and apses of these buildings, as well as furnishings and liturgical objects made from ivory, silver, and other precious materials. Representations of Christ enthroned or transcendent and depictions of the Madonna and the saints all became more common. As actual portraits began to emerge, biblical narratives became less frequent. These portraits were the predecessors of later Byzantine icons in that they represented their subjects in full frontal poses, with only enough additional detail to aid in identification.

Narrative imagery reappears, however, in the earliest existing illuminated biblical manuscripts of the fifth and sixth centuries. The oldest of these, the *Quedlingburg Itala*, consists of five leaves from the books of Samuel and Kings. Slightly later works include the *Cotton Genesis*, the *Vienna Genesis*, and the *Rabbula Gospels*. The two Genesis manuscripts offer previously unknown compositions, including a representation of Noah's flood showing the ark afloat in a swirling sea of dead or dying humans and animals and scenes from the story of Joseph. The *Rabbula Gospels* (c. 586) contains some of the earliest images of the crucifixion, Christ's ascension, and Pentecost. In the *Rabbula Gospels'* crucifixion scene, Christ appears fully clothed in a purple robe with two gold stripes (*clavi*), between the two thieves dressed only in loincloths. In both the ascension and Pentecost images, the Virgin Mary holds a central place among the disciples.

————

P. C. Finney, *The Invisible God: The Earliest Christians on Art* (1990); A. Grabar, *Christian Iconography: A Study of Its Origins* (1968);

R. Jensen, *Understanding Early Christian Art* (2000); E. Kitzinger, *Byzantine Art in the Making* (1977); J. Lowden, *Early Christian and Byzantine Art* (1997); R. L. Milburn, *Early Christian Art and Architecture* (1988); G. Snyder, *Ante Pacem: Archaeological Evidence of Church Life before Constantine* (1985); K. Weitzmann, *Late Antique and Early Christian Book Illumination* (1977); K. Weitzmann and H. Kessler, *The Frescoes of the Dura Synagogue and Christian Art* (1990).

ROBIN M. JENSEN

Art, Reformation During the Reformation, the perennial debate regarding the use and abuse of religious imagery raged with passionate intensity. Protestant reformers opposed works of religious art for various reasons. Some objected to the cost, and to using church funds that otherwise might help the poor. Others were scandalized that donors who commissioned religious art works believed that this action procured their own salvation. The strongest concern, however, and one that has triggered iconoclastic movements since the days of the early church, involved the fear of idolatry, the conviction that people would be tempted to worship the image itself.

The Reformers disagreed among themselves with regard to the limitation, prohibition, or destruction of religious images. Andreas Bodenstein von Karlstadt, who wrote *On the Abolition of Images* in 1522, urged that all religious imagery be removed from churches. Ulrich Zwingli convinced the people of Zurich in 1524 to destroy the religious statues, paintings, and altarpieces in their churches. John Calvin, who considered the mediation of images an unnecessary distraction in churches, and probably a temptation to idolatry, advocated the removal of religious imagery from the churches in Geneva. Martin Luther chose a more constructive position. At first skeptical about the value of the visual arts in religious experience, Luther gradually developed a defense for the pedagogical function of images and ultimately rejected the violence of the radical iconoclasts.

Luther proposed certain subject matter as appropriate for worship, thus inaugurating a major change of focus for northern European artists. As a result of Luther's influence, paintings of the Last Judgment or mariological themes were no longer in demand. Instead, the Last Supper and the crucifixion became particularly popular, as did images of the Prodigal Son, saved only because of his faith and thus reflective of the Lutheran message. A well-known example of Lutheran painting is Lucas Cranach's *Allegory of the Law and the Gospel* (1529), copied in many forms, including woodcuts for instruction manuals. Altarpieces, now considered a visual hindrance to the primacy of the pulpit, were commissioned less often, if at all.

The antipathy of the Reformers toward sculpted or painted images did not include the prohibition of prints, since images engraved on paper seemed to pose less temptation for idolatry. Moreover, because prints were inexpensive to manufacture and easy to disseminate, they offered the ideal medium for didactic purposes. Northern European artists produced prints of exceptional quality, utilizing sophisticated and expressive techniques, with superb chiaroscuro effects. Albrecht Dürer, Hans Baldung Grien, Lucas Cranach the Elder, and Hans Holbein, among many others, created acclaimed masterpieces of printmaking.

Another shift in focus for artists was a new interest in the natural world, the changing seasons, and the beauties of nonnarrative reality. A newly emerging pantheism is evident in the landscapes of Joachim Patiner and Albrecht Altdorfer, with their evocative receding panoramas of imaginary mountains, Danubian forests, and ephemeral atmospheric conditions. Pieter Bruegel further developed the interest in landscape with his realistic depictions of the subtle changes of the seasons. The growing prosperity of the mercantile class and the new importance of the private dwelling encouraged artists to paint for a new audience; thus, still lifes and genre scenes also became popular as embellishment for the home.

The most important change in the visual arts during the Reformation period involved the new prominence given to portraiture. Protestant emphasis on the faith of the individual and the Reformers' desire to replace images of the saints with those of another nature encouraged the rise of the portrait. Portraits from the sixteenth century are important political and social documents and herald a new age of modernity. Psychologically probing portraits from this period, with realistic details of clothing, jewelry, and professional attributes, include Jean Clouet's *Francis I* (c. 1525), Albrecht Dürer's *Philipp Melanchthon* (1526); Hans Holbein's *Sir Thomas More* (1527) and *Henry VIII* (1539); and Lucas Cranach's portraits of Luther.

The aniconic invectives of the Reformers effectively severed the medieval links between the visual arts and worship and caused the destruction of countless works of art. In their efforts to desacralize art, however, the Reformers stimulated artists to explore new avenues of expression and helped to transfer the art experience from the sacred into the secular sphere.

C. C. Christensen, *Art and the Reformation in Germany* (1979); J. Dimmick, J. Simpson, and N. Zeeman, eds., *Images, Idolatry, and Iconoclasm in Late Medieval England: Textuality and the Visual Image* (2002); C. Harbison, *Symbols in Transformation: Iconographic Themes at the Time of the Reformation* (1969); J. L. Koerner, *The Reformation of the Image* (2004); B. D. Mangrum and G. Scavizzi, *A Reformation Debate: Karlstadt, Emser, and Eck on Sacred Images: Three Treatises in Translation* (1991); S. Michalski, *The Reformation in the Visual Arts: The Protestant Image Question in Western and Eastern Europe* (1993); L. P. Wandel, *Voracious Idols and Violent Hands: Iconoclasm in Reformation Zurich, Strasbourg, and Basel* (1995).

PRISCILLA BAUMANN

Askew, Anne (1521–1546), English Protestant, gentlewoman, writer, and martyr. Askew was judged a heretic, tortured, and burned to death at Smithfield on July 16, 1546. Her *Examinations* is a spiritual autobiography and a dramatic account of her imprisonments, trials, and torture. She also wrote "The voyce of Anne Askewe out of the 54. Psalme of David" and "The Balade whyche Anne Askewe made and sange when she was in Newgate." Recent scholarship has concentrated on the theological, political, and social features of England near the end of Henry VIII's reign as the context in which Askew challenged church and court alike. Apparently close to Catherine Parr's circle at court, Askew held to a Protestant theology, in contrast to the conservative Catholic view of the court reflected in the Act of Six Articles (1539). Interpreters continue to debate the veracity and dating of several events in Askew's life, but her exemplary martyrdom and inclusion in Foxe's *Actes and Monuments* (1563) made her an inspiration for Protestants.

E. V. Belin, ed., *The Examinations of Anne Askew* (1996); R. Warnicke, *Women of the English Renaissance and Reformation* (1983).

JOHN E. GRISWOLD

Asterius the Sophist (d. after 341), Arian propagandist. Asterius, born in Cappadocia, was converted to Christianity before the perse-

cution of 303, during which he yielded and sacrificed. He was readmitted to communion but permanently excluded from the clerical state. As the Arian controversy flared up after 318, Asterius allied himself with the Eusebian bishops; he traveled to various churches and attended synods, where he read his theological compositions. Asterius is last mentioned in connection with the Dedication Council of Antioch in 341. Theologically, Asterius belonged to the generation of Eusebius of Caesarea and Eusebius of Nicomedia. These men, trained in an Origenist theology that was naively subordinationistic, naturally thought of Father and Son as distinct subsistents and rejected the innovative language of the Creed of Nicaea. Two of Asterius's works are known: the *Syntagmation* or "Little Treatise" that he wrote, probably in 320/321, in defense of the Eusebian theology (Athanasius preserves some fragments of it), and a letter, written c. 327, quoted by Marcellus of Ancyra. Marcellus's own work, for which he was condemned, was probably directed primarily against Asterius. Thirty-one homilies on the Psalms, once assigned to Asterius, are not his work.

W. Kinzig, *In Search of Asterius: Studies on the Authorship of the Homilies on the Psalms* (1990); M. Vinzent, ed., *Asterius von Kappadokien: Die theologischen Fragmente* (1993).

JOSEPH T. LIENHARD

Astrology and Numerology in Early Christianity Astrology is the belief that the stars and planets directly influence human lives. In antiquity professional astrologers, called *mathematicii* because they worked with numbers, diagrams, and tables, used birth date to determine a person's zodiacal sign. They then determined whether the stars were in an auspicious or inauspicious position for the person to undertake a particular course of action (e.g., make a voyage or purchase a farm). Sometimes astrology dealt with a person's whole life. Zodiacal signs intersected the horizon at twelve places called "houses." The twelve houses affected different spheres of life. For example, the first house dealt with the personality; the third, with education.

A pseudoscience today, in the ancient world astrology was a formidable intellectual enterprise and involved much astronomy, since the stars' positions had to be determined for their meaning to be interpreted. Although some intellectuals scoffed at the practice, most ancient people, including many Roman emperors, believed in astrology. Tiberius (14–37 CE) stopped worshiping the gods because his belief in astrology convinced him the world was ruled by fate.

Christians vigorously opposed astrology because its fatalism threatened the freedom of the will. Augustine of Hippo (354–430) provided a good summary of the Christian attitude toward astrology in his *City of God* (5.1–8). Many early Christians believed that the appearance of a star at Jesus' birth and the veneration of him by astrologers (magi) proved the inferiority of astrology to Christianity.

Numerology is the belief that numbers, individually or in combination, have mystical or symbolic significance, a view strongly supported by the ancient use of letters of the alphabet as numbers. The Jewish *Sibylline Oracles* represented Roman emperors by the numerical sum of the letters in their names, while the author of Rev. 13:18 says that the number 666 is the number of a man, the letters of whose name have that numerical value. Christians especially liked to interpret the mystical significance of numbers from the Old Testament in keeping with their view that the Old Testament's importance lay in its pointing toward the Christian revelation. In the second century the author of the epistle of Barnabas could claim that Abraham's 318 retainers, when the number was written in Greek, symbolized the cross of Christ. Later Christians believed they forecast the supposed 318 bishops at the ecumenical council of Nicaea in 325. Augustine believed the six-day creation symbolized the six ages of history and that numbers, being unaffected by world events, could well transport divine revelation. Numbers occurring in the natural world could also be used. Irenaeus of Lyon (c. 175) contended that there should be only four canonical Gospels because there were four regions of the world and four principal winds. The practice of numerology largely died out after the Reformation.

T. S. Barton, *Ancient Astrology* (1994); G. Ifrah, *From One to Zero: A Universal History of Numbers* (1985); H.-J. Klauck, *The Religious Context of Early Christianity* (2000); D. Lindberg, *The Beginnings of Western Science* (1991).

JOSEPH F. KELLY

Athanasian Creed

It also known as the *Quicunque vult*, from its opening phrase: "Whoever wishes to be saved." This Latin profession of faith is a Western product, dating almost certainly from the late fifth or early sixth century. Heavily dependent on the language of the *Excerpta* of Vincent of Lérins, who wrote in southern Gaul prior to 450, it first appears in a collection of sermons of Caesarius of Arles (c. 470–542). These circumstances make it likely that it emerged from the monastic environment of southern Gaul; Caesarius was also associated with the island of Lérins. The anachronistic association with the name of Athanasius is of unknown origin, but on the evidence of style and content it is certainly false.

The creed covers in broad scope a number of commonplaces in the doctrines of God, the Trinity, and the incarnation as articulated in the first four ecumenical councils, and adds a list of the most important events in the life of Jesus. Its account of the Trinity describes the Holy Spirit as proceeding not only from the Father but also from the Son (*et filio*), and the prestige of this creed appears to have influenced the Western addition of the *filioque* to the Nicene Creed. It is remarkable for its repeated assertion of the salvific necessity of belief in its doctrinal propositions and its anathemas upon those who do not concur with its assertions (e.g., "Whoever does not keep [the catholic faith] whole and inviolable will doubtless perish eternally").

The creed long held a prominent and authoritative role in Roman Catholic liturgical life. It enjoyed particular favor in the Anglican communion, as well as among some of the Lutheran churches. Both the Roman breviary and the Anglican Book of Common Prayer enjoined its use. Beginning in the nineteenth century many Anglicans called for its removal, and by the 1970s it had fallen into desuetude, owing primarily to the harshness of its language. It was not known to the Eastern churches before the twelfth century and has not been recognized as authoritative in the East, notwithstanding a brief appearance in Russian liturgical texts in the seventeenth century. It is not used in Orthodox worship but sometimes appears, without the *filioque*, in the *Horologion (Book of Hours)*.

J. N. D. Kelly, *The Athanasian Creed* (1964); V. M. Lagorio, "The Text of the *Quicunque vult* in codex Ottob. Lat. 663," *JTS* 25 (1974): 127–28.

THOMAS A. SMITH

Athanasius of Alexandria

(c. 295/300–373), theologian, bishop of Alexandria. Born in Egypt, Athanasius served as a deacon and secretary under Bishop Alexander of Alexandria with whom he attended the Council of Nicaea (325). On Alexander's death he was elected bishop in murky circumstances and had to spend considerable time strengthening his position. He traveled extensively through Egypt cultivating the growing monastic movement and trying to bring it under episcopal control.

When Arius was readmitted to communion by a council of Eusebian bishops as early as 327 under the command of Constantine, Athanasius refused to acquiesce. Moreover, his actions against the Meletians were ruthless and at times violent. In 334 he was summoned by Constantine to a synod at Caesarea in Palestine and in the following year to a synod at Tyre. He ignored the first summons and attended the second meeting only briefly, fleeing to Constantine's court when he saw the direction of events. Constantine followed Tyre's condemnation of Athanasius with exile to Trier. After Constantine's death Athanasius was allowed to return to Alexandria by Constantine II, in whose area of the empire he now found himself. During these years, Athanasius composed *Against the Nations* and *On the Incarnation*, a linked pair of treatises that sets out the essence of his soteriology. The latter focuses on the Word's assumption of the whole of humanity in the incarnation and describes the Word working through that union to restore humanity and bring it to share in divine perfections.

Deposed in 339, Athanasius fled to Rome. Bishop Julius held a small council that vindicated both Athanasius and the also deposed Marcellus of Ancyra. Athanasius presented the controversy solely in doctrinal terms (apparent in the first of his three *Orations against the Arians,* 339 or 340), and Julius accepted this account of events. A considerable rift with many prominent bishops in the East resulted (expressed in the texts of the "Dedication" Council of Antioch, 341). The Western emperor Constans and his Eastern counterpart Constantius summoned a joint council for 342 or 343 in Serdica (modern Sophia). This council never met as one; the Western bishops under the influence of Athanasius and Marcellus condemned the Easterners, and the latter responded in kind.

Athanasius at this time emphasized the distinction between Creator and creation (with the Son placed on the Creator's side of the divide) and upheld the principle that the Word or Son is "proper" to the Father (thus sharing the Father's attributes). To distinguish Father and Son, he relied on statements that the two are distinct (second and third *Orations*) and on an analogical base of a person and the person's

word or wisdom. Athanasius also made use of Nicaea's description of the Son as being "from the essence [*ousia*] of the Father." *Homoousios* was not yet an important term for him.

Constans persuaded his brother Constantius to allow Athanasius to return to Alexandria in 346, but after Constans's death in 350 the tide turned again. Athanasius may already have been condemned by a synod in 349, and Constantius, now in control of the whole empire, tried to insist that successive councils in the West agree to Athanasius's deposition. Athanasius escaped before troops could enforce these depositions. He hid in Egypt (356–361), spending much of the time with various monastic communities and composing several works, including his *Life of Antony* and the *Letters to Serapion*. The former text claims Antony as a supporter of Athanasius and sets out a vision of salvation that complements the earlier *On the Incarnation*. The latter text applies to the Spirit many of the arguments developed in conjunction with the Son's status. As the Son must be proper to the Father's being, so the Spirit must be proper to the Son; the Spirit, as dependent on the Son, is divine. Athanasius also began to articulate a fundamental principle for later pro-Nicene theology: because all three undertake the same actions, they must be one.

During this exile he composed his *On the Synods of Ariminum and Seleucia*, which attacks Constantius's religious policy, specifically the twin councils of 359 at and after which Constantius pushed for a homoian (*homoios* = like) creed. Athanasius attacked the theology of Acacius of Caesarea, one of the chief homoian leaders, but attempted to reach out to the homoiousian ("similar in essence") leaders. Throughout this text Athanasius also reiterated sections of his slightly earlier *On the Decrees of Nicaea* (c. 353), which offered his first explicit defense of Nicaea's terms. Here Athanasius defended *homoousios* and "from the essence of the Father" as terms that protect the status of the Son as truly "from God" and the "obvious" import of biblical terminologies such as "Word" and "Wisdom."

With Constantius's death Athanasius was once again able to hold his see openly. In 362 he summoned a council to Alexandria that took the momentous step of trying to find minimum conditions to allow all opposed to the homoian creed of 359–360 to come together. The council, under Athanasius's direction, asked only for a confession of Nicaea's creed and the divinity of the Spirit.

After brief exiles under Julian (362–363) and Valens (365–366), Athanasius spent the remaining years of his tenure undisturbed. He died in 373, having spent nearly eleven of his forty-five years as bishop in exile.

His theological influence on his contemporaries is unclear. Athanasius was somewhat out of step with the pro-Nicene theologies emerging in the 360s that articulated much clearer distinctions between persons and essence than he had done. The existence of translations into many of the languages of Eastern Christianity testifies, however, to the wide readership that he gradually began to have. The *Life of Antony* was perhaps the most influential of his works, as may be seen in book 8 of Augustine's *Confessions*.

K. Anatolios, *Athanasius* (1998); L. Ayres, *Nicaea and Its Legacy* (2004); T. D. Barnes, *Athanasius and Constantius* (1995); D. Brakke, *Athanasius and the Politics of Asceticism* (1995); R. C. Gregg and D. E. Groh, *Early Arianism—A View of Salvation* (1981); C. Kannengiesser, ed., *Politique et théologie chez Athanase d'Alexandrie* (1974).

LEWIS AYRES

Athenagoras (second cent.), apologist in Athens. Little is known of Athenagoras apart from two extant texts. The first, *Plea on Behalf of the Christians*, was addressed to the Roman emperors Marcus Aurelius and Commodus. Blending an array of references to ancient philosophers and poets with arguments common to the second-century apologists, Athenagoras demonstrates that Christians lead morally upright lives and that this morality is proof against pagan criticisms of the community, specifically atheism, cannibalism, and incest. Christians are no threat to the state but, rather, are faithful and obedient citizens of Rome. Devoting most of his attention to the accusation of atheism, he contrasts Christian monotheism with pagan polytheism. He suggests that pagan worship is an idolatrous contrivance inferior to worship of the Christian God. Though not fully developed in this text, Athenagoras's references to the Trinity are some of the earliest concrete explications of the doctrine of God. He argues for the Son as the eternal Word of God and the coinherence of Father and Son in the unity of the Spirit (chap. 10), as well as this triune God's economic role in the created order (chap. 24). In this regard, the apologist manifests his biblical and liturgical loyalties alongside his familiarity with the Greek poets and philosophers.

The second text of note, though dubious in its authorship, is *On the Resurrection of the Dead*. The question of authorship is due largely to the text's direct concern with third- and fourth-century concepts of the resurrection associated largely with Origen. Athenagoras does, however, mention a forthcoming discussion of the resurrection in the *Plea*'s final chapter and thereby lends credence to his authorship of *On the Resurrection*. The text contains two central arguments. First, God possesses both the power and the will to perform the noble and worthy act of resurrecting the human body. Second, God created humans as both soul and body and will eschatologically raise the body and reunite it with the soul, with the providential design of bringing either reward or punishment upon the human as both soul and body.

Athenagoras, *Athenagoras: Legatio and De resurrectione*, in OCuT, ed. W. R. Schoedel (1972); M. Marcovich, ed., *Athenagoris, Legatio pro Christianis* (1990); Marcovich, ed., *Athenagorae qui fertur De resurrectione mortuorum* (2000); L. W. Barnard, *Athenagoras: Study in Second-Century Christian Apologetic* (1972); B. Pouderon, *Athénagore d'Athénes: philosophe chrétien*, SC 378 (1989).

D. JEFFREY BINGHAM

Attila (d. 453), king of the Huns. In the late 430s, Attila and his brother Bleda, the nephews of king Rua, became kings of the Huns in the area of modern-day Romania. Around 445 Attila murdered his brother and became sole king. Truculent toward the Roman Empire, he required annual subsidies of 2,100 pounds of gold from the Eastern emperor Theodosius II (402–450). Subsequently, Attila's interests turned toward the West. In 451, he demanded half the Western empire and the hand of the princess Honoria. When the emperor Valentinian III (425–455) refused, Attila invaded Gaul. In July, the Huns were confronted by the Roman general Aëtius at the Mauriac Plain near Châlons. After heavy losses on both sides, the Huns were driven back to their camp, and Attila threatened to commit suicide rather than be taken captive. He withdrew across the Rhine and the next year invaded Italy, where, according to a pious legend, he was induced to withdraw by Pope Leo. Disease and starvation also intervened. In 453 Attila died of a hemorrhage on his wedding night. He subsequently obtained a reputation as a barbarian par excellence. Christian moralists referred to him as the "scourge of God" for his perceived role in punishing sinful Christians.

C. D. Gordon, *The Age of Attila: Fifth-Century Byzantium and the Barbarians* (1966); E. A. Thompson, *Attila and the Huns* (1948).

RALPH W. MATHISEN

Augsburg Confession (1530), Lutheran

statement of faith. When Emperor Charles V demanded that Lutheran principalities and municipalities justify their introduction of reforms at the imperial diet in Augsburg (1530), electoral Saxon officials prepared memoranda on their reforms (labeled since the eighteenth century "the Torgau Articles"). The Saxons were greeted in Augsburg by accusations of heresy (the 404 Articles of Roman Catholic theologian Johann Eck), so their leading theologian, Luther's colleague Philip Melanchthon, used Luther's Confession of Faith of 1528 and two other summaries of teaching, the Schwabach Articles and the Marburg Articles, to compose a statement demonstrating that Lutherans taught according to Scripture and the Catholic tradition. Melanchthon decided to label the document a "confession" rather than an "apology" or defense; it was to proclaim God's Word with the power Luther believed inherent in it. Twenty-one articles treat the core of Christian doctrine (Trinity, sin, Christ, justification by faith, the means of grace, new obedience, etc.); seven articles treat reform measures (Communion in both kinds, clerical marriage, the Mass, confession, fasting, monasticism, episcopal power). Charles rejected the confession, appointed a commission to compose a "Confutation," and refused to accept Melanchthon's written defense. He revised and published it as the *Apology of the Augsburg Confession* (1531). The Augsburg Confession remains the most important definition of Lutheran belief today.

R. Kolb and T. Wengert, *The Book of Concord* (2000); R. Kolb and J. Nestingen, *Sources and Contexts of the Book of Concord* (2001); W. Maurer, *Historical Commentary on the Augsburg Confession* (1986).

ROBERT KOLB

Augustine of Canterbury (d. c. 604),

saint and missionary to England. His feast day is May 26. Little is known of Augustine's early life. He was a Sicilian prior at the monastery of St. Andrew in Rome founded by Gregory the Great when in 596 the pope sent him on a mission to England with approximately forty men.

They traveled through Gaul, turning back once for fear of horrors they had heard concerning the English. Gregory provided them with Frankish interpreters. The group reached Kent in 597, landing on the Isle of Thanet. They were received civilly by King Aethelberht of Kent, whose wife, Bertha, was a Christian Frankish princess. After meeting outdoors, to protect himself from witchcraft, the king allowed them to settle in the queen's church, St. Martin's. He soon received baptism; ten thousand Englishmen were also said to receive baptism that Christmas day. After this Augustine settled in the old Roman city of Canterbury. He was made archbishop of the English. He attempted but failed to reach agreement with representatives of the Celtic church concerning their practices. The development of his cult did not begin until the eighth century. Most of what is known about Augustine is found in Bede's *Ecclesiastical History,* which includes Gregory's responses to Augustine's questions concerning such things as consanguinity and transferral of pagan sites to Christian ones.

R. Gameson, ed., *St. Augustine and the Conversion of England* (1999).

MARIANNE M. DELAPORTE

Augustine of Hippo (354–430), bishop

and theologian. A dominant figure in the North African church, Augustine was also one of the chief architects of the Christian tradition in the West. He is best known perhaps for his doctrines of grace and predestination. But these belong within his wider theology of love and his charting of the complex movement of the heart in which human beings turn from love of self to love of God. It is especially as a cartographer of the terrain of the heart that Augustine left his mark on Western Christianity and culture.

Augustine was born in Thagaste (Souk Ahras, Algeria), a small town in Roman Numidia, to a Christian mother (Monica) and a non-Christian father (Patricius), a town councilor of modest means with wider ambitions for his son. Through the support of a local dignitary Augustine received a classical education, which provided an avenue of escape from his provincial setting. He was trained in rhetoric (essential for political careers in the Roman Empire) at Carthage and taught rhetoric there, then in Rome, and finally in Milan, where he was appointed to the municipal chair of rhetoric.

But inspired by Cicero's *Hortensius,* an exhortation to philosophy he had read as a student, Augustine was also on a quest for wisdom and truth—which, under the influence of his mother, he sought in Christianity. In Carthage, repelled by the unsophisticated Christianity of the North African church, he had turned to the Manichees, who promised a reason-based faith. In Milan, now disillusioned with their pretensions, he discovered—through the preaching of Ambrose and his reading in Platonist philosophy—a form of orthodox Christianity that he could embrace. His famous "conversion" in 386 enabled him to give up his secular ambitions, to adopt a life of celibacy, and to commit himself wholeheartedly to a life of religious and intellectual pursuit of God. He was baptized in 387 and shortly thereafter returned to Africa to establish a religious community on a quasi-monastic model.

In 391, however, on a visit to Hippo Regius (Annaba), he was unexpectedly and forcibly ordained to the priesthood and in 396 made bishop of Hippo's catholic congregation. His ordination plunged him into an intense round of activities that lasted the rest of his life: preaching several times a week, hearing cases and mediating disputes in the bishop's court almost daily, debating and writing against competing sects and parties, administering church property, and trying to wean his congregation from the practices of Roman paganism. Augustine's mature theology is grounded, then, in the concrete life of the North African church. It was shaped by three great controversies.

The Manichees pictured the present world as the outcome of a cosmic struggle between a good principle and an evil power in which the evil force imprisoned human souls, themselves intrinsically good and particles of the divine, in material bodies. In contrast, Augustine insisted that the material world is the good creation of the one supreme God and that evil stems not from a cosmic power but from the exercise of free will. In debates with the Manichees in the early 390s, and especially in his study of Paul's letters in the mid-390s, however, he became convinced that the human will is indeed held captive—not by an external evil power but by its own habitual dispositions and desires. Its freedom consists only in an original ability to set its course, not a subsequent ability to overcome the desires that chain it to that course. Here lie the roots of both Augustine's doctrine of original sin and his conviction that only divine grace can ultimately shift the heart's deepest orientation. The first nine books of the *Confessions*, probably his best-known work, present this vision of the self in the form of an account of his own life up to the time of writing (c. 397).

The Donatists, a Christian separatist movement, maintained that only they constituted the true church because only they had preserved its purity in the face of Roman persecution and that, as a consequence, only their sacraments were valid. Augustine's counterattack emphasized unity expressed in love, not division expressed in exclusivism, as the mark of true Christianity and argued that the validity of the sacraments depends on Christ's presence in them, not on any purity of church or minister. In this context Augustine worked out his own understanding of the church as a "mixed body" of true and false Christians to be separated only at the last judgment, and even then not by any human criterion but only by God, who alone can discern the depths of the heart.

Pelagianism, a reform movement of the early fifth century, held that there is no excuse for failure to meet the full demand of obedience to God. Human beings are invested by God with ineradicable freedom of will and can direct their motives and desires if only they choose to do so. In response, Augustine reemphasized the visions of the human self and of divine grace that he had first set out in the 390s. Humans are inescapably entangled in their own past (now including the inherited past of original sin), they cannot dictate the direction of their own desire, and only divine grace can reorient the will from love of self to love of God. *The City of God*, the second of Augustine's two best-known works, portrays all history from creation to final judgment as a vast tale of the conflict, the intermingling, and ultimately the separation of two cities, the earthly and the heavenly. The earthly is constituted by love of self, chosen by humanity in its original fall; the heavenly by love of God elicited by divine grace.

In all three controversies, Augustine opposed forces threatening to splinter the Christian community on elitist grounds either of religious purity or of moral worth. For him, there is no form of human worth that wins divine grace, which is always sheer gift. The theological price of this doctrine of grace was the doctrine of predestination correlated with it, but even that represents an effort to ground the difference between the saved and the lost not in any human mode of distinction but solely in the ultimately mysterious workings of God.

———

W. S. Babcock, ed., *The Ethics of St. Augustine* (1991); P. Brown, *Augustine of Hippo* (new ed., 2000); J. Burnaby, *Amor Dei* (1938); H. Chadwick, *Augustine* (1986); C. Harrison, *Augustine*

(2000); R. A. Markus, *Saeculum* (rev. ed., 1988); F. van der Meer, *Augustine the Bishop* (1961); O. O'Donovan, *The Problem of Self-Love in St. Augustine* (1980); E. TeSelle, *Augustine the Theologian* (1970).

WILLIAM S. BABCOCK

Augustinianism This title is given to the influence of the great North African church father Augustine of Hippo (354–430) on the development of Christian theology and, to a lesser extent, Western philosophy. It is an imprecise term, since Augustine wrote on many and diverse topics, including homiletics. In the early Middle Ages, Christian scholars used Augustine primarily as an exegete, especially on the Gospel of John, the Psalms, and Genesis. "Augustinianism," however, does not include homiletics or exegesis. Even setting limits on the designation, however, does not call into question the immensity of Augustine's impact on Western Christian thought.

Augustinianism began shortly after Augustine's death when Gallic monks objected to the extremism of his later writings on predestination and grace. A controversy ensued for a century until the Gallic Second Council of Orange (529) implicitly accepted predestination, albeit in a greatly modified form. The question arose again in the ninth century when Gottschalk (c. 804–c. 869), a German monk, advocated a double predestination (to blessedness for the elect and damnation for others). Augustine had not taught the latter, and eventually Gottschalk's position was rejected. One of Gottschalk's opponents was the Irish philosopher, John Scottus Eriugena (c. 810–c. 875). John was unique in his day in his utilization of Augustine's Neoplatonic approach to philosophical questions.

Only in the High Middle Ages (twelfth–thirteenth centuries) did the philosophical Augustine become important. University-based scholastic theologians accepted his contention that we can know God from internal rather than external evidence. God illuminates our minds, thus directly aiding us in our process of learning. This approach greatly appealed to monks and other Christian thinkers who valued mysticism, since Augustine focused on interior experiences that may be similar to those of others but finally inexpressible. The earliest Franciscans, such as Bonaventure (1217–1274), accepted Augustine's teaching on illumination as well as his insistence that love is the foremost of virtues. This stance provided a counterweight to the growing Aristotelian rationalism represented by the Dominican friars, especially Thomas Aquinas (1225–1274).

Equally popular among the scholastics was Augustine's insistence on the primacy of faith over philosophy (an idea not original to him) and his belief that the soul is a substance, independent of the body, which can not only survive the body's demise but survive as a genuine subject.

Nevertheless, Aristotelianism triumphed in the universities. In the fourteenth century at both Paris and Oxford, 75 percent of the books read by the arts students were written by Aristotle. Yet as Augustine's Neoplatonism was losing its appeal, his theology enjoyed a strong revival.

In the fourteenth century there was a resurgence of Pelagianism among some scholastic thinkers. Their views were decisively overcome by Thomas Bradwardine (c. 1295–1349), archbishop of Canterbury, and Gregory of Rimini (d. 1358), a member of the Order of St. Augustine, who reasserted Augustine's teaching of the totally gratuitous nature of divine grace.

At the same time late scholastic scholars revived Augustine's theology, the Italian humanist Petrarch (1304–1374) rediscovered the Augustine of *The Confessions*, that most inward-looking spiritual autobiography, which he believed emphasized the moral and psychological elements of goodness rather than any unmerited gift of grace to a sinful person. Petrarch read Augustine selectively, but he showed a side of Augustine previously ignored in the Middle Ages.

Petrarch's conversion experience occurred when Augustine was becoming better known to Western thinkers, thanks to the publication in 1345 of Bartholomew of Urbino's *Milleloquium Sancti Augustini*, a compilation of 15,000 passages from Augustine's works. This remarkable work spread knowledge of Augustine for a century and a half until a printed edition of his work appeared in 1506.

Renaissance humanists loathed scholasticism, considering it petty and lifeless in its worn Aristotelianism. They turned to Neoplatonism and to its leading Christian exponent. The most important Italian Platonist, Marsilio Ficino (1433–1499), owed much to Augustine, whose influence he openly acknowledged.

The great Protestant Reformers, Martin Luther (1483–1546)—a member of the Augustinian order—and John Calvin (1509–1564), based their theories of sin, grace, and salvation on Augustine's theology, although adding their own interpretations. This proved especially true of Calvin, whose followers still hold to many of Augustine's basic ideas on the topics.

René Descartes (1596–1650) would prove to be the last great philosopher to rely heavily upon Augustine, although Descartes never acknowledged the debt. The Frenchman relied only on what his intellect could tell him, independent of external forces. Here he followed Augustine, who also believed one could develop a metaphysics based upon innate powers of reason that could determine points so convincingly true that they were beyond doubt. For Augustine, this knowledge came from God, something Descartes could not say.

Later philosophers used ideas of Augustine, but he became more and more one source among many. The Scientific Revolution and the corresponding rise in empiricism rendered his approach less relevant, except to philosophers who acknowledged a Christian background. His theology survived the Renaissance to play a role in the seventeenth-century Jansenist controversy in Roman Catholicism, but the revived Thomism of the nineteenth and twentieth centuries diminished Augustine's influence. Augustine impacted the New England Puritans and their spiritual descendants in evangelical churches, yet most Protestants have abandoned rigid predestinarian views and the automatic damnation of the unbaptized. Yet anyone familiar with his thought can see Augustine's ideas, unreferenced and maybe even unrecognized, in virtually every important theologian, even if that theologian is disagreeing with an African thinker who lived 1,600 years ago.

M. D. Jordan, "Augustinianism," in *The Routledge Encyclopedia of Philosophy*, ed. E. Craig (1998); E. King and J. Schaefer, *Saint Augustine and His Influence in the Middle Ages* (1988); H. Oberman and F. E. James, eds., *Via Augustini: Augustine in the Later Middle Ages, Renaissance, and Reformation* (1991); R. Weaver, *Divine Grace and Human Agency*, Patristic Monograph Series 15 (1996); A. Fitzgerald, ed., *Augustine through the Ages* (1999); G. Mathews, ed., *The Augustinian Tradition* (1999); M. W. F. Stone, "Augustine and Medieval Philosophy," in *The Cambridge Companion to Augustine*, ed. E. Stump and N. Kretzmann (2001), 253–66; G. Matthew, "Post-Medieval Augustinianism," in *The Cambridge Companion to Augustine*, 267–79.

JOSEPH F. KELLY

Augustinus Triumphus of Ancona

(1270/1273–1328), Italian Augustinian theologian. Augustinus defended the hierocratic doctrine of papal monarchy anticipating central conciliar arguments. After lecturing in Ancona, he served his last six years as a consiliarius/cappellanus at the court of King Robert of Anjou in Naples. Having defended Boniface in his *Tractatus contra articulos inventos ad diffamandum Bonifacium*, he dedicated to John XXII his *Summa de potestate ecclesiastica* (1326), a milestone work on papal supremacy and plenitude of power.

K. Walsh, "Augustinus de Ancona as a Conciliar Authority: The Circulation of His Summa in the Shadow of the Council of Basle," in *The Church and Sovereignty c. 590–1918: Essays in Honour of Michael Wilks*, ed. D. Wood (1991); M. Wilks, *The Problem of Sovereignty in the Later Middle Ages: The Papal Monarchy with Augustinus Triumphus and the Publicists* (1964).

KIRSI STJERNA

Aurelius, Marcus   *see Marcus Aurelius*

Auriol, Peter (c. 1280–1322), Conventual

Franciscan from Aquitaine, lecturer in Bologna (c. 1311) and Toulouse (c. 1314), regent master at Paris (1318–1321), a favorite of Pope John XXII, and archbishop of Aix-en-Provence (1321). Early in his career he wrote a treatise on Franciscan poverty, *Tractatus de paupertate et usu paupere* (*Treatise on Poverty and Poor Use*, 1311?) and two treatises in support of the Immaculate Conception of the Virgin Mary, *Tractatus de conceptione Beatae Mariae Virginis* and *Repercussorium* (*Treatise on the Conception of the Blessed Virgin Mary*, and *A Book of Retort*, both of 1314?). A historical theologian known to be rigorously systematic and critical of his predecessors and peers, Auriol wrote a *Sentence* commentary and a *Literal Compendium of the Whole of Sacred Scripture*, both of which had enormous influence on the late Middle Ages. The Apocalypse commentary of the *Compendium* advanced the literal historical method of interpretation and influenced Nicholas of Lyra, Wyclif, and Luther. He also defended the freedom of the will and criticized the late medieval doctrine distinguishing God's absolute and ordained powers. Auriol's soteriology influenced late medieval theologians such as Gabriel Biel: God offers his grace freely to all human beings, but salvation comes to those who passively accept this free offer of grace and do not put an obstacle before it. Auriol is noted as a conceptualist, that is, only singulars (i.e., individuals) have real, extramental existence; universals are mental phenomena, fabricated by the intellect.

P. Aureol, *Commentariorum in primum librum Sententiarum Pars Prima* (1596); P. Aureol, *Scriptum super primum sententiarum*, ed. E. M. Buytaert, 2 vols. (1952–1956); P. Auriol, *Compendium sensus litteralis totius sacrae Scripturae*, ed. P. Seeboeck (1896); P. Krey, "Many Readers but Few Followers: The Fate of Nicholas of Lyra's 'Apocalypse Commentary' in the Hands of His Late-Medieval Admirers," *CH* 64 (1995): 185–201; K. Tachau, *Vision and Certitude in the Age of Ockham: Optics, Epistemology and the Foundations of Semantics 1250–1345* (1988); R. L. Friedman, "Peter Auriol on Intellectual Cognition of Singulars," *Vivarium* 38, no. 1 (2000): 177–93; W. Duba, "The Immaculate Conception in the Works of Peter Auriol," *Vivarium* 38, no. 1 (2000): 5–34.

PHILIP D. W. KREY

Ausonius, Decimus Magnus (c. 310–
395), Gallo-Roman teacher, Latin poet, and imperial dignitary. In the mid-360s the emperor Valentinian I (363–375) called upon Ausonius, a teacher of literature and rhetoric at Bordeaux, to tutor his son. When Gratian (375–383) succeeded his father, the young emperor promoted his former schoolmaster through a series of high imperial offices, including the consulship (379). Ausonius used the positions to secure political appointments for family and friends. Apart from this remarkable display of the opportunities for political advancement still available to those who controlled the Latin literary and rhetorical traditions, Ausonius is best known for composing a topically and metrically diverse body of poetry that captures the dynamic cultural currents of the age. His most famous poem, the *Mosella*, celebrates that river valley while revealing the era's preference for intricate verbal patterning. Other works, such as his *Professores* and *Parentalia*, biographical sketches of teachers and family members, preserve distinct fragments of social history. Because his poetry ranges from erotic epigrams and a boldly descriptive wedding poem to Easter verses, a prayer, and an anxious exchange with the newly ascetic Paulinus of Nola (a former pupil), much discussion has centered upon the character and typicality of Ausonius's commitment to Christianity.

H. G. Evelyn White, trans., *Ausonius*, 2 vols. (1919–1921); R. P. H. Green, ed., *The Works of Ausonius* (1991); H. Sivan, *Ausonius of Bordeaux* (1993).

DENNIS E. TROUT

Austin Friars   *see* Hermits of St. Augustine

Authority in the Early Church
Authority is the legitimate power to command assent or obedience. In the early church, assent to the truth of the Christian faith was evoked principally by Scripture, the rule of faith or the creeds, and tradition. Bishops, presbyters, and others exercised authority in governing and ordering the Christian communities.

For Christians the only unconditioned authority for the truth was Christ himself. But after the first generation of disciples at least, the authority of Christ was always mediated. The earliest mediated or conditioned authority was Scriptures—that is, the Old Testament, usually read in the Septuagint translation and interpreted christologically. Phrases like "Scripture says" or "it is written" demonstrate the authority of Scripture for early Christian writers. Before a canon of New Testament books existed, the words of Jesus were authoritative, as quoted, for example, in the writings of the Apostolic Fathers and the Apologists. Once the New Testament was established, it enjoyed an authority at least equal to that of the Old Testament in the church. (A New Testament existed when a collection of Christian writings was accepted as equal in authority to the "Old Testament"; this happened, gradually, between 150 and 200.) This first New Testament contained twenty books: four Gospels, Acts, thirteen Pauline letters, 1 Peter, and 1 John; the other seven books gained authority during the third and fourth centuries. As soon as the New Testament was formed, disputes about its interpretation arose. To solve these disputes, appeal was made to the "rule of faith," beginning with Irenaeus and Tertullian. The rule of faith was a short summary of Christian beliefs, never verbally fixed, that expressed the chief doctrines of the faith; it was usually structured around the names of Father, Son, and Holy Spirit, but sometimes around Father and Son only. It was also called the "canon of truth" and various other names. Eventually, the creeds replaced the rule of faith as the concise statements of doctrine and the guide for interpreting Scripture. A baptismal creed is first found in Hippolytus of Rome's *Apostolic Tradition* (c. 220); the first conciliar creed is that of the Council of Nicaea (325). Later still, appeal is made to "tradition" as authoritative. Some Christian writers became authoritative for later writers. Augustine, for example, respected the authority of Cyprian, just as Augustine himself became an authority soon after his death. In the course of the christological controversy in the fifth century and later, florilegia, or collections of quotations from earlier Fathers, were made to support one position or another.

From the first days of its existence, the Christian community also had personal authorities, that is, leaders who organized the community and its worship, regulated the behavior of its members, and even excluded unwanted members. The earliest leaders, who were itinerant charismatics, had titles such as apostle, prophet, and teacher. They were soon replaced by stable, residential leaders, generally with the titles of bishop or overseer, presbyter, and deacon. Bishops gained their authority by "succession"— first, succession in doctrine or teaching, as in *1 Clement*, and then succession in office, as in Cyprian. As the church gradually became aware of its universal dimension, bishops, who were the leaders of local congregations, yielded some authority to metropolitans or archbishops, particularly the right to ordain a bishop and thus the right to refuse to ordain a candidate. The Council of Nicaea named three metropolitans "patriarchs" (the bishops of Alexandria, Antioch, and Rome; Constantinople and Jerusalem were added later). Finally, in the West, the patriarch of Rome gained authority over the whole Latin church, with the title "pope." Besides individual bishops, synods and councils of bishops enjoyed authority in doctrinal and disciplinary matters; noteworthy are the first four ecumenical councils (Nicaea, 325; Constantinople, 381; Ephesus, 431; and Chalcedon, 451). In addition to the urban hierarchy, others enjoyed authority over Christians. From the second century on, lay Christian teachers such as Justin Martyr and Clement of Alexandria exercised authority that was not strictly under the bishops. Later, the abbots and abbesses of monasteries and, more generally, those perceived as holy by the communities (for example, the stylite saints) exercised authority. Authority outside the "great church" was claimed by enthusiastic leaders such as Montanus, by dissident bishops, and by others.

H. von Campenhausen, *Ecclesiastical Authority and Spiritual Power in the Church of the First Three Centuries* (1969); R. B. Eno, "Authority," *Augustine through the Ages* (1999), 80–82; C. Munier, "Authority in the Church," in *Encyclopedia of the Early Church*, vol. 1 (1992), 103–4.

JOSEPH T. LIENHARD

Averroes (Ibn Rushd, 1126–1198), the exemplar of the Peripatetic philosophy in the Arabic tradition. He worked in Cordova under the patronage of the Almohad sultans, where he wrote three sets of commentaries on the works of Aristotle: epitomes, "Middle Commentaries" (paraphrases), and "Long Commentaries" (literal expositions). These commentaries, in their Latin and Hebrew translations, were the principal interpretative tools used by Christian and Jewish scholars of the Middle Ages for studying Aristotle. But Averroes's doctrines were also regarded as epitomizing the dangers to the revealed faith of Christianity posed by philosophical reason, especially in their arguments for the eternity of the world, the unity of the higher part of the soul (which implied that all human souls would lose their individuality after death), God's lack of knowledge of particulars, and the so-called double truth (in which reason and revelation were regarded as equally valid). Averroes provides his defense of the use of reason for achieving enlightenment in his *Destruction of the Destruction* (a response to al-Ghazali's attack on philosophers, which was also translated into Latin) and his *Decisive Treatise*. He also wrote influential works on medicine and Islamic law.

R. Arnaldez, *Averroès: Un rationaliste en Islam* (1998); G. Endress and J. A. Aertsen, eds., *Averroes and the Aristotelian Tradition* (1999).

CHARLES BURNETT

Avicebron (c. 1020–c. 1057), the Latin form of the name of the Jewish scholar Solomon ben Judah ibn Gabirol, a poet and philosopher from Arabic Spain. He lived for most of his short life in Saragossa. His poems, written in Hebrew, follow Arabic models and show a mystical tendency akin to Sufism. His major philosophical work, the *Fount of Life*, was written in Arabic but has survived complete only in a late-twelfth-century Latin translation made by Dominicus Gundissalinus and John of Spain. It is devoted to the description of matter and form, on both a spiritual and a corporeal level. It was meant to be followed by treatises on the science of God's will and on the First Essence (God Himself) respectively, but these, if they were written, have not survived. He adopted a Neoplatonic system that was independent of any revealed religion but that was meant to lead to knowledge of the divine world. The *Fount of Life* was almost forgotten by Jewish scholars but had a considerable impact on medieval latin Scholastic thought. In his *Crown for the King*, extant only in Hebrew, Avicebron gives poetic expression to the ideas in the *Fount of Life*.

H. Schlanger, *La philosophie de Salomon ibn Gabirol* (1968); Solomon ibn Gabirol, *A Crown for the King*, ed. D. R. Slavitt (1998).

CHARLES BURNETT

Avicenna (Ibn Sina, 980–1037), philosopher and medical writer. Avicenna, who was born in Bukhara in Central Asia, wrote voluminously on philosophy, partly in Persian, but mainly in Arabic. His principal work, the *Shifa'* ("Cure," i.e., from ignorance), is a self-sufficient exposition of logic, natural science, mathematics, and metaphysics that provided an alternative to studying the relevant works of Aristotle, Euclid, and Ptolemy. Several parts of the work were translated into Latin in the Middle Ages. His uncompromising belief in a philosophical way of explaining things was severely criticized in al-Ghazali's *Destruction of the Philosophers*, but the logical section of the *Shifa'* remained on the curriculum in Islamic schools until modern times. Notable among his contributions in this work is his demonstration of the entity of the soul (the "flying man" theory) and his delineation of the five "inner senses" involved in intellection. In other works he put his theories on the ascent of the soul into the form of allegorical tales. His *Canon of Medicine* provided a correspondingly comprehensive textbook on the theoretical and practical parts of medicine and became the principal text studied in medical schools both in the Islamic world and (through its Latin translation) in the West.

H. Corbin, *Avicenna and the Visionary Recital* (1960); L. E. Goodman, *Avicenna* (1992); D. Gutas, *Avicenna and the Aristotelian Tradition* (1988).

CHARLES BURNETT

Avignon Papacy From 1305 to 1378 seven popes lived at Avignon in what today is southern France but then was part of a territory owned by the papacy. This period, which the Italian poet Petrarch has stigmatized as, and which has since been called, "the Babylonian Captivity" of the papacy, was in point of fact a creative period for the papacy in terms of the ways it governed the Western church. After the French king Philip IV had humiliated Pope Boniface VIII (1294–1303), the popes were once again able to contribute to the political and religious life of Western Europe. Although having to live in the shadow of the French monarchy, the Avignon popes to some extent were able to act independently and partly avoid the dangers and defeats that involvement in Italian wars and politics had inflicted on their predecessors.

The first Avignon pope, Clement V (1305–1314), had been archbishop of Bordeaux. He gave way to pressure from Philip IV ("the Fair") and accepted Philip's savage persecution of the Knights Templar and the suppression of the order. His successor, John XXII (1316–1334), was a much stronger personality. He decided that the papal court for the time being was to remain at Avignon. His growing chancery bears witness to the fact that the papal court came to handle every kind of ecclesiastical business. It did so with relative efficiency. The Univ. of Paris regularly sent lists of graduates seeking church office, and papal notaries would provide positions for them all.

In the last years of his papacy John ruined his reputation by trying to establish as a doctrine that the souls of the just do not see God (the beatific vision) before Judgment Day. Theologians of the Univ. of Paris opposed him, and the pope had to back down. His successor, Benedict XII (Jacques Fournier, 1334–1342), was also interested in theology, but from a different point of view. A former Cistercian abbot, bishop of Pamiers, and inquisitor, Fournier is remembered for his meticulous protocols, which provided the sources for Emmanuel Le Roy Ladurie's *Montaillou* (1974), the story of Cathar peasants in a village in the Pyrenees.

While Benedict did his best to reform monastic orders, his successor, Clement VI (1342–1352), was more interested in art and high living. He is the only one among the otherwise efficient, dedicated administrators of Avignon who deserves the reputation that these popes acquired for neglecting the spiritual and pastoral life of the church. Innocent VI (1352–1362) returned to the agenda of reform of the religious orders, especially the Dominicans and the Franciscans, but met much opposition. His successor, Urban V (1362–1370), was devoted to literature and learning. He is said to have supported out of his own pocket fourteen hundred university students.

Under Gregory XI (1370–1378), the papacy returned to Rome, thanks in part to the urgings and warnings of holy women such as Catherine of Siena and Bridget of Sweden. Within months of Gregory's death, the Western church was split by schism, with one pope in Avignon and another in Rome. The relative stability and efficiency of the Avignon papacy were replaced by a period of conflict and controversy, but also of church reform.

———

Emmanuel Le Roy Ladurie, *Montaillou: The Promised Land of Error* (1979); G. Mollat, *The Popes at Avignon 1305–1378* (1963).

BRIAN PATRICK MCGUIRE

Ávila, Juan de (1499?–1569), Spanish preacher and saint of the Roman Catholic Church. After studies at Salamanca and Alcalá, Ávila was ordained a priest in 1526. By 1531 his popular preaching throughout Andalusia became the focus of the Inquisition, resulting in his imprisonment. After renewing his itinerant preaching in 1533, he gathered a considerable group of followers around an incipient movement of ecclesiastical renewal rooted in the foundation of educational institutions. He founded over fifteen schools for poor children and for the formation of the clergy, including the universities of Baeza and Jaén. His perspectives on the theological formation of the clergy were very influential for the Spanish delegation at the Council of Trent. In spite of the support that de Ávila had mustered in Spain and Portugal, his movement did not acquire definite institutional form. Instead, many of his followers eventually joined with his blessing the Discalced Carmelites and the newly founded Society of Jesus. Paul VI canonized him in 1970.

———

M. A. Martín, *San Juan de Ávila: Maestro de espiritualidad* (1997); R. Arce, *San Juan de Ávila y la reforma de la Iglesia en España* (1970); F. S. Bella, *La reforma del clero en San Juan de Ávila* (1981).

RADY ROLDÁN-FIGUEROA

Avitus of Vienne (d. c. 518), bishop (c. 494–c. 518). From a prominent Gallic family, Avitus succeeded his father Hesychius as bishop of Vienne. By then Germanic kingdoms had replaced imperial rule in the West. The diocese of Vienne lay within the realm of the Burgundians. Avitus championed the cause of Nicene Christianity in part by persistently encouraging the Arian ruler, King Gundovald (d. 516), to convert. His long effort reached fruition when the next monarch, Sigismund, converted to catholic Christianity. Avitus was an opponent of Semi-Pelagianism, an antipredestinarian position that most Gallic ecclesiastics had favored during the fifth century. Avitus is known for his eloquence and education. A collection of his let-

ters survives, which sheds light on Gallic ecclesiastics' theological and social sensibilities in the early sixth century. Perhaps the most famous among Avitus's epistles is the one sent to congratulate Clovis, king of the Franks, upon his baptism (c. 508?). Avitus's most noteworthy extant literary achievement is his five-book poem *On Acts of Spiritual History*, which addresses biblical history from Adam through the Hebrews' crossing of the Red Sea. Also surviving is a poem on chastity addressed by Avitus to his sister, the nun Fuscina.

———

Avitus, *The Poems of Alcimus Ecdicius Avitus* (1997); Avitus, *Avitus of Vienne: Letters and Selected Prose*, ed. I. Wood and D. R. Shanzer (2002).

ALLEN E. JONES

Babylonian Captivity of the Church

The period 1309–1374, during which the popes resided in Avignon (modern-day France) rather than Rome, is often called the "Babylonian Captivity of the Church" for the dominating influence France wielded over the church. Pope Clement V (1305–14) was elected with French support during a period of violent strife in Italy and rising nationalism across Europe. He moved to Avignon, a papal-controlled city bordering France, in 1309. Critics accused Clement of acting as a tool of French policy. When succeeding popes remained in Avignon, this reputation grew, alienating England and the HRE. Shocked contemporaries saw the popes' abandonment of their traditional Roman see as scandalous and increasingly associated the court with luxury and nepotism. Gregory XI (1370–78) reentered Rome in 1377 to popular rejoicing. While critics sometimes overstate French influence over the church during this period, and despite advances in ecclesiastical bureaucracy and finance, the Avignonese "exile" and the subsequent Western Schism (1378–1417) mark a period of decline in papal prestige after the high medieval zenith.

———

Y. Renouard, *The Avignon Papacy, 1305–1403* (1970); G. Mollat, *The Popes at Avignon, 1305–1378* (1963).

NATHAN BARUCH REIN

Bacon, Francis (1561–1626), British lawyer, philosopher, scientist. Bacon sought practical knowledge and fostered an optimistic vision of what science might achieve for humankind. An admired essayist, he wrote extensively in English and, when he sought an international audience, in Latin. He advocated empiricism (versus Cartesian rationalism), and envisioned an academy of sciences dedicated to "the knowledge of [the] causes, and secret motions of things; and the enlarging [of] the bounds of [the] human empire, to the effecting of all things possible." The founders of the Royal Society cited him as an inspiration, although modern science shed his disdain for mathematics and thus remedied his concomitant failure to advance any precise scientific method. Bacon is significant theologically for rooting science in biblical commandments and in his insistence that it be ethically driven. His famed remark that "knowledge is power" meant that knowledge would provide the power to improve the human condition. Likewise significant is his notion of the "idols of the mind," preconceptions that block the progress of knowledge. The French encyclopedist Diderot wrote of Bacon, "When it was impossible to write a history of what men knew, he drew up the map of what they must learn."

F. H. Anderson, *The Philosophy of Francis Bacon* (1948); P. Rossi, *Francis Bacon: From Magic to Science* (1968).

RODERICK MARTIN

Bacon, Roger (c. 1217–c. 1292), English philosopher, scientist, and polemicist. Bacon was a product of the universities of Paris and Oxford. Giving up a successful career as an arts teacher at Paris c. 1248, Bacon embarked on a multiyear study of science, mathematics, and languages; he also became a Franciscan (c. 1257). His profession of religion eventually brought him back into the classroom in some capacity, but there were also disagreements with his superiors that led to his being subjected to some measure of discipline. While it is possible that these disagreements were partly based on some of Bacon's scientific ideas, in particular those concerning astrology, the older view of Bacon as "a martyr for science," a kind of thirteenth-century Galileo, is untenable.

Bacon emerged from the above-mentioned period of study as a mature and innovative thinker with a novel program that criticized the scholastic enterprise and emphasized the utility of human knowledge. Bacon first gave coherent expression to this program in his *Opus maius* (c. 1267), written at the behest of Pope Clement IV. Other writings in this and the following decade elaborated on his basic message or dealt with specific scientific topics. With all due awareness of the danger of historical anachronism, one can say that what appears in full flower in Francis Bacon centuries later, we see in germ in Roger.

S. C. Easton, *Roger Bacon and His Search for a Universal Science* (1952); J. Hackett, ed., *Roger Bacon and the Sciences: Commemorative Essays* (1997).

STEVEN J. WILLIAMS

Baius, Michel (1513–1589), Roman Catholic theologian. At the Univ. of Louvain, where he worked as a teacher of theology, Baius wrote brief treatises on the doctrines of grace and justification. Based on a stern reading of Augustine, Baius's defense of innate depravity deviated from the official views of the church. In 1567 Pope Pius V condemned more than seventy theses taken from his writings. Baius submitted to Pius V and continued to work at the faculty in Louvain, which supported him despite continuing criticism from Jesuit quarters. Through his writings and students, Baius influenced the thought of Cornelius Jansen.

V. Grossi, "Michael Bajus," *TRE* 5 (1983): 133–37.

JORIS VAN EIJNATTEN

Baldung, Hans (1484/1485–1545), German Renaissance painter, draftsman, and designer of stained glass and woodblocks. The artist, known also as Hans Baldung Grien, was a member of Albrecht Dürer's workshop in Nuremberg from 1503 to 1506 or 1507, then settled in Strasbourg, where the civil unrest of peasant uprisings and religious controversy may have inspired the particularly expressive qualities of his art. Although Baldung completed several portraits and religious paintings, he is particularly renowned for his strange allegorical subjects with their obsessive stress on witchcraft, alchemy, sex, and death. Notable examples include the paintings *Death and the Maiden* (1509–1511), *Eve, the Serpent, and Death* (c. 1530), and *Three Ages of Women* (1540–1543); and the woodcuts *The Witches' Sabbath* (1510), *Aroused Stallion Approaching Mare* (1534), and *Sleeping Groom and Sorceress* (1544). Baldung's strikingly original and enigmatic work presents psychologically disturbing images that haunt the imagination.

J. L. Koerner, *The Moment of Self-Portraiture in German Renaissance Art* (1993); R. A. Koch, *Hans Baldung Grien—Eve, the Serpent, and Death* (1974); J. H. Marrow and A. Shestack, eds., *Hans Baldung Grien: Prints and Drawings* (1981).

PRISCILLA BAUMANN

Ball, John (d. 1381), English priest, popular preacher of radical social reform, and a leader of the Peasants' Revolt. Drawing on John Wyclif's ideas, Ball preached in York and Colchester before being excommunicated by Simon Islip, archbishop of Canterbury, between 1362 and 1366. Ball continued to preach radical social reform, such as murder of nobles and withholding of tithes from unworthy clergy, until his arrest in 1381 by Bishop Simon of Sudbury. The Peasants' Revolt of 1381 freed him from prison, and Ball was later among those who murdered Sudbury in the Tower of London. He was present during King Richard II's interview with Wat Tyler, the revolt's popular leader, at Smithfield. He later fled, was arrested in Coventry, and was executed for treason at St. Alban's by Richard II.

R. Dobson, *The Peasants' Revolt of 1381* (1983); A. Steel, *Richard II* (1941, 1963).

DAVID A. LOPEZ

Baltic Crusade This term primarily refers to crusading efforts in what are now Latvia and Estonia (medieval Livonia) and secondarily to activities in Finland, Prussia, and Lithuania. From the tenth century, Western European Christians had pushed eastward. As part of this effort, in the last half of the twelfth century, northern German merchants traded with the peoples of the eastern coast of the Baltic Sea. Missionaries, armies, and colonists followed.

In 1180, Meinhard, an Augustinian, established a mission on the Dvina River in Livonia, built a fortress at Uexküll, and died in 1196. Albert von Buxhövden was sent by his uncle Archbishop Hartwig II of Bremen to create an ecclesiastical government. In 1199, as bishop, Albert brought Saxon crusaders who enjoyed privileges from the pope and the German emperor. He established his headquarters in Riga, which became an important trading center. By 1207, Albert himself had become a prince of the German empire and, at the Fourth Lateran Council, answerable only to the pope. Annually, Albert returned to Germany to recruit pilgrims/crusaders because there was no adequate, permanent army. To help, he created a military order known as the Brothers of the Sword. They merged with the Teutonic Order

in 1237 after a devastating defeat by the Lithuanians at the Saule River.

The crusaders enjoyed initial success among the Livonians and Letts. Campaigns also were conducted against the Kurs, Semgallians, and Samogitians. Baptism was the symbol of conquest, and that act was followed by German laws and taxation. The Germans had some success in subjugating the Estonians. However, twelve years after Albert's death, the sainted Russian prince Alexander Nevski (1238–1263) defeated them on the ice of Lake Peipus in 1242, stopping their advance. Bishop Christian (1215–1245) followed Albert, and the crusade essentially concluded by about 1290.

The Teutonic Order began its conquest of Prussia in 1230. It lasted for the rest of the century. Large numbers of Germans colonized the monastic theocracy in Prussia, which lasted until it secularized in 1525. The ecclesiastical theocracy in Livonia saw small numbers of Germans in the ruling ranks of a primarily native society.

J. A. Brundage, trans., *The Chronicle of Henry of Livonia* (1961); E. Christiansen, *The Northern Crusades, the Baltic, and the Catholic Frontier, 1100–1525* (1980); E. N. Johnson, "The German Crusade on the Baltic," in *History of the Crusades*, vol. 3, ed. H. W. Hazard (1975); J. C. Smith and W. L. Urban, trans., *The Livonian Rhymed Chronicle* (1977); W. L. Urban, *The Baltic Crusade* (2nd ed., 1994); Urban, *The Teutonic Knights: A Military History* (2003); Urban, *The Samogitian Crusade* (1989).

ERHARD "ERIK" P. OPSAHL

Bancroft, Richard (1544–1610), archbishop of Canterbury (1604–1610) Bancroft was best known as a determined opponent of Puritans, Congregationalists, and recusants in Elizabethan England. He was an advocate for High Church views and tenacious in his orthodoxy. Educated at Cambridge, he took his BA in 1567, followed by an MA in 1570. In 1585 he was appointed treasurer of St. Paul's Cathedral, the same year he received his DD. It was on February 9, 1589, that he made a name for himself, preaching a sermon that openly attacked Puritanism. The sermon won him fame, as well as the attention of Lord Burghley and Elizabeth. During 1588–1589 he worked tirelessly to suppress the Marprelate Tracts, which he took as serious evidence of a "presbyterian plot" to overthrow High Church ecclesiology in the Church of England. He was named canon of Westminster in 1587 and prebendary of St. Paul's in 1590. He served as chaplain to Lord Chancellor Hatton, then Archbishop Whitgift. In 1597 he was consecrated as archbishop of London. Though he is best known as a tenacious opponent of any form of Puritanism, he had a genuine love of the church and sought to reform and rebuild the Church of England to his vision, attacking not only what he perceived to be heterodoxy but also clerical abuses within the Church of England itself. He was a major intellectual visionary and contributor to the 1611 Authorized Version of the Bible, on which he worked until his death at Lambeth Palace in 1610.

D. MacCulloch, *The Later Reformation in England, 1547–1603* (2nd ed., 2001).

ALDEN R. LUDLOW

Báñez, Domingo (1528–1604), Spanish theologian and philosopher, chief exponent of the Thomistic school of Salamanca. Born in Valladolid, Bañez studied liberal arts at the Univ. of Salamanca (1543–1546). In 1547 he joined the Dominicans. He obtained his doctorate in theology from the Univ. of Sigüenza in 1565. In 1552 Báñez began his distinguished teaching career at different learning centers, including his own convent of San Esteban (1552–1561), the Univ. of Ávila (1561–1567), the Colegio de Santo Tomás de Alcalá (1567–1569), and the Colegio de Santo Tomás de Ávila (1569–1570). In 1577 he was appointed to the prestigious chair of theology at the Univ. of Salamanca. Báñez played a central role in major disputes over grace involving the Jesuit Prudencio de Montemayor, the Augustinian Luis de León (1527–1591), and the Jesuit theologian Luis de Molina (1535–1601). Against Molina's doctrine of the efficacy of grace *ab extrinseco*, Báñez upheld the Thomistic doctrine of the efficacy of grace *ab intrinseco*. Báñez was also confessor of Teresa de Jesús (1515–1582).

J. A. G. Cuadrado, *Domingo Bañez (1528–1604): Introducción a su obra filosófica y teológica* (1999); Cuadrado, *La luz del intelecto agente: Estudio desde la metafísica de Bánez* (1998).

RADY ROLDÁN-FIGUEROA

Baptism In Greek, this word means "dipping in water," "immersion," or "drowning." From the first century of Christianity until today this central rite of initiation into the church has been conducted by affusion or aspersion of water (especially in "clinical baptism" of the sick who cannot be immersed) as well as by immersion, performed three times in succession. From the second century the water was often blessed with an invocation of the Holy Spirit, as it still is among the Orthodox, Roman Catholics, and some Protestants. The ritual gesture with water is accompanied by a Trinitarian formula, in keeping with Matt. 28:9. By the fourth century, two distinct formulas that remain today were apparent: in the West, "I baptize you in the name of . . ."; in the East, "N. is baptized in the name of . . ." Earlier communities utilized a threefold interrogation ("Do you believe in . . . ?") that is the source of the Apostles' Creed. Ancient Christian baptism took place in conjunction with gestures indicating conferral of the Holy Spirit—particularly anointing or laying on hands—and was immediately followed by first participation in the Eucharist (cf. Justin Martyr; *Trad. ap.*). Hence baptism, confirmation, and Eucharist are called the "sacraments of initiation." Mystagogy is the subsequent explanation of these rites. By the fourth century, Easter and Pentecost were preferred times for baptism. Nonetheless, the conviction that baptism is necessary for forgiveness of sins and entrance into the kingdom of Christ soon led to administration whenever death seemed imminent—at any age, including infancy, and at any time of year. Hence, the close association of Easter and Pentecost with baptism broke down in late antiquity, as the Christian population grew. These factors also contributed to the predominance of baptism by presbyters or deacons, since it was no longer possible for the bishop to be present for every baptism in his diocese. Even during the time of Tertullian laypeople could baptize, although the preference was clearly for the bishop to do so. Times of persecution led to the notion of "baptism by blood," applicable to those who died as martyrs for the faith before being baptized.

Early Christians saw baptism following upon repentance and belief (Acts 2:38) as death to sin and the beginning of new life in Christ (Rom. 6:2–11), as participation in the eschatological reward of the saints (Theodore of Mopsuestia), as presupposing and entailing a new set of moral demands (John Chrysostom), and as illumination (Cappadocians). According to Augustine, baptism is, along with faith and charity, necessary for salvation. Luther viewed baptism as a promise of the remission of sins, which is efficacious only insofar as it reflects faith in the one who receives it. He held that sin is only completely destroyed when baptism is fulfilled upon departing from this life. Calvin saw baptism as a confirmation and profession of faith that is efficacious only for the elect, and held that original sin remains after baptism. The Council of Trent taught that baptism confers grace that remits original and actual sin along with the punishment due to sin, infuses virtues into the soul, and incorporates one into Christ.

In the mid-third century, bishops Stephen of Rome and Cyprian of Carthage disagreed over the validity of baptisms performed by heretics. Stephen accepted the baptism of heretics and treated those entering his communion as penitents, by receiving them with a hand-laying. Cyprian rebaptized—or in his perspective, baptized for the first time—former heretics entering his fold. Donatists continued Cyprian's practice, and against them Augustine argued that baptism belonged to Christ alone, who ensured its validity regardless of the disposition of the human minister. Montanists and Arians introduced changes into the baptismal formula that caused further theological problems regarding recognition of their baptism. The attitudes of Eastern churches toward baptism among heretics and Western communions, based in part upon interpretations of the ninety-fifth canon of the Trullan Synod of 692 (Quinisext Council), have varied. Nicodemus of Mount Athos (*Pedalion*, 1800) appropriated Cyprian's arguments to convince many Orthodox theologians and clerics that non-Orthodox Christians should be rebaptized, although this position is far from being universally accepted. In the Middle Ages, some groups, such as the Petrobrusians in France (twelfth century), rejected the baptism of infants. This line of protest was continued by reformers who argued that only believers should be baptized, such as Anabaptists (sixteenth century), Baptists (seventeenth century), and numerous other Protestant groups to the present day. Pentecostals and many in the charismatic movement hold that "baptism in the Holy Spirit," manifested by glossolalia, or speaking in tongues (cf. Acts 11:15–17), as distinct from water baptism, is a mark of Christian discipleship.

Mutual acceptance of one another's baptism and convergence on biblical expressions of its meaning have been important cornerstones of ecumenical efforts since the twentieth century, as expressed in *Baptism, Eucharist, Ministry* (BEM), published by the World Council of Churches in 1982. Difficulties have arisen, however, because some local churches have introduced inclusive language Trinitarian formulas (e.g., "in the name of the Creator, and the Redeemer, and the Sanctifier"), which others have accused of modalism. Recent Western theological reflection often emphasizes the communal aspects of being "baptized into one body" (Gal. 3:27).

———

P. De Clerck, ed., *Baptême unique, églises divisées*, La Maison-Dieu, no. 235 (2003); J. D. C. Fisher, *Christian Initiation: Baptism in the Medieval West* (1965); Fisher, *Christian Initiation: The Reformation Period* (1970); A. Kavanagh, *The Shape of Baptism: The Rite of Christian Initiation* (1978); A. Schmemann, *Of Water and the Spirit* (1974); M. Thurian, ed., *Churches Respond to BEM*, 6 vols. (1986); E. C. Whitaker, *The Baptismal Liturgy* (2nd ed., 1981); E. C. Whitaker and M. E. Johnson, *Documents of the Baptismal Liturgy* (3rd ed., 2003); D. F. Wright, "How Controversial Was the Development of Infant Baptism in the Early Church?" in *Church, Word, and Spirit*, ed. J. E. Bradley and R. A. Muller (1987), 45–63.

DANIEL G. VAN SLYKE

Baradaeus, Jacob (c. 490–578), founder
of the Syrian Orthodox ("Jacobite") Church. His surname derives from his habit of wearing a horse cloth (Syriac, *barᶜdānā*). In 528 he accompanied Sergius to Constantinople to plead the Monophysite cause with Empress Theodora. Jacob was consecrated bishop of Edessa by Theodosius in 542, but his doctrinal position precluded his staying in the city. He traveled throughout the region, preaching and organizing the Monophysite church, and for this work later leaders named the church after him.

Jacob visited the Persian king Khusro I (559) to seek tolerance for the Syrian Orthodox. He consecrated Paul the Black as Syrian Orthodox patriarch (564), but eventually he was forced to agree to Paul's deposition in order to appease the Alexandrian party (575).

A few writings attributed to Jacob survive, though some doubt their authenticity: an *anaphora*, a few letters, canons, and statements of faith in Ethiopic. A *Syriac Life* by John of Ephesus is extant.

———

D. Bundy, "Jacob Baradaeus: The State of Research, a Review of Sources, and a New Approach," *Le Muséon* 91 (1978): 45–86; J. Baradaeus, "Epistolae," in *Documenta ad origines monophysitarum illustrandas*, ed. J. B. Chabot (1908, 1933); "Jacob Baradaeus," in *John of Ephesus: Lives of the Eastern Saints,* chaps. 49–50 in PO 18 (1924), 690–97 and 19 (1926), 153–58.

ROBERT A. KITCHEN

Barbarian Invasions   Since its inception the Roman Empire had been confronted by various northern neighbors, now commonly referred to as "barbarians." For over two centuries the Roman policy of "divide and conquer" successfully dealt with barbarian threats. The first sign of problems came during the reign of Marcus Aurelius (r. 161–180), who spent many years repelling barbarian assaults on the Danube frontier. The third century saw both the "Military Anarchy," a period of civil war, and the creation of barbarian "coalitions," such as the Franks, Alamanni, and Goths, who posed much more serious threats. Barbarian raids penetrated to Greece and Spain. Not until the Roman recovery under the emperor Diocletian (r. 284–305) were the frontiers restored.

Barbarian problems resurfaced in 376, when a large group of Visigoths (western Goths) fleeing from the Huns appeared on the Danube. The Visigoths offered military service in exchange for deserted farms inside the Roman frontier. Emperor Valens accepted the offer, on condition that the Visigoths turn over their weapons and the Romans provide them with provisions. Roman officials, however, failed to carry out these terms. Starving, armed Visigoths began rampaging about the Balkans. In 378, Valens met the Visigoths at Adrianople, where the Roman army was virtually annihilated and Valens was killed. His successor, Theodosius, unable to defeat the marauders, recognized the Visigoths as Roman federates (allies). This face-saving measure left the Visigoths free to roam about at will. The barbarian invasions had begun.

The invasions that initially affected the East soon impacted the West with even more devastating effect. In 401, Alaric's Visigoths invaded Italy. Troops were withdrawn from the north to defend Italy. On the last day of 406 a horde of barbarians including Vandals, Burgundians, and Sueves crossed the frozen, undefended Rhine River. Some made their way south into the fertile and largely ungarrisoned provinces of Spain. In the north, the emperor Honorius abandoned the isolated Britons, telling them to expect no help from Rome. Meanwhile, in 410 the Visigoths occupied Rome. The rather genteel sacking that followed lasted only three days. The churches were left untouched. The psychological damage was greater than the material destruction. *Invicta* ("unconquered") Rome, as it

had been called, was no longer unconquered. Honorius, who had retreated to the safety of Ravenna, rid himself of the Visigoths in 418 by granting them Aquitaine in southwestern France. The Western empire was beginning to fracture.

Technically, barbarian settlers like the Goths remained Roman federates, but many soon established their own independent kingdoms. In 429 the Vandals crossed to North Africa and soon occupied that richest of Western provinces. Thereafter the Burgundians were settled in Savoy, the Visigoths occupied Spain, and the Franks encroached into northern Gaul. Against fierce Romano-Briton resistance, Britain was gradually occupied by Angles and Saxons. In 451 an invasion of Attila and the Huns was defeated at the Mauriac Plain by a coalition of Romans, Visigoths, and Franks, but this was the last effective resistance against barbarian settlement. In 476, the last emperor in Rome was deposed by the barbarian chieftain Odovacar, who notified the Eastern emperor Zeno that Rome no longer needed its own emperor. Zeno responded in 489 by sending the Ostrogothic king Theoderic west. Theoderic established his own kingdom in Italy.

In general, the concept of barbarian "invasions" is misleading. The West was occupied by means of infiltration, peaceful settlement, and persistence rather than by military superiority or right of conquest. The real question is what made it possible for the barbarians to succeed in the fifth century when they had failed in the past. Economic problems and the inability of the Western Roman government to support an army provide one reason. The split of the empire, with the East and West going their own ways, suggests another. In many cases, Western Roman senators preferred a local barbarian king, who allowed them full autonomy, to a distant Roman emperor making exorbitant tax exactions.

Nor were these barbarians "foreign" in any real sense of the word. Most barbarian settlers already had assimilated much of Roman culture. By the time they created their own kingdoms on Roman territory, barbarian groups manifested a remarkably heterogeneous ethnic mix. Only a few of the "Visigoths" who settled in Aquitania in 418, for example, were descendants of those who had crossed the Danube in 376. They now included not only accretions from other barbarian groups but even Romans who had cast their lot with the barbarians.

In most regards, life in barbarian kingdoms differed little from that under Roman authority. Barbarians adopted Roman administrative practices, the Latin language, and classical culture with enthusiasm. One thing that did appear to set many barbarians apart was their adherence to the Arian form of Christianity. In practice, however, this distinction meant little, for Arians and Nicenes usually interacted freely, even attending each other's church services. Eventually, all the barbarian invaders became Nicene Christians. The pagan Franks were the first, when their king Clovis, influenced by his wife Clotilde, was baptized by Bishop Remigius of Reims in the late 490s, taking many of his people along with him. The Burgundian king Sigismund, influenced by Bishop Avitus of Vienne, espoused Nicene Christianity in 516, and the Visigoths in Spain belatedly converted in 589. In general, the Christian church thrived under barbarian rule.

Even though the Byzantine emperor Justinian (527–565) reconquered Africa, Italy, and part of Spain, the western part of the Roman Empire was never truly reintegrated into the Roman world. In 568 the Lombards invaded Italy, and by 711 the Muslims had acquired Africa and Spain. The barbarian invaders of the Western Roman Empire who left the greatest legacies were the Franks, Anglo-Saxons, Lombards, and Alamanni, who gave their names, respectively, to France, England, Lombardy, and (in French) Allemagne. Most others were amalgamated into other nations or peoples.

J. B. Bury, *The Invasion of Europe by the Barbarians* (1928); W. A. Goffart, "The Theme of 'The Barbarian Invasions' in Late Antiquity and Modern Historiography," in *Das Reich und die Barbaren*, ed. E. Chrysos and A. Schwarcz (1989), 87–107.

RALPH W. MATHISEN

Barclay, Robert (1648–1690), formative Quaker theologian. Barclay was born into an aristocratic Scottish family headed by a Quaker father. Distantly related to the Stuarts and a friend of James II, he used both his social connections and formidable intellect to help transform the followers of George Fox into a durable religious movement based upon a coherent system of thought. The latter is definitively presented in his *Apology* (Lat. 1676; Eng. 1678). Based structurally on the Westminster Confession but placing stronger emphasis upon immediate revelation as a source for knowledge of God, the work has found use both as a confessional statement of Quaker beliefs and as a tool for evangelism. Like many early Quakers, Barclay suffered imprisonment for his faith. Such experiences not only fortified the movement at

home, but they also led to its expansion abroad. Barclay traveled to Holland and Germany, where he sought the support of Princess Elisabeth of the Rhine. Later, with his friend William Penn, he involved himself in the colonization of North America, serving as governor of East New Jersey.

R. Moore, *The Light in Their Consciences: The Early Quakers in Britain, 1646–1666* (2000); D. E. Trueblood, *Robert Barclay* (1967).

KENNETH G. APPOLD

Bardaisan (154–222), Syriac philosopher, theologian, founder of a Christian sect. Bardaisan, a nobleman at the court of King Abgar VIII of Edessa, received a Syriac and Greek education, converted to Christianity, and strove to harmonize his faith with contemporary philosophy. Bardaisan rejected the teachings of Marcion but was soon labeled as a heretic himself. Only fragments survive of his writings. Some of his thought can be reconstructed from the *Book of the Laws of the Countries*, a dialogue written by a disciple in which Bardaisan is the main interlocutor, and from Ephrem's *Prose Refutations*.

Some scholars have linked Bardaisan to Gnosticism, but he was more influenced by Middle Platonism. He defended human freedom against notions of astrological determinism prevalent in late antique paganism, he incorporated current scientific models (e.g., atomism) into his cosmogony, and he is credited with inventing the Syriac hymn (*madrasha*). He is said to have denied the bodily resurrection and to have held a docetic Christology.

Bardaisan founded an influential community that received much support from the Edessan nobility. The Bardaisanites radicalized Bardaisan's teachings and flourished until at least the fifth century.

H. J. W. Drijvers, ed., *The Book of the Laws of Countries: Dialogue on Fate of Bardaisan of Edessa* (1965); Drijvers, *Bardaisan of Edessa* (1966); U. Possekel, "Bardaisan of Edessa: Philosopher or Theologian?" *ZAC* 10 (2006): 442–61.

UTE POSSEKEL

Bar Hebraeus (1226–1286), Jacobite bishop and scholar. Most of our knowledge about this person comes from remarks that he makes about himself. Even his name is confusing. He was born in Melitene to a Jewish father who was a convert to Monophysite

Christianity and was baptized John. At some point he adopted the name Gregory, possibly upon episcopal ordination. His mother may have been an Arab, and we also find the Arabic name for him, Abu al-Faraj. In 1244, Bar Hebraeus's father treated an ailing Mongol commander, who in gratitude took the family with him to the relative safety of Antioch. There Bar Hebraeus studied under both Jacobite and Nestorian teachers and entered a Jacobite monastery. Two years later, when he was scarcely twenty years old, he was ordained bishop of Gouba. A year later he was moved to Laqabin and became metropolitan of Aleppo in 1252. In 1264 he was made maphrain, a post second only to that of the catholicos.

As maphrain, Bishop Gregory was an energetic promoter of unity within the Jacobite community and of cooperation among all Christians living under non-Christian rule. His good relations with the Mongols allowed him to be the first maphrain to visit the see of Tagrit in over half a century. By 1284 he had successfully restructured the episcopacy and ordained a dozen new Jacobite bishops.

Bar Hebraeus's literary output is vast. It includes an encyclopedic compendium, *The Science of Sciences*, an extensive collection of scriptural commentaries, the *Storehouse of Mysteries*, and a *Nomocanon* that is an important canonical authority. Historians of the period most appreciate Bar Hebraeus for his *Chronicle*, which treats both secular and ecclesiastical history.

It is indicative of the respect in which he was held that his funeral was attended by Orthodox and Nestorians as well as Jacobites.

———

E. A. W. Budge, *The Chronography of Gregory Abu'l Faraj, the Son of Aaron, the Hebrew Physician, Commonly Know as Bar Hebraeus* (1932); W. Wright, *A Short History of Syriac Literature* (1894).

EUGENE M. LUDWIG, OFM CAP.

Barnabas, Epistle of

This ancient work comes from an unknown Christian author, likely Jewish in background, who wrote in the late first or early second century. The manuscript tradition attributes the text to Barnabas, presumably the wealthy, first-century Jewish Christian from Cyprus known from the book of Acts. In reality, both the author and any subsequent editors remain anonymous. While Asia Minor, Syria, and Egypt have all been offered as possible provenances for the work, the author's preference for the allegorical interpretation of Scripture, the early inclusion of the text in Codex Sinaiticus (fourth century), and its clear acceptance by Clement of Alexandria (*Strom.* 2.6–7) and Origen (*Cont. Cels.* 1.63) suggest the region of Alexandria as the most likely probability.

Classified among the Apostolic Fathers, this so-called epistle features three literary components. The core of the work is a general treatise or homily based upon Isaiah that illustrates Israel's forsaking of its covenant with God and the transference of that covenant to the true faith of Christianity (chaps. 1–17). The author, while familiar with the imagery and writings of Israel, vigorously condemns the shortfalls of Jewish faith. Another text has been added to this treatise from a second literary tradition, a brief excursus on the ways of light and darkness, commonly known as the "two ways" (chaps. 18–20). These two works were joined, either by the author or a later editor, into a rudimentary letter format with a general greeting (chap. 1) and farewell (chap. 21). The author's primary concern is to enhance the readers' faith with the knowledge of life, righteousness, and love (1.6).

———

L. W. Barnard, "The 'Epistle of Barnabas' and Its Contemporary Setting," *ANRW* 2.27.1 (1993): 159–207; R. Hvalvik, *The Struggle for Scripture and Covenant* (1995); R. A. Kraft, *Barnabas and the Didache* (1965); J. C. Paget, *The Epistle of Barnabas* (1994).

CLAYTON N. JEFFORD

Barnabites

The Clerks Regular of St. Paul, founded in 1532 by St. Anthony Mary Zaccaria, is known by the early association with the Church of St. Barnabas in Milan. The Barnabites were an innovative group of clerics whose affiliated communities eventually included noncloistered nuns and even married couples. Like other reforming groups (the Somaschi, Theatines, and Ursulines), Zaccaria and his companions were inspired by the Oratory movement, clergy and laity gathered together, seeking personal sanctification through prayer and practical charity. While still a layman, Zaccaria had sought to encourage a popular revival of faith in God and love of neighbor, conducting catechism classes for the young and Scripture study and meditation groups for adults. Zaccaria's community pledged to work for church renewal by self-reformation and by evangelizing the wider society through popular preaching, public penitence, devotion to the crucifixion, and love for the Eucharist. The Barnabites added to the traditional vows of poverty, chastity, and obedience a fourth vow never to seek ecclesiastical office or honors. Despite papal approval, the community did not escape misunderstanding and even accusations of heresy. Acquitted in at least two ecclesiastical trials, the community survived the premature death of Zaccaria in 1539. The Barnabites continue their ministry to this day.

B. Studi, *Rivista di ricerche storiche dei Chierici Regolari de S. Paolo (Barnabiti)* (1997); E. Bonora, *I conflitti della Controriforma: Santità e obbedienza nell'esperienza religiosa dei primi barnabiti* (1998); A. Montonati, *Fuoco nella città (Sant'Antonio Maria Zaccaria (1502–1539)* (2002); A. Wright, *The Counter-Reformation: Catholic Europe and the Non-Christian World* (1982).

PETER J. SCAGNELLI

Barnes, Robert (c. 1495–1540), early promoter of the Reformation in England. An Augustinian friar, Barnes attended Cambridge in the 1520s, where he was the prior of his order's house. It was at Cambridge that he encountered Lutheran theology. Subsequently, he introduced humanism, intensive NT study, and sharp criticism of clergy corruption, teaching with unflagging zeal. He encouraged study of Tyndale's English-language NT, an enterprise for which he nearly paid with his life and was forced to flee England for Wittenberg, where he studied Lutheranism at its source. It was from there, through his *Supplication* and other entreaties, that he tirelessly worked to convert Henry VIII and all England to Lutheranism. Though he failed to sway Henry, Thomas Cromwell took notice of him. Barnes returned to England in 1536, but Henry's theological stances tended to be fickle; he wavered between traditional and Reformation views depending on marital circumstances. By 1539, with the passage of the Six Articles, Catholicism was in favor again, and Barnes had lost his usefulness. He was branded a heretic and burned at the stake on July 30, 1540, just two days after Cromwell. Barnes's legacy to the English Reformation was extensive; his early studies and promulgation of Luther's writings were the seeds from which the English Reformation would flower. Though England eventually took the path of Calvinist reform, Barnes's zealous preaching, promulgation of the gospel in the English language, and tireless criticism of Catholic clerical corruption constitutes the important legacy of this "English Luther."

J. E. McGoldrick, *Luther's English Connection* (1979).

ALDEN R. LUDLOW

Baronius, Caesar (1538–1607), Italian ecclesiastical historian and cardinal. Baronius's *Ecclesiastical Annals [from the Birth of Christ to the Year 1198] (Annales ecclesiastici)*, published in twelve volumes (1588–1607), was the official Roman Catholic response to the *Magdeburg Centuries (Historia ecclesiae Christi)*, authored by Lutheran scholars (1559–1574) supervised by Matthias Flacius Illyricus. To the *Centuries'* portrait of the pope as the antichrist and the Roman church's doctrine as irrevocably alienated from the gospel, Baronius's *Annals* proposed a no less polemical interpretation, vindicating the claims of the papacy at every turn and portraying the institution of the Roman see as Christ's one true church.

Despite his bias as a papal apologist and reliance on documents later proved to be spurious, Baronius's history is unique as the fruit of a quarter century of unprecedented research in the previously inaccessible Vatican archives and through correspondence with sources all over Europe.

A lifelong member of the Oratory of St. Philip Neri, Baronius undertook the *Annals* in obedience to Neri (and the *Roman Martyrology* in obedience to the pope) and was continually subjected by Neri to the discipline of his reform-oriented Oratory to preserve Baronius's humility in the face of Vatican adulation. Often assigned to kitchen duty, Baronius finally posted a sign there: *Baronius coquus perpetuus* ("Baronius the perpetual cook"). Refusing promotion to the episcopacy, he was nevertheless named cardinal in 1596 and librarian of the Vatican.

Bouyer, *St. Philip Neri: A Portrait* (1995); Ponnelle and Bordet, *St. Philip Neri and the Roman Society of His Times* (1985); Pullapilly, *Caesar Baronius: Counter-Reformation Historian* (1975).

PETER J. SCAGNELLI

Baroque The principal style in the visual arts of Europe during the seventeenth and early eighteenth centuries. Baroque artists and architects attempted to impress the spectator with astonishment and admiration. The baroque style appeals directly to the emotions and is characterized by dynamic and energetic compositions, curved and irregular forms, unexpected lighting effects, and the sense of movement and immediacy.

The paintings of Michelangelo Caravaggio epitomize the baroque quest for moments of high drama and theatrical realism, as evident in *The Conversion of St. Paul* (c. 1601). Peter Paul Rubens, in *The Elevation of the Cross* (1610), creates a powerful image of the tortured Christ, defined by strong diagonals and dramatic lighting. Artemisia Gentileschi's *Judith and Maidservant with the Head of Holofernes* (c. 1625), employs a hidden light source to magnify the horror of the scene. The sculptor and architect Gianlorenzo Bernini utilizes similar techniques in the life-sized marble statue the *Ecstasy of St. Theresa* (c. 1645–1652).

Baroque architecture features curved walls, a preference for oval or polygonal spaces, concealed lighting, and effects of false perspective. The architectural designs of Francesco Borromini, Bernini, and Johann Dientzenhofer, among others, display these characteristics. Baroque art exerted a powerful impact on the viewer and was particularly popular during the Counter-Reformation.

––––––

I. Lavin, *Bernini and the Unity of the Visual Arts* (1980); A. Millon, ed., *The Triumph of the Baroque: Architecture in Europe, 1600–1750* (1999); R. Tolman, ed., *Baroque: Architecture, Sculpture, Painting* (1998).

PRISCILLA BAUMANN

Bartolomé de Las Casas   *see* Las Casas, Bartolomé de

Basel, Council of (1431–1449)   The Council of Basel was called by Pope Martin V, who died February 20, 1431, leaving his successor with the responsibility of actually presiding over the council and dealing with a host of thorny issues. On the one hand, there was the hostility of the college of cardinals toward the authoritarian administration of Martin V, expressed in the electoral capitulations the college imposed upon the new pope, Eugenius IV; on the other hand, there was the matter of reform, which was the overriding concern of church leaders. There was also the matter of the Hussite wars in Bohemia, which came on the heels of the condemnation of John Hus at the Council of Constance (1415), and the ongoing quest for reunion with the Greek church. Commencing in July 1431 and continuing intermittently until May 4, 1437, in some twenty-five sessions, Basel broke with the practice of Constance and abandoned organization by

nations, deciding instead to create four deputations or commissions to consider matters of faith, reform, reunion, and "common matters." As a consequence, the lower clergy and university masters played a much more influential role, resulting in sweeping reforms in such areas as the makeup of the college of cardinals, procedures governing papal elections, restrictions on the jurisdiction of papal courts, prohibitions against the practice of reservations of bishoprics and abbacies, and the payment of annates (connected with filling benefices).

The council renewed the decrees *Haec sancta synodus* and *Frequens*, which had been issued at Constance, reflecting the ongoing tension between the pope and other church officials. Eugenius responded by ordering the dissolution of Basel and the convocation of another council at Bologna. Faced with the opposition of fifteen of the twenty-one cardinals, Eugenius capitulated on December 15, 1433, and the council continued in Basel. By 1437 the council was breaking apart over various issues, and on September 18 of that year Eugenius transferred the council to Ferrara; in January 1439 it transferred once more to Florence. In 1443 the council was transferred to Rome, after which it simply faded away. Those who failed to comply with the papal actions in 1437 eventually declared Eugenius deposed and elected an antipope, thus causing a new schism, but when Frederick III of Germany and Charles VII, king of France, sided with Eugenius, their opposition was broken once and for all. On April 25, 1449, Basel declared its own dissolution, bringing to an end the "Conciliar Epoch" and the important efforts to reform the church "in head and members."

––––––

J. Gill, *Constance et Bâle-Florence* (1965); A. J. Meijknecht, "Le Concile de Bâle aperçu generale sur ses sources," *RHE* 65 (1970); H. Schneider, *Das Konziliarismus als Problem der neueren katholischen Theologie* (1976); J. W. Stieber, *Pope Eugenius IV, the Council of Basel, and the Secular and Ecclesiastical Authorities in the Empire* (1978).

PAUL B. PIXTON

Basil of Ancyra (d. after 363), bishop of the homoiousian party, which held that the Son is like the Father in essence. Basil, trained as a physician, was elected bishop of Ancyra in 336 to succeed Marcellus, who had been deposed. Basil himself was deposed and banished in 343, but Constantius reinstated him in 348 (or 353). Basil made his theological mark at the Synod of Ancyra (358). He and George of Laodicea, late adherents of the moderately Origenist Eusebian school, were shocked by the growth of anomoian sentiment (that the Son is unlike the Father) and the rejection of technical theological terms at the Synod of Sirmium (357) in its creed, called the "Blasphemy of Sirmium." Basil drafted a synodical letter and a profession of faith at the synod, which Epiphanius of Salamis preserved. The Son, Basil wrote, must be like the Father in essence (*homoios kat' ousian*), for the Father is the father, not the creator, of the Son. Basil rejected *homoousios* (same in essence) as synonymous with *tautousios* (identical in essence) since he understood both terms as Sabellian. As a result, Basil was deposed in 360. A long treatise on virginity has also been ascribed to Basil, partly on the grounds of the medical information it contains.

Letter and profession of faith in Epiphanius, *Panarion* 73; F. Williams, trans., *The Panarion of Epiphanius of Salamis*, 2 vols. (1987, 1994); Greek text of *De virginitate* in PG 30, 669–809.

JOSEPH T. LIENHARD

Basil of Caesarea (c. 330–379), monastic theoretician, theologian, bishop. One of nine children of a Christian and aristocratic family (including his older sister Macrina and his younger brother Gregory of Nyssa), Basil was educated at Caesarea in Cappadocia, as well as in Constantinople and Athens. In 357 he seems to have made a clear decision for an overtly Christian life. After visiting monastic communities in Syria, Palestine, and Egypt, he was baptized and joined the community at Annesi, founded by his sister Macrina, on a family estate. With his friend Gregory of Nazianzus, who briefly was a member of the community, Basil compiled an anthology of Origen's works, the *Philocalia* (distinct from the later Orthodox compilation of the same name).

Until around 361 he seems, like many Eastern bishops, to have favored the *homoiousian* theology of Basil of Ancyra. By the time of writing *Against Eunomius* (c. 363), his doubts about Nicaea's terminology had gone. His Trinitarian theology now focused around two poles: (1) an insistence that we must speak of unity among Father, Son, and Spirit at the level of common divine essence and of distinction at the level of personal particularities (*idiomata* or *idiotetes*); (2) an insistence that we know God by *epinoia*, by a process of reflection on the divine action in the world and not by knowing the divine essence. He was not the first to make these Trinitarian distinctions, but he was one of the first to offer an extended defense and account of them.

Basil became a priest in 362. In 368, as an auxiliary bishop to Eusebius of Caesarea, he was particularly active in the relief of suffering during famine. At Eusebius's death he was elected bishop (370). When the Eastern emperor Valens, who held to anti-Nicene homoian opinions, visited Cappadocia (372), he made use of Basil to help reorganize the church in Armenia. However, at the same time he divided the province of Cappacodia in two, giving the bishop of Tyana control over half of the area that Basil had previously controlled. Basil rushed to create new bishoprics in the old and new provinces to maintain influence (including forcing Gregory of Nazianzus into being consecrated as bishop of the small but strategic town of Sasima).

During the years of his episcopate the struggle against homoians and Eunomians continued. Basil sought to create alliances: throughout his immediate region; with the West, especially with Damasus of Rome; with Athanasius; and with his successor Peter of Alexandria. For the most part these attempts were not successful, in part because of disputes over Basil's support of Meletius, one of three bishops of the divided church in Antioch.

Evidence from Basil's *On the Holy Spirit* (375) and the third book of *Against Eunomius* suggests that Basil included the Spirit within the simple and unitary Godhead. He argued that Scripture speaks of the Spirit as undertaking each of the actions of Father and Son and that the Spirit completes each divine action that originates with the Father and occurs through the Son. Thus, the Spirit is due the same honor and worship as the other two persons. He also argued that many unwritten but essential practices and beliefs supported his position.

Through the 360s and 370s Basil produced texts that were fundamental to the development of Eastern asceticism and canon law. One of his central contributions to Eastern asceticism was to encourage the founding of monastic communities within cities that would be at the pastoral service of the wider church.

P. J. Fedwick, *Basil of Caesarea*, 2 vols. (1981); P. Rousseau, *Basil of Caesarea* (1994); B. Sesboüé, *Saint Basile et La Trinité* (1998); S. Elm, *"Virgins of God": The Making of Asceticism in Late Antiquity* (1994); L. Ayres, *Nicaea and Its Legacy* (2004).

LEWIS AYRES

Basilides (early to mid-second cent.), Christian gnostic in Alexandria of either Egyptian or Syrian ancestry. He was said by some to have been a disciple of Menander and to have served as a preacher to the Persians, though this cannot be historically validated. Among his works are a gnostic gospel known to Origen and the twenty-four-volume *Exegetika*, fragments of which Clement of Alexandria cited. The church fathers' accounts of his teaching are inconsistent. It would seem that Basilides believed in a multi-tiered universe with several gradations of deities. God could be divided into various distinct entities: the nonexistent God who is the source of all things; the God of the seven, called the Archon of the seven (Abrasax), who interacts with human beings and gives rise to the Son, Jesus; and the God of the eight who is the Archon over all the created universe, known as YHWH in the OT, and who has a son who instructed the Christ in *gnosis* (knowledge). In both instances the sons are greater than the fathers and reveal to them hidden *gnosis* about their status as begotten beings, the nature and purpose of the universe, and their roles in it. *Gnosis*, hidden until the time of Christ and revealed in the gospel, was the knowledge that there is a nonexistent God, that there is Sonship of the God of the eight and the God of the seven, and that there is a Holy Spirit who differentiates among "confused beings." Basilides' thought evidences a clear dualism between the body of Christ, which was mortal and suffered, and the "psychic part," which rose again to be reunited with the Archon of the seven.

———

W. Foerster, *Patristic Evidence*, vol. 1 of *Gnosis: A Selection of Gnostic Texts* (1972); R. Grant, *Gnosticism: A Source Book of Heretical Writings from the Early Christian Period* (1961); B. Layton, *The Gnostic Scriptures* (1987); K. Rudolf, *Gnosis: The Nature and History of Gnosticism* (1983).

RODNEY S. SADLER JR.

Baxter, Richard (1615–1691), Puritan pastor and theologian. Although Baxter never attended a university, he established himself as a leading Puritan through his writings, pastoral and polemical, and his fourteen years as minister at Kidderminster (1641–1660), interrupted by five years as an army chaplain. With the fall of the commonwealth and the return of the monarchy, Baxter was ejected from the established church under the terms of the Act of Uniformity. From then on, he was one of the two most senior figures in English nonconformity, the other being John Owen.

His pastoral writings, in particular his *Gildas Salvianus* (also known as *The Reformed Pastor*), were frequently reprinted after his death and have enjoyed considerable popularity over the years. His polemical works have generally been forgotten, though their major themes are discernible in his practical works.

———

N. H. Keeble, *Richard Baxter: Puritan Man of Letters* (1982); C. Trueman, "Richard Baxter," in *The Pietist Theologians,* ed. C. Lindberg (2003).

CARL TRUEMAN

Bay Psalm Book   This metrical Psalter, published in Cambridge, Massachusetts, in 1640 as *The Whole Booke of Psalmes*, was widely used in colonial New England. Puritans believed that church singing should be restricted to biblical texts, and leading ministers of Massachusetts, including John Eliot, Richard Mather, John Wilson, and John Cotton, dissatisfied with existing metrical versions, produced a new translation of the Hebrew Psalms. Other "spiritual songs" were added, and the poetry improved in its many later editions; in 1698, tunes were added. There were also editions in England and Scotland.

———

Z. Harastzi, *The Enigma of the "Bay Psalm Book"* (1956).

DEWEY D. WALLACE JR.

Bayle, Pierre (1647–1706), French philosopher. The son of a Huguenot pastor, he converted to Catholicism while studying at the Jesuit college in Toulouse. He reconverted to Protestantism and moved to Geneva to study theology. His exposure there to Descartes' writings stimulated his lifelong search for reliable knowledge in philosophy, history, and the natural sciences. Beginning in 1675, he taught philosophy at the Academy of Sedan. Religious persecution forced him to flee to Rotterdam in 1681, where he taught at the *Ecole Illustre* and published a monthly literary review. After the revocation of the Edict of Nantes in France, he wrote extensively in defense of toleration. In 1691 he lost his teaching post due to his skeptical views about religion. Thereafter, he focused on writing his *Historical and Critical Dictionary* (1696), which influenced many Enlightenment thinkers.

———

P. Bayle, *Historical and Critical Dictionary: Selections* (1991); E. Labrousse, *Bayle* (1983); T. Lennon, *Reading Bayle* (1999).

ERIC LUND

Beatrice of Nazareth (1200–1268), Cistercian nun and author of *The Seven Manners of Loving*. Born in Tienen, east of Brussels, Beatrice was sent by her father, after her mother's death, to live with a group of Beguines in the nearby town of Zoutleeuw (1207). At the age of ten she entered the monastic life at Bloemendaal, a monastery of Cistercian nuns. There she became a novice at the age of sixteen. While learning the art of manuscript writing in Rameya, south of Brussels, she grew very close to Ida of Nivelles, also a Cistercian nun and her spiritual mentor. Ida's guidance and friendship highly influenced Beatrice's spiritual growth as well as Beatrice's first mystical experience in early January 1217. Shortly thereafter Beatrice was recalled to Bloemendaal. Her father, Bartholomew, helped to organize three Cistercian monasteries, and it was in these three places that Beatrice lived out her life: first Bloemendaal, then Maagdendal, then Nazareth.

In May 1236, Beatrice transferred from Maagdendal to an abbey in Nazareth, newly built by her father and older brother, where she was eventually elected prioress. Beatrice's spirituality, as revealed in the text of *The Seven Manners of Loving*, is one of holy desire, pursued faithfully throughout her life. *The Seven Manners* offers insight on how this holy desire is directed, how it grows, and how it is rewarded. On August 29, 1268, Beatrice died in the monastery at Nazareth.

A. C. Bartlett, *Vox Mystica: Essays on Medieval Mysticism* (1995); R. De Ganck, *Beatrice of Nazareth and the 13th Century* Mulieres Religiosae *of the Low Countries: A Three-Volume Study* (1991); De Ganck, *Beatrice of Nazareth in Her Context* (1990); T. L. Vosper, *Spiritual Healing through Minne: A Reinterpretation of the* Seven Manners of Loving *by Beatrijs of Nazareth* (2002).

TODD M. RICHARDSON

Beatus Rhenanus (Rhinower) (1485–1547), German humanist. Beatus represents the shift in Renaissance Christian humanism toward pure scholarship and away from other humanists' educational, religious, and political engagements. Known as the best German textual critic of his era for his unbiased historical writing, critical editions, and commentaries on ancient texts, he studied with Parisian humanists (1503–1507) before collaborating (1511–1527) with Froben's press in Basel. He enjoyed Erasmus's esteem and oversaw the official biography and posthumous edition of Erasmus's works (1540). Beatus briefly considered Luther compatible with Erasmus but recoiled from Reformation upheavals. He therefore withdrew (1527) to his native Selestat in Alsace to pursue historical research. His masterpiece, *Rerum Germanicarum* (1531), avoided customary glorification of German history but advanced historical analysis using artifacts and nontextual materials. His editions of early Christian (*Autores historiae ecclesiasticae*, 1523; Tertullian, 1521, 1528, 1539) and Roman writers (Pliny, 1526; Tacitus, 1533; Livy, 1535) enjoyed renown. Although conservative in doctrine, even admitting the papacy's constructive potential, he apparently remained Protestant in a Catholic town.

J. D'Amico, *Theory and Practice in Renaissance Textual Criticism: Beatus Rhenanus* (1988); B. von Scarpatetti, "Beatus Rhenanus," in *Contemporaries of Erasmus*, vol. 1, ed. P. Bietenholz et al. (1985), 104–9.

JAMES MICHAEL WEISS

Becket, Thomas (c. 1120–1170), archbishop of Canterbury and martyr. Thomas was born in London to a prosperous merchant family. As a young man he entered Archbishop Theobald's household and in 1154 became archdeacon of Canterbury. But in December 1154 Theobald sent the personable Thomas to teach the new king, Henry II, English ways. In 1155 Thomas became chancellor of England and served the king well while living in great splendor. The English bishops protested when Henry chose Thomas as the next archbishop of Canterbury; he was considered too worldly and pro-royal. But Henry insisted, and Thomas was consecrated on June 3, 1162.

Thomas and Henry soon clashed. Henry demanded traditional royal rights over England's church, while Thomas fought for greater ecclesiastical independence. By 1164 royal pressure made Thomas flee England and appeal to the pope. Papal pressure led to a reconciliation of sorts in 1170, but Thomas's return to Canterbury was marked by bitterness and suspicion. His excommunication of his opponents seemed proof of bad faith. At this point Henry apparently fell into a rage, blaming his followers for allowing such insults to their lord. When Thomas refused to submit to a royal ultimatum, four of Henry's knights murdered him in his own cathedral. Papal and popular pressure forced Henry to make major concessions to the papacy and perform penance; Thomas himself was canonized as a martyr in 1173. His shrine attracted pilgrims until King Henry VIII ordered its destruction, blaming Thomas for England's subjection to the papacy.

F. Barlow, *Thomas Becket* (1986).

PHYLLIS G. JESTICE

Bede (673–735), Anglo-Saxon monk and scholar, honored with the title of "the Venerable." His feast day is May 25. Born in Northumbria and given by his family to St. Peter's monastery at Wearmouth at age seven, Bede was educated by abbots Benedict Biscop and Ceolfrith. He moved to the new monastery of St. Paul at Jarrow around 682 and remained there for the rest of his life, except for occasional visits to nearby monasteries such as Lindisfarne and York. Ordained deacon at 19 and priest at 30, Bede describes his monastic and scholarly vocation at the end of his most famous work, *The Ecclesiastical History of the English People* (731): "Amid the observance of the discipline of the Rule and the daily task of singing in the church, it has always been my delight to learn or to teach or to write."

Declaring his intention to follow "in the footsteps of the Fathers," Bede produced numerous works in a variety of fields for the benefit of fellow monks serving as pastors and teachers of the English church. Although he translated some prayers and biblical texts into English, only his Latin writings survive. Bede's works on grammar, natural history, and chronology were standard school texts throughout medieval Europe. His commentaries and homilies on the Bible attended both to historical and philological questions and to spiritual meanings derived through allegorical exegesis. He wrote several hymns and other poetic works, including the long poem "On Judgment Day," of which there is a tenth-century paraphrase in Old English. In the field of hagiography, he produced two lives of Cuthbert of Lindisfarne (one in verse and one in prose) and a history of the abbots of his own monastery.

The *Ecclesiastical History* includes hagiographical treatments of Roman, British, Irish, and Anglo-Saxon saints within a grand historical narrative depicting God's providential establishment of the English (and particularly the Northumbrian) church. Bede drew upon earlier histories, archives in Canterbury and Rome, eyewitness testimony, and legendary accounts—often noting the sources of his information and assessing their reliability. His purpose as a historian, however, was primarily didactic; a preface addressed to King Ceolwulf explains that history provides the reader with good examples to imitate and bad examples to avoid. The miracles and visions in Bede's account are portrayed as signs of God's special favor toward the saints and sources of inspiration for faithful Christians.

Near the end of his life Bede wrote a letter urging his pupil Egbert, bishop of York, to implement a program of reform in the Northumbrian church. He died on the eve of Ascension Day, declaring, "My soul longs to see Christ my King in all his beauty." In the eleventh century his body was moved from Jarrow to Durham Cathedral, and in 1899 Pope Leo XIII declared him a doctor of the universal church.

P. H. Blair, *The World of Bede* (1970); G. Bonner, ed., *Famulus Christi* (1976); G. H. Brown, *Bede the Venerable* (1987); N. J. Higham, *Re-Reading Bede* (2006); B. Ward, *The Venerable Bede* (1990).

ARTHUR G. HOLDER

Beguines Documented from the early twelfth century, Beguines were women who led semireligious lives, primarily in the Low Countries. Their male equivalents were known as "Beghards." As "semireligious," these women chose a form of life that was different from an enclosed monastic life with its communities governed by an abbess, a common rule, lifelong vows, and a renunciation of private property. Instead, Beguines took temporary vows that were renewable. They could leave at any time in order to marry, for example. They usually worked for a living, often in the textile industry. They might live alone, or together in neighborhoods, or in more established "Beguinages," some of which were large enough to house hundreds of Beguines. Beguine communities could become the center of local spiritual life, attracting the support and spiritual yearnings of nearby laity. Because of their popularity among laity and the fluidity of the forms of life associated with Beguines, they became suspect by the late thirteenth century, when ecclesiastical authorities were trying to regularize religious life. Restrictions were placed on their way of life by a series of synods held in the second half of the thirteenth century, and they were officially condemned in 1312 at the Council of Vienne, although this condemnation was mitigated in 1321 under John XXII. Some Beguine communities chose to adopt the Rule of the Third Order of St. Francis in order to regularize their life and thus legitimate it in the eyes of clerical authorities.

E. McDonnell, *The Beguines and Beghards in Medieval Culture, with Special Emphasis on the Belgian Scene* (1954); S. Murk-Jansen, *Brides in the Desert: The Spirituality of the Beguines* (1998); W. Simons, *Cities of Ladies: Beguine Communities in the Medieval Low Countries, 1200–1565* (2001).

DARLEEN PRYDS

Belgic Confession This sixteenth-century confessional statement was written mainly by the reformer Guy de Brès and was adopted by Reformed churches in the Low Countries. It was submitted to King Philip II in hopes of securing legitimacy and religious tolerance for Reformed Christians in the Habsburg-ruled Netherlands prior to the Dutch Revolt. The Confession was modeled after French Calvinism's Gallic Confession, but it softened that document's criticism of Rome and focused more sharply on a rejection of Anabaptists, who were viewed as a threat to the crown. Though its political project proved unsuccessful, the Belgic Confession nonetheless came to be adopted as a primary confessional statement of the Netherlandish Reformed as the region gained partial independence. It was first published in French in 1561, in Dutch in 1562, and edited frequently thereafter. Early versions were adopted at the Synods of Antwerp in 1566 and Emden in 1571; a revised edition was authorized at the Synod of Dordrecht in 1618–1619.

The Confession consists of thirty-seven articles summarizing the Christian faith from a largely Calvinist perspective. Its affirmations of presbyterian polity, the normative authority of Scripture, and justification by faith alone reveal a desire for ecclesial and doctrinal reform. Its positions on the sacraments (infant baptism, real but symbolic presence in the Eucharist) distance its adherents from Anabaptists and Lutherans, respectively.

A. Cochrane, ed., *Reformed Confessions of the 16th Century* (1966); K. Müller, ed., *Die Bekenntnisschriften der reformierten Kirche* (1903, repr. 1999); M. van Gelderen, *The Political Thought of the Dutch Revolt 1555–1590* (1992).

KENNETH G. APPOLD

Bellarmine, Robert (1542–1621), Italian Jesuit, theologian, and cardinal. Born in Montepulciano and the nephew of Pope Marcellus II, Bellarmine entered the Jesuit order in 1560. He taught at Florence, Mondovi, and Louvain before being recalled to Rome in 1576 to hold the chair of controversial theology in the Jesuit Roman College. From his experience as a teacher arose one of his most significant works, the *Controversies*. He served as rector of the Roman College and superior of the Jesuit Province of Naples before Pope Clement VIII named him cardinal in 1599. His career is notable for his role in a variety of theological and political controversies, including the conflict between the papacy and the Republic of Venice over clerical exemption from civil law, a debate with King James I of England over the nature of royal power, and a debate between Thomist and Molinist theologians over the relationship of grace and free will known as the *de Auxiliis* controversy. Bellarmine also became involved in the early stages of the Galileo affair. When Pope Paul V and the Congregation of the Index condemned the writings of Copernicus in 1616, it was Bellarmine who was delegated by the pope to inform Galileo of the condemnation. Pius XI canonized Bellarmine in 1930.

R. Bellarmine, *Opera omnia* (1870); R. J. Blackwell, *Galileo, Bellarmine, and the Bible* (1991); J. Brodrik, *Robert Bellarmine: Saint and Scholar* (1961); P. Godman, *The Saint as Censor: Robert Bellarmine between Inquisition and Index* (2000).

PAUL V. MURPHY

Benedict XII (1280–1342), Cistercian abbot, bishop, cardinal, and pope. Probably the son of a townsman of Saverdun (in the Ariège), Jacques Fournier rose to the church's highest office. But he is best known for the inquisition register he kept as a bishop, which served as the basis for the most famous book about a medieval village, Emmanuel La Roy Ladurie's *Montaillou* (1975). Jacques Fournier followed his uncle, Arnaud Novel, into the Cistercian order. When Novel became cardinal in 1311, he, with papal authorization, appointed Jacques as his successor as abbot of the Cistercian monastery of Fontfroide (in Languedoc). This began Jacques' rise in the church. Jacques left his studies at Paris and served as abbot for six years, when he was named bishop of Pamiers (March 19, 1317). He was later transferred to the see of Mirepoix (March 3, 1326), then soon named cardinal (December 18, 1327), and finally was elected pope (December 26, 1334), taking the name Benedict XII. That his scholarly pursuits continued as a cardinal is suggested by his large and little-studied commentary on Matthew's Gospel, published upon his papal election. His actions as pope included some attempts at reform (for example, the revocation of commends, that is, rights to benefice incomes, and an order that prelates resident at the papal court return to the places of their office). His negotiations with the emperor Ludwig of Bavaria were unsuccessful, and during his reign, the conflict over "Spirituals" in the Franciscan order seemed to drone on, in spite of his predecessor John XXII's condemnations and papal inquisitions. He constructed the fortified papal palace at Avignon (1336–1342). A resister of nepotism, he appointed only one family member to church office (his nephew Jean, a monk of Boulbonne, to the archbishopric of Arles). He also established a Franciscan vicariat in Bosnia, the most consistent Catholic presence there since the second quarter of the thirteenth century.

————

Benoît xii (1334–1342), lettres closes et patentes intéressant les pays autres que la France, ed. J.-M. Vidal (1950); *Benoît xii (1334–1342), lettres closes, patentes et curiales se raportant à la France*, ed. G. Daumet (1920); *Benoît XII (1334–1342), lettres communes analysées d'après les registres dits d'Avignon et du Vatican*, ed. J.-M. Vidal, 3 vols. (1903–1911); *Le registre d'inquisition de Jacques Fournier*, trans. and annotated by J. Duvernoy, 3 vols. (2004); B. Guillemain, *La cour pontificale d'Avignon* (1303–1376) (1962); A. Maier, "Der Kommentar Benedikts XII. zum Matthaeus-Evangelium," *Archivum historiae Pontificae* 6 (1968): 298–405; J. M. Vidal, "Les ouevres du pape Benôit XII," *RHE* 6 (1905): 557–65, 785–810; G. Mollat, *The Popes of Avignon* (1963).

CHRISTOPHER OCKER

Benedict of Aniane (c. 750–821), cloister founder, reformer, and counselor to King Louis the Pious. The son of the count of Maguelone, Benedict was born a Visigothic-Aquitanian noble and raised at the Frankish courts of Pippin the Younger and Charlemagne. His brother's death during Charlemagne's Italian campaign in 773–774 moved him to leave secular life. After a brief stay in the cloister St. Seine (near Dijon), he settled on his paternal inheritance in Aniane (near Montpellier), where he first lived as a hermit. Soon after, he adopted the Eastern rules of Basel and Pachomius for his community. Benedict subsequently turned to the Rule of St. Benedict, of which he became a resolute promoter. He spread the rule through Frankish noble cloisters and worked against softening the text through mixed rules, formulating the principle *una regula*, one rule.

In the year 792, Charlemagne placed the abbey of Aniane under his protection and elevated it to a royal abbey. At the same time, Louis the Pious, as king of Aquitaine, requested monks from Benedict to reform his cloisters according to the model of Aniane. Various visitations and legations were assigned to Benedict by commission of the Frankish rulers. When Louis the Pious became emperor (814), he took up, as part of his governmental program, cloister reform according to the ideal of the *una regula*. At three synods (816–819), through Benedict's decisive participation, the Rule of St. Benedict was imposed on all cloisters of the Frankish empire. A unified observance of the text of the rule was to be guaranteed by common "customs" (*consuetudines*) that shore it up and clarify it. By the emperor's will, he set up a model reformed cloister at the abbey of Kornelimünster (near Aachen) and supervised the implementation of the Aachen synodal decrees. As the emperor's counselor, he also influenced the reform of the life of the canons regular.

————

Concordia regularum, PL 103:703–1380; MGH. Epp. Karol. IV; *Corpus Consuetudinum Monasticarum* I, ed. J. Semmler (1963); *Vita Benedicti abbatis Anianensis*, MGH. Script. XV; J. Semmler, "Die Beschlüsse des Aachener Konzils i.J. 816," *ZKG* 74 (1963): 15–82; A. de Vogüé, *La règle de S. Benoît*, vol. 1 (1972); O. G. Oexle, *Forschungen zu monastischen und geistlichen Gemeinschaften im westfränkischen Bereich* (1972); A. Angenendt, "Kloster und Klosterverband zwischen Benedikt von Nursia und Benedikt von Aniane," *Vom Kloster zum Klosterverband*, ed. V. H. Keller (1997), 7–35; J. Hill, "Benedict of Aniane (d. 821)," in *Medieval England: An Encyclopedia* (1998), 117–18.

JÖRG OBERSTE

Benedict of Nursia (c. 480–c. 547), abbot of Monte Cassino and author of a monastic rule. According to the *Dialogues* of Gregory the Great, Benedict was born in the Italian village of Nursia and sent to Rome by his parents for a classical education. Scandalized by the decadent life in the capital, Benedict withdrew with his governess to the figurative "desert" of the town of Effide, and later to a cave at Subiaco, where he lived for three years as a hermit. After a brief, unhappy experience as abbot of a nearby monastery, where the monks tried to poison him on account of his strict discipline,

Benedict returned to Subiaco to establish twelve monasteries of twelve monks each.

Around 530 he took some companions to Monte Cassino southeast of Rome, where he destroyed a temple of Apollo, converted the inhabitants of the area through his preaching, and established a monastery. Gregory presents Benedict as working miracles similar to those of biblical saints and notes that his monastic rule was remarkable for its discretion and elegant language. The hagiographical account closes with Benedict's edifying visit with his sister Scholastica, his mystical vision of the whole world in a single ray of light, and his death after receiving Communion in the oratory at Monte Cassino.

Benedict's rule drew extensively on earlier sources, especially the early sixth-century *Rule of the Master*. Beginning with a prologue calling the monk to "listen carefully to the master's instructions," Benedict declares his intention to establish a "school for the Lord's service." The seventy-three chapters that follow deal with the kinds of monks (among whom cenobites are judged best); qualities of the abbot; monastic virtues of obedience, silence, and humility; and various practical matters such as the ordering of psalms in the Divine Office, reception of guests, forms of discipline, officers of the monastery, and the regulation of sleep, food, and work. Benedict concludes his "little rule for beginners" by exhorting the monks to mutual love and commending the reading of Scripture and the works of his monastic predecessors.

T. Fry, ed., *RB 1980: The Rule of St. Benedict* (1981); A. de Vogüé, *Gregory the Great: The Life of Saint Benedict* (1993); T. Kardong, *The Benedictines* (1988).

ARTHUR G. HOLDER

Benedictine Order   Named after Benedict of Nursia (c. 480–c. 547), founder of the monastery Monte Cassino (Italy) and author of the Benedictine rule. This monastic rule was first fully adopted by Anglo-Saxon monks who influenced the development of monasticism in the rest of Western Europe in the early Middle Ages, after it had coexisted for a time with a variety of different and often mixed rules. From the eighth century onward the Benedictine rule became dominant in Western Europe mainly through the support of secular rulers. Benedictine reform movements (e.g., Cluny since 910) exercised a strong influence on the Western church, with some reformed monasteries playing an important political role. In the following

period monasteries were primarily differentiated by the observance of different monastic customs, which formed the basis of a variety of Benedictine congregations. Only after the foundation of the new orders in the twelfth and thirteenth centuries can the Benedictine order be identified as an order in the full sense. From the sixteenth century onward the order expanded outside of Europe and also faced several crises due to the Reformation, the French Revolution, and the secularization in Europe and South America in the nineteenth century. In 1893 all Benedictine monasteries and congregations became united in the Benedictine Confederation. The history of the Benedictine nuns can be regarded as parallel to the history of the male branch of the order.

S. Hilpisch, *Benedictinism through Changing Centuries* (1958); P. Schmitz, *Histoire de l'Ordre de St.-Benoît*, 7 vols. (1942–1956).

ACHIM WESJOHANN

Benedictine Rule   The Benedictine rule is one of about thirty Christian monastic rules that were written at the transitional period from antiquity to the Middle Ages. It is not only the normative and spiritual basis of the Benedictine order and many other religious communities but also a unique witness to Christian spirituality. The exact time and place at which the author Benedict of Nursia (c. 480–c. 547) wrote his rule are not known. There is, however, evidence that it was during the last years of his life that he composed this complex text, created on the basis of numerous other texts.

The Benedictine rule explains various aspects of religious life. It gives clear and concrete instructions on everyday conduct, as well as hierarchy, offices, discipline, and penal law in the monastery. There are also detailed directions concerning the monastery's relation to the outside world and the integration of novices into the monastic community. A great part of the rule is dedicated to explanations of liturgy and monastic spirituality. The rule uses clear and simple diction. In all, it is not a treatise on radical asceticism but provides guidance for common religious life in the spirit of charity and mutual respect.

All these features helped to establish the Benedictine rule as the central text of Western monasticism. But also, two important figures of Western church history were responsible for the great success of the rule: Gregory the Great, who recommended it as a practicable and prudent instruction on religious life, and Benedict of Aniane, for whom the rule was a legal instrument for the renewal of monastic life in the course of the so-called Carolingian Reform.

———

A. de Vogüé, *Reading Saint Benedict: Reflections on the Rule* (1994); T. Fry, ed., *The Rule of Saint Benedict in Latin and English with Notes* (1981).

MARKUS SCHÜRER

Benefices The benefice (*beneficium*, "favor") originated with feudal lands granted for services. During the Carolingian period the practice expanded to include grants to clerics of revenues from church property in return for spiritual services, thus freeing recipients from manual labor (*Capitularies of Aachen*, 818, 819); income was derived from land and rights associated with it. Benefices were intended to be effective for the life of the beneficiary, and by the eleventh century, offices were inseparable from income. The *Codex Iuris Canonici* (1917) defined benefices as entities "perpetually constituted or erected by the competent ecclesiastical authority, consisting of a sacred office and the right to receive the income from the endowment connected with the office" (canon 1409). Secular benefices were available to clerics ranging from parish priests and chaplains to bishops and popes. Regular benefices adhered to offices in monasteries and could be apportioned to cellarers, almoners, sacristans, priors, and so forth. Canon law prohibited holding more than one benefice that involved the care of souls—a restriction honored in the breach as well as the observance.

Benefices continue to exist in the Church of England under the strict regulation of the Pastoral Measure (1968) and the Patronage (Benefices) Measure (1986). The Second Vatican Council called for discontinuation or reform of benefices; the *Codex Iuris Canonici* (1983) specifies supervision by the local Conference of Bishops for benefices still maintained (canon 1272). *See also* Prebends.

———

M. Bloch, *Feudal Society* (1961), 163–75; D. Luscombe and J. Riley-Smith, *New Cambridge Medieval History*, vol. 4, pt. 1 (2004), 143 ff.; G. Mollat, *Dictionnaire de droit canonique*, vol. 2 (1935), 406 ff.; N. Zacour, *An Introduction to Medieval Institutions* (1969), 93 ff.

LORNA SHOEMAKER

Beneficio di Christo This widely popular sixteenth-century Italian booklet, arguably the most famous text of the Italian Reformation, expresses Reformation ideas with allusions to and paraphrases of the writings of Luther, Melanchthon, Calvin, Valdes, et al. Its full title reads, *Trattato utilissimo del beneficio di Giesu Christo crocifisso verso i christiani* (*Useful Treatise on the Merits of Jesus Christ Crucified for Christians*). It was published anonymously at Venice in 1543, partly to avoid the sanctions of papal authority. Its origins are connected to the monastery of San Nicolo l'Arena and is perhaps the work of Benedetto da Montova, with editing help from Marcantonio Flaminio.

The *Beneficio*'s importance lay in its articulation of Reformation theology in the Italian context, along with its demonstration that the theological themes of the Protestant reformers (law and gospel, justification by faith alone, predestination, etc.) had a receptive audience there. The Inquisition condemned it in 1549, declaring that simply possessing a copy of it was evidence of the owner's heretical tendencies. The *Beneficio* was thus effectually suppressed in sixteenth-century Italy.

———

S. Caponetto, *The Protestant Reformation in 16th-Century Italy* (1999); E. Gleason, ed., *Reform Thought in 16th-Century Italy* (1981).

WILLIAM R. RUSSELL

Berengar of Tours (d. 1088), canon and archdeacon of Angers, with a controversial view of the Eucharist. Berengar was born near Tours and studied at Chartres; he became canon there in 1030 and taught liberal arts; in 1040 he became archdeacon of Angers.

Berengar continued the eucharistic doctrine of Ratramnus, for which he was declared a heretic. His contemporaries had developed the doctrine of real presence in a sensualistic manner, whereas Berengar held to an Augustinian idea of "sacred sign." He rejected the idea of a physical, real change of bread and wine, yet taught that the elements changed by mere consecration into the sacrament of the sacred flesh and blood of Christ. According to him, "sacrament" means neither an unsignifying mark of reference nor simply a hermeneutical device. To the contrary, a sign actually participates in that which it denotes because of a common similitude between sign and thing signified. Berengar combined the realism of his concept of image with sacramental symbolism in order to explain sacramental participation in Christ's real presence.

This was controversial. Ecclesiastical authorities urged Berengar to confess a realistic sacramental view. Especially at Roman synods of 1059 and 1079, one sees the intensity of the debate. Berengar's influence was to provoke a modernized eucharistic teaching that relied on the new philosophical realism to explain the character and meaning of the sacraments.

T. J. Holopainen, *Dialectic and Theology in the 11th Century* (1996); Holopainen, "Augustine, Berengar, and Anselm on the Role of Reason in Theology," in *Was ist Philosophie im Mittelalter?* ed. J. A. Aertsen and A. Speer (1998), 553–59; *RGG*[4] 1 (1998): 1306–7; *TRE* 5 (1980): 598–601.

RAINER BERNDT

Bernard of Chartres (d. c. 1124), French

teacher. Bernard of Chartres was the most famous master of the cathedral school of Chartres, France, and his career exemplifies education in Europe in the early stages of the twelfth-century renaissance. He was a great teacher but not an original thinker; Bernard's fame as a great Platonist scholar came from his modern misidentification with the intellectual Bernard Silvestris. Bernard of Chartres' importance came rather from the fact that he was in command of the learning of his age and made it accessible to a wider audience.

John of Salisbury told how his master Bernard compared his contemporaries to dwarves perched on the shoulders of giants, so that despite their personal deficiencies they could see further. This was the keystone of Bernard's teaching (and of twelfth-century education in general): devotion to ancient learning. He was a grammarian who explicated both poetic and prose classical Latin works, going from bare meaning to discussing the moral and philosophical teachings pertinent to his own time. John tells that Bernard was able to give even the dullest student a good grasp of Latin, the starting point of all learning. His teaching must, however, be regarded as a transitional phase in European education. Already considered old-fashioned in his lifetime, his method was abandoned by the 1150s as too slow.

R. W. Southern, *Medieval Humanism* (1970).

PHYLLIS G. JESTICE

Bernard of Clairvaux (c. 1090–1153),

French abbot and theologian. Bernard of Clairvaux is hailed as the last of the fathers of the church. He had a vast impact on twelfth-century religion, with echoes that continue to the present. Bernard was the son of a Burgun-

dian knight, intended for a secular career. But he became interested in the new reforming monastery of Cîteaux and as a young man decided to become a monk there. The first sign of Bernard's unbelievable charisma and power of persuasion is that he convinced no fewer than thirty-one friends and relatives to join him, including four of his brothers.

In 1115 Bernard went with a group of Cistercians to found a daughter house at Clairvaux. Initially Bernard's high notions of austerity caused difficulties, but soon he began attracting recruits and the Cistercian order began its astonishing rise to European prominence. Bernard is justly called the second founder of the order; by the time of his death Clairvaux had founded some sixty-eight daughter houses with the disciples Bernard attracted, while Clairvaux itself had seven hundred monks.

The fame of the Cistercians spread especially because Bernard spent surprisingly little time at the monastery where he was abbot. He was a man of immense ability and persuasive skill, by the end of his life reckoned as a living saint, and calls on his time were many. He mediated disputes, preached, took an important role in theological disputes, and advised. Bernard himself sometimes resisted spending so much time outside the cloister, calling himself the "chimaera" of his age, a strange beast neither secular nor monastic. But his is the greatest example of the twelfth century's greater emphasis on the inner spiritual state of a monk rather than outward observance. Although Bernard complained about his own lack of stability, the large volume especially of his mystical writings bears witness to an intense and profound monastic piety.

Besides spreading Cistercian monasticism and its values, Bernard played an important role in the history of the papacy. In the disputed papal election of 1130 he supported Innocent II's claims, eventually winning him recognition as the legitimate pope. Bernard's influence rose even higher when his former disciple became Pope Eugenius III in 1145. Until both died in 1153, Bernard was an important papal advisor, and his treatise for Eugenius, *On Consideration*, is a very important text for its suggestions on how to live a spiritual life in the midst of the overwhelming business of the papal court.

Not surprisingly, considering his intensely Christ-centered spirituality, Bernard was an avid advocate of the crusading movement, intended as it was to retake and maintain possession of the Holy Land. Bernard popularized the Knights Templar, a military order devoted to protecting the Holy Land. He wrote their rule, and his *In Defense of the New Knighthood* helped define a new religiosity that allowed a member of the fighting class to be godly without giving up arms. Even more importantly, Bernard was by far the greatest of the preachers of the Second Crusade, called after Edessa fell to the Turks in 1144. The greatest crisis of Bernard's life was the utter failure of this crusade, which called into question both his reputation and his own understanding of God's will.

Bernard's views were not always received favorably, whether by contemporaries or later historians. His defense of "pure" (or at least monastic) theology led him to attack two of the greatest scholars of his age, Gilbert of Poitiers and Peter Abelard. In the case of Abelard, Bernard's outrage or fear of his enemy's skill led him to override proper ecclesiastical procedures, arranging for Abelard to be sentenced unheard for theological views that were in reality orthodox. A similar outrage at the enemies of the church led Bernard to violent diatribes against heretics (although it should be noted that he protected Rhineland Jews from a pogrom at the time of the Second Crusade).

In his treatises and many letters, however, Bernard also presents the best of religious innovation in the twelfth century. He was a leader in the Cistercian "affective piety" movement, focusing on the events of Christ's life and encouraging worshipers to draw themselves into the emotional world of Jesus' original followers. Bernard's works on mystical prayer can still be read with great profit today.

Bernard was formally canonized in 1174 and was declared a doctor of the church in 1830.

Bernard, *Selected Works*, trans. G. R. Evans (1987); B. McGuire, *The Difficult Saint: Bernard of Clairvaux and His Tradition* (1991).
PHYLLIS G. JESTICE

Berquin, Louis de (d. 1529), French humanist admirer of Erasmus and Luther, early victim of efforts to suppress the Reformation in France. His case illustrates the determination of clerical and judicial authorities to pursue suspected heretics. Alarmed at the spread of Lutheran writings in France, the Paris Faculty of Theology and the Paris *Parlement* coordinated their attack on those suspected of harboring Luther's works. A search of Berquin's library in 1523 revealed translations of Luther, Melanchthon, and Karlstadt, along with Berquin's own writings. Berquin was about to be tried when Francis I intervened and obtained

his release. Rearrested in 1526, Berquin was found guilty of heresy but once again was set free on the king's orders. The matter lay unresolved, however, and Berquin's trial resumed in 1528. This time judges declared him guilty and sentenced him to life in prison on April 15, 1529. He appealed the decision to the *Parlement*, which sentenced him to death as a relapsed heretic. Berquin was burned at the stake two days later.

E. W. Monter, *Judging the French Reformation: Heresy Trials by 16th-Century Parlements* (1999); N. L. Roelker, *One King, One Faith: The Parlement of Paris and the Religious Reformations of the 16th Century* (1996).
SCOTT M. MARR

Bessarion of Nicaea, John (1403–1472), bishop, scholar, and humanist. Born in Trebizond and, under the patronage of its bishop, educated in Constantinople, he was tonsured a monk in 1423. After his ordination as a presbyter in 1431, he traveled to Mistra and studied with Gemistus Plethon. In anticipation of a reunion council between Latins and Greeks, he was named metropolitan of Nicaea and was part of the Greek delegation to the Council of Ferrara-Florence. At the council he became convinced of the compatibility of the Greek and Latin positions on the disputed points, particularly that of the procession of the Holy Spirit, and was instrumental in persuading most of the Greek delegation to vote for reunion. Mark Eugenicus of Ephesus opposed him. Bessarion continued to support the reunion even when it encountered strong popular resistance. Pope Eugenius IV named him a cardinal in 1440, and much of his subsequent career was spent in papal service. His residence in Rome was a meeting place for many Greek and Italian Renaissance figures, including Lorenzo Valla. He promoted the collection and translation of Greek classical and patristic literature and contributed an extensive collection to St. Mark's in Venice.

J. Gill, *Personalities of the Council of Florence* (1964); PG 160–161; L. D. Reynolds and N. G. Wilson, *Scribes and Scholars* (1974).
EUGENE M. LUDWIG, OFM CAP.

Bible in the Early Church For the Christians of the NT period, the Bible consisted of the Jewish Scriptures (albeit in Greek translation), but over the next few centuries it came to include the NT writings. The Bible was at the heart of the self-understanding and identity of the early Christians and was the foundation for all doctrinal development. For the church of the NT and patristic periods, indeed through the Middle Ages, theology and biblical exegesis were one and the same thing.

This intimate relationship between theology and exegesis is manifest in the NT. The Gospels' accounts of Jesus' ministry show that much of his teaching can be understood as a reinterpretation of the Jewish Scriptures (e.g., Matt. 5–7; Luke 24:13–27). Moreover, other NT writings begin the process of expounding both the Jewish Scriptures and Jewish institutions in the light of Christ (e.g., Acts 10:26–40; Hebrews).

Although early Christian writings often have an evangelistic thrust, just as often apologetics are also at work. As second-century authors responded to criticisms from outside the church (from Jews and pagans) and within (from gnostics and Marcionites, among others), they naturally turned to Scripture to defend their claims and thereby continued this process of reinterpreting it through the lens of Christ. This polemical context resulted in an ad hoc approach to the Bible insofar as the range of texts expounded was determined by these theological conflicts, and only passages germane to the particular issue under discussion were treated (e.g., Justin Martyr, *Dialogue with Trypho*, and Irenaeus, *Against Heresies*).

Despite this ad hoc approach, second-century exegetes such as Irenaeus of Lyon were guided by the premise of the Bible's unity. This is more than a little ironic: they were familiar with Scripture not as a single volume but as a series of discrete books or codices. Moreover, it would be several more centuries before the contours of the Christian canon would be set. Despite this, a general consensus about which writings were authoritative began to develop in the second century and appears to have been closely connected to the question of whether a particular book were regularly read in the liturgy. Nonetheless, despite this lack of a formal canon, and although scriptural texts existed as distinct books, Irenaeus and others affirmed the unity of the two Testaments: both were witnesses to Christ.

A major development occurred in the work of Origen, who insisted that, because Christ is the object of Scripture, the Christian exegete not only can but also ought to treat the Bible in its entirety, not merely as isolated passages. Preachers, Origen granted, are limited in what they can cover; commentators, however, should explain the text in detail, omitting nothing. Through this emphasis on exhaustive commentary on the Bible, Origen enabled the church to make the OT its own and thereby revolutionized Christian exegesis. Another important dimension of Origen's legacy lies in the notion that Scripture has multiple levels of meaning, the literal and the spiritual, because God's revealed word is intended not simply for those to whom it was first addressed. Rather, Scripture speaks to believers in all times and places (1 Cor. 10:11; *On First Principles*, bk. 4). While Origen emphasized the spiritual meaning, he did not neglect the literal, for he explored historical and philological aspects of the biblical text. This study, however, was never an end in itself but was always in order to discern a passage's theological significance for the church. Despite criticisms from some early Christians, Origen's method became the foundation for Christian biblical exegesis in East and West. His influence can be seen in the approach to Scripture of Gregory of Nyssa, Gregory of Nazianzus, Basil of Caesarea, Ambrose of Milan, Augustine of Hippo, and Gregory the Great.

————

Augustine, *De doctrina Christiana*, trans. R. P. H. Green (1995); Origen, *On First Principles*, trans. G. W. Butterworth (1936); P. Blowers, ed. and trans., *The Bible in Greek Christian Antiquity*; P. Bright, ed. and trans., *Augustine and the Bible* (1999); J. T. Lienhard, "Origen and the Crisis of the Old Testament in the Early Church," *Pro Ecclesia* 9 (2000): 355–66; H. de Lubac, *Exégèse médiévale* (1959); de Lubac, *Medieval Exegesis* (1998–); H. Y. Gamble, *Books and Readers in the Early Church: A History of Early Christian Texts* (1995); J. L. Kugel, *The Bible as It Was* (1997); T. Oden, ed., *The Ancient Christian Commentary on Scripture* (1998–); M. Simonetti, *Biblical Interpretation in the Early Church: An Historical Introduction to Patristic Exegesis* (1994); R. L. Wilken, ed., *The Church's Bible* (2003–).

ANGELA RUSSELL CHRISTMAN

Bible in the Early Medieval Church

The Greek church of the Byzantine era inherited an impressive body of patristic biblical interpretation—commentaries, homilies, and expository treatises—by Origen and Hippolytus (third century); by the Alexandrians: Athanasius, Eusebius, Cyril, Didymus, and the three Cappadocian fathers; and by the Antiochenes: Diodore of Tarsus, Theodore of Mopsuestia, John Chrysostom, and Theodoret of Cyrrhus (fourth and fifth centuries). Since the time of the emperor Justinian (d. 565) this heritage became accessible through exegetical chains, or *catenae*. *Catenae* were serial collections of Bible texts followed by explanatory excerpts from a limited number of sources. The earliest name connected with such compilations is Procopius of Gaza (c. 475–538). Original commentaries remained rare in the East. John of Damascus (d. c. 750) commented on the Pauline Epistles; Oecumenius and Andrew of Caesarea (sixth century), followed by Arethas (ninth century) on Revelation. In the eleventh and twelfth centuries, Theophylact of Ohrid and Euthymios Zigabenos were prolific commentators. The Syrian church had its own distinguished tradition of Bible interpretation. Tatian's Gospel harmony (late second century) was already a kind of commentary. Ephrem (d. 373), who also interpreted Genesis and Exodus, wrote a commentary on it. The school of Edessa, continued in Nisibis after 489, was a center of biblical scholarship in the Antiochian tradition. Narses (d. 503), Philoxenus of Mabbug (d. 523), and Ishodad of Merv (mid-ninth century) were its outstanding representatives.

In the West, after the fourth century, the disintegration of the Roman Empire and the conquests of the Germanic tribes altered the intellectual climate dramatically. Christian literary culture found a new home in the monasteries. Under Ostrogothic rule in Italy, Cassiodorus (485/90–c. 580) made the preservation of patristic writings a priority and left an influential Psalms commentary based on Augustine. In Visigothic Spain, Isidore of Seville (c. 560–636) kept patristic learning alive through numerous aids to Bible study, especially his encyclopedic *Etymologies*. Pope Gregory the Great (590–604) founded monasteries and wrote for his monks. His works, together with those of the other three "luminaries" of the Latin church (Ambrose, Augustine, and Jerome) formed the core of theological sources known to the medieval West. As an exegete, Gregory contributed his *Moralia in Job* and homilies on Ezekiel and Gospel passages. Irish Christianity, organized around monastic centers, produced a rich literature of translations and gloss commentaries, most of them anonymous. The Irish tradition was known to Bede (c. 673–735), the outstanding biblical scholar of the English realm. Bede used Greek for textual criticism and patristic sources for his numerous didactic commentaries on many biblical books and passages, among them accounts of Moses' tabernacle and Solomon's temple. His interests included chronology and natural sciences.

The Frankish cultural revival fostered by Charlemagne's educational legislation profited by the biblical scholarship of the British Isles. Charlemagne appointed Alcuin of York (c. 740–804), a prolific Bible scholar, head of his palace school and commissioned Wigbod to compile a commentary on the Octateuch. At his court, Theodulf of Orléans produced a scholarly revision of the Latin Bible using the two rival translations, the Old Latin and Jerome's Vulgate. Alcuin's redaction of 801, however, became the received text. By that time, a division of the scriptural senses into four, first formulated by John Cassian (d. after 430), had become the standard method of biblical interpretation: the literal sense was followed by the spiritual sense, which was subdivided into allegory, tropology, and anagogy. The Carolingian "Renaissance" led to a flowering of exegetical literature in the ninth and tenth centuries: Claudius of Turin wrote traditional commentaries on many books of the Bible; Hrabanus Maurus, a pupil of Alcuin, on almost all; Paschasius Radbertus commented on Lamentations and Matthew; Walahfrid Strabo on the Pentateuch, Psalms, and Catholic Epistles; Sedulius Scottus on Matthew and Paul; Angelomus of Luxueil on Genesis, Kings, and the Song of Songs; Haymo and Remigius of Auxerre on Genesis, Psalms, the Song, Isaiah, the Epistles, and Revelation. John Scottus Eriugena, one of the most brilliant minds of the time, drew on Greek sources for his exposition of John and of Gen. 1–3 in his *De rerum natura*. Knowledge of Eastern exegetes was rare, except for Origen and Chrysostom. For the Western fathers, several florilegia were in use, among them Paterius's exegetical excerpts from Pope Gregory I and Florus of Lyon's (d. c. 860) collection of Augustine on the Pauline Epistles. Preoccupation with the auxiliary disciplines of grammar, rhetoric, and dialectic became a major aspect of clerical education after the Carolingian era, but in the monasteries the study of the Bible remained central. It included memorization of biblical texts, especially the Psalter, exposure to expository homilies, and the practice of *lectio divina*, or personal meditation on the sacred text. Among the monastic writers of the eleventh and twelfth centuries, much interest focused on the Psalms and the Pauline Epistles (e.g., Lanfranc of Bec, Bruno of Segni, Bruno the Carthusian, Manegold of Lautenbach). Their main patristic authorities were Augustine, Cassiodorus, and the Ambrosiaster (Pseudo-Ambrose). Other biblical books were popular as well: Genesis, the Gospels, the Song of Songs (for which Rupert of Deutz [c. 1075–1129/1130] introduced a Marian interpretation instead of the usual equation of the bride with the church), and the Revelation of John. There was also a growing interest in history. Rupert's massive work, *On the Holy Trinity and Its Works*, is a commentary on the historical books of the Bible as the unfolding of God's history of salvation, a theme which became prominent in the School of St. Victor, with its concern for the literal sense, and in the teaching of the "masters of the sacred page" in the twelfth and thirteenth centuries.

M. M. Gorman, *Biblical Commentaries from the Early Middle Ages*, Millennio medievale 32 (repr. 2002); J. H. Hayes, ed., *Dictionary of Biblical Interpretation*, 2 vols. (1999); G. W. H. Lampe, ed., *The West from the Fathers to the Reformation*, vol. 2 of *The Cambridge History of the Bible* (1969); M. Saebo, ed., *The Middle Ages*, vol. 1:2 of *Hebrew Bible/Old Testament: The History of Its Interpretation* (1999), 135–236; B. Smalley, *The Study of the Bible in the Middle Ages* (3rd ed., 1983).

KARLFRIED FROEHLICH

Bible in the Reformation   On the eve of the Reformation, the Bible version known to Western Christianity was Jerome's (347–419/420) Vulgate (Lat., *editio vulgata*: "common version"). Despite traditional reverence for the Vulgate, the late medieval revival of Greek and Hebrew studies led to sharp philological and theological criticism of it by the linguists and theologians of the Renaissance and Reformation. In his major work, *In Novum Testamentum . . . adnotationes*, Lorenzo Valla (1407–1457) applied critical methods of philology to problems of biblical exegesis and translation, challenging the Vulgate's traditional authority. Desiderius Erasmus (1469–1536), inspired by Valla's *Adnotationes*, published his critical edition of the New Testament, *Novum Instrumentum* (1516), which included the Greek text of the NT with his own Latin translation, and provided an important impulse for vernacular translations throughout the West.

Humanists were also instrumental for several polyglot editions of the Bible. The Complutensian Polyglot Bible (*Complutum*, Lat. for "Alcalá de Henares") was printed between 1514 and 1517 at the University of Alcalá under the auspices of Cardinal Francisco Jiménez de Cisneros (1436–1517). The Old Testament consisted of a revised Masoretic Hebrew text and translations in Aramaic, Latin, and Greek; the New Testament appeared in Greek and Latin. The Antwerp Polyglot, *Biblia Regia*, published between 1569 and 1572, was sponsored by Philip II of Spain and supervised by the scholar Benito Arias Montano (1527–1598). The NT polyglot of Elias Hutter (1553–1609), published at Nuremberg in 1599, presented the NT in over eight different modern European languages.

Vernacular translations of the Bible were crucial for the Reformation. Martin Luther's (1483–1546) German translation of the NT marked both the evangelical movement and the development of the modern German language. Luther used Erasmus's *Novum Instrumentum* as a foundation for his translation of the NT, which first appeared in September 1522 and hence is known as the "September Testament." The translation of the OT, a Wittenberg group endeavor, appeared in 1534.

Among French translations, Lefèvre d'Etaples' (1455–1536) version of the New Testament appeared in 1523—condemned by the French Parliament in 1525—and his complete translation of the Bible, printed at Antwerp, in 1530. While he did not translate from the original languages of the Bible, d'Etaples did omit medieval glosses and supplemented the 1523 partial edition of the NT with two "epistres exhortatoires." Pierre-Robert Olivétan's (c. 1506–1538) translation from the original Hebrew and Greek was published at Neuchâtel in 1535 and became the basis for French-language Bibles printed in Geneva. In 1543 John Calvin (1509–1564) published a revision of Olivétan's NT, and in 1546 he published a revision of Olivétan's whole Bible. With Theodore Beza (1516–1605; discoverer of a fifth-century Greco-Latin text of the Gospels and Acts, the *Codex Bezae*), Calvin published a new revision of Olivétan's Bible in 1551. The last major revision of the French Geneva Bible was in 1588.

William Tyndale (1494?–1536) is widely recognized as the father of English biblical translation. His translation of the Greek NT first appeared in an incomplete edition in 1525, followed by a complete edition in 1526 and a translation of the Pentateuch in 1530. Tyndale also translated the OT to the end of Jonah by the time of his death. Myles Coverdale (1488–1568) authored the first complete English translation of the Bible (1535). Coverdale's Psalter, as revised for the 1539 edition of the Great Bible, later became the Psalter of the Book of Common Prayer. John Rogers (1500–1555, alias Thomas Matthew), editor and translator of the "Matthew Bible" (1537), employed Tyndale's translation of the OT, Tyndale's 1535 revision of the NT, as well as Coverdale's translation from Ezra to Malachi and the Apocrypha. The Great Bible—the work of Myles Coverdale—was the first English Bible formally authorized for public use and went through six editions between 1540 and 1541. William Wittingham (c. 1524–1579) headed the group of Marian exiles responsible for the English Geneva Bible of 1560. It incorporated massive marginal annotations that provided a "guided reading" of the biblical text and captured the imagination of the English readership. The Geneva Bible continued to rival the King James Version long after 1611. The Bishops' Bible (1568) was a response to the failure of the Great Bible and the exceeding popularity of the Geneva Bible. Initiated by Archbishop Matthew Parker (1504–1575), it became, after it was sanctioned by the Convocation of 1571, the second authorized version. By 1604 it was clear that the Bishops' Bible had also failed to surpass the Geneva Bible in popularity. Thus, when John Reynolds (1509–1607) asserted the need for a new translation at the Hampton Court conference, King James I (1566–1625) agreed. The "King James Version" was published in 1611.

In Spain biblical scholarship continued to flourish at the Universites of Alcalá and Salamanca. The Protestant Francisco de Enzinas (1518?–1552), however, did the first complete translation of the NT into Spanish from the original Greek (Antwerp, 1543). In reaction, the 1551 *Index* of the Spanish Inquisition censured vernacular Bibles. At Geneva, Juan Pérez de Pineda (d. 1567) published a revision of Enzinas's NT in 1556. Another exile, Casiodoro de Reina (c. 1520–1594), did the first complete translation of the Bible into Spanish (1569). Cipriano de Valera (d. c. 1602) issued another translation of the NT in 1596 (London) and a revision of the 1569 Spanish Bible in 1602 (Amsterdam).

Protestant Bible translations were condemned by Roman Catholic authorities from the outset for allowing "laymen and silly old women" to interpret Scripture, and for translations that undercut Roman Catholic doctrine and authority. Hence, the Council of Trent (1546) authorized only the old Latin Vulgate edition and condemned anyone who rejected the Vulgate or "presumes to interpret" it "con-

trary to that sense which holy mother Church . . . has held and holds."

———

I. Backus, *The Reformed Roots of the English New Testament* (1980); B. T. Chambers, *Bibliography of French Bibles: Fifteenth- and Sixteenth-Century French-Language Editions of the Scriptures* (1983); R. Griffiths, ed., *The Bible in the Renaissance: Essays on Biblical Commentary and Translation in the Fifteenth and Sixteenth Centuries* (2001); A. McGrath, *In the Beginning: The Story of the King James Bible* (2001); D. Norton, *A History of the English Bible as Literature* (2000); O. O'Sullivan, ed., *The Bible as Book: The Reformation* (2000); R. Roldán-Figueroa, *"Filius Perditionis*: The Propagandistic Use of a Biblical Motif in Sixteenth-Century Spanish Evangelical Bible Translations," *SCJ* 4 (2006): 1027–55.

RADY ROLDÁN-FIGUEROA

Bible, Lost Books   *see* Lost Books of the Bible

Bible Translations, Early Modern

Medieval translators rendered portions or all of the Bible into vernacular languages. The English translation by John Wyclif's "Lollard" followers (1380s) was suppressed, but, as in France, Iberia, and Bohemia, in Germany several renderings based on the Vulgate text and earlier, partial translations rendered from the ninth century on were in use (in print since 1466) when Martin Luther took the Greek text of Erasmus's *Novum Instrumentum* in hand to produce his "September New Testament" (1522). Ulrich Zwingli completed his "Zurich" Bible (1529; Leo Jud's revision, 1540) before Luther published his complete translation (1534; final revision, 1545), but Luther's set the standards and tone for the German Bible. Working largely alone on his first German NT but assisted by a committee of scholars on the OT, Luther used Greek and Hebrew texts and the Vulgate. He employed insights of humanistic scholars including Johannes Reuchlin, Jacques Lefevre d'Etaples, and Erasmus. His prefaces and marginal notes assisted the cultivation of readers' biblical literacy. Although scholars dispute the degree to which he actually forged a new public language, his linguistic and literary abilities enabled him to create a masterpiece of translation. Roman Catholic countertranslations appeared quickly (Jerome Emser, 1527; Johann Dietenberger, 1534; Johannes Eck, 1537), all dependent on Luther's expression. Kaspar Ulenberg revised Dietenberger's version in the

Mainz Bible (1630). Anabaptists Hans Denck and Ludwig Hätzer translated the OT prophets from Hebrew (1527).

The English tradition of translation continued with William Tyndale, who had become an excellent Greek scholar before leaving England for Germany, where he published his NT (1525) and was well along with the OT when arrested in 1535; he was executed for heresy in 1536. Luther's German translation heavily influenced his text; he also used Erasmus, the Vulgate, and recent scholarship. His version shaped subsequent English translations extensively, including the King James Version. Miles Coverdale continued Tyndale's work; John Rogers (alias Thomas Matthews), published his revision in 1537. The government-sponsored Great Bible of 1540 was essentially Coverdale's work; in 1557–1560 English exiles produced the Geneva Bible. Each had its own apparatus of aids for readers. In 1611 a special ecclesiastical commission produced the King James Version, which, with minimal nineteenth-century reworking, remained the "authorized" English Bible into the twentieth century. English Roman Catholic scholars produced the Reims translation of the Vulgate (1582), revised as the Douai Version (1609/1610).

Luther's influence strongly shaped translations into Danish (Hans Mikkelsen, 1524, 1529; a much improved translation by Christien Pedersen, 1529–1550; the Resen Bible, 1607; the Svanging Bible, 1647), Icelandic (NT, 1540; entire Bible, 1584), and Swedish (NT, 1526; Gustav Vasa Bible, 1541, revised 1549, 1560; Gustav Adolf Bible, 1641). Luther's student Mikael Agricola used his professor's translation and Erasmus in preparing his Finnish NT (1548) and psalms and prophets (1551/1552); the complete Finnish translation of Aeschylus Petraenus appeared in 1642. Partial translations into Estonian appeared in the sixteenth century; the first translations of the whole Bible into Estonian dialects appeared in 1686 and 1715. Johannes Bretken completed a Lithuanian translation in 1579–1590, and Ernst Glück used earlier partial translations in his Latvian Bible (1685–1689).

Lefevre d'Etaples based his 1530 French translation of the entire Bible upon the Vulgate. Theodore Beza edited earlier work by Pierre Robert Olivétan (1535) into the "Bible de Genève" (1588). The humanist Antonio Brucioli used the Latin of Pagninus and Erasmus to produce his Italian Bible of 1532, employed by exiled Protestants; the earlier Vulgate-based translation of Nicolao Malmeri (1471) remained standard for Italian Roman Catholics. The Spanish humanist Francisco de Enzinas used original-language texts for his Spanish NT (1543).

Students from Wittenberg and others built upon earlier Hussite translations as they translated the Bible in their own languages. Lutheran Jan Seklucyan produced a new Polish NT (1551/1552); Roman Catholic authorities published the entire Bible in Polish, edited by Jan Leopolita (1561); Polish Calvinists printed their version in 1563. Primus Trubar completed his NT in Slovenian (1557); Georg Dalmatin finished the Slovenian Bible in 1684. Jan Blahoslav of the Bohemian Brethren improved Hussite translations of the NT (1564). His church created the Kralice Bible (1579–1594), the standard for Czechs and Slovaks until the twentieth century. Caspar Helt and his associates produced a new Hungarian translation of most of the Bible (1552–1565).

Luther's belief that God as Creator engages his human creatures in conversation through the biblical text brought Protestants to lay great worth on the translation of the Bible, into vernacular languages so that all Christians could read it. This point of view, combined with the availability of printing technology, caused the new translations of the Bible produced in the sixteenth century to play a major role in the formation of early modern language and literature.

———

H. Bluhm, *Martin Luther, Creative Translator* (1965); Bluhm, *Luther, Translator of Paul* (1984); F. Büsser, *Early Printed Bibles* (1988–); S. Greenslade, ed., *The Cambridge History of the Bible: The West from the Reformation to the Present Day* (1987).

ROBERT KOLB

Bibliander, Theodor (1504/1509–1564), Swiss Reformation theologian, language scholar, and professor in the Zurich Academy. A native of Switzerland, Bibliander studied in Zurich and Basel. After teaching in Liegnitz (Legnica, Poland), he was appointed professor of Old Testament at the Zurich Academy upon Zwingli's death (1531). Bibliander's contemporaries recognized him as a premier biblical exegete and expert on languages. He regularly lectured on the OT, and transcripts were circulated widely among Swiss Reformed pastors. Among his twenty-five published books are exegetical, historical, polemic, and linguistic works, including a widely used Hebrew grammar. His most important contribution was a huge compendium of medieval and contemporary writings on Islam (*Machumetis saracenorum principis*, 1543), which included the first published Qur'an. His scholarship represents a type of evangelical Christian humanism reflecting the influence of Erasmus, although he believed he was faithful to Zwingli's theology. Bibliander came to hold a view of predestination that was at odds with his Reformed Swiss colleagues. Late in life (1560) Bibliander fiercely challenged the absolute double predestination teaching of his fellow Zurich professor Peter Martyr Vermigli. As a result of this conflict Bibliander was forced to resign his position, although he was given a pension.

R. S. Armour, "Theodore Bibliander's Alcoran of 1543/1550," *Perspectives in Religious Studies* 24 (1997); H. Clark, "The Publication of the Koran in Latin: A Reformation Dilemma," *SCJ* 15, no. 1 (1984): 3–12; E. Egli, *Analecta Reformatoria*, vol. 2 (1901); W. Holsten, "Reformation und Mission," *ARG* 44 (1953).

GREGORY J. MILLER

Biel, Gabriel (c. 1410–1495), scholastic theologian. He was born in Speyer and became a priest around 1432. After receiving degrees from the faculty of arts in Heidelberg in 1435 and 1438, he remained at the university as an instructor. Later he studied theology at Erfurt and Cologne and became cathedral preacher in Mainz. Because he was on the losing side of a dispute over who would become the next archbishop of Mainz, he was forced to flee to Marienthal, where he came into contact with the Brethren of the Common Life. He joined their community in 1462 and was appointed provost of their new house in Butzbach in 1468. He established the Württemberg chapter of the Brethren in 1477. At an advanced age, he was appointed to the theological faculty of the new university of Tübingen in 1484. Through his book, *On the Canon of the Mass,* and his commentary on *The Book of the Sentences,* he became one of the most influential representatives of nominalism (*via moderna*). Following William of Ockham, he stressed the freedom of God but suggested that God imposed an obligation upon himself to give justifying grace to anyone who first made an effort to love God. His stress on human initiative and divine-human cooperation made him the primary target of Martin Luther's attack on scholastic theology in the early sixteenth century.

G. Biel, *Canonis Missae expositio,* ed. H. Oberman and W. Courtenay (1963–1967); H. Ober-

man, *The Harvest of Medieval Theology* (1963).

ERIC LUND

Bishops, Early and Medieval The New Testament shows that in the first century, some Christian communities used the term "bishop" interchangeably with "presbyter" to designate administrative leadership. Not until Ignatius (c. 35–c. 107) is there testimony to the development of a three-tiered hierarchy of deacons, presbyters, and bishops. By the late second century this structure was a widespread and normative shield against heretical teaching. Also by this time the roles of apostles, prophets, teachers, women, and traveling evangelists had become subordinated to, or eliminated in favor of, this hierarchy. By the third century Christians around the empire were linked by a network of episcopacies based in cities. Bishops, according to *On Unity* by Cyprian (210–258), participated in collegial ministry with Rome, the first among equals. Cyprian's view of Rome's pivotal role is controversial because there are two versions of this treatise: one has a higher view of Roman authority than the other.

Early-fourth-century Christians within the Roman Empire experienced their greatest persecution yet, and bishops found themselves particularly targeted. By 313 however, Emperor Constantine declared himself a Christian, and soon returned confiscated property, built new churches, allowed bishops to judge certain civil cases, made some bishops respected advisors, and invited all bishops to a council at Nicaea (325). This council produced the famous creed and ruled, among other things, that bishops cannot leave one diocese to take another. It also ruled that the bishops of Antioch, Alexandria, and Rome have special authority. Jerusalem was also noted as having special honor but not authority. By the Council of Constantinople (381) this list of "patriarchs" expanded to include Constantinople with "prerogative of honor" second only to Rome.

By the early sixth century, Christianity had expanded beyond the empire's borders into places such as Armenia, Persia, Ethiopia, Ireland, and Germany. Key to these expansions were missionary bishops such as Patrick in Ireland, Ulfilas (c. 311–383) to the Goths, Frumentius (c. 300–c. 380) to Ethiopia, and Nestorius (d. after 451), the exiled bishop of Constantinople whose form of Christianity spread from Persia to China by the seventh century. From Rome, Pope Gregory I (540–604) positioned the papacy as the manager of a network of episcopacies that stretched across Europe. From his establishment of the archbishoprics at Canterbury and York, England, recorded in Bede's *History,* we see that the papacy had to carefully negotiate expansion with Frankish and already existing English episcopacies. With the Synod of Whitby (664) and the relationship that missionary bishops like Boniface (c. 675–754) and Willibrord (658–739) had with Rome, the pope became the central ecclesiastical authority in Western Europe.

In the East, the patriarch of Constantinople and other ancient patriarchs rejected the pope's claims to universal authority. The rise of Islam in the seventh century, however, severely limited the power of Antioch, Jerusalem, and Alexandria. Constantinople thus lost its eastern competition and a large amount of territory to compete for. Consequently, Constantinople sought expansion through its own missionary activities. The missionary activities of Cyril (826–869) and Methodius (c. 815–885) led to the conversion of Slavs and the establishment of episcopacies among them and the Russians by the tenth century.

Despite grand claims to authority by Rome and Constantinople, distance limited the ability of each to control other bishops. Thus bishops, as they ruled dioceses of various sizes and wealth, had a high degree of autonomous authority, particularly in the West. In the East at various times Constantinople could rely on some support from the emperor or empress. In the West, the rise of Carolingian power among the Franks offered an opportunity for bishops and the papacy to develop a similar sort of arrangement. Boniface and Pope Stephen transferred sacral kingship from the Merovingian clan to the Carolingians, then in 800 Pope Leo III crowned Charlemagne Holy Roman Emperor. Yet these relationships did not always run smoothly.

In the eleventh century Pope Gregory VII's reform movement advocating clerical celibacy, denouncing simony (selling of church offices), and asserting papal control over episcopal appointments led to conflict with Henry IV (1050–1106), the Holy Roman Emperor. Some bishops had become important feudal lords, with large dioceses, staffs (chapters), cathedral schools, and soldiers. Thus, rulers like Henry were interested in securing acceptable bishops as vassals. This dispute, known as the investiture controversy, was eventually resolved with the Concordat of Worms (1122), an appointment-sharing agreement that let emperors invest bishops with the scepter while popes

invested them with the crosier and the ring. The relationship between the interests of rulers and the interests of popes and bishops would continue to be difficult, however. Archbishop of Canterbury Thomas Becket (1120–1170), for example, was assassinated because of his opposition to his king, Henry II (1133–1189).

Most bishops did not meet such a fate. They were mainly occupied with the pastoral and administrative duties of their dioceses. By the thirteenth century, bishops were members of a monastic order (e.g., Franciscans, Augustinians) or they were "secular" (regular) clergy. In managing their affairs, bishops looked to church councils and models from the past such as Eusebius of Caesarea (c. 260–c. 340), Athanasius of Alexandria (299–373), Basil (330–379), Gregory of Nazianzus (330–390), Gregory of Nyssa (330–394), and John Chrysostom of Constantiople (c. 374–407) in the East. In the West they looked to Ambrose of Milan (337–397), Augustine of Hippo (354–430), Martin of Tours (316–397), and Patrick of Ireland (mid-fifth cent.). Writings and biographies of these figures were copied and studied. Particularly influential were Augustine's *On Christian Doctrine* and Chrysostom's *On the Priesthood,* as well as writings from later authors such as Gregory's *Pastoral Care* and Archbishop Hincmar of Reims's (c. 802–882) *The Office of a Bishop.*

P. Brown, *The Rise of Western Christendom: Triumph and Diversity, AD 200–1000* (2nd ed., 2003); H. Chadwick et al., *The Role of the Christian Bishop in Ancient Society* (1979); C. Morris, *The Papal Monarchy: The Western Church from 1050 to 1250* (1989); H. R. Niebuhr and D. D. Williams, *The Ministry in Historical Perspectives* (1983); R. W. Southern, *Western Society and the Church in the Middle Ages* (1970); J. M. Wallace-Hadrill, *The Frankish Church* (1983).

HORACE SIX-MEANS

Bishops, Late Middle Ages and Reformation

Since the early Middle Ages the crosier (staff) has symbolized the bishop's sacred role as shepherd of the church in the care of souls and the discipline of the clergy. But by the later Middle Ages many anticlerical voices maintained that bishop and clergy were not only miserable moral examples, but were also guilty of absenteeism, pluralism (holding multiple church offices), and simony (selling church offices). Moreover, given the temporal and ecclesiastical roles of many bishops as servants of crown and church, given their political lordship over cities and rural estates, and given their predominantly aristocratic origins, some critics charged that bishops were more vigilant princes than priests, that they preferred the sword to the crosier.

Such anticlerical sentiment reflects in part the complexity and difficulty of episcopal rule. During the later fourteenth and early fifteenth centuries, bishops contended with the disruption of episcopal government and pastoral care caused by papal schism. Politics—ecclesiastical and temporal—drew bishops away from their local responsibilities. In addition, they were often engaged in defending the lands and privileges of the regional church, leaving little time for pastoral work. Meanwhile, bishops relied more and more heavily on institutions and subordinate officers to oversee clergy and diocese. The cathedral chapter and archdeacons played a more active and independent role. The auxiliary or "assisting bishop" (also called a "suffragan bishop") was granted sacred authority to fulfill the liturgical and consecrating roles of the diocesan bishop. The official wielded legal authority, and the vicar general served as the bishop's chief representative. Some exceptionally reform-minded bishops did emerge in response to the criticism of the clergy and the robust conciliarism of the early fifteenth century. They composed reform mandates, convoked clerical synods, and made visitations to parishes and monasteries. Some bishops supported the work of humanist scholars and were patrons of the visual arts and education.

Although some bishops were active in correcting abuses, other reformers were also at work. Long before Martin Luther (1483–1546), territorial princes and city councils were encouraged to take matters of church reform into their own hands. In the HRE even the cathedral city, the capital of an ecclesiastical province or diocese, faced considerable lay encroachment. Indeed, by the end of the Middle Ages burghers had often wrested political, economic, legal, and some ecclesiastical control from their episcopal lords; many bishops were even expelled from their cathedral cities and forced to live elsewhere. The struggle over sacred spaces continued on to the eve of the Reformation, as the cathedral became an island of clerical power in a sea of lay dominion, and as bishop and citizens displayed their contested claims to urban lordship, pastoral oversight, and civic welfare during feast day processions, episcopal entries, and priestly burials.

During the sixteenth century, Protestant movements harnessed anticlericalism and drew

on the hardy reform impulses of the later Middle Ages, often with considerable implications for the episcopacy. In fact, in the empire those archbishops and bishops that maintained their political lordship in territory and cathedral city were most successful at strengthening their churches while controlling and marginalizing Protestants in their midst. Other bishops lost spiritual oversight of their cathedral cites, numerous parishes, and monasteries. Those territories and cities that came to embrace Lutheranism reshaped church structures, and after some experimentation replaced bishops with superintendents and consistories. Secular rulers took over much of the jurisdiction of the bishop.

Elsewhere in Europe the pattern varied. Calvinist churches often rejected the office of bishop, placing the oversight of the faithful in the hands of a presbytery (classis) of pastors and elders. Despite a considerable loss in land and the criticism of presbyterian-minded Puritans, the traditional episcopacy endured in England with the crown as supreme head of the church. But the virtuous example demanded of English bishops was often contradictory. They were expected to display a dignity and hospitality worthy of their aristocratic predecessors, and they were expected to embody the simple life of a Reformed pastor devoted to the preaching of the word and charity for the poor. Although at least twelve French bishops made public their conversion to Protestantism, in general the episcopacy of France remained faithful to Roman Catholicism. But most were less than ambitious in their pursuit of Calvinist Huguenots in their dioceses and provinces. Allegiance to the Roman Catholic kings of France proved to be the decisive factor in religious affiliation. The Concordat of Bologna (1516) had already ensured that royal authority, not papal, would be paramount in the appointment of French bishops.

Even as the episcopacy was besieged in some parts of Europe, it was renewed in others by the deliberations of the Council of Trent (1545–1563). The reforms of the council depended on a revitalized episcopacy that had to meet exacting expectations. According to Trent, bishops could only be absent from their sees for an extended time by special permission; they were to be active as preachers, conveners of diocesan synods, visitors to parishes and monasteries, and participants in provincial synods. Bishops were responsible for the quality of pastoral care in their dioceses and for the education and formation of their clergy; they were exhorted to create new seminaries for those purposes. Indeed, the Council of Trent provided a secure foundation for Roman Catholic bishops, which ensured the survival and vitality of the episcopacy until new challenges to church authority emerged at the end of the eighteenth century.

F. J. Baumgartner, *Change and Continuity in the French Episcopate: The Bishops and the Wars of Religion 1547–1610* (1986); *Die Bischöfe des Heiligen Römischen Reiches 1448 bis 1648*, ed. E. Gatz (1996); T. A. Brady Jr., "The Holy Roman Empire's Bishops on the Eve of the Reformation," in *Continuity and Change: The Harvest of Late-Medieval and Reformation History* (2000), 20–47; W. de Boer, *The Conquest of the Soul: Confession, Discipline, and Public Order in Counter-Reformation Milan* (2001); F. Heal, *Of Prelates and Princes: A Study of the Economic and Social Position of the Tudor Episcopate* (1980); J. J. Tyler, *Lord of the Sacred City: The Episcopus Exclusus in Late Medieval and Early Modern Germany* (1999).

J. JEFFERY TYLER

Black Rubric Appended to the text of the Lord's Supper in the second Book of Common Prayer (1552), the so-called Black Rubric is not a ceremonial directive but a doctrinal clarification of the significance of kneeling for the reception of Holy Communion. The Black Rubric seeks both to justify the traditional posture and to repudiate the doctrine of transubstantiation hitherto associated with it. Kneeling, according to the Black Rubric, expresses humble gratitude for Christ's benefits, safeguards the Eucharist from profanation, and ensures good order among communicants. Explicitly denied are both adoration ("idolatry") of the sacramental bread and wine and any "real or essential presence of Christ's natural flesh and blood," because Christ's natural body and blood are in heaven and cannot be in more than one place at one time. A clear concession to more radical Anglican reformers, the Privy Council mandated the Black Rubric over the objections of Archbishop Cranmer. Subsequent editions omit the Black Rubric or recast it as an alternative explanation of the mode of Christ's presence.

C. Jones, G. Wainwright, and E. Yarnold, *The Study of Liturgy* (1992); F. Proctor and W. H. Frere, *A History of the Book of Common Prayer with a Rationale of Its Offices* (1965); L. Pullan, *The History of the Book of Common Prayer* (1977).

PETER J. SCAGNELLI

Blandina (d. 177), martyr at Lyon. Blandina was a member of the earliest known Christian community in Gaul (southern France). The churches of Lyon and Vienne sent her story to Christians in Asia Minor and Phrygia (Turkey). Christians from that area probably had originally evangelized Gaul. Eusebius (*Hist. eccl.* 5.1.7–56) preserves parts of their letter.

The persecution in Gaul was a local one, unconnected to any others. Christians were accused of cannibalism and incest. Blandina, a young slave girl, was arrested with the deacon, the aged bishop Pothinius (predecessor of Irenaeus), other Gauls, and a number of people from Asia Minor. Also included in the group was Biblis, a woman representing Christians who had previously denied the faith.

Blandina's story is significant for several reasons. First, it provides an account of one of the earliest government-sponsored persecutions. Second, it is the record of a woman's leadership in a community of martyrs. She is deemed the mother of the community in faith, not unlike the mother of the Maccabees, and is compared to Christ in that she suffered by being hung in the form of a cross as she encouraged those martyred with her. Finally, her story provided literary patterns for that of Perpetua in North Africa.

W. H. C. Frend, *Martyrdom and Persecution in the Early Church* (1965), 1–22.

MAUREEN A. TILLEY

Blaurock (Cajacob), Georg (d. 1529), early Swiss Anabaptist leader and martyr. A priest in the diocese of Chur, he became convinced by 1525 that infant baptism was unscriptural and that the reform in Zurich, led by Zwingli, had come under the control of the civil government. Nicknamed "Blaurock" (blue coat), he was the first to receive rebaptism on his confession of faith from Conrad Grebel (c. 1498–1526). This historic event in the home of Felix Mantz (c. 1498–1527) is usually regarded as the origin of a separatist Swiss Brethren movement. Blaurock, Grebel, Mantz, and others began an underground ministry in homes and other locations, baptizing many and preaching the need for repentance and a morally changed life.

The Zurich Council took swift action against Blaurock and other Swiss Brethren, whom they considered a threat to religious and social order, and thus began decades of harsh persecution against the Anabaptists throughout Europe. Blaurock and a companion, Hans Langegger, were arrested in the Austrian Tyrol in 1529 and subsequently burned at the stake at Klausen, near Innsbruck.

C. A. Snyder, *Anabaptist History and Theology: An Introduction* (1995); G. H. Williams, *The Radical Reformation* (3rd ed., 1992).
                                                                    D. B. ELLER

Blood Libel The blood libel accusation against Jews emerged in the thirteenth century, about a century after the first accusations of ritual murder. Both accusations imputed to the Jew a desire to kill Christian children (predominantly young boys), but whereas the ritual murder accusation was understood as a reenactment of the crucifixion, the blood libel drew on several other elements in the image of the Jews. The blood libel is a tale of an annual conspiracy by which all Jewish communities chose one by lot charged with procuring a Christian child for the purpose of using its blood. This use could be medical—to rid Jews of a characteristic stench, to rid Jews of their pallor, as a love potion—or, and more commonly, ritual, for Christian blood was understood in some narratives to be a necessary ingredient for the Passover bread, the matzo, and for the central wine-drinking rituals of the Passover meal. Although the earliest cases, in eastern France and the Rhineland, did not gain official papal endorsement, bishops and monks colluded in its propagation, and the Inquisition conducted trials of the accused Jews. The case of Fulda in 1236 set the tone but also led the emperor to inquire into its veracity and to find it without truth. Pope Innocent IV issued a letter in 1247 to the bishops of Germany explaining that the crime attributed to Jews does not stand to reason and contradicts Jewish law. A famous and well-documented case is that of Simon of Trent, onto whose body the Jews of Trent (in northern Italy) were said to have inflicted a large number of blood-related and sexual pains. The inquisitorial trial wove a web into which all Jewish men were drawn. The images that accompanied pamphlets announcing the miracles worked by Simon's body spread the imagery of blood libel all over Europe and for generations to come.

A. Dundes, ed., *Blood Libel Legend: A Case-Book in Anti-Semitic Folklore* (1991); R. Po-chia Hsia, *The Myth of Ritual Murder: Jews and Magic in Reformation Germany* (1988); G. I. Langmuir, "Ritual Cannibalism," in *Towards a Definition of Antisemitism* (1990), 263–81.
                                                                    MIRI RUBIN

Blow, John (1649–1707), English composer and church musician. Blow was trained in the Chapel Royal, which he later served during the Restoration period in English church music (1660–1714). During the Civil War, the organs, music libraries, and choirs of many of the cathedrals in England were destroyed. After the Act of Uniformity (1662) these musical establishments again rose to prominence. The Chapel Royal, a group of musicians attached to the court, served as singers and instrumentalists for the round of daily services, wherever the monarch might be. John Blow sang in this choir as a child and then went on to take a succession of roles, becoming, in 1699, the first "composer of Chapel Royal." His music, an exemplar of the English sacred polyphonic style, consists mainly of service music and anthems written to fulfill his responsibilities at the Chapel Royal.

I. Spink, *Restoration Cathedral Music 1660–1714* (1995).
                                                                    LINDA J. CLARK

Bodin, Jean (c. 1530–1596), French philosopher and jurist. Initially sympathetic to Protestantism he soon returned to a liberal form of Catholicism. He avidly supported the French Renaissance and developed a new humanist curriculum in his *Oratio de Institutenda in Republic Juventate* (1559). Bodin practiced law in Paris before becoming counsel to Henry III in 1571, and then served briefly as royal secretary and delegate to the States-General before he fell into royal disfavor.

Bodin's chief fame came from his scholarship. His *Methodus ad facilem historiarum cogntionem* (1566) divided human knowledge into three branches: natural history (physics), divine history (theology), and human history (anthropology). His divine history, *Heptaplomeres sive colloquium de abditus rerum sublimium arcanus*, compared various religions and philosophies, and ultimately defended Judaism for the enduring wisdom of the Decalogue and Catholicism for its relative stability over time.

Bodin was most renowned for his writing on politics and political economy. His *Réponse aux paradoxes de Malestroit* (1568) provided a pioneering analysis of the history of prices and markets. His most important work was *Six Livres de la République* (1576, 1586), a detailed defense of absolute sovereignty as essential to the maintenance of a well-ordered republic. Absolute sovereignty lay with the hereditary monarch who had the absolute power of making laws, limited only by natural law. This included the monarch's power to establish that religion most conducive to a well-ordered society, and to suppress religions deleterious to the same. Bodin elaborated these latter views in *Demonomanie des sorciers* (1580), which advocated the suppression of witchcraft, though elsewhere he advocated toleration of peaceable religions, including Judaism and Protestantism.

———

J. Franklin, *Jean Bodin and the Rise of Absolutist Theory* (1973); P. Rose, *Bodin and the Great God of Nature: The Moral and Religious Universe of a Judaiser* (1980).

JOHN WITTE JR.

Boethius (c. 476–c. 525), writer, philosopher, translator, public official. Born to the Anicii (the family that would produce Pope Gregory I) and adopted by the Symmachoi, a family famous for its cultural achievements, Boethius received an exceptional education as a youth that included Latin and Greek literature, philosophy, and theology. Unlike his contemporary Cassiodorus, however, Boethius did not immediately pursue a public career under the Ostrogothic king Theoderic I but chose instead to devote himself to study and a different form of public service—that of a translator. After an initial set of translations in the quadrivium, of which *The Art of Arithmetic* and *Principles of Music* survive, he conceived an ambitious plan to translate into Latin all available works of Aristotle and the dialogues of Plato, intending in part to facilitate the reconciliation of the two schools of philosophy. In the end, he seems to have completed translations of Porphyry's *Isagoge* (a Neoplatonic introduction to logic) and all the works in Aristotle's logical corpus (the *Categories, Prior Analytics, Posterior Analytics, On Interpretation, On Topics, Sophistical Refutations*), as well as commentaries on the *Isagoge*, Aristotle's *Categories*, and *On Interpretation*, and glosses on several other Aristotelian works. He also produced textbooks on various aspects of logic that synthesized aspects of the earlier commentary tradition on Aristotle. Thus, in addition to providing the Latin West with translations of Aristotle's logical works and Porphyry's *Isagoge* that continued to be widely used throughout the Middle Ages, Boethius's importance also lay in providing the additional resources, both in his own commentaries and in his textbooks, that made these texts comprehensible to medieval readers.

Along with his work in logic, Boethius composed five short treatises on theological matters collectively known as the *Opuscula sacra*. Treating topics ranging from the catholic faith in general, the Trinity, and the nature of the good, to a refutation of the heretical Christologies of Eutyches and Nestorius, the treatises are noteworthy for their insistence on using philosophical terms and methods to solve theological questions. In the Middle Ages, these treatises continued to be read and, in the twelfth century, inspired thinkers such as Abelard and Gilbert of Poitiers to adopt a similar philosophically rigorous approach to theology.

After spending much of his life devoted to study, in 522 Boethius assumed one of the key posts in Theoderic I's court at Ravenna. Charged soon thereafter with treason, though more likely a victim of court intrigue, he was sentenced to death and exiled to Pavia. There, while awaiting execution, he composed *The Consolation of Philosophy*, a dialogue between Lady Philosophy and himself intended to heal the despairing Boethius. To do so, Lady Philosophy first led Boethius through an inquiry into the nature of the good and the nature and origin of true happiness. Next she addressed Boethius's sense of theodicy through a careful examination of the nature of Providence and its relationship with human affairs, a treatment that preserved human freedom even as it explained the omniscience of Providence. A masterpiece of literature as well as philosophy, *The Consolation* was read, commented upon, and imitated throughout the Middle Ages and early modern period.

———

Boethius, *The Consolation of Philosophy*, trans. P. G. Walsh (1999); M. Gibson, ed., *Boethius: His Life, Thought, and Influence* (1981); J. Marenbon, *Boethius* (2003).

WILLIAM NORTH

Bogomils   *see* Cathars; Dualism, Medieval

Bohemian   Brethren   (Unitas Fratrum)   The Brethren were a nonconforming Hussite community, spiritual ancestors of the Moravian Brethren. After the destruction of the Taborites, George, a nephew of the Utraquist archbishop-elect John Rokycana, and

Michael, a Utraquist priest, established a commune of some lower-class Hussites at Kunwald in northeastern Bohemia in 1457 or 1458. It soon had several thousand members. Influenced partly by the ideas of Peter Chelčický (c. 1390–1460), who advocated a withdrawal of believers from the world and strict adherence to the Sermon on the Mount, they called one another "brother" and "sister" and opposed oaths, military service, and the holding of public office. In 1464 they adopted a confession at Reichenau, and at Lehotka in 1467 they established their own priesthood and consistory and elected four elders with episcopal power. Despite persecution as Taborites, their numbers increased. But they remained a small percentage of the population. After Gregory's death (1473), Luke of Prague (c. 1458–1528) led the Brethren. They gradually forsook asceticism, pacifism, and social isolation, selectively accepting converts from higher social classes. A theological Augustinian, Luke differentiated between things "essential," "ministerial," and "accidental" to salvation. Differences over discipline and theology disturbed initial contacts of the Brethren with Luther and Zwingli. Jan Augusta (1500–1572), elected bishop in 1532, established better contacts with Luther, who wrote an introduction for and in 1538 published the Brethren's *Unitas Confession* of 1535. However, Augusta's efforts to obtain legal toleration for the Brethren and to broaden their international ties resulted in conflicts within the community, his imprisonment (1548–1564), the banishment of the Brethren from Bohemia, and his denunciation by a synod in 1561. Although a fellow bishop (Jan Blahoslav, 1523–1571) and other leaders sympathized with Calvin's theology, they also defended the autonomy of the Brethren. They thwarted Augusta's plans for a Czech national Protestant church uniting the Brethren, Utraquists, and Lutherans. Nevertheless, through the Consensus of Sendomiriensis (1570) and the Confessio Bohemica (1575), the Brethren did establish, at least formally, bonds with other confessional groups in Poland and Bohemia. They also published a six-volume translation of the Bible into Czech (Kralice Bible, 1579–1593). The involvement of the Brethren in the Bohemian revolt in 1618 led to the closing of their congregations and the conversion, banishment, or execution of their leaders. Their last regularly elected bishop, Jan Amos Comenius (1592–1670), went into exile in 1628. He observed but could not hinder the institutional death of the Unitas Fratrum.

P. Brock, *The Political and Social Doctrines of the Unity of Czech Brethren in the 15th and 16th Centuries* (1957); E. de Schweinitz, *A History of the Church Known as the Unitas Fratrum* (1885); F. G. Heymann, "The Impact of Martin Luther upon Bohemia," *Central European History* 1 (1968): 107–30; J. T. Müller, *Geschichte der Böhmischen Brüder*, 3 vols. (1922–31); Říčan, *The History of the Unity of Brethren* (1992); J. K. Zeman, "Responses to Calvin and Calvinism among the Czech Brethren," *Occasional Papers of the Society for Reformation Research* 1 (1977): 41–52.

DAVID P. DANIEL

Böhme, Jacob (1575–1624), German mystical writer. Born into a peasant family in Upper Lusatia, he received little formal education. He was apprenticed to a shoemaker at the age of fourteen and practiced this trade in Görlitz from 1599 until 1613, when he turned to making yarn in order to find more time for his speculative writing. In 1600, Böhme experienced a moment of intuitive awareness, which inspired him to seek a deeper understanding of the inner nature of God and the process of divine manifestation within the world. In 1612, he circulated a manuscript entitled *Aurora* among some friends. When it came to the attention of the local pastor, Böhme was investigated for heresy. To avoid imprisonment, he promised to stop writing. He kept his vow for five years but began the second period of his authorship in 1618, during which he wrote over twenty-five works. The publication of his book *The Way to Christ* (1624) provoked renewed hostility from Lutheran church leaders. He was summoned to appear before a consistorial court in Dresden but was allowed to return, unprosecuted, to Görlitz, where shortly thereafter he died. Although Böhme claimed that his thought came from inward illumination, it manifested the influence of Schwenckfeld, Paracelsus, and Weigel. He conceived of God as a primal Abyss whose will became manifest in the world as seven contrasting qualities. He wrote much about Wisdom or Sophia as a divine principle, in addition to the Father, Son, and Holy Spirit. To explain the existence of evil, he postulated a dialectic between God's love and wrath. Böhme's thought influenced many radical Pietists in Europe and also attracted much interest among English Spiritualists (the Behmenists and Philadelphians) and nineteenth-century German Romantics.

J. Böhme, *The Way to Christ*, trans. P. Erb (1978); D. Walsh, *The Mysticism of Innerworldly Fulfillment* (1983); A. Weeks, *Boehme: An Intellectual Biography* (1991).

ERIC LUND

Boleyn, Anne

Boleyn, Anne (1507–1536), second wife of Henry VIII of England, mother of the future Queen Elizabeth I. The daughter of Thomas Boleyn and Elizabeth Howard (descendants of Edward I), Anne, as Henry's wife since 1533, advanced the cause of the Reformation in England by protecting evangelical authors and acquiring their works—using Tyndale's New Testament herself—and supporting evangelicals for clerical and court appointments. Thomas Cranmer was instrumental in both making Anne's children the sole legitimate heirs and also annulling her marriage. She was beheaded along with five men in May 1536 on charges of sexual misbehavior and witchcraft, after giving birth to a dead male fetus.

E. W. Ives, *Anne Boleyn* (1986); R. M. Warnicke, *The Rise and Fall of Anne Boleyn: Family Politics at the Court of Henry VIII* (1989); P. F. M. Zahl, *Five Women of the English Reformation* (2001).

KIRSI STJERNA

Bolland, Jean

Bolland, Jean (1596–1665), Jesuit historian and founder of the *Acta Sanctorum*. In 1630, following the death of Héribert Rosweyde (1569–1629), Bolland was requested by his provincial to edit the *Acta Sanctorum*. The goal of this ambitious project, initiated by Rosweyde, was to provide a comprehensive compilation of hagiographies based on critical historical scholarship and ordered according to the liturgical year. Bolland settled in Antwerp to devote himself to what would turn out to be his lifework. In contrast to Rosweyde, who had already collected a vast quantity of source material, Bolland aimed to include all extant sources pertaining to the biography of any saint. The first two volumes, appearing in 1643, covered saints whose feast days occurred in January; the three volumes on February appeared in 1658. By then Bolland was collaborating with Godfrey Henschen (1601–1681) and Daniel Papebroch (1628–1714), who continued his work after his death. Bolland gave his name to the Jesuit historians—the "Bollandists"—who have carried out his project until the present day.

H. Delehaye, *L'oeuvre des Bollandistes à travers trois siècles, 1615–1915* (2nd ed., 1959); P. Peeters, *L'oeuvre des Bollandistes* (2nd ed., 1961); D. Knowles, *Great Historical Enterprises: Problems in Monastic History* (1963).

JORIS VAN EIJNATTEN

Bologna, Concordat of

Bologna, Concordat of Concluded by Francis I of France and Pope Leo X in 1516, the Concordat restored some measure of papal control over the appointment of bishops and abbots in the French church. The papacy had been pressuring the crown to reverse the principle of clerical election embodied in the Pragmatic Sanction of Bourges (1438), and Francis was anxious to improve relations with Rome in order to secure papal support for his foreign policy in Italy. The Concordat granted the king the right to nominate candidates for benefices and the pope the right to confirm nominations and protest any candidates who did not meet the qualifications for office. In addition, Rome was to receive one year's worth of revenues from the benefice (annates) upon confirming a nomination. The Concordat reintroduced papal control over offices in the French church and greatly enhanced Francis's political stature. Since the exercise of royal authority entailed the bestowal of favors and gifts, the power to make clerical appointments provided Francis an enormous source of patronage to ensure the fidelity of those placed in high positions of church office.

M. M. Edelstein, "The Social Origins of the Episcopacy in the Reign of Francis I," *French Historical Studies* 8 (1974): 377–92; R. J. Knecht, *Francis I* (1982).

SCOTT M. MARR

Bolsec, Jerome

Bolsec, Jerome (c. 1524–1584), French physician and critic of Calvin's predestinarian doctrine. A former Carmelite monk, Bolsec left Paris for religious refuge in the court of the duchess of Ferrara. By 1550 he had moved into the environs of Geneva and was attending the weekly Genevan Congregations, occasions on which exegetical and theological matters were discussed.

In one such meeting in October 1551, Bolsec challenged the orthodoxy and the biblical grounding of reprobation, an aspect of Calvin's teaching on predestination. Bolsec maintained that Calvin portrayed God as a tyrant and the author of evil; a theologically more sound position would emphasize God's prevenient grace, while giving greater weight to human freedom to respond to grace. Bolsec's charge implied that Geneva was disseminating erroneous doctrine and thereby tarnished the reputation of the political regime. He was arrested and tried by the city magistrates who sought advice from the churches of Bern, Basel, and Zurich, advice not strongly supportive of Calvin's doctrinal position. The magistrates, who had a history of tension with Calvin, imposed a relatively mild form of punishment: expulsion from Geneva.

Bolsec made his way to Bern and eventually returned to France and to the Catholic faith. In his last years he wrote scathing and scurrilous accounts of the lives of Calvin and Theodore Beza that supplied the basis for Catholic anti-Calvinist propaganda for generations to come.

P. C. Holtrop, *The Bolsec Controversy on Predestination, from 1551–1555*, 2 vols. (1993).
                              CHRISTOPHER ELWOOD

Bonaventure, St. (c. 1221–1274), Italian Franciscan friar, scholastic theologian, minister general of the Franciscan order, cardinal bishop of Albano, doctor of the church, known as the "Seraphic Doctor." Born in Bagnoregio, not far from Viterbo, Bonaventure was baptized with the name John of Fidanza. His earliest education was undertaken with the Franciscan friars in the town of his birth. After this, probably around 1234, he went to Paris, where he became a master of the arts. He entered the Franciscan order around 1243 and began the study of theology under Alexander of Hales, whom he described as his "master and father." In 1248, he became a bachelor of Scripture. By 1253, he had completed his commentary on the *Sentences* of Peter Lombard. Because of a conflict between the secular masters and the mendicants he was not recognized as a master until 1257. By that time, he had already been elected as minister general of the friars to replace John of Parma in that office.

This brought his academic career at Paris to an end, though in subsequent years he would give several series of lectures that dealt with problems confronting the friars in the context of the university. One set of problems came largely from the growing philosophical movement and dealt with the relation between philosophy and theology. A different set of problems was related to the influence of Joachim of Fiore's theology among the friars. Joachim's theology of history looked to a future age of the Spirit that would move beyond the age of the Son and the institutional church that played such a basic role in that age. The Joachite view tended to draw on apocalyptic themes to predict the end of the institutional church and the flowering of a church as a purely contemplative community. This raised both christological and ecclesiological problems that Bonaventure, as a theologian and minister general of the friars, had to address.

Beyond his early writings in the university context, he has left ascetical and mystical writings as well as a rich collection of sermons. In 1273, while he was delivering a series of lectures at Paris, *On the Six Days of Creation*, Pope Gregory X appointed him cardinal and bishop of Albano and called him to participate in the Council of Lyon. He was actively involved in the preparation of the council and in the work of the council itself, especially in the discussion with the Eastern Christians. Toward the end of the council, he became ill and died. He was canonized on April 14, 1482, by Pope Sixtus IV and declared to be a doctor of the church by Pope Sixtus V in 1588.

J. G. Bougerol, *Introduction to the Works of Bonaventure* (1964); E. Cousins, *Bonaventure and the Coincidence of Opposites* (1978); I. Delio, *Simply Bonaventure: An Introduction to His Life, Thought, and Writings* (2001); E. Gilson, *The Philosophy of St. Bonaventure* (1965); Z. Hayes, *The Hidden Center: Spirituality and Speculative Christology in St. Bonaventure* (1981); K. Osborne, ed., *The History of Franciscan Theology* (1994), 39–125.
                              ZACHARY HAYES, OFM

Boneta, Na Prous (d. 1328), a Beguine of Carcassonne. Arrested in 1325 with her sister Alisseta, she was accused of hiding Franciscan Spirituals and Beguines, who, like others, regarded Peter John Olivi as a saint and venerated his tomb at Narbonne. Her testimony before an inquisitor in Carcassonne provides a frank and vivid account of the radical adaptation of Olivi's views among Franciscan Spirituals, and evidence of the synthesis of an intense mysticism, religious poverty, and the conviction that Pope John XXII was the antichrist. She was executed in 1328.

D. Burr, *The Spiritual Franciscans* (2001); Burr, "Na Prous Boneta and Olivi," *Collectanea franciscana* 67 (1997): 277–300; B. Newman, *From Virile Woman to Woman Christ* (1995); "Na Prous Bonett" (David Burr's abridged translation of her deposition at Carcassone in August 1325), http://www.ford ham.edu/halsall/source/naprous.html (2007).
                              CHRISTOPHER OCKER

Boniface (c. 672/675–754), saint, missionary, cloister founder, and archbishop. Born "Wynfrith" in Exeter (Wessex, England), the future "Apostle of Germany" died as a martyr at Dokkum (Frisia) and is buried in Fulda (Germany). Wynfrith was born to an Anglo-Saxon noble and was given at an early age to the care of the cloister of Exeter. Around 700 he transferred to the Benedictine abbey of Nursling (at Winchester), where he rose to the position of school master and composed works of grammar and metrical composition.

Following the ideal of the *peregrinatio Christi*, the pilgrimage of Christ, he went in 716 on a mission to Frisia, which failed. In spite of his election as abbot of Nursling after his return, he left his homeland for good three years later, in order to follow his calling as a missionary. In Rome, on May 15, 719, he received from Pope Gregory II a commission to Germany and the new Roman name Boniface. His first missionary journey brought him to the Thuringians, to the Frisians again in 719 (together with Willibrord), and to the Hessians in 721. In Hessia, he established his first two cloisters, Amöneburg and Fritzlar. The opposition of the east Frisian clergy required him to journey again to Rome in 722, where the pope consecrated him the mission's bishop. An additional journey to the court of the Frankish ruler Charles Martel brought him Charles's protection. Boniface returned to the mission of the Hessians and Thuringians with increased authority.

In order to build up a church oriented toward Rome east of the Rhine, Pope Gregory III elevated Boniface to archbishop of the mission in the year 732. After additional cloister foundations in Ochsenfurt, Kitzingen, and Tauberbischofsheim and a third journey to Rome, Boniface, in 739, reformed the Bavarian dioceses of Freising, Passau, Regensburg, and Salzburg. In 741, he founded the bishoprics of Würzburg, Büraburg, and Erfurt. Under his leadership, the *concilium Germanicum* (743), a church synod sponsored by Carloman, the mayor of the palace, decided on a comprehensive reform program. Supported by Carloman, Boniface undertook the reform of the Frankish church, but he failed, especially after Carloman's retirement (747) and in the face of opposition by Frankish clergy. The bishopric of Mainz, which was given to him, he gave to his student Lul, and the cloister he founded at Fulda he placed directly under the pope before he returned again to the Frisian mission, this time as an old man, where he suffered the death of a martyr on June 5, 754. An important saint's cult developed at his grave in Fulda.

———

MGH, *Epp. select*, 1; MGH, *Script. rer. Germ. schol*, 57; MGH, *Concilia* 2; T. Schieffer, *Winfrid-Bonifatius und die christliche Grundlegung Europas* (1954); T. Reuther, ed., *The Greatest Englishman: Essays on St. Boniface* (1980); J. Wallace-Hadrill, *The Frankish Church* (1983); L. Padberg, *Bonifatius* (2003); F.-J. Felten, ed., *Bonifatius—Apostel der Deutschen* (2004).

JÖRG OBERSTE

Boniface I (d. 422), bishop of Rome (418–422). Born in Rome, Boniface emerged as victor in the struggle with Eulalius for the contested see in Rome. When the emperor Honorius learned that both men had been ordained on the same day, he ordered them to vacate the city until the issue was resolved. When Eulalius returned to the city at Easter, Honorius ejected him from Rome with the help of fifty-two bishops and appointed Boniface bishop of Rome.

During the Pelagian crisis, Boniface supported Augustine's efforts to counteract the spread of Pelagianism. Augustine expressed his gratitude by dedicating *Answer to the Two Letters of the Pelagians* to him. In this work Augustine recounts how Alypius's conversations with Boniface assured him of the pontiff's friendship. Boniface also upheld Zosimus's condemnation of Pelagius and Caelestius.

The matter was otherwise in the case of Antonius, the lector ordained bishop of Fussala, due to Augustine's own misjudgment. When Augustine resumed control of Antonius's jurisdiction because of his ineptitude, Antonius manipulated Boniface into reinstating him. After Boniface's death, Augustine appealed to his successor Caelestine for help. How the problem was resolved remains unknown.

———

J. H. Baxter, trans., *Select Letters (Letter 209)*, LCL 239 (repr. 1993); *CPL* (1995): 1648–49; R. Davis, trans., *The Book of Pontiffs* (2nd ed., 2000); R. Teske, trans., *Answer to the Two Letters of the Pelagians*, 1/24 of *Works of St. Augustine* (1998).

MARIANNE DJUTH

Boniface VIII (c. 1234–1303), medieval pope who clashed with the French monarchy. Boniface took his early training at Todi and Spoleto, became a canon at Paris and Rome, and joined the papal curia in 1276. He was appointed cardinal-deacon in 1281 and cardinal-priest in

1291. He encouraged the abdication of Pope Celestine V and was elected pope in 1294. He was concerned to pacify Europe under his spiritual leadership and liberate the Holy Land, in neither of which he succeeded. The conflict between Boniface and the French monarchy, however, overshadows all other aspects of his pontificate.

While Boniface proposed no novel doctrine of papal power, he asserted his position more intractably and less diplomatically than his predecessors. His conflict with King Edward I of England and especially King Philip IV of France over ecclesiastical property, taxation, and clerical immunities was defining and disastrous for Boniface. To articulate his position he promulgated the bulls *Asculta fili* (1301) and *Unam Sanctam* (1302), the most forceful statements of papal supremacy in the Middle Ages.

A coalition of Philip's supporters and alienated cardinals arrested Boniface on September 7, 1303, abused him, and attempted to secure his abdication. He died a month later, defeated by growing national sentiment and his own inflexible temperament.

———

T. Boase, *Boniface VIII* (1933); G. Digard et al., *Les Registres de Boniface* (1904–1939); W. Ullmann, *Medieval Papalism* (1949); C. Wood, *Philip the Fair and Boniface VIII* (1971).

LORNA SHOEMAKER

Book of Advertisements *see* Advertisements, Book of

Book of Common Prayer From its initial publication under Edward VI in 1549, the Book of Common Prayer, in different editions, versions, and languages, has served as a touchstone of ecclesial unity and liturgical continuity for the member churches of the Anglican Communion. Chief architect for the first edition in 1549, and the more radical one in 1552, was Thomas Cranmer, archbishop of Canterbury. Translating, revising, and creatively adapting, Cranmer shaped the English language as he appropriated diverse resources: the Sarum (Salisbury) Use (the Latin liturgy most widespread in England), Eastern liturgy, Lutheran and continental Reformed rites. Comprehensive and concise, the Book of Common Prayer replaced a virtual library of Latin service books that had been expensive for clergy and inaccessible to the laity. With its price regulated by the crown and its rubrics simplified by Cranmer, the Book of Common Prayer, with the Great Bible, provided everything necessary for a reformed English liturgy, as a composite of *Missal* (Eucharist), *Breviary* (daily office), *Processional* (litany), and *Manual* (pastoral offices). The Book of Common Prayer continues in use today, whether in a historical form supplemented by a separate volume as in England (*Book of Common Prayer 1662* and *Common Worship* [2000]), or in a periodically revised edition as in the United States (*Book of Common Prayer 1979*).

———

G. Cuming, *The Godly Order: Texts and Studies Relating to the Book of Common Prayer* (1983); D. MacCollouch, *Thomas Cranmer: A Life* (1996); L. Pullan, *The History of the Book of Common Prayer* (1977).

PETER J. SCAGNELLI

Book of Concord (1580), a collection of Lutheran confessions of faith. After Luther's death, controversies broke out among his followers over the precise definition of aspects of his thought, particularly regarding justification by faith and related questions (the role of the will in conversion and the use of the law in the Christian life), and regarding the Lord's Supper and related christological issues (1549–1577). With princely support and encouragement, theologians under the leadership of Jakob Andreae, Martin Chemnitz, David Chytraeus, and others composed a "Formula of Concord," which won acceptance by two-thirds of the German Evangelical churches (1577–1578). This document was published in 1580 together with the Apostles', Nicene, and Athanasian creeds, Philip Melanchthon's Augsburg Confession and Apology, Luther's Large and Small catechisms and Schmalkald Articles, and Melanchthon's *Treatise on the Power and Primacy of the Pope* as a standard for public teaching in the principalities that accepted it. Andreae interpreted the book's background and significance in its preface. Reformed theologians and some disciples of Melanchthon protested against it. It was later adopted as an official summary of belief by other German churches and by the Church of Sweden (and Finland) in 1663, as well as by some central European Lutherans and Lutheran immigrant and mission churches around the world.

———

I. Dingel, *Concordia controversa* (1996); G. Gassmann and S. Hendrix, *Introduction to the Lutheran Confessions* (1999); R. Kolb and T. Wengert, *The Book of Concord* (2000); G. Wenz, *Theologie der Bekenntnisschriften der evangelisch-lutherischen Kirche*, 2 vols. (1996, 1997).

ROBERT KOLB

Bora, Katharina von   *see* Katharina von Bora

Bordeaux Pilgrim The designation refers to the first recorded Christian pilgrim to the Holy Land from Western Europe. The *Itinerarium Burdigalense* is the record of this anonymous pilgrim's journey and is accepted as genuine. This short, dry account contains almost no personal or theological observations. The itinerary, prior to the Holy Land, is basically a listing of towns the pilgrim passed through (and where lodging may have been found) and the distances between them. Inside the Holy Land the itinerary often provides only a brief description of the biblical event which supposedly took place at that particular site.

The pilgrim set out in 333 from Bordeaux and traveled through Milan, the Adriatic coast, Macedonia, and across the Bosporous to Constantinople. The route then went through Asia Minor to Antioch, down the coast through Laodicea, Beirut, and Sidon, finally ending in Jerusalem. While in Jerusalem the pilgrim tried to visit every site mentioned in the Gospels, also making two side excursions: one to Jericho and the Jordan River and the second to Bethlehem and Hebron. Returning by way of Rome, the itinerary ends in Milan in 334.

L. Douglass, "A New Look at the *Itinerarium Burdigalense*," *JECS* 4 (1996): 313–33; A. Stewart, trans., *Itinerarium Burdigalense: Itinerary from Bordeaux to Jerusalem, the Bordeaux Pilgrim* (1887).

WILLIAM B. SWEETSER JR.

Borgia, Caesar (1475–1507), Italian prince and soldier. The illegitimate son of Pope Alexander VI, Borgia was appointed archbishop of Valencia and a cardinal while still a teenager. In 1499 he married Charlotte d'Albret, sister of the king of Navarre. Machiavelli is said to have based his portrait of *The Prince* upon Borgia, who was ruthless in reaching his goals. Nevertheless, he is also known for acting justly with his subjects. His father's papal successors were enemies of the Borgia family, and Caesar fled to Naples. Ferdinand of Aragon ordered his arrest, and he was brought to Spain but escaped to Navarre. There his brother-in-law employed him in military service and he was killed while besieging the castle of Vienna.

H. Jedin, ed., *History of the Church*, vol. 4 (1986); M. Mallett, *The Borgias: The Rise and Fall of a Renaissance Dynasty* (1987).

ELIZABETH GERHARDT

Borromeo, Charles (1538–1584), cardinal archbishop of Milan and a major proponent of the reforms mandated by the Council of Trent. The beginning of Borromeo's career coincided with his uncle's election as Pope Pius IV in 1559. In 1560 he was elevated to the cardinalate, appointed archbishop of Milan, and began to direct his uncle's administration, including oversight of the Council of Trent between 1561 and 1563. A turning point in his life was the death of his brother Federigo in 1562. Grief moved him to an austere form of life, the promotion of spiritual conversations among Vatican officials known as the *Noctes Vaticanae*, and attention to the pastoral needs of Rome. In 1565 he returned to Milan and convened the first provincial council of Milan to institute the reforms mandated by Trent. In 1566 he took up residence in Milan and turned his attention to his local church and the other dioceses of Lombardy. Through his own preaching, the convening of local synods, pastoral visitations, the establishment of a seminary in Milan, the promotion of religious orders, and the foundation of a variety of charitable institutions, Borromeo came to represent the ideal of the reformed bishop of the Tridentine era. The publication of the *Acta ecclesiae Mediolensis*, which recorded these activities, made Borromeo's the best-known model for diocesan reform in early modern Catholicism. Borromeo's career was not without political controversy, as he frequently entered into conflict with Philip II's Spanish governors over the independence of the church from temporal authority. He was canonized by Pope Paul V in 1610.

W. de Boer, *The Conquest of the Soul: Confession, Discipline, and Public Order in Counter Reformation Milan* (2001); J. M. Headley and J. B. Tomara, eds., *San Carlo Borromeo, Catholic Reform, and Ecclesiastical Politics in the Second Half of the Sixteenth Century* (1988).

PAUL V. MURPHY

Bossuet, Jacques-Bénigne (1627–1704), French bishop of Meaux, famed preacher, and tutor to Louis XV (r. 1670–1681). He drew up the Four Gallican Articles and secured the French clergy's support for them, advocated the Revocation of the Edict of

Nantes (1685), and supported French royal absolutism. His *Histoire des Églises protestantes* (1688) is the most significant of his numerous works against Protestantism, in part due to his use of primary sources and for his well-informed, if biased, theological arguments with the Reformers. Bossuet argued that Protestants are heretics, inevitably divided among themselves and perpetually reinventing Christianity, because they endorse individual judgment in contrast to the authority of the universal church. Bossuet contended that true Christianity, by contrast, is summarized in the Vincentian Canon: "what has been believed everywhere, always, and by all." He engaged in a long (though ultimately fruitless) ecumenical dialogue with the Lutheran philosopher Gottfried Wilhelm Leibniz.

———

E. E. Reynolds, *Bossuet* (1963).

RODERICK MARTIN

Bradwardine, Thomas (c. 1300–1349),
archbishop of Canterbury. Bradwardine was one of the most prominent English thinkers and ecclesiastics of the early fourteenth century. At Oxford, he was at the center of a group of masters affiliated with Merton College who came to be known for their quantitative approach in understanding motion (the "Oxford Calculators"). In his *De proportionibus velocitatum motuum*, Bradwardine provided an analysis of velocity in terms of the proportion of force to resistance ("Bradwardine's rule"). After his regency, he became part of the household of Richard of Bury, who advanced his ecclesiastical career. In 1337, Bradwardine became chancellor of St. Paul's and shortly afterward confessor to Edward III; in 1349 he was consecrated archbishop of Canterbury. His main theological work is the monumental *De causa Dei*, directed against allegedly contemporary adherents of the heretic Pelagius, such as William of Ockham and Thomas Buckingham. These theologians believed that human beings do not need grace in order to gain salvation. In contrast, Bradwardine emphasized the necessity of grace. In modern studies, Bradwardine has been presented as a supporter of Wyclif and as a precursor of the Reformation.

———

G. Leff, *Bradwardine and the Pelagians* (1957); H. A. Oberman, *Archbishop Thomas Bradwardine: A Fourteenth-Century Augustinian* (1958); J. E. Weisheipl, "Reportorium Mertonense," *Mediaeval Studies* 31 (1969): 172–224; E. W. Dolnikowski, *Thomas Brad-*

wardine, A View on Time and a Vision of Eternity in Fourteenth-Century Thought (1995).

J. M. M. H. THIJSSEN

Brant, Sebastian (1457–1521), Alsatian
poet, humanist, and satirist. He was born in Strasbourg, the son of an innkeeper and his wife. His father died when he was young, but he received a good education through the care of his mother. He moved to Basel in 1475 and attended the university there, ultimately earning his doctoral degree in both canon and civil law in 1489. He remained to teach literature and law and published a law textbook in 1490, also doing significant editorial work for Froben, Amerbach, and other publishers. His 1494 publication of the *Narrenschiff* won him considerable fame. Originally written in German, the book was widely translated into Latin and other languages.

Brandt was a lifelong conservative, loyal to the Holy Roman Empire and the Roman church. His critiques of immorality in the *Narrenschiff* reflect his deep piety as well as his learning. Other works include *Varia Carmina* (1498), based on an earlier collection in praise of the Virgin Mary, to whom Brandt was especially devoted. He was a friend of Reuchlin but did not defend him when in 1513 he came under attack by the Dominicans. In 1501 Brant returned to Strasbourg as legal advisor to the city after Basel joined the Swiss Confederacy; there he became a part of Jakob Wimpfeling's circle. He is significant for publishing in German as well as Latin, out of his sense of identity as a German and his desire to reach the masses.

———

S. Brant, *The Ship of Fools*, ed. and trans. E. H. Zeydel (1944); M. A. Rajewski, *Sebastian Brant: Studies in Religious Aspects of His Life and Works with Special Reference to the Varia Carmina* (1944); H. Vredeveld, "Materials for a New Commentary to Sebastian Brant's *Narrenschiff*" in *Daphnis* 26, no. 4 (1997): 553–651; E. H. Zeydel, *Sebastian Brant* (1967).

J. LAUREL CARRINGTON

Brenz, Johannes (1499–1570), the leading
reformer in southern Germany during the sixteenth century. Brenz studied in Heidelberg, where he was impacted by humanism and learned Greek from Johannes Oecolampadius. He also met Luther there in 1518 and was immediately attracted to the Reformer's emerging evangelical theology. In 1522 he was appointed preacher at St. Michael, the chief parish church in Schwäbisch-Hall, and began to introduce the Reformation by 1524. He proceeded deliber-

ately and diplomatically and did not celebrate the first evangelical mass until Christmas Day, 1526. In 1528 Brenz produced one of the first evangelical catechisms, a 1535 version of which appeared in more than four hundred editions. Brenz also began to serve as advisor to Margrave George of Brandenburg-Ansbach and to the city council of Nuremberg in 1528 as they promoted the Reformation in their territories. He attended the Marburg Colloquy in 1529, and he was a member of the margrave's entourage at the Diet of Ausburg in 1530. He married Margarethe Gräter Wetzel that same year and had nineteen children with her and his second wife, Katherine Eisenmenger (1550). When Duke Ulrich was restored to power in 1534, he invited Brenz to reform the church in Württemberg. This work continued under the patronage of Duke Christopher after 1550. Brenz published a church order for the duchy in 1536, taught at the Univ. of Tübingen in 1537–1538, and reorganized the university during that time. In 1548 he was compelled to leave Schwäbisch-Hall because of the Augsburg Interim and lived in exile until he was appointed provost of the collegiate church in Stuttgart in 1553. He now held the most important ecclesiastical position in the duchy as he continued to work closely with Duke Christopher in reforming the church. The "Great Church Order" of 1559 marks the culmination of Brenz's organizational efforts. However, he remained a tireless proponent of the Lutheran movement until the end of his life.

Brenz's contributions to the Reformation were diverse. While his writings deserve more careful study, he is generally recognized as one of the leading first-generation Lutheran thinkers. Like Luther, he was essentially a biblical theologian and produced commentaries on twenty scriptural books. The doctrine of justification was central to his theology, although, unlike Melanchthon, he did not stress the dialectic of law and gospel or a forensic understanding. Brenz was an early and persistent defender of the real presence in the eucharistic debates of the sixteenth century (Syngramma Suevicum, 1525). He developed his Christology in the context of his eucharistic thought and stressed the divine nature of Christ, the personal unity of Jesus with God, and the ubiquity of Christ's human nature in light of the communicatio idiomatum. Brenz was also one of the most important organizers of the evangelical church, and the organizational structures formulated in the "Great Church Order" became a model for other Lutheran territorial churches in Germany. He proposed a centralized polity under the ulti-

mate authority of the prince. A consistory of theologians and secular councilors administered the normal affairs of the church, including the appointment and dismissal of pastors, the payment of salaries, and the administration of church property. The consistory also constituted itself as the synodus in order to legislate and exercise discipline. Superintendents supervised congregations and pastors. With regard to ethical and practical matters, Brenz strongly opposed the Peasants' War, although he was empathetic to the demands of the peasants and criticized the unjust policies of the princes. He counseled leniency after the defeat of the peasants and rejected capital punishment when dealing with Anabaptists and other dissenters. While he was willing to criticize temporal authority, he respected it highly, especially the imperial office. Thus, he opposed the Wittenberg defense of the right of resistance.

With his biblical commentaries, theological writings, and postils, Brenz impacted the Lutheran community, especially in Würtemberg, for centuries. He may also be viewed as the chief architect of the territorial church in Germany.

———

M. Brecht, *Johannes Brenz: Neugestalter von Kirche, Staat und Gesellschaft* (1971); J. Estes, *Christian Magistrate and State Church: The Reforming Career of Johannes Brenz* (1982); H. M. Maurer and K. Ulshöfer, *Johannes Brenz und die Reformation in Württemberg* (1974).

KURT K. HENDEL

Brès, Guy de (1522–1567), reformer of the Low Countries and principal author of the Belgic Confession. Born in Mons and raised in an age of harsh religious repression in the Habsburg-ruled Netherlands, de Brès turned to the Reformation as a young man and embarked on a career of preaching punctuated by periodic exile in England, Switzerland, and France. His stays in London, Lausanne, and Geneva facilitated studies in Calvinist theology and led to important contacts within the internationally emergent Calvinist movement. Active mainly in the southern Netherlands and serving as pastor in and around Lille (1552–1556) and Tournai (1559–1563), de Brès organized Reformed "churches under the cross" in the region. While his efforts were marked by a conciliatory spirit toward the king, they were nonetheless viewed as acts of rebellion in the context of the Dutch Revolt. After exile in Sedan (1563–1566), de Brès returned to Valenciennes, where he became pastor and continued to promote church reform. Public demonstrations of Reformed faith in the city led to its siege by Margaret of Parma in 1566 and to de Brès' imprisonment and execution. His most durable legacy lies in the Belgic Confession, which became a primary doctrinal statement of Dutch Reformed churches. Further works include the apologetic *Le baston de la foy chrestienne* (1555) and a controversialist rejection of the rival Anabaptist movement, *La racine, source, et fondement des Anabaptistes* (1565).

E. M. Braekman, *Guy de Brès: Sa vie* (1960); T. Kaufmann, *Reformatoren* (1998).

KENNETH G. APPOLD

Brethren of the Common Life A medieval association, also known as the *Devotio Moderna*, founded to establish a Christian life of devotion and higher morality. The group was organized in 1374 by Geert Groote after being approached by a group of poor women who desired to live an exemplary Christian life. In 1379, Groote wrote guidelines for community life that required no vows and allowed members to continue in their ordinary vocations. Brethren communities emphasized a higher spirituality, a moral life, and the communal distribution of money and goods; they were also known for their obedience, charity, and poverty.

Brethren schools were established throughout the Netherlands and later in Germany. After the death of Groote in 1384, Florentius Radewijns became head of the Brethren. Radewijns had established the first community for men, and under his direction schools and communities flourished and the center of Brethren life moved to Zwolle. A group of Brethren adopted a rule and organized themselves as Augustinian canons. Thomas à Kempis, Pope Hadrian VI, and Gabriel Biel were widely known members of the Brethren, and the association was very influential in the area of education and the New Learning. The rise of universities and seminaries led to their demise in the late seventeenth century. *See also* Modern Devotion.

R. R. Post, *The Modern Devotion: Confrontation with Reformation and Humanism* (1968); J. Van Engen, *Devotio Moderna: Basic Writings* (1988).

ELIZABETH GERHARDT

Briçonnet, Guillaume (c. 1470–1534), reforming bishop of Meaux, France, and patron of scholars. The son of a wealthy family of Tours that served the king of France, Briçonnet received an education in humanism and law. He was made a bishop (1489) while still a student,

and his accomplished career in the church included being the queen's chaplain (1496), a canon of Paris (1503), and abbot of Saint Germain-des-Prés (1507). He held other titles, benefices, and revenues as well. In 1516–1517 he negotiated the Concordat of Bologna with Pope Leo X for King Francis I. Briçonnet is best known for his support of the French translation of the Bible by Jacques Lefèvre d'Étaples and promotion of vernacular biblical preaching. His short-lived "Meaux Group" of reformers, which included Gérard Roussel and Guillaume Farel, was protected by the sister of Francis I, Marguerite d'Angoulême. When it became obvious that Luther's teachings were present in Meaux, the theology faculty of Paris became alarmed and Briçonnet was challenged before the Parlement of Paris. He then withdrew his support of the "Meaux Group" and it disbanded.

M. Veissière, *L'evêque Guillaume Briçonnet, 1470–1534: Contribution à la connaissance de la Réforme catholique à la veille du Council de Trente* (1986).

JEANNINE E. OLSON

Brigitte of Sweden (1303–1373), patron saint of Sweden, founder of a religious order. Born in Finstad near Uppsala, daughter of Birgir Persson, a great landowner and governor and chief judge of Uppland, and niece of St. Ingrid, Brigitte was eleven when her mother Ingeborg Bengtsdotter died, who had experienced a vision of the Virgin foretelling Brigitte's birth and spirituality. At seven Brigitte began to experience visions of the crucified Christ and Satan. She was married at thirteen to Ulf Gudmarson, later governor of Nercia, with whom she bore eight children, including St. Catherine of Sweden. As lady-in-waiting to the queen, she enjoyed influence at the court. After a pilgrimage (1341/1343) to Santiago de Compostela, Ulf died at the Cistercian monastery of Alvastra and Brigitte entered the Cistercian monastery at Vadstena. Here she continued to receive revelations, largely during meditations on the passion of Christ, who recognized her as his bride. She wrote down these visions in Swedish (over six hundred), which dealt with such themes as the reform of the monastic life and the infant Jesus. They were translated into Latin by her confessor Matthias Magister and Prior Peter Olafsson. Brigitte founded the Order of the Most Holy Savior for both men and women (the Brigittines) under the rule of St. Augustine (confirmed in 1370 by Pope Urban V), which was well endowed by King Magnus II Eriksson and his wife. Several houses still exist in England, Germany, Rome, the U.S., and elsewhere. Brigitte traveled to Rome in 1349, where she established a hospice for Swedish pilgrims and students, and remained until 1373 as an informal papal advisor (urging the return of the papacy from Avignon), dying after returning from a pilgrimage to the Holy Land. In 1391 Brigitte was canonized by Pope Boniface IX following an extensive hearing, and on October 1, 1999, she was declared the protector of Europe by Pope John Paul II.

R. Ellis, ed., *The Liber Celestis of St Bridget of Sweden: The Middle English Version in British Library MS Claudius B i, Together with a Life of the Saint from the Same Manuscript* (1987); B. Gregersson and T. Gascoigne, *The Life of Saint Birgitta* (1991); M. T. Harris, ed., *Life and Selected Revelations: Birgitta of Sweden* (1990); B. Morris, *St. Birgitta of Sweden* (1999); C. L. Sahlin, *Birgitta of Sweden and the Voice of Prophecy* (2001).

MICHAEL GOODICH†

Browne, Robert (c. 1550–1633), English separatist. Born near Stamford in Lincolnshire and educated at Corpus Christi College, Cambridge, Browne was influenced by Thomas Cartwright and others advocating Presbyterian polity. He rapidly established a reputation as an extreme critic of the established church, particularly with regard to the matter of episcopal authority. He argued for an independent church government with congregations electing their own leaders. By 1581 he had become a separatist and established his own congregation in Norwich. His outspokenness led to imprisonment; upon release, he settled in the Netherlands, where he developed an understanding of the covenant that distinguished him from Puritan contemporaries.

In 1584 he traveled to Scotland, where he was imprisoned briefly. He then returned to England, submitted to the authority of the archbishop of Canterbury, and became master of St. Olave's School in Southwark in 1586. He was ordained in 1591 and installed as rector in Northamptonshire. In 1617 he was accused once again of failing to conform to the Book of Common Prayer. In 1631 he was excommunicated and died in Northampton in 1633.

A. Peel and L. H. Carlson, eds., *The Writings of Robert Harrison and Robert Browne* (1953).

CARL TRUEMAN

Bruegel, Pieter (the Elder) (c. 1525–1569), Dutch painter who worked in Antwerp.

Bruegel specialized in scenes of peasant life, which he observed with a sharp eye for detail and a mordant sense of irony. Typical examples include *The Wedding Feast* (c. 1566), *The Peasant Dance* (c. 1567), and *The Parable of the Blind* (1568). Popular proverbs provided the source for anecdotal activities in *Carnival and Lent* (1559), *Netherlandish Proverbs* (1559), or *Children's Games* (1560). His panoramic landscapes reflect humanist interest in the natural world. Bruegel depicted the changing seasons in a series of panels, with subtle tonal harmonies and visual evocation of atmospheric conditions. The two best known are *The Harvesters* (1565) and *Hunters in the Snow* (1565). Bruegel's terrifyingly apocalyptic *Triumph of Death* (c. 1562), with its scorched landscape and skeletal figures, depicts the devastation of war, surely a response to the religious wars raging in the Netherlands in the sixteenth century.

P. Freeman, *Images of the Medieval Peasant* (1999); E. M. Kavaler, *Pieter Bruegel: Parables of Order and Enterprise* (1999); E. Snow, *Inside Bruegel: The Play of Images in Children's Games* (1997); M. A. Sullivan, *Bruegel's Peasants: Art and Audience in the Northern Renaissance* (1994).

PRISCILLA BAUMANN

Brunfels, Otto (c. 1488–1534), German humanist, evangelical, teacher, botanist, and physician. Born in Mainz, Brunfels entered the Strasbourg Carthusian monastery about 1510. Sympathetic to Martin Luther, Brunfels fled the monastery in 1521 under the protection of Ulrich von Hutten, a knight and poet, and Johann Schott, a printer. With recommendation to Ulrich Zwingli, Brunfels traveled toward Zurich but halted en route and was appointed pastor at Neuenburg. Following a dispute with Erasmus in 1524 regarding Hutten, Brunfels returned to Strasbourg, opened a school, and married Dorothea Help. Brunfels, skilled in Greek, wrote biblical concordances and biographies of biblical figures. Theologically, Brunfels leaned toward the spirituality of Andreas Karlstadt rather than the theology of Martin Bucer and Wolfgang Capito. Around 1530 Brunfels turned to science and medicine, writing a botanical text listing plants and their medicinal uses. He moved to Bern, received a medical doctorate, and was appointed city physician in 1533 but died the following year.

O. Brunfels, *Herbarum vivae eicones ad naturae imitationem* (1530); M. U. Chrisman, *Lay*

Culture, Learned Culture: Books and Social Change in Strasbourg, 1480–1599 (1982); S. Weigelt, *Otto Brunfels: Seine Wirksamkeit in der frühbürgerlichen Revolution unter besondere Berücksichtigung seiner Flugschrift "Vom Pfaffenzehnten"* (1986).

SUZANNE S. HEQUET

Bruno the Carthusian (c. 1032–1101), founder of the Carthusian order. Bruno of Cologne, or Bruno the Carthusian, founded the monastery of La Grande Chartreuse in the Alps, mother house of the Carthusian order. Bruno, a native of Cologne, was educated there and at Reims. He became a canon in Cologne and then served as a master of the cathedral school of Reims for eighteen years, rising to the position of diocesan chancellor. However, Bruno became so disillusioned by the scandalous behavior of Archbishop Manasses of Reims that he returned to Cologne and decided to become a monk.

Like many monastic reformers of the eleventh century, Bruno could not find a religious life that suited him. He spent some time as a hermit under Robert of Molesmes, after which he and six companions decided to form their own monastery, with the assistance of Bishop Hugh of Grenoble. The monastic way of life Bruno established at La Grande Chartreuse in 1084 looked for inspiration to the early hermits and monks of Egypt and Palestine rather than the Rule of Benedict. Carthusian monks lived, for the most part, in separate cells, gathering only in the church for a liturgical round much reduced from that of contemporary monasteries. Thus, they emphasized contemplation and a more individual spiritual life than was available elsewhere at that time.

In 1090 Bruno's former student, Pope Urban II, called his old master away from the monastery he had created, demanding his advice on ecclesiastical affairs. So Bruno moved to Italy and served as a papal advisor. At first he settled in a hermitage among the ruins of the Baths of Diocletian, then with some new disciples founded the monastery of La Torre in Calabria, where he died in retirement.

B. Bligny, *Saint Bruno, le premier chartreux* (1984); C. H. Lawrence, *Medieval Monasticism* (2nd ed., 1989); G. Mursell, *The Theology of the Carthusian Life in the Writings of St. Bruno and Guigo* (1988).

PHYLLIS G. JESTICE

Bruno, Giordono (1548–1600), Italian Renaissance Neoplatonic philosopher. Born in Naples, he joined the Dominican order there in 1562 but abandoned it and fled when accused of heresy in 1576. Bruno then traveled extensively throughout Europe but encountered difficulties wherever he went. He was captured in Venice in 1592 and spent the remainder of his life imprisoned in Rome until he was burned at the stake for heresy on February 17, 1600. Bruno regarded Christ as a wizard and hoped to transform Christianity into the magical religion he thought was practiced in ancient Egypt. Bruno was a great admirer of the work of Raymond Llull (c. 1233–1315), and much of his work involved recasting ancient or modern texts through the medium of Hermeticism. He admired, for example, the cosmic truths that could be gleaned from the work of Nicholas Copernicus, whom he nevertheless regarded as a "mere mathematician." The frequent and simplistic depiction of him as a pantheist is inaccurate and misleading.

E. Cassirer, *The Individual and the Cosmos in Renaissance Philosophy* (1963); A. Koyré, *From the Closed World to the Infinite Universe* (1957); P. O. Kristeller, *Eight Philosophers of the Italian Renaissance* (1964); F. A. Yates, *Giordano Bruno and the Hermetic Tradition* (1964).

RODERICK MARTIN

Bucer, Martin (1491–1551), German reformer and church organizer. Born in Sélestat (Schlettstadt), Bucer entered the Dominican order at age fifteen and matriculated at Heidelberg Univ. in 1517. He attended Martin Luther's 1518 disputation and agreed with Luther's teachings. Obtaining papal dispensation from vows in 1521, Bucer became parish pastor under Franz von Sickingen and was married. He fled when von Sickingen was defeated in the Knights' War against ecclesiastical princes.

Bucer moved to Strasbourg in 1523 and joined reformers Matthew Zell, Caspar Hedio, and Wolfgang Capito in openly preaching reform. In 1524 Bucer was called—not appointed—by parishioners as pastor to St. Aurelien church in Strasbourg, marking the Strasbourg city magistracy's assumption of responsibility for pastoral appointments. Bucer and others continued to push for reform, and in 1529 city magistrates finally broke with the Roman church and abolished the mass.

Bucer's theology resembled Luther's, but with key differences. In an early publication, "That No One Should Live for Himself but for Others, and How We May Attain This," Bucer asserted that humans are justified by faith alone but each Christian is also responsible to serve others. As a reformer, Bucer attended many imperial diets and colloquies, including the

1529 Colloquy at Marburg, where Luther and Zwingli stated their differences concerning the nature of Christ's presence in the Lord's Supper. Luther held that Christ is physically present in the sacramental bread and wine. Bucer essentially agreed with Zwingli that Christ's body is spiritually present. Bucer's 1529 position came to vex Strasbourg at the 1530 Diet of Augsburg. To unify his German territories against invading Turkish armies, Charles V asked evangelical nobles to explain their religious positions. Their response was Philip Melanchthon's Augsburg Confession, which included Luther's teaching on the Lord's Supper. Since Strasbourg sided with Bucer against Luther on the Lord's Supper, their representatives could not sign Melanchthon's confession. Bucer and Capito hurried to Augsburg, where together they wrote the Tetrapolitan Confession for Strasbourg and three neighboring cities. The Tetrapolitan paralleled Melanchthon's confession but affirmed Christ's spiritual presence in the Lord's Supper. Later, both Bucer and Capito joined Protestants in signing the 1536 Wittenberg Concord, which mediated positions on the Lord's Supper.

In 1531 Bucer was appointed to the prestigious position of pastor at St. Thomas, the collegiate church in Strasbourg. In following years, he worked to organize the Strasbourg church. When dissident sects and radical groups attempted to establish independent churches, the city's 1534 church order set the confessional standard, bringing religious uniformity to a city that had been known for religious diversity.

In 1541 Charles V made his final attempt to resolve religious differences, calling for a colloquy at Regensburg. Bucer, together with Johannes Gropper, drafted the *Regensburg Book*, which was the focus for discussion. Collocutors reached tentative agreement on justification, but talks broke down over significant disagreements on transubstantiation, celibacy, authority to discern Scripture, and church reform.

Early in 1547, Bucer and other pastors called for parish discipline, particularly in preparation for the Lord's Supper. They established core groups, termed *ecclesiolae in ecclesia* or *christliche Gemeinschaften*, to instruct and discipline parishioners. Civil authorities and some church leaders objected to the groups. Following divisive debate, the city magistracy suppressed the movement.

In 1547 Charles V defeated the Protestant Schmalkald League. Bucer joined an attempt to block Strasbourg's reconciliation with Charles V, but when Jakob Sturm negotiated a settlement, Bucer fled, accepting the invitation of Thomas Cranmer to become Regius Professor of Divinity at Cambridge. After his death in 1551 he was buried in Great St. Mary's church at Cambridge. In 1556 Roman Catholic Queen Mary of England had his bones exhumed and burned. Queen Elizabeth I restored his tomb in 1560.

———

C. Augustijn, P. Fraenkel, and M. Lienhard, eds., *Martini Buceri Opera Latina*, 5 vols. (1982–2000); R. Stupperich, ed., *Martin Bucers Deutsche Schriften*, 17 vols. (1960–); J. Rott, ed., *Correspondance de Martin Bucer* (1979–). A. N. Burnett, *The Yoke of Christ: Martin Bucer and Christian Discipline* (1994); M. Greschat, *Martin Bucer: Ein Reformator und seine Zeit* (1990); J. M. Kittelson, *Toward an Established Church: Strasbourg from 1500 to the Dawn of the Seventeenth Century* (2000); C. Krieger and M. Lienhard, eds., *Martin Bucer and Sixteenth Century Europe: Actes du colloque de Strasbourg (28–31 août 1991)* (1993); V. Ortmann, *Reformation und Einheit der Kirche: Martin Bucers Einigungsbemühungen bei den religionsgesprächen in Leipzig, Hagenau, Worms und Regensburg 1539–1541* (2001); D. F. Wright, ed., *Martin Bucer: Reforming Church and Community* (1994).

SUZANNE S. HEQUET

Buchanan, George (1506–1582), Scottish humanist, neo-Latin poet, and tutor to Mary Queen of Scots and her son James VI. Born in a village in Stirlingshire, in his youth Buchanan studied and taught in Paris, where he was immersed in the circles of humanist poets and reformers. He returned to Scotland in 1534 and became tutor to James V's illegitimate son. From 1539 to 1547 he divided his time between Paris and Bordeaux, subsequently moving to Coimbra in Portugal to help establish the university. While there he was tried and condemned by the Inquisition; upon submitting to his judges he achieved his freedom in 1552. In 1561 he accompanied Mary Queen of Scots to Scotland, becoming a Protestant soon after. He joined forces with the anti-Marian faction subsequent to the murder of Darnley. His works, which made a major contribution to the development of a variety of genres, include the Psalm paraphrases, an assortment of tragedies, the *Rerum Scoticarum historia*, a group of anti-Franciscan satires, a set of love poems, the political treatise *De iure regni*, and the *Sphaera*, a scientific poem refuting Copernicus.

———

P. J. Ford, *George Buchanan: Prince of Poets* (1982); I. D. McFarlane, *Buchanan* (1981).

J. LAUREL CARRINGTON

Budé, Guillaume (1468–1540), French humanist, philologist, and legal scholar. Budé came from a respected family and received his education at Paris and Orleans. Originally intending to pursue a legal career, he changed course in 1491 and devoted himself to scholarship. A tireless worker despite ill health and a large family, Budé was regarded as the most accomplished Hellenist of his time, publishing an extensive commentary on the Greek language in 1529. His first major work was a philological study of Roman law, the *Annotations on the Pandects* (1508), followed by a study of Roman coinage, *The Whole and Its Parts* (1515).

A strong defender of French national glory, Budé is significant for participating in the developing national monarchy in France even as he devoted himself to the international community of scholars. He served at court and supported Francis I's crackdown on religious dissent following the Affair of the Placards in 1534, but wrote only one work in the vernacular, the *Education of the Prince* (1519). In 1530 Francis, at Budé's urging, established a group of regis professorships in classical languages that became the basis for the Collège de France.

G. Gadoffre, *La revolution culturelle dans la France des humanistes: Guillaume Budé et François Ier* (1997); M-M. de La Garanderie, *Christianisme et lettres profanes: essai sur l'humanisme français (1515–1535) et sur la pensée de Guillaume Budé* (2nd ed., 1997); D. O. McNeil, *Guillaume Budé and Humanism in the Reign of Francis I* (1975).

J. LAUREL CARRINGTON

Bugenhagen, Johannes (1485–1558), Pomeranian reformer and close colleague of Martin Luther. As an able theologian, interpreter of Scripture, pastor, educator, and organizer, Bugenhagen made crucial contributions to the Reformation, especially in northern Germany and parts of Scandinavia. He was born in Wollin, Pomerania, where his father was a city councilor. He studied in Greifswald for two years. In 1504 he became rector of the city school in Treptow on the Rega, and in 1509 he was ordained by the bishop of Cammin. Dissatisfied with medieval scholasticism, Bugenhagen was attracted to Erasmus and other humanist writers and was particularly interested in the study of the classical languages and of Scripture. In 1517 he was appointed biblical lecturer at the monastery school in Belbug and emerged as the leader of a circle of monks and priests interested in humanistic studies. When the Duke of Pomerania

requested that he write a chronicle, he published the *Pomerania* in 1518. In it he criticized abuses in the church, especially the neglect of scriptural studies. Bugenhagen became acquainted with Luther's works by 1520 and decided to study in Wittenberg. He arrived early in 1521 and began his studies in April, but he also lectured privately on the Psalms. Thereby he came to the attention of Melanchthon, who befriended him and encouraged him to give his popular lectures publicly. Luther was also impressed by Bugenhagen when he returned from the Wartburg, and Pomeranus, as he came to be known, quickly joined Luther's inner circle. When he married Walpurga in the fall of 1522, he became the first ordained Wittenberg reformer to take this audacious step. Three daughters and one son reached adulthood. In 1523 Luther supported Bugenhagen's election as pastor of the city church. In addition to his regular pastoral duties, Bugenhagen continued to teach at the university and to write. He also reformed the liturgy, reorganized the city school, established a poor chest, and participated in the visitation of the Saxon churches. In 1524 he rejected a call to Hamburg because of opposition from the city council. However, his pastoral concern for the people of Hamburg compelled him to write *Concerning the Christian Faith* for them in 1526. This seminal work not only addressed crucial theological themes but is also a precursor of his church orders. From 1528 to 1542 Bugenhagen traveled extensively, organizing and producing church orders for the evangelical churches in Braunschweig (1528), Hamburg (1528–1529), Lübeck (1530–1532), Pomerania (1534–1535), Denmark (1537–1539), Schleswig-Holstein (1542), Hildesheim (1542), and Braunschweig-Wolfenbüttel (1542). While in Denmark he crowned King Christian III, consecrated seven bishops, and reorganized the Univ. of Copenhagen. In 1532 Elector John Frederick appointed him superintendent of the Wittenberg region, and in 1533 he was awarded the doctorate and became a regular member of the theology faculty. Bugenhagen also assisted Luther in the translation of the Old Testament and produced a Low German translation of the Bible, which was published before the High German version. He was offered the bishoprics of Schleswig (1541) and Cammin (1544) but chose to remain in Wittenberg. The years after 1546 were difficult ones. The loss of Luther, the imperial siege of Wittenberg, the defeat of the Schmalkaldic League, the appointment of a new Elector, the controversy over the Interim, and the theological conflicts among the Lutherans affected Bugenhagen profoundly. Yet he continued to preach, teach, and write virtually to the end of his life.

Bugenhagen's contributions to the Reformation were multifaceted. He was Luther's pastor and *Seelsorger*, especially during Luther's persistent *Anfechtungen*. His numerous theological treatises and biblical commentaries focused on two major theological themes: the doctrine of justification, with the related topic of faith and works, and sacramentology, especially the defense of the real presence and infant baptism. His organizational contributions were truly formative. His detailed instructions in his church orders regarding the reform of the liturgy, education, and poor relief demonstrated a respect for the tradition, a sensitivity to local circumstances and needs, a deep commitment to the evangelical faith, and a conviction that theology must shape organizational structures. Both colleagues and opponents recognized Bugenhagen's impact upon the Reformation as a pastor, church leader, biblical interpreter, theologian, organizer, and social reformer.

A. Bieber, *Johannes Bugenhagen zwischen Reform und Reformation* (1993); G. Geisenhof, ed., *Bibliotheca Bugenhagiana* (1908, repr. 1963); V. Gummelt, *Lex et Evangelium: Untersuchungen zur Jesajavorlesung von Johannes Bugenhagen* (1994); H. H. Holfelder, *Solus Christus* (1981); Holfelder, *Tentatio et consolatio* (1974); R. Kötter, *Johannes Bugenhagens Rechtfertigungslehre und der römische Katholizismus* (1994).

KURT K. HENDEL

Bullinger, Heinrich

Bullinger, Heinrich (1504–1575), chief pastor (*Antistes*) at Zurich, Reformed theologian, and author of the Second Helvetic Confession. Bullinger, the youngest son of the parish priest at Bremgarten near Zurich, matriculated at the Univ. of Cologne in 1519. He received his MA in 1522 and in that same year embraced an evangelical position through his study of the church fathers and the New Testament. From 1523 until 1529 he lectured on the Bible to the monks at the Cistercian monastery at Kappel, near Zurich. In 1527 he attended lectures by Zwingli and studied Greek and Hebrew in Zurich. In 1529 he replaced his father as pastor of the church in Bremgarten, which had just embraced the Reformed teaching. In December 1531, after Ulrich Zwingli had died in the battle of Kappel, Bullinger was invited to become *Antistes* in Zurich, the position he held until his death more than forty-three years later.

Bullinger was the first reformer to develop an elaborate doctrine of the covenant, which became an extremely important theme in his theology. He used the concept of the covenant several times in his earlier writings, but he published his definitive work on the doctrine in 1534. In *The One and Eternal Testament or Covenant of God*, Bullinger argued that there was only one covenant in history. God first made the covenant with Adam, then renewed it with the Israelites through Abraham and Moses. When Christ fulfilled and renewed the covenant, the old rituals of circumcision and the Passover were replaced by baptism and the Eucharist. However, the conditions of the covenant—faith and love of the neighbor—never changed but remained the same in both OT and NT times. Baptism, like circumcision in the OT, enrolled the individual into the covenant and into the community of faith. Thus Bullinger, like Zwingli, held to the doctrine of the single sphere: the civil magistrate, whose laws enforce the conditions of the covenant, rules over the single Christian community, which includes all of those baptized into the covenant.

Bullinger's opposition to the Anabaptists is best understood within the context of his covenantal thought. He understood the source of their errors to be their rejection of the authority of the Old Testament. Thus, they not only rejected infant baptism, but they also refused to accept Bullinger's idea of the single sphere, a united covenantal community ruled by the Christian magistrate. Bullinger wrote two books specifically against the Anabaptists, one in 1531 and the other in 1561. Moreover, *The One and Eternal Testament or Covenant of God* was written at a time when he thought that they were an especially dangerous threat.

Bullinger and Calvin were two of the creators of the Reformed tradition, but they did not agree on all issues. In 1549 the two men finally came to an agreement on the Eucharist, with the *Consensus Tigurinus* (Zurich Consensus). But Bullinger, holding fast to his doctrine of the single sphere, could not agree with Calvin's concept of an independent church discipline and excommunication. Nor could they concur on predestination. Bullinger held firmly to his own carefully stated doctrine of single predestination, never accepting Calvin's concept of a double decree.

Bullinger had a great influence on the Reformed churches during the sixteenth century. He was a prolific writer of both letters and books; his extant correspondence numbers more than twelve thousand pieces, and he published 119 works in Latin and German. These books, commentaries on the Bible and theological works, found their way into every part of Europe. He was also a gracious host to exiles from Italy, Germany, and England during the 1540s and 1550s. He was the sole author of the Second Helvetic Confession (1566), which was widely accepted by the Reformed churches in Switzerland, elsewhere in Europe, and in England and Scotland. Along with Zwingli and Calvin, Bullinger was one of the principal architects of Reformed Protestantism.

J. W. Baker, *Heinrich Bullinger and the Covenant: The Other Reformed Tradition* (1980); P. Biel, *Doorkeepers at the House of Righteousness: Heinrich Bullinger and the Zurich Clergy, 1535–1575* (1991); B. Gordon, *Clerical Discipline and the Rural Reformation: The Synod in Zurich, 1532–1580* (1992); C. McCoy and J. W. Baker, *Fountainhead of Federalism: Heinrich Bullinger and the Covenantal Tradition* (1991); P. Rorem, *Calvin and Bullinger on the Lord's Supper* (1989); C. P. Venema, *Heinrich Bullinger and the Doctrine of Predestination* (2002).

J. WAYNE BAKER

Bünderlin, Hans (c. 1498–1533), early Anabaptist leader and spiritualist writer. Born in Linz, he studied at the Univ. of Vienna and became a preacher in Upper Austria. In 1526 he became acquainted with the Anabaptist leader Hans Denck (c. 1500–1527) under whose probable influence he joined the Anabaptist movement. Bünderlin was active as an evangelist in Linz and Nikolsburg in Moravia before appearing in Strasbourg in 1528. In Strasbourg Bünderlin published three of his four known writings, demonstrating an affinity for a spiritualized form of Anabaptism and challenging outward ceremonies such as water baptism and the Lord's Supper. His ideas were refuted in 1531 by the leader of the south German Anabaptists, Pilgram Marpeck (c. 1495–1556).

Bünderlin next appeared in Constance in 1529, hosted by the reformer of the city, Johannes Zwick (1496–1542), who was soon persuaded that Bünderlin's writings were heretical and unorthodox. From Constance, Bünderlin traveled to Prussia, perhaps under the influence of the Silesian nobleman Casper Schwenkfeld (1489–1561). After his expulsion from Prussia in 1531, all trace of Bünderlin is lost.

C. R. Foster, "Hans Denck and Johannes Buenderlin: A Comparative Study," *Mennonite Quarterly Review* 39 (1965): 115–24; C. A. Snyder, *Anabaptist History and Theology: An Introduction* (1995).

DAVID B. ELLER

Byzantine Church and the Jews

Reflecting the Augustinian attitude prevalent in Western Europe, the Byzantine church simultaneously defended the right of Jewish existence and sought to debilitate it. The Jews, for their part, opposed church politics with varying degrees of vigor throughout Byzantine history. Direct contact between church and synagogue usually confined itself to religious debate and literary rivalry, since the church had no jurisdiction over the Jews. Still, church attitudes found political and economic voice in the person of the emperor, the church's titular head, and imperial legislation regarding the Jews betrays enduring resentment rooted in Christian triumphalism.

Religious language suffused oppressive and sometimes violent decrees that punctuated the general, if inconstant, tolerance that characterized Byzantine-Jewish relations. Often citing Jewish insolence and Christian superiority, various emperors between Constantine I (r. 306–337) and Phocas (r. 602–610), especially Justinian I (r. 527–565), undermined Roman legal precedents protecting Jewish national autonomy. Most notably, the Jewish patriarchal office was abolished and building of synagogues severely limited. Many of these laws also attest to Jewish disdain for Christianity and churchmen, echoing some passages in the Palestinian Talmud of the same period.

Between the reign of Heraclius (r. 610–641) and Constantinople's occupation by the Latins in 1204 (the Fourth Crusade), four persecutions bore the stamp of religious zeal. The emperors Heraclius, Leo III (r. 717–741), Basil I (r. 867–886), and Romanus Lecapenus (r. 920–944) all executed forcible conversions, inspired by both spiritual and political motives. The Hebrew account of Basil's assault, in the *Chronicle of Ahima'az*, emphasizes the religious aspect, as it recounts an apocryphal disputation between Basil and the Jewish hero of the tale.

Occasionally church and synagogue encountered one another more directly, to both good and ill effect. The early synods sought to limit social contact between Christians and Jews for fear of heretical influence, even as church and ecclesiastically inspired decrees repeatedly outlawed or revoked forced baptisms. In 388 Ambrose, bishop of Milan, attempted to prevent Emperor Theodosius I (r. 375–395) from allowing the rebuilding of a synagogue destroyed in riots between Christians and Jews. In 1049 Emperor Constantine IX (r. 1042–1055) redirected the taxes of the Jews of Chios to the local monastery, bringing church and synagogue into rare economic contact.

More frequently, the ecclesiastical challenge came in the form of rhetoric and literature. The ideological questions raised by the very existence, and sometime opposition, of Judaism occupied Christian thinkers and shaped church policies, resulting in patent antipathy. Monasticism, which flourished in the early Byzantine period, wrought great influence on Byzantine society at large, and its adherents often attacked—and felt attacked by—Jews and Judaism. *Adversus Judaeos* literature, including imaginary debates, supersessionist tracts, and tales of miraculous conversion, flourished in all periods and among major authors such as Eusebius, John Chrysostom, and Nicholas of Otranto, among others. Clerics such as Theophanes and his successors, whose works count among the most informative historical sources, refer to Jews and their faith in the most negative terms. This rhetorical conflict between the Byzantine church and the Jews outlived the Byzantine Empire, only to reach an incomplete resolution in recent years.

Z. Ankori, *Karaites in Byzantium* (1959); M. Avi-Yonah, *The Jews under Roman and Byzantine Rule* (1976); S. Bowman, *The Jews of Byzantium 1204–1453* (1985); J. Juster, *Les juifs dans l'empire romain*, 2 vols. (1914); A. Külzer, *Disputationes Graecae contra Iudaeos* (1999); A. Linder,. *The Jews in Imperial Roman Legislation* (1987); Linder, *The Jews in the Legal Sources of the Early Middle Ages* (1997); J. Starr, *The Jews in the Byzantine Empire 641–1204* (1939); Starr, *Romania: The Jewries of the Levant after the 4th Crusade* (1949).

JOSHUA HOLO

Byzantine Monasticism *see* Monasticism, Byzantine

Byzantine Rite Also Greek Rite, this is the standard rite of Orthodox Christian and Byzantine Rite Catholic worship that developed between the sixth and fifteenth centuries at Constantinople and was based on earlier Palestinian, Antiochian, and Cappadocian rites. It gradually replaced the various local Eastern rites, while still allowing for local variations and translations into vernacular languages. The services are always sung a cappella; leavened bread is used in the Eucharist, according to both the Divine and "presanctified" (Lenten weekday) liturgies; and Communion to the laity is always given in both species, bread and wine (the body and the blood of Christ). The Eastern Catholic liturgy differs from the Orthodox in two ways: the Eastern Catholics occasionally include the *filioque* formula in the Nicene Creed and always give special prominence to the pope in the litanies. Although the eucharistic liturgy is the core of worship, many other services are included: other sacraments (baptism, confirmation, ordination, penance, matrimony, unction), the divine office (vespers, compline, matins [*orthros*], the "little" hours), and *akolouthia* (services) for specific congregational or individual needs (blessings and prayers, consecrations, exorcisms, monastic tonsure, funeral services, commemorations, and others). All of these elements are arranged in liturgical books. An adumbration of the liturgical books further reveals the level of complexity of worship. The most important books include the Great Euchologion, containing the eucharistic services (Divine Liturgies of John Chrysostom and Basil the Great, and the "presanctified" liturgy of Gregory the Great), the divine office, the sacraments (*mysteria*), the burial service, the services for tonsuring monks, the less-used services, special prayers, as well as instructions for administration of the sacraments and blessings; the Evangelion, the daily readings for the Gospel; the Apostolos, the daily reading of the Epistles; the Psalterion, the Psalms divided into 20 *kathismata* (sections); the Lenten Triodion for Great Lent, from the Sunday of the Publican and Pharisee through Holy Saturday; the Pentecostarion for Easter (*Pascha*) up to the first Sunday after Pentecost; the Parcletike (or Octoechos), services of the weekly cycle in their eight tones; the Menaeon, services for the saints and divided by month into twelve volumes; the Horologion ("hours"), the unchangeable/recurrent parts of services, the ecclesiastical calendar, the concluding festal hymns (*apolitikia*), the daily collects (*kontakia*); the Typikon ("decree"), for directions, order, and exceptions in conducting services; and the Archieratikon (technically part of the Great Euchologion) for the functions of a bishop. These books vary in name and content among the various traditions. The Byzantine Rite also encompasses the liturgical calendar (with jurisdictions and parishes divided between Gregorian and Julian), vestments, architecture, iconography, and music.

G. S. Bebis, "Worship in the Orthodox Church," *GOTR* 22 (1977): 429–43; G. A. Maloney, SJ, "Byzantine Rite," in *NCE*, vol. 2 (1967), 1000–1011; A. Schmemann, *Introduction to Liturgical Theology* (1966); R. F. Taft, "Byzantine Rite" in *The Oxford Dictionary of Byzantium*, vol. 1 (1991), 343–44; Taft, *The Byzantine Rite: A Short History* (1992); J. D. Zizioulas, "Symbolism and Realism in Orthodox Worship," *Sourozh* 79 (2000): 3–17.

MICHAEL D. PETERSON

Cabbala A transliteration of a Rabbinic Hebrew word for "tradition," Cabbala is a Jewish mystical school of biblical interpretation and commentary that emerged in late medieval and Renaissance Spain and France. Historically understood as a secret oral tradition originating with Adam and Eve, Cabbala was used by Christian thinkers to access hidden interpretations of the Bible. "Christian Cabbalists" (e.g., Cornelius Agrippa, Pico della Mirandola, and Johannes Reuchlin) found the esoteric method of the Cabbalist tradition conducive to deciphering biblical texts, particularly as they pointed to doctrines such as the incarnation, the atonement, and the Trinity. Christian Cabbala, with its complex mix of numerology, Neoplatonism, Christian theological presuppositions, and mysticism, allowed thinkers to interpret the Hebrew Bible (Old Testament) christologically.

Important in this movement were *Conversos*, the Spanish Jews whose conversion to Roman Catholicism brought Cabbala into Christian circles. Particularly influential here was Mithridates. His work connected Cabbala with Christianity as well as provided the translations of the primary sources used by Pico and Reuchlin. Postel then built upon this work and provided a systematic structure for Christian Cabbala of the fifteenth and sixteenth centuries. This project, however, was not well-received by sixteenth-century Protestant reformers such as Martin Luther, who found that the method departed too dramatically from the clear sense of the Scriptures.

J. Blau, *The Christian Interpretation of the Caballa in the Renaissance* (1965); E. Carlebach et al., eds., *Jewish History and Jewish Memory* (1998); D. Matt, *Zohar: Annotated and Explained* (2002).

WILLIAM R. RUSSELL

Caecilian (d. c. 345), bishop of Carthage. During the period immediately after the cessation of Diocletian's persecution (303–305), the episcopal see of Carthage, the primatial see of Africa Proconsularis, was vacant due to the martyrdom of its bishop. The archdeacon Caecilian was elected, but some Africans rejected his election. First, he was consecrated to the chief see in Africa, a sign of unity, without the usual participation of the primate of neighboring Numidia. Second, one of his consecrators, Felix of Abthugni, was reputedly a *traditor* (a Christian who surrendered Scriptures during the persecution of Diocletian). During the third and fourth centuries many considered the graced status of the minister of a sacrament essential to the sacrament's validity. Thus, Felix's participation cast doubt on Caecilian's consecration. Finally, Caecilian had disregarded the plight of confessors jailed during the persecution. The rejection of Caecilian and the election of Majorinus as rival bishop marked the formal beginning of the Donatist schism. While Caecilian was vindicated at councils at Rome (313) and Arles (314) and by the emperor (316), and Felix was exonerated (315), the schism continued for at least another hundred years.

"Optatus: Against the Donatists," "Proceedings before Zenophilus," and "Trial of Bishop Felix," in *Optatus: Against the Donatists,* ed. and trans. M. Edwards (1998), 1.16–20, 150–69, 170–80; "Acts of the Abitinian Martyrs" in *Donatist Martyr Stories: The Church in Conflict in Roman North Africa,* trans. M. A. Tilley (1996), 25–49.

MAUREEN A. TILLEY

Caesaria the Elder (d. c. 525), ascetic, monastic founder, abbess. Addressed by her brother Caesarius of Arles as "holy sister abbess" (*sancta soror abbatissa*) in a letter that dates before 512 (Caesarius, *Letter* 21), Caesaria headed a community of ascetic women in Arles. When warfare destroyed the monastery the bishop was building for them outside the city walls, it was relocated within the walls and dedicated on August 26, 512. Caesaria returned to Arles from the monastery in Marseille where she had been studying and presided over the institution until her death (*Life of Caesarius* 1.28, 35, 57–58). Caesarius endowed the monastery with church lands and funds (*Testament of Caesarius*) and composed a rule for it that emphasized strict enclosure, a simple lifestyle, independence from the bishop, and a demanding regime of prayer, fasting, and Bible reading.

W. E. Klingshirn, trans., *Caesarius of Arles: Life, Testament, Letters* (1994); M. C. McCarthy, trans., *The Rule for Nuns of St. Caesarius of Arles* (1960); A. de Vogüé and J. Courreau, *Oeuvres pour les moniales,* vol. 1 of *Césaire d'Arles: Oeuvres monastiques,* in SC 345 (1988).

WILLIAM E. KLINGSHIRN

Caesaria the Younger (d. c. 560), abbess. Raised in the monastery headed by her close relation Caesaria the Elder, the younger Caesaria became its abbess at the latter's death (c. 525). It was under her leadership that Caesarius issued the final version of his *Rule for Nuns* in 534 and at her urging that Cyprian of Toulon and four fellow clerics composed a *Life of Caesarius* in which her monastery prominently appears. She addressed a treatise on the monastic life to Richild (Agnes) and Radegund and played a prominent role in transmitting Caesarius's rule to their monastery in Poitiers. She is also the author of three monastic sayings and regulations for the church in which Caesarius, Caesaria the Elder, and the nuns of the monastery were buried. She was succeeded as abbess by Liliola.

W. E. Klingshirn, trans., *Caesarius of Arles: Life, Testament, Letters* (1994); M. C. McCarthy, trans., *The Rule for Nuns of St. Caesarius of Arles* (1960); J. A. McNamara and J. E. Halborg, with E. G. Whatley, trans., *Sainted Women of the Dark Ages* (1992), 114–18; A. de Vogüé and J. Courreau, *Oeuvres pour les moniales,* vol. 1 of *Césaire d'Arles: Oeuvres monastiques,* in SC 345 (1988): 470–74, 496–98.

WILLIAM E. KLINGSHIRN

Caesarius of Arles (469/470–542), monk, monastic founder, bishop, preacher. Documentation of his life and work is available through his writings, including over 250 sermons, the records of the church councils over which he presided, his correspondence, and the documents (his *Rule for Nuns,* his *Testament,* and the *Life of Caesarius*) created on behalf of St. John of Arles, the women's monastery that he and his sister Caesaria founded.

Born in Chalon-sur-Sâone, where he spent two years in the lower clergy, Caesarius went to Lérins in the late 480s for ascetic formation. In the mid-490s he moved to Arles, where he rose rapidly in the local ecclesiastical hierarchy with the support of his relative bishop Aeonius and the African rhetor and grammarian Julianus

Pomerius, whose reform ideas were to influence him. In 502 he succeeded Aeonius, although for a decade the local clergy sought to depose him. In 513 the support of Ostrogothic king Theoderic and of Pope Symmachus established Caesarius's control over the see.

Caesarius presided over a series of important councils, including the Council of Orange in 529, which attempted to settle the century-long debate over grace and free will sparked by Augustine's teaching. He promoted a wider pastoral role for the clergy (e.g., giving priests and deacons the authority to preach) and advocated an ascetic life for the laity.

He was buried next to his sister Caesaria, and his memory was kept alive by the women of St. John. A few of his possessions, including two *pallia* (symbols of papal favor), were retained as relics by the monastery until the French Revolution. Now divided between the Église St. Trophime and the Musée de l'Arles antique, they have recently been authenticated and restored.

M. Heijmans, "Césaire d'Arles, un évêque et sa ville," *Revue d'histoire de l'église de France* 87 (2001): 5–25; W. E. Klingshirn, *Caesarius of Arles: The Making of a Christian Community in Late Antique Gaul* (1994); Klingshirn, *Caesarius of Arles: Life, Testament, Letters* (1994); R. Weaver, *Divine Grace and Human Agency: A Study of the Semi-Pelagian Controversy* (1996).

WILLIAM E. KLINGSHIRN

Cainites   Not much is known about them besides that which Irenaeus (*Haer.* 1.31.1–2), Pseudo-Tertullian (*Adv. omn. haer.* 2), and Epiphanius (*Pan.* 38) record. Though called a Christian gnostic sect, the Cainites were peculiarly antiorthodox in their beliefs. The use of the name Cain, a biblical antagonist, to identify the group is indicative of their counterintuitive reasoning. Cainites championed biblical figures such as Esau, Korah, and the Sodomites, who were flawed, corrupted, even wicked because by their actions these characters had demonstrated their opposition to the creator of the heavens and earth. Cainites opposed the Creator God, called *Hystera* (uterus or womb) and all his works and considered followers of the creator to be obstructing the truth. They were accused of holding that salvation came not as a result of virtuous living but in the experience of all things, including every type of sinful act. Engaging in such acts without fear was the basis of their understanding of *gnosis* (knowledge). Chief among the biblical figures the Cainites venerated was Judas, the only one of the Twelve to have had *gnosis*. Judas, by betraying Jesus, destroyed all things in the heaven and on earth, facilitated the manifold benefits for humanity secured by Christ's death, and overcame the forces that sought to betray truth by preventing Jesus' suffering and death. Cainites held that it was only because of Judas's betrayal that salvation came to humankind; thus, they celebrated him in their sacred scripture, *The Gospel of Judas*.

W. Barnstone, ed., *The Other Bible: Ancient Alternative Scriptures* (1984); R. Grant, *Gnosticism: A Source Book of Heretical Writings from the Early Christian Period* (1961).

RODNEY S. SADLER JR.

Cajetan, Thomas de Vio (1469–1534),

Dominican theologian, prior general of his order, cardinal, reformer. Cajetan was born in Gaeta. He studied at Naples, Bologna, and Padua and then taught metaphysics at Padua, Brescia, Pavia, and Rome. Between 1507 and 1522 he expounded upon the *Summa theologiae* of Thomas Aquinas; an edited version of this work (the *Editio Leonina*) is still in use today and is considered one of the key classics of scholasticism. In the 1530s he wrote exegetical commentaries on virtually every book of the Bible.

As well as being a respected scholar, Cajetan was a leading figure in the church. He was made prior general of the Dominican order in 1508. In this position he served as a key diplomatic figure in affairs of church and state. He promoted the ecumenical Fifth Lateran Council (1512–1517). He was instrumental in granting to Ferdinand of Spain the first Dominican missionaries for the conversion of the natives of America. He was also involved in church negotiations with Luther. He interviewed Luther in 1518 at Augsburg, when he was a papal legate to Germany, without reaching an agreement. As a legate to Hungary in 1523, he had to support King Louis of Hungary in his resistance against the Turks. During the sack of Rome in 1527 Cajetan was seized but was ransomed for a large sum of gold. In 1534 he opted for the validity of the marriage of Henry VIII and Catherine of Aragon.

It was the common opinion of his contemporaries that had he lived, he would have succeeded Clement VII on the papal throne.

A. Krause, *Zur Analogie bei Cajetan und Thomas von Aquin* (1999); M. Nieden, *Organum deitatis: Die Christologie des Thomas de Vio Cajetan* (1997); J. Wicks, *Cajetan Responds: A Reader in Reformation Controversy* (1978); Wicks, "Thomas de Vio Cajetan (1469–1534)," in *The Reformation Theologians,* ed. C. Lindberg (2002), 269–83.

FRANZ POSSET

Calendar, Liturgical   *see* Liturgical Calendar

Calendar, Reform of   By the late Middle

Ages, a slight error in reckoning the length of the year of the Julian calendar put the date for the spring equinox ten days behind the true equinox, a problem for calculating the date for Easter. In 1572, a commission of astronomers appointed by Pope Gregory XIII proposed dropping ten days from the calendar to bring it back into alignment with the equinox. Accordingly, October 4, 1582, was followed by October 15, 1582. To prevent future problems, rules were established for suppressing the leap year in all century years except for those divisible by 400. The calendar was enacted in most Catholic European countries in 1582; Protestant regions were slower to accept the reforms.

G. V. Coyne, M. A. Hoskin, and O. Pedersen, eds., *Gregorian Reform of the Calendar: Proceedings of the Vatican Conference to Commemorate Its 400th Anniversary, 1582–1982* (1983).

SCOTT M. MARR

Calixt, Georg (1586–1656), Lutheran irenicist. After studies in Helmstedt, Calixt began to teach there (1614), finally consolidating the university around his program. He dedicated his life to the union of Christian churches, after 1629 arguing on the basis of the claim of Vincent of Lerin that consensus among the ancient church fathers, focused on the Apostolic Creed, existed in the church's first five centuries. During the Thirty Years' War he sought peace through an appeal to Roman Catholic theological faculties based on the Religious Peace of Augsburg (1555). Rebuffed in efforts to promote Protestant unity at the Colloquy of Thorn (Torun, 1645) by Abraham Calov, and criticized from many quarters, Calixt nonetheless found broad support even if his plans were not realized. He also wrote on eschatological and ethical topics.

I. Mager, *Georg Calixts theologische Ethik* (1969); H. Schüssler, *Georg Calixt, Theologie und Kirchenpolitik* (1961).

ROBERT KOLB

Callistus I, bishop of Rome (217–222). Born as a slave in Rome, Callistus was banished to the mines of Sardinia for reasons that are not entirely clear, although he had bankrupted his master's business and interrupted a synagogue service. Callistus returned to Rome after the amnesty of Commodus in 192. A few years later he entered into the service of Bishop Zephyrinus and rose quickly in the ecclesiastical hierarchy. Although Callistus is mentioned in Eusebius's *Ecclesiastical History* (6.21), the only information about his life and views comes from a rather hostile source, Hippolytus's *Refutation of All Heresies*. In fact, Hippolytus seems to have wanted his readers to consider Callistus's Trinitarian view as the climax of all ancient heresies. Callistus was accused of holding a modalist position, despite the fact that he excommunicated Sabellius. Callistus attempted to safeguard the oneness of God by denying the distinct existence of the Son before the incarnation. In pre-existence, Father and Son were "inseparable Spirit." Tertullian seems to have attacked Callistus's views under Praxeas's name. A rigorist Hippolytus also could not stand the leniency and inclusiveness of Callistus's ecclesiastical policy, as the latter admitted the fallen but penitent Christians, who were excommunicated from rigorist communities, back to the church. Evidently, he was also quite tolerant in regard to various marital issues. The two letters attributed to Callistus in Pseudo-Isidore's decretals are inauthentic. Callistus administered a cemetery, which later came to bear his name: the Catacomb of Callistus. The tomb of Callistus was discovered in 1960 under the ruins of an oratory in the cemetery of Calepodius.

M. Marcovich, *Hippolytus Refutatio omnium haeresium* in *Patristische Texte und Studien,* vol. 25 (1986), 9.11–13, 10.27; A. Brent, *Hippolytus and the Roman Church in the Third Century* (1995); R. Davies, ed., *The Book of Pontiffs (Liber Pontificales)* (2nd ed., 2000); R. E. Heine, "The Christology of Callistus," *JTS* 49, no. 1 (1998): 56–91.

TARMO TOOM

Calov, Abraham (1612–1686), Lutheran Orthodox theologian. After studying in Königsberg and Rostock, Calov taught in Königsberg (1630), then served as rector and pastor in Danzig (1643) and professor in Wittenberg (1650–1686). He strongly opposed the "syncretism" and plans for church union of Georg Calixt, particularly at the Colloquy of Thorn (Torun, 1645) and in *The Repetition*

of the *Consensus of the True Lutheran Faith* issued by the faculties of Leipzig and Wittenberg (1655). Calov was above all a biblical exegete (*Biblia Illustrata* [OT 1672, NT 1676]). His polemic against Roman Catholic, Calvinist, and Socinian theology is included in his twelve-volume *System of Theological Topics* (1655–1677), called "the climax of Wittenberg theology," although it is probably excelled by *The Theological System* of his son-in-law, Johann Andreas Quenstedt.

———

K. Appold, *Abraham Calov's Doctrine of Vocatio in Its Systematic Context* (1998); V. Jung, *Das Ganze der heiligen Schrift, Hermeneutik bei Calov* (1999).

ROBERT KOLB

Calvin, John (1509–1564), French evangelical teacher, interpreter of Scripture, and theologian. Born in Noyon, France, Calvin was initially educated in the aristocratic family of Charles de Hangest. Calvin's father sent him to the Univ. of Paris to prepare for the study of theology, but upon the completion of his undergraduate degree Calvin was instead sent to study law, first in Orleans, then in Bourges. Both Mathurin Cordier in Paris and Melchior Wolmar in Orleans awakened in Calvin a love of Latin and Greek literature, and upon his father's death in 1531 Calvin returned to the study of classical letters at the newly founded College of Royal Readers in Paris, under the influence of the French philologist Guillaume Budé. The fruits of these studies were published at his own expense in 1532 in his commentary on Seneca's *De Clementia*, which Calvin described as the first of a series of commentaries designed to restore the writings of Seneca to their rightful place in the world of the learned.

Sometime between 1533 and 1534, Calvin experienced a "sudden conversion to teachableness," more than likely under the influence of the 1520 treatises of Martin Luther, whom he described as his "father in the faith" and as a "distinguished apostle of Christ." Calvin's conversion to the gospel led him to dedicate his considerable gifts as a scholar to a new task, that of restoring the reading of Scripture to the unlearned Christians of Europe. Calvin's identification with the cause of the gospel led first to internal exile in France and then to exile in Basel, where he wrote his first "brief handbook" of catechetical instruction for the ordinary faithful in France, the 1536 *Institutes.* Though published anonymously, the book brought Calvin to the attention of many, including Guillaume Farel, who detained Calvin in Geneva on his way to Strasbourg, threatening God's wrath against him should he neglect the need of the Genevan church. Calvin was called by the Geneva City Council first to be a teacher of Scripture and then to be pastor, in company with Farel and Pierre Viret. However, Calvin and Farel soon found themselves at odds with the council and were expelled from Geneva in 1538.

Though Calvin had serious doubts about his call to public ministry, Martin Bucer called him to Strasbourg to minister to the French congregation there and to teach in the Strasbourg Academy newly founded by Johann Sturm. Calvin's work in Strasbourg brought him remarkable clarity with regard to his call to be a teacher and pastor. Under the influence of Philip Melanchthon's 1535 *Loci communes*, Calvin turned his own 1539 *Institutes* into a summary of godly doctrine for future pastors and ministers, to be used as a "necessary instrument" for the reading of his commentaries, beginning with Romans in 1540. Once instructed in the way to draw fruitful doctrine from the genuine meaning of Scripture, pastors were to teach their congregations the sum of godly doctrine in the catechism, and were to apply the genuine meaning of Scripture to their lives in their sermons, which followed the same *lectio continua* model as the commentaries. When Calvin was called back to Geneva in 1541, he set in place this new vision of the rightly ordered church, guided by teachers and pastors, culminating in the establishment of Geneva Academy in 1559. Calvin also set in place the Consistory, comprised of pastors and elected elders, to make sure that the congregation knew the rudiments of pious doctrine, attended sermons, and manifested their piety in their lives.

Calvin's theology centers on his understanding of God as the fountain of every good thing. God is essentially infinite and invisible, but God manifests God's self to us in the powers that God sets forth in God's works, such as goodness, wisdom, power, righteousness, and mercy. The powers of God are initially set forth in the living image of God in the universe, not only in the heavens above us but in humanity as a microcosm. We are to behold these powers as in a theater, and to experience and enjoy them within ourselves, so that we are drawn to the source of these powers in ecstatic admiration. However, given the fall into sin, we can no longer behold and enjoy these powers without the spectacles of Scripture and the illumination of the Holy Spirit. The fall into sin also means that the universe reveals God's wrath against our sin as much as it manifests the goodness of God toward humanity, due to the fact that God no longer recognizes God's image in us, apart from the lineaments of the image in our reason and intellect. God therefore manifests God's powers in the humanity of Christ, who is "God manifested in the flesh," so that Christ might communicate these powers to needy sinners. Christ does this by first taking on himself our sin, curse, death, and damnation in his crucifixion, and then by communicating to us his righteousness, blessing, life, and salvation in his resurrection and ascension. This work of Christ was first made known to the Israelites under the shadows and figures of the law, especially in the sacrifices, priests, and kings, and then in the clear light of the gospel in both preaching and the sacraments. Faith embraces Christ as clothed in the gospel and enables us to call on God with the confident assurance of children of God. Faith unites us with Christ, who forgives our sins, transforms us into the image of God, and leads us to full unity with God in eternal life.

A. Ganoczy, *The Young Calvin* (1987); B. A. Gerrish, *Grace and Gratitude* (1993); R. M. Kingdon, *Geneva and the Coming Wars of Religion in France, 1555–1563* (1956); W. G. Naphy, *Calvin and the Consolidation of the Genevan Reformation* (1994); T. H. L. Parker, *John Calvin* (1975); F. Wendel, *Calvin* (1963).
                          RANDALL C. ZACHMAN

Calvinism   The historical and theological movement associated with the views of John Calvin that spread through Europe in the sixteenth century and into the New World. It extends internationally to the present day in various forms.

The influence of Calvin beyond the city of Geneva, where he spent most of his years as a theologian, was substantial. Those drawn to Calvin's interpretation of Scripture and theological insights spread his views after his death. In a broad sense, Calvinism is a substantial part of the Reformed tradition, which includes perspectives of other important early reformers such as Bullinger and Zwingli. Calvinism is also a theological system which developed through the work of a number of Reformed theologians, particularly in the seventeenth century. Important figures in this development included Theodore Beza, Calvin's successor in

Geneva, and Francis Turretin, a later Geneva theologian. Prominent confessions of faith that reflect Calvin's views in various ways include the Scots Confession (1560), the Heidelberg Catechism (1563), the Second Helvetic Confession (1566), and the Westminster Confession (1647). Calvinism as a distinctive set of doctrines was epitomized in the "five points of Calvinism" promulgated at the Synod of Dort (1618–1619).

The spread of Calvin's thought was enhanced by his many writings, in which his overall understandings of Scripture and theological topics were expounded. Among these, Calvin's *Institutes of the Christian Religion* and his commentaries on most of the books of the Bible were highly influential. The Geneva Academy, which trained pastors, ensured there would be a steady stream of adherents to spread his understandings throughout Europe.

Theological development of Calvin's thought began with Beza and reached a zenith with the work of Turretin, whose *Institutio theologiae elenctiacae* (1679–1685) became the most important theological work produced in Geneva in the seventeenth century. Turretin developed Calvin's basic views in a much more detailed, "scholastic" form. His son, Jean-Alphonse Turretin, who succeeded his father as professor of theology at the Univ. of Geneva, did not continue this rigorous Calvinism. But Switzerland was the primary ground in which Calvinism took hold and developed.

Calvinist churches were planted in France, and a church polity developed. The Wars of Religion (from 1562) constrained the development of Calvinism, but the "Huguenots" represented the vitality of the Calvinist movement, even as thousands fled from persecution.

Calvinism penetrated the Netherlands and the Low Countries in pervasive ways. The "five points of Calvinism" of the Synod of Dort were framed against the counterviews of the Remonstrants, who followed James Arminius. These five points were: total depravity, unconditional election, limited atonement, irresistible grace, and the perseverance of the saints (acrostically designated as TULIP). Later important Dutch theologians who were Calvinist leaders in society and church include Abraham Kuyper and Herman Bavinck.

In addition to spreading through other nations in central Europe, Calvinism reached England and was embodied in various ways by the Puritan movement. Major theologians included William Perkins and William Ames. The Westminster Assembly's theological documents became highly influential in the following centuries as expressions of Calvinist thought. In Scotland, Calvinism became an even more potent theological and cultural force, with a succession of key theologians reflecting Calvinism in an array of shades.

The spread of Calvinism to North America came through a number of influences. Puritans who fled England and Calvinists persecuted in other lands emigrated to the New World and established several main church bodies with varying polities but with similar theological commitments to Calvinism. These included the Congregational, Presbyterian, Dutch and German Reformed, and some Baptist bodies.

Churches with a Calvinist heritage now appear on all continents. They reflect Calvin's own views as well as their further development in various ways. A strong characteristic of Calvinism has been its emphasis on highly articulated theology. This has led Calvinist (Reformed) churches to produce a number of confessions of faith. This practice continues in contemporary times.

———

P. Benedict, *Christ's Churches Purely Reformed: A Social History of Calvinism* (2002); W. Fred Graham, ed., *Later Calvinism: International Perspectives* (1994); J. T. McNeill, *The History and Character of Calvinism* (1954); M. Prestwich, ed., *International Calvinism 1541–1715* (1985); D. K. McKim, ed., *Encyclopedia of the Reformed Faith* (1992).

DONALD K. MCKIM

Camisards French Huguenot resistance movement. After the Revocation of the Edict of Nantes (1685), armed resistance to the suppression of their faith arose among Huguenots in the Cévennes. Inspired by ecstatic prophecies and visions of men and women of all ages, and led by a former shepherd and baker become "prophet," Jean Cavalier (1681–1740), as well as by Pierre Laporte, called Rolland, Abraham Mazel, and others, the secret societies of the Camisards (probably so designated because of their apparel) exchanged atrocities with the royal authorities, particularly in the period 1702–1705, with hostilities continuing until 1711. The subversion of Cavalier (1704) by the Marshal de Villars through unfulfilled promises of freedom of conscience and worship and of the release of arrested prisoners, along with the royal government's harsh military measures against the Huguenot population, finally reduced the movement. After Rolland's death (1704) and Mazel's execution (1710), the

Camisards faded from existence. Through efforts by Antoine Court (1695–1760) beginning in 1715, the all but eradicated Calvinist churches took on new life. He reorganized the institutions of congregation and synod and battled Camisard spiritualism with an emphasis on biblical authority.

P. Joutard, *Les Camisards* (1994).

ROBERT KOLB

Campeggio, Lorenzo (1474–1539),

lawyer, diplomat, cardinal, reformer, brother of Tommaso (1483–1564). Campeggio was born in Milan. He studied civil law under his father at Padua and Bologna, married, and had five children. After 1493 he was lecturer on law in Padua, after 1499 in Bologna. He entered ecclesiastical service in 1509 after the death of his wife. In 1512 he was given the bishopric of Feltre by Julius II and on July 1, 1517, he was appointed cardinal.

Campeggio took a leading part in some of the greatest events of the Reformation, especially in southern Germany and England. He considered the Roman Curia the chief source of all the evils of the age and spoke strongly against the reckless granting of indulgences, but he opposed Luther's reforms. For the reform of the German clergy he held a local reform council of twelve bishops of southern Germany along with Archduke Ferdinand and the Bavarian dukes. In 1518/1519 and in 1528/1529 he was papal legate in England. Together with Cardinal Wolsey he formed a court to try the so-called divorce suit of Henry VIII. Campeggio left the court when Pope Clement VII revoked the case to Rome. He was present at the coronation of Charles V by the pope (1530); afterward he accompanied the emperor to the Diets of Augsburg and Regensburg as legate. After Pope Clement's death in 1534, Campeggio returned to Rome and took part in the conclave in which Paul III was elected.

E. V. Cardinal, *Cardinal Lorenzo Campeggio, Legate to the Courts of Henry VIII and Charles V* (1935); G. Müller, ed., *Legation Lorenzo Campeggis 1532 und Nuntiatur Girolamo Aleandros 1532*, 2 vols. (1969).

FRANZ POSSET

Campion, Edmund (1540–1581), English

Jesuit missionary, saint, and martyr. Campion was born in London and educated at Oxford. In 1569 he went to Dublin to help found a university and wrote his *History of Ireland*

(published in 1587). His doubts about the Anglican Church led him to embrace Catholicism in 1571 at Douai. In 1573 he made a pilgrimage to Rome, where he entered the Jesuits. He was ordained a priest at Prague in 1578, where he taught and produced plays at the Jesuit college.

In June 1580 he, with Robert Parsons and Ralph Emerson, entered England in disguise and began the Jesuit mission there, mainly strengthening the faith of Catholic gentry families. His challenge to debate theology, known as "Campion's Brag," alarmed officials of Elizabeth I; Campion expanded his challenge in his *Decem rationes*, which was printed and distributed underground. Arrested in Berkshire in July 1581 after several close escapes, he was thrown into the Tower of London and racked repeatedly. On November 14 he was forced to debate three Anglican theologians; the government published its version of the debates. Campion was executed for treason on December 1. He was canonized in 1970.

E. Waugh, *Edmund Campion* (1935, 1946, 1980); T. McCoog, ed., *The Reckoned Expense: Edmund Campion and the Early English Jesuits* (1996).

JOHN PATRICK DONNELLY, SJ

Canisius, Peter (1521–1597), theologian

and preacher. Born in Nijmegen, Canisius attended the Univ. of Cologne, then entered the Jesuits in 1541. After brief spells teaching at Messina and the Univ. of Ingolstadt, he served as provincial superior of the German Jesuits from 1550 to 1567. Encouraged by Emperor Ferdinand I, he helped found Jesuit colleges at twelve cities of the empire. Canisius served as theologian at the Council of Trent (1547) and the Colloquy of Worms (1557).

From 1552 to 1555 he wrote his famous catechism, *Summa doctrinae christianae*, mainly for the use of priests. Ferdinand I made it the official Catholic catechism for the empire. There were twenty printings by 1559, and it remained popular into the nineteenth century. By 1615 there were editions in twelve languages. Canisius added shorter versions: one for adolescents and one for children. His catechisms stress practical piety and avoid polemics.

Canisius was a popular preacher, especially at Augsburg in the 1550s and 1560s, where he revived a dormant Catholic community. Five large volumes of his sermons have been published. In the 1570s he published lives of John the Baptist and the Virgin Mary, which tried to refute the Lutheran *Magdeburg Centuries*. He spent his last seventeen years at Fribourg, Switzerland, where he founded a Jesuit college and wrote books of popular piety. He was canonized in 1925.

J. Brodrick, *St. Peter Canisius, SJ* (1935, repr. 1950, 1962); O. Braunsberger, *Beati Petri Canisii Societatis Iesu epistulae et acta*, 8 vols. (1896–1921).

JOHN PATRICK DONNELLY, SJ

Cano, Melchior (1509–1560), Spanish Dominican theologian, leading light of the School of Salamanca, influential participant at the Council of Trent, and outspoken critic of the Society of Jesus. Cano gave shape to early modern Catholic thought by contributing to the development of positive, or fundamental, theology, a Thomistic theological method that stressed natural law and placed a greater emphasis on ethical concerns. Opposed to compromise with Protestantism, Cano upheld orthodox Catholic teachings on the sacraments at Trent, especially on questions concerning penance and the Eucharist. Aiming squarely against the paradigm of *sola scriptura,* Cano argued that religious truth could be found in a variety of sources, or *loci,* beyond the Bible: in oral traditions, the writings of the church fathers, the pronouncements of councils, bishops, and popes, and even the testimony of human history. A disciple of Francisco de Vitoria, whom he succeeded to the principal chair of theology at the Univ. of Salamanca, Cano joined his mentor in defending the rights of the American natives against abuses by Spanish colonists. Cano's summa, *De locis theologicis* (1563), became one of the most influential texts in post-Tridentine Catholicism and continued to have an impact for centuries, even among modern thinkers such as Joseph Marechal and Karl Rahner.

J. B. Plans, *La escuela de Salamanca y la renovación de la teología en el siglo XVI* (2000); A. Pagden, *The Fall of Natural Man* (1987); J. Sanz y Sanz, *Melchior Cano* (1959); J. Tapia, *Iglesia y teología en Melchor Cano* (1989).

CARLOS M. N. EIRE

Canon Law The body of ecclesiastical laws or rules for the government of the Christian church. The writings of the first generations of Christians described the customs of the early church. After the conversion of Constantine, church councils determined doctrinal and disciplinary matters. Such pronouncements were thought to have the binding force of law. The Council of Nicaea (325) issued twenty canons regulating a variety of issues. Collectors of conciliar canons added the decisions of other councils to those of Nicaea. Patriarch John Scholasticus of Constantinople organized the Greek canons systematically in his *Synagoge canonum* (c. 570). Dionysius Exiguus translated into Latin the canons of the Eastern councils and ordered them chronologically in his *Liber canonum* (several versions, early sixth century). In addition to conciliar canons, the decisions of popes (decretals) became another source of canon law and were included in Western collections. The work of Dionysius remained fundamental for centuries and was often rearranged and combined with other material. In 774, Pope Adrian I sent an expanded version, the so-called *Dionysio-Hadriana*, to Charlemagne.

Beginning in the seventh century, especially Irish authors produced penitentials, indicating the penance for different sins. Some of the contents of penitentials were received into canon law books. During the seventh century, the canons of Spanish and Gallic councils were collected in the *Hispana*, which became influential in Spain and Gaul. The chronologically organized collections of the early Middle Ages were cumbersome to use, and several attempts at systematic collections were made, especially in Gaul, such as the *Vetus Gallica* (c. 600) and the *Dacheriana* (c. 800).

In the mid-ninth century, members of the reform circles centered in the monastery of Corbie created the *Pseudo-Isidorian Forgeries*, which contain forged decretals claiming to be of the earliest popes alongside valid law. Their goals were to protect the church and its property against laypeople and the bishops against their archbishops. Pseudo-Isidore accomplished the latter by making appeals to the pope available to the lower clergy.

In the 1010s, Bishop Burchard of Worms produced a large and influential collection of canon law, systematically organized in twenty books. The papal reform movement of the late eleventh and the twelfth centuries required collections of canon law that took into account the goals of the reformers. This was a period of unprecedented activity. Among the many works that were produced, the following stand out for their popularity: the collection of Bishop Anselm of Lucca (1080s), the *Panormia* of Bishop Ivo of Chartres (1090s), the anonymous *Collectio Tripartita* (1090s), and the *Polycarpus* of Cardinal Gregory of St. Grisogono (1110s). These works introduced much new material into canon law, including excerpts from the writings of church fathers and from the Roman law of Justinian. In his *Prologue*, Ivo drafted guidelines for reconciling contradictory laws.

Gratian put Ivo's program into practice in his *Concordia discordantium canonum* (*Concord of Discordant Canons*, c. 1140), which in its second recension (c. 1150) became the accepted summary of the canon law of the first millennium. Gratian's work became a fundamental textbook in the law schools that it helped create, first in Bologna and soon after in most parts of Europe. Roman law was also studied in the schools, which strongly influenced the understanding of canon law as well as new legislation.

From Pope Alexander III (1159–1181), canon law was increasingly shaped by the growing number of papal decretals and the legislation of general councils. This legislation was collected in numerous compilations, many with official papal approval. At the end of the Middle Ages, a standard set of law books became known as the *Corpus iuris canonici*.

Without being included in the *Corpus*, the legislation of the reforming councils of Constance (1414–1418), Basel (1431), Ferrara-Florence (1438–1445), and, especially, Trent (1545–1563) circulated widely and influenced canon law. Papal acts, decisions of local and provincial councils, decisions of the Roman congregations and courts, and other legally interesting material were also collected in printed works.

After preparations during 1904–1917, Pope Benedict XV promulgated the *Codex iuris canonici* in 1917 to replace the *Corpus iuris canonici*. The new work used the nineteenth-century civil codes of Europe as a model and, unlike the *Corpus*, stated the law in abstract formulations cut off from the specific situations and cases in which the principles had been worked out. Legal changes, especially in the wake of the Second Vatican Council, led to the promulgation in 1983 of a new *Codex iuris canonici*.

The canon law of the Eastern church was summarized in the *Nomokanon* (several versions, the last by Theodore Bestes, c. 1090), which was partially based on the works of John Scholasticus and included conciliar canons as well as some imperial laws. A version of this work was translated into Slavonic at an early date and used in the Orthodox churches of Eastern Europe. Pope John Paul II promulgated a law book, the *Codex canonum ecclesiarum ori-*entalium (1991), for the eastern Uniate churches that have remained in communion with Rome.

Based on the *Corpus iuris canonici*, the law of the Anglican Church was modified by the *Canons* of 1604 and 1969.

J. A. Brundage, *Medieval Canon Law* (1995); *Codex iuris canonici Pii X Pont. Max. iussu digestus Benedicti Papae XV auctoritate promulgatus* (1917); *Codex iuris canonici auctoritate Ioannis Pauli PP. II promulgatus* (1983); E. Friedberg, ed., *Corpus iuris canonici*, 2 vols. (1879); C. Gallagher, *Church Law and Church Order in Rome and Byzantium: A Comparative Study* (2002); J. Gaudemet, *Église et cité: Histoire du droit canonique* (1994); R. H. Helmholz, *The Spirit of Classical Canon Law* (1996); W. Hartman and K. Pennington, eds., *History of Medieval Canon Law* (1999–); *Histoire du droit et des institutions de l'Eglise en Occident* (1955–); R. Metz, *What Is Canon Law?* (1960); R. Somerville and B. C. Brasington, *Prefaces to Canon Law Books in Latin Christianity* (1998); C. Van de Wiel, *History of Canon Law* (1991).

ANDERS WINROTH

Canons and Canonesses The first recorded appearance of the term "canon" (or "canonic") is in 535. The term is derived from the list, also called a canon, of clerics of a church who were entitled to support, or refers to a life lived according to the canons (*canones*). It designates the members of a chapter who celebrate liturgical services in cathedral or collegiate churches. They were distinguished from monks by the rule of Chrodegang of Metz in 755 and by the institutions of Aix-la-Chapelle in 816. Characteristic features of canons were, at first, communal living, ownership of private property by permission, and an internal organization according to degrees of dignity. The church reforms of the eleventh century brought a stricter interpretation of the rule by the canons regular. These were distinguished from secular canons, who gave up communal living, turning communal property into individual benefices as the core of the canonry and reducing the liturgical functions of canons. In the late Middle Ages, secular canons could be active in administration, diplomacy, jurisdiction, court life, academia, the service of the church, or secular rule.

The term "canoness," occurring from the fourth century in the Greek East and from the eighth century in the West, referred at first to all women who led a religious life not bound to a monastic community. In 816 they were defined as communities under abbatial supervision, of whom participation in masses and hours, meditation and the making of handicrafts, visits to the refectory and dormitory, and avoidance of contact with men were expected. Secular canonesses lived less strictly than the Augustinian canonesses and Premonstratensians.

———

G. P. Marchal, "Was war das Kanonikerinstitut im Mittelalter?" *RHE* 94 (1999): 761–807; 95 (2000): 7–53; I. Crusius, ed., *Studien zum Kanonissenstift* (2001).

OLIVER AUGE

Capito, Wolfgang (1478?–1541), German humanist, theologian, and reformer. Capito was born in Hagenau and studied in Pforzheim, Ingolstadt, and Freiburg im Breisgau. He returned to Hagenau in 1506, becoming a proofreader. After three years he enrolled at Freiburg where, following ordination, he continued theological studies, being taught in the nominalist tradition. Appointed preacher at Bruchsal in 1512, he began humanist studies that included Hebrew. Earning his doctorate of theology in 1515, he became cathedral preacher and professor in Basel, where he corresponded with Martin Luther and Ulrich Zwingli. Capito associated closely with Desiderius Erasmus, but this association did not last.

In 1520 Capito became cathedral preacher, confessor, and advisor to Archbishop Albert of Mainz, Germany's most powerful ecclesiastical prince. Capito mediated between Luther and the archbishop, asking Luther for moderation while blocking Albert's suppression of Luther. When Capito met with Luther in 1522 in Wittenberg, Capito essentially agreed with Luther that theological truths could be known independent of papal authorization. Capito left Mainz in 1523 to become provost of St. Thomas, the collegiate church in Strasbourg. Shortly thereafter, he openly embraced the Reformation. Leaving St. Thomas, he accepted a call to New St. Peter's church. In 1524 he, like other Reformation clergy, married. When his wife died several years later, he married Johannes Oecolampadius's widow.

In the late 1520s, when theological differences concerning the Lord's Supper threatened to split the evangelicals, a colloquy was convened at Marburg in 1529. Luther held that "This is my body" means Christ is physically present in the sacramental bread and wine. Zwingli and Martin Bucer asserted Christ's body is spiritually or symbolically present. Evangelical dissension continued, and when

Philip Melanchthon presented his *Augsburg Confession* to Emperor Charles V at the 1530 Diet of Augsburg, Strasbourg was placed in a difficult position. Strasbourg representatives had earlier repudiated the Roman church by abolishing the Mass, but they could not sign Melanchthon's confession because they disagreed with his article on the Lord's Supper. Capito and Bucer hurried to Augsburg, where together they wrote the Tetrapolitan Confession for Strasbourg and three neighboring cities. Although similar to Melanchthon's confession, the Tetrapolitan affirmed Christ's spiritual presence in the Lord's Supper.

Throughout his life Capito committed himself to church unity and public peace. In Strasbourg he worked with Bucer for a firmer ecclesiastical system that included some tolerance for dissident sects. Outside of Strasbourg he advised Bern, Basel, and Frankfurt on church orders. He and Bucer signed the Wittenberg Concord in 1536 and attended the 1540 Diet of Worms. Capito died of the plague the following year.

———

J. M. Kittelson, *Wolfgang Capito: From Humanist to Reformer* (1975); O. Millet, *Correspondance de Wolfgang Capiton, 1478–1541: Analyse et index* (1982); B. Stierle, *Capito als Humanist* (1974).

SUZANNE S. HEQUET

Cappadocians This title has traditionally been given to three great fourth-century theologians who came from Cappadocia in east central Roman Asia Minor (modern Turkey). They were Basil the Great (c. 330–379), his brother Gregory of Nyssa (c. 335–c. 395), and their friend Gregory of Nazianzus (330–390). They championed the theology of the Council of Nicaea (325), which taught that in the Trinity the Father and Son are *homoousios*, of the same divine nature or essence, in contradiction to Arius's insistence on the creaturely nature of the Son.

What distinguished the Cappadocians as a group from other theologians was that they had two great insights. First, they realized that Nicaea had not settled the question and that Arianism would grow and metamorphose into what scholars now call Neo-Arianism. Second, they realized that *homoousios* and other terms taken from Greek philosophy challenged many bishops who were not really anti-Nicene but rather uncertain as to exactly what the council had formulated. These bishops required education, not censure.

Basil spent some time as a monk (358–364) but eventually became bishop of Caesarea, capital of Cappadocia. His openness to Greek learning offended many strict Christians, but Basil believed in an educated hierarchy. Resolutely pastoral, Basil worked for the poor, including pagans and Jews, and tried to win Arian bishops to the Nicene position.

Convinced that Nicaea's opponents did not understand what had happened at the council, Gregory of Nazianzus worked to explain the meaning of *homoousios*. Countering the main argument against Nicaea, he insisted that doctrine could develop beyond the wording of the Scriptures. Late in his life he moved from Trinitarian theology to Christology. By insisting that Christ was fully human, he argued against Apollinaris of Laodicea, who believed the divine Son of God had no human mind or soul. Gregory used soteriology, the theology of salvation, to insist that "what was not assumed could not be saved," that is, Jesus could not redeem humans unless he himself were fully human. Orthodox tradition honors Gregory with the title "the Theologian."

Gregory of Nyssa was married and had a brief secular career before his brother Basil had him appointed bishop of an outpost named Nyssa. Gregory was a poor administrator but a great theologian. He provided the Nicenes with the formula that in the Trinity there is one *ousia* (nature) but three *hypostases* (persons). The Trinity consists of three distinct, equal persons all sharing the divine nature. The ecumenical council at Constantinople in 381 ratified Gregory's theology.

Modern scholars add a fourth Cappadocian to the original three: Macrina (c. 325–379), older sister of Basil and Gregory of Nyssa. When she was twelve, her parents arranged for a marriage, but her fiancé died. She decided upon a life of asceticism but not in the desert. She chose to stay home, where she created an ascetic family that welcomed women from all social classes, including ex-slaves. She valued virginity and transformed the meaning of the word to apply to women who withdrew from the world and thus from the obligations of procreation imposed by society (some "virgins" in her community were widows with children). Macrina significantly rethought the meaning of asceticism and of women's lives. Moreover, her brother Gregory speaks of her as his wise teacher, who instructed him in the nature of the soul and the resurrection.

———

Gregory of Nyssa, *Life of Saint Macrina*, trans. K. Corrigan (1989); S. Elm, *"Virgins of God":* *The Making of Asceticism in Late Antiquity* (1996); R. P. C. Hanson, *The Search for the Christian Doctrine of God* (1988); F. M. Young, *From Nicaea to Chalcedon* (1983); R. Van Dam, *Becoming Christian: The Conversion of Roman Cappadocia* (2003); Van Dam, *Families and Friends in Late Roman Cappadocia* (2003).

JOSEPH F. KELLY

Capreolus, John

Capreolus, John (c. 1380–1444), French scholastic theologian. He was born in the diocese of Rodez and became a Dominican friar affiliated with the province of Toulouse. In 1408, he began to lecture at the Univ. of Paris on *The Book of the Sentences*. He completed requirements for degrees from the Sorbonne in 1411 and 1415. Later he served as regent of studies for the Dominicans at Toulouse. He then returned to Rodez, where he completed work on the major project of his life, a commentary on the theology of Thomas Aquinas. His *Defense of the Theology of Thomas Aquinas* established his reputation as the "Prince of the Thomists." His declared purpose was to explain and defend Aquinas in response to nominalist critics, but occasionally he presented arguments that were different from his master's thought.

———

J. Capreolus, "On the Virtues" (*Defensiones, Book 3*), ed. and trans. K. White and R. Cessario (2001).

ERIC LUND

Capuchins

Capuchins After the Jesuits, the Capuchins were probably the most successful Catholic religious order of the Reformation era. Founded in 1522 by Matteo da Basceo as an offshoot of Observant Franciscans (under whose jurisdiction they remained until 1619), Capuchins were renowned for their strict adherence to St. Francis's ideal of radical poverty. Their name comes from the distinctive four-pointed cowl (*capuche* or *cappuccio*) that each member wore. They were extremely active and popular preachers and missionaries, and they devoted special attention to the poor and neglected. The austere Capuchins enjoyed especially high prestige among the Catholic laity and were regularly offered as a counterexample to the anticlerical caricatures of Protestants. The order was recognized by Pope Clement VII in 1529, and within twenty years it expanded from a handful of brothers to more than 2,500. The Capuchins suffered a severe though not fatal blow when their third general and most eminent member, Bernadino Ochino (1487–1564), defected to the

Protestant side in 1542. By the end of the sixteenth century, the order comprised over 17,000 members in 1,260 houses, with forty-two provinces in Europe, Asia, Africa, and the Americas. The severity of the order's Rule has been gradually mitigated, but the Capuchins remain a strict Franciscan order.

D. Nimmo, *Reform and Division in the Medieval Franciscan Order: From Saint Francis to the Foundation of the Capuchins* (1987).

JOEL F. HARRINGTON

Carmelite Order

Almost nothing is known about the origins of the Carmelite order. Probably in the course of the twelfth century, small communities of Latin hermits came to Mount Carmel in order to live in contemplation, poverty, and imitation of Christ. Between 1206 and 1214, Albert, patriarch of Jerusalem, gave these hermits their first rule, a so-called formula vitae with pronounced anchoritic features. During the thirteenth century, the hermits of Mount Carmel moved to Europe on account of the threat of the Muslims. This resettlement brought about fundamental changes in their characteristics. The modified rule (drawn up by Innocent IV in 1247) laid stress upon community life and cenobitical organization. As a result, the Carmelites became a mendicant order and spread all over Europe during the later thirteenth and the fourteennth centuries. After a period of decline, there were strong efforts at reform within the order from the second half of the fifteenth century onward: reform congregations, as well as a female branch (second order) developed, and also the first traces of the tertiary branch (third order) can be found. In the second half of the sixteenth century, the Discalced Carmelite order (*Ordo Fratrum Carmelitarum Discalceatorum*) emerged; it was separated from the Carmelite order in 1593. The protagonists of this development were Teresa of Avila and John of the Cross. During the seventeenth century, the Carmelites formed a wide network of missionary work that included Latin America and China. As a result of the French Revolution, the existence of the order was highly imperiled. Nevertheless, the attempt to revive Carmelite life during the nineteenth century succeeded.

J. Smet, *The Carmelites: A History of the Brothers of Our Lady of Mount Carmel,* 4 vols. (1988); *Medieval Carmelite Heritage: Early Reflections on the Nature of the Order*, ed. A. Staring (1989).

MARKUS SCHÜRER

Carmelites, Discalced

The Order of Discalced Brothers and Sisters of the Blessed Virgin of Mount Carmel grew out of the initiatives of Teresa of Jesus (1515–1582) in Avila, Spain, who introduced reforms, beginning with Spanish Carmelite nuns in 1562, designed to foster deeper lives of worship, prayer, and contemplation. She intended to follow the "Primitive Rule" of Carmel, together with her own Constitutions for Discalced Nuns. Teresa sought a return to the original disciplines of the order—abstinence from meat, fasting from September to Easter, emphasis on the spiritual life, devotion to the Virgin, daily Mass, recitation of the Divine Office, not wearing shoes (Lat. *dis*, "without," *calceus*, "shoe").

In 1567 the prior-general allowed Teresa to establish monasteries for men, one of which included John of the Cross (1542–1591), who became a coworker with Teresa. Under their leadership, the growing movement met resistance that led to the separation of Teresa's reform from the established Carmelite order in 1593 and the founding of the Discalced Carmelites as an independent order.

Today there are three branches of Discalced Carmelites worldwide: friars, nuns, and laypeople. Teresa and John were both canonized, in 1622 and 1726, respectively.

E. A. Peers, *Handbook to the Life and Times of St. Teresa of Avila and St. John of the Cross* (1964); J. Smet, *A Brief History of the Brothers of Our Lady of Mount Carmel,* 5 vols. (1988); A. Weber, "Spiritual Administration: Gender and Discernment in the Carmelite Reform," *SCJ* 31 (2000): 123–46.

WILLIAM R. RUSSELL

Carnival

The period of feasting and revelry that took place after Christmas and culminated in the riotous festivities of Fat Tuesday, or Mardi Gras, just before the start of Lent on Ash Wednesday. "Carnival" is derived from the medieval Latin expression *carne vale*, or "flesh, farewell," reflective of the abstentious dietary regimen that Catholics practice during the Lenten season. While originating in the Middle Ages, as first recorded in twelfth-century Venice and eventually observed across most of Europe, carnival may reflect the survival of the wintertime revels of the Romans known as the Saturnalia, when the social world was turned upside down and masters became slaves and slaves masters for three short days. Carnival culture as it emerged from the Middle Ages into the early modern era preserved such inversions of the social and moral order, such as the selection of Lords of Misrule and unholy bishops to preside over the tumult. Some scholars argue that these festivities served as a safety valve to release tensions inimical to communal cohesion, while others see them as ludic yet serious forms of social criticism from the underclasses of European society. The Catholic Church regarded these festivities as pagan and vainly tried to prohibit them. Sixteenth-century Protestant reformers also attacked carnival culture because of its reputed lewdness and superstitious character. Carnival nevertheless survives down to the present day, albeit now largely as a popular form of commercial entertainment.

E. L. R. Ladurie, *Carnival in Romans* (1979); M. Bakhtin, *Rabelais and His World* (1984); C. Humphrey, *The Politics of Carnival: Festive Misrule in Medieval England* (2001).

MICHAEL WOLFE

Carolingian Church The Christian church in Europe in the eighth and ninth centuries was characterized by great diversity, localism, conflict, and significant lay control. Paradoxically, for the first time since the Christian Roman empire of the fourth century, the church in Carolingian Europe played a socially and politically significant role. The Carolingian dynasty rose to power with the help and support of clergy, many of whom Carolingian rulers appointed to important ecclesiastical positions. Control of church land, primarily monasteries, was an important military and political asset for the Carolingians. Popes Zacharias (741–752) and Stephen II (752–757) participated in the deposition of the last Merovingian king and the installation of the first Carolingian king, Pepin III (751–768). Charlemagne (768–814) and Louis the Pious (814–840) saw themselves as leaders of the Christian community with ultimate responsibility for the health of the church and its members. While professing great reverence for St. Peter and his successors, Carolingian kings ran the church with little help from Roman popes. The conversions of the Saxons and the Northmen to Christianity, the last great conversions of pagan peoples, were orchestrated by Carolingian monarchs.

The church's institutional structure and intellectual underpinnings benefitted greatly from Carolingian patronage. Carolingian wealth helped to build and endow numerous church buildings and to create magnificently decorated books and liturgical utensils. Bishops and abbots were important leaders frequently called on to consult and support their kings. Royal leadership revivified conciliar governance of the church and, in turn, church councils served as vehicles for broadcasting the Carolingian vision of a biblically based Christian society. Royal mandates increased the number and quality of schools in monasteries and cathedrals. Church schools became seedbeds for religious reform and intellectual revival. The numerous convents for women are barely visible in the sources, except when they challenged efforts at strict regulation.

In the ninth century the Carolingian church was riven by systemic controversy. Bishops and abbots began to criticize Carolingian rulers, some even conspiring to depose monarchs such as Louis the Pious (see *Agobard of Lyon*). Clergy made good use of vision literature to criticize royal interference in church affairs, especially control of church property. Ingenious and elaborate forgeries of papal decrees portrayed a church in which bishops were independent of their archbishops. The episcopal vision of the church clashed with the monastic. Reformers criticized the venality and corruption of their clerical brethren. While the Carolingian church constituted the first significant audience for the works of the Latin church fathers, Carolingian interpretations of doctrine on issues such as predestination, the Eucharist, the use of images in worship, and Christology led to widespread controversy and accusations of heresy.

J. J. Contreni, "'By Lions, Bishops Are Meant; by Wolves, Priests': History, Exegesis, and the Carolingian Church in Haimo of Auxerre's *Commentary on Ezechiel*," *Francia* 29 (2003): 1–28; R. McKitterick, *The Frankish Church and the Carolingian Reforms, 789–895* (1977); R. E. Sullivan, "What Was Carolingian Monasticism? The Plan of St Gall and the History of Monasticism," in *After Rome's Fall: Narrators and Sources of Early Medieval History: Essays Presented to Walter Goffart*, ed. A. C. Murray (1998), 251–87; J. M. Wallace-Hadrill, *The Frankish Church* (1983).

JOHN J. CONTRENI

Carolingian Renaissance Carolingians ascribed the impetus for the noticeable quickening of artistic, cultural, and intellectual activity in Europe to reform, correction of abuses, and the moral regeneration of society. Carolingian monarchs, bishops, and abbots drove Europe's first deliberate effort to create a Christian, biblically centered society. The results were spectacular. Over six hundred new church buildings went up. Thousands of manuscripts bearing the religious and educational texts intended to support the reform were manufactured and studied. Hundreds of new texts were composed to address contemporary needs. Sophisticated painting, metalwork, and book illustration made visible the reform message and the skill of Europe's artisans. Despite the unitary focus of the cultural program, its results were as fragmented and localized as Carolingian Europe itself. When Carolingian authors and artists appropriated biblical and classical wisdom, they refracted ancient texts and models through their own individual lenses. Their messages were multiple and often contradictory. Among the signs the Carolingian age offers of its great intellectual vitality are numerous religious controversies ("heresies" to partisans), conflicts over the right social order, debates between political and religious authorities, and widespread forgery of key documents. Emulation was often professed, but messy innovation was the result.

J. J. Contreni, "The Carolingian Renaissance: Education and Literary Culture," in *The New Cambridge Medieval History*, vol. 2, *c. 700– c. 900*, ed. R. McKitterick (1995), 709–57.

JOHN J. CONTRENI

Carolingian Schools

The spiritual health of the Carolingian kingdoms depended on educated priests to transmit biblical lessons to Carolingian society. Priests also had to know proper liturgical practice to lead their flocks in correct worship. Cathedral and monastic schools were small, composed of perhaps a dozen students and a master. The talents of the priests, monks, and nuns who taught young members of their communities varied greatly, as did the supply of books that supported their pedagogy. Teachers were generalists who taught a broad curriculum that began with reading and writing, progressed through the liberal arts (both literary and mathematical), advanced to the Latin church fathers, and culminated in the study of Scripture. The reputation of any school depended on local resources and success in preparing a talented student to assume the reins of the teacher. Continuity and renown were episodic.

Parish schools provided basic religious and intellectual education for young lay children. These schools introduced the laity to a modicum of literacy and religious doctrine, but they were difficult to fund and staff. Palace schools were loosely organized and served royal and aristocratic pupils. Laymen and laywomen also received schooling in monasteries as external students.

J. J. Contreni, "The Carolingian Renaissance: Education and Literary Culture," in *The New Cambridge Medieval History*, vol. 2, *c. 700– c. 900*, ed. R. McKitterick (1995), 709–57.

JOHN J. CONTRENI

Carpini, Giovanni de Pian del *see* Giovanni de Pian del Carpini

Carpocratians

Founded by Carpocrates in the second century, the gnostic sect is known primarily from the critiques of Irenaeus (*Haer.* 1.25) and Clement (*Strom.* 3.1–2). Their more unusual practices receive an in-group justification from Epiphanes, the son of the founder. According to Irenaeus, Carpocratians posited a universe created by angels, chief among whom was the devil. This figure, they believed, delivered human souls to an angel who encased them in human bodies where they were imprisoned through a cycle of reincarnation. Only after having undergone all types of experience could souls be freed from their bodies. Carpocratian worship was similarly reputed to have been licentious.

According to Carpocratian thought, Jesus was a human being, the actual son of Joseph, who achieved a peculiar righteousness in his life and was, hence, elevated inasmuch as he abhorred the Jewish laws and despised the angels who created the world. Carpocratians are said to have portrayed Christ in the company of Greek philosophers, demonstrating their veneration of the Hellenistic wisdom systems. Though Jesus was a significant figure, Carpocratians believed that they could surpass Jesus in power by similarly opposing the forces that created the universe. A ritualized burning of the area behind the right earlobes served to identify some members of this community.

R. Grant, *Gnosticism: A Source Book of Heretical Writings from the Early Christian Period* (1961); B. D. Ehrman, *Lost Christianities: The Battles for Scripture and the Faiths We Never Knew* (2003); Ehrman, *Lost Scriptures: Books That Did Not Make It into the New Testament* (2003); W. Foerster, *Patristic Evidence*, vol. 1 of *Gnosis: A Selection of Gnostic Texts* (1972); K. Rudolf, *Gnosis: The Nature and History of Gnosticism* (1983).

RODNEY S. SADLER JR.

Carthage, Councils of Several councils that occurred in Carthage from 220 CE to 646 CE. The ancient North African port city of Carthage (modern Tunis), located at the crossroads of the Mediterranean, was founded and ruled by Phoenicians (eighth–second centuries BCE), then conquered successively by Romans, Vandals, Byzantines, and Arabs. During the Roman era numerous important church councils met at Carthage.

The first attested Council of Carthage convened c. 220–235 with Agrippinus, bishop of Carthage, presiding. The council condemned heretical baptism and stipulated that converts from heretical sects must be rebaptized. The next recorded council met c. 236–238, probably at Carthage, under the presidency of Donatus, to depose a bishop from southern Numidia for grave errors.

During his tenure as bishop of Carthage (248–258), Cyprian summoned an impressive seven councils. The first four conclaves ruled that apostasy (previously unforgivable) could be remitted upon completion of rigorous penance. In 254, controversy ignited over baptism administered by Novatian, who refused to readmit penitent apostates. Cyprian's final three councils rejected Novatianist baptism out of the conviction that a shismatic cannot possess the Holy Spirit and thus cannot confer it. Vehement disagreement with the bishop of Rome over the issue strained the normally cordial relationship of the two great sees. Cyprian's councils remain memorable for their frequency, organization, and controversial agendas.

The next attested conclave did not convene for another century, by which time the Donatist schism (originated 305) had indelibly changed the complexion of African Christianity. Imperial pressure against the Donatists caused a (short-lived) reunion between the two rival churches, and in celebration, Bishop Gratus of Carthage convened a council there in 345/348. With Donatism dominant by 390, low morale and passivity characterized the mood at a council summoned that year by Genethlius, catholic bishop of Carthage.

Each side's fortunes changed significantly in 391/392, upon Aurelius's ascent to catholic primacy at Carthage and the death of the Donatists' visionary leader, Parmenian. With his friend Augustine of Hippo, Aurelius embarked on an ambitious program to revitalize the catholic Church in Africa by instituting an annual plenary council to resolve pressing doctrinal, liturgical, and disciplinary matters. The plenary council convened almost always at Carthage,

with Aurelius presiding. Due to civil insurrection, no council met in 395, 396, and 398. Measures to repress Donatism and paganism (with imperial aid) consumed much of the council's attention. After 407, councils ceased convening annually to ease the burden on bishops. In 416 two conclaves assembled to alert the Roman church about the new heresy of Pelagianism. The council of 418 promulgated detailed theological canons against Pelagianism. In 419 concern over papal interference in the priest Apiarius's case prompted the council to send to Rome a large dossier of African canons, later incorporated into medieval canon law. No records remain for the council of 421. Circa 425 Apiarius's case resurfaced, and an exasperated council chastised the pope for further meddling in a strictly African matter. With the deaths of Augustine and Aurelius (430, 431), the golden age of African councils came to an end.

Almost no councils met (only in 484 and 525) during the Vandal occupation of Africa due to Arian oppression of catholicism. Under Byzantine rule, the African church's fortunes revived, though its glory days were past. Few councils convened (536, 554, and 646), with proceedings focused mainly on Eastern doctrinal issues. The Arab conquest of Carthage in 698 virtually extinguished Christianity in North Africa. The councils' legacy endures in medieval canonical collections invaluable to historians.

F. L. Cross, "History and Fiction in the African Canons," *JTS* 12 (1961): 227–47; G. Dunn, "Cyprian of Carthage and the Episcopal Synod of Late 254," *REAug* 48 (2002): 229–47; J. S. Kanyang, *Episcopus et Plebs* (2000); J. E. Merdinger, *Rome and the African Church in the Time of Augustine* (1997); C. Munier, ed., CCL 149 (1974); Munier, *Vie conciliaire* (1987).

JANE E. MERDINGER

Carthusian Order A religious order that grew from a monastery in the Alps of Savoy. Bruno of Cologne, master of the cathedral school and chancellor of the diocese of Reims, joined a band of hermits in the forest of Colan around 1080. After five years at the forest hermitage, Bishop Hugh of Grenoble gave Bruno and his companions an Alpine hermitage, a simple monastery consisting of an oratory and some cells. It was a fragile beginning, followed by organization and gradual expansion. Guigues (or Guigo) du Pin, dean of the cathedral in Grenoble, joined the community in 1106 and was elected prior in 1109. Guigues composed customs for the community by 1128, and, when the original hermitage was struck by an avalanche (1132), he built the complex known as La Grande Chartreuse. A friend of famous reformers, including Peter the Venerable and Bernard of Clairvaux, the fame of his community spread, attracting pilgrims to the Chartreuse and giving birth to daughter hermitages. The Grand Chartreuse was the model for all future Carthusian monasteries. It had a church; a small cloistered walk giving access to a refectory, chapter hall, and library; and a larger cloistered walk giving access to apartments (cells) for monks, with small walled gardens to the rear. The arrangement, like much of the Carthusian customary, is adapted from Benedictine practices. The new order, like the Cistercians and Premonstratensians, reflected the combination of Benedictine and eremitical ideals highly valued in the late eleventh and early twelfth century. Their own approximations of the life lived by hermits in ancient deserts included the prohibition of eating meat, strict limitations of contact between monks outside of the divine office, and, apart from prayer and the community meals celebrated on Sundays and feast days, silence and isolation, emphasizing contemplation and disengagement from the world. Thirty-seven Carthusian houses were established before 1200. The order's greatest medieval growth came in the fourteenth century, when half of the two hundred houses established before 1500 were founded.

C. H. Lawrence, *Medieval Monasticism* (1989); P. King, *Medieval Monasticism* (1999); J. Hogg, *Die ältesten Consuetudines der Kartäuser* (1973); *Analecta Cartusiana*, 66 vols. to date (1973–).

CHRISTOPHER OCKER

Cartwright, Thomas (1535–1603),

English Puritan reformer. Born in Royston, England, Cartwright matriculated in 1550 at St. John's College, Cambridge, where he continued even during the time of Mary Tudor, graduating in 1554. He became a Fellow of St. John's in 1558, and later took a Fellowship at Trinity. In the mid-1560s, he was already a significant figure, taking part in debates before the queen, and, in 1565, he sided with the Puritans against the wearing of clerical vestments.

After a short time as a chaplain in Ireland, Cartwright returned to Cambridge and took the Lady Margaret Chair in Divinity in 1569, a position he used to articulate and defend a form of Presbyterian church polity over against the Erastian episcopalianism of the Church of England. These controversial views placed him at odds with the authorities, and he was removed from his professorship that same year, precipitating a move to Geneva. In 1572 he attempted to return to Cambridge, where he enjoyed considerable personal popularity among the students, but was once again removed due to the interventions of John Whitgift, with whom he then engaged in a pamphlet war. With the tide now turning decisively against the Puritans in 1573, a warrant was issued for Cartwright's arrest, and he fled again to the Continent.

Throughout the 1570s and early 1580s, Cartwright traveled through Europe, spending time at Heidelberg and Basel and establishing himself as a leading figure in the European Reformed movement through his writings, his personal contacts, and his pastoral work among the Reformed communities in the Netherlands. Returning to England in 1586, he worked as master of a charitable hospital in Warwickshire; however, continued work on behalf of the Puritan and Presbyterian cause led to his arrest and imprisonment in 1590 for about eighteen months. In 1595 he moved to Guernsey as a chaplain, returned to Warwick in 1601, and died there in 1603.

———

A. F. S. Pearson, *Thomas Cartwright and Elizabethan Puritanism, 1535–1603* (1925); P. Collinson, *The Elizabethan Puritan Movement* (1967).

CARL TRUEMAN

Casiodoro de Reina *see* Reina, Casiodoro de

Cassian, John (c. 360–c. 435), early Latin

spiritual writer. Cassian may have come from Scythia (modern Romania) or southern Gaul. Around 380 he and his friend Germanus joined a monastery in Bethlehem. In 385 the two friends moved to Egypt, first exploring monastic sites in the Delta, then settling in Scetis (modern Wādi āl-Natrūn). He considered the monks of Scetis his spiritual masters, although he is strikingly silent about the one who influenced him most: the controversial Evagrius of Pontus. Germanus and Cassian left Egypt in 399 or 400, presumably because of the Origenist controversy. In Constantinople, John Chrysostom ordained Germanus as a presbyter and Cassian as a deacon. In 404 after Chrysostom's exile, the two joined the delegation sent to plead John's case before Pope Innocent I. Around 415 Cassian settled in southern Gaul, in the port city of Massilia (modern Marseilles).

Gennadius records that Cassian, now a presbyter, founded two monasteries there, one for men, another for women. Leading Gallic bishops and aristocrats sought him out as a respected authority on monasticism. To these men he dedicated his *Institutes* and *Conferences*.

The *Institutes* has a double focus. The first four books survey monastic basics: garb, psalmody, and instructions for newcomers. The remaining eight books survey the "eight thoughts" (gluttony, fornication, avarice, anger, sadness, *acēdia* [listlessness], vainglory, pride), a scheme Cassian drew from Evagrius.

The *Conferences* is Cassian's magnum opus. It purports to record twenty-four conversations with Egyptian spiritual masters. Individual conferences generally focus on a single theme, such as renunciation, prayer, chastity, or biblical interpretation. Conference 1 distinguishes between the "end" (*finis*) of monastic life, the kingdom of heaven, and its "goal" (*destinatio*), purity of heart. Conference 10 recommends unceasing recitation of Ps. 70:1 ("God, come to my assistance") and speaks of "fiery wordless prayer" and "ecstasies of heart."

In the 420s some read Cassian's Conference 13 as a veiled attack on Augustine's theology of grace. Augustine's friend, Prosper of Aquitaine, attacked Cassian directly in *Against the Conferencer*. This clash, named (or misnamed) the "Semi-Pelagian Controversy," would mar Cassian's long-term reputation. In 430 at the request of archdeacon (later pope) Leo, Cassian composed *On the Incarnation of the Lord, Against Nestorius*. Benedict, in his *Rule,* made Cassian required reading, thereby ensuring Cassian's influence on the spirituality of the medieval West.

———

A. M. C. Casiday, *Tradition and Theology in St. John Cassian* (2007); C. Stewart, *Cassian the Monk* (1998); R. H. Weaver, *Divine Grace and Human Agency: A Study of the Semi-Pelagian Controversy* (1996).

WILLIAM HARMLESS, SJ

Cassiodorus (c. 487–c. 585), public official, writer, monastic founder. Born of a Roman senatorial family based in southern Italy and highly educated in grammar, rhetoric, and law, Cassiodorus occupied a number of significant public offices under the Ostrogothic king Theoderic I and his successors. From this period (507–537) come the correspondence, official formulae, proclamations, and edicts assembled by Cassiodorus in his *Variae* as a mirror and eulogy of Gothic rule. Also from his time in public office stem two historical works dedicated to kings, the surviving *Chronicle* and a lost history of the Goths, both of which seem to have been intended to emphasize continuity between Roman and Gothic rule and to record Gothic achievements.

While summing up his secular career in the *Variae,* Cassiodorus also began to write on overtly religious themes, and his treatise *On the Soul* (537–540) offered a sustained analysis, philosophical in structure but based on scriptural and patristic authority, of the origin, nature, and future of the soul after death. The initial years of his retirement, first in Ravenna, then in Constantinople, saw him at work on a comprehensive commentary on the Psalms. Although he drew heavily on Augustine's interpretation of the Psalms, Cassiodorus also devoted extensive attention to the linguistic, grammatical, and rhetorical aspects of the text, making the Psalms serve, in effect, as a basic text for both theological and grammatical instruction. This work thereby embodied his ongoing preoccupation with Christian education, a concern expressed earlier in his career in the plan to found a Christian school in Rome with the help of Pope Agapetus (535–536) and later in his decision to found the monastery Vivarium on family lands in Squillace (554). A similar desire (or anxiety) inspired Cassiodorus's *Institutes* (562), a discussion in two parts of the proper course of sacred and secular reading, and his last work, *On Correct Writing* (577–584), composed at the request of the monks of the Vivarium.

———

S. J. B. Barnish, trans., *The Variae of Magnus Aurelius Cassiodorus Senator* (1992); Cassiodorus, *Explanation on the Psalms,* trans. P. G. Walsh (1991); Cassiodorus, *Institutes and On the Soul,* trans. J. Halporn (2004); J. J. O'Donnell, *Cassiodorus* (1979).

WILLIAM NORTH

Castellion, Sebastian (1515–1563), philologist and advocate for religious toleration. Castellion was born to a peasant family in Saint-Martin-du-Fresne in the duchy of Savoy. He embraced the Reformation in 1540 after viewing the persecution of Protestants and moved to Strasbourg, where he was appointed principal of the Latin school and produced his renowned text for teaching Latin and the Bible, the *Dialogi sacri* (1542). He moved to Geneva in 1542 to teach in the Geneva school, and sought to become a pastor to supplement his meager income. Calvin advocated for a larger salary for Castellion but opposed his call to the pastorate on the basis of his questionable doctrinal positions and his shocking biblical translations. Ironically, Castellion questioned the canonicity of the Song of Songs due to its obscene theme, to which Calvin replied by defending the Song's canonical status. By 1544 Castellion, frustrated by his inability to be ordained, called the Geneva pastors, and Calvin in particular, gluttonous, drunken, and wanton, and was expelled from Geneva by the City Council. He settled in Basel in 1545, first as an editor and then as professor of Greek (1553), where he produced Latin (1551) and French (1555) translations of the Bible. In 1553 the Spanish physician Michael Servetus was burned at the stake in Geneva. Calvin defended this action in his *Defense of the Orthodox Faith* (1554), in which he argued that the glory of God is greater than all feelings of human sympathy, which should lead us to kill all blasphemers in our midst, following the zeal of the Israelites. Castellion responded with his treatise *Whether Heretics Ought to Be Persecuted* (1554), in which he cited both patristic and contemporary sources to defend his claim that "to burn a heretic is not to defend a doctrine but to kill a man." In *Advice to a Desolate France* (1562), he applied the same argument to the outbreak of the religious wars in France. Castellion was accused of various heretical positions until the day of his death.

S. Castellion, *Concerning Heretics* (1965); H. R. Guggisberg, *Sebastian Castellio, 1515–1563* (2003).

RANDALL C. ZACHMAN

Catacombs The term is derived from the Latin *ad catacumbas,* which describes the topography of the site of certain underground burial chambers carved into the soft tufa rock along Rome's Via Appia Antica. *Catacumbas* ("at the hollows") probably originally referred to a depression in the ground or quarries at the site but came to describe the particular mode of burial found at this place from the second to the early fifth century: subterranean chambers (*cubicula*—in Lat. also "sleeping rooms") and narrow horizontal tombs (*loculi*) cut into the connecting tunnels—in contrast to the aboveground tombs or mausolea that lined the roads leading out of Rome in ancient times.

Although the Christian catacombs of Rome are the best-known examples, catacombs were also used by Jews and pagans in other parts of the Mediterranean world. The oldest Christian catacomb is the Catacomb of Callistus. It contains the Crypt of the Popes, with tombs of nine Roman popes from the mid-third century, as well as the "gallery of the sacraments," six small chambers with some of the earliest Christian paintings depicting funerary banquets and baptismal images. Other Roman catacombs include the Catacombs of St. Sebastian, Domitilla, Priscilla, St. Agnese, Praetextatus, SS. Peter and Marcellinus, and the Via Latina Catacomb.

The visual art found in the Roman catacombs is the earliest known Christian art and includes symbolic images as well as scenes from the Old and New Testaments. Plaques and inscriptions that covered or marked graves are an important source for knowledge about early Christian piety, family relationships, beliefs about death and the afterlife, and Christian social life.

The catacombs probably were never used as hiding places during persecution. They were places of pilgrimage and of limited liturgical celebrations in later centuries. In time many of their relics were translated to churches, and the catacombs themselves were forgotten until their rediscovery in the mid-fifteenth century by Antonio Bosio (1575–1629) and in the nineteenth century most prominently by Giovanni Battista DeRossi (1822–1894).

L. Hertling and E. Kirschbaum, *The Roman Catacombs* (1960); J. Stevenson, *The Roman Catacombs* (1978); M. Webb, *The Churches and Catacombs of Early Christian Rome* (2001).

ROBIN M. JENSEN

Cateau-Cambrésis, Treaty of This treaty of 1559 concluded over six decades of fighting, mainly in Italy, between France and the Spanish Habsburgs. Bankruptcy and growing religious dissent in their territories prompted the kings of France and Spain to end hostilities abroad. The treaty favored Spain more than France. Although France kept the cities of Metz, Toul, and Verdun, it had to relinquish claims to Milan and Naples and remove soldiers from the Italian peninsula.

The marriage of Elisabeth of Valois, daughter of Henry II of France, to Philip II of Spain in July 1559 sealed the peace. A jousting accident at the wedding celebration fatally wounded Henry. His death led to political and religious uncertainty in France as opposing court factions competed for influence in the government and control of the policy toward Protestantism, leading the way to over thirty years of civil conflict in France.

R. Bonney, *The European Dynastic States, 1494–1660* (1991); J. H. Elliott, *Europe Divided, 1559–1598* (2nd ed., 2000).

SCOTT M. MARR

Catechumenate   The term "catechumen" (*katēchoumenos*) means "one to be instructed" and appears in the New Testament itself (Gal. 6:6). In the early church, preparing candidates for baptism included not only catechesis but also a whole complex of ascetical and ritual exercises. However, this term generally covers the process of preparing candidates for baptism. Catechumens formed a distinct and sometimes sizeable order within the worshiping assembly. Recent scholarship has stressed the rich local diversity and gradual evolution in both the ancient catechumenate and the ancient rites of initiation.

The first clear evidence of an organized catechumenate appears in the early third century in accounts by Clement of Alexandria, Origen, and Tertullian. The earliest outline of rites and stages appears in the *Apostolic Tradition*, attributed to Hippolytus of Rome. It legislates an initial interrogation of new converts and their sponsors and decrees a three-year catechumenate during which catechumens "hear the word." Before baptism, catechumens were again examined, whether they "have done every good work." On Friday (before Easter?) they fasted, on Saturday were exorcised, and at the vigil were baptized. Recently questions have been raised about the authorship and provenance of the text and the dating of certain legislation.

The fourth-century catechumenate was carefully structured, both catechetically and liturgically. Entrance rites are described in Augustine's *On Catechizing Beginners*. Augustine expected catechists to examine converts' motives and offer an evangelical talk, surveying the biblical narrative and its import. Converts were then signed with the cross on the forehead and received a laying-on of hands and a taste of salt. These rites made them "Christians," Augustine insisted; they were now members of God's "household," though not yet "sons" or "daughters" worthy of full inheritance rights. The length of the catechumenate varied considerably. The Council of Elvira in Spain (305) decreed a two-year catechumenate. This was probably a minimum. Those from Christian families were typically made catechumens as children and not baptized until adulthood. Ancient sources list various complaints against catechumens: lax standards, suspect motives, delays of baptism. Nonetheless, the fourth-century catechumenate proved remarkably successful in Christianizing large segments of the Roman Empire's population. Ordinary catechumens did not attend classes or receive special instructions. They simply joined with the regular congregation for Sunday and daily liturgies where all would have pondered the same Scriptures and heard the same sermons. After the sermon, catechumens were formally dismissed; only the baptized were permitted to stay on for the Eucharist.

Lent marked a new stage in the catechetical process. A catechumen's conduct was publicly examined before formal enrollment for baptism. In the Greek East, these advanced catechumens were called *phōtizomenoi* ("those to be enlightened"); in Rome, *electi* ("the chosen"); and elsewhere in the Latin West, *competentes* ("petitioners"). They embarked on a six-week regimen of fasting, prayer, and almsgiving. Some churches required several, even daily exorcisms. Before Easter, bishops "handed over the creed," explaining it phrase-by-phrase in a sermon or sermon series. Candidates then memorized the creed and formally "handed it back." Similar rites of "handing over" and "handing back" the Lord's Prayer took place in some locales.

Initiation, which included baptism, chrismation, and Eucharist, typically (though not universally) took place at the Easter Vigil. The catechumenate officially ended with baptism, but during Easter Week the newly baptized received a form of catechesis known as *mystagogy* ("teaching of the mysteries"). The catechumenate as a living institution disappeared in the early Middle Ages, displaced, it seems, by the growing practice of infant baptism.

In the twentieth century, the catechumenate underwent a remarkable revival. It sprang from experiments by Roman Catholic missionaries in Africa and Asia and was much aided by pathbreaking research on the ancient liturgy. In 1963 the Second Vatican Council ordered that "the catechumenate for adults is to be restored and broken up into several steps" (*Sacrosanctum Concilium* 64). This mandate came to fruition with the Catholic Church's promulgation of the Rite of Christian Initiation of Adults (RCIA) in 1972.

The RCIA describes adult initiation as a "spiritual journey" and divides it into four periods: (1) evangelization, (2) catechumenate, (3) purification and enlightenment, and (4) mystagogy. Between the periods are "steps," or rites of passage that function as doorways to the next period. Evangelization is a time for hearing the gospel. It is meant to spark an initial conversion away from sin and toward God's love. The first step is the Acceptance into the Order of Catechumens, a rite in which candidates are signed with the cross on the forehead, ears, eyes, and so forth, and are invited to share "at the table of God's word." The second period, the catechumenate itself, involves an apprenticeship in Christian living, lasting "long enough—several years if necessary—for the conversion and faith of the catechumens to become strong." Catechumens attend Sunday liturgies of the Word, after which they are blessed and dismissed prior to the Eucharist. Once they are ready, a second step follows, the Rite of Election, held on the first Sunday of Lent. Here the church solicits testimony from sponsors and enrolls catechumens for baptism. The third period coincides with Lent and focuses on purification and enlightenment. The "elect," as candidates are now called, undergo an exorcism, or "Scrutiny," on the third, fourth, and fifth Sundays of Lent. They also receive Presentations of the Creed and of the Lord's Prayer. The third climactic step takes place at the Easter Vigil, where candidates are initiated via the sacraments of baptism, confirmation, and Eucharist. The fourth period, mystagogy, lasts from Easter to Pentecost; the newly baptized are to deepen "their grasp of the paschal mystery" and do works of charity (RCIA 244).

While designed for the unbaptized, the RCIA has prompted adaptations to other groups, such as baptized but uncatechized adults or adults seeking full communion. Since the late 1980s Episcopalians and Lutherans, especially in North America, have worked toward implementing the adult catechumenate for their respective communions.

The Rite of Christian Initiation of Adults (2nd ed., 1988); P. F. Bradshaw et al., *The Apostolic Tradition* (2002); A. Bugnini, *The Reform of the Liturgy 1948–1975* (1990); E. Ferguson, ed., *Conversion, Catechumenate, and Baptism in the Early Church* (1993); T. M. Finn, ed., *Early Christian Baptism and the Catechumenate*, 2 vols. (1992); Finn, *From Death to Rebirth* (1997); W. Harmless, *Augustine and the Catechumenate* (1995); M. E. Johnson, *The Rites of Christian Initiation* (1999); A. Kavanagh, *The Shape of Baptism* (2nd ed., 1991); E. Yarnold, *The Awe-Inspiring Rites of Initiation* (2nd ed., 1994).

WILLIAM HARMLESS, SJ

Cathars   The Cathars were dualist heretics of the twelfth and thirteenth centuries. They derived their beliefs and practices from the Bulgarian heresy of Bogomilism, which infiltrated Byzantium in the eleventh century and spread to the West, possibly aided by Frankish converts who set up a bishopric in Constantinople. The first indisputable evidence of the heresy comes from the Rhineland in 1143–1144, but it is likely to have had an influence elsewhere, and somewhat earlier. Cathars sought liberation from the world, which they believed to be wholly evil, the creation of an evil power. The incarnation was as a consequence denied: Christ was transmuted into an angel disguised as a man, come to earth to teach true doctrine. Sacraments, making use of evil matter, were rejected, and the church was stigmatized as the church of Satan. The *consolamentum*, conferred by the laying on of hands, enabled the candidate to secure escape at death from reincarnation and the evil world of matter, but only if onerous renunciations of marriage, of products of coition, milk, meat, and eggs, and frequent fasting on bread and water were sustained for a lifetime. There was an informal organization in houses of those who had received the *consolamentum*, known to inquisitors as the "perfect." Women had the same opportunity to become one of the perfect as men and to receive the ritual adoration of a genuflection known as the *melioramentum*, but they could not become deacons or bishops. Unlike the Bogomils, Cathars adopted a similar hierarchy to the Church plus a hierarchy of greater sons and lesser sons with automatic right of succession. Followers had limited duties and could not pray; being still in the power of evil they could not refer to God as "Our Father." Their hope lay in deathbed acceptance of the *consolamentum*. Conflicts spilled over from the Eastern founts of heresy after a visit c. 1167 by Nicetas, leader from Constantinople, followed soon after by a rival, Petracius from Bulgaria. Anxieties arose over the origins of evil, between those who accepted a moderate dualism in which the world was created by a fallen angel or son of God, and those who believed in creation by an eternal evil principle. Languedoc remained stable, but Italian Catharism split into denominations with rival episcopates. Catharism spread rapidly in the twelfth century, penetrating northern as well as southern France, the Low Countries, Italy, and parts of Spain. It reached England but only struck deep roots in Languedoc, aided by a tradition of toleration and political weakness, and in the Italian cities through conflicts between emperors and popes and disputes between bishops and civil governments. It died in the fourteenth century after a long struggle involving the summoning of the Albigensian Crusade by Innocent III in 1208, counterpreaching by friars, the development of lay confraternities, and the emergence of the papal inquisition. See also *Dualism, Medieval.*

M. Barber, *The Cathars* (2000); E. R. Ladurie, *Montaillou* (1975); M. Lambert, *The Cathars* (1998); R. I. Moore, *The Origins of European Dissent* (2nd ed., 1985); W. L. Wakefield and A. P. Evans, eds., *Heresies of the High Middle Ages* (1969).

MALCOLM D. LAMBERT

Cathedral Chapter

At the heart of the medieval diocese stood the first church of the bishop's see, staffed by the canons of the cathedral chapter. Although canons were originally dedicated to the celebration of the liturgy and the administration of the sacraments in the cathedral, they became increasingly involved in the affairs of the bishop and his diocese. During the eleventh century reformers sought to counter clerical corruption by forming cathedral chapters into monastic communities devoted to the apostolic life and in submission to their bishop or prior. But the administrative demands on the canons were not conducive to the cloistered life and instead encouraged the development of the chapter as an independent corporation with its own financial endowment, governing functions, and institutional identity apart from the bishop. Throughout the twelfth and thirteenth centuries canons became more and more involved in autonomous management of their endowed properties, protection of their legal rights and privileges, the election of bishops, and the administration of the diocese, especially during episcopal vacancies. As the power and influence of the chapter grew, its relationship to the bishop became increasingly complex and contested. Sworn legal agreements—capitulations—carefully defined the requisite rights of the chapter and bishop, thus providing a more secure foundation for the rule of the church and its lands.

E. U. Crosby, *Bishop and Chapter in 12th-Century England: A Study of the Mensa Episcopalis* (1994); L. G. Duggan, *Bishop and Chapter: The Governance of the Bishopric of Speyer to 1552* (1978).

J. JEFFERY TYLER

Cathedral Schools

In 789 Charlemagne ordered that all cathedrals and monasteries in his empire maintain schools to educate both clerics and members of the laity. This legislation standardized what was already common practice and ensured the continuity and even increase of European learning during the invasions and political turmoil of the ninth and tenth centuries. These schools perpetuated the central goal of the Carolingian renaissance: the ability to communicate fluently in Latin.

A cathedral school education consisted of advanced schooling specifically in the seven liberal arts (grammar, rhetoric, logic, arithmetic, geometry, music, and astronomy). Emphasis was placed particularly on Latin grammar, but beyond that the small size of these schools (usually with a single master, appointed by the bishop or cathedral chapter) meant that different schools specialized in one or two of the liberal arts. By the tenth century, diligent students traveled from school to school to get a complete education. The goal was mastery of ancient knowledge rather than new investigation; logic, which was one of the accepted liberal arts, had not yet assumed its twelfth-century role as the most important. Although they did not stress new ideas, the cathedral and monastic schools both had a massive impact on European learning, first by regaining classical Latin knowledge and then by using it as a platform for original work.

Until the middle of the tenth century cathedral and monastic schools were virtually indistinguishable: secular clerics studied at monasteries and monks studied at cathedral schools, while both accepted some lay students. By the mid-tenth century, however, cathedral schools began to flourish dramatically and to differentiate themselves from the more contemplative and otherworldly focus of monastic schools. In the tenth and eleventh centuries at least a dozen cathedrals, especially in Germany, were important centers of education, but with a much more secular stress. In Germany, a cathedral school education became almost a requirement for a position in imperial service. Thus, these schools emphasized the skills of the royal court: pleasant speech and a union of classical knowledge with manners. Most importantly in that regard, the historian Stephen Jaeger has traced how cathedral schools spread an ideal of *humanitas*, a strong sense of the dignity of the human being emphasizing gentleness and thoughtful kindness. These schools especially revived the study of the works of Cicero, with the great Roman's attention to philosophy used in the service of the state and the importance of ethics.

The well-rounded education of the cathedral schools gave way in the twelfth century to scholasticism, which focused above all on Aristotelian logic as the key to success. But cathedral schools paved the way for the universities of Western Europe by providing a critical mass of educated men as well as the first centers for higher education from which the universities grew.

C. S. Jaeger, *The Envy of Angels: Cathedral Schools and Social Ideals in Medieval Europe, 950–1200* (1995); C. Lutz, *Schoolmasters of the Tenth Century* (1977).

PHYLLIS G. JESTICE

Catherine de Médici (1519–1589), queen

of France, mother of the last three kings of the house of Valois. The daughter of Lorenzo de Médici, Catherine married Henry of Orléans in 1533, crowned Henry II in 1547. His death brought her fifteen-year-old son Francis II to the throne in 1559. After Francis's death the following year, Catherine became regent until her second son, Charles IX, came of age to rule.

The spread of Calvinism in France generated religious, political, and social divisions that imperiled the kingdom. Catherine's strategy to safeguard the monarchy for her sons by trying to conciliate Catholics and Protestants led to a colloquy at Poissy (1561) to reach a compromise on doctrinal differences. She next issued the Edict of January in 1562, granting Huguenots limited rights to public worship, but was unable to prevent the first of the Wars of Religion from beginning in March.

Catherine worked to reconcile the warring parties and establish a stable peace by arranging the marriage of her daughter, Marguerite of Valois, to the Protestant leader Henry of Navarre (later Henry IV of France). The wedding brought thousands of Huguenots to Paris and set the stage for the most notorious event in the religious wars, the St. Bartholomew's Day Massacre (August 24, 1572). Catherine's plan to assassinate a handful of Protestant military chiefs turned into the indiscriminate slaughter of Protestants in Paris and throughout France. During the reign of her third son, Henry III, she persisted in her efforts to preserve monarchical authority through an accommodation between royalist, Protestant, and Catholic League forces. Catherine died January 5, 1589, seven months before Henry III's assassination ended the Valois dynasty.

R. J. Knecht, *Catherine De' Medici* (1998); N. M. Sutherland, *Catherine de Medici and the Ancien Régime* (1966).

SCOTT M. MARR

Catherine of Alexandria, legendary mar-

tyr. There is no historical evidence of her existence and no mention of her prior to the tenth century. Early pilgrims to the sixth-century monastery on Mount Sinai do not know of her.

According to tradition, Catherine was born into a royal family and as a child was a renowned philosopher. After inheriting her father's kingdom, she refused to marry the eligible princes presented to her. She became the bride of Christ in a vision and rejected philosophy for Scripture. Challenged by the Roman emperor to defend her faith, Catherine reportedly argued with fifty pagan philosophers in Alexandria and converted them all to Christianity. When arrested, she converted her jailers and the empress. At her execution angels translated her relics to the eponymously named monastery on Mount Sinai.

The veneration of St. Catherine demonstrates the power of popular devotion. Returning crusaders and the *Golden Legend* spread her cult throughout medieval Europe. Joan of Arc claimed to have been directed by her voice; she was known in Germany as one of the Fourteen Holy Helpers in heaven; Renaissance painters depicted her as Jerome's female counterpart. Devotion to St. Catherine had largely disappeared by the eighteenth century.

K. J. Lewis, *The Cult of St. Katherine of Alexandria in Late Medieval England* (2000).

WILLIAM B. SWEETSER JR.

Catherine of Aragon (1485–1536), first

wife of Henry VIII. Catherine was the daughter of Duke Ferdinand of Aragon and Isabella of Castile, and aunt of the Holy Roman Emperor Charles V. She was married in 1501 to Arthur, Prince of Wales, who died the next year. Pope Alexander VI ordered a special dispensation so that she would be able to marry Arthur's younger brother, Henry, when he became King Henry VIII in 1509. They had five children, but only Mary (future Mary I) survived. In 1526, under the wiles and charm of Anne Boleyn, Henry began to question the validity of his marriage to Catherine. Pope Clement VII and Wolsey stalled on the issue of an annulment, but by 1532 the issue was presented to the universities for debate, and they upheld the invalidity of the marriage. Henry divorced Catherine and married Anne in 1533, with Thomas Cranmer delivering the annulment the pope had refused. Catherine lived out her life in exile in the English countryside and died in Peterborough in 1536.

J. J. Scarisbrick, *Henry VIII* (1968).

ALDEN R. LUDLOW

Catherine of Genoa (1447–1510), mystic and humanitarian. Caterinetta Fieschi Adorno, recognized for her vision of purgatory, modeled renewal of church and society through a return to ascetic apostolic life and selfless service of others. A watershed religious experience caused the married aristocratic lady to devote her life to serving the poor at the Pammatone Hospital in Genoa, which she directed from 1490 to 1496. Her husband since 1463, Giuliano of Adorno, followed her after his conversion experience. Catherine's ascetic, self-humiliating practices and her contemplation of the Eucharist were accompanied by visions and ecstasies from which she drew her experience-based, mystical theology. Ettore Vernazza, her disciple, and Don Cattaneo Marabotto, her spiritual director, edited her *Vita* as well as *The Treatise on Purgatory* and *The Spiritual Dialogue*, the latter presenting her distinctive vision for the spiritual stages of purgation, annihilation, and transformation of the soul toward loving God perfectly—the goal she attained in her painful death. Even though the nature of her love of mysticism, spiritual genius, authorship, and possible psychological pathologies have been debated, Pope Clement XII canonized Catherine on May 18, 1737. Catherine has inspired lay piety and mysticism among Catholics and Protestants alike.

S. Hughes, ed., *Catherine of Genoa, Purgation and Purgatory, Spiritual Dialogue* (1979); D. C. Marabotto, *The Spiritual Doctrine of St. Catherine of Genoa* (1989).

KIRSI STJERNA

Catherine of Siena (c. 1347–1380), Italian mystic and Dominican tertiary. According to her confessor and hagiographer, Raymond of Capua, Catherine chose at an early age to lead a penitential life. She joined the Dominican third order, an unusual choice for a young, unmarried woman. Her mystical experiences included a spiritual marriage and an exchange of hearts with Christ. Later she took on a public role of charitable activity and peacemaking

and began to gather a spiritual family around her. Her strong identification with Christ (as when she seemed to Raymond to take on Christ's features), her asceticism, and her reverence for the Dominican way of life supported her public apostolate.

Catherine traveled extensively, promoting a new crusade, the return of Pope Gregory XI from Avignon to Rome, and the reform of the church during the early part of the Great Schism. She wrote numerous letters and a *Dialogue on Divine Providence* (1377–1378). She was an important figure for the Dominican Observant movement and was canonized in 1461. She was made patron saint of Italy in 1939 and a doctor of the church in 1970.

Catherine of Siena, *Dialogue*, ed. Susan Noffke (1980); *The Letters of Catherine of Siena*, 2 vols., trans. Noffke (2000–2001); Raymond of Capua, *The Life of Catherine of Siena*, trans. C. Kearns (1980).

VICTORIA M. MORSE

Catholic League An alliance of French nobles and urban Catholics, clerical and lay, the League was fiercely dedicated to ensuring the Catholicity of the French crown. It was formed in 1584 in the late stages of France's religious wars (1562–1598) when Henry of Navarre, leader of France's Huguenots, became heir presumptive to the French throne and the prospect of a Protestant king alarmed most French Catholics. The leader of the League was the strongest of the anti-Huguenot nobles, Henry, Duke of Guise.

An alliance with Philip II of Spain added considerably to the League's military strength, and it moved quickly to preempt Navarre's succession by designating as heir presumptive his uncle, Charles, cardinal of Bourbon (1585). In Paris an uprising in support of Henry of Guise in May 1588 forced Henry III to flee. Despised by League partisans for his favorable treatment of Navarre and the Protestants, Henry III agreed to recognize the cardinal of Bourbon as his successor. But soon thereafter he engineered the assassination of Henry of Guise and the cardinal of Guise and imprisoned League leaders, including the cardinal of Bourbon. Catholic outrage expressed in sermons and pamphlets that borrowed heavily from earlier Protestant writings on the right of rebellion precipitated Henry III's assassination the following year (1589).

Henry of Navarre, pressing his claims to the succession, advanced on Paris and laid siege to it. The cardinal of Bourbon died in 1590, and Henry of Navarre's conversion to Catholicism (1593), coronation (as Henry IV), and triumphal entry into Paris (1594) effectively ended League power there and elsewhere in the kingdom.

D. Crouzet, *Les guerriers de Dieu: La violence au temps des troubles de religion*, 2 vols. (1990); M. Greengrass, *France in the Age of Henry IV* (1985); M. P. Holt, *The French Wars of Religion, 1562–1629* (1995).

CHRISTOPHER ELWOOD

Cecil, William (1520–1598), created Lord Burghley in 1571. Active in court, politics, and high office under Edward VI and Mary Tudor, Cecil became a prominent Protestant, political advisor, and chief secretary of state during the reign of Elizabeth I. A graduate of St. John's College, Cambridge, and private secretary to Edward Seymour (Protector Somerset), he was made secretary of state in 1550. Mary's accession in 1553 led him to lower his political profile; by 1558, under Elizabeth, he was once again secretary. He was Elizabeth's closest advisor and wielded tremendous power, yet he was respected throughout Europe. He aided in the authoring of the Acts of Supremacy and Uniformity of 1559, as well as the framing of the Thirty-Nine Articles of 1563, outlining a Protestant theology for the Church of England. A patron of moderate Puritanism, he was conciliatory in tensions between the Anglicans and the Puritans. His strongly Erastian views stressed the subservience of the Church of England to the crown; despite this, Cecil is responsible for establishing a strong Church of England.

S. Alford, *The Early Elizabethan Polity: William Cecil and the British Succession Crisis, 1558–1569* (1998); A. G. R. Smith, *William Cecil, Lord Burghley: Minister of Elizabeth I* (1991).

ALDEN R. LUDLOW

Cecilia (third cent.), Roman virgin and martyr. Little reliable information is known about her. According to her late-fifth-century *Acta*, she was an upper-class young Christian betrothed to a pagan, Valerian. She vowed to remain a virgin, converted her husband Valerian and his brother, Tiburtius, who also were martyred. Cecilia refused to sacrifice and converted her persecutors. An attempt to suffocate her failed. A soldier, after three blows, beheaded her. She was reported to have remained alive for

three days. Cecilia was highly honored in the tradition of the church. She is alleged to have been buried (c. 230) in the Callisto catacomb under Rome (the first early Christian communal underground cemetery). In 820 Pope Paschal I (817–824) moved her relics to the church bearing her name in Trastevere in Rome. In 1584 she was declared the patroness of the Academy of Music in Rome (she had always been depicted with a musical instrument). In 1599 when her church was renovated, it was reported that her remains were found complete and uncorrupted.

H. Delehaye, *Étude sur le légendier romain* (1936), 73–96; V. L. Kennedy, *The Saints of the Canon of the Mass* (1938), 178–82; L. V. Rutgers, *Subterranean Rome* (2000), 122–24.

DAVID M. SCHOLER

Celibacy of Clergy Clerical celibacy has been a divisive issue throughout the history of Christianity. The earliest sources suggest that a bishop, presbyter, or deacon was normally a married man, though "a man of one wife" (1 Tim. 3:2; Titus 1:6). In the earliest centuries this qualification was interpreted as a prohibition of marriage after ordination. The first evidence of an attempt to require celibacy of married clerics is the thirty-third canon of the Synod of Elvira in Spain (c. 305). The decree forbade "bishops, presbyters, and deacons, that is, all clerics placed in the ministry, to have sexual relations with their wives and to produce children." This canon would have had only local application.

At the end of the fourth century Siricius, bishop of Rome, issued several decretal letters in which he argued that higher clergy should observe celibacy after ordination (Letters 1.7.10, 5.8, 10.6). These letters, addressed to churches in Spain, Gaul, and North Africa, indicate that some bishops in those areas opposed the new requirement. Similar legislation by subsequent popes (e.g., Innocent I and Leo I) suggests that the requirement remained controversial, although most of the Latin fathers accepted it (e.g., Ambrose, Ambrosiaster, Jerome).

In the Eastern churches practices remained more fluid. Although many clergy were celibate, in the fourth century bishop Synesius of Cyrene insisted that he be allowed to keep his wife and marital privileges after ordination (Letter 105). By the sixth century Justinian's legislation required that candidates for the episcopacy be either unmarried men or men who had agreed to live apart from their wives. Presbyters and deacons were allowed to marry prior to ordination and to live with their wives, but marriage after ordination was forbidden. In 692 the Council in Trullo (Quinisext Synod) confirmed Justinian's legislation. The difference between Western and Eastern practice was a point of contention in the separation of 1054 and remains a dividing point today.

In the Western church, enforcement of clerical celibacy remained difficult, and throughout the medieval period the cohabitation of the clergy with women was widespread. The reforming popes of the eleventh century, especially Gregory VII, attempted to curb the abuses. The First and Second Lateran Councils of 1123 and 1139 declared clerical marriages invalid (not merely illicit). By the time of the Reformation, clerical concubinage had become rampant again, leading the Reformers to reject celibacy as a requirement for ministry. In 1563 the Council of Trent reaffirmed the celibacy requirement, although it allowed the possibility of exceptions. Such remains the practice in Roman Catholicism today.

W. Basset and P. Huizing, eds., *Celibacy in the Church* (1972); R. Cholij, *Clerical Celibacy in East and West* (1989); G. Denzler, *Die Geschichte des Zölibats* (1993); C. Cochini, *Apostolic Origins of Priestly Celibacy* (1990); R. Gryson, *Les origines du célibat ecclésiastique du premier au septième siècle* (1970); S. Heid, *Celibacy in the Early Church: The Beginnings of a Discipline of Obligatory Continence for Clerics in East and West* (2000); H. C. Lea, *History of Sacerdotal Celibacy in the Christian Church* (1907).

DAVID G. HUNTER

Celsus (second cent.), erudite pagan critic of Christianity. Celsus's identity is a mystery. Reconstructed fragments of his work *The True Doctrine* in Origen's massive refutation, the *Contra Celsum* (c. 245), provide some glimpses of his character. Celsus was an eclectic Middle Platonist, sympathetic with the Stoics' attempts to redeem the myths of the Roman gods through allegorical interpretation but also deeply committed to the Platonists' efforts to develop a sophisticated monotheism. Celsus affirmed that one high God, called by many names among many peoples, presided over the full pantheon of lesser deities and exercised providence to the ends of the inhabited earth.

The True Doctrine, perhaps composed in reaction to the apologetic works of Justin Martyr, indicted Christianity as a dangerous religious innovation, a secretive sect defiant of the religious tradition of Rome and even of its own mother religion, Judaism. Celsus demonstrated firsthand knowledge of the Gospels by caricaturing Jesus as an illicit magician who had duped and exploited his followers and after death had been exalted by them to the highest divine status. Christianity, Celsus charged, had abandoned acceptable notions of divine transcendence by asserting the incarnation and suffering of the one high God. Christian teaching on the resurrection of Jesus and ultimately of mortal flesh offended Greco-Roman sensitivities. Any virtuous features in Christian ethics, Celsus alleged, were plagiarized from Greco-Roman tradition.

Familiar with the Hebrew Scriptures, Celsus implicated the new religion in what he viewed as the Jews' fallacious cosmogony and prophecies and their outrageous claims to exclusive divine election. Origen answered Celsus's charges point by point, aspiring to best his pagan adversary on philosophical as well as biblical and theological grounds.

H. Chadwick, ed. and trans., *Origen: Contra Celsum* (1965); R. L. Wilken, *The Christians as the Romans Saw Them* (1984).

PAUL M. BLOWERS

Celtic Christianity The term generally refers to Christianity as developed by people in Scotland, Ireland, Wales, Cornwall, and Brittany, as well as the missionary activities of these people to East Anglia, Northumbria, and monastic centers in continental Europe until the reforms of the twelfth century, which tried to bring all of Europe into Latin unity. The Christianity of the Celts developed in the third century in Roman Britain and evolved its particular features when the Anglo-Saxons invaded Britain in the fifth century. Cut off from the European continent and Rome, the church turned westward and began to develop the traits that characterize it as Celtic Christianity. One of these was a strong tendency for mystical voyages, voluntary exile, or "white martyrdom." Among the earliest Celtic missionaries, Ninian (d. c. 423) voyaged to convert the Northern Picts. A contemporary of Ninian's, Pelagius, spread his heretical doctrine far enough to be Augustine of Hippo's adversary. The Briton Patrick (d. c. 490) strove to convert the Irish. By the end of the sixth century Ireland had replaced Britain as the center of Celtic Christianity. The early Irish missionaries include Colum Cille (d. c. 597), who settled at Iona in Scotland, and Aidan (d. 651), who settled on the island of Lindisfarne.

Other missionaries crossed the English Channel into Europe. Columbanus left Ireland c. 590 and established monasteries in Annegray, Luxeuil, and Fontaine before settling at Bobbio in northern Italy. The Celtic church in Brittany was founded by people such as Samson (c. 486–557). Born in Wales, the saint moved to Cornwall before becoming bishop of Dol.

Due to their separation from the rest of the Catholic world, the Celtic churches celebrated Easter at a different date than did the Roman church. Their monks also favored a different tonsure. These two points were the subjects of the Synod of Whitby (664), where it was decided that Northumbria should follow Rome. Many monasteries switched, but those Celtic monks who dissented left for Iona and later Ireland. Another difference was the hierarchical structure of the church. Unlike the Roman episcopal structure, the Celtic church developed around clan monasteries owned and run by a noble abbot or abbess who had complete authority, replacing, in this manner, the role of bishop, and indeed making the bishop beholden to the abbot. Columbanus exported this structure into Merovingian Gaul. Another particular characteristic that was successfully exported was that of private penance. The Irish traveled with their *penitentials*, books listing sins and a system of penance for each. This took the act of penance from the public square to the private sphere of sinner and confessor. Thus, Celtic Christianity influenced what became the more unified Christianity of the later Middle Ages.

J. P. Mackey, ed., *An Introduction to Celtic Christianity* (1989).

MARIANNE M. DELAPORTE

Cerdo

Cerdo (second cent.), Syrian gnostic. Not much is known about Cerdo. Irenaeus's account, an important source of information, is of questionable reliability. Cerdo is said to have been a Simonian who immigrated to Rome and taught during the rule of Bishop Hyginus in the mid-second century. He believed that the Father of Jesus Christ was an unknown deity distinct from the God of the Old Testament. This differentiation of deities was evident in the radical orientation of the Old Testament God toward justice, while the Father of the loving Christ was "good." Cerdo's belief in an alternate Father of the Christ is said to have won him an adherent in Marcion, although claims by the church fathers that he was Marcion's teacher cannot be substantiated.

R. Grant, *Gnosticism: A Source Book of Heretical Writings from the Early Christian Period* (1961); B. D. Ehrman, *Lost Scriptures: Books That Did Not Make It into the New Testament* (2003); K. Rudolf, *Gnosis: The Nature and History of Gnosticism* (1983).

RODNEY S. SADLER JR.

Cerinthus

Cerinthus (early second cent.), docetic gnostic from Asia Minor. Cerinthus posited a world created not by God but by a distinct power unaware of God's existence, perhaps an angel (Hippolytus, *Haer.* 1.26.1; Epiphanius, *Pan.* 28.1–8). He held the adoptionist view that Jesus was a particularly wise and righteous human being, born of natural relations between his mother Mary and father Joseph, who was elevated at his baptism by the descent of Christ as a dove. The spiritual Christ dwelt with him during his time of ministry and provided the knowledge of the Father and the ability to perform the miraculous feats that were evident in the Gospels. However, Christ departed from Jesus during the passion as he committed his spirit into the Father's hands. This was necessary inasmuch as the spiritual being, Christ, was not subject to human suffering or death. Jesus, the human entity, did suffer and die. He was later resurrected according to Cerinthus.

H. Bettenson, *Documents of the Christian Church* (1967); R. Grant, *Gnosticism: A Source Book of Heretical Writings from the Early Christian Period* (1961); K. Rudolf, *Gnosis: The Nature and History of Gnosticism* (1983).

RODNEY S. SADLER JR.

Chalcedon, Definition of

Chalcedon, Definition of Chalcedon, a city in Asia Minor, was the location of the Fourth Ecumenical Council in 451, at which the Definition of Chalcedon was produced. The council was called to address questions of Christology in response to the ongoing controversy between supporters of Dioscorus of Alexandria and those of Flavian of Constantinople.

After the Council of Ephesus (431) and the Formulary of Reunion between Cyril of Alexandria and John of Antioch (433), the question persisted of how Christ could be both fully God and fully human without separation of the humanity and divinity. Chrysaphius, a eunuch in the imperial court at Constantinople, was a supporter of extreme Cyrillian Christology and rejected the Formulary of Reunion. The bishop of Constantinople, Flavian, was Antiochene.

Chrysaphius, along with Dioscorus and Eutyches, a monk in Constantinople, sought to have the Formulary deemed unacceptable as a test for orthodoxy, as it was an adjunct to the Nicene Creed. Eutyches claimed that to confess two natures in Christ after the union was heresy. Flavian condemned him as an Apollinarian. Dioscorus condemned Flavian for using a standard other than Nicaea. Emperor Theodosius called a synod at Ephesus in 449.

This synod, later called the "Robber Synod," declared Flavian a heretic and Eutyches orthodox. In addition, the powerful bishop of Alexandria, Dioscorus, had not only Flavian but also Theodoret of Cyrus and Ibas of Edessa condemned. The twelve anathemas of Cyril of Alexandria were pronounced orthodox, and Eutyches was absolved of the charges of heresy. In 450 Emperor Theodosius died in an accident, and the throne was assumed by the dead emperor's older sister Pulcheria, along with her consort Marcian. They executed Chrysaphius, exiled Eutyches from the city, and called an ecumenical council to meet in Chalcedon in 451.

Considerable disagreement followed the Synod of Ephesus (449), both in the East and in Rome. Pope Leo I had sent a letter to the synod condemning Eutyches, but Dioscorus had not allowed it to be read. Besides the christological issues, political divisions also drove the continuing controversy among Rome, Constantinople, and Alexandria. Chalcedon was called in an attempt to create unity in the empire.

Theologically, Chalcedon sought to explain how the church can confess there to be only one subject in Christ while also confessing him to be fully God and fully human. The Definition of Chalcedon did this by acknowledging two complete natures in Christ while affirming only one person or *hypostasis*. The union in Christ was not to be thought of at the level of nature but at the level of person. The council sought to avoid the heresy of Eutychianism on the one hand and Nestorianism on the other. The Definition was widely received, though controversy continued as the Monophysites rejected the "two natures" language as too Nestorian.

ACO, vol. 2 (1932); A. Grillmeier and H. Bacht, *Das Konzil von Chalkedon* (1973); R. V. Sellers, *The Council of Chalcedon* (1953).

STEVEN A. MCKINION

Chambre Ardente   In 1547, shortly after his accession to the throne of France, Henry II established a special court of the Parlement of Paris to combat heresy. Known as the Chambre Ardente ("burning chamber") because of its reputation for efficiency and harshness, the court in a period of two years investigated and tried over three hundred heresy cases, handing down death sentences in approximately 12 percent of the total. Criticism from within the Parlement and the French church for the court's overextended jurisdiction and questionable constitutionality played a role in its dissolution in 1550.

Henry's use of this secular court to deal with heresy demonstrated his determination to pursue a rigorous policy of religious repression. It also underlined the principle of linking the religious charge of heresy and the political charge of treason. Although the Chambre Ardente had a relatively short life, it played a key role in the intensification of efforts to eradicate Protestantism in France and contributed to an increase in religious refugees in cities bordering France, notably Geneva.

F. Baumgartner, *Henry II: King of France 1547–1559* (1988); N. L. Roelker, *One King, One Faith* (1996); N. M. Sutherland, *The Huguenot Struggle for Recognition* (1980).

CHRISTOPHER ELWOOD

Chant   A term translated loosely from the Latin term *cantus*. Chant had a more specific and at the same time richer connotation in the Middle Ages than it does today, and for medieval music it reflects the position of music itself as a discipline. Dealing with the unseen *materia-substantia* of motion, sound, and time, music as an intellectual investigation was concerned with both visible properties that could be measured, such as arithmetic, geometry, and astronomy/physics, and the unseen *materia-substantia* of thought, memory, cognition, and emotion. Music, sharing in and using unseen *substantia*, provided a set of *exempla* that led eventually to the invisible *substantia* of God. *Cantus*, therefore, constituted a resource of *materia* to be used compositionally, as well as sung liturgically. It also exemplified the potentiality for, and properties of, invisible *materia*, preparing the way to understand the nature of God within the discipline of theology.

The word *cantus* is itself important within a medieval mentality. That neither this concept nor the analogical function of the discipline and practice of music is understood is indicated by the fact that *cantus* is typically not included in modern dictionaries of music except with qualification—that is, *cantus firmus, cantus planus, cantus coronatus*—an indication that points to a lack of understanding regarding aspects of the medieval mind upon which basis Western notated music has developed.

W. Apel, *Gregorian Chant* (1990); D. Hiley, *Western Plainchant: A Handbook* (1993).

NANCY VAN DEUSEN

Chapels This is a collective term for separate religious rooms attached to private houses or institutions and for individual churchlike rooms for Christian worship. With regard to architecture and the purpose of these rooms, a number of different types of chapels can be distinguished, such as side chapels, chantry chapels, and Lady chapels. The term "chapel" is derived from the description of the room where the cloak of St. Martin (*cappa*) was kept. As rooms for Christian services without the legal position of a parish church, chapels are collective places for donations, penance, and baptism.

Based on the model of the Frankish kings, a chapel is a room for the Christian service within a self-contained social unit such as a castle or palatinate. Such rooms developed into independent chapels attached to residences (e.g., palatine chapel). In the tenth century chapels became independent buildings as propriety churches or village churches.

The papal chapel developed after the model of the court chapel of the Roman-German kings/emperors within the scope of the extensive process of the formation of the Roman curia. In this context the name "chaplain" is applied to the entirety of clergymen who worked for the papal court (*capellani commensales*). The chaplains served the pope by performing religious services and liturgies, and they worked as secretaries, special commissioners, ambassadors, and since the thirteenth century even as judges and advocates. The term "capella" also includes the liturgical instruments, robes, and relics necessary for the ministry and denotes the pope's private chapel in the medieval papal palaces at Rome and Avignon.

G. Binding, *Architektonische Formenlehre* (1999); S. Haider, *Zu den Anfängen der päpstlichen Kapelle*, vol. 87 of *Mitteilungen des Instituts für Österreichische Geschichtsforschung* (1979); B. Schimmelpfennig, *Die Organisation der päpstlichen Kapelle in Avignon*, vol. 50 of *Quellen und Forschungen aus italienischen Archiven und Bibliotheken* (1971).

GESINE MIERKE

Charlemagne (748–814), king of the Franks (768) and, after 800, emperor who ruled most of Western Europe. Surprisingly little is known of Charlemagne the person, despite his being the subject of Einhard's near contemporary biography. His activities during his long life centered on cementing the authority of his family over the Franks and conquered peoples, military conquest, administrative and economic development, and the shaping and promotion of Christian religious culture. Charlemagne and Carloman, his brother, succeeded Pepin III, their father, in 768 as co-kings of the Franks. The tensions inherent in this dual kingship were alleviated when Carloman died in 771. Managing rivalries within the family and the opportunities those rivalries presented to nobles to operate independently of royal power remained a constant theme of Charlemagne's reign. In 785–786 Count Hardrad of Thuringia rebelled against the king, and in 792 Pepin "the Hunchback," one of the king's many illegitimate children, plotted against him. Charlemagne responded to these challenges by requiring personal oaths of loyalty from his subjects and by grooming his legitimate sons to maintain the family's hold on power.

Einhard's biography and Frankish annals document Charlemagne's constant military campaigns against Aquitainians, Lombards, Saxons, Bavarians, Bretons, and Iberian Muslims. Charlemagne's kingdom was a society organized for war. Hundreds of counts and dukes and their followers furnished the military and political muscle that made successful conquest and control possible. Charlemagne attempted to manage his far-flung realms through a lay and clerical administrative elite centered at his court, which in the 790s came to be fixed at Aachen. The prescriptive documents that issued from the court and the emissaries (*missi*) who traveled as circuit riders through the realm attempted to hold local centers of power accountable to the king's authority. In 800 Pope Leo III acknowledged Charlemagne as emperor. The meaning of the title and its political and religious ramifications were not clear at the time and proved to be an ambiguous legacy for his successors.

Although papal support was critical in the rise of the Carolingian family to political power, Charlemagne saw himself as the steward of right religion in his realms. He appointed bishops and abbots who often served as key political advisors and continued the Frankish policy of using church lands for political and military ends. Charlemagne's court was also a religious and intellectual center and the major source of patronage and inspiration for a movement some modern historians call the Carolingian renaissance. At the same time, Charlemagne's monarchy maintained many of the features of an early medieval warrior society with feasting, drinking, hunting, and casual sexual relations an important part of the mix. Einhard reported that out of paternal affection Charlemagne did not allow his daughters to marry, but he also may have wished to avoid the political complications of sons-in-law. He outlived all his legitimate sons but one, Louis (776–840), who after service as king of Aquitaine succeeded Charlemagne as emperor in 814. Under Charlemagne, the basic outlines of a new European civilization began to take shape.

D. Bullough, *The Age of Charlemagne* (2nd ed., 1973); R. Collins, *Charlemagne* (1998).

JOHN J. CONTRENI

Charles Martel (c. 688–741), Frankish warlord who established the platform upon which his family, called Carolingians after the Latin form of his name, *Carolus*, would rise to power in Western Europe. The details of his life are obscured by the partisan nature of eighth- and ninth-century sources. Martel, "the Hammer," emerged in 714–715 after Pippin II, his father and mayor of the palace for the Frankish kings, died. By 721 he triumphed over forces led by Plectrude, Pippin's widow, and by rival warlords to emerge as custodian of the king and sole mayor of the palace. He continued to lead military campaigns annually against Frankish rivals and independent nobles in Aquitaine, Burgundy, Provence, and Germany. In the process he extended the political and cultural influence of the Franks into new regions, enriched his allies, and substantially militarized Frankish society. His victory over Arab raiders from Spain near Poitiers in 732 or 733 enhanced his reputation, but its impact was exaggerated by later Carolingian writers and modern historians. Charles owed his success to his energy and his ability to command an enthusiastic fighting force. In 737 when King Theuderic IV died, Martel did not bother to create another king but continued to exercise power as de facto monarch until his own death.

P. Fouracre, *The Age of Charles Martel* (2002).

JOHN J. CONTRENI

Charles V (1500–1558), Holy Roman Emperor (1519 [1530]–1556), king of Spain (Carlos I, 1516–1556). His inheritance of the dynastic holdings of Aragon, Castile, Austria, and Burgundy, his election as Holy Roman Emperor, and the conquests of Mexico and Peru placed a concentration of power in the hands of Charles V not seen in Europe since the days of Charlemagne. Unfortunately, he possessed no effective central authority over his vast domains, and wars with France, Ottoman pressure on the eastern Habsburg domains, and the spread of Protestantism within the HRE severely strained his resources. Charles presided over Martin Luther's hearing before the Diet of Worms (1521) and resolutely sided with traditional Catholicism. Charles defeated the Protestant Schmalkald League at Mühlberg in 1547 and was able to impose a compromise religious settlement on the empire in the Augsburg Interim of 1548. The Princes' Revolt of 1551/52 undid the settlement and eventually led to the legalization of Protestantism in the empire in the Peace of Augsburg (1555). Charles was a conscientious and energetic Renaissance prince, an avid military campaigner, and a devout Catholic of a "preconfessional" mindset. He advocated reform of the clerical abuses, and his diplomatic efforts facilitated the convening of the Council of Trent. Charles sought to end Indian slavery and the worst abuses of the *encomienda* system in the New Laws of 1542, though enforcement of the legislation was only partially effective. Charles retired to a monastery in 1556, leaving the Spanish, Italian, and Dutch territories to his son Philip II while his brother Ferdinand I assumed the imperial title and retained possession of the central European Habsburg dominions.

M. F. Alvarez, *Charles V: Elected Emperor and Hereditary Ruler* (1975); K. Brandi, *The Emperor Charles V* (1939); W. Maltby, *The Reign of Charles V* (2002).

CHARLES D. GUNNOE JR.

Charron, Pierre (1541–1603), French preacher and philosopher. Charron studied law in Orleans and Bourges but turned to religion, becoming a famed preacher in Gascony and Languedoc. Refused admission to a religious order, he settled in Bordeaux and formed a close association with Montaigne. His *Les Trois Veritez* (1594) was an apology for the Catholic faith, and his major work, *De la Sagesse* (1601), unfairly dismissed as an imitation of Montaigne, developed a consistent ethic independent of religion, showing Stoic influences. Charron's ideas were developed more radically by libertine groups after his death.

F. Kaye, *Charron et Montaigne: Du plagiat à l'originalité* (1982).

JOHN TONKIN

Chartres, School of

The cathedral of Chartres in France sponsored a school in the Middle Ages, as did most cathedrals and monasteries. Chartres' school, however, has been the subject of an intensive modern debate involving the rise of the Univ. of Paris. Medievalists erected an image of Chartres as Paris's great rival, boasting a series of great teachers and especially noteworthy as a center for Plato studies (in contrast to Parisian Aristotelianism). This idea has been debunked in recent decades, especially in the work of Richard Southern. He has shown that Chartres never provided real competition for Paris and that most of the great schoolmasters associated with Chartres were never there at all. The school can take credit for only two great teachers: Fulbert in the tenth century and Bernard of Chartres in the early twelfth.

The School of Chartres is a good example of cathedral schools. It was small, normally with a single master. The purpose of the school was advanced study of the seven liberal arts, giving students a command of the learning of the age rather than pushing the boundaries of knowledge. With the rise of Paris, Chartres was soon relegated to an intellectual backwater.

N. Häring, "Chartres and Paris Revisited," in *Essays in Honour of Anton Charles Pegis* (1974); R. W. Southern, *Medieval Humanism* (1970).

PHYLLIS G. JESTICE

Chemnitz, Martin

(1522–1586), Lutheran theologian, coauthor of the Formula of Concord. Largely self-taught, Chemnitz's brief periods of study in Wittenberg produced a close relationship with Melanchthon, which dimmed as he supported the Gnesio-Lutheran critique of his teacher by his Braunschweig colleague, Joachim Mörlin. They became friends through their common opposition to Andreas Osiander's doctrine of justification while Chemnitz was librarian of Albrecht of Prussia (1550–1553) and Mörlin pastor in Königsberg. Mörlin drew Chemnitz to Braunschweig from Wittenberg (1554). The two led the Lower Saxon ministeria in defining Lutheran theology in their age, especially regarding the Lord's Supper and Christology (Chemnitz's *On the Lord's Supper* [1561] and *On the Two Natures*

in Christ [1570]), but also justification by faith, the use of the law in Christian living, original sin, and predestination. In 1567 Chemnitz succeeded Mörlin as superintendent of Braunschweig's church. His *Handbook of Christian Teaching* (1569) provided pastoral candidates an excellent introduction to theology. Having edited *corpora doctrinae* for three principalities (Prussia, Braunschweig-Wolfenbüttel, Braunschweig-Lüneburg), he played a critical role in composing the Formula of Concord (1573–1577) and the *Apology of the Book of Concord* (1583). His masterful critique of Roman Catholic theology in his *Examination of the Council of Trent* (four volumes, 1566–1573) laid the foundation for Lutheran polemic against Roman theology for centuries. His posthumously published *Loci theologici* (1591, 1592), a commentary on Melanchthon's dogmatic work of that name, shaped the Lutheran dogmatic tradition.

T. Mahlmann, *Das neue Dogma der lutherischen Theologie* (1969); J. Preus, *The Second Martin* (1994).

ROBERT KOLB

Children's Crusade

A misnomer for several outbreaks of popular religious hysteria in 1212, none of which was a crusade or composed primarily of children. The "Children's Crusade" was a result partly of the widespread medieval belief that poverty was virtuous, and partly of the fact that official crusading had been notably unsuccessful, something attributed to the sinful state of aristocrats and churchmen. Members of the lower classes became convinced that, being purer by reason of their poverty, they would be able to succeed where their superiors had failed.

One element of the Children's Crusade began in Germany, led by a youth named Nicholas, who collected a large group of lower-class followers, including a number of adolescents, and led them into Italy. There they broke up, unable to reach the Holy Land on their own. Most attempted to return home, though many died along the way, and some apparently managed to reach Marseilles, where they seem to have been betrayed, enslaved, and sold to Muslims in North Africa.

Similarly, in France a young shepherd named Stephen, accompanied by a smaller group of the same type as Nicholas, marched to Paris and presented a letter purportedly from Christ to King Philip II. His movement then dispersed without incident.

Our knowledge of these events comes from scattered references, mostly in monastic chronicles, where the primary participants were referred to in Latin as *pueri*. The word usually means "boy," and a tradition later grew up that these movements were constituted by children. However, the word can also refer to lower-class laborers such as shepherds and farmhands, and it almost certainly meant that in this context.

J. Hansbery, "The Children's Crusade," *CHR* 24 (1938): 30–38; P. Raedts, "The Children's Crusade of 1212," *Journal of Medieval History* 3 (1977): 279–323; N. Zacour, "The Children's Crusade," in *A History of the Crusades*, vol. 2, ed. R. L. Wolff and H. Hazard (1969), 325–42.

PAUL CRAWFORD

Chillingworth, William (1602–1644), English churchman and controversialist. About 1628, while studying at Oxford, Chillingworth converted to Catholicism and fled to the continent; he soon returned to England and eventually Protestantism, taking up his pen to oppose Catholicism. A proponent of social order, he sided with the royalists in the Civil War. In his writings, Chillingworth emphasized orthopraxis over orthodoxy and defended personal, Scripture-based rational inquiry as the only morally valid basis for an individual Christian's assent to a religious teaching. He advocated a universal church unified by common assent to an essential core of Christian beliefs with toleration of diversity regarding peripherals. He opposed all claims to absolute religious certainty (especially papal infallibility) as incompatible with human fallibility and as conducive to intolerance and schism.

R. Orr, *Reason and Authority: The Thought of William Chillingworth* (1967); Orr, *The Works of William Chillingworth*, 3 vols. (1838, repr. 1972).

DANIEL EPPLEY

Christian III (1503–1559), king of Denmark and Norway. Christian III followed the legacy of the reform-minded exile, Christian II. After the interim of his father, King Fredrick, Christian III and Queen Dorothea made Denmark a Lutheran kingdom with the help of the reformers Johannes Bugenhagen and Peter Palladius. After an encounter with Luther at the Diet of Worms in 1521, Christian enjoyed personal correspondence with Luther, Melanchthon, and Bugenhagen. The theologically invested and deeply Lutheran prince worked out an agreement (Speyer, 1544) with Emperor Charles V to protect his domestic and foreign interests, and kept out of the Schmalkald War. Having secured the throne by 1536 after a civil war, Christian imprisoned Catholic bishops and confiscated lands from the Catholic Church. Ordination of seven Lutheran superintendents ended apostolic succession in Denmark. Christian III's legacy was continued by two daughters and three sons, one of whom ruled as Fredrick II.

M. S. Lausten, *A Church History of Denmark* (2002).

KIRSI STJERNA

Christian Platonism Predominant philosophical system of patristic and early medieval periods adapted to give rational expression to core Christian doctrines. Christian Platonism has been called "a term . . . used, and misused, in a great variety of different ways, and applied to a great variety of different people" (Armstrong 1967). The inherent ambiguity of the term is rooted both in the diverse ways in which Platonic philosophy has been assimilated by Christian writers from the apostolic era up until the present day, and by the complexity of the pagan Platonic tradition itself, which underwent many changes from the time of Plato to the fifth-century CE Platonism of Proclus.

What is certain is that by the early Middle Ages the most influential Christian writers had already committed themselves to various Platonic doctrines, which they considered indispensable for a rational understanding of the truths of revelation, and had also composed philosophical and theological systems of their own that not only constitute some of the greatest works in the history of Platonism, pagan or Christian, but also became the main sources of Platonic doctrines up until the translations of Marsilio Ficino in the Renaissance. Thus, while acknowledging the genius of later developments in Christian Platonism, the term can be used primarily to signify certain writings of patristic and early medieval writers who assimilated Platonic doctrines in order to give a fuller rational expression to the truths of the faith embodied in Christian scriptural and oral traditions. Foremost among the authors of these texts were, in the Eastern church, Origen, the Cappodocians (especially Gregory of Nyssa), Pseudo-Dionysius and Maximus the Confessor, and in the Western church, Marius Victorinus, Ambrose, Augustine, Boethius, and John Scottus Eriugena.

Significantly, the direct sources for these Christian writers were not the dialogues of Plato but rather the exegetical and systematic writings of later pagan Platonists. These writings were marked by themes relating to the soul, the knowability of God, and the origin of the universe. In relation to the soul, these included the model of the tripartite soul composed of *nous*, "mind" (the guiding, rational part), *thumos*, "the spirited part," and *epithumia*, "the desiring part" (the *Phaedrus*); the notion of a divine eros as the driving force behind the soul's ascent to the divine (ultimately derived from Plato's *Symposeum* and *Phaedrus*); and the doctrine that the soul separated from the body is the true human being, so that in order to regain its prior existence in the intelligible world of the Ideas (the divine archetypes of natural beings) it must become a "likeness to God" by purifying itself of bodily passions and concerns (in its most radical form, the *Phaedo*). In relation to the knowability of God, these themes included the dialectical treatment of the simultaneous knowability and unknowability of the One, later to result in the Christian tradition of apophatic and cataphatic theology (the *Parmenides*); and a metaphysics of light involving the struggle of the soul to extricate itself from the darkness of material forms by training the "eye of the mind" to become receptive to the light of God, or the Good (the *Republic*). Finally, in relation to the origin of the universe, these themes included a cosmology of creation and of the divine origin of the harmony of the physical cosmos (the *Timaeus*).

While the reception of Platonic doctrines by Christian writers varied from piecemeal acceptance of select notions (e.g., Basil of Caesarea, c. 330–379) to wholesale adoption of entire theoretical systems (e.g., Pseudo-Dionysius, c. late fifth century), in no case did the pagan sources remain unchanged in the process. While such doctrines as the preexistence of souls, the eternity of the world, and the natural divinity of the soul were for the most part rejected by Christian writers, a profound tension continued to exist throughout the patristic era between, on the one hand, conceiving of the soul alone as the essential human being and, on the other hand, conceiving of the body as an inextricable part of the human person. In both Greek and Latin traditions, despite the eschatological exigencies of the doctrine of the resurrection of the body, there was a universal fascination with the dignity of the intellectual part of the soul, which alone was capable of true *theoria* or contemplative vision of the divine. Thus, while consistently maintaining the dignity of the body in regard to the overall salvation of the human person, the acknowledged power of the intellectual soul to become illumined by divine archetypes—now located in the divine mind or Logos, the second person of the Trinity—served to promote and conserve the Platonic bias against the body as impeding rather than aiding the soul's ascent to God.

The existence of the Ideas or "seminal reasons" and their participated presence in the soul was perhaps the most enduring and fundamental doctrine of Platonism to influence early Christian thought. Even Augustine, who was more critical of Platonic doctrines in his later years, never ceased to believe that human art could produce its symmetries and harmonies, figures and shapes, modulations and modes, only by a natural participation in the vision of art itself, which was nothing other than the immanent presence of the Word of God in the soul. This among many other Platonic motifs made Augustine the most influential Christian Platonist in the Western church up until the fascination of the late-twelfth and thirteenth centuries with the writings of Pseudo-Dionysius, who achieved the most thorough assimilation of pagan Platonism in the history of Christianity.

Controversial from their very appearance at the turn of the sixth century, these treatises were the main source for the transmission of the philosophy and theology of Proclus (d. 489), whose triadic ordering of the intelligible world and whose theories of the *energeia* (operation) of theurgic rites were altered respectively to conform to biblical accounts of the angelic ranks and to fifth-century ecclesiology and the liturgy of the Eastern church. Moreover, it is not an exaggeration to say that the Pseudo-Dionysian corpus was the main source for the most significant of pagan Platonic doctrines to influence medieval Western theology, such as the doctrine of participation to account for the relation between creature and creator, the division of theology into apophatic and cataphatic branches, and the metaphysical scheme of "remaining, procession, and return" to characterize respectively the immutability of God, the emergence of the created world from God, and its eventual return to God.

That so much unadulterated pagan Platonism formed the basis of the Dionysian corpus made the interpretive efforts of Maximus the Confessor (580–662) of great historical significance, for it was primarily Maximus who played the role of interpreter of the Pseudo-Dionysian corpus for subsequent Greek theologians, but even more significantly for the Latin West through

John Scottus Eriugena (fl. 860). While Eriugena was better known (and respected) for his translations of the great Eastern Christian Platonists rather than for his monumental synthetic treatise, the *Periphyseon* or *Division of Nature*, the latter exemplifies, perhaps more than any other Christian Platonic work, the degree to which Platonic thought could be elevated to serve the most profound of Christian speculative endeavors. But for the Middle Ages it was Boethius's (c. 480–524) *Consolation of Philosophy* that turned out to be the most influential work of Platonic philosophy, combining seminal Platonic notions of the soul and the cosmos with a lyricism that enchanted the Middle Ages. While the tradition of Christian Platonism is brilliantly represented in later ages, most notably in the twelfth-century glossators of the School of Chartres, in Bonaventure and Meister Eckhart, and in Marsilio Ficino and Nicholas of Cues in the Renaissance, one could say that all later Christian Platonic works are footnotes on the interpretive, critical, and synthetic works of these seminal Christian authors.

———

A. H. Armstrong, *St. Augustine and Christian Platonism* (1967); Armstrong, ed., *The Cambridge History of Later Greek and Early Medieval Philosophy* (rev. ed., 1970; repr. 1995); H. U. von Balthasar, *The Glory of the Lord: A Theological Aesthetics*, 3 vols. (1982, 1984, 1986); J. Dillon, *The Golden Chain: Studies in the Development of Platonism and Christianity* (1990); S. Gersh, *From Iamblichus to Eriugena: An Investigation of the Prehistory and Evolution of the Pseudo-Dionysian Tradition* (1978); B. McGinn, *The Foundations of Mysticism: Origins to the 5th Century* (1991); J. Pelikan, *Christianity and Classical Culture: The Metamorphosis of Natural Theology in the Christian Encounter with Hellenism* (1993); R. Roques, *L'univers dionysien: Structure hierarchique du monde selon le Pseudo-Denys* (2nd ed., 1983); L. Thunberg, *Microcosm and Mediator: The Theological Anthropology of Maximus the Confessor* (1965).

MARK DAMIEN DELP

Christianity in T'ang and Yuan China

T'ang China (618–908). Syriac-speaking traders were in China in the sixth century in large centers such as Chang-an and Loyang. Ecclesiastically they answered to the patriarch of the Church of the East at Seleucia-Ctesiphon. By 500 that church had been dubbed "Nestorian" by Chalcedonian Christians under Rome and Constantinople.

As an institution, Christianity in China dates from the 638 decree of the T'ang emperor T'ai-tsung (d. 649) issued some three years after the arrival at Chang-an of the Syrian monk Al-o-pen. That decree approved Al-o-pen's teachings and the erection in the capital of a monastery for twenty-one monks. This symbolized the monastic domination of the church throughout the T'ang dynasty.

A Buddhist reaction occurred under the dowager empress Wu-huo in 691. Mobs sacked a church/monastery in Loyang in 698 and the pioneer church in Chang-an in 712. Conditions for Christians improved under Hsuan-tsung (d. 756), despite communication problems with the church home base due to Arab conquests. A metropolitan was appointed and a second mission under Chi-ho arrived in 744. This was at the midpoint of the period of greatest growth of what in a 781 decree was called "the Luminous Religion." 781 is also the date of the famous Sian-fu stele (the so-called Nestorian Monument), which, inter alia, records the deeds of the monk Issu (Izd-buzid), who between 756 and 805 rendered great service to successive emperors in the area of military intelligence.

By 786 imperial decrees demanded that "clear" Buddhist and "muddy" Christian ways not be confused. By 800 the tide had turned against Christianity as the T'ang dynasty declined. In 845 a decree came out against all foreign religions, with Zoroastrians and Christians forced to leave monasteries and "to cease to confound the customs of China." Foreigners were to return to "their native places." A massacre of Christians, Muslims, and Parsis occurred in Canton in 888. To all intents and purposes Christianity was extinct in the China visited in 980 by a monk from Arabia.

As to the theology of these "Nestorians," neither epigraphical evidence from the Sian-fu stele nor documentary evidence from Tun-huang manuscripts supports the charge that they were heretics.

Yuan China (1279–1368). Well before the Church of the East ceased to flourish in China it had made inroads among key peoples of Central Asia. After the White Huns, around 500, converts were made among Sogdians and Uighurs. By early in the eleventh century these were joined by numbers of Keraits, Naimans, and Onguts. These became allies of the Mongols in the rise to power of Jinghis Khan (d. 1227). The Mongols came to depend on Christian kinfolk for help in administration and military leadership. Mongol leaders were also influenced by Christian wives. Chief among these was Sorghoqtani (d. 1252), a Kerait princess who was the mother of three great khans including Khubilai (d. 1294), who established his rule in China by 1261. Avowing loyalty to the god of Buddhists, Jews, Christians, and Muslims, Khubilai would not become a Christian lest it disrupt his new empire. Through the Polos he did ask the pope for 100 Latin priests, who responded initially by sending just one Franciscan, who arrived just after Khubilai's death.

Marco Polo noted the role of the "Nestorians" at court and in overall administration when he reached Khan Baliq (Beijing) in 1275. In 1289 Khubilai chose one of his "Nestorian" court physicians, Ai-hsueh, to oversee Christians and Manicheans in China. By 1275 the Church of the East had a metropolitan at Khan Baliq and, under the security provided by the great extent of Mongol rule through central Asia, contact with Baghdad was maintained via Christians in towns on the trade routes.

Monastics still played key intellectual and religious roles but did not dominate as they had in the T'ang period. While Christian literature was found in Chinese and Turkish, as well as in Syriac, Christianity remained a foreign religion to the Chinese populace. There was animosity in the Church of the East toward Catholics, especially when the latter established a parallel Latin episcopate in 1313. By 1330 Mongol rule in China was failing at a time when "Nestorians" numbered at least 30,000. Within four decades the dynasty had fallen. In its declining years, tantric Tibetan Buddhism influenced not a few Mongol leaders. So when the dynasty was replaced there disappeared with it its "running dog" associates, both "Nestorian" and Catholic.

J. Foster, *The Church of the T'ang Dynasty* (1939); I. Gillman and H. J. Klimkeit, *Christians in Asia before 1500* (1999); S. H. Moffett, *A History of Christianity in Asia*, vol. 1 (rev. ed., 1998); A. C. Moule, *Christians in China before the Year AD 1500* (1930); Moule, *Nestorians in China: Some Corrections and Additions* (1940).

IAN GILLMAN†

Christians under Islam
Within a century of Muhammad's death, most of the Christian East was under Muslim control. The Qur'an provided a special status for Jews and Christians, "the Peoples of the Book," who had also received a written revelation from God. Unlike idolaters, they were a *dhimmi*, a pro-

tected people. Muhammad himself had negotiated pacts with the Jews in Medina and with the Christians of Najran and Aqaba. These provided the precedents for the Umayyad Caliph Umar when he dealt with large Christian populations.

As Muslim society evolved, the *dhimmi* (or Persian, *millet*) system developed with it. While it always included some restrictive measures, practice was often determined by the needs of the moment. Local Christians were the bureaucrats; they were literate in Greek and they provided the needed artisans, scholars, and doctors. Many times personal relationships between Muslim officials and Christian leaders were as determinative as codified laws.

Initially Muslim conquest was not aimed at land settlement. In fact, under Umar Muslim Arabs were not allowed to own land, in order to preserve their character as a mobile military power. Christian and Muslim populations had little contact with one another. By the time of Caliph Abd al-Malik (r. 685–705) things had changed. Local converts had increased the Muslim population, Arab Muslims could own land, and the two populations were in more contact, whence arose the need to define religious boundaries.

Christians could not serve in the military and had to pay for their protected status with a head tax, the *jizya*, that could be very high. Escaping the head tax and the possibility of social advancement was frequently an inducement to conversion. The collection of the tax and the maintenance of order within the community fell to its leaders, the bishops.

By the time of the Muslim invasions, the Christological controversies had produced a divided Christian community. The Nestorian Christians in Sassanid Persia and the Jacobites in the Byzantine Empire experienced censorship and persecution. Melkite (Byzantine) Christians now lost their position of imperial favor and imperial financial support. The others found conditions at the outset of the Ummayad caliphate better than what they had experienced previously. For all of them the *dhimmi* system had the effect of shrinking and marginalizing all the Christian communities.

Christians (and Jews) eventually became segregated minorities with limited freedoms in Muslim lands. Christians could practice their religion within the boundaries of their communities, and their bishops were responsible for the administration of Christian law. They were forbidden to build new churches, and any church taken over as a mosque could not be returned to Christian use. Christian symbols, such as the cross, could not be displayed publicly. Proselytizing, even of non-Muslims, was punishable by death. Muslim women could not marry Christian men, and if a Christian woman married a Muslim man, their children had to be raised as Muslims.

R. B. Betts, *Christians in the Arab East: A Political History* (1978); K. Cragg, *The Arab Christian: A History in the Middle East* (1991).

    EUGENE M. LUDWIG, OFM, CAP.

Christology in the Early Church

Christology, the systematic reflection on the ontological status and personal identity of Jesus, has been central to Christian theological reflection since its beginning, although the term itself comes from the seventeenth century. The earliest Christian works composed after the New Testament emphasize Jesus' role as revealer of the transcendent God of Israel, as God's "beloved" foreseen by the Hebrew prophets (*Ascension of Isaiah* 8–11), or simply as God's "child" (*Didache* 9–10). Ignatius of Antioch refers to Jesus simply as "our God" in several places but also emphasizes the reality of his flesh and blood, even after his resurrection (e.g., *Smyrnaeans* 2–3). For Justin, Jesus was both the one in whom the figures of Hebrew Scripture came to fulfillment (*Dialogue with Trypho*) and the universal Logos or divine cosmic reason, in whom every reasonable creature participates, "who became human for our sakes, that by sharing in our sufferings, he might also heal us" (*Second Apology* 13).

In *Against Heresies*, composed around 185 to refute gnostic sects, Irenaeus of Lyon emphasized the paradoxical unity of Jesus as both the eternal Word and creative agent of the invisible God and a complete human being who is God's "formation" (e.g., 3.16.3). As "the visible of the Father," Jesus reveals the divine glory that communicates incorruptible life to intelligent creatures (4.6.3–6; 4.20.5–7), while as a full human being he "sums up" and so reshapes human history distorted by sin (e.g., 3.16.1; 3.19.3).

Origen of Alexandria, writing a generation after Irenaeus, understood Christ primarily as the Wisdom of God, eternally sharing God's substance, yet clearly second to the Father in rank; as divine Wisdom, Christ contains the "forms and principles" of all things that would be created according to his knowledge (e.g., *Princ.* 1.1.6). Although all other created intellects turned away from their original union with

God in knowledge and love, one remained inseparably united to God's Wisdom and eventually took on the fullness of human flesh, as the earthly Jesus, in order to reveal him (*Princ.* 2.6.5–7). In coming to know all the details of Christ's human and divine identity, intellectual creatures are restored to the unity with God that will be their final salvation (*Princ.* 3.6).

In the early fourth century, Arius of Alexandria drew on aspects of the Origenist tradition in urging that Christ, as Son of the Father, belongs essentially to the realm of what is produced or created and so must have had a beginning in time. In response, Athanasius insisted that if Jesus is truly the savior of fallen humanity, he must realize in his own person the irreducible paradox of being both fully God, "of the same substance as the Father," as the creed of Nicaea had declared in 325, and fully "embodied" in the world of fallen creatures. As God, the Son is "other" than all creatures, not limited by time and space, but as incarnate, he "makes a human body his own" (*Orationes contra Arianos* 3.32) in order to reveal God's splendor and remake the divine image in human creatures, allowing them to share again in incorruptible life (*On the Incarnation* 16, 18, 44, 54).

Like most Greek writers of the early fourth century, Arius and Athanasius both speak of the incarnation in terms of the divine Word's taking on and controlling a human body. In the third quarter of the century, Apollinarius of Laodicaea systematized this position by insisting that Jesus' role as Savior rested on his distinctive personal constitution: the divine Logos acting as the perfect mind and conscious governing principle of an animated human body. By the 380s, opposition to this conception of Christ had mounted, led by Gregory of Nazianzus and Gregory of Nyssa. The former enunciated what was to be the classical reason for rejecting the Apollinarian model: if Jesus is to be the savior and healer of human minds as well as human bodies, he must himself possess a complete human mind, "for that which he has not assumed he has not healed, but that which is united to his Godhead is also saved" (Letter 101).

In the late 420s, a new controversy over the personal constitution of Christ broke out in a polemical exchange of letters between Nestorius, bishop of Constantinople, and Cyril, bishop of Alexandria. A pupil of Theodore of Mopsuestia, Nestorius was convinced that the only way to avoid a relapse into Arianism was to make a careful distinction between the personal being of the divine Word or Son and the human Jesus, with whom he was uniquely united; otherwise one risked attributing limitation and even suffering to the transcendent God. Nestorius rejected the use of the title "God-bearer" (*Theotokos*) for Mary, the mother of Jesus; she could be called "Christ-bearer," since "Christ" was for him the proper title of Word and human being acting as one, but God, by definition, has no mother. Cyril, in response, insisted that the subject of Jesus' saving actions, in the Gospels and in the life of the church, is none other than God the Son, who accepted the limitations and even the possibility of human existence as his own.

After an abortive attempt to resolve the issue at Ephesus in 431, both parties reached agreement on the proper use of the *Theotokos* title in 433. Debate over the unity and distinction characteristic of the Savior, as Word made flesh, continued unabated, however. In 451, the Council of Chalcedon reached its celebrated formulation of the mystery, confessing "one and the same Christ . . . acknowledged in two natures without confusion, without change, without division, without separation," a rule for further orthodox speech about Christ that combined phrases from Cyril, Antiochene theologians, and Pope Leo I. After a century of even more heated conflicts about the reception of this formulation, the Second Council of Constantinople in 553 agreed on a set of canons interpreting it in a Cyrillian sense, particularly specifying that the one *hypostasis*, or individual, confessed to possess both human and divine natures in Christ is the second person of the Trinity, God the Son. In 680–681, the Third Council of Constantinople added further criteria for the orthodox interpretation of these conciliar formulations, adopting the arguments of Maximus the Confessor that the two natures united in Christ must each be recognized as having its own unimpaired operation and its own will. It is precisely in the personal integration of these two complete natural spheres of activity, Maximus insisted—in the Son's free subordination of his human mind, will, and actions to his Father's eternal saving plan—that the final transformation and divinization of all human nature begins.

———

K. Anatolios, *Athanasius: The Coherence of His Thought* (1998); H. U. von Balthasar, *Cosmic Liturgy: The Universe according to Maximus the Confessor* (2003); B. E. Daley, "'Heavenly Man' and 'Eternal Christ': Apollinarius and Gregory of Nyssa on the Personal Identity of the Savior," *JECS* 10 (2002): 469–88; Daley, "Nature and the 'Mode of Union': Late Patristic Models for the Personal Unity of Christ," in *The Incarnation*, ed. S. T. Davis, D. Kendall, and G. O'Collins (2002), 164–96; W. H. C. Frend, *The Rise of the Monophysite Movement* (1972); A. Grillmeier, *Christ in Christian Tradition*, vol. 1 (2nd ed., 1975), vol. 2/1 (1985), vol. 2/2 (1994), vol. 2/4 (1996); R. A. Norris, *Manhood and Christ: A Study in the Christology of Theodore of Mopsuestia* (1963); B. Studer, *Trinity and Incarnation* (1994); Studer, *The Grace of Christ and the Grace of God in Augustine of Hippo*; F. M. Young, *Nicaea to Chalcedon* (1983).

BRIAN E. DALEY, SJ

Chrodegang (c. 715–766), bishop of Metz and church reformer. Born of a high noble Frankish family in the region of Liège, Chrodegang was educated at the monastery of St. Trond before joining the court of the *major domus* Charles Martel, first as the *nutritus* (tutor) of Carloman, Charles's son, and from 737 as *referendarius* (director of the chancellery). Shortly after Charles's death (741), Carloman appointed Chrodegang to the bishopric of Metz (probably in 742), a position he held until his death. As the bishop of Metz, Chrodegang played an active role in the reform movement initiated by Boniface under the auspices of Carloman and Pippin III. He had close relations with the court of Pippin and consequently became Pippin's chief adviser on ecclesiastical matters. During the early years of the 750s Chrodegang composed a rule for canons, which had a wide circulation shortly after its composition and which was officially adopted by the Frankish church in 816 and subsequently implemented throughout the Frankish kingdom. Chrodegang also made an effort to replace the Gallican chant by importing and introducing Roman musical traditions to the church of Metz. Chrodegang was buried in the abbey of Gorze, which he had founded in 748.

———

M.-H. Jullien and F. Perelman, eds., *Clavis scriptorum latinorum medii aevi, scriptores Galliae 735–987*, vol. 1 (1994), 270–75; M. A. Claussen, *The Reform of the Frankish Church: Chrodegang of Metz and the* Regula Canonicorum *in the Eighth Century* (2004); Claussen, *Saint Chrodegang* (1967); J. M. Wallace-Hadrill, *The Frankish Church* (1988).

YITZHAK HEN

Chrysostom, John (c. 347–407), bishop. Given the name "Golden Mouth" (*chrysostomos*) almost immediately after his death because of his excellence in preaching, John Chrysostom is generally recognized as the greatest preacher of the patristic era. His preaching is marked by a "historical" reading of the scriptural text and by the pastoral concern of wanting his congregation to grow in their faith and service to God.

John was born and raised in Syrian Antioch. In his youth he studied under the pagan rhetorician Libanius, who also taught Theodore of Mopsuestia and Maximus of Seleucia. According to Sozomen (*Hist. eccl.* 8.2), Libanius later said that he had desired that John succeed him but that "the Christians have taken him." For his part, John later had nothing good to say about Libanius, calling him "that wretched and miserable man" (*Bab.* 105).

Around the age of twenty, John was baptized and began to study the Scriptures under Meletius, bishop of Antioch, and Diodore, later bishop of Tarsus. Three years later he became a lector and would likely have been ordained a priest shortly thereafter, but he left the city to practice a more ascetic Christianity. As he explains in *On the Priesthood*, his chief reason for leaving at this time was that he felt unfit for the priesthood. Though some scholars have doubted the veracity of this passage, it is evident from Chrysostom's writings that he highly valued the ascetic lifestyle. In any event, John spent four years under a Syrian monk and then spent two more years in a cave; his health forced him to return to the city.

In 381 John was ordained deacon by Meletius just before the bishop's death. In 386 Flavian, then bishop of Antioch, ordained John as presbyter, or priest, and for the next dozen years John was a popular speaker in the various churches of Antioch. He preached series on various books of the Bible (including Genesis, Matthew, John, and the letters of Paul).

His most famous occasional homilies from this time are the twenty-one *Homilies on the Statues*, preached in 387. In response to a new imperial tax, the Antiochenes had rioted and toppled statues of Emperor Theodosius and his family. While Bishop Flavian went to Constantinople to intercede for his people, John preached sermons that both comforted the people and held them accountable for the crisis.

John also delivered sermons on several liturgical feast days, including Christmas, Epiphany, Palm Sunday, Ascension, Pentecost, and the Transfiguration. His sermon for Christmas Day (delivered in 387) is the earliest extant Christmas Day sermon in Greek. In it John mentions that the celebration of Christmas in Antioch is less than ten years old; the bulk of the sermon defends this "new celebration" and shows that this is the proper time to celebrate the birth of Christ.

In 398 John was appointed bishop of Constantinople and reluctantly left Antioch. Although he continued to preach and to support the evangelization of the Gothic peoples in the area, the rest of his life was affected by both imperial and ecclesiastical politics. The "Synod of the Oak" in 403 brought several charges against John, including slandering the empress Eudoxia. John was deposed but was quickly recalled, partly due to the demands of the people. The respite, however, was temporary: John was soon deposed again and spent the rest of his life in exile. Several of his letters to the deaconess Olympias and two of his letters to Pope Innocent I date from this time. John died September 14, 407; his remains were later translated to Constantinople.

———

J. Chrysostom, *NPNF*,[1] vols. 9–14; R. C. Hill, *Homilies on Genesis* in FC 74, 82, 87 (1985–1992); Hill, *Commentary on the Psalms*, 2 vols. (1998); J. N. D. Kelly, *Golden Mouth: The Story of John Chrysostom—Ascetic, Preacher, Bishop* (1995); W. Mayer and P. Allen, *John Chrysostom* (2000); M. M. Mitchell, *The Heavenly Trumpet: John Chrysostom and the Art of Pauline Interpretation* (2002); Palladius, *Dialogue on the Life of St. John Chrysostom*, trans. R. T. Meyer, in ACW 45 (1985); R. L. Wilken, *John Chrysostom and the Jews: Rhetoric and Reality in the Late 4th Century* (1983).

MICHAEL COMPTON

Church and State in Early Christianity

In the ancient world, no distinction existed between religion and the state. Cultic rites and civic duties formed a seamless whole. The Romans believed that the gods had made Rome great; so long as proper worship was accorded them, the empire (31 BCE–476 CE) would flourish. Initially, the Romans regarded Christianity as simply a Jewish sect. Imperial officials grudgingly tolerated Jews, though they were monotheists, because of their ancient scriptures and tradition. By 64, Christianity was viewed as a new (and therefore suspect) religion; Emperor Nero blamed Christians for a devastating fire in Rome and executed them.

A marked ambivalence toward the state characterized the attitude of early Christians. Though Jesus recognized its necessity ("Render therefore to Caesar the things that are Caesar's . . ."), he also insisted that his kingdom was not of this world (John 18:36). In Rom. 13:1, Paul advised Christians to be subject to the governing authorities, yet he also maintained that Christ's second coming was imminent and urged believers not to concentrate on worldly matters. Their refusal to serve in the military (because of Jesus' injunction against bloodshed) contributed to their reputation for subversiveness. Christians also shunned the theater, gladiatorial games, and wild beast hunts because of their violence, immorality, and paganism. Gossip about Christians was lurid: they practiced cannibalism (partaking of the Lord's body and blood), incest ("brothers" and "sisters" exchanging the kiss of peace), and atheism (utter disbelief in the gods).

By the mid-second century Christianity attracted a few well-educated individuals who mounted an intellectual defense of the faith. These apologists (from Gk. *apologia*, "defense") argued that Christianity was philosophically superior to all other religions and fulfilled Hebrew Scripture. They emphasized that Christians were good citizens who prayed for the emperor and were highly moral, unlike many pagans.

Imperial policy against Christians long remained ill-defined. Persecution occurred locally and sporadically, instigated usually by mobs or merchants whose wares Christians shunned. Charged with keeping the peace, provincial governors did not deliberately seek out Christians but executed them if they appeared seditious. In 250 with the empire battered by war, famine, and political instability, Emperor Decius inaugurated the first empirewide persecution. Persecution from 303 to 311 saw Scriptures confiscated, churches burned, and Christians hideously tortured and executed.

Constantine inaugurated a new era in church-state relations when he became emperor in 312. Convinced that the Christian God had enabled him to defeat his rivals and must be duly reverenced, Constantine legalized Christianity in 313 and showered the church with favors. The euphoria felt by Christians after three centuries of fear and repression was expressed best by Eusebius, the historian-bishop who lauded Constantine as God's vicar on earth. When Donatism and Arianism erupted, Constantine himself summoned councils of bishops to resolve the controversies, including the First Ecumenical Council at Nicaea. His actions established a precedent for imperial intervention in ecclesiastical matters. Constantine's Arian successors ruthlessly imposed their beliefs on bishops everywhere, aided in the East by a submissive attitude engendered by Hellenistic and Persian influences.

By the late fourth century, strong catholic emperors emerged to secure victory for orthodoxy. In 380 Emperor Theodosius declared catholic Christianity the official religion of the empire and levied onerous sanctions against pagans, heretics, and Jews. Strong-minded bishops aided in the campaign. Mentor of emperors Gratian and Theodosius, Ambrose (bishop of Milan) did not hesitate to reprove them when the interests of the church were at stake. Ambrose's dogged resistance to imperial domination helped create in the West the legacy of separation of church and state. For Augustine, the state exists to curb the excesses and vices of fallen humankind. Laws and magistrates ensure some measure of stability for society, yet true peace and justice exist only in the heavenly city. Augustine's ambivalence toward institutions and his emphasis on the proper ordering of society also became part of the West's political heritage.

In the fifth century as the Western empire disintegrated under barbarian invasions, the papacy emerged as Rome's chief protector. Pope Leo I (440–461) himself dissuaded Attila the Hun from ravaging Italy. For centuries the moral authority and prestige of the popes would prove a formidable counterweight to Western rulers intent on dominating the church. The Eastern empire survived for another thousand years, but the church there remained under imperial control.

R. Dodaro and G. Lawless, eds., *Augustine and His Critics* (2000); E. Ferguson, ed., *Church and State in the Early Church* (1993); L. Strauss and J. Cropsey, eds., *History of Political Philosophy* (3rd ed., 1987); R. Wilken, *The Christians as the Romans Saw Them* (1984).

JANE E. MERDINGER

Church of the East in the Middle Ages

For the Church of the East, the Middle Ages fall between the decline of the T'ang Dynasty in China and the Abbasid Dynasty in Persia on the one hand, and the beginnings of the European colonial empires on the other, roughly the years 1000–1500.

Around the turn of the millennium, virtually the entire length of the Silk Road was in turmoil. Both the Abbasid Empire and the T'ang Empire were collapsing. The Mamluk slave soldiers of the Abbasids were becoming a power. Turkic invaders from Afghanistan were bringing Islam to the Punjab area of India, in what is now Pakistan. The turmoil brought both hardship and advantage to the Christian minority.

The jurisdiction of the Nestorian catholicos, or the patriarch of Baghdad extended through all of Asia, including China and India, without a clearly defined border with the Orthodox metropolitan of Kiev to his north. The Church of the East existed across this territory in geographically and culturally isolated pockets, some prosperous, most not. It was a church struggling for its survival, and documentation for this period is spotty.

The Christian mission under Al-o-pen that reached China in 635 had disappeared by the year 1000. No one knows how successful it was or what happened to it.

It appears that the Thomas Christians of India deliberately maintained their social and religious separateness and did not evangelize outside the bounds of their own social class. They were not a major social force in Indian society. They maintained Syriac as their liturgical language, and there is no known vernacular translation of the liturgy or of the Scriptures.

The Church in Persia, although divided into *dhimmi* communities, fared better, due in part to tensions within Islam between Sunni and Alid or Shi'ite Muslims. In the period 945–1055, a series of native Persian Shi'ite amirs known as the Buyids or Buwayhids held effective civil and military control under a nominal Sunni Abbasid caliph. The amir Abud (949–983) made a Christian his vizier and allowed him to rebuild and repair churches and monasteries. When Buyid power declined, so did the condition of Christians.

This same period was a time of missionary activity for the Church of the East among the nomadic tribes of Central Asia. Nestorian missionaries worked among several Mongol tribes, including the Kerait, Uighur, and Ongut tribes. Kerait women were the wives of some of the most powerful of the Mongol khans. When the Mongols overthrew the last Abbasid in 1258, the Mongol queen was a Christian.

The early Mongol Empire was a time of tolerance for Christians. The early khans in Persia were not Muslims. While few of them were Christians, frequently their wives were. Under Mongol rule, Nestorian Christians enjoyed more freedom than they had before or since. There exist accounts from this period of Christians publicly drinking wine during Ramadan and forcing Muslim merchants to stand in respect as Christians carried crosses through the public streets.

Khubilai Khan's China was another center for Nestorian Christians. A Nestorian Christian, Mar Sergius, was a governor of Gansu Province in the years 1278–1281. There was a Nestorian metropolitan in Beijing in the middle of the thirteenth century.

In 1279, a monk named Markos, probably an Ongut Mongol, stopped in Baghdad on a pilgrimage from Beijing to Jerusalem. Military hostilities prevented his progress or his return home. In 1281, he became the first and only Mongol elected patriarch of Baghdad and took the name Yaballaha III. That epoch of freedom for the Church of the East ended during his patriarchate with the conversion of the khans to Islam.

The Crusades had little direct impact east of the Euphrates. In their aftermath, however, western travelers, merchants, and missionaries started to arrive. The Franciscan Giovanni de Pian del Carpini came on an embassy to the Great Khan in 1246. The voyage of Marco Polo began in 1275. Another Franciscan, John of Montecorvino, arrived in 1294. Conversion of the Mongols for the sake of the security of Christian Europe was one motivation for their activity. Catholic missionaries even attempted with some success to convert Nestorian Christians to Catholicism.

The last synod of the Church of the East for which we have documentation met in 1318. That synod elected as patriarch Timothy II. There are virtually no records for the history of the Church of the East between then and the sixteenth century. With the fall of the Mongols in China, Christianity of either a Catholic or Nestorian variety vanished for those territories. In 1370, Timur, or Tamerlane as he is known in the West, began his campaign of conquest. By the time of his death in 1405, he had conquered most of Central Asia and almost extinguished the Church of the East. Most of the remaining Nestorian Christians fled northward into what is today the Kurdish area that straddles Iraq and Turkey.

W. Baum and D. W. Winkler, *The Church of the East: A Concise History* (2003); L. Brown, *The Indian Christians of St. Thomas: An Account of the Ancient Syrian Church of Malabar* (1982); S. M. Moffett, *A History of Christianity in Asia*, vol. 1, *Beginnings to 1500* (1982).

EUGENE M. LUDWIG, OFM CAP.

Church Offices In the early church, offices arose to meet the practical needs for authority and the distribution of charity (Acts 6:1–5; 1 Tim. 3:1–13; 5:3–22). With the growth and increasing complexity of the church, a hierarchy of church offices emerged from the basic roles of deacon, presbyter, and bishop. By the late medieval period the number of offices included porter, lector, exorcist, acolyte, subdeacon, deacon, priest, cardinal, and bishop. The bishop of Rome was the pope.

The sixteenth-century Reformers, seeking to return to the model of the early church, rejected a hierarchy of offices. Martin Luther (1483–1546) rejected ordination as a sacrament as well as the medieval church's vows of poverty, chastity, and obedience that designated the monastic and clerical life holier than lay life. Luther viewed the medieval distinctions between clergy and laity as unbiblical and claimed that all Christians by virtue of their baptism are ordained to priesthood, the universal priesthood of all the baptized. Article 14 of the Lutheran Augsburg Confession (1530) simply states "that nobody should publicly teach or preach or administer the sacraments in the church without a regular call." John Calvin (1509–1564), also claiming biblical precedent (Eph. 4:11–14) and rejecting the hierarchical ministries of the Roman Church, set forth four offices of ministry in his *Institutes of the Christian Religion* (1559): pastors, teachers, elders, and deacons. For the Protestant Reformers the office of ministry was primarily for the proclamation of the Word of God. The Church of England essentially retained the Roman Catholic form of church offices (bishops, archdeacons, deans, prebends, and parish clergy) with the exception of the papacy. The Roman Catholic Church at the Council of Trent (1545–1563) expressly rejected Reformation theologies of church office and reasserted its hierarchy of sacramentally based offices.

G. Dickens, *The English Reformation* (2nd ed., 1989); R. Henderson, *The Teaching Office in the Reformed Tradition* (1962); W. Lazareth, *Two Forms of Ordained Ministry* (1991); E. A. McKee, *Elders and the Plural Ministry* (1988); J. Olson, *Deacons and Deaconesses through the Centuries: One Ministry/Many Roles* (1992); M. Venard, ed., *Les Temps des Confessions, 1530–1620/30*, vol. 8 of *Histoire du Christianisme* (1992); G. Wingren, *Luther on Vocation* (1957).

JEANNINE E. OLSON

Church Order, Early "Church order" refers to the entire set of institutions that help constitute the church as a distinct social and religious reality at any one time. These institutions include practices of entrance into the church; the church's characteristic theological and ethical approach and the manner of inculcating it, especially through reading, explanation, and veneration of the Bible; celebration of religious unity in liturgy; offices, functions, and ranks that define groups within the church; schemes of collecting and distributing financial resources; managing failure through penance and excommunication; and ways of relating to people and social realities outside the church.

For its first five centuries, far from distinguishing church order as a disciplinary matter separate from dogmatic concerns, the church considered discourse on church order as a major part of church doctrine. Church order doctrine in this period exhorted Christians to practice church institutions properly and laid out the binding rules on how to do so. This hortatory and juridical institutional doctrine had to be drawn from church tradition and had to find support in references to Scripture and to the words and actions of Jesus and his apostles. Thus, at the heart of the early church order tradition, one finds a continuing effort to interpret Old and New Testaments as the prime witness of God's sanction for institutions the church had to cultivate in order to carry out its mission. Here the early church order tradition paralleled the interpretations of the Mosaic law behind the formulation of the Jewish Mishnah and Talmuds. Early church order teaching frequently adapted Jewish interpretive techniques and modes of prayer, even in the effort to underline the distinction between Jewish and Christian groups. Indeed, the early church order tradition was often concerned to strengthen the church's self-definition against outsiders—the classic trio of pagans, Jews, and heretics—whose views or practices threatened the church's identity by luring away Christians or by blurring the differences between these groups and the church.

Scholars label "church orders" as the surviving early literary sources given over in their entirety to this traditional doctrine on church institutions. These texts are all versions, adaptations, translations, or combinations of the *Didache*, the *Apostolic Tradition*, or the *Didascalia apostolorum*. Intended to put forth institutional doctrine valid for all churches and covering any cases that might arise, these documents explicitly treat a wide variety of institutions, and they include principles that can govern situations not mentioned in the documents themselves. These principles have also served to guide those who later modified these documents to adapt them to changed times. The traditional character of early church order doctrine fosters, rather than inhibits, innovations that develop new institutional elements or leave behind others. The last of the early church orders, the *Testamentum Domini Nostri Jesu Christi*, represents a version of the *Apostolic Tradition* written in the fifth century. One can also find early church order doctrine in letters circulated among the churches, such as the letter of Clement to the Corinthians, in sermons and catechetical and mystagogical instructions, in conciliar canons and canonical letters of bishops, and in other writings.

The texts of the *Didache* and perhaps the *Apostolic Tradition* seem to have circulated originally without explicit identification of their authors. However, because church order doctrine intended to witness to the living tradition of all the churches and anchored that tradition in the teachings of Jesus and the apostles, by the time of the *Didascalia apostolorum*, some Christians were explicitly attributing church order doctrine to the apostles. This pseudo-apostolic trend gained momentum in the fourth century as church order traditions previously thought to be optional were traced back to the apostles. Church orders such as the *Didascalia apostolorum* claim to have originated in a church council the apostles held, thus reflecting the influence of conciliar decisions on the church order tradition. The Edict of Milan in 313 increased the perennial influence of social forms outside the church on early church order as the empire began to protect the churches and to oversee their governance. The resultant huge influx of new Christians helped make the fourth century one of the most creative in the entire history of church order.

P. F. Bradshaw, *The Search for the Origins of Christian Worship: Sources and Methods for the Study of Early Liturgy* (2nd ed., 2002); A. Faivre, *Ordonner la fraternité: Pouvoir d'innover et retour à l'ordre dans l'Eglise ancienne* (1992); B. Steimer, *Vertex Traditionis: Die Gattung der altchristlichen Kirchenordnungen* (1992); E. M. Synek, *"Dieses Gesetz ist gut, heilig, es zwingt nicht . . .": Zum Gesetzbegriff der Apostolischen Konstitutionen* (1997).

JOSEPH G. MUELLER, SJ

Church Orders, Reformation

Church orders or ordinances are written documents that define and govern the life of the church, its leadership, and its members. Contemporary Protestant church orders typically govern worship, liturgy, discipline, clergy, polity, and property. Earlier church orders also dealt with marriage, education, burial, tithing, public morals, poor relief, and more. Today, Protestant church orders are almost always products of the church alone, whether issued by bishops, assemblies, synods, or councils. Previously they could just as well be part of the state's laws of religious establishment, whether drafted by theologians or jurists.

In the sixteenth century, Protestant churches developed these church orders to replace the canon law by which the Catholic clergy had governed Western Christendom for centuries. The medieval church's canon law was a pervasive legal system administered by a vast hierarchy of church courts and officials headed by the pope. The Reformation began as a call for freedom from this legal regime—freedom of the church from the tyranny of the pope, and freedom of the Christian's conscience from intrusive human traditions. Catalyzed by Martin Luther's burning of the canon law books in 1520, early Protestants denounced Catholic laws and authorities in violent terms and urged radical reforms of the church on the strength of the Bible.

When organizing their new churches, however, the Protestant reformers invariably drew upon Catholic canon laws and procedures. Particularly valuable were apostolic and patristic norms that were incorporated into Catholic canon law as well as selected later papal and conciliar laws grounded in Scripture. These canon laws were combined with new laws devised by Protestant theologians and jurists to form the new Protestant church ordinances. In Reformation Europe, these laws were variously labeled as reformations, ordinances, acts, statutes, mandates, articles, edicts, decrees, or instructions. At first they varied greatly in length, formality, and legal sophistication, ranging from a few sentences to hundred-page tomes. By the turn of the seventeenth century, most Protestant denominations had reduced these church orders to systematic legal codes.

The sundry Lutheran polities of Germany and Scandinavia had thousands of church ordinances in the sixteenth century, many of them drafted by Luther, Johannes Bugenhagen, Johannes Brenz, Martin Bucer, and Philip Melanchthon, among others. Typically these ordinances had separate sections on doctrine, worship, baptism, catechesis, liturgy, preaching, marriage, poor relief, and education. These sections on discrete subjects were sometimes split off and expanded into their own ordinances and then copied and further revised by neighboring polities. In most Lutheran polities, the city councilor or territorial prince had final authority over these church ordinances, in expression of the principle of *cuius regio, eius religio* set out in the Peace of Augsburg (1555) and Religious Peace of Westphalia (1648).

During John Calvin's day, Geneva passed more than fifty church ordinances to govern church polity, marriage, inheritance, education, catechesis, sumptuousness, public bathing, blasphemy, sexual crimes, and much else. These early ordinances were revised and systematized in the 1561 Ecclesiastical Ordinance and 1568 Civil Edict, whose prototypes Calvin had drafted. Primary jurisdiction over these subjects generally lay with the consistory court, with cases remanded or removed to the city council if they required more than spiritual sanctions. These early Genevan church ordinances and institutions set the standard for many early modern Reformed polities in Huguenot France, the German Palatinate, Pietist Netherlands, Presbyterian Scotland, and Puritan England and New England.

In Reformation England, the crown and Parliament claimed the authority to pass new ordinances for the Church of England. Parliament did eventually authorize the Book of Common Prayer (1559) and Thirty-Nine Articles (1571), which included modest changes to prevailing medieval canon law. Parliament made further small changes in several other discrete ordinances. But the expansive Reformation of Ecclesiastical Law (1552, 1571)—which contained detailed reforms of church law following Protestant Continental patterns—did not pass. Anglican England accordingly retained a great deal of the medieval Catholic canon law, though now under the ultimate authority of the monarch, not the pope. Medieval-style church courts retained their jurisdiction in England until the nineteenth century. Both Parliament and Convocation continued to make changes, particularly regarding liturgy, marriage, education, inheritance, charity, and poor relief. But many legal reforms that took three decades to take effect on the Protestant Continent took three centuries in Anglican England.

R. H. Helmholz, ed., *Canon Law in Protestant Lands* (1993); M. Hill, *Ecclesiastical Law* (2nd ed., 2001); R. M. Kingdon, ed., *Registers of the Consistory of Geneva in the Time of Calvin* (2000–); E. Sehling, ed., *Die evangelischen Kirchenordnungen des 16. Jahrhunderts,* vols.

1–5 (1902–1913), vols. 6–16 (1955–1968); J. Witte Jr., *Law and Protestantism: The Legal Teachings of the Lutheran Reformatim* (2002).

JOHN WITTE JR.

Church Visitations *see* Visitations, Church

Cicero, Marcus Tullius (106–43 BCE), Roman attorney, orator, and politician. After his education in philosophy and rhetoric in Athens and Rhodes, Cicero returned to Rome and was elected quaestor and subsequently consul. He was committed to the survival of the Roman republic at the time of its demise. Although he did not participate in the plot to kill Caesar, Cicero was present in the senate and approved of the assassination. His invectives before the senate against Anthony in his *Philippics* ultimately led to his own death.

Cicero's illustrious career as an attorney produced many orations, which are universally considered representative of the classical Latin language par excellence. In addition to his orations, Cicero's writings on rhetorical theory, as well as many of his letters, are still extant. Toward the end of his life, after the untimely death of his daughter Tullia in childbirth, Cicero turned his attention to philosophy.

Cicero considered himself a Platonist of the New Academy, which means that he was essentially a skeptic. In his *Academics* he overcomes the inevitability of the perpetual inaction that skepticism necessarily produces by adopting the probabilism of Chrysippus, which Cicero considered sufficient for action. Nevertheless, his fondness of Stoicism with its exaltation of virtue above all and its indifference toward pain and death is evident in his *Tuscullan Disputations.* His chief philosophical contribution, however, was the transmission of Greek thought into Latin.

His influence on the fathers of the church was enormous. Lactantius, the "Christian Cicero," inspired by Cicero's *The Nature of the Gods,* dealt with the Christian understanding of God. Ambrose modeled his *On Duties* upon Cicero's work with the same title and thus the Stoic cardinal virtues of prudence, justice, fortitude, and temperance became permanently Christian. In his *Confessions* Augustine describes how Cicero's *Hortensius* was a significant influence in his youth. His refutation of skepticism, *Against the Academics,* was a response to Cicero, as his *Christian Instruction* was influenced by Cicero's oratorical works.

Cicero, *Works*, trans. Harry Caplan et al., 29 vols., LCL (1913–); A. Everitt, *Cicero: The Life and Times of Rome's Greatest Politician* (2001); E. Rawson, *Cicero: A Portrait* (1975); M. Testard, *Saint Augustin et Cicéron*, 2 vols. (1958).

KENNETH B. STEINHAUSER

Cistercian Order The beginnings of the Cistercian order date from March 1098, when Robert, the abbot of Molesme, and a group of monks founded the cloister of Cîteaux near Beaune (Burgundy). They characterized their foundation programmatically as a "new cloister" (*novum monasterium*). There had been conflict in Molesme over observance of the Benedictine rule. The stricter part of the convent decided, under Robert's leadership, to start over, in solitude. Eremetical withdrawl, ascetic severity, and the literal observance of the Benedictine rule were the leading preoccupations of the new foundation. Thereby, the ideals of the first Cistercians rank themselves among the eremetical and cenobitic monastic reforms of the eleventh century.

In 1099 Abbot Robert returned to Molesme by order of Pope Urban II. The following year, the new abbot, Alberich (1099–1108), was confirmed by Pope Paschal II and formulated the tenets of monastic life begun at Cîteaux in the *Instituta monachorum cisterciensium de Molismo venentium* (*Precepts of the Cistercians Coming from Molesme*). Under his successor Stephen Harding (1109–1133), the community grew, enjoying the support of Duke Odo of Burgundy and the local nobility. Organization by filiations grew out of the bonds between the four first daughter monasteries— La-Ferté-sur-Grosne (1113), Pontigny (1114), Clairvaux (1115), and Morimond (1115)—an important feature of the order's constitution. Around 1125, the first Cistercian women's cloister was founded. Stephen Harding ordered a common liturgy and constitution in the *Ecclesiastica officia* (*Ecclesiastical Offices*), the *Usus conversorum* (*Exercise of Converts*), and the *Carta caritatis* (*Charter of Love*), this last approved by the pope in 1119.

The autonomy of the individual abbey competed with communal controls in the constitution of the Cistercian order. Until the late twelfth century, the order completely freed itself from episcopal control by means of papal privileges. The ideal of uniformity formulated in the *Carta caritatis* was to be guaranteed by an annual general chapter meeting at Cîteaux comprising all Cistercian abbots and by the regular visitation of each house. Decisions reached at the general chapter were binding on the entire order; since the early thirteenth century these decisions were arranged in systematic *libelli*. The abbots of the respective mother houses performed the visitations; for Cîteaux, it was the abbots of the primary abbeys or their representatives. The organizational model developed by the Cistercians prevailed in late medieval monasticism. The architectural style and liturgy of the Cistercians were oriented, in contrast to Cluny's richness of forms, toward the founding fathers' principles of uniformity and simplicity.

The rational constitution, strict form of life, and charismatic personality of the first abbot of Clairvaux, Bernard (r. 1115–53), ensured the great popularity of the order already in the first half of the twelfth century. The community quickly grew beyond its Burgundian and French core; noble and ruling houses throughout Europe tried to win the dispatch of convents to their territories. Outside of France, large filiations developed in Italy, Germany, England, Scandinavia, on the Iberian peninsula, and in Eastern Europe. During the time of Bernard's office alone, Clairvaux established 164 new foundations; around 1300, the order as a whole comprised more than 700 houses. In the church of the twelfth century Cistercians soon took up leading positions as bishops, cardinals, legates, and popes. The dominating influence of Bernard of Clairvaux is documented by his promotion of Pope Innocent II in the papal schism of 1130–1139 and the founding of the order of Templars, and by his commission from Pope Eugenius III (1145–1153), the first Cistercian upon St. Peter's throne, to preach the crusade.

Facilitated by nobility, the Cistercians advanced agricultural techniques and consistent self-management of cloisters by monks and the lay brothers (*conversi*) bound to a cloister led to rich economic gains. The Cistercians became specialists in the cultivation of wastelands, in iron extraction, fish breeding, and church building. These accomplishments endangered the original ideals of poverty and solitude. In the thirteenth century, the competition posed by the popularity of the mendicant orders aggravated the situation of the Cistercians. In the late Middle Ages, the Cistercians were carried by the undertow of the general crisis of monasticism, characterized by the increase of papal prebends, general economic depression, and the consequences of the Black Death and wars. Regional reforms in Italy, Spain, and Bohemia could not redress the crisis of the order; about a quarter of the convents disbanded. Reformation and secularization brought additional losses. After the Council of Trent (1545–1564), national congregations took shape in Catholic lands. In 1892–1894, as a result of its "strict observance," the French cloister La Trappe (Trappists) split off from the community. Today part of the Cistercian community belongs to the Trappist order.

Statuta Capitulorum Generalium Ordinis Cisterciensis ab anno 1116 ad annum 1786, ed. J. M. Canivez (1933–); *Les plus anciens textes de Cîteaux: Sources, textes et notes historiques*, ed. J. de la Croix Bouton, J. Van Damme (1974); *La codification cistercienne de 1202 et son évolution ultérieure*, ed. B. Lucet (1964); *Les monuments primitifs de la règle cistercienne*, ed. P. Guignard (1878); *Les Ecclesiastica officia des Cisterciens du XIIe siècle*, ed. D. Choisselet, P. Vernet (1989); K. Elm, ed., *Die Zisterzienser: Ordensleben zwischen Ideal und Wirklichkeit*, 2 vols. (1980, 1982); B. K. Lackner, *The Eleventh-Century Background of Cîteaux* (1972); L. J. Leclercq, "Die Intentionen der Gründer des Zisterzienserordens," *Cistercienser-Chronik* 96 (1989): 3–32; J. Lekai, *The Cistercians: Ideal and Reality* (1977); J. Mahn, *L'ordre cistercien et son gouvernement des origines au milieu du XIIe siècle (1098–1265)* (2nd ed., 1951); J. Oberste, *Visitation und Ordensorganisation: Zisterzienser, Prämonstratenser und Cluniazenser (12.–14. Jahrhundert)* (1996); M. Pacaut, *Les moines blancs: Histoire de l'ordre de Cîteaux* (1993); E. R. Elder, ed., *The New Monastery, Texts and Studies on the Earliest Cistercians* (1998).

JÖRG OBERSTE

Clare of Assisi (c. 1193–1253), considered to be the founder of the feminine branch of the Franciscan tradition, that is, the Order of the Poor Ladies, also known as Poor Clares or Clarisses. Like Francis, Clare's religious vocation turned on the issue of apostolic poverty. She fought throughout her life to secure for herself and her sisters the privilege of poverty.

Born into a wealthy family, Clare was inspired by the charismatic manner of Francis and embraced the religious life in a dramatic episode during a Palm Sunday liturgy in 1212. That night she ran away from her family and entered the religious life in a quiet ritual led by Francis. Temporarily housed with Benedictine nuns who could protect her from her father's rage and efforts to kidnap her, Clare was moved from convent to convent until she finally settled next to the small chapel of San Damiano just outside the walls of Assisi. Here she lived out her life with a small group of companions.

As an enclosed sister, Clare's life became focused on forging a rule that would allow the sisters to embrace the Franciscan charism as much as possible. Early rules written by popes were modeled closely on the Benedictine rule. On her deathbed Clare's rule, which secured poverty as a privilege, was finally approved. Her life's work is known from her rule, her letters of counsel, and hagiography written to support her canonization, which took place on September 26, 1255.

M. P. Alberzoni, *Clare of Assisi and the Poor Sisters in the Thirteenth Century* (2004); R. Armstrong and I. Brady, trans., *Francis and Clare: The Complete Works* (1982); M. Carney, *The First Franciscan Woman: Clare of Assisi and the Form of Her Life* (1993); I. Peterson, *Clare of Assisi: A Biographical Study* (1993).

DARLEEN PRYDS

Clarendon Code   Named for the Earl of Clarendon, this code consisted of a series of acts against the English Puritans following the restoration of the monarchy in 1660. The cumulative effect of the code resulted in dissenting denominations, including the Congregationalists, Presbyterians, and Baptists. Four acts made up the code. The Corporation Act of 1661 excluded Puritans from politics by requiring municipal officials to take the sacrament in the Anglican Rite. The Act of Uniformity of 1662 reasserted the sole use of the Book of Common Prayer in worship; this led to the Great Ejection of Puritan sympathizers in the clergy. The Conventicle Act of 1664 forbade congregational worship of more than five people using anything other than the Book of Common Prayer. The Five Mile Act of 1665 stipulated that former clergy must remain at least five miles from their former parishes.

G. Bray, *Documents of the English Reformation* (1994).

ALDEN R. LUDLOW

Clareno, Angelo (c. 1260–1337), one of the three principal Franciscan Spirituals, along with Ubertino da Casale and Peter John Olivi. Born Pietro da Fossombrone, he entered the Franciscan order around 1270 in Ancona, became embroiled, as a rigorist, in the emerging Franciscan conflict over religious poverty, and suffered numerous imprisonments during a largely itinerant career. He wrote a firsthand, polemical account of the persecution of Franciscan Spirituals.

D. Burr, *The Spiritual Franciscans* (2001); A. Clareno, *Expositio regulae fratrum minorum*, ed. L. Oliger (1912); Clareno, *Liber chronicarum sive tribulationum ordinis minorum*, ed. G. Boccali (1999); Clareno, *Opera*, vol. 1, *Epistole* (1999).

CHRISTOPHER OCKER

Classis A classis (plural, *classes*) is the assembly of clergy and representative lay elders in the Reformed churches, drawn from congregations in a particular local region, that meets regularly to provide oversight and offer mutual support and cooperation. The term was first used in 1537 in the churches in French-speaking Switzerland under the supervision of Bern. The French Reformed designated the analogous body a *colloquy*, while the Scottish church used the term *presbytery*. Dutch refugee churches, and the Reformed church established in the Dutch Republic in the late sixteenth century, adopted the term *classis*, and this remains the dominant designation for the regional ecclesiastical organization in Dutch Reformed contexts. English Presbyterians established classes within the Church of England in the 1570s but met with opposition from Elizabeth I.

In Holland especially, the classes were the key organizational element in the church and played a dominant role in the extension of Reformed influence over society at large. The classes supplied ministers to all churches, examined prospective ministers and provided remedial theological education when necessary, carried out regular parish visitations, and handled serious disciplinary matters. The business of many of the larger classes was sufficiently heavy that by the early seventeenth century standing committees—the *deputati classis*—were established to tend to matters arising between regular meetings.

A. Duke, G. Lewis, A. Pettegree, eds., *Calvinism in Europe, 1540–1610: A Collection of Documents* (1992); C. A. Tukker, *De classis Dordrecht van 1573 tot 1609* (1965).

CHRISTOPHER ELWOOD

Clement VII (1479–1534), papal advisor, diplomat, patron of the arts, elected pope in 1523. Clement was born into the Medici family and named archbishop of Florence and car-

dinal by the previous Medici pope, Leo X. He worked for Leo and then Adrian VI, strengthening the papacy's defensive alliance with Emperor Charles V against Francis I of France. Clement VII became pope after Adrian's brief, unpopular and, in terms of reform, disappointing reign. As pope, Clement seemed overwhelmed by the intrigue of secular politics, oblivious to the rising tide of the Reformation, and unwilling to admit the urgency of ecclesial reform. His continual vacillation between competing powers alienated all parties, neutralizing the Holy See's effectiveness in stemming the Turkish advance on Vienna, lending the Reformers renewed energy through the Diet of Speyer (1526), and finally inciting imperial wrath against Medici rule in Florence and his own pontificate in the horrific Sack of Rome (1527). Clement himself fled to the Castel Sant'Angelo, finally buying his freedom with a huge ransom and Charles's coronation. Still indecisive, Clement wavered over Henry VIII's divorce, unwilling to offend the emperor, Catherine of Aragon's nephew. The king then angrily led England into schism. Ironically, it was Clement who, just before his death, commissioned Michelangelo's *Last Judgment*, under whose ominous beauty and portentious warnings generations of conclaves have elected Clement's papal successors.

P. Crabites, *Clement VII and Henry VIII* (1936); E. Duffy, *Saints and Sinners: A History of the Popes* (1997); R. P. McBrien, *Lives of the Popes* (1997).

PETER J. SCAGNELLI

Clement of Alexandria (c. 150–c. 215), early Christian theologian and exegete in Egypt. A Platonic philosopher, polymath, and Christian apologist, Clement was the first Christian to attempt a thoroughgoing synthesis of the Bible and Greek philosophy. He is known primarily for a trilogy consisting of the *Exhortation* (*Protreptikos*), an invitation to the Christian faith directed at educated Greeks; the *Pedagogue* (*Paidagogos*), a moral treatise addressed to new Christians; and the *Miscellanies* (*Stromateis*), a work that treats philosophical, theological, and exegetical questions. This last is an enigmatic, diffuse work in which Clement both conceals and reveals, depositing "seeds" of his higher teaching for those who are able to appropriate them. His surviving works also include a treatise, *Who Is the Rich Man Who Shall Be Saved?* and an annotated collection of Valentinian gnostic texts, *The Excerpts from Theodotus*. Little is known of Clement's life or his role in the church. Eusebius describes him as the second head of the catechetical school at Alexandria (*Hist. eccl.* 6.6.1), but this has been doubted.

An optimistic and exuberant thinker, Clement thought of all truth as one. Christ, the divine Logos (Word) has a comprehensive plan for the education and salvation of all humanity; throughout the ages he has deposited seeds of truth in various cultures. Clement quotes widely from Greek literature and sees Greek philosophy as preparation for the gospel, given to the Greeks just as the Old Testament was to the Hebrews. He is at the beginning of a long tradition of Christian Platonism, in which the contrast between the sensible and the intellectual realms is important. The most complete revelation of truth, however, is in the Bible, which speaks of God's perfection and extravagant love. Because the immaterial God cannot be contained within sensible reality, even in the letters of Scripture, allegorical exegesis is required in order to grasp the transcendent realities of which biblical words are signs. Clement describes the ideal Christian as the "true" gnostic, who begins with the faith expressed in the church's "rule" (creed) and makes gradual progress toward perfect knowledge (*gnosis*). The ultimate goal of life is to ascend to the direct vision of God. Since "like is dear to like" (Plato, *Gorg.* 510B, cited in *Paed.* 1.6.28.2), Christian life is a pursuit of perfection, in which moral discipline, intellectual training, and imitation of the works of divine love go hand in hand.

J. Behr, *Asceticism and Anthropology in Irenaeus and Clement* (2000); A. C. Cox, ed., *ANF*, vol. 2, trans. W. Wilson (1885, 1994): 171–609; D. Dawson, *Allegorical Readers and Cultural Revision in Ancient Alexandria* (1992); J. Ferguson, FC 85 (1991); A. van den Hoek, "The Catechetical School of Early Christian Alexandria and Its Philonic Heritage," *HTR* 90 (1997): 59–87; J. L. Kovacs, "Divine Pedagogy and the Gnostic Teacher according to Clement of Alexandria," *JECS* 9 (2001): 3–25; S. R. C. Lilla, *Clement of Alexandria: A Study in Christian Platonism and Gnosticism* (1971); A. Méhat, *Étude sur les 'Stromates' de Clément d'Alexandrie* (1966); E. Osborn, *Clement of Alexandria* (2005); O. Stählin, L. Früchtel, U. Treu, eds., GCS, 4 vols. (1936–1985).

JUDITH L. KOVACS

Clement of Rome and Pseudo-Clementine Literature

Clement was the bishop of Rome at the end of the first century, as well as the reputed author of *1 and 2 Clement* and several other writings now identified as the Pseudo-Clementine literature. Both Tertullian (*Praescr.* 32) and Epiphanius (*Pan.* 27.6) report that the apostle Peter ordained Clement, while Eusebius (*Hist. eccl.* 3.15.34) and Irenaeus (*Haer.* 3.3.1) list him as the third bishop of Rome after Linus and Anacletus.

Though no author is named within the text, tradition has assumed that Clement's authority and reputation stand behind the composition of *1 Clement*. This late first- or second-century letter from Rome is addressed to the Corinthian church in response to power struggles there. The church at Rome stresses the desire of God for order and structure.

The text of *2 Clement* is a homily from the mid-second-century church, perhaps delivered in the context of a baptismal service. It is most unlikely that Clement was the author of this work, though Rome (together with Corinth and Alexandria) is often listed as a possible milieu for its composition. The primary theme of *2 Clement* is support in the face of false teachers.

The Pseudo-Clementine literature consists of texts that claim Clement as their author and are broadly concerned with the details of his life. They most likely are fourth-century works from Palestine or Syria based upon a third-century original. Included among this literature are the well-known *Recognitions* and *Homilies*, as well as spurious letters from Clement to James, Peter to James, and James to Peter.

B. Bowe, *A Church in Crisis: Ecclesiology and Paraenesis in Clement of Rome* (1988); D. A. Hagner, *The Use of the Old and New Testaments in Clement of Rome* (1973); F. S. Jones, "The Pseudo-Clementines: A History of Research," *SecCent* 2 (1982): 1–33, 63–96; W. Schneemelcher, ed., *NTApocr*, vol. 2 (1992), 483–541.

CLAYTON N. JEFFORD

Climacus, John (c. 570–c. 649), hermit, abbot, and writer on progress in the spiritual life. His Greek name means "John of the Ladder"; he is also referred to as "Klimax," "Scholastikos," and "Sinaites." He spent the majority of his life in or near the Monastery of St. Catherine in Sinai, arriving there in his early youth. He may have also spent short periods of time in Egypt, Scete, and Tabenesis. For many years he was under the obedience of an elder, and, after the elder's death, he became a cave-dwelling hermit. John was at a very advanced age when he was chosen to be abbot of the monastery, which office he held for only a brief time, then returned to the eremitic life. It was in this last period of seclusion that he composed *Heavenly Ladder* (also known as *Ladder of Paradise* or *Ladder of Divine Ascent*), subtitled, "a book called the spiritual tablets for the edification of the new Israelites, the people who have just come out of mental Egypt and from the sea of life." It is one of the most influential early medieval guides to the ascetic life, used by monastics and laity alike. The book had a profound effect on the hesychasts, and in particular Symeon the New Theologian. It has been translated into Latin, Syriac, Arabic, Armenian, Church Slavic, as well as all of the major modern languages. Exhibiting a profound psychological understanding of human behavior, it outlines a ladderlike scheme of thirty steps or chapters (derived from the thirty years of Christ's hidden life) that a monk must ascend to achieve the crown of glory from Christ. The pinnacle, the thirtieth level, is the chapter called "Faith, Hope, and Charity." At each step John describes the virtues and vices to be encountered and prescribes how to achieve or overcome them. In the thirty levels the monk will encounter virtues including obedience, meekness, chastity, temperance, poverty, humility, and discretion; he must conquer malice, slander, sloth, gluttony, avarice, vainglory, pride, and more—or be pulled from the ladder into the abyss.

J. Chryssavgis, *Ascent to Heaven: The Theology of the Human Person according to Saint John of the Ladder* (1989); J. Climacus, *The Ladder of Divine Ascent*, trans. C. Luibheid and N. Russell (1982); G. Florovsky, "St. John Climacus," in *The Byzantine Ascetic and Spiritual Fathers*, vol. 10 of *The Collected Works of Georges Florovsky* (1987), 241–52.

MICHAEL D. PETERSON

Cloister Gardens Monastic cloisters, large square yards surrounded by loggias and usually attached to the south flank of a church, had gardens that varied according to the monastery's geographical location and the taste and wealth of the monks who lived in them. Generally, cloisters featured a central basin or well, either dry or wet. In southern Europe (Spain, southern France, and Italy) cloisters were generally paved or of beaten earth, with

perhaps an evergreen tree and a few potted evergreen shrubs. In the moister climate of northern Europe, grass lawns were more common, often with crossing sanded or paved paths, with an evergreen tree, generally a pine or juniper, and sometimes evergreen shrubs such as boxwood.

Although monastic compounds often included orchards, herb gardens, and kitchen gardens, according to tradition the planting scheme of the cloister garden was kept very simple. In the Middle Ages it generally did not include colorful and distracting flowers. Rather, green was the central element; it was thought that the color green refreshed the mind and thus aided the monks and nuns in their meditation. The single evergreen tree featured in many cloister gardens symbolized the tree of life in Eden, the first paradise, and reminded monastics of the promise of everlasting life. Its branches were also useful for sprinkling holy water (aspersion) during church rituals. Today modern irrigation and plumbing and the wide availability of flowering plants via the nursery trade have led some monastic houses to plant more elaborate cloister gardens.

M. Hales, *Monastic Gardens* (2000); J. Harvey, *Mediaeval Gardens* (1981); W. Horn, "On the Origins of the Medieval Cloister," *Gesta* 12 (1973): 13–52; S. Landsberg, *The Medieval Garden* (1995); P. Meyvaert, "The Medieval Monastic *Claustrum*," *Gesta* 12 (1973): 53–59; Meyvaert, "The Medieval Monastic Garden," in *Medieval Gardens*, ed. E. B. MacDougall (1986), 24–53.

NANCY KATHERINE SPATZ LUCID

Clotilda (c. 470–544), Frankish queen (c. 496–544). Clotilda, a daughter of Chilperic II, a Burgundian king, married Clovis, king of the Franks, around 496. Gregory of Tours, whose *Histories* are the principal source for Clotilda, related that her uncle Gundobad had murdered the girl's father and sent her into exile, from which Clovis obtained her. The historian portrayed the subsequent Frankish and Burgundian wars of the 520s and 530s as a blood feud between Clotilda's sons and her uncle's family. This interpretation of events is unlikely. The marriage probably was intended to secure a Franco-Burgundian alliance, which later soured. Clotilda was a catholic, and the queen's encouragement was partly responsible for her husband's conversion to catholic Christianity. Of Clovis's four sons who proclaimed themselves king after their father's death (511), three were born of Clotilda. Upon her husband's demise, the queen relocated to Tours, where she lived as an ascetic. She remained a significant religious and political figure during her sons' reigns, an age marred by civil warfare among the siblings. Clotilda erected several churches, and she seems to have determined the selection of at least three bishops of Tours. From the seventh century Clotilda was venerated as a saint.

J. A. McNamara, J. E. Halborg, and E. G. Whatley, eds., *Sainted Women of the Dark Ages* (1992), 38–52.

ALLEN E. JONES

Clovis (c. 465–511), king of the Franks (c. 481–511). When Clovis (or Chlodwig) succeeded his father Childeric as king, he was but one of several Salian Frankish rulers who held territory in the northwest corner of Gaul. Clovis was a successful warrior who, by the end of his reign, controlled nearly the entirety of Gaul. He campaigned against other Germanic groups (Burgundians, Alamans, and Visigoths) and also against several Frankish kings. Clovis married the Burgundian princess Clotilda, and she influenced him to convert to catholic Christianity.

Sources for Clovis's life are contested. Gregory of Tours's *Histories* has traditionally been the principal source for information. However, Gregory wrote a century after the fact, and his writing is extremely stylistic. Scholars trustful of Gregory's chronology date Clovis's baptism around 496. Gregory contends that the king's conversion enabled him to turn a near disaster against the Alamans into a military victory. For Gregory, Clovis represents the exemplary faithful Christian monarch—a Gallic Constantine. More contemporary evidence for Clovis's career includes a letter written by Avitus of Vienne congratulating the Frankish ruler upon his baptism. Scholars relying principally upon this evidence support a date around 508 for the baptism.

In 507 Clovis and his Franks defeated the Arian king Alaric II and his Visigoths at the Battle of Vouillé. This episode marked the ascendance of Frankish, as opposed to Visigothic, control over Gaul. It also heralded the end of Arian practice in the region. In 511 Clovis summoned the bishops of his realm to a national synod, the Council of Orléans. Clovis died in the same year. His four surviving sons divided the realm among themselves. Clovis's dynasty, the Merovingians, would rule Gaul until 751.

I. N. Wood, "Gregory of Tours and Clovis," *RBPH* 63 (1985): 249–72; Wood, *The Merovingian Kingdoms, 450–751* (1994).

ALLEN E. JONES

Cluny   A Benedictine monastery, founded in 910 near Mâcon (Burgundy, France) by Duke William the Pious of Aquitaine. Cluny became—thanks to its reform activities, its spiritual influence, and generous donations—the center of a major monastic congregation which extended over all of Europe. A decisive impulse thereto was given under the rule of Abbot Odilo (994–1049). Cluny had its greatest social and spiritual role under abbots Hugh of Semur (1049–1109) and Peter the Venerable (1122–1156); the basilica "Cluny III" (for the third rebuilding of the monastery), completed in the twelfth century, was the largest church in Europe before the reconstruction of St. Peter's in Rome. After a serious crisis (the "schism" of Pontius of Melgueil), a legislative reform was undertaken by Peter the Venerable and was followed in the thirteenth century by profound institutional changes. These were initiated by the papacy and transformed the congregation into an order in the full sense of the word, for example, through the installation of a general chapter and of regular visitations in the abbeys and priories associated with Cluny. At the end of the Middle Ages, especially in the fifteenth century, the importance of Cluny was greatly reduced, although this decline should not be exaggerated. A reform was attempted several times at the end of the fifteenth and in the sixteenth centuries, but the Wars of Religion in France (1562–1598) dealt a devastating blow to Cluny and its order. Yet it survived into the seventeenth and eighteenth centuries, divided between an "old" and a "strict observance"; at this time, the order was strictly controlled by the royal power (Richelieu and Mazarin were among the abbots), which led to interminable internal conflicts. Cluny was suppressed by the French Revolution in 1790, and nearly all of the medieval buildings were destroyed.

G. Constable, *Cluniac Studies* (1980); Constable, *Cluny From the 10th to the 12th Centuries: Further Studies* (2000); N. Hunt, ed., *Cluniac Monasticism in the Central Middle Ages* (1971); D. Méhu, *Paix et communautés autour de l'abbaye de Cluny, X^e–XVe siècles* (2001); M. Pacaut, *L'ordre de Cluny (909–1789)* (1986); D. Riche, *L'ordre de Cluny à la fin du Moyen Âge: le "vieux pays clunisien", XIIe–XVe siècles*

(2000); B. H. Rosenwein, *Rhinoceros Bound: Cluny in the 10th Century* (1982).

SÉBASTIEN BARRET

Cocceius, Johannes (1603–1669), German-Dutch Calvinist Hebraist and theologian. A virtuoso of Hebrew and Greek, Cocceius successively held professorships in Bremen (Germany), in Franeker (Frisia), and in Leyden (Holland). He applied his exegetical skills to Reformed covenant theology, into which he systematically integrated the historical progression he observed in the divine economy of the Old Testament and New Testament. His two major works, the *Summa doctrinae* (1648/1653) and *Summa theologiae* (1662), reflect his antischolastic approach to theology, as well as a profound interest in the history of salvation. His historical reading of the OT led him to contend, among other things, that the commandment to observe the Sabbath had not been promulgated in paradise. These and other views gave rise to controversies that continued after his death. His followers later combined his theological system with Cartesian philosophy, the so-called Cocceio-Cartesian school, oriented to allegorical and typological exegesis. Cocceius's commentaries on various books of the OT and his Hebrew *Lexicon* (1669) were widely used in Reformed circles prior to the nineteenth century.

W. J. van Asselt, *The Federal Theology of Johannes Cocceius (1603–1669)* (2001); S. Strehle, *Calvinism, Federalism, and Scholasticism: A Study of the Reformed Doctrine of Covenant* (1988).

JORIS VAN EIJNATTEN

Cochlaeus, Johannes (1479–1552), humanist, priest, theologian. Cochlaeus was born in Raubersried near Wendelstein, Germany. After studies in Cologne he became the principal of the Latin school of St. Lawrence in Nuremberg in 1510, where his *Tetrachordum Musices* appeared in 1512. He continued with his humanistic, legal, and theological studies in Ferrara, where he earned his doctorate in theology in 1517. He was ordained to the priesthood at Rome in 1518. From there he went to Frankfurt am Main, where he became dean of the *Liebfrauenstift*.

Cochlaeus is best known as a vehement opponent of the Protestant Reformation. This opposition was sparked by Luther's *Babylonian Captivity of the Church*. In 1524 he accompanied Compeggio to the diets of Nuremberg and Regensburg. In 1527 he succeeded Emser as chaplain and secretary of Duke George of Saxony, an opponent of Luther. He attended the Diet of Augsburg with George in 1530. He worked on refuting the Augsburg Confession. After the Protestant Reformation was introduced in Saxony, he left for Breslau in 1539. In the 1540s he participated in the colloquies of Hagenau, Worms, and Regensburg. In 1544 he directed his *Philippicae* against Melanchthon. He composed approximately two hundred writings against German and Swiss reformers. One of them, *Commentaria de actis et scriptis M. Lutheri* of 1548, influenced the negative Catholic image of Luther up into the twentieth century.

D. Bagchi, *Luther's Earliest Opponents: Catholic Controversialists, 1518–1525* (1991); B. Peter, "Johann Cochlaeus," *Archiv für schlesische Kirchengeschichte* 57 (2000): 185–215; M. Samuel-Scheyder, *Johannes Cochlaeus, humaniste et adversaire de Luther* (1993).

FRANZ POSSET

Colet, John (1467–1519), English clergyman, scholar, dean of St. Paul's, son of Sir Henry Colet, the two-time Lord Mayor of London. Admired by Erasmus, Thomas More, and other humanists, Colet's criticism of the higher clergy in England became the foundation for later English Reformation anticlericalism. After graduating from Magdalen College, Oxford, he traveled to France and Italy, where he encountered Renaissance humanism. Influenced by humanism, Colet began to stress a return to an uncomplicated discipleship and evangelical piety reminiscent of the early church. In 1497 he returned to Oxford, where he gave a series of lectures on the Pauline epistles, in which he most clearly saw his own personal vision of the church. During this period he stressed literary-biblical exegesis and was often accused of Lollardy. He completed his doctorate in divinity at Oxford in 1504–1505. In 1505 he inherited his father's substantial estates, and it was his family connections and wealth that landed him the post of dean of St. Paul's school that year. Colet's focus on education made the school a significant center for educating the young. In 1512, called to give a sermon against Lollardy, Colet instead used the opportunity to attack the greed and worldliness of the clergy; he was brought up on heresy charges before Archbishop Warham, who dropped the charges. By 1515, very ill, he gave the sermon at Wolsey's elevation to cardinal.

Colet is remembered as a pioneer in education reform in Britain.

J. B. Gleason, *John Colet* (1989).
ALDEN R. LUDLOW

Coligny, Gaspard de (1519–1572),

Huguenot military leader. Gaspard de Châtillon, Lord of Coligny, served in the wars fought against Emperor Charles V. Named admiral of France in 1552 due to the influence of his uncle, Anne de Montmorency, Coligny commanded Saint-Quentin during the Spanish siege of 1557. Along with his two brothers, François d'Andelot (1521–1569) and Odet de Châtillon (1517–1571), Coligny converted to Calvinism and rose quickly as a leader of the Reformed movement in the 1560s. The Catholic Guise family suspected his involvement in the assassination of Francis of Lorraine, duke of Guise (1519–1563), and vowed revenge. Coligny also organized two unsuccessful colonies in the New World in 1555 and 1562. In 1569 Coligny was named commander of all Huguenot forces by the young Henry of Navarre (1553–1610). After the Peace of Saint-Germain (August 1570), which he helped to craft, Coligny went to the Valois court, where he soon exerted a powerful influence on the young king, Charles IX, whom he tried to persuade to declare war against Spain by forging an alliance with Dutch Calvinists. In a bid to end this relationship, Queen Catherine de Médici (1519–1589) formed a secret pact with the Guises to assassinate Coligny during the marriage festivities planned for Henry of Navarre and Marguerite of Valois (1553–1615) in late August 1572. Coligny narrowly escaped the first attempt on his life on August 22 but perished during the orgy of violence known as the St. Bartholomew's Day Massacre (August 24, 1572).

J. Shimizu, *Conflict of Loyalties: Politics and Religion in the Career of Gaspard de Coligny, Admiral of France, 1519–1572* (1970).
MICHAEL WOLFE

Collegiate Church A non-episcopal
church with a collegiate chapter of canons or canonesses led by a provost or dean, analogous to a cathedral chapter but with no say in the government of the diocese. It was the venue for masses and hours, to which the originally comprehensive community life of the canons increasingly limited itself. A collegiate chapter could be founded at any church that had enough assets to maintain a chapter of clergy. Such foundations were made throughout the Middle Ages; within Europe their number decreased markedly from west to east and from south to north (they were most frequently found in the south and the west). The first founders of collegiate chapters were bishops, who as heads of dioceses used them for spiritual and political purposes, in Germany particularly in the tenth and eleventh centuries as a consequence of the Ottonian-Salian imperial church system. Later, emperors, kings, and nobles founded collegiate chapters in their centers of power (palatinates, boroughs, residences) and used the institution to demonstrate their dominion, to provide pastoral care, or to serve a developing administration. In the late Middle Ages, towns or citizens then elevated parish churches to the status of collegiate chapters. Collegiate churches appear not to have developed specific artistic or architectural forms corresponding to their functions.

S. Lorenz, P. Kurmann, and O. Auge, eds., *Funktion und Form. Die mittelalterliche Stiftskirche im Spannungsfeld von Kunstgeschichte, Landeskunde und Archäologie* (2007); S. Lorenz and O. Auge, eds., *Die Stiftskirche in Südwestdeutschland* (2003); P. Moraw, "Über Typologie, Chronologie und Geographie der Stiftskirche im deutschen Mittelalter," in *Untersuchungen zu Kloster und Stift* (1980), 9–37.
OLIVER AUGE

Collegium Philobiblicum Since theology at Leipzig Univ. focused on dogmatics and homiletics, Professor Johann Benedict Carpzov suggested students form an academic society (*collegium*) devoted to biblical interpretation. In 1686 August Hermann Francke and Paul Anton began meeting weekly with six others to study selected Bible passages in the original Hebrew and Greek. Philipp Jacob Spener encouraged the group to aim at a living encounter with the Word, not mere historical acquaintance. By 1689 students began leading lay Bible studies and became the vanguard of the growing Pietist movement within Leipzig and beyond.

T. Kevorkian, "The Material of Faith: Religion and Society in Leipzig, 1685–1725" (PhD diss., Johns Hopkins Univ., 1997).
DOUGLAS H. SHANTZ

Colonna, Vittoria (1492–1547), acclaimed
Renaissance poet. Colonna was a daughter of a powerful Roman family associated with reforming voices in the Catholic Church in Italy and France and especially with ladies of

influence. She governed the papal city of Benevento, first with her military husband Ferrante Francesco d'Avalos, marquis of Pescara, and later on her own. She became entangled in papal politics and was suspected of heresy because of her Valdensian associations and the support she lent to the Capuchin cause. As a widow, Colonna traveled, cultivated literary circles, and sought repose in different convents in order to write *Love Poems* in memory of her husband. Her *Spiritual Poems*, characterized by a Neoplatonic mysticism of the crucified Christ, inspired her friend Michelangelo's art. Colonna's spiritual advisor, Cardinal Reginald Pole (and through him, Juan de Valdes) enhanced her interest in justification and faith, as evidenced in her poems and correspondence with Cardinal Contarini and other papal secretaries. These reforming interests as well as her connection to the notorious Capuchin preacher Bernardino Ochino (also a Pole), might have made her a candidate for the Inquisition had she not died first.

———

R. Bainton, *Women of the Reformation in Germany and Italy* (1971); F. Calabrese, *Vittoria Colonna: Corti e Paese reale al tramonto del Rinascimento* (1987); J. Gibaldi, "Vittoria Colonna: Child, Woman, Poet," in *Women Writers of the Renaissance and Reformation*, ed. K. Wilson (1987); R. Russell, "Vittoria Colonna," in *Italian Women Writers: A Bio-Bibliographical Sourcebook* (1998).

KIRSI STJERNA

Columba (c. 521–597), Irish saint. Born in Ireland of the O'Neill royal line, this "Dove of the Church" trained in monasteries under such teachers as St. Finnian. After participating in the battle of Cúl Drebene in 561, Columba was excommunicated for shedding blood in battle despite being a clergyman. He left Ireland as a penitential exile and settled in Iona in 565, according to tradition, because this was the first place from which he could no longer see Ireland. A mission to Bruide, king of the Picts, was one of his early activities in Scotland. He remained in Iona for thirty-four years, with occasional trips to Scotland and Ireland to plan churches. Over fifty monasteries in Ireland and Scotland claim to have been founded by him, beginning a new era of Irish Christianity. However, it is only certain that three—Derry (546), Durrow (founded before 565 according to Bede and c. 585 according to Adomnán), and Iona—were founded by Columba himself. A family descendant and later abbot of Iona, Adomnán wrote a *Vita Columba* (688–692), which together with Bede's *Ecclesiastical History* is our best source for the life of Columba.

———

D. Broun and T. O. Clancy, eds., *Spes Scotorum = Hope of Scots: Saint Columba, Iona, and Scotland* (1999); M. Herbert, *Iona, Kells, and Derry: The Life of St. Columba* (1988).

MARIANNE M. DELAPORTE

Columbanus (c. 540–615), Irish missionary. Born in Ireland, Columbanus spent most of his adult life in the monastery of Bangor before arriving at the Frankish kingdom in 590/591 in the company of twelve Irish monks. Under the auspices of the Merovingian kings, Columbanus founded a monastery at Annegray and subsequently at Luxeuil and Fontaines. Although Columbanus and his companions followed a rigorous regime of monastic discipline, he succeeded in attracting converts from all strata of society. After his fiery personality led him into conflict with the Gaulish bishops and the Merovingian queen Brunichilde, Columbanus was forced to leave the Frankish kingdom for Italy, where he founded the monastery of Bobbio. Columbanus was a prolific author. A small corpus of his letters and sermons, several treatises, and poems have come down to us, and they reveal a talented author of immense learning and impressive rhetorical skill. Apart from providing us with a panoramic view of the doctrinal and disciplinary issues that preoccupied him, Columbanus's writings also shed some light on the development of early medieval monasticism and penitential discipline, as well as on the Irish-Latin culture in which he was educated.

———

H. B. Clarke and M. Brennan, eds., *Columbanus and Merovingian Monasticism* (1981); M. Lapidge, ed., *Columbanus: Studies on the Latin Writings* (1997).

YITZHAK HEN

Comenius, John Amos (1592–1670), last bishop of the old Bohemian Brethren, leading educational reformer and ecumenist. While a school director in northern Moravia, Comenius suffered the loss of family and property at the start of the Thirty Years' War (1618–1648). He fled Moravia in 1628, spending most of his life as an exile. Many of his 150 books were published in Latin in Amsterdam, where he spent his last years. His allegorical, semiautobiographical work, *The Labyrinth of the World* (1623), is a classic of Czech prose and

Christian spirituality. Comenius's *Didactica Magna* (1657) is one of the most influential works in the Western pedagogical tradition. His encyclopedic educational program (Pansophism) aimed at practical improvement of humanity in preparation for an earthly millennium. Comenius's legacy includes the schools established by August Hermann Francke in Halle.

————

J. A. Comenius, *The Labyrinth of the World and the Paradise of the Heart*, trans. H. Louthan and A. Sterk (1998).

                              DOUGLAS H. SHANTZ

Comestor, Peter (d. 1178), French theologian and biblical interpreter. Born and raised at Troyes, Peter taught at the cathedral school of Notre Dame at Paris from 1160 and acted as its chancellor from 1168 on. In 1178 he took up residence at the abbey of St. Victor. During his teaching career he lectured on most books of the Old Testament using the ordinary gloss as a tool. He was also one of the first Parisian masters to lecture on Peter Lombard's *Sentences*, thus endorsing a topical approach to the teaching of theology. At St. Victor he composed his celebrated *Historia scholastica*, a compendium of biblical history from the creation to Christ's ascension, which soon became the basic textbook for beginning students of theology in the universities and the *studia* of the mendicant orders. Most manuscripts include an expansion by Peter of Poitiers (d. 1205), Comestor's successor at Notre Dame, which covers the story of the Acts of the Apostles. Following the example of Hugh of St. Victor and other Victorines, Peter pursued an active interest in Jewish scholarship. He used the OT commentaries by Andrew of St. Victor and drew freely on Josephus and perhaps even contemporary Jewish sources to support and verify historical details of his narrative.

————

D. Luscombe, "Peter Comestor," in *The Bible in the Medieval World*, ed. K. Walsh and D. Wood (1985), 109–29.

                              KARLFRIED FROEHLICH

Company of Pastors The institution of the Company of Pastors of Geneva in 1541 marked an important ecclesiological achievement in the Protestant Reformation. Comprising all the ministers of the city and its rural parishes, the company met regularly to conduct the church's business, provide for the calling of ministers, organize pastoral and preaching responsibilities, facilitate parish visitations, and arrange for the training of prospective ministers for other churches. Its broader mandate was to maintain the pure teaching of the gospel. To this end the pastors engaged in common study and discussion of biblical interpretation and provided regular occasions for mutual criticism and correction.

John Calvin was moderator of the company until his death (1564). Their work impacted not only Geneva but also the international network of Reformed congregations who looked to them for inspiration and support. Calvin and the company strove to model what they took to be a biblical pattern of collective church leadership while also working to enhance ministerial power and consolidate control over the church. The company thus posed a viable alternative to the monarchical model of episcopacy, as well as to Erastian experiments with civil governmental rule of the church and congregational proposals for an ecclesiastical democracy, and marked the way toward a presbyterian-synodical church polity.

————

P. E. Hughes, ed., *The Register of the Company of Pastors of Geneva in the Time of Calvin* (1966); W. G. Naphy, *Calvin and the Consolidation of the Reformation in Geneva* (1994).

                              CHRISTOPHER ELWOOD

Conciliarism Conciliar theory proposes that supreme ecclesiastical authority resides in general councils. This concept originated when thirteenth-century canonists could not reconcile papal monarchy and the possibility of heretical popes. Hugh of Pisa believed popes could err but that the church was inerrant (*Summa super Decreta*). During the conflict between Boniface VIII and Philip IV, John of Paris suggested the pope could be deposed by those who had elected him on behalf of all Christians (*De potestate regia et papali*). Marsiglio of Padua maintained the church's *plenitudo potestatis* was lodged in its whole body, represented by councils (*Defensor pacis*). These theories were supported by William of Ockham, Jean Gerson, and Pierre d'Ailly.

The Great Schism (1378–1417) elevated the controversy to its highest level. Conrad of Gelnhausen argued only a general council could act for the whole church (*Epistola concordiae*). The Council of Constance declared all Christians, including the pope, were subject to general councils, whose authority was directly from God. Martin V, however, attempted to prohibit appeals from papal decisions to general councils, and Pius II issued the bull *Execrabilis*, formally banning such appeals, negating the Constance decision.

In *De concordantia catholica*, Nicholas of Cues attempted a balanced approach to papal restraint, but conciliar theory failed after the fifteenth century, contributing to the reformations of the sixteenth century. The Second Vatican Council (1962–1965) reemphasized the corporate authority of general councils but did not suggest they had authority over popes.

B. Tierney, *Foundations of the Conciliar Theory* (1955).

LORNA SHOEMAKER

Concordat of Worms   *see* Worms, Concordat of

Confessionalization   The term refers to the historical process by which the great confessional groupings of Christian Europe—Catholic, Lutheran, Reformed, and Anglican—assumed cultural, political, religious, and geographical forms in the wake of the sixteenth-century Protestant Reformation; the term also refers to the historical period in which this process chiefly took place. Due to confessionalization's complex nature, it is difficult to give it fixed temporal boundaries, but most historians place its beginning sometime between the Augsburg Confession's composition (1530) and the Religious Peace of Augsburg (1555), and its end around the time of the Thirty Years' War (1618–1648). Confessionalization set in as the Reformation's early, uncontrolled spread drew to a close and as the changes it had effected were established, codified, and consolidated in new institutions and laws. In the confessionalization process, the interests of ecclesiastical and state authorities became ever more closely aligned, such that the end result was in some cases a near-total union between the two. Churches assumed new social functions, such as policing the citizenry's morals and inculcating the virtues of good subjects: obedience, loyalty, discipline, and respect for law and order. States became ever more tightly identified with particular religious identities and generally took on the role of guarantor of the established church's privileges. In some areas ministers became professional state employees; they underwent standardized training and state-supervised licensure. Parishioners often came to identify their pastors or priests with the state's authority. This period produced the "territorial church," in which a territorial ruler headed the church and all his subjects

were members. Unlike the medieval church, the confessional church no longer balanced the growing power of the territorial state but rather tended to bolster it.

The growth of the confessional church reflects a trend toward institutional and doctrinal consolidation. It tended to be rigid in its stance toward outsiders and toward the heterodox, acting to guard orthodoxy and enforce religious conformity. Its designation as "confessional" suggests the enormous significance of authoritative written statements of doctrine (i.e., confessions of faith) for the territorial churches of this period. Such documents, for example the Lutherans' Augsburg Confession (1530), were used as touchstones of orthodox belief. They possessed legal force, and formal acceptance was compulsory for all subjects.

Historians who define this period in terms of confessionalization tend to take a broad view of their subject, exploring not only religious but also social, cultural, and political developments. An analysis that centers on confessionalization attempts to avoid several traditional distortions: first, the distortions of an idealist view of history, which sees the new religious ideas of the Reformation as the main driving force behind the historical changes of the period and tends to ignore their social context; and second, those of a materialist view, which treats those ideas primarily as consequences of economic and demographic shifts. Heinz Schilling, one of the leading proponents of the confessionalization model, remarks in contrast that for the early modern period, "religious change was also social change," and the concept of confessionalization takes account of this by examining the sociology of early modern religion.

R. Po-chia Hsia, *Social Discipline in the Reformation, Central Europe 1550–1750* (1989); E. Koch, *Das konfessionelle Zeitalter: Katholizismus, Luthertum, Calvinismus (1563–1675)* (2000); B. Nischan, *Prince, People, and Confession: The Second Reformation in Brandenburg* (1994); W. Reinhard, "Reformation, Counter-Reformation and the Early Modern State: A Reassessment," *CHR* 75 (1989): 383–404; H. Schilling, *Religion, Political Culture, and the Emergence of Early Modern Society: Essays in German and Dutch History* (1992); E. W. Zeeden, *Die Entstehung der Konfessionen: Grundlagen und Formen der Konfessionsbildung im Zeitalter der Glaubenskämpfe* (1964).

NATHAN BARUCH REIN

Confessor   The term is from the Latin word *confiteor*, meaning both "I confess" and "I profess." At various times during the last two millennia Christians were persecuted simply for being Christians. During the third and early fourth centuries the government of the Roman Empire outlawed the practice of Christianity and held formal trials for practitioners. In that context, the word had a double but related meaning. At their trials Christians "confessed" in the sense of admitting their illegal adherence to Christianity. But their act was something more: it was a profession of their loyalty to their Christian commitments. In this sense, the primary translation of *confiteor* should be "I profess" and not "I confess."

The title has been applied to other groups of people. The first includes those who by their lives professed their Christianity in difficult circumstances but were not killed *in odium fidei* ("out of hatred for the faith"), for example, St. Paul the Hermit and Francis Xavier, the Jesuit missionary to Asia. Second, "confessor" is the title for priests who hear confessions, that is, who administer the sacrament of penance in private settings.

In the primary sense, all those who professed their Christianity, whether at arraignment, under pretrial torture, or at a formal trial, were confessors, as long as they did not later recant their profession. Some were eventually executed and became martyrs. Others survived and were eventually released.

Because of their witness, confessors enjoyed great prestige in the early church. Between incarceration and execution confessors interceded for those who had renounced their Christianity under pressure and later repented. Cyprian of Carthage and other bishops insisted that it was their prerogative as bishops to grant conditioned readmittance to Communion. However, confessors' letters of intercession for penitents often induced wavering presbyters to grant early or unconditional readmission, much to the bishops' frustration.

Upon release, confessors also enjoyed special status. In third-century Africa, some men who survived were admitted to the ranks of the clergy, except the episcopate, without an ordination ceremony.

———

Cyprian, *The Letters of St. Cyprian of Carthage*, ed. G. W. Clarke (1984–1989).

                                    MAUREEN A. TILLEY

Confirmation   In apostolic times, the laying on of hand(s) appeared as an act following baptism and in some way supplementing it with an outpouring of the Holy Spirit (Acts 8:17, 19:6; Heb. 6:2), although how normative this practice was remains an open question. From the early Christian centuries, hand laying, sealing with the cross, and anointing with oil followed baptismal washing in one continuous ritual of initiation. Tertullian sees the laying on of hands as the point at which the Holy Spirit is received. Ambrose speaks of a "spiritual seal," in which Christ gives the pledge of the Spirit and initiation is "perfected." Early Eastern authors described chrismation—so named because the oil is mixed with fragrant balsam to make chrism or myron—as the perfection or completion of the Christian soul regenerated in baptism.

In the West, confirmation developed as a distinct rite by the fifth century. Following the baptism of an infant performed by priests or deacons, sometimes in remote parts of a diocese, the bishop would confirm the newly baptized as soon as possible. This ideal was generally recognized by the Carolingian period. The separation of baptism from confirmation raised the question of how the gift of the Holy Spirit in confirmation differs from that same gift in baptism. In 1910 further theological complications arose as Roman Catholics began to administer confirmation at a later age than first reception of the Eucharist. In the East, priests have continued to administer chrismation and Eucharist to infants immediately following baptismal immersion in one integral liturgy of initiation; the bishop's unifying role is preserved through his blessing of the chrism.

From the twelfth to the twentieth century, the verbal formula used by Roman Catholics in the West was "I sign you with the sign of the cross and confirm you with the chrism of salvation, in the name of the Father and of the Son and of the Holy Spirit." Confirmation was predominantly seen as imparting, through a special grace of the Holy Spirit, the strength to persevere amid difficulties and proclaim the faith. The Council of Trent counted confirmation among the seven sacraments and affirmed that it imparts an indelible character (spiritual mark) and so cannot be repeated. The Reformers rejected confirmation as a sacrament on the grounds that it was not instituted by Christ. Anglican, Lutheran, and other liturgical books have retained rituals for confirmation, closely associating it with the completion of catechetical programs. In 1971, Pope Paul VI revised the Roman Catholic formula of the rite, in accordance with the ancient Byzantine practice, to "Be sealed with the gift of the Holy Spirit." At the same time he specified that the matter of the sacrament is anointing with chrism, traditionally prevalent in the East, rather than the laying on of hands, which was prevalent for many centuries in the West.

G. Austin, *The Rite of Confirmation: Anointing with the Spirit* (1985); B. Neunheuser, *Baptism and Confirmation* (1964); J. D. C. Fisher, *Confirmation: Then and Now* (1978); P. Turner, *The Meaning and Practice of Confirmation: Perspectives from a 16th-Century Controversy* (1987).

DANIEL G. VAN SLYKE

Confutation of the Augsburg Confession
Following the presentation of the Augsburg Confession in June 1530, Charles V and his advisors appointed a committee of traditional theologians to draw up a response. The committee included Johann Eck, Johannes Cochlaeus, and Julius Pflug. Cardinal Lorenzo Compeggio, the papal legate, assisted. Under Eck's lead, the committee first drew up a statement attacking all the heresies they found in the larger reform movement. Finding this excessively long and impolitic, Charles's advisors requested a revised statement, confined to the Augsburg Confession and stated on biblical grounds. The second document, which became the Confutation, was finished in late July and read in German before the diet on August 3. When Philip Melanchthon and the Lutheran theologians present refused to submit to the Confutation, they were denied a copy. On the basis of stenographic notes, Melanchthon prepared a refutation, his *Apology* to the Augsburg Confession. The Confutation has not been officially recognized as a Catholic statement of faith.

R. Kolb and J. A. Nestingen, eds., *Sources and Contexts of the Book of Concord* (2001).

JAMES ARNE NESTINGEN

Consilium de Emendanda Ecclesia
In May 1536, Pope Paul III announced a general council of the church to meet in Mantua, Italy, at Pentecost, 1537. In 1545, in order to prepare for the council, which did not convene at Mantua but at Trent, Paul appointed a commission of cardinals to draw up recommendations for reform. The expected report was to be used as a basis for the bishops' conciliar deliberations over the most pressing problems of the church.

Under the chairmanship of Gasparo Contarini, along with eight other prominent reform-minded prelates such as Reginald Pole (cousin of England's Henry VIII) and Gianpietro Carafa (the later Pope Paul IV), the commission met from November 1536 until February 1537. Their work produced the *Consilium* ("Proposal of a Select Committee of Cardinals and Other Prelates Concerning the Reform of the Church, Written and Presented by Order of His Holiness Pope Paul III in the year 1537").

On March 9, 1537, the report was delivered to the pope in consistory, with copies provided to the attending prelates. It notably places the problems facing the church directly at the door of the papacy. Specifically, the abuses and lack of discipline in the church are linked to exaggerated papal claims of far-reaching power to control all levels of churchly life. Although it was lacking in specific recommendations for reform and did not address basic doctrinal or structural concerns, it sharply divided the college of cardinals and, without papal support, it was not approved.

Soon printers obtained the *Consilium*, reprinting it thirteen times and publishing three different translations, between 1537 and 1557. In March 1538, Martin Luther publicly dismissed the document as duplicitous and shallow. When he provided a translation it was complete with derisive marginalia, preface, and illustrations.

S. Caponetto, *The Protestant Reformation in 16th-Century Italy* (1999); E. Gleason, ed., *Reform Thought in Sixteenth Century Italy* (1981); M. Luther, "Counsel of a Committee of Several Cardinals with Luther's Preface, 1538," in *The American Edition of Luther's Works*, vol. 34, ed. J. Pelikan and M. Lehmann (1955).

WILLIAM R. RUSSELL

Consistory of Geneva
The Consistory of Geneva was the creation of John Calvin, who insisted on its establishment as part of his agreement to return to Geneva in 1541. Calvin saw discipline as being the "sinews" of the body of Christ, even if he did not make it a mark of the church. Calvin drafted the legislation instituting the Consistory in the Draft Ecclesiastical Ordinances of 1541. Members of the Consistory included all Geneva pastors ex officio, one of the four magistrates as presiding officer, twelve elders elected annually, a secretary, and a summoning officer. The Consistory addressed several concerns Calvin had regarding the rightly ordered church. First, it protected the sanctity of the Holy Supper of the

Lord by excommunicating notorious sinners, a power not fully accorded the Consistory until 1555. Second, it examined members of the congregation to make sure that they were rightly educated in the rudiments of piety and that they were hearing sermons and reading Scripture for themselves. Third, it demonstrated in a concrete way the importance of living a life of piety according to one's profession of faith. Finally, it was a forum for pastoral care so that enmity between neighbors, or among spouses or family members, could be addressed and the persons involved reconciled before it erupted into more damaging behavior.

The structure of the Consistory, made up as it was of both pastors and elected lay elders, and the keeping of detailed minutes of its weekly proceedings reflected Calvin's criticism of what he considered the tyranny of the Roman practice of private confession, in which the priest and bishop could excommunicate without being accountable to the congregation for their decisions. Seen in this light, the Consistory was Calvin's way of seeking to reestablish the public, canonical penance of the patristic period while also respecting the privacy of members of the congregation.

R. M. Kingdon, *Registers of the Consistory of Geneva in the Time of Calvin*, vol. 1 (1996); R. A. Mentzer, *Sin and the Calvinists* (1994); W. G. Naphy, *Calvin and the Consolidation of the Genevan Reformation* (1994); J. R. Watt, *Choosing Death: Suicide and Calvinism in Early Modern Geneva* (2001).

RANDALL C. ZACHMAN

Constantine the Great (d. 337), Roman

emperor (306–337). Son of the emperor Constantius Chlorus (r. 293–305 as Caesar with Maximian; 305–306 as Augustus in the west with Galerius) and Helena, Constantine was proclaimed emperor at York in 306. During conflict with the emperor Maxentius, who controlled Italy, Constantine was said to have seen above the sun a cross of light accompanied by the words *In hoc signo vinces* ("In this sign you shall conquer"). Moreover, Christ is said to have appeared to Constantine in a dream that night and commanded him to create a standard bearing the Christogram, the overlapping letters X (chi) and P (rho), the first two letters in the Greek spelling of Christ. Constantine's victory at the Battle of the Milvian Bridge in October 312 was attributed to the support of the Christian God. By 324, Constantine had brought the entire Roman world under his control.

Like his eastern predecessor Diocletian (r. 284–305), Constantine believed that it was the emperor's responsibility to bring peace and stability, and he acted accordingly. His new gold coin, the *solidus*, was so successful that it provided a standard means of exchange in the Mediterranean world for nearly seven hundred years. Acknowledging the importance of the eastern part of the empire, Constantine established a second capital on the Bosporus on the site of Byzantium. It came to be called "Constantine's City," or Constantinople (modern Istanbul) and was modeled on Rome, save that it was intended as a Christian rather than a pagan city.

Constantine's most important legacy lies in his policies toward Christianity. In 313, he and his colleague Licinius issued the Edict of Milan, which decreed religious freedom for all and returned confiscated Christian property. Constantine also exempted Christian priests from taxation and made Sunday the official market day so that all could attend Christian services. The state benefited from the use of Christian churches to provide social services and the confiscation of pagan temple treasures.

Like previous emperors, Constantine thought that religion could provide a unifying element for the otherwise heterogeneous Roman world, but he saw Christianity, not paganism, as the unifying factor. Constantine soon discovered that Christianity itself was rent by disagreements involving questions of authority, organization, and belief. He therefore mobilized state authority in an attempt to create Christian unity, sometimes by issuing imperial regulations, and sometimes by summoning church councils.

In 314, Constantine convened the Council of Arles, which condemned the African Donatists. In 325, at the Council of Nicaea, Constantine persuaded 318 bishops to condemn Arianism. The council formulated an orthodox statement of belief, established the official date of Easter, and formalized an administrative hierarchy based on the Roman provincial model.

The personal piety of Constantine and his mother Helena is attested by their church building in Rome, Constantinople, and the Holy Land. But it was only on his deathbed that Constantine finally was baptized as a Christian, and that by an Arian bishop. He was buried in the Church of the Apostles in Constantinople and is a saint of the Greek Orthodox Church.

T. D. Barnes, *Constantine and Eusebius* (1981); H. A. Drake, *Constantine and the*

Bishop: The Politics of Intolerance (2000); A. H. M. Jones, Constantine and the Conversion of Europe (1948).

RALPH W. MATHISEN

Constantinople, First Council of

(381). The emperor Theodosius called the council following the death of his predecessor Valens at the battle of Adrianople (378). No acts survive from the council; thus, many of its details are unknown. It was probably not intended to be a universal council but to settle affairs in Constantinople and, perhaps more widely, in the civil administrative region or "diocese" of Oriens.

Meletius of Antioch presided. The council recognized Gregory of Nazianzus as bishop of Constantinople. An attempt to reach agreement with a group of "Macedonian" or "Pneumatomachian" bishops failed. When Meletius suddenly died, Gregory became president, but, being no diplomat, quickly lost the support not only of many at the council but also of Theodosius. Gregory resigned, and Nectarius, a former civil official, was quickly baptized and consecrated as bishop. Theodosius seems to have invited others to attend at this point: Acholius of Thessalonica (who had baptized the new emperor in 380), and Peter of Alexandria (an opponent of Gregory) arrived with supporters.

The council almost certainly issued a revised Nicene creed (although there is no clear reference to it until 451) and a statement of faith that does not survive. The creed is notable for its extra clauses on the status of the Spirit and for not saying directly that the Spirit is God or *homoousios* ("same substance") with Father and Son. The document probably represents an attempt at compromise with the "Macedonians" drawn up early in the meeting. While it is sometimes alleged that it represents the caution of the recently deceased Basil of Caesarea over against Gregory of Nazianzus's clear assertion of the Spirit's divinity, it has been argued convincingly both that Basil's "reserve" is something of an illusion and that the creed's clauses about the Spirit reflect the terminology of Gregory of Nyssa, who was important at the council. Although the creed tactically avoids certain terms, it uses a language that would have been very clear in intention to its architects. By 451 it seems that the council was gradually being recognized as an important turning point in the fourth-century controversies and was beginning to assume the status it now holds for creedal Christians.

L. Ayres, Nicaea and Its Legacy (2004); J. N. D. Kelly, Early Christian Creeds (3rd ed., 1972); A. Meredith, "The Pneumatology of the Cappadocian Fathers and the Creed of Constantinople," ITQ 48 (1981): 196–212; A.-M. Ritter, Das Konzil von Konstantinopel und sein Symbol (1965); R. Staats, Das Glaubensbekenntnis von Nizäa-Konstantinopel (1996).

LEWIS AYRES

Constantius II (317–361), Roman emperor (337–361). The dynasty established by Constantine I seemed to rest upon firm footing at the time of his death (337). His three surviving sons divided the empire among themselves. Constantine II ruled the West; Constantius II received the East (Egypt, Palestine, Syria, and Asia Minor); Constans obtained Italy, Africa, and Illyricum. While Constantine and Constans supported Nicene Christianity, Constantius II favored Arianism. Constantius probably was responsible for a purge of relations, of which two cousins survived. The imperial brothers soon turned against one another. Constantine died while invading Constans's territory in 340. In 350, supporters of a usurper named Magnentius murdered Constans. Constantius, in the meantime, had been defending the eastern territories against Persian invaders. Between 351 and 353 the emperor marched west and defeated Magnentius, thereby becoming the sole ruler of the empire. Constantius elevated his elder cousin Gallus as emperor in the east. When the latter claimed a greater share of authority, Constantius had him murdered (354).

Constantius was an ardent Christian, albeit an Arian. In 341 he and his brother Constans issued an edict that forbade pagan sacrifices. The two also legislated against destroying pagan temples. In 357 Constantius visited Rome on the occasion of the twentieth year of his rule. There he ordered that the altar of victory be removed from the Senate House, much to the consternation of the mostly pagan senators inhabiting the capital city. The Arian emperor proved a persistent opponent for the long-lived Nicene champion, Athanasius of Alexandria. Favoring the pro-Arian Eusebian faction, Constantius supported Athanasius's deposition as patriarch in 340. Athanasius traveled west, where he gained the support of Pope Julius and the friendship of the Nicene Constans. Around 344, Constantius even ordered that Athanasius would die should he try to reenter his see. The next year, however, Constantius permitted Athanasius's restoration, and the two even shared a cordial meeting at Antioch. Athanasius was exiled again in 356, however, and replaced by an Arian bishop. He would not return to Alexandria until after Constantius's death. Otherwise, after Constans's death Constantius strengthened his effort to spread Arianism by convening a series of church councils. At the double council, in Rimini and Seleucia (359), the Arian minority argued that the Son is *homoios* ("like") the Father. Constantius's acceptance of the term made it orthodoxy.

In 359 Constantius ordered his cousin Julian, emperor since 355, to lead his army east to aid against the Persians. Julian's soldiers mutinied and elevated their leader as Augustus. Civil war was averted, however, by Constantius's sudden demise. Julian, an apostate Christian, presided over Constantius's burial. Constantius was interred in the mausoleum his father had built for the Church of the Twelve Apostles. The pagan senators at Rome felt obliged to deem Constantius a god, while subsequent Nicene Christians, such as Jerome, regarded him a villain.

T. D. Barnes, *Athanasius and Constantius: Theology and Politics in the Constantinian Empire* (1993).

ALLEN E. JONES

Contarini, Gasparo (1483–1542), diplomat, cardinal, representative of the Italian *Evangelismo* (reform movement).

Contarini was born in Venice. From 1501 to 1509 he studied Greek, mathematics, philosophy, and theology at Padua. He had a conversion experience on Holy Saturday 1511 and afterward resumed his theological studies. In 1520 he was appointed as Venice's ambassador to the court of the emperor Charles V. At the Diet of Worms in 1521 he heard much about Luther but never met him in person. As a layman he wrote a book on the duties of a bishop. While still a layman he was created cardinal in 1535.

Contarini became a key figure in reforming the church from within. Ignatius acknowledged that he was largely responsible for the papal approbation of his Society of Jesus (1540). In 1541, he took part as the papal legate in the Colloquy of Regensburg between Catholics and Protestants, where his compromise formula on the issue of "justification" was rejected by both Rome and Luther. Because of his Regensburg formula he was accused of heresy but defended himself successfully with his *Epistola de iustificatione* (1541).

J. P. Donnelly, ed., *The Office of a Bishop (De Officio viri boni et probi episcope)* (2002); E. G. Gleason, *Gasparo Contarini: Venice, Rome, and Reform* (1993); P. Matheson, *Cardinal Contarini at Regensburg* (1972).

FRANZ POSSET

Controversial Theologians Sixteenth- and seventeenth-century Catholic polemicists and apologists, some four hundred in number, who argued, contrary to the Reformers, that Catholic doctrine and practice are consistent with Scripture and patristic tradition.

Robert Bellarmine's (1542–1621) three-volume *Disputationes* summarize the disputed issues: *God and the Church* (1586), *The Sacraments* (1588), *Grace and Justification* (1593). Early controversialists such as Johann Eck (1486–1543) and Sylvester Prierias (1456–1523) defended the church's mediating role and Roman primacy against Luther's challenge to the foundations of hierarchical authority and sacramental power. Johann Dietenberger (c. 1475–1537) responded to Luther's "Scripture alone" by emphasizing the perpetual and multiform presence of the Holy Spirit in the church, unfolding Scripture's deeper meaning through the Fathers, councils, and unwritten traditions. Cardinal Cajetan (1469–1534) affirmed Christ's unconditional sufficiency, but against "faith alone" posited an active role for Christ's members cooperating with grace and allowing Christ to work in and through their faith and good works. John Fisher (1469–1535) prepared a compendium of Lutheran errors and Catholic responses, while Thomas More (1477/1478–1535) published his own refutation of Luther and was principal author of Henry VIII's defense of Catholic sacramental doctrine that won the king the papal honor "Defender of the Faith"—though the king eventually ordered both apologists executed.

Later controversial theologians presented the doctrinal definitions of Trent as universal truths grounded in Scripture and tradition, and characterized Reformation teachings as dangerous and erroneous innovations. In their time, the controversialists checked the Reformation's advance and reversed some of its gains. Their influence endured to Vatican II, shaping Catholic piety, preaching, and pedagogy. While Vatican II addressed Reformation challenges, the *Constitution on the Sacred Liturgy* (1963) and the *Roman Missal* (1969, 2002) echo the controversialists in affirming the continuity of Catholic sacramental doctrine and liturgical practice. The *Dogmatic Constitution on Divine*

Revelation (1965) confirms their vision of the inseparability of Scripture, tradition, and the magisterium. Since Vatican II, the topics the controversialists debated have set the agenda for ecumenical dialogue, and issues they argued have reemerged in the agreements forged (e.g., *Joint Declaration on the Doctrine of Justification*, 1998–1999). Finally, their teachings reappear as clarifications in the most recent official publications of the contemporary Roman magisterium (e.g., *Catechism of the Catholic Church*, 1992, 1997; *Compendium of the Catechism*, 2005).

D. Bagchi, *Luther's Earliest Opponents: Catholic Controversialists, 1518–1525* (1991); L. Desgraves, *Réportoire des ouvrages de controverse entre catholiques et protestants en France, 1598–1685*, 2 vols. (1984–1985); E. Iserloh, ed., *Katholische Theologen der Reformationszeit*, 5 vols. (1984–1988).

PETER J. SCAGNELLI

Conversion   The term designates the turning of one's faith and allegiance to a religion in accordance with its teaching, rituals, and ethics. Christianity emerged as a prophetic religion that aspired both to satisfy natural human needs and to engender and articulate deeper needs that it also claimed to fulfill. Early on, conversion to Christianity paralleled conversion to Greco-Roman philosophical schools in that adherents were called to adopt the school's teaching and the way of life that embodied its worldview. Christianity, standing in the tradition of Judaism, also required the repudiation of idolatry while demanding obedience to the crucified and resurrected Christ and a life of service in expectation of eschatological judgment. The *Didache* envisioned two sharply defined alternatives for those at the threshold of converting to Christianity: the way of life and the way of death.

In the apostolic period a diversity of motivations for converting was the norm, such as intellectual conviction concerning the Messiah/Christ, contrition in response to the call for repentance, amazement at demonstrations of supernatural power, and the fear of judgment. Given the constraints on outright Christian evangelization in the pre-Constantinian era, new converts were often drawn by the exclusiveness of the Christian community manifested in its practices and sacramental rites and in its deep sense of a communal covenant. Into the fourth century apologists and preachers lauded Christianity's victory over the bankruptcy of pagan religion

and culture, yet the real successes were less public than private, achieved within communities that absorbed new converts largely through the influence and example of individual Christians or through the "domestic apostolate" of the household.

With the privileging of Christianity under Constantine and its ascendancy to the official imperial religion under Theodosius I, conversion for reasons of convenience or social advancement became an issue. The church responded with greater systematization of missionary activity and of the procedures of the catechumenate. Coerced conversions were discouraged, at least in principle. As John Chrysostom exhorted Christians, "Let us win the Greeks to us with good will. . . . Let us reason with Greeks just as fathers with children" (*Hom. 1 Cor. 5:6*). Augustine's conversion, made famous in his *Confessions* as an ascetic and mystical journey, was hardly typical. With the burgeoning of ascetic and monastic movements in the fourth and fifth centuries, numerous Christians embraced "conversion" to a higher and more radical Christian life, the heroics of which would profit the church for centuries to come as monks became the premier missionaries and exemplars of the devout life.

Although the miraculous had been an issue from the beginning (cf. Acts 13:6–12), it became critical in early medieval Europe as the church confronted a host of animistic cults with deeply entrenched magical practices. The *Life of St. Martin of Tours* and the sermons of Caesarius of Arles indicate the resilience of these pagan cults, as well as conversions "compelled" by Christian wonderworking. Uprooting the Arianism of certain barbarian tribes and Christianizing whole kingdoms produced further challenges. At the close of the fifth century, the Franks and their monarch Clovis were a test case; another, in the tenth century, was Prince Vladimir and the Russians. Forced conversions were not uncommon in later medieval Europe, as with the Jewish *conversos* beginning in the thirteenth century and the "conversion" of heretics to orthodoxy in the Inquisition.

With the rise of Protestantism, especially the Pietist and evangelical movements, preoccupation with the order of salvation generated introspective concern for the experiential aspects of conversion. Puritans, Methodists, and the revivalists of the American frontier sought to identify the precise effects of the Spirit's internal working in the soul to effect regeneration and transformation, though Calvinists and Arminians clashed over whether conversion was truly voluntary or intrinsically tied to divine predestination.

W. Conn, *Christian Conversion* (1986); L. Ferrari, *The Conversions of Saint Augustine* (1984); T. M. Finn, *From Death to Rebirth: Ritual and Conversion in Antiquity* (1997); R. Fletcher, *The Barbarian Conversion* (1988); R. Hefner, ed., *Conversion to Christianity: Historical and Anthropological Perspectives on a Great Transformation* (1993); A. D. Nock, *Conversion* (1933); A. Malherbe, "Conversion to Paul's Gospel," in *The Early Church in Its Context* (1998), 230–44; R. McMullen, *The Christianization of the Roman Empire* (1984).

PAUL M. BLOWERS

Conversion of Europe The problem with a discussion of the conversion of medieval Europe is a modern assumption about conversion. In the case of medieval European conversion, the emphasis was not on a spiritual, interior change for most people, but on a change in rituals and laws. The late Roman Empire had not been interested in the conversion of non-Romans; however, as others became part of the empire they adapted to it, accommodating by becoming Christians. Even outside the empire conversions occurred through seepage, as interchanges were made across frontiers, with traders, ambassadors, wives, slaves, and soldiers bringing their faith into other lands. While this is a very important phase of conversion, it is hard to document, as the thoughts of so many of these people went unrecorded.

A more overt, thought-out form of conversion was that of missionaries in their direct preaching, their conversion of rulers, and their establishment of monasteries. Patrick (d. 490), a Briton, left his native land to convert the Irish who had once enslaved him, and from Ireland would come many of the best-known missionaries of Europe, educated in the Celtic monastic systems. Missionaries to the British Isles also came from Rome. Pope Gregory the Great's greatest influence on northern European conversion was his sending of Augustine of Canterbury to the English (597), followed by letters of advice that were to be the hallmark of the style of missionary work done in the early Middle Ages. In these letters Gregory instructed that pagan shrines should not be torn down but rather rededicated to a saint: accommodation or syncretism was the style he favored.

On the Continent, paganism made way for both Catholicism and Arianism until, with the conversion of the Merovingian Franks to Catholicism, Catholicism took over with the aid of missionaries from the British Isles. The early missionaries began as pilgrims and were considered "green martyrs" according to Celtic thought, which considered exile from one's homeland a form of martyrdom. Among these early missionaries was Columbanus (d. 615), who established monasteries at Luxeuil and Bobbio and greatly influenced the Merovingian church. Their vision of missions marked a change in the perception of boundaries. Those missions that sprang from Roman conceptions of empire were aimed at controlling barbarian populations on the borders of the empire. For missionaries from the British Isles, the primary psychological barrier lay between one's own kin and tribe and everything outside of it. Once one made the decision to go beyond this small world, one could go anywhere.

A new concept of missions emerged in the British Isles in the eighth century. Gifted men who had grown up in monasteries faced a crisis when they reached their thirties. Either they became abbots in the midst of a culture that was marginally Christian or they sought a true Christian order as missionaries to other lands. Willibrord (d. 739) and Boniface (d. 754) were the first of this generation of missionaries. They traveled to Frisia (modern Netherlands), which was considered the gateway to Europe.

The missionary movement grew to its height in the ninth century, and with it missionary hagiography became very popular. Boniface's experiences were among those most cited. Boniface is best known for felling a sacred oak tree dedicated to Thor. He then used the wood to build a Christian chapel. Close to the papacy, he sought to establish a Roman-centered Christianity throughout northern Europe. Daniel of Winchester advised him to convince pagans through logical arguments about the strength of the Christian God over their pagan gods. These attempts at persuasion were not always successful. Boniface was martyred by an angry mob of Frisians in 754.

Missionary efforts to Scandinavia were not begun until relatively late due to its cultural isolation. Separated from the rest of Europe by the sea, this isolation was not breached until the Viking expeditions of the ninth century. Anskar (d. 865), like Boniface before him, used logical arguments in his mission work to the Swedes in the ninth century. The conversion of the Danes was precipitated by the baptism of Harald Klak, a Danish king, in 826. His godfather, Louis the Pious, was also a major political influence.

Political considerations were key in Iceland as well. Facing possible forced conversion from a neighboring king, Icelandic farmers adopted Christianity on their own terms in 1000.

Besides the missionaries, rulers were important in the conversion of Europe. They were often the ones missionaries sought to convert. There is a pattern in these conversions: first, the queen is often already a convert, and she, along with the missionary, aids in her husband's conversion. This is the case with the conversions of Clovis, king of the Franks (baptized c. 500 by Remigius); Aethelberht, king of Kent (baptized in 597 by Augustine of Canterbury); and Edwin, king of Northumbria (baptized in 627 by Paulinus). Second, the ruler must be convinced that Christianity will bring power, victory, and riches to his country. The ruler first hesitates; he must consult with his people and be assured of their continued support. Finally, the ruler converts and in turn aids in the conversion efforts of his people and neighbors.

Rulers generally found that nonviolent conversion was the most effective, primarily sponsored through the foundation of monasteries. Here the role of queens and noblewomen reached its apogee. Monasteries disseminated Christianity among the people surrounding them. As monasteries were founded, indigenous men were quickly trained as clergy, allowing Christianity to advance in the native tongue of the people: Christianity was not a religion of a fixed tongue. For example, the Byzantine brothers Constantine (d. 869) and Methodius (d. 885) translated the Gospel readings into Slavonic for the prince of Moravia.

As missionaries traveled and founded monasteries, they sent out their kin to do the same in neighboring monasteries, creating networks of monasteries throughout Europe. For example, Leoba (d. 779), abbess of Tauberbischofsheim, was a relative of Boniface, and Radegund, wife of Clothar, founded the monastery Saint-Croix de Poitiers (561), which was to become a center of noblewomen. Conversion by force was a controversial method in the early conversion of Europe. The primary example of this type is Charlemagne's conversion of the Saxons. Charlemagne's massacre of 4,500 Saxons at Verdun (782) was criticized by Alcuin (d. 804), who favored education and persuasion of converts.

With the twelfth century, attitudes toward conversion changed, as coercion and force began to be viewed less negatively. This shift was largely due to the ideology of crusade, which was applied to any non-Christian. Thus, the Wends revolted against what they perceived as a "German" religion when it was imposed upon them in the mid-eleventh century, and it was not until the end of the twelfth century that they were forced into conversion; this conversion was a forced cultural conversion. The change in attitude toward conversion was also due in part to a change in the meaning of conversion as educational reforms encouraged a search for unity in theology and practice that left less room for cultural differences. This search for uniformity can be seen in the increased reliance on papal directives and the establishment of new religious orders. The Franciscans and Dominicans, in their work against heretics, were also missionaries who not only went to pagan territory but converted people within their own lands, as they tried to turn Cathars, Jews, and Muslims alike into Catholics through preaching and, later, through the reinforcement of the Inquisition.

———

P. Brown, *The Rise of Western Christendom* (1996); R. Fletcher, *The Conversion of Europe: From Paganism to Christianity* (1997); J. N. Hillgarth, *Christianity and Paganism, 530–750: The Conversion of Western Europe* (1986).

MARIANNE M. DELAPORTE

Coornhert, Dirck (1522–1590), Dutch humanist and controversialist. Born of a wealthy Amsterdam family, Coornhert was self-educated and widely read. He translated a number of Latin classics into his native Dutch. He also expressed his sense of national pride by supporting William the Silent in his campaign to obtain independence from Spanish rule, and held political office in William's government. Coornhert developed distinctive religious views that paralleled his political outlook. He was a committed advocate of liberty of conscience and the freedom of the will. Influenced by contemporary humanism and classical Stoicism, he viewed the Christian faith primarily as an ethical system by which an individual could attain moral perfection. Since spirituality was a purely internal matter, he advocated external conformity to Catholicism (Nicodemism), and Coornhert himself never broke with the Roman church. He advocated religious freedom and tolerance but did not extend such tolerance to Calvinists. He virulently denounced the Reformed doctrines of predestination and original sin and personally attacked John Calvin in his 1560 work *Verschooninghe van de Roomsche afgoderye*

(*Apology for Roman Idolatry*). Calvin counter-attacked with his 1562 treatise *Reponse à un certain Hollandois* (*Response to a Certain Dutchman*).

M. van Veen, *"Verschooninghe van de roomsche afgoderye": De Polemiek van Calvijn met Nicodemieten in het bijzonder met Coornhert* (2001); G. Voogt, *Constraint on Trial: Dirck Volckertsz Coornhert and Religious Freedom* (2000).

RAYMOND A. BLACKETER

Copernicus, Nicholas (1473–1543), Polish clergyman, physician, and astronomer. He fomented the "Copernican revolution" when he rejected the hitherto prevailing geocentric cosmology of Ptolemy, devising his own heliocentric view. Copernicus argued that the empirically observable details of planetary motion were more apparent than real. Utilizing "Ockham's razor"—the teaching that the simplest solution to a given problem is probably the correct one—and mathematical calculations, Copernicus found the heliocentric system a simpler explanation for the movements of the planets than the geocentric one. His reliance on mathematics was important for the development of the scientific method, as was his defiance of commonsense empiricism. The theological significance of the Copernican revolution consists primarily in its having humbled the status of the earth and humankind vis-à-vis the cosmos. In wake of the Galileo affair, Copernicus's work was placed on the Papal Index in 1616.

T. Kuhn, *The Copernican Revolution* (1957); R. S. Westman, "The Copernicans and the Churches," in *God and Nature: Historical Essays on the Encounter between Christianity and Science*, ed. D. C. Lindberg and R. L. Numbers (1986), 76–113.

RODERICK MARTIN

Copts and Coptic Church Possibly the most resilient and viable of the ancient Christian communities still represented in the Middle East, the Coptic Church is an Oriental Orthodox church, with some six to eight million adherents. The Orthodox patriarch (or pope) of Alexandria leads the church, assisted by a legislative council or holy synod of abbots, metropolitans, and other bishops. Due to emigration, congregations of Copts may now be found all over the world, but the Coptic Church continues to be identified primarily with the historical experience of Christians in Egypt. Coptic worship traditions closely resemble the liturgical forms used in other Orthodox communions, while featuring the Coptic language and a unique style of hymnody.

The first century of Christian history in Egypt is not well documented, apart from the oft-cited tradition in Eusebius that credits St. Mark with the initial evangelization of the country. After 200 CE, despite periods of intense persecution that crested under Diocletian (r. 284–305), vigorous growth led to an increasingly influential role for the See of Alexandria within the wider Christian movement. Among the gifts of Egypt to the church universal during the patristic age were a host of brilliant theologians, including Origen, Athanasius, and Cyril of Alexandria; a surge of missionary energy that carried the gospel to the Pentapolis (Libya), Ethiopia, and eventually the Sudan; and the crucial institution of Christian monasticism (through Antony and Pachomius).

The Coptic Church differentiated itself from Melkite (Byzantine) Christianity in the aftermath of Chalcedon (451). Several factors contributed to the break in relations, not least a sharp rise of anti-imperial sentiment in Egypt and growing cultural differences, but the triggering issue was strictly theological: how to understand the two natures of Christ. After several efforts at compromise (e.g., the Henoticon of Zeno and monotheletism) and high-handed coercion failed to produce unity, rival patriarchates over Alexandria became permanently established. The non-Chalcedonian theology favored by the Copts and other Jacobites, which emphasizes the fullness of Christ's divine nature even after the incarnation, is commonly referred to as Monophysitism.

Following the Muslim conquest of Egypt in 642, the Coptic Church entered into a long process of Arabization, while learning to live as a minority population under Islamic rule. Although individual Copts have been able to assume positions of prominence, the community as a whole has had to endure unremitting economic and social discrimination, plus outbreaks of violent persecution. Since the mid-twentieth century, the Coptic Church has experienced religious revival, especially in monasticism, but has also had to contend with the threat posed by Islamic fundamentalism.

A. S. Atiya, ed., *The Coptic Encyclopedia*, 8 vols. (1991); N. van Doorn-Harder and K. Vogt, eds., *Between Desert and City: The Coptic Orthodox Church Today* (1997);

W. H. C. Frend, *The Rise of the Monophysite Movement* (1972); S. H. Griffith, *The Church in the Shadow of the Mosque* (2008); B. A. Pearson and J. E. Goehring, eds., *The Roots of Egyptian Christianity* (1986); Severus of Ashmunein, *History of the Patriarchs of Alexandria* (1910); D. Zeidan, "The Copts—Equal, Protected, or Persecuted? The Impact of Islamization on Muslim-Christian Relations in Modern Egypt," *Islam and Christian-Muslim Relations* 10 (1999): 53–67.

STANLEY H. SKRESLET

Cornelius (d. 253), bishop of Rome and martyr. Cornelius was elected bishop of Rome in 251 after a fourteen-month vacancy in the office due to the fury of the Decian persecution. Novatian had been the spokesman for the Roman church in those fourteen months and fully expected to succeed Fabian as bishop. Cornelius was elected primarily because of his support of a less rigorist position toward those who lapsed during the persecution. He, along with Cyprian of Carthage, advocated a policy of penance and restoration for those who had obtained, through imperial corruption, certificates of compliance (*libelli*) with the edict requiring sacrifice to the imperial cult. Those who actually sacrificed were to be restored to the church when and if they were in imminent danger of death.

Two letters of Cornelius to Cyprian are extant in Cyprian's corpus (Letters 49–50). Part of a letter to Fabius of Antioch is preserved by Eusebius (*Hist. eccl.* 6.43). Cornelius was exiled to Centum Cellae (Civitavecchia) during the reign of Gallus and died in 252. Cyprian referred to him as a martyr (Letter 61).

M. Bévenot, "Cyprian and His Recognition of Cornelius," *JTS* 28 (1977): 346–59; G. W. Clarke, *The Letters of St. Cyprian of Carthage*, vols. 2–3 (1984, 1986); H. L. Lawlor and J. L. Oulton, *Eusebius* (1927).

CHARLES A. BOBERTZ

Coronation Rites The ceremonies that legitimated European monarchs developed in the eighth and ninth centuries. Earlier precedents included acclamations by German or Roman troops. Coronation rites varied widely in the medieval West. The essential element was religious consecration of some sort, as when the bishop of Toledo anointed King Wamba of the Visigoths in 672 or when Frankish bishops consecrated Pippin III, the Carolingian king, in 751. The most famous medieval coronation took place in Rome when Pope Leo (795–816) crowned Charlemagne emperor on Christmas Day in 800. Little detail remains of these early rites. It is clear that their essential message was drawn from Old Testament accounts of the anointing of Israel's kings. The anointed medieval king became God's deputy in the manner of Solomon and David and thus could draw on a tremendous source of authority to bolster his secular power. As the anointed of God, a man became a God-man.

Coronation rites underscored the theocratic nature of medieval monarchy. But divine authority also brought responsibility. In the view of Pope Leo, Emperor Charlemagne had an obligation to defend the church. In the view of Archbishop Hincmar of Reims (845–882), kings were bound to uphold the law. The special status conferred by consecration obligated a king to produce heirs who, presumably, would also enjoy God's favor in due course. Coronation rites also reinforced aristocratic power. As witnesses and participants (leading magnates served the king at the coronation banquet), the king's loyal supporters, who received their authority from him, by extension also enjoyed divine approval.

Coronation rites took place in churches and were managed by clergy who developed elaborate liturgical rituals (*ordines*) for the ceremonies. In the thirteenth and fourteenth centuries canonists began to insist on the monarch's duty to protect the kingdom. Coronation made the monarch a guardian of the realm, not its lord.

R. A. Jackson, ed., *Ordines coronationis Franciae: Texts and Ordines for the Coronation of Frankish and French Kings and Queens in the Middle Ages* (1995); J. L. Nelson, "The Lord's Anointed and the People's Choice," in *The Frankish World, 750–900*, ed. J. L. Nelson (1996), 99–131.

JOHN J. CONTRENI

Corpus Christi This feast is celebrated on the Thursday following Trinity Sunday. The Feast of Corpus Christi celebrated the central sacrament of the Eucharist and its many manifestations in medieval Christian life, but it was a late addition to the Christian calendar. First promulgated as a local feast in the diocese of Liège in 1246 in response to local interest in eucharistic piety, it was ordained for general compulsory celebration when a member of the Liegois circle became Pope Urban IV in 1261. Urban IV died before the feast could take hold, and it was only fifty years later that the feast entered general observance, as Urban IV's bull was reissued as part of the important collection of papal letters and canonical authorities, the *Clementines*, in 1317 (see *Corpus Iuris Canonici*). The papal bull explained that the Christian calendar lacked a day for joyful celebration of the Eucharist's promise (as opposed to Maundy Thursday, which lamented in Christ's passion). It was also meant to be a feast that would encourage orthodoxy and confound heretics. Corpus Christi was to be celebrated at the very end of the Easter cycle, on the Thursday following Trinity Sunday (between May 21 and June 24). As parishes and religious houses established new traditions for the feast, they tended to place at the center a processional element in which clergy and laity could march in respect of the Eucharist contained in a precious vessel and treated majestically. In England cycles of biblical drama enacted by members of guilds developed. Throughout Europe interest in the feast was manifested by the creation of fraternities and by the elaboration of community celebrations. The centrality of the Eucharist prompted patrician groups to adopt it as a prestigious focus for social and religious activities. Conversely, the enthusiastic desire to see the Eucharist and gain access to its celebrations also elicited reforming criticism and, in the sixteenth century, rejection of the feast's tenor and message by Protestants.

V. A. Kolve, *The Play Called Corpus Christi* (1966); M. Rubin, *Corpus Christi: The Eucharist in Late Medieval Culture* (1991).

MIRI RUBIN

Corpus Iuris Canonici A collection of six ecclesiastical law books. The first five books are the *Decretum* (c. 1150) of Gratian, the *Liber extra* (also called the *Decretals*, 1234) of Gregory IX, the *Liber sextus* (1298) of Boniface VIII, the *Clementines* (1317), and the *Extravagantes of John XXII* (1325). The French legal scholar Jean Chappuis prepared an edition of these works as a set of three volumes in 1500–1507, adding his own collection of papal decretals issued 1261–1484, the *Extravagantes communes* of the sixth book. A papal commission working 1566–1580 edited the *Corpus*. Pope Gregory XIII published the resulting official edition in 1582 (the Roman edition), which he called "iuris canonici corpus" in his promulgation. This edition contains, as do most early editions, the standard university commentary (ordinary gloss) in the margins. The most recent

edition, by Emil Friedberg (Leipzig, 1879), contains a text of Gratian's *Decretum* based on eight medieval manuscripts, while for the rest of the *Corpus* the Roman edition is reprinted. The *Corpus iuris canonici* continued to be used in the Roman Catholic Church until 1917, when it was superseded by the *Codex iuris canonici* of 1917.

E. Friedberg, ed., *Corpus iuris canonici*, 2 vols. (1879); J. Tarrant, ed., *Extrauagantes Ioannis XXII* (1983).

ANDERS WINROTH

Corpus Iuris Civilis This collection of Roman civil law books consists mainly of the compilations of laws issued in 533–534 by Emperor Justinian: the *Institutes* (a brief introduction), the *Digest* (or *Pandects*, a large, systematic collection of excerpts from the writings of thirty-nine Roman jurists, mainly of the first to third centuries CE), and the *Justinian Code* (a systematic collection of imperial constitutions from 117 to 534). A fourth book, the *Novellae*, contains constitutions issued by Justinian and his successors after 534. The term *Corpus iuris civilis* appears from the thirteenth century.

Justinian's law books had limited influence until the eleventh century, when the growth of trade and government in Western Europe created a need for their sophisticated contents. The collection was studied at European law schools, especially in Bologna, from the twelfth century, generating numerous commentaries, most importantly the *Ordinary Gloss* (*Glossa ordinaria*) by Accursius (d. c. 1263). This commentary usually accompanied the texts in the margins of manuscripts and early-modern printed books. The doctrines of Roman law influenced legal thought and practice in the Western world until recent times.

T. Honoré, *Tribonian* (1978); H. Kantorowicz, *Studies in the Glossators of the Roman Law* (1938); T. Mommsen, P. Krüger, R. Schöll, and W. Kroll, eds., *Corpus iuris civilis*, 3 vols. (1872–1895); P. Stein, *Roman Law in European History* (1999); P. Vinogradoff, *Roman Law in Medieval Europe* (1968).

ANDERS WINROTH

Corro, Antonio del (1527–1591), Spanish Protestant reformer. In 1557 Corro fled from San Isidro, Spain, when the Inquisition began looking for Protestants in the city. After attending the Academy of Lausanne (1558–1559), he joined the court of Jeanne d'Albret, where he served as tutor to the future Henry IV of France. By 1564, Corro became, along with Juan Pérez de Pineda, chaplain of Renée de France. He left Renée's court after an invitation to minister in Antwerp. In Antwerp Corro published *Epistre aux pasteurs de l'Eglise Flamengue d'Anuers de la Confession d'Augsbourg* (1567) and *Lettre envoyée a la maiesté du roy des Espaignes* (1567). After arriving in England in 1567, Corro was confronted with skepticism by the Refugee Churches and was several times charged with heresy. In 1569, he published *Tableau de l'oeuvre de Dieu*, which led to a break with the Italian congregation that had harbored him since his arrival in England. By 1571 a clear transition to Anglicanism took place as he received several appointments at Inner and Middle Temples, and Oxford. Corro published his lectures on Romans, *Dialogus theologicus*, in 1574 and his commentary on Ecclesiastes, *Sapientissimi Regis Salomonis Concio*, in 1579.

P. J. Hauben, *Three Spanish Heretics and the Reformation* (1967); A. G. Kinder, "Antonio del Corro," in *Bibliotheca Dissidentium: Répertoire des non-conformistes religieux des seizième et dix-septième siècles* (1986).

RADY ROLDÁN-FIGUEROA

Councils, Later Middle Ages Five general councils took place in the late medieval, Western church between 1245 and 1445. The last two involved attempts to limit papal authority (see *Basel, Council of*). The other three are treated here.

During his conflict with Emperor Frederick II, Pope Innocent IV called a council at Rome in 1241 with the intent of declaring Frederick deposed. Frederick responded by capturing more than one hundred of the prelates en route and forcing the pontiff to flee Rome. Innocent took up refuge at Lyon on the Rhone River, where he convoked a general council that sat from June 28 to July 17, 1245. Although summoned to appear, Frederick refused and was condemned by the predominantly French, English, and Spanish bishops who attended. Having declared Frederick deposed as emperor, king of Germany, and king of Sicily, they thereupon instructed the electors to choose a new king. Among the twenty-two constitutions issued at the council were those that dealt with aid to the Latin Kingdom of Jerusalem, the threat of the Mongols, and stewardship of church property.

Gregory X summoned a second council at Lyon in 1274, which met in six sessions from May 7 to July 17. Among the items on its agenda were reunion with the Greeks and clerical reform. The Latin Empire had fallen, but Emperor Michael Palaeologus of Constantinople was amenable to the union of the two churches because of threats by Charles of Anjou, the ruler of Sicily. A revolutionary aspect of this council was the request sent out in advance for testimonials dealing with areas needing reform. The response was immense and sent a signal to the church hierarchy that changes were badly needed. The council issued thirty-one decrees, including *Ubi periculum*, which was intended to put pressure on the sacred college of cardinals to effect an election as soon as possible following the death of a pontiff by cutting the food ration after three days. The decree is still in force today.

Union with the Greeks was short-lived, owing to the death of Emperor Michael. Pope Clement V (1305–1314) summoned a council at Vienne in 1311. Some 132 fathers attended the three sessions held between October 16 and May 6 of the following year. The council confirmed the abolition of the Order of Knights Templar, intervened in the internal dispute of the Franciscans over the issue of poverty, and published reform decrees.

Not until a century later was the next council held, however, during which time the papacy languished at Avignon and, after 1378, experienced the crisis of the schism. The Council of Constance was convoked to end the schism, meeting in forty-five sessions between November 5, 1414, and April 22, 1418. Among other issues was the rejection of the doctrines of John Wyclif and the condemnation of John Hus. Refusing to recant, Hus was burned at the stake on July 6, 1415, together with his associate, Jerome of Prague. In dealing with the schism, the council accepted the abdication of the Roman pope, Gregory XII, deposed John XXIII, who had been elected by the council, and also deposed Benedict XII, the pope at Avignon. It then organized a conclave that elected Martin V (November 11, 1417). Giving expression to the views of the conciliarists of the day, the council then issued a decree declaring the superiority of a general council over the pope (*Haec sancta synodus*) and proposed that councils be held at fixed intervals in the future (*Frequens*). See also Basel, Council of.

D. J. Geanakoplos, *Emperor Michael Palaeologus and the West, 1258–1282* (1959); S. Kuttner, "Conciliar Law in the Making: The Lyonese Constitutions (1274) of Gregory X," in *Miscellanea Pio Paschini II* (1949); F. Oakley, *Council over Pope?* (1969); B. Roberg, *Die Union zwischen der griechischen und lateinischen Kirche auf dem II. Konzil von Lyon* (1964); M. Spinka, *John Hus at the Council of Constance* (1965); B. Tierney, *Foundations of the Conciliar Theory* (1955).

PAUL B. PIXTON

Courtly Love

A nineteenth-century term (coined in 1883) for values expressed in the love poetry of twelfth-century French troubadours and the literary traditions they inspired in later medieval Europe. This body of work was produced to entertain aristocrats at the royal and princely courts of Europe. The subject matter is a very specific sort of love: the love of a knight for an unattainable woman. The object of the hero's love in these works is almost exclusively a married woman of higher status. Such love did not normally end in happy marriage or even physical consummation. Instead, the poets of the courtly love genre explored their heroes' love as a means of self-realization.

The beloved objects of this courtly love bear little resemblance to real women of the later Middle Ages. They are always idealized—slim, red lipped, white breasted, etc.—and their characters are not normally well developed. Indeed, the troubadour Bertran de Bourn confessed in one poem that the ideal woman he described was a composite of desirable female features. Normally in courtly love literature the symbolic function of the lady is to stand very still on a pedestal, where she can be worshiped conveniently by her admirer. Indeed, the emphasis of the genre is a sort of gentle fantasy, a literary confection joined with certain behavioral conventions that everyone involved knew to be unreal. This point is often lost today, as modern critics have misunderstood satirical works such as Andreas Capellanus's *Art of Courtly Love*, with its careful rules and courts that sit in judgment on lovers, as fact rather than fiction.

Nonetheless, the literature of courtly love expresses some important truths about later medieval society. Courts were full of young men trying to win a place, unable to marry unless they could obtain the favor of their lord in the form of an estate. In this highly masculine atmosphere, one of the few aristocratic ladies present was the lord's wife, a key vehicle through which status could be transmitted. Actual adultery with the lord's wife was a heinous offense, but flattery and admiration in hope of assistance seem to have been common.

At a more symbolic level, the conventions of courtly love helped direct the development

of religious devotion to Jesus and especially to the Virgin Mary. Even as love of an unapproachable lady could lead to self-realization, love of God and Mary could be expressed in similar but transcendent terms, with emphasis on adoration and service by the mortal devotee. This is perhaps best expressed in Dante's *Vita Nuova (The New Life)*, in which the poet tells of a spiritual odyssey in which his love for the earthly woman Beatrice gradually opened his soul to love of supernal realities.

A. Capellanus, *The Art of Courtly Love*, trans. J. Parry (1960); Dante Alighieri, *Vita Nuova*, trans. M. Musa (1992); F. Gies, *The Knight in History* (1984); P. Potter, *Courtly Love in Medieval Manuscripts* (2003).

PHYLLIS G. JESTICE

Coverdale, Miles

(1488–1568), English translator of the Bible, bishop of Exeter. Born in Yorkshire and educated at Cambridge, Coverdale was ordained in 1514 and entered the house of Augustinian friars at Cambridge. He was among those who gathered at the White Horse Tavern to discuss theology and, especially, the reformist ideas increasingly prominent in Germany. Between 1528 and 1534 Coverdale was on the Continent. In 1529 he probably met William Tyndale in Zurich and, encouraged by Thomas Cromwell, produced an English Bible. Published in 1535, it was indebted to Tyndale's New Testament and Pentateuch, the Vulgate, and Luther's German translation. While Coverdale's efforts were dedicated to Henry VIII, they never received formal royal endorsement. Cromwell's injunction in 1536 that the English Bible should be placed in all churches supported Coverdale's work. In 1537 Coverdale's Bible went to a second printing. Attached to the court of Catherine Parr, Coverdale figured prominently in the Protestant reforms during the reign of Edward VI. In 1551 Coverdale was raised to the see of Exeter. With the succession of Mary Tudor, however, Coverdale was removed and imprisoned. He was released later, thanks in large part to the appeals of King Christian of Denmark. After seeking refuge in Denmark, Coverdale traveled to Geneva, where he contributed to the Geneva Bible of 1560. After Mary's death, Coverdale returned to England in 1559 but, perhaps owing to his sympathy for Calvinism, was never restored to his bishopric and returned to his role as an exceptional and popular preacher and was appointed to St. Magnus near

London in 1563. He resigned his living in 1566 rather than conform to the Act of Uniformity.

J. F. Mozley, *Coverdale and His Bibles* (1953); G. Pearson, ed., *Miles Coverdale, Writings and Translations* (repr. 1968).

JOHN E. GRISWOLD

Craig, John (1512–1600), Scottish preacher and reformer. Born in Aberdeenshire and educated at St. Andrews, Craig eventually became a Dominican. He traveled to Rome and befriended Reginald Pole, who made him master of novices in Bologna. Craig came upon Calvin's *Institutes* and was converted to the evangelical movement. He was sent to Rome and sentenced to be burned, only to be freed during the riot after the death of Pope Paul IV. Given safe conduct to England by Maximillian II, he returned to Scotland in 1560 and was soon appointed assistant to John Knox at St. Giles in Edinburgh. After being sent north to preach, he returned to Edinburgh as chaplain to James VI in 1579. He composed the National Covenant of 1580, assisted in the writing of the Second Book of Discipline, and also composed The King's Confession for ministers and Craig's Catechism of 1592.

T. A. Kerr, "John Craig, Minister of Aberdeen and King's Chaplain," in *Reformation and Revolution*, ed. D. Shaw (1967), 100–123.

RANDALL C. ZACHMAN

Cranach, Lucas (the Elder) (1472–1553), German artist and illustrator. Cranach named himself after his birthplace, Kronach; his family name is unknown. He began working in Vienna around 1501/1502, where he became acquainted with the humanist circle there. He was called in 1505 to Wittenberg to be the court painter of the Saxon Elector Frederick III. In 1508 he received from the Elector the famous logo of the winged snake. In the following years he was active as painter, illustrator, and book publisher. Married in 1512, he had at least two sons, one of whom was Lucas the Younger. Cranach became the most productive artist of his time through his large studio and rapid means of production. This also made him the wealthiest citizen of Wittenberg; in turn he served his town numerous times as a city councilor and mayor.

Cranach's personal relationship to Luther was apparently close but is not verifiable in detail. His first portraits of Luther, from 1520 onward, influenced the public's image of the reformer.

Through his captioned woodcuts and illustrations he promoted the spread of the Reformation.

Posterity owes its knowledge of Luther's appearance to Cranach's works alone, and his altar pieces and devotional images influenced Lutheran piety. However, the characterization of Cranach as the "Painter of the Reformation" is problematic, because until 1540 he also completed altar paintings for Catholic courts as well as for Cardinal Albert of Mainz in Halle. Cranach's artistic engagement in the Reformation was primarily due to the wishes of the Electoral Saxon Court, especially the last elector, John Frederick, with whom he had close ties. He voluntarily followed him into imprisonment after his defeat in the Schmalkaldic War.

C. Grimm and J. Erichsen, E. Brockhoff, eds., *Lucas Cranach: Ein Maler-Unternehmer aus Franken: Katalog zur Landesausstellung in Kronach* (1994); W. Schade, *Cranach: A Family of Master Painters* (1980); A. Tacke, *Der katolische Cranach* (1992).

MARTIN TREU

Cranach, Lucas (the Younger) (1515–1586), German artist. Born in Wittenberg, he entered the workshop of his father, Lucas Cranach the Elder, at an early age. Little is known of his life in this period, and any attribution of works to him before 1548 is uncertain because the ambition of the Cranach workshop was to produce a cooperative style that merged the participation of the individual artists. Cranach the Younger's work is regarded as lighter and more pleasing than that of his father. Shared works are not rare; one of the most well known may be the triptych on the main altar of the Wittenberg city church.

Next to portraits of princes and mythological themes, he dedicated himself above all to presentations of the Reformers. From 1547 at the latest, he took over the direction of the Wittenberg workshop while his father remained with the deposed Elector John Frederick first in imprisonment and then in Weimar.

The younger Cranach may rightly be regarded as the most significant propagandist of the Reformation. In contrast to the prior generation, it was no longer conceivable that his art would be placed in the service of Catholic courts. His images and graphic works influenced Lutheran piety just as much as hymns, catechisms, and prayers.

D. Koepplin and F. Tilman, *Lucas Cranach: Gemälde, Zeichnungen, Druckgraphik*, 2 vols.

(1976); W. Schade, *Cranach: A Family of Master Painters* (1980).

MARTIN TREU

Cranmer, Thomas (1489–1556), archbishop of Canterbury, reformer of England under Henry VIII and Edward VI. A Cambridge theologian, Cranmer assimilated the ideas of continental reformers. Lutheranism influenced him early in his career and Calvinism in his later years; both were an influence on his mature eucharistic theology. Born in Aslockton and educated at Jesus College, Cambridge, he was ordained in 1523 and received his doctorate in divinity in 1526. By 1529 he had secured an active role in using the English and continental universities to support Henry in his divorce proceedings against Catherine of Aragon. This initiative was highly successful, for Oxford, Cambridge, five French, and three Italian universities supported Henry's position that the marriage to Catherine was not valid. In 1530 Cranmer accompanied an embassy to Charles V in Rome to argue Henry's cause, traveling with Sir Thomas Boleyn. When William Warham died in 1532, Henry made Cranmer archbishop of Canterbury, consecrating him in 1533. Cranmer quickly acted to annul the marriage to Catherine. He is also responsible for the 1536 annulment of the marriage to Anne Boleyn, as well as the marriage (and subsequent divorce) between Henry and Anne of Cleves. Cranmer's actions in these matters clearly undermined papal authority in England. Also at issue for Cranmer was clerical celibacy, which he rejected. He was married twice; his first wife died in 1529, after which he married Andreas Osiander's niece. Despite problems with Henry on the issue of clerical celibacy, Cranmer's loyalty and devotion to the monarch was unquestioned, and Henry recognized this loyalty. Following Henry's death in 1547, Edward succeeded to the throne. Cranmer quickly worked to implement reforms blocked by Henry's traditionalism. Henry was the only stumbling block in a building wave of Protestantism surrounding the throne; upon Edward's succession, Cranmer, Latimer, Ridley, Queen Katherine Parr, and the Seymour family quickly and effectively brought the Reformation to England. The Book of Common Prayer appeared in 1549, which was largely conservative in tone; a revised edition appeared in 1552 reflecting the modified Calvinism that marks Cranmer's mature theology concerning the Eucharist and the liturgy. Cranmer was also largely responsible for the Forty-Two Articles of 1553, giving the Church of England a decidedly Calvinist tone. Mary Tudor's accession to the throne in 1553 posed problems for Cranmer; he was tried for treason and convicted, but his life was spared. In 1554, Convocation was called at Oxford for disputation; Cranmer, Ridley, and Latimer went head-to-head with traditionalists and were pronounced heretics. Cranmer was imprisoned once again; at issue during the disputation was his stubborn opposition to the traditional Roman Catholic doctrine of the real (corporeal) presence, a view he had rejected since his days at Cambridge. Following a period of imprisonment, he recanted his Protestant views several times under duress, and then renounced his recantations. By this point, Cardinal Pole had effected reconciliation with Rome, and papal delegates had presented their case against Cranmer, deciding against him and recommending that he be executed. He was burned at the stake at Oxford on March 21, 1556, days after the executions of Nicholas Ridley and Hugh Latimer; the account of his death is one of the most remarkable in Protestant martyrologies. Cranmer's legacy to the Church of England is tremendous. In addition to the Book of Common Prayer, Cranmer is responsible in large part for the first eucharistic liturgy in English (1548) and the Ordinal of 1550. Apart from his written legacy, other contributions are notable: he encouraged leading continental reformers to take refuge in England, spreading reform throughout the universities. Two notable reformers he sponsored were Martin Bucer and Peter Martyr Vermigli. Cranmer is the architect of the reformation Church of England; his voice is heard in the Book of Common Prayer used throughout the Anglican Communion to this day.

P. Ayris and D. Selwyn, eds., *Thomas Cranmer: Churchman and Scholar* (1993); C. F. Barbee and P. F. M. Zahl, *The Collects of Thomas Cranmer* (1999); G. R. Elton, *Reform and Reformation: England, 1509–1558* (1977); D. MacCulloch, *Thomas Cranmer: A Life* (1996); J. Ridley, *Thomas Cranmer* (1962).

ALDEN R. LUDLOW

Crespin, Jean (c. 1520–1572), Calvinist printer and martyrologist. After studying law in Louvain and serving as secretary to legal scholar Charles Du Moulin, Crespin fled France under suspicion of heresy in 1545, settling in Geneva in 1548. He established one of the city's largest publishing firms, producing above all religious literature, including the works of Luther, Melanchthon, Calvin, his friend Theodore Beza, and others, as well as Bibles, catechisms, and other works in several languages. Crespin composed his *History of Martyrs* in 1554, contemporaneous with John Foxe's *Book of Martyrs* and two years after the appearance of Ludwig Rabus's similar work in German (using material from both), and revised it as new stories of persecution, above all in France but also in the Netherlands and other areas, providing additional material. Unlike those other martyrologies, Crespin's did not treat martyrs of the early church but began with late medieval confessions and executions. His commentary did draw parallels between martyrdom in the early church and contemporary suffering for the faith, however. He believed that martyrdom must be seen within God's providential guiding of the church in his conflict against Satan's deceit. Crespin wove together juridical events with lengthy testimonies of belief in presenting the courage and the theology of the martyrs. His work substantially influenced French Protestant piety.

———

J.-F. Gilmont, *Jean Crespin, un éditeur réformé* (1981); B. Gregory, *Salvation at Stake: Christian Martyrdom in Early Modern Europe* (1999).

ROBERT KOLB

Cromwell, Oliver (1599–1658), English Civil War commander, Lord Protector. Cromwell was one of the most controversial figures of his era. He was born in Huntingdon, England, and entered Cambridge in 1616 as a fellow commoner. He left the university the following year after his father's death. In 1628 he represented Huntingdon in Parliament; later he represented Cambridge in the Short and Long Parliaments. During the decade of civil war to 1651, Cromwell distinguished himself primarily as an agile and successful military commander of increasing political importance. After 1651, Cromwell's military activity decreased, but his political power continued to rest on the success of the army. In 1649, after the execution of King Charles I, Cromwell became a member of the Council of State. Following the close of the National Assembly in 1653, Cromwell was installed as Protector. Committed to social, religious, and political reform, Cromwell was equally interested in postwar reconciliations. As the military leader of the revolution, Cromwell was politically positioned to lead the postwar recovery, suppressing military resistance in Britain and expanding British influence elsewhere in the world. Recent scholarship has emphasized this paradoxical feature of Cromwell's life— reforming revolutionary as military-dependent reconciling head of state—as the central feature of Cromwell's complicated life and ruptured reputation.

———

P. Gaunt, *Oliver Cromwell* (1997).

JOHN E. GRISWOLD

Cromwell, Thomas (c.1485–1540), a leading architect of the English Reformation. Born at Wimbledon, he was the son of Walter Cromwell (also known as Smyth), a successful brewer, smith, and fuller.

Thomas Cromwell first came to prominence as an able administrator and political confidant under the tutelage of Thomas Cardinal Wolsey during the reign of Henry VIII. Early in life he gained his education informally, through travel and experience, becoming competent in both business and law as he traveled throughout Europe, particularly Italy. Period sources suggest that after fleeing his tempestuous father, he served in the French army, fighting in Italy at the battle on the Gargliano (1503). Following this, it is believed that he served as a merchant in Italy, then Antwerp, and may have returned to Italy a second time. By 1512 he had returned to England and was in London acting as a solicitor and merchant. It was around this time that he married, and the versatility he showed in his work continued up to the early 1520s, when he began to gain recognition for practicing law; no mention is made of his wool and cloth business after 1524.

There is no documentation that reveals how Cromwell became acquainted with Wolsey, but it is likely the two knew each other from about 1520. Cromwell participated in the Parliament of 1523, though it is not clear how he got a seat; it was after his successes in Parliament that he became Wolsey's protégé and was preeminent among his many advisors. Following Wolsey's fall in 1529, Cromwell distanced himself from his former mentor and allied himself with a group of Henry's supporters who were tackling the issue of divorce from Catherine of Aragon.

Cromwell, always with an eye to the practical, managed not only to distance himself from Wolsey but also to make himself exceedingly popular at court. He quickly became a favorite in Henry's circle and was made privy councilor in 1531, in which role he served as an interme-diary ambassador between Henry and Charles V, master of the King's Jewel House in 1532, and principal royal secretary in 1534. This last position was the foundation of his power. He was made vicar general in 1535 and Lord Privy Seal in 1536; he used this power to suppress the monasteries on behalf of Henry and Wolsey. He was appointed Lord Chamberlain in 1539.

Though Cranmer was the architect of the English Reformation from a liturgical stand-point, Cromwell was its architect on the political side. He is responsible for the repression of Catholicism in England during this period: he supported the Ten Articles of 1536, as well as the Henrican Injunctions of 1536 and 1538. In effect, he engineered the dismantling of English Catholicism from its foundation, for these arti-cles and injunctions prohibited such traditional aspects of religion as worship of saints and relics, offerings for the dead, and pilgrimages.

Like Wolsey before him, Cromwell was then enticed into the private affairs of the king, arranging the marriage with Anne of Cleves. Cromwell, who had Protestant tendencies, had worn out his welcome in much of the royal court with his manipulations, and when Henry's mar-riage to Anne soured and was made useless through other alliances, the king also began to question Cromwell's usefulness as well as his loyalty. The first to turn on him were Bishop Stephen Gardiner and Thomas, Duke of Nor-folk, both staunch Catholics. Henry sided with Norfolk and others, and the resultant Act of Six Articles (1539) led to a restoration of Catholi-cism in England. After only six months the mar-riage to Anne of Cleves was dissolved and Henry was free to marry Catherine Howard, a Catholic. Factionalism led to treason and heresy charges against Cromwell. He was imprisoned and begged the king's mercy. Henry did noth-ing to support his faithful servant, and Crom-well was executed on July 28, 1540.

For scholars, Cromwell remains one of the best documented of Reformation-period per-sonages in England. The Calendars of State Papers from 1533 to 1540 are extensive and were seized from him prior to his execution. These papers contain communiqués, official documents, and letters to Cromwell, and remain the best source of information regard-ing this period of English history. The letters that he wrote, though not numerous, augment the information in the state documents. Over-all, it can be said that it is likely that Cromwell, not Henry, was the instigator of what Merriman calls "the secular and religious revolution of 1530 to 1540," though it was the political gain that was his central goal.

———

R. W. Beckingsale, *Thomas Cromwell: Tudor Minister* (1978); G. R. Elton, *The Tudor Revo-lution in Government* (1953); R. B. Merriman, *Life and Letters of Thomas Cromwell*, 2 vols. (1902).

ALDEN R. LUDLOW

Crotus, Rubianus

Crotus, Rubianus (1480–c. 1545), Ger-man humanist and satirist. Born Johannes Jaeger of a peasant family in Thuringia, he was ordained a priest and obtained a master's degree at the Univ. of Erfurt and a doctorate in theol-ogy at the Univ. of Bologna. He returned to Erfurt to teach in 1520, enjoying the company of a group of humanist scholars centered around Mutianus Rufus. He later served as chancellor to Albert of Brandenburg, archbishop of Mainz. Initially a supporter of Luther, he eventually turned against him and in 1531 published an *Apologia* criticizing the reformer. He is best known for his coauthorship with Ulrich von Hutten of the *Letters of Obscure Men*, published anonymously in 1515. This satirical, fictitious collection played a key role in the controversy between the German humanist and Hebraicist Johannes Reuchlin and his opponents, antihu-manist monks and theologians inspired by the converted Jew Johann Pfefferkorn, who aimed to suppress the study of Hebrew language and literature as a danger to piety.

———

E. Rummel, *Scheming Papists and Lutheran Fools: Five Reformation Satires* (1993); F. G. Stokes, trans., *Epistolae obscurorum virorum: The Latin text with an English Rendering, Notes, and an Historical Introduction* (1925, 1964).

J. LAUREL CARRINGTON

Crucifixion in Art in the Orthodox Church

Crucifixion in Art in the Orthodox Church In the East, the earliest known depictions of Christ's death on the cross date from the fifth century, while the earliest extant depictions are from the late sixth to the early seventh centuries. The latter include a leaf from the Syriac Rabbula Gospels of 586 (fol. 13r of MS Laur., Plut 1.56, in Florence); the cover of the Palestinian reliquary box in the Lateran Palace's *Sancta Sanctorum* (probably similar to the silver boxes [*capselloe argenteoe*] that in 519 Emperor Justinian I intended to send to Pope Hormisdas to obtain relics of St. Lawrence and other Roman saints [PL, vol. 18, 474]; and various Palestinian pilgrimage ampullae, which are in collections at Monza and Bobbio, Italy. These works normally show Christ surrounded by a crowd of figures, especially Mary the Mother of God, the apostle John, crucified thieves, and various soldiers. Christ tends to be open-eyed and holding himself up on the cross, even though the wounds in his side clearly indicate death. This image of Christ is an expression of the anti-Monophysite conception of the inseparability of Christ's corporeal and divine natures and is solely based on John's Gospel. Finally, he is dressed in a colobium tunic that covers all but his arms and feet. By about the eleventh century Byzantine iconographers created a fuller type of crucifixion scene based on John's Gospel supplemented with imagery from the other Gospels. Christ is dressed only in a loincloth and is clearly dead, with his head bent and body bowed. Here he is depicted in a much more natural human form than the early Syriac and Palestinian images. The Byzantine model also stresses the bare minimum of witnesses, namely, his mother, John, and the occasional holy woman and centurion. In what has become the classical composition, Christ's body is flexed to the right, with his head bowed and eyes closed to indicate death. His face is turned toward Mary and expresses a grave majesty in suffering. The overall impression is of one asleep and yet incorruptible in the face of death. Also, Christ's victory over death and hell is represented by a cleft or cavern rent in the base of Golgotha at the moment of Christ's death. The skull of Adam appears in the cavern opening, representing how Christ, the New Adam, has redeemed the first Adam. In 1054 this Byzantine conception of the crucifixion brought harsh criticism from Pope Leo IX's legates to Constantinople because Western art of the period preferred to show the living Christ crucified. However, the eleventh-century Byzantine model continues to be the classical presentation.

C. L. Chase, "A Note on the Theological Origins of the Iconography of the Dead Christ," *GOTR* 24 (1979): 58–64; R. Cormack, *Painting the Soul: Icons, Death Masks, and Shrouds* (1997); R. M. Jensen, "The Suffering and Dead Christ in Early Christian Art," ARTS, no. 1 (1995): 22–28; A. D. Kartsonis, *Anastasis: The Making of an Image* (1986); V. Lossky, "The Cross," in *The Meaning of Icons*, ed. V. Lossky and L. Ouspensky (rev. ed., 1983), 180–85; M. Quenot, *The Resurrection and the Icon* (1997).

MICHAEL D. PETERSON

Crusade, Albigensian   *see* Cathars; Crusades

Crusades   Generally, crusades were defensive wars fought on behalf of medieval and early modern Christendom and, in theory at least, authorized and directed by the papacy. Muslim powers had been attacking Christian territories since the seventh century, and Christians, particularly in Spain, Italy, and Byzantium, had been mounting defensive campaigns and minor counterattacks for almost as long. In this context, it is appropriate to see the Crusades as the first major Western Christian counterattack against Islam.

But crusading included many complicated social, theological, economic, and political aspects. By the eleventh century, Western Europe was recovering from the disintegration of the ancient world five hundred years earlier and was beginning to assert itself. Its economy was greatly strengthened, its towns were growing, its population was increasing, and its leaders were possessed of more disposable income. It also had better weapons and tactics at its disposal.

Moreover, after a century or so of church reform, laypeople believed that they ought to devote themselves more thoroughly to Christ and that society would benefit by imitating and absorbing monastic values. The church was seeking to tame aristocratic violence by initiatives known as the Peace and Truce of God. The advent of the year 1000 had stimulated popular religious fervor of both orthodox and heterodox varieties. Although there was firm agreement that society ought to be more thoroughly Christian, in ecclesiastical and political circles there was a raging dispute over who actually led Christian society—the pope, or the emperor or other secular authorities. Crusading addressed all these issues: it was considered an act of love in the tradition of laying down one's life for one's friends, it had a strong penitential aspect, it encouraged noble warriors to practice their craft in defense of Christendom and allowed the pope to demonstrate his capacity to lead the defense of Christendom. No wonder crusading held a predominant place in medieval Christianity from the late eleventh century on.

Many elements coalesced into the First Crusade in the late eleventh century, after the disastrous defeat of the Byzantines by the Muslim Turks in eastern Anatolia in 1071. The Byzantines appealed for help from Western Christians, particularly addressing the papacy. In 1095, Pope Urban II urged Christian noblemen to lead armed retinues to the aid of the Byzantines but also to go further and retake Jerusalem, which had been lost to Muslim attack in 638.

Neither Urban nor the Byzantines were quite prepared for the response. A popular movement, usually called the Peoples' Crusade, unsanctioned and undirected by the church, formed immediately and moved toward the East. Contrary to church law and teaching, elements of it persecuted Jews along the way and became such a nuisance that the king of Hungary defeated and dispersed part of it. The rest was quickly destroyed once it reached Muslim territory.

The First Crusade proper, led by experienced nobles and advised by a bishop, proceeded more slowly. Frictions with the Byzantines, who had wanted mercenaries, not Western armies under the control of Western leaders, developed early and plagued all subsequent crusades, but the First Crusade was successful beyond its own expectations and, on July 15, 1099, retook Jerusalem.

The few crusaders who stayed in the Holy Land thereafter set up four crusader states: the County of Edessa, the Principality of Antioch, the Kingdom of Jerusalem, and the County of Tripoli. These entities, along with the native Christian kingdom of Lesser Armenia and the Frankish Christian kingdom set up on Cyprus in the 1190s, constituted the "Latin East."

Urban II had intended to aid the Byzantines, recover Jerusalem, and demonstrate that the bishop of Rome was the effective leader of Christendom. He had asked Christians to emulate Christ in "taking up their crosses" and submitting to suffering in order to demonstrate their own penitence and to protect their brothers. He had not, however, presented a fully thought-out program of crusading (the word itself did not come into common use until the thirteenth or fourteenth centuries), and he was exploring theology that was still in the process of development.

This was particularly true regarding the penitential aspects of crusading and the complicated theology surrounding the indulgence. Put perhaps too simply, the church recognized two components to the consequences of sin: spiritual guilt and temporal consequences. While only God could forgive guilt, one had to work out the temporal consequences of one's sin, either on earth or in purgatory thereafter. Invoking the authority of the church, Urban offered remission of the temporal consequences of sin to those who went on a crusade. He was not very precise in the language he employed, and it seems likely that not everyone who heard him, or crusade preachers after him, understood the distinction between spiritual guilt and temporal consequences. But an age that was acutely concerned with the hereafter found his offer appealing.

The offer was open at first only to those who died on crusade to Jerusalem but was later expanded first to cover those who fought in other places or who went and survived and then to those who contributed materially but did not actually go.

Just as the indulgence was broadened in focus, so were the crusades. The Second Crusade in the mid-twelfth century included expeditions to Spain and to the Baltic area. The gnostic Cathars in southern France were the target of a crusade in the early thirteenth century. Crusading, created to defend Christendom from external enemies, was used periodically thereafter against internal enemies as well.

Of the seven major numbered crusades after the First, however, only the Third was even partly successful. By 1291, the Muslims had driven the Christians from the Holy Land once again, and over the next two centuries crusading focused, often without success, on preventing further Muslim inroads.

Many factors eventually tipped the balance of power in favor of the West and against the Muslim world, however; perhaps the last significant crusade occurred at the relief of the siege of Vienna by German and Polish forces in 1683. The word thereafter passed into the various Western languages as a synonym for a high moral endeavor against dangerous or powerful foes.

The Crusades have been controversial, their impetus given mistaken attribution in the past. Most notably, crusaders have been said to have been motivated by greed, a desire for conquest, or a desire to enforce conversion to Christianity. None of these was a major motivation. The Crusades were ruinously expensive, draining so much silver out of Western Europe that they helped cause a "silver famine" in the later Middle Ages. While some crusaders did indeed hope to acquire new lands in addition to serving their faith, most returned home, leaving the lands they had reconquered chronically short of manpower. Church law never countenanced forced conversion; although the language of crusading occasionally veered dangerously close to appearing to condone it (most notably during the Second Crusade), the idea never played a significant role and was usually explicitly rejected.

In modern times, historians have sought to define crusading. These attempts fall into three major schools: traditionalists, for whom a crusade has to be directed at the Holy Land; pluralists, for whom any defensive expedition authorized by a pope on behalf of Christendom constitutes a crusade; and generalists, who consider any Christian expedition mounted on behalf of the faith to be a crusade. Most crusade historians today have accepted the pluralist viewpoint. (See also *Baltic Crusade*; *Children's Crusade*; *First Crusade*; *Fourth Crusade*.)

P. Edbury, ed., *Crusade and Settlement* (1985); B. Kedar et al., *Outremer: Studies in the History of the Crusading Kingdom of Jerusalem* (1982); H. E. Mayer, *The Crusades* (2nd ed., 1988); J. Richard, *The Crusades, c. 1071–c. 1291* (1999); J. S. C. Riley-Smith, *The Crusades: A History*, 2nd ed. (2005); Riley-Smith, *The First Crusaders 1095–1131* (1998); Riley-Smith, *What Were the Crusades?* (3rd ed., 2002); K. Setton, ed., *A History of the Crusades*, 6 vols. (1969–1989).

PAUL CRAWFORD

Cruz, Juan de la

Cruz, Juan de la (1542–1591), Spanish mystic, Carmelite reformer, founder with Teresa de Jesús of the Discalced Carmelites. Born Juan de Yepes, he studied with the Society of Jesus but in 1563 joined the Carmelites. He studied at the Univ. of Salamanca (1564–1568), where he was ordained a priest. In 1568 he began, together with Teresa de Jesús (1515–1582), the reform of the Carmelites, aimed at restoration of the original rule of the order. That same year he adopted the name of Juan de la Cruz. He founded convents in Baeza (1579) and Granada (1582). Two years before his death he was elected prior of Segovia. His mystical works consist of three poems that were published posthumously: *Noche oscura del alma* (1618), *Llama de amor viva* (1618), and *Cántico espiritual* (1627). His works, in continuity with the Spanish mystical tradition, show the influence of the Franciscan Francisco de Osuna (1497–1540?). Juan de la Cruz was canonized in 1726 and proclaimed a doctor of the church in 1926.

J. C. Nieto, *El Renacimiento y la otra España* (1997); Nieto, *Mystic, Rebel, Saint: A Study of St. John of the Cross* (1979); M. A. Rees, ed., *Leeds Papers on Saint John of the Cross: Contributions to a Quartercentenary Celebration* (1991).

RADY ROLDÁN-FIGUEROA

Cuthbert

Cuthbert (c. 634–687), bishop of Lindisfarne. This English saint became a monk at the abbey of Melrose in Northumbria in 651. He was ordained a priest and traveled, preaching to the Anglo-Saxons. He founded an abbey at Ripon with Eata, his abbot, but when they refused to conform to Roman customs they were sent back to Melrose by the sub-king Alhfrith. Shortly after this the Synod of Whitby occurred and they gave up their Celtic usages. In 664 Cuthbert became prior of Melrose and then of Lindisfarne. He was later allowed to become a hermit on nearby Farne Island but was forced out of seclusion when he was made bishop of Lindisfarne in 685. After a brief episcopate he returned to Farne to die. He was buried on Lindisfarne. When his body was exhumed in 698 it was found to be uncorrupt, and a cult developed rapidly. By 720 three lives, including two by Bede, and the famous Lindisfarne Gospels, had been created in his honor. Due to the Scandinavian attacks of the ninth century the Lindisfarne monks took his relics and traveled with them until 995, when Durham Cathedral was built in his honor.

B. Colgrave, *Two Lives of Saint Cuthbert* (1940, 1985); G. Bonner, D. Rollason, C. Stancliffe, eds., *St. Cuthbert, His Cult and His Community to AD 1200* (1989).

MARIANNE M. DELAPORTE

Cydones, Demetrios

Cydones, Demetrios (1324–1398), Byzantine courtier, scholar, theologian. Born into a noble family in Thessalonica, he studied rhetoric under Nilus Cabasilas. He later became a partisan of John VI Cantecuzenus. Most of his life was spent in imperial service in Constantinople and in Italy. He was part of the revival of classical learning at Constantinople and was engaged in the debate within Byzantine circles about the proper place of philosophy and syllogistic reasoning within Orthodox theology. His pupil Manuel Chrysolaras was a major figure in the restoration of Greek studies in Italy.

Cydones was part of a group at court culturally and politically attracted to the West. He studied Latin and became impressed with the work of Thomas Aquinas, whose *Summa contra gentiles* and *Summa theologiae* he translated into Greek along with works of Augustine, Anselm, and other Latin theologians.

He and his brother Prochorus were among the opponents of Gregory Palamas and the hesychast movement and used Aquinas's theology in constructing their positions. When Palamism triumphed, Prochorus was excommunicated. Demetrios's imperial connections probably saved him from the same fate. Demetrios became a Catholic before 1365 and left Constantinople permanently in 1396.

R. J. Loenertz, ed., *Correspondence*, 2 vols. (1956, 1960); PG 109, 151, 154; D. M. Nicol, *The Last Centuries of Byzantium* (1972).

EUGENE M. LUDWIG, OFM CAP.

Cyprian of Carthage (c. 200–258),

bishop of Carthage (248–249). Cyprian is most noted for his strong stand on church unity and his opposition to the Roman church's practice of not rebaptizing those originally baptized by heretics or schismatics.

Cyprian, a classically educated rhetorician possibly of Roman senatorial status, was elected bishop of Carthage soon after his conversion to Christianity in 248. A dispute over his election, along with the outbreak of Roman persecution in 250, led to divisions within the churches of Carthage and Rome. Cyprian's influential writings on the role of the bishop and church unity were a direct result of this volatile situation.

At the outbreak of the Decian persecution in 250, Cyprian fled to a location outside Carthage and communicated with his clergy and people through letters that were later collected and preserved. The collection of writings usually attributed to Cyprian also includes thirteen formal treatises, although one, *Ad Quirinum*, is probably not his. These documents tell of a bishop who assumed the conventions of Roman patronage while setting out a middle course within the church at Carthage. On one side he was opposed by those who sought a pure and holy church and rejected any second chance for persons who had lapsed during the persecution. More influential in Rome than in Carthage, they were led by a Roman presbyter and schismatic bishop, Novatian. On the other side, he was opposed, most formidably in Carthage, by those who desired to grant immediate forgiveness to all who had lapsed during the persecution. In their view, forgiveness and restoration to the charity of the church was to be granted on the basis of the divine merits of confessors and martyrs. When the persecution ended in 251, Cyprian returned to Carthage. In concert with the Roman church, loyal clergy and laity in Carthage, and other African bishops, he announced a policy of gradual penitential reconciliation of the lapsed: those who had obtained a false certificate of compliance (*libellus*) would be restored after due penance; those who had actually sacrificed would be restored if they were in danger of death. One of Cyprian's most influential treatises, *On the Lapsed*, explains this position.

Cyprian's middle course could not prevent schism. Sometime between 251 and 253 each faction established its own church in Carthage. Cyprian's most famous treatise, *On the Unity of the Church,* was addressed to this problem. Its reflections on episcopal unity through the chair of Peter were later used by the Roman church to justify Roman primacy.

Cyprian came into conflict with Bishop Stephen of Rome, who threatened him with excommunication when he upheld the traditional position of the church in Carthage, that Christians baptized by schismatics and heretics had to be rebaptized inside the church. Cyprian's famous position that the Spirit could be found only within the church ("There is no salvation outside the church," *Letter* 73) was taken up by the African Donatist schismatics of the fourth century and Roman Catholic apologists in the Reformation. Cyprian became a martyr under the emperor Valerian in 258.

E. W. Benson, *Cyprian: His Life, His Times, His Work* (1897); M. Bévenot and R. Weber, eds., *Sancti Cypriani Episcopi Opera*, Pars I, CCSL (1972); C. A. Bobertz, *Cyprian of Carthage as Patron* (1990); C. A. Bobertz, "The Historical Context of Cyprian's *De Unitate*," *JTS* 5 (1990): 107–11; J. P. Burns, *Cyprian the Bishop* (2002); G. W. Clarke, *The Letters of St. Cyprian of Carthage*, vols. 1–4 (1984–1989); M. Sage, *Cyprian* (1975); J. J. Sebastian, *"Baptisma Unum in Sancta Ecclesia": A Theological Appraisal of the Baptismal Controversy in the Work and Writings of Cyprian of Carthage* (1997).

CHARLES A. BOBERTZ

Cyril and Methodius, known as "Apostles

of the Slavs." The brothers Constantine the Philosopher (827–869; Cyril was his monastic name) and Methodius (c. 815–885) were born in Thessalonica. Their father was a Byzantine official; their mother may have been a Slav. Educated in Constantinople, Constantine gained renown for his erudition and became a teacher of philosophy. According to his Life, he debated the iconoclast patriarch John Grammaticus, discussed Trinitarian theology with Muslims at the caliph's court, and learned the Hebrew language. On a diplomatic mission to Khazaria in 861 he debated with Jews before the Khazar khagan. Methodius began his career as an administrator of a Slavic principality in Macedonia. Around 850 he withdrew to the monastery of Mt. Olympus in Bithynia, where he became hegumen of the monastery. He may have accompanied his brother on the mission to Khazaria.

At the request of Prince Rastislav for missionaries who could teach his people in their native tongue, the Byzantine emperor Michael III sent Constantine and Methodius to Moravia in 863. Before setting out on this mission, Constantine devised a "Glagolitic" alphabet for the translation of the New Testament and Greek liturgical works into the Slavonic tongue, creating the literary language known as Old Church Slavonic. In Moravia the brothers established a church that worshiped in the Slavic language and trained native Slav priests. They faced opposition from Frankish clergy, however, and were called to Rome by Pope Nicholas I. Constantine died in Rome, after being tonsured and taking the monastic name Cyril. Methodius was consecrated archbishop by Pope Hadrian II in 869 and resumed his missionary work in Pannonia and Moravia. A change of rule and pressure from the Franks led to his arrest, imprisonment, and a journey to Rome to defend his orthodoxy. Warmly received in Constantinople in 881–882, Methodius returned again to Moravia with the support of Patriarch Photius to finish translating the Bible and other patristic texts.

The main sources on the brothers' lives are two Old Church Slavonic Lives. Constantine's Life may have been written by his brother, while Methodius's Life is ascribed to his disciple, Clement of Ohrid.

————

M. Kantor, *Medieval Slavic Lives of Saints and Princes* (1983); F. Dvornik, *Byzantine Missions among the Slavs: Ss. Constantine-Cyril and Methodius* (1970), 53–145.

ANDREA STERK

Cyril of Alexandria (c. 375–444), theologian and bishop of Alexandria. Little is known of Cyril's early life. In 412 he succeeded his uncle Theophilus as bishop of Alexandria. During Cyril's reign there was considerable conflict in Alexandria among the Jews, the pagans, and the Christians. While some have tried to connect Cyril to the death of Hypatia, a pagan teacher killed by a mob, there is no evidence to support such a position.

Early in his career as bishop Cyril wrote against the Arians. The majority of his extant writings are commentaries on the Bible. He is remembered primarily, however, for his participation in the so-called Nestorian controversy in the fifth century.

The controversy began when Nestorius, the young bishop of Constantinople, questioned the church's use of the appellation *Theotokos* ("bearer of God") for Mary, the mother of Jesus. Nestorius believed that the title implied that God was the subject of a human birth and thus had a beginning. In an effort to defend the eternity and impassibility of God, quite possibly in an anti-Arian context, Nestorius rejected the title.

Cyril wrote Nestorius to complain of his teaching. Nestorius initially refused to respond. Cyril gained the support of Celestine, the bishop of Rome. Cyril's *Third Letter to Nestorius* demanded his recantation under the threat of excommunication. It included twelve anathemas that Nestorius was called to affirm. Nestorius considered these to be Apollinarian and refused. The controversy that ensued resulted in the Third Ecumenical Council (431) in Ephesus. John of Antioch and the Antiochene delegation were delayed. The council, which Cyril convened without them, deposed Nestorius. When John arrived he convened another council, which deposed Cyril. The rift was healed in 433 when Cyril and John both agreed to a Formulary of Reunion. The formulary claimed that Christ was from two natures and softened Cyril's twelve anathemas. Many of Cyril's supporters felt betrayed. The continuing controversy led to the Fourth Ecumenical Council in 451.

Cyril's Christology sought to ensure only one active subject in Christ. Two subjects would result in adoptionism. He mistakenly used an Apollinarian confession of "one nature of God the Word Incarnate," believing it was Athanasian. He understood this statement to mean that although Christ possessed two complete natures, divine and human, God the Word was the only active subject. Cyril's teaching paved the way for the Christology of Chalcedon.

————

ACO 1 (1933); PG 68–77 (1859); W. J. Burghart, *The Image of God in Man according to Cyril of Alexandria* (1957); A. Kerrigan, *St. Cyril of Alexandria: Interpreter of the Old Testament* (1952); J. Liebaert, *La Doctrine chistologique de s. Cyrille d'Alexandrie avant la querelle nestorienne* (1951); J. A. McGuckin, *St. Cyril of Alexandria: The Christological Controversy* (1994); S. A. McKinion, *Words, Imagery, and the Mystery of Christ: A Reconstruction of Cyril of Alexandria's Christology* (2000); N. Russell, *Cyril of Alexandria* (2000); SC 97 (1964), 231 (1976), 237 (1977), 246 (1978), 372 (1991); T. Weinandy, *Theology of Cyril of Alexandria* (2003); L. R. Wickham, *Cyril of Alexandria: Select Letters* (1989); R. Wilken, *Judaism and the Early Christian Mind* (1971).

STEVEN A. MCKINION

Cyril of Jerusalem (c. 315–387), bishop.

Born in or near Jerusalem, Cyril became a deacon there probably before 335, then a priest around 342. The Arian metropolitan bishop of Caesarea, Acacius, had him appointed bishop of Jerusalem in 349 or 350, under conditions that some would later think canonically questionable. Cyril's orthodox faith and his promotion of Jerusalem's claim to episcopal authority over Caesarea and all Palestine soon led him to a public struggle with Acacius. Cyril was deposed, exiled, and brought back to his see three times (357–359, 360–361, and 367–379) during this conflict with Caesarea. The Council of Constantinople (381) seemed to solidify Cyril's victory by proclaiming his orthodoxy and listing him before Gelasius, who was Cyril's nephew and the bishop of Caesarea whom Cyril had appointed.

Four whole works of Cyril's remain: an allegorical sermon on the paralytic (John 5) seemingly from his presbyterate; a letter to the emperor Constantius, from 350 or 351, seeking his support for Jerusalem's claim to imperial favor and ecclesiastical authority; a series of Lenten instructions on repentance, baptism, and the creed delivered to candidates for baptism early in his episcopate (the prefatory *Procatechesis* and the *18 Catecheses*); and what seem to be preachers' outlines for a series of five Easter week explanations of the initiation rites to the newly baptized (*Mystagogical Catecheses*). Although some have attributed this last work to Cyril's successor, John, a convincing case has been made for assigning it to Cyril's ministry in the 380s. Some fragments of other works also survive. Cyril's writings express an orthodox theology centered on the glorious, saving cross of Christ, allegedly found in Jerusalem in Cyril's boyhood, and they show his integration of the cross and the holy sites of Jerusalem into his important development of that city's liturgy.

A. J. Doval, *Cyril of Jerusalem, Mystagogue: The Authorship of the Mystagogic Catecheses* (2001); E. Yarnold, *Cyril of Jerusalem* (2000); J. W. Drijvers, "Promoting Jerusalem: Cyril and the True Cross," in *Portraits of Spiritual Authority: Religious Power in Early Christianity, Byzantium, and the Christian Orient*, ed. J. W. Drijvers and J. W. Watt (1999).

JOSEPH G. MUELLER, SJ

Dadisho Qatraya (late seventh cent.), spiritual writer (Church of the East). Born in Bēt Qatrāyē (Qatar), Dadisho later became attached to the monastery of Rabban Shabur. His writings are of two genres: works on the solitary, spiritual life, and commentaries on large collections of ascetical literature and apophthegmata. The shorter works are *On Seven Weeks of Solitude,* a treatise on the progress of a monk toward a mature experience of solitude, and "Letter to Mar Abkosh on hesychia," written in response to questions on the practical aspects of the life of prayer.

One commentary is on the Syriac translation of the *Ascetical Discourses* of Abba Isaiah of Scete, a fifth-century Palestinian spiritual writer. Dadisho's comments are not a section-by-section analysis but a diverse discussion of Isaiah's understanding of the spiritual life of a cenobitic monk.

The second is on the Syriac *Paradise of the Fathers*, the compilation of the *Apophthegmata Patrum* (*Sayings of the Desert Fathers*) and similar stories of ascetics, compiled by ᶜEnanishoᶜ of Bēt ᶜAbē (seventh cent.). Dadisho uses the format of questions by monastic brothers to an elder who responds with answers.

L. Abramowski, "Dadisho Qatraya and His Commentary on the Book of the Abba Isaiah," *The Harp* 4 (1991): 67–83; Abramowski, "Treatise on Solitude and Prayer: On Seven Weeks of Solitude," in *Early Christian Mystics*, ed. and trans. A. Mingana (1934), 70–143; N. Sims-Williams, "Dadisho Qatraya's Commentary on the *Paradise of the Fathers*," AnBoll 112 (1994), 33–64; R. A. Kitchen, "Dadisho Qatraya's *Commentary on Abba Isaiah: The Apophthegmata Patrum* Connection," *Studia Patristica* XLI (2006): 135–50.

ROBERT A. KITCHEN

D'Ailly, Pierre (c. 1350–1420), a leading theologian of the Univ. of Paris, played a central role at the Council of Constance (1414–1418), which brought to an end the Western Schism of the Christian church. Already in the 1380s, he became well known when he saw to it that a university chancellor, Pierre Blanchard, was removed from office for taking excessive payments from students for granting

them their degrees. D'Ailly himself became chancellor in 1389 and did his best to involve the university in efforts to end the schism, in spite of a royal order that scholars refrain from discussing the matter in public.

The pope at Avignon, Benedict XIII, tried to win the support of d'Ailly and in 1395 gave him a bishopric. D'Ailly accepted the office but had by no means been bought. He saw to it that his star pupil Jean Gerson succeeded him as chancellor, and in the coming years the two theologians and friends cooperated in seeking to reform the church.

D'Ailly became a diplomat for the French court and was sent on missions to the popes in Avignon and Rome. At the Council of Constance, he was at the center of efforts to elect a pope acceptable to the entire Western church. D'Ailly spent his last years in Avignon, where he cultivated an interest in the sciences and in astrology. This fascinating figure, although long ignored, is now being rediscovered.

B. Guenée, *Between Church and State: The Lives of Four French Prelates in the Late Middle Ages* (1991); F. Oakley, *The Political Thought of Pierre d'Ailly* (1964).

BRIAN PATRICK MCGUIRE

Damasus I (c. 305–384), bishop of Rome (366–384). Damasus's pontificate began amid a schism whose origins lie in ecclesiastical alignments that emerged when Constantius II exiled and then recalled Damasus's episcopal predecessor Liberius (352–366). Damasus and his supporters, aided by the Roman civil authorities, violently suppressed the rival party of Ursinus, but charges of misconduct plagued Damasus throughout his episcopate. Nevertheless, as the emperors Gratian and Theodosius strengthened ties between the imperial throne and the church and disenfranchised the traditional cults of Rome, Damasus's policies and actions significantly enhanced the authority of the Roman church within and beyond Italy.

Damasus campaigned against *homoian* bishops (those who said the Son is like the Father), calling synods, promulgating statements of faith, and harboring Peter of Alexandria, though failing to dislodge Auxentius (355–374) from Milan. Damasus involved himself in the Antiochene schism on the side of the Nicene Paulinus against Meletius and Flavian, though he also took stringent measures against the rigorist Nicene followers of Lucifer of Cagliari. Damasus refused to receive Priscillian when the embattled ascetic bishop arrived at Rome and weighed in against Apollinarianism and other perceived heresies. In the first known pontifical decretal, addressed to the bishops of Gaul, Damasus pronounced on matters of church discipline that concerned virgins as well as the clergy. His quest for unity and leadership made Damasus a staunch advocate of Roman primacy. He consistently referred to Rome as the Apostolic See. After an imperial law declared official Christianity to be the doctrine transmitted by the apostle Peter to the Romans and now practiced by Damasus and Peter of Alexandria, Damasus first explicitly invoked Matthew 16:18 to justify Rome's claims.

At Rome Damasus developed the administrative and juridical institutions of episcopal government and enhanced the prestige and appeal of the Roman church. He commissioned Jerome to begin those revisions of the Old Latin versions of the Bible that would eventually yield the Vulgate. He accelerated the conversion of the Roman aristocracy, although he was chided for associating with wealthy, aristocratic ladies, and his intervention in the Altar of Victory affair further undermined support for the city's old cults. His construction of intramural churches jump-started the Christian transformation of Rome's topography and image, while his monumentalization of the suburban shrines of the martyrs, including initiation of the basilica of St. Paul on the Ostian Way, brought the burgeoning cult of the saints under episcopal control. His verse *elogia* (short commemorative poems), composed in classical meter and echoing classical poets, raised the profile of Christian poetry and, inscribed in the catacomb shrines of the saints, promoted a heroic vision of the church's past that facilitated a new sense of Romano-Christian identity. Damasus is the first Roman bishop whose works emerge with reasonable clarity; consequently his accomplishments have won him recognition as a seminal figure in the construction of the papacy.

A. Ferrua, *Epigrammata Damasiana* (1942); C. Pietri, *Roma Christiana* (1976); J. Fontaine, *Naissance de la poésie dans l'occident chrétien* (1981); J. Curran, *Pagan City and Christian Capital* (2000).

DENNIS E. TROUT

D'Angoulême, Marguerite *see* Marguerite d'Angoulême

David of Wales (sixth cent.), patron saint of Wales. David (Dewi) is an obscure figure historically, but legends about him abound. He lived during the dying days of Roman Britain when the pagan Anglo-Saxons were invading the island. David's monastery at Mynyw (later Tyddewi or St. David's) was on a peninsula in southwestern Wales and fostered seaborne relations with Irish Christians. Irish sources speak highly of David and refer to contacts between him and some of their own saints, such as Finnian of Clonard (d. 549). Such communication is historically probable, although specific contacts cannot be proven. David practiced a rigid asceticism and reputedly only drank water. Medieval Welsh sources made him a bishop in the manner of the Gallic St. Martin of Tours (d. 397). Gerald of Wales (1146–1223) credited him with having called the synod of Llanddewbref in 570. While historical facts are scarce, David's death probably occurred soon after this synod, as his widespread cult is attested from soon after this time. Britain's smallest Gothic cathedral bears his name.

W. Davies, *Wales in the Early Middle Ages* (1982); N. Edwards, *Early Medieval Settlements in Wales* (1988); N. Edwards and A. Lane, *The Church in Wales and the West* (1992); D. S. Evans, ed. and trans., *The Welsh Life of Saint David* (1988).

JOSEPH F. KELLY

Da Vinci, Leonardo *see* Leonardo da Vinci

De Haeretico Comburendo Act passed in 1401 by England's Parliament to suppress Lollardy. The statute initiated official persecution of heresy in England since up to this time the suppression of heresy had been the sole province of the bishops. Now heretics would be tried by canon law but sentenced to death by burning by the state. The act was repealed under Henry VIII, revived by Mary Tudor, and again repealed by Elizabeth I in 1559.

H. Bettenson and C. Maunder, eds., *Documents of the Christian Church* (1999), 198–202; E. Peters, ed., *Heresy and Authority in Medieval Europe* (1980); R. Rex, *The Lollards* (2002).

DAVID A. LOPEZ

Deacon and Deaconess Each term refers to a servant or minister, a subordinate church official. In classical Greek the *diakonia* family of words was used for intermediaries of various kinds. *Diakonos* ("deacon") in the New Testament, apart from being used in a nontechnical sense for a variety of occupations (waiters, government officials, apostles, etc.), is paired both with bishops and with presbyters.

Deacon. In early Christianity, deacons filled many functions, such as distributing the Eucharist in the Sunday assembly, assisting at baptism, and acting as ushers. The deacon stood in close relation to the bishop, serving him, carrying out his instructions, and reporting to him. Bishops were more often chosen from among the diaconate than from the ranks of the presbyters. The importance of the deacons became such that at Rome they considered themselves superior to the presbyters, causing some to oppose them.

Deaconess. The first extensive information on deaconesses is contained in the third-century *Teachings of the Apostles (Didascalia)* 16. They are described as assisting at the baptism of women (baptism was normally received nude and was accompanied by an anointing). Deaconesses gave postbaptismal instruction on Christian living to other women and guarded the women's entrance to the church. They conducted an examination of strangers, performed charitable deeds under the surveillance of both bishops and deacons, and acted as liaison between women and the clergy.

The fourth-century *Constitutions of the Apostles (Constitutiones Apostolorum)* demands that "as a deaconess, one should select a pure virgin; in absence of that, a widow married only once, faithful and honorable." The institution of the deaconess was at that time more closely linked to that of the widow (a social role that was a registered order within the church and entitled its members to material support but also demanded a particularly exemplary life) and to the newly emerging cultural role of virgins. In fact, the order of deaconesses evolved at a time when the order of widows had grown both powerful and unruly; on the basis of their personal charisma and aided by financial independence, many widows demanded a position similar to that held by members of the clergy. The creation of the office of deaconess—a new female ministry with clearly defined and easily enforceable boundaries but with a semi-public, quasi-clerical appeal—was an attempt on the part of ecclesiastical authorities to restrict the potential role of women.

This office also offered a way of regulating the problematic new category of women who declared themselves "virgins dedicated to God." The status of deaconess seems to have been actively promoted as a reward for socially active Christian women. As a result, "deaconess" became an honorable title, and its precise definition as deacon's helper was diluted. As a catchall category, "deaconess" absorbed the qualities of the widow and merged them with those of the virgin to provide a new social identity to a vast variety of women in late antiquity.

J. N. Collins, *Diakonia: Re-Interpreting the Ancient Sources* (1990); J. G. Davies, "Deacons, Deaconesses, and the Minor Orders in the Patristic Period," *JEH* 14 (1963): 1–15; U. E. Eisen, *Women Officeholders in Early Christianity*, trans. L. M. Maloney (2000).

SUSANNA ELM

Dead Sea Scrolls Between 1947 and 1956 approximately eight hundred documents, most of them written in Hebrew or Aramaic, and many consisting only of small fragments, were found in eleven caves located near Qumran on the northwestern shore of the Dead Sea. Paleographic evidence and a refined form of carbon 14 dating led scholars to conclude that the documents were copied between c. 250 BCE and 50 CE. The scrolls include copies, many of them extremely fragmentary, of all the books of the Hebrew Bible except Esther. There are also noncanonical Jewish writings from the Second Temple period such as *Enoch* and *Jubilees*, biblical commentaries, legal documents produced by the sectarians such as the *Rule of the Community* and the *Temple Scroll*, and liturgical writings.

The scrolls constituted the library of a sectarian Jewish group that opposed the Jewish religious leaders in Jerusalem. Anticipating the end of time, they established a community at Qumran, where they followed a lifestyle of strict obedience to the law of Moses and their own liturgical calendar under the initial leadership of a charismatic figure called the teacher of righteousness. Many scholars have identified the sectarians with the Essenes mentioned by Hellenistic Jewish writers Philo and Josephus, but this has been challenged by other scholars who stress the connections between the sectarians and the Sadducees. There is no evidence that links Jesus of Nazareth or John the Baptist directly with the Qumran sectarians.

The Dead Sea Scrolls are important witnesses to the diversity and vitality of the Jewish community during the Second Temple period. They also provide invaluable evidence for the text of the Hebrew Bible, since the scrolls predate previously known biblical manuscripts by approximately 750–1,000 years. The Dead Sea Scrolls illustrate the resilience and strength of early Judaism, which produced the rabbinic forerunners of modern Judaism and early Christianity.

J. Magness, *The Archaeology of Qumran and the Dead Sea Scrolls* (2002); L. H. Schiffman, *Reclaiming the Dead Sea Scrolls* (1995); J. VanderKam, *The Dead Sea Scrolls Today* (1994); G. Vermes, *The Complete Dead Sea Scrolls in English* (1998).

JAMES BRASHLER

Decius (201–251), Roman emperor. Gaius Modestus Quintus Decius, commander of Roman armies on the lower Danube, was proclaimed emperor by his soldiers in 249 after inflicting a defeat on the Goths. After disposing of the reigning emperor, Philip the Arab (244–249, according to some accounts a crypto-Christian), Decius was faced with a daunting task. The empire was in the midst of a "Military Anarchy" (235–284) marked by civil wars and barbarian invasions. No emperor had been able to bring stability. Decius began by adopting the name "Trajan," recalling the glorious Roman past. He then proposed to reunify the empire using religion as a common denominator. He required all citizens to revalidate their loyalty by sacrificing to the state gods. In return, they received a certificate, one of which reads, "I have always sacrificed to the gods, and now, according to the order, I have made sacrifice and libation, and tasted the victim's flesh." This was the first empirewide ruling that, potentially, could affect all Christians. Many Christians apostasized by sacrificing, but others, such as Pope Fabian, were martyred. The apostasies led to the Novatianist controversy.

In 251, Decius was killed in a battle against the Goths and Carpi in the Dobrudja. Rejoicing Christians saw this as the judgment of God.

J. B. Rives, "The Decree of Decius and the Religion of Empire," *JRS* 89 (1999): 135–54.

RALPH W. MATHISEN

Decretals These consist of papal answers to questions of church law or discipline. Formally, decretals bind only the recipient(s), but in practice their contents are taken to be normative for similar cases. While the first decretals were issued in the late fourth century, their number strongly swelled from the mid-eleventh century.

Decretals, or excerpts of their legally interesting passages, were collected from the fifth century onward. A selection of such texts appears in Gratian's *Decretum* (c. 1150), which was accepted as the standard summary of previous church law. Collections of more recent decretals were made from c. 1175. In c. 1190, Bernard of Pavia collected almost a thousand decretals in his *Breviarium extravagantium* and organized them into five books, which were subdivided into several thematic titles. This organization became standard in all later decretal collections.

Pope Gregory IX commissioned the canonist Raymond of Penyafort to compile a collection of recent law on the basis of the five collections of decretals known as the *Quinque compilationes antiquae*. The *Decretals of Gregory IX*, or the *Liber extra*, which collected almost two thousand papal decretals and conciliar decisions, was promulgated in 1234. Friedberg's edition of this work also contains, in italics, those parts of the originals that were excised in the editorial process.

In 1298, Pope Boniface VIII promulgated an official collection of decretals issued since 1234, called the *Liber Sextus*. Pope John XXII issued the *Constitutiones Clementinae* in 1317, collecting the decretals of Pope Clement V, especially the decisions of the council of Vienne (1311–1313). Two unofficial collections of decretals, the *Extravagantes Johannis XXII* (1325) and the *Extravagantes communes* (1500), were also accepted into the standard body of canon law, the *Corpus iuris canonici*.

Collections of decretals were part of the curricula of law schools and generated numerous commentaries, most importantly the *Glossa ordinaria*, which usually accompanied the texts in the margins of manuscripts and early modern printed books.

———

C. Duggan, *Twelfth-century Decretal Collections and Their Importance in English History* (1963); G. Fransen, *Les décrétales et les collections de décrétales* (1972); E. Friedberg, ed., *Decretalium collectiones*, vol. 2 of *Corpus iuris canonici* (1879); S. Kuttner, "Raymond of Peñafort as Editor: The 'Decretales' and 'Constitutiones' of Gregory IX," *Bulletin of Medieval Canon Law* 12 (1982): 65–80.

ANDERS WINROTH

Decretum Gelasianum   A compilation

also known under the title *De libris recipiendis et non recipiendis*, this document has been variously attributed in the ample manuscript tradition to popes Damasus I, Gelasius I, and Hormisdas. The work contains five parts and is clearly the product of at least two authors. The first part explicates the doctrine of the Trinity.

The second lists canonical scriptures. A third section stresses the primacy of the Roman see and places the sees of Alexandria and Antioch in the next two positions of prestige. The final two sections, different in style and tone from the first three, list other authorities of the faith, including orthodox fathers and the councils of Nicaea, Ephesus, and Chalcedon, and list "books to be received" and those *dubia* (uncertain)—both apocryphal scriptures and other writings—that should be rejected on various grounds. This last portion is responsible for the alternate title, noted above, found in several manuscripts. None of its cited authorities is later than c. 490, and it does not mention several controversies of the early sixth century. Scholarly consensus dates the completed work either in the late fifth or early sixth century. It is probably not a papal document, and arguments for an Italian (non-Roman) or a Gallic provenance have been advanced.

———

H. Leclercq, "Gélasien (Décret)," *DACL* 6 (1924): 722–47.

THOMAS A. SMITH

Defenestration of Prague   The open-

ing act of the Bohemian revolt that unleashed the catastrophe of the Thirty Years' War (1618–1648). Angered by the erosion of the religious liberties guaranteed by the 1609 Letter of Majesty, members of the Protestant-dominated Bohemian estates led by Count Matthias Thurn attempted to assassinate the chief Habsburg ministers by throwing them out a window of the Hradshin palace on May 23, 1618. The Bohemian revolt culminated in the deposition of Catholic Habsburg King Ferdinand II and the election of the Calvinist Frederick V of the Palatinate. The imperial victory at White Mountain (1620) led to the dispossession of rebels' estates and the establishment of Catholic orthodoxy in Bohemia.

———

G. Parker, ed., *The Thirty Years' War* (2nd ed., 1997); J. V. Polisenský, *The Thirty Years War* (1971); H. Sturmberger, *Aufstand in Böhmen: Der Beginn des Dreissigjährigen Krieges* (1959).

CHARLES D. GUNNOE JR.

Deism   This intellectual movement of the

seventeenth and eighteenth centuries sought to identify the universal principles of "natural religion" in contrast to the conflicting doctrines of historical religions based on supernatural revelation. Influenced by new developments in science and philosophy, which raised doubts about unverifiable traditional beliefs and the occurrence of miracles, Deists argued that true religion consisted only of the truths that all people could discover through the exercise of reason and direct empirical investigation. The Deists were also inspired to develop a simpler system of religious beliefs by the destructive effects of ecclesiastical intolerance and religious warfare in the early modern era. The common principles of Deism, first articulated in England by Lord Herbert of Cherbury (1583–1648) and Charles Blount (1654–1693) included belief in God as transcendent creator, the identification of true worship with living the moral life, and belief in divine recompense after death for the practice of virtue or vice. Early English Deists such as John Toland (1670–1722) and Matthew Tindal (1655–1733) tended to identify the core beliefs of Christianity with natural religion but honored Jesus primarily as a virtuous man and not as a resurrected savior. French Deists such as Voltaire (1694–1778) and Denis Diderot (1713–1784) suggested more explicitly that Christianity was a perversion of natural religion. Deism was defended in Germany by Hermann Reimarus and Gotthold Lessing, and in America by Thomas Jefferson and Benjamin Franklin.

———

P. Gay, ed., *Deism: An Anthology* (1968); K. Walters, *The American Deists* (1992); E. G. Waring, *Deism and Natural Religion: A Sourcebook* (1967).

ERIC LUND

De Labadie, Jean (1610–1674), French Reformed spiritualist and mystic. Born in Bourg near Bordeaux to a prominent family, de Labadie entered the Jesuit order. He soon came to hold Jansenist views that brought him into conflict with his Jesuit colleagues, and he left the order in 1639 and took up preaching in Bordeaux, Paris, and Amiens. Influenced by Calvin's writings, he joined the Reformed church at Montauban in 1650, where he served as a preacher and teacher of theology from 1652 to 1657. From 1659 to 1666 he preached in Geneva. He next took a pastorate in the Dutch city of Middelberg but was expelled after his sectarian tendencies came to light. In Amsterdam, de Labadie set up a conventicle and attracted numerous followers, including the polymath Anna Maria van Schurman. His spiritualist teachings included an emphasis on prophecy and interior divine inspiration, the rejection of infant baptism, the denial of original sin in children of believers, holding all goods in common, and separation from the

world. Unwelcome in Holland, the Labadists found sanctuary in Westphalia, Bremen, and Altona in Denmark, where de Labadie died. The Labadists founded abortive colonies in Dutch Surinam, Maryland, and New York. By 1732 the movement had died out.

———

T. J. Saxby, *The Quest for the New Jerusalem: Jean de Labadie and the Labadists, 1610–1744* (1987).

RAYMOND A. BLACKETER

Denck, Hans (c. 1500–1527), early southern German Anabaptist leader. Born in Upper Bavaria, he studied at the universities at Ingolstadt and Basel, becoming fluent in Hebrew, Greek, and Latin. In Basel he worked as a proofreader and became friends with the city's Protestant reformer, Johannes Oecolampadius (1482–1531), who recommended him as the principal of St. Sebald School in Nuremberg. Although Denck embraced Protestant reforms, he also had an independent spirit and was undoubtedly influenced by the revolutionary Thomas Müntzer (d. 1525). Called before the city council to explain his beliefs, Denck's unorthodox answers forced his banishment from the city in 1525, where he left behind a wife and child.

It is likely that he first met Anabaptists in the St. Gall region of Switzerland before his arrival in Augsburg in September, where he secured employment as a private tutor and may have been baptized into the Anabaptist faith by Balthasar Hübmaier (c. 1480–1528). His early leadership of the Augsburg Anabaptist circle is evidenced by his baptizing Hans Hut (d. 1527), who later became an Anabaptist leader in the Tyrol and Moravia. During this period he also wrote three important works: *Whether God Is the Cause of Evil, Of the Law of God*, and *He Who Truly Loves the Truth*. Discussions with the Lutheran clergy of the city, however, prompted him to leave Augsburg for Strasbourg before a public disputation could be held.

In Strasbourg, a debate with the Reformed leader Martin Bucer (1491–1551) in December 1526 led to his expulsion. For about six months Denck resided in Worms, working with Melchior Rink (c. 1493–c. 1553) for Anabaptist reforms while completing his most famous book, *Concerning True Love*. He also assisted Ludwig Hätzer (c. 1500–1529) in publishing a German translation of the Hebrew prophets. By August 1527 Denck was back in Augsburg, meeting with Hut and other Anabaptist leaders in the "Martyr's Synod" (so named because many of those present were killed within a short period of time). Leaving Augsburg, Denck set out for Ulm and Nuremberg, but after news reached him of the arrest of Hut and others, he resolved to return to Basel. When he arrived ill and exhausted in Basel in September, he sought the assistance of Oecolampadius, for whom he wrote a lengthy faith statement. Two years later Oecolampadius erringly published this document as Denck's *Recantation*. Denck died of the plague in November at the age of twenty-seven.

Although he is among the better-known first-generation Anabaptist leaders, Denck does not theologically fit the sectarian pattern of Hut or Michael Sattler (c. 1490–1527), whom he had met in Strasbourg. Moreover, Denck was disillusioned by divisions within the Anabaptist movement. Always more concerned for the inner word and spirit over external forms of practice, he was the least dogmatic of any early Anabaptist leader.

C. Bauman, *The Spiritual Legacy of Hans Denck: Interpretation and Translation of Key Texts* (1991); S. Ozment, *Mysticism and Dissent* (1973); W. Packull, "Hans Denck: Fugitive from Dogmatism," in *Profiles of Radical Reformers,* ed. H. Goertz (1982).

DAVID B. ELLER

Denis (mid-third century), bishop of Paris and martyr. Gregory of Tours recounts in his *Histories* the legend in which seven bishops were sent from Rome after Decius's imperial persecution (c. 250) to restore Christianity in Gaul. One of these seven was Dionysius, or Denis, who became bishop of Paris. A *Life of St. Denis* from the sixth or seventh century, once errantly ascribed to Venantius Fortunatus, further details Denis's effort to Christianize Paris. Aiding him were two companions, Rusticus the priest and Eleutherius the deacon. According to the Life, pagan priests orchestrated the arrest, torture, and execution of all three. A pious woman, Catulla, is credited with erecting a shrine over the martyrs' graves. In the mid-fifth century, Geneviève of Paris patronized construction of the basilica of St. Denis. The cult received royal promotion beginning with King Dagobert I (d. 639), who rebuilt the church on a grandiose scale and established its abbey. Henceforth, the saint was associated with Frankish royalty. By the eighth century the Parisian martyr was being identified with Dionysius the Areopagite and also

with Pseudo-Dionysius. Writings of Hilduin, abbot of St. Denis, and his pupil Hincmar of Reims helped secure the misidentification, which benefited the abbey. Belief in the erroneous combination of the three persisted throughout the Middle Ages.

S. M. Crosby, *The Royal Abbey of Saint Denis from Its Beginnings to the Death of Suger (475–1151)* (1987).

ALLEN E. JONES

Denis the Carthusian, *see* Denys van Rijkel.

Dentière, Marie (d. 1561), theologian and chronicler of the Genevan Reformation. Dentière's involvement in the Reformation began during her tenure as an Augustinian prioress in Tournai, Belgium, where she encountered Luther's thought and converted in 1521. Upon leaving Belgium, she married the Protestant pastor Simon Robert and moved to Aigle, Switzerland. After Robert's death, she married another Protestant minister, Antoine Froment, and moved to Geneva in 1535. Here she produced her best-known work, *La Guerre et delivrance de la ville de Geneve* (1536). The work chronicles the early Genevan Reformation and is notable for both historiographic insight and theological reflection. After Calvin's expulsion from Geneva in 1538, Dentière wrote a letter to the evangelically inclined Queen Marguerite of Navarre lauding the Calvinist reform movement and arguing theologically for a more prominent role for women in the church. While stopping short of calling for female clergy, Dentière nonetheless defended the right of women to publish theology and to participate in evangelism.

I. Backus, "Marie Dentière: Un cas de féminisme théologique à l'époque de la Réforme?" *Bulletin de la Société de l'Histoire du Protestantisme Français* 137 (1991): 179–95; J. D. Douglass, "Marie Dentière's Use of Scripture in Her Theology of History," in *Biblical Hermeneutics in Historical Perspective* (1991).

KENNETH G. APPOLD

Denys van Rijkel (c. 1402–1471), also known as Denis or Dionysius the Carthusian, Belgian Carthusian ascetic and mystic, biblical commentator, administrator, political and spiritual counselor, moral theologian, and reformer. After studying at the Univ. of Cologne he took vows at Roermond (1424) and began writing on spiritual, ecclesiastical, and theological topics around 1430, continuing to the end of his life.

Denys composed commentaries on all the canonical scriptures. The first (*Psalms*) contains his interpretation of the fourfold meaning of Scripture: the literal and historical senses support deeper exegesis of a text; this leads to its allegorical meaning—how words, figures, and actions communicate truth about the nature of Christ and his mystical body, the church; allegorical significance precedes the moral and ethical obligations intended by the text; finally, the anagogical meaning moves from earthly matters to contemplation of what is eternal. While Denys did not analyze the sources he employed in commenting, his approach to contemplation shows theological creativity and speculation, contrasting with the anti-intellectualism in much late medieval spirituality.

Denys also wrote on the subject of vocation, on the appropriate exercise of ecclesiastical office, and on the relationship between popes and councils. During 1451–1452 he accompanied Nicholas of Cues on reforming visitations to monasteries throughout the Rhineland, and in 1465 he assumed monastic administrative authority at Bois-le-Duc. Ill, he resigned that position in 1469 and returned to Roermond, where he died in 1471.

K. Emery Jr., *Corpus Christianorum, Continuatio Mediaevalis CXXI, Dionysii Cartusiensis Opera Selecta, vv. Ia and Ib* (1991).

LORNA SHOEMAKER

Descartes, René (1596–1650), French rationalist philosopher. He studied classics, philosophy, and mathematics at the Jesuit college of La Flèche and received a law degree from the Univ. of Poitiers in 1616. While serving in the army of Prince Maurice of Nassau, he benefited from contacts with Isaac Beeckman, a Dutch scientist. In 1619, he had a series of dreams, which determined his ambition to create a new system of thought. After traveling extensively throughout Europe between 1620 and 1628, he settled in Holland, where he found the seclusion he needed to work on his scientific and philosophical writings. In 1637, in addition to treatises on optics, meteorology, and geometry, he published his influential *Discourse on Method*. Seeking criteria for reliable knowledge, he argued that it was essential to begin with systematic doubt and to reject all ideas that are not clear and distinct. This meant that even empirical observations were not to be considered certain. Attempting then to move

beyond complete skepticism, he began to search for indubitable truths, beginning with his famous deduction, "I think, therefore I am." In 1641, he produced a more elaborate exposition of his thought entitled *Meditations on the First Philosophy*. Drawing conclusions from other innate ideas, he offered a proof of the existence of God and argued that the mind is an entity distinct from the body. Only after having established that God exists and is not a deceiver did he feel able to say that it is possible to rely on sense perceptions, at least to some degree. For his careful attention to methodology and his extensive questioning of traditional assumptions, Descartes has often been called the father of modern philosophy.

J. Cottingham, ed., *The Cambridge Companion to Descartes* (1992); J. Cottingham et al., trans., *Descartes: Selected Philosophical Writings* (1988); S. Gaukroger, *Descartes: An Intellectual Biography* (1995).

ERIC LUND

Devotional Images Christians have long recognized the ability of visual images to guide and intensify prayer, but communities have debated whether this potential should be cultivated or suppressed. Generally understood as a genre of Western Christian art, devotional images are typically portable representations of holy figures that encourage viewers toward contemplative engagement and emotional response. They were first identified by German art historians who coined the term *Andachtsbilder* in reference to a cluster of late medieval sculptures found in south German convents, but the term quickly acquired broader usage. Although the variety and circulation of devotional images peaked between 1300 and 1500, their appearance and use reflect much older traditions. Roman imperial and funeral portraiture exerted a powerful influence on Christian artists faced with the unique challenge of representing Christ's dual nature. By the sixth century, famous portraits of Christ, the Virgin Mary, and the saints began to appear, transmitting Greco-Roman pictorial conventions to Christian audiences. Legends describing the extraordinary and sometimes miraculous origins of these early icons helped legitimate their use in the absence of explicit scriptural support.

Eastern and Western visual traditions diverged following the Iconoclastic Controversy (c. 725–842). Early medieval devotional art in the West developed around the display of saints' relics. In the twelfth and thirteenth centuries, however, a resurgence of cultural contact with Eastern Christianity introduced expressive examples of icon painting to Western artists. Concomitant devotional trends, including Franciscan-influenced engagement with the passion narrative, the cultivation of individual and lay piety, and a greater emphasis on the contribution of emotion to prayer, provided a receptive climate for images influenced by Byzantine models. Popular panel paintings, including intimate half-length portraits of the Virgin and Child and of the crucified Christ, enabled viewers to enter into contemplative dialogue with the figure(s) represented and often featured models for devotees to emulate. North of the Alps, sculptures and paintings increasingly figured in the mystical experiences of contemplative nuns and the friars who attended them. Images such as the Pietà influenced private prayer and demonstrated the potency of visual experience as a means of communication with the divine.

Wealthy laypeople in the late Middle Ages eagerly commissioned images for their prayer books and private altars, and fifteenth-century technological improvements made devotional woodcuts readily available to laity of more modest means. By 1500, the practice of attaching papal indulgences to popular religious images—first introduced by Innocent III (r. 1198–1216)—had become widespread. Martin Luther objected forcefully to the trend, favoring pedagogical rather than devotional or cultic use of images. Other Protestant leaders sought to eliminate religious images regardless of function, and Catholic images were increasingly subject to institutional oversight. Devotional images in media such as holy cards, framed portraits of Christ and the Virgin, and depictions of Our Lady of Guadalupe have continued to influence Western Christians, though they have been largely supplanted by movies, television, and other popular media.

H. Belting, *The Image and Its Public* (1990); J. Hamburger, *The Visual and the Visionary* (1998); M. Miles, *Image as Insight* (1985); S. Ringbom, *Icon to Narrative* (1984); Henk van Os, *The Art of Devotion* (1994).

ADRIENNE NOCK AMBROSE

Díaz, Juan (c. 1515–1546), early Spanish evangelical martyr whose tragic death became standard in many martyrologies of the period. It appears that Díaz joined Protestant ranks through his acquaintance at the Univ. of Paris with Diego de Enzinas, brother of the Protestant humanist Francisco de Enzinas, translator of the New Testament (Antwerp, 1543). After a brief stay in Geneva in 1545 Díaz continued to Strasbourg, where he earned the trust of Martin Bucer, with whom he traveled to the Colloquy of Ratisbon (1546). In Ratisbon, the Catholic theologian Pedro Maluenda met with Díaz and, after failing to convince him to return to the Roman Catholic fold, notified Domingo de Soto, confessor of the emperor. De Soto then informed Juan's brother Alfonso Díaz, a jurist with the Roman Rota. Alfonso, also frustrated in his effort to change the mind of his brother, conspired with a servant and together they killed him. Immediately after Díaz's execution John Calvin, Francisco de Enzinas, and Philip Melanchthon wrote accounts of the sinister fratricide. Díaz's own *Christianae religionis summa* was published posthumously in 1546.

B. Gregory, *Salvation at Stake: Christian Martyrdom in Early Modern Europe* (1999); M. M. Pelayo, *Historia de los heterodoxos españoles*, in *Edición Nacional de las Obras Completas de Menéndez Pelayo*, vol. 37 (1948, 1964).

RADY ROLDÁN-FIGUEROA

Didache Known in antiquity as *The Teaching [Didache] of the Lord to the Gentiles by the Twelve Apostles*, this manual of ecclesiastical instructions was compiled in the late first or early second century from diverse sources. Current scholarship suggests an origin in Syria (perhaps Antioch) and multiple authors or editors.

The text may be roughly divided into three sections. The opening materials (chaps. 1–6) with the theme of "two ways," that is, of life and death, may have served as instructional materials for early catechumens. The Decalogue and ancient Jewish wisdom literature provide the foundation of an acceptable Christian lifestyle. The subsequent texts (chaps. 7–15) are concerned primarily with issues of liturgy and community life: instructions on baptism, fasting, prayer, prayers for worship (perhaps Eucharist), the reception of visitors, life with prophets, and respect for community officials. The final brief, concluding verses (chap. 16) are directed toward apocalyptic warnings about the coming of the Lord, as paralleled in Mark 13 and 1 and 2 Thessalonians.

The *Didache* has a decidedly Jewish perspective on the early church situation. The christological view of the authors is unclear: no titles of high Christology are employed, while vague allusions to "the Lord" often may be taken as references either to Christ or to God the Father. The traditions found in the text are distinctive within ancient Christian literature, though parallels to teachings within the Gospel of Matthew appear throughout. While the early influence of the *Didache* is unknown, traces of its teachings are evident in the *Rule* of Benedict and the *Apostolic Church Order*, and its structure clearly underlies the composition of book 7 of the *Apostolic Constitutions* (1.2–31.4).

J. A. Draper, *The Didache in Modern Research* (1996); C. N. Jefford, *The Didache in Context* (1995); K. Niederwimmer, *The Didache: A Commentary* (1998); H. van de Sandt and D. Flusser, *The Didache* (2002).

CLAYTON N. JEFFORD

Didymus the Blind (c. 313–398), theologian and exegete. Born in Egypt, Didymus lost his sight at a very early age but overcame this to become a noted exegete and scholar. He was appointed head of a catechetical school at Alexandria by Athanasius and numbered among his pupils Rufinus, Melania the Elder, and (briefly) Jerome. Exegetically he was a follower of Origen and was, like his master, anathematized following the Second Ecumenical Council of Constantinople in 553. Almost all his works perished as a result, with the notable exception of a treatise, *On the Holy Spirit*, translated by Jerome. He was staunchly Nicene, but a detailed estimate of his theology depends on which other works are considered his. The spurious fourth and fifth books of Basil's treatise *Against Eunomius* have been ascribed to him, as has a very interesting three-volume treatise, *On the Holy Trinity*. These ascriptions must be reconsidered in light of the rediscovery of several of his authentic works at the Toura oasis near Cairo in 1941. *On the Holy Trinity* is almost certainly not his, though this has been contested. The rediscovered works include commentaries on Genesis, Job, Psalms, Ecclesiastes, and Zechariah and are relevant to the textual history of the New Testament. Theologically Didymus laid particular emphasis on the full humanity of Jesus, including his soul, and the divine nature of the Holy Spirit.

CPG 2.2544–2572; J. Quasten, *Patrology*, 3.85–100; B. Ehrman, *Didymus the Blind and the Text of the Gospels* (1986); M. Ghattas, *Die Christologie Didymos' des Blinden von Alexandria in den Schriften von Tura* (2002); A. Heron, "The Holy Spirit in Origin and Didymus the Blind," in *Kerygma und Logos*, ed.

A. M. Ritter (1979), 298–310; Heron, "Some Sources Used in the *De Trinitate* Ascribed to Didymus the Blind," in *The Making of Orthodoxy*, ed. R. Williams (1989), 173–81.

RICHARD PAUL VAGGIONE, OHC

Diocletian (c. 245–313), Roman emperor (284–305). Having risen through the Illyrian military ranks, Diocletian became emperor and proved himself a most effective administrator. His reforms, alongside Constantine's, were largely responsible for the continuation of the Roman state. Diocletian divided imperial rule with another emperor (286), and he shared that with two caesars (293). He exercised his position as senior emperor of the East from his capital at Nicomedia in Asia Minor. Diocletian further stabilized governance by increasing the layers of imperial bureaucracy. Not all of his changes were successful. An attempt to control inflation with a maximum price edict failed in 301. Also problematic was his plan to impose religious unity by reviving paganism. In 303 Diocletian initiated the last imperial persecution of Christians. A first edict ordered the destruction of churches and Christian writings. A second called for arrest of clerics, and a third demanded that they be forced to make sacrifice to the Roman gods. A fourth edict ordered execution of Christians who refused to sacrifice. Eastern officials enforced the decrees more than did those in the western half of the empire. In 305 Diocletian abdicated, but his plan to effect a peaceful imperial transition failed. Civil warfare ensued, the ultimate winner of which was Constantine. The eastern persecution ended in 311. Diocletian, who had retired to Salona, died in 313.

T. D. Barnes, *The New Empire of Diocletian and Constantine* (1982).

ALLEN E. JONES

Diodore of Tarsus (fl. mid-fourth cent., d. before 394), monk, exegete, bishop of Tarsus. Due to christological controversies after his death that culminated in the condemnation of his student Theodore of Mopsuestia in the Three Chapters controversy, Diodore and his writings suffered the fate of obscurity and the taint of heresy. During his own lifetime, Diodore was both a champion of Nicene orthodoxy against Arians and Apollinarians and of Christianity itself against the emperor Julian (the Apostate). He was appointed bishop of Tarsus in 378 in which capacity he participated in the Second Ecumenical Council at Constantinople (381).

After completing his education at Athens, Diodore became a monk and priest in Antioch. He led a brotherhood of like-minded Christians with a special emphasis on studying the Bible. His "school" attracted many students, including Theodore of Mopsuestia and John Chrysostom. Diodore is known as the father of the Antiochene exegetical tradition, which reacted against the allegorical excesses of the Alexandrians, especially Origen. The few extant fragments (mostly in Syriac) demonstrate Diodore's attention to literal and historical interpretation. "History" (*historia*) in Late Antiquity referred to the basic sense of the narrative rather than verification of events.

Diodore's Christology, grounded in biblical terminology rather than philosophical, described the union of divine (Word) and human (often termed "flesh") as a union initiated by the Word who by grace bestows the humanity of Christ with gifts of divine honor and worship. Jesus is human by nature but Son of God by grace. Diodore and his followers carefully sought to preserve Christ's humanity in its fullness through distinguishing the creature from the Creator in the person of Christ.

———

G. L. Bray and T. C. Oden, eds., *Romans*, in ACCS 6 (1999; 2nd ed. 2005); K. Froehlich, *Biblical Interpretation in the Early Church* (1984), 82–94; R. A. Greer, "Antiochene Christology of Diodore of Tarsus," *JTS* 17, no. 2 (1966): 327–41; F. Young, "Alexandrian and Antiochene Exegesis," in *The Ancient Period*, vol. 1 of *A History of Biblical Interpretation*, ed. A. J. Hauser and D. F. Watson (2003), 334–54.

LISA D. MAUGANS DRIVER

Diognetus, Epistle to This ancient Christian apology offers limited clues concerning its authorship, context, or date. The only known witness to the work, a Greek manuscript destroyed during the Franco-Prussian War (1870), was preserved with certain writings of Justin Martyr, though Justin's authorship seems unlikely. Since the text is addressed to an otherwise unknown Diognetus, some scholars identify the intended recipient as the procurator Claudius Diogenes of Alexandria (197–203) and argue that the theologian Pantaenus should be considered as author. Otherwise, while various dates from the early second to mid-fourth centuries have been proposed, similar apologies by Melito of Sardis, Theophilus of Antioch, and Hippolytus suggest a probable mid- to late-second-century date.

The epistle has been fashioned from two separate works, an apology (chaps. 1–10) and a homily fragment (chaps. 11–12). The apology, which is primary, recounts the folly of both Jewish and pagan practices of worship and extols Christian faith and salvation through the Son of God. The homily, clearly secondary, focuses upon the coming of Christ as the Word of God, drawing upon Pauline thought and Johannine theology.

———

J. T. Lienhard, "Christology of the Epistle to Diognetus," *VC* 24 (1970): 280–89; H. G. Meecham, *The Epistle to Diognetus* (1949); A. L. Townsley, "Notes for an Interpretation of the *Epistle to Diognetus*," *RSC* 24 (1976): 5–20.

CLAYTON N. JEFFORD

Dionysius Exiguus ("the Small") (fl. 526–556), monk, translator, canonist, computist. Born in a region near the Black Sea then known as "Scythia," Dionysius received religious instruction from an early age. Fluent in both Greek and Latin, he moved to Rome c. 500, where he taught language and dialectic (to Cassiodorus, for example) and translated Greek theological and hagiographical texts into Latin at the request of a variety of patrons. In particular, his translations made available to Latin speakers important Greek theological and canonical texts, in an effort to ease ecclesiastical relations between East and West by improving access to a shared body of authoritative texts. His work as a translator and cultural mediator was particularly important in canon law, where he produced the first comprehensive canonical collection in the West, noteworthy not only for its completeness (it included both conciliar canons and papal decretals) but also for its strict chronological organization, attention to sources, and ease of use. Sent to Charlemagne by Pope Hadrian I, an expanded version of this work, the *Dionysio-Hadriana*, would become the dominant collection in the Carolingian period. Dionysius was also a distinguished computist, introducing the Eastern nineteen-year Easter cycle into the West and advocating the reckoning of historical time from the birth of Christ (*anno Domini*) rather than from the reign of Diocletian. Both became standard practices of medieval time-reckoning in the Latin West.

———

Dionysius Exiguus, *Praefationes*, ed. Fr. Glorie, vol. 85 of CCSL (1972), 28–81; H. Mordek, "Il diritto canonico fra Tardo Antico e Alto Medioevo—La 'svolta dionisiana' nella canonistica," in *La cultura in Italia fra Tardo Antico e Alto Medioevo*, vol. 1 (1981), 149–64.

WILLIAM NORTH

Dionysius the Pseudo-Areopagite
see Pseudo-Dionysius

Dioscorus of Alexandria (d. 454), controversial bishop of Alexandria (444–451). Dioscorus is remembered for his efforts to overthrow the Formulary of Reunion between Cyril of Alexandria and John of Antioch and to implement Cyril's infamous twelve anathemas. Dioscorus followed Cyril as the bishop of Alexandria and sought to reexert the ecclesiastical authority of the see.

Dioscorus, along with an archimandrite in Constantinople named Eutyches and a eunuch in the imperial court named Chrysaphius, plotted the overthrow of Flavian, bishop of Constantinople. In a council called by Flavian, Eutyches was condemned for rejecting two natures in Christ after the union. Dioscorus accused Flavian of using a test of orthodoxy other than the Nicene Creed, a practice that had been prohibited at the Council of Ephesus (431). This controversy led Emperor Theodosius to call a synod at Ephesus in 449 in which Dioscorus effected the deposition of Flavian from his see. The synod, later called the "Robber Synod," pronounced Eutyches orthodox and rejected the theology of the Formulary of Reunion.

The continuing controversy led eventually to the Council of Chalcedon (451). This council condemned and exiled Dioscorus. He died while in exile.

W. H. C. Frend, *The Rise of the Monophysite Movement* (1972); R. V. Sellers, *The Council of Chalcedon* (1953).

STEVEN A. MCKINION

Disciplina Arcani This Latin phrase means "rule of secrecy" and can be used to refer to the early church practices of keeping hidden from some people detailed knowledge of certain Christian doctrines and rites. Jesus commended the custom of keeping plain knowledge of certain teachings from outsiders who could not accept it (Mark 4:10–13; Matt. 7:6). Clement of Alexandria and Origen claimed that the church perpetuated the apostles' practice of reserving an unwritten doctrine on the deepest mysteries, including the spiritual meaning of the biblical text, for the most advanced Christians. By the fourth century, bishops commonly exhorted the faithful not to reveal plainly the actions, words, or meaning of certain rites and prayers, sometimes even of the creed, to the unbaptized. These bishops used scriptural typology to teach catechumens in veiled language about the sacraments. The bishops supposed that the privileges thus reserved for the fully initiated spurred to baptism those catechumens who were delaying full commitment until their deathbed. Bishops thought this progressive introduction to the deeper aspects of Christian life was pedagogically effective and respectful of the sacredness of the realities involved. This practice faded, along with the catechumenate, in the fifth century.

C. Jacob, *"Arkandisziplin," Allegorese, Mystagogie: Ein neuer Zugang zur Theologie des Ambrosius von Mailand* (1990); G. G. Stroumsa, *Hidden Wisdom: Esoteric Traditions and the Roots of Christian Mysticism* (1996).

JOSEPH G. MUELLER, SJ

Disputations The disputation was a medieval academic tradition that received new significance during the first two decades of the Protestant Reformation. Traditionally, this university forum involved a debate along the dialectical guidelines of assertion and repudiation. Beginning with Martin Luther's famous Ninety-five Theses in Wittenberg, most of the early evangelical criticisms of the Catholic Church took the form of open disputations, from Heidelberg (1518) and Leipzig (1519) to the famous disputation of Zurich (1523), where Huldrych Zwingli presented his oft-printed sixty-seven "Conclusions." When the imperial edict of Burgos (1524) prohibited public disputations, the names were simply changed to "dialogues" or "collations," and the forums continued to inspire Protestant legal reforms and help form confessional consensus in cities throughout the empire and the Swiss Confederation.

I. Backus, *The Disputations of Baden (1526) and Berne (1528): Neutralizing the Early Church* (1993).

JOEL F. HARRINGTON

Dissenters A term used to describe those who do not follow the doctrines and practices of an established church. Used in England after the Restoration (1660), it described those who would not adhere to the Act of Uniformity (1662) that prescribed adherence to the Church of England. Later, "Nonconformists" was used to describe primarily Baptists, Congregationalists, Presbyterians, and Quakers in England. The Act of Toleration (1689) later recognized these groups as legitimate. "Dissenting academies" to prepare candidates for the min-

istry were a feature of English Dissent, both before and after the Act of Toleration.

Dissenters may object to an established church for a number of reasons, including doctrinal incompatibility, differing views of church government, a varied perception of the nature of the Christian life, or the most valid form of authority for the church. Dissent may be tolerated, recognized as legitimate, or face various forms of persecution.

C. Burrage, *The Early English Dissenters in the Light of Modern Research, 1550–1641*, 2 vols. (1912); W. Clark, *History of English Nonconformity from Wiclif to the Close of the Nineteenth Century*, 2 vols. (1911); E. Routley, *English Religious Dissent* (1960).

DONALD K. MCKIM

Divination and Magic These are conventional terms for culturally specific ritual practices designed to extend the normal reach of human cognition and action. Although related, they have different aims. Divination is a "non-normal mode of cognition" (Peek) designed to uncover hidden knowledge, usually about the present but sometimes about the past or future. Inquirers seek out diviners to help them make decisions, diagnose misfortune, discern the wishes of gods or spirits, or solve other problems requiring normally inaccessible information. Magic is designed to solve problems through occult action, by (benignly or malevolently) controlling natural forces or human behavior. The term "magic" is sometimes used to classify what is not "science" or "religion" (and thus to include divination). With regard to early Christianity, the term refers to a narrower field of ritual in which recipes, substances, and spells are used for such purposes as binding, healing, protecting, and cursing. This is what the curse tablets, spellbooks, amulets, and magical papyri of Mediterranean antiquity show magicians doing.

Christianity took shape in a world in which divinatory and magical practitioners and practices were ubiquitous. Church leaders generally objected to these specialists and their activities, partly on the same philosophical and political grounds as did pagan intellectuals and government officials, but chiefly on the religious principle that all knowledge and power rightly come from God. Christians thus accepted some forms of nonnormal cognition or action, such as prophetic dreams or miraculous healings, as divinely granted, but rejected other forms as humanly fabricated or diabolic. A wide gray

area allowed the development in late antiquity of such phenomena as the divinatory consultation of the Scriptures (e.g., Augustine, *Conf.* 8.12.29–30), the copying of Christian divinatory and magical manuals, and the manufacture of Christian amulets by monks and clerics. Forms of divination authorized by the Bible, such as the astrological predictions of the magi (Matt. 2:1), were attractive—and problematic—for Christians.

In the Middle Ages as Christianity spread across northern Europe, divinatory and magical practices indigenous to the Irish, Germanic, and Slavic peoples were added to those already condemned by church authorities. In the West, Isidore of Seville's taxonomy of magicians and diviners (*Etymologies* 8.9) was used to classify this profusion of disapproved activity according to its degree of demonic influence, from the highest degree (witches, necromancers) to the lowest (lot diviners, astrologers). Byzantine classifications of divination and magic drew on such authorities as John Chrysostom, Basil of Caesarea, and the canons of church councils (e.g., canon 61 of the Quinisext council of 691/692). In West and East the practice of divination and magic was socially widespread, and ecclesiastical latitude toward it was considerable. In the Renaissance, the embrace of "natural magic" by intellectuals such as Marsilio Ficino (1433–1499) gave new respectability to the forces of stars, stones, herbs, and sacred words.

In the mid-sixteenth century Protestant and Catholic concern for church reform and fear of diabolic attack gave new urgency to the study and restraint of magic and divination. At the same time, European conquest and colonialism brought Christian concepts of magic and divination into confrontation with a new range of traditional practices. Although Reformation ideas coupled with advances in science, medicine, and technology are theorized to have initiated a decline of magic in Western Europe by the end of the seventeenth century—and the professionalization of data collection, economic forecasting, and personal counseling has reduced the appetite for divination in the developed world—there is still in traditional societies, and to some extent in secular ones, a steady operation of culturally powerful beliefs and practices perceived, whether by insiders or outsiders, as magical or divinatory.

V. Flint, *The Rise of Magic in Early Medieval Europe* (1991); D. Frankfurter, "Dynamics of Ritual Expertise in Antiquity and Beyond," in *Magic and Ritual in the Ancient World*, ed.

P. Mirecki and M. Meyer (2002), 159–78; F. Graf, *Magic in the Ancient World* (1997); R. Kieckhefer, *Magic in the Middle Ages* (1990); W. E. Klingshirn, "Isidore of Seville's Taxonomy of Magicians and Diviners," *Traditio* 58 (2003): 59–90; H. Maguire, ed., *Byzantine Magic* (1995); M. W. Meyer and R. Smith, *Ancient Christian Magic* (1994); P. Peek, *African Divination Systems* (1991); W. F. Ryan, *The Bathhouse at Midnight: An Historical Survey of Magic and Divination in Russia* (1999); P. M. Soergel, "Miracle, Magic, and Disenchantment in Early Modern Germany," in *Envisioning Magic*, ed. P. Schäfer and H. G. Kippenberg (1997), 215–34; K. Thomas, *Religion and the Decline of Magic* (1971).

WILLIAM E. KLINGSHIRN

Divine Office

The line in Psalm 119:164, "Seven times a day do I praise thee because of thy righteous judgments," may have provided impetus for the recurrence of the "offices" on a regular, periodic basis throughout the day. The early Christian church, apparently, from the earliest instances of organized meetings incorporated, according to the apostle Paul (Col. 3:16; Eph. 5:19), "psalms, hymns, and spiritual songs, singing with grace in your hearts to the Lord." The psalms of the Old Testament, together with the precedent set by the early church in the New Testament, can be seen to have set a pattern for worship, praise, and prayer as an organized community observance throughout the day, as well as manifesting a spirit of "watchfulness." It is to be noted, as well, that Christ, in the parable of the "householder" to whom he likens the kingdom of God, resumes his search for workers for his vineyard every three hours: at six in the morning, at nine o'clock, at noon, in the afternoon, and at the end of the day (Matt. 20:1–16). This habit of regular prayer hours is also reinforced by other passages in the New Testament, such as Mark 14:38, Matt. 26:41, and 2 Cor. 6:5.

The Divine Office complements the Mass in the following manner. The texts of the Mass include recombined portions, each summarizing a complete, self-contained, even modular, statement (*cento*, Lat. *punctum*), especially of the psalms, placed together in alternation with entire psalms, readings from the Old Testament, the Gospels, and the Pauline Epistles, as well as prayers. This series of events proceeds step by step leading to, and culminating in, the eucharistic celebration or the Lord's Supper (Canon of the Mass). On the other hand, rather than breaking up the psalms into portions and recombining them in a different order than what is found in the book of Psalms, the Offices present entire psalms in order, together with events specific to certain times of day, such as the canticles. During the hours of the Divine Office, not the Mass, hymns are also sung. At first these were limited to the hymns of Ambrose, fourth-century bishop of Milan, but later the repertory of hymns became greatly expanded, and it has continued to attract new compositions to the present. Hymns are sung during the most important of the hours, namely, morning and evening prayer.

Another practice, of the early church, of interrupting the work of the day by prayer was followed, either as individual and private or public and organized prayer. This scheme also brings to mind the two dimensions of time itself, that is, the contrast between specific, regular times of prayer, and Christ's observation that his disciples ought always to pray (Luke 18:1), as well as the Pauline injunction to "pray without ceasing" (1 Thess. 5:17). The prayer hours (*officium*), accordingly, point to the two simultaneous dimensions of experienced time, that is, measured time as it is lived moment by moment, and eternity as "timelessness" even as this dimension can be experienced in the world. These eight prayer hours begin at daybreak, at the start of the work of the day, and end with the invocation of blessing before retiring, with the following order of hours: Matins, originally known as Vigils, beginning after midnight, that is, c. 3 a.m., Lauds at daybreak, Prime, at 6 o'clock a.m., Terce, at 9 a.m., Sext, at noon, None, at 3 p.m., Vespers, at twilight or at the close of the day's activities, and Compline, before retiring for the night. Matins and Vespers are longer hours; Prime, Terce, Sext, and None are known as the "Little Hours." All of the hours bring together psalms framed by antiphons, lessons with responsories, and versicles with responses and prayers, arranged in a strict order, or course, that is, *cursus*. There are two primary versions of the *cursus*: the Roman *cursus,* followed by churches and cathedrals and regularized in the ninth century by Amalarius of Metz (c. 830), and the monastic *cursus*, followed by monasteries, which has its origin in the Rule of St. Benedict. Canticles are also sung as part of the unchanging aspect of the Divine Office— that is, the canticle *Benedictus Dominus Deus Israel* (Canticle of Zacharias, Luke 1:68–79) is sung at the close of the morning service, Lauds, and the *Magnificat* (Canticle of the Virgin Mary, Luke 1:46–55; cf. 1 Sam. 2:1–10) constitutes a high point of Vespers.

In spite of this strict, predictable organization of the structure of the Offices, there is a place for local usage, and a good deal of variation has apparently always been an aspect of the Offices, not only for the antiphons that are sung ("antiphonally" that is, in alternation between two groups) within the weekly cycle of the psalms, but also for the antiphons framing the *Benedictus* and the *Magnificat* and the antiphons for the invitatory or opening of Matins. This can be seen in liturgical books, or breviaries, which contain all of the texts for the entire church year, or antiphonals containing the musical portions, with texts, for the Offices. In addition, a "proper office," or service appropriate to a certain feast day or saint, may be substituted for a daily office ("ferial office") according to the particular usage at a specific place. The text of the *Magnificat* has more recently provided impetus to polyphonic composition, and one can observe other local differentiating features such as processions, or the singing of vernacular songs such as the Italian *Lauda* or *Laudesi* during the later Middle Ages at this point of the Vespers service. So the Divine Office not only projects two dimensions of time—that is, temporal, measured time, and "unceasing," unmeasured time—but also two dimensions of place, in which the universal is contrasted and combined with the specific and regional (see *Liturgical Music*).

J. M. Hanssens, ed., *Amarlarii episcopi opera liturgica omnia* (1948–1950); R. J. Hesbert, ed., *Corpus, antiphonalium officii* (1963–1970), i–iv; M. Righeri, *Manuale di storia liturgica*, vol. 1 (1964), vol. 2 (1969), 917–20; P. Salmon, "Divine Office, Roman," in *NCE* (1967); W. G. Storey and N. K. Paucher, *Medieval Liturgy: An Introduction to the Sources* (1986).

NANCY VAN DEUSEN

Divinization The term designates a doctrinal principle and spiritual ideal, developed principally but not exclusively in the Eastern Orthodox tradition, projecting the transformation of creatures to an exalted state of participation in the divine life. Certain Greek patristic writers identified the apostolic precedent for this principle in the summons of the faithful to become "partakers of the divine nature" (2 Pet. 1:4) and in discussions of "adoption" by grace (Rom. 8:23 and Eph. 1:5). The connection of deification with God's original plan for creation gave importance to the notions of "image" and "likeness of God" (Gen. 1:26–27) and the tra-

vail of creation in advance of its transformation (Rom. 8:18–25).

Theologically, for the Greek and Byzantine fathers, deification (*theōsis*, *theopoiēsis*) relied on the concept of the *vocation* of humanity as created in God's image and summoned to the highest assimilation to God. Irenaeus of Lyon (second cent.) argued that the fall frustrated but did not overturn God's plan for creation. Christ intervened not only to remedy the tragedy of sin but also to recapitulate God's original intention for humankind (cf. Eph. 1:10). Irenaeus, Clement of Alexandria, Origen, Athanasius, Gregory of Nazianzus, and others concurred that God became human in order for human creatures to become "divine," though perspectives differed on the dynamics of the projected transformation.

In the Alexandrian tradition, Clement and Origen associated divinization with transcendence of bodily limitations and recovery of the prelapsarian state of contemplation (*theōria*) of God and impassibility (*apatheia*). Later Origenists tended to view disembodiment or the sheer resolution of the human spirit into God as the goal. Athanasius, however, revived Irenaeus's concerns. Though the fall threatened a reversal of creation, the incarnate Logos inaugurated a new creation and the prospect of physical "incorruptibility" (*aphtharsia*). Cyril of Alexandria (fifth century) emphasized that through the grace of the incarnation and the presence of the Holy Spirit believers could become incorruptible "sons by participation [*methexis*]" in the Holy Trinity.

In the fourth century the Cappadocians articulated their asceticism and teaching on deification in the context of larger Trinitarian concerns. Gregory of Nyssa and Gregory of Nazianzus envisioned intimate participation in the Trinity short of direct knowledge. Nazianzus spoke of a sublime *theologia*, while Nyssa described a continuum of transformation, a perpetual striving (*epektasis*) of souls into the infinite mystery of God. Cappadocian mystical theology proved formative for Pseudo-Dionysius the Areopagite (sixth cent.), whose vision of "ecstatic" deification influenced both East and West.

Maximus the Confessor (seventh cent.) again focused the doctrine of deification through the lens of divine incarnation. In Jesus Christ the perfect concert of divine and human natures and wills in one *hypostasis* ("substance") held the key to the reintegration of the whole created universe. Maximus envisioned deification as an unprecedented "theandric" communion of God and human beings that perfected rather than violated creaturely dignity. His contemporary Anastasius Sinaïta explained, "To be divinized means to be uplifted to a greater glory, and certainly not to be altered from one's proper nature."

Later Byzantine theologians such as Symeon the New Theologian (eleventh century) and Gregory Palamas (fourteenth century) enhanced the experiential dimension of deification, especially the vision of the luminous divine glory rendered accessible through Christ's incarnational condescension. Contemporary Orthodox theology still draws from patristic teaching on divinization.

The doctrine of deification in the East developed concurrently in theological, ascetical, liturgical, and sacramental contexts. For monks deification was the ultimate goal of the practical, contemplative, and mystical disciplines. The Divine Liturgy was, from one perspective, a glorious dramatization of the mystery of incarnation and deification. Baptism was believed to effect a genuine ontological change, the new birth leading toward incorruptibility.

In the West deification never assumed a comparable theological status. Augustine affirmed the principle that God became incarnate in order to deify humanity, especially favoring the biblical notion of adoption by grace. Echoes of the theme appear even in Luther, but Protestant theological critics have consistently suspected the Eastern doctrine of deification of undermining the centrality of the cross and justification by faith. Adolf Harnack and other critical historians accused the Orthodox of turning salvation into a "physical" transformation grounded more in the incarnation than in the death of the Savior.

D. Balas, ΜΕΤΟΥΣΙΑ ΘΕΟΥ (1966); G. Bonner, "Augustine's Conception of Deification," *JTS* 37 (1986): 369–86; J.-C. Larchet, *La divinisation de l'homme selon saint Maxime le Confesseur* (1996); V. Lossky, *The Vision of God* (1963); P. Nellas, *Deification in Christ: Orthodox Perspectives on the Nature of the Human Person* (1987).

PAUL M. BLOWERS

Docetism

Modern scholars use the term "docetism" (Gk. *dokein*, "to appear") for the position that Jesus' human existence and experiences were merely "in appearance." However, the presence of a clearly defined sect of individual "docetists" in early Christianity is unclear. The term was used in the early third century: Serapion of Antioch uses "docetist" to describe a group in Rhossus advocating unspecified teachings based on the *Gospel of Peter* (Eusebius, *Hist. eccl.* 6.12); Clement of Alexandria claims that "docetism" originated with Julius Cassianus, though it is his encratism (see *encratites*) that Clement then criticizes (*Strom.* 3.13.91), and Clement asserts that "docetists" teach "peculiar doctrines," without specifying further (*Strom.* 7.17.108); finally, the *Refutation of All Heresies* ascribed to Hippolytus deals with the "docetists," although their teaching, a retelling of the story of Jesus in terms of a massive cosmic (and precosmic) drama involving numerous aeons, has much in common with Gnosticism (*Haer.* 8.1–11; 10.16). Theodoret of Cyrrhus used the term to speak of Marcion, Valentinus, and Manes (Letter 82). Although these and other gnostic figures exhibit docetic tendencies (denying to Christ an ordinary birth, or separating Jesus from the Christ as two distinct beings), by their time such claims were no longer simply docetic but resulted from a more comprehensive, usually dualistic, outlook. Possibly those mentioned in the letters of John who denied that Christ has come in the flesh (1 John 4:2; 2 John 7) were docetic. More certainly docetic were the opponents of Ignatius of Antioch, against whom he emphasized that Christ "truly suffered . . . not as some unbelievers say, that his passion was in appearance" (*To the Smyrnaeans* 2; cf. *To the Trallians* 10). Not only is the passion of Christ at stake but also his human nature: he was "truly of the family of David according to the flesh . . . truly born of a virgin" (*Smyrn.* 1). Again, it is unclear whether they were docetic, or simply struggling, as Christians always have, with how best to articulate the belief that Christ is human but also God, and that his death is at the same time the victory over death, the opposite of what it appeared to be.

J. Behr, *The Way to Nicaea* (2001), 77, 83–84; A. Grillmeier, *Christ in Christian Tradition*, vol. 1 (2nd ed. rev., 1975), 78–79.

JOHN BEHR

Dominic

(c. 1170–1221), saint, founder of the *Ordo Fratrum Praedicatorum* (the Order of Preachers, Dominicans). Born a Castilian noble (the family Guzmán), Dominic studied in Palencia, and around 1195 he entered the cathedral chapter of Osma as a regular canon. As subprior, he accompanied the bishop Diego of Osma in 1203 and 1205 on trips to Scandinavia, Rome, Aragon, and the southwest of France. In 1205/1206, Diego and Dominic received a commission from Pope Innocent III to support the preaching mission against the Albigensies in southwest France. In 1206 Dominic founded his first monastery at Prouille for converted heretics. His relationship with Simon of Montfort, the military leader of the Albigensian Crusade, cost him much popular sympathy.

In these years, Bishop Fulco of Toulouse appeared as Dominic's most important supporter, who committed a chapel in Toulouse to Dominic in 1215 and the right to preach freely in his diocese. In spite of Bishop Fulco's advocacy, Dominic was refused the confirmation of his community of preachers at the Fourth Lateran Council (1215). Only after the community took up the Augustinian rule and the canons' form of life, on the model of the Premonstratensians, did he receive full papal recognition by Pope Honorius III (1216/1219). On this basis, Dominic extended the preaching activity of his steadily growing community to other dioceses. In the year 1217, he sent the majority of his fellow friars to study and establish a convent at Paris. The founder himself modeled the ideals of the new community, that is, the bond between theological study, preaching, and a monastic form of life.

After 1217, Dominic received papal support to transform his community into a centralized order. New convents arose first in Spain and Italy, later in all of Europe. Dominic died a year after the first Dominican general chapter meeting in Bologna (1220), at which the Dominican constitution was laid down. By the time of his canonization (1234) by Pope Gregory IX, the Dominicans had become a pillar of the papacy in matters of pastoral care, scholarship, and persecution of heresy.

Monumenta Ordinis Fratrum Praedicatorum historica (1896+); B. Altaner, *Der heilige Dominikus: Untersuchungen und Texte* (1922); G. R. Galbraith, *The Constitution of the Dominican Order, 1216–1360* (1925); M.-H. Vicaire, *Histoire de Saint-Dominique*, 2 vols. (2nd ed., 1982); P. Timko, "Dominic, St. c. 1172–1221," *Encyclopedia of Monasticism*, vol. 1 (1998), 408–11; S. Tugwell, "Notes on the Life of St. Dominic," *Archivum fratrum Praedicatorum* 65–73 (1995–2003).

JÖRG OBERSTE

Dominican Order   The Order of Preachers (*Ordo fratrum Praedicatorum*; OP) emerged out of the religious community of canons founded in 1215 in Toulouse by the Regular Canon Dominicus Guzmán from Osma, with the declared aim to convert the Cathars in southern France by means of preaching and through an exemplary evangelical life of poverty. Gradually the community was reorganized and turned into a centralized religious order, receiving papal approval as one of the new mendicant orders in c. 1216. The Dominican friars follow the Augustinian rule.

Their foremost tasks were preaching and care of souls for the laity in towns. Training for preachers took place at the newly established universities, such as Paris and Bologna, where the friars founded their first houses in 1217. Under papal protection and with the support of the urban aristocracy—often against the opposition of the local secular clergy—the order spread rapidly throughout the whole of Europe. The number of houses gradually increased from 21 in 1221, to 404 in 1277, to 631 in 1357, to about 677 at the present day. In 1231 Pope Gregory IX assigned the office of the inquisition for Germany and France to the order. Unlike the Franciscan order, the Dominicans never promoted the idea of the absolute poverty of Christ and supported Pope John XXII in the poverty controversy against the Franciscans. From the days of Thomas Aquinas (d. 1274) they rejected the dogma of the Immaculate Conception, introduced as an official feast day in 1476 by the Franciscan pope Sixtus IV. In its organizational structures the order combined centralistic with democratic elements. The constitution (*Constitutiones antiquae*) dates back to the time of Dominic and his successors Jordan of Saxony (d. 1237) and Raymund of Penaforte (d. 1243). It is a masterpiece of medieval legislation, establishing the unified structure of the order to the present day. The female branch of the order was established by Dominic himself, with the first house in Prouille founded as early as 1217. From the beginning the friars also undertook missions to Asia. In the sixteenth century the Dominicans took a leading part in the missions to Latin America. The order produced numerous bishops, cardinals, and popes (Innocent V, d. 1276; Benedict XI, d. 1304). Among its most prominent members are Thomas Aquinas (d. 1274) and his teacher Albertus Magnus (d. 1280), Hugh of St. Cher (d. 1263, commentator of the Bible), Jacob of Voragine (d. 1298, author of the *Golden Legend*), Martin of Poland (d. 1278, historian), Bernard Gui (d. 1331, theologian, historian, and inquisitor), William of Moerbeke (d. 1286, interpreter), Vincent of Beauvais (d. 1264, encyclopedist), Meister Eckhart (d. 1328, theologian and mystic), Bartolomé de Las Casas (d. 1566, advocate of native peoples in

New Spain), and Luis de Granada (d. 1588, spiritual author).

E. T. Brett, *Humbert of Romans: His Life and Views of 13th Century Society* (1984); J. Dunbabin, *A Hound of God: Pierre de la Palud and the 14th-Century Church* (1991); G. R. Galbraith, *The Constitution of the Dominican Order* (1925); W. A. Hinnebusch, *The History of the Dominican Order*, 2 vols. (1966, 1972); C. H. Lawrence, *The Friars: The Impact of the Early Mendicant Movement on Western Society* (1994); M. O'Carroll, "The Educational Organisation of the Dominicans in England," *Archivum Fratrum Praedicatorum* 50 (1980): 23–62; S. Tugwell, *The Way of the Preacher* (1979).

ANNETTE KEHNEL

Donation of Constantine This forged document has Emperor Constantine I (r. 312–337) ceding wide secular authority over Italy and the West to Pope Silvester (314–335). Intense study by generations of scholars of the document's authorship, date, and purpose has yielded only approximate results. The consensus points to authorship by the papal entourage in late eighth-century Rome. The Donation grants the pope supremacy over all the churches in the world and hands over to the pope Rome, Italy, and the western regions. Such sweeping claims might have been inspired by the Lombard threat to papal Italy, the rise of the Carolingians, and the reorientation of papal influence from the Byzantine and Muslim East and North Africa to Europe. Whatever its original intentions, the earliest known uses of the Donation occur only in the ninth century in the writings of Carolingian bishops and in the Pseudo-Isidorian decretals. Carolingians appreciated the authority the Donation gave popes to recognize Western emperors. The Donation surfaced again in Rome in the eleventh century when popes Leo IX (1049–1054) and Gregory VII (1073–1085) used it to vindicate their own claims to papal authority. When it appeared in Gratian's twelfth-century *Decretum*, it was assured a fundamental role in papal and imperial controversies of the High Middle Ages and in the Reformation.

J. Muldoon, *Empire and Order: The Concept of Empire, 800–1800* (1999).

JOHN J. CONTRENI

Donatism and Donatus African Christian sect and its leader. During Diocletian's persecution (303–305), many Christians abjured their faith. Even bishops handed over the Scriptures to be burned, and thereby became traitors to the faith (*traditores*). Some who had fallen from the faith repented and sought readmission to the church. As in previous persecutions and schisms, the church had to provide some procedure for the reintegration of sinners. The general precedent was that those who repented would undergo a long period of penance and returning clergy would almost always rejoin as laity.

In 305 the Council of Cirta debated whether repentant bishops could participate in episcopal ordinations. With the paucity of nonlapsed bishops and the necessity of multiple bishops to ordain, the deeply divided council decided that those who returned might, of necessity, participate in ordinations.

At Carthage, in the first election after persecution (311), Caecilian was elected. Some impugned his election, primarily because one of his consecrators was supposedly a *traditor*, and they elected Majorinus instead. His successor, Donatus, gave the movement its name. Dual lines of episcopal authority grew up in major cities. Elsewhere, towns might have a single bishop of either group or bishops from both. Little is known of Donatus himself except that he was active from his election in 313 to his exile from Africa in 347.

In the period after the legalization of Christianity, Donatists were persecuted by the state with Catholic collusion in 317–321 and 346–348. Otherwise, the two groups continued in an uneasy truce until Augustine's time. By then sacramental theologies had developed independently. Donatists moved from placing the source of sacramental power in the person of the minister to the true church, while Catholics placed it in God. Augustine developed this idea in *De baptismo* where he differentiated valid, licit, and fruitful sacraments (Catholic) from those that were merely valid (Donatist). This difference allowed Catholics to request enforcement of legislation against Donatists as heretics. By 405 heavy fines were levied on Donatists and they were deprived of many civil rights, including inheritance.

In 411 the emperors Honorius and Arcadius called a judicial proceeding at which the two parties were to reconcile. The choice of presider and rules of discussion made the conclusion a *fait accompli*: Donatists were again proscribed. However, as in previous persecutions, the Donatists did not disappear. Their congregations flourished until the Vandal invasion (429), when the Arian administration persecuted Catholics and Donatists equally. By the Byzantine reconquest (530s), Donatism does not appear as a separate sect.

Optatus of Milevis, *Against the Donatists*, ed. and trans. M. Edwards (1997); W. H. C. Frend, *The Donatist Church: A Movement of Protest in Roman North Africa* (1952); M. A. Tilley, *The Bible in Christian North Africa: The Donatist World* (1997); Tilley, "From Separatist Sect to Majority Church: The Ecclesiologies of Parmenian and Tyconius," StPatr 33 (1997), 260–65; *Donatist Martyr Stories: The Church in Conflict in Roman North Africa*, trans. M. A. Tilley (1996).

MAUREEN A. TILLEY

Donne, John (1572–1631), English poet and dean of St. Paul's Cathedral. The most illustrious of the metaphysical poets, Donne was born a Catholic but joined the Anglican Church after his brother died in prison in 1593 for harboring a proscribed priest. As a young man he composed love poetry (later published as *Songs and Sonnets)* and the *Satires.* Beginning in 1596 he took part in naval expeditions to Cadiz and the Azores; on returning to England in 1598 he became secretary to the Lord Keeper of the Great Seal, Thomas Egerton. His secret marriage to Lady Egerton's young niece Anne More in 1601 led to his imprisonment and dismissal. After several difficult years, Donne regained favor for his *Pseudo-Martyr* (1610) and *Igantius his Conclave* (1611), attesting to his Anglican faith. He was ordained a priest in 1615 and was appointed dean of St. Paul's in 1621. Other works include *Devotions upon Emergent Occasions* and the *Divine Poems.*

J. Carey, *John Donne: Life, Mind, and Art* (1981); C. A. Patrides, *The Complete English Poems of John Donne* (1985); C. J. Summers and T.-L. Pebworth, eds., *"Bright Shootes of Everlastingnesse": The Seventeenth-Century Religious Lyric* (1987).

J. LAUREL CARRINGTON

Döring, Matthias (d. 1469). Franciscan reformer. Little is known of Döring's life. He lectured on theology from 1424 in the Franciscan House at the Univ. of Erfurt, Germany, and then became Franciscan minister provincial of Saxony (1427–1461). He was a reformer and Conventual Franciscan and a bitter opponent of the Observant Franciscans. He represented the Univ. of Erfurt at the Council of Basel, and there he was elected the minister general of the German Provinces (1443). He wrote an impressive *Exposition of the Rule* in 1451. Except for a massive *Commentary on Isaiah* and a continuation of the chronicle of Dietrich of Engelhausen (1420–1464), he is known only for his sharp *Replicae (Replies)* to Paul of Burgos's *Additions* to the Literal Postill of Nicholas of Lyra (1270–1349). The *Replicae* are bitter rejections, from a Franciscan perspective, of almost half of the 1,100 criticisms Paul of Burgos had made of Lyra.

S. Brant, ed., *Biblia Latina cum glossa ordinaria Walafridi Strabonis aliorumque et interlineari Anselmi Laudenensis et cum postillis ac moralitatibus Nicolai de Lyra et expositionibus Guillelmi Britonis in omnes prologos S. Hieronymi et additionibus Pauli Burgensis replicisque Mattiae Doering* (1498); P. Albert, *Matthias Döring, ein deutscher Minorit des 15. Jahrhunderts* (1892); L. Oliger, "Matthias Dörings Gutachten über die Franziskaner/regel (1451) und observantische Gegenschrift," in *Franziskanische Studien* 9 (1922): 203–36; J. Moorman, *A History of the Franciscan Order: From Its Origins to the Year 1517* (1968, 1988).

PHILIP D. W. KREY

Dorotheus of Gaza (c. 505–565), ascetical writer. After receiving a good general education, Dorotheus encountered the teachings of Barsanuphius and Evagrius and entered the monastery of Abba Serid in Gaza. Around 540 he founded his own monastery in Gaza and eventually became its archimandrite. The holy places of Palestine attracted monks from the entire Christian world and gave Palestinian monasticism a cosmopolitan character. This is reflected in Dorotheus's series of *Discourses,* which he wrote for his monks. They represent a synthesis of the sayings traditions of Egypt, the Cappadocians, and the teachings of Mark the Hermit. The emphasis of his spiritual teaching is the development of humility. Dorotheus is an important source for the texts of the earlier writers on whom he draws. Theodore the Studite was responsible for diffusing his works through Eastern monastic circles in the ninth century. The seventeenth-century Trappist reformer Abbé de Rance translated them into French for his monks.

PG 88; E. P. Wheeler, *Dorotheus of Gaza: Discourses and Sayings* (1977).

EUGENE M. LUDWIG, OFM CAP.

Dorothy (Schwartze) of Montau

(1347–1394), Catholic saint, visionary. Dorothy was born at Montau-on-the-Vistula, died at Marienwerder, and since the fifteenth century has been regarded as patron saint of Prussia and the Teutonic order.

At the age of six she began a life of mortification, including "invisible stigmata." Dorothy was married at sixteen at Gdansk (Danzig) to Adalbert of Prague, an older, wealthy, pious, but brutal swordsmith with whom she bore nine children, all but one of whom died in childhood. She dedicated a mystical tract to her surviving daughter Gertrude, a Benedictine nun at Kulm. After the deaths of four of her children from plague in 1383, Dorothy and her husband undertook pilgrimages to Aachen, Einsiedeln, Finsterwald, and Rome. Influenced by the life and visions of Brigitte of Sweden (whose relics came to Gdansk in 1374) and subject to visions, Dorothy began to take Communion every week. Prior to her husband's death in 1390, she undertook a life of chastity and in 1393 began living as a recluse at the cathedral of Marienwerder. She placed herself under the spiritual direction of John of Marienwerder (1343–1417), dean of the cathedral and professor at Prague, who began to record her supernatural experiences. In 1396 an abortive canonization procedure (renewed in 1955) began at the request of the head of the Teutonic order, detailing her miracles, cult, and spiritual ministry. John composed six works devoted to Dorothy's life and visions between 1396 and 1404, including three Latin biographies, a German biography, the *Septilium B. Dorotheae montoviensis*, dealing with the seven gifts of grace given to her, and the *Liber de festis*, a collection of her visions according to the liturgical calendar.

Johannes of Marienwerder, *The Life of Dorothea von Montau, a 14th-Century Recluse*, trans. U. Stargardt (1997); Johannes, *Liber de festis magistri Johannis Marienwerder: Offenbarungen der Dorothea von Montau*, ed. A. Triller (1992); R. Stachnik, ed., *Die Akten des Kanonisationsprozesses Dorotheas von Montau von 1394 bis 1521* (1978).

MICHAEL GOODICH†

Dort, Canons of

The doctrinal standard issued by the Synod of Dort rejecting the teachings of Jacob Arminius and the Remonstrant party in the Netherlands. The Canons function as a codicil to the Belgic Confession's teaching on predestination (article 16) and clarify five disputed points of doctrine: (1) that divine election and reprobation are unconditional, that is, not based on foreseen faith; (2) that Christ's atonement is intended and effective solely for the elect; (3) that sinful persons are unable to desire salvation or produce saving faith; (4) that divine grace effects salvation, and is thus irresistible; and (5) that all true believers are preserved in their faith to the end of their lives.

RAYMOND A. BLACKETER

Dort, Synod of

(1618–1619) The most important ecclesiastical assembly in the Dutch reformation and the only Reformed synod of the era that was international in composition and influence. The synod convened to deal with the controversy over the Remonstrant party in the Reformed Church in the Netherlands. The ultimate issue was whether the church would be able to maintain its character as a confessional church with a certain amount of independence from state interference in matters of doctrine, polity, and discipline. The synod was successful in achieving the doctrinal compromise that ensured the church's confessional integrity, but power struggles with the national and provincial governments continued.

Inspired by the teachings of Jacob Arminius and organized under the leadership of Johannes Uitenbogaert, the Remonstrant party had challenged the majority Reformed perspective on predestination and salvation that was represented in the Belgic Confession, article 16. They also envisioned a national church that made room for a diversity of theological views and that would be largely under state control. The Calvinists, for their part, were not about to surrender their hard-won right to exist as a confessional church. Fierce conflicts arose in the churches and universities that posed a serious threat to the unity of both the fragile alliance of Dutch provinces and of its fledgling national church.

The Remonstrants resisted a national synod. Prince Maurits, however, openly sided with the Calvinists, and the States-General convened the synod at Dort. The Remonstrant spokesman at the synod, Leiden professor Simon Episcopius, pursued a policy of dissemblance and obstruction, challenging the authority of the synod, leading to the Remonstrants' summary dismissal from the synod by its president, Johannes Bogerman. After strenuous doctrinal wrangling and compromise among the international gathering of doctrinally diverse but generally Calvinistic delegates, the synod produced its Canons, which refuted the five doctrinal points of the 1610 remonstrance and affirmed the more strictly Augustinian view of predestination advocated by the Calvinists. Some 200 Remonstrant clergy were deposed. The Heidelberg Catechism, the Belgic Confession, and the Canons of Dort became the basis for confessional unity in the Reformed Church in the Netherlands, and remain so for churches descended from it. Two further accomplishments of the synod include providing for a Dutch translation of the Bible (1637) and the drafting of a church order, which often met with resistance from the secular authorities but which remains the basis for polity in churches of the Dutch Reformed tradition.

P. De Jong, ed., *Crisis in the Reformed Churches* (1968); W. van't Spijker et al., *De Synode van Dordrecht in 1618 en 1619* (1987).
                                RAYMOND A. BLACKETER

Dositheus (1641–1707), patriarch of Jerusalem, convener of the Synod of Jerusalem. A native of Greece, Dositheus was placed in the care of the church at an early age. He was archdeacon of Jerusalem and archpriest of Caesarea prior to his appointment as patriarch of Jerusalem in 1669. His best-known achievement was the Synod of Jerusalem (actually held in Bethlehem), convened in order to combat the influence of Protestantism in the Greek Church (1672). Dositheus was the principal author of its decrees and summary statement (the Confession of Dositheus). Protestant influences had entered the church through the work of a previous patriarch of Constantinople, Cyril Lucar (1572–1638). Cyril took advantage of the undefined character of Eastern Orthodox dogma to graft aspects of Protestantism onto Byzantine theology (seeking an ally against the growing regional influence of Roman Catholicism) and in 1629 had supported the publication of a confession of faith that was thoroughly Calvinist. The Confession of Dositheus answered Cyril's confession point by point and is regarded as a document of primary importance in the history of modern Orthodox theology. In order to combat Protestantism, Dositheus drew heavily upon Roman Catholic sources in Orthodoxy's closest approximation to Tridentine Catholicism. Dositheus also published many theological and historical works.

H. M. Biedermann, "Die Confession des Dositheos von Jerusalem (1672)," in *Aus Reformation und Gegenreformation* (1974); Biedermann, *The Acts and Decrees of the Synod of Jerusalem, Sometimes Called the Council of Bethlehem, Holden Under Dositheus, Patriarch of Jerusalem in 1672* (1899, repr. 1969).
                                GREGORY J. MILLER

Douai, College of In the city in the Spanish Netherlands to which many Catholics fled during the English Reformation, this college was founded in 1568 by William Allen (later cardinal) to prepare learned clergy ready to return to England once Roman Catholicism was restored. As hope of restoration faded, hundreds of Douai priests returned to England to minister clandestinely and illegally. Of these, 160 were killed and are commemorated as the Blessed Douai Martyrs. The English translation of the Vulgate, for over three hundred years the only approved English version, bore the college's name.

P. Harris, "The English College, Douai, 1750–1794," *Recusant History* 10 (1969–1970): 79–95; M. Hodgetts, *Secret Hiding-Places* (1989); E. Rose, *Cases of Conscience: Alternatives Open to Recusants and Puritans under Elizabeth I and James I* (1975).
                                PETER J. SCAGNELLI

Doxology The word derives from two Greek words, δόξα (*doxa*), meaning in the ecclesial sense "glory," and λόγος (*logos*), meaning "word." A doxology is an expression of praise of God, especially one in liturgical use. Some scholars narrow the definition to insist that a doxology be brief or to specify that a doxology contain the word δόξα or an equivalent term. The Greek δόξα is the most frequent Septuagint translation of the Hebrew כָּבוֹד (*kābôd*), which carries the sense of a person's essence or intrinsic worth, thus suggesting that doxology ascribes to God God's worth.

In the broader senses of the word there are numerous doxologies in both the Hebrew and the Christian Scriptures and in Jewish and Christian worship. Doxology in the Christian Scriptures is almost exclusively of God, rather than of Christ, although occasionally of God "through" Christ (e.g., Rom. 16:27). The doxologies of 2 Peter 3:18 and Revelation 1:5–6, both late canonical writings, are unequivocally doxologies of Christ. The Christian Scriptures speak of Christ as a sublime expression of God's glory and essence (e.g., John 1:14; Col. 1:15; and Heb. 1:3), an understanding of the relationship of God and Christ that anticipates the church's eventual dogmatic assertion that Christ is fully divine.

Early Christian prayer frequently offers praise to God through Christ (e.g., *Did.* 9) and in or with the Holy Spirit (e.g., Hippolytus, *Trad. ap.*, 4 and 25). Most traditional and contemporary eucharistic prayers of formal Christian liturgy conclude in the same way. The Trinitarian controversy of the fourth century influenced Western doxology toward praise of God as the Father and the Son and the Holy Spirit, thus avoiding any possible subordinationist interpretation. The *Gloria in excelsis Deo*, a very early hymnic expansion of Luke 2:14, is called the Greater Doxology, and the *Gloria Patri*, the Lesser Doxology. The final verse of Thomas Ken's 1674 hymn "Awake My Soul and with the Sun," gave Christians the words of "The Doxology," probably the best-known doxology in Western Christian use today.

P. F. Fink, ed., *The New Dictionary of Sacramental Worship* (1990).

MARY CATHERINE BERGLUND

Dualism The term refers to a metaphysical or moral opposition between two entities or principles. The Bible acknowledges the duality of God and creation but not any intrinsic antagonism between them. Hebrew cosmology includes mythic elements celebrating the Creator's ongoing victory over the forces of chaos and an occasionally appearing Satan-figure, but God's transcendent lordship and love for the creation are not in question. The New Testament reflects the more developed dualistic imagery of intertestamental Judaism and significantly accentuates the antagonism between the Redeemer and the spiritual forces of evil and darkness, including the devil himself. Paul establishes an important moral dualism between "spirit" and "flesh" and an eschatological dualism pitting the present "age" against the "age to come." Yet the flesh remains redeemable, just as the new eschatological age entails the transformation, not the repudiation, of creation and history.

Early Christianity developed a sophisticated response to the severe ontological dualism of the gnostic schools and the less stringent metaphysical dualism of Platonism. Gnostic schools drew from Iranian-Zoroastrian religion, Jewish apocalyptic literature, and Platonic philosophy in elaborating their variant myths of the origin of the material world and conflict among divine principles. The "classic" gnostic myth not only pitted the supreme God against lesser powers but also extrapolated from this opposition an all-out cosmic conflict between the spiritual realm and the material, the latter subjected to a

ruthless subdeity (e.g., OT God). In the second and third centuries Christian writers, notably Irenaeus of Lyon, countered radical gnostic dualism by stressing the Creator's freedom, the continuity between creation and redemption, and the positive role of matter/flesh in the christocentric economy (*oikonomia*) of salvation. Gnostic dualism proved resilient, however, in Manicheism, which found adherents across North Africa and Asia even beyond the Middle Ages. Medieval sectarian groups (e.g., Bogomils, Paulicians, and Cathari) were condemned by the church for entertaining gnostic-type dualistic cosmologies.

Platonic dualism proved conducive to Christian philosophical exploitation. Plato had opposed the divine realm of "ideas" to the material realm but his speculation, as well as that of his commentators, on divine emanation mitigated this ontological dualism. The Greek fathers, and Latins such as Augustine, drew heavily from the Platonic bifurcation of reality, but in their repudiation of emanationist theologies developed the principle of a duality of the Uncreated (Trinity) and the creation bridged solely through the incarnation of the Son of God.

Christian orthodoxy has held to the fundamental spiritual opposition of God and the devil; however, this dualism has rarely provided the basis for a full-blown philosophical explanation of the origin of evil. The battle against gnostic cosmogonies largely inoculated Christianity against the temptation to pin the fallenness of creation on a spiritual power over and beyond human free will.

S. Pétrement, *A Separate God: The Christian Origins of Gnosticism* (1990); K. Rudolph, *Gnosis: The Nature and History of Gnosticism* (1987); S. Runciman, *The Mediaeval Manichee* (1947); W. Wakefield and A. Evans, trans. and eds., *Heresies of the High Middle Ages* (1969).

PAUL M. BLOWERS

Dualism, Medieval Medieval dualism refers to heresies, especially from the eleventh to the fourteenth centuries, based in doctrines that supported a fundamental notion that body and soul, matter and spirit, were so divided, so irreconcilable, that the universe was split by a vast cosmic chasm in which an active devil (or bad god) manipulated the earth and a passive, good god quietly dwelt in heaven. These heresies, as a consequence of this dualism, were described in varying detail as believing that the devil made the visible world, that souls were trapped in corrupting bodies, that marriage was polluting, that no flesh would be resurrected, that baptism was pointless, that the Eucharist was a lie, that the visible church was irrelevant, and that Christ never had a physical form but was pure spirit. These dualist heretics, scattered from the Mediterranean to the North Sea, from the Balkans to the Pyrénnées, were variously labelled "Manicheans," "Arians," "Publicani," "Paterini," "Albigenses," "gazars," "Cathars," and "good men." Modern scholars have, with very little justification, grouped all these dualist heretics under the confusing and misleading rubric of "Catharism." In the end, though, what Latin Christian descriptions of dualism reveal, powerfully and somewhat paradoxically, was an antidualism that saw the potential for heresy in almost anything and everything that was vaguely dissenting from the church.

The Benedictine Ademar of Chabannes, in the chronicle he wrote at the Abbey of St.-Cybard in Angoulême, noted in 1022, "Manicheans were discovered and destroyed at Toulouse." These Toulousain heretics, far from being historically alone, were the direct heirs of the third-century dualist heresiarch Mani and the corrupt allies of other "messagers of the Antichrist who appeared in various parts of the West." Ademar of Chabannes was one of a handful of eleventh-century Latin Christian intellectuals writing and worrying about heresy for the first time since late antiquity. The disturbing problem about this new awareness of heresy is whether such heterodoxy actually existed independently of the apocalyptic (and so historical) necessity of populating the world with heretics from the millennium onward. "There must be heresies," Rudulfus Glaber agreed with and quoted Paul around 1030, so "that they who are of the Faith may be proved." The apparent emergence of dualist heresies in the eleventh century was, more than anything else, the initial articulation of a literary and idealist model that saw all heretics as linked to each other through time and space, as hellish individuals connected to the divinely marvellous, and as an essential Christian phenomenon perpetually tinged with an apocalyptic and dualistic hue.

This is the temporal paradox of all medieval descriptions of heretical dualism (especially in the twelfth, thirteenth, and fourteenth centuries). As heretical events were narrated, as heterodox stories were told, time itself was flattened by the timeless audacity of dualism. A kind of heretical essentialism, immune to historical change, was actually confirmed, over and over again, by the very act of writing and talking about heresy. "For I do not recall having heard anything new or extraordinary in all their assertions," the great and severe Cistercian Bernard of Clairvaux preached about heretical dualist ideas in 1144, "but only trite commonplaces long vented amongst the heretics of old." Seventy years later, the Cistercian Pierre des Vaux-de-Cernay wrote that dualism in the Toulousain "was passed from father to son, one after the other," and so "infected with this ancient filth were the people of Toulouse" that nothing seemed capable of persuading the current "generation of vipers" to shed "their essential heretical tendencies" or overthrow "their natural disposition to embrace heresy." The historical truth revealed, and proved in every anecdote and in the repetitive use of ancient names like "Manichean," was the knowledge that heresy had always been with us and that heretics were never isolated, never unconnected to each other, but always organized, always threatening.

Crucially, although the learned medieval mind might classify a twelfth-century heresy as similar to a heterodox creed from the fourth, or adopt an ancient word to explain a thirteenth-century belief, or think that dualist errors had always lingered in the world, such explanations should not persuade modern scholars to adopt almost identical approaches. Admittedly, tracing the origins of medieval dualism all the way back to the Manicheans, though still to be found, is far less common than a century ago. A scholarly variation on this theme has the *gnosis* of Mani sneaking back into medieval Latin Christianity through the Byzantine Bogomils who, it is tacitly understood, were undoubtedly influenced by this dualist heresy. As for there being any genuine intimacy between the Bogomils and Western European dualism, it is neither obvious nor irrefutable that such a liaison ever existed. Indeed, the suggestion that Bogomil preachers were in Europe from the first millennium onward and that these Bosnian or Bulgarian seers were the cause of almost all eleventh-century heresy is simply untenable. A more nuanced vision imagines Balkan missionaries only coming to Europe in the twelfth century. Unfortunately, despite some allusions to dualism arriving from the eastern Mediterranean in the twelfth and thirteenth centuries, as well as the small number of questionable references to Byzantine heretical holy men, the efforts to truly link the Bogomils to Latin Christian dualists remain unconvincing. In the end, arguments about the influence of the

Bogomils upon Western European heresy, whether in the eleventh or in the twelfth centuries, rely upon detecting likenesses between ideas (or rituals or doctrines) irrespective of time and place.

In stark contrast to the articulate and coherent dualism described by Latin Christian intellectuals, especially in the thirteenth century, were the testimonies collected by Dominican and Franciscan inquisitors into heretical depravity in the same decades. Thousands of ordinary men and women confessed to intermittently dualist beliefs that were quite malleable, not always opposed to the church, and distinctly localized. The mistake has been to assume that these men and women, heretical or not, necessarily went through life with strict dualist structures shaping their minds and determining their actions, to the exclusion of all else. Dualist ideas, as far as they were understood, and the beliefs of priests or mendicants, as far as these were understood, frequently lived together in the thoughts of medieval persons. This seeming paradox makes the thinking of so many ordinary people in the Middle Ages appear, at least to modern eyes, as often shallow, equivocal, and incoherent. This contradiction between the articulate heresies condemned in learned sermons or histories and the halting inconsistent ideas recorded in inquisition trials necessitates, at the very least, more wariness than is usually given in the general interpretation of medieval dualism.

———

M. G. Pegg, *A Most Holy War: The Albigensian Crusade and the Battle for Christendom* (2007); Pegg, *The Corruption of Angels* (2001); Pegg, "'Catharism' and the Study of Medieval Heresy," *New Medieval Literatures* 6 (2004): 249–69; C. Taylor, *Heresy in Medieval France: Dualism in Aquitaine and the Agenais* (2005).

MARK GREGORY PEGG

Duns Scotus, John   *see* Scotus, John Duns

Duplessis-Mornay, Philippe (1549–1623), Huguenot military leader, diplomat, statesman, and theologian. Born into a confessionally divided family, Duplessis-Mornay completed humanist studies in Paris and in a tour of Europe before committing himself to the Protestant cause in France. He was in Paris in August 1572 for the royal wedding of Henry of Navarre and Marguerite of Valois but man-

aged to escape the St. Bartholomew's Day Massacre. He later entered Henry's service in 1577 and made diplomatic missions to England, the Netherlands, and Germany to raise military and financial support among foreign Protestant powers for the Huguenot struggle. Duplessis-Mornay also distinguished himself as a writer of several theological and polemical tracts. He likely had a hand in composing *Vindiciae contra Tyrannos* (1579), which advocated a people's right to resist their prince if he broke divine and natural law; such resistance, however, was legitimate only if directed by nobles and magistrates.

After helping to negotiate peace between Henry of Navarre and Henry III in 1589, Duplessis-Mornay was made governor of the town of Saumur. When Henry of Navarre succeeded to the throne of France (as Henry IV in 1589), Duplessis-Mornay became his most trusted advisor, offering counsel in military, diplomatic, and economic matters as well as shaping religious policy. He ceaselessly urged conciliation between Catholics and Protestants in France and warned Huguenots against taking up arms to defend their interests. However, his appeals for caution went unheeded, and with his authority among the Huguenot leadership waning, Duplessis-Mornay was removed from his governorship in 1621 and died two years later at his estate at La Forêt-sur-Sèvre.

———

H. Daussy, *Les Huguenots et le roi: le combat politique de Philippe Duplessis-Mornay, 1572–1600* (2002); A. Herman, "Protestant Churches in a Catholic Kingdom: Political Assemblies in the Thought of Philippe Duplessis-Mornay," *SCJ* 21 (1990): 543–57.

SCOTT M. MARR

Dura Europos   Mid-third-century city, situated on the eastern frontier of the Roman Empire, a military outpost and a port city on the Euphrates River. Although today in eastern Syria, it began as a Hellenistic colony and was held in succession by Parthians, Romans, and Sassanians. Excavations conducted jointly by French and American archaeologists from the 1920s through the 1940s unearthed the architectural remains that were either covered over or destroyed during the last battle between the Romans and their Persian enemies.

The most significant of the buildings excavated were thirteen separate pagan temples dedicated to a variety of traditional Roman and

Palmyrene deities, a mithraeum, a Jewish synagogue, and the earliest known and best-preserved Christian house church. All the buildings contained wall paintings that combined Eastern and Western styles and reflected the influence of Palmyrene or Parthian artisans. Both the Christian building and the synagogue had been converted from domestic structures.

The synagogue is particularly noted for its extensive, well-preserved, beautiful murals based on biblical narratives and some midrashic traditions. The Christian building, in addition to a large hall for assembly (like the synagogue), had a separate baptismal chamber that contained a rectangular basin at its western end, set under a vaulted canopy supported by heavy columns. The canopy and the side walls were covered with decorative, painted images. Behind the font the figure of the Good Shepherd appeared with Adam and Eve. The adjoining walls showed scenes from the New Testament, including Jesus stilling the storm, walking on the water, meeting the woman at the well, and an image that has been identified both as the woman arriving at the Christ's empty tomb, or the wise virgins arriving at the tent of the bridegroom.

C. Hopkins, *The Discovery of Dura-Europos* (1979); M. Rostovtzeff, *Dura-Europos and Its Art* (1938); A Perkins, *The Art of Dura Europos* (1973); L. M. White, *Building God's House in the Roman World* (1989).

ROBIN M. JENSEN

Dürer, Albrecht (1471–1528), magisterial and innovative German artist of Nuremberg, whose work consists of woodcuts, engravings, drawings, watercolors, and paintings, as well as treatises on human proportion, fortifications, and artistic theory. Dürer revolutionized the concept of the artist through his series of self-portraits and autobiographical writings. After traveling in Italy in 1494 and 1505, he introduced Renaissance ideals and forms in northern Europe. Dürer's greatest influence · was through his graphic work. His most famous woodcut series appears in the *Apocalypse* (1498), an oversized book that Dürer illustrated, printed, and published himself. Two of its full-page images are particularly creative and iconographically complex: *The Four Horsemen* and *John Devouring the Book*. Some of his other outstanding prints include *The Prodigal Son* (1497), *Adam and Eve* (1504), *Knight, Death, and the Devil* (1513), and *Saint*

Jerome in His Study (1514). Dürer's paintings include portraits and religious subjects, and the watercolors from his Italian voyages offer subtle evocations of atmosphere and superbly scientific depictions of animals and plants. He sought the company of humanists and scholars, like Willibrand Pirckheimer and Erasmus of Rotterdam. Compositional details of the *Last Supper* woodcut (1523) deviate from convention and emphasize Dürer's positive response to Luther's theology.

J. C. Hutchison, *Albrecht Dürer: A Biography* (1990); J. L. Koerner, *The Moment of Self-Portraiture in German Renaissance Art* (1993); E. Panofsky, *The Life and Art of Albrecht Dürer* (1943, 1971); D. Smith and L. Guenther, *Realism and Invention in the Prints of Albrecht Dürer* (1995).

PRISCILLA BAUMANN

Dyophysitism The term is a pejorative label referring to those who advocated the "Two natures" of Christ. It arose in the mid-fifth-century christological debates and was used by the Monophysite party, who advocated "one nature" of Christ, to identify what they perceived to be the essential fault of their opposition: that in the incarnation of Jesus Christ his person comprised two natures (*phūsis*), one human and one divine. Monophysites held that there was only one nature of Christ in one person, brought about by a *hypostatic* union of the divine and human natures, that is, a union of the natures in the *hypostasis* ("subsistence") of the Son. The Monophysites accused their opponents of creating two separate Christs, one human and one divine. Conversely, the Dyophysite advocates argued that the concept of a single nature of Christ obscured his humanity.

The term was initially targeted against Nestorius in the debates culminating in his condemnation at the Council of Ephesus (431). Nestorius reputedly had declared that Christ possessed two natures, each with its own distinct *prosōpon* ("person"). Nestorius would dispute this interpretation of his teaching, although he clearly saw the necessity of two natures in order to protect the human and salvific qualities of Christ.

During the controversy following the Council of Chalcedon (451), the term was applied from a different angle by the Monophysites to describe those who subscribed to the formula of Chalcedon. This formula said that Christ existed in two natures, human and divine, in one *hypostasis* or person. In early Monophysite polemic, authors such as Philoxenus of Mabbug and Severus of Antioch accused Chalcedonians of being essentially Nestorians.

The distinction between the Dyophysite positions is subtle but significant. Chalcedon declared that there was only one *hypostasis* in the incarnate Christ, the result of the hypostatic union of the divine and human natures; Nestorius and his successors, especially Babai the Great (d. 628), argued that a nature could not be separated from its *hypostasis*. Christ possessed two natures and two *hypostases*, coinciding and connecting in the one person of Jesus Christ, not by hypostatic union but by "the good pleasure" of God.

The Nestorian perspective, and to a lesser extent the Chalcedonian, is derived from Antiochene scriptural exegesis that stressed the literal and historical senses. It placed emphasis upon the humanity of Christ and his genuine moral decisions.

The Chalcedonian formula provides the theological legacy for most of Western Christianity. Nestorius and the Syriac-speaking churches that carried on his name identify Theodore of Mopsuestia (350–428) as their true theological and biblical teacher. The term "Nestorian" is understood as inappropriate today. The (Assyrian) Church of the East is the formal name for the descendant communities.

———

W. H. C. Frend, *The Rise of the Monophysite Movement* (1972); A. Grillmeier, *Christ in Christian Tradition*, vol. 1 (1965, 1975); D. S. Wallace-Hadrill, *Christian Antioch: A Study of Early Christian Thought in the East* (1982); J. Pelikan, *The Emergence of the Catholic Tradition (100–600)*, vol. 1 of *The Christian Tradition: A History of the Development of Doctrine* (1971).

ROBERT A. KITCHEN

Early Christian Apocalyptic Literature

Apocalypticism, a widely variegated worldview espoused by some Jews, Christians, and pagans in the Greco-Roman period, envisioned an imminent end to the world of time and space and a dramatic establishment of a new reality rooted in the transcendent plan of God. This eschatological vision came to expression in much of early Christian literature, but especially in a literary genre called "apocalypse" (from the Greek *apokalypsis*, "unveiling"). This genre typically includes several elements: pseudonymous authorship, reports of visions in highly symbolic language, a heavenly interpreter who explains the revelation, a dualistic worldview that distinguishes between the present evil age of this world and the world to come, a linear view of history that unfolds according to the divine plan, predictions of an imminent confrontation between the forces of evil and the forces of good, and symbolic descriptions of "a new heaven and a new earth."

The last book of the New Testament, Revelation, is the only NT example of an apocalypse, but much of the NT and other early Christian writings reflect an apocalyptic perspective on Jesus and the kingdom of God. Paul's letters, especially 1 Thessalonians, describe his apocalyptic expectation that "the day of the Lord will come like a thief in the night" (1 Thess. 5:2), and in 1 Corinthians Paul instructs his readers that "the appointed time has grown very short" (1 Cor. 7:29) and "the form of this world is passing away" (1 Cor. 7:31). The Synoptic Gospels, especially Mark, depict Jesus proclaiming that the kingdom of God is at hand. For the earliest Christians, the resurrection of Jesus marked the decisive victory in God's cosmic battle against the forces of evil. In their view, the present evil age had been overcome and was in its death throes. Faith in Jesus promised the believer eternal life in the world to come, when Jesus would render final judgment on sin and death and the powerful governments of this world. Before the end of the first century, many early Christians modified their expectations of the imminent return of Jesus as the Son of Man on the clouds of heaven into a generalized affirmation of God's control of history even though the timetable could not be precisely known.

The book of Revelation is dated by most scholars to the end of the first century CE and is attributed to John, although this is probably not the apostle John or the writer of the Gospel of John or the Johannine epistles. It manifests some of the most striking characteristics of early Christian apocalyptic literature. Its symbolic language describes dramatic visions of the cosmic struggle between God and the forces of evil. Scenes of worship in the heavenly Jerusalem where the resurrected Jesus reigns victoriously are juxtaposed with exhortations to endurance in the face of persecution as the present evil age moves toward its inevitable defeat.

Other early Christian apocalyptic expectations are reflected in the *Didache*, the *Shepherd of Hermas*, the Greek *Apocalypse of Peter*, and in several gnostic apocalyptic texts. A late first-century Christian writing, the *Didache* concludes with a short apocalyptic discourse similar to Mark 13 and Matthew 24. The *Shep-*

herd of Hermas, usually dated to early in the second century and linked with Rome, contains extensive vision reports and a pervasive apocalyptic eschatology that reflect the persecution of Christians and their ultimate redemption. Another document dated by most scholars to the second century, the Greek *Apocalypse of Peter*, contains a dialogue between Jesus and his disciples, especially Peter, on the Mount of Olives and vision reports featuring descriptions of the punishments of the wicked in hell and the heavenly redemption of believers.

Several gnostic writings dated to the second and third centuries are apocalypses containing gnostic interpretations of Jesus as the bearer of heavenly knowledge (*gnosis*). The *Apocryphon of John*, the Coptic *Apocalypse of Peter*, and two apocalypses attributed to the apostle James are among the gnostic texts from Nag Hammadi that were discovered in 1946. The gnostic apocalypses typically shift the focus from temporal eschatological speculation to descriptions of the heavenly world and the disclosure of secret knowledge as the key to personal salvation for the gnostic believer.

Speculation of the kind found in early Christian apocalyptic literature has had spokespersons throughout the history of Christianity, especially from those who perceive themselves to be alienated from the dominant culture or imbued with a radical new vision of the kingdom of God.

J. J. Collins, *The Apocalyptic Imagination* (2nd ed., 1998).

　　　　　　　　　　　　　　JAMES BRASHLER

Early Christian Architecture　*see* Architecture in Early Christianity

Early Christian Art　*see* Art in Early Christianity

Early Christian Ethics and Social Teaching　*see* Ethics and Social Teaching, Early Christian

Early Christian Hymns　*see* Hymns, Early Christian

Early Christian Rhetoric　By the first century CE in the Roman Empire, rhetoric had ceased to play a role in shaping policy but was still the capstone of a classical education among the elite. Christians' zeal to proclaim the good news and their need to defend themselves, to resolve theological differences, and to edify the faithful contributed to a revival of rhetoric as a powerful tool to shape hearts and minds. Recognizing the conventions of rhetoric in early Christian literature, indeed in the formation of biblical exegesis, is important for understanding the context and interpreting the theology of the period.

Christians held two basic positions regarding classical education and rhetoric. Taking a cue from Paul's comments about the foolishness of human wisdom, some Christians (e.g., Tatian, Tertullian) rejected worldly education, even while using their own training on behalf of Christianity. Others followed Justin's claim to all truth, regardless of its origin, for the use of true philosophy, or Christianity. Origen described this selective use of non-Christian culture as "plundering the Egyptians." Thus, Christian leaders such as Gregory of Nazianzus, John Chrysostom, Ambrose of Milan, and Augustine of Hippo made free use of the entire toolbox of classical rhetoric.

Rhetoric taught students strategies for oral and written composition. Christians came to describe their use of rhetoric as dedicated to speaking the truth with clarity, in contrast to the exaggerated language of secular rhetoric used to entertain or flatter. While Augustine followed the Ciceronian divisions of rhetoric into speech that instructs, delights, and persuades, Christian rhetoric also developed its own characteristics influenced by hymnody, prayer, the liturgical context of homilies, and emphasis on the lectionary and liturgical calendar. The most obvious shifts included incorporating biblical language (deemed barbaric by the intelligentsia) and preparing homilies that had to reach a variety of social and educational levels.

At the end of early Christianity the East continued to use classical Greek texts on rhetoric, while in the disintegrated western Roman world texts such as Augustine's *On Christian Doctrine* summarized classical theory for later preachers. Both East and West utilized homiletic and epistolary collections as models.

P. Brown, *Power and Persuasion in Late Antiquity* (1992); D. G. Hunter, ed., *Preaching in the Patristic Age* (1989); G. A. Kennedy, *Greek Rhetoric under Christian Emperors* (1983); J. L. Kinneavy, *Greek Rhetorical Origins of Christian Faith* (1987); H.-I. Marrou, *A History of Education in Antiquity* (1956); S. E. Porter, ed., *Handbook of Classical Rhetoric in the Hellenistic Period 330 B.C.–A.D. 400* (1997).

　　　　　　　　　　LISA D. MAUGANS DRIVER

Early Christianity and Paganism
see Paganism and Early Christianity

Early Modern Catholicism

Over the last century and a half Reformation historiography has hummed with efforts to characterize accurately "the Catholic side of things." Scholars have proposed and rejected a number of labels. For example, "Tridentine Catholicism" appropriately focuses on the continuities and changes embodied in the decrees of the Council of Trent but overprivileges episcopal reform and ignores dimensions such as Catholic missions. Recently enthusiasm has been growing for the phrase "early modern Catholicism." It is loose enough to hold the complex particularity of early modern Catholic experience without the baggage that vitiates other limiting terms. Its vagueness, in short, is its virtue. Constructively, it identifies a cultural system with four fundamental characteristics: it is local, dynamic, stratified, and complex.

First, the church experienced by early modern Catholics was incontestably local. With their particular saints, holy places, devotions, liturgical practices, and customs, local churches met the universal church of hierarchy and doctrine in the person of the parish priest, who mediated—sometimes uneasily—between them. Even matters of universal applicability were dependent upon secular governments for their local dissemination. Thus, the Tridentine decrees were not published in France until decades after the close of the council. "Early modern Catholicism" requires room for a Gallican Catholic Church as well as a Roman Catholic Church.

Second, early modern Catholicism was a dynamic system. Its structures and institutions proved resilient and adaptable. For example, the missions in Asia and the new world stimulated new pastoral practices and opportunities for reconsidering Catholic identity, and Catholic controversialists were as active in the new genre of catechetics as their Protestant counterparts. Sometimes this dynamism resulted in uncomfortable conflicts, when, for example, an older generation of priests came into conflict with a generation of successors trained in a different milieu and with different expectations. Nevertheless, "early modern Catholicism" is broad enough to capture the range of dynamism otherwise ignored or muted by narrower formulas.

Third, early modern Catholicism was stratified both horizontally and vertically. It admitted two fundamental distinctions: clergy and laity. The clergy, in turn, was divided horizontally into secular clergy, who provided pastoral ministry, and regular clergy who lived under a rule of life as monks and nuns or mendicants. The clergy were also vertically stratified, from parish priests who dressed, spoke, and looked like their parishioners, to the university-educated clerics who conducted the church's business, to the highest realms of the hierarchy. The laity too were stratified vertically, of course, but also horizontally. Members of confraternities enjoyed the responsibilities and privileges offered by such organizations, and men and women of all classes sought the intercession of spiritual patrons identified with issues and concerns pertaining to their social class, occupation, or gender. "Early modern Catholicism" requires the scholar to integrate, however uneasily, the richness of these dimensions into a single system.

Finally, early modern Catholics experienced their religion as a complex cultural system that included the dimensions of both practice and belief. Ritual relationships structured time, space, and reality itself. The sacraments, especially the Eucharist and penance, but also a penumbra of minor rituals, practices, devotions, prayers, and beliefs, textured the fabric of Catholicism for early modern Europeans and their converts around the world. But early modern Catholicism was also structured and given meaning by a theological framework into which most of that religious culture fit coherently. There were certainly points of conflict—as for example, when reforming bishops sought to impose social and religious discipline on their parishioners and curb "superstitious" practices and beliefs—but for the most part religious and theological culture interpreted and reinforced each other. Although the gulf between the church of correct belief and the church of proper devotional practice lessened in the latter half of the sixteenth century, both remained appropriate expressions of early modern Catholicism. "Early modern Catholicism" does not by itself capture the variety and complexity of the system sketched above. What it does is prevent other formulas from restricting the scope of scholarly inquiry and imagination. In that sense, the phrase does invaluable duty as a placeholder for scholars to fill with more and more nuanced meaning.

———

H. O. Evennett, *The Spirit of the Counter-Reformation* (1968); R. P. Hsia, *The World of Catholic Renewal, 1540–1770* (1998); H. Jedin, *Katholische Reformation oder Gegenreformation? Ein Versuch zur Klärung der Begriffe nebst einer Jubiläumsbetrachtung über das Trienter Konzil* (1946); J. O'Malley,

Trent and All That: Renaming Catholicism in the Early Modern Era (2000).

BENJAMIN W. WESTERVELT

Eastern Catholic Churches   *see* Uniate Churches

Ebionites

The term refers to a group of Jewish Christians attested from the second to the fourth century. Deriving from the Hebrew word for "poor," their name may reflect an asceticism of voluntary poverty, although Origen derides it as indicating their poverty of understanding (*De principiis* 4.3.8). Irenaeus provides the earliest testimony, noting that they used a version of Matthew's Gospel but rejected Paul (*Haer.* 1.26.2; 3.11.7) and did not admit the virgin birth (*Haer.* 3.21.1; 5.1.3). Hippolytus (*Haer.* 7.34) notes their adherence to Torah. Epiphanius (*Pan.* 30) offers extensive testimony, citing seven fragments of an otherwise unattested *Gospel of the Ebionites*. One of the extant fragments of the Gospel, probably a harmony of Synoptic materials, highlights the baptism of Jesus (*Pan.* 30.13.6) and uses the language of Psalm 2:7: "this day I have begotten you" (cf. Heb. 1:5; Luke 3:22). The language could imply adoptionism or, more likely, manifest the status of Jesus as Son of God (*Pan.* 30.13.7–8). This focus, and perhaps the language, may have led to the judgment of Tertullian (*Carn. Chr.* 14) that the Ebionites held a low Christology, maintaining that Jesus was a "mere man." Epiphanius, however, indicates that they were not simple adoptionists but held that Christ, though not begotten of the Father, was an angel or archangel (*Pan.* 30.16.4). Also, according to Epiphanius, they construed the saying about the true family of Jesus as a denial of his humanity (*Pan.* 30.14.5). Eusebius, perhaps reporting on another group of Ebionites, claims that they affirmed the virgin birth but denied the preexistence of Christ (*Hist. eccl.* 3.27.1–3). A focus on Israel appears in their account of the commission of the twelve apostles, as a "testimony for Israel" (Epiphanius, *Pan.* 30.13.2–3). They rejected the cultic system, attributing to Christ a saying that he had come to do away with sacrifices (*Pan.* 30.16.4; cf. Acts 7:41–50; Heb. 10:5–10). They also seem to have practiced vegetarianism, a stance reflected in their account of the Baptist's locust-free diet (*Pan.* 30.13.4) and a saying of Jesus that he did not come to eat flesh at Passover (*Pan.* 30.22.4).

A. F. J. Klijn and G. J. Reinink, *Patristic Evidence for Jewish-Christian Sects* (1973).

HAROLD W. ATTRIDGE

Ecclesiastical Centers of Early Christianity

Although in the first centuries—as for many centuries afterward—the vast majority of Christians lived in small towns or in the countryside, much of the church's organization and doctrine arose in large urban centers. This circumstance paralleled the political structure of the day: the emperor reigned in Rome and the provincial governors resided in capital cities. Some Christian centers took their importance from their founding; others from their size, intellectual influence, or political connections.

Jerusalem was the first Christian center. The earliest community, led by Jesus' closest disciples, experienced the Holy Spirit there at Pentecost and made the momentous decision to evangelize and proselytize. Leadership in this community passed to James, identified in the Acts of the Apostles as the brother of Jesus. He represented the conservative wing that wished to evangelize primarily if not exclusively among Jews. The importance of this community forced the apostle Paul to report to James, who, to his great credit, agreed that the faith should be preached to the Gentiles. James was martyred by hostile Jews c. 62. An ancient tradition says that the Jerusalem Christian community fled to the pagan town of Pella after the Romans destroyed Jerusalem in 70. Jerusalem did not become a major center of Christianity again until the fourth century under the leadership of a bishop named Cyril, but by then other centers had arisen, and Jerusalem never regained its original stature.

Antioch became the second center of Christianity. Paul began his missionary journeys from Antioch, the city where Jesus' followers were first called Christians, and possibly the home of both the Gospels of Matthew and Luke. In the early second century, letters by Antioch's bishop Ignatius show that the monarchical episcopate had emerged there, possibly as a way to counter factionalism, but this individual rule by the bishop would soon be the standard. A major port city in the important province of Syria, Antioch was the third city of the Roman Empire in size and stature, and its Christian community had considerable influence. It developed its own theological school, which focused on the historical exegesis of Scripture and on the independence of the persons of the Trinity, although these traits are noticeable mostly by contrast with the theological school of Alexandria. The greatest names of the Antiochene school were John Chrysostom, Nestorius, Theodore of Mopsuestia, and Theodoret of Cyrrhus.

By the 60s, the Roman community had enough stature to warrant from the apostle Paul his only letter to a church he did not found. Tradition claims Peter as the founder. Although Peter was resident there, he did not establish the community. Roman tradition reports that both Peter and Paul suffered martyrdom there, and Rome later claimed a double apostolic foundation. First in size and stature, the imperial capital gave the Roman church great influence, especially over other Western European churches. The community produced no great theological school. Indeed, many of Rome's most original thinkers (the Monarchians, Hippolytus, Novatian) were rejected by the community; only one bishop, Leo I, influenced doctrinal development. But the bishops of Rome began asserting a jurisdictional primacy as early as the third century, and Roman leadership of the Western European churches forced Eastern councils to seek Rome's agreement, thus making it a peripheral but significant player in doctrinal issues. In the fourth and fifth centuries, when the Roman Empire began to separate culturally and then later politically into a Western, Latin part and an Eastern, Greek part, the Roman church became even more important as the first church of the Latin European Christians.

Rome's only rival in the Latin West was Carthage, primal see of North African Christianity. No one knows how the faith arrived in Africa, but c. 180 Christians from Scilli became the first African martyrs. The Africans considered their church a gathering of saints, separated from the outside world of the pagans and also from those Christians who differed from the Africans on doctrine or practice. In the third century Tertullian disparaged the appropriation of pagan culture in some other churches, such as Alexandria, while Cyprian compared the church to Noah's ark: those not on board will drown. While these attitudes influenced many later Africans, such as the Donatists, the independent African bishops who met in yearly council guaranteed that Carthage never achieved the status of Antioch or Rome.

Brilliantly situated by Alexander the Great, the Nile-Mediterranean port of Alexandria was second only to Rome in size and stature. Christianity may have arrived there in the first century. By the second century we know of a catechetical school for the training of converts. This school developed into the leading intellectual center of the ancient church, including pioneering scholars such as Clement and Origen and major figures in the Trinitarian and christological controversies, such as Arius, Athanasius,

and Cyril. The Alexandrians emphasized the allegorical interpretation of Scripture and the unity of the persons in the Trinity, yet these traits stand out primarily in contrast to the Antiochene school. Alexandria had wealthy and powerful bishops, such as Theophilus and Cyril, who determined that their church would be the leader of the Christian East, and these bishops did not hesitate to use their wealth and power to maintain that leadership, especially against the upstart bishops of Constantinople.

There is no question when Christianity arrived in Constantinople because the emperor Constantine inaugurated it as a Christian capital in 330 and moved there himself. With easy access to the imperial court in an era when emperors routinely involved themselves in church matters, even doctrinal ones, the bishops of Constantinople soon gained great influence and engendered great resentment, especially in Alexandria. The city was host to the Second Ecumenical Council in 381. Its bishops included such great names as Gregory of Nazianzus (379–381) and John Chrysostom (398–404). Tellingly, the former resigned and the latter was deposed, among other reasons because of Alexandrian opposition. Two other bishops, Nestorius and Flavian, also fell victim to Alexandrian machinations. This imperial bishopric achieved real importance only after the Monophysite schism severely weakened Alexandria and the Eastern emperors increasingly relied upon the bishops of their capital.

G. W. Bowersock, ed., *Late Antiquity: A Guide to the Postclassical World* (1999); R. Krautheimer, *Three Christian Capitals: Topography and Politics* (1983); R. Wilken, *The Land Called Holy* (1992).

JOSEPH F. KELLY

Ecclesiola in Ecclesia   This term means "small church within the church." To address the low level of German piety, the Pietist founder Philipp Jakob Spener instituted a reform program in the 1670s centered on meetings in homes in addition to Sunday worship. Men and women, and nobles and artisans, met during the week for Bible study and encouragement.

H. Yeide, *Studies in Classical Pietism: The Flowering of the Ecclesiola* (1997).

DOUGLAS H. SHANTZ

Eck, Johannes (1486–1543), humanist, priest, theologian. Eck was born in Egg on the Günz, Germany. He studied first at Heidelberg, learning Hebrew and Greek. At Tübingen he received the degree of master of arts in 1501. At Cologne and Freiburg he studied philosophy, theology, jurisprudence, physics, mathematics, and geography and received his doctoral degree in theology at the age of twenty-four. He was ordained to the priesthood in 1508 with a papal dispensation from the age requirement. He became professor of theology in Ingolstadt. His *Chrysopassus* (1514) examines predestination, grace, and free choice. In 1519 he disputed with Luther and Karlstadt at Leipzig, an event that proved to be the turning point in his development and activities. Eck became a papal legate in 1520 in order to carry out the provisions of the bull of excommunication against Luther, which he had promoted in Rome. The *Enchiridion of Commonplaces of John Eck against Luther and Other Enemies of the Church* of 1525 became his most influential work with its 121 editions, including German, French, and Flemish translations. He spent his life opposing the Reformers in Germany and Switzerland, especially during the Diet of Augsburg in 1530 and the Colloquies in Worms and Regensburg in the 1540s. Eck also went on a mission to England and the Netherlands in the interest of the Catholic cause. In 1537 he published a German version of the Scriptures, translating the Old Testament from the original and adopting Emser's German translation of the New Testament. With his *Ains Judenbuechlins Verlegung* of 1541 he questioned Andreas Osiander's positive attitude toward the Jews.

F. L. Battles, trans., *Enchiridion of Commonplaces of John Eck against Luther and Other Enemies of the Church* (1978); D. V. N. Bagchi, *Luther's Earliest Opponents: Catholic Controversialists, 1518–1525* (1991); R. Rosin, trans., "John Eck's Four Hundred Four Articles for the Imperial Diet at Augsburg," in *Sources and Contexts of "The Book of Concord,"* ed. R. Kolb and J. A. Nestingen (2001), 31–82.

FRANZ POSSET

Eckhart, Meister (c. 1260–1328), German
theologian, philosopher, and mystic. Born in Tambach near Gotha (Thuringia), Eckhart entered the Dominican order as a young man. He studied philosophy and theology in Erfurt and Cologne, maybe while Albert the Great was still teaching there. In 1293/1294 Eckhart held a position as a lecturer on the *Sentences* at the Univ. of Paris. His order sent him to Paris two more times as a professor of theology

(*magister,* thus the name "Meister Eckhart"), first in 1302, then in 1311–1313. Between these periods of academic teaching, Eckhart held important offices in the administration of his order. He was prior of the Dominican convent in Erfurt and vicar of the Dominican province of Thuringia, provincial of the province of Saxonia, and in 1307 vicar general of Bohemia. Eckhart moved to Strasbourg in 1314, where he seems to have been involved with the tensions surrounding the local Beguine movement, and finally to Cologne (at the earliest in 1323). There an inquisitorial process was initiated by the local bishop in 1325, leading to the condemnation of seventeen sentences taken from his works as heretical and eleven as suspect of heresy. The papal bull condemning these sentences was published on March 27, 1329, several months after Eckhart's death.

In his works, mainly biblical commentaries in Latin, sermons in Latin and in the vernacular, and German treatises, Eckhart brings together a strong philosophical, theological, and spiritual interest. In the commentary on the Gospel of John he expresses the intent to read the Scriptures "in philosophical terms." Referring to the authority of Aristotle, Augustine, Averroes, Albert the Great, and their discussions about the nature of the intellect, he links a philosophical perspective to a strong emphasis on negative theology, on hermeneutics (quoting Maimonides extensively), and on the "birth of God in the soul," a concept he inherited from the church fathers. Arguing that the evangelical precept of poverty should be applied to the "ground of the soul" and read in terms of "detachment," Eckhart focuses on the "birth of God in the soul" in every person and on the unity between man and God. Based on these teachings, Eckhart has been read as a mystic since the nineteenth century, although he does not use the term or discuss personal mystical experience. Major German philosophers, among them Hegel and Heidegger, have been influenced by Eckhart's thought. In the twentieth century he became one of the key figures in comparative religious studies, especially in discussions of the relations between Eastern and Christian forms of mysticism (R. Otto, D. T. Suzuki).

Meister Eckhart, *The Essential Sermons, Commentaries, Treatise, and Defense* (1981); A. Hollywood, *The Soul as Virgin Wife: Mechthild of Magdeburg, Marguerite Porete, and Meister Eckhart* (1995); B. McGinn, *Meister Eckhart and the Beguine Mystics: Hadewijch of*

Brabant, Mechthild of Magdeburg, and Marguerite Porete (1994); B. McGinn, *The Mystical Thought of Meister Eckhart: The Man from Whom God Hid Nothing* (2001); B. Mojsisch, *Meister Eckhart: Analogy, Univocity, and Unity* (2001).

NIKLAUS LARGIER

Ecumenical Council The term refers to a "universal" assembly whose decrees have obtained the consent of the entire communion of Christian churches. Such assemblies provide binding definition concerning administration of sacraments, the formulation of doctrine, and the governance of the church. In Roman Catholic theory, the pope has the exclusive prerogative to convoke, preside over, and confirm the decrees of an ecumenical council. Orthodox churches historically looked to the emperor rather than the pope to convoke a council and confirm its decrees, and did not ascribe primacy to Rome in presiding over deliberations. Most Christian denominations recognize seven ecumenical councils, while the Roman Catholic Church acknowledges an additional fourteen. The seven ecumenical councils were convened between 325 and 787 and resulted in the definition of central doctrines concerning the nature of the Godhead and the union of divine and human natures in the person of Jesus Christ.

The earliest meeting of church leaders, described in Acts 15 and Galatians 2, is often referred to as the "Council of Jerusalem," and is adduced as apostolic precedent to conciliar assemblies. The biblical accounts, however, reflect significant differences in the conduct and purpose of the Jerusalem meeting from subsequent councils, and the origins of the ecumenical council are more directly rooted in the political developments of the fourth century. As the church became integrated into the government of the empire, the emperor promoted the ecumenical council as a vehicle to produce ecclesiastical consensus in support of imperial unity. Consequently, the seven councils employed precedents derived from practices of the Roman court and senate, and the theological deliberation aimed to establish concise formulas as the basis for a universal and imperially administered Christian confession.

After achieving sole power in 324 after a long civil war, Constantine convened the first ecumenical council in 325 in Nicaea, a suburb of Constantinople. The ecclesiastical world was divided over the proclamation, championed by the Alexandrian priest Arius, of a distinction in the Godhead between the persons of the Father and the Son. The Arians sought to protect strict monotheism by reserving unqualified status of divinity for a single member of the Godhead, the Father. Opponents to the Arians objected to the denial of equal divinity to the second person of the Godhead, the Son. The Nicene council rejected the Arian position, defining the Son as *homoousios* ("consubstantial") with the Father. The second council (Constantinople, 381) reaffirmed the formula of *homoousios* and implicitly extended it to include the third person of the Godhead, the Holy Spirit, promulgating the first complete definition of Trinitarian doctrine.

Defining the precise relationship between divine and human in Christ was the task of the third and fourth councils, Ephesus in 431 and Chalcedon· in 451. These two councils were dominated by fierce contention between rival Christologies, associated respectively with Antioch and Alexandria. The former developed a Christology that insisted upon the completeness and integrity of the two natures and defined the incarnation as the assumption of a self-sufficient human being by the divine Logos. The latter crafted a "single subject" Christology that insisted on the unity of the incarnate person and defined the activity of the indwelling Logos as the sole source of Christ's identity. Ephesus placed irrevocable limits on Antiochene Christology by condemning the teaching of Nestorius, who emphasized the integrity of the two natures of Christ by describing Mary as *Christotokos* ("Christ-bearer") while denying her the title *Theotokos* ("God-bearer"). The Council of Chalcedon sought to harmonize Alexandrian single-subject Christology with vocabulary more traditional to Antioch. This council agreed to a formula of Christ being known "in two natures," rather than an alternative phrase of "from two natures." The former was held to guarantee the persistence of both natures in the same subject and thus address Antiochene concerns that salvation necessitated the integrity of the human nature.

Many Eastern churches rejected the definition of Chalcedon as a reintroduction of Nestorianism and resisted the council's decrees. The fifth and sixth councils, Second Constantinople in 553 and Third Constantinople in 680–681, followed directly from this rift. The fifth council sought to conciliate opposition by condemning certain writings produced by three of the most controversial of the Antiochene theologians—Theodoret of Cyrrhus, Theodore of Mopsuestia, and Ibas—labeled as the "Three Chapters." Second Constantinople failed to achieve the desired reconciliation, and subsequent theological discussion was directed toward defining a compromise formula acceptable to both pro- and anti-Chalcedonian factions. The proposed formula asserted that the divine Logos supplies the single principle of activity in Christ, a position known as *monotheletism*. This compromise introduced new disputes and deepened an increasing divide between Greek and Latin churches. After the fall of the Eastern provinces to Muslim rule in the middle of the seventh century, the logic for finding a compromise formula collapsed. Third Constantinople condemned monotheletism and ended the attempt to reconcile the Eastern churches to Chalcedonian orthodoxy. The final council, Second Nicaea in 787, upheld the veneration (*proskynēsis*) of images of Christ, Mary, and the saints. This devotional practice, the source of sustained political and religious controversy in Byzantine society, seems at first glance to be removed from previous christological debates. The bishops at Second Nicaea, however, consciously defined their assembly as continuing the earlier deliberations, and declared icon veneration to be a necessary expression of the revelation of God in the union of two natures as defined by Chalcedon.

F. Dvornik, "Emperors, Popes, and General Councils," *Dumbarton Oaks Papers* 6 (1951): 1–23; J. A. Fischer, "Das sogennante Apostelkonzil," in *Konzil und Papst: Historische Beiträge zur Frage der höchsten Gewalt in der Kirche: Festgabe für Hermann Tüchle*, ed. G. Schwaiger (1975), 1–17; A. Grillmeier, *From the Apostolic Age to the Council of Chalcedon*, vol. 1 of *Christ in Christian Tradition* (1975); J. Meyendorff, *Imperial Unity and Christian Divisions* (1989); H. J. Sieben, *Die Konzilidee der alten Kirche* (1979); H. A. Slaatte, *The Seven Ecumenical Councils* (1980); N. P. Tanner, ed., *Decrees of the Ecumenical Councils*, 2 vols. (1990).

RICHARD A. LAYTON

Edit of Milan   *see* Milan, Edict of

Edit of Nantes   *see* Nantes, Edict of

Edict of Worms   *see* Worms, Edict of

Edward VI (1537–1553), Protestant king of England. The son of Henry VIII and Jane Seymour, Edward came to the throne in 1547 under the tutelage of an evangelically minded council of regency appointed by Henry in his last days.

Under the protectorate first of Edward Seymour, duke of Somerset (to 1549), and then of John Dudley, duke of Northumberland, Edward's reign brought accelerating religious reform under the guidance of archbishop Thomas Cranmer. An initial program of destruction of cultic images and appropriation of "superstitious" foundations was greeted by popular uprisings both for and against further reform. The repeal of censorship laws enabled open printing of Protestant literature in England including, in addition to vast polemical literature, the 1549 metrical psalter of Thomas Sternhold, beloved by Edward, and such official products as Cranmer's Book of Common Prayer (1549), approved by Parliament and further revised in 1552, and his Forty-Two Articles of 1553—documents that, in slight Elizabethan revision, defined English Protestant worship and identity for centuries to come. Continental theologians of Reformed cast helped shape Edwardian developments: after the defeat of the Schmalkald League in Germany, Martin Bucer, John a Lasco, and Peter Martyr Vermigli were all given refuge in Edwardian England; the Lutherans Melanchthon and Brentz were invited but declined. Formerly regarded as the mere puppet of his council, Edward is credited by recent scholarship with maturing Protestant convictions and policy, culminating in his ill-fated "devise for the succession" naming his Protestant cousin Jane Grey heir to the throne in place of his Catholic half-sister Mary shortly before his death of tuberculosis.

J. Loach, *Edward VI* (1999); D. MacCulloch, *The Boy King: Edward VI and the Protestant Reformation* (1999); J. G. Nichols, ed., *Literary Remains of King Edward the Sixth*, 2 vols. (1857).

CHRISTOPHER B. BROWN

Egeria (fourth cent.?), Christian pilgrim and writer. Our knowledge of Egeria comes exclusively from her description of a journey taken to the eastern provinces of the Roman Empire sometime in the late fourth or early fifth centuries. The document that has come to be known as the *Pilgrimage of Egeria* was discovered in 1884 in Italy and its author eventually identified with a pious woman named Egeria whose identical journey was summarized in a letter from a seventh-century Spanish monk, Valerius.

Possibly from Gaul or Spain, Egeria was of social status and wealth sufficient to sustain a prolonged visit to the Holy Land. Not only did she have the freedom to travel, but she was also greeted by clergy and monks of high standing within the church. In a conversational style she describes for her audience, whom she addresses as "my venerable sisters," her stay in Jerusalem and three excursions she made from the city to Egypt, the Sinai Peninsula, and Transjordan. She documents stops in Edessa, Antioch, and Seleucia as she made her way toward Constantinople and eventually home. Eager to make the Bible come alive for her readers, Egeria evaluates sites connected with the characters of the Bible and the ministry of Jesus. She also describes visits to the burial places of Christian martyrs and communities of monks and nuns that had grown up around the sacred sites.

In the second part of the document Egeria describes the liturgical practices of the foremost church in Jerusalem, which had been opened on the site of Golgotha in 348. She was particularly interested in the Sunday observances there and in the instruction received by candidates for baptism.

For modern readers Egeria provides important information about ancient liturgy and a unique description of biblical sites after the great age of Constantinian church building. She also adds to our growing body of knowledge about the position of women in the early church.

———

G. Gingras, *Egeria: Diary of a Pilgrimage*, ACW 38 (1970); J. Wilkinson, *Egeria's Travels* (3rd ed., 1999).

BARBARA J. MACHAFFIE

Elchasaites The name refers to Jewish-Christian apocalyptists active in the second and third centuries. Hippolytus (*Haer.* 9.13.1–17.2) reports that one Alcibiades from Apamea came to Rome under Pope Callistus, preaching a second baptism. He brought a book of revelations, written in the third year of Trajan, calling for repentance. The revelations had been delivered to Elchasai by two enormous angels, a male Son of God and female Holy Spirit. Hippolytus reports (*Haer.* 9.14.1) that the Elchasaites required circumcision and observance of the law and held that Jesus was born in ordinary human fashion. They believed that Christ had come to earth more than once and could do so again. Hippolytus ascribes this notion, as well as other heretical notions, to Greek philosophical roots, in this case, the Pythagoreans. In addition to calling for a second baptism of repentance, the *Book of Elchasai* apparently prescribed multiple baptisms for dealing with

physical ailments and demonic possession. It also contained astrological teaching (*Haer.* 9.16.1–4). Origen (Eusebius, *Hist. eccl.* 6.38) mentions "Helkesaites" as having recently begun preaching repentance in Caesarea. Origen also claims that the sect held denial of the faith in time of persecution to be a matter of indifference. The tenth-century Arabic *Fihrist* (9.1) reports that Mani's brother was a member of a sect founded by Elchasai. A third-century biography of Mani, the Cologne Mani Codex, confirms that report.

———

R. Cameron and A. Dewey, *The Cologne Mani Codex: Concerning the Origin of His Body* (1979).

HAROLD W. ATTRIDGE

El Greco (1541–1614), Greek Mannerist painter active in Italy and Spain. Trained in his native Crete as an icon painter, El Greco studied in Venice and Rome from 1568 to 1576, where he assimilated techniques and styles of Titian, Tintoretto, and Michelangelo. In 1577 he settled in Toledo, where he remained until his death. El Greco's portraits are noted for their astute assessment of character. A famous example is the painting of his close friend, Fray Félix Hortensio Paravicino (1609). His religious paintings include scenes of Christ's passion and many martyr-saints. The *Adoration of the Shepherds* (c. 1613), presents an almost hallucinatory night scene with flickering patterns of light. The symbolic cityscape, *View of Toledo* (1610), with its emphatic distortion of reality, seems to presage twentieth-century Expressionism. Noted for the exaggerated postures, features, and perspective in his work, as well as for violent extremes of light and color, El Greco created dynamically charged compositions. El Greco is considered one of the outstanding artists of the Counter-Reformation.

———

R. G. Mann, *El Greco and His Patrons: Three Major Projects* (1986); F. Marias, *El Greco* (1991); F. C. Seraller, *El Greco: The Burial of the Count of Orgaz* (1995).

PRISCILLA BAUMANN

Elisabeth of Brandenburg (1485–1555), niece of Frederick the Wise and John the Steadfast and sister of the exiled Danish king Christian II. She caused a major stir when in 1527 she received Communion in both forms from a Lutheran minister. Instead of returning to the faith of her husband Joachim, Elector of Brandenburg, who had banned Protestantism,

Elisabeth fled to Torgau. Protected by Elector John, she would not return without a guaranteed safety, resumption of marital relations, and the right to choose her own preacher. Years in poverty and separation from her children (Joachim, John, Anna, Elisabeth, and Margaret) caused her health to deteriorate, while she relied on the hospitality of friends such as the Luthers and the care of her newly Protestant daughter Elisabeth. She returned to Spandau as a widow after her son, Elector Joachim II, implemented the new faith.

———

K. Stjerna, *Women and the Reformation* (2008).

KIRSI STJERNA

Elisabeth of Braunschweig (1510–

1558), daughter of Elisabeth of Brandenburg. Married to Duke Erich of Braunschweig-Calenberg, she became zealous for the reform of the duchy. As a widow she reigned for her son, Erich, for five years with three conflicting guardians: her brother Joachim II of Brandenburg, and Duke Heinrich and Philip of Hesse, the anti- and pro-Protestant foes, respectively. With the help of Antonius Corvinus (from Hesse) she sponsored the writing of a Lutheran hymnbook, a church ordinance, and visitations. She wrote treatises on marriage and governance to Erich, who temporarily sided with the Catholics. Changing religious and political conditions led to her exile to Hannover. There, with no income, Elisabeth wrote hymns and letters, asking for money from her son-in-law, Albert of Prussia. Three years later she returned, was tricked into missing her daughter Katherine's wedding (to a Catholic), and as a result, became somewhat mentally unbalanced. Under the care of her second husband, Lutheran Duke Poppo of Henneberg, she wrote a book of consolation for widows.

———

K. Stjerna, *Women and the Reformation* (2008); M. Wiesner-Hanks, "Kinder, Kirche, Landeskinder: Women Defend Their Publishing in Early Modern Germany," in *Habent sua fata libelli*, ed. R. B. Barnes, R. A. Kolb, and P. L. Presley (1998), 143–52.

KIRSI STJERNA

Elisabeth of Schönau (1129–1165),

Benedictine nun, mystic, and author from the German monastery of Schönau, whose spiritual gifts were widely recognized by her contemporaries. She joined the monastery at age twelve and had her first recorded visions at twenty-three. Her brother Ekbert subsequently entered Schönau, a double monastery, and recorded her experiences, serving as her secretary and editor. Her revelations, in which the comforting presence of the Virgin Mary and the influence of communal worship were prevalent, occurred in the midst of considerable spiritual and physical suffering. Her Latin writings frequently advanced the interests of the official church, although her monastery's commitment to reform helped prompt her to identify and critique ecclesiastical corruption. Her most widely circulated work in the Middle Ages, *Revelations of the Virgin Martyrs of Cologne*, has perhaps done the most to undermine her appeal for modern readers. It describes her mystical encounter with Saint Ursula and eleven thousand virgins (scribal error was responsible for the implausible number); this experience was used by church leaders to authenticate recently discovered relics. Like her neighbor and correspondent Hildegard of Bingen, prophetic utterances were among Elisabeth's spiritual gifts; she considered herself a successor of the prophetic women in the Hebrew Scriptures. She died in the monastery at the age of thirty-six.

———

A. Clark, *Elisabeth of Schönau: A Twelfth-Century Visionary* (1992); *Elisabeth of Schönau: The Complete Works*, trans. A. Clark (2000).

ADRIENNE NOCK AMBROSE

Elizabeth I (1533–1603), Protestant queen of

England. The daughter of Henry VIII and Anne Boleyn, Elizabeth endured her mother's 1536 disgrace and execution to find a stable home after 1543 with her stepmother, Catherine Parr. Under Roger Ascham, Elizabeth received a distinctly evangelical humanist education in Latin, Greek, French, and Italian, translating Marguerite de Navarre's *Miroir de l'âme pécheresse* for Catherine. Henry's will named Elizabeth to the royal succession after Edward and Mary. Against probability, Elizabeth survived the scandal of Thomas Seymour's 1548 intrigues, the rebuke of Edward's plan of succession, which repudiated both Mary and Elizabeth as illegitimate, and imprisonment in the Tower of London under Mary to become queen upon Mary's death in 1558. The 1559 Act of Uniformity restored Edward's church order of 1552, including the Book of Common Prayer, though it retained Marian vestments; Cranmer's Forty-Two Articles were condensed into the Thirty-Nine Articles of 1563. But unlike the Edwardian reformers, Elizabeth regarded her religious settlement as permanent, placing her in tension not only with Presbyterians such as John Knox, whose ill-timed polemic against Mary had discredited him in Elizabeth's eyes, but also with most of her own bishops, including Archbishop Edmund Grindal, whose ideals, formed on the Continent in Marian exile, were more definitely Reformed. Elizabeth's policy was defended by a new generation that included Richard Hooker; those who pressed for continued reform in ritual and polity were labeled Puritans. Though Elizabeth preferred to punish religious nonconformity with fines and exclusion from office, Pius V's 1570 bull *Regnans in excelsis*, which excommunicated and deposed Elizabeth and absolved her subjects of their obedience, left English Catholics vulnerable to charges of treason, though Elizabeth executed fewer Catholics in forty-five years than Mary had Protestants in five. Mary Stuart, having resigned the throne of Scotland to her son James, was implicated in plotting with the Spanish and executed in 1587. The association of the Roman church with foreign military threat, turned back by the apparently miraculous defeat of the Spanish Armada in 1588, helped to consolidate English Protestantism and national identity under Elizabeth, reinforced by literature such as John Foxe's *Book of Martyrs* and Edmund Spenser's *Faerie Queen*.

————

P. Collinson, *The Elizabethan Puritan Movement* (1967); W. P. Haugaard, *Elizabeth and the English Reformation* (1968); W. MacCaffrey, *Elizabeth I* (1993); N. M. Sutherland, "The Marian Exiles and the Establishment of the Elizabethan Regime," *ARG* 78 (1987): 253–84.
CHRISTOPHER B. BROWN

Elizabethan Settlement Reached in 1559 under the authority of the English Parliament and queen Elizabeth I, the Settlement involved two parliamentary acts, the Act of Supremacy and the Act of Uniformity, as well as a set of Royal Injunctions. These collectively defined the Reformation-era official state religion of the Church of England. The Act of Supremacy reiterated the Act of Henry VIII, establishing, in this case, Elizabeth I as the "Supreme Governor" (rather than "Supreme Head," as in Henry's case) of the Church of England. The Act of Uniformity reestablished the Book of Common Prayer of 1552 as the only official book of worship in the church. The Royal Injunctions, based on those of Edward VI, provided guidelines for the church. The Settlement presented a problem to the Puritans and Presbyterians, who resisted it. This resistance, over time, led to the development of sep-

aratist Puritanism, various forms of dissenting denominations, and Anglo-Catholicism. The Settlement is a central tenet in the Church of England, defining the very character of the Church of England and the English religious identity.

————

G. Bray, *Documents of the English Reformation* (1994); P. Collinson, *The Religion of Protestants: The Church in English Society, 1559–1625* (1982); D. MacCulloch, *The Later Reformation in England, 1547–1603* (1990).
ALDEN R. LUDLOW

Emser, Hieronymus (1478–1527), humanist, priest, theologian. Emser was born in Ulm, Germany. He studied Greek and Latin in Tübingen in 1493 and law and theology at Basel from 1497 to 1499. In 1504, he lectured at Erfurt on Reuchlin's comedy *Sergius*; Luther was among his hearers. In 1505, he lectured on the classics at Leipzig, where he earned his licentiate in canon law and became chaplain and secretary to Duke George of Saxony in 1509. After witnessing the Disputation at Leipzig between Eck and Karlstadt, he upheld the papal supremacy.

Emser engaged in a very public, long-standing dispute with Martin Luther. In December 1520, Luther burned Emser's writings together with the papal bull of excommunication. Emser wrote eight polemical works in 1520 and 1521 and translated writings by Erasmus and Henry VIII. In 1527 he edited his revised version of Luther's German translation of the New Testament. Emser's version went through over one hundred editions over the next three centuries.

————

D. Bagchi, *Luther's Earliest Opponents: Catholic Controversialists, 1518–1525* (1991); B. D. Mangrum and G. Scavizzi, trans., *A Reformation Debate: Karlstadt, Emser, and Eck on Sacred Images* (1998); K. A. Strand, *Reformation Bibles in the Crossfire: The Story of Jerome Emser, His Anti-Lutheran Critique and His Catholic Bible Version* (1961).
FRANZ POSSET

Encratites This term (from the Greek *enkrateia*, "self-control") was used first by Irenaeus and later Hippolytus, Eusebius, and Epiphanius to describe Tatian and his version of Christianity, which required sexual abstinence and refusal of meat and wine for all followers. Their objection stemmed from their equation of Tatian's rejection of marriage (as well as other aspects of his theology) with a rejection of the goodness of God's creation. For this reason he was associated with Marcion and various gnostic heresies, an association that is the subject of scholarly debate. For example, Tatian's emphasis on asceticism, his "encratitism," was not as objectionable in his native Syria. The term "encratite" is currently used to denote a wide range of ascetic tendencies in second- and third-century Christianity. Orthodox Christians praised the self-control of some "perfect" Christians but did not condemn marriage or various eating practices (using the Pastorals). A more radical strain of "encratitism" (based on Matt. 22:29–30 and 1 Cor. 7:28) is apparent in heretical forms of Christianity, but these include both doctrinal and nondoctrinal heresies.

Irenaeus, *Against Heresies* 1.28.1; Hippolytus, *Refutation of All Heresies* 8.13; Eusebius, *Ecclesiastical History* 4.29; Epiphanius, *Panarion* 46.1.4–5, 8–9; 47.1.3, 5–8; G. S. Gasparro, "Asceticism and Anthropology: *Enkrateia* and 'Double Creation' in Early Christianity," in *Asceticism*, ed. V. L. Wimbush and R. Valantasis (1995), 127–46.

                                        REBECCA KRAWIEC

England, Reformation in While the church's power had been slowly eroded by the state from the late fifteenth century, it was during the reign of Henry VIII (1491–1547) that the legislative foundations of the English Reformation settlement were laid. While Henry was a convinced traditionalist in most areas of doctrine, and certainly took credit for the anti-Luther work *Assertio Septem Sacramentorum* (1521), his desire from 1526 onward to divorce his first wife, Catherine of Aragon, and solve the crown's financial difficulties led to a series of parliamentary acts which wrested control of the English church from the pope and placed it in the hands of the sovereign. Legally he found the basis for this in the series of fourteenth-century Acts of Praemunire (1353, 1365, 1393), designed to restrict papal power within England by carefully delimiting the involvement of the church in matters of state. Crucial to Henry's project was the appointment in 1532 of Thomas Cranmer to the archbishopric of Canterbury. With the Acts of Succession, Supremacy, and Treason in 1534, the break with Rome was complete and Henry was installed as "supreme head" of the Church of England.

In 1536, Henry's need for continental allies led him to pass the Act of Ten Articles, which

was intentionally vague on crucial issues and susceptible to a mildly Protestant interpretation, but in the years following the Catholic rebellion known as the Pilgrimage of Grace, Henry stepped back from pushing further theological reform, a policy that culminated in 1539 in the passing of the Act of Six Articles, which reimposed unambiguous Catholic dogma, particularly in the matter of the Lord's Supper. In subsequent persecution, high-profile religious and political figures were executed, including Thomas Cromwell, architect of the dissolution of the monasteries in the 1530s. Cranmer, however, managed to survive.

Edward VI's (1537–1553) accession to the throne in 1547 proved a major boost for the Protestant faction, with Parliament repealing Henry's Act of Six Articles. A boy-king, he ruled first under the protection of the Duke of Somerset, then the Duke of Northumberland, influenced not only by Cranmer but also by more radical Protestants such as John Knox and John Hooper. During his reign, Cranmer produced two Books of Common Prayer (1549 and 1552). The first was mildly Protestant, containing many elements that were also acceptable to traditional Catholics; the second was more avowedly Protestant, although the retention of kneeling at the Lord's Supper led to controversy with, among others, the Scotsman-in-exile John Knox and the insertion of the so-called Black Rubric, which denied that kneeling implied worship of the Real Presence.

Failure to secure Parliament for the Protestant cause or to seize the Catholic heir apparent, Mary, on Edward's death meant a return between 1553 and 1558 to a more Catholic policy. Nevertheless, ambivalence among the nobility concerning England's complete return to the Roman fold and antipathy to Mary's Spanish marriage meant that the religious policy of her reign was neither straightforward nor ultimately very successful. While scholars are divided over how successful Mary's attempts at re-catholicizing England were, there is no doubt that the execution of high-profile members of the Protestant church establishment, including Cranmer himself, proved useful propaganda to later Protestants, particularly as described in John Foxe's *Acts and Monuments*, and served to change the popular image of Protestantism from that of a politically corrupt movement to one of martyrdom and integrity.

With the advent of Elizabeth I in 1558, England returned once again to a Reformation based upon the second Book of Common Prayer (minus the Black Rubric), which was reintroduced by Parliament in 1559, although the royal title was now changed to "Supreme Governor of the Church of England." While the domestic and foreign policies of her reign until 1583 were broadly Protestant, she made a number of concessions toward more conservative opinion and successfully opposed the kind of presbyterian reformation policy being pushed by the Puritans, whereby discipline would have been placed unequivocally in the hands of the church courts. From 1583, however, fear of Catholic insurgency and problems with Spain meant that a stronger line against Catholic elements within England itself was pursued, in tandem with a vigorous anti-Puritan policy.

There are a number of points concerning the English Reformation about which there is no consensus in the scholarly literature: the importance of Lollardy, the Marian reaction, and the importance of doctrine.

It has been argued, most notably by A. G. Dickens and his followers, that Lollardy was a relatively healthy movement in the early sixteenth century and provided fertile soil for the popular reception of the Protestant Reformation. Others, such as Eammon Duffy, have argued that, on the contrary, Lollardy was only vibrant in a few places, that there was no widespread disillusionment with Catholicism, and that the Reformation should therefore be interpreted more as a state-imposed settlement than a popular phenomenon.

The Marian reaction has typically been seen as an ill-fated and ill-conceived scheme that was doomed in the face of popular resistance and the social and economic changes of the mid-sixteenth century. More recently, this picture has been nuanced and, while it is still clear that the attempt to reinvigorate monasticism was an anachronistic disaster, other evidence, such as the production of catechetical primers, indicates that Mary's reforms were not all so unpopular and that the reasons for the ultimate failure of her regime to effect long-term return to the Catholic Church are more complicated than once thought.

Scholars have typically sought to explain theological developments within English religion in the seventeenth century using the established terminology of "Calvinist" and "Arminian." Again, recent scholarship has demonstrated that the sixteenth-century roots of seventeenth-century religious conflict in England renders such bald terms as simply too unnuanced. Right from the inception of the English Reformation, issues of eccelesiology, soteriology, and worship cut across such puta-

tive party lines and made the whole situation of the English church far more complex.

———

P. Collinson, *The Elizabethan Puritan Movement* (1967); E. Duffy, *The Stripping of the Altars* (1992); A. G. Dickens, *The English Reformation* (1989); D. MacCulloch, *Thomas Cranmer* (1996); MacCulloch, *Tudor Church Militant* (1999); P. Marshall, ed., *The Impact of the English Reformation, 1500–1640* (1997).

CARL TRUEMAN

Ennodius, Magnus Felix (c. 473–521),

rhetorician, writer, and bishop of Pavia (c. 511–521). Born to nobility, probably in Arles, and orphaned, he was educated as the ward of an aunt in Pavia. After a conversion experience occasioned by severe illness, he took up the ascetic life and was ordained a deacon (c. 493) in Pavia by the bishop, Epiphanius. He was present in Rome at the "synod of the palm" in 502, taking up the side of Symmachus in a disputed papal succession. A treatise written in this context argued that the papacy was exempt from interference from any secular power. He was twice sent by Pope Hormisdas to the emperor Anastasius in an attempt to settle the lingering Acacian schism. In his writings Ennodius gives evidence of the struggle to find a rapprochement between the heritage of Greco-Roman classical learning and an authentically Christian culture. He wrote twenty-eight *Dictiones* (brief treatises on miscellaneous topics), two books of hymns, and nearly three hundred letters. His *Eucharisticum de vita sua* is a spiritual autobiography. His *Paraenesis didascalica* sets forth the need to counterpose a Christian literary culture to the old classics. He also wrote a panegyric for Theodoric, the Ostrogoth ruler of Italy, and Lives of Epiphanius and Antony, a monk of Lérins.

———

L. Navarra, "Contributo storico di Ennodio," *Aug* 14 (1974): 315–42.

THOMAS A. SMITH

Ephesus, Councils of (400, 431, 434,

447, 449) Ephesus, the metropolitan church of the Roman province of Asia and linked to the apostle John, was the site of several councils. The first, presided over by John Chrysostom, took place in 400 to review charges against clergy in Asia.

The next council (431), known as the Third Ecumenical Council, actually consisted of two rival councils. Disputes over prestige and jurisdiction among the foremost churches in the

Roman Empire overshadowed the theological conflict over appropriate language for the person of Jesus Christ.

Politically, Rome and Alexandria took offense that the Council of Constantinople (381) had elevated Constantinople as second in honor only to Rome. Rome bristled at assigning ecclesiastical "honor" for political purposes; Alexandria resented demotion to third place. Moreover, Constantinople's expanding jurisdiction diminished the status of Ephesus in Asia, and Jerusalem's quest for metropolitan status threatened Antioch's position among the Palestinian provinces. These rivalries would parallel the theological alliances at Ephesus in 431.

Theologically, the conflict was ignited when Nestorius, bishop of Constantinople (428), sought to correct popular devotion to Mary as *Theotokos* ("God-bearer" or "Mother of God"), which he thought blurred the divine and human in Christ. Cyril of Alexandria appealed to Celestine of Rome, and in 430 a Roman council condemned Nestorius. Cyril, as executor of the decision, did more than inform Nestorius. In his Twelve Anathemas, Cyril demanded adherence to an expression of Alexandrian Christology that was itself doctrinally suspect.

Emperor Theodosius II called for a church-wide council to be held at Ephesus beginning on Pentecost 431. Taking advantage of delays that beset the Syrians, Cyril convoked a council that was attended primarily by anti-Nestorians from Egypt, Asia, and Palestine. It condemned Nestorius for his refusal to attend and for his teachings against *Theotokos*. When the Syrians arrived, John of Antioch together with Nestorius's other adherents held a countercouncil. It voided Cyril's council and condemned both Cyril and Memnon of Ephesus. While not all were favorably disposed toward Nestorius's theology, the participants in the second council were even more concerned about Cyril's conduct and his Twelve Anathemas.

Theodosius II placed all parties under house arrest and accepted the depositions declared by both councils. The Roman delegates, when they arrived, approved Cyril's council. Finally, the emperor received Nestorius's resignation and rescinded the depositions of Cyril and Memnon.

John of Antioch and Cyril of Alexandria sought theological resolution through the Formula of Union (433). John condemned Nestorius and his teachings. Cyril withdrew his Twelve Anathemas and assented to an Antiochian Christology that allowed for calling Mary *Theotokos*. Egyptian outcry at Cyril's compromise would ultimately lead to the Monophysite crisis.

The third and fourth councils (434, 447) attempted unsuccessfully to resolve the case of Bassianus, a deacon at Ephesus who refused to accept the episcopacy of Evasa, preferring to seek election to the see of Ephesus. In 447 the bishops and clergy of Asia, with the support of the bishop of Alexandria, Timothy Ailurus, sought to restore the standing of Ephesus following the Council of Chalcedon, which had given Constantinople primacy over Asia.

The fifth council, called the "Robber Council," was called in 449 to resolve the dispute over whether the incarnated Christ had one nature (monophysite) or two. Under the presidency of Dioscorus of Alexandria, it was a triumph of sorts for Monophysite theology popularized by Eutyches, an abbot in Constantinople. The leading two-nature proponent, Theodoret of Cyrrhus, was forbidden from attending, and the Roman delegation was not allowed to present letters from Bishop Leo (who gave the council its name). The council's adoption of the Twelve Anathemas and its condemnations of the major two-nature theologians, as well as Nestorius's initial accusers, led to a riot in which Flavian of Constantinople was killed.

———

J. McGuckin, *St. Cyril of Alexandria: The Christological Controversy: Its History, Theology, and Texts* (1994); R. Norris, ed., *The Christological Controversy* (1980); N. P. Tanner, ed., *Decrees of the Ecumenical Councils: From Nicea I to Vatican II* (1990).

                                    LISA D. MAUGANS DRIVER

Ephrem the Syrian

Ephrem the Syrian (c. 306–373), poet, theologian, exegete, and apologist. Ephrem was born to Christian parents in Nisibis on the Roman-Persian frontier. In adulthood, he was ordained a deacon. After Julian's defeat in 363 and the cession of Nisibis to Persia, Ephrem immigrated to Edessa along with many other residents of Nisibis.

In his writings, Ephrem relies heavily on the use of symbols and types, parallels and paradoxes. His works can be subdivided according to genre into three groups: (1) *Prose works.* Extant in Syriac are biblical commentaries on Genesis, Exodus, and the *Diatessaron.* Also included in this group are the *Prose Refutations*, treatises refuting the teachings of Marcion, Bardaisan, and Mani; and the *Sermon on Our Lord*, an outstanding theological treatise. (2) *Metrical homilies (memre).* These include homiletical, pedagogical, and theological material. The *Memre on Faith* refute Arianism and show parallels with Greek theology. (3) *Hymns (madrashe)*. These poetic texts, based on syllable count and arranged in cycles, constitute the bulk of Ephrem's works. Many of these may have been composed for the liturgy, where they were recited by female choirs. The *madrashe* cover a variety of topics, ranging from events in Christ's life (nativity, crucifixion, resurrection) to theological subjects (Trinity, ecclesiology). Several *madrashe* address contemporary events, such as the Persian sieges of Nisibis and Julian's campaign. Translations of Ephrem's works into Greek were undertaken during his lifetime; however, the extant corpus of Greek texts ascribed to Ephrem is largely inauthentic. Various Ephremic texts survive only in Armenian.

Ephrem strongly influenced later Syriac Christian poetry and theology through the wealth of his symbolism, poetic form, and rejection of heterodox teachings.

————

S. Brock, *Hymns on Paradise* (1990); Brock, *The Luminous Eye: The Spiritual World Vision of Saint Ephrem* (1992); E. Mathews and J. Amar, *Selected Prose Works* (1994); K. McVey, *Hymns* (1989); S. Griffith, "Ephraem the Syrian's Hymns 'Against Julian,'" *VC* 41 (1987): 238–66; R. Murray, *Symbols of Church and Kingdom: A Study in Early Syriac Tradition* (1975; 2004); U. Possekel, *Evidence of Greek Philosophical Concepts in the Writings of Ephrem the Syrian* (1999).

UTE POSSEKEL

Epictetus

Epictetus (c. 50–c. 120 CE), philosopher. Epictetus was a Greek slave living in Rome and a pupil of Musonius. A master had broken both his legs, leaving him crippled. Freed by Epaphroditus during the reign of Nero, whom he served as secretary, Epictetus was exiled when Domitian banished the philosophers. He established a school at Nicopolis. His disciple Arrianus attended his lectures, took notes, and published them. Central to Epictetus's thought is *eudaimonism*, or "happiness," which is achieved through acknowledging the moral dimension of human nature. Each human being is endowed with four roles or identities. The first identity is as a human being. The common element, which all humans have, is a rational nature from which moral principles are derived. The second identity is individuality, namely, the particular human person with all his unique characteristics and idiosyncrasies.

The third identity relates to external circumstances, deriving from fortune rather than nature. The fourth and last identity is personal choice, which is by far the most important. Through understanding oneself, the human being is able to make moral judgments and carry them out in life. Epictetus considered only those things, which are subject to human control, ethically relevant, thus laying great emphasis on the will.

————

Epictetus, *Works*, ed. and trans. W. A. Oldfather, 2 vols., LCL (1979, 1985); A. A. Long, *Epictetus: A Stoic and Socratic Guide to Life* (2002).

KENNETH B. STEINHAUSER

Epicurus and Epicureanism

Epicurus and Epicureanism Epicurus (341–271 BCE), a moral and natural philosopher, founded a school in Athens that met in the garden of his home. He was a prolific writer, but most of his works are lost. Knowledge of him and his system comes primarily from a poem by Lucretius entitled *De rerum natura (On the Nature of Things)*. Epicurus divided philosophy into logic, physics, and ethics, with ethics playing the most important role. Epicureanism had pleasure as its guiding principle for achieving the happy life. Not to be confused with unqualified hedonism, Epicureanism sought to satisfy existing human desires, extolled pleasures of the soul over those of the body, and urged temperance. Often contrasted with Stoicism, which pursued virtue for its own sake, Epicureanism was much maligned in antiquity. Cicero, for example, called Epicureans animals. Among Christian writers they fared no better because of their emphasis on pleasure and for several other reasons. Epicureans denied the immortality of the human person. Following the atomist theory of Democritus, they held that the cosmos was an arbitrary arrangement of atoms without a creator. Denying divine providence, they held that the gods existed but were not interested in humans.

————

D. Clay, *Paradosis and Survival: Three Chapters in the History of Epicurean Philosophy* (1998); J. M. Rist, *Epicurus: An Introduction* (1972).

KENNETH B. STEINHAUSER

Epiphanius of Salamis

Epiphanius of Salamis (c. 315–403), bishop and heresiologist. Born in Palestine, Epiphanius joined the monastic movement and by the age of twenty had founded a monastery in his native province. In 367 he was elected bishop of Constantia (previously Salamis) on Cyprus. Epiphanius was an ardent defender of Nicaea and an opponent of heresy wherever he found it. In 392 he and Jerome began to attack Origenism. In 394 he visited Jerusalem, where he had a falling out with the bishop John, who was sympathetic to Origen. Jerome joined in the opposition to John, and Epiphanius ordained Jerome's brother Paulinian a priest, in violation of proper jurisdiction. In 400 Epiphanius traveled to Constantinople to support Theophilus of Alexandria, who had driven Origenist monks out of Egypt; he died at sea on the return voyage. Epiphanius's great work is the *Panarion* or *Medicine Chest*, an account of eighty heresies and their cure. The value of the work lies in Epiphanius's extensive citation of writings he considered heretical. He also composed the *Ancoratus*, a doctrinal treatise; *On Weights and Measures*, a rudimentary biblical encyclopedia; and *On Gems*, an interpretation of the high priest's breastplate. Epiphanius was a doctrinal positivist rather than a theologian.

F. Williams, trans., *The Panarion of Epiphanius of Salamis*, 2 vols. (1987, 1994); P. R. Amidon, trans., *The Panarion: Selected Passages* (1990).

JOSEPH T. LIENHARD

Erasmus, Desiderius

Erasmus, Desiderius (c. 1469–1536), Dutch humanist, reformer, and biblical scholar. Regarded as the most highly accomplished Latinist of his generation, Erasmus sought to bring his literary gifts to the service of a textual analysis of the New Testament in its original Greek, as well as to carry out a new Latin translation. In addition, he developed a program of reform from within the Catholic Church centered on Scripture and emphasizing the *philosophia Christi*, expressed in his *Enchiridion* (1501), stressing an inner focus on Christ over an outward appearance of piety through the observance of ceremonies. The son of a physician's daughter and a priest, Erasmus was orphaned in adolescence and entered the order of Augustinian canons at Steyn in 1487, where he remained until 1493. During these years he developed a passion for classical literature and devoted himself to what he called *bonae litterae*. He left in 1493 to serve as secretary to the bishop of Cambrai and in 1495 settled in Paris to study theology. He would never return to his monastery, and in 1517 was finally issued a papal dispensation granting him permission to remain in the world.

Erasmus pursued his humanistic studies in Paris, supporting himself as a private tutor. He was invited to travel to England in 1499 with one of his pupils and while there was befriended by Thomas More and John Colet. In the course of this visit and the period that followed, Erasmus discovered his deepest sense of vocation—to apply his knowledge and love of languages and literature to the study of Scripture. Commensurate with this discovery was his determination to learn Greek. He also developed a particular affinity for Jerome, whom he admired throughout his life for the saint's literary gifts as well as his holiness.

Following his return to the Continent in 1500, Erasmus published the first edition of a work that would grow to encompass a massive display of erudition: the *Adages*, a compilation of commonplaces from the Greek and Roman classics. Originally intended as an aid to writers and orators, it became a vehicle for Erasmus to express his views on a number of issues, as for example his philosophy of Christ in the *Sileni Alcibiadis* or his denunciation of war in *Dulce bellum inexpertis*. Other educational works include the *Colloquies*, the *De copia*, and the *De ratione studii*. He is most famous today for the *Praise of Folly* (1509), a satirical look at the various forms of irrationality adopted by humanity, ending in a lyrical tribute to the folly of the cross.

Erasmus's most significant contribution, however, was his New Testament, which involved an edition of the Greek text based on a literary analysis of the most ancient manuscripts he could find, a set of annotations explaining the original meanings of key terms and textual variations, and a new Latin translation intended not to displace or compete with the Vulgate but rather to offer an alternative rendering. He was influenced by the work of his predecessor Lorenzo Valla, whose *Adnotationes* he discovered in an abbey in 1504. The first edition of the New Testament was published in 1516; there were to be five altogether in his lifetime. Erasmus also applied himself to critical editions of Jerome, Cyprian, Arnobius, Hilary, Ambrose, and Augustine, editions and translations of Chrysostom and Irenaeus, and a translation of the works of Origen, whom he especially admired.

In response to Luther's first challenges against the abuses within the church, Erasmus was cautiously supportive; however, he soon became alarmed at the severity of Luther's attack and attempted to remain neutral. Eventually he took a stand in 1524 in his *De libero arbitrio*, and in the last decade of his life he remained embroiled in controversies both with

Catholic theologians who challenged his humanistic reform and with Luther's allies. As his own approach was a piety emphasizing reconciliation and concord, which he considered to be the essence of Christ's spirit, he ended his life believing his ideals were undone by the new spirit of relentless conflict that appeared to prevail.

C. Augustijn, *Erasmus* (1991); M. O. Boyle, *Rhetoric and Reform: Erasmus' Civil Dispute with Luther* (1983); *Collected Works of Erasmus* (1974–); M. Hoffmann, *Rhetoric and Theology: The Hermeneutic of Erasmus* (1994); J. B. Payne, *Erasmus: His Theology of the Sacraments* (1966, 1970); E. Rummel, *Erasmus' Annotations on the New Testament: From Philologist to Theologian* (1986); R. J. Schoeck, *Erasmus of Europe: The Making of a Humanist, 1467–1500* (1990).

J. LAUREL CARRINGTON

Erastianism   A doctrine which asserts the ascendancy of the civil authority over the ecclesiastical, named after Swiss theologian Thomas Erastus (1524–1583), sometimes known as Thomas Lüber. Identification with Lüber is somewhat arbitrary, since this doctrine was clearly articulated two centuries earlier by Marsiglio of Padua, reaffirmed by John Wyclif, and was implicit in the Lutheran and Zwinglian Reformation settlements and in the royal supremacy exercised by Henry VIII. The connection arose because Lüber, professor of medicine in Heidelberg, resisted the attempts of extreme Calvinists, led by Caspar Olevian, to introduce in Heidelberg a polity based on an independent ecclesiastical jurisdiction. By the time Lüber's major writing, *Explicatio gravissimae questionis*, was published six years after his death (with an English translation in 1659), the idea behind it had already taken firm root, most clearly in Richard Hooker's *Laws of Ecclesiastical Polity*. Originally conceived in the context of a state professing one religion, the doctrine survived the transition to a pluralistic and more secular state, restated by, among others, Thomas Hobbes.

W. S. Crowley, "Erastianism in England to 1640," *Journal of Church and State* 32 (1990): 549–66; R. C. Walton, "Der Streit zwischen Thomas Erastus und Caspar Olevian," in *Monatshefte für evangelische Kirchengeschichte des Rheinlandes* 37–38 (1988–1989): 205–46.

JOHN TONKIN

Eschatology   In Christian terms, eschatology is reflection on the "last things" that faith believes to await human beings in history, and on the final state of humans and the physical world beyond the limits of history, for which Christians hope. Although the term was first used in the nineteenth century, Christian preaching has emphasized the future expectations of faith since the New Testament, where Jesus proclaims, "The time is fulfilled, and the kingdom of God is at hand" (Mark 1:15), and portrays its coming as a time of cosmic disaster and universal judgment (Matt. 24–25; Mark 13; Luke 17). The earliest Christians seem to have thought that the resurrection of Jesus marked the beginning of history's end, as Jewish apocalyptic literature had portrayed it, and that Jesus would soon return in triumph to raise and judge all the dead (1 Thess. 4–5; 2 Thess. 1–2).

Second-century writers generally shared this vivid expectation of the end, although gnostic Christians often stressed that the final salvation promised to believers, including resurrection, had already occurred in their enlightenment by acceptance of esoteric doctrine. In response, Irenaeus of Lyon, around 185, insisted that the apostolic faith implies a strong hope for the immortality and physical transformation of the whole human person; included in this hope was the vision of a thousand years (millennium) of earthly peace and plenty for the just, which would take place after their resurrection but before Christ's final coming (*Haer.* 5).

In the early third century Origen responded to pagan critiques of the "materialism" of Christian hopes by presenting the future resurrection of the body and the circumstances of eschatological life in spiritualized terms, involving a radical change in quality of both the human soul's present bodily "vehicle" and of the cosmos itself. Origen's critics, such as the late third-century Methodius of Olympus, attacked his vision of the risen life as essentially gnostic and unscriptural, and even Origen's followers, such as Gregory of Nyssa in the late fourth century, carefully emphasized the material identity of the present human body with that of the resurrection. Although Augustine held a form of the millenarian hope in his early years as a Christian, he later adopted the view of the Donatist writer Tyconius in identifying this final, blessed period of history with the present age of the church.

The central themes of Latin eschatology through the Middle Ages were determined by Augustine as well as Gregory the Great. Augustine's influence was twofold. First, he portrayed the risen body in *The City of God* as this present body in a new, permanent form, reflecting either the holiness and moral freedom of the saved or the destructive self-alienation of the damned. Second, he emphasized the eternal existence of heaven and hell as Scripture portrays them. Gregory the Great's vision of the immediate judgment and purgative suffering of every individual at death, in *Dialogues* 4, was also a major influence.

Toward the end of the twelfth century, representatives of the new "scholastic" mode of theological discourse transformed the biblical and patristic images expressing Christian hope into a stable world of expectations. Death was seen as separating the soul from its body for the limited period of time remaining until the end of all history; the purgation of the faithful soul from the remaining traces of sin's effects came to be understood as a continuing state or "place" known as purgatory; heaven was seen primarily in terms of the eternal vision of God, which of itself confers ultimate knowledge and bliss; hell was conceived as both physical and psychological torment, resulting primarily from the loss of that fellowship with God for which humans are created; the resurrection was understood as the miraculous reconstruction of the whole human person in the fullest conceivable perfection of its qualities (see Thomas Aquinas, *Summa theologiae*, Supplement 69–99).

Opposition to some of the details of this medieval consensus about the "last things" played a role in the Reformers' critique of Western church practices, especially the promotion of indulgences to be "applied" to the souls in purgatory to win their release. Radical groups of Reformed Christians in the sixteenth and seventeenth centuries, in both England and continental Europe, revived the millenarian hope, which in the Middle Ages had been cherished by charismatic, anti-authoritarian movements such as the Joachimites and the "spiritual" Franciscans.

R. Bauckham and T. Hart, *Hope against Hope: Christian Eschatology at the Turn of the Millennium* (1999); H. U. von Balthasar, *Dare We Hope "That All Men Be Saved"?* (1988); C. W. Bynum, *The Resurrection of the Body* (1995); J. J. Collins, B. McGinn, and S. J. Stein, eds., *The Encyclopedia of Apocalypticism,* 3 vols. (1998); B. E. Daley, *The Hope of the Early Church* (2nd ed., 2003); Z. Hayes, *Visions of a Future: A Study of Christian Eschatology* (1989); C. E. Hill, *Regnum Caelorum: Patterns of Future Hope in Early Christianity* (1992);

J. LeGoff, *The Birth of Purgatory* (1984); J. Moltmann, *Theology of Hope* (1967); Moltmann, *The Coming of God* (1996); K. G. C. Newport, *Apocalypse and Millennium* (2000).

BRIAN E. DALEY, SJ

Ethics and Social Teaching, Early Christian

Throughout the early Christian period, ethical discourse was related to questions of identity, to the construction of a distinctive ethos within a wider culture, and to existing Jewish and pagan ethical models. Early Christian ethics was concerned with the representation of identity through behavior as well as with the relationship of the individual or the community to "the world." These themes are prominent in the New Testament, where the teachings of Jesus urge both a radicalizing of Jewish observance (Matt. 5:17–48) and a relativizing of social structures and obligations including marriage and procreation (e.g., Matt. 19:1–12; Luke 20:27–40), family (e.g., Matt. 10:34–39; Luke 14:26–27; Luke 23:29; Matt. 12:46–50), and wealth (e.g., Matt. 6:24–34; 19:16–30).

Two areas of tension dominated in early Christian ethics: the relationships of Christian behavior and belief to the broader culture and classical traditions of thought, and the role of perfectionism and elitism. In both of these areas, Christian writers, including Paul, were influenced by the dominant ethical theories of the period, including the concepts of virtue, vice, and the passions of the soul found in Stoicism and Platonism. Second-century apologists defended Christianity against charges of immorality; Justin Martyr noted that Christians value chastity, marry for procreation and not out of lust, do not expose their infants (abandon them in public places) avoid second marriages, pay their taxes, and obey authority (*Apology* 1.12–17, 27, 29). Justin and others, such as Clement of Alexandria (*Paedagogue, On Marriage* (Stromata III), *Who Is the Rich Man Who Will Be Saved?*), articulated a distinctive Christian identity and morality while emphasizing Christianity's continuity with the best of pagan philosophy and ethics. Tertullian, on the other hand (e.g., *Prescription Against Heresies* 7, *On the Shows, Apology*), used classical rhetoric and philosophical arguments yet insisted on Christianity's fundamental rejection of non-Christian society and the depravity of pagan morality. Yet both approaches demonstrate the need to define how a Christian should live distinctively in the context of a shared culture.

Ethical discourse also exhibited a tension between perfectionist notions of Christian identity and more accommodating expectations for behavior. This tension is evident in the New Testament (e.g., Paul's discussion of marriage in 1 Cor. 7), and it rises into high relief in later debates over postbaptismal sin, the value of martyrdom, the purity of the church, the legitimacy of marriage and sexual relations, free will, and the possibility of living without sin. Yet as vividly portrayed in sources such as the early fourth-century canons of the Council of Elvira or the late fourth-century sermons of John Chrysostom (e.g., *Homily 13 on Ephesians*, *Against the Circus Games and the Theater*), most Christians continued to marry, divorce, raise children, run households, and struggle with all of the moral dilemmas and failures that social existence entails.

The growth of monasticism, especially in the fourth century, created to some degree an institutionalized ascetic elite that tended to take on the weight of the ideal of perfection; yet this development was not without controversy. Some, such as Jovinian, criticized the spiritual elitism of ascetic theorists, such as Jerome, and argued for equality of virtue among Christians (Jerome, *Against Jovinian*). Pelagius likewise denounced spiritual hierarchy, but he argued rather that *all* Christians were called to be perfect and had been given the free will to choose the good and to resist the external habit of sin (e.g., *Letter to Demetrias*). In response to Pelagius and those influenced by him, Augustine argued not only that the will and ability to do good as well as the accomplishment of good are all dependent on grace (e.g., *Grace of Christ*), but also that sin exists not from external habit but from an internal tendency inherited from the disobedient first humans (e.g., *Marriage and Concupiscence*). The debate between Pelagius and his opponents encompasses all of the fundamental ethical questions of identity, human will, and ability implied in Jesus' directive, "If you would be perfect . . . come, follow me" (Matt. 19:21).

S. C. Barton, "The Relativisation of Family Ties in the Jewish and Graeco-Roman Traditions," in *Constructing Early Christian Families*, ed. H. Moxnes (1997), 81–100; R. L. Fox, *Pagans and Christians* (1987), 336–74; J. E. Grubbs, "'Pagan' and 'Christian' Marriage: The State of the Question," *JECS* 2 (1994): 361–412; R. Markus, *The End of Ancient Christianity* (1990); W. A. Meeks, *The Moral World of the First Christians* (1986);

E. Osborn, *Ethical Patterns in Early Christian Thought* (1976); T. M. Shaw, "Sex and Sexual Renunciation," in *The Early Christian World*, vol. 1, ed. P. F. Esler (2000), 401–21.

TERESA M. SHAW

Ethiopian Christianity

Ethiopian Christian tradition traces the origins of the faith there to the conversion of the royal eunuch by the evangelist Philip as recorded in Acts 8:26–29, yet this tradition asserts a much older biblical link, namely, that the queen of Sheba who visited the Israelite king Solomon (1 Kgs. 10:1–13) was an Ethiopian. She bore him a son, Menelik, a name later assumed by Ethiopian kings. These may be legends, but historically Semites from Arabia invaded Ethiopia between 1000 and 400 BCE, and the country's language, Ge'ez, is Semitic.

Determining the origins of Ethiopian Christianity is hindered by ancient Christian writers who confused Ethiopia with India and, more frequently, with Nubia (modern Sudan). History begins in approximately 330 CE when two Syrian Christian brothers, Adesius and Frumentius, were shipwrecked off the coast and were enslaved in Axum, as the Ethiopian kingdom was called. They managed to win the king's favor and became tutors to the crown prince. When their student became the ruler, Frumentius went to Alexandria to ask the bishop Athanasius to send a bishop to Ethiopia. Athanasius consecrated Frumentius, making him the founder of the Ethiopian church. The Alexandrian strongly supported the Council of Nicaea, and c. 356 the Arianizing Roman emperor Constantius II wrote to the king at Axum to try to replace Frumentius with an Arian. The king refused, and throughout the early Christian period, the bishop of Ethiopia was consecrated in Alexandria and was always an Egyptian monk. This practice guaranteed loyalty to Alexandria but also guaranteed that the bishop knew little of Ethiopian customs and traditions and thus knew little of the people, among whom Christianity spread slowly.

Egypt became Monophysite in the fifth century and Syria in the sixth. Monophysite missionaries from both countries worked in Ethiopia, the most important being the "Nine Saints," Syrians who traveled about the countryside. Also from this century came the first Ethiopic translation of the Bible. In the next century the Arab conquests cut the country off from the rest of Christendom, but this lone African Christian country struggled and survived for a millennium, an achievement that won no credit or even sympathy from later Catholic and Protestant missionaries who sought to "re-evangelize" the Ethiopians.

The Ethiopian church produced magnificently illustrated manuscripts of the Bible and preserved some biblical apocrypha not known elsewhere, such as the complete text of the Jewish *Book of Enoch*.

M. Heldman, *African Zion* (1993); B. Sundkler and C. Steed, *A History of the Church in Africa* (2000), chap 1; S. C. Munro-Hay, *Ethiopia: The Unknown Land* (2001).

JOSEPH F. KELLY

Eucharist   The term comes from the Greek verb *eucharistein*, "to give thanks." The Gospel writers used a form of it when quoting Jesus' words at the Last Supper, when he took the bread, gave thanks, broke it, and gave it to them. The church has taken that meal, eaten on the night before his crucifixion, to be the first Eucharist, Lord's Supper, or Holy Communion. "Do this," Jesus said, "in remembrance of me."

Scholars debate the meaning of "remembrance." Jesus is not asking his disciples simply to ponder nostalgic memories from the past. This remembrance is not a psychological act but rather evokes the Jewish image of memorial, namely, to hold up before God a reminder of God's pledge made to humankind in the death and resurrection of the Lord. That pledge is to defeat sin and death and bring into being a new creation, a new heaven and earth.

The Eucharist draws its significance not only from Jesus' last meal but also from accounts of meals during his ministry and after his resurrection. Forms of the same four Greek words recur in the meal stories: "took," "gave thanks" (or "blessed"), "broke," "gave." While the holy meal certainly re-presents Jesus' death, it also affirms his contemporary presence to those who share it and points forward to the consummation, the reign of God, in which people "shall come from east and west, and from north and south, and sit at table in the kingdom of God" (Luke 13:29).

Most likely the first Christians celebrated the Lord's Supper weekly on Sunday (the day of resurrection) as part of a common meal. When Jewish Christians were no longer welcome in the synagogue, they combined the synagogue service and the Lord's Supper into one service, which became the norm for Christian worship on the Lord's Day. From NT times, the church believed that the risen Christ became present to the assembly in the Eucharist. The Western church (based in Rome) encouraged philosophical speculation on the nature of that presence, how it was related to the bread and wine, and how and when it became manifest. Borrowing from Aristotelian philosophy, Thomas Aquinas articulated the doctrine of transubstantiation, which set the framework of discussion and debate for the Protestant reformers of the sixteenth century.

Martin Luther (1483–1546), Huldrych Zwingli (1484–1531), and others challenged the official doctrine and offered their own views. Basing his theology on the doctrine of ubiquity (Christ, after his ascension, is everywhere, and his humanity is inseparable from his deity), Luther maintained that in the Eucharist, the bread and wine do not change into Christ's body and blood but that the body and blood become present "in, with, and under" the bread and wine. Zwingli took a more radical view, arguing that the bread and wine simply represent Christ's body and blood. Forming a position similar to the Orthodox, John Calvin was reluctant to join the metaphysical speculation. Nor was he satisfied with Zwingli's reductionism. Calvin affirmed that Christ is truly present in the Eucharist, mediated by the Holy Spirit at work in and through the whole service, culminating in the acts of eating and drinking.

In pre-Reformation times, the Mass (Eucharist) was celebrated weekly and even daily, but few actually communed. Christians communed so rarely that the Fourth Lateran Council in 1215 ruled that all were obligated to receive Communion at least once a year, at Easter. The Reformers rejected the medieval practice of celebrating the Eucharist without communicants. Zwingli favored quarterly Communion, at which the whole assembly would share the meal. Quarterly Communion quadrupled the number of times most Christians communed. Both Luther and Calvin believed in restoring as the norm a service of both Word and sacrament. Luther achieved success for awhile, but weekly Eucharist died out in most of Lutheranism by the eighteenth century. The city council of Geneva overruled Calvin, favoring quarterly Communion as in Zurich. The Church of England ordinarily celebrated the Eucharist only a few times a year into the nineteenth century. Calvin used the word "defect" to describe the service of the Word alone, yet it has become standard in most Protestant churches until recently.

From the late nineteenth and into the twentieth century, Protestants and Catholics alike experienced a renewal of interest in worship. Biblical and historical scholarship uncovered dimensions of the early church's eucharistic worship. An ecumenical consensus emerged, becoming dramatically apparent in the reforms of Vatican Council II in the 1960s. Most contemporary service books of many denominations reflect that consensus. Word and sacrament are taken to be the norm for every Sunday. The eucharistic services are marked by a tone of solemn joy, rooted in the confidence of the risen Christ's presence, and turned toward his coming again in the eschatological consummation.

The new eucharistic prayers are most likely to follow the model of the West Syrian tradition of Antioch, descended from forms of Jewish prayer at table. These prayers are Trinitarian, beginning with thanksgiving for God's work of creation and redemption, concluding with the Sanctus and Benedictus. Then comes an *anamnesis*, with thanks specifically for Christ in his incarnation, holy life, death, resurrection, ascension, and coming again, with words of institution leading to a memorial acclamation; and finally there is the *epiclesis*, asking for the Holy Spirit to bless the assembly and the gifts of bread and wine. The Great Thanksgiving concludes with a Trinitarian doxology and the people's Amen. The Lord's Prayer follows. With slight variation, one can recognize the same prayer in Orthodox, Roman Catholic, Lutheran, Presbyterian, Methodist, and other churches.

L. Bouyer, *Eucharist* (1968); G. Dix, *The Shape of the Liturgy* (1982); C. Jones, G. Wainwright, E. Yarnold, P. Bradshaw, eds., *The Study of Liturgy* (1992); J. Jungmann, *The Mass of the Roman Rite* (1959); A. Schmemann, *Eucharist: Sacrament of the Kingdom* (1987); M. Thurian, *The Eucharistic Memorial* (1960).

RONALD P. BYARS

Eucharistic Controversies in the Reformation
Christ's words "This is my body" almost proved the downfall of sixteenth-century Protestantism. The debate over their meaning first emerged within the circle around Martin Luther when Andress Karlstadt, in 1524, interpreted the words of institution (Matt. 26:26) in a spiritual manner unacceptable to Luther. Following Karlstadt's expulsion from Saxony, Luther's *Against the Heavenly Prophets* (c. 1524) resolutely denounced Karlstadt's interpretation of the Lord's Supper. At this time Huldrych Zwingli was formulating his

own position on the Lord's Supper in response to a letter by the Dutchman Cornelius Hoen. What Zwingli drew from Hoen was the figurative interpretation (*est = significat*). In March 1525 Zwingli openly expressed his eucharistic position in his *Commentary on the True and False Religion*. The Basel reformer Johannes Oecolampadius laid down a similar position with a slightly different emphasis. It was at this point that warfare broke out. Luther entered the fray in 1526 with his *Sermon on the Body and Blood of Christ*, which inaugurated three years of bitter conflict between himself and Zwingli, marked by the exchange of increasingly vitriolic attacks. Zwingli attempted a *Friendly Exegesis* and sent a copy to Luther with a letter (April 1, 1527). Luther's reply, *That the Words of Christ, "This Is My Body," Stand Fast against the Fanatics*, denounced Zwingli, Oecolampadius, and Karlstadt in the same breath: all were minions of the devil. Against them Luther held that the meaning of the words of institution had to be interpreted literally. The polemical battle endured until the Marburg Colloquy (1529), called by Philip of Hesse in order to win religious unity for his political plans. The colloquy, though dramatic, did not reconcile the parties or even advance the debate. Following Zwingli's death in 1531, Heinrich Bullinger attempted to settle the dispute, but relations with Luther were poisoned and Bullinger eventually gave up hope of any reconciliation. By the mid-1530s the Eucharist had became a crucial symbol in the warfare between the confessional parties, dominated by Luther's condemnation of Zwingli. The Swiss could not accept the 1536 *Wittenberg Accord* because it was essentially Lutheran in its assertion of the corporal presence and oral manducation (process of assimilating a substance into oneself). A year and a half before his death, Luther went on the offensive again, to the grief of Melanchthon and other friends, in a vituperative attack on the "Sacramentarians" with his *Short Confession on the Holy Sacrament* (1544). By the time of his death there were no further negotiations between Lutherans and Zwinglians. Luther had famously remarked that he would rather drink blood with the papists than wine with the Zwinglians.

Luther had responded more favorably to the work of the young John Calvin. Calvin's eucharistic theology owed much to both Zwinglian and Lutheran theology, though he always accorded Luther the greater honor. The centrality of the Lord's Supper in Calvin's thought was reflected in his efforts to bring unity to the Protestant camp. He began by coming to an arrangement with Heinrich Bullinger (*Consensus Tigurinus*, 1549). This arrangement only fueled old hostilities, and Calvin was attacked by Gnesio-Lutheran Joachim Westphal, superintendent in Hamburg, during the mid-1550s. Calvin's defense of the *Consensus* formed a crucial stage in the emergence of Reformed teaching on the Lord's Supper. Calvin wrote his last tract against Westphal in 1557 (*Last Admonition to Westphal*), but the dispute between Bullinger and Calvin and the north German Lutherans raged on until the end of the decade.

The eucharistic controversies not only pitted established churches against one another, but they played an important role in the evolution of refugee churches across Europe. In communities such as London, Emden, and Wesel, under the leadership of men such as John Laski, the issue of the "sacramentarians" remained controversial. Even in the late sixteenth century, with the emergence of Calvinism in the HRE, the Eucharist remained central to hostilities between the Reformed and Lutheran parties.

———

M. Brecht, *Martin Luther*, 3 vols. (1985–1993); M. U. Edwards, *Luther and the False Brethren* (1975); B. A. Gerrish, *Grace and Gratitude: The Eucharistic Theology of John Calvin* (1993); B. Gordon, "Calvin and the Swiss Reformed Churches," in *Calvinism in Europe, 1540–1620*, ed. A. Pettegree, A. Duke, and G. Lewis (1994); B. Nischan, *Prince, People, and Confession: The Second Reformation in Brandenburg* (1994); A. Pettegree, *Marian Protestantism: Six Studies* (1996); P. Rorem, *Calvin and Bullinger on the Lord's Supper* (1989).

BRUCE GORDON

Eudoxia (d. 404), wife of Emperor Arcadius. Raised in Constantinople, Eudoxia was the daughter of the Frankish general, Bauto, who served Valentinian II. In 395 she married Arcadius and had five children, including the future Theodosius II. She was proclaimed Augusta in 400 and died following a miscarriage in October 404.

She is best known for her role in ruining the courtier Eutropius and, eventually, John Chrysostom, bishop of Constantinople. Initially her piety as a mother and venerator of martyrs drew John's praise. Even when his influence waned, he would still refer actions, such as the closure of the last pagan temple in Gaza (402), to Eudoxia's advisers and encourage the Tall Brothers (403) to seek her support against Theophilus of Alexandria. Neverthe-

less, Eudoxia overturned John's dismissal of Severian of Gabala in 401. She regarded John's homiletic references to Jezebel and Salome as insults to imperial dignity. Ultimately siding with Theophilus, she encouraged John's condemnation at the Synod of the Oak (403). While initially recalling him from exile, the next year she helped make that exile permanent when John complained in a homily about celebrations honoring her statue as Augusta.

———

K. Holum, *Theodosian Empresses* (1982); J. N. D. Kelly, *Golden Mouth* (1995); J. R. Martindale, ed., *The Prosopography of the Later Roman Empire*, vol. 2 (1980); F. van Ommeslaeghe, "Jean Chrysostome en conflit avec l'impératrice Eudoxie. Le dossier et les origines d'une légende," *Analecta Bollandiana* (1979), 131–59.

LISA D. MAUGANS DRIVER

Eugenius IV (c. 1383–1447), pope. Born in Venice to a merchant family, Gabriele Condulmaro's uncle, Pope Gregory XII (Roman pope, 1406–1415, during the papal schism) appointed him bishop of Siena in 1407 and cardinal in 1408. Gabriele succeeded Pope Martin V, otherwise known as Oddo Colonna, winning the support of cardinals by conceding papal incomes to them. As pope he managed, with some difficulty, to pacify the Colonna family while also confronting the ongoing Hussite revolt and an impending council, the Council of Basel, whose mandate could hardly have seemed less threatening. The council meant to continue the earlier Council of Constance's ongoing program of reform, and Eugenius did not. The council also intended to resolve the Hussite schism and end the schism between the Greek church and the papacy. Eugenius declared the Council of Basel dissolved in December 1431, soon after his rise to the papal throne, but after meeting relentless opposition, he withdrew the decision on February 15, 1433, and officially recognized the council. Anxious to control the assembly, he moved it to Italy in 1437. Those who remained at Basel deposed him on June 25, 1439, and elected a new pope, who took the name Felix V. Meanwhile, Eugenius and his supporters completed discussions with representatives of the Greek churches, who had followed him to Italy to continue negotiations at Bologna on May 24, 1437. The negotiations culminated in a formal declaration of reunion on July 5, 1439. The enormity of this accomplishment helped Eugenius eventually prevail over the continuing Council of Basel and its antipope Felix, winning the eventual support of the Holy Roman Emperor and the kings of Aragon and Scotland. Often judged harshly for his opposition to conciliarism, Eugenius reestablished the preeminence of papal government in the church and brought an end to the conciliar movement.

J. A. Gutwirth, "Eugenius IV," in *The Great Popes through History: An Encyclopedia*, ed. F. J. Coppa, vol. 1 (2002), 229–37; J. W. Stieber, *Pope Eugenius IV, the Council of Basel, and the Secular and Ecclesiastical Authorities in the Empire: The Conflict over Supreme Authority and Power in the Church* (1978); L. Vones, "Eugene IV," *Dictionary of Popes and the Papacy*, ed. B. Steimer, M. G. Parker (2001), 33–34; F.-C. Uginet, "Eugene IV," in *The Papacy: An Encyclopedia*, vol. 1, ed. P. Levillain, J. W. O'Malley (2002), 534–37.

CHRISTOPHER OCKER

Eugenius of Carthage (d. 505), bishop of Carthage from 479. Eugenius was a staunch supporter of orthodox Nicene theology during a time when anti-Nicene theology ("Arian" or "homoian") had the backing of the Vandal kings Huneric and then Thrasamund. During this time Christians who followed Nicaea and believed in the consubstantiality of the Father, Son, and Holy Spirit were persecuted and killed. Like earlier persecutions, these events produced a literature of acts of the martyrs that, like the previous *Acta*, survived primarily as episodes in larger church histories. Many early *Acta* are preserved in the *Ecclesiastical History* of Eusebius of Caesarea, while the *Acta* of Eugenius are preserved in the histories of Gregory of Tours. Persecution at the end of the fifth and beginning of the sixth century produced many Nicene martyrs (e.g., bishops Vindimialis and Longinus, the archdeacon Octavianus). It was during this time that Eugenius engaged in a series of public confrontations with the homoian bishop of Carthage, Cyrola, ranging from theological debate to miraculous healings. Eugenius was finally brought before the Vandal king, who sentenced him to exile in Gaul, where he died.

DHGE 15 (1912–), 1261–62.

MICHEL RENE BARNES

Eunomius of Cyzicus (c. 325–c. 395), anti-Nicene bishop of Cyzicus. Eunomius was born in Cappadocia of a free but poor artisan family. Almost all of his writings have been lost; what we know of his theology comes largely from his opponents, of which there were many. After the winter synod of Constantinople in 359–360, where homoian theology was established by the emperor as the official Trinitarian theology, Eunomius became bishop of Cyzicus. He held the office for only a few years before running afoul of, perhaps, both his parishioners and the emperor.

Eunomius's infamy springs almost entirely from his Trinitarian theology. He famously identified the essence of God with the state of unbegottenness: God is that who is by nature uncaused. God's nature, therefore, cannot be reproduced in any offspring, since reproduction is a kind of cause. The Son is the product of God's will, brought into being (created) through God's activity or operation. The Son is thus unlike God in essence but like God in activity or will. The Holy Spirit is a creature of the Son. It is not entirely clear whether Eunomius thought the Spirit exists as an essence or is simply the "activity" of the Son.

Eunomius supported this theology with a distinctive account of language, that is, that names express the essence of the thing named. The proper name of God is "Unbegotten," and all other titles must be understood either as synonyms of that name or as conditioned by that existence. For example, "Simple" is a divine title that expresses an aspect of Unbegotten existence, while a title such as "Light" has to be understood as "Unbegotten Light." (The Son, by contrast, is "Begotten Light," a different thing entirely.)

Eunomius, *The Extant Works*, OCuT, ed. and trans. R. P. Vaggione (1987); R. P. Vaggione, *Eunomius of Cyzicus and the Nicene Revolution* (2000).

MICHEL RENE BARNES

Eusebius of Caesarea (c. 260–339), East Roman apologist, bishop, exegete, and historian. Eusebius lived in Caesarea, where he was a disciple of Origen's student Pamphilus and where he made use of Origen's library. He came of age during the "Great Peace" of the church and then lived through the "Great Persecution," which began in 303. He witnessed the persecutions at Caesarea, Tyre, and Egypt; in Egypt he may have been jailed. After the end of the persecution he became bishop of Caesarea, perhaps in 314, and he worked with the emperor Constantine to restore the property and power of the church. In the Trinitarian debate Eusebius sought a middle ground. He was frequently attacked as insufficiently orthodox, despite his grudging adherence to the Nicene Creed in 325.

Of Eusebius's biblical commentaries, only his works on Isaiah and the Psalms survive. These books, not coincidentally, contain the largest number of passages understood to prophesy the coming of Christ. His approach was allegorical but more historical and less philosophical than that of Origen. He also wrote a concordance to the Gospels, which sought to harmonize the different accounts. His work *On Place Names in Holy Scripture*, drew on a variety of ancient and contemporary sources and is still used today to reconstruct the map of fourth-century Palestine.

Eusebius's treatise *Against Hierocles* was an early apologetic work, directed against the claim that the pagan holy man Apollonius of Tyana had performed miracles equivalent to those of Jesus. The *General Elementary Introduction to Christianity* was written for an interested pagan audience. The first five books, which do not survive, argued against paganism; the second five argued for the superiority of the Christian to the Jewish interpretation of the Bible, largely through detailed examination of OT messianic prophesies. Twenty-five books titled *Against Porphyry* do not survive, but their contents were recycled for the twenty books that comprise the *Preparation for the Gospel* and the *Demonstration of the Gospel*. These works feature long quotations from a very wide range of authors. In the *Preparation* Eusebius attempts to show that there is an essential harmony between Christianity and Greco-Roman civilization and that the best of Greek thought was derived from the older teachings of the Hebrews. The *Demonstration* argues by biblical citation that Christianity is the natural and superior heir to Judaism. Eusebius's *Divine Manifestation* is an abridged version of these two works in five books.

Eusebius's *Chronicle* survives in a Latin translation with an extension by Jerome and in an Armenian translation. The first part of this work, the *Chronography*, presents an outline of Near Eastern history. The second part, the *Canons*, presents this material in several columns to allow the chronological comparison of events and people from the histories of the Hebrews, Persians, Egyptians, Greeks, Romans, and many others. One goal of this work was to prove definitively the greater antiquity of the history of the Jews.

Eusebius's most important and original work is the *Ecclesiastical History*. In this work, which appears in several updated editions, he covers the period from the time of Jesus to the rise of Constantine. His work remains a major source for the first few centuries of Christian-ity. Eusebius included information about the bishops, writers, and teachers of the early church as well as discussions of persecutions, heresy, and the disasters that fell upon the Jews. Material that Eusebius used for his contemporary account *The Martyrs of Palestine* was incorporated into the latter books of the *Ecclesiastical History*. The work, despite some chronological and stylistic infelicities, served as the model for the future church histories of Rufinus, Socrates, Sozomen, Philostorgius, Theodoret, and Evagrius. History, for Eusebius, was the unfolding revelation of God's will. Divine punishment was visited upon persecutors, and the coming of Constantine was understood as the culmination of the divine plan for the uniting of church and empire.

Eusebius's works in numerous genres share a common understanding of Christianity as both ancient and as the culmination of Greco-Roman civilization. His theology of history was immensely influential and, after its adoption by the Spaniard Orosius, competed throughout the Middle Ages with the doctrine laid out in Augustine's *City of God*.

———

T. Barnes, *Constantine and Eusebius* (1981); G. Chesnut, *The First Christian Histories* (1986); A. Kofsky, *Eusebius of Caesarea against Paganism* (2000); D. Wallace-Hadrill, *Eusebius of Caesarea* (1960).

                                        DAVID ROHRBACHER

Eusebius of Nicomedia (d. c. 342),

bishop of Berytus (modern Beirut) and then of Nicomedia, the imperial capital in Asia Minor. Eusebius was a student of Lucian of Antioch and an early supporter of Arius in his battle with Alexander of Alexandria. He was not an "Arian," but one of a number who were opposed to Alexander even though they did not share all of Arius's views. At the Council of Nicaea (325) he may have presented a statement of faith that was rejected, but he eventually signed the Nicene Creed. Shortly afterward he was exiled for receiving into communion two of Arius's supporters. He was allowed to return in 328 or 329 and resumed his position of influence. Contemporary reports speak of his followers as "those around Eusebius" (*hoi peri Eusebian*), indicating that he was seen as the leader of an ecclesiastical party. He played some role in the deposition of Athanasius at the Council of Tyre in 335, although accounts of him as the mastermind of an "Arian" conspiracy are no longer sustainable. In 337 he baptized Constantine as the emperor lay dying. In 339 he became bishop of Constantinople.

Little of his writing survives: a letter to Paulinus of Tyre and some fragments. The letter gives the basics of his account of the Son: "[There is] one, the unoriginated, and one produced by him truly and not from his substance, not participating at all in the unoriginated nature nor in his substance, but produced as altogether different in his nature and in his power, being in complete likeness of disposition and power to him who made him."

CPG II (1974–), 2045–56; G. Bardy, *Recherches sur Saint Lucien d'Antioche et son école* (1936), 296–315; T. D. Barnes, *Constantine and Eusebius* (1981); R. P. C. Hanson, *The Search for the Christian Doctrine of God* (1988), 27–32.

LEWIS AYRES

Eusebius of Vercelli (d. 371), pro-Nicene bishop. Eusebius, a native of Sardinia, was elected bishop of Vercelli in northern Italy in 340. He was among the strongest opponents of Arianism in the West. Pope Liberius sent him and Lucifer of Cagliari on a mission to Constantius in 354. At the Synod of Milan (355), Eusebius refused to sign the condemnation of Athanasius and, as a result, was exiled to the East, along with Lucifer of Cagliari and Dionysius of Milan; he remained there until the accession of Julian in 362. In 362 in Alexandria, Eusebius signed the *Tome to the Antiochenes* that Athanasius drafted and brought it to Antioch. When he returned to Vercelli, Eusebius introduced the practice of having his clergy live a common life with him; hence, he is sometimes honored as one of the founders of canons regular. Upon Eusebius's death Ambrose of Milan wrote to the church at Vercelli to regulate the episcopal election and, in the letter, describes the clerical-monastic life at Vercelli. Three of Eusebius's letters survive. He wrote a commentary on the Psalms, which is lost. A work on the Trinity is attributed to him but is probably not authentic.

V. Bulhart, ed., *Eusebii Vercellensis Episcopi quae supersunt* (1957); J. T. Lienhard, "Patristic Sermons on Eusebius of Vercelli and Their Relation to His Monasticism," *Rbén* 87 (1977): 164–72.

JOSEPH T. LIENHARD

Eustathius of Antioch (fl. c. 325), bishop of Antioch and theologian. Born at Side in southern Asia Minor, Eustathius was elected bishop of Beroea and then, about 324, bishop of Antioch in Syria. He attended the Council of Nicaea in 325 and supported its definition but opposed the theology of Eusebius of Caesarea. He was deposed a few years later, for reasons variously reported, and exiled to Thrace. His supporters rioted and continued as a separately worshiping body through the early fifth century. Eustathius was accused of Sabellianism but was a strong supporter of the Council of Nicaea. His explanation of the council's teaching, however, inhibited his followers from accepting what eventually became the normative interpretation of its meaning (they are thus sometimes called "old" as opposed to "new" or "neo-" Nicenes). Eustathius rejected any so-called *Logos/sarx* (Word/flesh) Christology and emphasized the completeness of Christ's human nature, including his possession of a soul. Only one of his works survives in its entirety, an attack on Origen's interpretation of 1 Samuel 28:6–25 (the witch of Endor); all the rest are fragmentary. Eustathius is rarely mentioned after his deposition but is alleged to have died c. 360 in Thrace.

CPG 2 (1974–), 3350–98; J. Quasten, *Patrology*, vol. 3 (1963), 302–6; M. Spanneut, *Recherches sur les écrits d'Eustathe d'Antioche* (1948); R. P. C. Hanson, *The Search for the Christian Doctrine of God* (1988): 208–17.

RICHARD PAUL VAGGIONE, OHC

Eustochium (d. 418/419), Roman virgin, daughter of Paula, friend of Jerome. Jerome refers to Eustochium as "the first virgin of noble birth in Rome." The third daughter of the wealthy young widow Paula, Eustochium was dedicated to the virginal life from a young age. She and Paula were active with Marcella and other Roman women in the small groups of ascetic Christians who met in homes for prayer, instruction, and study of Scripture. Jerome addressed a long letter (*Epistula* 22), really a treatise on the topic of virginity, to Eustochium (384). He instructs the adolescent Eustochium on the best lifestyle, fasting, diet, seclusion, and behavior appropriate for her and other ascetics. Jerome describes virginity as marriage to Christ, using powerful erotic imagery that has been the subject of scholarly analysis, and offers only the most perfunctory approval of marriage. He vividly recalls his own ascetic struggles and fleshly desires, and condemns so-called heretical and false virgins. Eustochium accompanied her mother to Bethlehem, where they joined Jerome (385), and oversaw the women's monastery there after Paula's death

(404). Jerome notes that he translated the ceno-bitic rules of Pachomius into Latin so that Eustochium might use them in her monastery and reports that Eustochium, like Paula, learned Hebrew for biblical study.

Jerome, *Letters* 22, 31, 54.13, 108; Palladius, *Lausiac History* 41.2.

TERESA M. SHAW

Eutyches (370–451), controversial monk.

As the archimandrite of a monastery in Constantinople, Eutyches was a supporter of Cyril of Alexandria in the Nestorian controversy. Eutyches rejected the Formulary of Reunion between Cyril of Alexandria and John of Antioch, preferring to maintain the "one nature of God the Word incarnate" formula of the early Cyril. Eutyches was condemned by Bishop Flavian of Constantinople in 448 for refusing to affirm two natures in Christ after the union. Eutyches claimed that to do so would result in adoptionism. Bishop Dioscorus of Alexandria came to Eutyches' defense, and Emperor Theodosius called a synod in Ephesus in 449. At the synod, later to be called the "Robber Synod," Eutyches was rehabilitated and Flavian was deposed. Bishop Leo of Rome wrote to the synod denouncing Eutyches, but Dioscorus, who presided, refused to read the letter.

After the emperor's untimely death, his sister Pulcheria assumed the throne and called the Council of Chalcedon in 451. The council received as orthodox the letter from Leo (known as Leo's *Tome*) and condemned Dioscorus and Eutyches. Both died in exile.

A. Grillmeier and H. Bacht, *Das Konzil von Chalkedon* (1951); E. Schwartz, *Der Prozess des Eutyches* (1929).

STEVEN A. MCKINION

Evagrius of Pontus (345–399), an early theorist of Christian mysticism. Evagrius, the son of a country bishop, grew up in Pontus, near the Black Sea. In the 370s he moved to Constantinople, where Gregory of Nazianzus ordained him deacon. There he played an important role in the debate on the Trinity during the Council of Constantinople in 381. Soon after, he fell in love with a married woman and had to flee the capital. In Jerusalem, he befriended two Latin monastics, Melania the Elder and Rufinus of Aquileia. Under Melania's influence, he embraced the monastic life and moved to Egypt. In 383 Evagrius settled in Nitria, a cenobitic monastery forty miles from Alexandria, and

apprenticed under two leading desert fathers, Macarius the Alexandrian and Macarius the Egyptian. Two years later he moved to Kellia in Lower Egypt, where he spent the remaining fourteen years of his life. There he joined a circle of intellectual monks (led by the so-called Tall Brothers) and made his living as a calligrapher. Renowned for his gift of discernment of spirits, he attracted an influential circle of disciples, including Palladius. After his death, friends and disciples were persecuted and forced to flee Egypt during the Origenist controversy.

Evagrius was a prolific author. His writings are largely collections of terse proverblike sentences or brief paragraphs called "chapters" (*kephalaia*). His best-known work, the hundred-chapter *Praktikos*, focuses on "ascetic practice" (*praktikē*) and sets out his famous catalog of the eight evil "thoughts" (*logismoi*): gluttony, fornication, greed, sadness, anger, listlessness (*acēdia*), vainglory, and pride. Evagrius's disciple Cassian brought this scheme to the Latin West, where it became, with modification, the "seven deadly sins."

Other works by Evagrius are *The Gnostic* (*Gnostikos*), a work for advanced monks on spiritual fatherhood and exegesis; *On Prayer* (*De oratione*), a work that characterizes mystical prayer as ceaseless, wordless, and imageless; *Reflections* (*Skemmata*), a work that describes the human mind as an interior Mount Sinai, where one encounters the "sapphire light" of the Trinity; *Counter-Arguments* (*Antirrhetikos*), a compendium of 498 temptations; and *Scholia*, collections of brief commentaries on select biblical verses. Evagrius's most controversial work was the *Gnostic Chapters* (*Kephalaia gnostica*), an esoteric text of 540 chapters. Drawing on Origen, he sketched a bold cosmological vision that asserts both the preexistence of minds and a cosmic restoration of all things into God (*apokatastasis*).

Evagrius was posthumously condemned for Origenism by the Second Council of Constantinople in 553. His writings were preserved either under others' names (Basil of Caesarea, Nilus of Ancyra) or in Syriac and Armenian translations. In the twentieth century, scholars began rediscovering his works and recognized how profoundly Evagrius influenced mystical theologies in Byzantium, the Latin West, and the Syriac East. Evagrius is now counted among the most influential figures in the history of Christian spirituality.

A. Casiday, *Evagrius Ponticus* (2006); L. Dysinger, *Psalmody and Prayer in the Writings of Evagrius Ponticus* (2005); R. Sinkewicz, *Evagrius of Pontus* (2003); W. Harmless and R. R. Fitzgerald, "The Sapphire Light of the Mind: The *Skemmata* of Evagrius Ponticus," *TS* 62 (2001): 498–529.

WILLIAM HARMLESS, SJ

Evagrius Scholasticus (c. 535–c. 594), lawyer and church historian. Evagrius was born in the Syrian town of Epiphania. He received a classical education, which included study in rhetoric, probably at Antioch. His education culminated with four years of law at Constantinople, which qualified him as *scholasticus* ("advocate"). Evagrius apparently spent his adult life at Antioch. He supplemented a successful legal career with writing. His only extant work is the *Ecclesiastical History* in six books, which addresses the history of the church from 431 to 592. Evagrius was in the service of Gregory, patriarch of Antioch (570–592). The author defended this bishop's career as well as his religious agenda of doctrinal conciliation. As a historian, Evagrius gathered information from hagiography and histories such as the books of Procopius and Zosimus. Evagrius liberally quoted (and so has helped preserve) ecclesiastical documents such as the acts of various councils. His narrative highlights the Nestorian controversy, which raged in the Eastern empire during the fifth and sixth centuries. Although Evagrius regarded Nestorius as a heretic, he, like his patron Gregory, promoted conciliation among the different doctrinal contestants. Evagrius's view of history was providential. He considered the difficult doctrinal debates of his era disruptive but necessary; in the end, he believed, the church would be the stronger for them.

———

Evagrius, *The Ecclesiastical History of Evagrius Scholasticus*, ed. and trans. Michael Whitby (2000).

ALLEN E. JONES

Evergetinos   Around 1050, Paul Evergetinos founded a monastery dedicated to the Theotokos Evergetis in the outskirts of Constantinople. It was possible for lay commendatories (*charistikarioi*) to use or misappropriate monastic resources for personal or family gain. Some wealthy patrons had founded monasteries to provide a kind of retirement home for the founder, and perhaps some family members as well, who would not live the common life of the monastery. The founding of this monastery was part of a monastic reform movement in the eleventh century designed to secure a monastery's ability to control its own physical resources and membership. The monastery's *typikon* provided that the monastery was to be free of all outside control. The monks were not to have servants or private property and were to eat in common. The liturgy was to be celebrated daily, and contact between monks and their families was regulated. Evergetinos compiled a collection of traditional monastic texts and a significant number of anonymous hagiographies into a work that he called the *Synagoge* but that is generally called the *Evergetinos*. It is noteworthy for the way it uses traditional material discussing monks and their relations to family and the outside world to address the reformer's concerns.

———

M. E. Mullett and A. Kirby, *The Theotokos Evergetis and Eleventh-Century Monasticism* (1994).

EUGENE M. LUDWIG, OFM CAP.

Excommunication   This term refers to the exclusion of Christians from the fullness of ecclesial (especially eucharistic) communion with other members of their church. Churches have used exclusions of varying degrees and duration either as the first step in a penitential process aimed at provoking serious sinners to conversion, or simply as a penalty to protect the community's public order of faith or discipline from serious offenders. Thus, excommunication has evolved along with Christian penitential institutions and conceptions of church order, law, and authority.

The NT discipline in this area (e.g., 1 Cor. 5; Matt. 18:15–18; 2 John 7–11; 3 John 9–10) arose in the context of Jewish practices attested in the Old Testament, Dead Sea Scrolls, and rabbinical literature. Christians may hope for the excommunicate's conversion, reentry into community life, and salvation, but not always (Heb. 6:4–6).

From at least the mid-second century (*Shepherd of Hermas*, *Vision* 2.2, *Mandate* 4.3), the church tended to offer sinners only one chance at penitential excommunication and return to the community through ever more clearly defined, ritual, and public stages of conversion. The Carolingian reform confirmed the usage of a repeatable, private penitential excommunication for occult sins. The Latin schoolmen clearly differentiated between exclusion from the Eucharist lifted through the sacrament of penance and the juridical penalty of excommunication.

During the Quartodeciman controversy, Pope Victor furnished one of the earliest documented examples of the excommunication of whole churches by another church (Eusebius, *Hist. eccl.* 5.23–25). This practice was to solemnize many later schisms.

K. Hein, *Eucharist and Excommunication: A Study in Early Christian Doctrine and Discipline* (1975); W. M. Plöchl, *Geschichte des Kirchenrechts*, 5 vols. (1953, 1960–1969); C. Vogel, "Pénitence et excommunication dans l'Eglise ancienne et durant le haut moyen age," *Concilium* (French version) 107 (1975): 11–22.
JOSEPH G. MUELLER, SJ

Eznik of Kolb (fifth cent.), bishop of Bagrewand and author. He composed a treatise of theology and apologetic in Armenian, which modern editors and translators have titled *On God* or *Against the Sects*. It is a description of the God of the Christian religion and a polemic work against other religious ideas. Eznik addressed perceived threats to Christianity in Armenia from heretical and non-Christian movements, including Valentinian Gnosticism and the schools of Greek philosophy, Manicheism, Marcionism, and Zoroastrian Zurvanism. In his treatise can be found many earlier Greek and Syriac patristic sources. Eznik was one of the disciples of Bishop Maštocʻ (d. 440) charged with translating the Bible and church literature from Syriac and Greek into Armenian. Eznik traveled to Edessa (c. 429) and Constantinople (c. 430). This part of his life is described in Koriwn's *Life of Maštocʻ*, which, like *On God*, may have been composed in the mid-440s. In 449/450 as bishop of Bagrewand, Eznik participated in the Council of Artašat.

L. Mariès and C. Mercier, eds., *Eznik de Kolb: De Deo*, PO 28.3–4 (1959); M. J. Blanchard and R. D. Young, *A Treatise on God Written in Armenian by Eznik of Kolb (fl. c. 430–c. 450)*, in *Eastern Christian Texts in Translation*, vol. 2 (1998); G. Winkler, *Koriwns Biographie des Mesrop Maštocʻ: Übersetzung und Kommentar*, OrChrAn 245 (1994).
MONICA J. BLANCHARD

Family of Love   Also called "Familists," the group was founded c. 1539 by the German mystic Henry Nicholas in Emden, Holland. The Family of Love was concerned to aid the poor and convinced of the real presence of God in every human soul. Critics accused its adherents of enthusiasm and antinomianism. The group spread throughout Holland, Germany, and England. In England, Queen Elizabeth I's 1580 "proclamation against the sectaries of the Family of Love" ordered all adherents to be imprisoned and their books to be burned. This edict, however, had little effect. Familist influence can be felt in the work of John Everard, the English translator of numerous classics of continental mysticism. The teachings of the Family of Love contributed significantly to the development of England's Anabaptists and Quakers, into which groups the Familists were assimilated during the seventeenth century.

A. C. Thomas, *The Family of Love, or the Familists* (1893); R. M. Jones, *Studies in Mystical Religion* (1909).
RODERICK MARTIN

Farel, Guillaume (1489–1565), leading reformer of France and French-speaking Switzerland, colleague of John Calvin in Geneva. Born in Gap, France, Farel began in 1509 to pursue a course of humanistic studies in Paris. There he became a student of the noted biblical scholar Jacques Lefèvre d'Etaples, whose theological influence prompted Farel's gradual turn toward humanist Christian reform of the Erasmian mold. In the early 1520s, Farel joined the nascent reform movement around Bishop Guillaume Briçonnet in Meaux, became disillusioned with the group's tentativeness, and left to work with Huldrych Zwingli and Johannes Oecolampadius in Basel in 1523. His increasingly radical views led to a public break with Erasmus shortly thereafter and to a succession of evangelizing sojourns in France and Switzerland. Farel played a key role in establishing the Reformation in Neuchâtel, Lausanne, and Geneva during the 1530s. In Geneva, he recruited Calvin for the cause in 1536. Within a year, their cooperation produced articles of church order, a catechism by Calvin, and the Confession of Faith by Farel. The unpopularity of their measures led to their expulsion in 1538, with Farel returning to Neuchâtel to take a position as pastor. He held that post until his death twenty-seven years later, working toward a Calvinist-style institutionalization of the Reformation in the Neuchâtel area that culminated in church orders in 1562–1564. Farel also spent this last period of his life actively supporting Calvin's resumed initiatives in Geneva, promoting the Reformation in further parts of Switzerland and France and pursuing theological consensus with other Protestants.

Farel's significance to the Reformation lies above all in his tireless preaching and organizational efforts in France and francophone Switzerland. He was active at the very beginning of the movement and instrumental both to its definition and spread, often risking his life in the process. Part of Farel's influence arose through his writings, which, though few in number, were widely published in their day and played a foundational role for French-speaking Protestantism. Next to the Confession, these include his *Pater noster et le credo en français* (1524), a devotional commentary on the Lord's Prayer and the Creed adopted also by French Catholicism; the first Reformed liturgy in French, *La maniere et fasson . . .* (c. 1528); and his *Summaire et briefve declaration . . .* (c. 1529, rev. 1542), the first extended formulation of Reformed doctrine in French.

———

H. Wyrill, *Réforme et Contre-Réforme en Savoie* (2001); P. Barthel, ed., *Actes du colloque Guillaume Farel*, 2 vols. (1980, 1983).

KENNETH G. APPOLD

Fasting and Fast Days Fasting includes abstinence from all food for a period of time, temporary or permanent abstinence from specific foods (often meat and wine), or reduction of regular food intake. Christian fasting practices evolved in relation to Jewish piety, pagan religious and philosophical food abstinence, and contemporary understandings of diet and health. Within Judaism in the first and second centuries, fasting was interpreted as a form of individual or public penance, atonement or propitiation for sin, preparation for dreams and visions, a tool for purifying the soul, and an act of piety associated with prayer and almsgiving. Fasting figured in pagan religious practices, including preparation for ritual, divination, prophecy, or visions. Neoplatonic and Stoic philosophers such as Porphyry (*De abstinentia*) and Musonius Rufus (*Discourses* 7, 18) argued that food abstinence was valuable for the health and purity of the soul and the cultivation of virtues, especially self-control (*sophrosyne*). Medical writers considered diet and food restriction as essential influences on health, sexual function and desire, character, ethics, and the soul.

The representation of fasting in the New Testament is indicative of ambiguities and tensions that would continue through the early period. Fasting is a powerful tool of preparation and purification, as demonstrated by Jesus' forty-day fast prior to his endurance of temptations and the beginning of his public ministry (Matt. 4). The disciples observed regular fasting along with prayer (Acts 13:2–3; 14:23). Paul relativized food abstinence but argued that dietary freedom should not cause offense (Rom. 14:14–23; 1 Cor. 10:25–31). The author of 1 Timothy (4:1–5) warned of "liars" who will come in later times, forbidding marriage and insisting on abstinence from certain foods. Several elements shaped Christian fasting practices: continued recognition of the power of fasting in the religious life of the individual and the community; tension between acknowledgment of the effects of fasting as an insistently physical act of piety, on the one hand, and the relativizing of physical asceticism in favor of a "spiritual" fast, on the other; and disagreement on the requirement to fast and the related issue of ascetic elitism.

By the second century there is evidence for fasting before baptism (*Didache* 7.4; Justin, *1 Apol.* 61; Tertullian, *Baptism* 20), before Eucharist (Tertullian, *Ad uxorem* 2.5), and for some period before Easter (Eusebius, *Hist. eccl.* 5.24). *Didache* 8 reports that Christians fasted regularly on Wednesdays and Fridays. But these practices were by no means universal or even widespread before the fourth century. In the fifth century, Socrates the historian described the diversity of practices among Christians, especially in regard to the number of fast days before Easter, the types of foods avoided while fasting, and fasting on Saturdays (*Hist. eccl.* 5.22; also Jerome, *Epistula* 71.6). Regular fasting was a feature of monastic life, and extreme or miraculous abstinence was highlighted in hagiographical sources. Ascetic authors used philosophical, medical, and scriptural arguments for the benefits of fasting.

Tension over the intensity of fasting, the question of fasting as a requirement for all Christians, and the necessity of specific types of diets such as vegetarianism erupted in controversies involving the so-called Montanists, encratites, Priscillianists, Manicheans, and others. Nevertheless, fasting continued as a marker of Christian piety and observance. Over the centuries food abstinence came to be regularly practiced in preparation for feast days and sacraments, in observance of saints' days, during Lent and Advent, and at the change of seasons. Both lay and monastic Christians were encouraged to fast for spiritual and physical benefits. Fasting was interpreted as an imitation of the angelic life in paradise before the fall and redress for Adam and Eve's disobedient eating. It was a remedy for sin and a weapon against temptation, the bodily passions, and demons, and—especially when accompanied by prayer—an effective preparation for exorcisms, visions, or inspiration. Fasting not only improved health and tempered physical desire, but it helped to lighten the soul, purify the heart, and turn one's attention away from the world and toward God. Thus fasting was, in the words of John Chrysostom, the "mother of all good" (*Hom. Gen. 1*) and a key to the development of other virtues in the Christian life.

P. R. Arbesmann, *Das Fasten bei den Griechen und Römern* (1929, 1966); P. R. Arbesmann, "Fasting and Prophecy in Pagan and Christian Antiquity," *Traditio* 7 (1949–1951): 1–71; J. Haussleiter, *Der Vegetarismus in der Antike* (1935); H. Musurillo, "The Problem of Ascetical Fasting in the Greek Patristic Writers," *Traditio* 12 (1956): 1–64; T. M. Shaw, *The Burden of the Flesh* (1998).

TERESA M. SHAW

Fathers of the Eastern Church   The

name is given to revered theological authorities, many of them bishops or monks, in the Greek- and Syriac-speaking churches from the second through the eighth centuries. These pastors and teachers were dispersed geographically across the eastern Mediterranean basin, including Greece, Asia Minor, Syria, Palestine, Egypt, and Libya. Early on "fathers" often had a more generic usage, as in references to the convened bishops of ecumenical councils as fathers or guardians of the orthodox faith. In the fourth century, however, Christian authors began citing a more specific group of illustrious interpreters of the church's faith; by the fifth and sixth centuries their opinions began to circulate in *florilegia*, compilations of authoritative doctrinal statements, and in *catena* ("chain") commentaries on Scripture. In the fifth century too, Vincent of Lérins appealed to the "antiquity" of those "holy ancestors and fathers" who had long preserved the catholic faith.

The harbinger of the "patristic" period in the East was Ignatius of Antioch (d. c. 117), a transitional figure who depicted his tribulations still in the image of the apostolic martyrs while manifesting in his ministry the emerging system of monarchical episcopacy. Ignatius battled heresy, but Irenaeus of Lyon (fl. 180)—a bishop in Gaul honored among the Eastern fathers because he came from Asia Minor and wrote in Greek—joined that battle with new force, pro-

ducing a thorough refutation of Gnosticism and the first substantial theological exposition of the "economy" (*oikonomia*) of salvation.

Not all the Greek fathers were bishops or even ordained. Samaritan by birth, Justin Martyr (d. 165) was a "philosophical evangelist" and apologist who operated a school in Rome. The two early Alexandrian fathers, Clement (c. 150–215) and Origen (186–254), were likewise lay teachers, or *didaskaloi*, directing an academy that appealed to educated pagans. Origen had famous tensions with the bishop of Alexandria and relocated mid-career to Caesarea Palestinae, where he was ordained a presbyter and opened another school. Certain of his theological speculations, systematized by later disciples, were eventually condemned by the Council of Constantinople (553). Nonetheless, Origen's epic achievements in biblical scholarship and ascetical theology, even some of his doctrinal positions (e.g., the Trinitarian principle of the "eternal generation" of the Son from the Father, the defense of free will against gnostic determinism) guaranteed him an unofficial status among the Greek church fathers.

The rehabilitation of Origen's legacy already began in the fourth century with Athanasius of Alexandria (c. 295–373) and the Cappadocian Fathers of Asia Minor, architects of classical Trinitarianism. Athanasius championed the ontological identity of the Father and the Son in the wake of the Arian controversy and the Council of Nicaea (325), while the Cappadocian fathers—Basil of Caesarea (330–379), Gregory of Nazianzus (330–390), and Gregory of Nyssa (c. 335–395)—crafted much of the authoritative language of the eternal interrelation of the divine persons in the Trinity. Eastern patristic thought reached its first peak with the Cappadocians, whose collective writings reveal a profound integration of theology, liturgical and sacramental devotion, and asceticism.

Also prominent in this transitional fourth century was John Chrysostom (c. 340–407), the monk-turned-patriarch of Constantinople whose biblical exposition and preaching fortified Christian audiences against compromises with pagan culture. Meanwhile on the eastern frontier, Ephrem (d. 373), a deacon in Edessa, represented the fruition of a rich Syrian Christian culture affirmative of the Nicene faith but disposed, as Ephrem's writings illustrate, more to theological poetics than to dogmatic constructions per se.

The christological controversies of the fifth and sixth centuries included a number of patristic luminaries, none more formidable than Patriarch Cyril of Alexandria (c. 378–444), who led the opposition to Nestorius at the Council of Ephesus (431). Though the Council of Chalcedon (451) settled on a dyophysite ("two nature") christological definition, Cyril's strong defense of the unity of the person of Christ significantly impacted subsequent interpretation of Chalcedon in the Eastern churches.

The last two towering figures among the Eastern fathers, Maximus the Confessor (580–662) and John of Damascus (c. 665–749), were monastic theologians. Maximus produced the consummate synthesis of Greek patristic theology, taking the Chalcedonian Definition as the basis for a meticulously developed vision of the creation, redemption, and deification of humankind. Maximus spent his later career defending the doctrine of the two wills of Christ against the Monothelite Byzantine emperors, for which he was taken into imperial custody and exiled, eventually to have his Christology posthumously vindicated at the Council of Constantinople (681). In the eighth century, John of Damascus, denizen of a monastery in Arab-occupied Palestine, abundantly used *florilegia* to clarify and refine the Greek patristic synthesis for a generation faced with the expansion of Islam and the rise of Byzantine imperial iconoclasm.

Though traditionally considered the last of the Greek fathers, the Eastern Orthodox churches do not strictly end the "patristic" period with John. They have extended much the same prestige to later authorities such as Symeon the New Theologian (949–1022) and Gregory Palamas (c. 1296–1359).

G. Florovsky, *The Eastern Fathers of the Fourth Century* (1987); Florovsky, *The Byzantine Fathers of the Fifth Century* (1987); Florovsky, *The Byzantine Fathers of the Sixth to Eighth Century* (1987); J. Quasten, *Patrology*, 4 vols. (1950–1986).

PAUL M. BLOWERS

Fathers of the Western Church
The distinction between pastoral practice and academic theology was unknown until the rise of the medieval university. The fathers of the church were those individual bishops, simultaneously both teachers and pastors, who accurately taught the doctrine of Jesus Christ, faithfully transmitted the tradition of the church, and compassionately ministered to the faithful. It is unknown whether they were first identified as fathers because of their teaching or because of their pastoral activity. In any

event, there is certainly a pre-Christian basis in the *pater familias*, who wielded total power in the ancient Roman family. Used first in reference to those bishops who were present at the Council of Nicaea in 325, the designation "father" became by the end of the fourth century a customary term and was eventually extended to include priests, deacons, and laymen. True fathers of the church must have four characteristics: orthodox teaching, holiness of life, acceptance by the church, and antiquity. They were universally and spontaneously recognized by the community for their holiness and orthodoxy.

Chronologically the age of the fathers, or the patristic period, began with the end of the apostolic age and continued to the beginning of the Middle Ages. The first date is highly disputed and depends upon when one dates the last book of the New Testament or the death of the last apostle. Perhaps 125 would be an appropriate estimate. The second date is also highly disputed and depends upon when one dates the beginning of the Middle Ages. Certainly the fall of Rome to the Goths in 410 is too early, while the coronation of Charlemagne in 800 is too late. Gregory the Great is a transitional figure. During his lifetime Christianity ceased to be a Mediterranean phenomenon and became European. With a power vacuum created by the location of the imperial capital in Constantinople, the bishop of Rome began to assume wide sweeping political power in the West. Gregory's death in 604 marked the end of the patristic period. Traditionally, Isidore of Seville (d. 636) is considered the last father of the West. Some recent tendencies seek to extend the designation "father" to Bede the Venerable (d. c. 735). Nevertheless, the encyclopedic tendencies of Isidore and vulgar Latin of Bede place them both in the Middle Ages.

Geographically, the West is the western part of the Roman Empire, including Italy, Gaul, Spain, Mauretania, Numidia, and Africa Proconsularis. However, the West is really a linguistic rather than geographic designation. For example, because he wrote Greek, Irenaeus of Lyon is an Eastern father even though Lyon is located in the Rhone Valley. Because he wrote Latin, Jerome is a Western father even though he lived in Bethlehem. The oldest piece of Latin Christian literature is the *Acts of the Scillitan Martyrs*, and the first Christian author to write Latin was Tertullian, thus placing the beginning of Latin Christian literature in North Africa. Throughout the Middle Ages four great teachers were traditionally honored as fathers of the Western church well before they were proclaimed doctors of the church by Pope Boniface VIII in 1295: Ambrose of Milan, Jerome, Augustine of Hippo, and Gregory the Great. The continuity of Christian teaching was affirmed in iconography by the depiction of the four great Western fathers with the symbols of the four evangelists.

Further terminology developed from the word "father." "Patristics" refers to the theology of the fathers in contrast to biblical, scholastic, modern, or contemporary theology. "Patrology" refers to the study of the writings of the fathers. In the late twentieth century, the term "father" and its cognates began to be used less often, particularly in academic circles. Feminists considered the term "father" sexist, although it was bound to a certain historical period. As the expressions "early church" and "patristic period" were secularized into "late antiquity," the orthodoxy and personal status of the writers of the period became less important. While the church in its prayer and piety may still value the title "father of the church," many scholars treat the orthodox, heretical, and pagan literature of the period without differentiation.

J. Quasten, *Patrology*, 4 vols. (1950–1986); B. Ramsey, *Beginning to Read the Fathers* (1985); H. R. Drobner, *The Fathers of the Church: A Comprehensive Introduction* (2007).

KENNETH B. STEINHAUSER

Faustus (c. 405–c. 490), bishop of Reii (now Riez) in southern Gaul. Probably a Briton by birth and a Gaul by upbringing, Faustus entered the influential monastery of Lérins, rising to its abbacy c. 433. Translated to the see of Riez c. 457, he became perhaps the most revered Gallic preacher and theologian of the late fifth century. His extant works consist of a long treatise, *De gratia*; a shorter treatise, *De spiritu sancto*; eleven letters; and a large number of sermons.

De gratia has been taken by many scholars (Harnack, Loofs, Tixeront, Seeberg) as a clear statement of Semi-Pelagianism. Faustus regarded both the Pelagian assertion of free will and the predestinarian logic of Augustine's later anti-Pelagian works as extreme positions. Between these Faustus stressed the general availability of salvation and the perduring, though enfeebled, human endowments of intellect and will, while emphasizing the need for the grace of Christ to bring about authentic freedom. His anthropology, much like that of John Cassian, looks to pre-Augustinian and non-Augustinian sources. In the aftermath of the Pelagian controversy, Faustus had appropriated Augustine's anti-Pelagian sensibilities

and concern for the gratuity of grace. His account of the transmission of original sin clearly depended on Augustine, but he did not begin from a partisan Augustinian point of view. Rather, he attempted to produce a balanced account of the rapport between grace and the human free will, using many aspects of Augustine's thought without explicitly attaching Augustine's name to the seeming excesses of predestinarianism. Faustus was included in the Bollandist *Acta sanctorum*, and some local cult around Riez seems to have flourished into the eighteenth century.

M. Simonetti, "Il De gratia di Fausto di Riez," *Studi Storico-Religiosi* 1 (1977): 125–45; T. A. Smith, *De Gratia: Faustus of Riez's Treatise on Grace and Its Place in the History of Theology* (1990); C. Tibiletti, "Fausto di Riez nei giudizi della critica," *Aug* 21 (1981): 567–87; G. Weigel, *Faustus of Riez: An Historical Introduction* (1938).

THOMAS A. SMITH

Fawkes, Guy (1570–1606), English Catholic, Gunpowder Plot conspirator. Fawkes was born a Protestant in Yorkshire but converted to Catholicism in 1593, selling his property and joining the Spanish Army. Returning to England, he joined Catesby's conspiracy early on (1604) and was ultimately given responsibility for firing the powder to explode Parliament. Arrested in Parliament's cellar near several barrels of powder, he confessed under torture and was executed in January 1606. His role in the plot has made him the most famous of the conspirators.

H. Garnett, *Portrait of Guy Fawkes* (1962); E. Simons, *Devil of the Vault* (1963).

DAVID A. LOPEZ

Feasts of the Church A church feast is a joyful communal ritual celebration, properly eucharistic, centered on an aspect of the salvation of humankind that God has effected through the passion and glorification of Jesus Christ. The earliest, and primary, Christian feast is the celebration of the Lord's resurrection on Sunday. All other liturgical feasts celebrate the same paschal reality but from varied aspects of its multifaceted, mysterious significance.

It is not unreasonable to suppose that Jewish Christians, immediately after the death and resurrection of Jesus, began to look upon their cherished annual Passover observance as a commemoration also of an act of God greater than the exodus. Paul's words to the Corinthian community, "Christ our paschal lamb has been sacrificed" (1 Cor. 5:7), suggest this transformed content of the Jewish feast for Jewish Christians. Probably by the mid-second century Gentile Christians were observing a similar Christian Pasch, but on the Sunday following Passover, because Sunday was the day of the resurrection. The difference led to the bitter paschal controversy that was settled at the Council at Nicaea in 325. Observance of the Lord's nativity on January 6 in the East and December 25 in the West almost certainly predate Constantine and derive from determination of the precise date of the death of the Lord, identification of the days of his conception and of his death, and calculation of his nativity as nine months after his conception (Talley). Ancient calendar discrepancies account in part for the different dates of Eastern and Western celebration of the feast. Around each of the pivotal liturgical feasts, the resurrection and the nativity, a preparatory season and an extension of festivity arose.

A second cycle of Christian feasting focuses on saintly persons, that is, persons who, like Christ, were faithful to God to an exemplary degree and share now in Christ's glory. Christian literature perhaps from as early as the second century attests the honor the church accorded its martyrs, those who so strikingly claimed the passion of Christ as their own. The church soon honored also confessors, that is, persons who suffered persecution but were not killed, and, after the cessation of persecution, others such as virgins and ascetics who crucified their bodies less literally. The Council of Ephesus in 431 gave official sanction to the veneration of Mary as the mother of God, but her cult was already traditional. Through the centuries the church has honored many more holy persons. Many traditions observe a feast of All Saints, a day of rejoicing over all persons who live already with God in glory, countless in number and most unknown to us by name.

M. E. Johnson, ed., *Between Memory and Hope* (2000); P. Jounel, "The Year," in *The Liturgy and Time*, ed. A. G. Martimort, I. H. Dalmais, P. Jounel (1986); T. J. Talley, *The Origins of the Liturgical Year* (1997); R. Taft, "Toward a Theology of the Christian Feast," in *Beyond East and West* (1984), 15–29.

MARY CATHERINE BERGLUND

Fénelon, François (1651–1715), French archbishop of Cambrai and theologian, renowned for pastoral care and his novel, *Télé-*

maque (1699). He sought to convert French Protestants to Catholicism without resort to violence. In 1688 Fénelon began to defend the teachings of Madame Guyon. Nevertheless, he never shared her quietism, which he himself criticized in his *Explications des maximes des saints* (1697). Bossuet attacked this effort to distinguish true from false mysticism, and Fénelon was banished from court to spend the rest of his life exiled in his own diocese. He opposed absolutism, and in his capacity as tutor to Louis XIV's grandson, the Duke of Burgundy, he introduced ideas of alternative forms of government into the royal family. The Duke's premature death in 1712 left the French government staunchly absolutist until 1789. Fénelon's last years were spent disputing with Jansenism and dispensing charity.

P. Hazard, *The European Mind* (1963); J. L. May, *Fénelon: A Study* (1938).

RODERICK MARTIN

Ferrara-Florence, Council of (1438–1445) When the conciliarist Council of Basel opened (1431), many hoped for significant church reform, especially of the curia. Despite early success in attracting support among cardinals and secular princes, Basel's extreme attitudes against papal authority and compromise with the Greeks lost it that support. By 1438, Pope Eugene IV was able to transfer the council to Ferrara, and later Florence (1439) and Rome (1443). Eugene desired union with the Greeks, who would compromise for military aid against the Turks. Four main points were debated: the *filioque* clause (double procession of the Spirit), leavened versus unleavened bread in the Eucharist (azymes), purgatory, and papal primacy. With the support of Emperor John VIII, Palaeologus, and Archbishop Bessarion of Nicaea, essential agreement and recognition of differences was reached in July 1439 and issued in the bull *Laententur caeli*. This union, unpopular in the East, lasted until Constantinople's capture (1453).

The significance of this council is threefold: the success of papal authority over conciliar authority, the principle of union of faith with diversity of rite, and the definition of key doctrines.

G. Alberigo, ed., *Christian Unity* (1991); J. Gill, *Council of Florence* (1959); Gill, *Eugenius IV* (1961); Tanner, *Decrees* (1990), 513–91.

DAVID A. LOPEZ

Ficino, Marsilio (1433–1499), humanist and founder of the Florentine Academy. Ficino founded the academy under the patronage of the Medici family and became its head. The activities of the academy initiated a new interest in Platonic thought during the Italian Renaissance. Through the course of a productive scholarly life, Ficino provided the first complete Latin translation of all Platonic dialogues and wrote commentaries on Plato. In these writings he often manifests eclectic tendencies. For example, his theory of love draws upon Plato, Aristotle, Cicero, the Christian notion of *caritas*, and even courtly love. He conceives the universe as a hierarchy—not simply as tiered layers but rather as a dynamic unity wherein each level flows into the one above and below itself so as to give a picture of reality as a coherent unity. Like his theories of love and hierarchy, his understanding of contemplation, immortality, and religion draws on many ancient and medieval sources. Even though he was often under suspicion for his views on astrology, he firmly believed that Christianity was the most perfect of all world religions. He held these apparently conflicting views because in his mind all religions were ultimately related to the one true God. Ultimately for Ficino, true philosophy and true religion are never in conflict.

M. Ficino, *A Commentary on Plato's Symposium*; Ficino, *Theologica Platonica de Immortalitate Animarum*; Ficino, *De Christiana Religione* in *Opera Omnia/Marsilio Ficino*, 2 vols. (1962).

JOHN L. TRELOAR, SJ

Fifth Lateran Council   *see* Lateran Council, Fifth

Fifth Monarchy Men The most violent religious and political sect in a long history of British millenarianism. Taking their biblical warrant from Daniel 3:44, Fifth Monarchists regarded England at the time of the English Revolution and the Restoration as ripe for the imminent kingdom of Christ. They expected and pursued a theocracy in which "the saints" would provide a new order for the unregenerate prior to the second coming. Initially, Fifth Monarchists supported regicide and rebellion, but, ultimately, they opposed Oliver Cromwell and the Protectorate as unlikely to foster the awaited realm of Christ. Almost exclusively an urban movement, Monarchists were primarily journeymen and laborers led by a small but impressive group of military officers and clergy. After the Restoration, the Fifth Monarchists, once greeted by the people with fear and alarm, were then regarded with contempt. Impressive as a part of the history of millenarianism, the movement itself did not survive the seventeenth century.

B. S. Capp, *The Fifth Monarchy Men: A Study in Seventeenth-Century English Millenarianism* (1972).

JOHN E. GRISWOLD

Filioque This Latin word means "and from the Son." Not a part of the original Niceno-Constantinopolitan Creed (created at the First Council of Constantinople, 381), it was added in the Latin West to assert that the Holy Spirit proceeds not only from the Father but also from the Son. The earliest extant document that includes the *filioque* is found in the proceedings of the Third Council of Toledo (589). The addition of the term became a source of controversy and division between the Western churches and those of Eastern Orthodoxy, for as the Nicene Creed came to be considered a touchstone of the faith, it also came to be considered inviolate.

While not a part of the original creed, the procession of the Spirit from both Father and Son was indicated by early Latin theology, and in the early Middle Ages some Latin theologians asserted this double procession. Soon churches in Gaul and Spain began to use the word *filioque* in their professions of faith, as did Pope Martin I in 651 in a letter to the bishop of Constantinople, thus inadvertently alerting the Easterners about this new direction in Latin Trinitarian theology. Easterners accused the Latins of tampering with the Nicene Creed, and the legitimacy of unilateral creedal modification became the overriding issue. The Western debates about the *filioque* occurred mostly in the Carolingian Empire, fueled partly by a misunderstanding of the Eastern position. The bishops of Rome used the term circumspectly or not at all.

Its use spread in the West, however, and in the eleventh century the popes finally added it to the recitation of the creed in Rome. Each side drew upon patristic sources to justify its position. The Latins found passages in Greek fathers that could be interpreted as supportive of the *filioque*, but the term still continued to divide East and West throughout the Middle Ages and into the modern era.

Twentieth-century ecumenism changed this situation, as Western churches, including Rome but led by the Anglicans, retained the phrase but in dialogue with the Orthodox used it less and less, thus tacitly agreeing with a 1979 recommendation of the Faith and Order Commission of the World Council of Churches that the "normative" form of the Nicene Creed should not include the *filioque*. The question is not settled but is now being discussed ecumenically and not, as in the past, in terms of rival positions.

P. Gemeinhardt, *Filioque-Kontroverse* (2002); J. N. D. Kelly, *Early Christian Creeds* (1972); L. Vischer, ed., *Spirit of God, Spirit of Christ: Ecumenical Reflections on the Filioque Controversy* (1981); K. Ware, ed., *Anglican-Orthodox Dialogue* (1977).

JOSEPH F. KELLY

Finnian of Clonard (d. c. 549), founder of the monastery of Clonard in County Meath. This great Irish ecclesiastical hero was possibly not Irish but instead Romano-British, a Celt but one born in post-Roman Britain during years of the Anglo-Saxon invasions. Supporting this possibility are the medieval Irish traditions that he befriended two great Welsh monastic leaders, Cadoc and David. Against it is the easy seaborne contact between Ireland and Wales, which would have allowed for extensive cross-fertilization of ideas. Whatever his origin, Finnian made his career in Ireland as a monastic founder and a teacher. The monastery of Clonard sits on a tributary of the River Boyne and was accessible to the Irish students wishing to visit it. Finnian's most famous students became known as the Twelve Apostles of Ireland and included several prominent monastic founders. To Finnian is attributed a penitential, a book listing sins and the appropriate penances, a genre popular among the Irish. It deals primarily with monastic sins and modes of reconciliation, and it provides a unique insight into early Irish ascetic life.

L. Bieler, ed., *The Irish Penitentials* (1963); P. Byrne, "The Community of Clonard from the 6th to the 12th Centuries," *Peritia* 4 (1985): 157–73; T. M. Charles-Edwards, *Early Christian Ireland* (2002); D. Dumville, "Gildas and Uinniau," in *Gildas: New Approaches*, ed. Dumville and M. Lapidge (1984), 207–14.

JOSEPH F. KELLY

Firmicus Maternus (fourth cent.), Latin apologist. Firmicus Maternus is the author of two works that epitomize the tensions of the Constantinian age. A Sicilian of senatorial background known only through his works, Maternus was a pagan when he wrote his eight-book *Mathesis* (334–337), a handbook and defense of astrology dedicated to the pagan senator Lollianus Mavortius. Maternus's understanding of astral determinism, from which he exempted only the emperor (2.30.5), was drawn from Greek sources and influenced by Neoplatonic thought. But Maternus also affirmed the value of traditional religion (1.6.1–2) and ended his first book with a hymn to the sun and planets that blurs astral and cultic associations. Maternus was a Christian by the time he wrote *On the Error of Pagan Religions* (343–347). He now appealed unsubtly to the authority of Scripture, attacked paganism's mythology and worship, and called upon the emperors to eradicate its contagion. Motivated perhaps by political and religious interests, the work charts the rise of Christian intolerance. Despite their contrasts, Maternus's two treatises share a high moral tone (e.g., *Mathesis* 2.30.2; *On the Error* 12).

J. Bram, trans., *Ancient Astrology* (1975); H. Drake, "Firmicus Maternus and the Politics of Conversion," in *Qui miscuit utile dulci*, ed. G. Schmeling and J. Mikalson (1998); C. Forbes, trans., *The Error of the Pagan Religions* (1970); P. Monat, trans., *Mathesis*, 3 vols. (1992–1997).

DENNIS E. TROUT

Firmilian (d. 268), bishop of Caesarea in Cappadocia (c. 230–268). Following Firmilian's election, Caesarea evolved into one of the principal theological centers of its time. Firmilian was a close friend of Origen. He corresponded with Dionysius of Alexandria concerning Novatianism, which he opposed, and c. 250 he caused the abdication of Bishop Fabius of Antioch, who was sympathetic to Novatian's teachings.

Firmilian's only extant writing is a letter to Cyprian of Carthage (256), in which he supports Cyprian against Stephen I of Rome in favor of rebaptizing those who had been baptized by heretics and schismatics. The letter harshly criticizes Stephen's authoritarian behavior and contains the very interesting description of a local prophetess who had attracted a large following through her miracles. Firmilian was outraged by what he considered an "outbreak of demonic forces." Following this letter Stephen excommunicated Firmilian; nevertheless, Firmilian presided at the First Council of Antioch (264), which had gathered to investigate the orthodoxy of Paul of Samosata. During that investigation it transpired that Paul and members of his clergy cohabited with young women in a "spiritual marriage," described as *syneisaktoi*. On the way to the Second Council of Antioch, Firmilian died in 268.

Cyprian, Letter 75; Eusebius, *Hist. eccl.* 6.27, 6.46.3, 7.5, 14, 28, 30.4–5; S. Elm, "Perceptions of Jerusalem Pilgrimage as Reflected in Two Early Sources on Female Pilgrimage (3rd and 4th Century A.D.)," StPatr 20 (1989), 219–23.

SUSANNA ELM

First Crusade   The initial armed pilgrimage from Western Europe to Jerusalem, today called the First Crusade, was the result of Pope Urban II's (1088–1099) urging at the Council of Clermont-Ferrand in November 1095. A case for "just war" was made. There was a need to help the Byzantine Empire, which was trying to fight off the Muslim Seljuks and to return the Holy Land to Christian rule. Remission of sins (indulgence) was a powerful motivator for crusaders, who vowed to participate in the "holy war." As part of the First Crusade, spontaneous response among the lower classes led to the ill-fated Peasants' or People's Crusade brought to disaster by Peter the Hermit in September 1096.

Following the defeat of these unexpected armies, several armies led by various nobles and knights from different parts of Europe assembled and marched to Constantinople. Hugh of Vermandois was in charge of crusaders drawn mostly from the Ile de France. Duke Godfrey of Bouillon's contingent was from Lower Lorraine. The Normans of southern Italy followed Prince Bohemond of Taranto and his nephew Tancred. Raymond of St. Gilles, Count of Toulouse, brought the largest group, which also contained the papal legate, Bishop Adhémar of Le Puy. William the Conqueror's oldest son, Duke Robert of Normandy, William's son-in-law Stephen of Blois, and Robert's cousin Count Robert of Flanders led the Norman knights of Brittany, Normandy, and Flanders.

They left Constantinople in April 1097, restored Nicaea to Byzantine rule by June, and won a significant battle against the Turks at Dorylaeum on July 1. The long, difficult march across the hot, inhospitable Anatolian Peninsula took a toll on the Frankish fighting forces.

Baldwin of Boulogne separated from the main body and captured Edessa in March 1098.

After a nine-month siege, Antioch fell to the remaining crusaders in June 1098. Jerusalem was captured in a bloodbath on July 15, 1099. The small, crusading army was successful because the Muslim powers in the Middle East were distracted, until Saladin focused attention on the crusaders eight decades later.

Four feudal governments were established in the Levant. Godfrey was elected de facto king of Jerusalem and established a state that lasted in Palestine until 1291. The First Crusade generally is considered to be Western Europe's only successful crusade.

J. France, *Victory in the East: A Military History of the First Crusade* (1994); R. Hill, trans., *The Deeds of the Franks and the Other Pilgrims to Jerusalem* (1972); H. E. Mayer, *The Crusades*, trans. J. Gillingham (1988); J. Riley-Smith, *The First Crusade and the Idea of Crusading* (1986); Riley-Smith, *The First Crusaders, 1095–1131* (1997); S. Runciman, *The First Crusade* (1980).

ERHARD "ERIK" P. OPSAHL

Fishacre, Richard (c. 1200–1248), English theologian. Born to a knightly family in the diocese of Exeter, he joined the Dominicans within a few years of their arrival in England in 1221, studied at Oxford, and followed Robert Bacon as second Dominican master there probably around 1240. Although commentaries on the Psalms and Proverbs are attributed to him, Richard's reforms at Oxford led to a sharper distinction in method between systematic theology and biblical exegesis. Specifically, he introduced to Oxford in the early 1240s the custom of a master's lecturing *ordinarie* on Peter Lombard's *Sentences* (see *Four Books of Sentences*). Robert Grosseteste, from whom Fishacre otherwise drew many of his theological ideas, tried to prevent this typically scholastic innovation but was overruled by the intervention of Pope Innocent IV on Richard's behalf. The Oxford Univ. statutes of 1253, assigning this work to bachelors, did not prevent its continuation by later Oxford masters. Fishacre's extensive commentary, the first to originate in Oxford, did much to establish internationally the *status quaestionis* on a variety of theological issues from 1245 on. Bernard Gui reports Thomas Aquinas's interest in procuring a copy of this text, although Thomas progressively distanced himself from key positions (e.g., absolute predestination of Christ and the covenantal interpretation of Christian sacraments).

R. Fishacre, *In libros Sententiarum*, ed. K. Rodler, R. J. Long, et al. (2003/2008); T. Kaeppeli, SOPMA (1980, 1993), 3:303–6, 4:261–62; R. J. Long and M. O'Carroll, *The Life and Works of Richard Fishacre* (1999); *New Blackfriars* 80 (1999): 317–90; R. Sharpe, *Handlist of the Latin Writers of Great Britain before 1540* (1997), 476–78.

RICHARD SCHENK, OP

Fisher, John (c. 1469–1535), English theologian, chancellor of Cambridge Univ. (1504–1535), bishop of Rochester (1504–1535), and cardinal (1535). Fisher entered Cambridge from 1483, held several university offices, and was instrumental in the founding and endowment of Christ's and St. John's Colleges. As bishop, Fisher was very conscientious regarding his pastoral responsibilities. He was an active preacher, typically of sermons calculated to lead to repentance and improvement of life, and he was careful to ensure the competence of clergy within his diocese. Conjointly he advocated reform of clerical deficiencies, using his position at Cambridge to introduce curricular changes intended to enhance learning and piety. His concern for church reform, interest in biblical languages, and friendships with men like Erasmus link Fisher to early sixteenth-century humanism, but his works also indicate esteem for scholasticism and reliance on dogmatic authority that many humanists did not share. A strong advocate of papal primacy, Fisher believed that Christ willed ecclesiastical power to be concentrated in the hands of the clerical hierarchy, whose responsibilities included governing the church, performing the sacraments, and defining doctrine. While the Bible was the primary vehicle of revelation containing all truths necessary for salvation, it needed interpretation by church traditions (the teachings of church fathers and doctors as well as the pronouncements of popes and general councils) through which the Holy Spirit spoke. During the 1520s Fisher was active as a highly influential anti-Protestant polemicist. His controversial works show a heavy reliance on patristic sources and reflect deep concern for the pastoral implications of doctrinal innovations. Soteriologically, he balanced divine grace and human free will. While unmerited grace was primary in the order of salvation, it was not irresistible; to be saved, one needed to cooperate with grace by repenting, partaking of the sacraments, and pursuing good works. After 1527 Fisher was largely occupied in opposing Henry VIII's divorce and subjugation of the English church. He was executed on charges of treason for his unwillingness to deny the validity of Henry's first marriage or repudiate papal primacy.

B. Bradshaw and E. Duffy, eds., *Humanism, Reform, and the Reformation: The Career of Bishop John Fisher* (1989); M. Dowling, *Fisher of Men: A Life of John Fisher, 1469–1535* (1999); C. Hatt, ed., *The English Works of John Fisher, Bishop of Rochester: Sermons and Other Writings, 1520–1535* (2002); R. Rex, *The Theology of John Fisher* (1991); E. Surtz, *The Works and Days of John Fisher* (1967).

DANIEL EPPLEY

FitzRalph, Richard (c. 1300–1360), theologian, archbishop. Born in Dundalk, Ireland, FitzRalph was educated at Oxford (MA by 1325) and became regent master of theology (1331–1332) and chancellor (1332–1334). He was made dean of Lichfield Cathedral (1336) and finally archbishop of Armagh (1346). FitzRalph distinguished himself as a preacher and controversialist from early in his career until the time of his death. On each of four visits to the papal court in Avignon he participated in highly visible controversies there, and on the last two visits he was the main protagonist: 1334–1335 (Pope John XXII and the beatific vision), 1337–1344 (theological debates related to negotiations with the Armenian church), 1349–1351 and 1358–1360 (mendicant poverty). His most mature theological work, *Summa de questionibus Armenorum* (*Summa on the Questions of the Armenians*), was written in conjunction with the Armenian controversy; begun during his second visit to Avignon, the work was completed in Ireland. His most famous writings were against the friars: a *Proposicio* composed at Avignon in 1350, sermons against the friars preached at Oxford and London in 1356–1357, and the dialogue *On the Poverty of the Savior* (*De pauperie salvatoris*), completed in 1356. These works circulated widely in Central Europe. *De pauperie salvatoris* adapts a doctrine developed by Giles of Rome in defense of papal sovereignty and known as "dominion by grace." FitzRalph adapted the doctrine to deny the legitimacy of the mendicant orders. He provoked an investigation of the friars at the papal court in 1357, which failed to censure the mendicant orders. But John Wyclif learned the doctrine of dominion by grace from FitzRalph's dialogue (and he may have heard FitzRalph in person at Oxford). FitzRalph's anti-mendicant views were supported in Central Europe by the itinerant preachers Konrad Waldhauser and Jan Milič of Kroměříž and the anti-mendicant polemics of the Hussite Revolt.

K. Walsh, *A Fourteenth-Century Scholar and Primate: Richard FitzRalph in Oxford, Avignon, and Armagh* (1981); P. R. Szittya, *The Antifraternal Tradition in Medieval Literature* (1986).

CHRISTOPHER OCKER

Flacius Illyricus, Matthias (1520–1575), Lutheran theologian. Flacius fled his native Croatia in fear of the Venetian inquisition. After brief study in Tübingen, he came to Wittenberg (1541), where Luther's counsel brought his troubled spirit peace. Flacius quickly demonstrated his aptitude for theology and became Hebrew instructor on the Wittenberg faculty, a position he held from 1544 to 1549. Melanchthon expressed high regard for his student and colleague in the preface to Flacius's first work on biblical hermeneutics, *De vocabula fidei* (1549). By the time of its publication, however, the two had become alienated because of Melanchthon's efforts to stave off imperial invasion of Saxony and his suppression of the Lutheran movement, efforts Flacius interpreted as a betrayal of the gospel and Luther's heritage. Melanchthon reacted bitterly to what he considered Flacius's unfair criticism, and the two spent the last decade of Melanchthon's life in sharp conflict as Flacius fought for the integrity of the church over against secular government and for his interpretation of Luther, particularly in regard to the necessity of clear confession in times of persecution or suppression of the faith, the relationship of good works to salvation, and the bondage of the unconverted will. He defended a radical interpretation of Luther's theology, based upon his reading of Luther's writings, particularly in his definition of original sin as the formal (Aristotelian) substance of the fallen sinner, whose sin has recast the human creature into the image of Satan. Before and after a professorship in Jena (1557–1561), Flacius lived as an independent scholar, in Magdeburg (1549–1557), Regensburg (1562–1566), Antwerp (1566–1567), and Strasbourg (1567–1573), dying on the run in Frankfurt am Main. His criticism of Roman Catholicism and a variety of Protestant theologians, including Caspar Schwenkfeld, revealed the central position of biblical authority and salvation by grace through faith in his thought. He helped lay the foundations of Protestant church history through his *Catalogus testium veritatis* (1556), a collection of antipapal sources throughout the ages, and through his organization of the writing of the *Magdeburg Centuries* with its employment of Melanchthon's locus method for the presentation of the church's life and thought. He also composed the first Protestant hermeneutical work, *Clavis scripturae sacrae* (1567), as well as a New Testament commentary, *Glossa Novi Testamenti* (1570).

R. Keller, *Der Schlüssel zur Schrift* (1984); O. Olson, *Matthias Flacius and the Survival of Luther's Reform* (2002); W. Preger, *Matthias Flacius und seine Zeit*, 2 vols. (1859, 1861).

ROBERT KOLB

Flavian of Constantinople (d. 449), bishop during the christological controversy. In 448, an archimandrite in Constantinople named Eutyches denied that there were two natures in Christ after the incarnation. Bishop Flavian of Constantinople oversaw Eutyches' condemnation. The bishop of Alexandria, Dioscorus, responded with an accusation that Flavian had used a test for orthodoxy other than the Nicene Creed, a practice that had been prohibited by the Council of Ephesus (431). A synod met in Ephesus in 449. Dioscorus presided and Flavian was deposed. The synod was later called the "Robber Synod." Flavian was exiled and died on his journey, though probably not as a result of a supposed beating at the synod. At the Council of Chalcedon (451), Flavian was rehabilitated and Eutyches was condemned.

H. Chadwick, "The Exile and Death of Flavian," *JTS* 6 (1955); A. Grillmeier and H. Bacht, *Das Konzil von Chalkedon* (1951).

STEVEN A. MCKINION

Florence, Council of see Ferrara-Florence, Council of

Florimond de Raemond (1540–1601), humanist, lawyer, member of the parlement of Bordeaux, and polemical historian. Born in Agen of an old family, Florimond de Raemond studied at Bordeaux under a teacher of Protestant sympathies and subsequently in Paris under Pierre Ramus, a Protestant convert. Initially attracted to Calvinism, he closely followed the preaching and instruction of Beza but

reverted to Catholicism and devoted much of his work to a verbal assault on the Reformed faith and to a vindication of Rome, in the context of the continuing Wars of Religion. His major writing, *Histoire de la naissance, progrez et décadence de l'héresie de ce siècle*, was published posthumously in 8 volumes in 1605, though Pierre Bayle (1647–1706) casts doubt on the authorship of some volumes, as well as on Raemond's fitness to write such a work. Inaccurate at some points, heavily biased and lacking in balance, this work nevertheless provided valuable insights into early French Calvinism and was notable for the comprehensive sweep of Raemond's account of the various forms of Protestantism and for its interest in psychological dimensions.

B. S. Tinsley, *History and Polemics in the French Reformation: Florimond de Raemond, Defender of the Church* (1992).

JOHN TONKIN

Formula of Concord The central document of *The Book of Concord* (1580), this two-part document consisted of the Epitome and the Solid Declaration. It took final form in 1577, drafted by second-generation Lutheran theologians Jakob Andreae (1528–1590), Nicholas Selnecker (1528/1530–1592), Andreas Musculus (1514–1581), David Chytraeus (1531–1600), Christoph Körner (1518–1594), and Martin Chemnitz (1522–1586). The Solid Declaration went through a series of drafts from a set of six sermons (1573) by Andreae, who reworked them into the "Swabian Concord" (1574), through revisions by Chemnitz and Chytraeus for the Swabian-Saxon Concord (1575). Further revisions led to completion in 1577 of the Solid Declaration (called the "Bergen Book"), which Andreae summarized in the Epitome. It represented theological agreement among Lutherans on disputes arising after Luther's death and included articles on original sin, free will, justification, good works, law and gospel, third use of the law, adiaphora, election, and other (Anabaptist and spiritualist) factions. The ouster in the 1570s of theologians from electoral Saxony who propagated a more symbolic view of Christ's presence in the Lord's Supper led to the inclusion of articles on the Lord's Supper, Christology, and Christ's descent into hell. Over eight thousand pastors, preachers, and teachers from Germany subscribed to it. An appendix, *The Catalogue of Testimonies*, contained statements from the ancient church on Christ's natures.

R. Kolb, *Andreae and the Formula of Concord* (1977); R. Kolb and T. J. Wengert, eds., *The Book of Concord* (2000); R. Kolb and J. Nestingen, eds., *Sources and Contexts of "The Book of Concord"* (2001).

TIMOTHY J. WENGERT

Forty-two Articles This English document describes an extreme Reformation doctrine against conservative Catholic and moderate Lutheran positions. Archbishop Cranmer of Canterbury composed the list, drawing on the Augsburg Confession (1530) in its English form (Thirteen Articles, 1538), and on Henry VIII's Ten Articles (1536) and King's Book (1543). The articles were not intended as a comprehensive creed but rather as definitive statements on certain issues then considered most urgent.

The Forty-two Articles envisioned radical reform. Henry's conservatism had disinclined him to alter Catholic tenets such as the real presence, transubstantiation, auricular confession, clerical celibacy, and the efficacy of the Mass (Six Articles, 1539), but Edward VI's political weakness allowed Cranmer to spearhead an extensive reform of the church in England. Accordingly, the Forty-two Articles rejected not only the Six Articles but also moderate Lutheran ideas such as liturgical use of vestments and ceremonial.

Published with royal sanction by Edward (June 19, 1553), all clergy, schoolteachers, and graduates of Cambridge and Oxford were required to subscribe to these tenets. The articles were never enforced, however, because with Edward's death (July 6, 1553), the Catholic Mary Tudor gained power. Under Elizabeth I the articles were revived and modified to be less radical (Thirty-nine Articles, 1563, 1571). In this form they required explicit consent until 1865 and also influenced the Presbyterian Westminster Confession (1647).

G. Burnet, *History of the Reformation of the Church of England*, ed. N. Pocock (1865), 314–29; E. Gibson, *Thirty-nine Articles*, vol. 1 (1896), 12–29, 70–89.

DAVID A. LOPEZ

Four Books of Sentences The *IV Libri Sententiarum* (or *Sententiae in IV Libris Distinctae*) was begun by the Parisian scholastic Peter Lombard, the "Master of the Sentences," in the 1140s and completed before 1158. It was the culmination of his career as teacher in the Paris schools—indeed, it is the culmination of a century of theological and intellectual endeavor.

The work is a grand synthesis of patristic and contemporary thought, of biblical exegesis and systematic theology. Though profoundly traditional, it also engaged with the latest of scholarly debate and endeavor. Lombard revised it after 1154, taking account, for the first time in the West, of the newly translated *De fide orthodoxa* of John of Damascus. Characteristically, Lombard used it not only to bolster but also to revise and reject some of his own earlier arguments.

The largely successful goal of the *Sentences* is to give an orderly, rational, consistent, and, insofar as possible, complete account of the central questions of Christian theology. It comprises four books, originally arranged in chapters (*capitulae*) by Peter and later divided into "distinctions" by Alexander of Hales. The first book treats of God, divine actions and attributes, and the mystery of the Trinity; the second deals with the six days of creation (the Hexaemeron), angels, original sin, and grace; the third explores sin, virtue, the commandments, and the incarnation of God as Christ; the final book deals with "last things" (the end of the world, interim disposition of the souls of the dead, etc.) and the sacraments. Throughout, Peter applies the Augustinian distinction between "signs" and "things" and between "use" and "enjoyment," providing thematic unity and connecting the most abstract discussions of doctrine to the everyday lives of Christians. Questions raised during investigation of these matters demonstrate Peter's brilliant assessment of contemporary scholarly contention and are mainly resolved by judicious recourse to the Fathers, solid logical method, and a serene and magisterial moderation. Firmly decisive on most issues, Peter clearly delineates but prefers to leave unresolved those questions (such as the exact nature of the coinherence of the human and divine in Christ) that appear to him to be beyond the capabilities of the best of scholarship. There is nothing wildly speculative, dangerously original, or conspicuously idiosyncratic in the *Sentences*, an important factor in its subsequent popularity and usefulness.

It was not the first or the last *summa* of theology, but its comprehensiveness, clarity, and lack of extreme positions made it a reliable resource as well as a solid starting point for future discussion. One of its greatest contributions was its consistent terminology, by which Peter clarified the issues in contemporary debates; another was simply its demonstration

that the new systematic theology could be respectable and mainstream. In 1215 the Fourth Lateran Council pronounced orthodox Peter's teachings on the hypostatic union, as expressed in the *Sentences*, and in the same year the statutes of the Univ. of Paris mandated the *Sentences* for theology students. Its influence prevailed until the Reformation.

———

I. C. Brady, ed., *Sententiae in IV libris distinctae*, 2 vols. (3rd rev. ed., 1971–1981); M. L. Colish, *Peter Lombard*, 2 vols. (1994); P. Delhaye, *Pierre Lombard: Sa vie, ses oeuvres, sa morale* (1961).

THERESA GROSS-DIAZ

Fournier, Jacques. *see* Benedict XII.

Fourth Crusade   Preached by the powerful Pope Innocent III (1198–1216), the Fourth Crusade was intended to redirect Europe's attention to the retaking of Jerusalem, which had been left unaccomplished in the Third, or Kings', Crusade. In November 1199, a crusading army began to assemble at a tournament at a Champagne castle, Écry-sur-Aisne. The predominantly French crusaders wanted to book passage through the port of Venice. In 1201 Venetian doge Enrico Dandolo (c. 1193–1205) contracted with the crusaders for a sum of money to transport the crusaders to the Levant. By overestimating the size of the force, the crusaders had a significant money shortfall. As a result, the Venetians asked the crusaders to seize the city of Zara, recently lost by them to Hungary. The crusaders took Zara in November 1202, but this did not clear their full financial obligation to the doge.

At the same time, the deposed Byzantine emperor's son Alexius went to his brother-in-law, German king Philip (r. 1197–1208), for help in reclaiming the throne. The crusaders were convinced to go to Constantinople to assist the boy and, thereby, to pay off the remaining debt to Venice. They arrived in June 1203, attacked, and placed Alexius IV (r. 1203–1204) and his father Isaac II Angelus (r. 1185–1195, 1203–1204) on the throne. But Alexius angered the Franks by defaulting on his promises. Then a new emperor, Alexius V Ducas (1204), overthrew the co-emperors and opposed the crusaders. The outraged crusaders took Constantinople for themselves on April 12, 1204, and ravaged the city for three days.

The crusade ended and the Franks created the Latin Empire of Constantinople by electing Baldwin of Flanders and Hainault (1204–1205) as emperor. The Fourth Crusade has been called the turning point in Western Europe's efforts to regain the Holy Land because it crippled the crusaders' ally and the major Christian power in the eastern Mediterranean. A weakened Byzantine Empire was restored at Constantinople in 1261.

Historians long have argued the question of conspiracy in the Fourth Crusade. In the end, one may observe that the agendas of Innocent, Enrico, Philip, and some French nobles were advanced during the adventure.

A. J. Andrea, *Contemporary Sources for the Fourth Crusade* (2000); Andrea, trans., *The Capture of Constantinople: The "Hystoria Constantinopolitana" of Gunther of Pairis* (1997); Robert of Clari, *The Conquest of Constantinople*, trans. E. H. McNeal (1996); E. H. McNeal and R. L. Wolff, "The Fourth Crusade," in *History of the Crusades*, vol. 2, ed. R. L. Wolff and H. W. Hazard (1969), 153–86; D. E. Queller, *The Fourth Crusade: The Conquest of Constantinople, 1201–1204* (1997); M. R. B. Shaw, trans., *Joinville and Villehardouin: Chronicles of the Crusades* (1963, 1985).

ERHARD "ERIK" P. OPSAHL

Fox, George (1624–1691), Quaker founder and leader. Born in Drayton-in-the-Clay, Leicestershire, the son of a weaver, and apprenticed to a shoemaker, Fox left family and friends behind in 1643 in quest of religious awakening. By 1646 he had given up church attendance, and in 1647 he began preaching a message that truth was to be found through the inner voice of God speaking directly to the human soul. He was imprisoned on several occasions but attracted followers to his cause, known initially as "Friends of the Truth." From 1652 a stable organization began to emerge, based at Swarthmore Hall, near Ulverstone, in the house of Judge Thomas Fell, whose widow Fox married in 1669. To advance the work of his society, he undertook missionary journeys to Ireland in 1669, the West Indies and North America in 1671–1673, and northern Germany and the Netherlands in 1677. His journal was published posthumously in 1694, and the organization he founded became known as the Religious Society of Friends.

G. Fox, *Journal* (1924); Fox, *Works*, 8 vols. (1831, repr. 1975); H. L. Ingle, *First among Friends: George Fox and the Creation of Quakerism* (1994).

JOHN TONKIN

Foxe, John (1516–1587), Protestant martyrologist and historian, known primarily for his *Actes and Monuments*, popularly known as Foxe's *Book of Martyrs*. Foxe was born in Boston, Lincolnshire, and became a fellow of Magdalen College. As tutor to the Earl of Surrey's children, Foxe met John Bale, who encouraged his interest in history. With the accession of Mary Tudor, Foxe went into exile on the Continent. In 1555, in Frankfurt, he met Edmund Grindal, who had begun recording stories of Protestant martyrs. Foxe joined Bale in Basel, where he translated Grindal's stories into Latin. Foxe's book was published first in Basel in 1559. Following his return to England, Foxe worked with John Day, who published the first English edition of Foxe's book. Four editions were published in England during Foxe's lifetime. These editions had an enormous influence on popular piety and national self-consciousness in Elizabethan England. Until its most recent edition, most versions of *The Actes and Monuments* had been too abridged to bring out the breadth of Foxe's work.

P. Collinson, "Truth and Legend: The Veracity of John Foxe's *Book of Martyrs*," in *Clio's Mirror: Historiography in Britain and the Netherlands*, ed. A. C. Duke and C. A. Tamse (1985), 31–54; R. Helgerson, *Forms of Nationhood: The Elizabethan Writing of England* (1992).

JOHN E. GRISWOLD

France, Reformation in The French Reformation has roots in late medieval devotional trends that predate the inspiration of Luther and the Swiss reformers in France after 1517. Calls to increase the laity's role in matters of faith accompanied criticism of clerical abuses. The growing influence of the monarchy over the Gallican Church was also a factor. Most historians mark the beginning of the French Reformation with the reform activities of Guillaume Briçonnet (1472–1534), abbot of St. Germain de Prés and later bishop of Meaux, in the early 1500s. He and Jacques Lefèvre d'Étaples (c. 1460–1536) created a renowned center of academic study and personal piety that exemplified the Christian humanism of Erasmus. The circle of young reform-minded scholars that they attracted, known as the Cenacle of Meaux, profoundly shaped the course of the early French Reformation. They included Guillaume Farel (1489–1565), Guillaume Budé (1468–1540), Gérard Roussel (c. 1480–1550), and Louis Berquin (1485–1529). Their calls for reform and initial refusal to break with the church attracted the patronage and protection of Marguerite of Navarre (1492–1549), sister of King Francis I (1494–1547). However, mounting suspicion of their activities, particularly their vernacular translation of the Bible, eventually led to persecution by the powerful Faculty of Theology at the Sorbonne, which condemned Lefèvre d'Étaples of Lutheranism in 1521 and convinced the Parlement of Paris to execute Berquin for heresy in 1529.

The king's tepid sympathy for the reformers ended abruptly in the 1534 Affair of the Placards, when handbills touting reform were posted throughout the Louvre, including on the king's bedroom door. The ensuing persecution under Francis I and his son, Henry II (1519–1559), pushed the reformers in more radical directions, which attracted new followers. Among the new adherents was John Calvin (1509–1564). Born in Noyon, Picardy, Calvin studied law in Orléans and Bourges before pursuing a degree in letters at the Univ. of Paris. There he came into contact with Farel and the rector of the university, Nicolas Cop (1450–1532). Calvin and other reformers in Paris fled to Strasbourg in 1534, where Calvin published the first edition, in Latin, of the *Institutes of the Christian Religion* (1536). A revised French edition appeared in 1541 soon after he had moved to Geneva. In the *Institutes*, Calvin formulated his doctrines of grace, predestination, and divine majesty that formed the theological underpinnings of the ecclesiastical order he soon erected in Geneva. The key institution in the Genevan church was the consistory, which was made up of ministers of the Word, who interpreted Scripture, and elders in the community, who enforced God's law.

Calvin placed great importance on the proper training of pastors. Theodore Beza (1519–1605), Calvin's successor, took an early lead in this area in the late 1540s. The academies he set up soon attracted students from across Europe who fled to Geneva to escape persecution, eventually returning to their homelands in France, the Low Countries, the British Isles, and Germany to spread Calvin's teachings. A special affinity existed with the refugees from Calvin's native France, where the movement spread quickly in the 1550s. Catholics called Calvin's French followers "Huguenots," a word of uncertain origin. Calvinism attracted converts from artisan and professional groups in French towns as well as some noblemen and women, particularly in the southwest. The conversion of Jeanne d'Albret (1528–1572) in the early

1550s along with several members of the powerful Bourbon family gave the movement immediate clout. The movement's growth alarmed the monarchy and growing segments of the Catholic majority. The sudden death of Henry II in 1559 created instability, as none of the sons who succeeded him proved capable of containing the violent conflicts sparked by religious difference and political factionalism. The consequent series of civil wars over the next forty years profoundly shaped the course of the French Reformation.

In 1559, the first national synod of French Reformed congregations met in Paris. There and in ensuing meetings over the next decade, pastors and elders discussed different views of ecclesiastical discipline and organization. Antoine de la Roche Chandieu (1534–1591) spoke in favor of a presbyterian system of governance, while Jean Morelli (?–1572) represented a more decentralized congregationalist model. The Synod of Nîmes (1572) eventually supported Chandieu's views and condemned those represented by Morelli as heretical. The St. Bartholomew's Day Massacre later that year plunged the movement into decline and in even further radical directions as seen in the development of resistance theory against the crown by the Huguenot political theorists known as the Monarchomachs. The Huguenots eventually rallied to the royalist cause when their leader, Henry of Navarre (1553–1610), became presumptive heir to the throne in 1584 and then king in 1589. His conversion to Catholicism in July 1593 almost brought them back into conflict with the crown, however, until Henry IV granted them important but limited guarantees of security and freedom of worship in the 1598 Edict of Nantes.

The conditional toleration enjoyed by Huguenots over the next twenty years did little to stem further erosion of their ranks, particularly among the nobility, many of whom returned to Catholicism in order to advance in royal service. The French Calvinist church also split in the early seventeenth century, as did Calvinist communities across Europe, over the controversial views of the Dutch theologian, Jacobus Arminius (1560–1609), who conceded a greater measure of human free will in matters of salvation. The renewal of religious wars in the 1620s led to Huguenot defeat by Louis XIII (1601–1643) at the siege of La Rochelle in 1628. They still enjoyed a limited measure of religious freedom by the terms of the Peace of Alès in 1629 until Louis XIV (1638–1715) finally stripped that away when he revoked the

Edict of Nantes in 1685. Persecution led to forced conversions and emigration of the Huguenots abroad, though some fragments of the Reformed church continued to worship clandestinely over the next century until Louis XVI (1754–1793) granted them full religious liberty in 1787.

J. Garrisson, *A History of Sixteenth-Century France, 1483–1598: Renaissance, Reformation, and Rebellion* (1995); M. Greengrass, *The French Reformation* (1987); M. Holt, *Renaissance and Reformation France (1500–1648)* (2002); D. R. Kelley, *The Beginning of Ideology: Consciousness and Society in the French Reformation* (1981).

MICHAEL WOLFE

France, Wars of Religion in   *see* Wars of Religion in France

Francis I (1494–1547), king of France

(1515–1547).   Known as the "Father of Letters" for his appreciation of the Renaissance, Francis patronized many artists, writers, and architects, including Leonardo da Vinci, Benvenuto Cellini, Guillaume Budé, and Andrea del Sarto. His sponsorship of lectureships in Greek and Hebrew became the origins of the Collège de France. In foreign affairs, Francis invaded Italy in 1515 to secure his claim to the duchy of Milan and thereby launched France into several decades of war with the Habsburg Empire.

Francis's appreciation for Renaissance humanism led him to protect such reforming humanists as Jacques Lefèvre d'Étaples and the circle of reformers at Meaux associated with Bishop Guillaume Briçonnet. Francis withdrew his protection, however, when humanism seemed to be giving way to heresy. He became bitterly hostile toward Protestantism after the Affair of the Placards in October 1534 when broadsheets denouncing the Catholic Mass were posted in Paris and other cities in northern France. The Edict of Fontainebleau in June 1540 ceded control of heresy cases to the royal courts (*parlements*); thereafter, prosecutions for heresy in France increased dramatically.

R. J. Knecht, *Renaissance Warrior and Patron: The Reign of Francis I* (1994); E. W. Monter, *Judging the French Reformation: Heresy Trials by 16th-Century Parlements* (1999).

SCOTT M. MARR

Francis II (1544–1560), king of France

(1559–1560).   The first son of Henry II and Catherine de Médicis, Francis ascended the throne after his father's accidental death in July 1559. Francis, only fifteen years old, relied on his wife's uncles, Francis, duke of Guise, and Charles, cardinal of Lorraine. Ardent Catholics, the Guises took command of the government and continued Henry II's policy of repressing the Protestant movement in France. The Guises' program led to greater religious unrest, since it came just as the new faith was making its greatest inroads in France, especially among the nobility. Moreover, the Guises' domination of the government caused resentment among other nobles who felt excluded from power. A group of Protestant nobles, angered by religious repression, conspired to kidnap Francis (the Amboise conspiracy) in order to free him from his uncles' influence. Details of the plot leaked, however, and hundreds of the conspirators were arrested and executed. In the eyes of Catholics, the plot confirmed Protestantism's threat to the stability of France. Francis, who had never enjoyed good health, died December 5, 1560, and was succeeded by his brother, Charles IX.

J.-M. Constant, *Les Guise* (1984); N. M. Sutherland, *The Huguenot Struggle for Recognition* (1980).

SCOTT M. MARR

Francis de Sales (1567–1622), French

apologist, spiritual director, bishop of Geneva. Educated for a career in law, de Sales entered the priesthood instead and embraced the Tridentine reforms with enthusiasm and creativity. Named bishop while still under canonical age, he scrupulously eschewed the trappings and authority of office, and his legendary prowess in converting Calvinists is attributed as much to his openness to dialogue and courtesy in debate, so uncharacteristic of the time, as to the persuasiveness of his scripturally based preaching. With St. Jane Frances de Chantal he founded an innovative community of women, the Institute of the Visitation of the Blessed Virgin, without cloister, habit, or vows, witnessing in service to the poor. De Sales's enduring legacy is his insight that the laity have a unique, secular vocation to holiness. His classic *Introduction to the Devout Life* has remained in print since its publication in 1609. He was canonized less than fifty years after his death.

J. P. Camus, *The Spirit of Saint Francis de Sales* (2004); W. Wright, *Francis de Sales: Introduc-*

tion to the Devout Life and Treatise on the Love of God (1994).

PETER J. SCAGNELLI

Francis of Assisi (c. 1182–1226), founder of the Franciscan order. Born into an affluent merchant family, Francis eventually renounced his family's wealth in order to follow a life of apostolic poverty and itinerant preaching. Francis became a symbol for the renunciation of wealth and the embrace of a simple spirituality, a way of life that has remained popular through the centuries.

Francis's conversion took place in stages. After teenage years spent, by all accounts, frolicking, when he was about twenty, Francis joined his fellow Assisi townsmen in going to war against neighboring power Perugia. Captured and held prisoner for one year, Francis contracted a fever that, according to biographers, started the shift of his thoughts and concerns. Francis returned to Assisi in 1205 seeking a different life.

Two episodes of his life are especially noteworthy in leading to his conversion. The first is when he met a leper along the road and instinctively turned away in horror and disgust. Upon reflection, he returned and embraced the leper. The second is his exuberant display of largesse at his father's expense, when Francis threw clothes and valuables from his family home to passersby on the street below. In rage, his father dragged Francis to an ad hoc hearing in front of the bishop. Here Francis stripped his clothes and declared himself only the son of his Father in heaven.

Thereafter, Francis embraced a charismatic form of religious life centered on itinerancy, poverty, and humility. He became a model of religious life and attracted a small group of followers. While such a life had already become central to the lay revival known as the *vita apostolica*, Francis's innovation was that his way of life was supported and officially approved by Pope Innocent III, who, as a shrewd administrator, probably saw in Francis a way to rein in the popular exuberance of the movement through a vow of obedience directly to the pope. In 1209 or 1220 Innocent III orally approved a simple rule for the brothers, based largely on Gospel passages. A more formal rule was approved in 1223.

With a papally approved rule, Francis and his followers returned to Assisi, where their life attracted increasing numbers of followers. As the friars grew in number, the tendency to institutionalize changed the nature of the emerging order. While Francis had rigidly refused personal possessions, a growing number of friars saw a need for small items such as books so that they could say their prayers. Over the years, as the friars were enlisted for wider ecclesial tasks such as preaching, hearing confession, and inquisitorial duties, their need for higher education sharply affected the original intentions of the founder. Francis resigned as head of the order as it grew larger and as administrative responsibilities grew more complex. His final Testament is considered by many to be a plea to his friars to keep their life simple.

Although much sentimental piety surrounds Francis of Assisi, his spirituality was grounded in love and reverence for all of creation and an awareness of God's presence throughout creation. Hence, his famous "Canticle of the Sun," in which the natural elements are personified, reveals the closeness of the natural world and the unity of all divine creation. He is known for initiating the Christmas crèche in 1223, a tradition still practiced in many Christian denominations.

Because of the rigors of Francis's spiritual life, especially his dedication to poverty, his health was failing by the time he was forty. Blind and weak, Francis retreated to La Verna in September 1224, where he endured the closest identification with Christ by experiencing the stigmata.

He died on October 3, 1226, at the age of forty-five. This date is commemorated liturgically in Franciscan circles with a Transitus service, a liturgy that commemorates his passing from this life. He was canonized two short years later in 1228, and his feast day is October 4.

R. Armstrong, J. W. Hellman, W. Short, eds., *Francis of Assisi: Early Documents* (1999–2002); C. Frugoni, *Francis of Assisi: A Life* (1998); L. Landini, *The Causes of the Clericalization of the Order of Friars Minor, 1209–1260, in the Light of Early Franciscan Sources* (1968); R. Trexler, *Naked before the Father: The Renunciation of Francis of Assisi* (1989).

DARLEEN PRYDS

Franciscan Envoys to Medieval China

After missionary work in the Il-Khanate of Arghun in 1288–1290, John of Montecorvino (1246–1330) reached Beijing in 1294, just after the death of Khubilai Khan. Commissioned in 1291 to pursue the conversion of that emperor and to seek imperial help for Latin missionaries, John traveled by sea, spending thirteen months in southern India on the way. He had as a precedent the ground-breaking work of earlier Franciscans at the court of Jinghis Khan (d. 1227). The Polos, in China from 1271 to 1295, provided contacts, and John was welcomed by the new emperor, Timur Oljeitu (d. 1307). Regarded by the "Nestorians" at court as "a spy, magician, and deceiver of men," progress was slow at first.

An advance came in 1299 with the conversion, not long before his death while fighting rebels, of a leading "Nestorian" prince, George of the Onguts. George helped John erect a church and had "Nestorian" slanderers exiled. Having translated the New Testament and Psalms into the Tartar language, John claimed six thousand converts by 1305. Further progress among the Onguts stalled as the "Nestorians" reclaimed the loyalty of most of the royal family, and the conversion of the emperor was seen as an impracticable hope. A second church and a school were built in 1306, which church stood near the entrance to the royal court. There John was treated respectfully as a "legate of the lord pope."

In 1307 Clement V appointed John as archbishop of Beijing, and primate of the East with patriarchal authority. But it was 1313 before three of the seven bishops sent for the consecration reached Beijing and carried out the rite. As a result, a full Catholic episcopate was established in China, much to the chagrin of the "Nestorians," who in this paralleled the reactions of Greek Christians to the appointment of Latin patriarchs for Antioch, Jerusalem, Alexandria, and Constantinople, from 1100 to 1204.

Among the new bishops in China was Andrew of Perugia (d. 1332), who focused on central China and had his base in the southern port city of Zaitun. He had better relations with Armenian Christians than with the "Nestorians." No conversions of Jews or of Muslims were claimed, and those from Buddhism were deemed to be half-hearted. By 1322 Odoric of Pordenone (d. 1331) had arrived also, and he visited large centers such as Hangchow and Langchow. In the latter he found a Franciscan monastery, but there were no fewer than three "Nestorian" churches.

The death of John of Montecorvino in 1330 caused widespread grief, which was noted by a visiting Dominican, John of Cora. He commented on the continuing animosity of the "Nestorians," whom he thought numbered thirty thousand.

While contact between the Yuan dynasty and the papacy continued up to 1338, no immediate successor for John arrived. Then in 1342 John of Marignolli (d. 1357), with a party of thirty-two, reached Beijing to become archbishop. He stayed four years before returning to the pope at Avignon by 1353.

Urban V selected William of Prat as archbishop, and in 1370 he left for Beijing with a considerable number of Franciscan missionaries. There is no record of their arrival there. By 1368 the Yuan dynasty had been toppled and all things associated with the Mongols obliterated. This included both Catholic and "Nestorian" institutions. By 1400 isolated vestigial groups of Christians were all that remained of sustained evangelical endeavors by both Asians and Europeans.

K. S. Latourette, *A History of Christian Missions in China* (1966); W. W. Rockhill, ed., *The Journey of William of Rubruck to the Eastern Part of the World, 1253–55* (1941); C. W. Troll, "Die Chinamission in Mittelalter," in *Franzikanische Studien* 48 (1966) and 49 (1967); H. Yule, ed., *Cathay and the Way Thither* (1966).

IAN GILLMAN†

Franciscan Order This is the most numerous of the mendicant orders, with three independent male branches: *Ordo Fratrum Minorum* (OFM: Order of the Friars Minor, Grey Friars), *Ordo Fratrum Minorum Conventualium* (OFM Conv.: Friars Minor Conventual), *Ordo Fratrum Minorum Capuccinorum* (OFM Cap.: Friars Minor Capuchin). To the Franciscan family belong also the second, or female, order: *Ordo S. Clarae* (OSCl: Order of St. Claire, Poor Ladies, Poor Clares), and numerous third orders of brothers and sisters. The habit of the Friars Minor is brown (originally grey) with attached cowl and threefold knotted belt cord, symbolizing their dedication to poverty, chastity, and obedience.

The origin of this apostolic movement is closely connected with Francis of Assisi (d. 1226), who probably in 1207 felt the call to live literally according to the precepts of the Gospels and was, as a charismatic figure, soon joined by followers from Assisi. Absolute personal and communal poverty and the preaching of penance and peace were the guiding principles of his brotherhood. The universal character of the Franciscan mission became evident in 1209, when the first eight friars were sent from the Portiuncula in Assisi, the small chapel that was the headquarters of the order during Francis's lifetime, to the four parts of the world.

The simple Franciscan Proto-Rule (the text is not handed down) was orally approved by Innocent III in 1209. With Cardinal Ugolino of

Ostia (he became Pope Gregory IX) the order had its first protector and established a close connection to the Roman church. When the movement expanded in the 1220s from Umbria to the rest of Italy and then to nearly all of Europe, further regulation of the *vita minorum*, the life of the Friars Minor, became necessary. In 1223 the extensive *Regula non bullata* (1221) was replaced by the more pragmatic *Regula bullata* (the former was not confirmed by a papal bull, the latter was).

The first generation of friars consisted of laymen and clerics alike. The order's government was vertically structured with the minister general at the top, provincial ministers at regional levels (later sometimes divided into custodies), and the guardian as the head of the local friary. Both the central and regional level had chapters with legislative and executive powers and functions of control and oversight. The first statutes date from 1239; after additional constitutional texts had been promulgated, an important revision was made with the *Constitutiones Narbonnenses* (1260) during the generalate of Bonaventure.

The 1230s and 1240s saw changes both in the function and the character of the order. The brotherhood developed into a clerical order, which in exchange for material support offered professional spiritual leadership and became involved in university teaching, the Inquisition, and "secular" missions. Thus, the Franciscan friary became an integrative religious and political center of the town and also an institution in competition with the secular clergy. At the same time a serious internal controversy over the observance of the original ideals of Francis—centering on absolute poverty, simplicity, and the eschatological role of the Friars Minor in the process of the renovation of the church—divided the members of the order. Opposed to the main body of the Community or Conventuals, who supported the new orientation of the order, various parties of Spirituals (formerly known as Zealots) appeared, regarding themselves as the true keepers of original, radical Franciscan views and the practice of poverty. The conflict was decided in favor of the Community, with the final official exclusion of the Spirituals from the order and the Catholic Church by Pope John XXII in 1317.

Debates on the nature and practice of Franciscan poverty nevertheless continued, along with the formation of the well-organized and rather eremitic Observant reform movements. Attempts at reconciliation failed, and in 1517 the partition of the order into the two branches of the Conventuals and the Friars Minor (the former Observants) was finally confirmed by Pope Leo X. In modern times the order was again enlarged by new reforming groups. In 1619 the Capuchins, originating in Italy in 1525, were separated as the third autonomous branch of the Franciscan order.

———

R. J. Armstrong, J. A. W. Hellmann, and W. J. Short, eds., *Francis of Assisi: Early Documents*, 4 vols. (1999–2002); D. Burr, *The Spiritual Franciscans: From Protest to Persecution in the Century after Saint Francis* (2001); K. Esser, *Origins of the Franciscan Order* (1970); M. D. Lambert, *Franciscan Poverty: The Doctrine of the Absolute Poverty of Christ and the Apostles in the Franciscan Order, 1210–1323* (1998); E. Menestò and S. Brufani, eds., *Fontes Francescani*, in *Medioevo Francescano*, 2 (1995); J. Moorman, *A History of the Franciscan Order from Its Origins to the Year 1517* (1968).

ANNE MÜLLER

Franciscan Spirituals

Franciscan Spirituals   A name given to a party of Franciscan rigorists. The name was used polemically during the controversy over religious poverty c. 1300–1322, and it is often applied by scholars more broadly to what were two factions, one more radical than the other, that emerged among Franciscans in southern France and Italy in the 1270s and 1280s. In southern France, the controversy began over the interpretation of religious poverty and Peter John Olivi's doctrine of "poor use." In Italy, where rigorists were known as "fraticelli," the controversy began over the question of obedience to the pope (were Franciscans bound to obey a pope who ordered them to accept possessions, in apparent contradiction to a strict interpretation of the Franciscan rule?) and humility (were Franciscans living in a sufficiently impoverished way, in true conformity to St. Francis's rule?). Inspired in part by the exegetical method of Joachim of Fiore and encouraged by papal opposition to the most rigorous interpretation of the Franciscan rule, Ubertino da Casale, a friar who had been deeply impressed by the teachings of Peter John Olivi at Florence in 1287–1289, and Angelo Clareno, a friar from the March of Anconna, radicalized the union of the defense of poverty with apocalyptically framed criticisms of the papacy. Persecution of the Franciscan rigorists who defended the doctrine of "poor use" intensified at the beginning of the fourteenth century. Persecution was relieved by Pope Clement V

(1309–1314) in 1309, by which time the rigorists formed a definite faction within the Franciscan order. Nonetheless, agitation against the views of Peter John Olivi culminated in the condemnation of articles derived from his writings at the third session of the Council of Vienne (May 6, 1312). Clement's successor, Pope John XXII (1316–1334), in a sustained campaign that began soon after his coronation, destroyed the faction, condemning the doctrine of "poor use" in a series of bulls and constitutions from 1317 to 1322 and appointing inquisitors to prosecute supporters of the fraticelli and critics of the papacy. Yet ideas and ideals promoted by the Spirituals continued to influence, to one extent or another, Observant Franciscans, critics of the papal schism (1378–1417), Christopher Columbus, and others.

D. Burr, *The Spiritual Franciscans* (2001); *Nicolaus Minorita: Chronica*, ed. G. Gál and D. Flood (1996); R. Manselli, *Da Gioacchino da Fiore a Cristoforo Colombo: Studi sul Francescanesimo spirituale, sull'ecclesiologia e sull'escatologismo bassomedievali* (1997).

CHRISTOPHER OCKER

Francisco de los Angeles Quiñones
see Quiñones, Francisco de los Angeles

Francisco Jiménez de Cisneros   *see*
Jiménez de Cisneros, Francisco

Franck, Sebastian (1499–1542), German
spiritualist and historian. Influenced by Erasmus's humanism and by German mysticism, Franck became a Dominican in Heidelberg and later a priest in Augsburg. In 1524 he moved to the Nuremberg area where he joined the evangelical movement. Disillusioned with the magisterial reform, he separated from all forms of religious community. He advanced a spiritualist understanding of Christianity that emphasized the inner word of God modeled by Christ against all external expressions of religion. To support himself and his family he worked variously as a translator, printer, and soapmaker.

Franck primarily produced compilations and commentaries on the writings of others. His best-known work, *Chronica* (1531), reviewed the events and figures of world history, demonstrating the absence of God's true, inner word in all but the beliefs of a few individuals others had labeled heretics. His controversial ideas led to his expulsion from Strasbourg and then Ulm. He died in Basel.

S. Franck, "A Letter to John Campanus (1531)," in *Spiritual and Anabaptist Writers*, ed. G. H. Williams and A. Mergal (1957); Franck, *Paradoxes or Wondrous Sayings*, trans. E. J. Furcha (1986); P. Hayden-Roy, *The Inner Word and the Outer World: A Biography of Sebastian Franck* (1994).

MARY ELIZABETH ANDERSON

Francke, August Hermann (1663–
1727), Lutheran minister and principal organizer of Pietism. Born in Lübeck and educated at Erfurt, Kiel, Leipzig, and Hamburg, Francke was a pious and avid student with a keen interest in biblical languages. He completed his university education at Leipzig in 1685, where he had been part of a *collegium philobiblicum*, a group of students and occasional faculty that met for Bible study in the original languages. These group studies were patterned after the conventicles, or devotional circles, popularized by Philip Jacob Spener (1635–1705). In 1687 Francke underwent a profound conversion experience that changed his life and provided the foundation for his future ministry and social reforms. After meeting Spener the following year, Francke shaped his pastoral work to reflect Pietist reforms.

Francke taught briefly at the Univ. of Leipzig between 1689 and 1690, but his emphasis upon practical and devotional applications of the Bible led to disputes over Pietism. The next year he accepted pastoral work at Erfurt, but after fifteen months was dismissed there as well for his zealous preaching. In 1692 Spener recommended Francke for a faculty appointment in Greek and Oriental languages, without salary, at the newly created Univ. at Halle. At the same time he became pastor of a poor parish in nearby Glaucha. Francke proved to be a popular preacher and teacher, tasks that he tackled with enormous energy. The devotion he showed for his parishioners and the reforms he instituted at Glaucha raised the ire of some orthodox Lutheran clergy, but he was exonerated. In 1715 he became the senior pastor at St. Michael's Church in Halle, which served to enhance his influence. The following year he was appointed professor of theology at the university and in 1716 was made vice chancellor, a position he held until his death.

In 1695 Francke created the first of what would become several world-famous charitable institutes (the *Franckesche Stiftungen*) at Halle. It was a modest day school for poor children that at first met in his parsonage. Over the next few years several other schools were founded. These included a free boarding school for poor children, a Latin school for sons of the wealthy and the nobility, and a school to train teachers that greatly popularized his teaching methods. To train pastors in practical skills, a theological school was also begun, as well as a school for the study of biblical languages. Many older students were employed as teachers and house parents in the lower schools, in an orphanage begun in 1695, and in homes for widows, the aged, and the impoverished that began in 1698.

The formation of a Bible society in 1710 led to an active printing program, which was directed by Carl Hildebrand von Canstein (1667–1719). Halle presses produced thousands of inexpensive New Testaments and complete Bibles; the famous *Spiritual Hymnal* (1697) of Johann A. Freylinghausen (1670–1739), who became Francke's son-in-law; and other songbooks, devotional materials, and prayer books. Another great activity of the Halle institutes was missionary work. In addition to training a steady stream of pastors, Halle graduates, with books and medicines from the institute's pharmaceutical laboratory, were dispatched to mission work in India and elsewhere. Henry Melchior Muhlenburg (1711–1787), sent by Francke to America in 1742, shaped the organization and character of American Lutheranism.

Under Francke's guidance Halle became a world-renowned center for Pietism. Through its religious education and social outreach programs he and his supporters hoped that society could be transformed. Yet these efforts were not without controversy. Pietism stressed an inner, personal experience of Christ, a new birth (*Wiedergeburt*), an experience often preceded by an intense inner struggle of repentance (*Busskampf*). For Francke this event resulted in a changed life of active love and service in the world. Orthodox Lutherans, on the other hand, objected to the subjective emphasis on an inward repentance, insisting that salvation was through the means of grace (the preached Word, baptism, and the Lord's Supper). Francke's numerous writings include hymns, devotional pieces, and exegetical works. Among his better-known works are *Guide to the Reading and Study of the Holy Scriptures* (1693) and *Duty to the Poor* (1697).

———

K. Deppermann, *Der hallesche Pietismus und der preussische Staat unter Friedrich III* (1961); P. Erb, *Pietists: Selected Writings* (1983); M. Matthias, "August Hermann Francke," in *The Pietist Theologians,* ed. C. Lindberg (2003), 100–114; G. R. Sattler, *God's Glory, Neighbor's Good* (1982); F. E. Stoeffler, *German Pietism During the 18th Century* (1973).

DAVID B. ELLER

Francogallia A treatise on the right to resist tyranny written in 1573 by French Huguenot François Hotman. More humanist investigation than fiery polemic, *Francogallia* is an examination of the constitutional history of France. Based on meticulous documentation, Hotman argued that France was not an absolute monarchy. Rather, the kings of old were elected by the people and thus could be removed by the people. Hotman further argued that the ancient estates of France (monarchy, aristocracy, and people) provided a mechanism for the removal of a tyrannous king. According to Hotman, these three estates ordered the political and social life of the country and each provided a check to the excesses of the others. Conspicuously absent from this list is the church. Hotman's analysis of the estates served two purposes. First, by removing the church from the list of estates he undermined the government's claim to enforce religious conformity. Second, by highlighting the people's role in checking abuse by the other estates Hotman advocated a significant advance in resistance theory—popular sovereignty. The *Francogallia* was immediately popular because its analysis provided legal justification for Huguenot resistance to the crown's attempts to suppress Protestantism: according to the first premise, the actions of the king were unconstitutional and must, according to the second principle, be resisted by the aristocracy and the people. The *Francogallia* was expanded in 1576 and 1586, but its fundamental arguments remained unchanged.

———

F. Hotman, "*Francogallia,*" in *Constitutionalism and Resistance in the Sixteenth Century: Three Treatises by Hotman, Beza, and Mornay* (1969); D. R. Kelley, *François Hotman: A Revolutionary's Ordeal* (1973).

DAVID WHITFORD

Fraticelli   *see* Franciscan Spirituals

Frederick III (1463–1525), Elector of Saxony. Frederick, already called "the Wise" by contemporaries, came to the throne after the death of his father Ernst in 1486. The Saxon territories had been divided a year earlier. Frederick received the region without the traditional residence in Meissen and the established university in Leipzig. He therefore established both a new residence and a new university in Wittenberg, hiring Martin Luther as a professor of Old Testament. Provided with significant income from silver mines in the Erzgebirge mountains, he saw himself as the promoter of the arts and sciences, indicated by his appointment of Lucas Cranach as court artist in 1505. Frederick played an important role in imperial politics as the imperial marshall and representative of the emperor during his absence.

As evidenced by his great relic collection, Frederick adhered to a personal, traditional piety. He was also interested in the peaceful resolution of conflicts. Both aspects of his personality would play a role as the heresy trial against Luther commenced in Rome in 1518. Frederick prevented the extradition of his university professor and provided a "fatherly interrogation" for him in Germany. In 1521 he obtained a promise from the emperor that Luther would not be condemned without being heard at the Diet of Worms. After the consequent ban on Luther, he hid him in the castle of Wartburg.

On the other hand, Frederick always avoided openly declaring himself for Luther. He attached importance to the fact that he directly met Luther only once, in Worms. Luther's stay in Wartburg castle was organized by the electoral secretary, Georg Spalatin, so that Frederick could deny knowledge of Luther's whereabouts with a good conscience. Whether he really received the Lord's Supper on his deathbed under both species, thus in the Protestant manner, is not known with certainty.

R. Bruck, *Friedrich der Weise als Förderer der Kunst* (1903); I. Ludolphy, *Friedrich der Weise, Kurfürst von Sachsen, 1463–1525* (1984).

MARTIN TREU

Friends, Society of The movement commonly known as "Quakers" was founded by George Fox (1624–1691) amid the intense religious ferment of mid-seventeenth-century England. The label "Quaker," originally a pejorative term applied by a judge to George Fox, who had called on the judge to tremble at the Word of the Lord, is now proudly acknowledged. Though coinciding with Puritanism, the Friends' lineage is not so much Puritan as mystical and spiritual, based on the notion of a revival of NT Christianity. In addition to George Fox, theological leadership was provided by a number of prominent scholars trained in

other traditions, including Robert Barclay (1648–1690), who was trained at the Roman Catholic Scots College in Paris and whose "Apology" remains the major systematic statement of Friends' beliefs. From 1652 the movement enjoyed the protection of Judge Thomas Fell and his wife Margaret at Swarthmore Hall, near Ulverstone, from which center Fox and other preachers spread out across England, to various regions of Europe and to America, where William Penn (1644–1718) founded the colony of Pennsylvania on Quaker principles. From the beginning women were regarded as equal partners in every aspect of the enterprise.

While accepting the substance of the historic Trinitarian creeds, Quakers discarded the creeds as such because of their nonscriptural philosophical terminology and their use in enforcing doctrinal orthodoxy. The Bible was valued but regarded as subordinate to the Spirit. Theologically the movement was based on the notion of an immediate relationship between the living Christ and the individual soul, which rendered an ordained ministry, consecrated buildings, creeds, sacraments, and liturgical practices irrelevant. Worship took the form of silent and expectant waiting to apprehend the voice of God that, it was believed, would lead believers to unity and truth while working also on behalf of non-Christians. Notwithstanding this historic emphasis on silent waiting upon God, some modern Quaker meetings have "programmed" worship and appointed pastors.

The Friends' opposition to the swearing of oaths, tithing, and military service put them on a collision course with civil society. Persecuted under Cromwell and again under the Restoration monarchy, Quakers achieved religious freedom with the Toleration Act of 1688.

H. Barbour and J. W. Frost, *The Quakers* (1988); R. Bauman, *Let Your Words Be Few: Symbolism of Speaking and Silence among Seventeenth-Century Quakers* (1983); A. Lloyd, *Quaker Social History, 1669–1738* (1950); B. Reay, *The Quakers and the English Revolution* (1985).

JOHN TONKIN

Fulgentius of Ruspe (468–533), bishop, theologian, polemicist, saint. Fulgentius was born of a Catholic senatorial family of Carthage that had known persecution under Arian Vandal rule. He renounced the world to pursue the ascetic life after a brief career as procurator of Telepta. Fulgentius visited Rome, where he made lasting acquaintances among the elite, and then returned to North Africa, becoming bishop of Ruspe in 508. Exiled to Sardinia in 509 by King Thrasamund, Fulgentius was recalled to Carthage between 510 and 515 to engage the Arians in debate, but his defense of Catholic doctrine led to further exile in Sardinia until 523, when Thrasamund's successor, King Hilderich, adopted a more benign policy toward the catholic church. Fulgentius's life is known principally from the biography composed by his contemporary, Ferrandus of Carthage.

Fulgentius's writings fall into three groups: expositions of catholic doctrine against Arianism, synthetic discussions of Augustine's teachings on grace and predestination, and miscellaneous writings on a variety of religious issues. In later eras, Fulgentius remained important as an interpreter of Augustine's view of grace and predestination.

Fulgentius Ruspensis, *Selected Works*, trans. R. Eno (1997); Y. Modéran, "La chronologie de la vie de Saint Fulgence de Ruspe et ses incidences sur l'histoire de l'Afrique vandale," in *Mélanges de l'École française de Rome*, vol. 105 of *Antiquité* (1993), 135–88.

WILLIAM NORTH

Gaismaier, Michael (c. 1491–1532), military and political leader of the Peasants' War in the Tirol. Born to an upwardly mobile family in the southern Tirol, Gaismaier served as secretary to the region's vice-regent and advanced to a position serving the bishop of Brixen. Gaismaier's reasons for shifting from bureaucrat and landowner to a radically egalitarian revolutionary are obscure and continue to be debated. During the uprising against the nobility and prelates of Brixen, Gaismaier handed over the bishop's residence and was elected commander-in-chief of the insurgents. He and his cohorts presented their complaints against the feudal system in thirty articles. Imperial troops crushed the uprising in 1525, and Gaismaier fled to Zurich. There he wrote his famous Constitution (*Landesordnung*) for the establishment of a Christian society. The Constitution called for faithful biblical preaching and advocated the elimination of private commerce. When the Tirolers failed to join his invasion in 1526, Gaismaier retreated and sought asylum in Venice. His death came by assassination in Padua by an agent of Archduke Ferdinand.

A. Bischoff-Urack, *Michael Gaismaier: Ein Beitrag zur Sozialgeschichte des Bauern-*

krieges (1983); J. Bücking, *Michael Gaismaier: Reformer Sozialrebell Revolutionär* (1978); W. Klaasen, *Michael Gaismaier: Revolutionary and Reformer* (1978).

KEN SUNDET JONES

Gaius, bishop of Rome (282–295) and martyr. Born perhaps in Illyricum, later venerated as a martyr. He should not be confused with his second-century namesake, who wrote against millennialism and against a certain Montanist named Proclus. Gaius, the bishop, who is mentioned in Eusebius (*Hist. eccl.* 7.32) and by an epitaph in Greek, led the church during a peaceful period, right before the Diocletian persecution broke out at the end of the third century. Thus, the bishop had a brief opportunity to mobilize and organize the traumatized church. He encouraged the observance of the clerical hierarchy and evidently proposed a system of seven ecclesiastical districts in Rome. Gaius's name also figures in an early medieval text, *Passion of St. Sebastian*. The later tradition, which links him to the emperor Gaius (r. 37–41), is not credible. Bishop Gaius was buried in the catacomb of Callistus on the Via Appia but curiously not in the Crypt of the Popes.

R. Davis, ed., *The Book of Pontiffs (Liber Pontificales)* (2nd ed., 2000); R. Davis, "Pre-Constantine Chronology: The Roman Bishopric from AD 258 to 314," *JTS* 48 (1997): 439–70.

TARMO TOOM

Galen (c. 129–c. 200), Greek physician and philosopher. Born in Pergamum, Galen died in Rome, where he served as Marcus Aurelius's doctor. He wrote numerous treatises on various topics including physiology and anatomy, disease, foods and medicines, diet, sexual function, ethics and moral training, and previous and contemporary writers and debates. Galen saw himself as both a philosopher and a physician, and his writings assume the mutual connection of body, physical behavior, and constitution with the soul, personal character, and ethics. His system is based on concepts of the four principal elements (earth, air, fire, and water), the four humors of the body (blood, yellow bile, black bile, and phlegm), and the four qualities (warm, cool, dry, and moist). These combine differently in bodies, are subject to manipulation through regimen and diet, and affect both the condition of the body and the health of the soul. He also shared the Platonic concept of the tripartite soul but could not accept an incorporeal soul. Galen criticized

certain Christian beliefs but admired Christians' high moral standards. Christian ascetic authors used Galenic physiology and dietary theory to argue for the efficacy of physical disciplines such as fasting.

C. G. Kühn, ed., *Galeni Opera Omnia* (1964–1965); T. M. Shaw, *The Burden of the Flesh* (1998); P. N. Singer, *Introduction to Galen: Selected Works* (1997); O. Temkin, *Galenism* (1973).

TERESA M. SHAW

Galilei, Galileo (1564–1642), Italian astronomer, physicist, and mathematician.

Galileo was born in Pisa and educated, primarily, in the monastery of Vollombrosa near Florence. He lectured on mathematics at the Univ. of Pisa from 1592 to 1610, and in 1610 was appointed mathematician and philosopher to the grand duke of Tuscany, a position he held the rest of his life. Although he did not invent the telescope, he greatly improved it and thereby revolutionized the study of astronomy. He discovered the satellites of Jupiter and sunspots, and he proclaimed his support for the Copernican view of the solar system. Consequently, in 1616, he was forbidden to teach by the Roman church, which remained committed to the Ptolemaic system. Three features of his thinking are theologically noteworthy: he compared the cosmos to a vast book, written (by God) in the language of mathematics; his discovery of sunspots led him to regard the heavens as corruptible, just like the earth; and he distinguished his scientific work from his faith, arguing that the Bible was intended by God to teach faith and theology, not science.

M. Biagioli, *Galileo, Courtier: The Practice of Science in the Culture of Absolutism* (1993); M. Clavelin, *The Natural Philosophy of Galileo* (1974); W. R. Shea, *Galileo's Intellectual Revolution* (1972).

RODERICK MARTIN

Galla Placidia (c. 390–450), Roman empress. Daughter of Theodosius I (r. 379–395), Galla Placidia was captured during the Visigothic sack of Rome in 410. In 414 she married the Visigothic king Athaulf at Narbonne, but in 416, following Athaulf's murder, she was restored to the court of her half-brother Honorius (r. 393–423) at Ravenna. The next year Placidia married Honorius's general Constantius, who as Constantius III reigned briefly as Honorius's co-emperor (421). Their son,

Valentinian III, nominally ruled the West from 425 to 455. Placidia energetically conducted affairs of church and state. In 418–419, during the papal schism that disrupted Rome after the death of Pope Zosimus, she solicited Honorius's support for Eulalius against his (successful) rival Boniface I. Following Honorius's death she secured the imperial throne for the young Valentinian and managed his reign until Aetius rose to power in the 430s. Leo I's correspondence preserves letters written by Placidia to her nephew the Eastern emperor Theodosius II and his sister Pulcheria (Letters 56, 58). Both epistles adamantly support Roman primacy as well as Leo's condemnation of Eutyches. Placidia lavishly embellished her capital at Ravenna. Though she may have built her famous mausoleum there, she was probably buried at Rome where she died.

G. Mackie, *Early Christian Chapels in the West* (2003); S. Oost, *Galla Placidia Augusta* (1968); V. Sirago, *Galla Placidia: La Nobilissma* (1996).

DENNIS E. TROUT

Gallican Articles (1682), a declaration of the French clergy, composed by Jacques-Bénigne Bossuet, claiming autonomy from Rome on certain matters for the French church. Occasioned by a dispute between Louis XIV and Innocent XI over the appointment of French bishops, the four articles asserted that kings derive their authority over their subjects directly from God, not through the pope; proclaimed the authority of general councils over the pope; sought to reestablish the autonomy of the French church as an established tradition of the Catholic Church; and argued that the church, including the decrees and judgments of the pope, could be reformed via general councils.

P. Goubert, *Louis XIV and Twenty Million Frenchmen* (1970).

RODERICK MARTIN

Gallican Confession The forty articles of this "Confession of Faith Made by Common Agreement by the French Who Desire to Live according to the Purity of the Gospel of Our Savior Jesus Christ" were adopted by the first National Synod of the Reformed Churches of France meeting in Paris (May 1559). It ensured that French Reformed churches remained doctrinally united and was the first of similar confessions written where Calvinist churches organized. The seventh National Synod of La

Rochelle (1571) designated the Gallican Confession the True Confession of Faith of the Reformed Churches of France. It is known also as the Confession of La Rochelle. It became a standard for judging orthodoxy to which Reformed ministers, elders, and deacons subscribed. The text was solemnly read and reexamined at other national synods. Few changes were made. The seventeenth national synod (Gap, 1603) added the pope as the antichrist. Considered a summary of biblical teaching, the Confession affirms that Scripture alone legitimizes religious statements. Biblical references were attached. The Confession affirms the Apostles', Nicene, and Athanasian creeds and denounces heresy, mentioning Michel Servetus by name. It opposes "papal assemblies" (considered idolatrous), the intercession of dead saints, purgatory, auricular confession, and monastic vows. Converts from Catholicism were not to be rebaptized, as infant baptism was recognized as legitimate. It recognizes as biblical the Reformed offices of pastor, elder, and deacon, but not doctor.

———

P. Schaff, ed., *The Creeds of Christendom with a History and Critical Notes*, vol. 3, *The Evangelical Protestant Creeds, with Translations* (1919), 356–82.

JEANNINE E. OLSON

Gansfort, Johannes Wessel (c. 1419–1489), Dutch lay theologian and humanist.

Educated by the Brothers of the Common Life at Zwolle in the eastern Netherlands, Gansfort studied at the Univ. of Cologne and worked for a time at the Univ. of Heidelberg. In Paris around 1458, he gradually evolved from a Thomist into a nominalist and achieved great renown as a theologian. He returned to the Low Countries in 1475. Because he diminished the doctrinal authority of the church and stressed the Bible as the source of religious truth, Gansfort has often been regarded as a precursor of the Reformation; indeed, his *Farrago rerum theologicarum* was published in 1522 with a preface by Luther. It may be more to the point to regard him as an exponent of the northern Christian Renaissance.

———

H. A. Obermann, *Forerunners of the Reformation* (1966); F. Akkermann, *Wessel Gansfort (1419–1489) and Northern Humanism* (1993).

JORIS VAN EIJNNATTEN

Gardiner, Stephen (c. 1497–1555), bishop of Winchester (1531–51; 1553–55), diplomat,

statesman, prominent leader in the opposition to the Reformation in England. Though he was tradition minded, he supported Henry VIII and the Royal Supremacy over papal authority, citing the Old Testament as authority for his position. He was master of Trinity Hall, Cambridge, from 1525 to 1549. As secretary to Cardinal Wolsey, he tried to accommodate Henry VIII's antipapal legislation while restraining advocates of more radical reforms. Henry and Wolsey employed him as a diplomat to Rome regarding the annulment of Henry's marriage to Catherine of Aragon; in 1533 he acted as an assessor in the court that annulled the marriage. His opposition to Reformation influences led him to oppose Thomas Cromwell and Thomas Cranmer, with whom he disputed often on eucharistic theology. By Henry's death in 1547, Gardiner was the leading opponent of Reformation influences in England. His career following Henry's death took many turns; Edward VI imprisoned Gardiner in 1548 and deprived him of his bishopric in 1551. Upon Mary's accession in 1553, Gardiner was restored to Winchester; additionally, Mary made him Lord High Chancellor. Under Mary, Gardiner oversaw the reconciliation with Rome while also securing the ownership of church lands that had been confiscated under Henry and Edward.

———

D. MacCulloch, "Two Dons in Politics: Stephen Gardiner and Thomas Cranmer," *Historical Journal* 37 (1994): 1–22; G. Redworth, *In Defence of the Church Catholic: A Life of Stephen Gardiner* (1990).

ALDEN R. LUDLOW

Gaspard de Châtillon   *see* Coligny, Gaspard de

Gaul   This populous and prosperous Celtic-speaking territory beyond the Alps, conquered

by the Romans between c. 150 and c. 50 BCE, remained part of the Roman Empire until the fifth century CE, when it gradually came under the control of Goths, Burgundians, and other barbarian groups. By the mid-sixth century it was largely ruled by the Merovingian dynasty of the Franks. From the eightth century, when a new Frankish dynasty—the Carolingians—emerged, it was increasingly known no longer as *Gallia*, but as *Francia*.

The earliest detailed evidence for Christianity in Gaul comes from a letter preserved by Eusebius (*Hist. eccl.* 5.1–4) that recounts the martyrdom of about fifty Christians of every social class at Lyon, the provincial capital, in

177. By the mid-third century, there were Christian communities in Arles, Paris, Trier, and other cities in Gaul. By 314 when the emperor Constantine convened a council in Arles to deal with the Donatist controversy, there may have been as many as thirty bishoprics in Gaul. The most important fourth-century bishops in Gaul were Hilary, bishop of Poitiers (d. c. 367), defender of Nicene Christianity, and the ex-soldier and ascetic Martin, bishop of Tours (d. 397).

Literary and archaeological sources for Christianity in Gaul in the fifth and sixth centuries present the image of a stable Christian society in which bishops, mainly drawn from local aristocratic families, are firmly in command of religious power, benevolently controlling the mechanisms of ritual, shrines, relics, and cults of saints, and the extensive resources of patronage, land, and movable property in the interests of their communities. Some scholars uphold this image as essentially accurate; others have suggested that the written sources and to some extent even material evidence reveal (by attempting to mask) a messier scenario, in which local populations appeared indifferent, recalcitrant, and sometimes hostile to the demands of Christianization, especially when these conflicted with traditional ways of life. The career of Caesarius of Arles (469/470–542) represents a test case for these differences of opinion.

The works of Gregory of Tours (d. 594) vividly describe life in later sixth-century Gaul: the foibles and crimes of the Franks and Romans, the miracle-working powers of saints and their relics, the disasters and sufferings befalling Tours, Clermont, and other regions, and the prominence of his own family in those regions. By the seventh century, Gregory's late Roman Gaul began to give way to early medieval France.

———

D. Bertrand et al., *Césaire d'Arles et la christianisation de la Provence* (1994); P. Fouracre and R. A. Gerberding, *Late Merovingian France: History and Hagiography, 640–720* (1996); M. Heinzelmann, *Gregory of Tours: History and Society in the 6th Century* (2001); W. E. Klingshirn, *Caesarius of Arles and the Making of a Christian Community in Late Antique Gaul* (1994); A. C. Murray, *From Roman to Merovingian Gaul* (2000); R. Van Dam, *Saints and Their Miracles in Late Antique Gaul* (1993); I. Wood, *The Merovingian Kingdoms, 450–751* (1994).

WILLIAM E. KLINGSHIRN

Geiler of Kaisersberg, Johann

(1445–1510), German preacher, confessor, theologian. He was born at Schaffhausen on the Rhine and educated at Ammersweiher near Kaisersburg in Alsace and at Freiburg Univ. He lectured on Aristotle at Freiburg from 1465 to 1471 and then taught theology at Basel from 1471 to 1476, where he also preached at the cathedral. In 1478 the special office of preacher was created for him at the cathedral of Strasbourg. He then abandoned academic work to concentrate on preaching and on church reform. He was a renowned and popular preacher who admonished the masses to repent of their sins and attacked clerical luxury and corruption. He also preached against simony, indulgences, and relic worship. A remarkable stone pulpit was built for him and dedicated to him at Strasbourg. During the early Reformation, the reformer Matthew Zell (b. 1477) was forbidden by the authorities to preach from this pulpit. Geiler's publications included an edition of the works of Jean Gerson. Geiler never set out to publish his own sermons, for which he is most famous, but they were made available to the public via notes taken by his audiences.

———

E. J. D. Douglass, *Justification in Late Medieval Preaching* (1989).

RODERICK MARTIN

Gelasius I

(d. 496), bishop of Rome (492–496). Evidence for his birthplace—either in Rome or in Africa—is ambiguous. Upon coming to the papacy he immediately addressed the schism stemming from his predecessor's excommunication of Acacius, patriarch of Constantinople and author of the *Henoticon*, a formula of union between the Orthodox and Monophysite churches of the East. Gelasius essentially insisted on the continuation of Acacius's excommunication as the condition of reunion between East and West. Gelasius, who held a remarkably strong view of the power of the Roman episcopate, was the first to articulate the influential theory of two powers or "swords" on earth, arguing that sacred, or spiritual, power lay in the hands of the Roman pontiff, while kingly, or earthly, power lay in the hands of the emperor. He was the first pope accorded the title "vicar of Christ," at a Roman synod in 495. Pastorally, he argued (supposedly against Manicheans) for Communion under both species, and he opposed the celebration of the Lupercalia, a pagan winter festival, in Rome. His extant works consist of forty-two letters, fragments of forty-nine others, and six treatises. Neither the *Gelasian Sacramentary* nor the *Decretum Gelasianum* is from his hand.

J. Taylor, "The Early Papacy at Work: Gelasius I (492–496)," *JRH* 8 (1974–1975): 3–28.

THOMAS A. SMITH

Geneva Catechism (1541)

Calvin wrote his first vernacular catechism in Geneva (1536) together with a form of discipline as the foundation of the Reformed church in the city. The catechism was largely extracted from his *Institutes*. He then wrote a short confession of faith with twenty-one articles drawn from the catechism. He intended the catechism to be binding on all people in Geneva. After his return from Strasbourg, Calvin rewrote the catechism, expanding the text and rearranging the questions: the pupil gives the questions and the catechist provides the answers. Calvin had to produce the catechism quickly, and he often expressed the desire to revise it, but he never did. The catechism appeared in French (1542), Latin (1545), and thereafter was frequently reprinted. It was also translated into Italian (1551 and 1556), Spanish (1550), English (1556), German (1556), Dutch (1578), Hungarian (c. 1695), even into Greek (1551) and Hebrew (1554). It played a key role in the development of Reformed teaching and was especially used in France and Scotland. The catechism is a highly detailed work in five parts: faith (exposition of the Apostles' Creed, which, as in the Heidelberg Catechism, and in contrast to his first catechism, precedes the Ten Commandments); the law, or Ten Commandments; prayer; the Word of God; and the sacraments. The French divided the catechism into fifty-five lessons, for the fifty-two Sundays of the year and the three great festivals—a method followed in the later editions of the Heidelberg Catechism.

B. A. Gerrish, *Grace and Gratitude: The Eucharistic Theology of John Calvin* (1993); R. A. Muller, *The Unaccommodated Calvin* (2000).

BRUCE GORDON

Genevieve (c. 423–502)

virgin and patroness of Paris. According to her Life, Genevieve was born at Nanterre, about five miles from Paris. While she was still a child, Germanus of Auxerre, on his way to Britain, foretold her great service to the Lord. Consecrated prior to the time of organized monasticism in northern Gaul, she lived in Paris, perhaps with her godmother.

Genevieve was said to be known throughout Gaul for miracles: restoring sight and limbs, driving out demons, raising the dead, and uprooting trees to prevent shipwrecks. She also fed the poor and protected girls from arranged marriages. Her biographer claims that her fame was so widespread that Simon Stylites asked to be remembered in her prayers.

She was also a political force. Her Life records that she prevented Attila from capturing Paris in 451 by prayer and fasting and that she caused the bishop to begin construction of a basilica dedicated to St. Denis. During the siege of Paris (perhaps between 456 and 482) by Childeric I, she successfully interceded with this Frankish king on behalf of captives who were to be executed. Clovis, his successor, often acceded to her demands for mercy for criminals, and after her death he began construction of a basilica dedicated to her. This church decayed by the early eighteenth century and a new St. Genevieve's was begun in 1746. After the French Revolution it was renamed the Pantheon.

Nineteenth- and early twentieth-century scholars questioned Genevieve's existence and dismissed her Life as a fable. Her historical existence is now generally acknowledged, and her Life, written eighteen years after her death, is accepted as reliable in its outline.

J. McNamara, J. E. Halborg, with E. G. Whatley, eds. and trans., *Sainted Women of the Dark Ages* (1992), 17–37.

WILLIAM B. SWEETSER JR.

Gennadius of Marseilles (late fifth cent.)

priest and ecclesiastical writer. Little is known of Gennadius beyond his scholarship. There survives a list of the books that he wrote in opposition to various heresies, including those of Nestorius, Eutyches, and Pelagius. These books have been lost. Gennadius's sole surviving work is *On Illustrious Men*, a continuation of Jerome's work of the same title. It likely dates from the 490s. Following Jerome's example Gennadius provides short biographical sketches of prominent church writers. The ninety-eight entries detail persons from East and West and include many orthodox writers and a few heretical ones. Jerome and Gennadius's purpose was to emphasize the abundance and excellence of writings by those who were not heretics. Gennadius's text pertains to ecclesiastics of the fourth and fifth centuries. A good number were fellow inhabitants of Gaul (e.g., Sulpicius Severus and Sidonius Apollinaris). Like many prominent Gallic ecclesiastics of the fifth century, Gennadius would have espoused the so-called Semi-Pelagian position, as he offered high praise for Semi-Pelagians such as Hilary of Arles and Faustus of Riez. Additionally, he vaguely referred to the difficulty that Prosper of Aquitaine had with the thoughts of John Cassian, who upheld a moderate stance against predestination. Nevertheless, Gennadius did offer polite praise to Augustine for his voluminous literary achievement.

Gennadius of Marseilles, *Lives of Illustrious Men*, trans. E. C. Richardson, *NPNF*, 2nd series, vol. 3 (1953), 385–402.

ALLEN E. JONES

George (d. c. 303), martyr and patron saint of England and Greece. Although nothing is known of his life or martyrdom, his historical existence is generally accepted based on the early date of churches dedicated to him. His unreliable *Acta* (c. 490) relates how he, a Roman officer, refused to recant his faith before Diocletian (r. 284–305) and was executed at Lydda (Lod, Israel). The famous story of his slaying a dragon and saving a maiden, thereby bringing about the baptism of 15,000 men, is an invention of the *Golden Legend* (c. 1255).

George's fame spread relatively quickly, and he became one of the most venerated martyrs in the East from the fourth century on. In the West, Jerome knew of him (c. 400), and churches and monasteries were built in his honor beginning in the sixth century. He became firmly identified with England during the Crusades. He is supposed to have assisted the English at the siege of Antioch in 1098, and Richard I claimed his patronage in 1189. Edward III created the Order of the Garter with George as its patron in 1348, and English armies began to use the red cross on a white field, associated with George, as their emblem.

Acta Sancta Georgii, in CSCO 139 (1953); I. H. Elder, *George of Lydda* (1949); G. J. Marcus, *St. George of England* (1939).

WILLIAM B. SWEETSER JR.

Gerhard, Johann (1582–1637), professor at the Univ. of Jena and the leading theologian of Lutheran orthodoxy. His nine-volume *Loci Theologici* (1610–1622) remains the standard work of post-Reformation Lutheran theology and was republished as recently as 1863 by Eduard Preus. In his dogmatic method Gerhard adopted Aristotle's metaphysics, which he took over from Melanchthon, but without compromising Holy Scripture as the exclusive source of Christian doctrine. In presenting doctrines, he used Thomas Aquinas's categories of formal, material, instrumental, and final causes. In his early career he was superintendent in Heldburg and Coburg, for which he provided church constitutions. He anticipated German Pietism with his *Meditationes sacrae* (1606), and he wrote a polemic against the compromising Georg Calixtus, *Besuch in Jena* (1634), and another one against Roman Catholicism, *Confessio catholica* (1634–1637). In the latter work he argued that the Lutheran church was not only the authentic catholic church but also the true Roman church. His major exegetical work was a harmony of the Gospels, *Harmonia Evangelistorum* (1626–1627). His influence remained long after his death.

R. D. Preus, *The Theology of Post-Reformation Lutheranism*, 2 vols. (1970, 1972); D. P. Scaer, "Johann Gerhard's Doctrine of the Sacraments," in *Protestant Scholasticism*, ed. C. Trueman and R. S. Clark (1999).

DAVID P. SCAER

Gerhardt, Paul (1607–1676), German poet, active as a hymn writer during and after the Thirty Years' War (1618–1648). He was born at Gräfenhainichen, a small town between Halle and Wittenberg and studied theology at the Univ. of Wittenberg. Many of his hymns were published in Johann Crueger's *Praxis pietatis melica* (1647), the most influential chorale publication of the seventeenth century.

Gerhardt's texts, many of which were written during the Thirty Years' War, were used as a form of devotional literature. They displayed a warmth and a personal piety that would become the standard of the German Pietist movement in the last quarter of the seventeenth and early eighteenth centuries. As a mark of his popularity among people in the later Pietist movement, Freylinghausen's hymnal, *Geistreiches Gesangbuch* (1704), included fifty-two of his texts. The most famous text of his is the Lenten hymn "O Sacred Head, Sore Wounded," sung to the tune *Passion Chorale* by Hans Leo Hassler.

C. Bunners, *Paul Gerhardt: Weg, Werk, Wirkung* (1993); E. Hewitt, *Gerhardt as a Hymn Writer and His Influence on English Hymnology* (1918).

LINDA J. CLARK

Gerhoch of Reichersberg

Gerhoch of Reichersberg (c. 1092–1169), German Augustinian canon and reformer. The Bavarian Gerhoch was an important popularizer of the institution of canons regular (see *Regular Clergy*) in the twelfth century, devoting his life to clerical reform and especially advocating that all priests live in communities under a rule (as "regular" canons). After education at Hildesheim, Gerhoch became schoolmaster at Augsburg but fled after a conflict with the bishop. He went to Rottenbuch, a house of canons regular influential in southern Germany; there he made his profession after a brief return to Augsburg. In 1132 the bishop of Salzburg named Gerhoch provost of a canonry in Reichersberg.

For Gerhoch, regular canons did not comprise a new religious order but represented the generally valid form of life for all members of the clergy. His zeal to reform sinful priests won him the hatred of many clerics, who charged Gerhoch with heresy in 1130. Vindicated, Gerhoch became an extremely active reformer, visiting Rome several times, producing a large body of theological and polemical treatises, and proving to be a very effective preacher to the laity. Driven from Reichersberg by his enemies and exiled by Emperor Frederick I for his support of the papacy, Gerhoch returned to his post shortly before his death.

P. Classen, *Gerhoch von Reichersberg* (1960); G. Constable, *The Reformation of the Twelfth Century* (1996).

PHYLLIS G. JESTICE

Germanus of Auxerre

Germanus of Auxerre (d. c. 446), bishop (418–c. 446). Germanus was a Gallic aristocrat who served as an advocate and held a high Roman military position in Gaul before becoming bishop of Auxerre. He was intimately connected with ecclesiastics associated with the island monastery Lérins, including bishops Hilary of Arles and Lupus of Troyes. In 429 Germanus and Lupus traveled across the English Channel to combat Pelagianism in Britain. While there Germanus took the lead of an army and fended off a Saxon raid. Back in Gaul, Germanus used his social connections to negotiate tax relief in his diocese. Around 444 he made a second trip to Britain to combat Pelagianism. Upon his return Germanus mediated on behalf of the inhabitants of Brittany who were rebelling against rough treatment by Germanic soldiers stationed nearby. The bishop died at the imperial court at Ravenna. His body was returned amid much fanfare to Gaul. Germanus's Life, written around 480 by Constantius of Lyon, portrays the politically active ecclesiastic as a wonder worker. Alongside Sulpicius Severus's *Life of St. Martin of Tours*, the *Life of Saint Germanus* ranks among the most influential models for subsequent Western hagiography.

Constantius of Lyons, "The Life of Saint Germanus of Auxerre," trans. F. R. Hoare, in *Soldiers of Christ: Saints and Saints' Lives from Late Antiquity and the Early Middle Ages*, ed. T. F. X. Noble and T. Head (1995), 75–106.

ALLEN E. JONES

Germany (HRE, Austria, Prussia), Reformation in

Germany (HRE, Austria, Prussia), Reformation in On the eve of the Reformation, the German church possessed both a vibrant popular piety and deep-seated structural problems. Martin Luther's revolt began in 1517 with a controversy over indulgences. After a series of disputations with controversialists such as Johann Eck, Luther's message grew increasingly militant, and his *Address to the Christian Nobility of the German Nation* (1520) appealed to imperial princes to reform the church themselves. Though Luther enjoyed a groundswell of support among the citizens of the free imperial cities, the Diet of Worms placed Luther under an imperial ban and prohibited the Lutheran faith with the Edict of Worms (May 1521), although the edict was never vigorously enforced. While Luther took refuge in the Wartburg castle, full-fledged Protestant liturgical reforms were introduced at Wittenberg (1521–1522) by Luther's allies. The appearance of the Zwickau Prophets, three radical preachers who espoused direct revelation, was the first splintering of the nascent evangelical movement. More serious was the widespread upheaval represented by the Peasants' War (1524–1525). In treatises such as *The Twelve Articles,* the peasant leaders employed Protestant ideas such as the communal right to appoint ministers to ensure proclamation of the "pure gospel" to buttress their wide-ranging assault on feudal lordship. A few Protestant leaders, such as Thomas Müntzer, embraced the movement, though Luther himself repudiated it after mediation failed. Protestant and Catholic lords united to crush this "revolution of the common man."

While the failure of the Peasants' War dissipated some of the potential of the Reformation to become a mass social movement, the Protestant cause continued to attract adherents across the empire. Many imperial cities and territorial princes adhered to the evangelical faith and "protested" its continued legal exclusion at the 1529 Diet of Speyer. An attempt to forge a common Protestant confessional and political front failed at the Colloquy of Marburg (1529) when Luther and the Swiss Reformer Huldrych Zwingli could not agree on a common understanding of the Eucharist. Emperor Charles V resisted coming to terms with Protestantism, though the Augsburg Diet of 1530 saw the birth of the Lutheran Augsburg Confession authored by Philip Melanchthon, as well as an Upper German alternative in the Tetrapolitan Confession. Protestantism became more firmly entrenched in the wake of Charles's inaction, and the advent of the Schmalkaldic League in 1531, a Lutheran political alliance, threatened the maintenance of peace. However, the 1532 "Truce of Nuremberg" recognized the de facto legality of Protestantism until an anticipated council could settle the religious discord. The Protestant cause was blackened when a radical Anabaptist group led by Jan Matthijs and Jan of Leiden took control of Münster in 1534 and established an Anabaptist kingdom with a community of goods and polygamy. The prince-bishop and his Protestant allies brutally reconquered the city the following year.

A break in the Habsburg-Valois wars, a series of conflicts between the forces of Charles V and Francis I of France, and peace with the Turks in 1546 gave Charles the opportunity to seek a military solution to the religious discord. Charles's defeat of the Schmalkaldic League at the Battle of Mühlberg (April 1547) enabled him to force the restoration of Catholic practices on the defeated Protestants, although he conceded lay Communion and clerical marriage in a settlement known as the Interim (1548). However, the Princes' Rebellion of 1552 undermined the emperor's position and resulted in the Treaty of Passau (1552), which suspended the Interim and recognized the de facto legality of Lutheranism. Charles left it to his brother Ferdinand II to negotiate a definitive religious settlement. The Religious Peace of Augsburg (1555) established Lutheranism and Catholicism as the only valid confessions within the HRE and confirmed the prince's right to determine the religion of his territory.

The second half of the sixteenth century witnessed the spread of Reformed Protestantism, revitalization of Catholicism, and consolidation and retrenchment within Lutheranism. The "Second Reformation," in which a number of formerly Lutheran territories converted to Reformed Protestantism, began in earnest with the publication of the Heidelberg Catechism

(1563) by the Electoral Palatinate. Emperor Maximilian II regarded this development with hostility, since Calvinism had not been included in the terms of the Peace of Augsburg, but the Lutheran princes proved unwilling to exclude the Palatinate from the religious settlement. In Catholic lands, impetus for renewal gained force with the conclusion of the Council of Trent (1545–1563), though full implementation of the council's decrees would take decades. Jesuits such as Peter Canisius promoted the Catholic cause in Central Europe; they made their influence felt as princely advisors and worked to revitalize educational institutions in Ingolstadt, Vienna, and Cologne. In the Lutheran fold, those who claimed to adhere most closely to Luther's own teachings (Gnesio-Lutherans) won out over their Melanchthonian rivals with the adherence of the vast majority of Lutheran principalities and cities to The Book of Concord (1580). This development successfully consolidated the Lutheran movement and solidified adherence to core Lutheran doctrine, but it hindered future cooperation with Reformed Protestants.

Famine, disease, witchcraft persecutions and, above all, warfare made the first half of the seventeenth century one of the bleakest epochs in German history. Confessional tensions increased at the turn of the century with the advent of the Protestant Union (1608), a military alliance of Protestant states, and its counterpart, the Catholic League (1609). The Bohemian Revolt of 1618 ignited the Thirty Years' War. Early victories nearly brought about the complete triumph of the Catholic-Imperial party. The intervention in 1630 of the Swedish king, Gustavus Aldolphus, brought about a reversal in the Protestants' favor, but his premature death led to a relative stalemate in the mid-1630s. The direct intervention by the Catholic Bourbon monarchy of France against their Catholic Austrian and Spanish Habsburg rivals revealed that dynastic and state interests had triumphed over confessional concerns in the waning years of the conflict. The Peace of Westphalia (1648) confirmed the confessional pluralism of the HRE and legalized Calvinism, though the HRE remained a devastated realm in the shadow of its more illustrious neighbors. The late sixteenth and early seventeenth centuries also witnessed the apex of witch persecutions, a trend that transcended confessional divisions, though the most concentrated persecutions occurred in the ecclesiastical territories and cost approximately twenty thousand lives in the empire alone.

P. Blickle, *The Revolution of 1525* (1981);
H. A. Oberman, *Luther: Man between God and the Devil* (1989); J. Gagliardo, *Germany under the Old Regime* (1991); H. Holborn, *A History of Modern Germany* (1959); Geoffrey Parker, ed., *The Thirty Years' War* (1984).

DEBORAH FLEETHAM AND CHARLES D. GUNNOE JR.

Gerson, Jean (1363–1429), theologian of the later medieval church. His plans for reforming the church and limiting papal power have long been neglected or denigrated in descriptions of the period, but he is gaining recognition today as one of the leading spiritual and intellectual figures of his time. He was at the center of what rightly can be called the last medieval reformation of the Christian church.

Born in modest circumstances in a hamlet northeast of Reims, young Jean was sent at fourteen to study at the arts faculty of the Univ. of Paris. Here he took the name of his village, Gerson, as his surname, and later he discovered that the term in Hebrew means "pilgrim" or "wanderer." He soon established a reputation as a brilliant student. At the faculty of theology he was taught by Pierre d'Ailly, one of the leading theologians of his day and a consummate university politician. D'Ailly became chancellor of the Univ. of Paris and then, on accepting a bishopric, saw to it in 1395 that his star pupil succeeded him. Gerson, who in the meantime had become a favored preacher at the royal court and had acquired a doctorate in theology, became chancellor, an office he kept until his death.

In spite of his success, the young Gerson had doubts about his vocation as teacher, pastor, and administrator. In order to escape the politics of court and university life, in 1399–1400 he took up residence at Bruges, where the Duke of Burgundy had provided him with a prebend. Here he did his best to reform the chapter of the church where he was dean, but his efforts brought resistance from the privileged canons. Gerson returned to Paris and began fifteen productive and intense years of teaching, writing, and preaching in both Latin and French. He did his best to reach out pastorally and theologically to a new educated public, and especially to women whom he knew could read French and were devout Christians seeking a language with which to express their inner lives.

During these years Gerson became involved in efforts to bring to an end the schism that since 1378 had split the Western church, with one pope in Avignon and another in Rome. Gerson at first resisted calls for a general council of the church, but he eventually became convinced that such a meeting was the only way to end the schism and reform the church. In 1415 he left Paris to attend the Council of Constance, where he was one of the central figures in formulating proposals for the government of the church. The pope would remain head of the church, but he would be responsible to regular and frequent general councils, which would be able to depose him.

In the aftermath of Constance, Gerson saw that the papacy did its best to assert absolute power over the church. He spent the last decade of his life in exile, for the Burgundian party had captured Paris and killed some of his closest colleagues. Gerson became a political refugee of the Hundred Years' War between France and England. After traveling through Bavaria and Austria, he settled in Lyon, whose archbishop, a colleague from Constance, supported him and made it possible for Gerson to continue writing on theological and pastoral questions until his death.

B. P. McGuire, *Jean Gerson and the Last Medieval Reformation* (2005); B. P. McGuire, ed., *Jean Gerson: Early Works*, Classics of Western Spirituality (1998).

BRIAN PATRICK MCGUIRE

Gertrude of Helfta (1256–1301/1302), German mystic, also known as Gertrude the Great. She entered the Cistercian-inspired convent of Helfta at age five and grew to participate in the spiritual vitality and outstanding literary productivity of that institution. Her Latin writings, based largely on her mystical experiences, include book 2 of *The Herald of Divine Love*, a spiritual autobiography in which she described the visions and revelations she received beginning at age twenty-five; the remaining four books, which are anonymous, include biographical information and document the spiritual experiences of her closest companions at Helfta. Gertrude also produced a guide to mystical union later known as the *Teachings of the Spiritual Exercises*. She was regularly consulted for spiritual guidance by Dominican confessors and other visitors to the convent, and her spiritual authority in the cloister approached that of the clergy. Although strongly influenced by the earlier Mechthild of Magdeburg, Gertrude's spirituality remained more traditionally monastic, being grounded in the daily liturgical life of her community and in the scriptures and patristic writings she translated. She is recognized for her devotion to the Sacred Heart of Jesus, which she experienced along with the Eucharist as a site for encountering Christ's divine and human natures.

C. Bynum, "Women Mystics in the 13th Century," in *Jesus as Mother* (1982), 170–235; Gertrude of Helfta, *The Herald of Divine Love*, trans. M. Winkworth (1993).

ADRIENNE NOCK AMBROSE

Giberti, Gian Matteo (1495–1543), Italian reformer and bishop of Verona. Born in Palermo of a Genoese father, Giberti entered the service of Cardinal Giulio de Medici. He remained in his service when de Medici was elected Pope Clement VII in 1523. Clement appointed him datary and bishop of Verona. While in Rome he came to know Gian Pietro Caraffa, Gaetano da Thiene, and others associated with the Oratory of Divine Love, a confraternity that influenced the advance of reform in Rome. After the sack of Rome in 1527 Giberti took up residence in Verona, where his pastoral work made him a model bishop in Italy prior to the Council of Trent. He reformed his clergy, established a press for the publication of theological and spiritual works, and organized charitable care of the poor. He published his plan for reform in the *Constitutiones Gibertinae* (1542). His commitment to reform was widely recognized, and in 1536 Pope Paul III appointed him to the commission that produced the *Consilium de emendanda ecclesia*, a sharp critique of the papacy and the need for reform in Rome.

H. Jedin, *Bischofsideal der katolischen reformation* (1960); A. Prosperi, *Tra evangelismo e controriforma: Gianmatteo Giberti (1495–1543)* (1969).

PAUL V. MURPHY

Gilbert of Poitiers (c. 1080–1154), scholastic theologian, bishop of Poitiers. Among the greatest of the early scholastics, Gilbert studied in his native city of Poitiers before becoming a student of Bernard of Chartres, renowned master of advanced grammar and the classics. Gilbert then turned to the study of *sacra pagina* (Scripture) with Anselm of Laon (d. 1117) and wrote his *Commentary* on the Psalms. After Anselm's death Gilbert may have stayed in Laon; a single letter, once mistakenly attributed to Gilbert, is the sole evidence to support the claim that he taught in

Poitiers at this time. Gilbert returned to Chartres by 1124, as a canon of the cathedral, and by 1126 was chancellor of its school.

The evidence, however, suggests that he was seldom actually in Chartres. In fact, in the 1130s Gilbert achieved renown as one of the foremost masters available in Paris. Anecdotes reveal him teaching grammar and dialectic as well as the "new theology." He is associated with the cathedral school, the *vicus porretarum* (a street in the Latin Quarter and the source of his nickname *Porretanus*), and Mont Ste.-Geneviève. At this time manuscripts appeared of Gilbert's commentaries on the Psalms and on the Pauline Epistles, as well as the earliest manuscripts of the *Glossa ordinaria* on the Psalms, for which Gilbert was largely responsible and which his teaching certainly popularized. His biblical commentaries greatly influenced Peter Lombard and generations of scholars both secular and monastic. During this time he also composed his controversial commentary on the *Opuscula sacra* of Boethius. A prologue to a commentary on Revelation and a commentary on the Athanasian Creed also are convincingly attributed to Gilbert, but the *Liber de sex principiis* probably is not his. Among his students were Jordanus Fantasmus, Johannes Beleth, John of Salisbury, Ivo of Chartres, William of Tyre, Simon of Tournai, Alan of Lille and, if one believes contemporary reports, hundreds of others.

He was rewarded with the see of Poitiers in 1141 or 1142. The pastoral, reform-oriented influence of Laon is reflected in the care Gilbert lavished on his diocese: protecting it against lay appropriations, enriching its holdings, and of course preaching to its members. An extant Christmas sermon (*Sermo de natali domini*) probably dates from this period. It was another sermon, on the Trinity, which drew Gilbert into notoriety. At the consistory of Reims in 1148, presided over by Pope Eugene III, four theses allegedly upheld by Gilbert and his students were investigated by some of the greatest theologians of the day, including Peter Lombard. Despite Bernard of Clairvaux's powerful antipathy, Gilbert was vindicated. Many of his ideas passed into common acceptance in the schools.

H. C. van Elswijk, *Gilbert Porreta: Sa vie, son oeuvre, sa pensée* (1966); Gilbert of Poitiers, "Il commento ai Salmi di Gilberto della Porrée," in *Prologue and Commentary on Psalms 1–3*, ed. M. Fontana, *Logos* 13 (1930): 282–301; Gilbert, *The Commentaries on Boethius by Gilbert of Poitiers*, ed. N. M.

Häring (1966); T. Gross-Diaz, *The Psalms Commentary of Gilbert of Poitiers: From Lectio Divina to the Lecture Room* (1996); N. M. Häring, ed., "Epitaphs and Necrologies on Gilbert II of Poitiers," AHDLMA 36 (1969): 57–87; L. O. Nielsen, *Theology and Philosophy in the Twelfth Century: A Study of Gilbert Porreta's Thinking and the Theological Expositions of the Doctrine of the Incarnation during the Period 1130–1180* (1982).

THERESA GROSS-DIAZ

Gildas (sixth cent.), British monk and writer. Gildas is an enigmatic figure, but his *Ruin and Conquest of Britain* remains an indispensable source for the history of the island in the late Roman period. Though difficult and erroneous, Gildas's unique account of the Saxon conquest complements an unruly archaeological record. The work begins with a sketch of Britain's history from the Roman occupation to Gildas's own day. This narrative ends (chaps. 25–26) with Gildas's lament for the complacency and corruption that, he believed, characterized British society after the successful resistance led by the Roman "gentleman" Ambrosius Aurelianus, whom he credits with defeating the Saxons at Badon Hill (c. 500). Nevertheless, history writing was not Gildas's main objective. He portrayed early sixth-century Britain as a latter-day Israel, the Britons as a divinely chosen people, and himself as an OT prophet recalling his countrymen from sin and disobedience. The final three-quarters of his work castigate the British kings and clergy for their moral failure while cataloging OT parallels that support his denunciations. Gildas's report of Ambrosius Aurelianus is one strand underlying the later legends of King Arthur.

———

N. Higham, *The English Conquest: Gildas and Britain in the 5th Century* (1994); M. Lapidge and D. Dumville, eds., *Gildas: New Approaches* (1984); M. Winterbottom, trans., *Gildas: The Ruin of Britain* (1978).

DENNIS E. TROUT

Giles of Rome (c. 1246–1316), philosopher, theologian, and Augustinian Hermit. Giles of Rome, or Aegidius Romanus in Latin, was a member of the influential Colonna family. Giles joined the Augustinian Hermits at age fourteen and took his theological training at Paris, where he probably heard the lectures of Thomas Aquinas. While his work shows a deep familiarity with Thomas, Giles also differed from him, particularly in his insistence that *esse*

("being") and *essentia* ("essence") are completely different *res* ("things"). His own philosophical positions respecting existence and essence were condemned in 1277, and Giles was forced to leave Paris for Bayeux. When he returned to Italy in 1281 he became definitor, then provincial, and finally vicar general of the Roman province of his order. In 1285 Honorius IV directed that he be reinstated at Paris, where he became the first Augustinian master of theology and the tutor of King Philip IV of France.

Giles left Paris in 1291 and was elected general of his order in 1292. He was subsequently appointed bishop of Bourges (1295) by Boniface VIII. He was highly regarded by and advised Philip IV and Pope Celestine V, as well as Pope Boniface VIII. Giles wrote in support of Celestine's abdication and Boniface's election, and his *De ecclesiastica potestate* (*On Ecclesiastical Power*)—which describes papal theocracy as the most proximate reflection on earth of his vision of heavenly order—undoubtedly inspired Boniface's bull *Unam sanctam*.

———

F. del Punta, *Opera Omina*, in *Corpus Philosophorum Medii Aevi Testi e Studi* (1985); R. Dyson, *Giles of Rome on Ecclesiastical Power* (1986); C. Briggs, *Giles of Rome's* De regimine principum (1999).

LORNA SHOEMAKER

Giles of Viterbo (1469–1532), Italian scholar, preacher, cardinal, and reformer. Born at Viterbo, Giles joined the Augustinian Hermits and studied at Padua, Naples, Florence, and Rome. He was positively disposed to the work of Marsiglio Ficino, whom he met in Florence. Giles's academic interests included Latin poetry, Cabbala, and Scripture scholarship. He became known as an outstanding preacher. A high point in his career came when Pope Julius II chose him to deliver the opening address at the Fifth Lateran Council in 1512. The Augustinans elected Giles prior general in 1507. He held that office for over ten years and likely met Martin Luther on the latter's trip to Rome in 1510–1511. In 1517 Pope Leo X appointed him cardinal. Leo also called upon him for diplomatic services and sent him to the court of the emperor Maximilian in 1515 and to the court of Charles V in 1518.

———

F. X. Martin, *Friar, Reformer, and Renaissance Scholar: Life and Work of Giles of Viterbo, 1469–1532* (1992); J. W. O'Malley, *Giles of Viterbo on Church and Reform: A Study in Renaissance Thought* (1968); Convegno dell'Istituto Storico Agostiniano, *Egidio da Viterbo, O.S.A., e il suo tempo* (1983).

PAUL V. MURPHY

Giovanni de Pian del Carpini (1180–1252), Franciscan. Companion and disciple of Francis of Assisi (d. 1226), he was sent in 1245 as an envoy to the Mongol Great Khan. Pope Innocent IV entrusted to him an entreaty to the Mongol ruler to acknowledge Jesus Christ as Lord and to accept baptism. Thus it was hoped that Mongol inroads into Europe, as they had just occurred between 1240 and 1242, would cease. Giovanni (John) reached the Mongol capital at Sira Ordu in July 1246. Present when Kuyuk (d. 1248) was elected as the third Great Khan, John was impressed by the numbers of people at court. Among them, "Nestorian" Christians provided all the capital's clerks, maintained a chapel near the royal tent, and conducted regularly announced services. Strongly critical of these "Nestorians," John nevertheless received some assistance from them and did concede the orthodoxy of their baptism.

In November 1246, after an interview with Kuyuk, John set out with a sealed letter for the pope, holding hopes that the Great Khan was open to conversion. But Kuyuk's letter, the contents of which were kept secret, called on all Western powers to pay obeisance to him. He declared that he had no wish to "become a trembling Nestorian Christian, worship God and be an ascetic."

C. Dawson, *Mission to Asia* (1955); G. G. Guzman, "John of Plano Carpini," in *Dictionary of the Middle Ages*, vol. 7 (1986), 137–39; G. D. Painter, "The Tartar Relation," in *The Vinland Map and the Tartar Relation* (1995), 19–52; D. Sinor, "John of Plano Carpini's Return from the Mongols: New Light from a Luxemburg Manuscript," *Journal of the Royal Asiatic Society* (1957): 193–206; A. van den Wyngaert, *Itinera et Relationes Fratrum Minorum saec. XIII et XIV*, in *Sinica Franciscana*, vol. 1 (1929).

IAN GILLMAN†

Gnesio-Lutherans Following Luther's death some theologians took issue with what they saw as compromises of his teachings, especially by the Philippists, who saw Philip Melanchthon as their champion. For their unyielding position they were called Gnesio-Lutherans, literally "genuine Lutherans." Their leaders were Matthias Flacius Illyricus and Nicholas von Amsdorf. They opposed the Augsburg and the Leipzig Interims, agreements made by Melanchthon and his followers with Charles V, whose armies occupied Lutheran territories. These agreements allowed Lutherans to keep their essential teachings but required reinstituting certain Catholic practices. This dispute among Lutherans was called the adiaphoristic controversy, named for the Greek word for "indifferent things." In addition, they opposed the synergism they detected in Melanchthon's claim that along with the Word and the Holy Spirit the human will was a cause of salvation. They took issue with Osiander's view that justification was a process in the individual. In reaction to the teaching that good works were necessary for salvation, some held that works were detrimental to salvation. In spite of their extreme positions, some views of the Gnesio-Lutherans found a place in the articles of the Formula of Concord dealing with free will (II), righteousness (III), good works (IV), and adiaphora (X).

L. W. Spitz and L. Wenzel, eds., *Discord, Dialog, and Concord: Studies in the Lutheran Reformation's Formula of Concord* (1977); J. A. Nestigen, "Gnesio-Lutherans," in *The Oxford Encyclopedia of the Reformation*, vol. 2 (1998), 237–38.

DAVID P. SCAER

Gnosticism Modern scholarship has used this term as a label for a wide variety of religious phenomena of the second and third centuries. The ultimate basis for the category is the work of a series of heresiologists who combated movements that they considered problematic. The first attested work, the *Syntagma* of Justin Martyr, has been lost, but its influence survives in subsequent examples of the genre. The first surviving heresiological work is the *Adversus Haereses* (*Against Heresies*) of Irenaeus of Lyon, who was active in the last third of the second century. The first of his five volumes catalogues the teachings of, in the words of 1 Timothy 6:20, "falsely called knowledge." The chief opponents of Irenaeus are the disciples of Valentinus, a teacher who was active in Rome between 140 and 160. Irenaeus traces the teachings of one of these disciples, Ptolemy, through his master back to a variety of teachers of the early second century, prominent among them a group whom he labels the "Barbeloites" or "Gnostikoi" (*Haer.* 1.29).

Ptolemy and these earlier teachers share an interest in the exegesis of Genesis and in a philosophical cosmogony that maps a complex ideal, or noetic, world of spirit and its devolution into the world of matter. A key figure in the story is an element of the spiritual world, Sophia/Wisdom, whose "fall" generated the phenomenal world. In one account, her frustrated attempts to know the transcendent God produced the realms of soul and matter, over which rules an ignorant demiurge, the God of the Old Testament. Sophia's devolution from the Pleroma, or Fullness of Deity, scatters parts of divine spirit in the lower world, which the inferior creator god unknowingly infuses into the first human being.

Such an account of human origin scores many points. Among others, it frames the fundamental problem of human existence as alienation from God through ignorance. The problem is solved by the intervention of a revealer who brings salvific knowledge of the transcendent Father, enabling the spiritual elements to be reintegrated into the supernal world. Patristic critics such as Irenaeus, later heresiologists such as Hippolytus and Epiphanius, and theologians such as Origen (in his apologetic *Against Celsus* and particularly in the *Commentary on John*, which heavily criticizes a Valentinian teacher, Heracleon) objected to various elements of this type of teaching, including the distinction, sometimes a sharp opposition, between the transcendent God and the creator. The heresiologists particularly faulted the Valentinians for what they took to be a determinist soteriology and rigid anthropology. The Valentinians divided humanity into three classes: spirituals, psychics, and hylics. The heresiologists understood that division to imply that the relationship of human beings to salvation is determined by their "nature." The charge may be misguided. While these Gnostics had a strong sense of election, they seem to have recognized the potentiality for knowledge of God present in every human being. Later heresiologists such as Epiphanius (*Pan.* 26.3–4, on the Borborites) also condemned some gnostics as "libertines" who allowed or indeed encouraged immoral behavior, although most of these charges appear to be groundless polemic.

Modern study of the kinds of teaching to which the heresiologists objected has been aided by new discoveries. In the nineteenth century, individual codices from Egypt surfaced (Codex Askew, Codex Bruce) with teaching similar to the condemned teachings, containing lengthy tractates such as the *Pistis Sophia*, with complex discussions of cosmology and soteriology. A similar codex found its way to Berlin (Berlinensis Gnosticus 8502) in the early twentieth century and was partially published before the Second World War. In the early twentieth century scholars became aware of the Mandaeans, a group of Arabs in southern Iraq who traced their heritage to John the Baptist. The discovery in 1945 of a collection of fourth-century codices from Nag Hammadi has enriched the discussion of Gnosticism.

The heresiologists' picture of "knowledge falsely so called" as a heretical form of Christian theology came into question with some of the new discoveries. The *Religionsgeschichtliche Schule* ("history of religion school") in early twentieth-century Germany understood Gnosticism to be a world religion, developed from ancient Iranian myths of the Saved Savior. Unfortunately, the evidence for such mythology in the pre-Christian period is lacking, and the Iranian sources used to reconstruct such early myths are quite late. The discovery of Mandaean literature provided Rudolf Bultmann with data for his reconstruction of the gnostic background to the Fourth Gospel, but this literature seems to be rooted in late antique traditions at the earliest. The Nag Hammadi collection has provided new materials on the Valentinian school and on the kinds of literature that Irenaeus took to be its inspiration, now often identified as "Sethian."

Contemporary scholarship has become hesitant to offer large generalizations about "Gnosticism" as a religion or a religious phenomenon. The second century did see, both inside and outside Christianity, speculation on origins and radical exegesis of sacred texts. Some of this activity may have occurred first in Jewish circles, and many of the typical "gnostic" texts from Nag Hammadi indicate acquaintance with Jewish midrashic traditions. Much of this activity probably took place initially in small circles or study groups of Christian intellectuals in Egypt and Rome. Such speculative activity, seeking for a more intimate knowledge of God, may be labeled gnostic, but that label does not reveal what the speculative exegesis produced. Teachers embraced as "orthodox," such as Clement of Alexandria, could idealize the "true gnostic" (*Strom.* 8.3).

A paradigmatic case of gnostic literature of the sort to which the heresiologists objected is the *Apocryphon of John*, found in the Berlin Gnostic Codex and in three copies at Nag Hammadi and partially paralleled in Irenaeus. The text combines teaching about the divine world with a subversively literal exegesis of Genesis. Thus, the creator who prohibits Adam and Eve from eating of the "tree of knowledge," the ignorant deity who cannot find them in the garden and is jealous of his own standing, cannot be the true God. The work also contains catechetical material about the fate of different souls.

H. Jonas, *The Gnostic Religion: The Message of the Alien God and the Beginnings of Christianity* (2001); B. Layton, *The Gnostic Scriptures: A New Translation with Annotations and Introductions* (1987); J. C. Reeves, *Heralds of That Good Realm: Syro-Mesopotamian Gnosis and Jewish Traditions* (1996); K. Rudolph, *Gnosis: The Nature and History of an Ancient Religion* (1986); M. Williams, *Rethinking "Gnosticism": An Argument for Dismantling a Dubious Category* (1996).

HAROLD W. ATTRIDGE

Godescalc   *see* Gottschalk of Orbais

Golden Bull (1356)   A constitutional decree issued by Charles IV regulating the election of the Holy Roman Emperor by a majority vote of imperial electors. It set the number of electors at seven, comprising the archbishops of Mainz, Trier, and Cologne, and the secular rulers of Bohemia, the Palatinate of the Rhine, Saxony, and Brandenburg. Designed to consolidate Charles's power in Germany, it purposely excluded the pope, Austria, and Bavaria, Charles's dynastic rivals. Named for its seal of gold, rather than wax or lead, the Golden Bull remained in force through the Peace of Westphalia.

B. Heidenreich and F.-L. Kroll, *Wahl und Krönung* (2006); B.-U. Hergemöller, *Fürsten, Herren und Städte zu Nürnberg, 1355/56: die Enstehung der "Goldenen Bulle" Karls IV* (1983).

RAYMOND A. BLACKETER

Gomarus, Franciscus (1563–1641), Reformed theologian and a leading opponent of the synergistic teachings of Jacob Arminius. Gomarus's Flemish parents converted to the Reformed church and fled to the Palatinate in the face of persecution. Gomarus studied at Strasbourg, Neustadt, Oxford, Cambridge, and Heidelberg. Gomarus pastored a refugee church in Frankfurt before accepting a professorship at Leiden (1594), where he came into conflict with Arminius. After Arminius died, the university offered his position to the likeminded Conrad Vorstius, and Gomarus resigned in protest (1611). He went on to pastor another church in Middelburg and then to professorships at Saumur and Groningen.

Gomarus was a learned and accomplished theologian who, like his opponent Arminius, employed the best learning of humanism as well as the scholastic method of teaching and debate. His views on predestination were supralapsarian, a perspective shared by numerous Reformed theologians and not particularly extraordinary. But he was fiery and vehement in debate, and at Leiden Gomarus was less popular as a professor than Arminius. He was a delegate to the Synod of Dort but was not a vocal participant in the debate with the Remonstrants, except when he stood to deny the charge that the Calvinists taught absolute divine reprobation without any consideration of human sin. While the synod's *Canons* were infralapsarian in formulation, they did not condemn or exclude the supralapsarian position.

J. van Belzen, *Vroom, Vurig en Vreedzaam: Het Leven van Franciscus Gomarus* (1996); G. P. van Itterzon, *Franciscus Gomarus* (1930).

RAYMOND A. BLACKETER

Good Shepherd   The metaphor of a caretaking shepherd of a flock, applied to God in the Old Testament (e.g., Isa. 40:11; Ps. 23; Ezek. 34:11) and to Jesus in the New Testament (e.g., John 10:11–16; Heb. 13:20), was widely elaborated in early Christian literature and art. Christian art borrowed the image of a young male shepherd carrying a sheep or ram over his shoulders from a Roman representation of Hermes as a caretaker of souls. The Christian figure is distinguishable from the pagan primarily by its context or proximity to other Christian icons. The shepherd usually wears a short, belted tunic and boots and sometimes carries a purse, set of pipes, or bucket of milk. He appears frequently in catacomb frescoes, often at the apex of a domed ceiling, but also in relief sculptures on sarcophagi. Rare three-dimensional sculptures of the shepherd exist, probably discovered in or near early Christian tombs. The shepherd appears in nonfunerary contexts on ceramic bowls and plates, lamps, and glassware (cf. Tertullian, *Modesty* 7.1–4 and 10.12), and in the fresco over the baptismal font in the Christian building at Dura Europos.

Interpreters of these artworks have often taken the identification of the shepherd as Jesus for granted. However, some scholars have argued that the visual image of the shepherd refers to a general ideal of philanthropy or to the safety and caring of the whole Christian community. The iconographic parallels with non-Christian representations of the shepherd do suggest that Christians simply adapted a well-loved figure in order to communicate their particular message regarding divine care for the human soul.

―――

R. Jensen, *Understanding Early Christian Art* (2000); B. Ramsey, "A Note on the Disappearance of the Good Shepherd from Early Christian Art," *HTR* 76, no. 3 (1983): 375–78; G. Snyder, *Ante Pacem: Archaeological Evidence of Church Life before Constantine* (1985).
                                    ROBIN M. JENSEN

Gorzian Reform   Gorze was a monastery in Lorraine, originally founded in the eighth century but fallen into decay by the time the bishop of Metz gave it to a group of reform-minded clerics in 933. Under these reformers, Gorze was dedicated to a purification of monastic life under the Benedictine rule. Less famous than the contemporary French reform movement of Cluny, Gorze was a highly influential monastic center in Germany and Eastern Europe.

The Gorzians advocated a life of prayer and withdrawal from secular society similar to that of Cluny, although particular customs differed. There was an essential difference, though: Gorze grew in a land with a strong monarchy and reputable bishops who in general encouraged the monastic life. So the Gorzians never felt compelled to free themselves from outside "interference" and were also willing to spread their customs without assuming control of other monasteries. Gorze remained a single abbey rather than a monastic congregation. The Gorzian influence was particularly strong in central Europe because several German emperors planted Gorzian cells in regions they wished to influence; several Gorzians were important missionaries. By the early years of the eleventh century, when a "young Gorzian" movement succeeded the original reform, several hundred monasteries followed Gorzian customs, paving the way for the Gregorian reform.

―――

P. Jestice, "The Gorzian Reform and the Light under the Bushel," *Viator* 24 (1993): 51–78.
                                    PHYLLIS G. JESTICE

Gottschalk of Orbais (806/808–866/870), theologian, grammarian, and poet, and one of the most interesting characters among Carolingian intellectuals. Of his sacred poems, partly written in a surprisingly personal tone, a dozen are known today. The son of a Saxon count, he was given as a young boy to the royal monastery of Fulda (814) and educated

there, but his tragedy started when in later years he felt no vocation for the monastic life and asked for permission to leave Fulda. His abbot, Hrabanus Maurus, insisted on the legitimacy of the oblation. Gottschalk fled before receiving major orders. A decision in favor of Gottschalk by the Synod of Mainz in 829 was repudiated by Hrabanus, who appealed to the emperor (see his *De oblatione puerorum*). In the end, Gottschalk was allowed to leave Fulda for Orbais (in the diocese of Soissons) but not to leave the monastic estate. He served as a teacher there, then appeared as a traveling preacher in Upper Italy, was ordained priest (according to some, irregularly), and became a matter of controversy some years later with regard to his view of divine predestination. It seems that in the meantime Gottschalk had accepted his situation as a monk and translated it into theological terms. His theory about "double predestination," based on his reading of Augustine, was condemned by the synods of Mainz in 848 and Quierzy in 849. A further dogmatic debate evolved when Gottschalk attacked Hincmar for having replaced the formula *trina deitas* ("tripartite deity"), as written in the doxology of the hymn *Sanctorum meritis*, with the unproblematic *sancta deitas* ("holy deity"). Gottschalk was subsequently imprisoned at Hautvilliers by his metropolitan, Hincmar of Reims. He died a prisoner about twenty years later, but his issues continued to provoke a major debate among Carolingian theologians. His views were opposed by Hrabanus and Hincmar but supported by Rathramnus of Corbie, Florus of Lyon, some of Hrabanus's pupils (Walahfrid Strabo, Lupus of Ferrières), and for a time Pope Nicolas I, though for rather political reasons. Gottschalk's case showed the limitations of a theology based on the authority of Scripture and of the Fathers, yet John Scottus's audacious approach of introducing logic as an unconditioned analytical instrument to answer Gottschalk's questions was repudiated by all sides.

―――

C. Lambot, ed., *Oeuvres théologiques et grammaticales de Godescalc d'Orbais* (1945); J. Marenbon, "Carolingian Thought," in *Carolingian Culture: Emulation and Innovation,* ed. R. McKitterick (1994), 171–92; H. Maurus, *De oblatione puerorum*, in PL 107 (1864), 419–40; Maurus, *Die monumenta Germaniae historica poetae,* vol. 3 (1896, repr. 2000), 724–38; vol. 4 (1923, repr. 1998), 934–36; M.-L. Weber, *Die Gedichte des Gottschalk von Orbais,* vol. 27 of *Lateinische Sprache und Literatur des Mittelalters* (1992); J. Weitzel, "Oblatio puerorum: Der

Konflikt zwischen väterlicher Gewalt und Selbstbestimmung im Lichte eines Instituts des mittelalterlichen Kirchenrechts," in *Vom mittelalterlichen Recht zur neuzeitlichen Rechtswissenschaft: Bedingungen, Wege und Probleme der europäischen Rechtsgeschichte,* ed. N. Brieskorn et al. (1994), 59–74.

JOHANNES HEIL

Gratian (fl. c. 1140), author, teacher of canon law in Bologna, Italy. Practically nothing is known about Gratian's life, and statements that he was a monk or a bishop are poorly supported by evidence. In 1143, he may have served as an adviser to a papal judge in Venice.

Gratian's fame rests solely on his authorship of the *Concordia discordantium canonum* (*Concord of Discordant Canons;* also known as the *Decretum*), a comprehensive collection of laws covering most aspects of church discipline. Despite never being formally promulgated, the work became the first part of the *Corpus iuris canonici* and remained in use in law schools and courts until modern times. The *Decretum* collected the canon laws of the previous millennium, which mainly derived from general and provincial councils, papal decretals, patristic writings, the Pseudo-Isidorian forgeries, penitentials, and secular law. It was innovative in including brief comments (*dicta*) that use the methods of early scholasticism to reconcile apparently contradictory statements.

The *Decretum* is preserved in two recensions, perhaps produced by different authors. The first, finished shortly after 1139 probably by Gratian, contains most of the *dicta* and 1,860 chapters. The second, in use by 1150, contains 3,945 chapters.

E. Friedberg, ed., *Decretum magistri Gratiani,* vol. 1 of *Corpus iuris canonici* (1879); S. Kuttner, *Gratian and the Schools of Law* (1983); A. Winroth, *The Making of Gratian's Decretum* (2000).

ANDERS WINROTH

Gravamina Grievances against the papal hierarchy presented by the nobility of the German nation. A collection of complaints registered over decades, beginning at the councils of Constance (1414–1418) and Basel (1431–1445), most of the gravamina dealt with abuses among the clergy, especially in administrative contexts. At the Diet of Augsburg (1518), the first official form of these protests was presented to the emperor explaining why the German princes refused to pay ecclesiastical tithes.

Two years later Martin Luther's "An Open Letter to the Christian Nobility" (1520) reflects these concerns in the section "Abuses to Be Discussed in Councils." At the Diet of Worms (1521) both the new "evangelicals" (Lutherans) and the Catholic princes proposed ecclesiastical reforms. As a result of that diet, the famous "One Hundred Gravamina of the German Nation" was compiled against a variety of ecclesiastical abuses—from the immoral life of clergy to papal encroachments into political affairs. The Diet of Nuremberg (1522–1523) repeated these concerns, but no official response ever was offered. Although never recognized by the papacy, these statements provide significant insight into those issues that led to the reformations of the sixteenth century.

G. Strauss, ed., *Manifestations of Discontent in Germany on the Eve of the Reformation* (1971).

TIMOTHY MASCHKE

Great Schism (1054) Political and ecclesiastical rupture, traditionally dated from 1054, that occurred between the Eastern (Greek) and Western (Latin) churches. Deep-seated theological disputes—including the pope's claim to sole sovereignty, the Latin addition of the *filioque* to the Creed, and the Western use of unleavened bread in the Eucharist—came to a head when Pope Leo IX and Michael Cerularius, the patriarch of Constantinople, suppressed Greek and Latin usages in their respective sees. In 1054, Leo sent his representatives to Constantinople to demand that Cerularius refute his claim to the title of ecumenical patriarch and accept the pope's claim as sole head of the church. When Cerularius refused, Cardinal Humbert of the Latin legates anathematized and excommunicated him, and Cerularius reciprocated. However, the papal legates' actions remain controversial because Leo had died before their action was taken. Also, the mutual anathemas were limited only to the legates and the patriarch, rather than each church as a whole. When the legates of Pope Urban II visited Constantinople in 1089, the patriarch stated that the Byzantines had no record of formal schism and that the communion of the two churches could be restored once the pope made confession of the Orthodox faith. However, Latin and Greek cultures were drifting inexorably apart, and, after the Latins captured and sacked Constantinople in 1204 during the Crusades, there was little substantial hope of future union. Negotiations were irrevocably terminated when Constantinople fell to the Turks in 1453.

S. Runciman, *The Eastern Schism: A Study of the Papacy and the Eastern Churches during the XI and the XII Centuries* (1955); P. Sherrard, *The Greek East and the Latin West: A Study in the Christian Tradition* (2nd ed., 1995).

MICHAEL D. PETERSON

Great Western Schism (1378–1417)

After the return of the papacy from Avignon to Rome, the cardinals, under popular pressure, elected an Italian, Urban VI (1378–1389). Within months, they declared the election invalid and elected a cousin of the French king as Clement VII (1378–1394), who returned to Avignon. Each claimant and his successors attracted kings, clergy, and saints to his side; neither could suppress the other nor would yield to an arbiter. University theologians such as Pierre D'Ailly and Jean Gerson argued that in an emergency, a council might depose and elect popes. Though the Council of Pisa (1409) only established a third papal line, there was by 1415 wide political and ecclesiastical support for the Council of Constance, which accepted the Roman pope's resignation and deposed the claimants from Pisa and Avignon. Its election of Martin V (1417–1431) was accepted throughout nearly all of Western Christendom.

C. M. D. Crowder, *Unity, Heresy, and Reform, 1378–1460: The Conciliar Response to the Great Schism* (1977); R. N. Swanson, *Universities, Academics, and the Great Schism* (1979); B. Tierney, *Foundations of the Conciliar Theory* (rev. ed., 1998); W. Ullmann, *Origins of the Great Schism* (2nd ed., 1972).

CHRISTOPHER B. BROWN

Grebel, Conrad (c. 1498–1526),

humanist and founding member of the Swiss Brethren. Grebel earned the distinction of being the first Anabaptist because he rebaptized members of the Swiss Brethren on January 21, 1525. Grebel, the second son of Jakob Grebel, a prosperous iron merchant and influential member of the Zurich city council, was educated in the humanist tradition in Zurich and later at the universities of Basel, Vienna, and Paris. Much to the dismay of his family and his teachers, the two years Grebel spent in Paris were wasted on drinking and brawling in the local taverns. After much pleading, Grebel's father allowed him to return home to Zurich in 1520. In 1522, Grebel married Barbara, a woman of lower social standing, which displeased his family.

He and Barbara had three children, two of whom may have survived to adulthood.

The main source of information on Grebel comes from the extant letters written to his brother-in-law and a few others. Unfortunately, there are no known letters from the period in Grebel's life when he changed from a young humanist scholar to a fervent supporter of Huldrych Zwingli's Protestant reforms in Zurich. However, sources on Zwingli's activities in 1523 indicate that Grebel had joined the circle of young scholars interested in studying Latin, Greek, Hebrew, and the New Testament with Zwingli.

By the end of 1523, Grebel and Zwingli publicly disagreed over the pace of reform but not over theology. The Second Zurich Disputation, convened in October 1523 by the Zurich city council, ended with the conclusion that the Mass had to be reformed. Zwingli, however, did not ask for immediate reform. Instead, he declared he would wait for the city council to make its decision on when and how to change the observance of the Mass. It appeared to Grebel and his companions, including Felix Manz, Balthasar Hubmaier, Andreas Castelberger, Simon Stumpf, and others, that Zwingli and the city council had abandoned the true Christian church.

For more than a year, Grebel and his coreligionists, who would be known as the Swiss Brethren, continued to oppose Zwingli before the city council. In 1524, the Swiss Brethren worked to convince the city council to adopt their views on the church. It is tempting to assume that at this time many of the beliefs associated with the later Anabaptist movements were already held by the Swiss Brethren. It is only through Grebel's search for allies abroad that we know what the Swiss Brethren wanted to accomplish in Zurich. In his letter to Thomas Müntzer in 1524, Grebel outlined the following points: the Mass must be based on strict adherence to NT practice; Christian discipleship must be enforced by the ban (i.e., separation from the community; Matt. 18:15–18), not by execution; Christians must not resist violence; and only adults who make a confession of faith should be baptized. This letter, however, does not present a complete soteriology or ecclesiology. The only other source for Grebel's beliefs is a pamphlet only known through Zwingli's attack on it, *In Catabaptistarum strophas elenchus*.

The rift between Zwingli and the Swiss Brethren became permanent in January 1525 during the debate on infant baptism. Zwingli and the city council wanted to maintain the practice of baptizing infants into the church. Instead of an inclusive church, Grebel believed that the true Christian church could only comprise adults who freely chose to follow the Swiss Brethren's interpretation of the NT. Believing that they would never have the support of the city council, the Swiss Brethren confessed their faith to each other and baptized one another. For this act, Grebel and the others were imprisoned and exiled from Zurich. The exact date of Grebel's death is unknown, but he is reported to have died of the plague in July 1526.

H. Bender, *Conrad Grebel c. 1498–1526: The Founder of the Swiss Brethren* (1950); H.-J. Goertz, *The Anabaptists* (1996); Goertz, ed., *Profiles of Radical Reformers* (1982); L. Harder, ed., *Sources of Swiss Anabaptism: The Grebel Letters and Related Documents* (1985).

AMY R. CALDWELL

Gregorian Chant   A chant whose original distribution and allocation is attributed to Pope Gregory the Great. Gregorian chant is frequently substituted for the medieval term *cantus* (see *Chant*), based upon the hypothesis (1) that the original melodies associated with the texts of the Mass proper and the office liturgy originated by some indeterminate process in the city of Rome, (2) that these melodies were later modified within the Frankish territories and as such were transmitted throughout Europe, leaving only a small residue of manuscripts containing the so-called Old Roman chant within the city of Rome, and (3) that the association of this widespread "Frankish" revision chant, known in the English language as "Gregorian chant," is based on the widely circulated medieval attribution of the *cantus*, with respect to both the distribution and allocation of the texts as well as the melodies, to Pope Gregory the Great.

This attribution to Gregory has been attested in various ways. The familiar image of a dove dictating the arrangement of the psalmodic portions and the melodies to the pope is a conventional manuscript illumination, particularly for the beginning of the church year, the first Sunday of Advent. The attribution can be found as well in Paul the Deacon's ninth-century *Life of Gregory*, a biography concurrent with the appearance of music notation (*figurae*) in liturgical manuscripts, such as *graduals* containing the musical portions of the proper of the Mass, as well as within *antiphonals* containing the musical portions for the offices (antiphons and

responsories). Further, the name and activity of Gregory is emphasized in the introduction, *Gregorius presul*, that also appears before the opening of the church year and the beginning of the *temporale*, or significant events in the life of Christ. *Gregorius presul* is included in early graduals before the introit of the first Sunday of Advent, *Ad te levavi animam meam*, although the pope to which reference is made here could also be Gregory II (715–731), not Gregory the Great (590–604).

The perseverance, through centuries, of this attribution of *cantus* composition to Gregory the Great also led to hypotheses that attempted to explain the absence of musical notation in the texts that contain the chants up until the ninth century. This absence is striking considering the claim that Gregory the Great purportedly coordinated Scripture, primarily the Psalms, with musical notation before the beginning of the seventh century. The question has to do with the transmission and teaching of "Gregorian chant" for approximately three centuries from the beginning of the seventh to the last generation of the ninth century, without, so far as we know, the aid of the *figurae* of music notation. This question has invited responses that have appropriated the changing narrative models of the twentieth century—such as "oral transmission," "improvisation," "epic transmission"—as these models have appeared, one after the other. It is a moot issue, of course, if one discounts Paul the Deacon's attribution of the *cantus* to Gregory—for which there is little, if any, evidence. The term "Gregorian chant," primarily a twentieth-century usage, based on the above presuppositions, and requiring a good deal of qualification, should be discarded in favor of the medieval *cantus*.

W. Apel, *Gregorian Chant* (1958, rev. 1990); D. Hiley, *Western Plainchant: A Handbook* (1993); J. McKinnon, *The Advent Project: The Later-Seventh-Century Creation of the Roman Mass Proper* (2000); B. Stöblein, "'Gregorius Presul' der Prolog zum römischen Antiphonale," in *Musik and Verlag Karl Vötterle zum 65. Geburtstag*, ed. R. Baum and W. Rehm (1968), 537–61.

NANCY VAN DEUSEN

Gregory I (c. 540–604), monk, theologian, and bishop of Rome, known as "the Great." Son of an aristocratic Roman family, Gregory received an excellent education and was early marked for an administrative career. In 573 he was appointed prefect, the highest secular office in Rome. When his father died, Gregory gave up his secular career to become a monk. With his inheritance he founded monasteries in Sicily and converted his family home in Rome into a monastery dedicated to St. Andrew, where he lived with his fellow monks.

In 579 Gregory became one of the seven deacons of Rome and then papal ambassador to the imperial court in Constantinople. There he began to write the *Moralia* on Job, in which he set forth his teachings on prayer, penitence, humility, and self-denial as fundamental to the Christian life. Constantly troubled by stomach ailments provoked by strict asceticism, Gregory always empathized with suffering Job.

Following the death of Pelagius II in 590, Gregory became the first monk elected pope. The *Pastoral Rule*, written to explain his reluctance to undertake the papal office, became a standard manual for bishops on their ministry of preaching and pastoral care. When secular authority in Rome was too weak and the imperial government too unconcerned to deal with the problems of plague, famine, and threatened invasion by the Lombards, Gregory provided social services, negotiated treaties, and strengthened papal administrative procedures. Seeing civil disorder and natural disaster as signs of the world's imminent end, he believed it was his pastoral responsibility both to preserve the social fabric and to urge Christians to renounce the beguilements of a dying world.

As pope, Gregory worked to preserve monastic prerogatives, convert Jews by all means short of physical force, combat schismatic Donatists in Africa and heretical Arians and adherents of the "Three Chapters" in Italy, and evangelize the Anglo-Saxons through the mission of Augustine to Canterbury in 597. Although he asserted papal authority by denying that the patriarch of Constantinople should be called "ecumenical" (i.e., universal), Gregory refused that title for himself, preferring to be known as "servant of the servants of God."

Gregory wrote homilies on Ezekiel and the Gospels, dialogues about Italian saints such as Benedict, a commentary on the Song of Songs, and many letters. It has been said that he was responsible for shaping the theological legacy of Augustine into systematic formulas concerning penance, purgatory, the sacrifice of the Mass, angelic hierarchies, miracles, and the cult of saints. But that was largely the result of later generations' readings of Gregory; his own concern was to develop a theology of Christian spiritual experience in which polar opposites such as action and contemplation were carefully balanced through the characteristic monastic virtue of discretion.

———

J. C. Cavadini, ed., *Gregory the Great* (1995); G. R. Evans, *The Thought of Gregory the Great* (1986); R. A. Markus, *Gregory the Great and His World* (1997); J. Richards, *Consul of God* (1980); C. Straw, *Gregory the Great: Perfection in Imperfection* (1988).

ARTHUR G. HOLDER

Gregory VII (d. 1085), pope. Among the clerics who accompanied Pope Leo IX to Rome in 1049 was a Tuscan monk named Hildebrand who may have resided at Cluny in 1047–1049. He quickly rose to important positions, first as an assistant to Leo IX, then papal archdeacon in 1059, then chancellor of Pope Nicholas II sometime after 1060. Under Pope Alexander II (1061–1073) he became administrator of papal affairs. On the very day of the latter's funeral he was acclaimed pope at Rome, clearly contrary to the Election Decree of 1059; only later did a formal election occur.

Although he had spent much of his adult life in the reform atmosphere of Rome and Burgundy, he broke with both his predecessors and contemporaries in demanding a totally new reordering of the world, one that rejected the Carolingian theocratic emperor and elevated the pope alone to the leading role in Christendom. His principles were articulated in the *Dictatus papae* (*Dictates of the Pope*), published in the spring of 1075. This collection of twenty-seven sentences clearly stated his belief in the unquestioned supremacy of the Roman pontiff over all, including the German emperor. Indicative of this position is the fact that upon his elevation to the Roman see, Gregory merely informed the latter of his new office, similar to what had traditionally been done with other rulers in the Latin West.

Even before the *Dictatus papae*, however, Gregory had begun to challenge the existing order of things. At a synod in 1074 he declared priests guilty of simony deposed; he also forbade married priests from celebrating the Mass. The most serious threat to current practices occurred in February 1075 when he prohibited lay investiture of ecclesiastical offices, particularly those of bishop and abbot. This measure struck at the very heart of imperial administrative structure and, if carried out fully, would have undermined the emperor's control of his realm. Gregory had thus issued a challenge to Emperor Henry IV, which the young ruler took up with a vengeance.

Refusing to recognize the legitimacy of Gregory's election as pope, even addressing him as a "usurper and false monk," Henry summoned a council of German bishops at Worms in 1076 and declared Gregory deposed. Gregory in turn held a synod at Rome that anathematized Henry and suspended him from government, declaring that he now had four months to achieve reconciliation with Rome or else be declared deposed.

In the midst of this war of words, Gregory proceeded to move northward to Germany, where he intended to preside over that deposition and over the election of a new ruler. Stopping at the fortress of Canossa in Tuscany, he was joined by Countess Matilda of Tuscany, one of his staunchest supporters, and by Abbot Hugh of Cluny. Here too appeared Henry IV one day, standing in sackcloth and ashes as a humble penitent, seeking the pontiff's forgiveness. At the urging of Matilda and Hugh, Gregory relented and absolved Henry, fully expecting that the young German ruler would be more obedient and compliant in the future.

Unhappily for Gregory, Canossa gave Henry the opportunity to break the opposition of the German princes that was building at home, with the ultimate result that by 1080 he was in open defiance of the pope once more. A second excommunication proved ineffective, and that same year Henry secured the election of an antipope, Clement III (1080–1100), who prevailed for two decades against Gregory and his successors. Gregory's own support for the anti-emperor, Rudolf of Swabia, and his continued intransigence regarding Henry and various other issues led to the defection of no fewer than thirteen cardinals in 1083. Even the Cluniacs, who had been among the leaders in the reform movement of the tenth and eleventh centuries, found it difficult to give unqualified support to his actions.

When Henry IV invaded Italy in 1085, Gregory called upon his Norman allies from southern Italy to come to his aid. Under Robert Guiscard, the Normans rescued the pontiff and returned to the safety of their own lands; Gregory died at Salerno on May 25 that same year, an exile from the city of Rome that he loved with great passion and at odds with most of the secular rulers of his day.

Nevertheless, the pontificate of Gregory VII marks a significant turning point in the history of the medieval papacy. While he claimed to be enforcing old law (and he even had his priests search the old collections for precedents), there was little authority for his claims in the ancient canons. Neither a lawyer nor a skilled politician, he was motivated by the complete confidence that his commands were in fact those of God himself. His ambitions were thus not personal, but in behalf of God's holy church. Dispatching his legates throughout Latin Christendom, he paved the way for the universal dominion and absolute theocratic power that culminated in the pontificates of Innocent III and Boniface VIII.

G. Barraclough, *The Medieval Papacy* (1968); F. Eyck, *Religion and Politics in German History: From the Beginning to the French Revolution* (1998); A. Fliche, *La réforme grégorienne*, 3 vols. (1924–1937); J. H. Lynch, *The Medieval Church: A Brief History* (1992); G. Tellenbach, *Church, State and Christian Society at the Time of the Investiture Contest* (1940); B. Tierney, *The Crisis of Church and State, 1050–1300* (1964).

PAUL B. PIXTON

Gregory IX (c. 1170–1241), pope. Ugolino of Segni began his career at the universities of Paris and Bologna. He benefited from the patronage of Innocent III, a distant relative, and was among the first cardinals Innocent created (cardinal deacon of St. Eustache). Appointed cardinal bishop of Ostia in 1206, he served as an auditor and principal counselor in Innocent's curia. He was a trusted legate for Innocent III and Honorius III and served as cardinal protector for the fledgling Franciscan order, assisting in the development of the Third Order of Franciscans; unofficially he provided similar services for the Dominicans.

Upon the death of Honorius III, Ugolino was elected (the second choice) and consecrated as Pope Gregory IX in 1227. Like his predecessors, he immediately plunged into conflict with the Holy Roman Emperor, Frederick II, as Frederick vacillated between aiding Gregory and attempting to depose him. Gregory initially upheld the excommunication already imposed on Frederick, but withdrawing it later when Frederick seemed more tractable. Once it became evident that Frederick intended to take all of Italy after defeating the Lombards, Gregory excommunicated him again. The issues were not resolved in Gregory's lifetime.

During Gregory's pontificate the Inquisition became more focused, imposing death or life imprisonment on the unrepentant. The pope formally recruited both Dominicans and Franciscans into the ranks of inquisitors. He also initiated the systematic collection of papal and conciliar constitutions that would become the decretals.

L. Auvray, *Les Registres de Gregoire IX*, 4 vols. (1890–1955).

LORNA SHOEMAKER

Gregory of Elvira (fourth cent.), churchman, exegete, and preacher. He was a bishop of Elvira, a city in southern Spain, where the first-known church council had been held (c. 306). Gregory was a friend of a fierce anti-Arian, Lucifer of Cagliari, and a defender of Athanasius. He was also a convinced proponent of the Nicene faith and the term "consubstantial" (*homoousios*). In the two extant versions of his theological treatise, *On Orthodox Faith*, Gregory refutes the Arian Formula of Rimini (359), defends himself against the accusations of Sabellianism, and, most importantly, is one of the earliest to affirm the consubstantiality of the Holy Spirit. Gregory's ecclesiology lays great emphasis on the mystical union between Christ and the church. Some homilies and exegetical works of Gregory, which were previously attributed to Origen, Ambrose, or Gregory of Nazianzus, are still extant. Gregory's commentary on the Song of Songs in two recensions is one of the noteworthy early allegorical/christological interpretations of this book. His writings also provide valuable citations of old Latin versions of the Bible.

F. J. Buckley, *Christ and the Church according to Gregory of Elvira* (1964); R. P. C. Hanson, *The Search for the Christian Doctrine of God* (1988); F. J. M. Medina, *San Cecilio y San Gregorio* (2001).

TARMO TOOM

Gregory of Nazianzus (c. 329–390), bishop, known as "the Theologian." The work of Gregory of Nazianzus exerted singular influence on Christian thought in late antiquity and throughout the Byzantine period. Along with John Chrysostom and Basil of Caesarea, he is considered by the Eastern Orthodox to be one of the hierarchs of the faith. His works were translated into Latin, Syriac, and Armenian, and (exceptionally for a Christian author) included in the school curriculum of the Roman and Byzantine Empire.

Gregory was born into an elite, propertied family in Cappadocia. His father, Gregory the Elder, was bishop of Nazianzus (Diocaesarea), a station (*mansio*) on the major road between Constantinople and Antioch. However, it was Gregory's mother, Nonna, who, according to Gregory's autobiographical works, provided the family with its Christian grounding.

Gregory received an exceptional education, first at Caesarea in Cappadocia, then at Caesarea Maritima, Alexandria, and Athens. His teachers included Himerius and Prohairesius, and he studied and later cited a wide range of classical (pagan) authors. While in Athens he became a friend of Basil of Caesarea, his fellow student. After their return to Cappadocia, he briefly joined Basil at the latter's country estate at Annesi for the "philosophical life" of ascetic retreat.

Upon his return home in 358–359, Gregory taught rhetoric until his ordination as priest by his father in early 362. It was perhaps during occasional retreats with Basil that the two began to collect excerpts from Origen's works, the so-called *Philocalia*. Gifted as a writer, thinker, and preacher, Gregory continued to champion the advantages of the ascetic retreat. Nevertheless, he dedicated considerable effort to the affairs of the church, both at Nazianzus and beyond, although he never fully enjoyed the life and career of a major public administrator. In the early 370s his relationship with Basil deteriorated after the latter, now bishop of Caesarea, appointed him bishop of Sasima, a "hole in the wall," as a strategic move in his struggles with "Arian" bishops, who were seeking to expand their own influence after the division of the region into further dioceses. According to his celebrated funeral oration for Basil, Gregory viewed this ordination as a betrayal of their friendship.

Following the death of his parents in 374, he was offered the bishopric of Nazianzus but withdrew for four years to the monastery of St. Thecla in Seleucia. In 379 he took over the Nicene congregation in Constantinople and was made bishop of the capital in November 380. He resigned from the post in the following summer in protest against opponents at the Council of Constantinople (381) over which he was presiding. After retiring, he acted as bishop of Nazianzus until 384, when he moved to his country estate Arianzus, where he devoted his time to writing, especially poetry, and to publishing, including his collection of letters.

Gregory's posthumous renown as a philosopher and theologian was based on his prodigious literary oeuvre. It was his mission, to cite his own words, "to unite classical erudition with Christianity, and to place the glory of Athens's rhetoric at the feet of Christ." For Gregory, Christianity was heir to the true values of

Greek *paideia* (formation of elites through instruction in classical learning, a quintessential precondition for all leadership roles), and he remained convinced that truth could be found in the rigorous battle of thoughts in the arena of learning. To this end, he "rewrote" the canon of classical literature as a Christian one. His writings were enormously successful: throughout the Byzantine Empire, his writings were second only to the Scriptures in the frequency of citations, on a par only with those of Cyril of Alexandria. A masterful poet, he wrote more than 17,000 verses in a variety of meters that demonstrate an admirable command of the classical forms. Among his greatest achievements in verse is his poetic autobiography, remarkable both for its formal qualities and for its level of personal reflection. The strategy of self-marginalization that his autobiographical focus brings out served him both to convey an ascetic ethos and to voice an effective critique of the ecclesiastical establishment. Gregory's publication of his own correspondence at the end of his life marks another innovative step. Indeed, Gregory's ultimate success as a thinker was due not least to his dexterous use of the available literary media.

S. Elm, "A Programmatic Life: Gregory of Nazianzus' Orations 42 and 43 and the Constantinopolitan Elites," *Arethusa* 33 (2000): 411–27; F. W. Norris, L. Wickham, and F. Williams, *Faith Gives Fullness to Reasoning: The Five Theological Orations of Gregory Nazianzen* (1991); R. Van Dam, *Kingdom of Snow: Roman Rule and Greek Culture in Cappadocia* (2002); Van Dam, *Families and Friends in Late Roman Cappadocia* (2003); Van Dam, *Becoming Christian: The Conversion of Roman Cappadocia* (2003).

SUSANNA ELM

Gregory of Nyssa (335–395), bishop and theologian. Gregory was born in the region of Asia Minor called Cappadocia (in today's Turkey). He, his older brother Basil of Caesarea, and his brother's friend, Gregory of Nazianzus, constituted a close-knit and influential group of bishop-theologians known today as the Cappadocians. Gregory's reputation, however, has not been without controversy: his devotion to the teachings of Origen, his free use of philosophy, and even the region of his birth have figured in judgments against him. The twentieth century marked the great revival of interest in Gregory and in appreciation of his theology.

Historically, Gregory's theology began with asceticism and the theme of Christian perfection. The Genesis 1–3 account of creation and the fall dominated his thinking on the problem of human sinfulness. That sinfulness was transmitted by Adam and Eve to their progeny through the passion of sexual intercourse, an act that produces offspring who are themselves subject to passion. In this way passion is at the very root of our fallen existence. Christian perfection lies in freedom from our passions. Gregory's condemnation of passion was not total, for, like Origen, he recognized that some strong emotions described in Scripture are in the service of God, such as the anger of Phineas and Jesus. The most important example of such a "passion" is Jesus' suffering and death, which Gregory recognized as not truly passion but work done in God's will. Here Gregory's Christology guided his moral psychology.

Although it is not certain whether Gregory married, he was emphatic about the importance of virginity or celibacy and was a strong supporter of a monastic way of life. Monastic virginity is the first major change to turn us on the road back to human life before the fall, a life that was free of sexuality and sexual reproduction. Gregory's immediate model for this way of life was his sister, Macrina, who, he said, lived an "angelic" life here on earth, a life free of passion. Not every Christian is expected to obtain so perfect a life now, before death, although Gregory did follow Origen in the opinion that God will save all. Gregory, however, located this universal salvation in an afterlife process of coming to God that has its point of departure in this life. The moral perfection we attain in this life determines at what point we begin our spiritual pilgrimage to God in the next life, after death.

Gregory's Trinitarian theology represents the most developed expression of the theology of Nicaea (325) and Constantinople (381). In this Trinitarian theology the unity among the divine persons of the Trinity is found in their common power or operations, while the reality of the individuality of the three is found in the causal relationships among them: the Father uncaused but causing the Son and Spirit, the Son generated, and the Spirit spirated. Gregory's Trinitarian theology is thus roughly the same as Ambrose's or Augustine's. Gregory's writing on the Trinity began in his engagement with Eunomius of Cyzicus, the most important spokesman of anti-Nicene Anomoeanism. In his anti-Eunomius writings Gregory emphasized the divine power to create that the Father and Son have in common. Later Gregory argued against those who accepted the divinity of the Son but denied the divinity of the Holy Spirit. Against these "Spirit-resisters" Gregory emphasized the common operations the Spirit shares with the Father and Son (e.g., sanctification). Gregory's later description of the Trinity (in his *Great Catechism*) emphasized the power of moral perfection the three share, a moral perfection only attainable in the Divine.

Gregory had much to say about the character of the incarnation and, like his colleague Gregory of Nazianzus, he argued against the Christology of Apollinarius of Laodicea. Gregory's understanding of the incarnation included the full reality of the human nature of Jesus, but that nature was so overwhelmed by the divinity of the Son that it existed like "a drop of vinegar in the ocean." Such an opinion was not Gregory's alone, for his understanding of the glorified Lord was that the Son's body has now been completely absorbed by the divinity. This opinion shows Origen's influence on Gregory.

M. R. Barnes, *The Power of God: Dynamis in Gregory of Nyssa's Trinitarian Theology* (2001); R. Van Dam, *Becoming Christian* (2003); Van Dam, *Families and Friends* (2003); N. E. F. Harrison, *Grace and Human Freedom according to St. Gregory of Nyssa* (1992); A. Meredith, *Gregory of Nyssa* (1992); W. Moore and H. A. Wilson, eds., *NPNF*, series 2, vol. 5 (1893); H. Mursillo, ed., *From Glory to Glory: Texts from Gregory of Nyssa's Mystical Writings* (1961).

MICHEL RENE BARNES

Gregory of Rimini (c. 1300–1358),

scholastic scholar, general prior of the Augustinians. Gregory was born in Rimini, Italy. He studied theology at Paris from 1323 to 1329 before becoming lecturer (*lector*) at several Augustinian houses of study in Bologna, Padua, and Perugia. In 1341 or 1342 he returned to Paris to prepare his lectures on Peter Lombard's *Sentences* (see *Four Books of Sentences*), which he delivered in 1342–1343 or 1343–1344. In 1352, he became regent master at the Augustinian *studium* (see *Mendicant Schools*) of Rimini, where he taught until his election as general prior of the Augustinians in 1357.

Gregory's most important work is his lectures on books 1 and 2 of Peter Lombard's *Sentences* (*Lectura super primum et secundum Sententiarum*). If he ever composed lectures on books 3 and 4, they are now lost. His *Lectures* show familiarity with the views of many con-

temporaneous English philosophers, such as William of Ockham, Walter Chatton, Adam Wodeham, and Richard FitzRalph. The characterization of his doctrinal position has ranged from leader of the antinominalists to standard bearer of the nominalists. Recent scholarship perceives him as a nominalist (though distinctly different from Ockham) who derived much inspiration from the works of Augustine.

One of Gregory's best-known doctrines, possibly derived from Adam Wodeham, concerns the proper object of scientific knowledge. It is expressed in the context of the discussion of the status of theology as a science. According to Gregory, the object of scientific knowledge is neither the conclusion of a demonstrative syllogism, nor the things (*res*) signified by such a conclusion, but that which is being signified (*complexe significabile*). In this way, Gregory located the eternity and necessity of scientific knowledge in a state of affairs or mode of being, rather than in a mental proposition or extramental things.

Gregory of Rimini, *Lectura super primum et secundum Sententiarum*, D. A. Trapp et al., eds. (1979–1987); G. Leff, *Gregory of Rimini: Tradition and Innovation in Fourteenth-Century Thought* (1961); H. A. Oberman, ed., *Gregor von Rimini: Werk und Wirkung bis zum Reformation* (1981).

J. M. M. H. THIJSSEN

Gregory of Tours (c. 538–c. 594), bishop

of Tours, historian, and hagiographer. Gregory was born to a distinguished senatorial family from the Auvergne, a region of central France. After his father's death he was educated by his uncle Gallus and subsequently by bishops Avitus of Clermont and Nicetius of Lyon. In 563 Gregory was ordained deacon in Lyon, and on August 20, 573, he was consecrated as the bishop of Tours. Shortly after his ordination Gregory's political patron, King Sigibert I, died, and the city of Tours was seized by Chilperic, with whom Gregory had tense relations. He did not hesitate to criticize the king, and in 580 he even had to defend himself in court against charges of alleged treason and infamy. After Chilperic's death in 584, Gregory seems to have had good relations with Chilperic's Merovingian successors. He died on November 17 and was buried at the Tours cathedral next to St. Martin.

Gregory is best known for his prolific writing. He wrote *Ten Books of Histories* (misleadingly known as *The History of the Franks*), which are our main source on the history of the early Merovingian kingdoms. He also composed eight books of saints' lives, a commentary on the Psalms (now lost), as well as a short astronomical work (*The Course of the Stars*) for the use of the clergy.

W. Goffart, *The Narrators of Barbarian History* (1988); M. Heinzelmann, *Gregory of Tours: History and Society in the 6th Century* (2001); I. N. Wood, *Gregory of Tours* (1984); I. N. Wood and K. Mitchel, eds., *Gregory of Tours and His World* (2002).

YITZHAK HEN

Gregory Palamas (c. 1296–1359), monastic ascetic, Greek bishop, theologian, saint, and key proponent of *hesychasm*. He was born at Constantinople, the son of an aristocratic Anatolian family who had close ties to the court of Emperor Andronicus II. His father died when Gregory was only seven, but Gregory was able, at the imperial court's expense, to receive an excellent liberal education at the imperial university in Constantinople. In 1316, at the age of twenty-two and in the company of his two younger brothers, he was persuaded by Metropolitan Theolytus of Philadelphia to enter the monastic life on Mount Athos. He spent short periods there at the monasteries of Vatopedi and Great Lavra, finally settling for a lengthy stay as a hermit attached to Glossia Skete.

Gregory moved to Thessalonica in 1325 under threat of Turkish invasions of Athos. At the age of thirty he was ordained priest at Thessalonica in 1326. He moved to a mountain hermitage near Berrhea with ten companions, where for five years they practiced the life of hesychastic prayer that had been so strong on Athos. The hesychasm of Athos required intense solitude and inner quiet through the prayer of Jesus recited inwardly during the weekdays, followed by eucharistic celebration and spiritual fellowship with the whole community on Saturday and Sunday. When Berrhea came under Serbian attack in 1331, Gregory was forced to return to Athos, where he joined the hermitage of St. Sabas. Around 1335 he was made abbot of the Grand Laura, but the following year he returned to the solitude of St. Sabas.

At Pentecost in 1337 Gregory encountered the anti-Latin writings of Barlaam, a Greek-speaking philosopher-monk from Seminaria in Calabria, Italy. Much of the rest of Gregory's life was spent combating Barlaam's views, although he shared Barlaam's anti-Latin framework and borrowed from his methodology.

Barlaam disputed the Latin addition of the *filioque* to the creed and based his argument on the apophatic (negative) theology of the writings of Pseudo-Dionysius. He posited that the Latins should end their attempt to prove the doctrine of the procession of the Holy Spirit because God is unknowable. Since no direct knowledge of God is possible, the only alternative is a dialectic approach through Scripture and patristic statement. Furthermore, the doctrine of the procession should be relegated to the level of private theological opinions (*theologumena*) and should not be an obstacle to the unity of the church.

Gregory shared this anti-Latin view, but he reached different conclusions about the ability to know God. Around this time he wrote his two *Apodictic Treatises*, supported by the opinions of Patriarch Gregory of Cyprus (r. 1283–1289), to counter the Latin position on the procession. Using the same Aristotelian logical terminology as Barlaam, Gregory held that demonstrations showing God's existence are Orthodox. In short, he believed that theological discussion about the Trinity could lead to absolute truth. He established that Barlaam's argument—without directly naming Barlaam—constituted dogmatic relativism. Gregory came to the conclusion that Barlaam's extreme apophatic theology was agnostic and, therefore, not Orthodox.

There then followed a terse exchange between Gregory, Barlaam, and Gregory's former disciple Gregory Akindynos about the importance and meaning of the concept of demonstration. In the meantime, Barlaam took it upon himself to mock the practices of the hesychastic monks of Thessalonica, calling them "men with their soul in the navel" (*omphalopsychoi*) because they repeated the Jesus Prayer while focusing their eyes on a position below the chest. Barlaam held that the monks were guilty of Messalianism, the fourth-century dualistic heresy that held concentrated and ceaseless prayer as a way to envision the Holy Trinity. He was particularly offended by the monks' claim that the human body, not just the mind, could be divinely transfigured and thereby could contribute to the understanding of God's being. In 1338, while Barlaam persisted in condemning the hesychastic monks, the monk Isidore (later patriarch of Constantinople) recommended that the monks recruit Gregory to defend them. Gregory responded by returning to Thessalonica in order to issue the *Triads*, three treatises in defense of the hesychasts.

Barlaam sought to settle the dispute by organizing a council in Constantinople, but the move backfired. At the first council, held in June of 1341, Gregory was vindicated with the help of his childhood friend, Emperor Andronicus III. Barlaam confessed his position as heretical but then changed his mind and called for another council. Before the second council met in August, he realized that he would not be able to garner enough support to overturn the initial decision and left Byzantium for permanent residence in Italy. Gregory Akindynos, who had initially served as a mediator in the dispute, was condemned at the second council. Meanwhile, Barlaam continued to publish tracts against the monks, including rebuttals to points made in the first *Triad*.

Gregory continued the counterattack on Barlaam. He published a second *Triad* in which he included his definitive distinction that God's essence or being is unknowable although his energy or operation is perceptible. He later resoundingly condemned Barlaam's ideas in the *Hagioretic Tome*, which was solemnly supported by the Athonite authorities.

Gregory Akindynos then picked up the argument where Barlaam left off, albeit from an Orthodox position. Akindynos objected to Palamas's conception that although God is wholly transcendent, God can still be perceived as an uncreated and real presence. Palamas understood God as at once a transcendent divine essence and as uncreated yet revealed energies. Akindynos maintained that God is one with his essence, so that any vision of God—if that was even possible to begin with—was either a vision of the divine essence itself or of its created manifestations. Thus, according to Akindynos, it is impossible to make real distinctions in the uncreated nature of God's being.

However, councils of 1347 and 1351 endorsed Palamas's theology ("Palamism"), in spite of objections from Nicephorus Gregoras, the influential philosopher and historian who was a supporter of Akindynos. In 1347 Palamas was elected archbishop of Thessalonica, and his friends Isidore, Kallistos, and Philotheus Kokkinos were successively patriarch of Constantinople. From this period on, hesychasm exercised an enormous influence on the Orthodox Church as a whole. In 1354–1355 Palamas became a prisoner of the Turks when his boat was intercepted on a trip between Thessalonica and Constantinople. He was finally ransomed by the Serbs and returned to his bishopric at Thessalonica, where he died. He was canonized

in 1368. His relics continue to be venerated at the Cathedral of Thessalonica.

———

G. Florovsky, "St. Gregory Palamas and the Tradition of the Fathers," *GOTR* 5 (1960): 119–31; G. Palamas, *The Triads* (1983); G. I. Mantzarides, *The Deification of Man: St. Gregory Palamas and the Orthodox Tradition* (1984); J. Meyendorff, *A Study of Gregory Palamas* (1998); G. C. Papademetriou, *Introduction to Saint Gregory Palamas* (1973); H. Vlachos, *St. Gregory Palamas as a Hagiorite* (1997).

MICHAEL D. PETERSON

Gregory Thaumaturgus (c. 212–c. 272),

bishop. Eusebius mentions Gregory and a brother, Athenodorus, as students of Origen who later became bishops in Pontus, a Roman province on the Black Sea coast of Asia Minor, and tells us they participated in a synod at Antioch called to deal with heresy charges against Paul of Samosata (*Hist. eccl.* 6.30, 7.14, 7.28). A rich hagiographical tradition, beginning with a *Life* by Gregory of Nyssa, identifies him as a miracle worker (*thaumatourgos*) who effectively brought Christianity to Pontus. A large and disparate collection of written works has been attributed to him. Most scholars believe that he wrote the *Address* given by a student of Origen at his departure from his teacher. The work reflects Origen's theology and provides valuable insights into his teaching methods. Gregory may also have been the recipient of Origen's "Letter to Gregory."

———

R. L. Fox, *Pagans and Christians* (1987), 516–42; St. G. Thaumaturgus, *Life and Works*, trans. M. Slusser, FC 98 (1998); J. W. Trigg, "God's Marvelous *Oikonomia*: Reflections of Origen's Understanding of Divine and Human Pedagogy in the *Address* Ascribed to Gregory Thaumaturgus," *JECS* 9 (2001): 27–52.

JOSEPH W. TRIGG

Gregory the Illuminator (d. early fourth

cent.), missionary, bishop of Armenia. He is commemorated as founder of the Armenian church. The son of a Parthian noble, he was raised as a Christian in Caesarea of Cappadocia. He returned to Armenia when Trdat the Great claimed the Armenian throne (c. 298). He began to preach Christianity, and although he was persecuted and imprisoned, he eventually converted Trdat to Christianity. Gregory was ordained bishop of Armenia by Leontius, bishop of Caesarea of Cappadocia (c. 314). Gregory is associated with the organization of the church in Armenia and with Christian missionary activity in neighboring Georgia and Albania. He retired to a life of asceticism after the episcopal consecration of his son Aristakes, who represented Armenia at the Council of Nicaea (325). The major recension of Gregory's Life is found in the Armenian history of Agathangelos (late fifth cent.).

W. Seibt, ed., *Die Christianisierung des Kaukasus* [*The Christianization of Caucasus*]: *Referate des Internationalen Symposions (Wien, 9–12. Dezember 1999)* (2002); R. W. Thomson, "Mission, Conversion, and Christianization: The Armenian Example," *Harvard Ukrainian Studies* 12/13 (1988/1989): 28–45; Thomson, *The Teaching of Saint Gregory: Translation, Commentary, and Introduction* (rev. ed., 2001).

MONICA J. BLANCHARD

Grigor Tat'ewac'i (c. 1346–1409), Armenian theologian. Born in southeastern Armenia and baptized as Khut'lushah, Grigor became the most illustrious Armenian theologian and ecclesiastic of his day, and his works have established themselves as the most comprehensive distillation of medieval Armenian thought.

A pupil of Hovhannes Orotnets'i, he accompanied his mentor on a pilgrimage to Jerusalem, where he was ordained in 1371. Returning via the monasteries of Mount Sepuh in Eastern Anatolia, where he received his doctoral staff in 1373, he assisted Orotnets'i at the Monastery of Aprakunik' till the latter's death in c. 1386, editing his analyses of Aristotle and Prophyry's texts on logic. Soon afterward Grigor transferred his monastic academy to Tat'ew, where he assumed a leading role in refuting the proselytization of the Fratres Unitores, an Armenian brotherhood affiliated with the Dominican Order. Accordingly, his works oppose doctrines such as purgatory and defend the traditional Armenian interpretation of Christology. At the same time, his theological compendium, the *Book of Questions* of 1397, attests to the impact of Thomas Aquinas's sacramental theology and Hugh Ripelin's angelology and demonology.

His other main writings include two volumes of sermons and a *Oskep'orik* (potpourri) of 1407, which similarly reveal his familiarity with the views of Augustine, Isidore, and Ibn Rushd (Averroes). In addition to a series of biblical commentaries, Tat'ewac'i's versatility is manifest in studies on the scribal arts, music, and manuscript illumination. Inspired by a dream, he also strove to resolve the protracted

schism of the region of Vaspurakan, south of Lake Van. After his death on December 27, 1409, he was buried in Tat'ew, where his finely carved tomb can still be seen. (See *Latin Envoys to Medieval Armenia*.)

M. K. Krikorian, "Grigor Tat'ewac'i: A Great Scholastic Theologian and Nominalist Philosopher," *Medieval Armenian Culture*, T. J. Samuelian and M. E. Stone, eds. (1984), 131–41.

S. PETER COWE

Grindal, Edmund (1519?–1583), archbishop of Canterbury. Grindal was born in Cumberland and educated at Cambridge where he came under the influence of the Protestant theology popular at the time. He served as chaplain first to the English reformer Nicholas Ridley and then, beginning in 1553, to Edward VI. During the reign of Mary Tudor, Grindal went into exile. He was recording stories of Protestant martyrs when, in 1555, he met the historian John Bale and the martyrologist John Foxe in Frankfurt.

With the succession of Elizabeth I, Grindal returned to England while Foxe remained on the Continent to continue the work. Grindal's stories thus contributed substantially to Foxe's *Book of Martyrs*. Elizabeth made Grindal bishop of London in 1553, and he assumed the see of York in 1570 and the see of Canterbury in 1575. In 1576 Grindal rebuked the queen for ordering him to suppress clergy meetings known as "prophecyings." Despite several attempts at mediation, the rift between Grindal and the queen was never repaired. The queen restricted him from his ministry until he died as a blind and broken man.

Grindal's tenure has been regarded as a failure in several respects, especially in that Puritan pastors who remained in the church decreased use of the Prayer Book and emphasized holy and disciplined living. John Whitgift, however, who succeeded Grindal, regained the queen's support and, in keeping with the queen's resistance to Puritanism, advanced Calvinist Protestantism.

P. Collinson, *Archbishop Grindal, 1519–1583: The Struggle for a Reformed Church* (1979); Collinson, *The Elizabethan Puritan Movement* (1990).

JOHN E. GRISWOLD

Groote, Geert (1340–1384), Dutch preacher and organizer of the spiritual movement later known as the *Devotio Moderna*.

Born in Deventer (northern Netherlands), Groote attended the Univ. of Paris, where he studied subjects such as canon law, theology, and medicine. Afterward he pursued a clerical career and received two benefices in Aachen and Utrecht. An averted life crisis, possibly after recovery from a serious illness, led Groote to a "spiritual conversion" in 1374, after which he exchanged his career as a cleric for a life devoted to prayer and the Scriptures. He spent three years with the Carthusians at Monnikhuizen near Arnhem, then relinquished his benefice and opened his family home to poor women who wished to lead a communal life but without religious vows. By the end of his life in 1384 this group had become a distinct religious community known as "the Brothers and Sisters of the Common Life." Groote was ordained a deacon in 1377 and licensed to preach in the diocese of Utrecht. Important to Groote's spiritual direction was his visit in 1381 to the well-known Flemish mystic Jan van Ruusbroec at his community of canons regular (see *Regular Clergy*; *Ruusbroec, Jan van*) at Groenendael.

Through letters, sermons, and meditation tracts, Groote reemphasized the importance of developing the inward state of the believer's soul. He died of the plague on August 20, 1384. After Groote's death, the Brothers and Sisters of the Common Life grew rapidly, eventually coming to be known as the *Devotio Moderna*.

J. P. Arthur, *The Founders of the New Devotion: The Lives of Gerard Groote, Florentius Radewin, and Their Followers, by Thomas a Kempis* (1905); R. T. M. van Dijk, *Prolegomena ad Gerardi Magni Opera Omnia* (2003); J. van Engen, *Devotio Moderna* (1988); G. Epiney-Burgard, *Gérard Grote: Fondateur de la Dévotion Modern* (1998); H. Rijcklof, ed., *Prolegomena ad Gerard; Magni Opera omnia. Gerardi Magni contra Turrim Traiectensem* (2003); T. P. van Zijl, *Gerard Groote: Ascetic and Reformer* (1963).

TODD M. RICHARDSON

Grosseteste, Robert (c. 1168–1253), theologian and philosopher.

While there remain large gaps in our understanding of Grosseteste's early biography, we know that he came from humble parentage and that his path to the doctorate in theology went through the schools of Oxford and Paris. In a life exemplified by extraordinary energy, Grosseteste seems to have combined several careers in one; extraordinary, too, is the fact that the bulk of this activity seems concentrated in his final thirty-five years.

But it was as a scholar and writer that Grosseteste most distinguished himself. Learning Greek in his fifties, he prepared translations of both religious and philosophical texts, including the Pseudo-Dionysian corpus and Aristotle's *Nicomachean Ethics*. His commentaries on these and other texts, plus his original writings, reflect the impressive breadth of his interests and knowledge along with a precocious philological sophistication and an abiding pastoral concern. Noteworthy are his reflections on scientific method and his attempts to implement them in various scientific investigations, which would bear impressive fruit in the next two centuries. And while his theological work, with its celebrated "metaphysics of light," was in large measure conservative, it was nonetheless influential through the end of the Middle Ages. Finally, mention must be made of his allegorical poem, the *Chasteau d'amour*; written expressly for the laity, it was a medieval best seller.

J. McEvoy, *Robert Grosseteste* (2000); R. W. Southern, *Robert Grosseteste: The Growth of an English Mind in Medieval Europe* (2nd ed., 1992).

STEVEN J. WILLIAMS

Grotius, Hugo (1583–1645), Dutch jurist, theologian, and diplomat.

Born in Delft to a distinguished Protestant family, he served briefly as a diplomat, lawyer, and state historian before becoming attorney general of Holland in 1608. As representative of Holland in the Estates-General of the Netherlands (1613) he became embroiled in Calvinist and Arminian doctrinal debates. When Grotius's early attempts to forge a united Protestant confession for Holland failed, he defended the Arminian Remonstrants. Arminianism was ultimately condemned by both church and state, and Grotius was convicted for high treason and sentenced to life imprisonment in 1619. He escaped to France in 1621, where he held various academic and political posts.

Grotius's personal religious conflicts, together with his experiences of growing religious warfare throughout Europe, set him on a life-long quest for religious and political rapprochement. His biblical commentaries and his influential treatise *De veritate religionis Christianae* (1627) lifted up the pacific dimensions of Christianity and sought to prove the rational universality of core biblical teachings. His early legal treatise, *De Indiis* (1604), later published as *De iure praedae*, defended free trade on the high seas and denied nation-states from claiming exclusive rights to common property. His most influential work, *De jure belli ac pacis* (1625), laid the foundation for modern international law and just war theory. Based on classical and Christian sources, it detailed the rules of conduct, trade, and diplomacy obligatory on all nations in times of war and peace. He grounded these rules in a theory of natural law and natural rights that appealed first to reason and human nature, even while being consistent with the Bible and Christian tradition. Grotius's legal theories remained standard lore in Europe for more than two centuries thereafter.

———

C. Gellinek, *Hugo Grotius* (1983); D. Wolf, *Die Irenik des Hugo Grotius* (1969).

JOHN WITTE JR.

Grünewald, Matthias (1475/1480–1528), German Renaissance painter who worked for the archbishops of Mainz, then in Seligenstadt and Aschaffenburg. The monks of the Antonine hospice of Isenheim, in Alsace, who treated victims of ergotism (diarrhea, nausea, and hallucinations caused by the ingestion of ergot, a parasite found in grains of rye), commissioned Grünewald to paint nine panels for an altarpiece to be displayed in their chapel. Now known as the *Isenheim Altarpiece* (1510–1515), this work overwhelms the viewer with its pathos and physical details of acute suffering, as well as with its promise of redemption. The broken, tortured body of Christ on the cross is considered one of the most memorable interpretations of the crucifixion. The scene of Christ's resurrection depicts a gloriously diaphanous Christ dissolving in light. Influenced by the fourteenth-century mystical writings of St. Birgitta of Sweden, and exploiting color for its expressionistic power, Grünewald created a highly original and deeply visionary work, one of the most imposing and unforgettable altarpieces in northern Europe.

———

A. Hayum, *The Isenheim Altarpiece: God's Medicine and the Painter's Vision* (1989); R. Mellinkoff, *The Devil at Isenheim: Reflections on Popular Belief in Grünewald's Altarpiece* (1988).

PRISCILLA BAUMANN

Gualbert, John (c. 995–1073), Italian monastic reformer, founder of the Vallom-brosan order. John Gualbert was a Florentine nobleman who underwent a religious conversion one Good Friday when he forgave his brother's murderer—whereupon an image of Christ miraculously bowed to him. John became a monk at San Miniato in Florence but was so outraged when a new abbot flagrantly purchased his office (c. 1035) that he began a personal crusade against simony that would last the rest of his life. John tried to raise his fellow monks and the population of Florence against the simoniac bishop of Florence as well as his abbot. When this failed, he became a hermit.

John attracted like-minded disciples, and his hermitage grew into the monastery of Vallombrosa, mother house of a new religious order based on manual labor, eremitism, and opposition to simony. These Vallombrosans helped create a public consciousness that would later inspire the Gregorian reform movement (see *Reform Papacy*). They fought simony in northern Italy with vigor, sometimes drawing violence on themselves, as in 1066 or 1067 when the simonist bishop of Florence had a monastery assaulted. A papal council would probably have condemned John Gualbert as a radical in the 1060s if Hildebrand (the future Gregory VII) had not defended his friend so strongly. He was canonized in 1193.

———

P. Jestice, *Wayward Monks and the Religious Revolution of the Eleventh Century* (1997).

PHYLLIS G. JESTICE

Guibert of Nogent (c. 1053–1124), French abbot, historian, and theologian. Guibert was a noble Frenchman who joined the monastery of St.-Germer at age twelve. In 1104 he was made abbot of the small monastery of Nogent, where he remained until his death. Guibert took part in the ecclesiastical affairs of his day but is known today as an author of histories, biblical commentaries, and treatises; his style is derivative and often disorganized. He would be unimportant were it not for two highly unusual works: a critique of the cult of saints and the first true European autobiography since Augustine's *Confessions*.

Guibert's *On the Saints and Their Relics* has often been taken as a sweeping indictment of the medieval cult of relics, but closer reading shows it as on the one hand a diatribe of a rival monastery that claimed to have a baby tooth of Christ, and on the other hand a plea for supervision of relics cults. It is a valuable source on medieval popular religion. Of more sweeping interest are the memoirs written late in Guibert's life. Modeled on Augustine's work, the memoirs explore, sometimes morbidly, Guibert's troubled childhood and struggles to be a good monk. The work is an important primary source for twelfth-century France, valuable especially for understanding the rise of communes.

Guibert, *A Monk's Confession: The Memoirs of Guibert of Nogent*, trans. P. J. Archambault (1996); J. Rubenstein, *Guibert of Nogent* (2002).

                                                                PHYLLIS G. JESTICE

Gunpowder Plot An English Catholic attempt in 1605 by Robert Catesby, Guy Fawkes, and a few compatriots to assassinate King James I and members of Parliament by detonating casks of gunpowder they had stored in the cellars below Westminster Hall. The foiling of the plot further exacerbated decades-long English anti-Catholicism and reinforced the deeply rooted English Protestant national identity that celebrated God's defense of true faith and liberty against popish tyranny and Catholic treason exemplified by the Marian persecutions and the Spanish Armada.

D. Cressy, *Bonfires and Bells: National Memory and the Protestant Calendar in Elizabethan and Stuart England* (1989); A. Fraser, *Faith and Treason: The Story of the Gunpowder Plot* (1996); M. Nicholls, *Investigating Gunpowder Plot* (1991).

                                                                DAVID A. LOPEZ

Günzburg, Johann Eberlin von (1460?–1533), German reformer and publicist. Educated in the humanist tradition at the universities of Basel and Freiburg/Breisgau, he became a priest and an observant Franciscan. Influenced by Luther's early writings and convinced that the monastic life was against God's will, he left the monastery in 1521. He is best known for a series of influential pamphlets, *The Fifteen Confederates* (1521), critical of monasticism. One pamphlet, "Wolfaria," was among the first Protestant utopias. He studied in Wittenberg in 1522–1523 and later worked in southern Germany, Erfurt, and Wertheim. In later writings he shifted from anticlerical themes to clear explanations of Luther's theology aimed at lay readers; he also attended to practical reform issues. During the Peasants' War in 1524, he criticized the enthusiasts extensively. He died at Leutershausen.

S. G. Bell, "Johann Eberlin von Günzburg's 'Wolfaria': The First Protestant Utopia?" *CH* 36 (1967): 122–39; R. G. Cole, "Law and Order in the Sixteenth Century: Eberlin von Günzburg and the Problem of Political Authority," *LQ* 23 (1971): 251–56; Cole, "The Reformation in Print: German Pamphlets and Propaganda," *ARG* 66 (1975): 93–102; G. Dipple, *Antifraternalism and Anticlericalism in the German Reformation: Johann Eberlin von Günzburg and the Campaign against the Friars* (1996).

                                                                MARY JANE HAEMIG

Gustavus Adolphus (1594–1632), oldest son of King Charles IX of Sweden. Well educated, he acceded to the throne in 1611, at the same time inheriting the war against his cousin King Sigismund of Poland. He also took part in the fights over the throne of Russia. A third problem was Danish aggression. The peace of Stolbova in 1617 was the first victory for Sweden outside its own borders and established its dominions in the Baltics. One of Gustavus's main objectives was to build an alliance between the Protestant German princes against the Catholic emperor and his allies. In 1629 Sweden entered the Thirty Years' War. Swedish troops won the great victory of Breitenfeld in 1631, but in 1632 Gustavus was mortally wounded in the battle of Lützen.

Gustavus was a good king for his country; schools were reorganized, the Univ. of Uppsala received a large personal donation that raised its standards, the courts were established, and a new edition of the Bible was released. The Lutheran church flourished under his rule and the guidance of capable bishops.

O. P. Grell, ed., *The Scandinavian Reformation* (1995); M. Roberts, *Gustavus Adolphus* (2nd ed., 1992).

                                                                INGUN MONTGOMERY

Gutenberg, Johann (c. 1400–1468), German inventor of printing. A native of Mainz, Gutenberg (Gensfleisch) has long been credited with the invention of printing by moveable metal type, c. 1453. Contemporaneous attempts to invent printing were under way elsewhere in Europe. It had been invented centuries earlier in China, but it was only in sixteenth-century Europe, in the wake of Gutenberg's "invention," that the technology had momentous intellectual and sociopolitical consequences. Printing made the wide dissemination of Renaissance and Reformation writings possible. Gutenberg's career was initially financed by loans from Johann Fust (or Faust), a banker. They produced the forty-two-line Latin Bible (c. 1453–1456) together. By 1455 their partnership was over, but Gutenberg went on to produce another Bible, letters of indulgence, and a vocabulary called the *Catholicon* (c. 1460).

E. M. Eisenstein, *The Printing Press as an Agent of Change* (1979); D. C. McMurtrie, *The Life and Work of Johann Gutenberg* (1940); R. Barnes et al., eds., *Books Have Their Own Destiny* (1998).

RODERICK MARTIN

Guyon, Madame (1648–1717), French mystic and quietist. Upon her husband's death in 1676, Madame Guyon entered a life of devotion, inspired by the quietist works of Miguel Molinos. She attained influence in France by impressing Francois Fénelon and, through him, Madame de Maintenon, Louis XIV's wife. She taught that while God is incomprehensible, mystical union with him is possible through self-mortification and contemplation. Such mystical union would require complete indifference not only to the world but also to the church's teachings. Through Bossuet's efforts, the teachings of Madame Guyon and Molinos were declared heretical by the French church in 1695. For Bossuet, the visions and voices of Joan of Arc were genuine, but those of Madame Guyon were not. She was arrested and released in 1702 only after submitting to correction by the church. Her influence waned, and she lost even Fénelon's support in 1705.

P. Ward, "Madame Guyon," in *The Pietist Theologians*, ed. C. Lindberg (2004).

RODERICK MARTIN

Hadewijch of Brabant (thirteenth cent.), learned Beguine mystic from Flanders. Her vernacular writings include a variety of genres and are noted for their focus on the ways God loves and on the human response. Few biographical details survive, but according to her own account, her visions occurred early in life. References to classical Christian texts, including Scripture, and the use of courtly motifs in her writing are evidence of a noble education. Her oeuvre consists of poems, letters, and the *Book of Visions*, probably written in the 1240s, which appears to have been intended to guide

members of her community in their own mystical experiences. The role of love (*Minne*) in the encounters between herself and the divine is a central theme, and she adapts secular love poetry for its exploration. Encounters with Christ as her Divine Bridegroom and reflections on his life as the map for union with God are also prominent in her work. Hadewijch cites the privileged immediacy of her revelations in asserting her spiritual authority, a daring claim at a time when the sacramental authority of the clergy was being increasingly asserted. Her writings did not circulate widely in the thirteenth century but today are recognized for anticipating Meister Eckhart's understanding of mystical union.

Hadewijch of Brabant, *Hadewijch: The Complete Works*, trans. M. C. Hart (1980); B. McGinn, *The Flowering of Mysticism* (1998); E. A. Petroff, "Gender, Knowledge, and Power in Hadewijch's *Strofische Gedichten*," in *Body and Soul: Essays on Medieval Women and Mysticism* (1994), 182–202.

ADRIENNE NOCK AMBROSE

Hadrian (117–138), Roman emperor. Tied by kinship, tutelage, and marriage to Trajan (98–117), Hadrian was acclaimed in Cilicia amid uncertainties provoked by Trajan's death. Hadrian dealt swiftly with opposition to his promotion and, already experienced in military and political affairs, proved a diligent emperor and administrator. He tempered Trajan's aggressive foreign policy, abandoning recently annexed territories, restoring the Euphrates as Rome's eastern frontier, and constructing defense works in Germany and Africa as well as Hadrian's Wall in Britain. He toured the provinces regularly, frequenting cities and military camps. A proponent of Greek culture, Hadrian practiced and patronized the arts. He built lavishly in Rome (e.g., the Pantheon), Italy (e.g., Tivoli), and the provinces (e.g., Athens). His decisions to refound Jerusalem as Colonia Aelia Capitolina and to ban circumcision apparently sparked Judea's Bar Kokhba revolt (132–135), with whose suppression rabbinic activity definitively shifted north to Galilee. Tertullian thought Hadrian not unfriendly to Christianity (*Apol.* 5.7), while Justin Martyr preserves a Hadrianic law, of debated authenticity, ordering that Christians be tried for actual crimes (not merely for profession of the name) and that calumnious informers be punished (*1 Apol.* 68; cf. Eusebius, *Hist. eccl.* 9).

H. Benario, *A Commentary on the Vita Hadriani* in *Historia Augusta* (1980); A. Birley, *Hadrian: The Restless Emperor* (1997); M. Boatwright, *Hadrian and the City of Rome* (1987); Boatwright, *Hadrian and the Cities of the Roman Empire* (2000).

DENNIS E. TROUT

Hagenau Conference Called by Emperor Charles V at Speyer in June 1540 with the intent to settle differences between Catholics and Protestants that had festered since the Augsburg Confession a decade earlier. The plague caused the meeting to be moved to Hagenau. When Charles sought to serve as mediator, the Protestant princes of the Schmalkaldic League demanded Scripture alone as their authority. The critical issue was the nature of the church. Present among the Protestants were Johannes Brenz, Martin Bucer, Wolfgang Capito, John Calvin, Caspar Cruciger, Justus Menius, Oswald Myconius, Andreas Osiander, Johannes Pistorius, and Urbanus Rhegius. Philip Melanchthon could not attend because of illness, and Martin Luther was not allowed to go out of concern for his safety. The emperor sent his brother, Ferdinand, along with a papal representative. The papal legate (Morone) also attended, but only as an aid to the Catholic delegation made up of Johannes Cochlaeus, Johannes Eck, Peter Faber, and Friedrich Nausea. The Catholic contingent wanted to proceed beyond the Augsburg Confession, claiming the controversial issues had been resolved. The Protestants rejected that assertion, requesting a full and free discussion of their beliefs. The meeting ended on July 28, 1540, with no resolution, except a plan to meet later that year in Worms.

G. Müller, ed., *Die Religionsgespräche der Reformationszeit* (1980).

TIMOTHY MASCHKE

Hagia Sophia (Gk. "Holy Wisdom") The term "sophia" is used in the Pauline epistles as an appellation of Christ. In the Old Testament, especially in the eighth chapter of Proverbs, it is used as a personification of God and—by Christian interpreters—as a foreshadowing of Christ. In particular, it is the memorial name of the Great Church at Constantinople (now Istanbul). The present edifice was built during the reign of Justinian I by Anthemius of Tralles and Isidore of Miletus between 532 and 537. It was consecrated by Patriarch Menas on December 27, 537. It is an outstanding example of Byzantine architecture and is a transitional type of the domed basilica. Its massive dome is supported by four huge piers. Its four arches are connected by four pendentives. The apices of the arches and the pendentives support the circular base that holds the main dome. The dome has a band of forty single-arched windows that illuminate the interior and create a sense of infinite space. Additional light comes from the twelve large windows in the tympana of the north and south arches above the arched aisle and gallery colonnades. In addition to the large dome, which has a circumference of almost 33 meters at a height of 62 meters above the floor, there are two half-domes opening east and west. These, along with smaller conchs of the bays at the four corners of the nave and the huge external north and south buttresses, act to counter the thrust of the great dome. Cross vaults cover the inner and outer narthexes, while two roofed inclined ramps to the north and south of the inner narthex give access to the galleries. Because of the clever architectural means employed to mask the dome's bearing structure, one gets the impression that it is free-floating in space. From 1204 on, Hagia Sophia began a serious decline from ill treatment at the hands of Western crusaders. The final blow came on May 29, 1453, when Sultan Mehmet and his army captured Constantinople and, shortly thereafter, directed that the Great Church be converted into his imperial mosque. In response to the Islamic prohibition of images, the church's many mosaics were either covered or eradicated. The surviving mosaics were uncovered during restoration work in 1847–1849 and were restored during the twentieth century. Hagia Sophia, now officially called Ayasofya Muzesi, has been a museum since 1935.

G. Downey, "The Name of the Church of St. Sophia of Constantinople," *HTR* 52 (1959): 37–42; G. Florovsky, "The Hagia Sophia Churches," in *Aspects of Church History*, vol. 4 of *The Collected Works* (1987), 131–35; L. J. James, "Byzantine Aesthetics, Light, and Two Structures," *St. Vladimir's Theological Quarterly* 29 (1985): 201–19; R. J. Mainstone, *Hagia Sophia: Architecture, Structure, and Liturgy of Justinian's Great Church* (1988); R. Mark and A. S. Gakmak, eds., *The Hagia Sophia: From the Age of Justinian to the Present* (1992); J. Meyendorff, "Wisdom-Sophia: Contrasting Approaches to a Complex Theme," *Dumbarton*

Oaks Papers 41 (1987): 391–401; E. H. Swift, *Hagia Sophia* (1940); T. Whittemore, *The Mosaics of St. Sophia at Istanbul*, 4 vols. (1933–1952); E. Yucel, *Hagia Sophia* (2003).

MICHAEL D. PETERSON

Hagiography   The term refers to Christian literature that pertains to saints and to the modern study of saints. Stories of saints were one of the most common forms of writing from late antiquity through the Middle Ages. Varieties of hagiography include saints' Lives (*vitae*), miracle stories, lists of holy persons according to the dates of their festivals, vision stories, and tales of the translation of holy relics. Hagiography can be found in sermons, liturgical texts, histories, and other kinds of clerical writing. Medieval Christians believed that saints were holy persons who had ascended to heaven upon their death. The very composition of a text that extolled the holy virtue of an individual was an important criterion for regarding that person a saint. Throughout the early Middle Ages bishops commonly promoted the cults of local saints, and it often was they who commissioned the composition of saints' Lives. By the thirteenth century the papacy had secured full authority over the canonization process in Western Christendom.

Hagiography is not to be equated with biography. Whereas a biographer focuses upon a person's distinctive traits, hagiographers (writers of saints' Lives) generally attempt to portray their subject bearing virtues, and performing deeds and miracles, that were thought common among all holy persons and not unique to the individual. As a consequence of such stylization, saints' Lives can seem to the modern reader rather repetitive. Additionally, hagiographers often did not restrict their writing to factual material. Their intent was not to offer historical material but to provide a model for living the Christian life. One who produced a *vita* expected faithful readers of the text (and listeners, since saints' Lives often were intended for reading aloud in churches and monasteries, especially during saints' festivals) to seek to emulate the holy figure. Despite much that is conventional, one finds great variety among the details within particular hagiographies, in the kinds of person being portrayed, in the different subgenres of hagiographic literature, and in the purposes for which different accounts were commissioned. An investigation of hagiography over time also reveals changing interpretations for sanctity itself.

The earliest form of hagiography was writings about the martyrs. Probably the oldest surviving authentic story of Christian martyrdom is that of Polycarp, bishop of Smyrna. Polycarp was burned at the stake c. 155. The account's inclusion of the fact that friends gathered the bodily remains is evidence for Polycarp's immediate reverence as a saint.

Constantine's conversion to Christianity in 312 helped effectively end the age of persecution for orthodox Christians. Increasingly, they considered sanctity to rest among persons who lived a distinctive lifestyle for Christ. First among the famous confessors were hermits and monks who practiced extreme asceticism, braved privation, and confronted demons in the solitudes of the Egyptian and Syrian deserts. Bishop Athanasius of Alexandria wrote a most influential text, the *Life of Saint Anthony of Egypt* (c. 360). This *vita*, quickly translated from Greek into Latin, played an important role in the transmission of monasticism to Western Europe.

Late antiquity was the great age for the proliferation of saints, their cults, and hagiography. During the fourth through eighth centuries bishops and monks especially were touted as saints, as were many nuns. Around 394 the Gallic aristocrat Sulpicius Severus was so taken by the holiness of Martin, a bishop of Tours who had not relinquished his ascetic tendencies, that he wrote the *Life of Saint Martin* three years before the bishop's death. This *vita* provided a template for much subsequent Western hagiography.

Perhaps the most prolific hagiographer of the early Middle Ages was Gregory of Tours (d. 594). His output attests to the great variety within the genre. His book *On the Miracles of the Bishop Saint Martin*, consists primarily of a catalog of posthumous miracles occurring at the saint's tomb. The *Life of the Fathers* is a compendium of twenty *vitae* proper, three of which promote the holiness of Gregory's own relations. *The Glory of the Confessors* contains brief anecdotes of miracles performed by more than a hundred saints, most from Gaul. Gregory's hagiography was intended to reveal that his Gaul continued to participate in salvific history.

About 20 percent of medieval saints' lives pertain to women, especially founders of convents and abbesses. A saintly acquaintance of Gregory of Tours was Queen Radegund (d. 589), who abandoned her husband and established a nunnery at Poitiers where she lived out her life. Not long after Venantius Fortunatus had written a first *Life of St. Radegund*, Baudonivia wrote a second one more appropriate for the edification of her fellow nuns.

The vitality of the High Middle Ages is reflected in an even greater variety of subjects for the hagiography of the age. From the twelfth century devout women of the Low Countries began to pursue spiritually fulfilling lives beyond the convent. The notable priest (and eventual bishop) Jacques de Vitry wrote a *vita* about Mary of Oignies (d. 1213) in order to promote the novel Beguine cause.

Around 1260 Jacobus de Voragine composed his famous compilation, *The Golden Legend*. Part of the work's popularity owed to the fact that many of Jacobus's legends indeed bordered on the mythological. Also popular in the late Middle Ages were fantastical accounts such as those about the giant, St. Christopher, noted for bearing the infant Christ over a river. Texts such as *The Golden Legend* were the subject of ridicule by Renaissance humanists and subsequent Protestant reformers. In the early seventeenth century, John Bolland gathered a group of Jesuits who applied a critical method to hagiography to distinguish fact from fiction. The Bollandists' effort can be said to mark the beginning of modern scholarship in hagiography. While many remained suspicious of saint's Lives until the mid-twentieth century, today's scholars recognize the study of hagiography as integral for an understanding of Christian mentalities. See also *Medieval Saints' Lives*.

———

D. Attwater, *The Penguin Dictionary of Saints* (1965); H. Delehaye, *The Legends of the Saints* (1961); T. J. Heffernan, *Sacred Biography: Saints and Their Biographers in the Middle Ages* (1988); M. Stouck, *Medieval Saints: A Reader* (1999).

ALLEN E. JONES

Haimo of Auxerre (c. 810–c. 870), monk,

perhaps of Spanish heritage, in the monastery of St. Germanus in Auxerre (France) and later abbot of a nearby monastery at Cessy-les-Bois. Haimo was one of the most original biblical scholars of the Carolingian age. In a genre that encouraged creative compilation of texts from the patristic age, Haimo's exegesis was characterized by personal reflection on the biblical text. He wrote at least seventeen commentaries on biblical books, including interpretations of Ezekiel and Isaiah, books rarely tackled by medieval exegetes. Haimo's exegesis was characterized by grammatical analysis of the text and concern for the life of monks. Haimo also wove ancient history into his comments and related biblical history to contemporary ninth-century society. The commentary on Ezekiel offers a scathing indictment of the Carolingian church from a monastic perspective. His comments on the three orders (clergy, warriors,

peasants) also reflect his concern for social structure. Haimo wrote sermons for monks and may have compiled a précis of early church history. Heiric of Auxerre (841–c. 875), Haimo's only known pupil, preserved in his *Scolia quaestionum* a record of Haimo's pedagogy.

———

J. J. Contreni, "'By Lions, Bishops Are Meant; by Wolves, Priests': History, Exegesis, and the Carolingian Church in Haimo of Auxerre's *Commentary on Ezechiel*," *Francia* 29, no. 1 (2003): 1–28.

JOHN J. CONTRENI

Half-Way Covenant This term refers to

a practice that resulted from controversy over admission to baptism in the congregational churches of colonial New England. In most early congregations of Massachusetts and Connecticut, full membership was granted only to those "visible saints" who had undergone an experience of conversion and "owned" the church covenant, and only they could have their children baptized. This was ratified by the Cambridge Synod of 1648, though not without opposition. Increasingly there were many who had been baptized as infants but had never qualified for church membership, yet they wanted their children baptized; many ministers favored this so that a larger community would be included in the nurture and discipline of the churches. In the 1650s, some congregations adopted such a wider baptismal practice. A synod of laymen and ministers meeting in Boston in 1662 approved this extension of baptism to the children of nonmembers if they lived uprightly and accepted the covenant of their congregation. These persons were not, however, admitted to the Lord's Supper. Opponents rejected the change as an unwarranted departure from earlier practice and later derisively dubbed it the Half-Way Covenant. Many congregations in Massachusetts and Connecticut long failed to implement the policy of the "Half-Way Synod," and there were many local conflicts over it. Where adopted, it was a step in the direction of a more inclusive church.

———

S. Foster, *The Long Argument* (1991); E. S. Morgan, *Visible Saints* (1963); R. G. Pope, *The Half-Way Covenant* (1969); W. Walker, *The Creeds and Platforms of Congregationalism* (1893, 1960).

DEWEY D. WALLACE JR.

Haller, Berchtold (1492–1536), reformer

of Bern, Switzerland. Born near Rottweil, he

attended the Univ. of Cologne. He moved to Bern in 1513 to teach, in 1519 became preacher at the Münster, and was ordained in 1520. Haller was heavily influenced by Huldrych Zwingli, whom he first met in 1521. Evangelical preaching began in Bern in the early 1520s, but the Council kept the canton officially Roman Catholic. At times, Haller was isolated in his support of reforms. He quit saying mass in 1525. At the Baden Disputation (1526) he opposed Johannes Eck's efforts to consolidate opposition to reform. The Bern Council ordered that a disputation occur in January 1528 to determine the nature and extent of reforms. The ten theses issued by Haller and Franz Kolb for this "Bern Disputation" reflect dependence on Zwinglian ideas. The Bern reform accordingly resembled Zurich's. In 1532 Haller cooperated with Capito to write a new order for the church of Bern (*Berner Synodus*). Haller corresponded with Bullinger on questions of how to deal with Anabaptists.

B. J. Wayne. "Church, State, and Dissent: The Crisis of the Swiss Reformation, 1531–1536," *CH* 57 (1988): 135–52; D. L. Hendricks, "The Bern Disputation: Some Observations," *Zwingliana* 14, no. 10 (1978): 565–75.

MARY JANE HAEMIG

Hamilton, Patrick (c. 1504–1528), the

"first martyr of the Scottish Reformation." Studying at Paris and Louvain, Hamilton came under the influence of Luther's theology and Erasmus's humanism. When he returned to Scotland, he became associated with John Major. Hamilton professed open sympathy with Lutheran ideas, and Archbishop James Beaton charged him with heresy, whereupon Hamilton fled to the Continent, eventually arriving in Wittenberg, where he visited Luther and Melanchthon in 1527. During his visit he also visited Marburg's newly established university, where Reformation doctrines were being taught. He again returned to Scotland, where Beaton caught up with him; Hamilton was burned at the stake February 29, 1528. His conviction for heresy was based on Hamilton's violations of the 1525 ban on the importing of Lutheran literature into Scotland. His only surviving work is his *Loci communes*, also known as *Patrick's Places*, a Lutheran reflection on faith and good works, published originally in Marburg in 1527.

I. B. Cowan, *The Scottish Reformation: The Church and Society in Sixteenth-Century Scot-*

land (1982); J. E. McGoldrick, *Luther's Scottish Connection* (1989).

ALDEN R. LUDLOW

Hampton Court Conference Called

by James I of England in 1604, this conference of English bishops and Puritan leaders met in January to address ecclesiastical reforms. The prominent Puritan representative John Rainolds, dean of Lincoln, debated with Archbishops Bancroft and Bilson. Rainolds and the Puritans presented the Millenary Petition, demanding reforms to the liturgy and discipline of the Church of England. James reportedly responded, "No bishop, no king," effectively supporting the bishops. Minor concessions were made to the Puritans, and James promised changes to the Book of Common Prayer and a new Bible translation. The translation, delivered in 1611, became known as the Authorized, or King James, Version.

P. Collinson, "The Jacobean Religious Settlement: The Hampton Court Conference," in *Before the English Civil War*, ed. H. Tomlinson (1983).

ALDEN R. LUDLOW

Hardenberg, Albert (c. 1510–1574),

Dutch-born reformer active in the Low Countries and in Germany, notable for his involvement in Bremen's eucharistic controversies. Educated by the Brethren of the Common Life in Groningen, Hardenberg went on to study at universities in Louvain and in Mainz, where he received his doctorate (1539) and met the noted reformer Jean à Lasco. Returning to Louvain, he was arrested for espousing Reformation theology and organizing dissent, but he managed to negotiate his release with a fine. Hardenberg moved to Wittenberg (1543/1544), where he studied with and befriended Philip Melanchthon. After a number of pastoral and advisory positions that included travels to southern Germany and Switzerland, Hardenberg took a post as cathedral preacher in Bremen (1547). Here his independent eucharistic theology, which integrates aspects of Melanchthon, Calvin, and Bucer, drew fire from Lutheran colleagues and embroiled him in a decadelong controversy. Despite Hardenberg's popularity, the dispute ended with his dismissal in 1561 after he refused to sign the Augsburg Confession. In later years, Hardenberg found a home in Reformed circles, spending the final seven years of his life as a pastor in Emden.

W. Janse, *Albert Hardenberg als Theologe: Profil eines Bucer-Schülers* (1994).

KENNETH G. APPOLD

Hätzer, Ludwig

Hätzer, Ludwig (c. 1500–1529), Swiss mystic and translator. Hätzer studied at Univ. of Basel from 1517 to 1518. He was drawn by Zwingli's reform movement to settle in Zurich in 1523 and quickly became a leading advocate of reform, publishing an attack on images that same year. In the fall of 1524, he associated with the radicals who had begun to attack infant baptism. Because he was not rebaptized when the other radicals introduced adult believer's baptism in January 1525, the Zurich authorities treated him somewhat more leniently. After expulsion from Zurich, Hätzer went to Augsburg, where he was also expelled. He found a temporary haven in Basel in 1525, where he worked closely with Oecolampadius. After more time in Zurich and a stay in Strasbourg, he made his way to Worms in 1527, where he encountered Hans Denck.

This relationship led to a lasting contribution to biblical scholarship, namely, the translation of the Hebrew prophets that Hätzer had begun in Zurich. Their translation, which appeared anonymously in Worms in 1527, was the first Protestant translation of those biblical books and it saw no fewer than twelve printings by 1529. After travels throughout southern Germany, he came again to Constance in 1528, where he was imprisoned by the city authorities at the request of the city council of Augsburg, which had charged him with adultery but was more concerned with his unorthodox theology. Convicted, Hätzer was beheaded in 1529.

J. F. G. Goeters, *Ludwig Hätzer c. 1500 bis 1529: Spiritualist und Antitrinitarer* (1957); S. Ozment, *Mysticism and Dissent* (1973).

D. JONATHAN GRIESER

Healing, Religious

Healing, Religious The basic types of healing correspond to the various types of sickness that afflict the human person as a whole: physical (disease or injury), moral or spiritual (especially sin), and psychological (a category of which Christians became more acutely aware in the twentieth century). From the perspective of ancient Christians, sickness was intertwined with diabolic activity, such that healing and exorcism, or deliverance from demonic power, could be seen as one and the same thing. Both played prominent roles in Jesus' ministry (e.g., Matt. 8:16; Mark 1:34) and in that of his disciples (e.g., Mark 6:13; Luke 9:1). Deliverance, physical healing, and spiritual healing were effected by the same ritual means: laying on of hands, anointing with oil, and uttering Christ's name, accompanied by faith and prayer and preceded by fasting. Deliverance and healing could be the function of a charismatic gift (1 Cor. 12:9) or of a ritual entrusted to presbyters (Jas. 5:14–15). Until the ninth century, lay Christians also anointed their sick, often using oil blessed by the bishop according to a formula such as that found in the Hippolytan *Apostolic Tradition*. The effectiveness and accessibility of Christian healing was a key factor in the spread of Christianity, although ancient writers avoided centralizing such miraculous occurrences within Christian experience. Since apostolic times miraculous cures have been associated with saints' relics, including body parts or objects that touched their bodies (Acts 19:12). Miracles of healing have been the marks of and an expectation from those honored as saints. They are also associated with holy places and apparitions, a good example being the volume of reported healings that have taken place at Lourdes. Nonetheless, local churches which deny that such miracles take place after biblical times have not been lacking. The practice of caring for the sick with ordinary means is a perennial witness of Christian charity and has often taken the form of institutionalized health care services organized by parishes, regional faith communities, or religious orders.

Catholics call penance and anointing of the sick the "sacraments of healing." In the Middle Ages they were administered together with the Eucharist (then called *viaticum*, connoting food for the journey) as the "last rites" for those near the point of death. By the twelfth century, anointing was exclusively administered to the dying; this circumstance, added to the fact that it was the last sacrament of healing to be administered, is why "extreme unction," a title first used by Peter Lombard, became its common name. There was a corresponding shift in emphasis from physical healing to spiritual healing. Luther, and especially Calvin, severely criticized the value of smearing with "oil, not the sick, but half-dead corpses." Included in the first Book of Common Prayer (1549), a rite of visiting and anointing the sick was left out of subsequent editions from 1552 until the twentieth century, when it reappeared in several regional (or national) versions of the book. The Second Vatican Council encouraged "anointing of the sick" for those gravely ill and aged, not only for those in immediate danger of death. This change was made in deference to the stress on the possibility of actual physical healing that was evident in ancient Christian practice. In the East from the eleventh to the thirteenth centuries, the liturgical service of anointing the sick, often called the *euchelaion*, or "prayer of oil," developed. One of the most lengthy and complex rites in the Euchologion (the main Byzantine liturgical book), it involved seven priests and obviously was not intended for those in immediate danger of death. In current practice the rite is often abbreviated and celebrated by fewer priests, or even one.

"Spiritual healing" usually designates attempts to combine psychological and physiological treatments with prayer and ritual in order to effect cures of the whole person. It plays a prominent role in Pentecostal and charismatic groups.

———

H. Avalos, *Health Care and the Rise of Christianity* (1999); R. J. S. Barrett-Lennard, *Christian Healing after the New Testament* (1994); A. Cuschieri, *Anointing of the Sick: A Theological and Canonical Study* (1993); J. T. Carroll, "Salvation and Healing in the New Testament Gospels," *Interpretation* 29, no. 2 (1995): 130–42; M. T. Kelsey, *Healing and Christianity* (1973); M. J. O'Connell, trans., *Temple of the Holy Spirit: Sickness and Death of the Christian in the Liturgy* (1983).

DANIEL G. VAN SLYKE

Heidelberg Catechism Among Reformation catechisms, the Heidelberg Catechism (1563) is second in influence only to Luther's Small Catechism. Commissioned by Elector Frederick III of the Palatinate, it offered a moderate Calvinism to attract his Lutheran subjects. Its authors, Caspar Olevianus (1536–1587), pastor of the main church in Heidelberg, and Zacharius Ursinus (1534–1583), professor of theology at the university, were students of Calvin and Melanchthon. Its 129 questions were divided into fifty-two parts to facilitate Sunday preaching. These were grouped into three sections: human misery, redemption, and gratitude. Human misery dealt with humankind's sinful predicament in the inability to do good and being under God's wrath. Redemption covered the Apostles' Creed and the sacraments. Gratitude covered the Ten Commandments and the Lord's Prayer. Worship and good works are done out of gratitude to God. Missing from the catechism is Calvin's

doctrine of predestination, but its doctrines on Christ and the sacraments are his. Christ's human nature is in heaven, and he is present on earth only in his divine nature and the Holy Spirit. Baptism is God's pledge to wash us with the blood of Christ and the Holy Spirit. Eating Christ's body means believing in him and receiving the forgiveness of sins. For children, baptism is a sign of the covenant to which they belong with their parents. The Heidelberg Catechism is still widely used among Reformed churches in Germany and America.

———

M. A. Noll, *Confessions and Catechisms of the Reformation* (1991).

DAVID P. SCAER

Helena (d. 329), mother of Emperor Constantine and a Christian pilgrim. Little is certain about Helena's life prior to 306 when Constantine was proclaimed emperor. Of humble origin, she may have been legally married to Constantius Chlorus, Constantine's father, although he left her to contract a politically advantageous marriage to Theodora, the stepdaughter of Maximian.

Constantine, who made Helena "Augusta," glorified his mother's position as a means of securing the legitimacy of his own. Her journey to the eastern provinces, including Palestine, in 327 and 328, which Eusebius (*Hist. eccl.* 3.42–47) attributes to her devotion, was likely made to consolidate her son's power. Constantine was undertaking an aggressive program of Christianization in the East, which included the construction of churches, the unification of dogma, and the devaluation of non-Christians and non-Christian cultic sites.

Helena was exceedingly generous with treasury gifts to the poor, the cities, and the soldiers of the Roman army. Although she did help forge a link between the government of Rome and the Christian faith, she is better remembered because of a late fourth-century legend that claimed she had been guided by heaven to the discovery of the cross of Jesus Christ in rubble beneath a status of Venus.

———

J. W. Drijvers, *Helena Augusta: The Mother of Constantine the Great and the Legend of Her Finding of the True Cross* (1992).

BARBARA J. MACHAFFIE

Heliand ("Savior") The first epic in German literature, this poem consists of almost six thousand verses in Old Saxon. Writing c. 830, the unknown author based the story of Christ's life loosely on Tatian's *Diatessaron*, a hybrid version of the Gospels. The poet also knew Latin biblical commentaries and vernacular German traditions. In its complexity, originality, and artistry, *Heliand* complements *Beowulf*. The poet worked in the generation after the Franks defeated the Saxons and forcibly converted them to Christianity following a century of brutal conflict. The poet aimed to introduce Christ to the Saxons in terms they could appreciate and to bolster their new faith. The poem's language and images prove that the poet knew and cherished Saxon culture. Rather than simply transcribing in the vernacular a biblical or Roman and Mediterranean Christianity for the Saxons, he blended basic Christianity with Saxon culture to produce a "Saxon Savior" or a "North Sea Gospel." The sea, rivers, and beaches provide essential background. James and John's boat is described as a "well-nailed" northern craft. Fate is omnipresent. Christ appears as a chieftain and generous mead giver, his disciples as Thanes. The popular poem's new image of Christ resonated with medieval feudal culture.

G. R. Murphy, SJ, *The Saxon Savior: The Transformation of the Gospel in the Ninth-Century Heliand* (1989).

JOHN J. CONTRENI

Hellenization
In the early Christian world charges abounded that one's opponent was dependent on Greek philosophy (frequently Aristotle) rather than on the Christian faith or Scripture. Similar charges may be found in medieval authors and in the Reformation (where frequently Plato is the philosopher detected). Within modern classical and archaeological scholarship the term "hellenization" has also been used to describe the process whereby Greek culture became dominant around the Mediterranean, particularly after the conquests of Alexander the Great.

Within the study of early Christianity, however, "hellenization" refers to a nineteenth-century thesis associated particularly with the German historian and theologian Adolf von Harnack. Harnack argued that the break of the earliest Christians with the Jewish community and the inherent universal appeal of the Christian gospel drew the early Christians to recognize the gospel's natural home in the cultural and philosophical world shaped by Hellenism. The adoption of this new "home" radically conditioned the way Christians used and interpreted their Jewish and OT heritage. Harnack

did not see this process as a simple passive falling of the church into Greek hands; rather, it was the result of the active nature of the Christian mind and community searching for ways to articulate its universal message. In many ways Harnack saw this shift as positive; for example, the adoption from Greek philosophy of the idea of the Logos gave the gospel a new coherence and revealed that Christianity might have a philosophical and universal form. Harnack understood the production of Christian dogma as a result of hellenization but also as a stage through which Christianity has had to pass as awareness of its universal character has grown. The existence of dogma both reflects the philosophical universality of Christianity and, at the same time, easily becomes part of a hierarchical ritualistic system of superstition. Indeed, Harnack saw Gnosticism as itself a form of acute hellenization: even though its mythical and ritualist systems (systems that abandoned the OT) were rejected, they are recapitulated within Catholicism. With this last sentence it becomes clear that Harnack's account is highly teleological: the culmination of the process of hellenization in its best sense is reached with the work of the liberal Protestant theologian who is able to penetrate to the core of the gospel in its universal character and move beyond the need for dogma.

While aspects of this understanding of hellenization are still repeated, the theory as a whole has been increasingly discredited in recent scholarship. First, although Harnack rightly saw the spread of Greek culture subsequent to Alexander the Great's conquests as the beginning of hellenization, and although he saw this influence as already present in the Judaism of Jesus' time and in the NT, he operated with a strongly essentialist notion of "Jewishness." For Harnack, the thought-world of Hellenism could never truly intermingle with Judaism as such. This picture of the nature of cultural interaction and of Jewish thought in particular is no longer sustainable. Second, the complex evolution of early Christian dogma has been the subject of much study in recent decades. Increasing realization that those developments were both continually exegetical and yet involved the constant piecemeal adoption of ideas from a variety of non-Christian traditions has rendered very problematic any one grand narrative about the quality of the shifts that occurred, especially a narrative inattentive to the continuing centrality of the scriptural texts and imagery in Christian thought. Third, the teleology of Harnack's account has come under much suspicion. Nineteenth-century suspicion of a simple Enlightenment agenda such as Harnack's already raised questions about his account, and recent postmodern critiques and attempts at Christian *ressourcement* have only increased the suspicion that his account too directly serves the purpose of promoting a form of Christianity with few connections to the classical faith of Christians.

D. Martin, "Paul and the Judaism/Hellenism Dichotomy: Toward a Social History of the Question," in *Paul beyond the Judaism/Hellenism Divide*, ed. T. Engberg-Pedersen (2001), 29–61; W. V. Rowe, "Adolf von Harnack and the Concept of Hellenization," in *Hellenization Revisited*, ed. W. Hellman (1994), 69–98; A. von Harnack, *The History of Dogma*, vol. 4 (1958).

LEWIS AYRES

Heloise (c. 1100–1164), abbess. Raised at the monastery of Argenteuil and educated in the arts by her uncle, Fulbert, canon of Notre Dame, Paris, Heloise had a strong knowledge of classical authors. She was later taught by Peter Abelard, with whom she fell in love. After the birth of their son Astrolabe and subsequent marriage, Abelard was castrated (1117). She entered Argenteuil and later became prioress. When this monastery was taken over by Suger of St. Denis (1129) the convent moved to the Paraclete, founded by Abelard, where she became prioress and abbess (1135). She posed questions to Abelard concerning religious life (*Problemata*) and wrote a letter to Peter the Venerable after Abelard's death. She was also in friendly contact with Bernard of Clairvaux.

The authenticity of the letters she exchanged with Abelard was long disputed but is now generally accepted. Heloise continued to regard Abelard as her "only love," while displaying her high intellectual stature by her writing style. A second collection of 113 letters copied in the fifteenth century as *Letters of Two Lovers* also seems to be authentic.

Ep. 167 in *Letters of Peter the Venerable*, ed. G. Constable (1967); C. Mews, *Abelard and Heloise* (2004); C. Mews and N. Chiavaroli, *The Lost Love Letters* (2001); J. T. Muckle, ed., *Mediaeval Studies*, vol. 15 and vol. 17 (1953, 1955); *Problemata*, in PL 178 (1855), 677–730; B. Radice, trans., *The Letters of Abelard and Heloise* (1974); J. Verger, *L'amour castré* (1996); B. Wheeler, ed.,

Heloise (1999); B. Wheeler, ed., *Listening to Heloise* (2000).

RALF M. W. STAMMBERGER

Helvetic Confessions The First Helvetic Confession, the earliest common Reformed confession of faith, was adopted on February 4, 1536, in Basel by delegates from the Swiss Reformed churches. Not only did it encourage unity among the Swiss churches, but it also provided a model for more extensive confessions of faith. One of its principal authors was Heinrich Bullinger of Zurich.

Twenty-five years later, while severely ill, Bullinger crafted a personal confession of faith. Having survived his illness, Bullinger showed the confession to others, including Peter Martyr Vermigli, who endorsed it. In 1565 Bullinger sent Frederick III, elector of the Palatinate, a copy of the confession, which Frederick used to defend his own orthodoxy. Published in 1566, it soon came to be known as the Second Helvetic Confession.

The Second Helvetic Confession was the first comprehensive declaration of the Reformed faith. It was Bullinger's most important bequest to the Reformed churches. Except for the Heidelberg Catechism, it was the most authoritative and widely accepted Reformed creed of the sixteenth century. The confession was first accepted by the Swiss Reformed cantons and the Palatinate. Geneva only agreed to the confession after Bullinger, at the insistence of Theodore Beza, revised the wording of the article on predestination to reflect more closely the Calvinist understanding of the doctrine. It was also later approved by the Reformed churches of Scotland (1566), Hungary (1567), France (1571), and Poland (1571 and 1578), and it was well received in Holland and England. It was translated into nine languages, including Magyar, Polish, and Arabic.

E. Koch, *Die Theologie der Confessio Helvetica Posterior* (1968); J. Rogers, *Presbyterian Creeds: A Guide to the Book of Confessions* (1992); P. Schaff, *Creeds of Christendom*, vol. 1 (6th ed., 1990); J. Staedtke, ed., *Glauben und Bekennen: Vierhundert Jahre Confessio Helvetica Posterior* (1966).

J. WAYNE BAKER

Helvidius (fourth cent.), Roman theologian. Reacting to the spread of ascetical ideals in the church at Rome, Helvidius wrote a book addressed to a monk named Carterius. In this work, which is no longer extant, he argued that marriage and celibacy were equally virtuous vocations for Christians. To support his position Helvidius appealed to the example of Mary the mother of Jesus. While Mary remained a virgin at Jesus' conception, Helvidius maintained, she and her husband Joseph lived a normal married life after Jesus' birth. Together they are the parents of the "brothers" of Jesus mentioned in the Gospels. In addition to his arguments from Scripture, Helvidius also cited previous authors in the Christian tradition, such as Tertullian, who held similar views. Helvidius was the object of a bitter polemic by Jerome in 383. Ambrose, likewise, responded to his ideas, though he never mentioned Helvidius by name. According to Augustine, in the early fifth century a sect of *Helvidiani* survived that followed the teaching of Helvidius.

———

Jerome, *De perpetua virginitate b. Mariae adversus Helvidium*, in PL 23 (1845), 193–216; D. G. Hunter, "Helvidius, Jovinian, and the Virginity of Mary in Late Fourth-Century Rome," *JECS* 1 (1993): 47–71; G. Jouassard, "La personalité d'Helvidius," in *Mélanges J. Saunier* (1944), 139–56; C. W. Neumann, *The Virgin Mary in the Work of Saint Ambrose* (1962), 181–204; G. Rocca, *L'Adversus Helvidium di san Girolamo nel contesto della letterartura ascetico-mariana del secolo IV* (1998).

DAVID G. HUNTER

Hemmingsen, Niels (1513–1600), Danish theologian. Hemmingsen, the son of a peasant, was educated in Roskilde, Lund, and finally Wittenberg, where he studied with Melanchthon. As a pastor in Copenhagen and a professor of Greek, dialectics, exegetics, and eventually theology, Hemmingsen became a leader at the Univ. of Copenhagen and in Scandinavian theology during the sixteenth century, attracting attention beyond Denmark. His influence continued even after his suspension in 1579 over his view of the Lord's Supper. Although he initially adhered to the Augsburg Confession in regard to the Lord's Supper— drafting a statement with his colleagues to that effect—he eventually moved from a Philippist to an openly Calvinist view of the Lord's Supper. He contributed significantly to the rejection of the Formula of Concord as a confessional text in Denmark. Trained in biblical humanism and scholastic theology and deeply influenced by the views and methods of Melanchthon, with whom he corresponded for years, Hemmingsen wrote groundbreaking works in theology (*Enchridion theologicum*), homiletics (*Evan-*

geliepostil), and pastoral theology (*Pastor*), all of which became textbooks in their fields.

———

E. M. Madsen, *Niels Hemmingsens Etik: En idehistorisk Studie* (1946); T. R. Skarsten, "The Reaction in Scandinavia to the Formula of Concord," in *Discord, Dialogue, and Concord*, ed. L. W. Spitz and W. Lohff (1977).

KIRSI STJERNA

Henoticon This policy statement of the Byzantine emperor Zeno was issued in 482. Most of the clergy, monks, and faithful in the eastern Roman Empire rejected as heretical the formulation of the person of Christ by the Council of Chalcedon (451). After subduing the revolt of the usurper Basiliscus (475–476), who had courted dissident groups in Syria and Egypt by renouncing the Chalcedonian decree, Zeno sought an imperial policy that would allow for an understanding of Christ more congenial to anti-Chalcedonians without explicitly disowning Chalcedon. In a letter to the faithful of Egypt of 482, apparently drafted by Patriarch Acacius of Constantinople and known afterward as the *Henoticon*, or "formula of unity," Zeno professed his concern to maintain the orthodox tradition as set forth by the councils of Nicaea (325), Constantinople (381), and Ephesus (431). He repeated earlier condemnations of Nestorius and Eutyches and recognized as normative the Christology of Cyril of Alexandria. Insisting that the faith accepted by the imperial government had never changed, he added, "Everyone who has held or holds any other opinion, either at the present or at some other time, whether at Chalcedon or in any synod whatever, we anathematize." The statement remained the basis of a kind of church unity in the Greek-speaking world for thirty-seven years but was regarded in the West as deficient. As a result, Rome broke communion with Constantinople from 483 to 519, a rupture known as the "Acacian schism."

———

Evagrius, *Church History* 3.14; E. Schwartz, ed., *Codex Vaticanus 1431: Eine antichalkedonische Sammlung aus der Zeit Kaiser Zenos* (1927), 52–54; W. H. C. Frend, *The Rise of the Monophysite Movement* (1972), 169–83; A. Grillmeier, *Christ in Christian Tradition* 2/1 (1987), 247–317.

BRIAN E. DALEY, SJ

Henry IV of France (1553–1610), also known as "Henry of Navarre," leader of the French Protestants during the Wars of Religion.

He was the son of Jeanne d'Albret, queen of Navarre and a devout Protestant, and Antoine de Bourbon, first prince in line for the French throne. Henry's religious allegiance shifted back and forth between Protestantism and Catholicism, depending on his context. While living at the Valois court he became Catholic (1562), but he reconverted to Protestantism after leaving the court (1567). An excellent cavalryman and tactician, Henry became king of Navarre (1572). In August 1572 Henry married Marguerite of Valois, the daughter of Catherine de Médicis, queen mother of France. After the wedding in Paris and the ensuing St. Bartholomew's Day Massacre (August 24, 1572), Henry was forcibly reconverted to Catholicism. After leaving the court he again renounced Catholicism (1576). Upon the assassination of Henry III (1589), he became king of France, inaugurating the Bourbon dynasty that ruled in the nineteenth century except for the years 1792–1814. Unable to overcome the resistance of Paris and other major cities to the idea of a Protestant king, Henry again converted to Catholicism in 1593. He thereby secured his throne, and in time he sought to placate French Protestants, most notably by the Edict of Nantes (1598), which granted them a number of garrisoned towns in southwestern France. A pragmatic ruler, Henry sought to develop the nation, renew the French Catholic Church, and provide safety for the Protestants in order to prevent the return of religious conflicts and promote the well-being of the kingdom.

D. Buisseret, *Henry IV* (1984, repr. 1992); M. Greengrass, *France in the Age of Henry IV: The Struggle for Stability* (2nd ed., 1995).

JEANNINE E. OLSON

Henry VIII (1491–1547), king of England (1503–1547) and controversial founder of the Church of England. Henry, the second son of the first Tudor monarch, Henry VII, was engaged to his brother Arthur's widow, Catherine of Aragon, daughter of Ferdinand and Isabella of Spain, in order to maintain an alliance with Spain. Henry married her shortly after his accession to the throne.

By 1525 it was clear that Catherine would have no more children beyond their surviving child, Mary Tudor. Henry, obsessed with the notion that England would never accept a woman ruler, appealed through Cardinal Thomas Wolsey to Pope Clement VII for an annulment and permission to remarry. Catherine opposed the divorce as did her powerful

nephew, Charles V, king of Spain and Holy Roman Emperor.

As the case dragged on, the king dismissed Wolsey and summoned the "Reformation Parliament" (1529–1536). Guided by his new chief minister, Thomas Cromwell, Parliament repudiated papal power over England and declared Henry and his successors to be "the only Supreme Head on earth of the Church of England." Those who defied the will of the king, including Lord Chancellor Thomas More, were executed. In 1539 Parliament, at the king's behest, passed the Six Articles, which reaffirmed traditional Catholic doctrines.

In 1533 Henry's new archbishop of Canterbury, Thomas Cranmer, granted Henry's divorce from Catherine and ratified his marriage to Anne Boleyn, who gave birth to a second daughter, Elizabeth (r. 1558–1603). Anne was soon replaced by another lady of the court, Jane Seymour. Seymour died shortly after giving birth in 1536 to Henry's only legitimate son. Henry married three more times but never embraced Protestantism. The flowering of English Protestantism began with the reign of his son, Edward VI (1553–1558). Almost every aspect of Henry VIII's life and career remains the subject of enormous debate among historians.

———

K. Lindsey, *Divorced, Beheaded, Survived: A Feminist Reinterpretation of the Wives of Henry VIII* (1995); R. Rex, *Henry VIII and the English Reformation* (1993); J. Scarisbrick, *Henry VIII* (1968); D. Starkey, *The Reign of Henry VIII: Personalities and Politics* (1985).

JONATHAN W. ZOPHY

Henry of Ghent (c. 1217–1293), a scholastic theologian in the Augustinian tradition. Henry was born in Ghent and pursued his early studies at the cathedral school of Tournai, where he became a canon of the cathedral in 1267. He was named an archdeacon at Bruges in 1276 and at Tournai in 1278. In 1276, he became a master of theology at the Univ. of Paris and was one of the most influential theologians at Paris until he retired in 1292. Called the "Solemn Doctor," his strongest works are his *Summa quaestionum ordinariarum* (*A Summa of Ordinary Questions*) and his fifteen *Quodlibeta* (his formal responses to questions posed arbitrarily by his university audiences). He died in Tournai.

In his early days at Paris, Henry was a strong participant in the theologians' efforts to control the influence of the Arabic philosopher Averroes's interpretation of Aristotle. These efforts resulted in the condemnation of 219 propositions at Paris in 1277 by Bishop Etienne Tempier. Among the condemned statements: (1) There is no more excellent state than to study philosophy. (2) The only wise men in the world are the philosophers. (3) In order to have some certitude about any conclusion, one must base oneself on self-evident principles. (4) One should not be content with authority to have certitude about any question. This was the intellectual challenge theologians such as Henry had to face when students from the arts faculty at Paris, which had become an Aristotelian philosophy faculty, came to the study of theology.

In dealing with this challenge of philosophy, Henry did not ignore Aristotle's teachings but confronted them. Thomas Aquinas tried to use Aristotle's model of a subalternated science (such as optics, which borrows principles of geometry on the authority of the geometrician and uses them to arrive at scientific conclusions) to show how the study of sacred doctrine is science. Henry criticized Thomas's position in a detailed examination of Aristotle's teachings. He argued that none of the instances of Aristotle's subaltern sciences is truly parallel to theology. And if theology does not fit into the Aristotelian theory of science, then Aristotle's theory is not ample enough and the theologian should not force Christian revelation into its limited framework. Henry likewise criticized his other contemporary at Paris, Godfrey of Fontaines. Godfrey argued that theology is not a science because science is based on evidence. Henry responded that in every other faculty, teachers praise their discipline; it is only in a theology faculty that masters criticize their own discipline in order to elevate the status of philosophy. Henry pointed to the theological activity carried out by Augustine, Gregory the Great, Hugh of St.-Victor, and Bonaventure as models to be imitated, embracing the Augustinian rather than the Aristotelian view of science.

Henry's *Summa of Ordinary Questions* is his equivalent to Thomas's *Summa of Theology*. Yet this work is not an explicit attempt to cover all the themes of theology. It is an enormous treatise dealing with the triune God, for Henry the most important teaching of the Christian faith. However, throughout this work Henry indirectly covers almost every aspect of Christian doctrine, always emphasizing the relation of doctrine to the Trinitarian center of Christian belief.

———

Henry of Ghent, *Summa quaestionum ordinariarum* (1520, repr. 1953); Henry, *Quodlibeta* (1518, repr. 1961); Henricus de Gandavo, *Opera omnia* (1979–); R. J. Teske, *Quodlibetal*

Questions on Free Will (1993); R. Macken, H. de Gand, *Maître en théologie à l'Université de Paris, archdiacre de l'évêché de Tournai* (2002); S. P. Marrone, *Truth and Scientific Knowledge in the Thought of Henry of Ghent* (1985); G. Guldentops and C. Steel, *Henry of Ghent and the Transformation of Scholastic Thought* (2003); J. C. Flores, *Henry of Ghent: Metaphysics and the Trinity* (2006).

STEPHEN F. BROWN

Herbert, Edward (1583–1648), first baron of Cherbury, active in English diplomatic and military life under James I and Charles I. A soldier of fortune, he worked as Charles's ambassador to France to arrange a marriage between the king and Henrietta Maria. In the civil war he attended the king but resisted his summons. He surrendered the castle given him by the king to parliamentary forces in 1644. As a religious philosopher, he stood at the dawn of rationalism. He combined psychology with a method of investigating the truth and a certain understanding of natural religion. This approach appeared in *De veritate*. Herbert was a Deist, as is evident in his history of religion, *De religione Gentilium*. He believed that God has implanted truth in the mind and hence human beings need no special revelation to guide their behavior. His position is summarized in five ideas: belief in a supreme being, worship of him, a virtuous life as the best form of worship, repentance for misdeeds, and rewards in the afterlife based on behavior. These can be found in institutionalized religions throughout the world.

———

E. Herbert, *The Life of Edward, Lord Herbert of Cherbury* (1764); Herbert, *Pagan Religion*, ed. J. A. Butler (1996).

DAVID P. SCAER

Heresy in Early and Medieval Christianity

Heresy is a conscious deviation from an established and publicly formulated teaching of the church or, since the Great Schism of the eleventh century and the Reformation of the sixteenth, of the churches. Heresy must be distinguished from heterodoxy, a deviation from a widely accepted, but not yet established, teaching. Most in the earliest Christian community believed that the gospel should go only to Jews. The apostle Paul held a heterodox view for which he was reviled, but later generations of Christians believed that Paul's view was the work of the Holy Spirit. The Docetists believed that Jesus did not have a body but only seemed (Gk. *dokeō*) to have one, a heterodox view at the time. They were seeking to defend the divine Son of God from fleshly corruptibility. Unlike Paul's views, theirs did not win communal acceptance and were considered heretical by later generations.

Authority was the great problem Christianity faced in the second century. In mid-century, Marcion of Pontus, who was offended by materiality, argued that the God of Scripture (at that time the Greek version of the Old Testament) had acted wrongly in creating a material world and proclaiming it good. Somewhat later, Montanus claimed authority from the Holy Spirit and launched the New Prophecy, or Montanism. In light of these challenges, Christians needed criteria for making judgments. Irenaeus of Lyon (c. 130–c. 200) argued that Christians should base their views on the reliable authorities of Scripture and tradition. As Scripture, Irenaeus cited not only the OT but also Christian books such as the Gospels and Pauline epistles. Irenaeus saw tradition (Scripture interpreted through the rule of faith by the bishops) as something organic, a living connection from the apostolic age to his own. Every generation added to tradition. Irenaeus carried the day, and theologians continue to cite support for their views in the Scriptures and in previous Christian thinkers.

The third and fourth centuries saw general, although not yet final, acceptance of the NT canon, a standard from which one could not deviate and still claim to be a Christian. Yet Christians still debated how to interpret Scripture. Many local churches also drew up creeds or professions of their basic beliefs. As monarchical bishops came to dominate local church structures, they too became sources of authority.

In 325 the First Ecumenical Council met at Nicaea to deal with Arianism. Only bishops voted at Nicaea, and they tried to base their arguments on Scripture but eventually felt the need to employ a nonscriptural term, *homoousios* ("same substance"), to refute Arius. Ecumenical councils came to be sources of authority, deviation from which was heresy, a view accepted in the Middle Ages when a hierarchical church was the norm and "heresy" extended to even minor deviations from church teachings. Since the Reformation, many churches no longer accept ecumenical councils as sources of authority, while other churches restrict the number of valid councils to the first four, that is, those before the medieval period. Both these groups of churches insist upon the primacy and sufficiency of Scripture. Roman Catholicism considers all of its councils to be authoritative, and Eastern Orthodoxy accepts the first seven councils, from Nicaea I to Nicaea II in 787. A limitation of the emphasis on tradition is that it has often left Christians in succeeding centuries unable to deal with new realities. For example, when Copernican astronomy and Darwinian evolution challenged the accepted literalist interpretation of Scripture, a static view of tradition caused those Christians who initially accepted these scientific advances to be considered heretics.

In the Middle Ages when churchmen enjoyed great wealth and power, heresies were often social or national, dealing with the role the church should play in society. For example, the French Cathars of the twelfth and thirteenth centuries censored the lifestyles of aristocratic bishops and led lives of rigid poverty, while in the fifteenth century the Bohemian patriot Jan Hus wanted to liberate his people from the imperialist dominance of Western European churchmen. Both Cathars and Hus were condemned as heretics. Many modern Christians feel uncomfortable with the term "heresy," but every church assumes the right to define its teachings and to repudiate divergence.

———

R. P. C. Hanson, *The Search for the Christian Doctrine of God* (1988); A. J. Hultgren, *The Rise of Normative Christianity* (1994); A. J. Hultgren and S. Haggmark, eds., *The Earliest Christian Heretics* (1996); F. Young, *The Making of Creeds* (1991).

JOSEPH F. KELLY

Hermann of Wied (1477–1552), elector and archbishop of Cologne, supporter of the Protestant Reformation. He was chosen early on for ecclesiastical office and became archbishop in 1515. He supported Charles V in the imperial election of 1519, and after the Diet of Worms (1521) he actively suppressed the followers of Luther. However, as a result of influence by Erasmians, starting in 1536 he moved increasingly closer to Protestantism. Noted for his piety but not his intellect, he relied on advisors such as John Gropper and Philip Melanchthon. The city council and the majority of his subject peoples opposed him. The anticipated support of the Schmalkald League failed to materialize, and he was deposed in 1546. Afterward, Cologne became an important center for the Counter-Reformation. He died a Lutheran.

———

A. Franzen, *Bischof und Reformation: Erzbischof Hermann von Wied in Köln vor der*

Entscheidung zwischen Reform und Reformation (1971).

GREGORY J. MILLER

Hermas The narrator of the *Shepherd of Hermas*, a second-century text from the area of Rome. Though the figure may be a literary creation, suggestions of his identity range from the apostle Paul (see Acts 14:12), to the Hermas of Rome mentioned in Romans 16:14 (so Origen), to the brother of Bishop Pius of Rome (c. 141–154) as identified by the Muratorian Canon. Dates for the text have ranged accordingly from the 70s until the earliest mention of the work by Irenaeus (c. 175).

The *Shepherd of Hermas* itself contains three types of literature: prophetic visions, ethical exhortations, and extended parables. From the outset, Hermas tells of his life as a freedman in Rome who encounters the reality of the church through the figure of a woman in successive scenes. In this process Hermas gains instruction from a divine shepherd about the nature of the spirit of God, an ethical lifestyle, and the need to reform his view of life according to Christian virtues.

It is difficult to determine whether the final text comes from a single author or, more likely, is the product of various literary traditions that have been edited together. Mention of the name of Clement (8.3), if a reference to Clement of Rome, may place at least a portion of the text at the end of the first century. In either case, the text was well received and widely used among early churches, and it found its way into the work of authors from Clement of Alexandria to Eusebius of Caesarea to Jerome.

C. Osiek, *Shepherd of Hermas* (1999); L. Pernveden, *The Concept of the Church in the Shepherd of Hermas* (1966); G. F. Snyder, *The Shepherd of Hermas* (1968); J. C. Wilson, *Toward a Reassessment of the Shepherd of Hermas* (1993).

CLAYTON N. JEFFORD

Hermits of St. Augustine The order of the Hermits of St. Augustine belongs to the larger movement of mendicant orders. It arose from a merger of several eremitical and radically reform-oriented groups in northern Italy (Tuscany). To establish control and discipline Innocent IV in 1244 directed these groups and ascetic individuals to accept the rule of St. Augustine and to found communities of Augustinian religious. In 1256 Pope Alexander IV again forced these eremitical groups into one mendicant order, which became widely dispersed in the cities of Western Europe.

After 150 years of expansion the need for reform occurred, and several observant congregations were locally established. The Wittenberg reformation was initiated by Martin Luther (1483–1546), who belonged to the observant congregation of Saxony. Several members of his communities in Erfurt and Wittenberg supported the evangelical movement, and some became the first Protestant martyrs in the early sixteenth century. Effects of the Reformation and the secularization of later times, especially in early nineteenth-century France, affected the order considerably. Numbering nearly thirty thousand members in the late fifteenth century, the number of friars declined to less than three thousand by 1977, notably working in Europe, the Americas, and the Philippines.

It is still a matter of discussion whether the Augustinian Hermits developed a unique "Augustinian" theology. A group of famous members in the late Middle Ages belonging to the *via antiqua* (see *Nominalism*) proposed a clear Thomistic branch of scholastic theology that provoked the theory of a close connection to Dominican theology. Another group of Augustinian friars (e.g., Gregory of Rimini, d. 1358) returned the anti-Pelagian writings of Augustine to the fore. It is still debated whether this latter trend attracted Luther and others. Still belonging to the old faith, members of the "Augustinian" school within the order (e.g., Girolamo Seripando, d. 1563) became quite influential at the Council of Trent. After 1600, theologians of the order concentrated their interests in pastoral care and the establishment of new provinces in the colonies of Latin America and Asia. After Trent new reform movements were established, which for a long time remained subject to the jurisdiction of the prior-general of the Augustinian Hermits, until they became independent orders during the twentieth century.

N. Teeuwen et al., *Bibliographie historique de l'ordre de saint Augustin 1945–1975*, in *Augustiniana* 26 (1976), 39–340; T. Kolde, *Die deutsche Augustiner-Kongregation und Johann von Staupitz* (1879); R. Arbesmann, *Die Augustiner in Deutschland* (1934); D. A. Perini, .*Bibliographia Augustiniana*, 4 vols. (1929–1937); A. Kunzelmann, *Geschichte der deutschen Augustinerremiten*, 7 vols. (1969–1976); E. Gindele et al., *Bibliographie zur Geschichte und Theologie des Augustiner-Eremitenordens* (1977); D. Gutiérrez, *Los*

Agustinos, 3 vols. (1971, 1977, 1980; ET 1979, 1983, 1984); I. R. Rodrígues, ed., *Agustinos en America y Filipinas* (1990).

MARKUS WRIEDT

Hesshus, Tilemann (1527–1588), Lutheran theologian, controversial figure following Luther's death. For his unyielding Lutheran stance, especially in opposing Calvinism and laxity in practice, he was expelled from many positions, including court preacher in Neuberg, professor in Rostock, Heidelberg, Jena, and Helmstedt, superintendent in Goslar, and bishop of Samland. He led Lutheran opposition to the Calvinists in the Palatinate and removed some from their posts in Neuberg. In defining Christ's presence in the Lord's Supper, he insisted that the words "in" and "with" were essential, but he made no use of Luther's understanding of the ubiquity of Christ's human nature. In the synergistic and adiaphoristic controversies, he took the side of Flacius against the Philippists, who had become dominant in Wittenberg. Later he opposed Flacius's view that sin was part of human substance and not an accident. As professor in Helmstedt, he kept Brunswick from accepting the Formula of Concord. In a book on the office of the ministry, he argued that obedience to the pastoral office was a mark of the church. He was firmly committed to his beliefs, but his narrowness in some cases tragically made him unnecessarily combative.

———

D. C. Steinmetz, "Calvin and His Lutheran Critics," *LQ* (1990): 179–94.

DAVID P. SCAER

Hesychasm This term comes from the Greek word relating to quiet or rest. It is a monastic contemplative tradition of inner quietness most frequently centered on the perpetual use of the Jesus Prayer ("Lord Jesus Christ, Son of God, have mercy on me, a sinner"). At its pinnacle in the fourteenth century, it was practiced and developed in particular by the monks of Mount Athos. The ultimate goal of the hesychast is to achieve communion with God, while the more immediate task is to achieve prayer of the heart by uniting heart and mind. Through spiritual discipline and grace the hesychast may achieve an encounter with the divine light that surrounded Christ at his transfiguration on Mount Tabor. Gregory Palamas defined this spiritual condition as participation in God's uncreated energies (as distinguished from his essence).

The hesychastic tradition can be traced back to the desert fathers, in which context "hesychast" is often synonymous with a hermit or anchorite in the process of desert retreat. The words "hesychia" and "hesychast" appear frequently in fourth- and fifth-century monastic and patristic literature, especially of Gregory of Nyssa, Evagrius Ponticus, and the homilies associated with St. Macarius of Egypt. The fifth-century *One Hundred Chapters of Spiritual Perfection* by Diadochos, bishop of Photike in Epiros, is an example of an important early work involving hesychastic prayer. St. Catherine's Monastery in Mount Sinai was a particularly influential center of hesychasm, in large part because of John of Climacus's *Heavenly Ladder*. John, who had been abbot of St. Catherine's, composed his work in the seventh century as a handbook to guide monks through the virtues and pitfalls of the spiritual life. It contains many echoes of *The Sayings of the Fathers*, a compilation of the sayings of the desert monks living in Egypt, Syria, and Palestine in the fourth to the sixth centuries. Other important writers on hesychasm from the seventh to the tenth centuries include Maximus the Confessor and Symeon the New Theologian.

Hesychasm received its fullest treatment in the fourteenth-century monastic writings of Gregory of Sinai, Nicephorus of Mount Athos, and—most importantly—Gregory Palamas. The essential texts on hesychasm and the Jesus Prayer are included in the *Philocalia*, compiled in the eighteenth century by Macarius Notarus and Nicodemus of the Holy Mountain. From the fourteenth to fifteenth centuries in Byzantium the term "hesychasm" implied both the narrower sense of the monastic movement at Athos, whose main defender was Palamas, and the broader meaning of political, social, and religious movements involving hesychasts. In late Byzantium, there is record of physical exercises—consciously controlled aspiration, head bowed, eyes focused on the chest—attached to hesychastic prayer and intended to enhance concentration. These physical exercises must be understood as no more than supplementary tools to the crucial task of contemplative prayer.

———

L. Gillet, *The Jesus Prayer* (1987); Gregory Palamas, *The Triads* (1983); J.-Y. Leloup, *Being Still: Reflections on a Forgotten Mystical Tradition* (2003); G. A. Maloney, *Russian Hesychasm: The Spirituality of Nil Sorskij* (1973); J. Meyendorff, *Byzantine Hesychasm: Historical, Theological, and Social Problems:*

Collected Studies (1974); K. Ware, "The Hesy-
chasts: Gregory of Sinai, Gregory Palamas,
Nicolas Cabasilas," and "The Hesychast
Renaissance," in *The Study of Spirituality*, ed.
C. Jones, G. Wainwright, and E. Yarnold
(1986), 242–58.

MICHAEL D. PETERSON

Hilary (c. 401–449), bishop of Arles. Born to
a noble family, Hilary was converted to the
ascetic life by his older contemporary and relative Honoratus, founder of the monastery of
Lérins. Around 420 Hilary became a monk of
Lérins, then followed his mentor to Arles in
Gaul, where Honoratus became bishop for the
last few years of his life. Hilary succeeded
Honoratus as bishop c. 430 and presided over
regional episcopal councils at Riez (439),
Orange (441), and Vaison (442). In 444, exercising his role as metropolitan of Gaul, he
deposed a bishop, who then appealed to the
pope, Leo I, who in turn deprived Arles of
metropolitan status. Over vigorous opposition
from Hilary and his fellow bishops, including
a face-to-face appeal, Leo obtained from the
emperor Valentinian III a decree ceding jurisdiction over Gaul to the bishop of Rome. Gennadius (*On Illustrious Men* 70) notes that
Hilary wrote "few things." His Life attributes
to him several works, including homilies, letters, and an explanation of the creed. He is the
author of the *Life of St. Honoratus*, no doubt
delivered upon the death of his predecessor.

O. Chadwick, "Euladius of Arles," *JTS* 46
(1945): 248–80; R. W. Mathisen, "Hilarius,
Germanus, and Lupus: The Aristocratic Background of the Chelidonius Affair," *Phoenix* 33
(1979): 160–69.

THOMAS A. SMITH

Hilary (c. 300–367), bishop of Poitiers.
From a few autobiographical allusions, we
know only that Hilary converted from paganism to Christianity in his adult years. The
beginning of Hilary's episcopate is usually
placed c. 350, coinciding with the emergence
of anti-Nicene domination of religious politics
in the West.

Hilary's *Commentary on Matthew*, his
earliest known work, recalls the thought-world
of Tertullian, Novatian, and Cyprian and
shows little sign of the Trinitarian controversies that would later characterize his career. For
reasons that are still not clear, Hilary was
arraigned before a local council in Béziers
(Biterrae) in 356 where, he later said, false

charges were brought against him and he was
banished to Asia Minor. Just before Béziers,
Hilary claimed, he first heard the Nicene Creed
recited.

During his four-year exile, Hilary gained
much insight into the dynamics of those theological tensions which divided East and West.
In a diplomatic letter (*On the Synods*) written
to his episcopal brethren in the West, Hilary
sought to establish harmony between Eastern
and Western notions of orthodoxy. He stated
that *homoiousios* ("similar in essence") can be
faithfully interpreted so as to be compatible
with the Nicene watchword *homoousios*
("same in essence"), although the latter must
not harbor modalist applications, which had
been the ongoing cause of Eastern suspicions
of Western theology.

Hilary seems to have attended the Eastern
council of Seleucia in 359. In Constantinople
he sought unsuccessfully to block the official
ratification of the Homoian creed promulgated
at Ariminum and Seleucia. Sometime during
the first half of 360, he returned to Poitiers
without imperial permission. From there he
vigorously opposed Constantius II as an enemy
of the true faith.

Now back in the West, Hilary published
scriptural commentaries and at least three
polemical works: a dossier of creedal and epistolary documents, now in fragmentary form,
which served to implicate two leading
Homoian bishops, Valens and Ursacius, with
doctrinal duplicity and heretical intentions; a
document accusing Auxentius, the Homoian
bishop of Milan (355–374), of Arianism; and a
composition in twelve books, the so-called *On
the Trinity*. In this last work, most of which was
written in the East, Hilary argued that the Son
is ontologically equal to the Father: they share
the same divine substance and have the same
divine attributes. The Son, as always begotten,
is also truly distinct in origin from the unbegotten Father. As in *On the Synods*, Hilary
charted a middle course between the extremes
of subordinationism and modalism. To refute
the "Arian" argument that the passion of the
incarnate Son was proof of his inferior divinity, Hilary argued that Christ's body, while feeling the impact of suffering, felt no pain because
his soul, of divine origin, was unaffected by the
consciousness of suffering. Some scholars have
seen in this view a christological docetism.

P. Burns, *Hilary of Poitiers' Commentary on
Matthew* (1967); Burns, "Hilary of Poitiers'
Road to Béziers: Politics or Religion?" *JECS* 2

(1994): 273–89; D. H. Williams, "A Reassessment of the Early Career and Exile of Hilary of Poitiers," *JEH* 42 (1991): 212–17; Williams, "The Anti-Arian Campaigns of Hilary of Poitiers and the 'Liber Contra Auxentium,'" *CH* 61 (1992): 7–22; P. Smulders, *Hilary of Poitiers' Preface to His "Opus Historicum"* (1995).

D. H. WILLIAMS

Hildegard of Bingen (1098–1179),

abbess, scholar, musician, and mystic. Wielding extraordinary spiritual authority during a turbulent period in the medieval church, the visionary Hildegard of Bingen also served as the founding abbess of two convents and wrote voluminously on subjects from cosmology to medicine. Her most famous work, *Scivias*, transcribes and interprets twenty-six visions she had experienced beginning in childhood; its understanding of Christian life and dynamic images of the divine were embraced by church officials eager for a fresh affirmation of orthodoxy, and the work was endorsed by Pope Eugene III. *The Life of St. Hildegard*, begun before her death as part of an ultimately unsuccessful campaign for canonization, is the most complete source for her biography. The youngest of ten children and of noble birth, Hildegard received no formal education and was pledged to religious life at age eight. Her young adulthood was spent under the tutelage of the celebrated ascetic Jutta of Sponheim. Their cell, attached to a newly reformed Benedictine monastery, gradually expanded to house an elite community of observant women, which in turn formed the nucleus for Hildegard's new monastery at Mount St. Rupert. A smaller house at Eibingen followed. From her dual abbatial post, Hildegard composed liturgical music and dramas for the sisters, corresponded with prominent Christians including protégé Elisabeth of Schönau and abbot Bernard of Clairvaux. She was frequently consulted for her prophetic gifts by powerful leaders, including Emperor Frederick Barbarossa. Committed to Benedictine ideals and alarmed by widespread corruption in the church, Hildegard boldly urged reform. She admonished negligent church leaders of every rank both in letters and in person, and warned clerical and lay audiences in apocalyptic sermons. Her writings, including *Scivias*, *Book of Life's Merits*, *Book of Divine Works*, and a vast correspondence, develop a unique theological language that employs light imagery as well as organic and musical metaphors. Paintings, possibly under-

taken by Hildegard herself, accompany two early manuscripts and convey the visual nature of her revelations. Even in the context of a contemporary increase in women's participation in institutionalized religious life, Hildegard remains exceptional for her accomplishments and influence. Despite frequent and debilitating illnesses, possibly including optical migraines, Hildegard was active until her death at age eighty-one.

B. Newman, ed., *Voice of the Living Light: Hildegard of Bingen and Her World* (1998); S. Flanagan, *Hildegard of Bingen, 1098–1179: A Visionary Life* (1989).

ADRIENNE NOCK AMBROSE

Hincmar of Reims (c. 806–882), one of

the most prominent members of the Frankish clergy in the second half of the ninth century. The descendant of a Frankish noble family, he was educated in the royal monastery of St. Denis, near Paris, and at the court of Emperor Louis the Pious. Louis' son, Charles the Bald, called him into permanent service in 840 and appointed him archbishop of the west Frankish metropolis Reims in 845, from where Ebbo, an intimate of Louis the Pious, had been deposed in 835 and again in 841. Doubts over his appointment remained, and several examinations were undertaken by papal order (Nicholas I) until 866, especially by demand of clergy whom Ebbo had ordained and who consequently had been deposed. In the end Hincmar was able to maintain his see. The circumstances of his beginning are significant for his whole career: Hincmar worked at the very center of government, but in a position of permanent self-defense. Most of his works derive from debates in which he was personally involved or to which he contributed, such as his dossier against Emperor Lothar's divorce and marriage to Theutberga. His most important contribution to dogmatic matters are the result of the debate about the Trinity and predestination, in which he defended the concept of free will against the view of Gottschalk of Orbais. Hincmar had a considerable impact on church matters and the development of canon law, especially with regard to ecclesiastical property, ecclesiastical discipline (*Capitula episcoporum*), and the defense of archiepiscopal authority regarding suffragans. The deposal of Rothad of Soissons and his conflict with his nephew Hincmar of Laon caused major conflicts, especially with Pope Nicholas I, who restricted the right of episcopal deposition to the apostolic see. The case of Laon contributed substantially to one of the most audacious forgeries in church history, the "Pseudo-Isidorian Decretals." Hincmar remained throughout his entire reign a critical supporter of King Charles the Bald. He organized the resistance of the west Frankish episcopate against the invasion of King Louis "the German" and supported Charles's policy to gain hegemony over Lotharingia, yet he remained reserved toward the kings' Italian and imperial aspirations.

C. Chazelle, "Archbishops Ebo and Hincmar of Reims and the Utrecht Psalter," *Speculum* 72 (1997): 1055–79; J. Devisse, *Hincmar, Archevêque de Reims, 845–882*, 3 vols., in *Travaux d'histoire ethico-politique*, vol. 29 (1975–1976); Hincmar, *De divortio Lotharii Regis et Theutberga reginae*, ed. L. Böhringer, MGH Concilia 4, suppl. 1 (1992); *Epistolae karolini aevi* 6/1, ed. E. Perels, MGH Epistolae 8/1 (1985); *De ordine palatii*, ed. and trans. T. Gross, R. Schieffer, MGH Fontes iuris Germanici 3 (1980); *Collectio de ecclesiis et capellis*, ed. M. Stratmann, MGH Fontes iuris Germanici 14 (1990); *De cavendis vitiis et virtutibus exercendis*, ed. D. Nachtman, MGH Quellen zur Geistesgeschichte des Mittelalters (1998); M. Stratmann, "Zur Wirkungsgeschichte Hinkmars von Reims," *Francia* 22 (1995): 1–44.

JOHANNES HEIL

Hippolytus (c. 170–235), Roman presbyter, born in the East, later venerated as a martyr. He is known for his involvement in ecclesiastical and Trinitarian controversies. As a rigorist proponent of the purity of the church, Hippolytus had serious disagreements with the more lenient Callistus, bishop of Rome, about readmitting fallen Christians into the church. Although he may have been elected as a rival bishop to Callistus, because monoepiscopacy was a later phenomenon, Hippolytus cannot be regarded as the first antipope. Hippolytus was a Logos theologian, who attributed a distinct existence to the Father and the Son from all eternity, in opposition to Callistus's alleged monarchianism. Representing a minority view in Rome, Hippolytus was accused by Callistus of being a worshiper of two Gods. There are three main lists of Hippolytus's works: Eusebius's *Ecclesiastical History* 6.22, Jerome's *On the Lives of Illustrious Men* 61, and a list on a mutilated statue. Although the corpus is impressive and available in various ancient languages, few works have survived in the original Greek. Furthermore, Hippolytus is increasingly regarded as a mere

coauthor or editor of the most famous works attributed to him: *Refutation of All Heresies*, *Apostolic Tradition*, and *Against Noetus*. The presbyter also wrote several exegetical works, including *The Commentary on Daniel*, some doctrinal expositions, such as *The Antichrist*, a few treatises on chronology, and homilies. Hippolytus's life ended in the mines of Sardinia, but he is buried in a catacomb in Rome, which now bears his name.

A. Brent, *Hippolytus and the Roman Church in the Third Century* (1995); Hippolytus, *Works*, trans. J. H. Macmahon, ANF 5; J. Mansfeld, *Heresiography in Context: Hippolytus' Elenchos as a Source for Greek Philosophy* (1992); C. Osborne, *Rethinking Early Greek Philosophy: Hippolytus of Rome and the Presocratics* (1987); L. E. Phillips et al., eds., *The Apostolic Tradition: A Commentary* (2002); A. Stewart-Sykes, ed., *Hippolytus: On the Apostolic Tradition* (2001).

TARMO TOOM

Historiography, Early Christian The early Christian view of history rejected the cyclical vision of time common in pagan thought and instead drew from Judaism the idea of a progressive movement from a datable creation to an awaited end of days. For Christians, as for Jews, God had acted in history, suffusing historical events with providential significance, and Christians, in addition, saw the dramatic intervention of God on earth as Christ as dividing history into two distinct epochs. While pagan historians had written to commemorate the great deeds of the past and provide moral and political lessons for the future, Christian historians necessarily grappled with the theological import of historical events.

In the first Christian centuries, Christians did not produce their own forms of history but often used history for apologetic or apocalyptic purposes. Pagan charges of the novelty of Christianity, for example, were parried by chronological research that linked Christianity to Judaism and then demonstrated the antiquity of Judaism as compared to Greco-Roman history. This sort of history can be seen as early as the introductory genealogy in the Gospel of Matthew and figures prominently in second- and third-century apologists, such as Tertullian and Hippolytus. The *Chronography* of Sextus Julius Africanus, known only through later sources, chronicled history from creation to 221, synchronizing the birth of Jesus with the cosmic year 5500 as part of an eschatological framework that expected the end time in the seventh millennium. Lactantius's *On the Deaths of the Persecutors* spelled out in gruesome detail the punishments God exacted upon the anti-Christian emperors who preceded Constantine.

The fourth century marked the true birth of Christian history at the hands of Eusebius of Caesarea, who provided models for its two characteristic forms: the chronicle and the church history. Eusebius's *Chronicle* continued the apologetic project of demonstrating the antiquity of Christianity. His *Ecclesiastical History* was more novel. He listed the following as his subjects: apostolic succession, significant people and events in church history, heresy, the divine punishment of the Jews, persecution, martyrdom, and the final victory of Constantine and Christianity. He incorporated official letters and documents into his *History* verbatim, a departure from the elegant paraphrasing employed in classical historiography. Eusebius's works portrayed history as progressive and providential. He had linked the coming of Christ with the rise of the Roman Empire as early as his *Chronicle*; in his later works he argued that Constantine's conversion marked a crucial step in God's plan that united the universal Roman Empire with the universal religion of Christianity.

In the West, Rufinus of Aquileia translated and extended Eusebius's *History* in 402. This Latin version sought to assuage concerns about barbarian raids by demonstrating that Eusebius's triumphalist understanding of history and empire was still valid a century later. Rufinus portrayed the emperor Theodosius I as a new and better Constantine, who had ensured the defeat of paganism and the spread of Christianity throughout the world.

Eusebius's *History* was continued in the East by four Greek historians of the 430s and 440s: Philostorgius, Socrates, Sozomen, and Theodoret. All focused on the struggles over the relationship between the three persons of God that divided the church in the fourth century. These historians included more secular material than Eusebius had, revealing the extent to which imperial and church history had become connected in the Christian empire. This trend reaches its peak in Evagrius, the last of the Greek church historians, who continued his predecessors' work up to 594 and who fully integrated both secular and ecclesiastical material in his work. The histories of Socrates, Sozomen, and Theodoret were translated into Latin under the direction of Cassiodorus in the

sixth century and combined into a "Tripartite History" that was popular in the medieval West.

Jerome translated Eusebius's *Chronicle* into Latin and brought it up to his own day, and in general the *Chronicle* continued to serve as a vehicle for Christian as well as secular history. Prosper of Aquitaine, for example, continued Jerome's work in Latin up to 455, and the Spaniard Hydatius brought Jerome's work up to 468. Hydatius's gloomy account of fifth-century Spain was influenced by his apocalyptic belief that the world would end in May 482.

Orosius's *Seven Books against the Pagans* was a polemical and apologetic work that followed the Eusebian tradition of historical theology. He wrote his work in 418 at the suggestion of Augustine, who sought historical details to rebut pagan accusations that the sack of Rome in 410 had resulted from the suppression of paganism. Orosius explored the parallels between the Babylonian, Carthaginian, Macedonian, and Roman empires, which he identified with the four empires in the book of Daniel and connected by a complex numerological schema. To absolve Christianity of responsibility for recent disorder, he dwelled extensively on the violence and disasters of the Roman past and argued that the world had improved regularly and continually since the coming of Christ and Augustus. He both minimized barbarian invasions and celebrated them as the method by which God would bring non-Romans to Christianity.

Orosius's work met with the disapproval of Augustine, who criticized it obliquely in his *City of God* (426). His doctrine of the two cities rejected both apocalyptic and Eusebian, triumphalist readings of history. Instead, he argued that the Roman state, even in Christian times, was necessarily imperfect in a fallen world. The incarnation provided hope for the individual believer but did not and could not fundamentally change the nature of human society. The tension between Eusebian/Orosian readings of history, which found triumphalist or apocalyptic meaning in human events, and the Augustinian reading, which denied such meaning, continued in the historiography of the medieval West.

G. Chesnut, *The First Christian Histories* (1986); R. M. Grant, *Eusebius as Church Historian* (1980); R. A. Markus, *Saeculum* (1970); S. Mulhlberger, *The 5th Century Chroniclers* (1990); J. Neusner, ed., *The Christian and Judaic Invention of History* (1990); G. J. P. O'Daly, *Augustine's City of God* (1999); D. Rohrbacher, *The Historians of Late Antiq-*

uity (2002); G. W. Trompf, *Early Christian Historiography* (2000).

DAVID ROHRBACHER

Historiography, Medieval For most of the European Middle Ages, the study and writing of history was largely restricted to ecclesiastical circles, and was practiced at several levels. At the simplest, historical writing took the form of annals or chronicles, bare recitals of the most important events in a year. Most monasteries, convents, and cathedrals appear to have kept an annal, a large number of which have survived. For each year, the author would record, in a sentence or two, the most important events, usually emphasizing occurrences of immediate concern to the community, although also including notable regional or even international matters. Thus the annals of the German bishopric of Hildesheim gave pride of place in the 993 entry to the consecration of Bernward as their new bishop, but also recorded under the same year the end of a Slavic rebellion, where the king celebrated Christmas, and that there was a drought in summer and fall, succeeded by heavy snows, disease, and many deaths. Such chronicles were often continued for many generations, religious foundations sometimes borrowing the annals of other houses to fill out their own accounts or to serve as the basis for a new annal.

Of greater interest to modern historians are a number of more extensive chronicles that add colorful detail, sometimes providing paragraphs or even pages of information for each year. Such works are particularly valuable when penned by an author about events in his or her own lifetime. Thus the chronicle of Bishop Thietmar of Merseburg (d. 1018) is our best single source for Germany around the turn of the millennium, and the "Greater Chronicle" of the Benedictine monk Matthew Paris (c. 1200–1259) is invaluable for understanding the mid-thirteenth century.

The case of Matthew Paris, however, is cautionary, because the St. Albans monk was anything but objective, especially in his clear partiality for Frederick II in the emperor's long struggle with the papacy. But it is doubtful that any of Matthew's contemporaries expected objectivity. Rather, the writing of history through the Middle Ages appears to have been regarded as a branch of rhetoric. Annalists were not only selective, but certainly shaded events to reflect their own views. The more extensive chronicles, while still maintaining a year-to-year description of great events, are filled with opinion, the authors often subtle in expressing their own or their communities' point of view. Thus it is unsurprising that the annalist of Quedlinburg (probably a canoness of that house) expressed the greatness of her abbesses and of the Ottonian dynasty that founded the community—and said very little positive about Emperor Henry II, who "stole" some of Quedlinburg's privileges. Other authors wrote to prove a point. For example, Rudolfus, who wrote the "Deeds of the Abbots of St. Trond" (Belgium) in the early twelfth century, was deeply concerned to show his brethren that the monks' own greed and a resulting influx of pilgrims had ruined the community.

A rhetorical, persuasive approach to historiography is particularly strong in the works that modern scholars have labeled "histories" rather than "annals," "chronicles," or "deeds" (although it should be noted that the distinction between the various genres is frequently unclear). In general, the "histories" of the Middle Ages are extended pieces of writing that attempt to tell a whole, self-contained story, often with a high degree of analysis, and often to prove a particular point of the author's. Medieval authors inherited this "high" history, most akin to our modern understanding of the genre, from both the Bible and the Romans. Besides scriptures, medieval historians had above all late antique historians but also a few Roman works such as those of Suetonius to use as models.

These grander historiographical works could take two basic forms: universal histories and particular histories. Universal histories often followed the practice of the fourth-century Christian historian Eusebius in dividing human history into six ages, the sixth of which began with the incarnation of Christ (Christ will come again at the dawn of the seventh age). In their general plan, they tend to stress the unfolding of human salvation. A particularly fine example is the work of the polymath Hermann of Reichenau (1013–1054), whose history created a single narrative of events of the first Christian millennium.

Histories of particular times or events, usually approximately contemporaneous to the author, also relied on ancient exemplars. Certain general rules of practice emerged. There was a concern for accuracy, or at least its appearance. Bede in his *Ecclesiastical History of the English People* (completed in 731) includes transcripts of letters and reports of where he obtained other information, and many historians did the same—admittedly sometimes inventing their "sources" in the process.

Yet it was also expected that good history should have a point, should go beyond what happened to an explanation of why it happened. This goal is especially plain in the great ethno-histories of the early Middle Ages, including Bede's *Ecclesiastical History*, Gregory of Tours' sixth-century *History of the Franks*, and Paul the Deacon's eighth-century *History of the Lombards*. Over the centuries, historical writers wrestled repeatedly to understand historical causation and the implications of events for their own times. Historians like Adhemar of Chabannes (d. 1034), Sigebert of Gembloux (d. 1112), Bishop Otto of Freising (d. 1158), and Christine de Pizan (d. c. 1434), to name just a few, took a stand on contemporary events, while dozens of authors sought to commemorate and understand the crusades. And hundreds of lesser historians, both ecclesiastical and secular, writing in poetry and prose, Latin and the vernacular languages, told the stories of individuals, events, and causes, giving meaning to their own world and preserving the knowledge of medieval people—and how they regarded the past—for future ages.

E. Breisach. *Historiography: Ancient, Medieval, and Modern* (3rd ed., 2007); R. H. Davis and J. M. Wallace-Hadrill, eds., *The Writing of History in the Middle Ages* (1981); L. Kramer and S. Maza, eds., *A Companion to Western Historical Thought* (2002); G. Spiegel, *The Past as Text: The Theory and Practice of Medieval Historiography* (1997).

PHYLLIS G. JESTICE

Historiography, Reformation Eyewitness reports and vivid records of the world-changing Reformation era were quickly disseminated during the sixteenth century through the recently developed printing press. Luther's writings and autobiographical reflections provided powerful fodder for contemporary and future foes and friends. Catholic pamphleteer Johannes Cochlaeus (1479–1552) wrote a *Commentary on the Acts and Writings of M. Luther* that mirrored Philip Melanchthon's deferential biography of Luther but with a decidedly different emphasis and purpose.

Birthed by the Renaissance, humanistic interest in the sources fueled the desire of theologians to reconnect the present with the past. Lutheran theologian Matthias Flacius Illyricus (1520–1575), seeing the benefit of linking Luther's reformation with the early church, coordinated the publication of *Ecclesiastica Historia* (1557–1574), a thirteen-volume sourcebook of primary church documents. Called "the Magdeburg centuries" because it was developed in Magdeburg and arranged by centuries, this encyclopedic work describes doctrinal developments of the church until Luther's reformation. Catholic scholar Caesar Baronius (1538–1607), encouraged by Philip Neri, authored a work rivaling Flacius's opus. His twelve-volume *Annales Ecclesiastici* (1588–1607) surveyed ecclesiastical and papal history until 1198 yet served as a storehouse for future Catholic historical study.

During the rise of rationalism and Pietism, Gottfried Arnold (1666–1714) prepared an *Impartial History of the Church and Heretics* that viewed church history from the perspective of the so-called heretics. A century later, Leopold von Ranke (1795–1886), the father of modern historiography, drew political and theological dimensions together, attempting an "objective" history by utilizing memoirs, letters, diaries and other eyewitness accounts in his *German History of the Reformation Era* (1845–1847), through which he also popularized the term "Counter-Reformation."

Scottish church historian Thomas Lindsay (1843–1914) provided in his *Luther and the German Reformation* (1900) and two-volume *A History of the Reformation* (1906–1907) an ecumenical approach to Reformation history by exploring the universal faith-issues that led to religious revival. As the ecumenical twentieth century proceeded, Catholic historians Joseph Lortz (1887–1975) and Hubert Jedin (1900–1980) presented more tolerant perspectives on Luther's reform and the Council of Trent as churchly activities with ecumenical dimensions.

Theological issues, which excluded broader contexts, dominated Reformation historiography until the middle of the twentieth century, although Ernst Troeltsch (1865–1923) and Karl Holl (1866–1926) viewed the Reformation from sociological perspectives that had cultural as well as religious significance. Roland Bainton (1894–1984), prolific popularizer of Reformation history, introduced the Reformation's "left wing"—Anabaptists, Hutterites, Schwenckfelders, and Socinians. He also addressed a rising feminist concern with a series on women of the Reformation. Both topics continue in contemporary Reformation research. George William's encyclopedic *The Radical Reformation* gave the problematic though popular label "radical" to the same movements Bainton termed "left wing." Since then some scholars speak of "reformations" in the plural, recognizing the multiplicity of reforms that occurred throughout the sixteenth century.

Historiography in the late twentieth century enlarged its purview by adopting the designation "early modern period," a phrase that goes beyond the decades between 1517 and 1555. Renaissance and Reformation studies are grouped together to show continuity with earlier movements that gave rise to early modernity. Heiko Oberman (1930–2001) gave impetus to an expanded understanding of the Reformation—with roots in the Middle Ages and ramifications in the Enlightenment—thus providing a non-confessional perspective on the Reformation.

The anniversary of Luther's birth in 1983 provided a renewed interest in his life and influence. Coupled with this revival, research on his wife, Katharina von Bora, produced several studies on her influential involvement in the Protestant Reformation. Feminist interests have given rise to increased awareness of the impact women have had on the Reformation. Confessionalization, a rather nebulous concept of developing denominational identity creating modern society, became a research focus toward the end of the twentieth century.

At the beginning of the twenty-first century, Reformation scholars influenced by social historians recognize that multiple disciplines increase their understanding of the historical contexts and the effects of the Reformation. Reception of Reformation principles with social and political consequences are being scrutinized in public civil records, church records, sermons, devotional writings, and private letters and diaries. Scholars throughout the world, including China, Korea, and Japan, are studying the impact or appropriation of the Reformation on other institutions as well as the interplay of other institutions on the Reformation from a variety of political, sociological, and cultural perspectives.

A. G. Dickens and J. M. Tonkin, *The Reformation in Historical Thought* (1985); H. J. Hillerbrand, ed., *Historical Dictionary of the Reformation and Counter-Reformation* (2001); C. Lindberg, *The European Reformations* (1996); W. Maltby, ed., *Reformation Europe: A Guide to Research II* (1992); J. O'Malley, ed., *Catholicism in Early Modern History: A Guide to Research* (1988); O'Malley, *Trent and All That* (2000); S. Ozment, ed., *Reformation Europe: A Guide to Research* (1982); A. Pettegree, ed., *The Reformation World* (2000); R. Scribner, *The German Reformation* (1986).

TIMOTHY MASCHKE

Historiography of Early Christianity (Contemporary)

Recent decades have seen an explosion of scholarly interest in the early church. David Brakke points out that modern work in the field has come to be dominated not by the dwindling ranks of "church historians" but by historians, classicists, and others who consider themselves specialists in "late antiquity." Early Christianity is thus most often considered in close comparison with late antique Judaism and varieties of paganism, as in the collection of Richard Valantasis, *Religions of Late Antiquity in Practice* (2001).

A wide variety of critical methods have been brought to the study of the early church. Some scholars, such as Rodney Stark and Peter Brown, have drawn upon modern work in sociology and anthropology to illuminate questions of Christian conversion and sexual renunciation. Modern scholarship emphasizes the existence of a diversity of Christian beliefs from the very beginning and rejects the notion of a "pure" early church challenged by heresy and schism. Drawing in part upon theorists such as Pierre Bourdieu and Michel Foucault, some scholars have therefore investigated the "construction" of orthodoxy and heresy as labels applied after the fact for reasons of power as much as of theology. The indeterminacy of the label "Arian," applied to a wide variety of different theological positions, provides a useful example of this phenomenon.

The theoretical approaches that have become increasingly prevalent in the humanities have influenced the study of early Christianity in numerous ways. The drive to understand texts not as transparent evidence of reality but as rhetorical and self-referential documents informs the work of scholars such as Averil Cameron and Elizabeth Clark. Theoretical approaches to textual interpretation that stress the indeterminacy of texts and their dependence upon particular communities of readers for understanding have also inspired neo-traditionalist, avowedly Christian readings of the church fathers. The work of Christopher Hall, for example, is predicated upon the usefulness of a Christian perspective for the appreciation of patristic exegesis.

Feminist scholarship has increased exponentially in recent years. Feminist approaches have been particularly prevalent in the study of the historical role of women in the early church, the creation of ideologies of gender in early Christian thought, and female martyrdom and asceticism in late antiquity. Future scholarly work in early Christianity will likely continue to emphasize the social and historical environment of the early Christians and to reflect broader trends in the humanities.

M. Barnes and D. Williams, *Arianism after Arius* (1993); D. Brakke, "The Early Church in North America," *CH* 71 (2002): 473–91; P. Brown, *The Body and Society* (1988); A. Cameron, *Christianity and the Rhetoric of Empire* (1991); E. Castelli, "Heteroglossia, Hermeneutics, and History," *JFSR* 10 (1994): 73–98; E. Clark, "The Lady Vanishes: Dilemmas of a Feminist Historian after the 'Linguistic Turn,'" *CH* 67 (1998): 1–31; C. Hall, *Reading Scripture with the Church Fathers* (1998); R. Stark, *The Rise of Christianity* (1996); R. Valantasis, *Religions of Late Antiquity in Practice* (2000).

DAVID ROHRBACHER

Historiography of Medieval Christianity (Contemporary)

The study of medieval Christianity was transformed in the second half of the twentieth century. Before then, most scholars of medieval religion were Roman Catholics who studied doctrine and the mainstream of Christianity, affirming tradition and reinforcing the idea of a monolithic authoritative church governed by the popes. The few Protestants who wrote on the subject tended to follow their own confessional bias, viewing medieval religion as an oppressive preface to the Reformation. By the 1930s, however, scholars were beginning to explore a wider range of topics and questioning simple views of medieval Christendom, heralded by authors like the Germans Gerd Tellenbach (*Church, State and Christian Society at the Time of the Investiture Contest*, 1936) and Herbert Grundmann, whose pathbreaking *Religious Movements in the Middle Ages* first appeared in 1935.

The trickle of innovative studies of medieval Christianity became a flood in the 1960s when the Second Vatican Council relaxed censorship rules, leaving Catholic scholars freer to consider the implications of their sources. Also, as the scope of study broadened, increasing numbers of non-Catholics and non-Christians began to examine medieval Christendom. Thus the field in the period 1960 to the present has seen a gradual shift away from the study of dogma and the white male ecclesiastics who created it. Such work was and is still produced, including brilliantly insightful works like Sir Richard Southern's several studies of St. Anselm and Jean LeClercq's voluminous

works, including his *Love of Learning and Desire for God*, a study of medieval monastic scholarship that first appeared in French in 1957. The work of authors like Southern and LeClercq, with its tender appreciation of medieval religious life, has found fewer and fewer emulators, however. The cutting edge of the discipline is now dominated by four major issues that had rarely been considered before the 1960s: (1) the Christianization of Europe; (2) lay spirituality; (3) heterodoxy; and (4) women's spirituality.

The French historian Jean Delumeau opened a major debate over how Christian the medieval "age of faith" was with his publication of *Le catholicisme entre Luther et Voltaire* (1971), in which he argued that Europe was only superficially Christian until the Reformations of the sixteenth century. A number of studies succeeded Delumeau's work, including *The Pagan Middle Ages* by Ludo Milis (1998) and James Russell's provocative *The Germanization of Early Medieval Christianity* (1994). The great weakness of many such studies is that the authors have weighed medieval practice against an ideal normative Christianity that owes more to nineteenth-century positivist historians than to historical reality. The most recent scholarship in this area, though, has increasingly called into question the whole notion of a single monolithic Christendom, instead pointing to enormous diversity over time and place, including much hybridization of Christianity as it spread through Europe and beyond.

Such studies have been fed by a new fascination with religiosity, the actual religious practices and beliefs of the many, rather than the theological ponderings of the few. Etienne Delaruelle in his many works, some of the most interesting of which were collected in his *La piété populaire au Moyen Age* (1980), was a pathbreaker in applying the methods of the French *Annales* school to study the lives of ordinary Christians. Others have explored many issues of lay spirituality, including André Vauchez (*Religion et société dans l'Occident medieval*, 1980) and, recently, Eamon Duffy, whose work has transformed understandings of the Reformation by demonstrating the rich spiritual life of late medieval Christians (e.g., *Marking the Hours: English People and Their Prayers 1240–1570*, 2006). More specific studies have gone far in rehabilitating the cult of the saints as a valid expression of popular piety, including Donald Weinstein and Rudolph Bell's *Saints and Society* (1982), Patrick

Geary's *Furta Sacra: Thefts of Relics in the Central Middle Ages* (1978), and Arnold Angenendt's magisterial *Heilige und Reliquien* (1994). Thanks to these and many other works, scholars now have a much clearer notion of ordinary folks' religious beliefs and practices.

Growing from interest in lay religion is a third issue: medieval heterodoxy. Again, the French *Annales* school helped push scholarship in this direction, most notably with Le Roy Ladurie's *Montaillou: The Promised Land of Error* (published in French in 1975), a brilliant microhistory of a Cathar village in Languedoc. Two of the most influential works on medieval heresy came from the pen of R. I. Moore, *The Origins of European Dissent* (1977) and *The Formation of a Persecuting Society* (1987). Moore tells of the development of a rule-oriented and repressive Christian hierarchy in the high Middle Ages, increasingly devoted to expunging dissent. Moore's arguments have been refined in a number of studies, including the work of Malcolm Lambert and Heinrich Fichtenau.

Recent work on heterodoxy points to perhaps the most radical transformation of recent historiography on medieval Christianity: it includes women. Three factors account for this new sensitivity to gender and the differences between men's and women's experience of religion. First is the simple fact that many more women are becoming professional historians, adding their insights to the topic. Second is a recent fascination with the mysticism of the later Middle Ages, best exemplified by Bernard McGinn's magnificent studies (e.g., *The Flowering of Mysticism*, 1998). Many of the great mystics of the medieval West were women; they transcended gender divides in their own lifetimes, and their writings have helped to do the same in studies of medieval Christianity today. A third factor behind the current fascination with medieval women's spirituality is the immensely influential work of Caroline Walker Bynum, whose works, including *Jesus as Mother* (1982) and *Holy Feast and Holy Fast: The Religious Significance of Food to Medieval Women* (1987), have inspired many.

In short, the study of medieval Christianity has seen many new doors open in recent decades. Much valuable work has been done, opening still more vistas for future scholarship. The result has been the beginning of a new understanding of medieval Christianity as something stranger, deeper, and far more diverse than earlier historians had imagined.

C. Berman, ed., *Medieval Religion: New Approaches* (2005); N. Cantor, *Inventing the Middle Ages* (1991); J. Van Engen, "The Future of Medieval Church History," *CH* 71 (2002): 492–522.

PHYLLIS G. JESTICE

Historiography of the Reformation (Contemporary)

Until recently the construction of the narrative of the Reformation was mainly the domain of church historians who tended—consciously or not—to select those historical sources that buttressed their denominational and/or theological commitments. Their church-historical categories of the Reformation still in use are "magisterial" (in the double sense of led by academics, *magistri*, and with the political support of magistrates), which broadly led to Lutheran, Calvinist, and Anglican establishments; "radical" or "left wing," which included Anabaptist and dissident movements; and "Catholic Reformation" or "early modern Catholicism" (in pre-ecumenical days, the "Counter-Reformation"). By the latter half of the twentieth century there was a growing realization that the Reformation was too significant a subject for the development of the modern world to be left to the church historians and theologians. Political and social historians have since provided a multitude of insightful perspectives informed by political history, Marxism, psychology, sociology, anthropology, religious studies, and women's studies. This is not to suggest, however, that the historical interpretations of these latter scholars are value free or "objective." Indeed, Heisenberg's "indeterminacy principle" applies to historical studies as well as subatomic physics: what is observed is influenced by the observer. In the words of the great French historian Fernand Braudel: "History is the child of its time." This should not be understood negatively, for personal commitments and social contexts may serve to sharpen perspectives and insights. An example is early Marxist historiography informed by Friedrich Engels's (1820–1895) study of the German Peasants' War (1524–1525) that perceived religious commitments and expressions primarily as vehicles for socioeconomic struggles against the early modern development of capitalism. Other examples are the works of the great German scholars Leopold von Ranke (1795–1886), Ernst Troeltsch (1865–1923), and Karl Holl (1866–1926), which in one way or another strove to relate the modern German identity and state to the Reformation. For Ranke, the Reformation was a unique epoch of history bracketed by Luther's Ninety-five Theses (1517) and the "Religious Peace" of the Diet of Augsburg (1555). Troeltsch, on the other hand, viewed the magisterial Reformation, especially in its Lutheran form, as the last gasp of the Middle Ages. For Troeltsch, the break from the unified, authoritarian medieval culture and the initiation of the modern world came with the Calvinist and even more so the Anabaptist decoupling of church and state, and in the quest for individual freedom of conscience. Holl strove to refute Troeltsch's position by focusing upon Luther's theology and ethics as the key to the integration of German culture. Responses to these and other historiographical orientations have stimulated research into the social, political, and economic as well as the theological bases of the Reformation. Informed by constructs denoting church-state partnership such as "social disciplining" and "confessionalization," as well as growing interest in ritual and "popular religion," there has been a growing sense that "the Reformation" consists of a number of messily intertwining movements given such labels as "princes' Reformation" and "urban Reformation" (reform from the top down) and "communal Reformation" and "peoples' Reformation" (reform from the bottom up) that extend back to medieval renewal movements and forward into the modern period. The debate shows no sign of slackening.

P. Benedict, "Between Whig Traditions and New Histories: American Writing about Reformation and Early Modern Europe," in A. Molho and G. S. Wood, eds., *Imagined Histories: American Historians Interpret the Past* (1998), 295–323; T. A. Brady Jr., *The Protestant Reformation in German History* (1998); Brady, "New Studies on the Protestant Reformation," *Journal of Modern History* 71 (1999): 431–44; A. G. Dickens and J. M. Tonkin, *The Reformation in Historical Thought* (1985); W. K. Ferguson, *The Renaissance in Historical Thought: Five Centuries of Interpretation* (1948); C. Harline, "Official Religion—Popular Religion in Recent Historiography of the Catholic Reformation," *Archive for Reformation History* 81 (1990): 239–57; S. Hendrix, *Recultivating the Vineyard: The Reformation Agendas of Christianization* (2004); C. Lindberg, *The European Reformations* (1996); S. C. Karant-Nunn et al., "Focal Point/Themenschwerpunkt: Post-Confessional Reformation History," *Archive for Reformation History* 97 (2006), 276–306; R. O'Day, *The Debate on the English Reformation* (1986); J. W. O'Malley, *Trent and All That: Renaming Catholicism in the Early Modern Era* (2000).

CARTER LINDBERG

Hobbes, Thomas (1588–1679), philosopher.

Hobbes's connections with the Cavendish and other noble families made possible his European travel and contact with such prominent thinkers as Francis Bacon and Galileo. At the threat of civil war he fled to Paris in 1640, where he became tutor to the future Charles II. In *Leviathan* he argued that all human beings are self-serving and that a state with absolute power is the only solution to prevent them from devouring one another. Such moral virtues as right, liberty, and justice are derived from human self-interest and social agreement to avoid inflicting harm on others. He argued that government authority is derived from its subjects, who are bound to their monarch, who in turn cannot injure his subjects. This displeased the parliamentarians, who argued for the rights of the people over the king, and the royalists, for whom the king's authority was divinely given. His absolutist views on the state were seen as a challenge to personal morality. He spent his last years with the Cavendish family, where he translated *The Iliad* and *The Odyssey*.

T. Hobbes, *The English Works of Thomas Hobbes of Malmesbury*, ed. W. Molesworth (1962); R. Tuck, *Hobbes* (1989).

DAVID P. SCAER

Hoburg, Christian (1607–1675), radical

disciple of Johann Arndt, active in Lutheran churches in northern Germany and among Mennonites in the Netherlands. Unable to afford university, the young Hoburg read works by Caspar Schwenckfeld and Arndt. Hoburg advocated a lay Christianity marked by new birth and mystical renewal. A critic of the Lutheran state church and its theology, Hoburg's best-known writing was *Der unbekandte Christus* (1669): "The Unknown Christ. A thorough demonstration that the Christianity of today in its various sects does not truly know Christ." Later German Pietists highly valued Hoburg's works.

J. Wallmann, *Der Pietismus* (1990).

DOUGLAS H. SHANTZ

Hoen, Cornelius (c. 1469–1524), Dutch scholar who persuaded Huldrych Zwingli that the word *est* ("is") in the institution of the Eucharist means *significat* ("signifies"). As a consequence, the Eucharist became a focus of dissension between Luther and his followers, on the one hand, and Zwingli and his (including the Reformed tradition generally), on the other. At the Marburg Colloquy (1529) Luther insisted on the literal interpretation of the statement "This is my body," but he was opposed by Oecolampadius, whose *De Genuina Verborum Domini* (1525) drew upon citations from the church fathers, particularly Tertullian, to support Hoen's view.

H. O. Oberman, *Forerunners of the Reformation* (1981).

RODERICK MARTIN

Hoffman, Melchior (c. 1495–1543), lay preacher and reformer in northern Europe. Hoffman preached justification by faith but combined it with apocalyptic themes, rejection of the real presence in the Eucharist, and congregational polity. He believed that the Bible was interpreted by a direct revelation from the Holy Spirit, and he opposed images. These views brought him into conflict with both Catholics and Lutherans, and he was expelled from Livonia in 1526. He made his way to Strasbourg, where several visionaries convinced him that the second coming was near and that he himself was Elijah, the first of the two witnesses predicted in Revelation 11:3. His radical ideas led to his imprisonment by the Strasbourg authorities. After escaping, he fled north and pursued a successful ministry in East Frisia and the Netherlands. After his followers came under persecution, he announced the suspension of adult baptism for two years, until the second coming took place, an event he prophesied for the year 1533. After further missionary journeys, he returned to Strasbourg in 1533 and was imprisoned until his death.

Combining Anabaptism, apocalypticism, and spiritualism, Hoffman created a potent theology that attracted a wide following in the Netherlands and northern Germany. Although the movement collapsed in the wake of the defeat of the Anabaptist Kingdom of Münster, many of his ideas, especially his Christology, continued to influence Dutch Anabaptism.

K. Deppermann, *Melchior Hoffman: Social Unrest and Apocalyptic Visions in the Age of the Reformation* (1987); W. Klaassen, *Anabaptism in Outline* (1981).

D. JONATHAN GRIESER

Holbein, Hans (the Younger) (c. 1498–1543), renowned German portraitist of the northern Renaissance. Born in Augsburg, Holbein moved to Basel, where his reputation became established with *Christ in the Tomb* (1521), a gruesomely realistic depiction of a prone body, frozen in rigor mortis, identified only by lance and nail wounds. Holbein became a friend of Erasmus and painted three portraits of the great humanist. Between 1523 and 1526 Holbein illustrated the Luther Bible and published the *Dance of Death* woodcuts. He fled the religious unrest in Basel for Antwerp, then England, where he joined the household of Thomas More. Holbein's portrait of More (1527) is an astoundingly penetrating portrayal of personality. Holbein received commissions from merchants of the Hanseatic League, as well as from members of the court. *The French Ambassadors* (1533), an iconographic masterpiece of realism and allusion, dates from this period. Holbein ended his career working for Henry VIII, completing portraits, among others, of the king, Jane Seymour, and Anne of Cleves.

O. Bätschmann and P. Griener, *Hans Holbein* (1999); M. Roskill and J. Hand, eds., *Hans Holbein: Paintings, Prints, and Reception* (2001); J. North, *The Ambassadors' Secret: Holbein and the World of the Renaissance* (2002).

PRISCILLA BAUMANN

Holcot, Robert (c. 1290–1349), Dominican theologian, Bible commentator, and teacher at Cambridge and Oxford. Holcot studied theology at Oxford. One of Holcot's contributions to theology were his 1331–1332 lectures on Peter Lombard's *Sentences*. Their revision was completed around 1336. In the 1330s, he also wrote a series of quodlibetal questions and a work called *Six Articles* (*Sex articuli*). Particularly influential were his biblical commentaries, among which was the *Book of Wisdom*. In the older literature he has been labeled a nominalist and an Ockhamist, but it is more adequate to characterize him as a thinker who was deeply involved in the debates of his time. These debates involved Franciscan thinkers such as William of Ockham, Walter Chatton, and Adam Wodeham, and his fellow Dominican William Crathorn.

Noteworthy is Holcot's discussion of the status of theology as a science (*scientia*). According to his understanding, theological truths cannot be acquired during this life, and thus theology does not qualify as a science, for its truths are not demonstrable. We cannot, for instance, demonstrate the existence of God. The universe, from which God's existence can be inferred, is contingent: there always is the possibility that God interferes with the natural order. From such possibilities Holcot draws the skeptical conclusion that our empirical beliefs are not absolutely certain, even though we should not discard them either.

Another interesting view concerns Holcot's application of logic to the discussion of the Trinity. Debates with Scotus and Ockham led him to a different conception of how things can be said to be distinct (such as the Father and the Son in the Trinity) and eventually led him to the view that theology requires a special kind of logic, a *logica fidei*.

H. Gelber, *Exploring the Boundaries of Reason: Three Questions on the Nature of God* (1983); F. Hoffman, *Die theologische Methoden des Oxforder Dominikanenlehrers Robert Holcot* (1972); L. A. Kennedy, *The Philosophy of Robert Holcot, Fourteenth-Century Skeptic* (1993).

J. M. M. H. THIJSSEN

Holy Sepulcher, Church of the

Certainly since the early fourth century the site of the Church of the Holy Sepulcher in Jerusalem has been regarded by Christians as the location of Jesus' crucifixion, burial, and resurrection. The emperor Constantine desired to build the most splendid church in the world at this location and provided lavishly for its construction. It was dedicated in 335.

The design of the sepulcher flowed from the more public to the more private worship space. An atrium on the eastern side opened to a basilica with five aisles and a small apse for congregational worship. To its west was the colonnaded court of Calvary, which contained the traditional rock of the crucifixion. At the end of this court was the rotunda of the Anastasis ("resurrection"), the focal point of veneration within the complex. Its exterior wall was semicircular with three apses, within which was a circle of columns surrounding the tomb of Jesus.

The Anastasis was destroyed and rebuilt in the eleventh century. Crusaders completely rebuilt the church in the twelfth century but incorporated much of the fourth-century structure.

S. Gibson and J. E. Taylor, *Beneath the Church of the Holy Sepulchre* (1994); P. W. L. Walker, *Holy City, Holy Places* (1990), 235–81; J. R. Wright, *The Holy Sepulchre: The Church of the Resurrection: An Ecumenical Guide* (1995).

EVERETT FERGUSON

Homoians

The fundamental doctrine of homoian Trinitarian theology is that the difference that distinguishes the Son from the Father is a difference that reveals the Son to be less than the Father—specifically, less divine than the Father. Homoian theology arose out of the debate over the Nicene (325) use of "essence" (*ousia*) and is a phenomenon of the late fourth and fifth centuries. Although often called "Arian," homoian theology may owe little to Arius and more to the anti-Marcellus (antimodalist) theology of the 340s that emerged after Arius's death. Primitive homoian theology may be found in the Creed of Sirmium from 357. For homoianism, the Son is "son" by adoption and is more appropriately called "perfect servant."

In the East, Greek-speaking homoians argued that the Son is the product of the Father's will and not of his nature. In the West, Latin-speaking homoians argued that scriptural descriptions of God as unbegotten and invisible necessarily exclude the Son from being truly divine, since he is both "begotten" and visible (either in the OT theophanies or in the taking on of flesh). The "visibility" of the Son still had significance for Latin Trinitarian theology, while since the time of Origen it had none for Greek theology, and in these different understandings we find the difference in fundamental logic between Latin and Greek homoian theology.

The center of anti-Nicene theology in the East shifted after 361 to anomoean theology: Greek homoian theology was replaced rather than vanquished. Suppressed in the West in 388 by the emperor Theodosius, Latin homoian theology nonetheless continued. Its fortunes were closely tied to renewed political patronage. The rise of separate post-Roman kingdoms in the West during the fifth and sixth centuries signaled a high-water mark for the establishment of Latin homoian theology. In 505, for example, Eugenius, the Nicene bishop of Carthage, was exiled by King Huneric at the hand of Cyrola, the homoian bishop of Carthage. The years 533–589 saw a strong push to defeat the Visigoths of Spain and the Vandals of North Africa and in so doing to return them to rule under a catholic (Nicene) king or emperor. The famous *filioque* addition to the creed of Constantinople (the

Nicene-Constantinopolitian Creed)—"the Holy Spirit proceeds from the Father *and the Son*"— was added in Spain around 589 as part of the rehabilitation of the formerly homoian Goths.

R. P. C. Hanson, *The Search for the Christian Doctrine of God* (1988).

MICHEL RENE BARNES

Honoratus of Lérins (c. 350–430), Gallic nobleman and monk. Honoratus and his brother Venantius practiced asceticism first in their home, then in Greece (where Venantius died). Honoratus then lived as an ascetic in Italy. Finally, on the island of Lérins in the Bay of Cannes, he founded a monastery c. 410. What we know of life at Lérins during his abbacy comes from a funeral panegyric composed after Honoratus's death by his cousin and successor as abbot, Hilary of Arles. The panegyric dwells upon Honoratus's virtues and not upon the biographical information of value to historians. We do know that Honoratus was a priest in an age when many monks were not. His greatest achievement was to convince the Gallic bishops of the value of monasticism, often viewed as spiritually elitist and indifferent to episcopal authority. Indeed, Honoratus turned his monastery into a school for the Gallic episcopate; Lérins alumni included Eucherius of Lyon, Salvian of Marseilles, Fautus of Riez, and Caesarius of Arles. Honoratus himself became bishop of Arles in 428 but died in 430. Nothing is known of his episcopate.

A. de Vogüé, "Les Débuts de la vie monastique à Lérins," *RHE* 88 (1993): 5–53; Hilary of Arles, *The Life of Saint Honoratus*, in *The Western Fathers*, ed. and trans. F. R. Hoare (1954); R. Van Dam, *Saints and Their Miracles in Late Antique Gaul* (1993).

JOSEPH F. KELLY

Hooker, Richard (1554–1600), English churchman, theologian, and controversialist. Hooker attended Oxford Univ. and from 1584 enjoyed a series of minor clerical appointments. Theologically, Hooker was in the Reformed tradition, as illustrated by his soteriology. Beginning with a fallen humanity incapable of meritorious action, Hooker argued that salvation was consequent upon the reception of justifying righteousness, attained through faith, on account of which God forensically declared the possessor worthy of salvation and which was inevitably accompanied by sanctifying righteousness that led to holiness of life. Faith, jus-

tification, and sanctification were all utterly gratuitous gifts of God to the elect. Hooker differed, however, from Elizabethan Puritans on several points, including his assertion that God was merciful to save even some Catholics provided their heretical views were held ignorantly, not obstinately. These points of difference sparked a dispute between Hooker and the Puritan Walter Travers, with whom Hooker shared a pulpit in the mid-1580s as master of the temple.

Hooker is known primarily for his magnum opus, *Of the Laws of Ecclesiastical Polity*, a rhetorically, theologically, and philosophically sophisticated defense of the Elizabethan church. The work's preface and first five (of a projected eight) books were published in the 1590s; drafts of the remaining books were published posthumously. Hooker's intention was to justify the Elizabethan settlement to Puritan detractors by demonstrating its consistency with the dictates God had provided regarding ecclesiastical affairs. Following the preface, the *Laws* open with a discussion in the Thomistic-Aristotelian tradition of the hierarchy of divinely ordained laws that govern existence. Key are (1) natural law, a standard of right and wrong perceived by human reason; (2) divine law, provided in Scripture to lead fallen humanity to salvation; and (3) human laws, derived from natural and divine law and necessary to maintain order in human societies. While granting that Scripture is a perfect guide in matters essential to salvation, Hooker denies the Puritan claim that God intended it to provide detailed guidance for the ordering of all aspects of life, or even of the church. Consequently, as a human society the visible church requires regulation by human laws in matters not directly ordered by Scripture or natural law. The power to formulate such laws is held in theory by the church as a whole and in practice by representatives speaking on behalf of the church community. Because in Hooker's view even wicked persons and obstinate heretics are rightly called Christians if they have been baptized and outwardly profess Jesus as the Christ, he argued that in England essentially every person is also a Christian. Thus, church and realm are equivalent in terms of membership, and it is natural that the crown in connection with the convocation, representing the whole realm, should create ecclesiastical laws.

Hooker did concede that laws contrary to the dictates of Scripture were invalid, so in order to secure obedience to church laws he needed to address hermeneutics. He did so by identifying reason as the standard by which one could distinguish between valid and invalid interpretations of the Bible, and then maintaining that private determinations of what constituted reasonable interpretations must be subordinated to public determinations rendered by the church authorities both because the latter were more likely to be correct and because such subordination was necessary to preserve order in the church. In addition to legitimating the authority of the crown in Parliament (i.e., the influence of the king) to devise ecclesiastical laws, Hooker also defended the quality of the laws established by the church authorities in England, arguing that the episcopal polity, prayer, and sacrament-centered liturgy of the Elizabethan church provided a context in which Christians could grow in grace and holiness. The prescribed prayers of the church taught Christians "to pray as we ought" and through their uniformity brought the church into conformity with the heavenly host. The sacraments (baptism and the Eucharist) were not mere signs of divine favor but effective means through which God actually communicated grace. Through prayer and sacraments the visible and invisible churches merged as members were taken up into a supernatural society, uniting as the mystical body of Christ through common union with Christ.

W. S. Hill, ed., *The Folger Library Edition of the Works of Richard Hooker*, 7 vols. (1977–1998); Hill, ed., *Studies in Richard Hooker* (1972); W. J. T. Kirby, *The Theology of Richard Hooker in the Context of the Magisterial Reformation* (2000); A. S. McGrade, ed., *Richard Hooker and the Construction of Christian Community* (1997); P. Secor, *Richard Hooker: Prophet of Anglicanism* (1999).

DANIEL EPPLEY

Hooper, John (c. 1500–1555), English theologian and bishop of Gloucester and Worcester (1551–1554). Hooper's theology reflects strong Zwinglian influence. He identified the Bible alone as the ultimate religious authority, taught salvation by faith, emphasized that true faith must issue in holy living, and viewed the Eucharist as a memorial in which Christ was present spiritually but not corporeally. Hooper initially declined his bishopric because he refused to wear episcopal vestments; he capitulated after months of controversy and was consecrated wearing the prescribed dress. A zealous preacher and bishop, Hooper vigorously promoted purity and holiness in doctrine and lifestyle. Following Mary Tudor's ascension he was imprisoned and ultimately executed for heresy.

———

S. Carr, ed., *Early Writings of John Hooper, D.D.* (1843); E. W. Hunt, *The Life and Times of John Hooper (c. 1500–1555), Bishop of Gloucester* (1992); C. Nevison, ed., *Later Writings of Bishop Hooper* (1852).

DANIEL EPPLEY

Hosius of Cordova (c. 257–357), bishop and imperial advisor. Bishop of Cordova in Spain from before 300, Hosius was a confessor during the persecution of Maximian and attended a council at Elvira at some point about that time. He came to the attention of the emperor Constantine about 312 and was one of his principal religious advisors. Influential in distributing imperial largesse, he was instrumental in the condemnation of the Donatists in North Africa in 316. In 324, after Constantine conquered the East, he was sent to try to mediate between Alexander of Alexandria and Arius. When that failed, he played a major role in the condemnation of the latter at the Council of Nicaea the following year. He helped develop the council's principal formulary, which asserted that the Son is "of one essence" with the Father. After Constantine's death in 337 he retained considerable prestige and presided at the Council of Serdica in 342 or 343. In extreme old age he was induced by Constantine's son Constantius to sign the so-called Blasphemy of Sirmium (357), which rejected the word "essence" altogether. Hosius's signature was used by opponents of Nicaea to try to establish a new, non-Nicene imperial "orthodoxy." Hosius himself died not long after.

———

CPL, 537 (1940/1), 538 (1916), 539 (1930), 539a (1930), 540 (1990), 540a (1990), cf. 449, 578; V. C. De Clercq, *Ossius of Cordova* (1954); J. Quasten, *Patrology*, vol. 4 (1986), 61–62.

RICHARD PAUL VAGGIONE, OHC

Hosius, Stanislaus (1504–1579), Polish humanist theologian, Counter-Reformation bishop, and Roman curial official. Educated among Erasmus's disciples in Cracow and sent to study law and theology in Italy, he served the Polish king, Sigismund, from 1534 to the king's death in 1548. Appointed bishop by Sigismund II in 1549, Hosius spearheaded anti-Protestant efforts in Poland. His *Confessio fidei catholicae* became the most widely used of his many writings supporting Catholicism and refuting Protestantism. Called to advise the papacy (1558), he reconverted Maximilian, heir to the HRE, to Catholicism. Created cardinal (1561), he was president of the Council of Trent in its stormy final year, 1562–1563. In Poland, 1564–1569, he stabilized Catholic influence. In Rome, 1569–1579, he represented Polish interests and directed Catholic reforms in the empire, Scandinavia, and Poland.

H. Kowalska, "Stanislaus Hosius," in *Contemporaries of Erasmus*, vol. 2, ed. P. Bietenholz et al. (1986), 206–7; H. Wojtyska, *Cardinal Hosius, Legate to the Council of Trent* (1967).

JAMES MICHAEL WEISS

Hospitallers This military order (known at various periods in history as Knights of the Hospital of St. John of Jerusalem; Knights of Rhodes; Knights of Malta; and Sovereign Military Order of Malta) was founded between c. 1050 and c. 1080 and, in modified form, still exists today.

The Hospitallers began as an Italian hospice in Jerusalem. By the 1120s they had begun to assume military responsibilities as well, responding to the manpower needs of the Latin East and expanding their definition of "charitable" to include defending as well as healing.

Like the Templars (q.v.), the Hospitallers' foundation reflects the growth of lay piety and revived attention to just war theory as propounded by Augustine and Ambrose. Also like the Templars, the Hospitallers (though not technically monks) took monastic vows, were answerable directly to the pope, and distinguished themselves repeatedly in defense of the Holy Land.

Unlike the Templars, the Hospitallers had an alternate vocation—hospital care—that they never abandoned. After the Holy Land was lost in 1291, the Hospitallers based themselves on Rhodes, resisting Muslim encroachments by sea. Driven from Rhodes by the Turks in 1523, they found a new home on Malta and continued to play a key role in Christian attempts to hold back the Muslims. In 1565, they survived a siege by the Turks—a victory celebrated across Europe, riven though it was by sectarian conflict.

Thereafter, as the Turkish threat declined, so did Hospitaller activity. By the eighteenth century they were enfeebled. Napoleon captured Malta in 1798 almost without opposition. The order was scattered and barely survived. It managed to reconstitute itself, however, and still exists today, concentrating on its charitable and spiritual vocations.

H. Nicholson, *The Knights Hospitallers* (2001); J. S. C. Riley-Smith, *The Knights of St. John in Jerusalem and Cyprus, c. 1050–1310* (1967); H. J. A. Sire, *The Knights of Malta* (1994).

PAUL CRAWFORD

Hospitals Classical antiquity had already known various kinds of hospitals, for example, for the poor, the sick, foundlings, and so forth. While the autonomous hospital continued to exist in Byzantium, the Western hospital of the early Middle Ages was not an independent establishment but belonged to an abbey obligated to receive the poor, pilgrims, and the ill.

Since about 1130, hospitals increasingly appeared as largely independent institutions. André Vauchez has called this increase a "revolution of the love of neighbor." The cause of this development was, on the one hand, the influence of or its contemporaneousness with new religious movements (especially, by the early thirteenth century, the mendicant orders) and an essentially spiritual orientation to suffering and, on the other hand, the role of the laity and rise of ruling elites (princes, urban elites) and the formation of independent communes.

In the late Middle Ages there arose a great number of specialized institutions, such as orphanages, houses for the mentally ill, and large hospitals. They were increasingly used by the propertied social ranks, and by the beginning of the fifteenth century they were hardly seen any longer as answering the needs of the rising numbers of poor. The differences between late medieval and early modern hospitals grew. Not only was there increased diversity among the inhabitants of hospitals (pilgrims, the poor, the elderly, the sick, prebendaries, foundlings) but also the parties controlling them (now orders, confraternities, communes). In addition, the functions assumed by hospitals increased. For example, they were used as homes for the elderly, poor houses, schools, financial institutions, or even wine cellars and beer cellars. Because of the diversity of functions and controlling parties surrounding "hospitals," social historians currently question the soundness of the concept of the hospital. They are not alone, as scholars in the fields of archaeology and architectural history also contest the concept. The various forms of hospitals could stand in competition with each other, as well as complement one another. Considering their institutional diversity, many methodologically diverse subjects (constitution, the concept of the foundation, finances, norms, memorialization, medicine, nutrition, festivals) are relevant to their study. From this perspective, the hospital presents itself, on the threshold of the modern period, as a reflection, but also a producer, of socioeconomic processes.

N. Bulst and K.-H. Spiess, *Sozialgeschichte mittelalterlicher Hospitäler* (2002); G. Drossbach, *Christliche Caritas als Rechtsinstitut: Hospital und Orden von Santo Spirito in Sassia (1198–1378)* (2005); Drossbach, ed., *Hôpitaux en France, Allemagne et Italie au Moyen âge et aux Temps modernes: Une histoire comparée* (forthcoming); J. Dufour and H. Platelle, *Fondations et oeuvres charitables au Moyen âge: Congrès national des sociétés historiques et scientifiques (121e, Nice, 26–31 octobre 1996): Section d'histoire médiévale et philologie* (1999); M. Matheus, ed., *Funktions- und Strukturwandel spätmittelalterlicher Hospitäler im europäischen Vergleich* (2004); F.-O. Touati, ed., *Archéologie et Architecture Hospitalières de l'Antiquité tardive à l'aube des temps modernes* (2004).

GISELA DROSSBACH

Hotman, François (1524–1590), French humanist, jurist, and historian. A Huguenot, Hotman is best known for his tract on the right to resist tyranny, *The Francogallia*. Born in Paris, he attended the Univ. of Paris and received his licentiate in law from the Univ. of Orléans in 1540. Though his father was a key figure in the suppression of Protestant "heresy," Hotman converted sometime in the early 1540s. In 1548 he left France for exile in Geneva. There he became John Calvin's secretary and later professor of law at Lausanne and Strasbourg, where he came into contact with English exiles fleeing Mary Tudor. From that point forward Hotman used his pen to defend the right to resist government tyranny. In the *Tiger of France* (published anonymously in 1560), he argued against the tyranny of the French crown and church and further hinted that tyrannicide might be an acceptable remedy. In his 1567 *Antitribonian*, Hotman begins to sketch the constitutional thesis that France was not an absolute monarchy and that the king ruled on behalf of the people. This thesis would be expanded in the *Francogallia*. In 1572 Hotman narrowly escaped the St. Bartholomew's Day Massacre. He never returned to France and died in Basel.

D. R. Kelley, *François Hotman: A Revolutionary's Ordeal* (1973).

DAVID WHITFORD

Hrabanus Maurus (c. 780–856), Benedictine, abbot of Fulda, and archbishop of Mainz. In 791 his parents, from a Frankish noble family in the Rhine area, gave the boy as an oblate to the monastery of Fulda. There he was educated and served as teacher and abbot (822–842). He was deposed for political reasons, for his support of the emperor Lothar and his opposition to Louis the German. He lived for some years in exile near Fulda and was installed as archbishop of Mainz by Louis the German in 847, a position he held until his death. His canonization is limited to the former territory of Mainz, today the dioceses of Limburg, Fulda, and Mainz.

Hrabanus's importance goes far beyond ecclesiastical and political matters. He was the most prolific and one of the most important writers of the ninth century. His exegetical work, as far as it is known today, covers almost all books of the Bible, among which the most important were the interpretations of the books of Kings and the books of Maccabees. All these works were written not out of personal ambition but upon the demand of monks at Fulda, bishops, and secular powers. The letters of dedication for these works reflect his many ties to the leading circles in the empire during the reigns of Louis the Pious and his sons. The surviving number of manuscripts of his exegetical works, however, is rather low. It seems that his extensive works inspired other exegetes of his time but were simply too long to become standard commentaries in their time. Hrabanus composed many poems, obituaries, and hymns (but the attribution of *Veni creator spiritus* to him remains doubtful), as well as a series of works for use in churches (homilies, penitential books, etc.). His most influential works were those that reflect his work as a teacher: *De institutione clericorum* (*On the Institution of the Clergy*) and the revision of Isidore's encyclopedia in *De rerum naturis*, or *De universo* (*On the Nature of Things*, or *On the Universe*). Another work of special importance is his *De laudibus sanctae crucis* (*Praise for the Cross*), written 814 or earlier as a composition of twenty-eight figurative poems in hexameters and prose decorated with illustrations of outstanding quality. With this work Hrabanus paved the way to fill the theoretical gap left open by the previous debates in the East and West about the legitimacy of visual images.

Hrabanus was an innovative conservative. His concerns were teaching and providing the necessary tools for advancing knowledge. He strongly defended the ideal of unity of the empire, since it should guarantee the unity of the church. Shortly after 800 he was for some time a pupil of Alcuin, and he followed Alcuin's principles as teacher and politician throughout his life. He used tradition, which to him meant mainly the authority of the church fathers, and he tried to remodel it. The texts that he wrote were mostly compilations of citations of the fathers, yet his process of composition was highly selective and followed the needs of his own time. Some of the most important scholars of the middle of the ninth century studied with him at Fulda: Walahfrid Strabo, later abbot of Reichenau, Otfried of Weissenburg, and Lupus of Ferrieres. It is, however, indicative of the rapid changes which the intellectual landscape underwent in the ninth century that some of his pupils refused to follow the conservatism of their teacher. Such were the supporters of Gottschalk, the rebel against monastic discipline and traditional teachings about free will.

In the sixteenth century there arose renewed interest in Hrabanus, yet his modern title, *Praeceptor Germaniae*, teacher of Germany, is misleading, since it neglects the European dimension of his education, work, and influence. His *Opera omnia* were first published by Colvener in three volumes in 1626–1627, but though a considerable number of his works have been re-edited in the CCCM during the last decades, the modern edition is still far from complete.

———

M.-A. Aris, "'Nostrum est citare testes': Anmerkungen zum Wissenschaftsverständnis des Hrabanus Maurus," in *Kloster Fulda in der Welt der Karolinger und Ottonen: Kultur—Politik—Wirtschaft*, ed. G. Schrimpf (1996), 437–64; G. Cavallo, *The "De rerum naturis" by Rabanus Maurus: Cod. Casin. 132, Archives of Monte Cassino Abbey* (1994); M. C. Ferrari, "Il *"Liber sanctae crucis"* di Rabano Mauro: Testo—immagine—contesto (1999); E. Heyse, "Hrabanus Maurus' Enzyklopädie" *"De rerum naturis"* (1969); H. Maurus, *Opera omnia* in PL 107–12 (1851–52); Hrabanus, *Liber de laudibus sanctae crucis*, in *Vollständige Faksimile-Ausgabe des Codex Vindobonensis 652 d. Österreichische Nationalbibliothek Wien*, ed. K. Holter (1972); Hrabanus, *Rabani Mauri Martyrologium*, ed. J. McCulloh, and *Rabani Mauri De computo*, ed. W. M. Stevens, in CCCM 44 (1979); Hrabanus, *In honorem sanctae crucis*, ed. M. Perrin, CCCM 100 (2000); Hrabanus, *Expositio in Matthaeum*, ed. B. Löfstedt, in CCCM 174–174A (2000); R. Mauro, *La cena di Cipriano* (2002); H. Spels-

berg, *Hrabanus Maurus: Bibliographie* (1984); H.-G. Müller, *Hrabanus Maurus, De laudibus sanctae crucis: Studien zur Überlieferung und Geistesgeschichte mit dem Faks.-Textabdruck aus Codex Reg. Lat. 124 der Vatikanischen Bibliothek* (1973); H.-C. Picker, *Pastor Doctus: Klerikerbild und karolingische Reformen bei Hrabanus Maurus* (2001); M. Rissel, *Rezeption antiker und patristischer Wissenschaft bei Hrabanus Maurus: Studien zur karolingischen Geistesgeschichte*, in *Lateinische Sprache und Literatur des Mittelalters* (1976); D. Zimbel, *Hrabanus Maurus: De institutione clericorum libri tres: Studien und Edition* (1996).

JOHANNES HEIL

Hubmaier, Balthasar (c. 1480–1528),

German Anabaptist theologian and martyr. Hubmaier studied under Catholic controversialist theologian Johannes Eck at the universities of Freiburg and Ingolstadt and was the only early Anabaptist leader with a doctorate in theology. He became chief preacher in Regensburg in 1516 and soon took control of the anti-Semitic movement there. Under his leadership, the Jews were driven out of the city, their synagogue torn down, and a Christian chapel built in its place. Named in honor of the Virgin Mary, this chapel, with Hubmaier as its first chaplain, became a popular pilgrimage site where many miracles were reported.

In 1521, Hubmaier left Regensburg for the town of Waldshut on the Upper Rhine in an area under the Austrian Archduke Ferdinand I (1503–1564). Here he came under the influence of Zwingli, the Zurich reformer, sometime in 1522. In 1524 Hubmaier, full of zeal for his new theology, began instituting religious reforms in Waldshut and took a wife. He went into temporary exile in Schaffhausen during the tensions leading up to the Peasants' War (1524–1525).

Hubmaier returned to Waldshut and was converted to Anabaptism the next Easter, 1525, receiving baptism from Wilhelm Reublin. Hubmaier proceeded to baptize three hundred others. With the support of a majority of the town council, Hubmaier instituted what amounted to magisterial Anabaptism in Waldshut.

There is much debate as to the extent of Hubmaier's involvement in the Peasants' War, but it seems likely that he either authored or edited socially radical peasant documents. When Austrian troops pacified Waldshut in December 1525, Hubmaier sought refuge in Zurich only to be imprisoned and tortured until he recanted his Anabaptist views. He was released and made his way eventually to

Nikolsburg in Moravia (present-day Mikulov, Czech Republic) in 1526, where he again set up a state-sponsored Anabaptism, authorized and protected by the secular ruler, Leonhard von Lichtenstein, who allowed himself to be (re)baptized. Not long after Hubmaier arrived in Moravia the region came under the rule of his old enemy, Archduke Ferdinand. Reluctantly, Hubmaier's protectors handed him over to the Austrian authorities in July 1527. He was imprisoned and put on trial in Vienna for heresy and sedition. Hubmaier's motto was "The truth is immortal." Unfortunately, Hubmaier was not. He was burned at the stake March 10, 1528. His wife, Elsbeth, was drowned in the Danube River three days later.

Hubmaier's theology is characterized by extreme biblicism and radical ecclesiology. He argued for voluntary church membership and religious toleration in an age of state churches and persecution. His *On Heretics and Those Who Burn Them* (1524) is one of the earliest and most eloquent arguments for religious toleration. While he accepted a Zwinglian view of baptism's symbolic nature, Hubmaier argued strongly against infant baptism and for the baptism of adult believers only. His treatise *On the Christian Baptism of Believers* (1525) is the most important early defense of believer's baptism. Through believer's baptism one joins the church and becomes a part of the body of Christ. He linked baptism so closely with conversion that some modern interpreters have accused him, probably unjustly, of teaching baptismal regeneration. Despite this radical ecclesiology and believer's baptism, some modern scholars see Hubmaier's theology closer to Catholicism and less radical than Luther's because discipleship, free will, and nominalism are all important features of Hubmaier's thought.

Hubmaier taught a Neoplatonic, tripartite anthropology, in which the spirit is free from original sin, but not the body and soul. In addition to his unique anthropology, Hubmaier's teaching on the sword distinguishes him from other Anabaptists. His position, worked out in the aftermath of the peasants' unsuccessful war and outlined in his pamphlet *On the Sword* (1527), represents a *via media* between Anabaptist nonresistance and the crusading militarism of the day. Because of his moderate militarism and insistence on believer's baptism, modern Baptists claim Hubmaier as a prototype for their own tradition.

───────

T. Bergsten, *Balthasar Hubmaier: Anabaptist Theologian and Martyr*, ed. W. R. Estep (1978); B. Hubmaier, *Balthasar Hubmaier: Theologian of Anabaptism*, ed. and trans. H. W. Pipkin and J. H. Yoder (1989); D. C. Steinmetz, "Scholasticism and Radical Reform: Nominalist Motifs in the Theology of Balthasar Hubmaier," *Mennonite Quarterly Review* 45 (1971): 123–44.

J. TRAVIS MOGER

Hugh of St. Cher (c. 1190–1263), Dominican theologian and churchman, provincial general for France (1227), first Dominican cardinal (1244). Hugh was papal legate in Germany (1251–1253), primarily residing at the papal court (after 1253) in the capacity of Grand Penitentiary (from 1256), an office of the papal court that examined cases of conscience and delivered decisions and dispensations. He died at Orvieto.

Hugh's main scholarly contributions were in the field of biblical studies. As the second Dominican master at the university (1230) and prior of the Dominican study house at St. Jacques in Paris, he organized and supervised three major collaborative projects for the benefit of students and preachers: a *Correctorium Bibliae* (*Correctory of the Bible*), which listed alternative readings mainly from patristic sources as aids to establishing a reliable Latin text for interpretation; the *Concordantiae S. Jacobi* (*Concordance of St. Jacques*, named after the Dominican convent and school at which it was created), the first comprehensive verbal concordance to the Bible; and the *Postillae*, a massive commentary on the whole Bible that supplemented and expanded the *Glossa ordinaria*. The *Concordantiae* (first ed., Lyon 1540, 2 vols.) and the *Postillae* (first ed., Basel 1498–1502, 7 vols.) were repeatedly printed prior to 1800. His authorship of some short treatises has been demonstrated recently, but other works remain unpublished, among them the innovative commentary on Peter Lombard's *Sentences* and more than 420 sermons.

───────

L.-J. Bataillon et al., eds., *Hugues de Saint-Cher (+ 1263), bibliste et théologien* (2004); J. Paulsell, "Hugh of St. Cher," in *Dictionary of Major Biblical Interpreters*, ed. D. K. McKim (2007), 554–57.

KARLFRIED FROEHLICH

Hugh of St. Victor (d. 1141), canon, philosopher, and theologian. He is one of the most influential figures involved in the ecclesiastical reform movement of his time. Hugh was born most probably in Hamersleben, near Halberstadt (Germany) and was canon regular in the abbey of St. Victor in Paris, although the exact date of his arrival in Paris is unknown. Hugh was considered a pupil of William of Champeaux (d. 1121), the founder of the community and later bishop of Chalons-sur-Marne (1113–21).

Hugh's philosophical and theological works reveal great intellectual breadth. His writings made an important contribution to the methods of intellectual production in his generation. His main theological work, *De sacramentis christiane fidei* (*On the Sacraments of the Christian Faith*), but also his *Dialogus de sacramentis legis scripte* (*Dialogue on the Sacraments of the Written Law*) and the *Sententie de divinitate* (*Sentences on Divinity*), uniquely synthesized exegesis, law, and theology. Hugh relied on Neoplatonic (Augustinian-Dionysian) tradition, despite the twelfth-century controversy over its relationship to biblical revelation. In his philosophy of law and doctrine of state, Hugh based his views mainly on the OT. This allowed him, on the one hand, to develop a strong doctrine of natural law, and on the other hand, to formulate his conception of government according to the example of prophetic criticisms of OT royalty in contrast to the royalty of Christ taught in the NT.

R. Berndt, "The School of St. Victor in Paris," in *Hebrew Bible/Old Testament: The History of Its Interpretation*, ed. Magne Saeboe (2000), 469–75; Berndt, "Hugo von St. Victor: Theologie als Schriftauslegung," in *Theologen des Mittelalters: Eine Einführung*, ed. U. Köpf (2002), 96–112; Hugh of Saint-Victor, PL 175–177 (1854); "Hugh of St. Victor," ed. R. Berndt in *Corpus victorinum*; Hugh of St. Victor, *On the Sacraments of the Christian Faith*, trans. R. Deferrari (1951); Hugh of St. Victor, *Soliloquy on the Earnest Money of the Soul*, trans. K. Herbert (1956); Hugh, *Selected Spiritual Writings* (1962); *LTK* 5 (1996): 311–2; R. Moore, *Jews and Christians in the Life and Thought of Hugh of St. Victor* (1998); D. Poirel, *Hugues de Saint-Victor* (1998); I. Van't Spijker, "De wereld en de ziel: Tropologie in Hugo van Sint-Victor's *De sacramentis*," *Bijdragen* 58 (1997): 56–78.

RAINER BERNDT

Huguenots   French Calvinists were named Huguenots. The first Calvinist church was established at Paris in 1555, and soon evangelical groups from across France were petitioning the Genevan Company of Pastors to send pastors to their communities. The first national synod of Reformed churches, held secretly at Paris in 1559, drew up a confession of faith, based largely on the Genevan model, and an ecclesiastical discipline, which provided institutional structure for the French churches. Calvinism made great headway in France until the outbreak of the Wars of Religion in 1562. By the early 1560s, Huguenots made up around 10 percent of the total population, with a strong presence in Normandy and the west and a heavy concentration in the south. They were represented at every social level, with artisans and urban professionals their social basis. It is estimated that around one-third of the French nobility also embraced Calvinism by the eve of the religious wars, providing political and military leadership to the movement. Sustained repression and persecution in a Catholic kingdom helped to fashion Huguenot identity. Although the French Wars of Religion, and especially the St. Bartholomew's Day Massacre, took their toll on the Huguenots, persecution only strengthened the conviction of those who remained Calvinist that Divine Providence would bring their eventual triumph. The Edict of Nantes (1598) issued by Henry IV granted them religious freedom and privileges.

P. Benedict, *The Faith and Fortunes of France's Huguenots, 1600–1685* (2001); R. Kingdon, *Geneva and the Coming of the Wars of Religion in France, 1555–1563* (1956); M. Prestwich, "Calvinism in France, 1559–1629," in *International Calvinism, 1541–1715*, ed. M. Prestwich (1985), 71–107.

SCOTT M. MARR

Humanism   An intellectual movement affecting European culture from about 1350 until the 1600s and well beyond. This humanism should not be confused with unrelated twentieth-century movements carrying similar names such as "secular humanism."

The humanism of the Renaissance, Reformation, and early modern period was an educational movement spreading from Italy throughout all Europe, beginning with Francesco Petrarca (1300–1374). The word "humanism" comes from *studia humanitatis*, a program of studies based on grammar, rhetoric, history, poetry, and moral philosophy. Humanists took ancient authors—Greek and Latin, pagan and Christian—as models who prepared students for lives of intelligent public service better than did the scholastic curriculum of the trivium and quadrivium that stressed philosophical logic.

Humanist education flowed from a distinctive perception of human nature, linking humanity's intellectual growth to its moral, emotional, and aesthetic potential. Its goal was practical rather than theoretical. Humanism could, of course, pursue pure scholarship: it initiated modern textual criticism and contributed to the origins of modern science. Typically, however, it sought to shape lives.

Within humanism was a strand known as "Christian humanism," originating before but completely pervading the Reformation. Christian humanists sought to renew theology, clerical education, church life, and public piety by a fresh appreciation of the Bible and early Christian writers. They also found moral and literary models in ancient non-Christian writers such as Cicero, Plato, and others. Christian humanism invigorated a spirituality for the laity that influenced, or converged with, sixteenth-century Catholic developments, as well as Protestant teachings on the priesthood of all believers.

Before the Reformation, Christian humanists such as Lorenzo Valla, Thomas More, and Jacques Lefevre d'Etaples proposed improvements for a decadent church, but the humanists were hardly alone in their criticisms. As the Reformation proceeded, humanists varied widely in their styles of theology and church leadership. They did not—this point deserves emphatic restatement—they did not agree in their views on key Reformation debates, such as those on free will, justification, and sacraments. What they did agree on were shared methods of argument: emphasis on the Bible and patristics above medieval thinkers, rhetorical strategies in interpretation and argumentation, and the demand for an educated clergy and better preaching.

The epitome of Christian humanism was Desiderius Erasmus of Rotterdam (1467–1536), who made fundamental contributions to almost every branch of humanism and church reform. Virtually every reformer, humanist, and reformation program after 1520 absorbed some aspect of Erasmus's heritage. Debates between Erasmus and Luther did not stand in the way of an emerging Lutheran humanism, which was spearheaded by Philip Melanchthon. In Switzerland and Strasbourg, all the first- and second-generation reformers showed humanist or Erasmian influence, including Huldrych Zwingli, John Calvin, Martin Bucer, Wolfgang Capito, Oswald Myconius, Theodore Beza, and Johannes Sturm. The Church of England also was deeply influenced by Erasmus's spiritual-

ity, Scripture commentary, and his desire to find a middle way in church debates, granting tolerance on nonessentials. Some Anabaptist and radical reformers resembled or drew from his humanism in their spiritualized view of sacraments, and perhaps in some anti-Trinitarianism. On the Catholic side, well through the 1500s, Spanish, Portuguese, Italian, and Jesuit spiritualities and church reforms showed either Erasmian or broader humanist influences, even though the Council of Trent rejected some popular humanist initiatives such as the replacement of the Vulgate Bible. The Habsburg and Germanic Catholic domains remained hospitable to humanistic renewals in education, flowering in a "late humanism" around 1600.

Even as non-Latin literatures emerged toward 1600, with towering figures such as Michel de Montaigne, William Shakespeare, Hans Sachs, Miguel de Cervantes, and Torquato Tasso, the influence of humanist concern with regularized language, style, genres, and syntax remained.

For religious, civic, literary, and educational purposes, Europeans from the late 1500s forward could take for granted a range of skills and a canon of readings established by the humanist movement. This gave them a culture transcending religious and geographical divisions, drawing from humanist educational models and enduring into the twentieth century. Indeed, humanism provided a unity that religion could no longer offer.

A. Goodman and A. MacKay, *The Impact of Humanism on Western Europe* (1990); J. Kraye, ed., *The Cambridge Companion to Renaissance Humanism* (1996); C. Nauert, *Humanism and the Culture of Renaissance Europe* (1995); A. Rabil, ed., *Renaissance Humanism*, 3 vols. (1988); Z. Schiffman, ed., *Humanism and the Renaissance* (2002).

JAMES MICHAEL WEISS

Hunain ibn Ishaq

Hunain ibn Ishaq (809–873), scholar, physician, and translator. Arab scholars in the early Abbasid period became very interested in Greek science and philosophy. Educated Christians had already begun translating Greek classical works, especially Aristotle, into Syriac and had become significant figures in the transmission of Greek learning to the Arabs. Hunain was born in Hira into a Nestorian Christian family. He studied medicine and spent most of his career as a court physician in Baghdad. He became the supervisor of the caliph Maimun's school, which gave him responsibility for the caliph's translation projects. Greek texts were generally translated first into Syriac and then into Arabic. He himself translated Galen and Hippocrates. Hunain's son, Ishaq, was also known as a talented translator and Arabic stylist. The tenth caliph, Mutawakkil, named Hunain his personal physician. There is a story that he was imprisoned by the caliph after he refused to poison one of his courtiers but that the caliph was, in fact, merely testing his ethical behavior and later released him. The translators of the mid-ninth century, mostly Christian, were instrumental in the formation of medieval Arab culture and ultimately for the transmission of Aristotle to the medieval West (see *Aristotle, Translations of*).

A. Baumstart, *Geschiche der syrischen Literatur* (1922); L. O'Leary, *How Greek Science Passed to the Arabs* (1979).

EUGENE M. LUDWIG, OFM CAP.

Hungary, Reformation in

Reports about Luther and the reform efforts in Germany as well as pamphlets of the Reformer began to circulate in the royal free cities of northeastern Hungary and in the mining cities of north-central Hungary shortly after Luther's publication of the Ninety-five Theses. Support for Luther was expressed already in northern and eastern Hungary by 1521. In 1522 the first of 1,018 students from Hungary to study at Wittenberg during the sixteenth century enrolled at the university. The Catholic hierarchy and nobility adopted harsh laws in 1523 and 1525 to try to halt the tide of the Reformation. But on August 29, 1526, the Turks annihilated the Hungarian army at Mohács. King Louis II, two archbishops, and five bishops were killed. John Zápolya and Ferdinand I Habsburg struggled for the Hungarian throne. The Turks occupied central Hungary, and the country was divided into three parts. Only northern Hungary (roughly analogous to modern-day Slovakia) and the western borderlands were under Habsburg control. This situation enabled the Reformation to spread rapidly into royal Hungary and almost autonomous Transylvania.

While both rivals for the throne alternately hounded or courted evangelicals in Hungary, after the 1530s the Reformation spread more quickly in the cities and towns of the kingdom where Germans comprised the majority of the population. Members of the high nobility, magnates, and some of the lesser nobility also converted and frequently took over the administration of vacant church property. High secular officials who supported both Ferdinand and the Reformation included Peter Perenyi, Thomas Nádasdy, Francis Révay, Alexius Thurzo, and Christopher Ország. Among the lesser nobles were numbered the Balassy, Nyáry, Radvan, and Benický families. Nobles and cities employed their right of ecclesiastical patronage to call evangelical pastors to churches they had built. Many cities, towns, and noblemen established schools at which evangelical humanists, often graduates of Wittenberg, taught. By the end of the sixteenth century well over a hundred evangelical schools functioned in Hungary. Even mercenaries in the service of Ferdinand I inclined to Protestantism and had Protestant preachers in the fortresses along the Turkish border. Some captains in the Habsburg army, such as Lazar Schwendi, John Rueber, and John Ungnad, supported the Reformation.

Most reformers in Hungary were moderates. They respected but did not slavishly follow Luther. In Hungary there were Erasmian humanists such as John Henckel from Levoča, evangelical humanists such as Leonard Stöckel of Bardejov and John Honter of Brasov, and Helvetic Reformed humanists such as Martin Kálmáncsehi and Peter Melius Juhasz. A number of former Franciscans such as Matthias Bíro Devay and Michael Szátari became evangelicals. There were a few, such as Wolfgang Schustel in Barejov and Andreas Fischer, a Sabbatarian Anabaptist active in Spiš county, who advocated radical reform. They were either forced to leave or, like Fischer, were executed. Unique among them was Francis Dávid from Cluj in Transylvania, who was a bishop first among the Lutherans, then the Reformed, and finally became a leader of the Antitrinitarians.

Nobles, town councils, and leagues of cities wanted to maintain control of the process of religious change, as did the regional pastoral fraternities. At regular consultations or synods they defined what teachings and practices would be acceptable.

The decisions of the Council of Trent, the attempt to revitalize Catholicism in Hungary, the defeat of the Protestant League of Schmalkald in Germany, and the 1548 edict of the Hungarian Diet against religious innovations led to the definition and differentiation of the reform movements in Hungary. Lutherans believed the edict did not apply to them since Ferdinand had tacitly recognized the Confession of Augsburg. But the Roman bishops held that the law forbade all religious innovations and sought to enforce it in the area under their ecclesiastical jurisdiction. They organized visitations to identify and expel religious innovators.

The various Reformation communities responded by preparing confessions of faith that defended their orthodoxy and right to toleration. But the scores of confessions produced highlighted differences among the reformers. The second half of the sixteenth century was characterized by theological controversy between and within each confessional group. As they sought to establish their identity and integrity, the reform movement in Hungary fractured into three distinct groups: the Evangelical or Lutheran (to which the German townspeople, many magnates, and the Slovaks adhered), the Helvetic Reformed (which attracted the Magyars in central Hungary and Transylvania), and the Antitrinitarian (supported largely by the Szekely and some Magyars in Siebenbürgen).

Although in Torda in January 1568 the Transylvanian diet proclaimed religious toleration for Catholic, Evangelical (Lutheran), Reformed, and Antitrinitarian communities, in the rest of Hungary religious toleration was achieved only in 1608. After fifteen years of war and the revolt of Stephen Bocskai (1604–1606) the Hungarian diet approved articles that made possible the establishment of independent ecclesiastical administration for both the Lutherans and the Reformed.

———

M. Bucsay, *Der Protestantismus in Ungarn 1521–1978: Ungarns Reformationskirchen in Geschichte und Gegenwart*, vol. 1, *Im Zeitalter der Reformation, Gegenreformation und katholischen Reform* (1977); D. P. Daniel, "Hungary," in *The Early Reformation in Europe*, ed. A. Pettegree (1992), 49–69; Daniel, "Calvinism in Hungary: The Theological and Ecclesiastical Transition to the Reformed Faith," in *Calvinism in Europe: 1540–1620*, ed. A. Pettegree et al. (1994), 205–30; W. Tóth, "Highlights of the Hungarian Reformation," *CH* 9 (1940): 141–56.

DAVID P. DANIEL

Hus, Jan (c. 1369–1415), central figure of the Czech Reformation. Of peasant stock, he obtained his MA degree at Charles Univ. in 1396, where he then lectured. In 1402 he became dean of the philosophical faculty. Ordained as a priest in 1401 and named Czech preacher at Bethlehem Chapel in Prague, he attacked the avarice and debauchery of clerics. He opposed the condemnation of Wyclif's views by the German majority of the university. After the Council of Pisa (1409) Hus, Czech professors, and King Václav IV (Wenceslas) supported the Pisan pope. Arch-

bishop Zajíc Zbyněk and the Germans supported the Roman. After the king granted the Czech nation four votes on the board of Charles Univ. and the Bavarian, Saxon, and Polish nations only one, the Germans left to establish a new university in Leipzig. Hus was then elected rector. He and Jerome of Prague vigorously challenged the authority and attitudes of the Roman church. He defied attempts by Archbishop Zbyněk to implement papal decrees. Excommunicated four times, Hus lost royal sufferance when he condemned the sale of indulgences. After Prague was placed under an interdict in 1412, Hus withdrew to Kozí Hrádek and Krakovec, where he wrote fifteen tracts. In November 1414 he arrived in Constance to defend his views. Despite a guarantee of safe conduct from Emperor Sigismund, Hus was imprisoned, interrogated, condemned, and executed as a heretic on July 6, 1415.

———

M. Spinka, *John Hus at the Council of Constance* (1965); Spinka, *John Hus' Concept of the Church* (1968); Spinka, *John Hus, a Biography* (1965); F. Seibt et al., eds., *Jan Hus— Zwischen Zeiten, Völkern, Konfessionen: Veröffentlichungen des Collegium Carolinum*, vol. 85 (1997).

DAVID P. DANIEL

Hussites This is a collective term for Czech reform movements that trace their origins back to Jan Hus. The burning of Hus (1415) and Jerome of Prague (1416) as heretics by the Council of Constance coalesced the ecclesiastical, national, and socioeconomic reform movements under way in the Czech kingdom. Hussites held that God's law and the Scriptures were to govern both ecclesiastical and public life. They rejected the authority of the Roman pontiff, advocated the reception of both bread and wine at Communion, and sought to increase the number of Czechs in position of importance in public life. To a greater or lesser degree they accepted the Four Articles of Prague (1420): freedom to preach the Word of God, Communion in both kinds, clerical poverty, and severe punishment for mortal sins. The Hussite movement was not monolithic but comprised different, often mutually hostile groups, such as the Utraquists, neo-Utraquists, Taborites, and Bohemian Brethren. More radical Hussitism came to be represented by the Unitas Fratrum. During the sixteenth century Utraquism split into pro-Catholic and Protestant parties. Through the Confessio Bohemica (1575), the neo-

Utraquists and Bohemian Brethren sought to create a Czech national Protestant church. Although its church order was recognized in 1609, the Bohemian revolt of 1618 began the destruction of Reformation Hussitism.

F. M. Bartoš, *The Hussite Revolution, 1424–1437* (1986); R. Říčan, *The History of the Unity of Brethren* (1992).

DAVID P. DANIEL

Hut, Hans (c. 1490–1527), German Anabaptist leader who combined the ideas of Andreas Bodenstein von Karlstadt, Hans Denck, and Thomas Müntzer into a volatile theology. In late 1524 he arranged for the publication of Müntzer's *Ausgedrückte Entblössung* in Nuremberg. He joined Müntzer and was present at the Battle of Frankenhausen, somehow escaping arrest and death. In 1526, he was baptized by Hans Denck and began extensive missionary work throughout southern Germany, Austria, and Moravia. His preaching focused on the coming end times, which he expected in the summer of 1528. He marked the elect not with water baptism but by making the sign of the cross on the forehead with a wet finger. Among his most distinctive doctrines was the "gospel of all creatures." Based on Mark 16:5, Hut argued that creation serves humanity by suffering. By observing the suffering of creatures on behalf of humanity, one can see the need to be ready to suffer in the service of God. Hut was less interested in establishing and organizing congregations than other Anabaptist leaders because of his intense apocalyptic expectation. He was arrested in Augsburg in 1527. Sentenced to death, he died on December 6, 1528, of smoke inhalation during a failed escape attempt. The movement he began did not long survive his death, but his mystical-spiritualist writings had a lasting influence on other Anabaptist groups, especially the Hutterites.

H.-J. Goertz and W. Klaassen, eds., *Profiles of Radical Reformers* (1982); W. Packull, *Mysticism and the Early South German–Austrian Anabaptist Movement, 1525–1531* (1977).

D. JONATHAN GRIESER

Hutchinson, Anne (1591?–1643), colonial American dissident who sparked a New England conflict known as the Antinomian Controversy. Arriving in Massachusetts in 1634, Hutchinson tended the sick and joined the Boston church in which John Cotton, whose message she had admired in England, was

"teacher." She held home meetings for the discussion of sermons, maintaining that the elect could be certain of God's grace by an immediate awareness of it apart from the evidence of good works. She claimed this was the covenant of grace as taught by Cotton, while she and her supporters, who constituted a political faction, denounced other ministers for teaching a covenant of works. Accused of heresy, in 1637–1638 she was examined by civil and church authorities who banished and excommunicated her for theological errors, fomenting disorder, and claiming immediate revelations from the Holy Spirit. She went to Rhode Island in 1638 and then to Long Island, where she was killed in an Indian uprising. She exemplified the mysticism and antinomian Calvinism that appeared on the fringes of seventeenth-century English and American Puritanism, and also the desire of women to engage in theological instruction.

D. D. Hall, *The Antinomian Controversy, 1636–1638* (rev. ed., 1990); M. P. Winship, *Making Heretics* (2002).

DEWEY D. WALLACE JR.

Hutten, Ulrich von (1488–1523), German humanist and patriot. Hutten studied at German and Italian universities and was drawn into the humanist movement. He wrote against the enemies of Emperor Maximilian, including Pope Julius II, for which he was honored as poet laureate. In the service of Albert of Brandenburg, archbishop of Mainz, he condemned celibacy and attacked the excesses of the papal court. After the Leipzig Debate in 1519 he attached himself to Luther. This cost him his position and he found refuge in the castle of his friend Franz von Sickingen, where he wrote treatises urging the German populace to depose the pope. When a campaign against Richard von Greifenklau, archbishop of Trier, failed, he fled to Basel and then to Zurich, where he died in 1523. Next to Luther, Hutten personified the aspirations of the Germans against Rome. His posthumously published *Arminius* provided inspiration for German nationalism in plays, stories, and operas. It has been surmised that Luther incorporated some of his thinking in his *To the Nobility of the German Nation*.

S. Fussel, ed., *Ulrich von Hutten* (1989).

DAVID P. SCAER

Hutter, Jacob (c. 1500–1536), Austrian Anabaptist leader and martyr. Born in Moos,

Tirol (in present-day Italy), Hutter received some basic formal education in Bruneck and then moved to nearby Prags, where he learned hat making. After leaving Prags, Hutter traveled widely, plying his trade. Details of his conversion and baptism are unknown, but he probably first encountered the Anabaptists while in Klagenfurt.

Though not the first to bring Anabaptism to the Tirol, Hutter served as spiritual leader for a small congregation at Welsperg, which began to suffer under severe government persecution. He became the leader of Tirolean Anabaptism when the Swiss Anabaptist George Blaurock, who had led the movement briefly, was captured and executed in September 1529.

While Anabaptism spread covertly in Tirol, it flourished in Moravia (present-day Czech Republic) under the protection of the lords of Liechtenstein. Soon after Hutter assumed the leadership of the Tirolean Anabaptists, he visited Anabaptist communities in Moravia and arranged for the emigration of refugees from Tirol. Hutter returned to Moravia several times over the next few years, settling there in 1533 to help resolve conflicts within and among the Anabaptist communes. Having gained both moral authority and a sizeable constituency among the displaced Tiroleans, Hutter was elected their leader and reestablished the group on a firm ideological base with a well-organized communal structure.

Although Hutter's followers were peaceful, they were persecuted and then expelled in 1535 and became pitiful wandering refugees. Many left the movement and returned home. The remnant splintered into smaller groups, which continued to live communally after settling in various places. Following a letter Hutter wrote to the governor of Moravia on behalf of his beleaguered and displaced flock, the authorities increased their efforts to capture him. Consequently, Hutter voluntarily relinquished leadership of the group in July 1535 and returned to Tirol to evangelize. There he was captured and taken to Innsbruck for trial. In spite of torture and theological coercion, Hutter did not recant; he was burned at the stake on February 25, 1536. His followers celebrated him as a martyr. The survival of the Hutterian Brethren, or Hutterites, for almost half a millennium is in part a testament to Hutter's organizing genius.

H.-J. Goertz, ed., *Profiles of Radical Reformers* (1982); Hutterian Brethren, *The Chronicle of the Hutterian Brethren, 1525–1665*, vol. 1 (1987); W. O. Packull, *Hutterite Beginnings: Communitarian Experiments during the Reformation* (1995).

J. TRAVIS MOGER

Hutterites This Anabaptist group named for Jacob Hutter, an early leader and martyr, are characterized by communalism ("community of goods"). Hutterites are direct heirs to the original Swiss Anabaptism that began in Zurich among Zwingli's followers in 1525. In 1526, Anabaptist theologian Balthasar Hubmaier led a congregation of Anabaptists in Nikolsburg, Moravia (in present-day Czech Republic), which later divided into two camps after Hubmaier's execution in 1528. The *Schwertler* ("sword-bearers") accepted Hubmaier's defensive militarism, while the *Stäbler* ("staff-bearers") were pacifists. Led by Jacob Wiedemann, the *Stäbler* instituted communalism when they left the Nikolsburg area and moved to Austerlitz. The next year another group settled in Auspitz. As more refugees flooded into Moravia, new communities began to form.

In 1533 complaints about corruption and strife caused Hutter, the Tirolean Anabaptist leader, to move to Moravia to stabilize the situation. Hutter became head of the Auspitz community after its leader was discredited for having hidden money for his personal use. Hutter reorganized the community on a firm ideological base and complete economic sharing.

In 1535 local authorities expelled the Hutterites under intense governmental pressure. After a period of homeless wandering, some found sympathetic landlords in Moravia while others moved to nearby Slovakia (then in Hungary). During the Schmalkald War (1547–1548) Hutterites were expelled from Moravia and moved briefly to Hungary before being banished. After four years of wandering and deprivation, Hutterites were again permitted to settle in Moravia.

Hutterites enjoyed a period of peace and prosperity—the "golden years" (1565–1578)—under the leadership of Peter Walpot; however, during the Thirty Years' War (1618–1648), many Hutterites were killed and many Hutterite communities destroyed. In 1621, almost two hundred Hutterites were forcibly moved to Transylvania (in present-day Romania). In 1622 the Hutterites were again expelled from Moravia. Many went to Slovakia and Transylvania.

Hutterite communities gave up their communal living at various times, but the practice was deeply rooted in their traditions and foundational writings. Even when communalism was abandoned, it was later revived, though there are noncommunal groups (e.g., Prairieleut) that survive today. During an intense persecution in the late eighteenth century, Hutterites fled to Wallachia (in present-day Romania). They continued to move east with each new persecution, eventually settling northeast of Kiev, Ukraine, and the area just north of the Black Sea in Russia.

Beginning in 1874 many Hutterites, both communal and noncommunal, emigrated to the United States in order to escape the government's attempts at Russification. During World War I many moved to Canada to avoid military service and harassment. Since a change was made in U.S. law allowing for conscientious objection, many Hutterites have returned to the United States. At the beginning of the twenty-first century there are approximately forty thousand Hutterites living in over four hundred communal colonies on both sides of the Canadian and U.S. border.

L. Gross, *The Golden Years of the Hutterites* (1980); Hutterian Brethren, *The Chronicle of the Hutterian Brethren* (1987); R. Janzen, *The Prairie People* (1999); W. O. Packull, *Hutterite Beginnings: Communitarian Experiments during the Reformation* (1995).

J. TRAVIS MOGER

Hymns, Early Christian By Augustine's classic definition of a hymn as "a song of praise of God" (*Enarrat. Ps.* 148.11), Christians have long been singing hymns, although precisely how the earliest Christians praised God in song is not clear. One difficulty is a tendency to associate a contemporary concept of music with a distant culture that did not make the same distinction between singing and speech as did later Western culture.

As inheritors of Jewish tradition, Christians continued to use the psalms, although most likely originally as prophetic reading rather than sung prayer. The first evidence for the latter use comes from the later second century. The canticles of Luke 1–2 are psalmlike compositions with strong biblical grounding and clear messianic, easily christological, interpretation. With significant disagreement scholars isolate other NT texts as hymns or hymn fragments (e.g., Phil. 2:5–11; Rom. 6:1–11), some of which are specifically christological. Paul may suggest that individual Christians composed songs spontaneously at worship (1 Cor. 14:26). Efforts to identify the "psalms, hymns, and spiritual songs" of Ephesians 5:19 and Colossians 3:16 as specific hymn categories are not convincing.

The pre-Constantinian church gives numerous references to assembly singing (one occurs in the famous letter of Pliny the Younger to the Roman emperor Trajan, *Letter* 10.96) and attests lively Christian hymn writing (e.g., Eusebius, *Hist. eccl.* 5.28). The *Phos hilaron*, the core of the *Gloria in excelsis*, and the *Te Deum laudamus* are precious remnants from a once significant treasury of early Christian psalmlike but nonbiblical texts, most of which fell victim to periodic efforts of the church to eliminate from its worship hymns of merely human provenance.

The hymns of Hilary of Poitiers (all lost), Ambrose of Milan (known as the father of Latin hymnody), the Spaniard Aurelius Prudentius, and Venantius Fortunatus of Merovingian Gaul all contributed to a growing tradition of metrical Latin hymnody of enormous influence. In the East the great hymnographer Ephrem the Syrian and the Greek poets Romanos ("the melodist") and Andrew of Crete composed richly lyrical hymns of outward form quite different from that of the West. The earliest extant record of the tonal shape of a Christian hymn appears in the third-century Oxyrhynchus papyrus 1786.

E. Foley, *Foundations of Christian Music: The Music of Pre-Constantinian Christianity* (1996); J. Gelineau, "Music and Singing in the Liturgy," in *The Study of Liturgy*, ed. C. Jones, G. Wainwright, E. Yarnold (1992), 493–507.

MARY CATHERINE BERGLUND

Hypatia (c. 370–415), mathematician and philosopher. Hypatia was the daughter of Theon, a mathematician attached to the museum in Alexandria. Like her father, she wrote works on mathematics and astronomy. Hypatia taught philosophy, perhaps publicly but more likely privately. Her students included prominent pagans and Christians. Notable among the latter was Synesius of Cyrene, a devoted follower who addressed several letters to her. Unfortunately, none of Hypatia's writings survive; thus, the kind of philosophy that she espoused is a matter open to conjecture. Although commonly regarded as a Neoplatonist, she may have followed a Middle Platonic position. Hypatia's claim to fame is the occasion of her murder. Alexandria was rife with religious tension, owing largely to the machinations of its patriarch Cyril. His abusive treatment of local Jews had caused a breach with the city's prefect, Orestes, a friend of Hypatia. She was drawn into the fray not by virtue of her paganism but on account of her prominent social connections. John of Nikiu writes that rumors spread that Hypatia was practicing witchcraft. In 415 a band of Cyril's henchmen (overly zealous monks?) dragged her from a carriage into the street, where they murdered and mutilated her. Cyril's complicity in the affair is not beyond dispute. What is certain is that Hypatia's story has fired the imaginations of modern litterateurs and feminists.

M. Dzielska, *Hypatia of Alexandria* (1995); J. M. Rist, "Hypatia," *Phoenix* 19 (1965): 214–25.

ALLEN E. JONES

Iamblichus (c. 245–330), Hellenic Neoplatonic philosopher. Born in Calcis, Syria, Iamblichus was a defender of apophatic Neoplatonism and a vigorous proponent of theurgy. He wrote a defense of theurgy (*On the Egyptian Mysteries*), a biography of Pythagoras (*On the Pythagorean Life*), an exortation to philosophy incorporating extracts from the works of Plato and Aristotle (*Protrepticus*), and a criticism of earlier philosophers (*On the Soul*).

In reaction to Porphyry's treatment of the Plotinian *hypostases*, Iamblichus restored the One to a radically transcendent status. Following Plotinus, he located the One above Mind, which now consists of an Intelligible Triad, and Soul. Soul is viewed as a separate self-subsistent *hypostasis*, dependent upon and inferior to Mind. It is intermediary between the intelligible and sensible worlds. Although the human soul contains all the *logoi* operative within Soul, it is fallen and in need of salvation.

Iamblichus argued that theurgy alone unites the human soul with the gods. Through ritual the theurgist taps into the cosmic sympathy that links all reality, and through theurgy the soul is purified and saved. It ascends to the intelligible order by the will of the divine. Salvation is not within human power alone but is dependent upon theurgy and divine grace.

R. M. Berchman, "Rationality and Ritual in Neoplatonism," in *Neoplatonism and Indian Thought* (2002), 229–68; J. Dillon, ed. and trans., *Iamblichi Chalcidensis [In Platonis Dialogos Commentariorum Fragmenta]* (1973); J. Dillon and J. Heshbell, eds. and trans., *On the Pythagorean Way of Life* (1992); J. Finamore, *Iamblichus and the Theory of the Vehicle of the Soul* (1985); S. Gersch, *From Iamblichus to Eriugena* (1978); T. M. Johnson, trans., *Iamblichus,*

Exortation to Philosophy (1988); S. Ronan, ed., T. Taylor and A. Wilder, trans., *Iamblichus on the Mysteries* (1989); G..Shaw, *Theurgy and the Soul: The Neoplatonism of Iamblichus* (1995); C. Steel, *The Changing Self: A Study on the Soul in Later Neoplatonism: Iamblichus, Damascius, and Priscianus* (1978); R. T. Wallis, *Neoplatonism* (1972).

ROBERT M. BERCHMAN

Ibas (d. 457), Syriac bishop of Edessa (Urfa; 435–457), teacher, and translator. Ibas taught at the School of the Persians in Edessa and translated from Greek into Syriac the works of Diodorus of Tarsus and Theodore of Mopsuestia.

He succeeded Rabbula (d. 435) as bishop of Edessa. Ibas had supported Nestorius at the Council of Ephesus (431) and wrote a letter to the Persian bishop, Mari of Rew Ardashir, critical of that council and of the ideas and tactics of Cyril of Alexandria. This letter would become part of the "Three Chapters" condemned at the Council of Constantinople (553). Ibas was eventually imprisoned, deposed, and excommunicated in absentia at the Second Council of Ephesus (449). He was reinstated at the Council of Chalcedon in exchange for formally anathematizing Nestorius.

None of his literary works are extant. According to the *Chronicle of Edessa*, Ibas built the Church of the Twelve Apostles in Edessa and the Church of St. Sergius outside of Edessa.

J. B. Segal, *The Blessed City* (1970), 93–95, 130–35, 183; A. Vööbus, *History of the School of Nisibis* (1965), 12, 15–17; W. H. C. Frend, *The Rise of the Monophysite Movement* (1972); M. Van Esbroeck, "Who Is Mari, The Addressee of Ibas' Letter?" *JTS* 38 (1987): 129–35.

ROBERT A. KITCHEN

Icon The term comes from the Greek word meaning image or portrait. An icon is a sacred depiction of Christ, his mother, saints, angels, or holy events. The modern understanding of the term is typically applied to portable images on wood, but according to the definition of the Fifth Ecumenical Council (Constantinople II, 553) it signifies any sacred image "upon sacred vessels and garments, on walls and panels painted with colors, made in mosaics, or out of any other material." The definitive pictorial terminology and content of icons were established by iconographers of the Byzantine period. The principal figures in Byzantine icons are typically laconic, face forward, in distinctive colors, and shadowless and flat in perspective. The pictorial language is essentially a development within the spiritual and liturgical life of the church, that is, an expression of Orthodox theology in color. Moreover, icons are viewed by the Orthodox not as replicas or portraits of specific individuals, but as an image of Christ's incarnation and of what he calls his followers by grace to be. Also, Orthodox theology requires the important distinction that icons are always venerated and never worshiped because only God is worthy of worship. The earliest extant examples of icons date from the fifth and sixth centuries; however, mention is made of their veneration in Christian literature of the second to fourth centuries.

P. Evdokimov, *The Art of the Icon: A Theology of Beauty* (1990); P. A. Florenski, *Iconostasis* (1996); L. Ouspensky and V. Lossky, *The Meaning of Icons* (1982); L. Ouspensky, *Theology of the Icon*, 2 vols. (1992); E. N. Trubetskoi, *Icons: Theology in Color* (1973).

MICHAEL D. PETERSON

Iconoclasm An "iconoclast" (Gk. *eikon*, "image," and *klastes*, "breaker") is someone who destroys images, especially those that embody religious meaning. Throughout Christian history iconoclasm has surfaced sporadically, usually in response to the biblical prohibition of images (Exod. 20:4–5; Lev. 19:4), but two dramatic outbreaks dwarf the rest. The first took place in the Byzantine Empire during the eighth and ninth centuries, and the second in Western Europe during the sixteenth and seventeenth centuries.

The Byzantine iconoclastic controversy began around 725 when Emperor Leo III ordered the removal of all religious images, setting off waves of violence against images and the *iconodules* who defended them. In Syria, John of Damascus responded by writing an immensely influential defense of image veneration in 726–730. Although iconoclasm stopped in 787, when the veneration of images was affirmed at the Second Council of Nicaea, it was renewed in 814 by Emperor Leo V. This second phase of iconoclasm lasted until 843, when Empress Theodora and Patriarch Methodius reinstated images.

In the West, medieval dissidents such as the Cathars, Lollards, and Hussites rejected images and sometimes destroyed them, but their iconoclasm was relatively limited in scope and duration. The most dramatic iconoclastic period in the West began in 1521 with the advent of the Protestant Reformation. Despite some disagreements, most Protestant churches rejected religious images and called for their removal. Lutherans normally objected to wholesale iconoclasm, but they removed many images, retaining only those that illustrated biblical stories and themes. Anglicans also adopted an ambivalent attitude toward images and their place in the life and worship of their church, but they still got rid of a great deal of religious art. Reformed Protestants—followers of Huldrych Zwingli and John Calvin—rejected not only images but the whole symbolic structure of Catholicism as "idolatry." Consequently, iconoclasm followed the spread of Reformed Protestantism throughout Switzerland, France, the Netherlands, Germany, and the British Isles, sometimes wiping out much of the artistic heritage of medieval Catholicism. Radical Protestants tended to oppose religious imagery, but they varied in their attitude toward iconoclasm: pacifists such as the Swiss Brethren and the Mennonites shied away from all violent acts, including the breaking of images, but militant revolutionaries, such as those at Münster in 1534, attacked images along with anything else they deemed ungodly. Though it eventually became a footnote in Protestant history, iconoclasm came to be regarded as a defining characteristic of Protestantism by Catholics.

Iconoclasm has continued to surface sporadically since the Reformation, often as an expression of revolutionary anticlericalism or atheism, especially in the French Revolution (1789), the Russian Revolution (1917), and the Spanish Civil War (1936–1939).

A. Besançon, *Forbidden Image: An Intellectual History of Iconoclasm* (2000); C. M. N. Eire, *War against the Idols* (1986); H. Feld, *Ikonoklasmus des Westens* (1990).

CARLOS M. N. EIRE

Iconography Iconography is the study of assessing the meaning inherent in pictorial representations. In the modern technical sense it is a tool used to help determine the meaning of an artwork by gathering, classifying, and analyzing pertinent data. The practical emphasis of iconography is to document the generation and evolution of motifs, themes, and types related to figurative images and architectural works. Proper historical context is an overriding factor to prevent distortion through anachronistic imposition. In this way iconography is similar to archaeology, focusing on careful collection and cataloging in order to aid historians.

Although the terms "iconography" and "iconology" are frequently used interchangeably, the two are in fact distinctive fields of study. Iconology investigates and explains the meanings of the representations established by iconography. In short, iconology is explanatory and picks up at the point where the descriptive work of iconography leaves off. In the West, iconography originally meant a collection of portraits, as in van Dykes's seventeenth-century series of portraits of his contemporaries. It became a serious field of study in the sixteenth century through writings of Cesare Ripa (whose work *Iconologia* [1593] deals with personifications and was the first book to use the word), Fulvius Ursinus (*Imagines et elogia virorum*, 1570), Joannes Molanus (*De picturis et imaginibus sacris*, 1570), Giorgio Vasari (*Ragionamenti*, 1588), and Achilles Statius (*Inlustrium virorum*, 1569). The seventeenth-century proponents included Antonio Bosio (*Roma sotterranea*, 1632) and Giovanni Bellori (*Le vite*, 1672). In the eighteenth century, Anne-Claude-Philippe de Tubierres (*Recueil*, 1752–1767) played a prominent role, whereas Johann Joachim Winckelmann laid the foundations for iconography as a scientific field of study when he proposed a detailed and objective examination of ancient monuments as a prerequisite to understanding their fuller importance. In the nineteenth century the French scholar Adolphe Didron made a considerable contribution to the field, and in the twentieth century the most influential scholars were Emile Male, Erwin Panofsky, and Aby Warburg.

A significant role of iconography is determining the symbolic and allegorical content of artworks. A symbol is an object that, within a given context, signifies a general idea. Allegory uses symbols as well as the personification of abstract ideas to communicate complex messages in simpler form. In the area of Christianity, iconography investigates the pictorial or symbolic meaning of persons, ideas, and history. It seeks to recover and express the context that fosters a representative convention, especially when the convention assumes symbolic value. Early Christian art is viewed as primarily typological, where Christ, his church, and Christian concepts are signified by contemporary idealized images. These images are intended to be at once catechetical and inspirational in the face of enormous adversity.

From the time of Emperor Constantine on, Christian art became an established form wherein images relating to liturgy and doctrine became more fully developed and popular. The essential element in the development of Byzantine iconography is the icon. The iconography of medieval Christian art in later centuries is relatively easy to treat because the artist thought in symbols that were easily understood. However, Western Christian art from the Renaissance on presents the greatest difficulty in that it looks to a new emphasis on perspective—as in naturalistic realism. Symbolism is now presented in a veiled form that makes it almost impossible to distinguish where symbol begins and reality ends.

C. Cavarnos, *Guide to Byzantine Iconography* (1993); A. Cutler, *Transfigurations: Studies in the Dynamics of Byzantine Iconography* (1975); A. N. Didron, *Christian Iconography*, 2 vols. (1851–1886, repr. 1965); A. Grabar, *Christian Iconography* (1968); E. Male, *Gothic Image* (1958, repr. 1973); C. R. Morey, *Early Christian Art: An Outline of the Evolution of Style and Iconography in Sculpture and Painting from Antiquity to the Eighth Century* (1942); E. Panofsky, *Meaning in the Visual Arts* (1974); Panofsky, *Studies in Iconology* (1939); L. Safran, ed., *Heaven on Earth: Art and the Church in Byzantium* (1998); G. Schiller, *Iconography of Christian Art* (1971); C. Walter, *Art and Ritual of the Byzantine Church* (1982); A. Warburg, *The Renewal of Pagan Antiquity* (1999).

MICHAEL D. PETERSON

Ignatius Loyola (1491?–1556), mystic and founder of the Society of Jesus (the Jesuits). Much of the success of the society he founded can be attributed to his own charismatic and administrative gifts. Born Iñigo Lopez de Loyola, a Basque aristocrat, he began calling himself Ignatius after 1537.

He was terribly maimed in 1521 during the defense of French-besieged Pamplona. Convalescing in Loyola, he began a conversion, prompted by pious works such as *The Golden Legend* and *The Life of Christ*. These chivalric romances, much beloved by his social class, and the saintly examples provided by his bedside reading led him to reimagine himself as a courtier-servant of Christ.

On pilgrimage to Jerusalem in 1522, he stopped at the monastery of Montserrat. After an all-night vigil, he left his sword and dagger on the altar, replaced them with a pilgrim's garb, and retired to nearby Manresa to take stock. In the knightly tradition, the vigil ought to have been the beginning of his new identity; in fact, it was the end of the old Iñigo. At Manresa he surmounted a spiritual crisis, but the experience completed his conversion and solidified his new spiritual identity. He resolved doubts about the efficacy of his confessions and their accompanying spiritual desolation by learning to discern spirits—to identify the source of the consolation and despair that visited him. Once he learned to distinguish these spiritual experiences he was filled with confidence, serenity, and mystical knowledge that remained with him for the rest of life. Ignatius arrived at Manresa a pious and enthusiastic Christian romantic; he left eleven months later a new creation, ready to begin his life's work.

He returned to Catalonia from Jerusalem by the spring of 1524 and began both his ministry and his education for ministry. After two years of preparatory study, he matriculated at the Univ. of Alcalá de Henares. Thereafter, his life fell into a familiar pattern: at Alcalá (1526–1527), Salamanca (1527–1528), and Paris (1528–1535), he "helped souls" (as he defined his ministry), studied logic, philosophy, and theology—and ran into trouble with the ecclesiastical authorities. His unorthodox behavior repeatedly attracted the Inquisition, but in each encounter he and his companions were examined, affirmed, and released. The authorities in Salamanca found no error in his life or teaching but insisted that he not discuss mortal and venial sin until further studies, which he pursued at the Univ. of Paris.

The nucleus of the Society of Jesus also formed in Paris. From his earliest days of helping souls, Ignatius had also attracted and inspired devoted followers, whom he guided in holiness and "spiritual exercises." The latter, based on his own experiences at Manresa, written down and amplified over time, became the basis for his *Spiritual Exercises*. In 1533, Ignatius and six fellow students bound themselves to lives of poverty and ministry in Jerusalem, or in the service of the pope. As war with the Turks precluded traveling to Jerusalem, the companions took holy orders and headed for Rome.

The subsequent phase of Ignatius's life revealed his administrative talents. He was a natural leader. Anticipating the election of a superior while he was away, Francis Xavier, on the eve of his departure for the Indies in 1540, cast a sealed vote for "our old leader and true father, Don Ignacio, who since he brought us together with no little effort, will also with similar effort know how to preserve, govern, and make us advance from good to better, since he knows each of us best." Moreover, Ignatius attracted powerful patrons for the Society (e.g., Cardinal Gasparo Contarini) and deflected the hostility of powerful enemies (e.g., Cardinal Gian Pietro Contarini). In 1540 Pope Paul III formally established the Society with the bull *Regimini militantis Ecclesiae*, and in 1541 his companions elected Ignatius superior general, a position he held until his death.

In Rome, he initiated diverse projects devoted to helping souls. He also took the leading role in organizing the Society for its mission, drafting (with collaborators) its *Constitutions*, overseeing the activities of its far-flung members, and advocating for it in the corridors of Roman power. His tenacity, flexibility, self-confidence, adaptability, and his harnessing of spiritual goals and human means ensured the nascent society's survival and success. On the morning of his death, Romans spread the word saying, "The Saint has died." In 1622, the Catholic Church confirmed their judgment by canonizing him.

———

C. de Dalmases, *Ignatius of Loyola, Founder of the Jesuits* (1985); G. E. Ganss, ed., *Ignatius of Loyola: The Spiritual Exercises and Selected Works* (1991); J. W. O'Malley, *The First Jesuits* (1993); A. Ravier, *Ignatius of Loyola and the Founding of the Society of Jesus* (1987); W. J. Young, ed., *Letters of St. Ignatius Loyola* (1959).

BENJAMIN W. WESTERVELT

Ignatius of Antioch

Ignatius of Antioch (d. early second cent.), bishop of Syrian Antioch, either immediately after the apostle Peter (Origen, *Homiliae in Lucam* 6) or following Euodius (Eusebius, *Hist. eccl.* 3.22). Ignatius is known from the letters he wrote to the churches of Asia Minor as he was taken for martyrdom in Rome late in the reign of Trajan (98–117). Ignatius (known also as Theophorus) embodied the church's movement away from its Jewish roots at the turn of the century.

Of the thirteen letters associated with his name, the seven that are usually accepted as authentic (*Ephesians, Magnesians, Trallians, Romans, Philadelphians, Smyrnaeans, Polycarp*) identify the primary issues of his theology and ecclesiology. Ignatius successfully argued for a triple-tiered hierarchy (bishop, presbyter, deacon) as a reflection of the divine order (God, apostolic council, Jesus Christ). He wrote passionately against the dangers of Jewish tradition and the influences of docetism upon Christian practice and theology. He saw these threats in numerous churches, either as separate perils or as a united movement. In these efforts, Ignatius employed certain variations on early creeds to establish an acceptance of Jesus Christ as both human and divine (*Eph.* 7:2; 18:2), born of a virgin (*Smyrn.* 1:1–2), and truly raised from the dead (*Trall.* 9:1–2).

Ignatius mentions numerous church leaders within his correspondence. He directs one letter to his friend Polycarp, bishop of Smyrna, and elsewhere mentions Onesimus, bishop of Ephesus, who was perhaps the slave mentioned by Paul (Phlm. 10–18). The impact of Ignatius and his ideas upon subsequent church theology and ecclesiology is inestimable.

V. Corwin, *St. Ignatius and Christianity in Antioch* (1960); P. J. Donahue, "Jewish Christianity in the Letters of Ignatius of Antioch," *VC* 32 (1978): 81–93; J. Rius-Camps, *The Four Authentic Letters of Ignatius* (1979); W. R. Schoedel, *Ignatius of Antioch* (1985).

CLAYTON N. JEFFORD

Index of Prohibited Books The official list of forbidden books issued by the Roman Catholic Church. Such prohibited books were deemed contrary to the church's teaching on faith and morals, and with a few exceptions, members of the church were forbidden to read them. The Congregation of the Inquisition (1557) under Pope Paul IV issued the first Index. Pius V created a "Congregation of the Index" (1571) that revised the list as needed and provided oversight. In 1917, Benedict XV disbanded the Congregation and transferred its duties to the Holy Office. In modern times, the control of controversial literature rested with the diocesan bishops. Leo XIII delineated their duties in 1897 in *Officiorum ac Munerum*, and these duties were subsequently included in the *Codex iuris canonici* in 1917. The Index became less prominent in the twentieth century, and many books found contrary to the church's teaching on faith and morals were not included. In addition, the Holy Office issued an "Index Expurgatorius" of books that were permitted to be read only after certain egregious passages were removed from them. In 1966 the Index ceased to have the force of ecclesiastical law. Nevertheless, the Congregation for the Doctrine of the Faith stated that it retains its moral force.

P. F. Grendler, *The Roman Inquisition and the Venetian Press, 1540–1605* (1977); J. O'Malley, ed., *Catholicism in Early Modern History: A Guide to Research* (1988).

ELIZABETH GERHARDT

Indulgences According to a doctrine established in the thirteenth century, an indulgence is the complete or partial remission by the church of temporal punishment for sins that have already been forgiven, if certain conditions have been fulfilled. The debt of punishment is paid off from the treasury of merit that has been acquired by Christ, the Blessed Virgin, and the saints. The practice is related to the high medieval establishment of sacramental penance, in which the priest absolved the truly contrite penitent from the guilt of sins but stipulated an appropriate penance of punishment. If the penance is incomplete for any reason, the remainder could be fulfilled in purgatory. Therefore, an indulgence offered remission from purgatory to a person. The power of giving indulgences was vested primarily in the pope, who alone could grant remission from all temporal punishment. The merits acquired from a plenary indulgence might also be applied for the benefit of souls who were already in purgatory. The pious practice and the doctrine were the product of a complicated historical process reaching back to the third century, even though it has no direct biblical basis. Indulgences were invented in the High Middle Ages for the reasons of pastoral care to ensure the forgiveness of sin for the faithful.

With their popular origin in ecclesiastical and pious practice, the roots of problems with indulgences easily can be found. They quickly became prone to abuse and fraud, and although attempts were made to limit them and to obviate abuses, indulgences became devalued in the minds of the faithful. Preachers such as Raimondo Peraudi and Johannes Tetzel obscured important distinctions and insinuated that indulgences were a means to salvation. The popes themselves encouraged this impression by declaring that plenary indulgences gave remission from guilt as well as from punishment.

Martin Luther's critique of indulgences objected to the avarice associated with them and to the tendency to suppose that one could buy one's own salvation or the release of deceased persons from purgatory. He regarded the practice as symptomatic of a profound depravation within the church, which he later associated with the reign of the antichrist. Thus, his Ninety-five Theses of October 1517 became the starting point for a broad criticism of ecclesiastical practice combined with complaints about the secular dominance of the pope. Even though Luther's stepping out was interpreted as the beginning of the Reformation and—partially—as the dawn of a new epoch, little in his early publications was really new. Criticism of indulgence practice arose much earlier, and even his opponent in Augsburg, Cardinal Cajetan, wrote a treatise to examine the legitimacy of ecclesiastical penance and indulgence.

The history of indulgences in the Middle Ages can be seen as a striking example of the depravation of a well-intended, but incompletely legitimated, ecclesiastical practice in that period. The Reformers gathering around Martin Luther did not so much focus on the wrong practice as argue for a new and ultimate authority to legitimate religious practice and ecclesiastical doctrine.

J. E. Campbell, *Indulgences* (1953); B. A. R. Felmberg, *Die Ablasstheorie Kardinal Cajetans* (1998); J. le Goff, *The Birth of Purgatory* (1984); A. H. M. Lepicier, *Indulgences* (2nd rev. ed., 1928); M. Ohst, *Pflichtbeichte* (1995); N. Paulus, *Geschichte des Ablass im Mittelalter*, 3 vols. (1923); B. Poschmann, *Der Ablass im Licht der Bussgeschichte* (1948).

MARKUS WRIEDT

Innocent I of Rome (mid-fourth cent.–417), pope from 402, advanced papal claims to preeminence more than any of his predecessors. The son of Pope Anastasius, Innocent was a deacon in the Roman church before acceding to the papacy. His efforts to negotiate a peace with the Visigoths proved fruitless, and in 410 they sacked Rome.

Competition from the great Eastern sees during the fourth-century Arian controversy and a growing self-awareness on Rome's part had caused Innocent's immediate predecessors to extol the preeminence of the Roman church (i.e., Rome was the sole apostolic see in the West and claimed Peter, the greatest apostle, as its founder). Innocent went further by declaring that all decisions about major cases should be confirmed by Rome.

During the Pelagian controversy, Augustine and the African church enlisted Innocent's aid to combat Eastern sympathy for the heresy. Innocent affirmed the African councils' condemnation of Pelagius, but the pope's response clearly demonstrated that he regarded himself not as the Africans' colleague but as their superior. Regarding John Chrysostom's deposition and exile from Constantinople, Innocent vigorously defended his wronged colleague, ultimately severing relations with Antioch and Alexandria. Denouncing a vicious attack (possibly by Pelagians) on Jerome's monastery in Bethlehem, Innocent upbraided the local bishop for negligence in security. Innocent reimposed papal control on churches in the Balkans, although the civil administration there had recently been taken over by Constantinople.

Especially in liturgical and disciplinary matters, Innocent encouraged Western churches to seek guidance from the Apostolic See, since he believed that Christianity in the West had been disseminated solely from Rome. Thirty-six letters from Innocent are extant.

G. Ellard, "How Fifth-Century Rome Administered Sacraments: St. Innocent I Advises an Umbrian Bishop," *TS* 9 (1948): 3–19; R. Eno, *The Rise of the Papacy* (1990); J. N. D. Kelly, *The Oxford Dictionary of the Popes* (1986).

JANE E. MERDINGER

Innocent III (c. 1160–1216), medieval pope. Lotario de' Conti di Segni began his career as a student of theology and law at Paris and Bologna. He was created cardinal-deacon of St. Sergio and St. Bacco in 1190 by his uncle, Pope Clement III; unanimously elected pope January 8, 1198, the day Celestine III died; and consecrated bishop of Rome six weeks later, taking the name Innocent III. He successfully asserted, more than any other medieval pope, the aspirations to universal and ultimate authority of the papacy, effectively intervening as spiritual head of Christendom in imperial controversies (Emperors Otto IV, Frederick II), national controversies (Kings John of England and Philip II of France), and regional politics throughout the West, while protecting the interests of the Papal States.

Among Innocent's consuming interests were reformation of the church, eradication of heresy, and recovery of Jerusalem. Toward these ends he employed various strategies, including support for the nascent mendicant orders, restructuring of the Roman curia, and crusades for Jerusalem (the catastrophic Fourth) and against the Albigensians (in contrast to the reconciliation of the Humiliati and Poor Catholics with the Catholic Church).

The Fourth Lateran Council, called by Innocent in 1215, defined Western Christianity until the sixteenth century. It articulated the core of belief (including the doctrine of transubstantiation) and practice, established the Inquisition, limited new religious orders, circumscribed clerical activities, and defined Jewish-Christian relations.

PL 214–217 (1855); C. Moore, *Pope Innocent III (1160/61–1216): To Root Up and to Plant* (2003); J. M. Powell, *The Deeds of Pope Innocent III by an Anonymous Author* (2004).

LORNA SHOEMAKER

Innocent IV (c. 1200–1254), medieval pope. A protégé of Pope Gregory IX, Sinibaldo Fieschi began his career as a canon lawyer at Bologna, where he both studied and taught; he is considered among the most capable medieval canonists to have become bishop of Rome. He was elected pope in 1243, after an eighteen-month, imperially engineered vacancy of the position, and consecrated as Pope Innocent IV. Immediate and continuous conflict with Emperor Frederick II ensued, leading in part to Innocent's flight for safety to Lyon in 1244. In the following year he convened an ecclesiastical council to address the Hohenstaufen threat. Innocent endorsed Frederick's excommunication, announced the emperor's deposition, and declared a crusade against him. After Frederick's death, the papal-imperial conflict extended to encompass the entire Hohenstaufen family, especially Frederick's sons Conrad IV and Manfred, with particular reference to the security of the Papal States.

Innocent's use of crusade as a political tool, extension of the Inquisition to include torture during inquests, and great expansion of papal provisions and benefices to advance personal interests diminished the moral authority of the papacy; his constant conflict with the Hohenstaufens reduced his efficacy as an administrative leader and spiritual guide.

S. Runciman, *The Sicilian Vespers* (1958); D. P. Waley, *The Papal State in the Thirteenth Century* (1961); J. A. Watt, *The Theory of Papal Monarchy in the Thirteenth Century: The Contribution of the Canonists* (1964).

LORNA SHOEMAKER

Inquisition, Early Modern Inquisitorial processes had occurred in Europe from the thirteenth century through individual inquisitors commissioned by the pope or through the prosecution of heresy in ecclesiastical courts. These processes expanded and acquired increased importance during the early modern period partly, but not exclusively, because of the threat of Protestantism. The circumstances,

targets, and processes varied significantly from country to country.

The Spanish Inquisition predated Protestantism, having been set up in 1478 by monarchs Ferdinand and Isabella to deal with *conversos*—converts from Judaism and Islam accused of continuing or reverting to their previous practices. Protestantism remained a marginal preoccupation until the mid-sixteenth century when local Protestant groups were suppressed and foreign Protestants persecuted.

In the HRE the traditional office of inquisitor remained into the sixteenth century but had been damaged by the fallout from the Reuchlin dispute, and the absence of any effective inquisitorial process enabled the early Lutheran movement to flourish unchecked. In response to this failure in Germany, Charles V's introduction of an inquisition to the Netherlands in 1522 was specifically directly against Protestantism and was responsible for the deaths of the first Protestant martyrs. England and France had no viable inquisition, and secular courts provided an alternative avenue for the pursuit of heresy which avoided the issue of papal authority.

Protestantism provided the specific reason for the institution of the Holy Office (or Roman Inquisition) in 1542. Set up by Pope Paul IV (Caraffa), it was run by a committee of six cardinals under the presidency of the pope. Those brought before it included not only Protestants but supporters of the heliocentric hypothesis of the universe, most notably Galileo. In addition to individuals, books deemed to be heretical were targeted and indices of prohibited books were drawn up by both the Spanish and the Roman Inquisitions.

P. F. Grendler, *The Roman Inquisition and the Venetian Press, 1540–1605* (1977); G. Henningen and J. Tedeschi, eds., *The Inquisition in Early Modern Europe: Studies on Sources and Methods* (1986); H. Kamen, *Inquisition and Society in Spain in the Sixteenth and Seventeenth Centuries* (1985); W. Monter, *Frontiers of Heresy: The Spanish Inquisition from the Basque Lands to Sicily* (1990); E. Peters, *Inquisition* (1988); J. Tedeschi, *The Prosecution of Heresy: Collected Studies on the Inquisition in Early Modern Italy* (1991).

JOHN TONKIN

Inquisition, Medieval "Inquisition" (*inquisitio*) was, in Roman law of the imperial period, the name for a procedure of inquiry initiated by a magistrate (who acted as the emperor's deputy) or initiated by the magistrate's official, rather than by an accuser. A semblance of ancient Roman procedures of inquiry survived in the Carolingian and post-Carolingian West. After, "synodal witnesses" (*testes synodales*) sometimes undertook investigations, in the tenth and eleventh centuries, in cases involving church personnel and property. As the study of law and the institutions of government developed in Europe, and anxiety over religious dissent grew, the ancient procedure was adapted and promoted by the papacy and others.

Intensifying reactions of bishops and other church reformers to religious dissent over the course of the twelfth century culminated in a sweeping condemnation of heretics and their supporters in 1184 in Pope Lucius III's bull *Ad abolendam*. This bull called on bishops to visit parishes where heresy had been reported, to take sworn testimony from local people, to impose church sanctions on the guilty, and to hand the guilty over to secular tribunals for punishment: the clergy were not permitted to do violence directly themselves (this provision had appeared sporadically in church councils over the course of the previous century, and it later meant that religious inquisitions always required the cooperation of temporal authorities). Those secular authorities who failed to cooperate were threatened with excommunication and interdict (an interdict prohibited religious services in a specified place and forbade the faithful to have contact with the place). Lucius's provisions were expanded by Pope Innocent III in his bull *Vergentis in senium* of 1199. He identified heresy with *lèse majesté*, ordered the confiscation of the property of heretics, and disinherited their children.

In the thirteenth century, popes, and sometimes other rulers, assigned powers of investigation to specially appointed officers (*inquisitores*, "inquisitors"). After the Albigensian Crusade, which was summoned by Pope Innocent III in 1208 and took place from 1209 to 1229 (the first crusade directed to a region within Europe), the church acquired a laboratory for the eradication of heresy in southern France. The regional Council of Toulouse in 1229 assigned powers of inquiry to bishops and abbots, who were ordered to nominate a priest and two or three laity in each parish (as "synodal witnesses") to inspect places where heretics could hide. The French crown, which had won control over most of Languedoc in the crusade, ordered its officials to find heretics in 1229. A similar, if less organized, development occurred in the north. During the 1220s Conrad Dorso, John the One-eyed, and Conrad of Marburg, without papal or episcopal license, solicited accusations against heretics in the Rhine valley. Pope Gregory IX, in 1231, then appointed the Dominican prior of Regensburg as delegate judge to seek out heretics in Germany and empowered him to appoint his own proxies to the task. Numerous, periodic papal appointments of Dominicans, Franciscans, and other friars as "inquisitors of heretical depravity" to France, Germany, and other parts of Europe followed in the next decades. This continued until the national and papal reorganizations of inquisition in the late fifteenth and sixteenth centuries.

Papal inquisitors make up the popular image of medieval inquisition, for example, the Dominican Bernard Gui, a character in Umberto Eco's novel *The Name of the Rose*. Gui was an actual papal inquisitor in Toulouse in the early fourteenth century. He left behind a handbook on the conduct of inquiry, and his notaries' register survives. Medieval inquisition was not a particular organization (the Spanish Inquisition, a peculiar national institution, was authorized by the papacy in 1478; and the "Roman Inquisition" was established by Pope Paul III in 1542 and organized as a curial "Congregation" in 1588). Medieval inquisition was a procedure of inquiry. It was an extension of a bishop's pastoral office, his administration of the sacrament of penance and the care of souls, with the pope recognized as the juridical chief of all bishops. The pope could thus appoint inquisitors to regions anywhere in Christendom especially suspected of holding heretics. But significant inquisitions were also conducted by bishops, for example, Jacques Fournier, the bishop of Pamiers.

Although medieval inquisition can hardly be called a benevolent institution, it was not as bloody as it is often portrayed. Gui, for example, is known to have prosecuted 647 heretics over twenty years. Only 45 were executed. The vast majority were assigned penances. Nevertheless, it was more than a corrective institution. It was repressive, if for no other reason than that there was a tremendous imbalance between interrogators and the accused. Inquisitors were trained in scholastic theology, logic, and disputation. They kept, by all appearances, careful records and employed sophisticated interrogation methods to detect and exploit a suspect's inconsistencies. Witnesses and plaintiffs were often uneducated. They could hold uncertain beliefs, which an inquisitor clarified by a battery of questions meant to lay bare vital theological distinctions hidden in a suspect's mind, presumably willfully hidden, and possibly too minute to be comprehended by the suspect. The process of interrogation recontextualized popular belief into the framework of theological tradition and canon law. Uncertain beliefs could in certain circumstances be clarified by torture applied by officers of a cooperating temporal government. Accordingly, scholars periodically have wondered where, in the testimonies, eccentric religious opinion or casual anticlericalism ended and self-conscious adherence to a sect began. Was it in the mind of the interrogator or in actual fact? In at least some times and places, inquisitors surely gave better doctrinal and social shape to a deviant opinion than plaintiffs could have done if left alone. Such issues notwithstanding, the records of inquisitions provide historians with remarkable evidence. Surviving records are detailed, display care in the recording of testimony, and include vivid first- and second-hand reports from ordinary people whose record would otherwise be completely silent.

J. Douvernoy, *Inquisition à Pamiers, interrogatoires de Jacques Fournier, 1318–1325* (1966); J. B. Given, *Inquisition and Medieval Society: Power, Discipline, and Resistance in Languedoc* (1997); B. Gui, *Manuel de l'inquisiteur*, ed. and trans. G. Mollat (1926–1927); R. I. Moore, *The Formation of a Persecuting Society* (2nd ed., 2007); M. G. Pegg, *The Corruption of Angels: The Great Inquisition of 1245–1246* (2001); A. Patschovsky, *Die Anfänge einer ständigen Inquisition in Böhmen: Ein Prager Inquisitoren-Handbuch aus der ersten Hälfte des 14. Jahrhunderts* (1975); E. Peters, *Inquisition* (1988).

CHRISTOPHER OCKER

Interdict This was a sanction of the Catholic Church that prohibited the sacraments, divine offices, and ecclesiastical burial. Its usage became regular in the twelfth century but declined after the sixteenth century. It was imposed on places and communities but rarely on individuals, for whom excommunication was the more usual canonical penalty. It usually punished violations of ecclesiastical liberty by secular rulers and affected their subjects together with them. Popes often exploited it as a political weapon, even imposing it on whole kingdoms, notably England in 1208. Bishops and lesser prelates also imposed it on smaller units within their own jurisdiction. It was meant to make the innocent compel the guilty to come to terms, since otherwise an interdict might not be relaxed. But often it made the innocent hostile to the church and the guilty even more defiant. Hence, medieval popes increasingly reduced its severity for the innocent, permitting infant baptism, final absolution and Communion, preaching, and certain other ministrations during interdicts.

C. R. Cheney, "King John and the Papal Interdict," *BJRL* 31 (1948): 295–317; P. D. Clarke, *The Interdict in the Thirteenth Century: A Question of Collective Guilt* (2007); E. B. Krehbiel, *The Interdict* (1909).

PETER D. CLARKE

Interims The Augsburg Interim refers to the imperial statute of 1548 that attempted to provide a provisional settlement of the religious affairs of the HRE until the conclusion of a general council. With his victory over the Protestant Schmalkald League at the battle of Mühlberg in 1547, Emperor Charles V (1519–1556) was in a position to construct a religious settlement for the empire in keeping with his reformist Catholic convictions. Catholic bishops Julius Pflug and Michael Helding composed the preliminary drafts of what became the Augsburg Interim, but the document went through many stages and received input from the Protestant court preacher Johann Agricola before it was ratified by the "armored" Diet of Augsburg on June 30, 1548. A confessional document of twenty-six articles, the Interim was Catholic in its basic theological orientation and endorsed traditional views of papal authority and the seven sacraments, though the document's teaching on justification allowed a possible Protestant interpretation. The chief concessions to the Protestants were the sanction of clerical marriage and Communion in both kinds to the laity. The Interim was widely disdained by Catholics and Protestants alike and not uniformly enforced in the empire. Although Charles had sought a settlement that would embrace both his Catholic and Protestant subjects, the Catholic principalities balked and were not included in the settlement; thus, the largely Catholic document applied only to Protestant territories. The only states in which it was rigorously imposed were those under direct imperial occupation such as Württemberg, Constance, Augsburg, and Ulm. The introduction of the Interim forced some prominent reformers such as Johannes Brenz and Martin Bucer to abandon their posts. Lands such as the Palatinate and Brandenburg promulgated the Interim but did not actively enforce it, and many North German states refused it altogether. Charles's chief Protestant ally, Elector Maurice of Saxony, likewise hesitated in executing the Interim and commissioned a compromise settlement more in keeping with Protestant teaching with the cooperation of Philip Melanchthon. Excerpts from these proposals were published and derisively labeled the "Leipzig Interim" by Matthias Flacius Illyricus in Magdeburg. The Leipzig proposals had a limited impact on church life, but the controversy surrounding them had tremendous significance for the internal development of Lutheranism. Melanchthon's willingness to tolerate traditional practices he dubbed "things indifferent" (*adiaphora*), such as extreme unction and vestments, split the Lutheran camp between his followers (Philippists) and Gnesio-Lutherans such as Flacius Illyricus who claimed to adhere more closely to Luther's doctrine. Enforcement of the Interim ended with the 1552 Treaty of Passau. The dogged resistance that the Interim encountered from Protestants and Catholics alike signaled the end of the era of religious dialogue and the hardening of confessional camps.

J. Mehlhausen, ed., *Das Augsburger Interim von 1548* (1970); H. Rabe, *Reichsbund und Interim* (1971); G. Wartenberg, "Interims," in *The Oxford Encyclopedia of the Reformation*, vol. 2 (1996), 319–21.

CHARLES D. GUNNOE JR.

Investiture This ceremony centered on the bestowal of symbols (a sword for a vassal, a ring or shepherd's crook for a bishop) and invested officials with the authority appropriate to their offices. Bishops, abbots, and abbesses welcomed royal investiture and protection of their property from local interference. Henry I (918–936) and Otto I (936–973) used appointment and investiture of religious leaders to rebuild a strong monarchy in the face of resistance from German nobles. German prelates performed important political, legal, and military functions and helped establish the revival of the empire in 962. But the reforming popes of the eleventh century challenged secular control of ecclesiastical offices and personnel arguing that the liberty and integrity of the church required spiritual control of spiritual offices. The so-called investiture controversy erupted when Gregory VII (1073–1085) challenged the authority of Emperor Henry IV (1056–1106) to invest bishops in Italy and Germany. The ensuing debate between pro-papal and pro-imperial parties produced numerous pamphlets and treatises, heightened interest in Roman and canon law, and strengthened the German aristocracy. An agreement reached at Worms (1122) amounted to a compromise between emperor and pope and offered only a respite in an enduring struggle between religious and secular authorities over right order in Christian society (see *Reform Papacy*).

U.-R. Blumenthal, *The Investiture Controversy: Church and Monarchy from the Ninth to the Twelfth Century* (1988).

JOHN J. CONTRENI

Irenaeus (c. 130/140–c. 200), bishop of Lyon. Despite his importance as the most profound and influential theologian of the second century, we know very little about Irenaeus. What we do know comes from his own works. He was probably born in Asia Minor, for in his early youth he had listened to Polycarp at Smyrna (*Haer.* 3.3.4; his letter to Florinus, in Eusebius, *Hist. eccl.* 5.20.4–8). Polycarp had known the apostles, and this connection to apostolic times was important for Irenaeus in his later defense of Christian practice and teaching. Eventually he traveled west, probably stayed in Rome and learned from such teachers as Justin, and then went to Gaul. After the violent persecutions of 177, a controversy developed regarding the teaching of Montanus in Asia Minor. Irenaeus was sent to Rome on a mission of peace, bearing the *Letter of the Churches of Vienne and Lyons to the Churches of Asia and Phrygia* (Eusebius, *Hist. eccl.* 5.1–3) and another letter to Bishop Eleutherius of Rome (175–189). The latter describes Irenaeus as a "presbyter," a term often used interchangeably with "bishop." Irenaeus was probably the leader of the community in Vienne and also had responsibility for Lyon, whose imprisoned bishop, Pothinus, Irenaeus would succeed. He later made another peace mission to Rome, urging Bishop Victor (189–198) to be tolerant of the Asian (Quartodeciman) practice of celebrating Pascha on 14 Nisan (see Eusebius, *Hist. eccl.* 5.23–24). Although he is commemorated as a martyr, the evidence is late.

Eusebius mentions a number of works written by Irenaeus and preserves extracts from several letters (see *Hist. eccl.* 5.20, 24, 26), but there are only two extant works: *The Refutation and Overthrowal of Knowledge Falsely So-called* (the title given by Irenaeus), or more concisely, *Against the Heresies* (Eusebius, *Hist. eccl.* 3.23.3), which survives in an almost complete Latin translation, an Armenian translation of the fourth and fifth books, and a number of Greek fragments; and *The Demonstration of the Apostolic Preaching*, which survives only in an Armenian translation discovered at the beginning of the twentieth century.

Irenaeus's pivotal importance for subsequent Christian theology and history lies in his defense of "catholic," "orthodox," or simply "normative" Christianity against, especially, Gnosticism and Marcion but, importantly, on a basis that rests on the manner in which the Gospel was proclaimed, "according to Scripture" (see 1 Cor. 15:3–4), by the apostles from the beginning. Irenaeus is the first Christian writer to use extensively the apostolic writings as Scripture, but he does so within the context of a Christian tradition defined by the elements of the "rule [*canon*] of truth" (belief in one God, one Son, one Spirit—the basis of later creeds), a canonical body of Scripture (largely the same as used thereafter), a sense of apostolic tradition (the preservation of the teaching of the apostles delivered "once for all"), and a claim to a continuity of apostolic succession (a visible witness to the preservation of the teaching). Irenaeus's genius is found in how he develops this matrix, not merely as ad hoc measures to support his episcopal position, arbitrarily excluding others as rhetorically constructed "heretics," but as a means of preserving the Christ proclaimed by the apostles. Scripture is, in his analogy, a mosaic image of a king, the stones of which have been rearranged by the gnostics to produce a picture of a dog; those who know the canon of truth, delivered in baptism, within the tradition, are able to restore the image to contemplate Christ (*Haer.* 1.8–10; 3.1–5).

Preserving this coherence of the Scriptures, Irenaeus is also able to affirm the bodily reality of the human being against the devaluation of the body resulting from the gnostic mythologies. For Irenaeus, the human being is essentially and profoundly earthy, made from mud and animated by the breath of God. The creation described in Genesis already looks forward, according to Irenaeus, to Jesus Christ. The hands of God, the Son and the Spirit, are continuously at work fashioning the earth creature into the image of God, which is attained, finally, only through death and resurrection in Christ, vivified by the Spirit. The martyr, the one no longer living by the flesh but by the Spirit, in confession of Christ, is therefore "the glory of God, the living human being" (*Haer.* 4.20.7).

J. Behr, *Asceticism and Anthropology in Irenaeus and Clement* (2000); J. Behr, *The Way to Nicaea* (2001), 29–48, 111–33; R. M. Grant, *Irenaeus of Lyons* (1997); D. Minns, *Irenaeus* (1994); E. Osborn, *Irenaeus of Lyons* (2001).

JOHN BEHR

Irene (c. 752–803), Byzantine empress and saint. Irene was born in Athens between 750 and 755 into the prominent Sarantapechos family but was subsequently orphaned. In 769 she was brought to Constantinople by Emperor Constantine V to marry his oldest son and heir Leo IV. They were betrothed on November 1; on December 17 she was crowned, followed by marriage. Their only child, Constantine VI, was born on January 14, 771. Leo succeeded his father in 775, and on Easter Sunday, April 14, 776, he crowned his five-year-old son as successor. After Leo died on September 8, 780, Irene ruled for ten years as regent for her son. Irene proved herself to be a convinced iconodule—in opposition to her husband and the policy of the church—and, thus, in 787 she convened the second ecumenical council to be held at Nicaea (the Seventh Ecumenical Council), which restored the veneration of icons. She was deposed in 790 when the army refused her demand for precedence over Constantine. She spent two years in suburban exile until she was recalled on January 15, 792. In 797 she became the first female Byzantine autocrat after having her son Constantine, now twenty-six years old and still the rightful emperor, blinded and deposed. On October 31, 802, she was deposed and succeeded by Nicephorus, her finance minister. She died in exile on the island of Lesbos on August 9, 803. In the twelfth century her remains were transferred to the Church of the Holy Apostles in Constantinople.

Overall, Irene weakened the empire administratively, militarily, and financially because of her distrust of the established aristocratic families, many of whom were iconoclasts. Instead, her government was entrusted to two eunuchs, Stauracius and Aetius, both of whom seriously compromised her position. In 802, Aetius prevented Irene from acting on a proposal to marry Charlemagne and thus unite the two halves of the empire. To her credit, Irene was a very active philanthropist who founded old-age homes, hospices for the poor, and traveler hostels. She also established a number of churches, including St. George the Victorious at Ramla in the Holy Land (784), St. Sophia in Thessalonica, Bizye in Thrace, and several monastery churches in Bithynia. She was canonized for reestablishing the veneration of icons.

C. Diehl, *Byzantine Empresses* (1963); L. Garland, *Byzantine Empresses: Women and Power in Byzantium, AD 527–1204* (1999); Garland, "Constantine VI (780–797 A.D.) and Irene (797–802 A.D.)," in *De Imperatoribus Romanis: An Online Encyclopedia of Roman Emperors* (http://www.roman-emperors.org/irene.htm); S. Runciman, "The Empress Irene the Athenian," in *Medieval Women*, ed. D. Baker (1978); W. Treadgold, "The Empress Irene's Preparation for the Seventh Ecumenical Council," *Patristic and Byzantine Review* 7, no. 1 (1988): 49–58.

MICHAEL PETERSON

Irish Monasticism (sixth–twelfth cent.)

In Ireland, a land never conquered by the Romans, monastic communities dominated the ecclesiastical organization. The most prominent monastic communities were founded by Patrick (Armagh), Cierán (Clonmacnoise), Columba (Kells, Derry, Iona in Scotland), and Kevin (Glendalough). The monks lived under the rule of their respective founder. Seeking exile (*peregrinatio*) counted as the ultimate ascetic practice, and it was voluntary exile that initiated many Irish missions to continental Europe (e.g., Columban the Younger's mission to Merovingian Gaul in 591, where he founded the monasteries of Annegray, Luxeuil, Fontaines, and Bobbio). Lay abbots (*abbas, princeps*) ruled the monastic communities in hereditary succession and in close alliance with secular rulers. Spiritual jurisdiction over the monastic community, including huge numbers of lay brothers (called *manaig* in Old Irish) who lived and worked with their families on monastic lands, fell to the local bishop. The monasteries functioned as proto-urban places of trade and learning and produced invaluable cultural treasures, such as the Book of Kells. Monastic Ireland came to an end when the Irish Church was reorganized, a process completed by the Norman invasion in the twelfth century.

L. M. Bitel, *Isle of the Saints: Monastic Settlement and Christian Communities in Early Ireland* (1990); C. Etchingham, "The Implications of Paruchia," *Ériú* 44 (1993): 139–62; M. Herbert, *Iona, Kells, and Derry: The History and Hagiography of the Monastic Familia of Columba* (1988); A. Kehnel, *Clonmacnois— The Church and Lands of St. Ciarán* (1997); A. MacShamhráin, *Church and Polity in Pre-Norman Ireland: The Case of Glendalough* (1996); R. Sharpe, "Some Problems Concerning the Organization of the Church in Early Medieval Ireland," *Perita* 3 (1984): 230–70.

ANNETTE KEHNEL

Isaac of Nineveh (c. 630–700), spiritual writer.

We know little of Isaac's life prior to his ordination as bishop of Nineveh in 676. He was born along the Persian Gulf and entered the monastery of Bet-Qatraye. He resigned the episcopate after only five months and retired to Kurdistan and the monastery of Rabban Shaphur. His literary activity dates from this period, and legend says that he went blind from a combination of asceticism and study. His ascetic treatises are written in apothegmatic style and became well known and accepted even outside the Nestorian Church (see *Church of the East, Middle Ages*). Various tripartite schemas of spiritual growth are common in the Christian East. Isaac's is more practical than theoretical and articulates the way of the body, the way of the soul, and the way of the spirit, leading to wonder and continual praise of God. The spiritual teaching of Isaac emphasizes the primacy of God's love and mercy. His expressions raised some controversy about his orthodoxy since they were perceived as displaying Origenistic tendencies.

P. Bedjan, *De Perfectione Religiosa* (1909); S. Brock, *Isaac of Nineveh (Isaac the Syrian): The Second Part Chapters IV–XLI,* in CSCO Scriptores Syri (1995), 224–25; Brock, *The Syriac Fathers on Prayer and the Spiritual Life* (1987).

EUGENE M. LUDWIG, OFM CAP.

Ishu-Yab II, Catholicos (patriarch) of Seleucia-Ctesiphon (628–646).

The Shah Khasro II (589–628) prevented the Nestorians in Persia from electing a catholicos. His successor, Kovad II, allowed an election, and after Mar Babai declined the office, the choice fell on the bishop of Balad, Ishu-Yab. This was a period of political instability in Persia and a time of growing military threat not from the Byzantines but from the Arabs.

The Zoroastrian royal family chose Ishu-Yab to lead a delegation to Constantinople to negotiate terms of peace with the Christian emperor Heraclius. Their meeting took place in Aleppo, and Ishu-Yab was even able to persuade Heraclius of his christological orthodoxy. The two received the Eucharist together and concluded a peace agreement beween Persia and the Roman Empire. During Ishu-Yab's tenure as catholicos, missionaries from the Church of the East reached the capital of the T'ang dynasty in China in 635 (see *Al-o-pen* and *Christianity in T'ang and Yuan China*). He has been credited with establishing an independent metropolitan see in India, but that more likely took place under Ishu-Yab III. Ishu-Yab's diplomatic skills were in evidence again in 637 when the Arabs took Seleucia-Ctesiphon and he was able to negotiate favorable terms of treatment for Christians.

———

S. Moffet, *A History of Christianity in Asia*, vol. 1, *Beginnings to 1500* (1992).

EUGENE M. LUDWIG, OFM CAP.

Ishu-Yab III, catholicos (patriarch) of Seleucia-Ctesiphon (649–659). Ishu-Yab III was the third catholicos of Seleucia-Ctesiphon during the Arab conquest, the first two being Ishu-Yab II and Marama. Prior to becoming catholicos he had been bishop of Nineveh-Mosul and metropolitan of Irbil. He was a member of the embassy to Heraclius led by Ishu-Yab II. The favorable treatment of Christians negotiated by Ishu-Yab II held through his reign, and he even wrote of the respect shown to Christians by the Muslims. When the Muslims moved their capital from Damascus to Baghdad, only the Nestorians were permitted to locate their catholicos there.

Ishu-Yab had to contend with a secessionist movement centered in Fars along the Persian Gulf coast. His own position was secure enough that he was able to deal successfully with the challenge to his authority. It was probably during his reign that jurisdiction over India was removed from the Persian bishop of Riwardashir and given to an Indian metropolitan subject only to the catholicos. According to the eleventh-century *Chronicle of Seert*, Ishu-Yab was a major influence in the formation of the liturgy of the Church of the East.

———

R. Duval, ed., *Scriptores Syri*, vols. 11 and 12, CSCO (1904); P. Scott-Moncrieff, *The Book of Consolation, or the Pastoral Epistles of Mar Isho-yabh of Kuphlana in Adiabene* (1904).

EUGENE M. LUDWIG, OFM CAP.

Isidore of Seville (c. 560s–636), renowned bishop, theologian, and younger brother of Leander of Seville, whom he succeeded as bishop in Seville in 599 or 600. Isidore served as bishop for about thirty-seven years. He played a major role in the promotion of the religious and political unity of Iberia, already formally started at the Third Council of Toledo in 589. He also presided over two influential provincial councils: the Second Council of Seville (619) and the Fourth Council of Toledo (633). In the first he led the bishops of Seville in a forceful defense against Monophysite views being propagated in the Visigothic kingdom. In the second council, he led the way to establishing liturgical uniformity in Iberia, in a rite that later was called the Mozarab Rite. He also decreed at this council the establishment of intense instruction of the clergy in each diocese. The gifted were to be ordained, while the less academic were directed to monasteries. Significantly, the council under his leadership condemned any attempts to convert the Jews by force, an action that went against the policies of the Visigothic monarchs. These and other reforms had a profound and salutary effect on the life of the church, so much so that some scholars have even called this period the "Isidorian Renaissance."

Isidore was by far the most prolific author of the Visigothic church, with approximately seventeen major treatises to his credit. His works reveal a profound knowledge of Scripture and the fathers of the church, a tribute to the teaching he received from his brother Leander as well as by his own initiative. During the medieval centuries he became one of the most quoted authors; his works were read in Ireland, Gaul, North Africa, the Greek East, and even in the Muslim world in Arabic translation. His writings span the full range of topics: commentaries on the Old and New Testaments, doctrine, ecclesiology, liturgy, asceticism, penance, cosmology, biblical numerology, allegorical insights into over three hundred Bible figures, heretical sects, Christian formation and spirituality, a history to 615, a work against Judaism (not anti-Semitic), lives of illustrious men (thirty-three African-Iberian), a second commentary of the OT, and a history of the Germanic invasion and settlement of Iberia, where he presents the invaders as the heirs of Rome. His most famous work is the *Etymologies*, a didactic encyclopedia. It is a synthesis of learning that includes fifty-two ancient authors and twenty-one Christian ones from the Bible and the church fathers. Wherever it was read it encouraged the reading of classical writers and a deeper understanding of the Christian faith. He began the work in 615 and was circulating it by 621 under title *Origins* before the final version was completed. Collaborators under his guidance expanded the work significantly.

Isidore's remains were taken in 1063 to León for safekeeping—in the face of the Muslim invasion—where they remain to this day. He was declared a doctor of the church in 1722, and as recently as 2001 he was proposed as the patron saint of the Internet.

M. C. Diaz y Diaz, "Introducción," in *San Isidoro de Sevilla: Etimologías*, ed. J. Oroz Reta (1982), 1–257; J. Fontaine, *Isidore de Séville et la culture classique dans l'Espagne wisigothique*, 3 vols. (1983); M. Reydellet, *La royauté dans la littérature latine de Sidoine Apollinaire à Isidore de Séville* (1981).

ALBERTO FERRERIO

Islam and the Western Church

According to Richard Southern, Islam was medieval Christendom's greatest problem. Christian attitudes toward Islam were characterized from the beginning by ambivalence and repulsion, on the one hand, and baffled admiration for and fascination with Islam's military and cultural achievements, on the other. Confidence in the superiority of Christianity was regularly challenged by the inescapable realization that Islam was also the leading religion of a thriving, flourishing rival. The defensive military position of Western European Christians and the capital punishment awaiting proselytizers in Islamic lands deterred missionary efforts and helped shape the complexity and variety of Western attitudes toward Muslims. These attitudes ranged from crusade to mission, from conflict to dialogue and scholarly exchange.

Both conflictual and less conflictual responses evolved over time, but the blueprint was conflictual and shaped by the encounter of Eastern and Spanish Christians with Islam. When Christians first encountered Muslims in the seventh century, they tried to fit them into one of the categories they had established for the religious other: Jew, pagan, and heretic. An inimical portrait of Islam was painted by authors as diverse as Bede (673–735), who depicted Muslims as a divinely ordained, pagan scourge, Joachime of Fiore (c. 1135–1202), and Nicholas of Lyra (1270–1340), who continued an earlier Eastern debate about the link between Islam and the forces of the antichrist. The Third and Fourth Lateran Councils extended restrictions on Jews, which prohibited them from owning Christian slaves and excluded them from public office, to Muslims, while Lateran IV regarded members of both faiths as blasphemers and hostile to Christianity. Vernacular literature employed the established tropes. The authors of *chansons de geste* viewed Saracens as pagans. Dante viewed Muhammad as a

heretic. According to John Tolan, Western writers "ignored or distorted" those "uncomfortable facts" that challenged established views. Current scholarship has stressed the role of typifying and defining the other as a path for self-definition for Christians (Neumann, but see also Kedar). Distortions of Islam were accompanied by a growing sense of Christian superiority. By the twelfth century, European writers, many of whom were churchmen, fell back "on the hermeneutical and exegetical weapons . . . presenting Islam as a new variety of one of the well known and thoroughly despised enemies of old: pagan idolatry, heresy, the cult of Antichrist, or a confused blend of all of these" (J. V. Tolan, *Saracens: Islam in the Medieval Imagination*).

Given the prevailing view of Islam in the West, conquest seemed a reasonable response; it was in due course complemented by efforts at conversion. Popes from the eleventh century on mobilized crusaders (seen as defenders of the faith) against Muslims (the most important being Pope Urban II and Pope Innocent III). The Crusades adopted conversion as their objective by the mid-twelfth century according to Kedar (and, more often than not, scholarly interests appear to have been shaped by missionary goals). Pope Gregory VII and Abbot Hugh of Cluny advocated conversion of newly conquered Sicilian and Spanish Muslims. Prelates such as Jacques de Vitry (c. 1160–1240, bishop of Acre) and mendicant friars missionized (Francis of Assisi, who visited the sultan of Egypt; the Dominican master general, Humbert of Romans [c. 1194–1277], set conversion as one of the order's goals, and called for missions to the Holy Land). Missions extended from Seville to Morocco and Jerusalem, and some friars were martyred—for example, the missionaries to Tana, who were sentenced to death after telling the Muslim judge that "in no way is [Muhammad] a prophet, but rather a diabolical man who carried out the ministry of the devil" (Tolan, *Saracens*, 230). To support missionary efforts, the Council of Vienne (1311/1312) accepted Ramon Lull's proposal to establish chairs of Oriental languages in the universities of Paris, Oxford, Bologna, Avignon, and Salamanca. Ironically, Lull, a layman, was heeded more than the friar Roger Bacon, who had campaigned for the philological and philosophical training of missionaries before him.

The twelfth century saw the awakening of a European interest in Islam, too, which continued into the thirteenth century. Peter the Venerable and Robert Ketton, the astronomer and translator of the Qur'an, for example, tried to understand Islam on its own terms to a far greater degree than had been customary before them. Modern scholars have differed in their interpretation of the motives of this interest. Was Robert Ketton's translation of the Qur'an (1140s) part of a campaign to refute and convert Muslims, or was it part of a scholarly trend to synthesize learning by studying the Qur'an and Arabic translations of ancient texts? Either way, one fact stands out: European Christians viewed Islam through theologically tinted eyes. The opinions of diplomats, merchants, artists, and any European Christian who had connections with the East, however much they contributed to the tempering of early type-casting, were shaped by the overarching Christian view of Islam, which by the thirteenth century had crystallized around a European portrayal of Muhammad as a false prophet and precursor of the antichrist, evil and dangerous enough to Christians to justify *reconquista* and crusade, mission and conversion.

D. R. Blanks and M. Frassetto, *Western Views of Islam in Medieval and Early Modern Europe: Perception of Other* (1999); N. Daniel, *Islam and the West: The Making of an Image* (1960); L.-A. Hunt, "'Excommunicata Generatione': Christian Imagery of Mission and Conversion of the Muslim Other between the First Crusade and the Early Fourteenth Century," *Al-Masâq: Studeia Arabo-Islamica Mediterranea* 8 (1995): 79–153; B. Z. Kedar, *Crusade and Mission: European Approaches toward the Muslims* (1984); J. Kritzeck, *Peter the Venerable and Islam* (1964); I. B. Neumann, *Uses of the Other: "The East" in European Identity Formation* (1999); J. V. Tolan, *Medieval Christian Perceptions of Islam: A Book of Essays* (1996); Tolan, *Saracens: Islam in the Medieval European Imagination* (2002); W. M. Watt, *Muslim-Christian Encounters* (1991).

VARDA KOCH OCKER

Islam, Reformation Understanding of

During the reign of Sultan Sulaiman the Magnificent (1520–1566), the Ottoman Empire reached the height of its military power. Throughout Europe the "Turk" became a catchword for popular fear and anxiety. To a large degree, the Turkish threat was so terrifying because many Germans understood the conflict between the Habsburg and Ottoman Empires to be a struggle not between two political powers but between the forces of Christendom and that

of its archenemy, Islam. Although noticeably less among Calvin and his successors, early modern interest in Islam is clearly evident through the hundreds of sermons, pamphlets, and broadsheets that were printed concerning the Turks. (Among most central and northern Europeans, "Turks" and "Mohammedans" were synonymous terms.)

While continuities with the medieval period remained, during the Reformation important alterations occurred in Western interpretations of Islam. Even though he did not systematically analyze Islam, the categories of understanding that Martin Luther established served as the framework for later Protestant thinking on Islam. Luther viewed Islam as fundamentally a religion of works righteousness. In contrast to medieval writers, Luther avoided designating the faith of the Turks as heresy. According to Luther, Muslims worship a different God than Christians; they worship the devil himself. At times Luther grudgingly did praise the Turks for their piety. However, this was done primarily as an attack against Roman Catholic "works." But if the Turks were the tool of the devil, why does God not stop them? It was clear to all confessions that the seemingly unstoppable Ottoman advance was not due to any innate Turkish advantages. Rather, God was permitting the continued Ottoman victories because of the internal failings of Christendom. Despite Luther's reliance on a call to repentance against Islam, he also advocated a military response. However, the Lutheran military response to Islam differed significantly from the sixteenth-century Roman Catholic continuation of the medieval crusading ideal. Christians as Christians were not to lead or even participate in battle. Furthermore, ecclesiastical attempts at military leadership angered God. Luther's argument was quickly criticized by Roman Catholic theologians, but his unequivocal denunciation of the traditional crusade was highly influential and is one of the most important developments in Western understandings of Islam during the Reformation. According to Luther, military action was still necessary, however, because Christians were not only citizens of heaven but also citizens of an earthly kingdom. War against the Turks was justified on the basis of God's dual political commands: governments must preserve peace and order, and Christian subjects must obey established authority. The Turks also played a significant role in early Lutheran interpretations of the eschaton. The most direct references to the Turks in prophetic scripture were understood to be the "little horn" of Daniel 7 and Gog and Magog in Revelation 20 and Ezekiel 38–39. Both Daniel and Revelation were interpreted to prophesy that the Turks would be allowed dominion for a time but then would be destroyed by God immediately before the Last Judgment.

Luther's understanding of Islam was widely influential, but his was not the only new voice on the subject during the Reformation. An interest in linguistics and missions led the Zurich reformer Theodor Bibliander to study Arabic and to publish the first-ever printed Qur'an in Latin translation in 1543. There were a variety of responses among the radical reformers. Some spiritualists used the Turks as an example of those who possessed a separate but equally valid revelation from God. The threat of Islam provided a striking worst-case scenario for Anabaptists to demonstrate their absolute rejection of all violence and war, even in the self-defense of Europe against the "cruel and bloody Turk." Various Protestant responses to the Ottomans shattered the dominant medieval unity within Christendom concerning the understanding of and the response to Islam. Although much of the medieval heritage remained, Reformation understandings of Islam would provide the seeds for linguistic interest that would culminate in the development of the scholarly field of Orientalism and a secularized approach to relations with the Turks that would gradually allow the Ottoman Empire to be integrated into the European state system.

D. R. Blanks and M. Frassetto, *Western Views of Islam in Medieval and Early Modern Europe: Perception of Other* (1999); H. Bobzin, *Der Koran im Zeitalter der Reformation: Studien zur Frühgeschichte der Arabistik und Islamkunde in Europa* (1995); C. Göllner, *Turcica: Die Türkenfrage in der öffentlichen Meinung Europas im 16. Jahrhunderts* (1978); G. J. Miller, "Luther on the Turks and Islam," *LQ* 14 (2000): 79–97.

GREGORY J. MILLER

Italy, Reformation in In and around the sixteenth century, a varied and extensive set of initiatives for the reform of church and society arose in the territories of modern-day Italy. These initiatives flowed from a variety of sources. One source was the generalized desire for reform inherited from the medieval and Renaissance periods. This desire energized the efforts of numerous would-be reformers such as the fiery Florentine Girolamo Savonarola (1452–1498), the peripatetic Anabaptist Camillo

Renato (c. 1500–c. 1575), and the conciliatory Cardinal Gasparo Contarini (1483–1542), who were active from Sicily in the south to Milan in the north—and beyond. Their messages, sometimes infused with apocalyptic imagery, sometimes charged with emotional fervor, and sometimes focused on the politics of institutional reform, emphasized a common critique of the power and immorality of the papal court, which had reached infamous depths of pastoral neglect under the pontificates of Alexander VI (1492–1503) and Julius II (1503–1513).

A second source of the Reformation in Italy flowed from the rich cultural diversity on the peninsula. The social, geographic, climatic, economic, and cultural differences among the Italian states during this period make the designation "Italy" little more than a convenient geographic designation. The lack of unified Italian culture allowed numerous reformers to appear and reformation programs to be initiated, but these attempts remained rather localized and isolated from one another. The disparate social settings in which the message was proclaimed (e.g., local churches, convents, artisans' shops, academies, confraternities, universities, monasteries, workplaces), together with the diversity of local circumstances, produced a multiplicity of reformation movements while simultaneously making a unified reformation difficult if not impossible.

A third source of the Reformation in Italy was the flow of Protestant ideas from reformers north of the Alps—preeminently Martin Bucer, John Calvin, Martin Luther, Philip Melanchthon, and Huldrych Zwingli. As the Reformation made its way to Italy, ideas of these men (and the movements they represented) found receptive audiences—providing useful biblical and theological underpinnings for the efforts of reformers in Italy. Particularly in the 1520s, Reformation theological emphases such as the Word of God, the dialectic of law and gospel, the priesthood of all believers, and the reform of the Mass were well received and closely watched by Italians. These emphases were expressed well in the widely popular booklet *Beneficio di Christo*, published in 1543 and infused with references to and paraphrases of various German and Swiss reformers.

A fourth source of the Reformation in Italy flowed from the reformist groups within the Roman Catholic curia itself. Primary here is the group known as *Spirituali*—those priests and prelates who entertained Reformation ideas and sought a degree of conciliation with Protestants, while maintaining their positions within the

Roman Catholic Church's hierarchy. Other reform-minded groups who stayed within the Catholic Church (e.g., "catholic evangelicals" and "Nicodemites") expressed their ideas in diverse ways, sometimes hiding their convictions, sometimes tailoring them for acceptance by the hierarchy, sometimes accepting modest reforms as sufficient progress. This fourth source of the Reformation in Italy is exemplified by Cardinal Gasparo Contarini, who represented Rome at the Regensburg Colloquy in 1545 and whose activities eventuated in his appointment to head a select commission of prelates charged with making recommendations for church reform to the general council of the church that was eventually to meet at Trent from 1545 to 1563. In 1537 the commission produced the document *Consilium de emendanda ecclesia*, which is notable for its candid and stern critique of the church, especially its placing of responsibility for the corruption and immorality of the church squarely at the feet of the papacy. Even though it offered little in the way of innovative recommendations for reform, the document pointed at the concentration of churchly power in the pope as the fundamental cause for the church's current state.

A fifth source of the distinctive character of the Reformation in Italy was the powerful presence of the papacy, in particular the consistent unwillingness of the popes during this period to allow reform in "head and members." They successfully used their political power (upon which many weaker Italian states and princes depended) to suppress calls for reform, but they could not silence them. Popular interest in a viable moral protest against church corruption continued until it was variously marginalized (e.g., the Waldensians), given an institutional voice at the Council of Trent (1545–1563), and suppressed by the Inquisition (reinstituted in 1542).

Finally, these sources flowed together to provide the Reformation in Italy with its distinctive character. As the ideas of northern European reformers met existing desires for reform in Italy, they were given variable expressions and took on various local permutations. This diversity did not provide sufficient influence in any one place for any rulers in Italy publicly to support Protestant Reformation initiatives. Neither did any Italian states become Protestant. After 1542, a strengthened and reorganized Inquisition (patterned after Spain, with its authority centralized in the papacy) began to deal effectively and decisively with dissenters, after a period of relative inactivity, so that inquisitors eventually repressed unacceptable reform initiatives. Furthermore, the Council of Trent gave institutional expression to many aspects of the Catholic reform impulse and firmly established the Counter-Reformation, particularly after 1580. Finally, a revitalized late-sixteenth-century Roman Catholic Church spawned growing religious uniformity and supplanted the diversity of reform thought on the peninsula.

S. Caponetto, *The Protestant Reformation in 16th-Century Italy* (1999); F. C. Church, *The Italian Reformers, 1534–1564* (1974); D. Cantimori, *Italian Heretics of the 16th Century* (1979); E. Gleason, ed., *Reform Thought in 16th Century Italy* (1981); G. Hanlon, *Early Modern Italy: A Comprehensive Bibliography of Works in English and French* (2002); H. Jedin, *A History of the Council of Trent*, 2 vols. (1957); Jedin, *Papal Legate at the Council of Trent: Cardinal Seripando* (1947); J. A. Marino, *The Short Oxford History of Italy: Early Modern Italy, 1550–1796* (2002); J. Tedeschi, ed., *Italian Reformation Studies in Honor of Laelius Socinus* (1965).

WILLIAM R. RUSSELL

Jacob of Edessa

Jacob of Edessa (640–708), Syrian Orthodox bishop, scholar. Born at En Debha near Antioch, Jacob studied as a monk at Qenneshrē, then at Alexandria under Greek scholar John Philoponus. He served as bishop of Edessa twice (684–687, 708). The first occasion he resigned when the patriarch failed to support his efforts to reform monastic discipline. Retirement allowed him to devote himself to scholarship, especially the transmission of Greek science, philosophy, and theology into the Syriac realm.

He is considered perhaps the greatest scholar of Syriac letters. His primary contributions include a complete revision of the Peshitta (Syriac) Old Testament based upon the Hebrew and the first Syriac grammar, in which he utilized Greek vowel points and diacritical marks for pronunciation. It became the basis of the Syriac grammar of Bar Hebraeus (1225–1286) and of Semitic grammar generally. He wrote a historical *Chronicle* in 692 and a commentary on the Hexameron (six days of creation) that included much scientific material from Greek sources. It was completed after his death by George, bishop of the Arab Tribes (d. 724). He also translated homilies of Severus of Antioch from the Greek into Syriac, the former now lost.

S. Brock, "Jacob of Edessa's Discourse on the Myron," *Oriens Christianum* 63 (1979): 20–36; Jacob of Edessa, *Chronicle*, ed. E. W. Brooks, *ZDMG* 53/54 (1899–1900): 261–327, 100–102; "Canons" in A. Vööbus, *The Synodicon in the West Syrian Tradition*, vol. 1 (1975), 206–47.

ROBERT A. KITCHEN

Jacob of Serug (449–521), Syriac poet, biblical expositor, bishop. An anonymous life describes Jacob as a child prodigy who recited homilies and theological treatises and at the age of twenty-two began formal writing for the church. He studied at the School of Edessa (c. 470) and was ordained a priest, then appointed chorepiscopus (502), and finally consecrated bishop of Batnan in Serug by Monophysite champion Severus of Antioch (518).

Jacob reputedly wrote 760 *mēmrē*, or metric homilies (approximately 300 survive), on biblical and ascetical themes, earning him the title of "the Flute of the Holy Spirit." These homilies, 300–400 verses long, were read or sung during worship in a distinctive twelve-syllable meter. There are forty-three letters extant, eight festal homilies, a saint's life, and liturgical works.

Living in the turbulent post-Chalcedonian era, Jacob did not enter the christological debates and appeared to criticize those who dwelt upon these issues. His position is still debated. Most have judged Jacob to be Chalcedonian, but his letters indicate a disapproval of Dyophysite Christology.

M. Hansbury, *Jacob of Serug: On the Mother of God* (1998); S. A. Harvey, "Jacob of Serugh's Homily on Simeon the Stylite," in *Ascetic Behavior in Greco-Roman Antiquity*, ed. V. Wimbush (1990), 15–27; T. Kollamparampil, *Jacob of Serugh: Select Festal Homilies* (1997).

ROBERT A. KITCHEN

Jacobite Church   Jacobite is a name for the non-Chalcedonian Syrian Orthodox Church. It is derived from Jacob Baradeus, who was sent by Empress Theodora as bishop to the monophysite Ghassanids. Jacob ordained and organized a non-Chalcedonian hierarchy that gave institutional stability to the Syrian Orthodox Church. Today the term is used officially only in India, and in many circles it is considered pejorative. In the seventh through the ninth centuries, Syrian Orthodox scholars such as Jacob of Edessa and Gregory Bar Hebraeus were active

with their Nestorian counterparts in the transmission of classical Greek texts to the Arabs. Liturgically, the Jacobite Church belongs to the West Syrian family, and the official liturgical language is Syriac. The patriarch's title is "patriarch of Antioch and all the East." The patriarchal residence is in Damascus, as are those of the Melkite and Orthodox patriarchs. Complex political and religious realities make it easier for patriarchs of Antioch to live in Syria than in Turkey.

In the year 2000, the Syrian Orthodox population in the Middle East was around 200,000, with about an equal population in diaspora. The Syrian Orthodox Church of India has about two million members.

R. B. Betts, *Christians in the Arab East: A Political Study* (1978); J. Meyendorff, *Imperial Unity and Christian Divisions* (1989).

EUGENE M. LUDWIG, OFM CAP.

James I of England (1566–1625), king of Scotland from 1567 (as James VI) and king of England from 1603. James was the only son of Henry Stuart, Lord Darnley, and Mary, Queen of Scots (who abdicated in 1567). As king of Scotland, he sought an alliance with England, which he obtained in 1586. He married Anne of Denmark in 1589. As king of Scotland, he generally supported the clergy over against the nobility, but he resented the political influence of the Presbyterian clergy; from 1598 forward, he supported and actively sought the restoration of the episcopacy. In 1603 he took the throne of England by right of his mother's descent from Henry VII, and at the Hampton Court Conference of 1604 he effectively upheld the divine right of kings and clerical apostolic succession. His leniency toward Roman Catholics led to a peace with Spain in 1604, and during his reign the influence of the clergy at court increased dramatically. His reign, successful in many ways, a failure in others, paved the way for the disasters of Charles I and the English Civil War.

I. Carrier, *James VI and I, King of Great Britain* (1998); J. Doelman, *James I and the Religious Culture of England* (2000).

ALDEN R. LUDLOW

Jane Grey (1537–1554), Protestant queen of England. The daughter of Henry, duke of Suffolk, and grandniece of Henry VIII, Jane received an exemplary humanist and evangelical education, learning Latin, Greek, French, Italian, and Hebrew. She admired Martin Bucer (then at Cambridge) and corresponded in Latin with Heinrich Bullinger. The sickly Edward VI, supported by Jane's new father-in-law, John Dudley, duke of Northumberland, named Jane heir to the throne instead of Edward's Roman Catholic half-sister Mary. With Edward's precipitous death on July 6, 1553, the sixteen-year-old Jane was acclaimed queen. Mary, however, rallied popular pro-Tudor sentiment to herself and by July 20 had seized the throne. Jane was imprisoned; after her father's support of Thomas Wyatt's failed rebellion, she was sentenced to death. She steadfastly resisted conversion to Catholicism, eloquently defending her Protestant faith. Jane was beheaded for treason on February 12, an ambiguous martyr for Elizabethan Protestants.

R. Bainton, *Women of the Reformation in France and England* (1973); Bainton, *The Chronicle of Queen Jane, and of Two Years of Queen Mary*, ed. J. Nichols (1850); J. Foxe, *Acts and Monuments*, vol. 6 (1837); P. Zahl, *Five Women of the English Reformation* (2001).

CHRISTOPHER B. BROWN

Jansenism A movement within Roman Catholicism in the seventeenth and eighteenth centuries that emphasized the Augustinian doctrines of predestination and sovereign divine grace. It is named for Cornelis Otto Jansen (1585–1638), a Dutch theologian and bishop of Ypres influenced by Michel Baius (de Bay, 1513–1589). Jansen immersed himself in the study of Augustine's writings and came to embrace a form of Augustinianism radically opposed to the Jesuit and Molinist emphasis on human free will, the merit of works, and conditional predestination. Jansen concluded that the Jesuits and many of the theologians of the Catholic Reformation had been driven to the extremes of Semi-Pelagianism in their controversies with the Protestants. His major controversial work, *Augustinus* (published posthumously in 1640) found considerable readership and approbation in the Low Countries and even met with initial, yet short-lived, approval by some theologians of the Sorbonne. In 1653 Innocent X condemned Jansen's views in the bull *Cum occasione*. The papal bull condemned five propositions derived from *Augustinus*: (1) that special grace is required to fulfill God's commands; (2) that interior grace is irresistible; (3) that the only freedom required to obtain merit is freedom from compulsion, not freedom from

necessity; (4) that to claim that the human will is free to comply with or resist divine grace is Semi-Pelagianism; and (5) that it is Semi-Pelagian to teach that Christ died for every human person. There are intriguing similarities between Jansen's opposition to the Molinist Jesuits and the Calvinists rejection of Arminius's views at the Synod of Dort. Despite further papal condemnations the Jansenist movement continued under the leadership of Antoine Arnauld. Blaise Pascal was its most famous adherent. The movement also challenged the authority of the pope and the church's sacramental theology. Clement IX's *Unigenitus* (1713) harshly condemned the Jansenist views of Pasquier Quesnel, giving rise to persecution of Jansenists in France. Jansenism was tolerated in the Netherlands, and a schismatic Jansenist bishop was consecrated in Utrecht in 1723.

Henri de Lubac, *Augustinianism and Modern Theology* (1969); C. Maire, *De la cause de Dieu à la cause de la nation: Le Jansenisme au XVIIIe siecle* (1998); J. Orcibal, *Jansenius d'Ypres* (1989); A. Sedgwick, *Jansenism in Seventeenth-Century France: Voices from the Wilderness* (1977).

RAYMOND A. BLACKETER

Jeanne of Navarre (1528–1572), Calvinist queen of Navarre, daughter of Marguerite d'Angoulême (sister of King Francis I of France) and Henry d'Albret of Béarn and the remnant kingdom of Navarre. Raised by a governess in Normandy, Jeanne saw little of her parents. She resisted an arranged marriage and married Antoine de Bourbon, first prince of the blood, heir to the French throne after the Valois. Both converted to Protestantism, but he returned to Catholicism. She remained steadfast, raising their son Protestant, the future Henry IV, king of Navarre (1572–1610) and France (1589–1610). She corresponded with the Reformed leaders of Geneva. Pierre Viret and then Nicolas Des Gallars were sent as resident pastors to help her establish the Reformed church in Béarn. She and her son became leaders in the Huguenot cause during the Wars of Religion. Shortly before her death from tuberculosis, she agreed to his marriage to Marguerite of Valois, daughter of Henry II and Catherine de Médicis, regent mother for Charles IX, king of France (1560–1574).

N. Roelker, *Queen of Navarre, Jeanne d'Albret, 1528–1572* (1968).

JEANNINE E. OLSON

Jeremiah II (1530/1535–1595), patriarch of Constantinople. He was recognized early on for his administrative skills and was appointed patriarch in 1572. Although he suffered due to internal Turkish politics, he was noted for combating simony and encouraging education among the clergy. He played an important role in the establishment of the Patriarchy of Moscow (1588–1589). It was during his patriarchy that Lutheran theologians from Tübingen wrote to Constantinople in an attempt to receive acknowledgment and support. In the answer he authorized (1576), Jeremiah praised several Lutheran doctrines, including the marriage of priests, but opposed any deviation in the creed. Jeremiah's answers are the first clear and authoritative critique of the doctrines of the Reformation from an Orthodox point of view.

E. Benz, *Wittenberg und Byzanz* (1949); G. Mastrantonis, *Augsburg and Constantinople: The Correspondence between the Tübingen Theologians and the Patriarch Jeremiah II of Constantinople on the Augsburg Confession* (1982).
                                    GREGORY J. MILLER

Jerome (c. 347–419), biblical scholar and controversialist. Jerome was born in Stridon in Dalmatia of Christian parents. He studied grammar, rhetoric, and philosophy in Rome and was baptized there in 366. From Rome he went to Trier and then, after a visit to Stridon, through Asia Minor to Antioch (374). He then went to the desert of Chalcis to undertake an ascetical life (375–377), but he also continued his studies of the Bible and began to learn Hebrew from a converted Jew. From Chalcis he went back to Antioch, where he heard lectures on the Bible by Apollinaris of Laodicea; by this time he was fluent in Greek. The bishop Paulinus ordained him a priest there on the condition that he would not be bound to a church. He then went on to Constantinople, where he heard Gregory of Nazianzus and began to translate homilies by Origen. In 382 Jerome returned to Rome and became secretary to Pope Damasus and spiritual director to ascetically minded noblewomen. Damasus asked Jerome to revise the Latin translation of the Gospels on the basis of old Greek manuscripts; thus Jerome began the most important work of his life. He also revised the translation of the Psalms at this time. Damasus died in 384, and the Roman populace turned against ascetics. In 385 Jerome left for Bethlehem, where he lived for most of the rest of his life, although he traveled to Egypt

and heard Didymus the Blind lecture on the Prophets. Others, including Paula and her daughter Eustochium, joined Jerome in Bethlehem, and two monasteries were built there, one for men and one for women.

The principal work of Jerome's life was the translation of, and commentary on, the Bible. After correcting the Latin Gospels and the Psalter, he began work on the Old Testament. He first attempted to revise the Latin books against the Septuagint but soon realized that this procedure was inadequate. In 391 he began a wholly new translation from the original Hebrew text.

Besides his translations, Jerome wrote prefaces to the books he translated or revised, as well as several glossaries of Hebrew names and place names. He wrote commentaries on many books of the Bible, often drawing on Origen, Eusebius, or other sources. His earliest commentaries (386–387) are on Pauline letters (Ephesians, Galatians, Philemon, and Titus); he also wrote on Ecclesiastes (389), the twelve Minor Prophets (393–406), Matthew (398), and the four Major Prophets (407–420).

Jerome was a controversialist all of his life. His controversial works are marked by invective and sarcasm, which mar his defense of his beliefs. The most bitter controversy of his life concerned Origen. Before he turned against Origen, Jerome had shown great enthusiasm for him and had translated many of his homilies (on Isaiah, Jeremiah, Ezekiel, the Song of Songs, and Luke). Later, principally for political reasons, Jerome turned against Origen and against anyone who favored him, particularly his one-time friend Rufinus of Aquileia. In other controversial works, Jerome wrote against Helvidius in defense of Mary's perpetual virginity, against Jovinian and Vigilantius in defense of asceticism, and against the Origenist John of Jerusalem and the Pelagians.

Besides Origen's homilies, Jerome translated Eusebius's *Chronicon*, Didymus the Blind's *On the Holy Spirit*, and a body of Pachomian writings on monasticism. Finally, a collection of 150 letters (not all by Jerome) survives, as well as many homilies, three highly imaginative lives of monks, and a survey of 135 Christian writers (*On Illustrious Men*).

Jerome was the most learned Christian of his day. Besides Latin, Greek, and Hebrew, he also knew Aramaic and Syriac. For his time, he had a good sense of textual criticism and an acute sense of style; his translations of the Bible were well received partly because of their elegant Latin. It is more difficult to speak of Jerome as a theologian. Although he presented reasonable arguments against the Pelagians, the "Cappadocian formula" of "one *ousia*, three *hypostases*" for the Trinity baffled him. The Bible and the ascetical way were the great loves of his life.

Jerome, *Works*, trans. W. H. Fremantle, *NPNF*, vols. 2, 6 (1892, repr. 1975); Jerome, *Letters 1–22*, trans. T. C. Lawler, ACW 33 (1963); Jerome, dogmatic, polemical works, and sermons, in FC 48 (1964), 53 (1965), 57 (1966); J. N. D. Kelly, *Jerome: His Life, Writings, and Controversies* (1975).

JOSEPH T. LIENHARD

Jerome of Prague (c. 1370/1380–1416),

Bohemian philosopher, burned at the stake at the Council of Constance on May 31, 1416. In 1399 he went to Oxford to acquire Wyclif's theological works. He returned to Prague in 1401 and went to Jerusalem in 1403. From 1404 he studied at Paris, Cologne, Heidelberg, and Prague and was granted four master's degrees in arts, the first from Paris in 1406. He was forced to flee from three of these universities because of controversies based on teachings of Wyclif, among others. In Prague he joined the reform movement alongside Hus, and his role was considerable. A traveler and diplomat, Jerome was imprisoned in Hungary, tried for controversies in Vienna, and examined in Cracow. In Lithuania he caused confusion with favorable remarks on the Orthodox Church. These activities led to accusations of heresy.

Jerome followed Hus to Constance to offer assistance. Advised to flee upon arrival, he was arrested and returned in chains. Under examination, Jerome renounced the teachings of both Wyclif and Hus, hoping that he would be released. When he found that he would stay in prison for life, he renounced the recantation and was consigned to the flames.

V. Herold, "Der Streit zwischen Hieronymus von Prag und Johann Gerson—eine spätmittelalterliche Diskussion mit tragischen Folgen," in *Société et Eglise, Textes et discussions dans les universités d'Europe centrale au moyen âge tardif*, ed. Z. Wlodek (1995), 77–89; Z. Kaluza, "Le chancelier Gerson et Jerome de Prague," *Archives d'histoire doctrinale et littéraire du Moyen-âge* 59 (1985): 81–126; F. Šmahel, "Leben und Werk des Magisters Hieronymus von Prag," *Historica* 13 (1966): 81–111.

DAVID R. HOLETON, OTA PAVLÍČEK

Jerusalem, Destruction of David

captured Jerusalem (Jebus), a Canaanite city-state in the central highlands west of the Dead Sea and made it the capital of Israel in approximately 1000 BCE (2 Sam. 5:6–9). When David's son Solomon constructed the first temple in Jerusalem (966–959, 1 Kgs. 6:1–38), Jerusalem became Israel's cultic center. Various adaptations, such as broader walls and an advanced water system, were made to the growing city (2 Chron. 32:1–8), but even so, Jerusalem was not impregnable. In 587–586, the Babylonians conquered Jerusalem, deported its inhabitants to Babylon, and demolished the city and its temple (2 Kgs. 25:1–21).

The Edict of Cyrus in 538 allowed the people of Jerusalem to return to their homeland (Ezra 1:1–4), and they constructed the Second Temple and rebuilt the city walls under the leadership of Zerubbabel and Nehemiah (Ezra 5:1–6.18; Neh. 3–6). Jerusalem was the region's cultural, political, and religious center throughout the rest of the Persian period, the subsequent rule of the Greeks (333–141), a short period of self-rule (141–63), and the Roman occupation (starting in 63 BCE).

Despite every Roman attempt to mollify the local population, the Palestinian Jews despised their Roman overlords, and civil unrest grew until it led to a rebellion in the summer of 66 CE. The Romans responded by sending 60,000 troops to quell the revolt. The Romans quickly reconquered Galilee and moved southward toward Jerusalem. According to Flavius Josephus, a Jewish general who realigned himself with the Romans, the Roman troops commanded by Vespasian prepared to lay siege to Jerusalem. When Vespasian was called to Rome to become emperor, command of his troops was assumed by his son, Titus, who surrounded the city and attempted to starve it into submission. Intrigue and infighting among the various Jewish groups sapped Jerusalem's defensive strength and resolve, and in August–September of 70 CE the Romans breached the walls, killed or captured the remaining Jewish rebels, looted the city's riches, and burned the temple to the ground (Josephus, *B.J.* 4.486–7.20). Titus's victory was commemorated in Rome by the erection of a gigantic arch decorated with images of the captured rebels being led away in chains and the army, laden with the spoils of war, returning to Rome.

In approximately 130 CE, the Roman emperor Hadrian visited Jerusalem and decided to raze the remnants of the city and build a new

Roman city in its place that would be called Aelia Capitolina (named after himself, Publius Aelius Hadrianus, and the major Roman deity, Jupiter Capitolinus). Under the leadership of Simeon bar Kosiba, known as Bar Kochba or Son of the Star, the citizens of Jerusalem revolted in an attempt to resist Hadrian's plans. The rebellion was finally quashed in 135. The Romans then built Aelia Capitolina and adorned the area where the temple once stood with statues to Jupiter and Hadrian. Because of their resistance to Hadrian's plan, the Jews were subsequently forbidden from entering the city (Eusebius, *Hist. eccl.* 4.6.1–4; Dio Cassius, *History of Rome*, 69.12).

R. L. Wilken, *The Land Called Holy* (1992); G. W. Bowersock, "A Roman Perspective on the Bar Kochba War," in *Approaches to Ancient Judaism* (1980).

J. DAVID CASSEL

Jesus in Early Christianity The early church was hardly monolithic in its teaching regarding Jesus. Even in the New Testament divergent, if not contradictory, views are evident. Emphasis on his Davidic descent, as in the genealogies of Matthew (1:1–17) and Luke (3:23–38), point to the humanity of the Messiah. Other passages also take the humanity for granted (Mark 6:2–3; 10:17–18; Matt. 11:18–19; 21:11–12; Luke 2:52; 7:34; John 6:14).

On the other hand, there are passages that point to the divinity of Jesus: the hymn in Philippians (2:5–11) of the self-emptying of one in the form of God; Colossians 1:15–18, which speaks of the one through and for whom all was created; the Prologue to the Gospel of John, in which the Word, who is with God and is God, becomes flesh (1:1–18); and references to Jesus as Son in relation to the Father (Matt. 11:25–27; Mark 13:32).

The presence of passages that presuppose Jesus' humanity along with passages that point to his divinity contributed to a wide variety of convictions regarding the Savior. At extremes were two groups, both ultimately rejected. At one extreme were Ebionites, Jewish Christians who believed that Jesus was entirely human but was adopted by God because of his perfect obedience to the Jewish law, which all Christians were obligated to keep. At the other extreme were Marcionites, Gentile Christians, who believed that Jesus was entirely divine. Marcion saw a radical disjunction between the Old Testament and the gospel. The God of the Jews

was both creator of the material world and lawgiver. The God from which Jesus had come was unknown to and superior to the Jewish God. A Docetist, Marcion taught that Jesus, as nonmaterial, had only appeared to be human and to suffer.

The gnostics, a diverse collection of groups, typically held somewhat similar views. For them it was significant that the Savior (often docetic) brought *gnosis*, secret knowledge that enabled escape from the material realm.

Ebionites, Marcionites, and gnostics, although eventually rejected by the church, provided the useful service of forcing Christians who disagreed with them to clarify their own beliefs.

In contrast, perhaps deliberately, to the elaborate teaching of the gnostics, the claims of the apostolic fathers regarding Jesus were decidedly nonspeculative. Ignatius of Antioch (d. early second cent.) spoke, without elaboration, of Jesus' suffering as "the suffering of my God" and claimed him to be both God and human.

Apocryphal literature from the second century and later fed the pious imagination. It tended toward docetism and the fabulous, particularly in its presentation of the nativity and infancy of Jesus.

In the mid-second century Justin, an apologist in Rome, developed an explanation of the person and work of Jesus that could cohere with monotheism. He spoke of Jesus as teacher, reason itself, Logos, Son and messenger of God, second in place to the Father but above the Spirit, leader of the good angels, and fulfillment of Old Testament prophecy. The effect was to provide a clear hierarchy of Father and Son (and Spirit), with the Son as mediator between the immaterial God and the material world.

Justin's hierarchy, modified by both Irenaeus and Origen, would seem to have proved satisfactory until the early fourth century, when the question of just how divine Jesus was forced the church to clarify the Son's relationship to the Father (Council of Nicaea, 325; Council of Constantinople, 381) and the relationship of the divine nature and the human nature in Christ (Council of Chalcedon, 451).

B. D. Ehrman, *Lost Christianities* (2003); R. M. Grant, *Jesus after the Gospels* (1989); R. P. C. Hanson, "The Doctrine of the Trinity Achieved in 381," *SJT* 36, no. 1 (1983): 41–57; W. Schneemelcher, ed., *New Testament Apocrypha*, 2 vols. (1991, 1992).

REBECCA H. WEAVER

Jewel, John (1522–1571), English controversialist, author of *An Apology in Defense of
the Church of England* and *A Defense of the
Apology*, and bishop of Salisbury (1560–1571).
Jewel was educated at Oxford following a curriculum that emphasized Reformed and
humanist studies, which provided him with a
thorough grounding in patristics and rhetoric
that served him well in later controversies. He
was pressured into signing Catholic articles in
1554 but soon fled to the Continent anyway. He
spent time at Frankfurt, where he publicly
repented his subscription to Catholicism, and
Zurich, whence his definition of Christian
purity was largely derived, returning to England in 1559. While he recognized and at times
emphasized the importance of a pure church,
Jewel's religious thought centered on (1) the
distinction between fundamentals of the faith
and things indifferent and (2) the value of unity
and peace within the church. Responsibility for
preserving unity Jewel assigned to the godly
prince, who was authorized to enforce requisite
elements of the faith as well as set standards for
the community concerning adiaphora. Regarding essentials, allegiance to the monarch was
limited by prior obedience to God; regarding
nonessentials, the prince's authority was absolute. This understanding of royal authority
explains Bishop Jewel's enforcement of church
policies requiring liturgical vestments despite
his personal disapproval of "popish" garments.
Whatever his private tastes, he considered vestments matters of adiaphora, and thus it was sinful to disorder the church by resisting the prince
over them. The distinction between fundamentals and things indifferent was central to
Jewel's defense of the English church against
Catholic charges of heresy and disunity. In his
controversial writings Jewel minimized the
essentials of the faith to a small core of doctrine, by which standard the English church
was clearly orthodox and regarding which he
could plausibly claim that all Protestants
agreed. To defend this reduction of necessary
Christian doctrines, Jewel pointed to the Bible
as the sole authoritative source of Christian
truth and to the early church (prior to 600 CE)
as the model of pure scriptural Christianity. He
argued that a doctrine should be deemed necessary only if it was grounded in Scripture,
taught by a consensus of the church fathers, and
considered essential to the faith by the fathers.
Jewel then interpreted the patristic writers in a
way that strictly limited the teachings they
deemed essential and on which there was consensus. Thus, while his controversial writings

evince heavy reliance on the fathers, his use of
them was overwhelmingly negative (showing
that they did not support Romanist teachings)
rather than positive (arguing that they supported doctrines of the English church). In his
later years Jewel defended the Elizabethan
church against Puritan critics, challenging their
claim that the innovations they promoted were
scriptural and denouncing their defiance of the
queen in matters he considered adiaphora.

J. Ayre, ed., *The Works of John Jewel*, 4 vols.
(1845–1850); J. Booty, *John Jewel as Apologist
of the Church of England* (1963); W. M. South-
gate, *John Jewel and the Problem of Doctrinal
Authority* (1962).

DANIEL EPPLEY

Jewish Christianity, Early

The imme-
diate followers of Jesus were Jews and understood the significance of Jesus in terms of
categories at home in Jewish tradition (e.g., the
kingdom of God, the Messiah). Within a generation of the death of Jesus, non-Jews joined the
movement in significant numbers. Tensions
soon arose over what traditional Jewish practices would be expected of these new converts.
Paul's Epistle to the Galatians and the book of
Acts both indicate tension between followers of
Jesus in Jerusalem, where James, the brother of
Jesus, was revered, and the Christians of Antioch. Conflict focused on the rite of circumcision
and the observance of *kashrut* (dietary laws).
Paul maintains that the authorities in Jerusalem
and representatives of Antioch had agreed on
the issue of circumcision, which was not to be
required of non-Jews. He also indicates that the
issue of prerequisites for table fellowship
remained controversial. Yet Galatians as a
whole indicates that some followers of Jesus
still maintained the necessity of circumcision.

While some NT texts celebrate the elimination of distinctions between Jew and Gentile
(Eph. 2:11–18), others insist that the followers
of Jesus constitute the true Israel, opposed to
the "synagogue of Satan" (Rev. 3:9). Followers
of Paul continued to struggle with Christians
who insisted on some traditional practices (cf.
Col. 2:16–17).

The NT thus strongly suggests the presence
of followers of Jesus, whether ethnic Jews or
not, who continued to observe traditional Jewish practices. "Jewish Christianity" is usually
used as a label for such Christians and is attested
in the centuries following the destruction of
Jerusalem by the Romans in 70 CE. Eusebius
(*Hist. eccl.* 3.5.3) reports that the community of

observant followers of Jesus in Jerusalem left the city just before its destruction and fled to Pella in the Transjordan. Whether reliable history or mere legend, the account attests the self-understanding of one community of Syrian Christians in the second or third century.

Whatever their origins, there were apparently groups practicing circumcision and maintaining some form of purity and dietary regulations in the second and third centuries, bearing names such as Nazoreans, Ebionites, and Elchasaites. The patristic sources reporting on these groups charge them with having a low Christology, understanding Jesus to be a mere human being or denying the Virgin Birth. Irenaeus describes in such terms the teachings and practices of Cerinthus, the Ebionites, and the Nicolaitains (*Haer.* 1.26.1–3). Hippolytus (*Haer.* 7.34) and Eusebius (*Hist. eccl.* 3.27) report on the Ebionites. Epiphanius (*Pan.* 29) discusses the Nazoreans at length. Such reports probably oversimplify. The evidence for the beliefs of such groups suggests that their Christology was more complex and that they maintained strong apocalyptic hopes.

Fragments of second- and third-century Gospels preserved in patristic sources provide some meager evidence for Jewish-Christian groups. The number of such Gospels and the relationships among them are highly problematic. A *Gospel of the Hebrews* is attested in Clement of Alexandria (*Strom.* 2.9.45; 5.14.96), Origen (*Comm. Jo.* 2.12), and Eusebius (*Hist. eccl.* 3.25.5; 3.27.4). Eusebius suggests that Papias (*Hist. eccl.* 3.39.17) and Hegesippus (*Hist. eccl.* 4.22.8) in the second century knew the text. A *Gospel of the Ebionites* is attested solely in Epiphanius (*Pan.* 30). Jerome in numerous places (e.g., *Vir. ill.* 2) provides evidence of the *Gospel of the Nazoreans* and indicates acquaintance with the sect in Beroea, near Aleppo.

An important potential source for Jewish Christianity is found within the Pseudo-Clementine *Homilies* and *Recognitions*. These romances, dating in their current form from the fourth century but probably dependent on an earlier source, perhaps of the third century, tell a story of Christian origins inimical to Paul, who represents a form of apostasy from the correct version of the faith. Thus, the introductory *Epistle of Peter to James* (2.3) castigates the "lawless and absurd doctrine" of the one who is Peter's enemy. The narrative portrays the opponent to be Simon Magus, who, as missionary to the Gentiles (*Hom.* 2.17.3), is a transparent cipher for Paul (*Hom.* 17.19). The narratives emphasize

the role of the "true prophet," manifested throughout history in a series of figures culminating in Jesus (*Ep. Pet.* 2.5; *Hom.* 3.17–19). The true prophet can recognize false passages in Scripture, including those that refer to sacrifice (*Hom.* 2.44.2; 3.52.1) and temple (*Hom.* 2.44.1). The Christology recalls the Elchasaites known to Hippolytus (*Haer.* 9.14.1); the repudiation of sacrifice is attested among the Ebionites (Epiphanius, *Pan.* 30.16.4).

Despite considerable variety, there is a generic resemblance among such Christian groups, intent on observing Torah, albeit selectively, and understanding Jesus in less metaphysical terms than some of their contemporaries.

A. F. J. Klijn, *Patristic Evidence for Jewish-Christian Sects* (1973); Klijn, *Jewish-Christian Gospel Tradition* (1992); G. Lüdemann, *Opposition to Paul in Jewish Christianity* (1989).

                                    HAROLD W. ATTRIDGE

Jewish Martyrdom   Martyrdom played a negligible role in the earliest stages of Jewish history. The Hebrew Bible narrative core follows the emergence and development of an Israelite religious polity. While often engaged in conflict, this religious polity did not create the circumstances for religious persecution and martyrdom. Indeed, the Hebrew phrase for martyrdom—*kiddush ha-Shem*, "sanctification of God's name"—indicates any action that enhances God's glory in the world, although with the passage of time the term became increasingly restricted to dying on behalf of God and in that extreme way enhancing divine glory in the world.

The Hebrew Bible includes three major sets of figures destined to play a major role in the development of Jewish notions of martyrdom. The simplest of these were Daniel and his companions, who were exposed to persecution by the Persian authorities and prepared to die for their faith. More important was the patriarch Abraham, willing to sacrifice his beloved son to divine command. Likewise critical was the Suffering Servant of Isaiah 52–53, fated to suffer gratuitously and grievously and emerge victorious. All three sets of figures became central to both Jewish and Christian thinking and were claimed by the two religious communities.

The first significant instance of religious persecution came during the reign of the Seleucids in Palestine, in the second century BCE. At that point, the commitment to dying rather than abandoning Judaism first seems to have emerged, and the first Jewish martyr figures were bequeathed to posterity. Subsequent Roman overlordship in Palestine set the framework for yet further development of Jewish martyrdom. In particular, as the Hadrianic edicts of the second century outlawed key elements in Jewish practice, major communal leaders accepted death rather than these restrictions. These rabbinic martyrs were subsequently embedded centrally in Jewish liturgy and thought. All these early instances of Jewish martyrdom involved governmental repression and Jewish defiance of such repression.

The First Crusade generated a new-style Jewish martyrdom. While the traditional church policy vis-à-vis Jews demanded toleration of Jewish existence in Christian society, and while the call to the crusade by no means repudiated that traditional policy, maverick crusading bands in Germany transformed the crusading message into a warrant for forced baptism of the Jews, with the alternative of death. Rhineland Jews, sharing the religious exhilaration of the period and faced with the stark alternatives of baptism or death, embraced the latter in activist ways, regularly taking their own lives and the lives of their family members. This activist stance constituted a distinctly new phase in the history of Jewish martyrdom. In taking this activist stance, the Rhineland Jews regularly invoked the biblical imagery of Daniel and his associates and of the patriarch Abraham.

The ubiquity of religious persecution and Jewish martyrdom through the latter centuries of the Middle Ages moved Jewish polemicists to apply insistently the biblical imagery of Isaiah's Suffering Servant to the Jewish people, contesting vehemently Christian ascription of that image to Jesus.

With the disintegration of the medieval order, optimists saw the end of the saga of religious persecution and Jewish martyrdom. The new world order, however, maintained many of the anti-Jewish themes bequeathed from the Middle Ages, and new-style persecution emerged on a mammoth scale in the Holocaust. While the new persecution did not offer the option of conversion and thus seemingly eliminated the element of choice critical to martyrdom, observers have come to depict the Jewish victims of the Holocaust as martyrs to their Jewish identity.

D. Boyarin, *Dying for God: Martyrdom and the Making of Christianity and Judaism* (1999); R. Chazan, *European Jewry and the First Crusade* (1987); S. Spiegel, *The Last Trial* (1967).

ROBERT CHAZAN

Jewish Polemic against Christianity

According to the New Testament, first-century Jews were much involved in polemical interchange with Jesus and followers such as Peter and Paul. The earliest of these exchanges took place within the Palestinian Jewish community. Only with the slow parting of the ways between Jews and Christians does it become possible to speak of interreligious polemic. For Christians, anti-Jewish polemic was a staple, beginning with the New Testament itself and continuing with the church fathers. The *adversus Judaeos* literature was rich from early times down through the Middle Ages. For Jews, a parallel early *adversus Christianos* literature, however, does not exist; such a literature developed only during the second half of the Middle Ages.

The classics of early rabbinic Judaism—the Mishnah and the two Talmuds—have strikingly few references to Christianity. These few references are slim and unsophisticated, in sharp contrast to the anti-Jewish writings of the early church. The sages of the Mishnah and the two Talmuds were not preoccupied in any theoretical way with Christianity, and actual Christian spiritual pressures do not seem to have unduly affected them. There is a folk Jewish anti-Christian literature, broadly identified as the *Toldot Yeshu* tradition, which seems to have its roots in antiquity, although very early exemplars of this literature have yet to be found. This fluid corpus consists of a counter-history of early Christianity, patterned on the Gospels, but subverting major Gospel themes into an unflattering portrait of Jesus and his adherents.

Through the first half of the Middle Ages, the bulk of world Jewry was concentrated in Muslim countries, where Christian spiritual pressures were nearly nonexistent. The Jews in the sphere of Islam were brilliantly creative in a number of cultural spheres, some traditional and some innovative; however, religious polemic—whether anti-Muslim or anti-Christian—was not a significant preoccupation. The Jews of the Muslim world bequeathed one major work of anti-Christian polemic: the recently edited and translated *Qissat Mujadalat al-Usquf*. While groundbreaking in its marshalling of extensive anti-Christian materials, the argumentation of the *Qissat* is neither sophisticated nor couched in an appealing literary format.

As the Jewish population in western Christendom began to grow, starting in the eleventh century, the Jews of this rapidly developing area had to address the spiritual pressures exerted by their vibrant Christian environment. Evidence of reactive anti-Christian thrusts can be found in the impressive Jewish Bible commentaries composed in northern Europe from the close of the eleventh down through the early thirteenth century. Especially noteworthy is the emergence of a genuine polemical literature in southern France and northern Spain during the closing decades of the twelfth century and into the thirteenth. This new anti-Christian polemical literature revealed deep Jewish anxiety over the spiritual pressures exerted first informally and then formally by an increasingly aggressive Christian majority. Jewish intellectual and spiritual leaders took upon themselves the tasks of identifying the major Christian challenges and fashioning persuasive Jewish responses.

The most traditional Christian challenge involved biblical proof texts for the truth of Christianity. Jewish polemicists argued extensively against the Christian understanding of key biblical verses adduced by Christian tradition and cited by Christian contemporaries. Jewish authors claimed that Christians: misread and mistranslated the Hebrew verses; failed to perceive the original contexts of the cited verses; conducted readings that led to contravention of stances central to the thinking of the Hebrew Bible; conducted readings that led to contradiction of well-known Christian views; and conducted readings that led to irrational and thus unacceptable conclusions.

As philosophical thinking penetrated ever deeper into Western Christendom, Christian intellectuals attempted to harness philosophical truth to that of Scripture, arguing that Christian doctrine is consonant with both the Bible and philosophy. Dispute over the rationality of Christian doctrine thus entered the realm of Jewish polemical literature, with Jews arguing vigorously that core Christian doctrines—especially the incarnation and the Trinity—are utterly inconsistent with principles of reason.

A line of Christian argumentation that deeply concerned the Jews of Western Christendom focused attention on the historical reality of Christian ascendancy and Jewish degradation, which was taken to corroborate the true messianic role of Jesus and the Jewish error of rejecting him. Jewish polemicists put these claims regularly in the mouths of the Christian protagonists they created, and they devoted considerable attention to rebutting these demoralizing allegations. The rebuttals included insistence that the current dire circumstances of the Jewish people had been fully predicted in Scripture, as had eventual redemption from these circumstances. According to medieval Jewish polemicists, present Jewish pain must be seen as expected, and eventual redemption of the Jewish people was a certainty. In addition, Jewish polemicists argued that the achievements of Christianity, while impressive, by no means fulfilled the biblical imagery of messianic redemption. These Jewish writers pointed increasingly to the power of Islam, urging that biblical imagery suggested a messianic redemption that would involve submission of the entire world to the divinely appointed Messiah and to the true religious vision he embodied. Yet another hallmark of messianic times was to be permanent peace, and Jewish polemicists noted regularly the ubiquity of warfare on the medieval scene, arguing that Christendom was rife with strife and violence—hardly an indication of messianic advent.

Related to this last theme in Jewish polemical literature was the introduction of the moral element in the assessment of religious truth. Truth claims, urged medieval Jewish polemicists, must be assessed in terms of the moral achievements of religious communities. In this vein, Jewish polemicists pointed to a variety of moral failures and social injustices in Christian society, claiming that the smaller and weaker Jewish communities achieved in contrast a remarkably high level of moral purity and social equity.

The Jewish polemical enterprise was hardly a sterile intellectual exercise. Jewish leaders understood that their followers lived under the constant pressure of a missionizing Christian society and a proselytizing Roman Catholic Church. By the middle decades of the thirteenth century, the pressures had progressed from the informal to the formal, as the church began to commit considerable resources to mission work in general and proselytizing among the Jews in particular. Jewish leaders used the widest possible variety of literary formats for carrying their anti-Christian argumentation to the Jewish community. Sermons, theological and philosophical treatises, and mystical tracts were yoked to the effort to rebut Christian views and to reinforce Jewish belief. Because of the centrality of the Hebrew Bible to the Christian case, Jewish Bible commentaries were replete with anti-Christian polemical thrusts. Indeed, by the late thirteenth century Jewish authors were penning Bible commentaries completely devoted to polemical issues. As was true in the Christian sphere, the dialogue format was especially favored for conveying polemical argumentation. The give-and-take of the dialogue allowed nicely for the presentation of Christian views and their rebuttal. In addition, appealing characters could be created, along with a narrative flow that would reinforce the sense of Jewish superiority and ultimate victory in debate.

R. Chazan, *Fashioning Jewish Identity in Medieval Western Christendom* (2004); D. J. Lasker, *Jewish Philosophical Polemics against Christianity in the Middle Ages* (1977); F. E. Talmage, ed., *Disputation and Dialogue: Readings in the Jewish-Christian Encounter* (1975); H. Trautner-Kromann, *Shield and Sword: Jewish Polemics against Christianity and the Christians in France and Spain from 1100–1500* (1993).

ROBERT CHAZAN

Jews and the Western Church see *Western Church and the Jews*

Jiménez de Cisneros, Francisco

(1436–1517), Spanish prelate and statesman, cardinal of the Roman Catholic Church. After studies at Salamanca and Rome, Jiménez was appointed archpriest of Uceda (1471). In 1484 he joined the Observant Friars Minor and in 1492 was elected confessor of Queen Isabel. Three years later he was appointed archbishop of Toledo. As archbishop, two times regent (1505, 1516), and later cardinal (1507) and inquisitor general (1507), Jiménez had an active role in the government of the Hispanic kingdoms and in the reform of the church. His pastoral concerns motivated his diocesan synods in 1497 and 1498, which foreshadowed broader reforms adopted at the Council of Trent. In addition to pastoral reforms, Jiménez also restored the use of the Mozarabic rite in the Cathedral of Toledo. He headed the forced conversion of the population of Granada, which led to the insurrection of the Alpujarras (1500–1502). Jiménez founded the Universidad Complutense de Alcalá de Henares. Jiménez also sponsored the production of the Complutense Polyglot Bible, which included the first printed Greek New Testament. This Bible was printed between 1514 and 1517 but only distributed after 1520 because of a privilege granted to Erasmus.

J. G. Oro, *El Cardenal Cisneros: Vida y empresas* (1992–1993); E. Rummel, *Jiménez de Cisneros: On the Threshold of Spain's Golden Age* (1999).

RADY ROLDÁN-FIGUEROA

Joachim of Fiora (c. 1135–1202), monk,

abbot, biblical interpreter. Joachim was born at Celico, in Calabria, probably as the son of a notary, eventually coming himself to work in the chancery of the Norman king of Sicily at Palermo. As a pilgrim to Jerusalem when he was in his early thirties, he experienced a revelation on a mountain. He then returned to Sicily as a hermit to reside near Mount Etna, finally moving to Cosenza, becoming a priest, and entering the nearby Benedictine monastery of Corazzo. Within five years, by 1176, he was abbot and had begun making prophetic calculations from the Bible. His efforts to see Corazzo incorporated into the Cistercian order brought him to the Cistercian house of Casamari (1183–1184), where he wrote his *Concordances of the Old and New Testaments* and a commentary on the Apocalypse of John. There he also experienced two revelations, both related to his biblical and theological scholarship and his concept of history. The first occurred during matins on Easter, when he enjoyed a sudden comprehension of the Apocalypse and of the agreement of the Old and New Testaments. The second occurred during the divine office on the next Pentecost, when he experienced a sudden comprehension of the Trinity. Joachim sought and received permission from Pope Lucius III (1181–1185) to publish his discoveries, which now included the beginning of *The Psalter of Ten Strings*, a work he completed after his return to Casamari in 1184.

The abbot's life was marked by frequent travel: to the papal court at Verona, Rome, and elsewhere; to Naples with Staufen emperor Henry VI in 1191, to Palermo in the now Staufen kingdom (where he heard the empress's confession in 1196), to Messina, where he was summoned in 1190/1191 by Richard the Lionheart while the king returned to England from a crusade, and other places. Throughout his life he tried to establish a rigorous monastic order and to pursue the hermit's life—the former task's administrative requirements not always consistent with a hermit's aspirations—and he published his theological discoveries. In 1188, traveling to ask the new pope, Clement III (1187–1191), for yet another permission to publish, he finally accomplished the incorporation of Corazzo into the Cistercian order. The pope released him from his office as Corazzo's abbot and ordered him to complete his *Concordances* and Revelation commentary. He then established his own monastery, San Giovanni in Fiore, in the mountains above the Sila plateau. Joachim was a respected figure at the Staufen court, and Henry VI and his son Frederick became important patrons of the new community, which quickly developed daughter houses. But hermitage continued to lure Joachim, and in 1201 he withdrew from San Giovanni to a church near Petrafitta, high in the Silla, to build the hermitage of San Martino di Giove. There he died on March 30, 1202.

Joachim became famous, and long remained famous, for his prophetic interpretations of Scripture and his correlation of biblical narratives and the phases of history. He believed that the narratives of the OT prefigured the entire history of the church—past, present, and future. Similarly, the book of Revelation in the NT continued, he showed, patterns found in the OT. His method allowed him to calculate the time of the antichrist's appearance (1260) and led him, in his *Psalter of Ten Strings*, to describe history as a Trinitarian arrangement of three overlapping "statuses" of the Father, the Son, and the Holy Spirit. Equally important was Joachim's conclusion that the millennium described in Revelation 20 referred to a future time of sabbath rather than the present church as Augustine had taught and as was universally believed. The discovery made Joachim the first medieval millennialist.

B. McGinn, *The Calabrian Abbot: Joachim of Fiore in the History of Western Thought* (1985); R. E. Lerner, *The Feast of St. Abraham: Medieval Millenarians and the Jews* (2001); R. Manselli, *Da Gioacchino da Fiore a Cristoforo Colombo: Studi sul Francescanesimo spirituale, sull'ecclesiologia e sull'escatologismo bassomedievali* (1997); M. Reeves, *The Spirit of Prophecy in the Later Middle Ages: A Study of Joachimism* (1969); V. de Fraja, *Oltre Cîteaux: Gioacchino da Fiore e l'ordine florense* (2006).

                    CHRISTOPHER OCKER

Joan of Arc (c. 1412–1431), visionary, military figure, saint. Born at Domrémy, an obscure village in the duchy of Bar in eastern France, Joan began hearing voices at the age of thirteen. During the war of the allied forces of England's Duke of Bedford (uncle and regent of the English child-king Henry VI) and Duke Philip the Good of Burgundy against the Dauphine Charles VII, Joan traveled to Charles's court, at Chinon, wearing a male disguise. Charles was struggling for recognition in northern France, which was controlled by the English and their Burgundian allies during this phase of the period of French-English conflict

known as the Hundred Years' War. Eventually received by the king on March 6, 1429, Joan was examined twice by theologians attached to the court, accepted as a visionary, fitted with armor, and allowed to accompany a successful expedition that ended the English siege of Orléans on May 8, 1429. Joan then joined the French campaign to regain control of the Loire valley and, having demanded a proper anointing for the king, accompanied Charles to the cathedral of Reims on July 17, 1429. After participating in Charles's brief siege of Paris (September 8, 1429), she organized another campaign against the Burgundians without Charles's support, was captured at Compiègne on May 23, 1430, and subsequently was handed over to the English and tried between January 9, 1431, and May 24, 1431. At the conclusion of the trial she abjured her errors but within days resumed male dress (May 28, 1431) and was immediately tried again as a relapsed heretic. This resulted in her execution by burning in the old market of Rouen on May 30, 1431. Over a decade later, Charles VII, close to completing the Valois reconquest of northern France, requested a new trial (1449), but it was only authorized by Pope Calixtus III in 1455. The subsequent "nullification trial" was based on the recollections of numerous witnesses to Joan's childhood, deeds, and previous examinations and trials. The nullification trial (July 7, 1456) declared the 1431 judgment null. A final procedure for canonization began in 1869. Joan was beatified by papal decree on April 11, 1909, and canonized on May 9, 1920.

Joan became a symbol of Valois claims to the French throne, and of resistance to the English more generally, already at the siege of Orléans. Many things have contributed to her status as a national symbol in the fifteenth century and beyond: the peculiar combination of innocence and tenacity displayed in the records of her heresy trial, the cruelty and overtly political nature of the trial, her cross-dressing (first when she traveled from Vaucouleurs, near Domremy, to Chinons, and then when she wore the armor fitted for her before the expedition to free Orléans), her flamboyant harrowing of enemy troops at Orléans and Paris, her visions and prophetic exhortations, her sincere appeal to common symbols of French ruling authority (e.g., royal annointing at Reims) and, finally, her tragic execution. She is the subject of all manner of scholarly and popular rumination. Although some have considered her a military genius, most recent scholarly interest has focused on the surprising role assumed by this religious visionary—a young woman and a mystic—and on the shaping of representations of her in the fifteenth century and in modern times.

———

P. Doncoeur and Y. Lanhers, eds., *Documents et recherches relatifs à Jeanne la Pucelle*, 5 vols. (1952–1961); P. Duparc, ed., *Procès en nullité de la condamnation de Jeanne d'Arc*, 5 vols. (1977–1989); P. Tisset, ed., and Y. Lanters, trans., *Procès de condemnation de Jeanne d'Arc*, 3 vols. (1960–1971); W. S. Scott, trans., *The Trial of Jeanne d'Arc* (1956); T. D. Murray, ed., *Jeanne d'Arc, Maid of Orleans, Deliverer of France* (1907; English trans. of the nullification trial); D. A. Fraioli, *Joan of Arc: The Early Debate* (2000); I. Raknem, *Joan of Arc in History, Legend, and Literature* (1971); B. Wheeler, ed., *Fresh Verdicts on Joan of Arc* (1996); R. Pernoud and M. V. Clin, *Joan of Arc: Her Story*, trans. and rev. J. duQuesnay Adams (1998); C. T. Wood, *Joan of Arc and Richard III: Sex, Saints, and Government in the Middle Ages* (1988); *The Trial of Joan of Arc.* trans. D. Hobbins (2005); *Joan of Arc: La Pucelle*, trans. C. Taylor (2006).

CHRISTOPHER OCKER

Johann von Staupitz *see* Staupitz, Johann von

Johannes Trithemius (1462–1516),

abbot. Born at Trittenheim, Johannes received a basic education in the schools of Trier, Cologne, the Netherlands, and Heidelberg; there is, however, no evidence for higher academic studies. In January 1482 he entered the novitiate at Sponheim; the monks elected him abbot on July 29, 1483. Because of his intellectual interests he paid special attention to the library, which grew to a collection of two thousand books. The abbey became a center of humanist learning. Johannes became an important participant in the reform movement that affected Germany in the second half of the fifteenth century. He was invited to visit monasteries and to give sermons to monastic chapters all over Germany.

He is best described as a monk and a learned writer. He composed Scripture commentaries and Lives of the saints; he also composed an important catalogue of ecclesiastical writers (1494). More ambiguous seem to be his historiographical works, where he often argued on the basis of spurious documents. In 1506 Johannes had to retire at the abbey of St. James in Würzburg, where he continued writing in difficult circumstances. His works show a person who emphasized more the collection of knowledge than penetration and understanding.

———

Biographisch-Bibliographisches Kirchenlexikon, vol. 19 (2001), 1446–54; N. L. Brann, *Trithemius and Magical Theology: A Chapter in the Controversy over Occult Studies in Early Modern Europe* (1999); M. Embach, *Überlieferung der Werke Hildegards von Bingen* (2003).

RAINER BERNDT

John XXII (c. 1244–1334), pope. Trained in

law at Montpellier, Jacques Duèse's advance through higher offices came relatively late in life. He became bishop of Fréjus in 1300, chancellor to two kings of Naples, Charles II and Robert of Naples, bishop of Avignon in 1310, and cardinal bishop of Porto in 1313. He was finally elected to succeed Pope Clement V (1305–1314) in the spring of 1316 and was crowned as John XXII on August 7 of that year. In 1309 Clement had moved the apostolic see to Avignon, a southern French enclave held by the king of Naples, a papal vassal. Intended to provide temporary refuge from Rome's political turmoil, John, like his predecessor, took up residence in Avignon's Dominican priory but later moved into the episcopal palace (the famous papal palace of Avignon was not begun until 1335, by John's successor, Benedict XII). Yet John's authority and aggressive fiscal policy helped establish the Avignon papacy.

His authority was first demonstrated just after he assumed office, when the Franciscan minister general, Michael of Cesena, asked for his help in suppressing Franciscan Spirituals. John condemned the most radical form of Franciscan poverty (1317), then appointed inquisitors to persecute the Spirituals in Italy and France (four were executed by burning in 1318). But the main body of the order soon felt its own interpretation of Franciscan poverty under threat. When John declared in March 1322 that the use of property and ownership were indistinguishable (undermining the Franciscan doctrine of "poor use," which allowed Franciscans to use property without actually having possession of it), the order, under Michael of Cesena's leadership, at its general chapter in June of that year insisted that Christ and the apostles (the models of religious poverty) owned nothing. John responded with a series of papal bulls (1322–1324) that intended to impose ownership on the Franciscans. His opinion on poverty and property was abetted, if not shaped, by the Franciscan Bertrand de la Tour, whom he appointed cardinal in 1320. John was soon antagonized further when the principal advocates of a moderate, Bonaventuran view of religious poverty—the minister general Michael of Cesena and the friars Bonagratio of Bergamo and William of Ockham—turned to John's enemy, Ludwig of Bavaria, in the disputed election of the Holy Roman Emperor (1314). Cesena, Bergamo, and Ockham, with Marsiglio of Padua, became Ludwig's defenders when Ludwig appointed a counterpope and had himself crowned Holy Roman Emperor at Rome in 1328. They were all excommunicated by John in 1329. John also condemned twenty-eight propositions derived from the works of the Dominican mystic Meister Eckhart in that year. By then, Franciscan Spirituals and the circle around Michael of Cesena alike had considered John a heretic for what they regarded as his repudiation of evangelical poverty. When in 1331–1332 John preached a series of sermons arguing that the souls of the blessed will only enjoy the beatific vision after the final judgment, Ludwig tried and failed to arrange for a general council to depose the pope, supported by the polemical writings of William of Ockham and strengthened by the Univ. of Paris's condemnation of John's opinion.

His fiscal policy extended papal control of benefices pursued by popes of the thirteenth century, especially Innocent IV (1243–1254), and he contributed to the continuing trend of centralization of church government, but rather than limit himself to the control of bishoprics and abbacies, John pursued a policy of the "methodic colonization of minor benefices" (Caillet), a centerpiece of the late medieval papacy's encroachment on religious life. His cardinal appointments increased French control of papal government, but he also created episcopal sees in Anatolia, Armenia, India, and Iran.

"John XXII," in *The Oxford Dictionary of Popes*, ed. J. N. D. Kelly and M. Walsh (2006); L. Caillet, *La Paupauté d'Avignon et l'Église de France* (1975); G. Mollat, *The Popes at Avignon* (1963); P. Nold, *Bertrand de la Tour and the Apostolic Poverty Controversy under Pope John XXII* (2004).

CHRISTOPHER OCKER

John of Antioch (428–441), bishop of Antioch, defender of Nestorius. John was consecrated bishop of Antioch (428) at the same time that his friend Nestorius became patriarch of Constantinople. The latter denounced the concept of the Theotokos (Mary as "Mother of God") as entailing a confusion of the two natures, human and divine, in the incarnate Christ. John supported Nestorius against Cyril of Alexandria, who presided over the Council of Ephesus (431) called by Emperor Theodosius II to mediate the controversy. Without waiting for John, leader of the Syrian bishops, to arrive at the council, Cyril declared Nestorius deposed. When John and his forty-three bishops arrived a few days later, he held a countercouncil that reversed the decision against Nestorius and condemned Cyril. Using bribes and public opinion, Cyril prevailed and Nestorius spent the rest of his life in exile.

John and Cyril reconciled by means of a compromise "Formula of Reunion" (433), in which both were required to cede some of their principles. John had to assent to the reaffirmation of Nestorius's condemnation and to accept the legitimacy of the Theotokos. Yet the formula forced Cyril to rescind the "twelve anathemas" against Nestorius and to agree to the Antiochene concept of the union of Christ, "out of two natures." The formula functioned as a precursor to the definition of Chalcedon, but both John and Cyril were severely criticized at home for their perceived capitulations.

W. H. C. Frend, *The Rise of the Monophysite Movement: Chapters in the History of the Church in the Fifth and Sixth Centuries* (1972), 16–24; Frend, *The Rise of Christianity* (1984), 752–62; J. N. D. Kelly, *Early Christian Doctrines* (5th ed., 1978), 325–30; R. V. Sellers, *The Council of Chalcedon: A Historical and Doctrinal Survey* (1961), 6–27.

ROBERT A. KITCHEN

John of Damascus (c. 655–c. 750), Greek monastic, theologian, compiler of theological sources, and doctor of the church. There is little definitive information about his life because the first biography was not composed until the eleventh century. He was a native of Damascus, where his father and grandfather held important government posts, first under the Byzantines, then, after 636, under the Arab rulers. His father, Sergius (Ibn-Serjun), served the caliph as "great logothete," or administrator. According to legend, as a youth John was a student of Cosmas Melodus, who later became bishop of Maiume. John succeeded his father as logothete to the caliph. He left the caliph's service to join St. Sabas's Monastery near Jerusalem sometime prior to the beginning of the Iconoclastic Controversy (c. 725). In contrast to his worldly and complicated situation at the caliph's palace, in the monastery he devoted himself to a life of prayer, obedience, and writing. He was ordained priest by Patriarch John of Jerusalem around 734. His greatest written work is the *Fount of Knowledge*, dedicated to Cosmas of Maiuma and comprising three independent sections: (1) "Philosophical Chapters," (2) "Briefly on Heresies," and (3) "Exposition on the Orthodox Faith." The last section, the most important of the three, is largely christological and based on post-Nicene Eastern writers, especially Gregory of Nazianzus, Nazianzus's fellow Cappadocians, and the works of Pseudo-Dionysius. Pope Leo I is the only Western author used. Overall the work is a dogmatic code rather than a systematic theological treatise. The "Exposition" was very influential in both the East and the West. However, the Latin translation was not made until the twelfth century and was extremely faulty. Unfortunately, it was the translation used by Peter Lombard and Thomas Aquinas. John's other significant writings include three *Discourses against the Iconoclasts* (between 726 and 730), *Against the Jacobites*, *Sacred Comparisons*, and a number of poems still incorporated in Orthodox services. His exegetical works tend to be of little interest, but his extant sermons have considerable merit. His authorship of *Barlaam and Joaseph* continues to be much disputed. In 1890, Pope Leo XIII declared him a doctor of the church.

———

G. Florovsky, "St. John of Damascus," in *The Byzantine Fathers of the Sixth to Eighth Centuries*, vol. 9 of *The Collected Works* (1987), 254–92; John of Damascus, *On the Divine Images,* ed. and trans. D. Anderson (1980); A. Louth, *St. John Damascene: Tradition and Originality in Byzantine Theology* (2002); J. H. Lupton, *St. John of Damascus* (1882).

MICHAEL D. PETERSON

John of Ephesus (507–589), Syrian

bishop, evangelist, historian of Monophysite persuasion. Born in Ingilene district under Amida jurisdiction, John was healed by the stylite Maro at age two and became his spiritual son at four. After the death of Maro, he moved to the monastery of Mar John Urtaya in Amida. Ordained deacon by John of Tella in 529, he moved to Constantinople under the protection of Empress Theodora, who was sympathetic to Monophysitism. John was consecrated bishop of Ephesus (558) by Jacob Baradaeus, the chief organizer of the Syrian Orthodox Church (Jacobites).

Ironically, John was commissioned by the emperor Justinian to undertake extensive evangelization among the pagans and heretics of Asia Minor, even though Justinian's Chalcedonian position was opposed to John's Monophysitism. John claimed to have converted eighty thousand and to have established numerous churches and monasteries.

John divided his *Ecclesiastical History* into three parts: from Julius Caesar to the death of Theodosius II (d. 450); from 450 to 571; from 571 to John's death in 589. Sections of this history were incorporated into the important *Chronicles* of Pseudo-Dionysius of Tell Mahre (d. 845) and of Michael the Syrian (d. 1199).

John's other major work is *Lives of the Eastern Saints*, a collection of fifty-eight stories of Monophysite Mesopotamian and Syrian ascetics, most of whom he had known and found inspiring. The most famous were Jacob Baradaeus, Habib, John of Tella, Mary and Euphemia, Mary the Anchorite, and Paul of Antioch.

———

John of Ephesus, "Lives of the Eastern Saints," ed. E. W. Brooks in PO 17–19 (1923–1925); R. P. Smith, trans., *The Third Part of the Ecclesiastical History of John, Bishop of Ephesus* (1860); S. A. Harvey, *Asceticism and Society in Crisis: John of Ephesus and The Lives of Eastern Saints* (1990).

ROBERT A. KITCHEN

John of Leiden (1509–1536), Dutch

Anabaptist. A traveling tailor, he visited Münster in the summer of 1533 after hearing that Reformation ideas were being proclaimed there. Whether or not he had already been introduced to Melchiorite apocalypticism, he was convinced of it on this visit. Around November 1533, John was baptized by Jan Matthijs and commissioned to spread the gospel in Holland. In mid-January he returned to Münster and participated in the Anabaptist takeover of the city. He worked alongside Matthijs, and then after Matthijs's death in 1534, John assumed the mantle of leadership. In July 1534 he introduced polygamy, taking as his second wife Davira, Matthijs's widow. Eventually he acquired sixteen wives. In September, he proclaimed himself a new King David. When the deliverance of the city he had promised did not take place by Easter 1535, his hold on power became tenuous. The city was retaken in June 1536, and Jan was captured. He was paraded through the region for several months, interrogated, and then executed. His body and that of two colleagues were displayed for centuries in cages hanging from Münster's St. Lambert's Church.

J. Stayer, *Anabaptism and the Sword* (2nd ed., 1976); G. H. Williams, *The Radical Reformation* (3rd ed., 1992).

D. JONATHAN GRIESER

John of Montecorvino   *see* Franciscan Envoys to Medieval China

John of Plano Carpini   *see* Giovanni de Pian del Carpini

John of the Cross   *see* Cruz, Juan de la

John the Grammarian of Caesarea

(fl. 510–520), presbyter, schoolmaster, and theologian. John the Grammarian was an early member of the Neo-Chalcedonian movement, which sought a theological reconciliation between the dyophysite (two *physeis*, or natures) definition of the Council of Chalcedon (451) and the traditional monophysite (one *physis*, or nature) formula propounded by Cyril of Alexandria. Later references to him as a bishop are probably the result of confusion with one of his contemporaries, John the Khozbite, bishop of Caesarea in Palestine.

A grammarian was a teacher of language and literature at a secondary level, beyond basic literacy but not yet at the level of rhetorician. The work of a grammarian was the analysis and definition of words. John brought this method to the christological discussion by examining the way in which Cyril of Alexandria and the Council of Chalcedon used their christological terms. He argued that Chalcedon used the term *physis* with the meaning of *ousia*, whereas Cyril sometimes used the word in that sense and sometimes in the sense that Chalcedon used the word *hypostasis*. Hence, he concluded, Cyril and the Council of Chalcedon were not really opposed to one another and that christological orthodoxy required the acceptance of both Cyril and the council.

M. Richard and M. Aubineau, *Iohannis Caesariensis presbyteri et grammatici opera quae supersunt*, CCSG 1 (1977).

EUGENE M. LUDWIG, OFM CAP.

John Scottus

(c. 810–c. 875), the most learned of the many Irishmen (*scotti*) who populated the courts, cathedrals, and monasteries of Carolingian Europe in the eighth and ninth centuries. John also called himself "Eriugena," or "born of Ireland." Biographical details are sparse. His Irish handwriting and reminiscences in his work of Irish culture indicate that he came to the Continent after his first intellectual formation as a mature individual perhaps in his early thirties. As a scholar in the palace of King Charles the Bald (r. 840–877), he was drafted in 850/851 to combat views of predestination deemed heretical. His own contribution to the controversy, *On Predestination*, was itself controversial and drew episcopal censure. That John continued to teach and write suggests that he enjoyed substantial royal support throughout his life. He dedicated major works to Charles and wrote poems for his court. John's scholarship and teaching were wide ranging. He explained Priscian's grammar and difficult biblical vocabulary to his students. He commented on Martianus Capella's *On the Marriage of Philology and Mercury*, a complex treatise on the liberal arts. He may have commented on Virgil and on Bede's computistical works as well. John's interests also embraced exegesis, especially the Gospel of John, for which he composed a commentary and a homily. He may also have commented on Matthew. John's intellectual outlook was inspired by four sources: the Bible; his deep understanding of the liberal arts, both the trivium and the quadrivium; his profound Augustinianism; and a Neoplatonism nourished by Byzantine Greek theology. John's encounter with the works of Pseudo-Dionysius, Maximus the Confessor, Gregory of Nyssa, and Gregory of Nazianzus was transformative. His translations of their works, the most significant body of translation from Greek to Latin since Boethius and before the High Middle Ages, enriched his thought. The *Periphyseon* (*On Nature*) combined all four elements of John's intellectual formation in a masterful synthesis that is at once rigorously argued, highly original, and a literary tour de force. Presented as a dialogue between a master and his student, the *Periphyseon* explores both creation and the Creator. A polymath and prolific author like many during the Carolingian renaissance, John's familiarity with Byzantine sources set him in a special category. But he was no isolated scholar. His knowledge of Greek developed on the Continent, probably as a result of contact with Byzantines. He had many students who copied his works and passed elements of this teaching and thought on to subsequent generations. He was a familiar figure at court and in the ecclesiastical provinces of Reims, Soissons, and Laon in northern France. It is not known if he held clerical rank. Nothing in his work suggests that he was a monk. One of his short poems celebrates the companionship of fellow Irishmen.

G. Van Reel, C. Steel, J. McEvoy, eds., *Iohannes Scottus Eriugena: The Bible and Hermeneutics* (1996); J. McEvoy and M. Dunne, eds., *History and Eschatology in John Scottus Eriugena and His Time* (2002).

JOHN J. CONTRENI

Jonas, Justus (1493–1555), Lutheran reformer. He studied at the Univ. of Erfurt and received doctorates in law and theology from the Univ. of Wittenberg. He was influenced by humanism through Erasmus, whom he visited in 1519. As rector at Erfurt he added Greek and Hebrew to the curriculum. He became a follower of Luther at the 1519 Leipzig Disputation and accompanied him to the Diet of Worms in 1521. He was then appointed professor of canon law at Wittenberg and provost of the Castle Church. He lectured on the Scriptures and from 1523 to 1533 was dean of the theological faculty. He attended the Marburg Colloquy (1529) and the Diet of Augsburg (1530) and helped provide church orders for Anhalt, Zerbst, and Halle, where he was superintendent before being forced out in 1546 by imperial troops. Upon his return in 1547 he removed the last vestiges of Roman Catholic worship. Jonas opposed Osiander's doctrine that humans are justified by the indwelling of Christ's divine nature. His opposition to the Leipzig Interim led to a falling out with Melanchthon.

W. Delius, *Lehre und Leben Justus Jonas, 1493–1555* (1955); M. Lehmann, *Justus Jonas: Loyal Reformer* (1963).

DAVID P. SCAER

Joris, David (c. 1501–1556), Dutch Anabaptist and spiritualist leader. He was attracted to Luther's writings around 1524, but his 1528 distribution of an anticlerical broadsheet led to his arrest, torture, and imprisonment for three years. Exiled to East Frisia, he became acquainted with the apocalyptic teaching of Melchior Hoffman. He was baptized in 1534/1535 and ordained an elder by Obbe Philips. After the fall of the Anabaptist kingdom of Münster, during which Joris advocated nonviolence, his standing among Dutch Anabaptists was enhanced. In 1536, Joris had a series of visions concerning the coming of a third David and the advent of a new spiritual kingdom of God. Persecution of his followers (some one hundred executions in 1539) sent him underground first to Antwerp (1539), then to Basel (1544), where he lived under the name Johann van Brugge. He continued to write to his supporters in the Netherlands, and it was only in 1559, three years after his death, that his identity was learned and his remains were exhumed and burned at the stake.

G. K. Waite, *David Joris and Dutch Anabaptism: 1524–1543* (1990); Waite, ed., *The Anabaptist Writings of David Joris, 1535–1543* (1994).

D. JONATHAN GRIESER

Joselmann of Rosheim (1478–1554), a leader of the Alsatian Jewish community and advocate for Jews. Born Joseph ben Gershom in Alsace, Joselmann represented Jewish interests in various venues within the HRE of early modern Europe. A calm and convincing pragmatist, Joselmann was an effective advocate, respected by Christians and Jews alike. In 1507, he successfully appealed the ordered expulsion of the Jews from Obernai, Alsace. He was then elected a leader of the Alsatian Jewish community in 1510. Thereafter, Joselmann spent his public career advocating for Jewish concerns before various local, provincial, and imperial authorities. He was an advocate for Jewish communities confronted with expulsion as well as charges of desecrating the Host (abusing stolen, consecrated Communion bread) and ritual murder (the so-called blood libel accusing Jews of killing Christian children and using their blood ritualistically).

His most important political contribution was the sweeping guarantee of Jewish rights obtained from Emperor Charles V in 1544, gaining the highest degree of tolerance awarded to medieval German Jewry. In addition to advocacy, he published several short works and, most importantly, his memoir, *Sefer ha-Mikne*, which spans the years 1541 to 1547.

E. Carlebach et al., eds., *Jewish History and Jewish Memory* (1998); H. Fraenkel-Goldsmith, ed., *Rabbi Yosef Ish Rosheim, Sefer ha-Mikne* (1970).

WILLIAM R. RUSSELL

Joseph Hazzaya (710–late eighth cent.), monastic, ascetical writer, and abbot in the Church of the East. Born of Persian Zoroastrian parents in Nimrud, Joseph ("the Visionary") was captured following a rebellion and sold as a slave to a Christian in Qardu (Iraq).

Impressed by the life of monks, Joseph entered the monastery of Abba Sliwa (Bēt Nūhādrā), became a solitary, and later served as abbot of the monastery of Rabban Bakhtisho^c.

Joseph was reputed to have written 1,900 works, but few survive. His most significant work is *Letter on the Three Steps of the Monastic Life*, until recently falsely attributed to Philoxenus of Mabbug. Joseph utilized Evagrius Ponticus's three stages of the spiritual life—body, soul, spirit—but adapted them to the progression of a novice monk working to become a solitary outside the monastery.

Joseph was condemned in a synod (787) convened by Patriarch Timothy I for supposed Messalian tendencies—that one needs to reject prayer and worship in order to receive the gifts of the Spirit and that one who has attained perfection no longer has need of prayer, worship, reading, or manual labor—none of which appear in any of his writings.

J. Hazzaya, "Treatise on the Workings of the Grace of God," in *Early Christian Mystics*, ed. A. Mingana (1934), 145–84, 262–81; S. Brock, *The Syriac Fathers on Prayer and the Spiritual Life* (1987), 314–25; E. J. Sherry, "The Life and Works of Joseph Hazzaya," in *The Seed of Wisdom: Essays in Honour of T. J. Meek*, ed. W. S. McCullough (1964), 78–91.

ROBERT A. KITCHEN

Joseph of Volokolamsk (1439–1515),

Russian monastic and saint. Born Ivan Sanin to a family of gentry in Volokolamsk, near Moscow, at twenty Joseph entered monastic life at Borovsk under the tutelage of the abbot St. Paphnutius. Paphnutius demanded unquestioning obedience, to which Ivan acquiesced. In 1477 following Paphnutius's death, he was chosen abbot, but he left sometime after to return to Volokolamsk to found his ideal monastery. The new monastery grew large and incorporated strict obedience, work, and long liturgical services. He became the dominant spiritual leader of his day by supporting monastic possession of property and by subordinating monasteries under the immediate control of the czar. He put great stock in ritualism, property, and the letter of the law, in stark contrast to Nil Sorsky and the Trans-Volga hesychastic hermits. Although his disciples eradicated these northern hermitages, Russian hesychasm made resurgences in subsequent centuries.

G. P. Fedotov, "St. Joseph of Volok," in *The Russian Religious Mind*, vol. 2 of *The Middle Ages: The Thirteenth to the Fifteenth Centuries* (1966); D. M. Goldfrank, ed. and trans., *The Monastic Rule of Iosif Volotsky* (1983); S. Hackel, "Late Medieval Russia: The Possessor and the Non-Possessors," *Christian Spirituality* (1987): 223–35; M. Raeff, "An Early Theorist of Absolutism: Joseph of Volokolamsk," *American Slavic and East European Review* 7 (1949): 81ff.

MICHAEL D. PETERSON

Josephus (c. 37–c. 100), Jewish historian.

Joseph ben Matthias was born in Jerusalem to an aristocratic priestly family. An education befitting his status equipped Josephus for diplomatic service in the tense period leading up to the Jewish revolt against Rome (55–73 CE). During that revolt he led Jewish forces in Galilee in a brief struggle for independence. Captured alive at Jotapata after a siege, Josephus predicted that the Roman general Vespasian would become emperor (*Jewish War* 3.401). He was spared by the Romans and used as a translator during the siege of Jerusalem.

After the revolt, the emperors Vespasian and Titus rewarded Josephus with an imperial appointment in Rome, where he wrote several important works. The seven-volume *Jewish War*, completed around 80, recounts the struggle of the Jews against Rome. The work, which also highlights the role of Josephus in Galilee, attempts to elicit sympathy for the Jewish people while condemning the "brigands" who led the futile revolt.

The twenty-volume *Jewish Antiquities* recounts the history of the Jewish people from creation until the period just before the great revolt. The first ten books paraphrase Scripture, introducing motifs that present Jewish history in terms comprehensible to a Hellenistic audience. The latter half of the work derives from various sources, including some works of Second Temple Judaism (1 Maccabees, *Letter of Aristeas*) as well as lost works such as the *Universal History* of Nicolaus of Damascus, a scholar employed by Herod the Great. This lengthy work attempts to elicit understanding of the Jewish nation by presenting its past in highly moral terms. Particularly important for early Christians were passages on John the Baptist (*Ant.* 18.116–19), Jesus (*Ant.* 18.63–64), and James, the brother of Jesus (*Ant.* 20.200). Many suspect that the passage on Jesus, the *Testimonium Flavianum*, is an interpolation, though it may be an original report embellished by Christian scribes.

Against Apion, a frankly apologetic work, quotes various sources, primarily from

Hellenistic Egypt, about the Jews. Josephus argues that such sources demonstrate the venerable antiquity of the Jewish people even if their tales of origins are biased and false. Finally, the brief *Life,* composed as an autobiographical appendix to the *Antiquities,* retells the story of Josephus's activity in Galilee, defending his behavior at the time. Eusebius cites Josephus extensively for historical data about the time of Jesus.

—

S. J. D. Cohen, *Josephus in Galilee and Rome: His Vita and Development as a Historian* (1979); L. H. Feldman, *Josephus' Interpretation of the Bible* (1998); S. Mason, *Josephus and the New Testament* (1992); Mason, *Understanding Josephus: Seven Perspectives* (1998); T. Rajak, *Josephus: The Historian and His Society* (2002).

HAROLD W. ATTRIDGE

Jovinian, fourth-century monk and polemicist. In the late 380s the monk Jovinian preached in Rome against the excessive praise of asceticism. He denied that celibacy merited Christians a special reward in heaven and argued that fasting is no more virtuous than receiving food with thanksgiving. He also rejected the idea that Mary the mother of Jesus remained a virgin while giving birth to Jesus. Jovinian's central theological principle was that baptism initiated all Christians into a holy community that rendered individual ascetic merit irrelevant. Jovinian and a few followers were condemned in 393 by episcopal synods at Rome and Milan. The most extensive response to Jovinian came from Jerome, who composed two books *Against Jovinian.* An imperial edict of 398 decreed that Jovinian should be flogged and banished (*Codex Theodosianus* 16.5.53). Despite these measures, Jovinian's teachings continued to spread in the fifth century, when they were opposed by Augustine, Pelagius, and other ascetical teachers.

—

A. Budzin, "Jovinian's Four Theses on the Christian Life: An Alternative Patristic Spirituality," *TJT* 4 (1988): 44–59; D. G. Hunter, *Marriage, Celibacy, and Heresy in Ancient Christianity: The Jovinianist Controversy* (2007); J. Nolan, *Jerome and Jovinian* (1956); F. Valli, *Gioviniano* (1953).

DAVID G. HUNTER

Juan de Torquemada (1388–1468), Spanish theologian, cardinal of the Roman Catholic Church. He was born in Valladolid of a mixed marriage between an Old Christian father and a New Christian mother. He joined the Dominican order and entered the Convent of St. Paul in Valladolid around his sixteenth birthday. In 1424 he received his licentiate in theology and within a year his master's degree from the Univ. of Paris. After his return to Spain, he became prior of the Convent of St. Paul in Valladolid and eventually of the Convent of Pedro Mártir in Toledo. He attended the councils of Constance (1414–1418) and Basel (1431–1449). At Basel he became a defender of the principle of supreme papal authority against conciliar theory. In return Eugene IV made him cardinal in 1439. He died in Rome.

—

B. Netanyahu, *The Origins of the Inquisition in Fifteenth Century Spain* (1995).

RADY ROLDÁN-FIGUEROA

Jud, Leo (1482–1542), Swiss reformer, scholar, and translator. The son of a parish priest, Jud studied theology at the Univ. of Basel, where he became close friends with Huldrych Zwingli. Ordained to the priesthood in 1507, he served in several positions before becoming pastor of St. Peter's in Zurich (1523), where he was Zwingli's closest colleague. Jud was with Zwingli during his confrontation with the Anabaptists in 1525. He was one of the two clerical judges on the Zurich Marriage Court (*Ehegericht*) from its inception in 1525. Jud is best known as the leading translator of the Zurich Bible into the local German dialect (1525–1529). He also translated several Latin works by Zwingli and by Heinrich Bullinger into German.

In December 1531 Jud recommended Bullinger as Zwingli's successor. However, in March 1532 Jud broke with Bullinger on the nature of the Christian community. Under the influence of Johannes Oecolampadius and Kaspar von Schwenckfeld, Jud rejected the Zurich concept of the single sphere society with coterminus ecclesiastical and civil jurisdictions and advocated a church discipline separate from the civil jurisdiction. In December 1533 Jud finally made peace with Bullinger, and the two worked closely together until Jud's death.

—

J. W. Baker, "Church, State, and Dissent: The Crisis of the Swiss Reformation, 1531–1536," *CH* 57 (1988): 135–52; K. Deppermann, "Schwenckfeld and Leo Jud," in *Schwenckfeld and Early Schwenckfeldianism,* ed. P. C. Erb (1986), 211–36; L. Weisz, *Leo Jud, Ulrich Zwinglis Kampfgenosse, 1482–1542* (1942).

J. WAYNE BAKER

Judaizers A pejorative term that hearkens back to the controversy in the early church over how far Gentile converts to Christianity should be required to observe the ceremonial laws of Israel (see Acts 15; Gal. 2:14). In the Reformation era, the term was applied somewhat indiscriminately to any interpretation of Christianity that seemed wrongly to diminish distinctively Christian elements of faith or practice in favor of presumably Jewish ones. The prevalence of this criticism indicates the church's continuing struggle to appropriate Israel's faith while insisting on the finality of Jesus Christ as the Messiah. How was the new covenant of Christ to be related to the old one of Moses?

In the sixteenth century, from Spain and England to Germany and beyond, a startlingly diverse group of persons faced the charge of "judaizing," ranging from the Czech reformer Jan Hus to the Lutheran Andreas Osiander, and from the Spanish Antitrinitarian Michael Servetus to the Sabbatarian Oswald Glaidt. Early in his reforming career, Martin Luther, too, seems to have been accused (falsely) of "judaizing" the faith by denying the perpetual virginity of Mary. At the same time, Luther also frequently criticized others for "judaizing," including the medieval Franciscan biblical scholar Nicholas of Lyra and the sixteenth-century Hebraist Sebastian Muenster. More broadly, Protestant criticisms of the rituals and icons of the Roman church struck some as "judaizing" because of their similarity to criticisms previously voiced by Jews. For Protestants, on the other hand, "judaizing" most often denoted confusing the allegedly Jewish notion of salvation by good works with the presumably authentic Christian gospel of salvation by grace through faith alone, a fault they not infrequently associated with the Roman church. However, they also used the argument against one another, notably the Lutheran Aegidius Hunnius, who unfairly accused John Calvin of "judaizing" the faith exegetically when he denied the Trinitarian interpretation of certain NT texts. Among the Polish Brethren, a tiny faction did actually "reform" their faith to the point of becoming Jews, but their case was the exception.

———

J. Friedman, *The Most Ancient Testimony: Sixteenth-Century Christian-Hebraica in the Age of Renaissance Nostalgia* (1983); D. C. Steinmetz, "The Judaizing Calvin," in *Die Patristik in der Bibelexegese des 16. Jahrhunderts* (1999), 135–45; R. Dán, "*Judaizare*—The Career of a Term," in *Antitrinitarianism in the Second Half of the Sixteenth Century* (1982).

MICKEY L. MATTOX

Julian (331–363), Roman emperor. After his father Julius Constantius and his older brother were killed during the ascension of Constantius II (337), Julian and his brother Gallus were raised and tutored by Christian leaders outside of Constantinople. By all accounts Julian was a serious and pious young man attracted to the Christian monastic lifestyle, but his love of pagan religion and philosophy, particularly Neoplatonism, continued to deepen. He studied in Athens, where he met Basil of Caesarea and Gregory of Nazianzus. In 355 Julian was named Caesar and served as military leader in Gaul. When Constantius died (361), Julian as Augustus began a remarkable effort to reform the empire and revitalize pagan religion and philosophy. He reopened temples, reinvigorated sacrifice, returned exiled bishops, attempted to rebuild the Jerusalem temple, and ordered that only pagan believers could teach classical literature. His lifestyle was rather ascetic and his appearance and mannerisms awkward. Julian died during a battle against Persian forces. Both pagan and Christian authors attempt to account for Julian's early "deception" concerning his conversion to paganism, his piety and character, and his claim of Greek *paideia* (elite culture and education) and the classical heritage for pagan believers.

———

Julian, *Works*, LCL, 3 vols. (1913–1923); Ammianus Marcellinus, *History* (books 14–25) LCL, 3 vols. (1935–1939); Libanius, *Julianic Orations*, LCL (1969); Claudius Mamertinus, "Speech of Thanks to the Emperor Julian," in *Julian: Panegyric and Polemic*, ed. S. N. C. Lieu (1989), 13–38; Gregory of Nazianzus, *Orations* 4–5, SC 309 (1983); Socrates, *Ecclesiastical History* 2.34, 3; *NPNF*, series 2, vol. 2 (1979); Sozomen, *Ecclesiastical History* 5, 6.1–2, *NPNF*, series 2, vol. 2 (1979).

TERESA M. SHAW

Julian of Eclanum (c. 380–c. 454), Italian bishop and Pelagian controversialist. The son of Bishop Memorius and his wife Juliana, Julian was born in Apulia in south-central Italy. Well trained in rhetoric and dialectic, he embarked on a distinguished career. His wife Titia was possibly the daughter of the bishop of Beneventum. Around 408 Julian visited Augustine's friend, Honoratus the Manichean, in Carthage. In 416 he was consecrated bishop of Eclanum.

Julian's success ended abruptly in 418. His strong opposition to Pope Zosimus's *Epistula tractoria* excommunicating Pelagius and Caelestius led to his exile along with eighteen other bishops. During this period his objection to Augustine's doctrine of original sin, because it denied the good of marriage, ignited a controversy with Augustine that lasted until Augustine's death (430). In *To Turbantius* and *To Florus*, Julian defended the goodness of God and creation and accused Augustine of reverting to Manicheism. He was the most intellectually formidable opponent Augustine faced during the Pelagian controversy. Though at times openly hostile and mean-spirited toward Augustine, he relentlessly sought a philosophical and scriptural basis for the central tenets of Pelagianism. Against Augustine, he maintained the soundness of human nature, the natural effectiveness of the will's choice of good and evil, and the natural goodness of concupiscence in procreation when not in excess.

An accomplished exegete, Julian wrote commentaries, perhaps during his exile, on Job and the Minor Prophets. They are extant, as is a Latin translation of Theodore of Mopsuestia's *Commentary on the Psalms*.

In 428–429 Julian was forced to leave Cilicia, where Theodore of Mopsuestia had granted him refuge. In Constantinople, he unsuccessfully sought the aid of Nestorius and the emperor Theodosius II. After his condemnation by the Council of Ephesus in 431, he returned to Italy. A final appeal to Pope Sixtus in 439 ended in failure.

CPL (1995), 773–777a; M. Lamberigts, "Julian of Aeclanum on Grace: Some Considerations," StPatr 27 (1993), 342–49; A. E. McGrath, "Divine Justice and Divine Equity in the Controversy between Augustine and Julian of Eclanum," *DRev* 101 (1983): 312–19; R. Refoulé, "Julien d'Éclane, théologien et philosophe," *RSR* 54 (1964): 42–84, 233–47.

MARIANNE DJUTH

Julian of Norwich (c. 1343–1416),

English anchoress and mystic who occupied a cell adjoining what is now the parish church of St. Julian in Norwich. Julian is known as the author of *Revelations of Divine Love*, writings that describe and interpret the series of sixteen revelations or "showings" she experienced following an illness at age thirty. Confident that the visions were granted on behalf of fellow Christians, Julian persisted in recording them despite fourteenth-century impediments to female authorship. She composed two accounts of her experiences: the so-called short text, written soon after the visions in 1373, and the long text, a revised and expanded account produced after approximately twenty years of prayer and reflection. Written in polished Middle English prose, Julian's *Revelations* convey a message of God's supreme love for humankind and present a unique, post-Augustinian understanding of sin which emphasizes its pedagogical purpose in the lives of the saved rather than its origins in a flawed human will. Her theology is built upon compassion for Christ's suffering on the cross and is influenced by visual representations of the scene and on her conviction that salvation was achieved by this loving act. Her revelations led her, in the long text, to reintroduce and build upon the neglected concept of Christ as mother, allowing traditionally maternal attributes such as tenderness and mercy to be integrated into her understanding of the Trinity. The timing of her visions, which occurred after her sudden recovery from a life-threatening illness, shaped their reception. The healing and relief Julian experienced readied her to receive God's repeated reassurances that "all will be well," an insight valued by contemporaries struggling with the consequences of war, disease, famine, and corruption in the church. She was consulted as a spiritual advisor and designated a beneficiary in several wills; fellow mystic Margery Kempe recounts a visit to Julian in her *Book*. Virtually no information about Julian's childhood or education survives, but her familiarity with the Vulgate and especially the Pauline letters is evident from her writing, as is her knowledge of contemporary devotional and theological texts. Although no evidence indicates that Julian's writing was well-known during her lifetime, it began to attract considerable interest in the twentieth century and is now valued for the freshness of its theological vision.

Julian of Norwich, *Showings,* trans. E. Colledge and J. Walsh (1978); D. Baker, *Julian of Norwich's* Showings: *From Vision to Book* (1994); G. Jantzen, *Julian of Norwich: Mystic and Theologian* (new ed., 2000).

ADRIENNE NOCK AMBROSE

Julius I, bishop of Rome (337–352). He

became bishop just weeks before the emperor Constantine died and the empire entered into a new phase of political and religious foment. With the emperor's death, an amnesty was declared for exiled bishops, including Athanasius of Alexandria and Marcellus of Ancyra, enabling them to return to their sees. Now tensions long smoldering among Eastern bishops over ecclesiastical and theological issues flared into open conflict, including the contention that Athanasius and Marcellus had been condemned by previous councils and should not be allowed to resume their sees. The two made separate appeals to Julius as a way out of the impasse, and he invited the Eastern bishops to a council in Rome in order to resolve the matter. The Council of Antioch (341) brushed off this suggestion as Western meddling. A Roman council was held, and Julius's stern reply to the Easterners is the only document of the Roman bishop to survive in its entirety (Athanasius, *Apol. sec.* 21–35). Besides exonerating the two exiles, Julius accused the Easterners ("Eusebians") of fomenting schism within the church. For his unrelenting support for Athanasius, Julius was named seventy years later by Cyril of Alexandria among the select bishops whose writings should be given special preference. Unfortunately, we know of no works of importance attributed to him.

———

R. P. C. Hanson, *The Search for the Christian Doctrine of God* (1988); Socrates, *Church History* 2.8, 15, 17, 20, 23, 34.

D. H. WILLIAMS

Julius II (1443–1513), papal nephew, soldier, patron of the arts, elected pope in 1503. Julius II epitomizes the Renaissance papacy as the irascible patron of Raphael, Michelangelo, and Bramante. As the warrior called *Il terribile* by his contemporaries, Julius II rampaged up and down the Italian peninsula leading his own troops. Laden with high-revenue benefices and a cardinal's hat at twenty-eight, this father of three daughters would see three conclaves before being unanimously elected in a conclave lasting mere hours, secured by bribery and a portfolio of broken promises including the convocation of a reforming council. Only when threatened by the Council of Pisa did Julius finally interrupt his military campaigns to convoke Lateran V, but by then he had already laid the cornerstone for the new St. Peter's and, in the indulgence sales to finance it, a cause for the Reformation. Lampooned in life and death by Erasmus (*Praise of Folly, Julius Exclusus*), Julius is memorialized by Michelangelo's Moses in the Church of St. Peter in Chains, a symbolically apt title for the church of which this warrior-pope had been cardinal-priest.

———

E. Duffy, *Saints and Sinners: A History of the Popes* (1997); C. Shaw, *Julius II: The Warrior Pope* (1993).

PETER J. SCAGNELLI

Justin Martyr (c. 100–c. 165), apologist, martyr. Details of his life, including his roots in Syrian Palestine and his conversion, are found in his own works. Having sought truth in four major philosophical schools (Stoic, Peripatetic, Pythagorean, Platonist), he was ultimately convinced that Christianity alone led to complete, unambiguous truth. After his conversion, he founded an influential school in Rome and became an ardent defender of and educator for Christianity. During the reign of Marcus Aurelius he was martyred for his beliefs.

Only two of his many works are completely extant. The *Apologies*, two books addressed to an imperial and senatorial audience, criticize the manner in which the state was punishing Christians, expose the false accusations being brought against Christians, and describe the actual history, doctrine, and practice of Christians. In the second work, the *Dialogue with Trypho*, Justin explains the Old Testament from a Christian point of view through a conversation with Trypho, a Jew. It is the earliest extant work to present a defense of Christian claims against the claims of Judaism. These works, as well as a fragment from *Concerning the Resurrection* and references to lost works by Eusebius and Irenaeus, contain an extensive and eclectic array of details about Christian faith and practice in the second century.

Justin employs both philosophical and biblical arguments in each work to clarify the misconceptions about Christianity and to describe accurately its doctrine and ethics. He begins the *Dialogue* by demonstrating that Christianity is not only the superior philosophy but also the source for all others. Because the Logos is present within every person, even ancient pagan philosophers extolled some truth. Only Christianity, however, contains the whole truth because it is rooted in the Logos himself, Christ, the source and fulfillment of all truth. Justin also appeals to NT prophecies in each work. In the *Dialogue*, by seeking to demonstrate that the prophecies apply to Jesus directly, Justin contends that Christianity is the proper successor to Judaism. In the *Apologies* he argues that Christ's fulfillment of prophecies validates the testimony of the NT prophets, the antiquity of Christianity, and the truth claims made by Christ and the apostles.

———

L. W. Barnard, *Justin Martyr: His Life and Thought* (1967); E. R. Goodenough, *The Theology of Justin Martyr* (1923, repr. 1960); Justin, *Dialogus cum Tryphone*, ed. M. Marcovich, in PTS 47 (1997); Justin, *Dialogue with*

Trypho, ed. M. Slusser, trans. T. B. Falls, rev. T. P. Halton (2003); Justin, *The First and Second Apologies*, ed. W. J. Burghardt (1997); Justin, *Justini Martyrs Apologiae pro Christianis*, ed. M. Marcovich (1994); Justin, *Justin Martyr, The First and Second Apologies*, trans. L. W. Barnard, in ACW 56 (1996); D. Rokeah, *Justin Martyr and the Jews* (2002).

D. JEFFREY BINGHAM

Justinian I (c. 483–565), emperor of the East from 527 to 565. Flavius Anicius Julianus Justinianus was a Latin-speaking Illyrian born at Tauresium (Taor) near Uskup. He was the son of the emperor Justin's sister Vigilantia and one Sabatius. As a youth he moved to Constantinople, where his favorite uncle was a military commander of high rank. Although he received a very good education there, it is reported that he never achieved fluent Greek. When Justin became emperor in 518, Justinian became a trusted and influential advisor to his uncle—even to the point of being legally adopted by the childless emperor. In 525 Justinian was given the title Caesar, then two years later, on April 4, 527, was made coemperor with the rank of Augustus. Simultaneously, his wife Theodora was made Augusta. Justinian became sole emperor at his uncle's death on August 1, 527. As emperor, Justinian's primary goal was to regain the Western territories of the Roman Empire, and at this he was largely successful. He succeeded in recapturing Italy, North Africa, and parts of Spain—albeit at a financial and physical toll that seriously weakened the empire after his death. After 565, the various territories of the empire fell prey to the Slavs, Persians, and Muslims.

He also focused great attention on integrating church and state by refining Eusebius of Caesarea's theology of the church-state relation. In particular, he developed the concept of "symphony" in the balance maintained between imperium and the sacerdotal role of the church. Justinian elaborated this balance in his legal reform, codified in the Code of Justinian (*Codex Iustinianus*). Not until the Isaurian dynasty of the eighth century did any emperor come as close as Justinian to realizing complete dominance of both church and state, although even he would occasionally defer to the judgment of church leaders. Primarily it was the emperor's born calling to ensure the stability of church government and to promote Orthodox teachings, and Justinian was an unstinting champion of the Orthodox faith. He almost completely exterminated the Montanists, closed the Athe-

nian philosophy schools (a campaign against paganism rather than Greek philosophy), and forced the conversion of many pagans. The crucial doctrinal crisis of Justinian's time was the conflict between the christological definition of the Council of Chalcedon (451) and the doctrine of Monophysitism. Chalcedon determined that Christ's divine and human natures coexist uncomingled, while the Monophysites—to whose theological doctrine the empress Theodora subscribed—appeared to emphasize his divine nature at the expense of his humanity. Justinian attempted to reconcile the two parties by calling the Fifth Ecumenical Council in 553 (Constantinople II). However, the attempt to unite the Chalcedonian and non-Chalcedonian parties was a failure, which may ultimately have contributed to the loss of Egypt and Syria to Islam in the next century. Among his successes, Justinian spearheaded a magnificent building program that created monuments throughout the empire from Ravenna to Jerusalem. In particular, the great church of Hagia Sophia at Constantinople continues to be one of the outstanding works of world architecture. Although Justinian's government was legendary for its heavy taxation (largely spent on his visionary enterprises), he was renowned for his Christian beneficence in time of dire need. He is considered one of the greatest of Roman Caesars. His likeness can be seen in the mosaic in St. Vitale Church at Ravenna.

J. W. Barker, *Justinian and the Later Roman Empire* (1966); R. Browning, *Justinian and Theodora* (rev. ed., 1987); J. A. S. Evans, *The Age of Justinian: The Circumstances of Imperial Power* (1996); W. G. Holmes, *The Age of Justinian and Theodora*, 2 vols. (1905); Justinian I, *On the Person of Christ: The Christology of Emperor Justinian* (1991); J. Meyendorff, "Emperor Justinian, the Empire, and the Church," in *The Byzantine Legacy in the Orthodox Church* (1982), 43–66; W. Schubart, *Justinian and Theodora* (1943); P. N. Ure, *Justinian and His Age* (1951); A. A. Vasiliev, *Justinian the First: An Introduction to the Epoch of Justinian the Great* (1950).

MICHAEL D. PETERSON

Juvencus, Gaius Vettius Aquilinus (fl. 330), Hispano-Roman presbyter and poet. Little is known of Juvencus's life, but late in the reign of Constantine (306–337) he composed his *Evangeliorum libri quattuor*, an epic poem on the "life-sustaining deeds of Christ." Based primarily upon Matthew's Gospel,

Juvencus's narrative begins with the annunciation and concludes with the risen Christ's appearance in Galilee. Apologetic, exegetic, and aesthetic aims not only encouraged Juvencus to proclaim the "glory of the divine law" (4.804) in four books of Virgilian-style hexameters, a literary form highly respected by educated Romans, but also to present Christ as the true fulfillment of OT prophecy, to recast Israel as bucolic Italian countryside, and to Romanize the poem's hero. Jerome (Letter 70.5) approved of Juvencus's audacious submission of the gospel story to the laws of meter, while subsequent Latin poets viewed his work as seminal. Modern scholars debate the poem's literary qualities, especially its relationship to the art of rhetorical paraphrase, but the *Evangeliorum libri quattuor* remains important as first in a series of biblical epics blending Christian content and the conventions of classical poetry. Juvencus was read throughout late antiquity and the Middle Ages.

J. Fontaine, *Naissance de la poésie dans l'occident chrétien* (1981); J. Huemer, ed., *Evangeliorum libri quattuor*, CSEL 24 (1891); M. Roberts, *Biblical Epic and Rhetorical Paraphrase in Late Antiquity* (1985).

DENNIS E. TROUT

Kappel, Peace of   The first peace of Kappel (1529) averted looming hostilities between the Christian Civic Union, an alliance of Reformed cantons and cities, and the Christian Union, a rival alliance of Catholic states linked with Austria, on terms generally favorable to Zurich. By 1531, economic pressures forced on the Catholic cantons by Zurich and Bern led to war, a decisive victory for Catholic forces, and the death of Zwingli. The terms of the second peace of Kappel confirmed political and legal arrangements prior to the conflict and allowed each canton to choose the Reformed or Catholic faith. In the Common Territories the principle of parity in most cases guaranteed freedom for minorities, while the Independent Districts were recatholicized.

G. R. Potter, *Zwingli* (1976, repr. 1984), chaps. 14–16; J. Rilliet, *Zwingli: Third Man of the Reformation* (1964).

JOHN TONKIN

Karlstadt, Andreas (1480–1541), theologian, dean of the theological faculty and Luther's senior colleague at the Univ. of Wittenberg, itinerant priest and pastor, and archdeacon of Castle Church of All Saints in Wittenberg. Karlstadt studied at the universities of Erfurt and Cologne prior to being called to teach at the Univ. of Wittenberg in 1505. In 1510 he received the degree of doctor of theology at Wittenberg and was chosen archdeacon of the Castle Church of All Saints.

In 1515 Karlstadt traveled to Rome, where he completed a dual doctorate in civil and canon law within a year. As a result of Karlstadt and Luther's public debate with Johannes Eck at Leipzig in 1519, Karlstadt's name was appended to the same papal edict that threatened Luther with excommunication the following year. On Christmas Day 1521, Karlstadt celebrated the first evangelical Communion service of the Reformation at All Saints Church before two thousand people, in defiance of the Elector Frederick's prohibition against liturgical innovations. Dressed in plain clothes, Karlstadt distributed the sacrament in both kinds (bread and wine), disregarding whether or not communicants had confessed or fasted. For the first time in the Reformation, the words of institution were spoken in the vernacular German instead of Latin. On the following day, Karlstadt became engaged to a fourteen-year-old girl. His marriage and lavish wedding celebration on January 19, 1522, created a public furor but lent theological legitimacy to the Wittenberg theologians' rejection of clerical celibacy.

During Luther's absence while in hiding at Wartburg Castle, Karlstadt seized the opportunity for initiating evangelical reforms in response to growing demands for them. On January 24, 1522, the town council of Wittenberg endorsed changes in public worship modeled on Karlstadt's Christmas Day mass. At Karlstadt's urging, they also demanded the removal of images in churches and established a common chest for poor relief. Luther returned to Wittenberg and preached his famous eight "Invocavit" sermons against Karlstadt's rapid pace of reforms. Karlstadt subsequently severed his formal academic ties with the Univ. of Wittenberg and All Saints Church. In February 1523, Karlstadt renounced his academic titles and liturgical duties and became "Brother Andrew (Andy)," taking on the garb of the peasants and lay commoners whom he admired. Karlstadt then took a parish at Orlamünde, where he could introduce similar reforms to those he began at Wittenberg without Luther's interference.

Despite the adamant refusal of both Karlstadt and his Orlamünde congregation to support Thomas Müntzer's call to revolution, Karlstadt's former association with Müntzer at Wittenberg implicated him. Luther charged Karlstadt with having the same "rebellious and murderous spirit" as Müntzer in his sarcastic diatribe "Against the Heavenly Prophets" (1525), which was partly to blame for the princes' expelling of Karlstadt from Electoral Saxony altogether. Forced to seek refuge in city after city, Karlstadt finally found refuge at the Univ. of Basel in 1534, where he was made professor of Hebrew and resumed the calling he had publicly repudiated ten years before. He joined the victims of the plague, among whom he had ministered in Basel, on December 24, 1541.

Karlstadt was the first reformer to implement the full equality of all believers. Like Luther, Karlstadt strongly affirmed the centrality of Scripture and the mediation of grace via the external word of God, as well as the freedom of the laity to read and interpret Scripture for themselves. Yet Karlstadt never compromised the priority of the internal witness of the Spirit. It was Karlstadt's stress on the "inner Word of God" that led to Luther's notorious association of Karlstadt with Müntzer. Karlstadt is now recognized as the first proponent of a theology unique to the various Baptist movements of continental Europe, including Anabaptism, making him the "Father of the Baptist movements." The predominant Protestant understanding of the Lord's Supper as a memorial can be attributed largely to Karlstadt's liturgical legacy.

E. J. Furcha, trans. and ed., *The Essential Carlstadt: Fifteen Tracts by Andreas Bodenstein (Carlstadt) from Karlstadt* (1995); C. Lindberg, "Karlstadt's 'Dialogue' on the Lord's Supper," *Mennonite Quarterly Review* 53 (1979): 35–77; C. A. Pater, *Karlstadt as the Father of the Baptist Movements: The Emergence of Lay Protestantism* (1984); C. A. Pater, "Lay Religion in the Program of Andreas Rudolff-Bodenstein von Karlstadt," in *Leaders of the Reformation*, ed. R. L. DeMolen (1984); R. J. Sider, *Andreas Bodenstein von Karlstadt: The Development of His Thought, 1517–1525* (1974); R. J. Sider, ed. and trans., *Karlstadt's Battle with Luther: Documents in a Liberal-Radical Debate* (1978).

MARVIN L. ANDERSON

Katharina von Bora (1499–1552), wife of Martin Luther. Sources for Katharina's life are plentiful only for the period of her marriage (1525–1546). We have twenty-one letters to her from Luther, and eight of her own letters, although only one is from Luther's lifetime.

Katharina came from an old, impoverished noble family. In 1509 she entered the Marienthron Cloister at Nimbschen and in 1515 was dedicated as a nun. In 1523, influenced by Luther's writings, she and eight other nuns fled to Wittenberg. In 1525 she married Luther. From 1526 to 1534 they had six children, four of whom reached adulthood. After 1530, under her direction, the one-time cloister of the Augustinian Eremites was renovated to become the Luthers' home. Katharina instituted a dwelling for students (a so-called *Burse*) from which she received considerable income. With this income Luther at her request acquired numerous gardens and fields in the vicinity of Wittenberg from 1538 on, and in 1540 the property of Zölsdorf near Leipzig. At the outbreak of the Schmalkald War in 1546, she fled Wittenberg. She died in Torgau, where her gravestone remains.

R. Bainton, *Women of the Reformation in Germany and Italy* (1971); R. Markwald, *Katharina von Bora: A Reformation Life* (2002); M. Treu, ed., *Katharina von Bora: Die Lutherin* (1999).

MARTIN TREU

Katherine of Alexandria   *see* Catherine of Alexandria

Kempis, Thomas à   *see* Thomas à Kempis

Kempe, Margery (c. 1373–c. 1438), English lay author and mystic. Neither formally educated nor affiliated with a religious order, Margery independently pursued a life that included visionary prayer, pilgrimage, and close contact with her parish. Her mystical experiences displayed degrees of religious intensity and intimacy increasingly available to the laity in the late Middle Ages. Her unconventional life is known only through *The Book of Margery Kempe*, the spiritual autobiography she dictated to two male scribes. Margery was born to a politically prominent family in Lynn; around age twenty she married a local citizen named John, eventually giving birth to fourteen children. At forty, she persuaded her husband to accept a chaste marriage and increased her religious activity. Shaped by late medieval emphases on the passion, and on the use of emotion as a devotional tool, Margery was criticized by contemporaries for an effusive style of prayer that frequently included tears. Others prized her devotional sensitivity as evidence of divine favor; anchoress Julian of Norwich affirmed her vocation, as did members of the clergy. Concern over Lollardy and her public notoriety encouraged Margery's critics to accuse her of heresy; although imprisoned, she was never convicted. She died sometime after 1438. The immediate influence of Margery's writings was minor, but her work survived in a single fifteenth-century manuscript. Its rediscovery in 1934 has resulted in new appreciation for her contribution to Christian mysticism.

L. Staley, ed. and trans. *The Book of Margery Kempe: A New Translation, Contexts, Criticism* (2001); C. Atkinson, *Mystic and Pilgrim: The Book and the World of Margery Kempe* (1983).

ADRIENNE NOCK AMBROSE

Kilian (d. 689), Irish bishop and martyr. Born in Mullagh, Ireland, Kilian was consecrated bishop before he set off for a mission to East Franconia and Thuringia in Germany. Tradition associates him with the monastic *familia* community of Columban the Younger. Kilian traveled to Rome to secure papal permission for his mission. Back in Würzburg, he converted the local ducal family and urged Duke Gozbert to separate from his wife Geilana, the widow of his brother (although licit according to Roman and Germanic law, such a marriage was prohibited by canon law). Geilana, unhappy with this demand, had Kilian and his companions Kolonat (or Colman) and Totnan murdered in a horse stall. A cult of the martyrs soon developed in Franconia. Charlemagne is said to have been present when Burchard I, first bishop of Würzburg, had the relics transferred to his cathedral on July 8, 752. Tradition links Kilian with the foundation of the Irish monastery of St. Jacob in Würzburg. In Ireland a cult developed only later. Kilian appears in early ninth-century martyrologies.

A. Wendehorst, "Die Iren und die Christianisierung Mainfrankens," in *Die Iren und Europa im frühen Mittelalter*, vol. 1, ed. H. Löwe (1982), 319–29; J. Erichson and E. Brockhoff, *Kilian, Mönch aus Irland, aller Franken Patron* (1989).

ANNETTE KEHNEL

Kilwardby, Robert (c. 1215–1279), Dominican academic and churchman. Kilwardby was born in England and died at Viterbo. In the 1230s and 1240s at Paris, he studied, taught, and published widely on Aristotelian logic. Entering the Dominican order and residing at Oxford, during the 1250s he developed

into a proponent of a more patristic (increasingly neo-Augustinian) and ever less Aristotelian form of theology, just as the paradigm for understanding Aristotle was shifting from logic to natural philosophy. His popular reference works on patristic sources (*capitula, tabulae, concordantiae*)—both in the original and mediated by Peter Lombard—stood in the service of this theological program. He also published questions on Lombard's *Sentences*, turning his reflections on book 4 into a theology of non-Christian religions in the ambivalently philo-religious tradition of Hugh of St. Victor. As provincial of the English Dominicans (1261–1272) and archbishop of Canterbury (1272–1278), he maintained his interest in theological developments, culminating in his censure of Thomistic anthropology (March 18, 1277) and an open letter against Thomas's central thesis (*anima unica forma corporis*). The ensuing reaction against him did much to shape the reception of Thomism for centuries to come. Following his refusal to tax his clergy, Kilwardby was called as cardinal of Porto to the papal court, where he died half a year after his arrival.

R. Kilwardby, *Quaestiones in libros Sententiarum*, ed. J. Schneider et al., 6 vols. (1982–1995); Kilwardby, *On Time and Imagination*, 2 vols. ed. P. O. Lewry (1987, 1992); T. Kaeppeli, *Scriptores Orindinis Praedicatorum Medii Aevi*, vol. 3 (1980), 320–25, vol. 4 (1983), 267–69; Lewry, *Robert Kilwardby's Writings on the Logica vetus* (1978); I. Rosier, *La parole comme acte* (1994); R. Sharpe, *A Handlist of the Latin Writers of Great Britain and Ireland before 1540* (1997), 560–64.

RICHARD SCHENK, OP

King's Book (1543)   Popular name for *The Necessary Doctrine and Erudition of a Christian Man*, a revised edition of *The Institution of a Christian Man*, or "Bishop's Book" (1537). The preface is by King Henry VIII. The revisions were few but significant, emphasizing the English king's primacy in the hierarchy of the Church of England (versus Rome's claims), and expounding various articles of faith (versus the interpretations of Luther or Calvin). For example, the work asserts that justification is "the making of us righteous before God," which requires strenuous moral effort and does not occur "by faith alone."

T. A. Lacey, ed., *The King's Book* (1932).

RODERICK MARTIN

Knights of the Temple *see* Templars

Knights' Revolt (1522–1523) Revolt of the free imperial knights against the territorial princes of the HRE. Led by Franz von Sickingen (1481–1523), the revolt was the result of the marginalization of the knights in imperial society due to expanding princely control over territories. Military reforms further lessened their importance in favor of cannon and infantry. Finally, in 1521 an imperial peace was declared that outlawed private warfare. Since many knights depended upon private feuds for their financial security, this was a grave threat to their livelihoods. At the same time, many knights believed they had an ally in Martin Luther's condemnation of abuses in the church and his calls for reform and greater freedom for the German people. Ulrich von Hutten (1488–1523) prominently connected Luther's movement to the knights' cause. The revolt reached a crescendo in August 1522 with the attack on the city and bishop of Trier. Sickengen took Trier for a short time but was ultimately forced to retreat; he died in April 1523 from wounds suffered in battle.

W. R. Hitchcock, *The Background of the Knights' Revolt, 1522–1523* (1958); H. Holborn, *Ulrich von Hutten and the German Reformation* (1965).

DAVID WHITFORD

Knox, John (1513–1572), Scottish preacher and reformer. Born in Haddington, in East Lothian, Knox was educated briefly at Glasgow (1522) and then at the Univ. of St. Andrews. He was ordained a priest in 1536. He seems to have joined the cause of reform through the influence of George Wishart (c. 1513–1546), for he first appeared in public view in 1546, defending Wishart with a sword before Wishart's arrest and execution by Cardinal David Beaton (c. 1494–1546). Beaton was in turn slain by Wishart's supporters, and Knox next appeared in 1547 when he joined them in their safe haven in the castle of St. Andrews, where he preached his first sermon, a dramatic indictment of the papacy. This sermon reveals Knox at his fieriest; his sermonic zeal to uproot and destroy what he viewed as papal tyranny enabled him to inspire others to do the same. When the French took the castle in July 1547, Knox was captured and spent nineteen months in the French galleys. He was released in 1549 and departed for England, where he became preacher at Berwick and Newcastle. While at

Berwick, Knox instituted a form of Communion at which members of the congregation sat at table. When Thomas Cranmer was revising the Book of Common Prayer, Knox persuaded him to give an evangelical explanation for the practice of kneeling for Communion, called the "Black Rubric."

When Mary Tudor became queen, Knox fled first to Frankfurt and then to Geneva, which he described as "a perfect school of Christ." Knox ministered to the English congregation in Geneva and wrote a *Genevan Service Book* based in large part on Calvin's *Form of Prayers*. Knox was deeply influenced by Calvin's understanding of the sacraments and of the rightly ordered church. However, unlike Calvin, Knox made discipline a third mark of the true church. While in Geneva, Knox wrote two tracts encouraging both the nobles and the common people of Scotland to take up arms to overthrow the "tyranny" of rulers devoted to the church of Rome. Frustrated by the rule of queens with ties to the Roman church, especially Mary Tudor and Mary of Guise, Knox published from Geneva his infamous *First Blast of the Trumpet against the Monstrous Regiment of Women* (1558), which was published just in time for the succession of Elizabeth I to the throne in England.

Unable to return to England, Knox traveled instead to Scotland in 1559 and preached a series of fiery sermons in Dundee and Perth, with the latter inciting an iconoclastic riot. Upon the departure of both the French and the English from Scotland in the summer of 1560, Knox led a public service of thanksgiving in his church, St. Giles Cathedral, Edinburgh, thanking the English for their help in freeing the Scots from the French. Knox then joined the efforts at national church reform begun by Parliament in the absence of Mary of Guise. Knox encouraged the work of Parliament in a series of sermons on Haggai, urging the restoration of the church after its return from Roman captivity. Knox was a member of a commission of six men who wrote the Scots Confession, a document that strongly links the Kirk to the history of Israel, and was also the author of the influential *First Book of Discipline* (1560). Though the latter lacked state sanction and was later superseded by the *Second Book of Discipline* (1581), the work did influence the direction of the Protestant community in Scotland, especially its concern for the education of children and the attention it devoted to the poor.

In spite of the return of Mary of Guise to Scotland in 1561, Knox was able to continue the reform of the church, securing in 1561 the free right of assembly for provincial synods, famously stating, "Take from us liberty of assemblies and you take from us the gospel." Much of Knox's *Genevan Service Book* was implemented in the *Book of Common Order* of 1564, including the singing of psalms, which became a distinctive mark of Reformed worship, and the celebration of Communion while seated at table. The last work produced by Knox was a *History of the Reformation* (1572), which once again reveals his undying passion for the reform of the church according to the Word of God and his deep enmity for all remnants of the "papal tyranny."

J. Cameron, *The First Book of Discipline* (1972); G. Donaldson, *The Scottish Reformation* (1960); J. Knox, *History of the Reformation in Scotland* (1949).

RANDALL C. ZACHMAN

Konrad of Megenberg (1309–1374),

medieval theologian. Born in Mäbenberg, Konrad began his studies at Erfurt and taught philosophy in the Cistercian college of St. Bernard at Paris, while completing the *studium generale* at the university (c. 1330–1334). He then taught at the university for eight years, during which time he also visited the papal court (1337). At Paris, he wrote both versions of his *Planctus ecclesiae in Germaniam* (*Lamentation of the Church in Germany*, 1337, 1338), examining the conflict between *imperium* and priesthood and the conflict between Ludwig of Bavaria and Pope Benedict XII. His participation in the controversy over theses of William of Ockham at the Univ. of Paris in 1340–1341 brought him a brief suspension from teaching. At Paris he also produced a commentary on Peter Lombard's *Sentences* (not extant) and a disputation against Walter Burleigh.

Konrad became rector of St. Stephen's School in Vienna (1342–1348) and was responsible for all education in the city. At Vienna, c. 1342, he wrote his *Expositiones* and the *Quaestiones super speram* (*Questions on the Spheres*), commenting on the standard textbook of astronomy, John of Sacrobosco's *Spaera*, which he later expanded and translated into German between 1347 and 1350. He also began work on a German version of Thomas of Cantimpré's *Liber de natura rerum* (*Book of Nature*, 1348–1350), based on Thomas's third recension, attributed by Konrad and by his contemporaries to Albertus Magnus. A second version of Konrad's *Book of Nature*, containing a three-part introduction, was

dedicated to the young Rudolf IV of Austria, although there is some dispute over Konrad's authorship of the addition.

In 1348, Konrad settled in Regensburg as cathedral canon and served from 1359 to 1363 as the cathedral pastor of St. Ulrich. There he probably completed his *Speculum felicitates humane* (*Mirror of Human Happiness*, also called the *Monastica,* 1348, and dedicated to Rudolf IV) and composed his *Yconomica* (1348–1352) in three books. The latter work examined simple households, the household of the German king and Roman emperor, as well as church institutions, with digressions on the structure of offices at court, the conflict between secular and ecclesiastical power, and the 219 theses condemned at Paris in 1277. Konrad's later political tractates, *De translacione imperii* (*On the Transfer of the Imperium*, 1354) and *Contra Occam* (*Against Ockham*), are largely derived from the second book of the *Yconomica*. His *Tractatus de moralitate in Alamannia* (*Treatise on Morality in Germany*) deals with the 1348 outbreak of the plague, rejecting, among other common explanations of its outbreak, the accusation of Jewish well-poisoning (he also condemns the persecution of Jews), and searching for the causes of the plague among the intellectual currents of his time; he also demands a reform of liberal arts study and the universities. In 1357 Konrad visited the papal court on behalf of the city of Regensburg and in 1361 on behalf of the Holy Roman Emperor Charles IV.

Konrad also wrote a *Tractatus contra mendicantes ad papam Urbanum V* (*Treatise against the Mendicants to Pope Urban V*), also known as the *Lacrima ecclesiae* (*Tears of the Church*, around 1364), which was never printed; a *Commentarius de laudibus Beatae Virginis Mariae* (*Commentary on the Praises of the Blessed Virgin Mary*), his most important theological work, written after 1364 and never published; *Statuta capituli ecclesie Ratisponensis* (*Statutes of the Chapter of the Church of Regensburg*, 1355/1359), intended to reform the cathedral chapter; a *Tractatus de limitibus parochiarum civitatis Ratisponensis* (*Treatise on the Parish Boundaries in the City of Regensburg*, 1373), on church order in the city; and *Historia Sancti Erhardi* (*History of St. Erhard*), in which he contributes to the history of music.

Lexikon des Mittelalters, vol. 5 (1991), columns 1361–62; W. J. Courtenay, "Conrad of Megenberg: The Parisian Years," *Vivarium* 35 (1997): 102–24; G. Hayer, *Konrad von Megenberg:*

Das Buch der Natur: Untersuchungen zu seiner Text- und Überlieferungsgeschichte (1998); G. Drossbach, *Die "Yconomica" des Konrad von Megenberg: Das Haus als politische und soziale Norm* (1997).

GISELA DROSSBACH

Labarum The term was first applied in the mid-fourth century to the military standard adopted by Constantine and his successors. Its design, a combination of the Greek letters *chi* and *rho* (the first two letters, or monogram, of the Greek word *Christus*), usually within a wreath, is based on the story of a vision Constantine had before his victory over Maxentius at the Milvian Bridge in 312.

According to Lactantius (*Mort.* 44.3–6), Constantine was told in a dream that he would be victorious if he put the "heavenly sign of God," a cross-shaped letter X, on his soldiers' shields. Eusebius (*Vit. Const.* 1.26–29) recounts a vision shared by Constantine's army, in daylight, of the "trophy of a cross of light" in the heavens with the inscription "Conquer by this." In Eusebius's version, Christ appeared to Constantine in a dream telling him to use this sign in all his military engagements.

From 315 the labarum became the primary Constantinian military insignia. It eventually became a standard Christian motif, especially associated with victory over death. It appears in the earliest passion imagery on fourth-century Christian sarcophagi, as well as in mosaics in churches and baptisteries, and is etched on funerary plaques.

R. Jensen, *Understanding Early Christian Art* (2000); P. Bruun, "The Christian Signs on the Coins of Constantine," *Arctos*, NS 3 (1962): 6–34.

ROBIN M. JENSEN

Lactantius (d. c. 325), African Christian writer. Lactantius was a convert to Christianity and a student of Arnobius of Sicca. Due to his fine Latin style, he was first called the "Christian Cicero" by the Renaissance humanist Pico della Mirandola. His chief work, *The Divine Institutes*, inspired by Cicero's *The Nature of the Gods*, was the first attempt at a Christian *summa* in Latin. The apologetic character of the work is evident as Lactantius moves from criticism of error to exaltation of truth, ever toward the Stoic goal of happiness. Especially important is the section where he deals with passions (6.14–16). Siding with the Peripatetics against the Stoics, Lactantius insists that passions are

constitutive of humanity. He considers the Stoic ideal of *apatheia* ("passionlessness") unrealizable and dangerous. An epitome of *The Divine Institutes*, written by Lactantius himself, also exists. *The Wrath of God* criticizes Epicureans for considering God inert and Stoics for not distinguishing between just anger and unjust anger. For Lactantius, God does become genuinely angry but always acts out of love for human beings. His other extant works include *The Workmanship of God*, *The Death of the Persecutors*, and *The Phoenix*.

Lactantius, *Works*, trans. W. Fletcher, in ANF, 1st series, vol. 7 (1950); J. M. Hallman, "The Mutability of God: Tertullian to Lactantius," *TS* 42 (1981): 373–93.

KENNETH B. STEINHAUSER

Laínez, Diego (1512–1565), second general of the Jesuits, preacher, theologian. Laínez was born at Almazán, Spain, and studied at Soria, Sigüenza, and Alcalá. He and his good friend Alfonso Salmerón decided to continue their studies at the Univ. of Paris, where they quickly became friends with Ignatius Loyola, who introduced them to his other companions, notably Francisco Xavier and Pierre Favre. After he made Loyola's Spiritual Exercises, Laínez, along with Ignatius and five other companions, vowed in 1534 that after completing their studies they would go to Palestine and work as missionaries. If they could not go to the Holy Land, they would put themselves at the pope's disposal. In 1537 the seven companions and some new recruits gathered in Venice, where Laínez was ordained a priest. Almost all of the rest of Laínez's life was spent in Italy. When war between Venice and the Turks prevented their sailing, Laínez preached in Venice and Vicenza. In 1538 and 1539 Paul III assigned him to teach at the Univ. of Rome. The companions gradually decided to start a religious order, the Society of Jesus, or Jesuits. Paul III gave his approval in 1540. Meanwhile Laínez spent 1539 to 1544 preaching and reforming convents with great success in northern Italian cities. His greatest preaching success came in Florence in 1547 when some of his sermons drew nine thousand people. Later he preached in Sicily and Genoa. He was chaplain of a Spanish-Italian expedition that captured Tripoli from the Turks in 1550.

Laínez was the best theologian among Loyola's early companions, and for years he worked on a large catechism for use in Germany, but he never completed it. He served as theologian at all three phases of the Council of

Trent (1545–1547, 1551–1552, and 1562–1563). There he generally took a conservative stance, arguing against Communion with both bread and wine and against a doctrine of twofold justification that went far toward accommodating Lutherans. In 1561 at the Colloquy of Poissy, sponsored by Catherine di Médici, he defended Christ's real presence in the Eucharist against the Calvinist theologians Theodore Beza and Peter Martyr Vermigli.

Ignatius died in 1556, but the General Congregation to elect his successor had to be postponed because Paul IV and Philip II were at war. Meanwhile Laínez served as vicar general of the order. The General Congregation met in 1558, approved Loyola's Constitutions, and elected Laínez general. He served until his death in 1565. Jesuit numbers tripled during those few years. Paul IV admired Laínez and wanted to make him a cardinal, but Ignatius successfully resisted this. Later Laínez as general had to accept certain oral demands from Paul IV contrary to the Jesuit Constitutions. When Paul IV died in 1559, the Jesuits returned to their previous practices, solemnly approved by previous popes.

J. Fichter, *James Laynez, Jesuit* (1944); J. O'Malley, *The First Jesuits* (1993); F. Cereceda, *Diego Laínez en la Europa de su tiempo, 1512–1565* (1945–1946).

JOHN PATRICK DONNELLY, SJ

Laity Scripture uses the Greek word *laos* ("people") to refer to the "people of God," meaning both Israel and the Christian church. It embraces the whole community without distinguishing one member from another. First Peter 2:9 identifies the church as "a chosen race, a royal priesthood, a holy nation, God's own people."

As early as the New Testament, a variety of offices and functions had begun to emerge in the nascent church (Acts 6; 1 Cor. 12:28; 1 Tim. 5:17). Distinctive offices, particularly those of bishop and presbyter, developed in the early centuries and were nearly always associated with liturgical roles. Nevertheless, the church in the patristic age continued to think of itself in terms of a shared ministry in which there might be distinctions of role but no substantial distinctions of status. By baptism (and particularly in baptismal anointing), all shared the "royal priesthood" that had begun with Israel's kings and priests and now, in Christ, included all the faithful. Even when the term "priest" began to be used, it was generally understood that the individual's priesthood derived from the priesthood of the whole community.

Particularly after Constantine (274–337), a sharp distinction began to develop between "clergy" and "laity." Prerogatives long associated with the laity—to approve or disapprove of leaders, to baptize, to share in corporate discipline, to hear confessions, and to participate in synods and councils—started to wither. Even though most monastic orders began as lay movements, lay influence rested almost exclusively with royals. When they began to interfere with ecclesiastical appointments, the Gregorian "reforms" of the eleventh century resulted in redefining the laity's role in passive terms. "The church" meant the hierarchy.

The Protestant reformers launched a salvo against hierarchical authority under the slogan "priesthood of all believers." Particularly in Reformed churches, significant roles were given to lay officers in synodical and congregational governance, and some prerogatives were guaranteed to congregational assemblies. In reaction, the Council of Trent (1545–1563) assigned to laity an inferior status. Although one of the impulses leading to the Reformation had been lay dissatisfaction with clericalism, the Protestant churches soon invented their own versions of it.

From as early as the colonial era, Protestant churches in the United States have tended to be lay driven. In Virginia, Episcopal vestries presumed powers that made authorities in England nervous. In sparsely settled areas, seldom visited by ordained ministers, Protestant churches often relied upon lay leadership. A strong strain of populism has contributed to the power of laity. Nevertheless, American Protestantism presents a curious mixture of clericalism (even in free churches) and lay power (even in more centralized churches).

Y. Congar, *Laity, Church, and World* (1960); H. Kraemer, *A Theology of the Laity* (1958); Second Vatican Council, *Decree on the Apostolate of the Laity* (1965); S. Neill and H.-R. Weber, eds., *The Layman in Christian History* (1963).

RONALD P. BYARS

Lambeth Articles (1595)   Nine propositions written by William Whitaker, a Puritan professor of divinity at Cambridge. They were originally written in Latin with double predestination as the central focus, reflecting the dispute between Calvinist orthodoxy and Anglican Calvinism prevalent in the English universities at this time. The archbishops of

Canterbury and York approved of these articles, which were intended to act as a supplement to the Thirty-nine Articles of 1571. Elizabeth took offense to the clergy acting without her support and approval, and she disputed the articles on both political and theological grounds. As a result, they never carried any official authority.

G. Bray, *Documents of the English Reformation* (1994).

ALDEN R. LUDLOW

Lanfranc (c. 1010–1089), Benedictine monk, archbishop, and theologian. Born at Pavia, Lanfranc received his intellectual training in northern Italy (until 1130). He then taught in Burgundy and later on at the cathedral school of Avranches in Normandy. In 1042 he entered the Benedictine monastery of Le Bec, where he acted as prior (1045–1063) before being named abbot of the monastery of St. Stephan at Caen and then archbishop of Canterbury (1070–1089) by Duke William.

Lanfranc achieved an important work of reform among the Benedictines of Bec and Caen as well as within the English church. He visited Rome at various times (1050, 1067, and 1071). Popes Alexander II and Gregory VII charged him with legations. He urged the English bishops to promise oaths of allegiance to Rome, but he could not convince Duke William, despite their close relation, to do the same. Lanfranc authored several important theological and canonistic works. His commentaries on the Psalms and the Pauline Letters were considered innovative by his contemporaries. He wrote a treatise against Berengar of Tours, in which he insisted upon the physical aspects of Christ's real presence in the Eucharist. Lanfranc also composed an abbreviation of the Pseudo-Isidorian Decretals. His sixty letters reveal the everyday business of an ecclesiastical dignitary.

G. R. Evans, "Lanfranc, Anselm, and a New Consciousness of Canon Law in England," *English Canon Law* (1998): 1–12; LTK³ 7 (1997), 636; RGG⁴ 5 (2002), 67; J. Rubenstein, "Liturgy against History: The Competing Visions of Lanfranc and Eadmer of Canterbury," *Speculum* 74 (1999): 279–309.

RAINER BERNDT

Langton, Stephen (1150/1155–1228), English theologian, cardinal, and archbishop of Canterbury. Langton taught in Paris from 1180 to 1205 and left numerous biblical commentaries and study aids, theological treatises, and sermons. His exegetical lectures covered most of the Bible, progressing methodically from the literal to the spiritual senses. His division of the biblical books into numbered chapters is still in use today. In 1206, Pope Innocent III called him to Rome and consecrated him archbishop of Canterbury (1207) in the midst of fierce controversy with King John (Lackland). Barred from entering England, Langton stayed at the abbey of Pontigny in France until 1213, when John's capitulation allowed him to take possession of his see. His sympathy with the baronial grievances and the Magna Charta earned him the ire of the king and a temporary suspension from office. He was, however, able to attend the Fourth Lateran Council in Rome (1215). After his reinstatement by Honorius III in 1218, he crowned young King Henry III in 1220 and, starting with a provincial council at Oxford in 1222, began to implement constitutions aimed at improving clerical discipline and education. His reformatory actions deeply affected church life in England.

G. Lacombe and B. Smalley, "Studies on the Commentaries of Cardinal Stephen Langton," in *Archives d'historie doctrinale et littéraire du moyen âge*, vol. 5 (1930), 5–220; R. Quinto, *Doctor nominatissmus: Stephen Langton (+ 1218) e la tradizione delle sue opere*, Beiträge zur Geschichte der Philosophie und Theologie des Mittelalters 39, NS (1994).

KARLFRIED FROEHLICH

La Rochelle, Synod of   see Rochelle, Synod of

Las Casas, Bartolomé de (1474–1566), Spanish Dominican missionary, defender of the rights of aboriginal Americans. Las Casas traveled to the New World as a colonist in 1502, but after becoming a priest in 1510 he turned his attention to the plight of the natives. Traumatized by the atrocities he witnessed as a military chaplain during the Spanish conquest of Cuba (1512–1514), Las Casas began to denounce colonial abuses and to call for the abolition of the land grants (*encomiendas*) that allowed Spanish settlers to demand labor from natives on their estates. In 1515 he returned to Spain to plead his case before Emperor Charles V. After a failed experimental settlement supposed to grant natives more autonomy, Las Casas joined the Dominicans and devoted his life to advocate for human rights. His efforts had mixed success. The *New Laws of the Indies* (1542) curbed some of the worst abuses in the *encomienda* system but led to increased importation of African slave labor to the Spanish colonies. In 1550–1551 he took part in a public debate at Valladolid in which he and fellow Dominicans Francisco de Vitoria, Melchior Cano, and Domingo de Soto attacked the notion that New World natives were inferior beings worthy of enslavement, arguing that levels of cultural development are relative and cannot be used to determine the superiority or inferiority of human beings. Las Casas wrote numerous books influential in his own day, the most famous of which, *The Destruction of the Indies* (1552), went through many editions and translations. Known as "the Apostle of the Indies" and hailed as one of the world's first ethnographers and cultural relativists, Las Casas stands out among all those who pricked the conscience of the Spanish colonists. Ironically, his exposés of the sins of his own nation were long used by Spain's rivals—especially the English, French, and Dutch—to prove that the Spanish were a twisted, cruel people, obviously "inferior" to other Europeans.

R. Adorno, *The Intellectual Life of Bartolome de las Casas* (1991); J. Friede and B. Keen, eds., *Bartolomé de las Casas in History* (1971); A. Huergo, *Vida y obras de Bartolomé de las Casas* (1998).

                                        CARLOS M. N. EIRE

Lasco, Jean à (1499–1560), Polish Calvinist reformer. Born of nobility and having received a humanist education in Italy, à Lasco (Jan Łaski) was on his way to a promising career in the Roman Catholic Church when he converted to Protestantism. He met Erasmus in 1524 and stayed at his home in Basel for a year. There he came into contact with Zwingli and Oecolampadius, who had a lasting impact on his thought. In 1529 he became titular bishop of Veszprém in Hungary, and in 1538 he was appointed archdeacon of Warsaw. Mysteriously, perhaps for love or out of religious conviction, he left Poland and his ecclesiastical offices. He married in 1540 and by 1543 was in Emden as superintendent of the Protestant church of East Frisia. By this time he had adopted a Reformed outlook and attempted to impress a Calvinist stamp upon the East Frisian church. The Augsburg Interim forced his departure to England, where he oversaw the French and Dutch refugee ("stranger") churches in London. He composed important works of church polity, which had clear affinities with the polity of the Zurich reformers. He also penned a confession of faith, catechism, and a treatise on the sacraments. Upon the accession of Mary Tudor, à Lasco was again forced into exile. He eventually returned to Poland (1556), where he ended his days as superintendent of the Reformed churches in southern Poland.

A. Kuyper, ed., *Joannis a Lasco Opera*, 2 vols. (1866); H. P. Jürgens, *Johannes à Lasco in Ostfriesland: Der Werdegang eines europäischen Reformators* (2002).

                                RAYMOND A. BLACKETER

Lateran Council, Fifth   Convened by Julius II in 1512 and concluded by his successor, Leo X, in 1517, this council was held at the palace near St. John Lateran, the pope's cathedral. It had been urgently sought by many and would prove to be the last chance to deal with church reform before the Reformation. Though Julius had promised at his election in 1503 to summon a council, he acted only when confronted by dissident cardinals supported by Emperor Maximilian and King Louis XII of France. But with only about a hundred, mostly Italian, bishops present, Lateran V was a missed opportunity. Far from serious reform, papal authority was reasserted, conciliarism condemned, and denunciations issued against the growing autonomy of national churches. The bishops did not sense the ground of ecclesial unity shifting beneath them. Lateran V opened with the Augustinian Giles of Viterbo's apocalyptic challenge for pope and prelates to mend their ways lest Christendom cease to exist. Mere months after the council adjourned, another Augustinian, Martin Luther, would propose a debate on indulgences, and that would initiate a reform of apocalyptic proportions.

E. Duffy, *Saints and Sinners: A History of the Popes* (1997); N. Minnich, *The Fifth Lateran Council: Studies on Its Membership, Diplomacy, and Proposals for Reform (1512–1517)* (1993).

                                PETER J. SCAGNELLI

Lateran Councils   Between 1123 and 1215, four ecumenical councils were convoked in the basilica of St. John Lateran in Rome by Popes Calixtus II, Innocent II, Alexander III, and Innocent III, respectively. Their purpose was primarily to celebrate the papacy's victories over its foes, but also to deal with matters of grave concern, such as reform and the Crusades. The First Lateran Council convened from March 18 to April 6, 1123. It formally ended the investiture controversy and ratified the Concordat of Worms (1122). Its twenty-five decrees condemned simony, lay interference in ecclesiastical affairs, and clerical incontinence; they were copied into twelfth-century canon law manuscripts and thereby made their way into Gratian's *Decretum* (c. 1140/1141). Some of the thirty decrees of Lateran II are also found in the *Decretum*: like its predecessor, this council condemned simony and clerical lapses, and it affirmed the Truce and Peace of God (see *Truce of God*). It also anathematized the antipope Anacletus. Reflecting the growing attraction of the schools, it forbade monks and canons regular to abandon their religious vocations in favor of studies in medicine or Roman law.

Following a bitter conflict with Emperor Frederick Barbarossa and a papal schism that began in 1159, Pope Alexander III convened the most splendid council that careful planning could produce. Consisting of three sessions that ran March 5–19, it confirmed the peace treaty concluded with the emperor at Venice in 1177; issued decrees requiring a two-thirds majority of votes within the college of cardinals in papal elections, hoping thereby to avoid future schisms; condemned the schismatics of recent memory; and pronounced anathema against the Cathars, dualistic heretics whose strength, especially in southern France, had grown to alarming proportions. In matters of church governance, Lateran III stipulated the age of thirty for the appointment of bishops, and it decreed that a prebend or stipend be given to a master of arts who was to provide instruction at the cathedral school.

Pope Innocent III announced Lateran IV two years in advance, citing his intention to reform the church and promote crusade. Over 1,200 participants filled the basilica for the three sessions held during November 1215, and they dealt with such matters as aid to the Holy Land, the revolt of the English barons against King John, the civil war in the German Empire, and various ecclesiastical disputes. The crowning achievement of the council was the publication of seventy decrees that addressed doctrinal matters such as transubstantiation, the Trinity, and the heretical teachings of Joachim of Fiore, plus reform of the clergy through a reinvigoration of diocesan and provincial synods, problems with the policy regarding consanguinity, confession and the Eucharist, and the Jews. Lateran IV marked the high point of medieval papal legislation and was the most important Western council before Trent. Its decrees passed into the *Decretales* of Pope Innocent IV in 1234, ultimately becoming part of the *Corpus iuris canonici*.

———

C. R. Cheney, "The Numbering of the Lateran Councils in 1179 and 1215," in *Medieval Texts and Studies,* ed. C. R. Cheney (1973); R. Foreville, *Latran I, II, III et IV* (1970); M. Gibbs and J. Lang, *Bishops and Reform, 1215–1272* (1934); P. B. Pixton, *The German Episcopacy and the Implementation of the Decrees of the Fourth Lateran Council, 1216–1245* (1995).

PAUL B. PIXTON

Latimer, Hugh (c. 1490–1555), early English Reformation preacher, bishop of Worcester, and martyr. The son of a Leicestershire farmer, Latimer was educated at Cambridge and elected Fellow of Clare Hall in 1510. Ordained a priest in 1515, he initially opposed Reformation ideas, though not the need for church reform. By 1522, his eloquence and zeal against ecclesiastical abuses gained him the privilege of preaching throughout England; he became known for a straightforward, homely style of speaking and a deep understanding of human nature.

Gradually, Latimer's attitudes toward the Reformation began to change. In 1524, his disputation for his bachelor of divinity degree still rejected Melanchthon's ideas, but soon after, he began to change his attitude toward the Reformation. In 1525, he refused a request by Bishop West of Ely to preach against Luther and was banned from preaching in that diocese, though his privilege was restored on his successful defense before Cardinal Wolsey. In Lent 1530, he gained Henry VIII's favor when he delivered a sermon on the limits of using royal powers to defend orthodoxy; afterward he was granted a benefice in Wiltshire. In March 1532 he was censured by Convocation for spreading Reformation ideas. He submitted, signing the bishops' articles of faith. Henry's break with Rome in 1534 helped Latimer's standing. He became royal chaplain that year and bishop of Worcester the next. He supported Henry's dissolution of monasteries and approved the execution of Cardinal Pole's family in 1538. However, he opposed Henry's doctrinally conservative Six Articles in 1539 and resigned his see under pressure from Thomas Cromwell.

He was banned from preaching in 1540 and imprisoned in the Tower of London by 1546 but released on Edward VI's accession the next year. Under Edward, he was again a popular court preacher, continuing to support both reform of church abuses and reformation of doctrine. On Mary's accession in 1553, he was again imprisoned in the Tower. In 1554, he was chosen with Archbishop Cranmer and Bishop Ridley to dispute at Oxford about Reformation ideas, especially on transubstantiation and the sacrifice of the Mass. He rejected the Catholic position and was excommunicated. Reexamined later, he again rejected Catholicism, and with Cranmer and Ridley was executed as a heretic on October 16, 1555.

A. Chester, *Hugh Latimer* (1954); G. Corrie, ed. *Sermons*, 2 vols. (1758); H. Darby, *Hugh Latimer* (1953); C. Hammer, "The Oxford Martyrs in Oxford," in *JEH* 50, no. 2 (1999): 235–50; M. Skeeters, *Community and Clergy* (1993); C. Stuart, *Latimer: Apostle to the English* (1986).

DAVID A. LOPEZ

Latin Envoys to Medieval Armenia

Relations between the Latin church and Armenia unfolded against the backdrop of the Crusades and attempts to draw the various "schismatic" Eastern churches into union under Roman primacy. The first overtures were extended to Catholicos Grigor II the Martyrophile in 1080 by Pope Gregory VII in the aftermath of the fall of the principal kingdoms of Greater Armenia to the Seljuks and the inauguration of an independent Armenian principality south of the Taurus Mountains. Over the next century the frequency and intensity of those contacts increased as the papal legate Alberich accompanied Catholicos Grigor III to the Jerusalem Synod of the Cenacle in 1141/1142, other intermediaries conveyed the mitre and pallium to Catholicos Grigor Tghay in 1183 from Lucius III, and the process culminated in Innocent III's dispatch of Conrad of Wittelsbach, archbishop of Mainz, to officiate at the coronation of Levon I as king of Cilicia in 1198 in response to Armenian initiatives acknowledging papal supremacy.

The inauguration of the Dominican and Franciscan orders in the early thirteenth century greatly impacted papal communications with the Armenians. However, Cilicia's strong geopolitical situation and the Armenian submission to Mongol suzerainty led to a cooling of relations with the papacy in the middle decades of the thirteenth century. In the 1230s the Dominican Simon de St. Quentin drew up a list of Armenian errors, while the Franciscan Dominic of Aragon acted as emissary to King Het'um I to invite an Armenian presence at the First Council of Lyon (1245). This provoked a refutation of fifteen points of Latin dogma and ritual by the scholar Vardan Arewelts'i. An even more acerbic encounter over Petrine primacy took place between the legate Thomas Agni de Leontino and the Armenian representative Mkhit'ar Skewrats'i at Acre in 1262. Gregory X's invitation for an Armenian delegation to attend the Second Council of Lyon (1274) met with a similar rebuff.

Nevertheless, the Franciscans, in particular, began to gain influence at the Armenian court as well as among Armenian merchant communities on the Near Eastern trade routes where the order maintained centers (Erzurum, St. Thaddeus, Salmast, Karpi, Tiflis, Sultaniya, and Tabriz). At the end of the thirteenth century King Het'um II set a trend followed by certain other noblemen of requesting a complement of six friars as counselors and was so impressed by the intrepid Fr. John of Montecorvino (see *Franciscan Envoys to Medieval China*) that he assumed the latter's monastic name when he joined the order on his abdication some years later. Meanwhile, the Dominicans expanded their Armenian mission in 1318 with the creation of a new archdiocese by Pope John XXII centered on the Il-Khanid capital of Sultaniya, with suffragans in the cities of Sivas, Tabriz, and Maragha. The Franciscan brother Peregrine's correspondence of the same year also indicates a lively rapport with the Armenian colony in the Chinese port city of Zaytun. As already noted, the Franciscans established a community at the monastery of St. Thaddeus in the Maku region in what is now northwestern Iran, the seat of the Armenian exarch, Archbishop Zak'aria Artazets'i. Under Franciscan influence presumably, the latter adopted Catholicism in the late 1310s and received two letters from the pope in 1321 commending him for enduring persecution for the faith and empowering him to ordain clergy locally. Under his auspices a school of translation was founded with the participation of Yovhannes Tsortsorets'i and other former pupils of the major Armenian monastic academy of the time at Glajor, which began with the rendition of Thomas Aquinas's commentary on the fourth book of Peter Lombard's *Sentences* (see *Four Books of Sentences*) with the assistance of the new Dominican bishop of Tabriz, Bartolomeo Abbagliati. Most of the other texts selected were Franciscan in background, such as Bonaventure's *Life of St. Francis* and Nicholas of Lyra's commentary on John. Indeed, in the early 1330s St. Thaddeus became a temporary bastion of the Franciscan Spirituals under the leadership of Fra Pontius, who inveighed against papal infallibility, attempted to remove Thomist teaching from the region, and for a time resisted the authority of the Dominican bishop of Tabriz. After Zak'aria's death and the onset of the Black Death (1347/1348) the community ceased to maintain its momentum, and the site passed to the Dominicans in the last quarter of the century.

The Dominican mission to Greater Armenia was significantly advanced by the see of Maragha and its hierarch Bartolomeo da Poggio. In 1328 a small group of Armenian monks headed by Yovhannes Krnets'i established another translation school there, which moved with the bishop to the monastery of K'rna in the Ernjak district of the Siwnik' region in 1330. The following year it was given over to the order, and by January 31, 1356, the community received papal recognition as the Fratres Unitores of the Congregation of St. Gregory the Illuminator, the baptizer of the Armenian court in the early fourth century. Bartolomeo was assisted in these activities by other Dominican representatives: Peter of Aragon, John of Swineford, and John of Florence. Their translations introduced Armenians to contemporary Latin theological and philosophical thought and gained currency in both uniate and nonuniate circles. Although greatly attenuated, the Fratres Unitores continued until 1583, at which point they were reorganized as a regular Dominican province. Thereafter the new Armenian mission associated with the Counter-Reformation was primarily entrusted to the Jesuits, Theatines, and Capuchins.

———

B. Hamilton, "The Armenian Church and the Papacy of the Time of the Crusades," *Eastern Churches Review* 10 (1978): 61–87; J. Richard, *La papauté et les missions d'orient au moyen âge (xiiie–xve siècles)* (2nd ed., 1998).

S. PETER COWE

Latin Kingdom of Jerusalem

After Jerusalem had been captured and ravaged by the first armed pilgrimage of the crusading era on July 15, 1099, a feudal kingdom was established. The victors elected Duke Godfrey of Bouillon as "Advocate of the Holy Sepulcher," de facto king of Jerusalem. Three other Frankish states were established: the county of Edessa, the principality of Antioch, and the county of Tripoli. Edessa and Tripoli became vassals of the king. By 1153 all the Mediterranean ports had come under Frankish control.

Because many knights returned to their European homes, defense of the new kingdom depended on a small number of soldiers who settled and who began to adopt a native way of life. Society evolved with the Western Christians on top, Eastern Christians next, and Jews and Muslims on the bottom. The Western lords in manor houses, castles, or villages were supported by the native economy, which included crops and crafts such as dye and glass making. International trade provided items such as spices from the Orient to Europe and brought in vast tax revenues.

King Guy of Lusignan (r. 1186–1192) led his army to defeat by Saladin at Hattin on July 4, 1187. Jerusalem fell shortly thereafter. The kingdom's capital moved to Acre, where the Franks finally were forced to leave the mainland in 1291. A "king of Jerusalem" existed on Cyprus and elsewhere in Europe for centuries afterwward.

———

B. Z. Kedar, H. E. Mayer, and R. C. Smail, ed., *Outremer: Studies in the History of the Crusading Kingdom of Jerusalem* (1982); J. Phillips, "The Latin East, 1098–1291," in *The Oxford Illustrated History of the Crusades*, ed. J. Riley-Smith (1995); J. Prawer, *The Latin Kingdom of Jerusalem, European Colonialism in the Middle Ages* (1972); J. Riley-Smith, *The Feudal Nobility and the Kingdom of Jerusalem, 1174–1277* (1973).

ERHARD "ERIK" OPSAHL

Latin Poetry, Early Christian

Christian Latin poetry from the fourth through the sixth centuries is generally distinguished from classical Latin poetry and contemporary non-Christian poetry by content rather than form. While liturgical poetry and hymnody in Latin existed before the fourth century, these are poorly known. The rising surge of Latin Christian poetry that began in the Constantinian period, however, is overall characterized by the adoption, manipulation, and modification of classical quantitative meters, poetic language, and genre for the expression of Christian doctrine, history, and legend. With the public success of Christianity in the fourth century came a desire to read and write poetry that was aesthetically pleasing as well as spiritually satisfying. For Christianizing elites in Italy, Gaul, Spain, and Africa this meant honoring traditions of verse composition that arose from, recalled, and alluded to Virgil, Horace, and Ovid while eschewing pagan gods and myths. At the same time, the Christian poets of late antiquity apparently shared with their non-Christian counterparts aesthetic values that distinguished them all from the Augustan poets. Less concerned about narrative thrust and integrity, and enamored of exquisite description and lexical repetition and variation, late antique poets generally display a revised aesthetic sensibility that is also evident in the visual arts. Likewise they challenge the generic boundaries of earlier poetry by extending and mixing genres. Late Latin poetry, therefore, is vital on its own terms and not simply a devolution from classical antecedents.

No single taxonomy can encompass the richness of this poetry. From Lactantius's poem on the phoenix and Juvencus's gospel epic in the early fourth century through the complex corpus of Venantius Fortunatus in the late sixth, Christian poets worked in a wide range of genres. This breadth is most pronounced from the late fourth through the late fifth century, when the institutions and traditions of literary and rhetorical education were still relatively strong. Between Damasus's epigrams for the Roman saints and the collected works of Sidonius, for example, stand the exemplary figures of Paulinus of Nola and Prudentius. Their adaptation of such traditional forms as the marriage poem, epic, and the hymn—like their employment of poetry to praise the martyrs, express doctrine, and denounce heresy and paganism—illustrates well the range and power of late Latin verse. The Latin epic tradition especially gave rise to a productive and long-lived stream of composition. Initiated for us by Juvencus's epic and Proba's Virgilian cento retelling OT and NT episodes, the series of biblical epics rolls on into the sixth century and includes the works of Cyprian of Gaul, Sedulius, Claudius Marius Victorius, Alcimus Avitus, and Arator. The same desire to teach and delight informs Fortunatus's hagiographic epic celebrating Martin of Tours. Much of this poetry continued to be read through the Middle Ages even as the use of rhythmic meters and rhymes already manifest in late antique hymnody enjoyed great popularity.

J. Fontaine, *Naissance de la poésie dans l'occident chrétien* (1981); M. Roberts, *The Jeweled Style* (1989); C. White, *Early Christian Latin Poets* (2000).

DENNIS E. TROUT

Latin Rite "Rite" indicates a liturgical family, or a broad pattern of observance belonging to an ethnic, linguistic, or cultural group. Thus, "Rite" should be distinguished from "rite," which indicates how a particular ceremony is conducted (e.g., the rite of marriage). The Latin Rite originated in the third and fourth centuries, when Western Christians began to worship in the Latin tongue. Another important step was taken when the prayers and ceremonies celebrated were written down; from the fourth century numerous little books, or *libelli*, circulated, containing instructions on how to celebrate particular feasts or rites. Scribes gathered them into collections such as the *Veronensis* (sometimes erroneously called the *Leonine Sacramentary*) of the mid-sixth century, which represents the phase of transition to liturgical books properly so-called. Liturgical books proved a primary means by which local Latin liturgies influenced one another. In this early period, Carthage, Milan, and Rome were important centers of development. By late antiquity the Latin Rite included several major regional variations: Roman, Ambrosian, Gallic, Hispanic, and Celtic.

Owing to the prestige with which the church of Rome was regarded in the medieval West, the influence of the Roman Rite gradually spread. Augustine of Canterbury brought it to the British Isles with his mission at the close of the sixth century, thereby setting in motion the decline of the ancient Celtic Rite, which Eastern practices had influenced at a very early period. The North African Rite disappeared with the Muslim incursion, although it is thought to have influenced Spanish and Italian practices. From around 700, *ordines Romani* describing the ceremonies for numerous rites penetrated Gaul. In the eighth and ninth centuries, Carolingian rulers used the Roman Rite as a basis for standardizing worship throughout the Frankish realms. They made considerable adaptations in order to accommodate the needs of Christian communities north of the Alps. The result was an amalgamation of Roman and Gallic influences that were synthesized in the *Romano-Germanic Pontifical* (RGP), compiled under Archbishop William of Mainz (r. 954–968). In the same century Emperor Otto the Great imposed the RGP on the Roman see, and it came to be regarded as authentically Roman. These initiatives demonstrate how the Roman Rite influenced and was influenced by other liturgical families throughout Europe, resulting in some degree of standardization.

Nonetheless, much diversity remained in the medieval period, such that the Latin Rite can be divided among particular "uses" on the regional level (e.g., the uses of Sarum and York in England), on the diocesan level (e.g.,

Aquileia, Ravenna, and Braga), and on the level of religious families (e.g., Cluniac and Dominican). Following the Council of Trent (1545–1563), Roman liturgical books spread throughout Catholic Europe, and many local uses were displaced. Several factors led to the predominance of the Roman Rite: intermittent papal initiatives; the spread of the Franciscans, whose liturgy was closely modeled on that of the Roman curia; and the market dynamics occasioned by the rise of the printing press. On the other hand, the use of vernacular languages characterized Protestant worship from its origins; thus, it is improper to speak of it as belonging to the Latin Rite. Here and there some continuity of structure and text with previous uses was preserved, particularly in the Book of Common Prayer and the Lutheran liturgies.

Within contemporary Catholicism, the term "Latin Rite" has both a juridical and a liturgical significance. In its liturgical meaning it encompasses principally the Roman Rite but also the rites of some local churches (e.g., Ambrosian or Milanese, Old Spanish or Mozarabic) and religious orders (notably the Carthusian, Cistercian, Premonstratensian, Carmelite, and Dominican). The Latin Rite does not include the rites of Eastern groups that are in communion with Rome, including the Maronite, Malankar, Chaldean, Malabar, Coptic, Ethiopian, Ukrainian, Croatian, and Ruthenian. In its juridical meaning, "Latin Rite" is synonymous with the "Latin Church" (*Ecclesia latina*), which is subject to the bishop of Rome and has its own highly developed system of ecclesiastical discipline and governance, particularly expressed in the 1983 Code of Canon Law. From this perspective, the history of the Latin Rite is tied to the development of canon law and the gradual centralization of authority in the office of the bishop of Rome.

J. Harper, *The Forms and Orders of Western Liturgy from the Tenth to the Eighteenth Century* (1991); A. Herman, "De conceptu ritus," *Jurist* 2 (1942): 333–45; A. King, *Liturgies of the Primatial Sees* (1957); A. King, *Liturgies of the Religious Orders* (1955); C. Vogel, *Medieval Liturgy: An Introduction to the Sources* (1986).

DANIEL G. VAN SLYKE

Latitudinarianism   Pejorative term applied to the seventeenth-century movement of some Anglican clergy whose reaction against divisive doctrinal disputes minimized doctrine and promoted reason and personal judgment.

The Latitudinarians were generally sympathetic to Arminian theology and open to contemporary intellectual trends such as those advanced by the Cambridge Platonists. Latitudinarianism elevated the transforming personal experience of Christ above corporate worship, prayer and Bible study above liturgy and doctrine.

M. Griffin, *Latitudinarianism in the Seventeenth-Century Church of England* (1992); W. M. Spellman, *The Latitudinarians and the Church of England, 1660–1700* (1993).

DAVID A. LOPEZ

Laud, William (1573–1645), archbishop of Canterbury. Born in Reading and educated at St. John's College, Oxford, Laud was highly influential beginning with the reign of Charles I. As an Arminian, he opposed Calvinist doctrines in the Church of England and maintained a conception of Roman Catholicism and the Church of England as two parts of the "church catholic." Despite these apparent Romanist views, he never recognized the authority of the pope and always asserted his Protestantism. These positions, as well as his seeking to establish pre-Reformation liturgy, brought him into conflict with Puritans as well as many Anglicans. He was made bishop of Bath and Wells in 1626, and in 1630 became chancellor at Oxford. He was named archbishop of Canterbury in 1633. Laud stressed ceremonial uniformity, with the Communion table, not the sermon, as the focus of the service; this view led him to bar Puritans from the pulpit, though he supported Puritan lecturers. Attempts to enforce a new liturgy in Scotland (1637) led to a convocation in 1640 during which he proclaimed the divine right of kings and introduced the infamous "et cetera oath" that forced those taking the oath to swear to never alter the governance of the Church of England; the oath effectively bound the church to the government. This oath was met with hostility, and Parliament imprisoned him in the Tower of London as part of its plan to dismantle Charles's royal absolutism; he was tried in 1644 for high treason, and beheaded the following January. Laud was the foremost Anglican high churchman, broad on doctrinal matters to stress unity, narrow on liturgy and ceremony, stressing uniformity.

E. C. E. Bourne, *The Anglicanism of William Laud* (1947); C. Carlton, *Archbishop William Laud* (1987).

ALDEN R. LUDLOW

Laurentius Norvegus (c. 1540–1622), Norwegian Jesuit, leader of the Counter-Reformation in northern Europe. He spent most of his life outside Norway. In 1575 he returned to Scandinavia as a Catholic missionary, appointed by Rome as a chaplain to the Catholic Polish wife of the king of Sweden, Johan III. However, the king appointed him to lead the theological school he was about to establish in Stockholm. Eventually, in the summer of 1580, the Jesuits fell out of favor with the king and most of the order left the country.

Laurentius then stayed for three years in Olmütz as a teacher before moving to Prague, where he received his doctoral degree in 1587. In 1589 he was deported to Graze, where he studied moral theology for the next nine years. He then moved to Braunsberg in 1601 to teach Scandinavian students. From 1610 he lived in Riga, and in 1621 he met King Gustavus Adolphus when his army captured Riga and forced the Jesuits to leave the city. They went to Vilna in Lithuania, where Laurentius died in 1622.

O. Garstein, *Rome and the Counter-Reformation in Scandinavia*, 4 vols. (1963–1992); V. Heik, *Laurentius Nicolai Norvegus S.J.* (1966).

INGUN MONTGOMERY

Laus Perennis This Latin term meaning "perpetual praise" refers to a monastic form of prayer that was used c. 400–816. By the fifth century most monastic observances called for prayer eight specific times a day interspersed with work, eating, and sleeping. Against this formalization, Alexander (who abandoned the study of rhetoric in Constantinople to pursue the monastic life) founded a group of ascetics at Zeugma (present-day southeastern Turkey) where, according to his Life, God told him to institute continuous praise. Alexander divided his monks into *turmae* ("choirs"), according to their nationalities, to chant the Psalms night and day without interruption. The continuous singing of the Psalms and the division of monks into *turmae* to accomplish this purpose became the two definitive characteristics of the *laus perennis*.

After moving to Constantinople around 425, Alexander's monks became known as *acoemetae*, or Sleepless Ones, and the *laus perennis* came to symbolize Catholic orthodoxy.

Between 515 and 816 the *laus perennis* was observed at eight monastic establishments within Neustrian Gaul. It was first established in Burgundy as the symbol of King Sigismund's Catholic conversion from Arianism. Between 585 and 650, it was instituted at four royal monasteries as a symbol of monarchial power and patronage and at two female monastic establishments unconnected to the Merovingian court. In 797 it was instituted at one monastery to pray for Charlemagne. Louis the Pious abolished it in favor of the Benedictine *Rule* in 816.

At the present time, Greek Orthodox monks at Mount Athos take turns chanting the Psalms. This observance is not, however, the *laus perennis* because these monks are not divided into choirs and they work when not chanting.

G. Gindele, "Die Gallikanischen 'laus perennis'—Klöster und Ihr 'ordo oficii,'" *RBén* 69 (1959): 32–48.

WILLIAM B. SWEETSER JR.

Law, Protestant *see* Protestant Law

Lawrence (d. 258), deacon and martyr. Lawrence was one of seven deacons under Sixtus II in Rome. Virtually nothing is known about him. He was beheaded under Emperor Valerian (253–260), who had issued edicts in 257–258 outlawing Christian clergy. A tradition, probably unreliable, noted by Ambrose (*Off.* 1.41.204–6; 2.28.140–41; *Ep.* 37.36–37) and Prudentius (*Perist.* 2), notes that Lawrence was roasted to death on a gridiron. The tradition reports that Lawrence, asked by a Roman official to turn over the treasures of the church, brought forward a group of the poor, to whom he had ministered, and said, "These are the treasure of the church." Lawrence was highly honored in subsequent years; he became one of the saints of the Canon of the Mass. He is portrayed in a mosaic in the Galla Placidia in Ravenna. In the fourth century a church was built over his tomb, to which pilgrims came. In the sixth century it was expanded to the basilica of St. Lawrence-outside-the-Walls. Bede (*Hist. eccl.* 3.29) reports that Pope Vitalian (657–658) sent some of his relics to Oswy, the Saxon king of Northumbria.

V. L. Kennedy, *The Saints of the Canon of the Mass* (1938), 124–28; W. McCarthy, "Prudentius, Peristephanon 2: Vapor and the Martyrdom of Lawrence," *VC* 36 (1982): 282–86; M. T. Tavormina, "A Liturgical Allusion in the *Scottish Legendary*," in *Notes and Queries* 33 (1986): 154–57.

DAVID M. SCHOLER

Lectionary A lectionary may be either a list of scriptural texts to be read weekly or daily, or a book for liturgical use in which those texts are printed. While most Protestant churches using a lectionary read the assigned texts from a Bible, some churches (particularly Roman Catholic and Orthodox, but often Anglican and sometimes Lutheran) read them from the lectionary book.

The public reading of Holy Scripture has been a significant part of Christian worship since before the canon was fixed. Christians inherited the practice from the synagogue. It is probable that at least a century before Christ, Jewish practice was to read in sequence through the books of the Torah over a period of from one to three years. Over the next four centuries they gradually added a reading from the Prophets (the *haftarah*) judged to be relevant to the Torah reading for the day.

One of the earliest references to the reading of Scripture in Christian worship is from Justin Martyr, who, about 150 CE, wrote to the emperor that in worship, Christians read from the "records of the apostles" or "the writings of the prophets." Early Christian practice was *lectio continua*, that is, beginning with the first chapter of a biblical book and reading it in course over a period of Sundays, or "Lord's Days." The church began to develop an annual cycle of celebrations, beginning with Pascha, near the time of the Jewish Passover, marking both Jesus' passion and his resurrection. The readings for Pascha interrupted the *lectio continua* in order that the church might hear the gospel accounts of Jesus' death and rising.

Perhaps as early as the second century, the church normally baptized at Easter. Lent developed as a period of preparation for baptism. Later came Christmas and the cycle of Advent-Christmas-Epiphany. As the church year developed, customary readings—*lectio selecta*—began to be associated with each day or season. From Advent to Pentecost, the church focused specifically on the life of Christ, seen particularly through the lens of the paschal mystery, the resurrection of the Lord.

The lectionaries of the Eastern churches have remained more or less consistent since early centuries. In medieval times, the Roman lectionary became increasingly complicated by the addition of readings for saints' days. During the Reformation, Luther took a conservative stance, maintaining many of the lections, while Calvin and others rejected them entirely, reverting to *lectio continua* except at Christmas, Easter, and Pentecost. After Vatican II, many Protestant churches adopted, with modifications, the revised Roman lectionary. This lectionary combines principles of *lectio continua* and *lectio selecta*.

H. Allen, "Introduction" to *Common Lectionary* (1983); A. Bugnini, *The Reform of the Liturgy, 1948–1975* (1990); J. Reumann, "A History of Lectionaries," *Interpretation* 31 (1997): 116; *The Revised Common Lectionary* (1992); T. J. Talley, *The Origins of the Liturgical Year* (1991); E. Werner, *The Sacred Bridge* (1960).

RONALD P. BYARS

Lefèvre d'Étaples (1455/1460–1536), the leading French humanist of the early sixteenth century and a promoter of ecclesiastical reform. Lefèvre was born in Étaples, Picardy. He studied at Paris and lectured there from about 1490 until 1509. In 1492 he traveled to Italy where he met both Ficino and Pico della Mirandola. The chief focus of his early scholarly endeavors was Aristotle, whose works he edited and annotated. He also read and edited patristic writings. His mystical tendencies evoked an interest in Pseudo-Dionysius and in the medieval mystics. Hence, he published works by Hildegard of Bingen, Ramon Llull, Jan Ruysbroeck, Richard of St. Victor, and Elizabeth of Schönau, as well as the first significant edition of the writings of Nicholas of Cues. After 1509 he turned his attention almost exclusively to Scripture. During the next two decades he produced the Quincuplex Psalter (1509) and commentaries on the Pauline Epistles (1512), the Gospels (after 1522), and the Catholic Epistles (1527). In 1530 he also published a French translation of the Vulgate, which impacted the famous translation of Pierre Robert Olivétan. While the significance of his humanistic scholarship is widely recognized, his relationship to the Reformation remains a matter of debate. Lefèvre clearly favored renewal of the church and was part of the reform circle of Guillaume Briçonnet. He read works by various reformers, including Luther. His doctrine of justification was similar to Luther's, and he used such theological terminology as *solus Christus* and *sola gratia*. His works also raised the suspicion of the Sorbonne. Yet he never left the church and did not ally himself openly with the Reformation.

G. Bedouelle, *Lefèvre d'Étaples et l'intelligence des écritures* (1976); Bedouelle, *Le Quincuplex Psalterium de Lèfevre d'Étaples: Un guide de lecture* (1979); P. E. Hughes, *Lefèvre: Pioneer of Ecclesiastical Renewal in France* (1984).

KURT K. HENDEL

Leibniz, Gottfried Wilhelm (1646–1716), German rationalist philosopher and mathematician. He studied philosophy at Leipzig and received a doctorate of law from Altdorf in 1667. Thereafter he served as a diplomat for the Elector/archbishop of Mainz. While on missions to France and England, he met many of the leading scholars of his day. He also consulted with Spinoza, whose philosophy he strongly repudiated. After 1676, he worked as the librarian for the duke of Brunswick-Lüneburg. He discovered infinitesimal calculus during this period and published his findings in 1684, three years before Isaac Newton revealed his own work on this topic. While living in Hanover, Leibniz also began to publish his most important philosophical writings. He wrote a detailed reply to Locke's critique of the existence of innate ideas. His *Theodicy* (1710) discusses the goodness of God and the origin of evil. He argued that evil is not a positive entity and that God permits evil only as a means to a good end. He asserted that this world is the best of all possible worlds. He was preoccupied throughout his life with the idea of the cosmos as a universal harmony. In *Monadology* (1714), he attempted to show how apparent multiplicity of substances within the world could be reconciled with this notion. He also participated in many efforts to promote reunion between the various branches of Christianity and proposed the formation of a Christian alliance between all the states of Europe.

R. M. Adams, *Leibniz: Determinist, Theist, Idealist* (1994); N. Jolly, *The Cambridge Companion to Leibniz* (1995); G. M. Ross, *Leibniz* (1984).

ERIC LUND

Leo I (d. 461), pope. "Leo the Great" became pope in 440 during an extremely turbulent time in the history of the church. From without, the empire was threatened by barbarian invasions; from within, the christological controversy was at its peak. The events of Leo's pontificate are recorded in his letters and in the *Liber Pontificalis*. The first pope to be called "the Great," an honor he shares only with Gregory the Great (590–604), Leo was instrumental in developing the concept of papal authority both in practice and in theory. His frequent preaching encouraged his flock to avoid heresy, particularly Arianism, Manicheism, and paganism, which persisted in some quarters. By maintaining close contacts with bishops in northern Italy and by means of an annual Roman synod, he coordinated ecclesiastical life in Rome and most of Italy. His influence stretched to other dioceses in the West and the East. He urged adoption of the Roman view concerning the date of Easter. In his preaching he presented a theology of papal primacy explicitly citing Matthew 16:13–20 and John 21:15–19.

Leo also played a significant role in the Monophysite controversy. His *Tome to Flavian,* written in response to Eutyches, an adamant defender of the one-nature Christology of Cyril of Alexandria, clarified the matter theologically through a distinction between person and nature. The one-person Jesus had two complete and unmixed natures, human and divine, that operated in communion with each other. Despite this theological insight, political and ecclesiastical wrangling persisted. Although he considered the problem solved, Leo sent delegates to the Council of Ephesus in 449. His tome was never read, as Monophysite monks took over the proceedings, beating some bishops and forcing a decision in their favor. Leo later dubbed the proceeding a *latrocinium* ("robber synod"). The Council of Chalcedon was called in 451 to rectify the matter, and the bishops adopted the terminology of Leo's tome, which Leo considered a middle road between Eutyches and Nestorius.

Leo also exercised political influence in the West, although he was less successful in the East. When Attila the Hun entered Italy and was about to attack Rome, Leo was instrumental in convincing him to spare the eternal city, although some consider Leo's journey to Mantua with the imperial delegation and his personal meeting with Attila to be legend. Several years later Leo also convinced the Vandal king Gaiseric not to destroy the city. In his dealings with the emperor in Constantinople and with bishops in the East, he was very firm in asserting the primacy of Rome. He refused to subscribe to canon 28 of the Council of Chalcedon, which attributed second rank to the see of Constantinople over the sees of Antioch and Alexandria, which through Peter had a special relationship to Rome.

T. Jalland, *The Live and Times of St. Leo the Great* (1941); Leo, *Works*, trans. C. L. Feltoe, *NPNF*, 2nd series, vol. 12; Leo, *Letters*, trans. E. Hunt, FC 34 (1957); P. McShane, "Leo the Great, Guardian of Doctrine and Discipline," *EgT* 14 (1983): 9–24.

KENNETH B. STEINHAUSER

Leo X (1475–1521), ecclesiastical politician and patron of the arts, elected pope in 1513. Upon his accession to the papacy, Giovanni de Medici, who had been tonsured a cleric at seven and named cardinal at thirteen, is said to have exclaimed, "Now that God has given us the papacy, let us enjoy it!" Thus, it is hardly surprising that, as pope, he was utterly ill-suited even to comprehend, much less cope with, the fervor for reform that, long smoldering throughout the European church, burst into flame during his reign. Leo's interests were neither scholarly nor spiritual but involved the supremacy of the Medici family; personally his time and energy were dissipated on art, music, the theater, lavish banquets, and massive hunting expeditions. Such decadence, together with the building of St. Peter's, emptied the papal treasury, which Leo sought to replenish by augmenting the indulgence sales begun under Julius II. The theological bankruptcy and financial corruption attending this endeavor sparked Martin Luther's call for reform, which Leo's response in the bull *Exsurge Domine* failed to extinguish.

E. Duffy, *Saints and Sinners: A History of the Popes* (1997); M. Gilmore, ed., *Renaissance Princes, Popes, and Prelates: The Vespasiano Memoirs: Illustrious Men of the XVth Century* (1963); R. P. McBrien, *Lives of the Popes* (1997).

PETER J. SCAGNELLI

Leonardo da Vinci (1452–1519), Italian Renaissance painter, sculptor, scientist, and inventor. Leonardo studied in Florence with Andrea del Verrochio and became a master in the painters' guild in 1472. After 1483 he worked in Milan for Duke Lodovico Sforza, where he painted the *Virgin of the Rocks* (c. 1485) and the famous *Last Supper* (c. 1496). After returning to Florence, Leonardo completed the enigmatic *Mona Lisa* (c. 1504). In 1507 he was appointed court painter for Francis I of France.

Leonardo's sculptural work is lost, but his paintings and many notebooks of anatomical sketches and aeronautical theory attest to his multiple talents. This polymath genius, with his insistence on direct observation and experiment, helped bring about scientific specialization. He anticipated later inventions, including the tank, the submarine, and the airplane. Perhaps because of his many interests, Leonardo left many commissions unfinished. Leonardo remains the embodiment of the universal Renaissance genius.

D. A. Brown, *Leonardo da Vinci: Origins of a Genius* (1998); K. Clark, *Leonardo da Vinci* (2nd ed., 1967); M. Kemp, *Leonardo da Vinci: The Marvellous Works of Nature and Man* (2nd ed., 1988); A. R. Turner, *Inventing Leonardo* (1993).

PRISCILLA BAUMANN

Leontius of Byzantium (c. 500–c. 544), monk and controversial theologian. Although the manuscripts of his six extant works give his name simply as "Leontius the Monk," it is likely he is the "Leontius of Byzantium" known from Cyril of Scythopolis's *Life of Sabas* as a leader of the "Origenist" party in the Judaean desert monasteries of the early sixth century. He went to Constantinople with Sabas, the monastic leader, in 531. He remained there at least until 536, acting as representative of the Palestinian monks at court and participating in intense, technical debates about the christological formula of the Council of Chalcedon (451).

Leontius participated in a fruitless conference with the anti-Chalcedonians, led by Severus of Antioch, in 532 and attended the local synod of 536 that broke communion with Severus and his followers, ending Justinian's efforts at reconciliation. Leontius then returned to Palestine. There, according to Cyril, he played an inflammatory role in the disputes between the defenders of Chalcedon, among which he and the other "Origenist" monks belonged, and its opponents. Around 540, he returned to Constantinople, where he continued his theological activity until his death, sometime before 545.

Leontius's works use the language and techniques of contemporary school philosophy to show that Chalcedon's symmetrical conception of Christ, as a single *hypostasis* or person existing in two fully operative natures, is the only adequate formulation of orthodox faith.

B. E. Daley, "The Origenism of Leontius of Byzantium," *JTS* 27 (1976): 333–69; "'A Richer Union': Leontius of Byzantium and the Relationship of Human and Divine in Christ," StPatr 24 (1993), 239–65; A. Grillmeier, *Christ in Christian Tradition*, vol. 2 (1995), 181–229.

BRIAN E. DALEY, SJ

Leontius of Jerusalem (sixth cent.), Palestinian monk, theologian, and defender of Chalcedonian Christology. For some time scholars believed Leontius of Jerusalem to be identical with Leontius of Byzantium. Modern scholars, however, recognize the former as an important figure in the christological controversies following the Council of Chalcedon. He was a Palestinian monk who eventually made his way to Constantinople, hence the obvious connection to the Byzantine Leontius. He perhaps participated in the dialogue between Monophysites and Chalcedonians in Constantinople between 532 and 536. Leontius rejected both Monophysitism and Nestorianism and confessed Chalcedonian Christology. He is the author of *Against the Monophysites* and *Against the Nestorians*. Important to note is his defense of the definition of Chalcedon from the side of the Christology of Cyril of Alexandria. Thus, while he denied Apollinarianism and Eutychianism, he also maintained that Christ's humanity did not possess its own *hypostasis*, or individuality. To explain his Christology, Leontius coined the term *enhypostasis*, wherein humanity received its *hypostasis* ("subsistence") from the Word. By considering the human nature to be hypostasized through its union with the Word, Leontius believed he could maintain a Cyrillian Christology while avoiding the heresies anathematized at Chalcedon.

P. T. R. Gray, *The Defense of Chalcedon in the East (451–533)* (1979); D. Krausmiller, "Leontius of Jerusalem, a Theologian of the Seventh Century," *JTS* 52 (2001): 637–57.

STEVEN A. MCKINION

Liberal Arts   The name goes back to Cicero and describes the education of the free Roman citizen. The liberal arts (*artes liberales*) were first systematized by Varro (in *Disciplinarum libri IX*, a lost work) and adapted by the church fathers. Through Latin Christian writers, mainly Augustine, they were brought to the medieval West (of Augustine's own writings on the arts, only *De musica* survived). Augustine argued for the compatibility of the liberal arts with a Christian education based on Scripture. The liberal arts comprise the *quadrivium* (*quadruvium* in medieval Latin: arithmetic, geometry, music, and astronomy) and the *trivium* (grammar, rhetoric, and dialectic). Boethius wrote the most important works on the *quadrivium* and dialectic: they were studied throughout the Middle Ages. Martianus Capella provided the first synthesis of all seven liberal arts. Influential were the accounts by Cassiodorus and Isidore of Seville. The liberal arts saw a revival in Carolingian times (writings by Alcuin, Hrabanus Maurus) and then again in the cathedral schools in the tenth and eleventh centuries. Thierry of Chartres compiled a collection of forty-five basic texts for their study. Hugh of St. Victor saw them both as an end in themselves and as necessary for the study of Scripture. Through the introduction of new Greek and Arabic texts into the Latin world in the twelfth and thirteenth centuries, the study of the arts was renewed. Dominicus Gundisalinus built them into an Aristotelian system of sciences. The faculty of arts was one of the four faculties at the Univ. of Paris and provided the basic education needed for the study of theology, law, and medicine.

Arts libéraux et Philosophie au Moyen Âge (1969); I. Hadot, *Arts libéraux et philosophie dans la pensée antique* (1984); U. Lindgren, *Die Artes liberales in Antike und Mittelalter* (1992); D. L. Wagner, ed., *The Seven Liberal Arts in the Middle Ages* (1986).

RALF M. W. STAMMBERGER

Liberius (d. 366), elected bishop of Rome in 352. Thirteen of his very brief letters survive and provide some points of the process by which he, a confessor of Western orthodoxy, signed a supposedly Arian creed and then recanted.

After the Council of Arles (353) reaffirmed the condemnation of Athanasius and also suggested the imposition of an Eastern formula hostile to the Western settlement at Serdica (342–343), Liberius pressed Constantius II to call another council. The Council of Milan (355) reiterated the decisions made at Arles and resulted in the exile of several leading Western bishops who refused to sign the decisions of the Council of Milan. Liberius, not present at the council, foresaw his own fate. Accepting exile rather than sign, he was banished to Thrace.

Within a year's time (c. 357), he agreed to renounce communion with Athanasius and the decisions of Serdica and signed the same formula of faith (probably the creed of Sirmium, 351) forced upon the Westerners at Arles and Milan. He was returned to his see and remained in quiet complicity with the emperor's policies until the latter's death (361).

Liberius thereafter favored the church's acceptance of penitent bishops who had signed the Ariminum Creed (359). Whereas his vacillation may have undermined the authority of the Roman episcopacy, his lapse contributed to a political pliability that paved the way for smoother relations between Western and Eastern churches. Nevertheless, Liberius has never been canonized along with the other confessors and theologians of his time.

T. D. Barnes, *Athanasius and Constantius* (1993); D. H. Williams, *Ambrose of Milan and the End of the Nicene-Arian Conflicts* (1995); Socrates, *Church History*, 4.12.

D. H. WILLIAMS

Libertines Calvin is the best known of those reformers who applied the pejorative label "libertines" to a circle of spiritualist Christians active in the Netherlands, France, and Lower Germany. Calvin's focus was a group originating in Flanders, present in the 1540s at the court of Marguerite d'Angoulême, queen of Navarre, which included the acknowledged leader, Quintin of Hainaut. The spiritualism of the Quintinists may be related to doctrines of Loy Pruystinck of Antwerp, whose followers underwent severe persecution in 1545. Libertines held a strict anthropological dualism according to which flesh and spirit are independent and the spiritual or regenerate person is sinless. Calvin attacked these and other views, such as a pantheistic determinism and a denial of the reality of evil, that he believed eviscerated moral agency and resulted in moral license.

The term "libertine" is sometimes, though improperly, applied to the Perrinist faction in Geneva (after their leader Ami Perrin), who opposed Calvin and the company of pastors, especially over the practice of ecclesiastical discipline, until their defeat in 1555. The motivations of the Perrinists were political rather than explicitly religious.

J. Calvin, *Treatises against the Anabaptists and against the Libertines*, ed. B. W. Farley (1982); G. H. Williams, *The Radical Reformation* (3rd ed., 1992).

CHRISTOPHER ELWOOD

Library of Alexandria *see* Alexandria, Library of

Libri Carolini *see Opus Caroli Regis Contra Synodum (Libri Carolini)*

Lindisfarne This small island (later known as Holy Island) off the eastern shore of northern England is linked to the coast of Northumbria by a causeway at low tide. It became a religious center in 635 CE when St. Aidan (d. 651), an Irish monk from Iona, founded a church and a monastery near King Oswald's stronghold of Bamburg with the aim to convert the Northumbrians. Soon the monastery constituted a flourishing center of Christian scholarship, producing masterpieces of Anglo-Celtic calligraphy and illumination such as the famous Lindisfarne Gospels, made by a monk named Eadfrith around 700. The monastery owed much of its prestige to St. Cuthbert (d. 687), who was Lindisfarne's sixth bishop and one of the most venerated English saints.

In 793, the Danish invaded the island and destroyed the church. Their continuing raids forced the monks to flee inland with the shrine of St. Cuthbert. The monastery was reestablished by the Benedictine community of Durham in 1082, without ever regaining the status of a see (the see was first transferred to Chester-le-Street and finally to Durham in 995). In the mid-fourteenth century, the buildings were fortified against the Scots. Economically depressed and depleted in numbers of monks, the priory was dissolved during the Reformation in 1537. The extensive ruins of the priory and the Norman church date from around 1100, still symbolizing in architecture and decoration its close connection with Durham.

J. Backhouse, *The Lindisfarne Gospels* (2000); G. Bronner, D. Rollason, and C. Stancliffe, eds., *St. Cuthbert, His Cult and His Community to A.D. 1200* (1989); D. O'Sullivan and R. Young, *English Heritage Book of Lindisfarne* (1995).

ANNE MÜLLER

Litany The word derives from the Greek λιτανεύω (litaneuō), which means "to pray" or "to entreat," especially for protection. A litany in the contemporary ecclesial sense is a prayer composed of a series of short repeated invocations or intercessions, or of invocations or intercessions alternating with responses. Psalm 139, with its repeated refrain "for [God's] steadfast love endures forever," and the Song of the Three Youths in the Fiery Furnace of Daniel 3 provide ancient classic models of a litany. As a form of public prayer a litany alternates between a leader or a group of leaders, such as a choir, and the congregation. The *Kyrie eleison* is a litany from the early church that survives in the worship of many Christian traditions. Intercessory prayer in public worship often takes the form of a litany, with a simple congregational response, such as "Lord, have mercy" or "Lord, hear our prayer," to petitions voiced by a leader.

After Constantine's legalization of Christianity the church began frequently to conduct public outdoor processions, sometimes to coincide and compete with established pagan festivities. There is evidence from the fifth century that the term "litany" designated supplication spoken during such liturgical procession, and the term came to designate the procession itself. The Greater Litanies on April 25, opposing the pre-Christian Roman agricultural festival Robigalia with its prominent procession, and the Lesser Litanies on the three days preceding Ascension Thursday, with fifth-century origins in Gaul, are traditional occasions for Christian processions accompanied by fervent prayer for God's mercy and protection and for the fruitfulness of the earth. In Rome the processions on these four Rogation Days came to include the ancient Litany of the Saints.

Numerous Christian litanies developed in medieval times, often for use in processions, but public recitation of most of them has disappeared. The Litany of the Saints, whose precise provenance is not known, begins with invocation of the persons of the Trinity and of the saints and continues with extensive supplication for God's mercy, protection, and blessing. The Litany of the Saints is the most important litany for Roman Catholic Christians. The Great Litany of the Book of Common Prayer is similar to the Litany of the Saints but does not include invocation of saints. Litanies are more significant in the worship of the East than of the West.

———

C. Jones, G. Wainwright, and E. Yarnold, eds., *The Study of Liturgy* (1978).

MARY CATHERINE BERGLUND

Liturgical Books

The Bible, or more specifically the parts of it possessed by a Christian community, was the only liturgical book well into the fourth century. The *libelli precorum* (little books of prayers), local booklets with texts for a presider to use, served in the ordered improvisation of worship. The *Sacramentary of Serapion* (Egypt, 350) is the earliest example of a complete collection. Church orders circulated widely, with directions for the bishop's use rather than texts for prayer, and without official status beyond claims to apostolic authority. Official approval for central liturgical texts began to be expected in North Africa in the fourth century.

Books for the Roman Rite developed in the fifth to sixteenth centuries: the sacramentary, lectionary, antiphonal, and calendar. A sacramentary contained texts for the presider for Mass and other services. Lectionaries ranged from marginal marks in a Bible to indicate readings, to lists of readings in order of liturgical use (capitulary), to books of full readings in order of

their use (epistolary and evangeliary). The book of Gospel readings received artistic and ceremonial reverence. The chant for Mass (gradual psalm, offertory response, introit, Communion antiphon) was contained in the antiphonal (*liber antiphonarium*). Collections of chants by type, and for seasons and feasts, tended to be combined into a single volume over time. The calendar developed unevenly from the ninth to twelfth century both in book form (*comes*) and as text inserted into other liturgical books. Distinctions among types of books were not rigid.

The *Missale Romanum* (1570) was promulgated as a uniform liturgy. In the medieval period, the word "missal" could mean a sacramentary or several masses bound in a *libellus*. From the eighth to the tenth century, missals included the content of the sacramentary, antiphonal, and lectionary. The missal encouraged uniformity, provided convenience, and accommodated a priestly piety that said all the texts of the mass. Following Vatican II the missal has been translated into vernacular languages, and multiple books have reappeared to serve varied liturgical ministries. The sacramentary (not a full missal) guides the presider at Mass. Seasonal booklets for the people at Mass (missalettes) are still common.

Daily prayer was served by books for song (psalter, antiphonal, and hymnal), for prayers by the presider (*collectar*, but terminology varied greatly), and readings (scriptural lectionary, patristic homilary, hagiographical passionary or legendary). From the twelfth through the thirteenth century, the breviary combined former books, though less systematically than did the missal. Since Vatican II, the *Liturgy of the Hours* (4 vols.), with various psalters and hymnals serves congregational, monastic, and clerical prayer.

Roman books for sacraments and other rites include the pontifical (for bishop) and ritual (for priest). The ceremonial (whether papal, episcopal, monastic, religious, or for a non-Roman Western rite) guides the liturgical practices of a community through the year. An ordinal is also a guide to local ceremonial practice.

Books for the Eastern churches, whether Orthodox or Catholic ("Uniate"), are many and varied according to rite: Armenian, Byzantine, Coptic, Ethiopian, East or West Syrian. The Eastern Christian books are predominantly of a medieval type, given the era of standardization. Byzantine Rite books, as an example, include those that contain biblical readings (lectionaries and compilations) and the books of commentaries on them, books for the Eucharist and for sacraments and other rites, books for the daily office (prayer), and various books of directions and ceremonial guidance. There are vernacular translations from the official languages and Western translations that also include various abridgements and combinations of these books. Many of these are unofficial but in popular use. Until Vatican II, many Eastern Catholic churches produced missals and breviaries for private reading.

P. Bradshaw, ed., *The New Westminster Dictionary of Liturgy and Worship* (2002); A. J. Chupungco, OSB, ed., *Handbook for Liturgical Studies*, vol. 1 of *Introduction to the Liturgy* (1997); E. Palazzo, *A History of Liturgical Books, from the Beginning to the Thirteenth Century*, trans. M. Beaumont (1998); C. Vogel, *Medieval Liturgy, An Introduction to the Sources*, rev. and trans. W. G. Storey and N. K. Rasmussen, OP (1986).

STANLEY R. HALL†

Liturgical Calendar The Christian church began early in its history to observe the major events of the life of Christ and to celebrate on a weekly basis the day of Christ's resurrection, that is, Sunday, rather than the Jewish Sabbath. Thus, the *temporale,* or principal events marking Christ's life and earthly ministry, became standardized, with the most important events, such as Christ's birth and his resurrection, belonging to the oldest stratum of observance. To these two events were added the Advent season of anticipation and penance, as well as Epiphany, Lent and Holy Week, Ascension and Pentecost, and finally the Sundays following Pentecost (Trinity Sundays). These seasons and specific celebrations vary from year to year; a category of tables and treatises, the *computationes,* developed through the course of the Middle Ages to determine accurately when, for example, Easter would occur each year. But these events did not vary from location to location. Easter, again as an example, was celebrated on the same date in a given year throughout Europe.

Interspersed with the *temporale* were celebrations of saints' days. For example, the Nativity season included the celebrations of Christmas on the 25th of December; St. Stephen, the first Christian martyr, on the 26th; St. John, the apostle and evangelist, on the 27th; Holy Innocents on the 28th, St. Thomas, bishop and martyr, on the 29th; St. Silvester on the 31st; the Circumcision of the Lord on January 1; and Epiphany on January 6. Using the

example of the Nativity season, one observes how the *temporale* and *sanctorale* (the cycle of fixed feast days of saints) interlock, and this was the case to a greater or lesser extent throughout the liturgical year. Although certain of the saints' days were—and are—widely and consistently celebrated, the *sanctorale* nevertheless offers opportunities for local practice, so that manuscripts can even be geographically located according to the particular saints that are celebrated or given special observance. Another occasion for local practice is the celebration of the dedication of a church or cathedral. Hence, we can see that the *temporale* remains geographically stable but varies as far as its specific date from year to year, whereas the *sanctorale* is celebrated in a given location on the same day each year but with a good deal of variation from place to place with regard to this series of saints' celebrations. Details of both *temporale* and *sanctorale* have been revised many times throughout the history of the church, as well as from place to place.

W. H. Frere, *Studies in Early Roman Liturgy* (1940); A. A. King, *The Liturgy of the Roman Church* (1957); K.-H. Bieritz, *Das Kirchenjahr: Feste, Gedenk- und Feiertage in Geschichte und Gegenwart* (1994).

NANCY VAN DEUSEN

Liturgical Calendar, Significance of All liturgical worship is celebration of the paschal mystery, the life-giving death/death-defying resurrection of Jesus Christ. The liturgical year is an annual cycle of feasts and seasons that, from a variety of interdependent perspectives, gives expression to this primary Christian manifestation of God's saving action. The cycle has roots in biblical history, communal and individual human experience, and cosmic phenomena, such as the daily, monthly, and yearly cycles of earthly existence. Through its yearly celebration of God's salvific work, the church seeks both to know itself by remembering its past and to render God's saving action present and operative in the lives of all persons of all times. In so doing, it transforms itself into the community of faithful disciples mandated by the Lord Jesus and facilitated by his continuing presence through the Holy Spirit.

From apostolic times the church has kept a weekly commemoration of the Lord's death and resurrection on Sunday. By the early fourth century Christians were supplementing their weekly celebration with yearly commemorations of specific events in the life of Jesus. First, and probably beginning shortly after the death of Jesus, at least among Jewish Christians, the church observed Easter, or Pascha, the celebration of Jesus' death and resurrection. Observance of Christmas/Epiphany, the celebration of the incarnation of the Word of God as a human person, developed somewhat later. In each case a preparatory season evolved (Lent and Advent) and an extension of the celebration over several weeks (the Easter and Christmas seasons). The remaining weeks of the church year are called "Ordinary Time." The adjective derives from Latin *ordino* ("to arrange" or "to order") and indicates that these Sundays are counted. The weeks of Ordinary Time celebrate the paschal mystery in all its richness.

The church year is more than historical remembrance. Its every aspect flows from and points to the passion and glorification of the Lord and intends to effect the conformity of Christian life to this pattern. In Advent and Christmas the church commemorates and anticipates the coming of the Lord Jesus both as the child, whose sacrificial death and glorified life inaugurate the reign of God, and as the sovereign Lord, whose final coming will bring the reign of God to fullest reality. Lent both looks to the continuing conversion of faithful Christians not yet completely conformed to Christ and also prepares aspiring new members for acceptance into the body of believers by their own baptismal identification with Christ's death and resurrection at Easter. In Eastertide the church deepens its relationship with its risen Lord, living as if already experiencing the perfect joy of the new era that God is bringing into existence by the paschal mystery. In Ordinary Time Christians strive to model their daily lives in accord with the sacrificial life of Jesus.

A. Adam, *The Liturgical Year* (1981); M. E. Johnson, ed., *Between Memory and Hope* (2000); T. J. Talley, *The Origins of the Liturgical Year* (1986).

MARY CATHERINE BERGLUND

Liturgical Music In the Eastern, Byzantine tradition, as in the Western liturgical tradition, the liturgy centers around the Eucharist and the eucharistic prayers of consecration that surround that celebration. There are three Byzantine liturgies, of which two contain prayers attributed to St. Basil (primarily used until c. 1000) and St. John Chrysostom. The two are similar. Most of the music for these liturgies is to be found in the Akolouthiai

manuscripts compiled by Joannes Koukonzeles (fourteenth century and later).

In the Western medieval tradition, music constitutes an integral component of the liturgy, since, as Augustine states in *De ordine* and *De musica*, both speech, or the spoken text, and music use a material in common known as the *materia-substantia* of sound. Three results proceed from this observation: first, tone and syllable are bonded together as they share in a common substance bringing about an integral fusion of text and tone within liturgical time-lapse. Second, a body of *cantus* (commonly translated as "chant") develops, essentially complete for the entire church year by the end of the ninth century, in which utmost care is taken to closely coordinate text and music so that both would fit aptly together, reinforcing each other. Third, again, influenced by Augustine's program of education in *De ordine,* as well as the observations he makes concerning the nature and usefulness of music in *De musica,* music within the predictable, programmed time-lapse of the Mass not only shares fully in the delivery of the texts, mainly extracted and rearranged from the Psalms, but also by its very material presence articulates the function of making comprehensible unseen, invisible realities, thus providing a way of understanding the nature of the unseen, triune God.

Nothing could be understood without music, wrote Augustine, since music by the use of the invisible "substance" of sound, time, and motion exemplified the properties of invisible substance itself, thus enabling comprehension of theological-philosophical realities. This ministry, as well as potential, constituted ultimately the reason for music within the liturgy of both the Mass as well as the cycle of the Divine Offices and was concurrently the reason for the inclusion of music as the exemplary discipline among the material and measurement disciplines. Music, by means of individual tones, made clear the abstract concept of particularity and individuation. By an appropriate, well-modulated succession of tones, music made manifest the concept of relationship. By its inexorable movement, music also made the nature of movement itself plain.

Having understood these basic concepts by means of musical exemplification, one was then equipped, as Roger Bacon stated, to proceed to a study of the nature of God in terms of material, individuality, relationship, and movement. Day by day, week by week, year by year, by means of the Mass and Divine Office, as one sang the texts of the *temporale* (events in the life of Christ) as well as the *sanctorale* (events in the lives of saints and martyrs), one not only reinforced the language of the Psalms in alternation with the readings of Old Testament, the Gospels, and the Pauline Epistles, but one also reinforced the most basic principles of life on this earth, applying them to the study of the nature and work of God, for example, in the creation of the world. In principle, practice, and experience came understanding. One understood by *doing*. Music, which must be practiced and experienced, again, according to Augustine, was also attractive—sweet to the taste, even delectable. Music, then, in the Latin liturgy, was inseparable from doctrine, discipline, and education. (See *Divine Office, Liturgy of the Mass*.)

Augustine, *De musica*, FC 2 (1948); Augustine, *De ordine*, FC 1 (1948); N. van Deusen, "Roger Bacon on Music," in *Roger Bacon and the Sciences*, ed. J. Hackett (1998), 223–41; "Music, Rhythm," "*Musica, De*," and "*Ordine, De*," in *Augustine through the Ages: An Encyclopedia*, ed. A. D. Fitzgerald (1999); W. Hubner, "Die 'Artes liberales' in zweiten Buch von 'De ordine,'" in *Augustinus Charisteria Augustiniana Josepho Oroz Reta dicata* (1994), 317–43; V. Pacioni, *L'unita teoretica del De ordine di S. Agostino* (1996).

NANCY VAN DEUSEN

Liturgies   *see* Reformation Liturgies

Liturgy of the Mass   *Principle of Alternation (alternatim)*. The liturgy of the Mass sets forth a logical progression of events, each accompanied by corresponding, delineating, recognizable, and characteristic *figurae* (schemata) and proceeding to the Mass's climax, the Eucharist. In the Middle Ages, the logical progression with respect to each event and the entire ritualized order were described in expositions of liturgy. In fact, the thirteenth-century *Rationale* of Durandus (or William Durand, c. 1230–1296), arguably the most complete, as well as the most influential of these expositions, was reissued in early printed versions.

The individual components of the Mass were carefully combined, based on the principle of *alternatim* found in both the Old and New Testaments, in which a process of constantly shifting *modi* (or manners of movement) indicated by characteristic *figurae* generate various and diverse means for bringing to mind facets of the theme at hand, for example, the birth of Christ. There are four groups of four *modi* each: melodic *modi* (commonly known as Dorian, Phrygian, Lydian, and Mixolydian, each with an "authentic" and "plagal"), four textual *modi* (historical, allegorical, tropological, and anagogical or eschatological), four syllable-tone *modi* (syllabic, neumatic, psalmodic, and melismatic), and four action-contemplation *modi* having to do with the read/sung portions of the Mass, that is, action with both text and music (such as the Introit of the Mass), contemplation with both text and music (such as the Gradual of the Mass), action without music using only text (Canon of the Mass), and contemplation (such as *orations* or prayers) using only text. All four groups of four *modi*, or as they are often designated, *senses,* are alternated, imparting freshness, detail, and dynamism to the Mass liturgy and focusing the attention of the participants on a distinctive aspect of the liturgical theme of the day. An example of this, *Puer natus est,* the Introit for the third Mass of Christmas:

> melodic mode: mixolydian
> text mode: historical
> syllable-tone mode: neumatic (that is, one to three notes per syllable)
> action/contemplation mode: action, namely, an introit

For both textual as well as melodic *modi* there is room for difference of interpretation as to classification, but there is agreement concerning the fact that there were salient, observable, differences—*differenciae* deliberately indicated by characteristic *figurae*, and that the *alternatim* structure of the Mass was based upon these *differenciae*.

Structure of the Mass Liturgy. Little is known concerning the development of the Roman Mass in late antiquity. But by c. 700, the *Ordo Romanus,* which describes the pontifical Mass, a model for this celebration, is available. Gradually through the Middle Ages, the structure of the Mass liturgy accrued its present progression with its logical directionality toward and then away from the eucharistic celebration. The Mass liturgy comprises the Proper chants, which vary from day to day according to the season of the year (*temporale*) or the saint celebrated (*sanctorale*), the ordinary chants, which remain the same for the most part throughout the year, and the prayers and readings. This complementary, alternating structure can be summarized in this way:

Proper Chants	Ordinary Chants	Prayers and Readings
Introit		
	Kyrie	
	Gloria	
		Collect
		Epistle
Gradual		
Alleluia/tract		
Sequence		Gospel
	Credo	
Offertory		
		Preface
	Sanctus	
		Eucharistic prayer
		Pater noster
	Agnus Dei	
Communion		
		Post-Communion
	Ite missa est	

Compositional Method. The compositional method for the liturgy of the Mass involved the arrangement of *centones* ("pieces" or "chunks"), translated into the Latin *puncta*, in which portions from the book of Psalms and other texts were disengaged from their customary context and resituated, thus achieving a new associative framework. These *centones* were approximately the length of what could have been spoken comfortably on one breath. Thus, the essentially declamatory aspect of the biblical text must be kept in mind, also as a way of selecting tempi for singing within the liturgy today, the main consideration being that the text must be comprehensible. This compositional method of placing together "chunks," primarily of the Psalms, was carried out with artfulness and sense of appropriateness so that attention was trained onto the many facets of the liturgical topic of the day. The sequence, sung between the Alleluia and the reading of the Gospel, as a transition from Old Testament to New Testament, however, does not use the above-described method of composition. This liturgical category, in as many ways as possible, brings together instances of the "Old" versus the "New" in preparation for the reading of the Gospel. These include, for example, the comparisons *synagoga* and *ecclesia*, Eve and Virgin Mary, the Old Testament law of the Ten Commandments and the New Testament law of love, Adam and Christ, the "old man" and "new man" in Christ, and the letter and the spirit, as well as other comparisons between the Old and

New Testaments in preparation for the Gospel reading. All of these features point to very careful attention to detail on the part of mostly anonymous medieval composers who placed together in ever new combinations the component parts of all of the Mass texts and who wrote sequences. Even today, centuries later, there are well over three thousand extant graduals and missals, copied between c. 900–1600, containing the music and texts of the Mass proper (texts and music appropriate to the changing daily liturgical situation, that is, the *temporale* or events of the life of Christ, and the *sanctorale*).

———

P. Wagner, *Geschichte der Messe* (1913); W. Apel, *Gregorian Chant* (rev. ed., 1990); T. Georgiades, *Musik und Sprache*: *Das Werden der abendländischen Musik dargestellt an der Vertonung der Messe* (1954, ET 1982); N. van Deusen, "The Use and Significance of the Sequence," *Musica disciplina* 40 (1986): 1–46.

NANCY VAN DEUSEN

Llull, Ramon (c. 1232–1316), theologian. Llull's significance lies in the fact that he, like the great theologians of the twelfth century (and the later philosophers of the Enlightenment) held to a strongly rationalistic program and thus claimed to establish rationally the specific Christian dogmas of the Trinity and Christology. This establishment of dogma was based on a new method of the combination of the basic concepts (such as "greatness" or "goodness") from which all possible derived complex concepts should be created and which should alert one to possible contradictions between concepts.

Llull was not a member of the clergy but a father with a family. He played an important role at the court of James I of Aragon as tutor of the king's son, the later king of Mallorca James II. He decided, probably in 1263, by reason of a conversion experience, to convert unbelievers. He was especially interested in converting the many Muslims still on the island of Mallorca, to write a book that should achieve this end by arguments, and to stimulate the foundation of language schools in which missionaries would receive an appropriate education. He himself learned Arabic, which he apparently knew better than Latin, but composed most of his more than 290 works in Catalan, which through him became the first European vernacular to be used for philosophy. The religious dialogue *Libre del gentil e los tres* savis (*Book of the Pagan and the Three Wise Men*), in which the representatives of the three monotheistic religions try to convert a pagan to their position and which has an open ending, along with his most extensive work, the *Libre de contemplació en Déu* (*Book of the Contemplation of God*), were written before the development of his combinatory method, which he believed God had revealed to him on Mount Randa, probably in 1273. He published his method in various versions (the last is the *Ars generalis ultima* of 1308) and took pains to reconceive the sciences of his day on the basis of it (for instance, in the *Logica nova* of 1303). His purely literary works, for example, the novels *Blaquerna* and *Fèlix* and the autobiographical poem, *Lo Desconhort*, are superb. He worked inexhaustibly in the Mediterranean region to promote his plans with popes, religious orders, and universities. He made three trips to North Africa, where he was imprisoned because of his missionary work and, in the end, allegedly stoned. In 1376, on account of his rationalism, he was condemned by Pope Gregory IX. Often listed on the Index, Llull nevertheless profoundly influenced Nicholas of Cues, Giordano Bruno, Gottfried Wilhelm Leibniz, and many lesser thinkers.

_____

A. Bonner, ed. and trans., *Doctor Illuminatus: A Ramón Llull Reader* (1993); Bonner, ed., *Selected Works of Ramón Llull (1232–1316)* (1985); *Obres de Ramon Lull*, 21 vols. (1906–1950); E.-W. Platzeck, *Raimund Lull*, 2 vols. (1962–1964); *Raimundi Lulli Opera Latina*, 27 vols. (1959–).

VITTORIO HÖSLE

Locke, John (1632–1704), English philosopher. He grew up during the era of the English Civil War and attended Christ Church, Oxford. Through reading Descartes, he became interested in philosophical issues. While a tutor at Oxford in the 1660s, he pursued further studies in medicine and experimental science. He was elected a fellow of the Royal Society in 1668. Beginning in 1666, he served in several capacities as an advisor to the Earl of Shaftesbury, a prominent statesman during the era of the Restoration. When Shaftesbury fell from power in 1675, Locke fled to France. After another brief period of government service, he was forced to take refuge in Holland, but he returned to England in 1688 after the Glorious Revolution. He then began publishing his philosophical treatises. In *An Essay Concerning Human Understanding* (1690) he argued

that knowledge was based on sensation and reflection on sense perceptions, not on innate ideas as Descartes had argued. His conviction that knowledge is at best only probable made him an opponent of dogmatism and constraint of individual freedom by either church or state. In *Letters on Toleration* (1689–1692), he argued that matters of religion should be outside the jurisdiction of the state. In *Two Treatises on Government* (1690), he refuted the doctrine of the divine right of kings and insisted that the power of the state must rest on the consent of the governed. In *The Reasonableness of Christianity* (1695), he argued that some truths are above reason but never contrary to it. He espoused a simple latitudinarian faith that stressed morality and Christ as the Messiah sent to reveal God's true nature.

_____

V. Chappell, *The Cambridge Companion to Locke* (1994); J. Marshall, *John Locke: Resistance, Religion, and Responsibility* (1949); N. Wolterstorff, *John Locke and the Ethics of Belief* (1996).

ERIC LUND

Logos The Greek word *logos* is a noun derived from the same root as the verb "to speak" (*legō*). It is primarily intended to describe ordered speech, and its range of meanings extends from "argument" to "concept" to "treatise" to "oration" and beyond. In English it is conventionally translated by "word" but rarely refers to a single word or expression. As early as the fifth century BCE, the philosopher Heraclitus used it to describe the rational principle that produces order in the universe, a principle discernible by the mind. This is the sense of *logos* that underlies most Jewish and Christian usage.

The Septuagint uses *logos* to describe God's prophetic word and, by extension, God's creative commands in history and creation. Thus, it is possible to imagine God's "almighty word" as a warrior leaping to Israel's defense (Wis. 18:15). The *logos* similarly imagined is also found in the New Testament (Rev. 19:11–16), but the passage underlying most Christian usage is the Prologue of John's Gospel (John 1:1–18). There the One encountered in Jesus is the Word or *Logos* which made the world now become "flesh." Parallels to this idea have been sought in the works of Philo Judaeus and in early Aramaic paraphrases of the Hebrew Scriptures. The *logos* as imagined and *logos* as a philosophical concept have both played important roles in Christian thought.

The *logos* as instrumental Creator gave theologians a conceptual tool to link the Jesus of earthly experience with the divine Creator active in Israel's history and perceived in the rational order of the universe. By emphasizing Jesus as the *logos* become flesh, the source of all human goodness, Justin Martyr and other second-century apologists were able to affirm the goodness of much in non-Hebraic thought: the divine *logos* prefigured in the OT and fully present in Jesus was dimly visible in the works of Plato and other Greek philosophers. This view was rejected by non-Christians such as Celsus (who wrote a work entitled *The Real Logos* to rebut it), but *"logos* theology" remained attractive to Christians, especially those such as Origen who affirmed the value of human reason apart from direct divine revelation. The *logos* doctrine helped these theologians bridge the gap between the Word of God proclaimed in the OT and the divine Word seen incarnate in the NT. The *logos* "made flesh" in Jesus was identical with the pre-incarnate *logos* encountered centuries earlier by Moses and Abraham. Moreover, the contrast between a word or concept present in human minds (the *logos endiathetos*) and same word or concept as expressed in speech (*logos prophorikos*) afforded an attractive (if dangerous) metaphor for divine generation.

There were difficulties, however. One of the major issues in the Trinitarian controversies of the fourth century was the difficulty in reconciling the absolute unity of God with the creative and historical roles ascribed to the pre-incarnate *logos*. A consensus was eventually reached when the *logos* came to be seen as one in a triad of persons subsisting within the single Godhead. A parallel difficulty was experienced in trying to conceptualize the incarnation; some theologians thought that the *logos* functioned within Jesus the way souls do in other human beings. The great majority of Christians rejected this view and insisted that though Jesus was indeed the *logos* made flesh, he possessed a true human mind and soul.

In the Christian East, theologians such as Maximus the Confessor and Symeon the New Theologian made participation in the *logos* a focal point of their mystical theologies. In the West *logos*, both in the person of Christ and in the human mind, has been seen primarily as a font of rational structure and order—sometimes in opposition to the charismatic unpredictability of direct inspiration, the divine "foolishness" that is wiser than human wisdom (1 Cor. 1:25). This polarity runs from Tertullian

in the third century through the scholastic and monastic theologians of the thirteenth to Barth and Tillich in the twentieth. Philosophical challenges to the possibility of human knowledge not determined by personal subjectivity suggest the continuing debate will be a lively one.

———

J. Daniélou, *Gospel Message and Hellenistic Culture* (1973), 39–73 and passim; V. Karayiannis, *Maxime le Confesseur* (1993), 283–332; W. Kelber, *Die Logoslehre: Von Heraklit bis Origines* (1976); C. Kock, *Natürliche Theologie: Ein evangelischer Streitbegriff* (2001); J. Meyendorff, *Christ in Eastern Christian Thought* (1975); P. Perkins, "Logos Christology in the Nag Hammadi Codices," *VC* 35 (1981): 379–96; H. A. Wolfson, *The Philosophy of the Church Fathers*, vol. 1 (1970), 177–286.

RICHARD PAUL VAGGIONE, OHC

Lollardy   A pre-Reformation movement influenced by John Wyclif (c. 1329–1384), also known as "Wyclifism." The origin of the term "Lollard" is unclear, perhaps deriving from "chanter" or referring to someone as a "mumbler of prayers." Lollardy was characterized by an emphasis on personal faith, the authority of the Bible, and a belief in divine election; it was marked by simplicity of doctrine and worship. The movement was notable in its gains in Kent and the Midlands. In addition to the personal faith elements, Lollards were noted for their rejection of clerical celibacy, oral confession, veneration of saints and icons, indulgences, pilgrimages, and, in particular, transubstantiation. Wyclif's teachings at Oxford on the Eucharist split the university into "Lollards" and "Catholics" in 1379; the term was first used officially in 1387. In 1382 Archbishop Courtenay condemned Wyclif's teachings at Oxford, but the beliefs prevailed, and by 1395 Lollards were an organized sect with representatives in Parliament. They opposed church hierarchy and wealth, as well as ownership of property by the church. Importantly for the later Reformation of the church in England, they emphasized Bible reading in the vernacular. Henry IV ostensibly destroyed the sect in 1401 with his injunction *De haeretico comburendo*, but the sect persisted and posed problems for Henry V; both kings used royal forces to persecute Lollards for heresy. There is evidence of Lollard resurgences in 1414 and 1431, but the history of the Lollards post-1430s is unclear, though their influence during the later reforms in England is keenly evident: in the Church of England, Puritanism, and in later Pietism. The connections between Lollardy and later Lutheranism and other continental reform movements is one of the most hotly debated topics in current English Reformation studies.

M. Aston, *Lollards and Reformers: Images and Literacy in Late Medieval Religion* (1984); A. G. Dickens, *Lollards and Protestants in the Diocese of York, 1509–1558* (1959); A. Hudson, *The Premature Reformation: Wycliffite Texts and Lollard History* (1988); J. A. F. Thomson, *The Later Lollards, 1414–1520* (1965).
                                            ALDEN R. LUDLOW

Lombard, Peter   *see* Peter Lombard

Lord's Prayer   To show his disciples how to pray, Jesus taught them the words Christians have come to call the Lord's Prayer. Both Matthew (6:9–13) and Luke (11:2–4) record the prayer; Matthew gives essentially the version familiar to later Christian tradition, while Luke gives a shorter form. Precisely why the two versions differ is not clear. One possibility is that the prayer is part of the Q tradition, which Matthew and Luke incorporated into their Gospels in different ways that reflect their different theological and pastoral emphases. Another possibility is that liturgical usage in the distinct communities in which the two Gospels arose shaped the prayer. The doxology that the King James Version includes and that concludes the prayer in many Christian traditions appears in some inferior manuscripts of Matthew and, in a shorter form, concludes the prayer in the *Didache* (8.2).

After its opening invocation of God as "Father," the Lord's Prayer presents a series of petitions, the first ones asking in different ways for the perfect realization of God's rule and the remaining ones looking to the needs of the petitioners. Scholars debate whether the petitions focus on the present or the future or dimensions of both; the last understanding offers the most compelling resolution of the difficulties. Thus, the prayer prays for the manifestation now of God's powerful transforming presence and seeks help for Christians in meeting their constant need for food, reconciliation, and security. At the same time, it looks to the final coming of God's kingdom and requests readiness for participation in that kingdom through proleptic sharing in the kingdom feast, forgiveness of sin in view of the coming judgment, and deliverance from the powers of evil that threaten to sever the Christian from the final blessings of God.

The *Didache* (8.3) urges recitation of the Lord's Prayer three times daily, perhaps in Christian imitation of classical Jewish thrice-daily prayer. At least by the time of Tertullian Christians were interpreting the prayer's request for bread not only as food for their bodies but also as the spiritual bread that is the Lord's body (*De oratione* 6). By the late fourth century we are certain of use of the prayer in the eucharistic liturgy, in which it has assumed a privileged place in preparation for Communion as a request both for eucharistic food (Ambrose, *De sacramentis* 5.4.24–25) and for forgiveness of sin (Augustine, *Sermones* 229.3).

The ancient church treasured its prayer in the Lord's own words (e.g., Cyprian, *Dom. or.* 1–3) and was acutely conscious of its boldness in repeating his words (*Apost. Const.* 7.24). The church's respect for the prayer was reflected in its practice of keeping the prayer secret from its catechumens until shortly before their baptismal transformation into children of God with the attendant privilege of sharing with the Lord Jesus the intimate address of God as "Father."

J. Jeremias, *The Prayers of Jesus* (1978).
                                 MARY CATHERINE BERGLUND

Lost Books of the Bible   These are not a uniform set of texts but variously construed eclectic collections of early noncanonical Christian books also called either the Christian Pseudepigrapha or the Apocrypha. The "lost books of the Bible" bear testimony to the transitional nature of the first Christian canons, for many of the "lost books" were sacred to various communities. These texts were composed, often under the name of apostolic figures, to explore matters of theological significance as adherents of different sects in nascent Christianity sought to define the nature of the emergent faith.

Ideas espoused in these texts frequently diverge substantially from more conventional expressions of Christianity. For this reason, over time the church suppressed many of these texts as it struggled toward orthodoxy and formulated a canon of Scripture in keeping with its understanding of authentic Christian thought (367 CE). It is more difficult to discern why other texts failed to make the Christian canon, for some of these lost books closely resemble biblical materials in content and form. In fact, the genres of many of the lost books recall those with which we are familiar among the twenty-seven NT canonical books.

For instance, there are a number of Gospels (e.g., the *Gospels of Peter, Mary, Philip, Thomas, the Nazareans, the Ebionites, the Hebrews, the Egyptians*), several Acts (e.g., the *Acts of Paul [and Thecla], Thomas, Andrew, John, Peter*), numerous epistles (e.g., *Didache,* Paul's *Letter to the Laodiceans, 1–2 Clement, 3 Corinthians, Paul and Seneca*), and even a few Apocalypses (e.g., the *Shepherd of Hermas*, the *Apocalypse of Peter*, the *Apocalypse of Paul*, the *Secret Book of John*).

However contemporary readers assess the authenticity of these texts, the lost books clearly provide valuable vantage points from which to understand the conceptual controversies and theological battles that characterized early Christianity. They continue to be significant to the church as artifacts that provide a window into the ideological world of early Christianity, allowing the voices silenced by orthodoxy to speak on their own terms and represent their understanding of the faith in language that they chose.

W. Barnstone, ed., *The Other Bible: Ancient Alternative Scriptures* (1984); W. Barnstone and M. Meyer, eds., *The Gnostic Bible* (2003); B. D. Ehrman, *Lost Scriptures: Books That Did Not Make It into the New Testament* (2003); J. M. Robinson, *The Nag Hammadi Library in English* (4th ed., 1996).

RODNEY S. SADLER JR.

Lucian of Antioch (d. 312), priest and martyr. The figure of Lucian of Antioch stands in shadows that have only grown deeper with the advance of historical research. Near the end of the third and last general persecution, Lucian was brought to Nicomedia and interrogated in the presence of the emperor. He suffered martyrdom on January 7, 312. That much is certain. In addition, Arius, in a letter addressed to Eusebius of Nicomedia and preserved by Eusebius, refers to himself as a *sylloukianistēs*, a "fellow Lucianist," although the word itself is a conjecture by modern text critics. Beginning from that word, some theorists have tried to discover the roots of Arianism in Lucian's theology, of which, however, almost nothing is known. Lucian is sometimes called the founder of the Antiochene school of exegesis, but this attribution, too, is anachronistic. The Second Creed of the Dedication Council of Antioch is sometimes called the Lucianic Creed. The creed is certainly not Nicene, but it is difficult to associate a creed so well developed with a pre-Nicene presbyter. Finally, there is speculation about a "Lucianic

recension" of the Septuagint and of the New Testament, the latter of which forms the basis of the *textus receptus* of the NT, but, again, a direct association with Lucian is dubious.

G. Bardy, *Recherches sur saint Lucien d'Antioche et son école* (1936).

JOSEPH T. LIENHARD

Lucian of Samosata (c. 120–before 200), Greek satirist. Born in Samosata in northern Syria, Lucian traveled throughout the empire, spending several years in Athens. Under Commodus (r. 180–192) he accepted a teaching post in Egypt, where he died.

Lucian studied rhetoric and philosophy. He soon gave up philosophy, except to make fun of it in his writings (see especially his *Philosophies for Sale*). The Cynic school, and Menippus in particular, were favorite targets of Lucian.

Lucian is of special interest for his *On the Death of Peregrinus* (*De morte Peregrini*), which describes the career and death of Peregrinus, a Cynic philosopher who, true to his nickname "Proteus," became many things during his life, including, briefly, a Christian, "after learning about that cult in Palestine." Lucian states that Peregrinus quickly became a leader among the Christians, "interpreting their books and composing his own," and that the Christians gave him second place of honor after "that crucified sophist." After Peregrinus was imprisoned, the Christians provided lavishly for his needs, calling him "the new Socrates."

Lucian portrays the Christians as naive wretches who are easily deceived. While Lucian was a satirist rather than a historian, there is likely some truth to his rather unflattering description of Christianity.

Lucian, in LCL, 9 vols., trans. A. M. Harmon (1913); C. P. Jones, *Culture and Society in Lucian* (1986).

MICHAEL COMPTON

Lucifer of Cagliari (d. 370), radical anti-Arian bishop. Lucifer is first known in 354/355 as bishop of Calaris (later Cagliari) in Sardinia. Liberius of Rome sent Lucifer on a delegation to Constantius in 354. In 355 Lucifer, who held radically pro-Nicene views, refused to sign the condemnation of Athanasius at the Synod of Milan and, as a result, was exiled to the East, along with Eusebius of Vercelli and Dionysius of Milan. His exile lasted until the amnesty of Julian in 362. Lucifer then went to Antioch, where he consecrated as bishop Paulinus, who belonged to the paleo-Nicene party that continued the tradition of Eustathius of Antioch. Lucifer thus exacerbated the schism at Antioch, which now had three bishops (Melitius, the Arian Euzoius, and Paulinus). Lucifer continued to refuse Communion to anyone he suspected of Arianism and perhaps died in schism. While in exile, Lucifer composed five tracts addressed to Constantius; several of his letters also survive. The importance of Lucifer's writings is more philological than theological; he wrote in colloquial or vulgar Latin and had no speculative skills but was a master of invective. Jerome attacked Lucifer's followers in his *Dialogue against the Luciferians.*

Lucifer of Cagliari, *Luciferi Calaritani Opera quae supersunt,* ed. G. F. Diercks (1978); W. Tietze, *Lucifer von Calaris und die Kirchenpolitik des Constantius II* (1976).

JOSEPH T. LIENHARD

Lucilla (fl. c. 305–311), influential Christian in Carthage. Originally from Spain, Lucilla was a prominent community leader in the origins of the Donatist schism. She is remembered for two reasons. First, she is reported to have kissed the relic of a martyr before receiving Communion. Optatus notes that the archdeacon Caecilian reproached her for this practice. Optatus does not focus on her veneration of a relic per se but for honoring a saint whose cult was not ecclesiastically sanctioned. Thus, we have early evidence of attempts by ecclesiastical authorities to control popular veneration of martyrs.

Second, she led a group of Carthaginians who repudiated Caecilian's election as bishop of Carthage. It had been irregular because he was not yet a presbyter when ordained bishop, he was ordained by Felix of Abthugni who was reputed to have been a *traditor,* and no Numidian bishops had been present, as was customary. According to Optatus, Lucilla's money, given under the guise of donations for the poor, bankrolled Majorinus's election. This member of Lucilla's household had been subdeacon when Caecelian was deacon. Thus, Lucilla was responsible for the genesis of a second line of bishops at Carthage. This was the formal beginning of the Donatist schism.

Optatus of Milevis, *Against the Donatists* 1.16, and *Proceedings before Zenophilus,* ed. and trans. M. Edwards (1997).

MAUREEN A. TILLEY

Ludmila (c. 860–c. 921), Slavic princess, later venerated as a saint, who facilitated the conversion of Bohemia to Christianity. Born c. 860, Ludmila lived during a turbulent period in the political and religious history of Bohemia. She married the Czech duke Bořivoj in 873, and the couple soon converted from paganism to Christianity. The Czechs had recently received the Byzantine form of Christianity with the Slavic Rite created by Constantine-Cyril (see *Cyril and Methodius*), and some sources even affirm that Bořivoj and Ludmila were baptized by Methodius. However, with the dissolution of the Great Moravian Empire, Bohemia reallied itself with German Bavaria in 895.

Ludmila's life is known to us primarily through hagiographical accounts. After Bořivoj's death, her sons Spytihněv and Vratislav reigned. Vratislav married Drahomira, reputed to be a pagan, and Ludmila was entrusted with the education of their son Wenceslas. Probably more from jealousy of her mother-in-law's influence than from alleged anti-Christian ambitions, Drahomira had Ludmila murdered in her castle by two Czech noblemen c. 921. As part of her canonization process, Wenceslas had Ludmila's relics moved to the Church of St. George in Prague in 925. Her cult spread rapidly in Bohemia, and she is the subject of several medieval lives in both Old Church Slavonic and Latin. She is remembered as a model mother and widow, a patron of the poor, and the first Christian martyr of Bohemia.

M. Kantor, *The Origins of Christianity in Bohemia: Sources and Commentary* (1990).

ANDREA STERK

Luis de Molina *see* Molina, Luis de

Luther, Martin (1483–1546), German theologian and reformer. Luther was the son of an entrepreneurial miner who sent him to school to become a lawyer. In 1505, having sworn to become a monk amid the mortal peril of a thunderstorm, Luther abandoned the university to take vows in the Augustinian cloister, where he was ordained a priest. The Augustinians, however, sent Luther back to study theology. He received his doctorate at the new university of Wittenberg in 1512 and there took up his lifelong post as lecturer on the Bible.

Luther's struggles (*Anfechtungen*) for assurance of God's mercy through monastic discipline and exegetical study, especially of the Psalms and Romans, led finally to the breakthrough expressed in his *Sermon on Two Kinds of Righteousness* of 1518. Based on Romans 1:17, Luther identified God's righteousness as the righteousness of Christ given to sinners, which could only be received, passively, by trusting in God's promise (*sola fide*), as distinguished from the active righteousness with which a person strove to fulfill God's law and serve his neighbor.

Luther had already come onto the public stage in 1517 with his Ninety-Five theses criticizing the abuse of indulgences, which others quickly published throughout Germany. In defending himself, Luther came to articulate more clearly the unique authority of the Scriptures over against fallible ecclesiastical traditions and papal judgments. Excommunicated by Pope Leo X, Luther refused to recant before the imperial Diet of Worms in 1521; only the protection of Saxon elector Frederick the Wise saved him from execution.

Luther's university training in arts and theology was based on the nominalism of William of Ockham. Though firmly rejecting Ockham's soteriology as Pelagian, Luther's theology built on Ockham's emphasis on divine promises as the primary relation between God and creation. Though not educated as a humanist himself, Luther used Erasmus's Greek New Testament in his lectures and supported humanist reforms of the Wittenberg curriculum, aided by Philip Melanchthon. Luther's cause received wide early support from German humanists, but after 1521, the older generation fell away. The break was made public with Erasmus's 1525 critique of Luther's theology, *On the Freedom of the Will*, to which Luther responded in his *Bondage of the Will*, reasserting human impotence in spiritual matters.

Erasmus noted with dismay Luther's skill in setting his theology before a wide public. In the early 1520s, Luther's works dominated the German presses. The theology that answered the struggles of a devout monk was not irrelevant to laity who had been taught in their own piety to aspire to the monastic ideal. In addition to sermons and treatises, Luther published catechisms and some forty hymns which, along with his German translation of the Bible (the NT was published in 1522, the OT in 1534) laid the foundation of Lutheran lay piety; he also arranged a vernacular liturgy (1526) that was widely imitated. Luther's academic work as professor of Bible continued throughout his life; his commentaries on Galatians (1531) and Genesis (1535–1545) exemplify his mature thought.

Luther rejected a special sacerdotal estate, teaching that all baptized Christians were priests before God; he emphasized, however, the dignity of the divinely established office of the public ministry of preaching and administering the sacraments, called through the congregation or its representatives (in practice, the prince or town council). It was as leading Christian laymen that Luther appealed to German rulers to assume the role of "emergency bishops" in supporting religious reform; he taught subjects that a ruler who sought to suppress the gospel must be disobeyed. The institutions of secular life, common to Christians and unbelievers, were God's "left hand" for maintaining moral order in the world, distinct from God's "right hand" rule over believers through the proclamation of the gospel. Thus, though Luther agreed with many of the peasants' claims of injustice in 1525, he denounced their appeal to the gospel, rather than natural right, as a basis for social change. Luther's ethics centered on the freedom afforded by God's promise of justification to serve the neighbor according to one's vocation within the estates of state, church, and family. Luther's 1525 marriage to the former nun Katharina von Bora and their six children exemplified his teaching on the dignity of the married estate.

The distinctive emphases of Luther's theology were sharpened in conflict with other versions of reform. For Luther, the scriptural word was not merely an intellectual or moral authority but the means by which God crushed the sinner with the law and revived him through the gospel promise, conveyed by preaching, baptism, the Lord's Supper, and absolution. Luther's insistence on the efficacy of the scriptural promise and on the real fulfillment of Jesus' words ("This is my body") in the Lord's Supper led him to condemn reformers such as Müntzer, Karlstadt, or Zwingli who instead emphasized the direct action of the Spirit apart from external words or elements, a position Luther labeled "enthusiasm" (*Schwärmerei*). Unlike these other reformers, Luther also defended the use of religious art and especially music in Christian teaching and devotion. Against Johann Agricola, Luther insisted that not only the gospel but also the law was to be preached to Christians, carefully distinguished in their roles. The harsh writings of Luther's last years against false (Protestant) brethren, the pope, and the Jews echo in another key his lifelong hostility to all who, in his judgment, denied or undermined the biblical promises pointing to justification by faith in Christ alone.

D. Martin Luthers Werke, 81 vols. (1883–); *Luther's Works*, 55 vols. (1955–1986); M. Brecht, *Martin Luther*, 3 vols. (1985–1993); P. Althaus, *The Theology of Martin Luther* (1966); B. Lohse, *Martin Luther: An Introduction to His Life and Work* (1986); Lohse, *Martin Luther's Theology: Its Historical and Systematic Development* (1999); *Luther Digest* (1993–); *Lutherjahrbuch* (1919–).

CHRISTOPHER B. BROWN

Lutheranism A designation for the beliefs, practices, and institutions of followers and theological descendants of Martin Luther. Opponents such as Johann Eck (*Expurgatio adversus criminationes F. Martini Lutter [1519]*) first coined the term "Lutheran" to distinguish Luther's supporters in his dispute with Rome over indulgences from those loyal to the papacy. The contours of Lutheranism first became clear over the course of the sixteenth century. Starting in 1524 Luther and his followers argued with Huldrych Zwingli and others over the presence of Christ in the Lord's Supper, revealing doctrinal distinctions that eventually led to Reformed and Lutheran branches of Christianity. The 1527 visitation of Saxon churches not sanctioned by ordinary bishops heightened the religious crisis within the HRE and led Charles V to convene the imperial diet in Augsburg in 1530. Some argue that Lutheranism officially began when the Saxon elector Frederick the Wise and his "evangelical" allies presented the Augsburg Confession on June 25, 1530. Others view that document as a reform proposal that only defined Lutheranism as an entity separate from the Roman church after the Roman faction presented its *Confutation* in August 1530. Publication of the Confession and its Apology (defense) in 1531 transformed it into the doctrinal touchstone for Lutheranism.

The Wittenberg Concord of 1536, an agreement on the Lord's Supper between Luther and the Strasbourg reformer Martin Bucer, along with their allies, broadened Lutheran alliances. In his Schmalkald Articles of the same year, Luther rejected the papal call for a general council. Colloquies between adherents to the Augsburg Confession (using Philip Melanchthon's heavily edited version, the *Variata*) and supporters of Rome ended in failure, despite tentative agreement on justification.

The defeat of evangelical princes in the Schmalkald War of 1547 resulted in a spate of controversies among Luther's followers and their successors in the following decades and included renewed controversy over the Lord's Supper. In 1555, the Peace of Augsburg gave important but limited constitutional legitimacy within the empire to churches of the Augsburg Confession. During the same period, territories outside the empire subscribed to the Augsburg Confession (and sometimes to Martin Luther's Small Catechism), including Slovakia, Denmark, Sweden, and Finland.

The Formula of Concord (1576) published in *The Book of Concord* (1580) united about two-thirds of German-speaking Lutherans within a variety of territorial churches. Besides the Augsburg Confession in its original form (the *Invariata*), the book contained the three ecumenical creeds, the Apology, the Formula, Luther's catechisms, and the Schmalkald Articles. Non–German-speaking churches did not generally accept it. What united all these churches, besides a special respect for Luther and his writings, was the Augsburg Confession and its commitments to justification "by grace through faith on account of Christ" and to the real presence of Christ in the Lord's Supper.

The late sixteenth and seventeenth centuries saw the development of Lutheran orthodoxy—a systematization of theology using various Aristotelian methods. Orthodoxy carefully demarcated Lutheran theology from its Reformed and Roman Catholic equivalents. Although sometimes described as dry and intellectualized, this period was accompanied by a rich Lutheran piety, reflected in the production of a Lutheran hymnody and edifying literature (especially Johann Arndt's *True Christianity* of 1610) and by the maintenance of a vivid eschatology.

In 1675 Philip Jakob Spener (1635–1705) published *Pia desideria*, a proposal for reform of the church. Orthodox Lutherans, sensitive to synergism and legalism, often attacked so-called Pietists such as Spener and his spiritual successor, August Hermann Francke (1663–1727), professor of theology at the Univ. of Halle. Reacting to the perceived decline in church life and morals in the wake of the Thirty Years' War (1618–1648), Pietists championed the formation of smaller groups of committed Christians among territorial churches whose members gathered to read the Bible and edifying literature. They advocated the renewed spiritual life of the universal priesthood (the laity) and established charitable institutions that cared for the sick, published inexpensive Bibles and other literature, and trained pastors for work in other countries. Similar movements arose in Scandinavia and Slovakia in the eighteenth and nineteenth centuries.

C. Bergendoff, *The Church of the Lutheran Reformation: A Historical Survey of Lutheranism* (1967); Bergendoff, *The Encyclopedia of the Lutheran Church* (1965); G. Gassmann, *Historical Dictionary of Lutheranism* (2001); E. W. Gritsch, *Fortress Introduction to Lutheranism* (1994).

TIMOTHY J. WENGERT

Macarius Magnes (fl. 400), Greek apologist. He composed the five-book *Apocriticus*, which survives incomplete. The work presents itself as the record of a debate between a pagan and a Christian. The format is literary artifice, and Macarius apparently drew his pagan interlocutor's objections from an unidentified tract that itself recapitulated earlier anti-Christian polemics. The pagan sources behind Macarius's intermediary source are now commonly identified as the anti-Christian writings of the third-century Neoplatonist Porphyry, although it cannot be ruled out that Macarius (or his source) also incorporated material from the lost works of Porphyry's contemporary Sossianus Hierocles. The *Apocriticus*'s pagan interlocutor derides the "absurdity" of various NT verses, discrepancies among the Gospels, the unreliability of the disciples, and the indefensibility of the doctrines of the incarnation and bodily resurrection. Jesus is unfavorably contrasted with the first-century neo-Pythagorean sage and miracle worker Apollonius of Tyana. Macarius's Christian finds truth in congruity of sentiment not phraseology, harmonizes Scripture through allegorical exegesis, and, with Christian readers in mind, sets all interpretation within a single economy of salvation. Macarius is, perhaps, to be identified with a homonymous early fifth-century bishop of Magnesia.

T. Barnes, "Porphyry *Against the Christians*," *JTS* 24 (1973): 424–42; T. Crafer, trans., *The Apocriticus of Macarius Magnes* (1919); R. Waelkens, *L' économie, thème apologétique et principe herméneutique dans l'Aprocriticos de Macarios Magnès* (1974).

DENNIS E. TROUT

Macarius the Great (c. 300–390), Egyptian monk. Evidence about Macarius appears largely in forty-one sayings attributed to him, as well as in descriptions in the *Lausiac History* (17.1–13) and *History of the Monks of Egypt* (21.1–17). Macarius was the first to establish ascetic withdrawal in Scetis, where he then served as a teacher to many disciples who gathered around him in a loose organization of cells, with two or three monks in each. A monastery bearing his name remains active in this region of Egypt today. His sayings emphasize freedom from the passions (*apatheia*), a common goal in this type of monasticism. A monk was to strive to become a "dead man." The sayings also show significant interaction among the monks, spanning from gossip to Macarius's spiritual direction.

Scholars have recently debated the nature and historical reliability of these sources. They note the important influence of the editors, who collected the sayings, in shaping the presentation of Macarius. Another difficulty is the association between Macarius and Pseudo-Macarius, the author of fifty spiritual homilies that have an entirely different provenance (Syria) and context (the Messalian controversy) from Macarius the Great.

W. Harmless, SJ, *Desert Christians* (2004); G. A. Maloney, trans., *Pseudo-Macarius: The Fifty Spiritual Homilies and the Great Letter* (1992); C. Stewart, *Working the Earth of the Heart* (1991); B. Ward, trans., *The Sayings of the Desert Fathers: The Alphabetical Collection* (1980), 501–21.

REBECCA KRAWIEC

Machiavelli, Niccolo (1469–1527), Renaissance Italian humanist, philosopher, statesman. Born in Florence, Machiavelli served as a government diplomat until the Florentine Republic was overthrown. He was exiled from Florence by the Borgias, whom he despised, when they seized power. Nonetheless, he dedicated his most famous work, *The Prince* (1513), to Cesare Borgia. While he has been maligned as an advocate of cruel and dishonest government, his work as a political commentator and theorist has often been misunderstood. His depictions of government in *The Prince*, in which rulers who are feared are preferred to those who are loved, and those who "seem" virtuous are preferred to those who actually are virtuous, are intended not as descriptions of how government ought to be (the traditional procedure among political theorists), but of how successful governments actually operate. *The Prince*, therefore, concerns "successful," not "good," government. Machiavelli also wrote *Discourses on Livy*, which shows his interest in history as a means of interpreting the present. This work and his published *Letters* display his profound sense of the humanity of the past and his strong personal approval of republicanism and distaste for every other form of government.

S. de Graza, *Machiavelli in Hell* (1987); J. R. Hale, *Machiavelli and Renaissance Italy* (1960); Q. Skinner, *Machiavelli* (1981).

RODERICK MARTIN

Macrina the Younger (327–380), founder

of a community of "virgins of God." Macrina was the oldest of nine children of Basil the Elder and Emmelia, of the wealthy Christian Cappadocian elite. Her grandmother, Macrina the Elder, had endured the persecutions of Maximinus Daia, and Macrina herself had been given the name of Thecla. Her brothers were Basil the Great, Gregory of Nyssa, and Peter of Sebaste.

At age twelve Macrina became engaged to a young man who died before the engagement was complete. She refused a second engagement and began to lead the life of a "virgin dedicated to God." She remained in her family home but altered her daily routine. She began to pray and recite psalms at regular intervals, and, undertaking a task strictly reserved for household slaves, she baked her mother's bread.

In the late 340s, Macrina and Emmelia retreated to the family estate at Annesi, where both practiced a strict ascetic regimen of prayer, frugal nourishment, and manual labor. Emmelia, persuaded by Macrina, abolished all difference of status between herself and her slaves and subdivided her possessions among her children. At Annesi the nuclear group consisting of family members and slaves was augmented by other well-born women as well as by women and orphaned girls who sought succor during a famine (368–369). Macrina now became head of the household and of a community of female ascetics who, whether widowed, mothers, or physically virgins, became "virgins" in the spiritual sense.

Our main sources for Macrina and her ascetic community are from her brother Gregory of Nyssa: her biography (the earliest hagiography), Letter 19, and the dialogue *On the Soul and the Resurrection*, in which he portrays his sister as teaching him, from her deathbed, about the nature and destiny of the human soul—a move that recalls another classic female teaching figure, namely, Diotima. If Gregory did not reproduce her words faithfully (and there is no way in which we can ever know what Macrina herself said), he at least used Macrina to voice important theological notions that he might not have dared to claim during

times of heightened orthodox and heterodox debates. Macrina was also praised by another famous Cappadocian, Gregory of Nazianzus (Letter 163). She is a saint of the Orthodox Church.

S. Elm, *Virgins of God* (1994); R. Van Dam, *Families and Friends in Late Roman Cappadocia* (2003).

SUSANNA ELM

Magdeburg Centuries The *Magdeburg*

Centuries (or *Ecclesiastica Historia*) are the first comprehensive Protestant history of Christianity and began publication in 1559. This eleven-volume, twelve-thousand-page project took shape under the combined leadership of the scholar and controversialist Matthias Flacius Illyricus and the diplomat Kaspar von Niedbruck, both committed Protestants. The work, written in Latin, was the first to use hundred-year-long periods as a principle of organization. It represents an innovative departure from medieval historiography, which focused on saintly or heroic individuals. For each century, the authors collected data describing the various loci or themes of church history: doctrines, customs, church polity, geographical extent of the church, persecutions, schisms and heresies, and the like. Its authors sought to portray the church holistically, as a unity, and to demonstrate the historical continuity and antiquity of true (i.e., Protestant) teaching, as well as the sources of religious errors. The project continued until the publication of the eleventh volume, covering the thirteenth century, in 1574.

R. E. Diener, "The Magdeburg Centuries: A Bibliothecal and Historiographical Analysis" (ThD thesis, 1978); O. K. Olson, *Matthias Flacius and the Survival of Luther's Reform* (2002); H. Scheible, *Die Entstehung der Magdeburger Zenturien: Ein Beitrag zur Geschichte der Methode* (1966).

NATHAN BARUCH REIN

Magdeburg Confession (1550) The

"Magdeburg Confession" is the name commonly given to a Lutheran confession of faith from the city of Magdeburg, Germany, giving religious justification for the city's refusal to submit politically to its Catholic overlords. The *Confession, Instruction, and Warning of the Pastors and Preachers of the Christian Church of Magdeburg* (the work's full title) bore the signatures of the city's clergymen but was almost certainly written by the pastor Nikolaus Gallus (1516–1570). In the years following the Protestant Reformation, the Schmalkald War (1546–1547), the first of the German religious wars, pitted the Catholic Holy Roman Emperor Charles V and his supporters against an alliance of Protestant princes and cities, including Magdeburg. The war ended in a Catholic victory, but Magdeburg refused to make a formal surrender unless its religious freedom was guaranteed. The Magdeburg Confession argued that the city government, as a "lesser magistrate," was obligated by Christian love and German law to protect its subjects from tyrannical rule imposed from above, particularly the religious tyranny of forced Catholicization. The Confession influenced the development of similar doctrines among Calvinists and contributed to the modern conception of limited political rule.

I. Höss, "Zur Genese der Widerstandslehre Bezas," *ARG* 54 (1963): 198–214; O. Olson, "Theology of Revolution: Magdeburg 1550–1551," *SCJ* 3 (1972): 56–79; C. Schoenberger, "The Development of the Lutheran Theory of Resistance," *SCJ* 8 (1977): 61–76; D. M. Whitford, *Tyranny and Resistance: The Magdeburg Confession and the Lutheran Tradition* (2001).

NATHAN BARUCH REIN

Maimonides (1135/1138–1204), rabbi, codifier, philosopher, and physician. Maimonides' early years in Spain were disrupted by the Almohade conquest in the late 1140s and the concomitant persecution of Jews. After some time his family fled to Fez, and from there he eventually made his way to Egypt, where he became a physician in the royal court and leader of the Jewish community. His sense of communal responsibility extended beyond Egypt; thus, he responded to the beleaguered Jews of Yemen with a classic letter of encouragement in much the way that he had written on an earlier occasion to shore up the morale of a community that had been converted as a result of the Almohade persecution.

He did pathbreaking work in many fields. In medicine, his rationalistic outlook made him wary of empirically untested remedies and led him to appreciate the value of preventive measures, such as a healthful diet, and to understand the impact of psychological factors on somatic conditions. In talmudic studies, his commentary on the Mishnah was the first comprehensive explication of that classic work. His *Book of the Commandments* was the first book

to enumerate the traditional 613 commandments of Judaism within the context of a careful explication of the principles governing such an enumeration. His *Mishneh Torah* is a magisterial, unprecedented, almost breathtaking codification of the totality of Jewish law. While most of his works were written in Arabic, this one was written in a lucid Hebrew style that he had virtually created. In philosophy, his *Guide of the Perplexed* and the philosophical sections of his talmudic works set the agenda for all subsequent Jewish philosophers in the Middle Ages. In the Mishnah commentary, he had constructed a list of thirteen dogmas that he presented as the indispensable building blocks of Judaism. These included a rejection of anthropomorphism, a theme that recurs in his code and again in the early chapters of the *Guide*. The *Guide* goes on to provide a critique of the kalam school of Muslim thought; present proofs of the existence of God; analyze the arguments for and against creation *ex nihilo;* discuss the parameters of providence, theodicy, miracles, and prophecy; and suggest historical reasons for many commandments of the Torah.

Precisely because he bestrode both talmudic and philosophical studies like a colossus, Maimonides became a figure of intense controversy in his lifetime and beyond. Critics objected to the general omission of sources in his code and saw it as an effort to supplant the Talmud. The *Guide* clearly contained controversial assertions on central issues of faith, and some readers in both medieval and modern times have argued that even more radical views can be discerned through an esoteric reading of the work. At the end of his life, Maimonides was impelled to write a *Treatise on the Resurrection* in response to accusations that he denied this cardinal doctrine. None of this, however, undermined his standing as a figure of almost peerless influence and reputation.

M. Maimonides, *The Code of Maimonides*, books 3–14 (1949–); Maimonides, *The Guide of the Perplexed*, trans. S. Pines (1963); I. Twersky, *Introduction to the Code of Maimonides* (1980); D. Yellin and I. Abrahams, *Maimonides, His Life and Works* (1903, repr. 1972).

DAVID BERGER

Major, Georg (1502–1574), Lutheran reformer, preacher, and professor of theology in Wittenberg. During the Schmalkald War, he sided with Melanchthon to support Elector Moritz of Saxony and defended the Leipzig Interim that required Lutherans to continue certain Roman Catholic practices. He lent his name to the Majoristic Controversy, a debate over his statement "Good works are necessary for salvation." He denied that he had ever said it and went on to explain that good works included faith and the entire Christian life. Matters were resolved in 1577 by article four of the Formula of Concord. After the deaths of Bugenhagen and Melanchthon, he became the leader of the Wittenberg faculty in 1560 and was a fringe figure in the Crypto-Calvinist controversy at the university. In his essay on the word of God in 1550, he developed a concept of verbal inspiration. Another of his works traces the doctrine of the Trinity from Adam through the church councils down to his own time.

———

R. Kolb, "Georg Major as Controversialist: Polemics in the Late Reformation," *CH* 45 (1976): 455–68; Kolb, "Major, Georg," in *The Oxford Encyclopedia of the Reformation*, vol. 2 (1998), 237–38; T. Wengert, "Georg Major (1502–1574): Defender of Wittenberg's Faith and Melanchthonian Exegete," in *Melanchthon in seinem Schülern* (1997), 129–56.

DAVID P. SCAER

Major, John (1470–1550), Scottish theologian and historian. Born near Haddington, Scotland, Major studied at Cambridge and Paris, where he became a doctor of theology in 1505. He first taught theology and logic at Paris from 1505 to 1518, where he produced his *Commentary on the Four Books of the Sentences of Peter Lombard* (1509). He taught at Glasgow from 1518 to 1523 and had John Knox as a student. While at Glasgow, he wrote a commentary on Matthew (1518) and his *History of Greater Britain, both England and Scotland* (1521). He taught at St. Andrews from 1523 to 1525. He returned to Paris from 1525 to 1530, where he produced a commentary on the four Gospels (1529). In 1530 he was named provost of St. Salvator's College at St. Andrews, where he remained until his death. Major sought to bring together England and Scotland in his history, and nominalism and realism in his theology.

———

A. Broadie, *The Circle of John Mair: Logic and Logicians in Pre-Reformation Scotland* (1985).

RANDALL C. ZACHMAN

Mandeism Along the rivers of Iraq and Iran can be found traces of the last extant group of gnostics, the Mandeans (from *mandayi*, Mandaic word meaning "gnosis" or "knowledge") who hold that Christ was a false Mes-

siah. Mandeans actually call themselves the "elect of righteousness" or the "race of life" and consider themselves to be chosen possessors of secret knowledge. In their beliefs, the cosmos is divided into a World of Light, ruled by the Great Spirit or the Great Life, and the World of Darkness, governed by the evil dragon Ur and the evil spirit Ruha. These two latter evil forces produced a number of offspring, among which are the Seven (planets) and the Twelve (signs of the Zodiac). Mandeans also believe in four distinct lives, the fourth of which, Ptahil, created the world in conjunction with seven planets, the twelve signs of the zodiac, and Ruha. They also believe that humans are dualistic beings formed of physical Adam, corrupt like the world in which he lives, and secret Adam, a spiritual essence derived from the World of Light. It is this secret part of humanity that can be redeemed in Mandaean thought. Their sacred literature includes the *Ginza*, or *Sidra Rabba*, the *Drasha Dyahya*, and *Qolasta*.

———

W. Barnstone, ed., *The Other Bible: Ancient Alternative Scriptures* (1984); W. Barnstone and M. Meyer, eds., *The Gnostic Bible* (2003); W. Foerster, ed., *Coptic and Mandean Sources*, vol. 2 of *Gnosis: A Selection of Gnostic Texts* (1974); K. Rudolf, *Gnosis: The Nature and History of Gnosticism* (1983).

RODNEY S. SADLER JR.

Mani (216–277), founder of Manicheism, a world religion, and a religious author and missionary. Born in Babylonia during the Persian occupation, at ages twelve and twenty-four Mani received divine revelations that convinced him that he was to bring to completion the religions of Buddha, Zoroaster, and Jesus. His followers identified him with the Paraclete, the messenger that was to be sent to complete Jesus' mission on earth. Mani referred to himself as the Apostle of Jesus Christ.

Around 242 he traveled to India, then returned to Persia where, with the help of King Shapur, he proclaimed his Religion of Light. For the next thirty years, Mani's religion spread throughout Mesopotamia and the adjacent regions, east and west. After the death of Shapur he fell into disfavor with Bahram I and was executed in 277.

The canon of Mani's writings contains seven books. Though none of these works have survived intact, extracts preserved in the polemical writings of Christian, Syriac, and Arabic authors long made possible a fragmentary knowledge of them. In the twentieth century, the number of authentic, extant Manichean texts increased enormously. Manuscript discoveries in China, Algeria, and Egypt have enabled scholars to reconstruct the main tenets of Manicheism.

Mani's teaching on salvation explains the origin of evil in terms of a radical dualism. The cosmic drama of salvation unfolds within the framework of three moments. The initial moment, Former Time, consists of a period prior to the existence of heaven and earth in which the two co-eternal principles of light and darkness are separated from each other. The light principle, identified with God, the Father of Greatness, possesses characteristics such as goodness, tranquility, and wisdom and dwells in the realm of light. The dark principle, composed of matter, is Satan. Inherently evil, it governs the realm of darkness with qualities antithetical to those of light.

The second moment, Present Time, constitutes a period of constant conflict between light and dark particles that, in a mixed state, comprise the temporal world. This mixture arose when the principle of darkness attacked the kingdom of light and imprisoned some of its particles in the darkness. The light principle fought back to rescue the light particles. Initially unsuccessful, it then sent Jesus to Adam and Eve to reveal the light of divine knowledge (*gnosis*).

The Manicheans refused to identify Jesus with the incarnate Christ who died on the cross, because they regarded the human body as the evil fruit of satanic copulation. Instead, they differentiated Jesus the Splendor, light particles gathered in the sun and the moon and awaiting transfer to the kingdom of light, from the Suffering Jesus, the light (soul) trapped in the demonic matter of the human body, groaning for release.

Salvation consists in the separation of the light and dark particles. The Manichean clergy, the Elect or perfect ones, effect this release through digestion of prescribed foods containing light particles. The Auditors, or lay catechumens, supply the food from which the light particles are expelled into the air. This process continues until the third, and final, moment occurs—the end of the world, or The Future Time, when a conflagration will erupt, ending the mixture of particles. The world will vanish. The original state of separation will emerge, though some of the light particles will remain trapped forever in darkness.

In the years following Mani's death, Manicheism spread throughout the Roman Empire, where it was regarded as a virulent form of Christian heresy. By the sixth century, it had almost entirely ceased to exist in the West, though some scholars have conjectured that during the Middle Ages the Cathars in Western Europe were the descendants of the Manichees. Augustine of Hippo, the most famous adherent of Western Manicheism, remained an Auditor for nine years until his conversion to Christianity.

In the East, Manicheism established a foothold in eastern Iran. From there, travelers carried the religion along the Silk Road to China. In the eighth century, Manicheism became the official religion of the Uighur Turks, who disseminated it throughout China. It later flourished in the Tarim Basin until the time of Jinghis Khan. Traces of Manicheism can be found in Fukien until the sixteenth century.

R. Cameron and A. J. Dewey, *The Cologne Mani Codex (P. Colon. Inv. nr. 4780): Concerning the Origin of His Body* (1979); I. Gardner, *The Kephalia of the Teacher* (1995); S. N. C. Lieu, *Manichaeism in the Later Roman Empire and Medieval China* (1985); G. B. Mikkelsen, *Bibliographia Manichaica: A Comprehensive Bibliography of Manichaeism through 1996* (1997).

MARIANNE DJUTH

Manicheanism   see Cathars; Dualism; Dualism, Medieval; Mani

Mantz, Felix (d. 1527), leader and first martyr of Zurich Anabaptism. Mantz, an illegitimate son of a Zurich canon, received a humanistic education and became one of Huldrych Zwingli's most avid initial supporters. He soon joined the radical opposition and signed the 1524 letters to Thomas Müntzer that articulated the radicals' dissatisfaction with the pace of reform in Zurich. After seeing to the publication of several radical works of Andreas Bodenstein von Karlstadt, Mantz presented Zurich's city council with his *Protestation*, in which he argued against infant baptism. Mantz, along with Conrad Grebel and the rural pastor William Reublin, participated in the disputation on baptism held before the city council on January 17, 1525. When the council declared its support for Zwingli's position and forbade the radicals from meeting, Mantz and his associates made the final break with the magisterial reformation by rebaptizing one another.

In the following two years, Mantz worked energetically to popularize the movement. He was active in Swiss territory and was seen especially in the Zurich countryside during or immediately after the Peasants' War of 1525. Early on, he articulated the position on nonresistance that would come to characterize much of Swiss Anabaptism. In 1526 the Zurich authorities captured him along with Conrad Grebel and Georg Blaurock. After escaping, Mantz was recaptured in December 1526. Because he had broken his solemn oath to baptize no one else, he was punished with execution by drowning on January 5, 1527, in the River Limmat.

L. Harder, *The Sources of Swiss Anabaptism* (1985); C. A. Pater, *Karlstadt as the Father of the Baptist Movements* (1984); G. H. Williams, *The Radical Reformation* (3rd ed., 1992).

D. JONATHAN GRIESER

Mar Aba I (fl. 540–552), Catholicos (patriarch) of Seleucia-Ctesiphon. The Church of the East was caught in a bitter schism in the years 524–539, with rival claimants to the office of catholicos appointing rival bishops in many places. The schism was ended with the election of Mar Aba in 540. He immediately set out on a tour of the disputed sees and quickly settled questions of episcopal succession. His decisions were ratified by the Synod of Mar Aba (c. 544). This same synod officially accepted the decrees and canons of the Council of Chalcedon. He inaugurated a reform program that included founding a school in Seleucia-Ctesiphon based on the model of Nisbis, and he advocated monastic revival and moral reform.

In 544, there was a fresh outbreak of hostilities with the Roman Empire, which precipitated fresh hostility against Christians. The Zoroastrians denounced Mar Aba to Khusro I for being a convert from Zoroastrianism and for proselytizing. Because of his respect for Mar Aba's leadership of the Christian minority, Khusro sentenced him to prison and then exile in Azerbaijan, rather than to death. After seven years of governing his see from exile, he was able to return but continued to face difficult circumstances.

R. Duval, *Synodicon Orientale* (1902); S. H. Moffett, *A History of Christianity in Asia* (1992).

EUGENE M. LUDWIG, OFM CAP.

Mar Thoma (St. Thomas) Church
The term is a general name for the group of churches originating in southern India from Syrian missionaries. According to tradition, the apostle Thomas arrived at Kodungalur (state of Kerala) in 52 CE. The fourth-century Syriac *Acts of Judas Thomas* provides a legend of how Thomas introduced an ascetical Christianity into India.

Syrian merchants and missionaries settled in southern India early in the millennium. They established a church with strong Near Eastern connections and used Syriac in the liturgy and vernacular. Although the bishops were generally Syrian, indigenous priests and deacons were the rule. The church adapted itself to Indian culture and found a place in the caste system.

Conflict for control of the Indian church has been continual, first with the Near Eastern church, then starting in the 1500s, with European missionaries and Rome. The Synod of Diamper (1599) forcibly united the East Syrians with Rome, but after the Dutch replaced the Portuguese, most Christians joined the Syrian Orthodox Church. There are about seven million adherents, divided among numerous communions.

L. W. Brown, *The Indian Christians of St. Thomas* (1956, 1982); A. F. J. Klijn, trans., *The Acts of Thomas* (1962); J. Vellian, ed., *The Malabar Church* (1970).

ROBERT A. KITCHEN

Marburg Colloquy (1529), a dialog between Huldrych Zwingli and Martin Luther, along with followers of each. Since 1525 Zwingli and Luther had engaged in sharp polemical exchange over the definition of the presence of Christ in the Lord's Supper. Zwingli's views rested upon the Neoplatonic presumptions he had learned in Basel and Vienna, above all—that matter could do no more than symbolize the spiritual, and that Christ's human body was restricted to one location in heaven after his ascension. Luther's nominalist training enabled him to believe that God was able to determine that material elements, such as bread and wine, could convey Christ's body and blood and effect God's forgiveness, and that a literal interpretation of the words of institution was thus proper. Their series of published polemical exchanges frustrated efforts at establishing a united political front among evangelicals in the German Empire against the suppressive religious policies of Emperor Charles V. Therefore, Landgrave Philip of Hesse invited representatives of the Swiss and the Wittenberg Reformation movements to his castle in Marburg for a three-day meeting on October 1–4, 1529. Luther, Melanchthon, Johannes Brenz, and three others represented the Lutherans; Zwingli and Johannes Oecolampadius of Basel led the delegation of Swiss and Strasbourg theologians. The two sides reached agreement on fourteen articles touching the doctrines of God, justification, God's Word, baptism, good works, confession and absolution, secular government, and tradition, but they failed to come to agreement on the presence of Christ in the Supper. They rejected the medieval doctrine of the Mass and the refusal to provide laypeople with Communion in both kinds; they agreed that the Supper is a "sacrament of the true body and blood of Christ, and the spiritual reception of the body and blood is particularly necessary for every Christian," but they disagreed on the bodily presence of Christ. The polemic between Wittenberg and Zurich did not resume before Zwingli's death (1531).

W. Köhler, *Zwingli und Luther*, 2 vols. (1924, 1953); R. Kolb and J. Nestingen, *Sources and Contexts of the Book of Concord* (2001); H. Sasse, *This Is My Body: Luther's Contention for the Real Presence* (1959).

ROBERT KOLB

Marcella (d. c. 410), Roman ascetic, friend of Jerome. Most of our knowledge of Marcella is based on Jerome's letters, especially Epistle 127, written to her companion Principia after Marcella's death. Jerome identifies Marcella as the first "high-born" woman in Rome to take on the monastic life. After a short marriage and the death of her husband, Marcella made her home the center of a small circle of ascetic women. Jerome credits her with Eustochium's ascetic training. She was an avid scholar of Scripture who convinced Jerome, shortly after his arrival in 382, to study with her and the others. After his departure in 385 their correspondence continued; in Rome Marcella became a sought-after authority on Scripture. So insistent were Marcella's questions on scriptural interpretation and Hebrew vocabulary that Jerome complained of her torments and called her his "task mistress" (Letters 28.1; 29.1) He credits her with leading the refutation of the Origenists in Rome. She and her cousin Pammachius were among Jerome's strongest supporters and among the most active opponents of the Origenists. Despite an invitation from Paula and Eustochium (Letter 46), she did not join them and Jerome in Bethlehem. She died days after being physically attacked during the invasion of Rome.

Jerome, *Letters*; E. A. Clark, *The Origenist Controversy* (1992), 27–30; J. N. D. Kelly, *Jerome* (1975), 91–103.

TERESA M. SHAW

Marcellus of Ancyra (c. 285–374), defender of Nicaea and reputed heretic. By 314 Marcellus was bishop of Ancyra in central Asia Minor. In 325 he took part in the Council of Nicaea and became one of its staunchest defenders, opposing the Arian teaching of Asterius the Sophist. His theology was unacceptable to the majority of Eastern bishops. He was deposed at a synod in Constantinople in 336. In 339/340 he was in Rome, as Athanasius was. He accompanied the Western bishops to the Synod of Sardica in 343, in which the Eastern bishops refused to participate because Athanasius and Marcellus were to be seated. Around 345 Athanasius broke off communion with Marcellus, probably only temporarily. Marcellus was still alive in 371 when his deacon Eugenius sought to maintain communion with Athanasius. He died in 374.

Apart from a letter addressed to Julius of Rome, Marcellus's only certainly authentic writing is his *Against Asterius*, extant only in fragments. The heart of Marcellus's theology is his adherence to the phrase "one *hypostasis*" ("one substance," "one reality") to describe God. He may have proposed a kind of economic Trinitarianism, in which the Son and the Holy Spirit emerge to carry out the work of redemption and sanctification. His failing was probably due more to theological naiveté than to Sabellianism, of which he was often accused. The phrase "of his kingdom there will be no end," found in the Creed of Constantinople (381) and many other creeds, is directed against Marcellus, because he wrote that in the end Christ would hand over the kingdom to the Father (1 Cor. 15:24).

J. T. Lienhard, *Contra Marcellum: Marcellus of Ancyra and Fourth-Century Theology* (1999); M. Vinzent, ed. and trans., *Die Fragmente; Der Brief an Julius von Rom* (1997).

JOSEPH T. LIENHARD

Marcian (r. 450–457), Roman emperor. The Eastern emperor Theodosius II was succeeded by Marcian, an elderly senator whose nominal marriage to Theodosius's sister Pulcheria made him part of the established imperial dynasty. Marcian decided to terminate the payment of the weighty annual subsidies to the Huns and was rewarded when they turned their attentions to the West. Marcian also addressed the religious divisions caused by the christological controversy and exacerbated by the Monophysite-dominated "Robber Synod." To deal with the problem, Marcian summoned the Fourth Ecumenical Council in 451, which was held at Chalcedon, south of Constantinople. The council disallowed Monophysite teachings, but the Monophysites continued to have a wide following in Egypt (where they survive as the Copts), in Syria, and in the New Persian Empire. The Council of Chalcedon also sowed the seeds of contention between East and West by making the bishop of Constantinople equal in status to the bishop of Rome. Pope Leo and his successors refused to accept this, and the offensive clause was omitted from proceedings of the council that were used in the West. Marcian died in early 457 and was succeeded by Leo (r. 457–474), who commenced a new dynasty.

B. Croke, "The Date and Circumstances of Marcian's Decease, A.D. 457," *Byzantion* 48 (1978): 5–9; E. A. Thompson, "The Foreign Policies of Theodosius II and Marcian," *Hermanthena* 76 (1950): 58–75.

RALPH W. MATHISEN

Marcion (c. 85–c. 160), teacher widely condemned as a heretic. Marcion's life and work are known only from writers who sought to refute and discredit him, but he still emerges as an impressive figure. A merchant from Sinope on the Black Sea coast of Asia Minor, Marcion seems to have arrived in Rome sometime after 140. When his teaching led to a breach with the main Christian community there, he founded his own church, which spread quickly throughout the Roman world and lasted at least four centuries.

Marcion sharply distinguished Jesus' loving God and Father from the angry and jealous God of the Old Testament who had said, "I create evil" (Isa. 45:7). He accepted the OT's account of creation, of the giving of the law, and of the history of Israel, along with its prophecies of a coming warrior messiah, but he denied the identification of that messiah with Jesus Christ. Rather, a previously unknown God, alien to our world and not responsible for it, mercifully took pity on humanity and sent Jesus in the appearance of a man to proclaim a gospel of grace. Marcion denied that Jesus had implicated himself in the Creator God's world through human birth and fleshly resurrection, but he affirmed the

crucifixion, which gave Jesus the opportunity to preach the gospel in Hades. In keeping with his rejection of the Creator God, Marcion taught abstinence from marriage and procreation.

Rejecting the continuing validity of the OT, Marcion pioneered the notion of a distinctively Christian Scripture. He edited the Gospel of Luke and ten epistles of Paul (excluding the Pastorals and Hebrews) to make them consistent with his theology. (He saw this as a necessary reconstruction of works that had been corrupted by the Judaizers whom Paul condemned as preaching a "different gospel.") He also composed *The Antitheses*, a book in which he contrasted the God of the OT with the God Jesus proclaimed.

Marcion's place in the history of Christianity is disputed. At the very least, seminal thinkers such as Tertullian and Origen developed their own thought, in large measure, in reaction to his. Ancient Christian writers such as Irenaeus, for whom the primary criterion of heretical gnosis was the denial of the identity of the God and Father of Jesus Christ with the God of the OT, stressed the affinity of Marcion's ideas with gnostics such as Basilides and Valentinus. Modern writers are more inclined to stress his distinctiveness. Harnack's work on Marcion remains essential eighty years after its final edition, although contemporary scholars are skeptical of his interpretation of Marcion as a precursor of his own liberal Protestantism.

A. von Harnack, *Marcion: The Gospel of the Alien God* (1990); G. May, "Marcion in Contemporary Views: Results and Open Questions," *SecCent* 6 (1987/1988): 129–51; G. May and K. Greschat, eds., *Marcion und seine kirchengeschichtliche Wirkung/Marcion and His Impact on Church History* (2002); *Texte und Untersuchungen*, vol. 150 (2002).

JOSEPH W. TRIGG

Marcus Aurelius (121–180), Stoic philosopher and Roman emperor (161–180). His writings include letters to his tutor Fronto and his masterpiece, *To Himself*, later titled the *Meditations*. Themes addressed here include a history of Stoic philosophy, the desire for reflection, political and social obligation, the inevitability of death and resignation toward it, and the implausibility of immortality. Anger, like all emotions, is forbidden. He advocates compassion for the weak and evil and love for humanity. Happiness lies in patient acceptance of the will of a pantheistic Stoic God, the material soul of a material universe.

A supporter of traditional Roman religion, Marcus Aurelius thought Christianity a danger to the state. Although he did not support a general persecution of Christians, he held that they were to be executed unless they sacrificed to the gods.

E. V. Arnold, *Roman Stoicism* (1911); E. Asmis, "The Stoicism of Marcus Aurelius," in *ANRW* 2.36.3 (1989): 2228–52; P. A. Brunt, "Marcus Aurelius and the Christians," *Studies in Latin Literature and Roman History* 1 (1979): 483–520; L. Edelstein, *The Meaning of Stoicism* (1966); M. Grant, *The Antonines: The Roman Empire in Transition* (1994); A. A. Long, *Hellenistic Philosophy* (1986); Marcus Aurelius, *Meditations*, trans. G. M. A. Grube (1963); J. M. Rist, *Stoic Philosophy* (1969); S. Sambursky, *The Physics of the Stoics* (1959).

ROBERT M. BERCHMAN

Marguerite d'Angoulême (1492–1549), queen of Navarre, woman of letters, and an influential supporter of evangelical reform in sixteenth-century France. Her close relationship with her brother, King Francis I, accounted for her extraordinary leverage in religious matters. Her support of Bishop Guillaume Briçonnet's efforts to reform the diocese of Meaux, and her protection of evangelically oriented reformers such as Jacques Lefèvre d'Etaples, Gérard Roussel, and Clément Marot, pitted her against the theologians of the Sorbonne who were determined to stamp out every hint of the "Lutheran" heresy. Marguerite's sponsorship in Paris of the enormously popular 1533 Lenten sermons of Roussel prompted the Sorbonne to question the orthodoxy of her devotional poem *The Mirror of the Sinful Soul.*

Marguerite then fostered a circle of reformists in her territories in the southwest of France and focused on her own literary efforts. A series of her novellas was published posthumously as *The Heptameron.* Those in her orbit tended to reject a schismatic solution to the church's troubles. Marguerite's own religious position is hard to identify with precision. She seems to have melded influences from Lefèvre, Luther, Calvin, Neoplatonist writers, and sixteenth-century spiritualists with her own mystical inclinations in a unique religious synthesis.

C. Thysell, *The Pleasure of Discernment: Marguerite de Navarre as Theologian* (2000).

CHRISTOPHER ELWOOD

Marguerite Porete (d. 1310), Flemish mystical author of *The Mirror of Simple Souls.*

Little is known about the life of Marguerite Porete except from the records of the heresy trial that resulted in her death. Her accusers labeled her a Beguine—a member of a women-only lay community that required no vows and dedicated itself to charity and devotion—but they meant it as an insult because of the association of unorthodox mystical beliefs with them. Her writing suggests that she was well educated in courtly literature, as well as biblical and other religious texts. In the early 1300s she lived in the Hainaut region in eastern Belgium, and sometime before 1306 *The Mirror of Simple Souls* was condemned by the bishop of Cambrai and publicly burned. When asked to make concessions regarding her book and beliefs, Marguerite refused. She even added seventeen chapters, sought its approval by another bishop, John of Châlons-sur-Marne, and continued to circulate it. She was tried by the Inquisition at Paris, condemned as a relapsed heretic, and burned at the stake on June 1, 1310.

The Mirror of Simple Souls influenced mystics for centuries, most importantly Meister Eckhart. One of its central tenets is that annihilation of the will is a form of freedom and that it is only through this abandonment of the will that all separation between humans and their creator will be removed.

E. Z. Brunn and G. Epiney-Burgard, *Women Mystics in Medieval Europe* (1989); E. Colledge, trans., *The Mirror of Simple Souls by Marguerite Porete* (1999); A. Hollywood, *The Soul as Virgin Wife: Mechthild of Magdeburg, Marguerite Porete, and Meister Eckhart* (1995).

TODD M. RICHARDSON

Marian Devotion The foundation for devotion to the Virgin Mary, mother of Jesus, was first laid during the second century. It was one aspect of the growing veneration for the saints, especially the martyrs. The apocryphal *Early Gospel of James* appeared by the latter part of the century. Written to fill in the gaps left by the canonical Gospels, it told of Mary's remarkable conception, granted as an answer to the prayer of her aging and childless parents, Anne and Joachim. This writing already asserted Mary's perpetual virginity, including her virginity *in partu,* or in childbirth. Taught by several theologians of the late second and early third centuries, this belief is certainly one of the main reasons that Mary became an inspiration for the early monastic community. Prayers and hymns to Mary began to be written by the beginning of the fourth century when

Marian devotion truly blossomed, particularly in the Eastern church.

The earliest doctrinal statements regarding Mary occurred in connection with councils called to decide christological issues. Ephesus (431) declared the Virgin to be Theotokos, or "God-bearer," and Chalcedon (451) declared her perpetual virginity when it adopted Pope Leo I's *Tome*, which included this belief. The dogmas of Mary's assumption into heaven and her immaculate conception were also generally popular, though not universally accepted, in the early medieval church. They were not declared official Catholic dogmas until the modern period—the immaculate conception in 1854 and the assumption in 1950. The immaculate conception stirred the greatest controversy due to opposition by significant theologians, including Thomas Aquinas.

The highest level of Marian devotion in the West was reached in the twelfth century. Inspired by the courtly love tradition of the troubadours, the Virgin became "Our Lady," honored with love songs and poetry. During this time, devotion to Mary, like the official doctrines, focused on her bodily relationship with Christ and her participation in the mystery of the incarnation. She had given her flesh to become the body of the Son of God. For nine months God had dwelt within her. The mystical unity of their shared flesh ensured her special ability to suffer with her son at the cross and made her the ultimate source of the body of Christ received in the eucharistic host. It also ensured her place in heaven as intercessor with her son on behalf of sinners.

A shift in Marian piety began to occur, however, in the late medieval and early modern period. Because of a growing emphasis on interior religion fostered by increased literacy, a new focus on the individual, new forms of piety such as the rosary, and the impact of the Protestant Reformation, preachers and artists began to highlight Mary's soul and her spiritual motherhood of Jesus and to downplay her physical role. This trend has generally continued into the modern era.

———

D. S. Ellington, *From Sacred Body to Angelic Soul: Understanding Mary in Late Medieval and Early Modern Europe* (2001); H. Graef, *Mary: A History of Doctrine and Devotion* (1963, 1994); J. Pelikan, *Mary through the Centuries: Her Place in the History of Culture* (1996); A. Winston-Allen, *Stories of the Rose: The Making of the Rosary in the Middle Ages* (1997).

DONNA SPIVEY ELLINGTON

Mariana, Juan de (1536–1624), Spanish historian and political philosopher. Educated at Alcalá, he joined the Jesuit order in 1554 and began a teaching career, first in Rome, then Sicily and Paris. In 1574 he returned permanently to Toledo for health reasons. He wrote two important works: *Historiae de rebus Hispaniae* (*A History of Spain*, 1592) and *De rege et regis institutione* (*On the King and the Institution of Kingship*, 1599). He wrote *De rege* for Phillip II of Spain. In it Mariana attacks royal absolutism, advocates a constitutional monarchy through the consent of the governed, and supports the right to assassinate a tyrannous king. His advocacy of tyrannicide made the work and Mariana famous and controversial. After the assassination of Henry IV of France in 1610, Mariana's work was widely condemned and became a source of anti-Jesuit polemic.

———

G. Lewy, *Constitutionalism and Statecraft During the Golden Age of Spain: A Study of the Political Philosophy of Juan De Mariana, S.J.* (1960).

DAVID WHITFORD

Marie de l'Incarnation (1599–1672), French missionary and educator in New France (Quebec), beatified in 1980. A widowed mother before she was twenty, Marie Guyart, strong and self-reliant, supported herself and her young son as manager of her brother-in-law's business. Claiming mystical visions, she left her son in her sister's care and became an Ursuline nun. Then as Marie de l'Incarnation, she left France to evangelize the natives of what later became Quebec. She opened the first Ursuline school there, learned the Algonquin and Iroquois languages and prepared dictionaries for both, and resolutely maintained her order's independence when the local bishop sought greater control. Respected both for strong-willed competence and selfless compassion, she was much sought after as a counselor, leaving behind a living chronicle of life in New France in a correspondence of over twelve thousand letters.

———

M.-F. Bruneau, *Women Mystics Confront the Modern World: Marie De L'Incarnation (1599–1672) and Madame Guyon (1648–1717)* (1998); G.-M. Oury, *Marie de l'Incarnation*, 2 vols. (1973).

PETER J. SCAGNELLI

Maronite Church (Antiochian Syrian Maronite Church) The designation refers to a religious community of Syrian origin in formal communion with the Roman Catholic Church. The Maronites trace their origin to Maron, a fourth-century ascetic whose life story is recorded in the *Historia Religiosa* (16) of Theodoret of Cyrrhus. His disciples formed the monastery of Bet Maroun in Syria Secunda in 452. Because they accepted the Council of Chalcedon, the monks found themselves in opposition to the Monophysites.

The Maronites adhered to the formula of Monotheletism that affirms one will in the two natures of Christ, in line with Emperor Heraclius's attempt at doctrinal unity of 638. When the doctrine was eventually condemned at Constantinople in 681, the Maronites did not change their position. The resulting persecution forced them to migrate to isolated mountains in Lebanon.

During the Crusades, many Maronites joined the Crusaders and abandoned their Monotheletism. Others resisted the alliance. Patriarch Jeremiah al-'Amshiti (1199–1230) visited Rome and was formally recognized by the pope as head of the Maronite Church (1215). Pope Gregory XIII founded the Maronite College in Rome (1584) to educate Maronite clergy in the Roman Catholic tradition.

As a Uniat church, Maronites have their own liturgy, conducted in Arabic and Syriac. A new liturgy (1993) resembles closely the original Syrian Mass.

———

S. J. Beggiani, *Early Syriac Theology, with Special Reference to the Maronite Tradition* (1983); M. Moosa, *The Maronites in History* (1986).

                                        ROBERT A. KITCHEN

Marot, Clément (c. 1496–1544), French

Renaissance poet and author of the first collection of metrical psalms in French. Trained in law, Marot became a favored poet in the royal court. Arrested and imprisoned in 1526 for heresy, he was protected by his royal patrons, Marguerite d'Angoulême and her brother, King Francis I. After the affair of the placards (1534) and the ensuing religious repression, Marot left France for the court of the duchess of Ferrara, Renée de France. He responded to Francis's offer of pardon to all exiles who abjured heresy and returned home in 1536. But when proceedings against heretics escalated in 1542, Marot left France for Geneva, since his opponents associated him with Calvin. Marot's versification of the Psalms, begun in 1530, had been adopted by Calvin in his earliest liturgy. While Marot did not remain long in Geneva, the fifty-two metrical psalms he created

became a centerpiece of the Reformed piety Geneva exported to many parts of Europe. The success of the French Psalter, completed in 1562 by Theodore Beza, made Marot's psalms by far the most popular French poetry of the sixteenth century.

———

M. A. Screech, *Clément Marot: A Renaissance Poet Discovers the Gospel* (1994).

                                        CHRISTOPHER ELWOOD

Marpeck, Pilgram (c. 1495–1556), leader

of the South German Anabaptists after 1530. Marpeck was born at Rattenburg, in the Austrian Tirol, where he became a mining engineer. By 1525 he was both a mining magistrate and member of the city's upper council. In 1528 he abruptly resigned his offices and left Rattenburg, leaving behind considerable property. Undoubtedly these actions reflected his conversion to Anabaptism.

After brief stops in the mining regions of Bohemia and Moravia, Marpeck settled in Strasbourg, where he became a city engineer. He assumed leadership of Strasbourg's Anabaptist community around 1529. His caustic public criticisms of church affairs in the city eventually compelled Strasbourg's leading reformer, Martin Bucer (1491–1551), to move against him, and he was exiled in 1532.

For the next several years he probably lived in Switzerland, traveling to and from Austrian territories and Moravia. In the early 1540s he engaged Caspar Schwenckfeld (1489–1561) in a printed debate regarding baptism. He settled in Augsburg in 1544, where he lived the rest of his life. He was employed again as a city engineer and also assumed leadership of the city's Anabaptist congregation. Marpeck was threatened with prosecution for his Anabaptist activities several times, but he managed to retain his civil position. Although not a trained theologian, he was a prolific writer.

———

S. B. Boyd, *Pilgram Marpeck: His Life and Social Theology* (1992); W. Klassen, *Covenant and Community: The Life, Writings, and Hermeneutics of Pilgram Marpeck* (1968).

                                        DAVID B. ELLER

Marprelate Tracts   These writings were a

series of extreme Puritan tracts by various English authors, published in 1588–1589 under the pseudonym Martin Marprelate. These pamphlets violently attacked Elizabeth I's moderate Protestantism and cooperative episcopacy, which were fundamental to royal policy. The authors felt that Elizabeth's Protestantism was still too conservative, especially in its reliance on episcopal hierarchy, and advocated a more presbyterial organization. Archbishops John Whitgift and Richard Bancroft both vigorously, but unsuccessfully, used the archbishopric's coercive judicial powers to suppress the tracts. The principal authors were probably Job Throckmorton, a politician; John Udall, a curate from Surrey; and John Penry, a London Separatist. Throckmorton successfully denied the accusations. Udall was arrested and sentenced to death in 1590; he died in prison in 1592. Penry fled to Wales to avoid arrest; returning to London in 1592, he was hanged for treason. Significant replies were published by Bancroft, Bishop Cooper of Winchester (the tract *Hay any Work for Cooper* attacks him specifically), and Thomas Nash.

L. Carlson, *Martin Marprelate* (1981); D. McGinn, *John Penry and the Marprelate Controversy* (1966); R. McKerrow and F. Wilson, eds., *Works of Thomas Nashe*, vol. 5 (1958), 34–65; W. Pierce, ed., *Marprelate Tracts* (1911, 1967).

DAVID A. LOPEZ

Marranos Pejorative Iberian reference to Jewish and Muslim converts to Christianity, especially to Jewish converts who continued to practice their old religion in secrecy. While belief in widespread apostasy among Jewish converts (also known as *conversos*, or *Cristianos nuevos*) stood behind the establishment of the Spanish Inquisition (1478), the incidence of this practice remains a matter of intense historiographical debate. Some scholars argue that Jewish converts were fully assimilated into Christian society, while other scholars hold that the observance of Jewish religious rites and festivities was common among new Christians.

B. Netanyahu, *The Marranos of Spain: From the Late 14th to the Early 16th Century* (3rd ed., 1999).

RADY ROLDÁN-FIGUEROA

Marriage Courts, Reformation *see* Reformation Marriage Courts

Marriage, Early Christian From its inception, Christian teaching on marriage was decidedly rigorous. The Synoptic Gospels preserve traditions of Jesus' prohibiting divorce (Mark 10:5–9; Luke 16:18). Matthew's Gospel,

however, adds the important qualification "except on account of unchastity" (Matt. 5:32; 19:9). Paul confirms that this tradition is based on a saying of the Lord (1 Cor. 7:10–11). While Paul expresses his preference that Christians remain unmarried, he allows that it is no sin to marry (1 Cor. 7:39). Later NT writings evince more positive attitudes. The Letter to the Ephesians (5:22–33) teaches that the love of husband and wife can reflect the love of Christ and the church, and the Pastoral Epistles assume that a church overseer (*episkopos*) should be a "man of one wife" (1 Tim. 3:2; Titus 1:6) who has proved his suitability for office by managing his household properly (1 Tim. 3:4–5).

In the second century the question of remarriage after the death of a spouse was widely discussed. Although Paul had allowed Christians to remarry (1 Cor. 7:39), some regarded remarriage as merely "well veiled adultery" (Athenagoras, *Supplication* 33). Rigorist groups, such as the Montanists, made single marriage the centerpiece of their moral practice (e.g., Tertullian, *On Monogamy*). But most Christians followed Paul's advice and regarded second marriage as an acceptable, if inferior, alternative to perpetual widowhood (Hermas, *Mandates* 4.32).

In the second century some radical Christian groups forbade marriage altogether. Marcion believed that an evil creator-god made the world; therefore, he considered procreation to be evil. Others, such as Tatian, the reputed founder of the "Encratites," accepted the created world as good but regarded sex and marriage as symptoms of the "original sin" of Adam and Eve. By the end of the second century, Christian leaders such as Irenaeus of Lyon and Clement of Alexandria responded to the views of Marcion and Tatian and defended sex and marriage, at least for the purpose of procreation. Following the lead of the Pastoral Epistles, Clement envisioned the Christian household as the ideal context for the practice of virtue (*Miscellanies* 3).

When Christianity gained legal toleration in the early fourth century, the situation of the church in relation to the social and political world changed dramatically. Bishops and other church leaders were faced with the question of how to Christianize the marital mores of new converts. John Chrysostom, presbyter at Antioch and later bishop of Constantinople, was the first to acknowledge that the Christian family was the place where Christian moral formation should begin (e.g., *On Vain Glory and the Proper Way to Raise Children*). At the same time the spread of the monastic movement increased the popularity of the ascetic ideal. Many Christians began to see marriage as greatly inferior to celibacy. Although some Christians resisted this development, a moral hierarchy eventually was established: faithful Christian marriage was regarded as occupying a third rank, below perpetual virginity and widowhood.

In the fourth century there was a movement toward the Christianization of marriage by means of Christian rituals. For example, in late fourth-century Rome it was common for a bishop to pronounce a blessing over the couple and to cover the bride's head with a veil (Siricius, Letters 1.4.5 and 7.3). Official formulas for nuptial blessings, however, are not found until the seventh century (*Verona Sacramentary*). In the East, clergy in the fourth century were also starting to participate in weddings by bestowing crowns on the married couple and pronouncing a blessing. Such rituals, however, were not required for the validity of a marriage until a much later date.

The writings of Augustine of Hippo (354–430) provided the first true Christian theology of marriage. Rejecting the dualism of the Manichees and the extremes of some Christian ascetics, Augustine insisted that Christian marriage consisted of three "goods": the procreation of children, sexual fidelity, and indissolubility. Augustine regarded the last of these goods as the true "sacrament" in marriage. Augustine's emphasis on the role of original sin in corrupting sexual desire, however, has tended to obscure this positive teaching.

J. Evans Grubbs, *Law and Family in Late Antiquity: The Emperor Constantine's Marriage Legislation* (1995); D. G. Hunter, *Marriage in the Early Church* (1992); T. Mackin, *The Marital Sacrament* (1989); P. L. Reynolds, *Marriage in the Western Church: The Christianization of Marriage During the Patristic and Early Medieval Periods* (1994); K. Ritzer, *Le mariage dans les Églises chrétiennes du Ier au XIe siècle* (1970); K. Stevenson, *Nuptial Blessing: A Study of Christian Marriage Rites* (1983).

DAVID G. HUNTER

Marriage, Medieval Church

There was a tension in early Christianity between asceticism and marriage. From its beginnings, Christianity emphasized the mutual relationship between husband and wife. Yet Paul viewed chastity as the superior Christian way of life and marriage as a vehicle to harness human sexuality and prevent adultery. Augustine stressed the procreative purpose of marital sexuality. Early theologians such as John Chrysostom and Jerome were especially moved to develop a highly critical view of marriage. But the early analogy of the relationship between husband and wife to the relationship of Christ and the church (Eph. 5:22–33) persisted. Ultimately, the increasing sway of the church and its institutions over European society allowed a certain tempering of early ascetic zeal and led to the church's primary transregional role in defining the ritual and legal contours of marriage. The church defined marriage as a sacrament by the thirteenth century (according to some, as early as the ninth century), a sacrament unique insofar as it was administered by the couple themselves through the free exchange of vows. In its turn, the ceremony of marriage informed central ecclesiastical rites, such as the investiture of bishops and the taking of vows by nuns. Canon law defined (1) the marital bond as legally indissoluble (except for extreme cases and in contrast to Jewish and pagan practices), (2) the kinship boundaries of the marriage pool (couples must be no less than four degrees of kinship removed from each other, according to the Fourth Lateran Council), (3) the minimum age of the couple (fourteen for men and twelve for women, as had already been the case in Roman law), (4) the free consent required of the couple, and (5) the relative equality of wives and husbands. It also condemned polygyny and divorce, discouraged remarriage, and tried to control sexual pleasure. Two cumulative effects of these understandings have been famously argued by Jack Goody: the promotion of the nuclear family at the expense of wider domestic groups of kin and the church's accumulation of property. By the end of the eleventh century, the church claimed exclusive jurisdiction over marital cases. But it is important to remember that the church's claims evolved over centuries of theological thinking, synodal and conciliar decision-making, and the changing relationships between popes, theologians, and temporal rulers. And local customs and practices often contradicted the church's norms.

C. Brooke, *The Medieval Idea of Marriage* (1989); J. Brundage, *Law, Sex, and Christian Society in Medieval Europe* (1987); C. Donahue, "The Canon Law on the Formation of Marriage and Social Practice in the Later Middle Ages," *Journal of Family History* 8 (1983): 144–58; J. Goody, *The Development of the Family and Marriage in Europe* (1983); Goody, *The European Family: An Historical-Anthropological*

Essay (2000); R. Helmholz, *Marriage Litigation in Medieval England* (1974); M. M. Sheehan, "Marriage Theory and Practice in the Conciliar Legislation and Diocesan Statutes of Medieval England," *Medieval Studies* 40 (1978): 408–60.

VARDA KOCH OCKER

Martin of Braga (c. 520–c. 579), bishop, missionary, and monastic founder in the Roman province of Galicia in what is now northern Portugal and northwestern Spain. He was a native of the province of Pannonia, in present-day Hungary, who also lived the ascetic life in the Holy Land. From there he traveled westward, very likely via Rome, to Tours, where he went to venerate the relics of his namesake Martin of Tours. From Tours he traveled the maritime route to Galicia, where he focused on the Sueves, a Germanic tribe that had settled and established a kingdom whose capital was in Braga, Portugal, and who were at that time adherents of the Arian heresy. He successfully led the Sueves to the Catholic-Nicene profession of faith and maintained a close relationship with four successive Sueve monarchs spanning from about 550 to 579. He also preached with positive results against Priscillianism, Arianism, and paganism.

Under his pastoral care he convened two important councils in Braga in 561 and 572. In the Second Council of Braga he chaired the meeting as the metropolitan bishop of Braga. It was there that he introduced into the Galician church a large collection of Eastern conciliar canons known as the *Capitula Martini*, which undoubtedly solidified his missionary labors. Several contemporaneous writers testify that he established an extensive network of churches and monasteries throughout Galicia, thus earning him (posthumously) the title "Apostle of the Sueves."

Unfortunately, Martin's abundant epistolary correspondence has not survived. His few extant works experienced wide circulation well beyond Iberia and the Middle Ages. *Formula vitae honestae*, on the four cardinal virtues and based loosely on Seneca, was still being read in the Italian Renaissance. His sermon *De correctione rusticorum* against paganism, modeled after Augustine's *De catechizandi rudibus*, was translated and used in Iceland, Anglo-Saxon England, and Germany to convert pagans. Finally, two collections of the wisdom of the desert fathers that he brought with him from the East were translated from Greek into Latin and greatly influenced monasticism in the Iberian Peninsula.

C. W. Barlow, ed., *Martini Episcopi Bracarensis Opera Omnia* (1950); A. Ferreiro, "The Missionary Labors of Martin of Braga in 6th century Galicia," StudMon 23, no. 1 (1981): 11–26; Ferreiro, "Braga and Tours: Some Observations on Gregory's *De virtutibus sancti Martini* (1.11)," *JECS* 2 (1995): 25–35.

ALBERTO FERREIRO

Martin of Tours (c. 316–397), monk, bishop, missionary, saint. Martin was born in Pannonia to a military and non-Christian family and was raised in Pavia. While serving in the military (until the late 350s) and still a catechumen, he performed the act for which he became best known as a saint: he divided his military cloak to clothe a naked and freezing beggar (later revealed to be Christ). Once baptized, Martin devoted himself to ascetic practice and missionizing, particularly in the milieu of Hilary of Poitiers, where he established a monastery that would become the important monastery of Ligugé. He was elected bishop of Tours in 370. Known to posterity primarily through the writings of his contemporary admirer, Sulpicius Severus, Martin, as bishop of Tours, represented the rise of an alternative episcopal ideal, in which power and charisma flowed not from membership in the region's social and intellectual elite, and from the wealth and power this membership implied, but from a systematic, sustained, and recognized regime of asceticism and spiritual practice. As bishop, Martin was particularly remembered for his powers as an exorcist of demons, his efforts at converting the countryside around Tours, and his willingness to oppose imperial power, as when he intervened with the emperor Maximus to prevent the execution of the heretic Priscillian. Martin's monastic retreat at Marmoutier also became a leading center of asceticism in the region.

J. Fontaine, ed., *Sulpicius Severus, Vie de saint Martin* (1967); B. Peebles, *Sulpicius Severus: Writings* (1949); C. Stancliffe, *Saint Martin and His Hagiographer: History and Miracle in Sulpicius Severus* (1983).

WILLIAM NORTH

Martyrios (Sahdona) *see* Sahdona Martyrius

Martyrology The Greek root for the term *martyr* means "witness." During the persecutions of the early church, Christians who testified to their faith often suffered torture and execution. Hence, martyrdom came to mean accepting punishment for the confession of the Christian faith. Such "witnessing" to the faith was understood in light of the biblical mandate to take up one's cross and follow Jesus (Luke 14:27; Matt. 10:33). However, as alternative interpretations of the faith arose, it became apparent that one person's martyr was another person's heretic. Augustine (354–430) distinguished true from false martyrs with his dictum: "Not the punishment but the cause makes a martyr." With the fragmentation of Christendom in the Reformation period, it became increasingly difficult to apply Augustine's phrase. Hence, each of the Christian communities arising in the Reformation movements of sixteenth-century Europe developed its own martyrology as a witness to the truth of its convictions and as support and encouragement to its members to resist efforts to break their faith. At the same time, martyrologists of different confessions borrowed material from each other as well as from writers of the early church and medieval martyrologies.

The many martyrologies as well as their numerous reprintings and editions reflecting every Reformation position testify to the universal embrace of the witness of the martyrs. Lutheran martyrologies began with Luther's ballad commemorating two of his martyred followers, "A New Song Here Shall Be Begun" (1523), followed by his tract *The Burning of Brother Henry* (1525), and then were expanded in Ludwig Rabus's (1524–1592) *Historien der Heyligen Ausserwölten Gottes Zeügen, Bekennern und Martyrern* (1552–1558). The Huguenot martyrs were celebrated by Jean Crespin's (1520–1572) *Histoire des martyrs persecutez et mis à mort pour la verité de l'evangile . . .* (1554, 1555; Latin, 1556, 1560; six further French editions 1555–1619; German extracts, 1587; English, 1602) and Simon Goulart's (1543–1628) *Mémoires de l'estat de France sous Charles IX* (1576). The Dutch book of martyrs, more historically and geographically comprehensive than other Protestant martyrologies, was initiated by Adriaan Corneliszoon van Haemstede's (1520–1562) *History and Death of the Devout Martyrs* (twenty-three Dutch editions, 1559–1671). English Protestants were bolstered by John Foxe's (1516–1587) *Book of Martyrs, or the Acts and Monuments of the Christian Church . . . from the Commencement of Christianity to the Present Period* (Latin, 1554; English, 1563, many subsequent editions). The Anabaptists,

persecuted by both Catholic and Protestant communities, were not included in the above martyrologies. Anabaptists remembered their martyrs in hymns until publication of the major Anabaptist martyrology by Tieleman van Braght (1625–1664), *The Bloody Theater, or Martyrs' Mirror* (1660, 1685). Braght included a large amount of Mennonite pamphlet material as well as material from the earlier Mennonite *The Sacrifice unto the Lord* (eleven publications, 1562–1599). The Hutterite *Chronicles* remained in manuscript form until the nineteenth century, with an English translation in 1987. There were also innumerable Catholic martyrologies of individuals such as John Fisher, Thomas More, and Edmund Campion, as well as broader national martyrologies and republications of the medieval lives of the saints in all the European languages. Also, Catholic orders such as the Franciscans celebrated the martyrs of their order.

Martyrologies imparted courage and legitimacy to those suffering for their faith, reinforced the shared conviction that only a church "under the cross" is the true church and that therefore persecutors witnessed to the false church of the devil. Martyrologies hardened confessional identities and diminished doctrinal reconciliation; they were thus works of polemic as well as edification. As such, the martyrologies were expressions of developing Reformation historiography that both shared and individualized the self-understanding of various communities.

———

A. G. Dickens and J. Tonkin, "Weapons of Propaganda: The Martyrologies," in *The Reformation in Historical Thought* (1985), 39–57; B. S. Gregory, *Salvation at Stake: Christian Martyrdom in Early Modern Europe* (1999); R. M. Kingdon, *Myths about the St. Bartholomew's Day Massacres, 1572–1576* (1988); R. Kolb, *For All the Saints: Changing Perceptions of Martyrdom and Sainthood in the Lutheran Reformation* (1987); D. Loades, *The Oxford Martyrs* (1970); D. Watson, "Jean Crespin and the Writing of History in the French Reformation," in *Protestant History and Identity in Sixteenth-Century Europe*, vol. 2, ed. B. Gordon (1996), 39–58; D. Wood, ed., *Martyrs and Martyrologies* (1993).

CARTER LINDBERG

Mary of Egypt (fourth–fifth cent.), legendary desert mother. The early traditions associated with Mary (whom later tradition often confused with the Magdalene) are preserved in three widely varying versions of her hagiography. The most well-known narrative (attributed to Sophronios and modeled on Jerome's *Life of Paul the Hermit*) presents Mary as living a life of sexual promiscuity, not for financial gain but for sheer pleasure. After making a pilgrimage to Jerusalem (seducing other pilgrims along the way), Mary, unable to enter a church, converts through the intercession of the Virgin. Afterward, Mary retreats to the Judean desert. The description of her interaction with Zosimas, a priest who encounters her, presents Mary as spiritually gifted (levitating during prayer and walking on water) and independent of church authority (self-baptized). Her humility exposes to Zosimas the pride he derives from communal monastic practice. This gender reversal reinforces the Life's valorization of anchoritic spirituality. In the end, however, (male) ecclesiastic authority (apparent in Mary's request for the Eucharist and Zosimas's orthodox burial of her body) is reasserted. Various versions of Mary's hagiography were popular in medieval Western traditions as a tale of repentance; and her Life is part of the Lenten liturgy in the East, where she appears as a female counterpart to male tales of repentance.

B. Ward, *Harlots of the Desert* (1987); L. Coon, *Sacred Fictions: Holy Women and Hagiography in Late Antiquity* (1997); E. Walsh, "The Ascetic Mother Mary of Egypt," *GOTR* 34 (1989): 59–69.

REBECCA KRAWIEC

Mary of Hungary (1505–1558), Habsburg archduchess of Austria, queen of Hungary and Bohemia, governor of the Netherlands. Daughter of Philip the Fair and Joanna "the Mad," her siblings included Charles V, Ferdinand I, and Eleanor of France. She was raised by her aunt Margaret, governor of the Netherlands. In 1515 her grandfather, Maximilian I, married her to Louis II Jagiello (1506–1526) in order to secure Habsburg claims to the Hungarian crown. In Hungary she encountered the hostility of many Magyar nobles. After the death of Louis at Mohacs (August 29, 1526) she used her position and influence to secure the election of Ferdinand I as king of Hungary and Bohemia, despite the prior election of John Zapolya. In 1528 she left for the Netherlands and "temporarily" assumed its governorship in 1531. But she adamantly refused all entreaties to marry again. For twenty-five years her administrative and diplomatic skills were employed to raise money for the wars of Charles, to enforce but also to lessen the severity of his anti-Protestant edicts, and to secure the borders, autonomy, and unity of the Netherlands. She was also a knowledgable patron of the arts. Prior to 1525 she demonstrated an interest in the views of Erasmus and Luther. After being widowed she received treatises from Luther (*Four Comforting Psalms*, 1526) and Erasmus (*A Christian Widow*, 1530). Until her death she subordinated her person and religious views to the dynastic interests of her family, as she had promised to her brothers in 1527.

D. Daniel, "Piety, Politics, and Perversion: Noblewomen in Reformation Hungary," in *Women in Reformation and Counter-Reformation Europe*, ed. S. Marshall (1989), 68–88; J. de Jong, *Mary of Hungary, Second Regent of the Netherlands* (1959).

DAVID P. DANIEL

Mary Stuart (1542–1587), queen of Scots. The daughter of Mary of Guise and King James V of Scotland (r. 1513–1542), Mary wed Francis of Valois, heir to the French throne, in 1558 and was queen of France for a short time. Following Francis II's death in 1560, Mary returned to Scotland as queen. Presbyterianism, led by John Knox, had become a strong force in the country, but Mary did not check the Protestant ascendancy.

In 1565 she married Henry, Lord Darnley, a fellow Catholic with a claim to the English throne. Mary soon became disenchanted with the witless Darnley and caused a great scandal by marrying James, Earl of Bothwell, who was widely believed to have participated in the murder of Darnley in 1567. Widespread outrage led to a revolt against them, and Bothwell fled the country. Mary languished in jail before escaping to England, where her royal cousin, Elizabeth of England, kept her under house arrest from 1568 on and refused to allow Mary to come to court. Increasingly frustrated, Mary entered into a number of plots with Catholic sympathizers who wanted her to replace Elizabeth as England's queen. Finally in 1587, Elizabeth signed her death warrant, and Mary died bravely as a Catholic martyr. Her Protestant son James succeeded Elizabeth as king of England in 1603.

G. Donaldson, *Mary Queen of Scots* (1974); A. Fraser, *Mary Queen of Scots* (1969); J. Wormald, *Mary Queen of Scots: A Study in Failure* (1988).

JONATHAN W. ZOPHY

Mary Tudor (Mary I) (1516–1558), queen of England (1553–1558). Daughter of Henry VIII and Catherine of Aragon, she was excluded from succession to the throne due to Henry's annulment of his marriage; in effect, the annulment made her an illegitimate child. The situation was deeply humiliating to her, particularly because she was a devout follower of traditional Roman Catholicism. In 1544 she was restored to the line of succession, albeit following Edward VI. Despite this, Edward, during his reign (1547–1553), colluded with his Protestant advisors and attempted to have Lady Jane Grey put in the line of succession before her. Roman Catholics welcomed her accession to the throne in 1553, and she was crowned by Bishop Stephen Gardiner. Her marriage to Phillip II of Spain ended as a failure, a marriage in name only. By 1555 she had sent Reginald Pole (named cardinal in 1556) to reconcile with Rome; Pole, a traditionalist fanatic, restored the heresy laws in England, and trials began. Gardiner died in 1555, and it was from 1555 to 1556 that Thomas Cranmer, Hugh Latimer, Nicholas Ridley, and John Hooper were put on trial and burned at the stake. Following the trials, Mary's reign met with parliamentary disapproval and her prestige generally declined. She died at St. James Palace.

———

D. M. Loades, *Mary Tudor: A Life* (1989); J. Loach, *Parliament and the Crown in the Reign of Mary Tudor* (1986).

ALDEN R. LUDLOW

Masses for the Dead A type of votive Mass (one with a special intention) performed to benefit the soul(s) of the departed. Eucharistic memorials for the dead appear as early as 170 CE in Asia Minor. Since the fourth century, they evolved alongside the panoply of other types of votive Masses (to alleviate sickness, provide a personal or collective benefit, mark a special occasion, etc.). In the fourth century, they were commonly performed on set days after a death (e.g., the seventh and thirtieth days, or the fourth and fortieth). By the sixth century, the practice of performing Masses on successive days by a celebrant, without any other participants, appears, and there is evidence at least since the late sixth century of such Masses being performed in some stipulated number. During the seventh century in the West, it became common to pledge prayers and Masses for the deceased in churches and monasteries. Those so memorialized were often associated with the

aristocratic families who established the churches or monsteries to begin with. Masses, along with prayers, thus became a central feature of personal memorialization in medieval Europe. With the expansion of the European population after the tenth century and buttressed by an ever more sophisticated theology of eucharistic sacrifice, Masses for the dead were increasingly endowed by all social ranks. They came to occupy an important place in the ministry of monsateries and churches, and they became a vital part of the late medieval religious economy. What was the theoretical basis of these Masses? Although the sacrifice of Christ was of infinite virtue, Archbishop of Canterbury John Pecham (d. 1292) once noted, it is effective in the sacrament only by a finite quantity; hence, the repetition of the sacrament could multiply the finite quantity for the benefit of particular soul(s). The Mass applied the benefits of the passion within space and time, and the intention of the priest could point those benefits to specific individuals. By the late Middle Ages, testators commonly requested such Masses in wills for their own souls (e.g., about one-third of English wills from 1500 to 1546 did so), and the requests, which accompanied donations, were sometimes extravagant (e.g., one thousand Masses for a soul). Likewise, late medieval funerary rites often included two professionals: a mourner (this was often a member of a religious order, a Beguine, or a nun) and a priest (this was normally one's confessor). The prayers of the Office of the Dead were said by mourners and family through a vigil that culminated on the following day in a requiem Mass pledged to the deceased's soul.

———

P. Binski, *Medieval Death: Ritual and Representation* (1996); J. A. Jungmann, *The Mass of the Roman Rite: Its Origins and Development*, 2 vols. (1951); P. Marshall, *Beliefs and the Dead in Reformation England* (2002); Marshall, *The Catholic Priesthood and the English Reformation* (1994).

CHRISTOPHER OCKER

Mather, Cotton (1663–1728), Congregationalist minister in colonial Massachusetts. Born in Boston, he was the son of Increase Mather and Maria Cotton, daughter of John Cotton. A precocious boy, he entered Harvard College in 1674, received a BA in 1678, an MA in 1681, and was ordained in 1685 as his father's colleague at Second Church, Boston, where he remained for the rest of his life. As a pastor, he supported the Half-Way Covenant but opposed the broad admission to the Lord's Supper promoted by Solomon Stoddard. He aided the overthrow of Sir Edmund Andros, the royal governor, in 1689. Although troubled by the disorderly proceedings and the use of "spectral evidence" in the Salem witchcraft trials, his vindication of the reality of witchcraft in *Wonders of the Invisible World* (1693) brought criticism upon him. Mather's scientific interests (he reported on the flora and fauna of America to the Royal Society in London, which granted him membership in 1713) also led to controversy because of his support for smallpox inoculation. But his deepest commitments were religious, and these found expression in almost four hundred published books, many impressively learned. *The Everlasting Gospel* (1700) proclaimed an evangelical Calvinism characteristic of the later English and American Puritans. *Magnalia Christi Americana* (1702) celebrated the earlier generations of New England in order to renew their sense of mission. *Bonifacius* (1710), later republished as *Essays to Do Good*, encouraged practical benevolence. *The Christian Philosopher* (1721) was an exposition of natural theology. Mather's piety, rooted in Puritan spiritual introspection, was also influenced by European Pietism (he corresponded with A. H. Francke) and was expressed in long hours in prayer and fasting, ecstatic spiritual raptures, and occasional angelic visitations. Cotton Mather was a transitional figure, exemplifying a late stage of New England Puritanism but also prefiguring aspects of the Great Awakening and the Enlightenment.

D. Levin, *Cotton Mather: The Young Life of the Lord's Remembrancer, 1663–1703* (1978); R. F. Lovelace, *The American Pietism of Cotton Mather* (1979); R. Middlekauff, *The Mathers: Three Generations of Puritan Intellectuals* (1971); K. Silverman, *The Life and Times of Cotton Mather* (1984).
DEWEY D. WALLACE JR.

Mather, Increase (1639–1723), Puritan minister in colonial Massachusetts. Increase, born in Dorchester, Massachusetts, was the son of Richard Mather, one of the first New England ministers. In 1656 he received a BA from Harvard College and in 1658 an MA from Trinity College, Dublin. Back in Massachusetts in 1661, the next year he attended the synod that approved the Half-Way Covenant, which, unlike his father, he opposed (but later supported). In 1664 he was ordained teacher of

Boston's Second Church, serving until his death. He was a leader in the Reforming Synod (1679) that denounced the sins of the colonists. In 1685 he accepted the presidency of Harvard, without resigning at Second Church. He was in England from 1688 to 1692, attempting unsuccessfully to restore Massachusetts's charter that had been revoked in 1684. After his return to Massachusetts he defended the new charter, questioned the evidence used in the Salem witch trials, denounced emergent liberalism at Harvard, defended the autonomy of congregational churches, and opposed Solomon Stoddard's advocacy of more inclusive admission to the Lord's Supper. He wrote more than one hundred books, including many published sermons.

M. G. Hall, *The Last American Puritan: The Life of Increase Mather* (1988); R. Middlekauff, *The Mathers: Three Generations of Puritan Intellectuals, 1596–1728* (1971).
DEWEY D. WALLACE JR.

Matilda of Tuscany (1046–1114), Italian ruler and papal supporter. Matilda was the most important secular supporter of the papacy during the Investiture Controversy that rocked Italy and Germany from 1076 to 1122. She was sole heiress of Count Boniface of Tuscany and his wife Beatrice of Lorraine, and upon her father's murder in 1053 became one of Europe's greatest landholders. Matilda was well educated and notably pious; these attributes, added to the influence of her stepfather, Duke Godfrey the Bearded of Lorraine, encouraged her to support the papacy's centralizing efforts against the German emperors.

Matilda became sole ruler of an extensive territory on both sides of the Alps in 1076, when both her mother and her husband (Godfrey the Hunchback, her stepbrother) died. When relations between Pope Gregory VII and Emperor Henry IV completely broke down, Matilda mediated between the two at her castle of Canossa in early 1077.

When efforts at peace failed, Matilda provided Gregory with military support. She was one of the few medieval women to lead an army, most notably in 1087 when she marched against the antipope in Rome. In c. 1090 Matilda, at Urban II's request, married Duke Welf of Bavaria, but when Welf went over to Emperor Henry in 1096, she remained faithful to her papal alliance. Finally, the childless Matilda willed her extensive personal lands to the Roman church, a bequest disputed by successive emperors and not settled in the papacy's favor until 1213. In the seventeenth century Matilda's body was removed to St. Peter's, Rome, in recognition of her major role. (See *Reform Papacy*)

H. E. J. Cowdrey, *Pope Gregory VII* (1998); I. S. Robinson, *Henry IV of Germany* (1999).

PHYLLIS G. JESTICE

Matthias of Janov (c. 1350/1355–1393),

Bohemian theologian and reformer. Matthias was profoundly influenced by his contact with the "Jerusalem" community of Milíč of Kroměříž before he began theological studies in Paris (1372–1381). There, through the Parisian masters and his study of Augustine and Jerome, Matthias "discovered" Scripture. His monumental *Regulae Veteris et Novi Testamenti* (*Rules of the Old and New Testament*) is the most significant theological treatise of the fourteenth-century Bohemian reform movement. Foundational to the implementation of his reforms (perfecting the true Christian life, elimination of clerical abuse, a more balanced view of the veneration of images) was the restoration of frequent (best daily, at least weekly) Communion for all adult lay Christians.

A Prague Synod (1389) forced Matthias to retract his teaching on frequent Communion (and the veneration of images), placing him under ecclesiastical discipline, but he was vindicated in 1391 when Archbishop Jan Jenštejn reversed his opposition and the synod allowed lay Communion as often as desired. The texts Matthias assembled in his *Regulae* justifying frequent Communion were foundational for the restoration of the lay chalice (1415) and infant Communion (1417), both of which were fundamental to the later reforms of the Utraquists.

Matthiae de Janov dicti Magistri Parisiensis Regulae Veteris et Novi Testamenti, 6 vols., ed. V. Kybal (I–IV), O. Odložilík (V), J. Nechutová, H. Krmíčková (VI) (1908–1993); J. Nechutova, "Matěj of Janov and His Work *Regulae Veteris et Novi Testamenti*," BRRP 2 (1998), 15–24.

DAVID R. HOLETON

Matthijs, Jan (d. 1534), Dutch Anabaptist

leader. Little is known of his early life, except that he lived in Haarlem and was a baker by trade. He probably converted to Melchiorite Anabaptism in the early 1530s. After Melchior Hoffman had instructed his followers to sus-

pend the practice of adult baptism, Matthijs announced to the faithful in November 1533 that it should be reinstated in preparation for the coming millennial reign of Christ. After Anabaptists gained control of the city council in Münster in February 1534, Matthijs and other Dutch Anabaptists came to the city. Matthijs gained effective political control of the city on February 23, 1534, and announced that only those residents who had been rebaptized would be permitted to live there. He also proclaimed that the faithful could take up arms to defend themselves against the godless. In the next month, he introduced a number of measures, including the establishment of a community of goods, which may have been a response to the siege of the city undertaken by Franz von Waldeck, the bishop of the city. In response to a vision that promised him victory over the bishop's forces, on Easter Sunday 1534 Matthijs took a small band of armed men out of the city to attack the bishop's forces. He was killed in the ensuing battle, but the radical movement he began in Münster survived until June 1536.

J. Stayer, "Christianity in One City: Anabaptist Münster, 1534–1535," in *Radical Tendencies in the Reformation*, ed. H. J. Hillerbrand (1988), 117–34; G. H. Williams, *The Radical Reformation* (3rd ed., 1992).

D. JONATHAN GRIESER

Maulbronn Colloquy (1564), a Lutheran-

Reformed dialogue. As Elector Frederick III of the Palatinate introduced a locally adapted version of Calvin's theology into his lands, his Lutheran neighbors challenged him. His theologians, led by Kaspar Olevianus and Zacharias Ursinus, met theologians from Württemberg, led by Jakob Andreae and Johannes Brenz, in a six-day exchange of views on the Lord's Supper and related christological issues. The Palatine representatives rejected the Lutheran defense of the true presence of Christ's body and blood in the Lord's Supper through the concepts of the oral partaking of Christ's body and blood and the partaking of them by the impious, a position based on the Lutheran belief that the Word of God establishes the reality of Christ's presence. The Palatine rejection of the christological support for the Lutheran position on the basis of the communication of the attributes of Christ's human and divine natures with each other initiated the use of the term "ubiquitarian" as a polemical charge against the Lutherans. The failure of the two sides to reach agreement marked an important stage in the political and theology antagonism of the two confessions in Germany.

E. Bizer, *Studien zur Geschichte des Abendmahlsstreits* (1940).

ROBERT KOLB

Maximus the Confessor (c. 580–662),

monk and theologian. Maximus wrote extensively on doctrinal, monastic, liturgical, and exegetical matters. Among scholars, Maximus was long known as an opponent of Monotheletism (see *Monothelites*). In the past half-century, he has drawn more attention as a spiritual writer. Competing Lives, a friendly Greek one and a hostile Syriac one, give divergent accounts of his early years. His writings attest to a broad education, and the tradition that he became the secretary to Heraclius (Byzantine emperor, 610–641) is well founded. He left imperial service in 614 to become a monk. After the Avar, Slav, and Persian invasions of 626, Maximus fled Constantinople for Africa. After 630, he became an opponent of monotheletism, which was being promoted, especially within imperial circles, as a means of reconciling Chalcedonians and anti-Chalcedonians. He was instrumental in its condemnation by synods in Africa and at Rome.

He was arrested in 653, brought to Constantinople, tried for treason, and banished. When that did not silence his opposition to monotheletism he was brought back to Constantinople in 662 and his tongue and right hand were cut off. He was exiled to Lazica, where he died of his injuries.

The influence of the Cappadocians and the monastic tradition of Evagrius and Pseudo-Dionysius can all be seen in Maximus's works. Maximus's Christology and spiritual theology are of a piece. Essential human nature (*logos*) was created for communion of life with the Trinity (deification). Human will has brought about a mode of being (*tropos*) where God and humanity are divided from one another. The incarnation unites the extremes of humanity and divinity, not to destroy human *logos* but to restore it to a *tropos* that enables human beings to practice virtue—hence the significance of the two wills of Christ.

P. M. Blowers, *Exegesis and Spiritual Pedagogy in Maximus the Confessor: An Investigation of the Quaestiones ad Thalassium* (1991); A. Louth, *Maximus the Confessor* (1996); PG 90, 91 (1860); L. Thunberg, *Microcosm and Mediator: The Theological Anthropology of Maximus the Confessor* (2nd ed., 1995).

EUGENE M. LUDWIG, OFM CAP.

Meaux Circle In 1521 Bishop Guillaume

Briçonnet of Meaux invited the humanist biblical scholar Jacques Lefèvre d'Étaples and a circle of protégés, including Gérard Roussel, Guillaume Farel, Michel d'Arande, Martial Mazurier, and Pierre Caroli, to help introduce evangelical reform in his diocese. Thus began one of the earliest sustained attempts at reform of the church in sixteenth-century France.

The "circle of Meaux" focused on preaching, conveying the message of the Bible to the laity, and reforming lay piety. With the support of the French king, Francis I, and his sister Marguerite d'Angoulême, the Meaux reform was envisioned as a model for ecclesiastical renewal, along humanist lines, throughout the kingdom. However, hostile religious conservatives, notably the theologians of the Sorbonne who detected Lutheran influence in the reformers' evangelism, pressured Briçonnet to condemn Luther's errors, affirm elements of traditional Catholicism, and distance himself from those in Lefèvre's circle whose teaching most closely approximated the positions of German and Swiss reformers. But by 1524 popular radicalism had spread in the diocese of Meaux, discrediting Briçonnet in the eyes of conservatives and provoking the Parlement of Paris to move against the spread of heresy while Francis I was held captive in Spain following a military defeat. In 1525 Briçonnet was brought to trial, while Lefèvre, Roussel, d'Arande, and Caroli fled to Strasbourg.

Francis I's return to France in 1526 restored royal protection to those in Lefèvre's circle, but the conservatives' actions ended the official diocesan reformation in Meaux. Those who had been active in the Meaux reform tended toward either the moderate Catholic evangelism exemplified by Roussel, made bishop of Oloron in 1536, or the uncompromising Protestantism of Farel, who from exile became an architect of the French Reformed movement.

H. Heller, *The Conquest of Poverty* (1986); M. Veissière, *L'Evêque Guillaume Briçonnet, 1470–1534* (1986).

CHRISTOPHER ELWOOD

Mechthild of Magdeburg (c. 1208–

c. 1282), German mystic and author. A Beguine who later resided at Helfta, Mechthild's vernacular writings influenced the representation of

God in the late Middle Ages and are examples of the unprecedented opportunities for female religious expression in thirteenth-century Europe. According to her own account, Mechthild's first revelations occurred at age twelve; approximately a decade later, she joined the Beguines in Magdeburg. Her extraordinary spiritual experiences led her Dominican confessor to encourage her to write. The resulting work, *The Flowing Light of the Godhead*, was completed in sections over thirty years; its seven books utilize poetry, visionary accounts, allegory, and dialogue in describing encounters with God. Mechthild's familiarity with courtly literature and fondness for nuptial imagery, especially from the Song of Songs, are apparent throughout. Her extended reflections on Christ's wounds and descriptions of stringent ascetic practices reflect the desire, found in much contemporary Christian spirituality, to imitate Christ's passion. Criticism of decadent clergy may have prompted relocation to the convent of Helfta, where she spent her final years. Though her writings did not circulate widely in her lifetime, they were well known at Helfta and were translated into Latin around 1290.

———

C. Bynum, "Women Mystics in the Thirteenth Century," in *Jesus as Mother* (1982); A. Hollywood, *The Soul as Virgin Wife* (1995); Mechthild of Magdeburg, *The Flowing Light of the Godhead*, trans. F. Tobin (1998); F. Tobin, *Mechthild von Magdeburg: A Medieval Mystic* (1995).

ADRIENNE NOCK AMBROSE

Medieval Kingship This ever evolving political form was one of the Middle Ages' enduring contributions to Western civilization. While Romans abhorred even the name "king" (*rex*), their German successors in the West embraced kingship. In the fifth and sixth centuries a series of powerful kings such as Theodoric the Great in Italy and Clovis in northwestern Europe ran substantial monarchies. By the mid-eighth century Christianity had become a constitutive element of medieval monarchy. Papal approval sanctioned the Carolingian overthrow of the Merovingians in 751, and in 800 Pope Leo III crowned Charlemagne emperor. While religious ties helped kings to rule theocratically, competing claims of authority often meant endemic conflict with religious leaders. The eleventh-century controversy over investitures attempted to establish spiritual supremacy over secular power but ended in a compromise. Pope Innocent III (1198–1216) dramatically intervened in the kingdoms of Frederick II (1212–1250) of the HRE, Philip II (1180–1223) of France, and John (1199–1216) of England. For most of the Middle Ages, however, kings resisted the theoretical claims of religious leaders and, in effect, ran national churches.

Monarchical power rested on control of the kingdom and its resources, which the king administered through a consensual system of authority. Nobles, in theory, helped the king to rule and shared the kingdom's wealth and royal authority. Kings also established politically powerful links through marriage. Their queens brought substantial political and financial resources with them. As dispensers of gifts, mediators of access to their husbands, and guardians of personal treasure, queens were an indispensable part of effective monarchy. But family politics could be fractious, especially when ambitious royal heirs joined with ambitious nobles to subvert royal power. The family politics of Henry II (1154–1189) of England and Eleanor of Aquitaine, his queen, offer but one example of how family feuds influenced the course of kingdoms.

At first arbiters of relationships among their nobles, kings extended their legal reach throughout their realms and even into ecclesiastical institutions. The king's law became the law of the land. Royal authority was never absolute but depended on negotiations among an ever widening community of the realm. The king's first partners were churchmen and nobles, but after the eleventh century, monarchs allied with the emerging towns. Towns provided revenue and political support in exchange for protection from local nobles. Effective management of the competition between traditional aristocratic power and the new power of wealthy towns enhanced royal power. The new monarchies of the High Middle Ages were negotiated monarchies involving kings, religious leaders, nobles, and urban dwellers. New assemblies such as *parlements* provided the settings where kings attempted to manage competing interests. Europe's kings propelled the discovery and exploitation of the New World.

J. Nelson, "Kingship and Empire," in *The Cambridge History of Medieval Political Thought, c. 350–1450*, ed. J. H. Burns (1988), 211–51; S. Reynolds, *Kingdoms and Communities in Western Europe, 900–1300* (1984); P. H. Sawyer and I. N. Wood, eds., *Early Medieval Kingship* (1977).

JOHN J. CONTRENI

Medieval Mysticism *see* Mysticism, Medieval

Medieval Papacy *see* Papacy, Medieval

Medieval Preaching *see* Preaching, Medieval

Medieval Saints' Lives The biographies of medieval saints were based on the rhetorical precedents of Roman *laudatio* ("funeral orations") and Scripture and the *passiones* ("passions") of the early martyrs, and were meant to serve the didactic role of philosophy (or religion) of "teaching by example." The cardinal virtues were reflected in the life of the saint, illustrated by specific examples. Those who had witnessed his or her life and ministry, experienced the miracles, read or heard the biography, gazed at frescoes, icons, or other works of art based upon it, or participated in the liturgical office commemorating a feast day were to be edified and encouraged to imitate the heroic virtues personified by the saint.

Medieval hagiography was a form of polemical literature. The hero or heroine is portrayed battling against the internal and external enemies of the faith: the temptations sent by Satan; the ideological foes of Christianity such as Judaism, paganism, heresy, and Islam; or more mundane dynastic foes of the church. The lives of the saints were typically presented in a number of literary genres: (1) the *Vita et miracula*, which summarizes the chief stages of the saint's life, including virtues and miracles performed, both in life and posthumously; (2) legendaries, such as the *Lives of the Desert Fathers* (c. 400) or Jacob of Voragine's *Golden Legend* (1260), which contain shortened biographies based on the liturgical calendar; and (3) sermons preached on the occasion of the saint's feast day. For example, a sermon delivered by Caesarius of Heisterbach in commemoration of Elizabeth of Thuringia (d. 1231) presents her life as a reflection of Matthew 5:14: "A town that stands on a hill cannot be hidden." Most lives were produced under the auspices of a patron such as a religious order or bishop and may have been intended to legitimize political authority or the establishment of a new monastery, dynasty, or church. New orders such as the Cistercians, Dominicans, Franciscans, and others were particularly keen to document their early history through the publications of biographies of their founders.

In the prologue the author identifies his informants and cites his scriptural models or literary predecessors, such as the *Life of Martin of Tours* by Sulpicius Severus (d. c. 420) or Pope Gregory the Great's *Dialogues* (593). The hagiographer often relied on firsthand evidence of the saint's life, although a large number of *vitae* were written considerably later or were summaries or rewritings of earlier versions (e.g., the lives of Martial of Limoges or Francis of Assisi), tailored to fit the needs of a particular audience. In the central Middle Ages, the formulation of canon law, the requirements of papal canonization of saints, and the demand for greater accuracy in the reports of the saint's virtues and miracles led quasi-judicial inquiries in which trained notaries recorded the testimony of witnesses who had personal knowledge of the saint and his or her miracles. Such hearings became the raw material of saints' lives, and enhanced their reliability. The rise of scholastic learning resulted in greater citation of Scripture, the fathers of the church, and classical sources in the composition of medieval hagiography. A larger number of biographies, such as those of Angela of Foligno and Margaret of Cortona, appear to have been based on reports by their confessors, and more biographies were written or translated into the vernacular in order to satisfy a lay (largely female) audience.

T. Head, ed., *Medieval Hagiography: An Anthology* (2000); T. Heffernan, *Sacred Biography: Saints and Their Biographers in the Middle Ages* (1988); T. F. X. Noble and T. Head, eds., *Soldiers of Christ: Saints and Saints' Lives from Late Antiquity and the Early Middle Ages* (1995); G. Philippart et al., eds., *Hagiographies: Histoire internationale de la littérature hagiographique latine et vernaculaire en Occident des origines à 1550*, 2 vols. (1994, 1996).

MICHAEL GOODICH†

Medieval Satire The embryonic development of a satirical literature based loosely on the forms of *trovaritz* and *Minnesang*, in both epic and lyric genres, coincided with the rise of other forms of satire. The satirical versions of these high art forms, as well as later prose developments, once thought to be inferior epigones, were—like their "serious" models—aimed at an aristocratic audience and often ridiculed the peasantry. With the beginning of communal revolts around the same time, that is, in the later twelfth and early thirteenth centuries, a new stratum of urban commoners, burghers, expressed itself in the *fabliaux*, short stories told in lines of eight syllables. These relatively harmless and pleasant tales were designed to be amusing rather than challenging or didactic. The characters in these tales are drawn from the burgher milieu: craftsmen, traders, and the like, male and female. They perform all manner of adventures, and their vices are pilloried, sometimes in quite indelicate terms. Irony and cross-talk inform this genre, rather than the courtly or "gentle" ethos of aristocratic poetry. Laughter, not aesthetic enjoyment or didactic value, was the purpose of the *fabliaux*.

The *Roman de Renart*, a kind of bastard sired by the *fabliaux* on the memory of the *chansons de geste* in the early thirteenth century, was a disjointed compilation of stories in verse, counting around thirty thousand lines. It was not the work of a single writer but rather a general and constantly expanding collaboration produced by the medieval *bourgeoisie*, or rather, its literary representatives. Renart (the fox), Ysengrin (the wolf), Noble (the lion), and Chantecler (the cock) are the core characters, who give the compilation some unity and represent various types in a satirical view of noble and courtly society and feudal institutions. In this genre, both nobles and clerics receive rough satirical treatment regarding their morals and way of life.

In the fourteenth century, bands of merry companions amused themselves in groups such as the *basoche*—a society of lawyers—and the *sots* or the *enfants sans souci*. They composed and played comic pieces, especially farces, morality plays, and "follies" (*soties*) until the time of the Reformation. The form and themes of these pieces were simply those of the *fabliaux*. An example is the 1470 *Farce de l'Avocat Panthelin*, a duel of wits between two rascals, a lawyer and a cloth merchant. The morality was didactic; the *soties* were dramatic pamphlets or squibs. Anticlerical and anti-Semitic elements form obligatory set-pieces in these and other satirical genres. Italian, German, Dutch, and English burghers had their own versions of such literary and dramatic satires; the French example is used here because it refers to the largest and most easily identified body of such texts. The Italian *commedia del'arte* and its offspring, the English Punch-and-Judy show, date from this period. The German *Fastnachtsspiele*, such as the *Spil von dem Herzogen von Burgund* (c. 1486–1494, by Hans Folz), an orgy of fecality, anti-Semitism and violent degradation, demonstrates that the French did not have a monopoly on coarse humor and violent satire.

Chaucer has traditionally been seen as the high point of medieval vernacular (satirical) literature, serving as a kind of bridge between the tradition of the *fabliaux* and *Roman de Renart* on the one hand, and the realism of the vernacular genres already developing in Italy (and which modernist scholars, enamoured of literary and other genealogies, took to be the roots of Italian humanist literature) on the other. His "satire of estates" (including his attacks on clerics of all sorts) is strongly reminiscent of the *fabliaux*. However, his simultaneously rollicking and sophisticated humor place him more in the line of later satirists such as Rabelais, Pope, and Voltaire.

A related genre is the Latin parody or satire, which is almost always on religious topics: biblical parody, drinkers' masses, bawdy litanies, lives of saints such as Nemo (Nobody) and Invicem (One Another). These texts, written by and for clerics, mirror the tastes and interests of contemporary vernacular/lay audiences.

———

J. V. Alter, *Les origines de la satire anti-bourgeoise en France: Moyen Age—XVIe siècle* (1966); M. Bayless, *Parody in the Middle Ages: The Latin Tradition* (1997).

ANDREW GOW

Megander, Casper (1495–1545), Swiss

Reformed theologian and educator. A native of Zurich, after receiving his master's degree in Basel (1518) Megander returned to Zurich as hospital chaplain and preacher in the Grossmünster. He was a principal theologian in Zurich's abolishing of the Mass and the celibacy of priests. He represented Zurich at the Bern disputation in 1528 and subsequently served as the principal theologian in the state of Bern. Megander founded the theological academy in Bern and wrote several biblical commentaries. In conjunction with Leo Jud, he edited Zwingli's biblical commentaries and sermons. He was suspended in the wake of the Second Kappel War due to his opposition to the moderate position of Bern. Following his reinstatement he fought every attempt to reconcile the Swiss with the German Lutherans. He was uncompromising and stubborn, and this isolated him from his colleagues and made him a political liability to the rulers of Bern. His primary objective was to preserve the heritage of Zwinglian theology. He was forced by the Council to leave Bern in 1537 and lived thereafter in Zurich.

———

B. Gordon, "Switzerland," in *The Early Reformation in Europe* (1992); G. Locher, *Die*

Zwinglische Reformation im Rahmen der europäischen Kirchengeschichte (1979).
GREGORY J. MILLER

Melanchthon, Philip

Melanchthon, Philip (1497–1560), son of the electoral Palatine armorer, Georg Schwartzerdt (d. 1508). Melanchthon attended Latin school in Pforzheim and lived with the sister of Johannes Reuchlin, the humanist and Hebraist to whom Philip was related by marriage and who in 1508 gave him the hellenized form of his name (*melan*, "black"; *chthon*, "earth"). Trained there in Greek, he attended the Univ. of Heidelberg (BA, 1511) and the Univ. of Tübingen (MA, 1514).

In 1518 Reuchlin nominated him for the newly established professorship of Greek at the Univ. of Wittenberg, where he remained for the rest of his life. There the humanistically trained Greek scholar, who also taught courses in rhetoric and dialectics (logic), came under Martin Luther's theological influence. In 1519 he received under Luther a bachelor of Bible (*baccalaureus biblicus*), which allowed him to teach not only on the Greek text of the New Testament but also the Bible's content. At the same time, instead of preparing lectures on the *Sentences* of Peter Lombard, Melanchthon composed his own theological overview, based upon the topics in Romans and titled the *Loci communes rerum theologicarum* (*Commonplaces of Theological Matters*, 1521). That year he was among the first laypersons in Wittenberg to receive communion in both kinds. In 1523, as the first married rector of a European university, he revised the curriculum for the arts faculty according to humanist and Reformation principles. In 1533 he revised the theological curriculum.

By 1527 he and Luther had received special positions at the university that allowed them freedom to teach any subject. As a result, he lectured in both the arts and the theology faculties and distinguished throughout his life between the righteousness and knowledge of this world and the divine righteousness imputed to believers because of Christ. He produced two more Latin editions of the *Loci communes* (1536 and 1543) and a final German version in 1555. His biblical work included influential commentaries on Romans (1532, 1540, and 1556) and Colossians (1527, 1528, 1534, and 1559), in which he used humanist methods, especially rhetorical analysis and the identification of the authors' commonplaces. His textbooks on Greek and Latin grammar, rhetoric, and dialectics were used throughout Europe. He produced commentaries on such authors as Cicero, Terence (1516), and Aristotle. His work on a history of the world reached the period of Charlemagne. He also wrote occasional pieces on law, medicine, and astrology and maintained an enormous correspondence (of which over nine thousand pieces have survived).

He was a leading representative of Wittenberg's theology. In 1519, he accompanied Luther to the Leipzig Debates and wrote the earliest account of them. He also participated in the Marburg Colloquy with Luther and Huldrych Zwingli. Besides the *Loci communes* and biblical commentaries, he wrote many of Wittenberg's official theological opinions. In 1530, as the leader of the Saxon theologians at the Diet of Augsburg, he drafted first the Augsburg Confession and then wrote its *Apology* (published twice in 1531). Later he penned an appendix to the Confession, the *Treatise on the Power and Primacy of the Pope* (1537).

He was also involved in colloquies and discussions with those who disagreed with Wittenberg. He successfully mediated an agreement between Luther and Martin Bucer of Strasbourg on the Lord's Supper (the Wittenberg Concord of 1536). In 1540–1541 he was the chief spokesman for evangelicals at colloquies with the Roman party in Worms and Regensburg. In 1551, to prepare for possible Protestant participation in the Council of Trent, he composed the Saxon Confession.

His theological career was not without controversy. In 1527 he clashed with John Agricola of Eisleben over penitence and the law. In the mid-1530s, Nicholas von Amsdorf and others challenged views expressed in the second edition of the *Loci communes* on the necessity of good works and the role of the human will in salvation. In 1543, working with Martin Bucer on a reform of the archbishopric of Cologne, his position on Christ's presence in the Lord's Supper came under suspicion.

After Luther's death in 1546 and in the aftermath of the defeat of the Schmalkald League in 1547, he became embroiled in disputes over adiaphora. While rejecting the emperor's interim decree on religious matters, imposed at the 1548 Diet of Augsburg (the Augsburg Interim), he framed an alternative that preserved evangelical theology while compromising on matters of practice viewed as adiaphora. Amsdorf, Matthias Flacius, and other "genuine Lutherans" (Gnesio-Lutherans) attacked him and Wittenberg's faculty. Later, other issues involving free will, original sin, and good works also became matters of dispute, pitting

Gnesio-Lutherans against Melanchthon and his students (Philippists). An attack against Melanchthon's view of forensic justification in the early 1550s by Andreas Osiander brought Lutherans of both camps to Melanchthon's defense. At the same time, debates over Christ's presence in the Lord's Supper and the relation of Christ's human and divine natures arose. An opinion penned for the Elector of the Palatinate on this question in 1559 came to light shortly after Melanchthon's death, leading to fights over his legacy to this day.

S. Kusukawa, ed., *Philip Melanchthon: Orations on Philosophy and Education* (1999); C. Manschreck, *Melanchthon: The Quiet Reformer* (1958); Melanchthon, *Loci communes 1543*, trans. J. Preus (1992); Melanchthon, *Commentary on Romans*, trans. F. Kramer (1992); Melanchthon, *Corpus Reformatorum*, vols. 1–28 (1834–1860); H. Scheible, *Melanchthon: Eine Biographie* (1997); Scheible, ed., *Melanchthons Briefwechsel*; R. Stupperich, ed., *Melanchthons Werke in Auswahl*, 7 vols. (1951–1975); T. Wengert, *Human Freedom, Christian Righteousness* (1998).

TIMOTHY J. WENGERT

Melania the Elder (c. 342–c. 410), Roman noblewoman, ascetic, monastic founder, grandmother of Melania the Younger. Widowed and having lost two sons as a young woman, Melania entrusted her remaining son, Valerius Publicola, to a guardian and took up the ascetic life. She visited the monks in Egypt, supported exiled monks during the rule of the Arian Valens, converted Evagrius of Pontus to the ascetic life, and founded a women's monastery on the Mount of Olives, close to Rufinus's monastery for men. Both Palladius and Paulinus of Nola praise the "manliness" she displayed through her ascetic discipline, and Paulinus calls her "the perfect dove of the Lord." She was wealthy, self-confident, assertive, and generous. A friend and intellectual comrade of Rufinus, Evagrius, Palladius, John of Jerusalem, and the Egyptian monks known as the "Tall Brothers," Melania along with them fell under suspicion for her support of "Origenist" theology and ascetic theory. Jerome, who writes glowingly of Melania's renunciations, maligns her after his falling out with Rufinus, and her name is glaringly absent from Gerontius's biography of her granddaughter.

Palladius, *Lausiac History* 10, 38, 46, 54, 55; Paulinus of Nola, *Letters* 28.5, 29.5–14, 31.1, 45.2–3; Jerome, *Letters* 3.3, 4.2, 39.5, 45.4,

133.3; E. A. Clark, *The Origenist Controversy* (1992).

TERESA M. SHAW

Melania the Younger (c. 385–439), wealthy Roman woman turned ascetic, founder of monasteries, granddaughter of Melania the Elder. According to her biography, written by Gerontius in the mid-fifth century, Melania's family forced her to marry Valerius Pinianus and opposed the couple's decision, after a few years of marriage, to renounce both the world and sexual relations. Their renunciation took place in stages and was complicated by their enormous wealth as well as the political situation in Rome. They first withdrew to property outside of Rome and began to divest themselves of wealth, free their slaves, and give property to the church and monasteries. After a period in North Africa, where they met Augustine and practiced increased physical renunciations, they traveled to Jerusalem and visited the monks in Egypt. Following the death of her mother and Pinianus, Melania built monasteries for both women and men on the Mount of Olives, where her grandmother had established communities more than fifty years earlier. She traveled to Constantinople in order to convert her uncle Volusian and was on familiar terms with the empress Eudocia. Her biographer attempts to separate Melania from her grandmother's Origenist background, but evidence from Palladius suggests otherwise.

Augustine, *Letters* 124–126; E. A. Clark, *The Life of Melania the Younger* (1984); Gerontius, *Vita Melaniae Junioris*, SC 90 (1962); Palladius, *Lausiac History* 54, 61.

TERESA M. SHAW

Melchiorites Followers of the lay preacher Melchior Hoffman (1495?–1543). Initially an advocate of Luther's reform ideas, Hoffman itinerated through major Baltic cities, Stockholm, and northern Germany preaching fiery sermons flavored with apocalypticism, spiritualistic-allegorical biblical interpretations, and occasional advocacy of civil disobedience. Both Catholics and Lutherans soon rejected his radical preaching, and he was expelled from area after area until he reached Strasbourg, where he came under Anabaptist influence. After further wanderings in the Netherlands, he returned to Strasbourg in 1533, convinced he was Elijah and that Strasbourg would be the site of Christ's imminent return. The last years of his life were spent in prison in Strasbourg expecting liberation upon the end of the world.

Melchior's preaching and writings influenced Anabaptist groups in northern Europe and England. Although some of his followers, such as Obbe Philips (c. 1500–1568), embraced Anabaptist pacifism, Melchiorites became notorious for their takeover of the city of Münster (1534–1535). In 1533 Bernhard Rothmann (c. 1495–1535), the reformer of Münster, the capital city of the territory of Münster in northwestern Germany, accepted Hoffman's prophecies and embraced Melchiorite Anabaptism. Jan Matthijs (d. 1534) from Amsterdam soon displaced Rothmann as leader of the Münster Melchiorites. Gaining control of the city, the Melchiorites proclaimed it the New Jerusalem, to be defended by the sword. Combined Catholic and Lutheran forces retook the city and executed the Melchiorite leaders. The Melchiorite movement per se ended with the Münster debacle. Some of the remnants found new leadership and direction from Menno Simons (1496–1561), others joined the Swiss Brethren, and others returned to the main Reformation churches.

K. Deppermann, *Melchior Hoffman: Social Unrest and Apocalyptic Visions in the Age of the Reformation* (1987); C. Krahn, *Dutch Anabaptism: Origin, Spread, Life, and Thought, 1450–1600* (2nd ed., 1981); J. Stayer, *Anabaptists and the Sword* (2nd ed., 1976); G. H. Williams, *The Radical Reformation* (2nd ed., 1992).

CARTER LINDBERG

Meletian Schisms There were two contemporaneous Meletian schisms in the fourth century, one named after Meletius of Lycopolis in Egypt and one named after Meletius of Antioch. The Egyptian schism began in 304 during a persecution and had as its major causes Meletius's ordination of priests in Alexandria and his claim to its bishopric in the absence of Bishop Peter, who had fled for safety. Also, Meletius argued for a longer period of repentance for those who lapsed during persecution. After the persecution (during which Meletius was arrested, although he was freed in 311, and Peter was eventually martyred) the schism continued between two groups with competing claims to the bishopric. Athanasius, the victor against the group he labeled "Meletians," largely suppressed the movement among the urban laity over whom he had control. Meletians were tolerated, indeed active, in monastic settings for some centuries and may even have

been the first Christians to establish communal monasticism in Egypt.

The schism in Antioch centered on Bishop Meletius, exiled three times between his appointment in 360 and death in 381 while presiding over the Council of Constantinople. His evolving orthodoxy during the Trinitarian controversy was a factor in both exiles and schism. His eventual recognition as the rightful bishop was due in part to support by the Cappadocian Fathers, who in this matter were at odds with their ally Athanasius (whom Meletius had refused Communion) and with Rome, both of whom backed Paulinus (associated with the party of Eustathius) as bishop of Antioch.

Athanasius, *Defense against the Arians, History of the Arians*, ed. and trans. A. Robertson, vol. 4 of *NPNF*, 2nd series (1986); H. I. Bell, *Jews and Christians in Egypt* (1924), 38–99; J. Goehring, "Monastic Diversity and Ideological Boundaries in Fourth-Century Christian Egypt," *JECS* 5 (1997): 61–83; Gregory of Nyssa, *On Meletius*, ed. and trans. W. Moore, vol. 5 of *NPNF*, 2nd series (1986); K. M. Spoerl, "The Schism at Antioch since Cavallera," in *Arianism after Arius*, ed. M. R. Barnes and D. H. Williams (1993), 101–26.

REBECCA KRAWIEC

Melito (later second cent.), bishop of Sardis. According to Eusebius (*Hist. eccl.* 5.24), Polycrates of Ephesus referred to Melito as "the eunuch whose conversation was always in the Holy Spirit." Eusebius presents him as a major writer of the later second century, the author of the treatise *On the Passover*, an *Apology*, and numerous other works. Eusebius (*Hist. eccl.* 5.26) also cites Melito's list of OT books and quotes a passage from his *Apology* in which Melito argues that the birth of Jesus during the reign of Augustus was a good omen for the compatibility of Christianity with the Roman Empire.

Eusebius gives the misleading impression that *On the Passover* defends the practice, traditional among Christians from the Roman province of Asia, of celebrating Passover (that is, the Christian Easter) along with the Jews on the fourteenth of their month of Nisan. *On the Passover* has now been recovered and edited from ancient copies on papyrus. The work is evidently a sermon, written in a florid Asiatic style, that reflects on the Passover lamb of Exodus 12 as an image, planned in advance, of Christ. In the process, Melito reflects on other OT prefigurations of Christ, on Christ as God and man, and on the supersession of Judaism by Christianity.

Melito of Sardis, *On Pascha and Fragments*, trans. S. G. Hall (1991).

JOSEPH W. TRIGG

Melville, Andrew (1545–1622), Scottish Presbyterian leader and scholar. From 1559 Melville attended successively the universities of St. Andrews, Paris, and Poitiers, whence he proceeded to Geneva. Upon returning to Scotland in 1574 he was appointed principal of the College of Glasgow, and in 1580 he was translated to St. Mary's College at St. Andrews. At both institutions he introduced educational reforms that greatly enhanced the prestige of the Scottish universities. Melville was a zealous religious reformer; his ecclesiastical ideals, largely embodied in the *Second Book of Discipline* (1578), centered on (1) coordinate independent jurisdictions for church and state and (2) the establishment of a presbyterian polity. He championed the abolition of episcopacy, opposed royal pretensions to supremacy over the church, and claimed for ecclesiastical courts broad jurisdiction independent of the civil authorities. While ministers could not exercise civil jurisdiction, they were nevertheless authorized to teach the magistrate how it ought to be exercised according to God's word. Melville's views were not popular with the civil authorities, and because he continued to press vehemently for reform from the pulpit, in the general assembly, and even before king and court, he often faced powerful opposition. Ultimately he was incarcerated in the Tower of London (1607). His release was secured in 1611 to teach at the university at Sedan in France, where he died.

T. McCrie, *The Life of Andrew Melville* (1824); S. Mechie, "Andrew Melville," in *Fathers of the Kirk*, ed. R. Wright (1960).

DANIEL EPPLEY

Mendicant Orders The mendicant orders appeared in the thirteenth century, representatives of a new spirituality and way of life. At the bottom of this way of life was absolute poverty, an indispensable foundation of the newly founded communities—and an object of heated debate. Absolute poverty implies not collecting tithes but living from one's own work or from alms. The mendicants were consequently allowed to beg—hence their name, from the Latin *mendicare*, "to beg"—and were not bound by the vow of stability; they saw their role as in the world and not only within the walls of a clois-

ter. Unlike previous orders, they settled mainly in cities, which they saw as their natural sphere of activity. After a dramatic surge in the number of such communities, the papacy felt the need to control the movement. Only four orders were officially authorized by the Second Council of Lyon (1274): the Dominicans, the Franciscans, the Carmelites, and the Austin Friars (also known as the Augustinian Hermits). The Servites became the fifth official mendicant order in 1487; the Minims (1567) and various orders in the sixteenth, seventeenth, eighteenth, and even twentieth centuries were granted the corresponding juridical status by the papacy without always being closely related to the "traditional" mendicant orders: Jesuats, a fourteenth-century lay order also known as the *Clerici apostilici S. Hieronymi* (1567), Crosiers (1591), Jesuits (1571), Trinitarians (1609), Piarists (1622), Hospitalers of St. John of God (1624), Mercedarians (1690), Scalzetti (1784), and the Teutonic Order (1929). Furthermore, branches of the older orders were considered as mendicants, such as Tertiary Franciscans, Capuchins, and Récollets. The Hieronymites of the community of the Hermits of Peter of Pisa may also be added to the list. Due to their orientation, the mendicant orders, especially Dominicans and Franciscans, were active, and still are, in preaching and missionary work, and formerly, in the Inquisition.

L. Barbaglia and F. Dal Pino, *Mendicanti, Ordini*, vol. 5 of *Dizionario degli istituti di perfezione*, ed. G. Pellicia and G. Rocca (1978), 1163–1212; H. Grundmann, *Religious Movements in the Middle Ages* (1996); W. A. Hinnebusch, *The History of the Dominican Order: Origins and Growth to 1500*, 2 vols. (1966); C. H. Lawrence, *The Friars: The Impact of the Early Mendicant Movement on Western Society* (1994); J. R. H. Moorman, *A History of the Franciscan Order from Its Origins to the Year 1517* (1968); B. Rano, *The Order of Saint Augustine* (1975).

SÉBASTIEN BARRET

Mendicant Schools Like most religious orders, the mendicants lent great importance to study. However, their internal system of education differed substantially from those of the "old" orders. Whereas the Dominicans developed an extensive and well-organized educational system from the very beginning, Francis of Assisi had concerns about the sciences as sources of pride and arrogance. Nevertheless, the Franciscans also founded a thought-out system of studies, as did the Carmelites and Austin

Friars. Their educational system was organized on three levels. The basic educational institutions were the convent schools, the so-called *studia conventualia*, which formed an integral part of almost every convent. Normally there was a lector or study leader responsible for the reading and for the teaching of preaching skills. Scholars and teachers were allocated from the provincial chapter to the separate houses. The next level constituted the custodial and provincial schools, which were established on the level of the province or custody. In these schools the novices were taught in the arts, and members of the order were prepared for the next education level, the so-called *studia generalia*, or general schools. Mostly these establishments were founded in university towns. Here the students got an extensive theological education. The general chapter was directly responsible for those *studia generalia*. Many of them were later incorporated into the universities. This educational system was highly differentiated, decentralized, and efficient. Since the fifteenth century, corresponding to the spread of universities, the mendicant schools gradually lost importance. The number of monks who preferred to study at the university increased. During the Reformation the so-called teaching orders emerged (Jesuits, Oratorians, Doctrinarians, etc.). Similarly, the mendicant orders opened their schools to laymen and laywomen. Mendicants founded or took charge of schools in both urban and rural territories.

The curriculum within the *studia* system was hierarchically arranged. The course of study started with grammar, followed by the *studia naturalium*, and the highest level consisted of theological studies. Many of the provincial schools developed their own academic profile.

———

M. M. Mulchahey, *"First the Bow Is Bent in Study . . .": Dominican Education before 1350* (1998); B. Roest, *A History of Franciscan Education (c. 1210–1517)* (2000).

MIRKO BREITENSTEIN

Menius, Justus (1499–1558), Lutheran pastor and "Reformer of Thuringia." He translated Luther's Galatians commentary and other Latin works by him and Melanchthon and abbreviated the Small Catechism. Menius participated at the Marburg Colloquy (1529) and the assemblies that adopted the Wittenberg Concord (1536) and the Schmalkald Articles (1537). He provided ethical guidance for the family in his *Oeconomia Christiana* (1529). His commentary on *I Samuel* (1532) provided arguments

for resisting civil authorities and established a basis for the Lutheran princes to resist Charles V in the Schmalkald War. An opponent of the Augsburg Interim (1548), he wrote a confession for the sons of John Frederick, who had been imprisoned and deposed as elector of Saxony. Though he opposed the Interim, he supported the inclusion of the exorcism in baptism. Menius wrote against Osiander's doctrine of justification, but his concern for the moral dimension of the Christian faith surfaced in his refusal to condemn Major's teaching that good works are necessary for salvation. Amsdorf, an opponent of Major, forced Menius from Saxony. His last years were spent in Leipzig, where Melanchthon secured a post for him.

———

R. Kolb, *Nikolaus von Amsdorf, 1483–1565: Popular Polemics in the Preservation of Luther's Legacy* (1973).

DAVID P. SCAER

Mennonites The Mennonites emerged out of the Anabaptist movement of the early sixteenth century as followers of the Dutch leader Menno Simons. Mennonite scholars of the mid-twentieth century argued that the Mennonites were the descendants of the strict biblicist Anabaptists, specifically the Swiss Brethren from Zurich, Michael Sattler in southern Germany, and Menno Simons in the Low Countries. For these scholars, led by Harold Bender, normative Anabaptism was peaceful and centered on the Bible. This view was meant to overthrow more than four centuries of anti-Mennonite scholarship that portrayed the Anabaptists as violent enthusiasts. Since the 1970s, this revisionist approach to Mennonite history has been itself revised, with the polygenesis theory of Anabaptist origins. According to this theory, the Mennonites can trace their origins not only to the nonviolent Anabaptists but also to mystical, millenarian, and violent reformers popular in the early sixteenth century. These include the spiritualist Hans Denck, the apocalyptic Thomas Müntzer, who was involved in the German Peasants' War (1524–1525), his disciple Hans Hut, and others. The polygenesis theory has been widely accepted by Anabaptist scholars, both Mennonite and non-Mennonite. It was through the work of Menno Simons, Dirk and Obbe Phillips, and others in the second half of the sixteenth century that the mystical, violent, and millenarian branches of the Anabaptist movement were either expelled from the church or converted to a more moderate form of Anabaptism.

After decades of persecution and the defeat at Münster (1535), the surviving members of the Anabaptist movement adapted certain beliefs and practices that would characterize the Mennonites for most of their history. These beliefs include: baptism is for adults only after they have made a confession of their faith; church discipline must be enforced by the ban as outlined in Matthew 18; true Christians must be separated from the world; Christians must not use violence; the true church suffers persecution; the church is for those who are willing to live according to a strict interpretation of discipleship based on the New Testament; salvation is found not only in faith but also in practicing that faith by following Christ. These characteristics, which define the Mennonites as well as the other descendants of the Anabaptists—the Hutterites and the Amish—set the Mennonite Church apart as neither Protestant nor Catholic. In the eighteenth and nineteenth centuries, the Mennonite Church experienced many schisms. Most Mennonite schisms have occurred over the interpretation and practice of the aforementioned beliefs.

In the seventeenth and eighteenth centuries, many Mennonites left Western Europe to found communities in the North American colonies, Poland, and Russia. Even though executions for heresy were rare after 1648, Mennonites were subject to exile, confiscation of property, and branding. In their new homes, Mennonites were free of persecution for the first time in their history. This precipitated changes in Mennonite church government and their relationship with the world.

The earliest form of Mennonite church government was basically congregationalist. That is, authority for the church was invested in the local leaders of the congregation. Beginning in the 1700s, the Mennonites began to adopt larger systems of church government. Ministers from across a region, such as Lancaster or Franconia, would agree to meet regularly to discuss issues of relevance for the Mennonite community at large. Gradually these meetings became synods that had the authority to set standards for discipline and to codify Mennonite beliefs but that lacked the ability to enforce these standards without the consent of the individual congregations.

C. J. Dyck, *An Introduction to Mennonite History* (3rd ed., 1993); W. Klaassen, ed., *Anabaptism Revisited* (1992); J. Stayer, *Anabaptists and the Sword* (1976); J. Stayer, W. Packull, and K. Deppermann, "From Monogenesis to Polygenesis," *Mennonite Quarterly Review* 53 (1979): 175–218.

AMY R. CALDWELL

Merovingian Church The church as it developed in the Frankish kingdom during the Merovingian dynasty began with the baptism of Clovis. Clovis chose a Catholic wife, Clothild, niece of Gondebaud, the Burgundian Arian king. Prior to his conversion Clovis was already in contact with the church and respectful of its power. The turning point for Clovis's conversion, however, was the battle of Tolbiac (496), in which he invoked the god of Clothild and won the battle against the Alemani. Clothild then called Bishop Remigius of Reims to counsel and later baptize Clovis.

The Merovingian church developed both from within, largely by the nobility, and from without, by missionaries. Among the best known of the first is Radegund of Poitiers (c. 518–587). The captured daughter of a Thuringian king, she was raised in the court of Clothar I (d. 629), who later married her, despite her preference for an ascetic, religious life. When Clothar had her brother murdered, Radegund fled to Noyon, begging Bishop Médard to make her a deaconess, then proceeded to Poitiers, where she founded a monastery of nuns with Clothar's permission. The monastery had Venantius Fortunatus (c. 530–c. 610), the poet and later bishop of Poitiers, as its chaplain. Radegund was one among many powerful religious women figures of the Merovingian era who founded and supported monasteries and had hagiographies written for them. Indeed, the Merovingian hagiographical renaissance is known for the richness of its lives of contemporary aristocratic saints who mingled the worldly and spiritual.

Martin of Tours was the primary patron saint of the Merovingians, and under Dagobert I (d. 639) the Abbey of St. Denis became the burial place of Merovingian kings and a central holy place. Dagobert purportedly had the abbey built for the saint who was to become the protector of the Frankish kings. Its customs may have been similar to those of the abbey of Martin of Tours, which had no written rule or vows. Under Dagobert's son Clovis II, the queen, Balthildis, attempted to impose a more rigid monastic rule upon the abbey, with little success. A mixing of rules was common among Merovingian monasteries, and there was great variety until the reforms of the Carolingian age.

Under the reign of Clothar's sons, religious life changed with the arrival of Columbanus from Ireland. Prior to Columbanus, the Gallic church had been primarily urban, after the Roman model. Columbanus's Celtic monasticism appealed to the Merovingian aristocracy, adapting to rural life and their kinship ties. The monks following in Columbanus's steps re-Christianized Normandy and northeastern Francia, bringing life back to ruined villages. Missionaries also moved outward: under Dagobert, Frankish missionaries strove to convert the Rhineland and northern Francia; Amandus (d. c. 684) went as far as to attempt to convert the Basques, mostly unsuccessfully. Unlike with the Irish, however, bishops were the central figures of the Merovingian church. Coming from the aristocracy, these bishops had close ties with rulers and held vast amounts of land. One example is Gregory, bishop of Tours (538–594), who wrote a *History of the Franks* covering both political and religious history. Born of a Gallo-Roman senatorial family, Gregory also wrote many lives of saints. Another major historical source is Fredegar's chronicles (c. 642–660).

Dagobert I was the last influential figure for the Merovingian church as well as the last Merovingian king to rule over the three kingdoms that the Carolingians later reconstituted. As king of the Franks, he surrounded himself with episcopal counselors, including the saints Ouen of Rouen, his chancellor (d. 684), and Eligius of Noyon, his chief counselor (d. 660). After Dagobert, the power of the Merovingian kings waned, causing the decline in popularity of many of the abbeys and saints they had supported.

J. K. McNamara and J. Halborg, trans. and ed., *Sainted Women of the Dark Ages* (1992); I. Wood, *Merovingian Kingdoms, 450–751* (1994).

MARIANNE M. DELAPORTE

Messalianism At the end of the fourth century, ascetic "Pray-ers" (trans. from the Syriac) drew criticism that led to condemnations at the Council of Ephesus (431). Messalianism spread from Syria into Asia Minor. Flavian of Antioch and Amphilochius of Iconium reacted to exaggerated ascetic practices (e.g., refusal to undertake manual labor in an attempt to pray ceaselessly) and spiritual elitism. Messalians were accused of believing that the sacraments and even the church are unnecessary to those purified through ceaseless prayer and ineffective to those not so purified. The accusation stemmed from their belief that each person suffers from the indwelling of evil, which is dis-

placed only when the Holy Spirit possesses the monk through strenuous prayer. In his *Ecclesiastical History* (mid-fifth cent.), Theodoret of Cyrrhus provides an early description of Messalianism at a synod in Antioch where a Messalian leader gave testimony about the movement to Flavian.

The Messalians found some sympathy from Gregory of Nyssa, who extolled the virtues of Mesopotamian monks and sought to protect ascetic enthusiasm even while reconciling it to the church. Gregory adapted Pseudo-Macarius's *Great Letter*, which was read in Messalian circles and was likely a precursor to the radicalization evident in Theodoret's history. Later the title "Messalian" was used with other equally loaded descriptors to attack various ascetic movements, such as the Bogomils in the tenth century.

J. Meyendorff, "St. Basil, Messalianism, and Byzantine Christianity," *St. Vladimir's Theological Quarterly* 24, no. 4 (1980): 219–34; M. Plested, "A Survey of Recent Research on Macarius-Symeon (Pseudo-Macarius)," *St. Vladimir's Theological Quarterly* 47, nos. 3–4 (2003): 431–40; C. Stewart, *"Working the Earth of the Heart": The Messalian Controversy in History, Texts, and Language to A.D. 431* (1991).

LISA D. MAUGANS DRIVER

Methodius (later third cent.), teacher and author. Evidence about Methodius's life is scanty and inconsistent. Modern scholars dismiss claims by Jerome (*Vir. ill.* 83) that Methodius was a bishop and martyr. His works indicate that he was a Christian teacher, probably from Olympus in Lycia (southwestern Asia Minor). He wrote dialogues, a peculiar genre for a bishop. The *Symposium*, his only work surviving in Greek, frequently alludes to Plato's dialogue of the same title and to other Platonic dialogues. In it ten virgins discuss chastity, to a large extent by interpreting biblical passages. It became an important source for ascetic theology.

Other works by Methodius survive as fragments and in translation into Old Church Slavonic. The *Symposium* shows that Methodius's thought—in particular his approach to the Bible—was heavily influenced by Origen. In later works he became more critical of what he took, sometimes mistakenly, to be Origen's views.

G. N. Bonwetsch, *Methodius*, in GCS 27 (1917); H. Musurillo, trans., *The Symposium:*

A Treatise on Chastity, in ACW 27 (1958); L. G. Patterson, *Methodius of Olympus: Divine Sovereignty, Human Freedom, and Life in Christ* (1997).

JOSEPH W. TRIGG

Metropolitan Bishops Certain bishops in the Latin church presided over an ecclesiastical see that was designated as the head of a province, exercising some degree of actual jurisdiction over the suffragan bishops of that province. Tradition associated the apostles and their disciples with many of the metropolitan churches that were established in the principal cities of the various Roman provinces. Those churches that grew up in the provincial hinterland quite naturally became subordinate to them. Provincial cities hosted meetings of regional bishops (synods), and the bishop of that city usually convoked and presided at the sessions. The first certain and official designation of these bishops as "metropolitan" is found in the fourth canon of the Council of Nicaea (325), which presupposed their existence and attributed to them the right to confirm the election of the bishops of the province. Rome remained the lone metropolitan see in Italy until about 350 when Milan and L'Aquila were raised to that status. By the thirteenth century there were metropolitan sees throughout the Latin church, including York, Lund, Salzburg, Magdeburg, Trier, and Besançon.

Over the centuries the power of the metropolitans waxed and waned: Charlemagne required metropolitans to be archbishops. From the eleventh century, as the papacy began to assume ever greater control over all aspects of Latin church life and organization, the metropolitans became increasingly ceremonial, though they did retain the right to summon provincial synods, hear appeals, conduct visitations of suffragan bishoprics, and assume administration of vacant sees in their province. Their dependency on Rome was symbolized in the necessity of their obtaining the pallium following their election before they could exercise the full powers of their office. Some metropolitans had quasi-political functions as well, such as those of Canterbury, Cologne, and Reims, who maintained the right to consecrate the respective rulers of England, the HRE, and France. Lateran IV (1215) briefly enhanced the metropolitans' role by demanding that they gather their provincial clergy together annually in a synod where the decrees of Innocent III were to be proclaimed anew. The extensive use of papal legates and provisions by thirteenth- and fourteenth-century popes stripped away most metropolitan prerogatives; by the time of Trent they had lost even the right to confirm suffragan bishops. *See also* Provinces, Ecclesiastical

G. Barraclough, *Papal Provisions* (1935); R. Brentano, *Two Churches: England and Italy in the 13th Century* (1968); K. Ganzer, *Papsttum und Bistumsbesetzungen in der Zeit von Gregor IX. bis Bonifaz VIII: Ein Beitrag zur Geschichte der päpstlichen Reservationen* (1968); J. Heydenreich, *Die Metropolitangewalt der Erzbischöfe von Trier bis auf Balduin* (1938); E. O. Kehrberger, *Provincial- und Synodalstatuten des Spätmittelalters* (1938); J. Wenner, *Die Rechtsbeziehungen der Mainzer Metropoliten zu ihren sächsischen Suffraganbistümern bis zum Tode Aribos (1031)* (1926).

PAUL B. PIXTON

Michael VIII Paleologus (1224–1282), Byzantine emperor from 1259 until his death. Michael VIII was the first emperor of the Paleologan dynasty, which lasted until the fall of Constantinople in 1453. After the death of the Nicaean emperor Theodore II Laskaris, he conspired to become regent for his son John IV, and was crowned co-emperor in 1259. After his army retook Constantinople from the Latins, he entered the city and had himself crowned again and took his son Andronicus as his colleague, thus effectively eliminating young John IV whom he later had blinded. Patriarch Arsenios excommunicated him for this act. Michael moved quickly to solidify his control over imperial territory. Although he had several significant military and diplomatic triumphs, he was unable to gain solid control against the Turks in Anatolia. His concern to protect his empire against further Latin invasion led him to accept the union between the Greek and Latin churches negotiated at the Council of Lyon in 1274 (see *Councils, Later Middle Ages*). At the end of his reign he was involved in the plot against the Angevins known as the Sicilian Vespers. Michael remained loyal to the unpopular reunion and the unionist hierarchy until his death and was refused burial by the Orthodox Church.

D. Geanakoplos, *Emperor Michael Paleologus and the West* (1959); W. Treadgold, *A History of the Byzantine State and Society* (1997).

EUGENE M. LUDWIG, OFM CAP.

Michelangelo Buonarroti (1475–1564), Italian Renaissance sculptor, painter, architect, and poet, active in Florence and Rome. One of the world's most famous artists, Michelangelo was nicknamed *Il Divino* by contemporaries and commissioned for major projects by Medici dukes and several popes. His sculptural work includes Madonnas, figures from classical mythology, and biblical personages, most notably, the colossal David (1501–1504) and the dramatic Moses (c. 1515). His architectural designs include the Laurentian Library reading room and vestibule, and the dome of St. Peter's in Rome. As a painter Michelangelo excelled as well. His encyclopedic and visionary images on the ceiling of the Sistine Chapel at the Vatican (1508–1512), recently restored to their original brilliant color, and the sixty-foot-high mural of the Last Judgment on the chapel wall (1534–1541) broke new ground for their depiction of the human body, as well as for their cosmic message. Working furiously until his death at age seventy-nine, Michelangelo left his imprint of passionate genius in all the arts.

———

G. C. Argan and B. Contardi, *Michelangelo: Architect* (1993); H. Hibbard, *Michelangelo* (1985); C. H. Smyth, ed., *Michelangelo Drawings* (1996); E. Wind and E. Sears, eds., *The Religious Symbolism of Michelangelo: The Sistine Ceiling* (2001).

PRISCILLA BAUMANN

Micron, Marten (1523–1559), Dutch Reformed pastor, theologian, and physician. During his short life Micron exerted significant influence on the early Reformed movement in the Netherlands, primarily through his works of polemical theology and church polity. Together with Jan Utenhove, Micron revised à Lasco's church order for the exile churches in London. He published a Dutch version in 1554. That same year he debated Menno Simons at Wismar on the topic of Christ's incarnation. Micron was a skilled polemicist and apologist, writing two works against Simons's Anabaptism and a treatise defending the Reformed understanding of the Lord's Supper against the attacks of Joachim Westphal, a Lutheran.

———

W. F. Dankbar, ed., *Marten Micron, De christliche ordinancien der Nederlandscher Ghemeinten te London (1554)* (1956); O. P. Grell, "Exile and Tolerance," in O. P. Grell and B. Scribner, eds., *Tolerance and Intolerance in the European Reformation* (1996), 164–81; A. Pettegree, *Foreign Protestant Communities in Sixteenth-Century London* (1985).

RAYMOND A. BLACKETER

Milan, Edict of   After Constantine's victory at the Milvian Bridge in October 312, he openly supported Christianity. The following spring Constantine met his fellow emperor Licinius at Milan for the latter's marriage to Constantine's daughter Constantia. Constantine also impressed upon Licinius, then engaged in a war with the pagan emperor Maximinus, the need to support their Christian subjects. The two reached an agreement providing not only for freedom of worship for Christians, as in the emperor Galerius's Edict of Toleration of 311, but also for the restitution of Christian property that had been confiscated by the imperial treasury or acquired by private persons, with the latter being provided compensation by the state. This marked the first time that the imperial government recognized the Christian church as a lawful institution.

The ruling survives only in the form that Licinius forwarded to Eastern officials for promulgation later in 313. As a result, some have asserted that it was "not an edict, and not issued at Milan." But the term is correct. The document clearly was drafted at Milan by both emperors and was intended to apply to the entire empire. Presumably it was circulated in a like manner by Constantine in the West.

———

T. D. Barnes, *Constantine and Eusebius* (1981), 39–75; Eusebius, *Hist. eccl.* 10.5; Lactantius, *On the Deaths of the Persecutors*, 48.

RALPH W. MATHISEN

Military (or Military-Religious) Orders   These orders were fusions of the military and religious callings and first appeared in the early twelfth century. Many military orders adopted, or evolved out of, a hospitaller vocation. The three major military orders were the Templars, international in membership and the most single-minded of the military orders; the Hospitallers, international and involved in hospital work as well as military activity; and the Teutonic Order, which drew its membership from German-speaking areas and operated hospitals in addition to fielding knights. There were many lesser military orders as well.

The impetus behind the military orders came from several sources, including a wave of lay piety sparked by eleventh- and twelfth-century efforts at church reform to raise the spiritual level of society by adapting aspects of monasticism to other areas of life; a desperate need for pilgrims in the newly liberated Holy

Land for physical defense; and a changed attitude toward warfare that was more consistent with the thought of Ambrose and Augustine and that emphasized defensive warfare on behalf of Christendom as a self-sacrificial act of love.

Though military orders arose in a context of crusading, their members, who took monastic vows, were prohibited from also taking Crusade vows. Their activities were viewed, in theory at least, as defensive. They answered only to the pope, a fact that typically created tension between them and local ecclesiastical authorities but that enhanced their flexibility and effectiveness.

Though a few theologians sometimes questioned the validity of the military orders' joint calling, their effectiveness was amply demonstrated. Various military orders protected pilgrims, defended Christian states in the Latin East against Muslim attacks, and operated hospitals. Some provided financial services to pilgrims and kings, or played a key (if controversial) part in the pacification of the pagan Baltic region in the later Middle Ages. Their Muslim enemies reserved a special hatred for them because of their fierce dedication to the protection of Christian interests. Most used at least some part of their resources charitably.

By the eighteenth century, many of the military orders had become mere decorations. Few still exist today as religious entities. Of those that do, the most notable are the Sovereign Military Order of Malta (descendant of the Hospitallers) and the Teutonic Order. None retains its military mission.

A. Forey, *The Military Orders from the 12th to the Early 14th Centuries* (1992); D. Seward, *The Monks of War: The Military Religious Orders* (2nd ed., 1995).

PAUL CRAWFORD

Mill, John (1645–1707), English biblical scholar. Having earned distinction as a classical scholar at Queen's College, Oxford, he was ordained in 1670. He later served as chaplain for the bishop of Exeter and King Charles II. In 1685, he was elected principal of St. Edmund Hall, Oxford. For the rest of his life, he worked on a new Greek edition of the New Testament. The work listed all variant readings and clearly described the manuscripts he consulted, thereby significantly advancing the discipline of textual criticism.

A. Fox, *John Mill and Richard Bentley: A Study of the Textual Criticism of the New Testament, 1675–1729* (1954).

ERIC LUND

Miltitz, Karl von (c. 1490–1529), German nobleman and papal diplomat. After studying in Cologne and Bologna, Miltitz went to Rome. In 1518 Pope Leo X sent him to give Frederick the Wise the Golden Rose, symbolic of certain privileges, and to facilitate action against Luther. Miltitz negotiated with Luther in 1519, but his attempts were interrupted by events leading to the Leipzig Disputation. Miltitz met with Luther several more times; Luther published an open letter to Leo X and *On the Freedom of the Christian* in response. After 1521 Miltitz played no important role.

M. Brecht, *Martin Luther: His Road to Reformation 1483–1521* (1985).

MARY JANE HAEMIG

Minucius Felix (c. second–third cent.), Latin apologist, likely in Rome or Africa. Minucius Felix is known for one primary text, *Octavius*. (A second text, *De fato*, mentioned in *Octavius*, was either never written or is simply not extant.) The *Octavius* is a hypothetical discussion among Minucius Felix, another Christian (Octavius), and a pagan (Caecilius).

Against Christianity, the pagan Caecilius argues that the world is not providentially ordered and that it is better to rely upon the beliefs of antiquity. The novelty of Christianity is its impiety, and Christians are atheists whose religion exhibits various forms of perversity and absurdity. Octavius's rebuttal seeks reasonable grounds for belief in the unity, providence, invisibility, and transcendence of God. He argues for the high moral standards and social sensitivity of Christians. The *Octavius* ends with the participants cheerful and Caecilius convinced of the fundamentals. Employing philosophical material to find common ground with its assumed audience, the *Octavius* does not cite Scripture but uses Stoics such as Cicero and Seneca the Younger as sources.

H. J. Baylis, *Minucius Felix and His Place among the Early Fathers of the Latin Church* (1928); Minucius Felix, *Octavius*, trans. G. W. Clarke, ACW 39 (1974); Minucius, *Octavius*, ed. B. Kytzler (1982); Minucius, *Octavius*, ed. M. Pelligrano (1950); S. Price, "Latin Christian

Apologetics," in *Apologetics in the Roman Empire*, ed. M. Edwards et al. (1999).

D. JEFFREY BINGHAM

Miracles in the Middle Ages

The term *miraculum* is derived from *mirus*, "something to wonder at," a phenomenon that confounds or even appears to contradict the normal rules governing nature or society. Such a "sign" often serves the larger purpose of signifying God's greatness or the order that underlies creation, such as the considerable catalog of divine wonders found in Ecclesiasticus 42:15–25 and 43:1–33. The efficacy of relics as repositories of the sacred also received legitimacy in 2 Kings 13:21, which recounts the revival of a dead man through contact with Elisha's bones, and was later confirmed in the cure of the sick through contact with clothes touched by the apostle Paul (Acts 19:11–12). The biblical miracle stressed God as the underlying cause of both order and disorder in the universe. The most common miracles include cures and healings, visions, unanticipated changes in nature (e.g., the transformation of water into wine), rescue from danger (such as unjust imprisonment or military defeat), and exorcism.

The Old Testament also offers a distinction between sorcery or magic, and miracle. As Deuteronomy 13:1–5 suggests, such portents or signs that are intended to drive believers away from God are performed by heretics, charlatans, or sorcerers, like the magicians who confronted Moses with their secret arts. They are performed by the agents of Satan, himself a fallen angel who may perform supernatural acts. The need to establish criteria for distinguishing such demonic acts from divine miracles therefore became the focus for discussions by medieval theologians. The angelic or saintly performer of miracles was regarded merely as an intermediary through whom God acts and whose mission is to lead to the recognition of God's greatness, uniqueness, and power against his (usually pagan) foes. As Pope Innocent II said in his 1139 canonization of Abbot Sturmo of Fulda, "God has performed miracles by means of his [i.e., Sturmo's] merits," as attested by the evidence of eyewitnesses.

The prototypical miracles had been publicly performed by Moses, Elijah, and Jesus, and later miracles were regarded as the necessary means of bringing Jews and other nonbelievers to the faith, as both Justin Martyr (d. 163/167) and Origen (d. c. 254) noted. Augustine's treatment of the miracle (largely in the *De trinitate*), although not always consistent, remained the *locus classicus* for both medieval canonical and theological sources. He essentially regarded miracles as an acceleration of the normal processes of nature whereby the seeds (*semina seminum*) inherent in nature are activated. These phenomena occur in a manner contrary to the normal course of nature, confound nonbelievers, and arouse surprise and wonder among unlearned observers.

In *De potentia* and the *Summa theologiae* Thomas Aquinas (thirteenth cent.) provided a more systematic distinction between miracles outside of, contrary to, and beyond the normal course of nature. In the face of the proliferation of events labeled supernatural by ordinary believers (and which were mocked by heretics, Jews, and other foes of the church), Thomas attempted to distinguish between phenomena that may be explained by learned experts, and those the untrained eye regards as supernatural. Other medieval theologians who dealt with this subject were Hugh of St. Victor, William of Auvergne, Albertus Magnus, and Engelbert of Admont. The scholastic effort to deemphasize the number of supernatural phenomena is epitomized by Hugh of St. Victor's argument that Psalm 39:6—"Thou hast multiplied Thy wonderful works, O Lord"—suggests that all the works of God's creation are wonderful and should bring one closer to God. John Locke later provided a succinct definition of the miracle: "A miracle then, I take to be a sensible operation, which, being above the comprehension of the spectator, and in his opinion contrary to the established course of nature, is taken by him to be divine." At the same time, canon lawyers developed legal criteria to determine the credibility of any alleged miracle. Beginning in the early thirteenth century, papal canonization proceedings were initiated with a list of questions to be posed to persons claiming to have witnessed or experienced a miracle attributed to a putative saint. Testimony concerning a miracle should have provided information concerning the time and place of the event and the identity of the witnesses. If a medical problem existed, the witnesses were asked about its symptoms, how long they had lasted, what natural means had been attempted to cure the condition, and what evidence there was that health had been restored to the victim. Inquiry was made concerning words of the evocation to the saint or sacred relics, the vow undertaken and its fulfillment, and the reaction of those who had seen or heard about the miracle. The evidence of each miracle (many posthumous) was then studied by members of a commission of inquiry and members of the curia before being included in a papal bull of canonization. Were the testimony presented by reliable, trustworthy witnesses proven to have been based on hearsay, been contradictory, or been insufficiently precise or amenable to a natural explanation, the miracle would have been rejected. Such internal discussions survive in the cases of King Louis IX of France, Pope Celestine V, and Bishop Thomas of Hereford.

Thousands of miracles are to be found in medieval sources, most frequently in miracle collections (attributed to a particular shrine or saint) and saints' lives. These miracle tales were communicated to a wider audience through sermons, liturgy, and the visual arts. To cite one example, the life and miracles of Bishop Richard of Chichester (d. 1253) were investigated by a papal commission. The pope then issued a bull of canonization (1262), and a sermon was delivered in Richard's honor by Cardinal Odo of Châteauroux. Both the bull and the sermon cited miracles that had passed learned scrutiny. The judicial testimony was turned into a narrative biography by the Dominican Ralph Bocking (1268/1272). This biography was transformed into an Anglo-Norman French poem (1276/1277) by Pierre d'Abernon of Fetcham in order to reach a wider lay audience. These sources then became the foundation for the offices and lives of Richard that circulated until the sixteenth century. In a similar way, visual cycles of the lives and miracles of the saints were based upon individual biographies (e.g., Thomas of Celano's life of Francis of Assisi) or collections such as Jacob of Voragine's *Golden Legend* (c. 1260).

B. Bron, *Das Wunder: Das theologische Wunderverständnis im Horizont des neuzeitlichen Natur- und Geschichtsbegriff* (2nd ed., 1979); P. R. L. Brown, *The Cult of the Saints: Its Rise and Function in Latin Christianity* (1981); R. C. Finucane, *Miracles and Pilgrims: Popular Beliefs in Medieval England* (1977); M. Goodich, *Violence and Miracle in the 14th Century: Private Grief and Public Salvation* (1995); A. Kleinberg, *Prophets in Their Own Country: Living Saints and the Making of Sainthood in the Later Middle Ages* (1992); P.-A. Sigal, *L'homme et le miracle dans la France médiévale, XIe–XIIe siècles* (1985); R. Van Dam, *Saints and Their Miracles in Late Antique Gaul* (1993); A. Vauchez, *Sainthood in the Later Middle Ages*, trans. J. Birrell (1997); B. Ward, *Miracles and the Medieval Mind* (1982).

MICHAEL GOODICH†

Mithraism

Mithraism   Religion of Hittite, Iranian, and Indic origins containing some rituals that were similar to Christian rituals. The earliest manifestation of "Mithras" was as a semi-divine hunter and keeper of the plains. He was later associated in the Persian pantheon with Ahura-Mazda. Then in the *Vedas* he is associated with Veruna, Lord of the Heaven. In the Hindu *Vedas* and the Zoroastrian *Avesta* he is called "Mitra" or "Mithras." His early symbols were sun, light, and the bull, all associated with life and fecundity.

Mithraism entered the Greco-Roman world in the first century BCE. Mithras's older attributes were combined with Hellenistic astrological and mystery symbolism associated with salvation. As "Mithras the Invincible Sun" he was life-giver and savior.

Initiates went through symbolic ascents of suffering and struggle through seven planetary spheres, whereby they advanced toward Mithras and salvation. Central to Mithraic rites was a communal meal. This meal was similar enough in its details to the Christian Eucharist that Tertullian claimed it was inspired by the devil to undercut the validity of the Christian rite. The cult of Mithras was popular in the Roman military and was sanctioned by several emperors. It excluded women and had neither clergy nor public festivals. It was superseded in the fourth century by Christianity.

E. Cumont, *The Mysteries of Mithras* (1956); J. R. Hinnels, ed., *Mithraic Studies*, 2 vols. (1975); A. S. Geden, *Mithraic Sources in English* (1990); M. P. Speidel, *Mithras-Orion: Greek Hero and Roman Army God* (1980); D. Ulansey, *The Origins of the Mithraic Mysteries* (1989); M. J. Vermassen, *Mithras, the Secret God* (1963).

ROBERT M. BERCHMAN

Modern Devotion   see Brethren of the Common Life; Groote, Geert; Radewijns, Florentius; Ruusbroec, Jan van; Thomas à Kempis; Windesheim Congregation

Mohács, Battle of   Near the town of Mohács on the Danube River, about 115 miles south of Budapest, a battle took place on September 1, 1526, between Hungarians, led by King Louis II, and Ottomans, led by Suleiman. After capturing Belgrade (1521), Suleiman attempted to expand Turkish power by attacking Hungary. After less than two hours of battle, the Hungarian force was destroyed due to its direct frontal charge against a superior force. King Louis was drowned as he attempted to flee. This battle has been considered the greatest national catastrophe in Hungarian history and marks the beginning of Habsburg rule. Following Mohács, the Ottomans controlled the southern one-third of Hungary until 1687.

G. Dávid and P. Fodor, *Ottomans, Hungarians, and Habsburgs in Central Europe: The Military Confines in the Era of Ottoman Conquest* (2000); G. Perjés, *The Fall of the Medieval Kingdom of Hungary: Mohács 1526–Buda 1541* (1989).

GREGORY J. MILLER

Molina, Luis de (1535–1600), Jesuit theologian. Born in Cuenca, Spain, he studied law at Salamanca and philosophy at Alcalá. After entering the Jesuits in 1553, he studied philosophy and theology at Coimbra and theology at Évora in Portugal. He taught philosophy at Coimbra (1563–1567) and theology at Évora (1568–1588). He spent his last twelve years in Madrid writing and publishing. External events played only a little role in his life as a scholar.

His most famous work, *Concordia libri arbitrii cum gratiae donis, divina praescientia. providentia, praedestinatione et reprobatione* (1588), treats the interaction of human nature, divine grace, and predestination. His stress on human freedom in the process of salvation (known as Molinism) rejected the teachings of Protestants as well as contemporary Dominicans, notably Domingo Bañez. To protect human freedom from being effectively destroyed by God's foreknowledge and predestination, Molina invented a "middle knowledge" of God concerning human actions midway between God's knowledge of all past and future events and his knowledge of mere possibilities. God's distribution of grace derives from this middle knowledge. Molina hoped to steer a middle course between determinism and Pelagianism. Controversy over Molinism poisoned relations between Jesuits and Dominicans for centuries.

Molina's writings include a two-volume commentary on book 1 of Thomas Aquinas's *Summa theologiae*, and *De justitia et jure* on personal and social morality.

F. Costello, *The Political Philosophy of Luis de Molina, S.J., 1535–1600* (1974); G. Smith, *Freedom in Molina* (1966).

JOHN PATRICK DONNELLY, SJ

Monarchianism A prevalent Trinitarian doctrine in second- and third-century Rome. Monarchianism emphasized the singleness of the divine being. The word "monarch" comes from the Greek *monos* ("alone") and *archein* ("to rule"). Tertullian was the first to call the opponents of the preferred Logos Christology "monarchians" (*Prax.* 10.1). The views of the latter are known primarily through Tertullian's treatise *Against Praxeas* and Hippolytus's tract *Against Noetus*. Scripture teaches that "God is one" (Deut. 6:4; 1 Cor. 8:6), and philosophers had argued that there could be only one First Principle and Prime Mover. God is by definition one, simple, and immutable. However, the author of *2 Clement* reminded his audience, "Brethren, we must think of Jesus Christ as God" (1:1). Thus, Monarchianism emerged because the oneness of God seemed to be threatened by the Christian belief in the divinity of Jesus Christ.

Two obvious but ultimately heretical solutions suggested themselves to some of the early theologians: modalism and adoptionism. Either Christ is the Father (Isa. 45:5; John 10:30) or Christ is completely other than the Father (John 14:28). Both options had a legitimate and honorable goal: to rescue the oneness and the monarchy of God. Adolf von Harnack, a church historian of the late nineteenth and early twentieth centuries, distinguished between Modalist Monarchianism and Dynamic Monarchianism. The Modalist Monarchians (or Sabellians in the East), such as Noetus, Sabellius, and Callistus, sought the solution on the side of God. The one divine being had revealed itself as Father, Son, and Holy Spirit, but these names refer only to temporary modes of God's economic activity and are not eternal entities within the one Godhead (Hippolytus, *Haer.* 10.27). The scriptural attestation for this position was John 14:10: "I am in the Father and the Father is in me." According to their critics, Modalist Monarchians completely confused the roles of the Father, Son, and Holy Spirit in the history of salvation. The Dynamic Monarchians sought the solution on the side of Christ's humanity. Theodotus the Leathermaker, Theodotus the Banker, Artemon, and Paul of Samosata defended the oneness of God by teaching that Christ was a human being who received the divine power (*dynamis*). "[He] was declared to be the Son of God with power" (Rom. 1:4). The unity of God was rescued by making the divinity of Christ an impersonal power empowering the human Jesus (cf. Ps. 45:7; Mark 1:9). Dynamic Monarchians either separated Jesus into two beings (Hippolytus, *Haer.* 7.23) or called him a "mere human" (Eusebius, *Hist. eccl.* 5.28). Dynamic Monarchianism is also known as "psilanthropism," because it taught the empowerment of a "mere human" (*psilos anthropos*) and denied the preexistence of Christ. An unqualified Monarchianism, which promoted the "simple unity" of God, was ultimately rejected, because the Christian God was perceived to be one in a new way—including the three persons of the Trinity.

G. U. Bilbao, *Monarquía y Trinidad* (1996); M. Slusser, "The Scope of Patripassianism," StPatr 17, no. 1 (1982): 169–75; A. von Harnack, *History of Dogma*, vol. 3 (repr. 1997).

TARMO TOOM

Monasteries, Dual-Sex The "double monastery" still lacks an exact definition: either one should understand it as referring to monks and nuns living together in one monastery under one rule, sharing among themselves their possessions and incomes (the narrow view), or the phrase should also include separate male and female houses that are simply joined because they are ruled by one superior (the broader view). In any case, one should consider the original intention of the foundation rather than simply its external features. It seems that the controversy can partially be explained by the very different development in Eastern and Western Christianity. Symbiotic forms of monastic living in the East date back to late antiquity, where the women apparently fulfilled the everyday economic tasks of the community while the men predominately took over religious service. Very likely such organizational patterns resulted out of the structures of the early ascetic communities. Only later do we find evidence concerning the contemplative life of the *sanctimoniales*, the nuns (Schenute, Ep. 7). With men and women living that close, it was also recognized that there were dangers with regard to the common vow of chastity. The concern to guard chastity thus accounts for the often-repeated ban of this form of monastic life (in the *Corpus iuris canonici*, and in the *Corpus iuris civilis, Codex* 1.3.43 and Novellae 123.36). Nevertheless, we find references to dual-sex communities in the East well into the fourteenth century.

In contrast, dual-sex monasteries in the Western church developed in various ways. Apart from some early attempts in England, Spain, and France to implement the Eastern form of the double monastery (John Cassian, *Institutiones*), what is striking is the richness of forms of monastic life in the period of the eleventh- and twelfth-century reform movements. Galatians 3:28 often provided a model for such monastic life, but to discover what was intended one must analyze the circumstances of particular monastic foundations. The foundation of Vallombrosa (1056–1090) appears to have been clearly intended for a common life without any recognizable hierarchy. Robert of Arbrissel, the founder of Fontevraud (1119), considered it a sign of special humility to place himself under the direction of a woman, following the model of the apostle John, who had served the Virgin Mary. At Fontevraud, the normative difference between the men and women was that the nuns lived under the Benedictine rule, while the brothers lived according to the Augustinian rule. Another pure form of double monastery—the Gilbertines (1147)—appears not to have been the result of a deliberate plan. When the original plan to incorporate his female community into the Cistercian order failed, Gilbert of Sempringham recruited a number of male Premonstratensians for the education and pastoral care of his nuns.

None of the Western dual-sex monasteries managed to find stable institutional forms. The privileges enjoyed by these monasteries contradicted ecclesiastical decisions (the Second Lateran Council, Gratian's *Decretum*, the Fourth Lateran Council). Dual-sex monasteries adapted to the values propagated by the church and then gradually disappeared. The process is clearly to be seen in the development of the Premonstratensian order. In contrast to the explicit intention of the founder Norbert of Xanten (1120), who envisaged every house to be a double monastery, the spatial and legal separation of male and female communities was commanded in 1140. The reception of women in the order was completely forbidden in 1198.

M. Bateson, "Origin and Early History of Double Monasteries," *Transactions of the Royal Historical Society, NS* 13 (1899): 137–98; U. Berlière, "Les monastères doubles aux XIIe et XIIIe siècles," *Académie royale de Belgique, Classe des Lettres et des Sciences morales et politiques, Mémoires*, vol. 18, fasc. 3 (1923); K. Elm and M. Parisse, eds., "Doppelklöster und andere Formen der Symbiose männlicher und weiblicher Religiosen im Mittelalter," *Berliner Historische Studien* 18 (1992); S. Hilpisch, *Die Doppelklöster: Entstehung und Organisation* (1928).

LARS-ARNE DANNENBERG

Monastic Schools Monastic schools were, in addition to the cathedral schools, the most important educational institutions in the early and the High Middle Ages. Already in late antiquity, some religious men and women had educational backgrounds, but systematic monastic education is not to·be found before Irish monasticism in the sixth and seventh centuries (e.g., monasteries at Bangor and Clonmacnoise). In the eighth century, Irish and Anglo-Saxon monks contributed much to the foundation of monasteries in Central Europe, where scholars were formed (Fulda, Reichenau, and St. Gall monasteries). The decision of the Synod of Aachen (817) that monastic schools should be open only for oblates was no impediment for laymen to attend such a school. Education was organized in so-called interior schools for oblates and in exterior schools for laymen and clerics.

With the expansion of cathedral schools from the eleventh century onward, monastic schools were gradually called into question, as was the practice of oblation. With the rise of the universities in the twelfth to thirteenth centuries the importance of monastic schools decreased. Their functions were now limited to the education of novices, which meant imparting religious knowledge and the basics of monastic life. Nevertheless, in the late Middle Ages laymen and novices sometimes were still taught together in monastic schools.

With the religious schism that took place during the Reformation, the educational system was divided along confessional boundaries. In Catholic territories, monasteries offered again an education for external scholars. The so-called teaching orders (Jesuits, Oratorians, Doctrinarians, etc.) took an eminent position in post-Tridentine Catholicism. The Jesuit college—often connected with a boarding school—was a new type of school. There the studies were systematically structured within a strict curriculum. Today the character of monastic schools has radically changed: whereas the interior school is an exclusive institution for educating novices, the exterior school is subject to government regulation.

The curriculum in the monastic schools comprised, in addition to reading, writing, and mathematics, the *trivium* (grammar, rhetoric, logic) and often also the *quadrivium* (arithmetic, geometry, astronomy, music). Generally there was no homogeneous curriculum.

G. Ferzoco and C. Muessig, eds., *Medieval Monastic Education* (2000); M. M. Hildebrandt, *The External School in Carolingian Society* (1992); P. Riché, *Education and Culture in the Barbarian West, Sixth Through Eighth Centuries* (1976); Riché, *Écoles et enseignement dans le haut moyen âge* (1989).

MIRKO BREITENSTEIN

Monasticism, Byzantine

Origins. From the Greek word μονάζειν ("to live alone"), monasticism denoted a life of separation from the world and commitment to prayer and asceticism. Diverse forms of ascetic life were practiced by Christians both in and beyond the Roman Empire, and the unique Egyptian origin of Byzantine monasticism can no longer be affirmed. Nevertheless, tradition looks back to Anthony the Great and Pachomius as fathers of eremitic and cenobitic monasticism, respectively. Anthony went out to the Egyptian desert toward the end of the third century to pursue a life of Christian perfection. The *Life of Anthony*, attributed to Athanasius of Alexandria, was particularly important in spreading monastic ideals and fostering ecclesiastical support for the movement. It presented the hermit's life as a model of monasticism in the service of the orthodox church and provided an ideal for monks and nuns of future generations. Although Pachomius wrote an early rule for communal monasticism in Egypt, the so-called Long Rules of Basil the Great (d. c. 379) provided the foundation for Byzantine monasticism. Basil favored cenobitic over eremitic or solitary monastic life. He emphasized moderation in ascetic practices, obedience to superiors in the community, manual labor, and charity to the poor. Basil's monastic writings influenced Benedict's composition of a rule for the West, and the Basilian form of monasticism has continued to shape Greek and Slavic traditions of monastic life. From the middle of the fourth century monasticism spread rapidly in both the countryside and cities of Byzantium. By the middle of the sixth century there were almost seventy monasteries in Constantinople alone.

History. Monasticism was integral to the social, political, economic, cultural, and religious life of Byzantium. Building on the canons of the Council of Chalcedon, the legislation of Emperor Justinian I (482–565) gave Byzantine monasticism its official and uniform character and its full institutional significance in the life of the state. Monasticism as an institution was firmly subordinated to the church hierarchy, and the oversight of monasteries was relegated to bishops. In keeping with his general enthusiasm for monastic life, Justinian conferred on monasteries many economic privileges, including the right to inherit from private citizens, protection from confiscation of property, and exemption from payment of state taxes. During outbreaks of iconoclasm in the eighth and ninth centuries many monasteries may have lost their property, but in the tenth century monasteries began to acquire significant wealth in land and precious objects. Later imperial legislation attempted to curb the acquisition of monastic estates, as monasteries became the major landowners in the late Byzantine period.

The Studios monastery in Constantinople rose to prominence at the end of the eighth century under the leadership of the iconodule monastic reformer Theodore the Studite. With as many as 700–1000 monks under Theodore's authority, Studios demonstrated an ideal of the monastery as a working community. Holy Mountains arose in different regions of the Byzantine Empire, where cenobitic and semi-eremitic forms of monasticism were practiced side by side. The monastic settlement of Mount Athos, an international religious community comprising Italian, Georgian, Russian, Serbian, Bulgarian, as well as Greek monasteries, helped to spread Byzantine monasticism to the medieval Slavic world. Also influential in the development of Byzantine and Orthodox monasticism was the eleventh-century monastery of the Theotokos Evergetis in Constantinople. Central to the monastic reform movement that swept Byzantium in the late eleventh century, Evergetis offers an unrivaled collection of texts on administration, economy, daily life, liturgy, spirituality, and instruction in the Byzantine monastery.

Monasticism was particularly important in the history of Byzantine theology and spirituality. Monks played leading roles in the ecumenical councils of the fourth through sixth centuries, and their writings helped to shape orthodox doctrine on the Trinity and Christology as well as on liturgy and mysticism. Monks were also among the primary supporters of icon veneration in the iconoclastic controversies of the eighth and ninth centuries. The mystical theology of Symeon the New Theologian, a monk of the early eleventh century, was extremely influential in shaping what became the Eastern Orthodox tradition. The triumph of hesychasm, championed by Gregory Palamas and the Athonite monks in the fourteenth century, shows the authority and popularity of monastic opinion in matters of faith. In keeping with their reputation as defenders of orthodoxy, Byzantine monks consistently opposed attempts at reunion of the churches.

Distinctive Features. In contrast with the West, Byzantine monasticism developed no orders. Each monastery was independent and had its own rule or *typikon*, though many rules were based on earlier models. Cenobitic monasticism dominated, but forms of eremitic and semi-eremitic monasticism continued to flourish. Wandering holy men might migrate from one monastery to another despite the canonical principle of *stabilitas*, and cenobitic communities were often interspersed with the cells of hermits. As in the West, a tradition of double monasteries persisted despite legislation prohibiting the practice.

The focus of Byzantine monastic life was contemplation (*theoria*) and pursuit of the perfect life. Despite an emphasis on solitude and withdrawal, however, Byzantine monasteries had several important social and cultural functions. They served as places of refuge for the poor and oppressed, for social outcasts, and for those in need of protection or aid. They were used as places of imprisonment or exile for rebels, failed political rivals, and deposed emperors and patriarchs. Monasteries often established philanthropic institutions such as hospitals, orphanages, and hospices (xenodochia). They had small but influential scriptoria and libraries, and though education was never a primary aim of Byzantine monasticism, monks and nuns comprised a significant percentage of the literati of the empire throughout its history. As major beneficiaries of both imperial and private patronage, the construction and decoration of monasteries also helped to preserve the rich artistic and architectural heritage of Byzantium.

Byzantine monasticism played an important role in at least two other spheres. As in the West, it was primarily monks who led the church's missionary thrust. Also, monasteries were often the source of leadership for the church as a tradition of monk-bishops spread throughout the Christian East. Monks were increasingly promoted to bishoprics and patriarchates where they influenced imperial as well as ecclesiastical policy.

Byzantine Monastic Foundation Documents: A Complete Translation of the Surviving Founders' Typika and Testaments, 5 vols., *Dumbarton Oaks Studies* 35, ed. J. Thomas and A. C. Hero (2001); P. Charanis, "The Monk as an Element of Byzantine Society," *DOP* 25 (1971): 61–84; R. Morris, *Monks and Laymen in Byzantium, 843–1118* (1995); A.-M. Talbot, "An Introduction to Byzantine Monasticism," *Illinois Classical Studies* 12 (1987): 229–41.

ANDREA STERK

Monasticism, Early Egyptian and Palestinian

Monasticism is a way of Christian living marked by a renunciation of the "world" (family, property, marriage, career) and a quest for communion with God in prayer. Early monks joined ascetical disciplines (fasting, vigils, poverty, celibacy) with a life of manual labor. Most recited psalms at fixed hours, especially dawn and sunset; they also took to heart Paul's admonition to "pray unceasingly" (1 Thess. 5:17), exploring methods of interior meditation and contemplation. The two classic forms of monasticism emerged early: the anchoritic, or solitary life of the hermit; and the cenobitic, or life within an organized (and often secluded) community. The Greek term for "monk," *monachos*, means "solitary one." Its earliest application to a Christian appears in a recently discovered Egyptian papyrus, dated 324, which speaks of "Isaac the monk" rescuing a farmer caught in a violent village dispute. Although fourth-century Egypt has often been called the birthplace of Christian monasticism, other regions—Syria, Palestine, Cappadocia—had their own traditions as old as those of Egypt, if less well documented and perhaps less influential.

One of the earliest monks was Antony (d. 356), an anchorite whose life was celebrated in Athanasius of Alexandria's popular and influential biography. He helped define early monasticism by his "withdrawal" (*anachōresis*) into the desert. His disciples, in Athanasius's famous phrase, "made the desert a city."

There were other pioneers. In Upper Egypt, near the bend of the Nile, Pachomius (d. 346) created a remarkable confederation of nine cenobitic monasteries, called the Koinonia ("fellowship"), which at its peak housed several thousand monks. He also composed the first known monastic rule. In Lower Egypt, west of the Nile, Macarius the Egyptian (d. 390) founded the monastic settlement of Scetis (modern Wādi āl-Natrūn). The wisdom of the monks of Scetis was collected in *Sayings of the Fathers* (*Apophthegmata Patrum*), an anthology containing over a thousand sayings and anecdotes. The work has been preserved in Greek, Latin, Syriac, Coptic, Ethiopic, and Armenian and in two distinct recensions: the Alphabetical, which lists its numbered sayings under individual abbas, and the Systematic, which organizes these same sayings under various headings (e.g., humility, compunction, discernment). Amoun (d. 347) founded two prominent monastic centers in Lower Egypt:

Nitria, a cenobitic monastery, and Kellia (the Cells), a settlement for anchorites.

Egyptian monasticism attracted an intellectual elite who helped broadcast its traditions to the wider Roman world. Evagrius of Pontus (d. 399) put together the classic analysis of human vice (the "seven deadly sins") and plotted out the classic map of the soul's journey to God. John Cassian (d. c. 435) helped translate desert spirituality for the Latin West. Benedict made Cassian's *Institutes* and *Conferences* required reading in monasteries under his *Rule*.

Recent scholarship has stressed the rich diversity of ancient experiments in ascetic Christianity. It also has uncovered texts, figures, and movements unfairly ignored. For example, Shenoute of Atripe (d. c. 466), whose works were preserved only in Coptic, served for decades as abbot of the White Monastery and oversaw some 2,200 monks and 1,800 nuns. Ancient definitions of orthodoxy and church order meant certain groups got dropped from the historical record. The schismatic Melitians had thriving monasteries in the 330s, a fact not appreciated until papyrus discoveries in the early twentieth century. Women established ascetic households, served as superiors of double monasteries, embarked on arduous pilgrimages, and played vital roles as benefactors.

Monasticism in Palestine was, from the beginning, international in character. Certain pilgrims to the Holy Land stayed on, establishing or joining local monastic communities. In the 370s, Melania the Elder and Rufinus of Aquileia founded a Latin-speaking double monastery on the Mount of Olives; Jerome and Paula founded a similar one in Bethlehem. Chariton, a Cappadocian by background, is credited with creating the *laura*, a unique amalgam of the anchoritic and cenobitic. Famous *lauras* sprang up in the Judean desert east and south of Jerusalem. The best-known account of Palestinian monasticism comes from Cyril of Scythopolis (d. after 559), who composed seven Lives celebrating figures such as Euthymius (d. 473) and Sabas (d. 532). Another prominent center was Gaza. Its distinctive spirituality appears in the letters of spiritual direction composed by two sixth-century solitaries, Barsanuphius and John of Gaza.

D. Brakke, *Demons and the Making of the Monk* (2006); D. Burton-Christie, *The Word in the Desert* (1993); D. Chitty, *The Desert a City* (1966); E. A. Clark, *The Origenist Controversy* (1992); S. Elm, *Virgins of God* (1994); J. E. Goehring, *Ascetics, Society, and the Desert*

(1999); W. Harmless, *Desert Christians* (2004); Y. Hirschfeld, *The Judean Monasteries in the Byzantine Period* (1992); J. L. Hevelone-Harper, *Disciples of the Desert* (2005); C. Stewart, *Cassian the Monk* (1998).

WILLIAM HARMLESS, SJ

Monasticism, Medieval Western

Largely based on Eastern Christian models of asceticism, hermitage, and a communal religious life of withdrawal from the world, monasteries of one kind or another began to assume an important role in the church in the Western Roman Empire by the beginning of the fifth century. The prominence of monasticism in the European church continued through the tribal kingdoms that followed the Roman Empire and in Catholic Europe up through the Reformation and into modern times. By the end of the fourth century, a communal religious life of men and/or women living in groups (even anchorites often lived in groups) was widely regarded as the highest form of Christian religiosity. During the fifth and sixth centuries, particularly in Gaul, Catholic bishops were routinely recruited from monasteries, while some monasteries also served as conduits of the flourishing culture of the Byzantine East and as preservers of Roman culture—in the peculiar fusions of Latinity and Christian doctrine represented by the likes of Jerome, Augustine, Hilary of Poitiers, Caesarius of Arles, and Cassiodorus. In the seventh and eighth centuries, monasteries became instruments of European Christianization (in distinct ways, at different times and places) in all the kingdoms of the West, while many of the most learned scholars were, or had been, monks (for example, Bede and Pope Gregory the Great). In the Frankish kingdom, due to the patronage of all manner of nobles (it was sometimes lavish), monastery landholdings vastly multiplied and grew, while in Ireland monasteries comprised communities of clergy and laity (including families) ruled by lay abbots closely tied to tribal kings. When the descendants of Charles Martel ruled the Frankish kingdom, their success rested in part on monasteries, which they patronized, exploited for their property, and employed in order to achieve their plan for a Christian society and government. The Carolingians favored the Rule of Benedict of Nursia, which had been written two centuries earlier for the community Benedict had founded at Monte Cassino (c. 530), but groups of canons who lived according to a rule ("regular canons," whom the Carolingians formally distinguished from

monks) multiplied too. Carolingian monasteries operated schools, as cathedrals did, provided material support to the Frankish military (this included the production of military hardware), and formed part of the Carolingian administrative apparatus. Monastic schools promoted learning, adapting fourth-century ideals that prized the liberal arts as prelude to the study of Scripture and theology. Monastic scholars emphasized the interpretation of Scripture by authoritative writers of antiquity ("church fathers"), and they posed as models for the clergy overall, as a body of celibate and literate, learned people.

The turmoil that followed the ninth-century breakup of the Carolingian empire temporarily dented the progress of monasticism, but Carolingian precedents contributed to the roles of monasteries in religion, learning, and government in the various states of the tenth to twelfth centuries. Monastic reform swept Europe in the tenth and eleventh centuries, and soon the forms of monastic life further diversified, from the eleventh through the thirteenth centuries, in a long wave of monastic re-adaptation. The tenth-century revival rested largely on Benedictine standards promoted earlier by the Carolingians. It radiated out from the monastery at Gorze in Lorraine to Central and Eastern Europe, from the monastery of St. Victor at Marseille to all of Provence, and from the monastery of Cluny to most of Western Europe. Cluniac influence was tremendous and encompassed the Continent. It contributed to growing interest in the asceticism of Christian antiquity and hermitage, which in the late tenth and eleventh centuries gave rise to new religious orders. Some of these new orders combined strict observance of the Benedictine Rule with ascetical rigor (the Cistercians) or were deeply influenced by Benedictine models (the Premonstratensian canons and canonesses). Others saw ancient Christian asceticism as an alternative to Benedictine models (e.g., the Carthusians). A monastic form of life became more common among canons and canonesses, who in the twelfth century saw the "canonical order" as rooted in antiquity, and they were sometimes committed to religious poverty (and like the monastic reform movements, they grew regional and transregional networks). Monastic norms increasingly impacted the laity, a fact most astonishingly displayed in the rise of military orders in the twelfth century but also displayed in the twelfth-century growth of a lay spirituality based on the apostolic life, which could be seen as a popular adaptation of a monastic religious culture. Finally, in the wake of European urbanization, the Mendicant orders emphasized both communal and personal observance of religious poverty combined with an active life of preaching. Although the Fourth Lateran Council (1215) prohibited the founding of new religious orders, the papacy approved a rule composed by Francis of Assisi and allowed Dominic of Guzman's order to adapt the Augustinian Rule. The pope seems to have promoted these orders in part as an antidote to heretical forms of religious poverty. An ideal of poverty inspired semimonastic communities of beguines too. Male and female orders of Franciscans and Dominicans, followed by the Carmelites and Augustinian Hermits, spread rapidly in cities throughout Europe from the various times of their creation in the thirteenth century to the European pandemic of 1348/1349 (the "Black Death"). Few new religious orders arose in Europe between 1350 and 1500 (the Brigittines, founded by Brigitte of Sweden and approved by the papacy in 1370, is an important exception). But in the fourteenth and fifteenth centuries some orders did expand (e.g., the Carthusians). Others endured, or enjoyed, movements of reform (e.g., Benedictines, Franciscans, Dominicans, Augustinian Hermits), and new semimonastic organizations emerged (e.g., the Windesheim Congregation and the Brothers and Sisters of the Common Life).

The history of monasticism in the West is marked by a certain irony. What distinguishes monastics from the sum total of Christians is their withdrawal from the world, pursued in an organized way within a community of persons who live under religious vows. Yet these ideals vested such prestige in the monks and nuns of Europe that monasteries achieved a very worldly success, not least as property-holders (consider that protected property could survive the ups and downs of monastic recruitment), and they were vital contributors to the social and political histories of Europe, up to the secularizations of 1780–1830. The irony of renunciation and success may account, in part, for the tendency of religious orders, together with their historians, to organize monastic history into cycles of corruption and reform, just as the religious public tended to measure monks and nuns against a perception of their rigor or laxity. But whatever one's judgment of some monastery at any given time may have been, the historian cannot deny that monasticism was a fixture of European society in the Middle Ages.

P. King, *Western Monasticism: A History of the Monastic Movement in the Latin Church* (1999); C. H. Lawrence, *Medieval Monasticism* (2nd ed., 1989).

CHRISTOPHER OCKER

Monica (c. 331–387), North African laywoman, mother of Augustine of Hippo. She is known exclusively through the writings of her eldest son (she also had a second son, Navigius, and a daughter whose name is not known), chiefly the *Confessions*. Born into a Christian family, Monica held strongly to her Christianity throughout her life, going to notable lengths to try to draw Augustine into the orbit of catholic Christianity as well. In 383 she followed him from North Africa to Milan, where he was finally converted in 386. In book 9 of the *Confessions*, Augustine gives a brief account of her life, including such vivid details as her early weakness for wine, her sometimes difficult marriage to Patricius (a pagan who became Christian only late in life), her awkward relations with her mother-in-law, and her unwillingness to repeat malicious gossip. The account culminates in the mystical experience she and Augustine shared in Ostia, outside Rome, just before Monica's death, in which (Augustine reports) they were carried beyond the temporal realm to a momentary touch of the eternal. Monica was buried in Ostia, where part of the inscription on her tomb was discovered in 1945. A cult of St. Monica emerged in the late Middle Ages.

P. Brown, *Augustine of Hippo* (new ed., 2000); M. M. O'Farrell, "Monica, the Mother of Augustine: A Reconsideration," *Recherches Augustiniennes* 10 (1975): 23–43; W. Wischmeyer, "Zum Epitaph der Monica," *RQ* 70 (1975): 32–41.

WILLIAM S. BABCOCK

Monophysitism The term, from Greek, refers to the christological position that Christ has "only one nature." Monophysites were those Christians who rejected the Definition of Chalcedon (451), which affirms that Christ has two natures: human and divine. These non-Chalcedonian Christians spoke of Christ as having one nature after the union of deity and humanity in the incarnation. They preferred the terms Henophysites or Miaphysites ("one nature"). They accepted the Council of Nicaea, which affirmed that the Son, "begotten of the Father" and "of one substance with the Father," had become incarnate. The Council of Ephesus (431) had prohibited any addition to the Nicene Creed, and the Monophysites viewed the Definition as a violation of that prohibition.

Monophysitism was originally associated with the city of Alexandria, and today's Monophysites claim to be the theological descendents of Cyril of Alexandria. Monophysites find any talk of two natures in Christ after the union unacceptable, although they do not specifically deny the fullness of the humanity, as they have often been charged with doing.

Severus of Antioch was perhaps the most notable Monophysite theologian of the fifth and sixth centuries. His correspondence with Sergius the Monophysite reveals the differences between moderate Monophysites, represented by Severus, and extreme Monophysites, represented by Sergius. Severus held that the nature (*physis*) and identity (*hypostasis*) of Christ is that of the divine Logos united with full and complete humanity. The humanity is not itself a nature, for Severus understood "nature" to mean a concrete being with its own identity. Nevertheless, Severus upheld the unconfused reality of the humanity such that Christ's body was mortal. Sergius's view of the incarnation resulted, in Severus's estimation, in a mixture of the two natures.

Following the Council of Chalcedon (451) the Monophysite controversy led to several attempts at reconciliation, all of which failed. In 482, Emperor Zeno offered his *Henoticon*, which described the union in Christ without the "two natures" language of Chalcedon. The Western church rejected the document because it did not take seriously Leo's *Tome*, which had factored so prominently at Chalcedon. In 553, the Council of Constantinople condemned Theodore of Mopsuestia, Theodoret of Cyrus, and Ibas of Edessa in a further effort at reconciliation with the Monophysites. That attempt, also opposed by the Western church, failed to satisfy the Monophysites as well.

Monophysite churches today are frequently referred to as Oriental Orthodox Churches. They include the Coptic Church in Egypt, the Jacobite Church in Syria, and the Armenian Orthodox Church.

W. H. C. Frend, *The Rise of the Monophysite Movement* (1979); A. Grillmeier, *Das Konzil von Chalkedon* (1951); J. Lebon, *Le Monophysisme severien* (1909); I. R. Torrance, *Christology after Chalcedon* (1988).

STEVEN A. MCKINION

Monothelites

The doctrine claims that the divine person of Christ acted with one energy. Desire for religious harmony within an embattled empire led successive emperors to propose compromises between dyophysite (two *physeis*, or natures, in the person of Christ) Chalcedonians and monophysite (one nature) anti-Chalcedonians throughout the sixth and seventh centuries. Unlike Monophysitism, Monotheletism does not represent a well-established local theological tradition. It is an imperial concoction, and its history is as much political as theological. In the 620s Emperor Heraclius and Sergius, patriarch of Constantinople, proposed a refinement to the current christological understanding—one divine person with two complete natures united hypostatically—by adding the affirmation that this person acted with one energy. This locates the source of Christ's activity in the one hypostasis, not in the dual natures.

The compromise attempt had some significant but short-lived success in Alexandria in 633. When Patriarch Sergius reported it to Honorius of Rome, the pope responded with an affirmation of "the one will of our Lord Jesus Christ." This became the standard terminology and is found in the imperial decree or *Ekthesis* promulgated by Heraclius in 638. Among the opponents of Monotheletism were Sophronius of Jerusalem and Maximus the Confessor, who argued for the necessity of the functional as well as the metaphysical reality of the dual natures in Christ. The Sixth Ecumenical Council (Constantinople III, 680–681) condemned Monotheletism as a heresy.

J. Meyendorff, *Christ in Eastern Christian Tradition* (1969); J. Pelikan, *The Spirit of Eastern Christendom (600–1700)* (1974).

EUGENE M. LUDWIG, OFM CAP.

Montaigne, Michel

(1533–1592), French philosopher and essayist. His famed *Essays* explore a wide range of themes but offer above all an exploration of the man himself. His skeptical motto was "Que sais-je?" ("What do I know?") A professing Catholic, his sincerity in that regard has been alternately affirmed and denied by students of his writings. Montaigne was mortified by the religious wars and theological battles of his day, and his work can be seen in part as an effort to find intellectual peace in a profoundly bellicose world. He had a profound sense of the differences between his own culture and that of alien peoples such as those of the "New World." His work also conveys a strong connection to ancient moral philosophies, including Stoicism, Epicureanism, and Cynicism, which he helped to make comprehensible to his own and subsequent generations as autonomous ethical systems on their own terms. Famed for citing Socrates' dictum that "to philosophize is to learn to die," Montaigne also remarked "our great and glorious masterpiece is to live appropriately." His influence can be seen in the works of Francis Bacon, Blaise Pascal, and Pierre Bayle.

D. Frame, *Montaigne: A Biography* (1965); M. A. Screech, *Montaigne and Melancholy* (1983).

RODERICK MARTIN

Montanus, Montanism (fl. c. 160–170), with Maximilla and Priscilla (or Prisca), founded the "New Prophecy," a spiritual renewal movement subsequently called "Montanism." Anti-Montanist claims that Montanus was a castrated former priest of Cybele or Apollo may be accurate but charges that he equated himself with the Paraclete (Holy Spirit), practiced infanticide and ritual cannibalism, and eventually hanged himself are unfounded. Montanus established the movement's center at Pepouza in West-Central Phrygia, expecting the "New Jerusalem" to descend out of heaven between Pepouza and Tymion, a settlement 12 kilometers due north.

Montanus and his cofounders wanted to bring the church of their day into line with what they believed to be the ultimate ethical demands of the Paraclete revealed through their prophetic utterances. No Montanist books but thirty or so oracles, including those of later Montanists, have survived. About the same number of authentic Montanist inscriptions are extant.

Local bishops, such as Apolinarius of Hierapolis and the anonymous bishop whose letter to Avircius Marcellus is Eusebius of Caesarea's main source about Montanism, were convinced by the ecstatic phenomena which accompanied Montanist oracular utterances that the New Prophecy was a pseudoprophecy with unwarranted novelties, an unacceptable eschatology, and a heretical pneumatology. Montanists at Rome were also accused of Modalistic Monarchianism. A synod convened in Iconium, in Phrygia (c. 233), mandated that Montanists wishing to join the catholic church be (re-)baptized.

Montanism threatened traditional Christianity by claiming that the Paraclete had come fully only through the revelations communicated via the New Prophecy, by producing "new scriptures," by elevating prophecy over apostolic succession, by including women in all ranks of ministry, by establishing an alternative hierarchy, and by teaching a stricter penitential discipline. There is no warrant, however, for the widely held assumption that Montanists had a greater emphasis on voluntary martyrdom.

Many of Montanism's main features were attractive to early Christians. The movement spread rapidly throughout Asia Minor and to Syria, Italia, Gaul, and Africa Proconsularis, where Tertullian became the New Prophecy's most famous adherent. There is no evidence, however, that anyone at Carthage in Tertullian's day left the catholic church to join or form a separatist Montanist community. The later "Tertullianists," who ceded their basilica to the catholic church in Augustine's time, probably adhered to the New Prophecy as explained and defended by Tertullian's writings. Whether they should be designated either as the true embodiment of North African Montanism or as a Montanist subsect is debatable.

While Montanists saw themselves merely as Christians favorably disposed toward the New Prophecy, their earliest opponents referred to them as "members of the sect named after the Phrygians." "Phrygians" in this context meant Montanus, Maximilla, Priscilla, or subsequent Phrygian leaders of the movement, such as Miltiades and the prophetess Quintilla. This was later misunderstood as a race of people, spawning terms such as "the Phrygian heresy," "Cataphrygians," or simply, "Phrygians" to designate Montanists.

The earliest extant reference to the term "Montanists" comes from Cyril of Jerusalem (c. 250). By 375, Montanists were also known as "Pepouzians." Epiphanius took this to be an alternative for "Quintillians," who, according to him, originated from the "Cataphrygians," as did the "Artotyrites" and "Tascodrougitans." Artotyrites, allegedly, used cheese as well as bread in their Eucharists, and Tascodrougitans (also known as "Passolorinchites") supposedly prayed with their index fingers alongside their noses. The connection between Montanism and these sects is unsubstantiated. Additional charges leveled at Montanists in the post-Constantinian era include sorcery and black magic, mixing the blood of infants with flour to bake Communion bread, holding drunken orgies at Eucharists, and baptizing "in the name of Montanus."

The readiness of catholic clergy and state officials to believe these charges produced increasingly more severe anti-Montanist legislation. From the time of Constantine onward, Montanist books were burned, places of worship confiscated, adherents deprived of basic civil rights, and clergy beaten, exiled, or executed. The final blow came in 550 when John of Ephesus, on Justinian's orders, came with soldiers to Pepouza, took over the Montanist churches, and burned the bones of Montanism's founders.

R. E. Heine, *The Montanist Oracles and Testimonia* (1989); W. Tabbernee, *Montanist Inscriptions and Testimonia* (1997); Tabbernee, "Portals of the Montanist New Jerusalem: The Discovery of Pepouza and Tymion," *JECS* 11 (2003): 87–93; Tabbernee, *Fake Prophecy and Polluted Sacraments* (2007); Tabbernee and P. Lampe, *Pepouza and Tymion* (2008); Tabbernee, *The New Prophecy* (2008); C. Trevett, *Montanism: Gender, Authority, and the New Prophecy* (1996).

WILLIAM TABBERNEE

Montbéliard, Colloquy of

The colloquy was an attempt in 1585 by the German Lutheran Count Frederick of Montbéliard to deal with the request of his Francophone and Reformed subjects to worship according to Reformed principles. The Peace of Augsburg (1555), which established the principle *cuius regio ejus religio* (a territory's ruler determines its religion), provided religious options for Lutherans and Catholics within the HRE but not for Reformed Protestants, whose primary disagreement with Lutherans concerned the Eucharist. While the Lutherans asserted the real, bodily presence of Christ in the Lord's Supper, the Reformed followed Calvin's interpretation that Christ is truly and spiritually but not bodily present.

The Genevan theologian Theodore Beza represented the people of Montbéliard, a minority in the Lutheran duchy of Württemberg. The Lutheran side was advanced by the Tübingen theologian Jakob Andreae, an adviser to the duke of Württemberg and one of the authors of the Lutheran Formula of Concord. Discussion ranged across a variety of theological subjects beyond the Eucharist, but aside from some common understanding on images and music, theological agreement eluded the participants. In an era of hardening confessional divisions, the quest for a broader conception of Christian unity was thoroughly frustrated.

J. Raitt, *The Colloquy of Montbéliard* (1993).

CHRISTOPHER ELWOOD

Moravians

This Christian community traces its history through three major phases. The "first birth" occurred in fifteenth-century Bohemia and Moravia under the name of the *Unitas Fratrum* (Unity of the Brethren). Dissatisfied both with Roman Catholicism and alternative forms of developing Protestantism, they gathered around obedience to the "six small commandments" of the Sermon on the Mount. The earliest remembered congregation emerged in 1458 and was organized into three groups: clergy and the voluntarily impoverished, the main body of farmers and other producers, and those seeking membership, called "penitents." Clergy were elected but also consecrated by bishops; the chain of bishops was held to link them to the early church. Initially suspicious of infant baptism and requiring rebaptism of new members, infant baptism was reintroduced in 1478 and rebaptism eliminated in 1534. Synods in the 1490s relaxed earlier pacifism, permitting participation in government and the military. Conversations with emerging sixteenth-century Protestant groups produced understanding but no mergers. Persecutions ended the community's presence in its homeland in 1628, after which it enjoyed a diaspora existence in many places.

The "second birth" occurred via interaction with Count Zinzendorf in the eighteenth century. A portion of the community found refuge on Zinzendorf's Saxon estate, renamed "Herrnhut" (the Lord's refuge). It was shaped by the eighteenth-century Pietist movement and created new forms of pietism under Zinzendorf's leadership. Other religious refugees had also come to Herrnhut, and Zinzendorf hoped to form a community that would live within the Saxon Lutheran Church. A high point occurred in a spirit-filled Communion on August 13, 1727, a date remembered as the founding of the *Herrnhuter Bruedergemeinde*, or Renewed Unitas Fratrum.

Thereafter, in the third phase, this community sent groups to many places and mounted a vigorous program of world missions. The goal of remaining within the Lutheran Church collapsed, but some Moravians continued to claim membership in other churches, keeping alive the vision of the Renewed Unitas Fratrum as an *ecclesiola*, a small renewal group within the larger church. Often Moravians became a denomination beside other denominations. This is true of the American branch of the church, despite Zinzendorf's 1730s visits to the colonies when he tried to unify various Protestants. Moravians did mission work with Native Americans.

Early settlements in Winston-Salem, North Carolina, and Bethlehem, Pennsylvania, survive as centers of church life in America.

———

J. Taylor and K. Hamilton, *History of the Moravian Church* (1967); J. R. Weinlich, *The Moravian Diaspora* (1959).

HARRY YEIDE JR.

More, Thomas (1478–1535), English lawyer, humanist, controversialist, and lord chancellor (1529–1532).

More attended Oxford briefly and proceeded to study law at the inns of court in London. He was active in politics much of his life but had little influence on government policies. More was an avid humanist, undertaking and championing the study of Greek and basing his religious views on ancient Christian sources to the exclusion of the scholastics. He favored rhetoric as key to discerning Christian truth, believing that such truth was grasped by human minds through dialectical historical processes that elicited intellectual striving while making people aware that absolute doctrinal correctness was an illusory goal. More was also an advocate of reform; his best-known work, *Utopia*, features a critique of contemporary Christian culture, including moral failures among the clergy who ought to serve as exemplars for the laity.

Exceptionally devout and theologically sophisticated for a layman, More was a staunch opponent of heresy, which he considered a grave threat not only to souls but also to civil order. He vigorously supported both in theory and in practice the enforcement of antiheresy laws. He was a prolific controversialist, and in his polemics More employed all of his skills as a rhetorician and lawyer to discredit Protestantism, emphasizing the connection between heresy and sedition and attacking the character of Protestants, especially Luther's marriage in violation of his celibacy vow, as well as their doctrines.

He considered predestination blasphemous (making God responsible for the sins of malefactors) as well as a menace to souls and to civil order, since it robbed people of the incentive to strive to attain salvation by living virtuously. While acknowledging that even virtuous acts were tainted with sin and that people were incapable of earning salvation without the assistance of grace, More also believed that God made the requisite grace available to all people and that consequently none were excluded from salvation except those who culpably failed to cooperate with grace. Primary sources of grace were the sacraments, especially the Eucharist,

that, far from being mere signs, were effective means through which the faithful received grace on account of Christ's merits. While repudiating predestination, he did have a strong sense of providence, seeing God as actively integrating even wicked people and their deeds into the divine plan that included punishing vice and exercising virtue through tribulation.

In contrast to the Protestant doctrine of *sola scriptura*, More argued that revelation was an ongoing process expressed through the divinely inspired church as well as through Scripture. He also highlighted the need for a strong disciplinary infrastructure to regulate the faith and for an authoritative interpreter to ensure that Scripture was rightly understood. Consequently, the individual Christian conscience was sovereign only when aligned with church dogma, never against it. Within the church the ultimate authority was the universal community of the faithful, whose will was articulated in church traditions and general councils. Papal primacy More felt to be legitimate but not crucial, based on the will of the universal church and revocable by the same.

Through the late 1520s and into the 1530s More fell increasingly out of step with government policies. He was eventually driven to resign as lord chancellor and later was imprisoned for refusing an oath that affirmed royal supremacy over the English church, renounced papal authority in England, and declared Henry VIII's first marriage invalid. Following his fall and especially during his imprisonment he penned meditations on suffering that are considered classics of devotional literature. More did not pursue the essentially suicidal course of openly denouncing Henry's divorce and supremacy over the church, but his highly visible refusal to support them and a handful of veiled statements made his disapproval obvious. He was executed on a charge of treason for allegedly stating that Parliament did not have authority to establish the king as head of the English church contrary to the consensus of the universal church.

———

A. Fox, *Thomas More: History and Providence* (1982); J. Guy, *Thomas More* (2000); R. Marius, *Thomas More* (1984, repr. 1999); L. Martz, *Thomas More: The Search for the Inner Man* (1990); C. Miller et al., eds., *The Complete Works of St. Thomas More* (1963–97).

DANIEL EPPLEY

Moritz of Saxony (1521–1553), Duke and elector of Saxony who dramatically impacted

the German political and religious context of his time. He became duke of Albertine Saxony in 1541 and supported the newly introduced Reformation. To enhance his duchy's and his own importance, Moritz pursued a potentially dangerous, often unpopular, but ultimately successful policy of alliance with the Habsburgs. Although a nominal member of the Schmalkald League, he pledged neutrality during the Schmalkald War in the Regensburg Agreement of 1546. He quickly abandoned neutrality and invaded the territories of his cousin and rival, Elector John Frederick of Ernestine Saxony, after Emperor Charles V promised him the electoral title and Ernestine lands in October 1546. Moritz received both in the Wittenberg Surrender of May 19, 1547. Branded as the "Judas of Meissen" and eager to promote princely and territorial freedom against centralized imperial authority, he decided to become a defender of Lutheranism and to oppose the emperor. Hence, he resisted the Augsburg Interim of 1548, forged a military alliance, and marched against Charles V in 1552. Charles agreed to the Passau Agreement of 1552, which anticipated the Religious Peace of Augsburg of 1555. Moritz enjoyed his dynastic and ecclesiastical achievements only briefly, since he succumbed to injuries sustained in the battle of Sievershausen in July 1553. However, Albertine Saxony's future leadership role in German political and ecclesiastical affairs was assured.

K. Blaschke, *Moritz von Sachsen* (1983); G. Wartenberg, *Landesherrschaft und Reformation: Moritz von Sachsen und die albertinische Kirchenpolitik bis 1546* (1988).

KURT K. HENDEL

Morone, Giovanni (1509–1580), Roman

Catholic Italian cardinal, papal envoy, and diplomat. Born in Milan to an aristocratic family, Morone was appointed bishop of Modena, Italy, at age twenty and named cardinal at thirty-three. Papal nuncio to the Habsburg court (1536–1542), he participated in colloquies at Worms and Hagenau (1540), Regensburg (1541), and Speyer (1542), where he promoted Protestant participation in what was to become the Council of Trent (1545–1563).

Returning to Modena as cardinal in 1542, he encountered Protestant and/or heretical tendencies in his diocese. Dealing sensitively with these movements, Morone was accused of "Lutheran" sympathies, partly because he continued his association with a group of reform-minded Roman Catholics (Contarini, Cortese, Flaminio, Pole, et al.). Pope Paul IV imprisoned Morone in 1557 on suspicions of heresy, but Morone was vindicated by Paul's successor, Pius IV, who freed him and appointed him secretary of state. His greatest accomplishment was his chairmanship of the final session of the Council of Trent (1563). Morone led the council to a conclusion that the various parties, even the secular rulers, could endorse. He thereby helped establish normative Roman Catholic teaching for the next four hundred years. In his later years, his ongoing interest in Germany led him to found the German College in Rome (1552). He also continued his diplomatic efforts, participating in ecclesiastical negotiations at Genoa (1575), Augsburg (1555), and Regensburg (1576).

E. G. Gleason, *Gasparo Contarini* (1993); H. Jedin, *Crisis and Closure of the Council of Trent* (1967).

WILLIAM R. RUSSELL

Moschus, John (late sixth to early seventh

cent.), Byzantine monk and author. He is best known as the author of the *Pratum Spirituale* (*Spiritual Meadow*), a collection of monastic stories and sayings. This text illuminates the religious and social history in the East in a time of continued conflict between the followers of Chalcedon and the Monophysites as well as of significant social turmoil caused by a Persian invasion. John had his own monastic training in Palestine. After his formation there he traveled widely, along with his companion Sophronios, to learn about other monks, especially in Egypt. His collection reflects this geographic diversity. The *Pratum* recalls the dedication and ascetic feats that were part of the early monastic movement. John wrote it in order to stimulate revival during what he believed to be a time of monastic decline. The tales, therefore, focus on extreme ascetic achievements. John, still with Sophronios, spent the later part of his life fleeing from Persian invasions, first to Syria, then to Alexandria, and finally to Rome, where he wrote the *Pratum* shortly before his death.

N. Baynes, "The Pratum Spirituale," in *Byzantine Studies* (1955), 261–70; H. Chadwick, "John Moschus and His Friend Sophronios the Sophist," *JTS*, NS 25 (1974): 41–74; John Moschus, *The Spiritual Meadow (Pratum Spirituale)*, trans. J. Wortley (1992).

REBECCA KRAWIEC

Moses ben Maimon   *see* Maimonides

Moses ben Nachman (1194–1270), known as Ramban to the Jewish world and Nachmanides to the non-Jewish world, one of the most impressive communal leaders and creative thinkers on the medieval Jewish scene. A native of Catalonia, Nachmanides lived through the turbulent decades of the thirteenth century, as Christian forces conquered ever larger tracts of the Iberian peninsula and the Roman Catholic Church intensified its missionizing efforts. The Jews of Spain found themselves under increasing pressure, and the creativity of Spanish Jewry expanded and deepened.

Nachmanides led an extremely active life. He served as rabbi in the important Catalan Jewish community of Gerona; he clearly had ties of some sort to the court of the king of Aragon. He served as mediator in the destructive strife that erupted within European Jewry over the writings of Maimonides. In 1263 he was chosen to represent the Jews in the important missionizing engagement arranged by the Dominicans in Barcelona. At the same time, Nachmanides wrote one of the most perceptive commentaries of the Middle Ages on the five books of the Torah, as well as important glosses on the Babylonian Talmud. He was a central figure in the emergence of the new style of Jewish mysticism that eventuated a generation later in the composition of the *Zohar*, the classic of medieval Cabbala.

The activism and intellectual acuity of Nachmanides combined to make him one of the most effective Jewish polemicists of medieval times. Serving as Jewish spokesman at the Barcelona disputation, Nachmanides erected Jewish defenses against the new missionizing argumentation that sought to demonstrate Christian truth from rabbinic writings. In the wake of the public engagement in Barcelona, Nachmanides harnessed his considerable literary skills to the composition of three important works: a vigorous and beguiling narrative account of the disputation, a close exegesis of the Suffering Servant passage in Isaiah (Isa. 53), and a treatise on the inevitability of divine redemption of the Jews, all intended to strengthen Jewish defenses against aggressive Christian proselytizing.

I. Twersky, ed., *Rabbi Moses Nahmanides (Ramban): Explorations in His Religious Virtuosity* (1983); R. Chazan, *Barcelona and Beyond: The Disputation of 1263 and Its Aftermath* (1992).

ROBERT CHAZAN

Moses Khorenac'i (eighth cent.?), historian. He wrote a *History of the Armenians* in three books. It begins with the Adamic genealogy of Hayk, eponymous founder of the Armenian (*hay*) nation, and ends with the deaths of the founders of the Armenian literary tradition: Maštoc' (d. 440), inventor of the Armenian alphabet, and patriarch Sahak (d. 439), translator and exegete of the Armenian Bible. Drawing upon classical, Jewish, and Christian writings and other sources, the *History* describes the great antiquity of the Armenian people, the emergence of Armenia as a Christian nation, and its course through the first part of the fifth century. Moses identified himself as a pupil of Maštoc'. However, modern scholars have suggested that Moses flourished in the eighth century rather than the fifth century, based on internal evidence in his *History*. Armenian tradition accords him the title "father of history" (*patmahayr*).

D. Kouymjian, ed., *Movsēs Xorenac'i et l'historiographie arménienne des origines* (2000); R. W. Thomson, *Moses Khorenats'i, History of the Armenians: Translation and Commentary on the Literary Sources* (1978); A. Terian, "Xorenac'i and Eastern Historiography of the Hellenistic Period," *Revue des etudes arméniennes* 28 (2001–2002): 101–41; C. Toumanoff, "On the Date of the Pseudo-Moses of Chorene," *Handes Amsorya* 75 (1961): 467–76; B. L. Zekiyan, "Moïse de Khorène (saint)," in *Dictionnaire de Spiritualité, Ascétique et Mystique*, vol. 10 (1980), 1473–75.

MONICA J. BLANCHARD

Mount Athos   Mount Athos, or the Holy Mountain, is a peninsula of about 135 square miles in the Chalkidi region of Greece. It contains twenty independent monasteries and numerous smaller dependent houses. In the year 2000 there were 1,610 monks on the Holy Mountain. It is respected for its exemplary monastic life and is famous for its collection of rare manuscripts and art. While technically a part of Greece, in practice Mount Athos is a self-governing monastic republic. Every permanent resident of Athos is a monk subject to one of the twenty governing monasteries. Representatives of these twenty monasteries constitute the Holy Community, the legislative body for the monastic communities.

Although eremitical foundations existed earlier, the first documented cenobitic foundation on the peninsula dates from 961 and the foundation of the Great Lavra by Athanasius of

Athos. Since its foundation, Athos was the subject of special imperial privileges and legislation such as the *Tragos* of John Tzimiskes (972) and the *Typikon* of Constantine XI Monomachos (1045). The monasteries survived both the period of the Frankish kingdoms and the Ottoman Empire, but not without difficulty. It is currently governed under the provisions of a charter ratified by the Greek state in 1926.

C. Cavernos, *The Holy Mountain* (1973); S. Kadas, *The Holy Mountain* (1993); G. Speake, *Mount Athos: Renewal in Paradise* (2002).

EUGENE M. LUDWIG, OFM CAP.

Mozarab Rite An early Iberian liturgy that developed mainly in the Visigothic era and was made uniform at the Fourth Council of Toledo (633). This was achieved by the brothers and bishops Leander and Isidore of Seville under the careful watch of Pope Gregory the Great. The liturgy has the notable distinction of invoking frequently the Trinity, likely a natural reaction to Arianism, which rejected the Trinitarian creed of Nicaea. The liturgy continued to flourish during the long Muslim occupation of Iberia—hence the name "Mozarab"—until the middle of the eleventh century. In the pontificate of Gregory VII (1073–1085) there was a continent-wide liturgical reform intended to establish a uniform liturgy for the West. In a letter dated March 19, 1074, the pope wrote to the monarchs of León-Castilla, charging that the Mozarab liturgy was tainted with Arian and Priscillian influences. The pope ordered them to adopt the liturgy of the Cluniac reform better known as the Roman Rite. In 1080 at Burgos the Roman Rite officially replaced the Mozarab in León-Castilla, following in the steps of the rest of the peninsula. The Mozarab Rite was allowed to flourish in Toledo, but in 1504 its celebration was limited to a chapel in the Cathedral of Toledo. In our time it is still celebrated there and in the Calatrava chapel of the Cathedral of Salamanca.

M. Férotin, *"Le "Liber ordinum" en usage dans l'église Wisigothique et Mozarabe d'Espagne du V au IX siècle,"* in *Monumenta Ecclesiae Liturgica*, vol. 5 (1904); D. M. Hope and G. Woolfenden, "The Medieval Western Rites," in *The Study of the Liturgy*, ed. C. Jones et al. (1992), 264–85.

ALBERTO FERREIRO

Müller, Heinrich (1631–1675), gifted preacher, song and devotional writer. Like Johann Arndt, Müller criticized a religion of externals that relied upon the "four idols" in the church: the baptismal font, pulpit, confessional, and altar. He pointed Christians instead to the "school of cross, repentance and prayer." Müller's pictorial devotional books encouraged family prayers, and his hymns drew upon Catholic mystics such as Bernard of Clairvaux. J. S. Bach had many of Müller's books in his library.

G. R. Sattler, *Nobler Than the Angels, Lower Than a Worm: The Pietist View of the Individual in the Writings of Heinrich Müller and August Hermann Francke* (1989).

DOUGLAS H. SHANTZ

Münster Revolt (1534–1535) An Anabaptist revolt in the "Kingdom of Münster." In 1532 Bernhard Rothmann organized the first Protestant congregation in Münster, in northwestern Germany, and soon began to preach against infant baptism. He allied with the followers of the Anabaptist Melchior Hoffman (Melchiorites), including Jan of Leiden. In January 1534 Melchiorite followers of Jan Matthijs from Amsterdam baptized Rothmann. A week later Jan of Leiden arrived in the city and baptized 1,400 people. The city council refused the bishop's demand to arrest the Anabaptist preachers and endorsed religious freedom. When Matthijs heard of the city council's action, he proclaimed Münster to be the New Jerusalem. Rumors spread that the bishop was preparing to lay siege to the city, and the gates were closed. Calls went out for all true believers to come to Münster to defend the city and await the immanent return of Christ. Two thousand inhabitants who refused to be rebaptized were expelled. In April Matthijs attacked the bishop's forces and was killed. Jan of Leiden replaced him and appointed a council of twelve to oversee the defense of the city. In September Jan was crowned king on the throne of David. Meanwhile the bishop and Philip, Landgrave of Hesse, undertook a blockade of the city. The city fell in June 1535, and Jan of Leiden was executed in January 1536.

K.-H. Kirchhoff, *Die Täufer im Münster, 1534–1535* (1973); J. Stayer, *Anabaptists and the Sword* (1972).

DAVID WHITFORD

Münster, Sebastian (1488–155?) Lutheran Hebrew scholar and cartograph Born in Ingelheim in the Rhenish Palatinate was trained in the arts and theology at Heidelberg. Entering the Franciscan order in 1505, he studied Hebrew, Greek, cosmography, and mathematics under the Renaissance humanist Konrad Pellikan. In Tübingen, he studied geography and mathematics with Stoffler and Hebrew with Reuchlin. Münster embraced Lutheranism in the 1520s after editing several of Luther's writings. He moved to Basel in 1529, where he taught Hebrew and OT exegesis. He produced a two-volume *Biblia Hebraica* (1534–1535) with a Latin translation, several Hebrew grammars, a Chaldean (Aramaic) dictionary and grammar (1527), and a trilingual dictionary in Latin, Greek, and Hebrew (1530). In 1539, he published a "missionary" approach for Jewish evangelism entitled *Mashiach* (*Messiah*). In Basel, Münster became renowned for his work in geography and cartography, publishing the standard geography text in German for over a century, *Cosmographia universalis* (1544). The definitive edition of the *Cosmographia*, including pictures of cities and portraits of various costumes, was printed in Basel two years before his death from the plague.

———

J. Friedman, *The Most Ancient Testimony: Sixteenth-Century Christian Hebraica in the Age of Renaissance Nostalgia* (1983).

TIMOTHY MASCHKE

Müntzer, Thomas (1489–1525), theologian and spiritual leader in the German Peasants' War. Müntzer probably studied theology at the universities of Leipzig and Frankfurt. He most likely met Luther during his stay at the Univ. of Wittenberg from 1517 to 1519, but he was more intrigued by Luther's senior colleague Andreas Karlstadt. In 1519 Müntzer immersed himself in the mystical sermons and writings of Johannes Tauler and Henry Suso at Orlamünde. In May 1520 Luther recommended Müntzer to be the preacher of St. Mary's in Zwickau, to replace the humanist Johannes Egranus. Upon Egranus's return, Müntzer moved to St. Catherine's in Zwickau, where he 'et Nicholas Storch, one of the notorious 'vickau prophets," who personified Müntzer's anticlerical ideal of the uneducated and 'yman. Forced to leave Zwickau in April 'intzer traveled to Prague, where he 'l December 1521. In his "Prague '; stressed that only those who hear 'd of God directly from God's 'om books, can be truly taught

After being expelled from Prague and wandering for several months in Thuringia and Saxony, Müntzer accepted the post of preacher at St. John's Church in Allstedt, where he served from late March 1523 until August 8, 1524, and there married a former nun. The popularity of Müntzer's liturgical innovations at Allstedt attracted huge crowds from adjoining villages and territories and led to his decision to publish the first comprehensive version of the Mass in the German language.

On March 24, 1524, members of Müntzer's League of the Elect, a secret military alliance, burned down a small chapel at Mallerbach renowned for its veneration of Mary, thus implicating Müntzer. Under growing political pressure, Müntzer delivered his famous "Sermon to the Princes" to Duke John, brother of the Elector, and Crown Prince John Frederick on July 13, 1524. Müntzer warned them that if they refused to defend the commoners in destroying the "godless tyrants," the sword would be taken away from them and given to the "elect." Müntzer secretly fled Allstedt in August 1524 and made an unsuccessful bid for radical reform in the free imperial city of Mühlhausen with a former monk, Heinrich Pfeiffer. Müntzer returned to Mühlhausen in February 1525, and the citizens of Mühlhausen chose him to be the preacher at St. Mary's Church, the largest church in the city. When Luther demonized Müntzer as "the Satan of Allstedt" in his *Letter to the Princes of Saxony Concerning the Rebellious Spirit* in July 1524, Müntzer vehemently refuted Luther's caricature of him as a crazed fanatic inciting the rabble to violence.

Since his days in Prague, Müntzer was convinced that he was a prophet called by God to establish the kingdom of God on earth. On the eve of the battle at Frankenhausen on May 12, 1525, Müntzer reassured the commoners that because God was on their side and the rebellion was a "justified uprising," victory was theirs. The bloody slaughter, however, proved otherwise: the princes' army of Hessian and Saxon mercenaries, who lost only six men, killed over 6,000 rebels. Although Müntzer managed to escape, he was found, arrested, and interrogated. After his "confession," extracted under torture, Müntzer was returned to Mühlhausen, where he and Pfeiffer were beheaded on May 27, 1525. Luther subsequently vindicated the public execution of this "murderous spirit" as a warning to all who contemplate rebellion.

The historical picture of Müntzer has been distorted by a historiographical tradition beginning with Luther and Melanchthon that has blamed him for instigating insurrection. Whether recognized primarily as a theologian of revolution or as a Reformation theologian, Müntzer's seminal imprint on southern German and Austrian Anabaptism remains his most significant historical legacy. In addition to his profound influence on the spiritualists Hans Denck and Sebastian Franck and on his follower Hans Hut, Müntzer's influence continued through Conrad Grebel and Melchior Rinck, as well as Valentin Weigel and his followers, who became radical Pietists.

H.-J. Goertz, *Thomas Müntzer: Apocalyptic Mystic and Revolutionary*, ed. P. Matheson (1993); Matheson, ed. and trans., *The Collected Works of Thomas Müntzer* (1988); T. Scott, *Thomas Müntzer: Theology and Revolution in the German Reformation* (1989); J. Stayer, *The German Peasants' War and Anabaptist Community of Goods* (1991); J. M. Stayer and W. O. Packull, eds. and trans., *The Anabaptists and Thomas Müntzer* (1980).

MARVIN L. ANDERSON

Murner, Thomas (1475–1537), German satirist, moral reformer, and opponent of the Reformation. Born in Oberehnheim, Alsace, he joined the Franciscans in 1490 and was ordained in 1494. While earning doctorates in theology (1506) and canon and civil law (1519), he taught in several Franciscan institutions. His pugnacious nature and sharp tongue, as well as his literary gifts, are evident in a series of satirical writings in the tradition of Sebastian Brant's *Narrenschiff* that criticized abuses in society and called for ethical reform. After 1520 Murner became one of the first and most persistent critics of the Reformation. He rejected the Lutheran themes of Scripture alone and of the universal priesthood and defended papal authority and the sacrificial nature of the Mass. In 1523 he traveled to England and supported Henry VIII when the latter challenged Luther's sacramentology. From 1525 until 1529 Murner was preacher and teacher in Lucerne and opposed Zwinglianism. When threatened with legal action, he fled to the Palatinate in 1529 and returned to Oberehnheim in 1530 to serve as pastor.

J. M. Miskuly, *Thomas Murner and the Eucharist* (1990); H. Smolinsky, *Eine Persönlichkeit an der Zeitenwende: Thomas Murner zwischen Spätmittelalter und Moderne* (1988).

KURT K. HENDEL

Mystery Religions Flourishing during the Hellenistic and Roman periods, the mysteries involved the worship of deities from Greece, Asia Minor, Egypt, and Persia, including Demeter and Kore, Dionysus, the Great Mothers Kybele/Atargatis and their lovers Attis/Adonis, Isis and Osiris, and Mithras. The ancient heritage of associations with nature and agrarian festivals helps explain the prominent place of goddesses and dying and rising deities. These mothers, as cosmic matriarchs and universal sources of life, embodied the forces of life and death. Religious concern was for fertility and protection of a divine mother. Their consorts, in dying and rising, symbolized "rebirth." Followers of the mysteries were convinced that the cycles of nature and human life were related.

The mystery religions were a response to the need among people for new and more satisfying religious experiences. They emphasized an inwardness and privacy of belief and worship within closed communities.

The secrets of ritual death and rebirth remain obscure. In the mysteries associated with Demeter-Kore, Kybele-Attis, Isis-Osiris, Dionysus, and Mithras, followers underwent rituals of darkness and light to emerge "reborn." Initiates took sacraments of food and drink, if not the raw body and blood of the god incarnate. In this way the sacrificed god was brought within. Practices included fasting, abstinence from sex, prayers, observation of sacred works of art, and participation in the sacred drama of the sufferings and joys of deities and saviors. Here "blessed ones" performed, spoke, heard, saw, and tasted death and rebirth.

U. Bianchi, *The Greek Mysteries* (1976); W. Burkert, *Greek Religion* (1985); J. Campbell, ed., *The Mysteries* (1955); F. Cumont, *The Oriental Religions in Roman Paganism* (1956); J. Godwin, *Mystery Religions in the Ancient World* (1981); M. W. Meyer, *The Ancient Mysteries* (1987); R. Reitzenstein, *Hellenistic Mystery-Religions: Their Basic Ideas and Significance* (1978).

ROBERT M. BERCHMAN

Mysticism, Medieval What monastics called *contemplatio* and later medieval and early modern authors identified as *theologia mystica*, mysticism was first designated as everything connected with the mysteries of faith, but in the late Middle Ages it came to be associated with the direct, unmediated experience of God. Modern scholars discuss medieval mysticism as an element of religion that refers to a process or way of life whose desire is to attain, through divine grace, an encounter with God. The central paradox of the divine presence described by mystical writers is that because of God's transcendence of language and comprehension, God's presence is also an absence, something that can be expressed but is also inexpressible. Mysticism is not just one event but is a succession of insights and revelations about God that gradually transforms the devout. This developing mystical path is typically described as having three stages—purgation, illumination, and union—which are at times not completely distinct categories.

The use of language connected to "mystery" is dependent on the conviction that biblical interpretation, Christian doctrine, and knowledge of God involve matters known only by revelation. The initial layer of Christian mysticism was linked to reading and praying the biblical message with the aim of penetrating beyond the literal sense so that its mystical core could be revealed. Exegesis and mysticism were inseparable. Fourth-century monastic authors utilized this contemplative theology in their ideal of flight from the world in order to lead a specialized life of penance and prayer. Writers such as Ambrose (340–397) and Augustine (354–430) sought to express their understanding of mystical transformation through biblical exegesis and a theoretical exposition designed to lead the devout into the mystery of the consciousness of God's presence. The writings of Gregory the Great (540–604) on the mystical life are also exemplary of the interrelationship of the Bible and mysticism in the medieval period. While Gregory's letters provide some insight into his teaching and experience, it is in his Bible commentaries (on Job and the Song of Songs) and in his homilies (on Ezekiel and the Gospel readings for Mass) that Gregory offers his most descriptive statements about the life of asceticism, the stages of prayer/experience, and the fleeting experiences of the "uncircumscribed light" of divinity. In the writing of later authors such as Pseudo-Dionysius, God remains mysterious even in revelation and, therefore, description is possible only in terms of what God is not.

In the first half of the twelfth century, Bernard of Clairvaux (1090–1153) expanded the "contemplative" tradition by emphasizing the need for personal experience as a criterion almost equivalent to the biblical text. Bernard, along with William of St. Thierry (1085–1148), described the spiritual life as a search for union with God based on love. It was this emphasis on experience along with new forms of religious life created around the year 1200, such as the Mendicant orders of Franciscans and Dominicans and the independent groups of women known as Beguines, that mark a shift in Christian mysticism. Previous forms of mysticism, based on withdrawal from the world and programs of ascesis and contemplative prayer, did not dissolve. Rather, they were challenged to a certain degree by what Bernard McGinn describes as new lifestyles encouraging types of mysticism that were democratic (practically possible for all Christians, not just the religious elite, to enjoy immediate consciousness of God's presence) and secular (flight from the world was not a necessary precondition for attaining such divine grace). As a result of the growing conviction that God could be found anywhere and by anyone if the proper dispositions were present and grace was given, personal encounters with God, such as visionary experiences, were increasingly documented, especially those of women.

Through newly established avenues of religious affiliation and expression, women began to take a more prominent place in the mystical tradition and play a larger role in helping to form mystical practices and the teaching they entailed. For example, it has been argued that Mechthild of Magdeburg's (1210–1285) *The Flowing Light of the Godhead* and Marguerite Porete's (d. 1310) *The Mirror of Simple Souls* had significant influence on the thought of Meister Eckhart (1260–1327), one of the most profound mystical writers of the thirteenth and fourteenth centuries.

In the thirteenth century, several women wrote, often in the vernacular, of the visions and ecstatic states they had experienced. Beatrice of Nazareth (d. 1268), a Cistercian nun, described the "seven ways of love" that led the mystic to become "one spirit" with God. Mechthild described her mystical experience by composing scenes of dialogue between God and the soul, between Dame Soul and Dame Love.

The most notable of the changes in mystical practice was an emphasis on ecstatic experience, which also entails a concept of union of identity, or indistinction, with God. According to Eckhart, whose preaching was frequently addressed to Beguines and nuns, though God is completely other than humanity, there exists in the soul a "something" where the image of God is in some way imprinted. Contact between the divine essence and the devout can spring from this on the condition that one acknowledges one's nothingness in the face of being. When the soul has attained renunciation, God comes to it and transforms it into the divine essence. By the end of the Middle Ages, "mysticism" described a process or desire for renewal of the whole religious life. The meditation on Christ's humanity and the ideal of *imitatio Christi*, the use of affectionate language to describe spiritual realities, and the greater value given to individual experience and the interiorization of religious behavior were phenomena that were not limited to devout circles but concerned all the faithful.

Because of the personal, experiential nature of mysticism in the later Middle Ages, whose ultimate aim consisted in merging with God at the exclusion of any institutional intermediary, ecclesiastical space and hierarchy were implicitly called into question. Often religious experiences and teaching were deemed by the church to be heretical. For example, when Marguerite Porete rejected all clerical mediation and refused to make concessions regarding her book and beliefs, her mystical treatise was declared heretical and she was burned at Paris in 1310. Likewise, Eckhart's teaching was condemned by Pope John XXII in 1311 and 1329.

K. Armstrong, *Visions of God: Four Medieval Mystics and Their Writing* (1994); A. C. Bartlett et al., eds., *Vox Mystica: Essays on Medieval Mysticism in Honor of Prof. Valerie M. Lagorio* (1995); O. Davies, *God Within: The Mystical Tradition of Northern Europe* (1988); W. Harmless, *Mystics* (2008); B. McGinn and P. F. McGinn, *Early Christian Mystics: Divine Vision of Spiritual Masters* (2003); B. McGinn, *The Flowering of Mysticism: Men and Women in the New Mysticism (1200–1350)* (1998); W. F. Pollard and R. Boenig, eds., *Mysticism and Spirituality in Medieval England* (1997); E. R. Wolfson, *Through a Speculum That Shines: Vision and Imagination in Medieval Jewish Mysticism* (1994).

TODD M. RICHARDSON

Mysticism, Medieval Women's

Though it is difficult to define a mystical experience that is solely applicable to women, it may be possible to discern patterns of presentation of mystical consciousness—both of the immediate experience of God as well as of the path to it and the effects it produces—that are first found in the writing of women mystics and

that remain more consistently realized in the case of women than in that of men. Though mystical experiences can take place through various media, mystical visions, or "visualizations," form a large part of divine illuminations communicated by female mystical writers. Medieval women mystics engaged powerful imaginative creations, primarily visual and affective in nature, based on intense meditation on the imagery of the Bible and the liturgy, as well as artistic representations of Christ, the angels and saints, and heaven and hell, and they were flooded with love or sorrow for what they saw. The emotions were so powerful that these women felt compelled to share them with others, and in so doing they discovered and invented new ways to communicate mystical experiences and insights.

Beginning in the twelfth century, women came together to form new religious communities. These women—called Beguines in northern Europe, Franciscan or Dominican tertiaries in southern and northern Europe—lived together in groups, supporting themselves by manual labor and devoting their lives to serving others and growing spiritually. Many well-known medieval mystical writers, among them Hadewijch of Antwerp, Mechthild of Magdeburg, Angela of Foligno, and Catherine of Siena, belonged to these informal communities. Spiritual practices recommended to, or invented by, medieval women in these settings facilitated the kind of devotion and mental concentration that often led to visions and mystical experiences. These practices were shared by religious women, as well as the laity, but not usually by the men in religious communities, who had a more systematic intellectual education.

During this period, literature concerning women who imitated the Magdalene, not only in penitential weeping but also in seeking out and attaining loving union with Christ, grew significantly. Many of the visionary texts of mystical women contain descriptions of direct encounters with Jesus that signal a new form of mystical consciousness, or mystical knowing—more direct, more excessive, more bodily in nature than older forms. Madness of love, infinite longing, and annihilation of the will are constant motifs in the women mystics in the later Middle Ages. Directly influential to the development of amorous mystical descriptions by female mystical writers was Scripture, specifically the Song of Songs, and commentaries, notably the Bernardine and Cistercian commentaries on the Song of Songs, along with meditative texts on the life and crucifixion of Christ.

F. Beer, *Women and Mystical Experience in the Middle Ages* (1992); E. Z. Brunn and G. Epiney-Burgard, eds., *Women Mystics in Medieval Europe* (1989); C. W. Bynum, *Holy Feast and Holy Fast: The Religious Significance of Food to Medieval Women* (1987); A. Hollywood, *The Soul as Virgin Wife: Mechtild of Magdeburg, Marguerite Porete, and Meister Eckhart* (1995); B. McGinn, *The Flowering of Mysticism: Men and Women in the New Mysticism (1200–1350)* (1998); E. R. Obbard, ed., *Medieval Women Mystics: Gertrude the Great, Angela of Foligno, Birgitta of Sweden, Julian of Norwich* (2002); E. A. Petroff, ed., *Body and Soul: Essays on Medieval Women and Mysticism* (1994); U. Stölting, *Christliche Frauenmystik im Mittelalter: historisch-theologische Analyse* (2005).

TODD RICHARDSON

Nachman, Moses ben; Nachmanides *see* Moses ben Nachman

Nadere Reformatie A movement in post-Reformation Dutch Calvinism that sought to apply the doctrines of the Reformation to the everyday moral and religious life of believers, the church, and Dutch society. The Dutch term *nadere* means "nearer" or "closer" and refers to the application of Reformed doctrine in practical piety, Christian discipline, and public morals. Leading figures in the movement, such as Willem Tellinck (1579–1629) and Gisbertus Voetius (1589–1676), were learned scholastic theologians who emphasized the experiential and practical relevance of confessional Reformed doctrine. English Puritan piety, with its dual emphasis on doctrinal integrity and experiential piety, provided much of the inspiration for the movement; the works of William Perkins and his student William Ames were widely read in the Netherlands. Unlike the later German Pietism of P. J. Spener, the Nadere Reformatie was not antagonistic to scholastic theology but in fact was its counterpart. A later leader in the movement, Wilhelmus à Brakel (1635–1711), attacked the antidoctrinal, anticonfessional tendencies of German Pietism. Moreover, the Nadere Reformatie did not focus exclusively on the individual's interior spiritual experience but sought to transform family, church, and societal life in line with the teachings of the Reformed faith.

J. R. Beeke, *Assurance of Faith: Calvin, English Puritanism, and the Dutch Second Reformation* (1991).

RAYMOND A. BLACKETER

Nag Hammadi This town in Upper Egypt is near the site of the discovery in 1945 of a hoard of ancient religious texts. The collection, consisting of thirteen codices, wholly or partially preserved, contains fifty-two texts representing various genres, including apocalypses, academic treatises, biblical paraphrases, and collections of sayings. The texts survive in various dialects of Coptic, although most were probably composed in Greek, a few fragments of which survive. The codices date to the mid- to late-fourth century, but the original works come from the second to the fourth centuries.

Many texts in the collection exhibit strongly ascetical tendencies and reflect the tastes of fourth-century Egyptian ascetics. Scholars originally associated the texts with Pachomian monasteries in the vicinity of ancient Chenoboskion, but study of the *cartonage* (used papyri used for backing) in the bindings of the codices provides no firm evidence of a close connection with monasticism.

Apart from their ascetical concerns, the texts range widely in their religious interests. Some provide evidence for movements labeled heretical or "gnostic" in second- and third-century Christian sources. One group of texts (e.g., *Gospel of Truth* 1.3; 12.2; *Epistle to Rheginos* or *Treatise on Resurrection* 1.4; *Tripartite Tractate* 1.5; and *Exposition on Anointing, Baptism, and Eucharist* 11.2) shares important affinities with the teachings of Valentinian Christians active in Rome, Alexandria, and in the Rhone Valley in the late second century. Other texts (*Apocryphon of John* 2.1, 3.1, 4.1; *Hypostasis of the Archons* 2.4) resemble the teachings labeled Barbeloite by Irenaeus (*Haer.* 1.29) and may be part of a larger corpus, often now labeled "Sethian" (*Apocalypse of Adam* 5.5; *Trimorphic Protennoia* 13.1; *Zostrianos* 8.1; *Marsanes* 10.1; *Allogenes* 11.3). Others (*Discourse on the Eighth and the Ninth* 6.6; *Prayer of Thanksgiving* 6.7; *Asclepius* 6.8) have affinities with Hermetic literature. Still other texts have no demonstrable sectarian affiliation but reflect general tendencies of early Christian piety and moral teaching (*Teachings of Silvanus* 7.4). There is at least one small bit of classical literature, a garbled translation of Plato's *Republic*.

Perhaps the best-known text is the *Gospel of Thomas*, a collection of 114 sayings of Jesus. A product of Syrian Christianity, it enigmatically celebrates the work of the living teacher Jesus. Other "Gospels" represent different genres: the *Gospel of Philip* is an anthology, the *Gospel of Truth* is a meditative homily, and the *Gospel of the Egyptians* (3.2; 4.2) is an esoteric account of salvation history.

———

J. M. Robinson, *The Nag Hammadi Library in English* (3rd ed., 1996); J. D. Turner and A. McGuire, *The Nag Hammadi Library after Fifty Years: Proceedings of the 1995 Society of Biblical Literature Commemoration* (1997).

HAROLD W. ATTRIDGE

Nantes, Edict of Recently crowned but still facing resistance from Protestants and ultra-Catholics, Henry IV issued the Edict of Nantes in April 1598 in order to appease the Huguenots, obtain their allegiance to his rule, and bring an end to the religious wars that had devastated France for over thirty years. The full edict, which incorporated elements from previous peace edicts, guaranteed freedom of conscience for everyone; Protestant worship, however, was restricted to certain towns and the private residences of nobles. The edict awarded Huguenots full civil rights, access to schools and universities, and rights to hold public and royal offices. There were numerous clauses designed to reduce any ill will arising from religious difference. For example, the edict enjoined Huguenots from disrupting Catholic religious festivals, priests and pastors were prohibited from using abusive language to describe the rival faith, and special law courts were created to hear cases involving Protestants. Royal *brevets*, issued separately from the articles as personal concessions made by the king, agreed to give annual sums to the Reformed church to pay pastors' salaries and permitted the Huguenots to maintain towns with fortified garrisons for a measure of military security.

———

J. Garrisson, *L'Édit de Nantes: Chronique d'une paix attendue* (1998); R. Whelan and C. Baxter, eds., *Toleration and Religious Identity: The Edict of Nantes and Its Implications in France, Britain, and Ireland* (2003).

SCOTT M. MARR

Na Prous Boneta   *see* Boneta, Na Prous

Narsai (c. 399–c. 502), poet of the Church of the East. Born in 'Ain Dulba in Ma'alta (Persian Empire), Narsai was orphaned and raised by an uncle who was the superior of the monastery of Kfar Mari, near Bēt Zabdai. He studied ten years at the School of the Persians in Edessa and later became a teacher and eventually the head. Conflict with Bishop Cyrus forced him to move to Nisibis, where he helped

reestablish the school (c. 471). When the Edessene School was closed by Emperor Zeno (486), Narsai's school took in many of its students and faculty.

All his extant works are in verse that utilizes both seven- and twelve-syllable meter. Most of these verse homilies treat biblical topics in both the Old and New Testaments, although a number are commentaries on the baptismal and eucharistic rites. Narsai is the most important poet of the Church of the East, yet very few of his verse homilies are available in modern translation.

———

F. G. McLeod, trans., Narsai's *Metrical Homilies on the Nativity, Epiphany, Passion, Resurrection and Ascension*, PO 40 (1979); S. P. Brock, trans., "On the Sacrifice of Isaac," in *A Brief Outline of Syriac Literature* (1997), 186–88; J. Frishman, "Narsai's Homily for the Palm Festival—Against the Jews," in *IV Symposium Syriacum 1984* (1988), 217–29.

ROBERT A. KITCHEN

Nativity, Church of the From the second century there are references to Jesus' birth occurring in a cave at Bethlehem. In the fourth century, Helena, mother of Emperor Constantine, dedicated a church on the site. It consisted architecturally of three elements: a square colonnaded atrium on the west, a nearly square basilica with five aisles (the central nave had a clerestory with four lower side aisles), and an octagonal apse to the east over the grotto of the nativity (the circular plan marking a sacred spot). The Church of the Nativity and the Church of the Holy Sepulcher combined a meeting place for worship with a memorial (*martyrion*) of salvation history.

The Constantinian building was replaced in the sixth century by enlarging the basilica, adding a narthex, removing the octagon, extending the presbyterial area to enclose the cave (which was provided with two stepped entrances), and adding three apses (on the north and south end of the nave and at the eastern extension of the church). The Crusaders restored the church in the twelfth century to its sixth-century condition, and it survives to this day.

———

G. T. Armstrong, "Imperial Church Building in the Holy Land in the Fourth Century," in *BA* 30 (1967): 90–102; R. W. Hamilton, *The Church of the Nativity, Bethlehem* (1947); R. Krautheimer, *Early Christian and Byzantine Architecture* (4th ed., 1986), 59–60, 266–67.

EVERETT FERGUSON

Negri, Paola Antonia (1508–1555), Italian Roman Catholic sister and deposed leader of Barnabite and Angelic orders in mid-sixteenth-century Milan. Negri rose through the Order of the Angelics of St. Paul (founded in Milan in 1535) to exert authority over the corresponding male house (Barnabites). As both a spiritual and institutional leader, she emphasized social service and study, meditation and work. Her "Spiritual Letters," written to her followers, 1542–1551, articulate her program: *imitatio Christi*, spiritual mediation, and the seeking of "perfection" through community. Eventually her strong leadership of a "mixed" group (her followers called her "divine Mother") brought her to the attention of Roman Catholic authorities, who removed and imprisoned her for life. As followers distanced themselves, they disparaged her as scheming and supercilious. However, because her writings were eventually judged to be orthodox by the Inquisition in 1576, historians attribute her demise to various factors, such as a mid-century trend toward the cloistering of women religious, androcentric stifling of strong women, and reinvigorated Roman Catholic authority.

P. R. Baernstein, *A Convent Tale* (2002); E. S. van Kessel, ed., *Women and Men in Spiritual Culture, XIV–XVIIth Centuries: A Meeting of South and North* (1986), 71–90.

WILLIAM R. RUSSELL

Neochalcedonians This anachronistic term refers to those supporters of the Council of Chalcedon who were followers of Cyril of Alexandria. Although they accepted the Definition of Chalcedon, they did so by interpreting it in a Cyrillian fashion. These writers rejected both Nestorianism and Eutychianism. They disliked the Chalcedonian phrase that Christ was one "in two natures," preferring the phrase "from two natures," as found in Cyril. However, for the sake of rejecting the Eutychian heresy, the Neochalcedonians approved of the Definition.

Although the Neochalcedonians were opposed to Eutychianism and Apollinarianism, they employed the Theopaschite Formula, accepted the *Three Chapters* of Emperor Justinian I, and approved the anathemas of the Council of Constantinople (553). Important Neochalcedonian thinkers include John of Scythopolis, John the Grammarian, and Leontius of Jerusalem.

A. Grillmeier and H. Bacht, *Das Konzil von Chalkedon* (1951); S. Helmer, *Das Neuchalke-*

donismus (1962); J. Lebon, *Le Monophysitism severien* (1909); I. R. Torrance, *Christology after Chalcedon* (1988); L. R. Wickham, *After Chalcedon* (1985).

STEVEN A. MCKINION

Neoplatonism A development in Platonic philosophy, Neoplatonism began with the teachings of the philosopher Plotinus (c. 204–270). Its pivotal authors were Plotinus, Iamblichus (d. 326), and Porphyry (c. 232–c. 304), an anti-Christian polemicist who was Plotinus's student and publicist. Neoplatonism was opposed to the materialism of Stoicism and to the radical dualism of Gnosticism and Manicheism.

The term, originally meant to distinguish the philosophy from that of Plato and his immediate successors, was used in some older modern scholarship to cover not only any Platonic philosophy after Plato but any set of ancient ideas that seemed to presume real participation. In contemporary scholarship Neoplatonism names a specific body of Platonic teachings that is distinguished from early Platonism, the skeptic Platonism that followed (129 BCE–c. 85 BCE), and the return of dogmatic Platonism now referred to as Middle Platonism.

The distinguishing features of Middle Platonism and Neoplatonism are most easily recognized in doctrines that are best described as cosmological or theological, that is, they pertain to the origin of existence and the nature of the good (or virtue). Middle Platonism emphasizes Plato's creation theory in the *Timaeus* and so features a hierarchy of Mind, Demiurge (Maker), and World Soul. The causal relationship among these three is only thinly described. Neoplatonism teaches a first principle—the One—that existed beyond Mind and was the source of Mind and Soul. The One generates Mind and Soul through a process called "emanation." Emanation is a difficult mechanism to describe, but it is analogous to the way fire produces heat or odor arises from a scent.

A list of other influential Neoplatonic doctrines includes (1) a notion of divine simplicity, (2) a division of reality into immaterial and material, (3) certain notions of cause, (e.g., that the cause is greater than its effect), (4) an emphasis on the role of "vision" for platonic thought, and (5) a strong emphasis on spiritual "ascent" and doctrinal details of that ascent. Some Neoplatonic doctrines played a special role in the theology of specific Christians. Augustine, for example, attributed his realization that God cannot be material to his reading of the works of the Platonists. Augustine's understanding of immaterial beauty probably drew upon Neoplatonic sources. The allegorical reading of Scripture he encountered in Ambrose and attributed to Neoplatonism was actually dependent on Philo and Origen, both of whom were prior to Neoplatonism. It was only with Gregory of Nyssa, Ambrose of Milan, and Augustine of Hippo that Neoplatonism entered the mainstream of Christian thought.

A minimum reading acquaintance with Plotinus begins with *Enneads* 1.6, 5.1, and 6.9. *Ennead* 5.1 is especially important, for it seems to have been one of the few works by Plotinus known by all the Cappadocians. Furthermore, portions of this *Ennead* are quoted by Eusebius of Caesarea and were known to Cyril of Alexandria, suggesting that *Ennead* 5.1 was one of the first texts by Plotinus to have any influence on Christian teaching.

T. Finian and V. Twomey, eds., *The Relationship between Neoplatonism and Christianity* (1992); S. Lilla, "Neoplatonism" and "Platonism and the Fathers," in *Encyclopedia of the Early Church*, vol. 2, ed. A. Di Berardino (1992), 585–93, 689–98; J. M. Rist, *Platonism and Its Christian Heritage* (1985).

MICHEL RENE BARNES

Neopythagoreanism

Neopythagoreanism A revival of the Pythagorean school dating from the first century BCE. Neopythagoreanism flourished in the second century CE under Moderatus, Nicomachus, and Numenius. The Neopythagoreans combined metaphysical, ethical, and psychological theories from Platonic, Stoic, and Aristotelian sources. They regarded the universe as a harmonious world order based on numbers and arithmetical relations. The soul, as part of that order, attained happiness when in harmony with it.

Neopythagoreans were metaphysical monists. They postulated a triadic hierarchy of Gods: the One, the ground of reality; the Dyad, the creator of the world; and the World-Soul, the universe. A procession and return from the highest level of reality to the lowest was postulated.

Neopythagoreans were also metaphysical dualists. They claimed reality has two distinct parts: the intelligible and the sensible. This dualism explicitly emerges in their theory of the soul's heavenly fall into materiality. Hence, the soul has two parts (rational and irrational), two natures (good and evil), and two possibilities (immortality or transmigration). The soul could be reincarnated as a higher daemon or a lower animal. The aim of philosophy is to "salvage and free our separable intellect from the snares and bonds of bodily life." The good soul knows the virtues of moderation, courage, gentleness, self-control, and perseverance and is purified through ascetic and dietary rules to attain salvation. Members had strict ethical, religious, and dietary norms to follow; they met for religious worship and cultic meals.

C. J. De Vogel, *Pythagoras and Early Pythagoreanism* (1966); J. Dillon, *The Middle Platonists* (1972); R. M. Grant, "Dietary Laws among Pythagoreans, Jews, and Christians," *HTR* 73 (1980): 299–310; D. O'Meara, *Pythagoras Revived* (1989); G. R. S. Mead, *Apollonius of Tyana: The Philosopher-Reformer of the First Century AD* (1966); H. Thesleff, *An Introduction to the Pythagorean Writings of the Hellenistic Period* (1961).

ROBERT M. BERCHMAN

Neri, Filippo (1515–1595), Roman Catholic Italian priest, reformer, and founder of the Congregation of the Oratory. Born in Florence, Neri, under the lingering influence of Savonarola, left his family's business and moved to Rome permanently in 1533. Appalled by Roman decadence, he felt called to reform the city. The pious Neri frequented the catacombs, where he fasted, meditated, and prayed. He also gathered with others to tend the sick and pilgrims of Rome (founding what became the hospital of Santa Trinita). An informally educated layman, he studied philosophy and theology at the Sapienza. Neri was ordained in 1551.

The "Apostle of Rome," known for his joyful and creative demeanor, hosted lay and clergy gatherings for studying the Bible, discussing theology, praying, and singing hymns in "the Oratory," a residential community through which many leaders of the Catholic Reformation passed (e.g., Jacopo Sadoleto, Francis de Sales, Ignatius Loyola). Neri's influence was extensive, mediated by his advice, so frequently sought by cardinals, bishops, and other notables. Gregory XIII granted the Oratory "religious congregation" status in 1575. Neri was canonized in 1622.

L. Bouyer, *St. Philip Neri: A Portrait* (1995); M. Trevor, *Apostle of Rome: A Life of Philip Neri* (1966).

WILLIAM R. RUSSELL

Nero (54–68), Roman emperor. The last Julio-Claudian emperor, Nero acceded to the throne upon the death of his adoptive father, Claudius (41–54). His reign began moderately under the influence of Seneca and the praetorian prefect Afranius Burrus. After Nero's murder of his mother, Agrippina, in 59 and the death of Burrus and retirement of Seneca in 62, Nero displayed the impetuosity and excess that earned him the animosity of contemporaries and the disdain of later writers. Though Nero's liberality placated the Roman plebs, senators objected to his disregard of their prerogatives. The city's propertied classes suffered from the megalomania and confiscations that followed the great fire of 64. A failed conspiracy in 65 inspired a reign of terror that, together with disregard of the army, set the stage for military revolt. Meanwhile, misjudgments in Judea contributed to the outbreak of the Jewish War in 66. Nero's despairing suicide only facilitated the civil wars that brought Vespasian (69–79) to the throne. Casting blame for the fire of 64 upon the city's Christians and instigating persecution (*1 Clement* 5–6; Tacitus, *Annales* 15.44) won Nero infamy among Christians (e.g., Tertullian, *Apol.* 5.3–5; Sulpicius Severus, *Chron.* 2.29). Early literary traditions imply Peter and Paul's martyrdom at Rome during Nero's persecution (c. 64–67; e.g., *1 Clement* 5–6; Ignatius, *Rom.* 4).

M. Griffin, *Nero: The End of a Dynasty* (1984); Suetonius, *Life of Nero*; Tacitus, *Annales* 13–16.

DENNIS E. TROUT

Nestorian Missionary Enterprise In the thirteenth and fourteenth centuries, the Church of the East was represented across 5,000 miles west to east from Tarsus to China's coastline, and from north to south across 3,500 miles from Siberia's Lake Baikal to the southern tip of India. It contained at least twenty-five archbishops, two hundred bishops, and many monasteries, priests, and parishes. It was regarded as Nestorian by Christians who answered to Rome and Constantinople. But this was a church that, from its patriarchal seats (Seleucia-Ctesiphon to 775 CE and then Baghdad) dwarfed all others in jurisdiction and endeavor across vast distances.

The base for Nestorian missionary efforts was located in what is now modern Iraq. Forbidden to proselytize in their homeland, first by Sasanian Zoroastrians and then by Muslims after 652, Nestorian Christians concentrated their evangelical efforts among "heathens" across Central Asia and into Tibet. First contacts were made by Syriac-speaking merchants moving along trade routes such as the Silk Road, via

centers such as Merv, Herat, Samarkand, Bokhara, and Kashgar. Such pioneer work was consolidated by monks, who also brought education, medicine, and agricultural skill. These monks stressed an asceticism like that of their contemporaries, the Celtic missionaries in Europe (see *Irish Monasticism*).

Within three decades of the death of Augustine of Canterbury (in 604) the Church of the East, led by Al-o-pen, was established in China under the tolerant T'ang dynasty. Central Asian peoples heard the gospel between 500 and 1000. Converts among Sogdians, Keraits, and Uighurs were faithful disciples for centuries. Their influence on the Mongols, who rose to prominence under Jinghis Khan (d. 1227), was noted by early Franciscan envoys (see *Giovanni de Pian del Carpini*).

In the years after the Muslim conquest of Parthia the Church of the East had reasonably good relations with the new rulers. Church leaders assisted the rulers with administration, medical knowledge, and education through their translations of Greek classics into Syriac and then into Arabic. Patriarch Timothy I (d. 823) engaged in friendly but serious debate with the caliph Mahdi (d. 785) on the relative merits of Islam and Christianity. Through Kerait and Uighur relationships with the Mongols there was a positive but reserved attitude toward the church by Jinghis Khan and by Khubilai Khan (d. 1295). The Poles were aware of lay-led "Nestorian" strength in their time in China (1271–1295), but at no time did the Church of the East have support such as Charlemagne (d. 814) gave to Catholic expansion in Europe.

The possibility of an alliance between the Mongol Il-Khanate in Persia and Western Christians against the threat of Muslim Turks disappeared with the conversion of the Il-Khanate to Islam by 1335. Exhaustion, the plagues of 1337–1339, and the depredations of Timur Leng (d. 1405) combined to reduce the Church of the East in the early fifteenth century to but a shadow of its former self. It was restricted to an enclave in the mountains of northeastern Syria and to southwestern India. So ended the most impressive missionary endeavor of the first 1,500 years of Christian history.

———

I. Gillman and H.-J. Klimkeit, *Christians in Asia before 1500* (1999); W. Hage, *Syriac Christianity in the East* (1988); S. H. Moffett, *A History of Christianity in Asia*, vol. 1 (rev. ed., 1998); A. Mingana, "The Apology of Timothy the Patriarch before the Caliph Mahdi,"

Bulletin of the John Rylands Library 12 (1928): 137–227.

IAN GILLMAN†

Nestorius (c. 351–452), patriarch of Constantinople (428–431). His reputed ideas sparked a christological controversy and an ecclesiastical tradition. Following consecration as patriarch, Nestorius, an Antiochene monk and student of Theodore of Mopsuestia (350–428), rejected the use of the term *Theotokos* ("God-bearer," "Mother of God") for the Virgin Mary. He believed the term would denigrate the humanity of Christ as well as improperly elevate Mary's status to divinity. He preferred *Christotokos* ("Christ-bearer"). His blunt language incited vigorous response from theologians and laity.

Nestorius described the relationship between the humanity and deity of Christ as that of two distinct *phūses* ("natures"), human and divine, which require two *hypostases* ("subsistences"), coinciding and joined in one *prosōpon* ("person") at the "good pleasure" of God. The divine Logos had entered into the human Jesus, an action of "indwelling." Nestorius stressed that the human Jesus underwent a process of moral development that demonstrated his function as both Redeemer and personal example for humanity.

Cyril of Alexandria took particular issue with Nestorius, arguing that Christ possesses only one nature, derived from two natures, united in one *hypostasis*. This teaching became the classical Monophysite doctrine. Both sides believed the other's position led to serious error: Nestorius argued that in Cyril's thought the divine nature obscures the human nature; Cyril accused Nestorius of advocating two separate Christs.

When the Council of Ephesus (431) was convened to mediate the controversy, Cyril assumed the position of chair. Without waiting for John of Antioch and other Antiochene supporters of Nestorius to arrive, the council condemned Nestorius's ideas and deposed and excommunicated him. When Nestorius's supporters did arrive, a countercouncil reversed the decisions and condemned Cyril. However, following the compromise document, the Formula of Reunion (433), Cyril emerged the victor while Nestorius remained in exile for the rest of his life.

The Council of Chalcedon (451) reaffirmed the condemnation of Nestorius so that the Nestorian party was now opposed by two factions: the signers of the Definition of Chalcedon (who affirmed two natures in one person and one *hypostasis* "without confusion") and the Monophysites (who declared one nature, derived from two natures, united in one *hypostasis*). So close were the Chalcedonian and Nestorian definitions that the dissenting Monophysites denounced those who subscribed to Chalcedon as Nestorians. Both were labeled "Dyophysites" (two-nature advocates).

Reexamination of Nestorius's thought, particularly after the discovery of his *Book of Heracleides* early in the twentieth century, has raised serious doubt whether Nestorius was ever a "Nestorian" and whether the Nestorianism of the councils really existed in a religious community. Nestorius and the churches bearing his name have always identified Theodore of Mopsuestia as the source of their biblical and theological teaching.

Following Chalcedon, the Nestorians were driven eastward into the Persian Empire (present-day Iraq), which was not friendly toward Christians in general. The famed School of the Persians in Edessa (Urfa), long the Syriac intellectual center in the tradition of Theodore of Mopsuestia, was forced to close in 486 by Emperor Zeno but was subsequently moved to Nisibis inside the Persian realm. Nestorian missions continued to venture eastward and established churches in southern India, central Asia, and in China.

In the wake of the Islamic conquest, the heirs of the Nestorian label thrived, mostly in Iraq and in southern India. The church produced a number of theologians whose writings were accepted readily across Syriac church doctrinal lines: the poet Narsai; the systematizer of Nestorian theology, Babai the Great; and spiritual writers Isaac of Nineveh, Martyrius Sahdona, Joseph Hazzaya, Dadisho Qatraya, and John of Dalyatha. Currently the heirs of the Nestorian church are found throughout Europe and North America. Lesser numbers remain in the Near East and India. In response to the negative historical image of Nestorius, the title "Nestorian" is generally rejected in favor of the (Assyrian) Church of the East.

J. F. Coakley and K. Parry, eds., "The Church of the East: Life and Thought," *Bulletin of the John Rylands Univ. Library of Manchester*, 78, no. 3 (1996); W. H. C. Frend, *The Rise of the Monophysite Movement: Chapters in the History of the Church in the Fifth and Sixth Centuries* (1972), 16–49; J. N. D. Kelly, *Early Christian Doctrines* (5th ed., 1978), 310–43; J. Pelikan, *The Emergence of the Catholic Tradition*

(100–600), vol. 1 of *The Christian Tradition: A History of the Development of Doctrine* (1971), 251–77; J. Pelikan, *The Spirit of Eastern Christendom (600–1700)* (1977), 39–49; D. Wilmhurst, *The Ecclesiastical Organization of the Church of the East, 1318–1913* (2000).

ROBERT A. KITCHEN

Netherlands, Reformation in the

Reformist ideas began filtering into the Lowlands as early as 1520, when Dutch versions of Luther's works were being printed at Antwerp and Leiden. Substantial trade with Germany ensured that Luther's works would make their way into the region. The earliest manifestations of Protestantism were diffuse and not part of any organized movement. But Charles V zealously defended the Catholic faith and sought vigorously to uproot all heresy in his ancestral Netherlands. Three Augustinian monks were executed for holding Lutheran opinions in the 1520s. The persecution of Protestants and Anabaptists only intensified over the years; more persons were put to death for heresy in the Lowlands than in any other region of Europe. The unintended effect of this persecution was increasing resentment among the local magistrates and the populace. This resentment increased still further after the abdication of Charles V, when his son Philip II of Spain pursued a policy of burdensome taxation and brutal persecution of religious dissenters. Philip, who spoke neither French nor Dutch, was widely seen as a foreign despot, raising the ire of local magistrates and reform-minded religionists alike.

By the 1530s Anabaptists were gathering numerous adherents in the Lowlands, but they were also acquiring a very negative reputation for militancy and violence. In 1535 Anabaptists unsuccessfully attempted to take over cities such as Leiden and Amsterdam and turn them into bastions of the kingdom of God, such as Melchior Hoffman (d. 1543) had done at Münster. Anabaptists came to be seen as a serious threat to social stability and were severely persecuted. Menno Simons (1496–1561) managed to steer Anabaptism in a peaceful and less threatening direction.

In the 1540s, many Protestants fled the Lowlands under the pressure of persecution. These exiles founded refugee or "stranger" churches in Wesel, London, Frankfurt, and Emden; many Walloon (francophone Dutch) Protestants sought refuge in Huguenot churches in France. The refugee churches also provided support for underground churches in the southern provinces, the "churches under the cross." Antwerp, with both a French- and Dutch-speaking congregation, became an important center for these underground churches. The doctrine and polity of these churches was decidedly Calvinist. By 1561 the churches had their own Belgic Confession, penned by Guide de Brès. The exile synod in Emden (1571) endorsed this and other Calvinist symbols, as well as advocating Calvinist church polity and discipline.

The year 1566 was crucial for the future of religious reformation and political independence in the Netherlands. The government of Margaret of Parma, regent of the Netherlands, was faltering as hundreds of noblemen petitioned her to relax the persecution of Protestants. She dismissed them as "beggars," a term embraced by Dutch patriots. But when a wave of iconoclastic riots broke out across the region, Margaret was forced into a compromise with William of Nassau, Prince of Orange (1533–1584), allowing limited freedom of religion as long as the iconoclasts were stopped. But this iconoclasm was counterproductive. Philip appointed as governor-general the cruel and brutal Duke of Alva (or Alba), who arrived in 1567 with an army of ten thousand, initiating a campaign of terror that would further fuel resentment and nationalist sentiments. His "Council of Troubles," popularly called the "Council of Blood," rooted out political and religious dissent by dispensing summary executions and instilling fear into the populace. Alva followed up with a program of oppressive taxation, which precipitated a political revolt under the leadership of the Prince of Orange. The Eighty Years' War (1568–1648) resulted in the division of the Lowlands. The northern provinces gained independence as a Protestant nation, the United Netherlands; the south remained Catholic and under Spanish dominion.

The Calvinist churches and the leaders of the nationalist revolt formed a fruitful but increasingly tense alliance. French Calvinism allowed magistrates and princes to rebel against tyrants, but it also conceived of the church as a doctrinally confessional community, with relative independence from the state, and in which members submitted to church discipline. Many Dutch magistrates envisioned a national church that would embrace the whole populace under a latitudinarian civic Protestantism and would remain largely under state control. When the Reformed Church was recognized as the official ecclesiastical body in the Netherlands, Calvinists comprised only 10–20 percent of the population. Lutherans and Anabaptists eventually acquired the status of tolerated minorities. The Synod of Dort (1618–1619) maintained the confessional basis of the Reformed Church, but provincial governments frequently blocked the implementation of the Dort church order and continued to assert their authority in ecclesiastical matters. The Calvinists had fought for the right to exist as a confessional church; the political leaders had championed the cause of religious liberty. This inherent tension between church and state was never reconciled.

P. M. Crew, *Calvinist Preaching and Iconoclasm in the Netherlands, 1544–1569* (1978); A. Duke, *Reformation and Revolt in the Low Countries* (1990); C. Kooi, *Liberty and Religion: Church and State in Leiden's Reformation, 1572–1620* (2000); A. Pettegree, *Emden and the Dutch Revolt* (1992); H. Schilling, *Civic Calvinism in Northwestern Germany and the Netherlands* (1991).

RAYMOND A. BLACKETER

Newton, Isaac (1642–1727), English scientist. He studied mathematics and philosophy at Trinity College, Cambridge (1661–1665), but left Cambridge to avoid the plague. While studying at home in Lincolnshire, he began to develop the insights that led to important advances in the fields of optics, astronomy, physics, and calculus. He returned to Cambridge as a fellow and became the Lucasian Professor of Mathematics. His *Mathematical Principles of Natural Philosophy* (1687) set forth his three laws of motion and his universal law of gravitation. He became active in politics after the Glorious Revolution and served two terms in Parliament. In 1693, he suffered a breakdown that forced his retirement from research. Thereafter, he moved to London, where he served as warden (1696) and master of the Royal Mint (1699). In 1703 he was elected president of the Royal Society, and in 1705 he became the first scientist to be knighted.

Newton's description of a universe operating according to a set of fixed mathematical laws inevitably raised questions about many traditional Christian beliefs. Newton related religion to science by portraying God as a clockmaker who initially created the world and subsequently had to intervene occasionally to repair it. He doubted the doctrine of the Trinity but devoted much time near the end of his life to the interpretation of biblical prophecy.

B. Dobbs, *The Janus Face of Genius: The Role of Alchemy in Newton's Thought* (1991); F. Manuel, *The Religion of Isaac Newton* (1974); R. Westfall, *The Life of Isaac Newton* (1993).

ERIC LUND

Nicaea, First Council of   In retrospect, the Council of Nicaea (325) is generally considered the first "ecumenical" or worldwide council, which set the pattern for all later ones. It led to the gradual development of what is now called the Nicene Creed and was a direct result of the reunification of the Roman world, or *oikoumenē*, under Constantine in 324. In that year Constantine, the first Christian Roman emperor, became ruler of the Eastern as well as Western halves of the Roman Empire. As the East had more Christians than the West, Constantine also inherited a number of very divisive ecclesiastical controversies, such as the date of Easter or how to deal with persons who lapsed under persecution.

Two of the most contentious concerned Egypt and its primate, Alexander of Alexandria: a rigorist bishop, Melitius, had set up an alternative episcopate, and Alexander had excommunicated the presbyter Arius on theological grounds (318). Since Arius and Alexander both appealed to bishops outside Egypt, their dispute was "ecumenical" before Constantine arrived. After an attempt at mediation, Constantine referred the matter to a church council, a tactic used earlier in the West. Constantine called the council to coincide with a celebration of the empire's reunification and his own twentieth anniversary as emperor; he thus brought together bishops from the entire Roman world and beyond. Most were from the East, but the 318 or so bishops who gathered at Nicaea on May 20, 325, were diverse enough to justify the title "ecumenical." The bishop of Rome was represented by legates; the emperor took part in person.

The minutes of the council have been lost, but surviving documents include a synodical letter, twenty canons, and a "faith" or creed. This "faith" is *not* the Nicene Creed in use today but a creedlike manifesto intended for episcopal professionals. It establishes what might (or might not) be said about issues raised by Arius and concludes with four anathemas condemning his teaching. The creed called "Nicene" today appeared fifty years later, about the time of the Council of Constantinople (381). It was called "Nicene" because it was thought to represent Nicaea's teaching; in fact, it represents a half-century of consensus building after the council.

Arius taught that the Son, the "Only-begotten God" (John 1:18), is not identical with the uncreated Source of all things and thus cannot be "God" in the same sense. Hence, by inference from Proverbs 8:22 (LXX), the word "creature" can be applied to this Only-begotten God, albeit in a unique sense. The original creed or "faith" of Nicaea sought to exclude this position by introducing nonscriptural terms from philosophy: the Son is said to be "begotten, not made" and begotten from the "essence" (*ousia*) of the Father; he is therefore "of one essence" (*homoousios*) with the Father. The word *homoousios* was controversial even among those who opposed Arius but was explained by its proponents in a very restricted sense. All but a few of the bishops accepted it on that basis, and the few who did not were exiled, as was Arius.

A compromise was achieved with the Melitians, the date of Easter was established, and other issues were addressed. Unfortunately, on the main theological issue the bishops were clearer as to what they rejected (Arius) than what they meant by *homoousios*. Constantine used the council's written "faith" to achieve external uniformity, but opposition continued in private. When Constantine died in 337, that opposition became public, and the emperor Constantius tried to establish a new uniformity by rejecting *homoousios* and "essence language" altogether. Athanasius, Alexander's successor, a participant at Nicaea, objected and began to use *homoousios* to symbolize a "Nicene" faith that went beyond the teaching of the council itself.

After the death of Constantius in 361, the work of Athanasius and others led to a new consensus that described the Spirit as well as the Son as *homoousios* with the Father. In the 360s and 370s, Meletius of Antioch, Basil of Caesarea, and others developed an understanding of *homoousios* that spoke of three divine *hypostases* (entities or persons) subsisting in a single divine essence or *ousia*. This understanding of *homoousios* prevailed and became the basis of later theological development. Nicaea remained a symbol of the starting point of this development, but this specific language became the norm only about the time of the Nicene Creed of 381:

Mansi 2.635–1082, in *ANF* 14 (1869), 1–56; L. Ayres, *Nicaea and Its Legacy* (2004); P. F. Beatrice, "The Word 'Homoousios' from Hellenism to Christianity," *CH* 71 (2002): 243–72; R. P. C. Hanson, *Search for the Christian Doctrine of God* (1988), 152–207; S. Parvis, *Marcellus of Ancyra and the Lost*

Years of the Arian Controversy 325–345 (2006); R. P. Vaggione, *Eunomius of Cyzicus and the Nicene Revolution* (2000); F. M. Young, *From Nicaea to Chalcedon* (1983).

RICHARD PAUL VAGGIONE, OHC

Nicene Creed What is today referred to as the Nicene Creed is actually not the product of the First Council of Nicaea (325), the first ecumenical council, but of the First Council of Constantinople (381). There is no extant official record of the former council, but unofficial sources, most significantly a letter of Eusebius of Caesarea, report the actions of the council. Its creed, especially the anathemas, was designed to disallow the Arian subordination of the Son. The Son is of the "same substance" as the Father.

As was the case of the council of 325, there are no extant records of the council of 381. The creed associated with it, technically known as the Niceno-Constantinopolitan Creed, was first used officially seventy years later at the Council of Chalcedon (451), the fourth ecumenical council. There it was presented as an elaboration of the faith of 325 made necessary by theological questions that had arisen subsequent to the Council of Nicaea. Thereafter the creed of 381 was generally viewed as an enlarged yet trustworthy expression of the faith expressed at Nicaea.

Recent textual studies have demonstrated that the creed of 381, although in accord with the creed of 325, was not simply an expansion of it. Instead, the latter creed was derived from another, perhaps liturgical, source, which the members of the council likely amended. Most significantly, it addresses the person and work of the Holy Spirit, leaving no doubt that the Spirit is to be worshiped as God, although the language of "same substance" used with regard to the Son is not repeated.

Language about the origin of the Spirit became a source of controversy between Christians in the East and those in the West. The creed states that the Spirit "proceeds from the Father." The West latter added the *filioque*, thereby amending the creed to read "proceeds from the Father and the Son." That unilateral change contributed to the eventual split of the church in the East and the West.

R. P. C. Hanson, *The Search for the Christian Doctrine of God* (1988); J. N. D. Kelly, *Early Christian Creeds* (3rd ed.; 1972); J. Pelikan and V. Hotchkiss, *Creeds and Confessions of Faith in the Christian Tradition*, 4 vols. (2003).

REBECCA H. WEAVER

Nicephorus I (c. 750–815), patriarch of Constantinople (806–815). Nicephorus was born to a family in imperial service. His father served at the court of Constantine V Copronymos until he was dismissed and exiled to Nicaea during the Iconoclastic Controversy. He founded several monasteries on the Asian side of the Bosphorus without ever becoming a monk himself. He was a layman in imperial service when he was appointed patriarch in 806. He faced two major challenges during his episcopate. The first was dealing with the priest Joseph who had blessed an irregular fourth marriage of Emperor Constantine VI. After some vacillation, he supported the emperor and this earned him the permanent opposition of Theodore the Studite and his followers. Nicephorus's second challenge came from Emperor Leo V, the Armenian whom he crowned in 813. When Leo revived iconoclasm, Nicephorus was exiled in 815 and died in his monastery of St. Theodore.

He authored a *Major Apology*, a *Minor Apology*, and *Three Antirhettics* in support of icons. His *Breviarium* is an important source for the history of the seventh and eighth centuries.

PG 100 (1860); A.-M. Talbot, ed., *Byzantine Defenders of Images: Eight Saints' Lives in English Translation* (1998); J. Travis, *In Defense of the Faith: The Theology of Patriarch Nikephoros of Constantinople* (1984).

EUGENE M. LUDWIG, OFM CAP.

Niceta of Remesiana (c. 340–c. 414), bishop and writer. Little is known of Niceta. By 370 he had become bishop of Remesiana (now Bijelo Polje in Montenego). The city was part of the ecclesiastical patriarchate of Rome, but Emperor Theodosius placed it within the political confines of the eastern part of the Roman Empire. Thus, although Niceta wrote in Latin, he also spoke Greek and had to deal with Eastern problems. His two trips to Italy (398 and 402) are known from *Poems* (17, 27) that Paulinus of Nola (c. 353–431) wrote in his honor. These affectionate, elaborate verses, wishing Niceta Godspeed, praise his virtues but offer little biographical information. Niceta's own writings, first edited critically by A. E. Burn, include a treatise for catechumens that attacks Arians, Pneumatomachians, and astrology. Niceta also wrote about liturgical matters. During his episcopate, barbarians invaded the region. Presumably he had to deal with the disruption they caused. He may have tried to evangelize them. Letters of Innocent I (401–417) dated 409 and 414 mention Niceta. No reference to him occurs after 414.

A. E. Burn, *Niceta of Remesiana* (1905); A. di Berardino, *Patrology*, vol. 4 (1986); K. Gamber, ed., *Textus patristici et liturgici* (1964–1969); G. Walsh, trans., "Works of Niceta of Remesiana," in FC 7 (1949), 1–76.

JOSEPH F. KELLY

Nicholas, Henry (1502–1580), Dutch mystic, founder of the sect of Familists. Nicholas was the son of a merchant and a native of Münster. From the time he was a young boy he experienced mystical visions. Arrested for heresy, upon his release (c. 1531) he made for the more hospitable religious climate of Amsterdam, where by 1540 he had founded the Familia Charitatis (Family of Love), having been commanded to do so in a vision. This community of love was made up of Nicholas's followers and was restricted to those who also had had life-changing mystical experiences. One of the unique aspects of this community was its service of worship, where Nicholas welcomed those who were led by the Spirit to make prophetic utterances. He believed that the eschaton was imminent and that the community was charged with the responsibility to prepare for it. He encouraged members to serve each other in love. Special respect was given to elders, who were thought to be more deeply filled with the Spirit.

Nicholas wrote numerous works, the most famous of which was the anonymously published *Mirror of Justice*. He was forced into exile in 1560 and spent the remainder of his life wandering from town to town throughout Holland and Germany. His mystical teachings were regarded by Roman Catholic and magisterial Protestants alike as dangerously pantheistic and antinomian, and his group as representing another variety of Anabaptism. His followers became most numerous in England, ultimately becoming Anabaptists or Quakers there during the seventeenth century.

A. Hamilton, *The Family of Love* (1981); G. H. Williams, *The Radical Reformation* (3rd ed., 1992).

RODERICK MARTIN

Nicholas of Autrecourt (c. 1296–1369), theologian who originated from Autrecourt in the diocese of Verdun and probably attended the arts faculty at Paris. In the 1330s, he studied theology and belonged to the Collège de Sorbonne. It is unclear, however, whether Autrecourt ever became a full-fledged master of theology. One of the striking features of Autrecourt's academic career is his condemnation in 1346, after a trial in Avignon that dragged on for six years. In 1347, upon his return to Paris, Autrecourt had to repeat his recantation of selected theses (*articuli*) for the academic community and burn a treatise, most likely the *Exigit ordo*. Autrecourt has become best known for his correspondence with Bernard of Arezzo and one Master Giles dating from the year 1336/1337. He has often been portrayed as a skeptic because of his view that it is unwarranted to infer knowledge of the effects from knowledge of the causes, or knowledge of substances from knowledge of the accidents. Actually, Autrecourt attacked the "Academics" or ancient skeptics and their school of philosophy. His philosophical stance can be more accurately characterized as a challenge to the prevailing Aristotelian position that substances and causal relations really exist. He also was an atomist.

Nicholas of Autrecourt, *The Universal Treatise*, trans. L. Kennedy, et al. (1971); Autrecourt, *His Correspondence with Master Giles and Bernard of Arezzo: A Critical Edition and English Translation*, ed. L. M. de Rijk (1994); Z. Kaluza, *Nicolas d'Autrecourt: Ami de la vérité*, vol. 42/1, *Histoire littéraire de la France* (1995).

J. M. M. H. THIJSSEN

Nicholas of Cusa (1401–1464), cardinal, bishop, reformer, and philosopher. The son of a Mosel shipper and merchant, he studied the liberal arts at Heidelberg (1416) before going to Padua, where he learned canon law (earning the doctorate in 1423), was exposed to the conciliarism of Francisco Zabarella, and began a friendship with the mathematician, physician, and astronomer Paolo Toscanelli. His ecclesiastical career was launched in 1424 when he became secretary to Cardinal Orsini for a short time. He continued his studies and teaching in canon law and theology at Cologne, a center of theological studies then dominated by the metaphysics of Albert the Great. He was also introduced to the writings of Pseudo-Dionysius and Ramon Lull at Cologne.

After service at the court of the bishop of Trier and ordination as a priest (1430), he went to the Council of Basel as an advocate for Count Ulrich von Manderscheid, whose bid for the vacant see of Trier failed. However, Nicholas became a member of the council's collegium in 1432, winning the favor of the council's president, the cardinal legate Julian Cesarini, and becoming an important participant in the council's many and complex deliberations. In 1433 he presented to Cesarini and the emperor Sigismund his own reform program, *De concordantia catholica* (the *Catholic Concordance*), which marked him as a conciliarist. When the confrontation between the council and Pope Eugenius IV culminated in the latter's relocation of the council to Italy, Nicholas left with Cesarini and the papal party. He soon found himself in the papal embassy to the Byzantine emperor, which planned the reunion of Eastern and Western churches intended to establish a Christian block against the advancing Ottomans. The trip aroused his interest in Greek philosophy, which was further nurtured by his friendships with Bessarion of Nicaea and Gemisthos Plethon, by the acquisition of Greek books (Proclus), and by the ensuing East-West negotiations at Ferrara and Florence. He remained busy, polemicizing against the conciliarists who remained at Basel (he accused them of introducing a new schism in the church, an accusation confirmed by the council's election of an antipope) and performing papal service (he represented popes Eugenius IV and Nicholas V at the imperial diets of 1441, 1442, and 1444, trying to draw the German princes from their neutrality to support the papal party against the council). At the same time, Nicholas wrote Neoplatonic philosophical treatises, beginning with his famous *De docta ignorantia* (*On Learned Ignorance*, 1440). Over the next two decades he continued to develop a unique philosophy around a concept of the coincidence of opposites, and he continued his political and reforming activities. Greek Platonists in the emperor's entourage to Italy influenced Nicholas's Platonism, as did the writings of Meister Eckhart, and he commissioned a copy of Eckhart's most important metaphysical work, the *Opus tripartitum*, in 1444. (In 1449 the Heidelberg theologian Johannes Wenck accused Nicholas of pantheism, which was condemned in Eckhart's writings in 1329.)

After Pope Eugenius IV abandoned the Council of Basel in 1437, support for the conciliarists who remained at Basel steadily declined. In 1447 the German princes, then the emperor Frederick III, having won various useful privileges and concessions from the papacy, endorsed the papal party. The antipope Felix V soon resigned, and the Council of Basel dissolved itself in 1448.

That same year Nicholas was named cardinal. He received his insignia in 1450, when he was also appointed bishop of Brixen, in the southern Tirol (March 23, 1450, a papal appointment against the cathedral canons' elected nominee). By the end of the year he was named papal legate to Germany (December 24, 1450). He assumed the office of bishop in 1451 on the strength of imperial investiture, and as papal legate he began a two-year journey through Germany to announce the jubilee indulgence of 1450, holding special plenary powers to reform the German church. The journey's fanfare was not matched by lasting reforms. After the tour, he settled at Brixen, where he brought the cathedral out of debt and won confirmation of privileges and temporal rights at the expense of the Tirolian duke Sigmund. He reformed the cathedral's bookkeeping, visited cloisters, took measures against simony and clerical concubinage, and continued to write philosophy, developing his unique approach to questions of divine being, its relation to human being, intellect, and the critique of Aristotle.

In 1457 he fell into open conflict with the duke, who was resentful of the interference of this foreign, nonnoble bishop with his own designs on the cathedral and its holdings. In 1458, Nicholas fled to the papal court, from which he campaigned for restoration to his see. There, in Rome, as general vicar over temporal matters (appointed January 11, 1459), he tried to reform the court (by holding a reform synod on February 10, 1459). A final ecclesiastical appointment came in 1463, when he was made abbot of the Benedictine monastery at Orvieto. He tried and failed to reform the monastery. A settlement with Duke Sigmund soon allowed the diocese of Brixen to be administered by Nicholas's delegate, but the frustrated bishop died on August 11, 1464. His body was buried in the cathedral of Brixen, except for his heart, which by his prior instruction was removed and interred in the chapel of the hospital he had established at Kues in 1458, which also became home to his personal library. The library survives there largely intact to this day.

———

K. Flasch, *Nikolaus von Keus in seiner Zeit* (2004); J. Hopkins, *A Concise Introduction to the Philosophy of Nicholas of Cusa* (3rd ed., (1986); Hopkins, *A Miscellany on Nicholas of Cusa* (1994); S. Meier-Oeser, *Die Präsenz des Vergessenen: Zur Rezeption der Philosophie des Nicolaus Cusanus vom 15. bis zum 18. Jahrhundert* (1989); E. Meuthen, *Nikolaus von Kues, 1401–1464: Skizze einer Biographie* (1976); N. Winkler, *Nikolaus von Kues: Zur Einführung* (2001).

CHRISTOPHER OCKER

Nicholas of Lyra (1270–1349), Franciscan, biblical exegete, "the plain and useful doctor," regent master in Paris (1308–1309), and Franciscan minister provincial of France (1319) and Burgundy (1325). Born in Lyre, Normandy, in the diocese of Évreux, a center of Jewish learning, Nicholas may have learned Hebrew there. He became acquainted with the Talmud, Midrash, and the works of Rashi (Rabbi Solomon ben Isaac, 1045–1105). In 1300 during the reigns of Boniface VIII and Philip the Fair, Nicholas became a Franciscan and immediately moved to the *studium generale* in Paris, where he flourished in the university setting despite a period of conflict over evangelical poverty between the papacy and the Franciscan order. He was one of the Franciscan bachelors of theology at the affair of the Templars (1307) and participated in an academic disputation, or quodlibet, "On the Advent of Christ" (1309). He participated in the ecclesiastical hearing at Paris for the Beguine mystic Marguerite Porete (1310). A moderate within the order concerning absolute poverty, he maintained close relationships with the Franciscan hierarchy, the papacy, and the French royal family. His magnum opus, the *Literal Postill on the Whole Bible* (1322/1323–1331) was a running commentary on the Old and New Testaments, intended for theologians and known for its double literal sense, affirmation of history and literary context, and Jewish interpretations of the OT. The double literal sense served as his key to interpret OT prophetic passages, allowing the exegete to draw two interpretations from the passage: one for the prophet's own time and another (usually christological) for the future. His *Moral Postill on the Whole Bible* (1333–1339) was a handbook for lectors and preachers, that is, a typological and allegorical series of notes on passages of Scripture that could be given a moral or spiritual interpretation. There are hundreds of manuscripts, some beautifully illustrated, and early modern printed editions of the Postills. Other works that are extant are *Quaestio de adventu Christi* (*Question on the Advent of Christ*, 1309); a treatise summarizing the *Literal Postill*, entitled *De Differentia nostre translationis ab hebraica littera veteris testamentis* (*On the Difference of Our Translation from the Hebrew Letter of the Old Testament*, 1333); a treatise against the Jews, *Responsio ad quendam Iudeum ex verbis Evangelii secundum Matthaeum contra Christum nequiter arguentem* (*Response from the Words of the Gospel according to Matthew to a Certain Jew Who Argues Badly against Christ*, 1334); a treatise on the beatific vision, *De* *visione divine essentie* (*On the Vision of the Divine Essence*, 1333). His last work (c. 1339) was the *Oratio ad honorem S. Francisci*, an acrostic devotional text spelling the name of St. Francis while commenting on the literal sense of ten psalms.

K. Froehlich and M. Gibson, "Introduction," facsimile reprint of the Rusch 1480–1481 edition of *Biblia Latina cum Glossa Ordinaria* (1992); E. A. Gosselin, "A Listing of the Printed Editions of Nicolaus of Lyra," *Traditio* 26 (1970): 399–403; D. Klepper, *The Insight of Unbelievers: Nicholas of Lyra and Christian Reading of Jewish Text in the Later Middle Ages* (2007), 297–312; P. Krey and L. Smith, eds., *Nicholas of Lyra and the Senses of Scripture*, Studies in the History of Christian Thought 90 (2000); P. Krey, "Nicholas of Lyra: Apocalypse Commentator, Historian, and Critic," *Franciscan Studies* 52 (1992): 53–84; P. Krey, "Many Readers but Few Followers: The Fate of Nicholas of Lyra's Apocalypse Commentary in the Hands of His Late Medieval Admirers," *CH* 64 no. 2 (1995): 185–201; C. Ocker, *Biblical Poetics before Humanism and the Reformation* (2002).

PHILIP D. W. KREY

Nicholas, St. (fourth cent.), bishop of Myra (Mugla, southwestern Turkey). Accounts of his life are fictitious. The only certainty is that he was bishop of Myra in the first half of the fourth century. His shrine is in Bari, Italy.

Nicholas was venerated in the East from the sixth century, but his *Acta* were not written until the ninth. Supposedly orphaned when he was young, he used his considerable inheritance for charity, notably saving three virgins from prostitution by providing each a bag of gold for her dowry. He is also credited with resurrecting three dead children, saving an unjustly condemned man, and opposing Arianism. Nicholas may have been buried in his cathedral, but Christian traders stole his relics and translated them to Bari in 1087. Pope Urban II dedicated his shrine in 1095, and the popularity of Nicholas in the West dates from this time.

In the Middle Ages northern Europeans gave children presents on his feast day (December 6). The Dutch brought this custom to America, where the gifts came to be given on Christmas Day. Washington Irving was the first to popularize the figure of "Santa Claus," around 1808, and Thomas Nast's cartoons of "Santa," which appeared in *Harper's Weekly* between 1863 and the 1890s remain the standard depiction.

C. W. Jones, *Saint Nicholas of Myra, Bari, and Manhattan: Biography of a Legend* (1978).

WILLIAM B. SWEETSER JR.

Nicodemism   This label derives from the biblical example of Nicodemus, who in John 3 visits Jesus under cover of darkness. It was applied particularly to those with Protestant leanings in sixteenth-century France and Italy who hid their true orientation and publicly conformed to Catholic practices, such as attending Mass. French Protestants such as Calvin and Guillaume Farel, who suffered exile rather than compromise with "idolatry," argued strenuously that faith commitment required external expression; thus, for the faithful who faced persecution the only alternatives were flight or martyrdom. Geneva was the center of opposition to Nicodemism; between 1537 and 1562 its presses produced no fewer than thirteen polemical titles devoted to the subject.

There is little evidence that Nicodemism generated a body of literature or constituted an organized movement with a coherent ideology. Spiritualist and irenicist emphases—regarding external rites and particularities of doctrine as things indifferent, since the real substance of religion is internal and invisible—may have influenced some labeled Nicodemite by Calvin. But, in fact, his targets were a diverse lot whose views reflected a variety of theological outlooks.

C. Ginzburg, *Il Nicodemismo* (1970); G. H. Williams, *The Radical Reformation* (3rd ed., 1992).

CHRISTOPHER ELWOOD

Nicolai, Philipp (1556–1608), Lutheran pastor and hymn writer, best remembered for the hymns "How Lovely Shines the Morning Star" ("the queen of chorales") and "Wake, Awake, for Night Is Flying" ("the king of chorales"). He studied at the universities of Erfurt and Wittenberg, receiving a theological degree from the latter in 1579. After four years ministering near his family home in Waldeck, he was installed as pastor of a Lutheran congregation at Herdecke. While serving there and afterward as preacher at court in Waldeck, Nicolai defended the Formula of Concord against denunciations by both Roman Catholic and Calvinist opponents, particularly over sacramental theology. These public disputes reached such fervor that the landgrave forbade the Univ. of Marburg from awarding Nicolai his doctorate in 1594. While serving a congregation at Unna (1596–1599) he composed a series of theological meditations published under the title *Gladsome Mirror of Eternal Life*, written for comfort after death by plague had taken 1,300 of his parishioners. Installed as pastor of St. Catherine's Church in Hamburg in 1601, Nicolai enjoyed a reputation as the "second Chrysostom" for the vitality and influence of his preaching.

N. Philipp, *Freudenspiegel des ewigen Lebens* (1599, repr. 1963); A. C. Piepkorn, "Philipp Nicolai, 1556–1608," *CTM* 39 (1968): 432–61.
DONAVON L. RILEY

Nil Sorsky (1433–1508), Russian monastic and contemplative. The son of a Muscovite nobleman surnamed Maikov, he began his monastic calling at the monastery of St. Cyril in Beloozero, northern Russia. He later visited Mount Athos, where he encountered the contemplative tradition known as hesychasm ("mystical quietness"). He returned to Russia to establish a hermitage at the Sora River in the forest near Beloozero. Here he introduced a form of ascetic monasticism that involved a small community (*skete*) guided by a spiritual father (*starets*). The members lived in hut-cells surrounding a wooden chapel. Nil compiled a monastic rule for the settlement that embodied poverty, simplicity, and contemplative prayer. The rule, which has survived, is a compendium of writings on asceticism by church fathers from the fourth to the fourteenth century. At the time his ideas were overshadowed by the "possessor" approach of Joseph of Volokolamsk, but his hesychastic, "nonpossessor" principles became very influential beginning in the eighteenth century.

G. P. Fedotov, "St. Nilus Sorski," in *The Russian Religious Mind*, vol. 2, *The Middle Ages: The 13th to the 15th Centuries* (1966); "St. Nilus Sorsky: The Teacher of Spiritual Prayer," in *A Treasury of Russian Spirituality*, ed. and comp. G. P. Fedotov (1965); S. Hackel, "Late Medieval Russia: The Possessor and the Non-Possessors," in *Christian Spirituality* (1987); G. A. Maloney, *Russian Hesychasm: The Spirituality of Nil Sorskij* (1973).
MICHAEL D. PETERSON

Nîmes, Synod of The eighth national assembly of Reformed congregations in France since the inaugural session in Paris (1559). The synod met in Nîmes in May 1572, with Theodore Beza, Calvin's successor in Geneva, in attendance, along with eighty-five other notable pastors and deacons. The assembly took up several important issues, chief among which was the ongoing controversy over the confession of faith of the French Reformed Church. Antoine de la Roche Chandieu (1534–1591) spoke for the group in favor of a Presbyterian system of organization, while Jean Morelli (d. 1572) articulated the views of those advocating a more decentralized congregationalist model. The assembly eventually voted in support of Chandieu's views and condemned those represented by Morelli as heretical. Furthermore, the Synod of Nîmes affirmed the inclusion of lay deacons in the consistory, though it underscored the leadership of the pastors in all doctrinal matters.

R. A. Mentzer and A. Spicer, eds., *Society and Culture in the Huguenot World, 1559–1685* (2002); G. Sunshine, *From French Protestantism to the French Reformed Churches: The Development of Huguenot Ecclesiastical Institutions* (1992).
MICHAEL WOLFE

Ninian (c. 360–c. 420), traditional apostle of Scotland. Ninian was a Romano-British Christian known only from a brief passage in the Venerable Bede's (673–735) *Ecclesiastical History of the English People* (3.4.1). An eighth-century poem and a miraculous Life by the English monk Ailred of Rievaulx (c. 1110–1167) add nothing of biographical value. Ninian built a church, which he dedicated to Martin of Tours (d. 397), on the peninsula at Whithorn in modern Dumfries and Galloway. Made of white stone, the church was called Candida Casa or "White House" by the English. Most likely Ninian was a cleric who worked with the local Romano-British population, but Bede tells us that he also evangelized the Picts of what is now southern Scotland. Both the medieval church and Scottish tradition exaggerated his role to make him the national apostle, but modern scholars limit his work to southwestern Scotland, no small achievement for that day. Archaeological excavations have uncovered a medieval ecclesiastical complex and an early Christian cemetery at Whithorn, while place-name evidence supports the tradition of Romano-British attempts to evangelize the Picts.

C. W. S. Barrow, "The Childhood of Scottish Christianity: A Note of Some Place-Name Evidence," *Scottish Studies* 27 (1983): 1–15; P. Hill, *Whithorn and St Ninian: The Excavation of a Monastic Town* (1997); J. MacQueen,

St. *Nynia* (1990); C. Thomas, *Whithorn's Christian Beginnings* (1992).

JOSEPH F. KELLY

Nizzahon Vetus This work is an anonymous late thirteenth- or early fourteenth-century Jewish polemic against Christianity of northern European, probably German, provenance. It is in large measure an anthology drawing upon *Sefer Yosef ha-Meqanne* (a polemic written in France in the 1260s) and similar compositions, roughly divided into three sections. The first follows the order of the Hebrew Bible, citing and refuting christological interpretations. The second generally follows the order of the Gospels, pointing out contradictions and other difficulties as well as inconsistencies with later Christian belief. The third subjects Christian doctrines and behavior to an extended, often withering critique.

The work reflects its Ashkenazic environment in its deemphasis of philosophical argumentation, in the eclectic character of its critical stance toward Jesus, who can be either a sinner or an observant Jew depending on the exigencies of the argument, and in its sharp, confrontational style. Unlike Jewish polemicists from southern Europe, the author counsels his readers to pursue an aggressive posture in their debates with Christians, preventing their adversaries from changing the subject when they find themselves in dire polemical straits.

While not all the reported exchanges can be considered historical, the book probably reflects the reality of lively religious discussion on the streets of northern Europe in which Jewish participants familiar with Christian texts expressed their views with remarkable candor.

D. Berger, *The Jewish-Christian Debate in the High Middle Ages: A Critical Edition of the* Nizzahon Vetus *with an Introduction, Translation, and Commentary* (1979, 1996).

DAVID BERGER

Noetus of Smyrna (fl. c. 200), "heretic" in Asia Minor. Information about Noetus comes from his opponents: Hippolytus rebutted his supposedly Heraclitean views, which had lately spread to Rome with Cleomenes (*Refutation* 9.2–6); Epiphanius and Theodoret refuted Noetians a few centuries later (*Panarion* 57 and *History of Heresies* 3.3). The treatise *Against Noetus* (c. fourth cent.), traditionally attributed to Hippolytus, refutes the "heresy" from the point of view of later orthodoxy. Noetus was excommunicated by the "blessed presbyters" of Smyrna because of his antitrinitarian views. He was accused of being a modalist or patripassianist, as he taught that it was not the second person of the Trinity but the one and only God who was born, suffered in the flesh, and died. This incarnated mode of God was called "the Son." Substantially speaking, God was one; nominally speaking, God was Father, Son, and Holy Spirit. Evidently upholding strict monotheism and attempting to avoid introduction of any plurality into the Godhead, Noetus rejected the prevalent Logos doctrine as gnostic.

J. Behr, *The Way to Nicea* (2001); J. Frickel, "Hippolyts Schrift Contra Noetum: Ein Pseudo-Hippolyt," in *Logos: Festschrift für Luise Abramowski*, ed. H. C. Brennecke et al. (1993), 87–123; R. M. Hübner, *Der Paradox Eine: Antignostischer Monarchianismus in zweiten Jahrhundert* (1999).

TARMO TOOM

Nominalism A label used to characterize a specific philosophical orientation. What that orientation is, and how it should be evaluated, is contested. The term "nominalists" (*nominales*) was used as early as the twelfth century and was then linked to the debate over universals. During the fifteenth century, however, the label was used within the context of the struggle of the different philosophical schools, the *via moderna* (nominalists) and the *via antiqua* (realists), and its meaning extended beyond a concern with universals. Important documents in this respect are the edict issued in 1474 by the French King Louis XI against the nominalists, and their response. These documents list a number of fourteenth-century thinkers, among whom were numbered William of Ockham, Adam Wodeham, John Buridan, Gregory of Rimini, Marsilius of Inghen, Albert of Saxony, Pierre d'Ailly, and Jean Gerson. They were not, however, themselves labeled as nominalists but were considered to be the sources behind the nominalist movement at the time of the controversy. No doubt, this fifteenth-century perspective has influenced historians in discovering nominalist strands in medieval thought, even in those periods, such as the fourteenth century, when authors neither identified themselves as nominalists, nor were designated in that way by their opponents.

But were there distinctive nominalist doctrines? It seems that a clear answer is only possible in the context of the medieval debate over universals. Nominalists challenged the view that universals are real things other than names. A nominalist ontology typically insists that only particulars exist and that universals have to be identified with common terms. In other words, the universal term "man," for instance, signifies the concept "man," but it has no ontological equivalent in reality, except the singular men to which it refers. Realists deny such a view and claim that universal concepts refer to mind-independent universal constituents in the singular things. The best-known nominalists in this debate were Peter Abelard and William of Ockham. They diverge, however, as to their theory of conceptual representation, that is, as to how universal concepts can signify individual things.

In a broader sense, "nominalism" is associated with a method of doing philosophy. It is a reductive approach toward metaphysical questions that aims at eradicating unnecessary entities in the explanation of philosophical problems (the principle of parsimony). This approach is often based upon the application of logic and semantics as tools of analysis within the realms of metaphysics, theology, and natural philosophy. In particular, the medieval semantic theory of the properties of terms (*proprietates terminorum*) plays a pivotal role in this type of philosophical analysis. Historians have often misconstrued the semantic approach in philosophy and the program of ontological reductionism as a reduction of metaphysics to the study of words and to logic-chopping. Within this context, medieval nominalism has been misunderstood as the cradle of a strongly critical intellectual climate and as the start of the decline of scholasticism.

W. J. Courtenay, "In Search of Nominalism: Two Centuries of Historical Debate," in *Gli studi di filosofia medievale fra otto e novecento*, ed. R. Imbach and A. Maierù (1991), 233–51; M. J. F. M. Hoenen et al., eds., *Philosophy and Learning: Universities in the Middle Ages* (1995); *Vivarium* 30, no. 1 (1992).

J. M. M. H. THIJSSEN

Nonconformity
Refusal to conform to the policies of an established church, often applied more specifically to Protestants unwilling to conform to the standards of the early modern English state church. Nonconformity rose to prominence in English religious life during the reign of Elizabeth I especially through the Vestiarian controversy and the Presbyterian movement. Some Nonconformists, including moderate and Presbyterian Puritans, supported a comprehensive national church and remained in communion with the Church of England, dissenting only from certain perceived abuses that they sought to reform. Other Nonconformists, often referred to collectively as "Separatists," formed autonomous congregations, rejecting the national church either on principle or as beyond hope of reformation. In the later seventeenth century, government policies pressed dissenters to choose between full conformity and separation from the national church. The Act of Uniformity (1662) required that all Church of England clergy declare their "unfeigned assent and consent" to everything contained in the Prayer Book. The Toleration Act (1689) legalized the formation of separate Nonconforming Protestant churches. Among the groups commonly identified with Nonconformity are Baptists, Congregationalists, Quakers, Methodists, and English Presbyterians.

C. Durston and J. Eales, eds., *The Culture of English Puritanism, 1560–1700* (1996); M. Watts, *The Dissenters*, vol. 1 (1978).

DANIEL EPPLEY

Nonjurors
(late seventeenth cent.), mostly clergymen in England who, because of their belief in the divine right of kings, regarded the Stuarts as legitimate monarchs and therefore refused to submit an oath of allegiance to William and Mary in 1688. The Nonjurors regarded themselves as the "faithful remnant," and they held secret religious gatherings, although some had reservations about these illegal gatherings. Altogether, the Nonjurors included eight bishops, including Sancroft of Canterbury, about as many laymen, and about four hundred priests. Their theology influenced the Oxford movement of the nineteenth century.

L. M. Hawkins, *Allegiance in Church and State* (1928); J. H. Overton, *The Nonjurors* (1902).

RODERICK MARTIN

Norbertines
see Premonstratentian Order

Norvegus, Laurentius
see Laurentius Norvegus

Novatian
(d. 258), Roman presbyter, theologian, and first antipope. An intellectual of considerable talent, Novatian was appointed presbyter by Bishop Fabian of Rome and became the de facto spokesman and leader of the Roman church in the months between the

martyrdom of Fabian in 250 and the election of Cornelius as bishop of Rome in 251. Novatian disputed the election of Cornelius, primarily on the question of the treatment of those who lapsed during the Decian persecution. Novatian was a rigorist who upheld the purity of the church by not allowing for the penance and readmission of the lapsed and calling for the excommunication of those caught in other grave sins. After garnering the support of three southern Italian bishops, Novatian had himself consecrated as bishop of Rome and proceeded to establish like-minded churches in Italy, Spain, Africa, and Syria in the east. Novatian was excommunicated by a synod of sixty bishops held at Rome, but the rigorist schism he established lasted until the fourth and fifth centuries. According to the later church historian Socrates, Novatian was martyred in 258 during the Valerian persecution.

Novatian was the first Roman Christian author to write in Latin. According to Jerome (*Vir. ill.* 70), Novatian wrote a great many treatises, of which four are extant: *De cibis Judaicis* (*On Jewish Foods*); *De bono pudicitiae* (*On the Advantage of Chastity*); *De spectaculis* (*On Shows*) and *De Trinitate* (*On the Trinity*). By far Novatian's most important contribution to the origins of Latin orthodox theology is *De Trinitate*. It is the real beginning of Latin dogmatic theology on the subject and established much of the form and content of later doctrinal development. Influenced by Stoic philosophy, especially the idea of the Logos, the treatise develops the three articles of the creed on Father, Son, and Spirit, and defends the eternal relationship of the Trinity (though Novatian does not use the word *Trinitas*) against various heresies.

G. W. Clarke, *The Letters of St. Cyprian of Carthage,* vol. 2 (1984); G. F. Diercks, *Opera quae supersunt nunc primum in unum collecta ad fidem codicum qui adhuc extant necnon adhibitis editionibus veteribus* (1972); Novatian, *Treatise on the Trinity,* trans. H. Moore (1919); Novatian, *The Trinity, The Spectacles, Jewish Foods, In Praise of Purity, Letters,* trans. R. J. DeSimone (1974).

CHARLES A. BOBERTZ

Observant Movements These were monastic reforming and observant movements during the late Middle Ages, the result of a general monastic decline that included almost every religious order since the mid-fourteenth century: monastic, canonic, mendicant, knight, and hospital. Their common concern was to renew the life of each order by effecting radical reforms in its social and economic structure. However, due to the variety of medieval orders these shared efforts diverged significantly in their aims. By reviving the original monastic ideal and spiritual life of the orders, and by calling for the strict observance of vows, rules, and statutes, all reforms were geared to rehabilitating an order's economy, to reorganizing and modernizing its structure as well as reinstituting laws and obedience. Consequently, during the fourteenth and fifteenth centuries, both congregations and observances formed in already existing orders (e.g., Windesheim Congregation, Franciscan Observants, Paulaner, Birgitts) and altogether new orders came into being.

The initiative for these reforms lay in most cases with the order's members. But the congregations also responded to external impulses. On the one hand the popes, the councils, and the episcopacy fostered and encouraged the enforcement of these reforms, while on the other hand they sought to hinder or altogether prevent them. Established secular authorities such as provincial rulers and town councils also took an interest in this process of reshaping, as it offered them greater opportunities for political encroachment in order to keep a strict check on the orders and secure pastoral work for the community.

Monastic Orders. Since the end of the fourteenth and the beginning of the fifteenth centuries there were reforming efforts within these orders that resulted in the creation of congregations. Centers of reform in the German Empire were Kastl (Upper Palatine) since 1380, later Melk and Bursfelde, the most important Benedictine center of reform. In France continued efforts can be traced to Cluny and Chezal-Benoit. In Italy ancient monastic centers of reform developed in Subiaco, Camaldoli, Vallombrosa, and San Giustina in Padua.

Canonical Orders. An active revival of spiritual life took place in the canonical orders beginning in the second half of the fourteenth century. Centers of reform were San Frediano near Lucca, San Salvatore in Laterano, and Windesheim near Deventer. The latter two were the founding places of the Windesheim Congregation, or Congregation of the Lateran; both embodied a reforming spirit inspired by the Devotio Moderna, leaving its distinctive mark on canonical reforming activities.

Mendicant Orders. By the middle of the fourteenth century mendicant orders were also characterized by reforming movements. Due to the intensive work of its preachers, especially

Bernardius of Siena, the most successful and lasting attempts at observant reforms were accomplished within the Franciscan orders. Although other mendicant orders (Dominicans, Augustinian Hermits, Carmelits, Servits) strove for reforms too, they never reached the dimensions of the Franciscan observant movement, which even produced the independent order of the Franciscan Observants toward the end of the fifteenth century.

M. Richards, "The Conflict between Observant and Conventual Reformed Franciscans in Fifteenth-Century France and Flanders," *Franciscan Studies* 50 (1990): 263–81; N. Rubinstein, "Lay Patronage and Observant Reform in Fifteenth-Century Florence," in T. Verdon and J. Henderson, eds., *Christianity and the Renaissance: Image and Religious Imagination in the Quattrocento* (1990), 63–82; K. Elm, ed., *Reformbemühungen und Observanzbestrebungen im spätmittelalterlichen Ordenswesen* (1989); *Il rinnovamento del Francescanesimo: L'Osservanza* (1985); P. L. Nyhus, "The Observant Reform Movement in Southern Germany," *Franciscan Studies* 32 (1972): 154–67.
SUSANNE CONRAD

Observantism

A reform movement within the monastic and Mendicant orders of the Western church emphasizing unqualified "observance" of the religious rule and a return to the spirit of the founder. Those resisting reform were known as "Conventuals." First appearing within the Franciscan order from 1368 with a drive to observe the original rule of St. Francis (1223), similar movements developed in most monastic and Mendicant orders over the late fourteenth and fifteenth centuries, producing such notable leaders as the Franciscan Bernadino of Siena, the Dominican Vincent Ferrer, and the Augustinian Martin Luther. Observant houses emphasized austerity and simplicity in food and clothing, devotion to prayer, study, manual labor, and pastoral ministry, and rejected dispensations from the rule, private possessions, and the holding of external offices. The movement was most successful where strong leaders were able to enforce central discipline through vicars, especially among the Dominican and Augustinian friars, or through visitors, among the Benedictines, but it failed among the Franciscans, who split into two separate orders. The movement culminated with the decree on religious orders at the twenty-fifth session of the Council of Trent (1563).

D. Knowles, *Christian Monasticism* (1977); D. Nimmo, *Reform and Division in the Medieval Franciscan Order from St Francis to the Founding of the Capuchins* (1987).
JOHN TONKIN

Ochino, Bernardino

(1487–1564), Italian reformer, Lutheran preacher. Born in Siena, he entered the Observantine (Franciscan) Friars and rose to become their vicar-general. Desiring a stricter rule, he entered the very austere order of Capuchins in 1534. That same year he was elected their vicar-general and was reelected in 1541. Ochino was such a popular preacher that at one point the pope had to limit his preaching during the Advent and Lenten seasons. Influenced in Naples by the Spanish nobleman Juan de Valdés and the Calvinist reformer Peter Martyr Vermigli, Ochino questioned the efficacy of works for salvation and heeded Protestant teachings.

After a series of sermons on justification by grace through faith alone that he preached in Venice in the late 1530s, his Catholic orthodoxy became suspect. He publicly embraced Lutheranism in 1541. During the Inquisition in 1542, he was summoned to Rome on suspicion of holding heretical "Lutheran" views. Warned by Cardinal Contarini, who was sympathetic to his evangelical teachings, Ochino fled to Florence and then to Geneva, where he married.

Serving Italian refugees there for two years, he published several volumes of controversial tracts, known as *Prediche (Sermons)*, which explained his change in theological emphasis—articulating Luther's view that justification was the article upon which the church stands or falls. In 1545 he served an Italian congregation in Augsburg, but within a year he had to flee to England when imperial troops occupied the city during the Schmalkald War. He accepted an invitation in 1547 from Thomas Cranmer in Canterbury, where he published several works that some believe influenced Milton's *Paradise Lost*. Most significant was a tract he authored against the papacy, *Tragedy or Dialogue on the Usurped Primacy of the Bishop of Rome* (1549), in which Ochino asserted that the papacy's existence was the consequence of Satan's horrendous power.

With the accession of Queen Mary I in 1553, Ochino fled to Zurich. There he served as pastor for a congregation of Italian Protestant refugees. Publishing a work entitled *Labyrinth*, he attacked Calvin's teaching on predestination in favor of an interpretation more in line with

Lutheran teachings. Engaging in doctrinal conflict with the reformers Theodore Beza and Heinrich Bullinger, Ochino was finally banished by the Zurich council for his views on divorce, polygamy, and his purported Socinian view of the Trinity, which he expressed in *Thirty Dialogues* (1563), a catechism-type pamphlet. He departed for the more tolerant Poland, where three of his four children died of the plague. He himself died the following year in the small Hutterite community of Slavkow (Austerlitz), Moravia.

R. Bainton, *The Travail of Religious Liberty* (1951); D. Cantimori, *Italian Heretics of the Sixteenth Century* (1979); B. Ochino, *Tragedy of the Unjust Usurped Papacy of the Bishop of Rome* (1960).

TIMOTHY MASCHKE

Ockham, William   *see* William of Ockham

Odo of Cluny (c. 879–942), French abbot,
reformer. Odo was one of the great reformers of the tenth century and responsible for the early stages of Cluny's growth from a single monastery into an influential monastic congregation. He became a monk at Baume in 909 after being a canon at Tours. Berno, abbot of Baume, went on to found Cluny; Odo succeeded him as abbot of Baume in 924 and of Cluny three years later. When Odo became abbot, Cluny was already a monastic reform center. Odo continued the process, emphasizing monastic purity and separation from secular society. To that end, he kept Cluny free from any secular control by obtaining both royal and papal charters of immunity and liberty.

Odo was renowned as a holy man, famed for silence and contemplation. These qualities, combined with political astuteness, led to many calls on his time to act as a mediator in both France and Italy. He was also called upon to reform other monasteries; by the time of his death Odo had reorganized at least twenty abbeys in France and Italy, while many other monasteries imitated Cluniac customs.

C. H. Lawrence, *Medieval Monasticism* (2nd ed., 1989); G. Tellenbach, *The Church in Western Europe from the Tenth to the Early Twelfth Century* (1993).

PHYLLIS G. JESTICE

Oecolampadius, Johannes (1482–
1531), Hebrew scholar, humanist, Reformed theologian, and reformer of Basel. Oecolampa-

dius studied theology at Heidelberg, Tübingen, and Basel. He embraced Protestantism in 1520, and in 1522 he became preacher at St. Martin's in Basel, where, inspired by Huldrych Zwingli's reformation in Zurich, he worked arduously for the reform of the church. In 1525, based on his own symbolic understanding of the Eucharist, which was close to Zwingli's, Oecolampadius celebrated the first Reformed Communion service in Basel. But it was not until April 1, 1529, that the Basel magistrates published the Reformation ordinance that established a state church, including a Marriage (or Morals) Court to establish Christian discipline in the community. The ordinance was based on the common assumption, shared by Zurich and Bern, that there was only one jurisdiction in the Christian community, governed by the civil magistracy.

Rejecting this assumption, Oecolampadius presented a plan to the Basel council for a new form of discipline in 1530. Although Oecolampadius agreed that the church and civil society formed a Christian commonwealth, he was also certain that there should be a church jurisdiction independent of the civil authority. He asserted that the church discipline of excommunication was an absolute necessity as a remedy for sin. Instituted by Christ (Matt. 18:15–18), its purpose was spiritual edification and it should be exercised in love. Oecolampadius also proposed the formation of an ecclesiastical court composed of twelve presbyters chosen from the pastors, the magistrates, and the congregation. The court would excommunicate the sinner, after proper warnings, until the sinner repented publicly, at which time the individual could be reconciled with the church.

When Oecolampadius wrote to Zwingli to gain his support, Zwingli was temporarily persuaded, but soon he reverted to his concept of a single corporate Christian community. When in 1531 Oecolampadius approached Heinrich Bullinger, his idea was utterly repudiated. Nor was Oecolampadius's plan put into effect in Basel. Only with John Calvin would Oecolampadius's approach to Christian discipline be implemented.

J. W. Baker, "Church Discipline or Civil Punishment: On the Origins of the Reformed Schism, 1528–1531," *Andrews University Seminary Studies* 23 (1985): 1–18; H. R. Guggisberg, *Basel in the 16th Century* (1982); O. Kuhr, *"Die Macht des Bannes und der Busse": Kirchenzucht und Erneuerung der Kirche bei Johannes Oekolampad (1482–1531)* (1999).

J. WAYNE BAKER

Oikonomia   The origins of this word lie in household management. It comes from the Greek verb *oikonomeō*, which is itself a combination of the words for "house" and "governance" (*oikos* and *nomeō*, the latter a cognate of *nomos*, the word for "law"). Governance in this sense can be considered either from the point of view of structure (the way a household is organized) or from the point of view of process (the means used to achieve that structure in a specific context). From either perspective the parallel between household management and the governance of a city or empire is obvious. As a result, *oikonomia* came to be applied first to royal or imperial governance and then to the divine governance of the world: God's supervision of the universe was likened to the *oikonomia* of an earthly household manager.

Oikonomia in this sense was not unrelated to the parallel idea that God exercises a *pronoia* ("providence") over the world that can be discerned in the lives of individuals and in current events. However, *oikonomia* differs from providence in that its managerial focus allows a greater emphasis on adaptation to an existing set of circumstances—that is, there is a difference between a nature, law, or principle considered in itself and the way an action based on that nature, law, or principle is dispensed or administered in an actual case. Thus, while the principle remains the same, its application may vary radically.

This emphasis on adaptability meant that, already in the New Testament, it was possible to speak of a divine *oikonomia* or "economy" that would be expressed completely only in the "fullness of time" (Eph. 1:10). *Oikonomia* in this sense became more important once the majority of Christians were not ethnically Jewish. It became necessary to account for a perceived difference between God as portrayed in the Hebrew Scriptures and God as proclaimed in the Christian writings that were then starting to become canonical. For some Christians the "god" behind the Hebrew Scriptures had to be a different god from the God proclaimed by Jesus Christ. Mainstream Christian writers such as Irenaeus and Tertullian sharply rejected this idea and replied that it was not "God" who was different in either case but rather God's *oikonomia* or mode of acting—the divine "management" was different before and after the coming of Christ. The Latin equivalent of *oikonomia* is *dispositio* or *dispensatio*; thus, in English it is possible to speak of one God but two "dispensations" or systems of management, the one characteristic of the OT, the other of the NT.

Since the turning point in the entire process is the coming of Christ, in some authors *oikonomia* is used as more or less equivalent to "incarnation." The focus of *oikonomia* in this sense is obviously process, but it can also be applied to God from the perspective of structure. As Christians reflected on the way the divine management was described in Scripture, they were brought to recognize in it three divine subsistences or persons (*hypostases*), all of whom were in some sense to be considered the one God. Some writers (such as Tertullian) were prepared to describe the relations among these subsistences as an *oikonomia* or economy. In this economy the Father could be seen as the Fount of the Godhead who "generates" the Son and is the Source from whom the Spirit "proceeds." Eastern and Western Christians have differed very sharply over whether (as in the East) the Spirit proceeds from the Father only or (as in the West) from the Father and the Son. *Oikonomia* in this sense defines the structure of the Divine in terms of relationship.

One school of Christian thought (known as modalist or Sabellian) took the biblical words "Father," "Son," and "Holy Spirit" to refer *solely* to relationships, not entities. This way of speaking is sometimes said to describe a purely economic rather than an ontological Trinity. It was sharply rejected by the wider church.

The divine *oikonomia* can be seen either in terms of the internal structure of the Godhead or in terms of its outward expression in the divine management or plan of salvation. After the fourth century, especially among Eastern Christians, this distinction began to play a major role in theology and devotion. Increased emphasis on the unknowability of the divine essence made it important to distinguish between theology proper (God's being as considered in itself) and the *oikonomia* or economy (God's actions in human history). Yet if God's being considered in itself is unknowable, in what sense is the God revealed by the economy the real God? The accepted resolution of this difficulty, associated with the name Gregory Palamas, was to assert that the actions of God (*energeiai*) were distinct from God's essence but still "uncreated" and genuinely revelatory.

Other uses of *oikonomia* lay in the moral sphere. The managerial contrast between a particular principle and the way that principle worked out in specific instances made it possible to apply the concept of economy to moral action. The negative connotation of the Latin equivalent, "casuistry" (the moral law as applied to particular "cases"), points to some of the dangers (e.g., it was possible to speak of "economizing" the truth). Nonetheless, *oikonomia* in this sense plays an essential role in easing the tension between the human aspiration to moral righteousness and the actual imperfections of lived experience. In a related sense, *oikonomia* (like "dispensation" in the West) has come to occupy an important place in the canon law of the Orthodox East.

P. Burns, "The Economy of Salvation: Two Patristic Traditions," *TS* 37 (1976): 598–619; K. Eden, "Economy in the Hermeneutics of Late Antiquity," *Studies in the Literary Imagination* 28 (1995): 13–26; R. J. Kees, *Die Lehre von der Oikonomia Gottes in der Oratio catechetica Gregors von Nyssa* (1994); W. Marcus, *Der Subordinatianismus als historiologisches Phänomen* (1963); R. A. Markus, "Trinitarian Theology and the Economy," *JTS* 9 (1958): 89–102; G. L. Prestige, *God in Patristic Thought* (1969), 55–75 and *passim*.

RICHARD PAUL VAGGIONE, OHC

Old Believers (Raskolniki)

From the Russian word for a schismatic or dissenter, *Raskolniki* refers to a fundamentalist minority of Russian Orthodox who rebelled when Patriarch Nikon of Moscow changed the style of popular forms and ceremonies (including the sign of the cross and the spelling/pronunciation of "Jesus") to bring the Russian church into closer conformity with the Greek usages of Constantinople (1654). In general the Raskolniki came from northern Russia and were anti-intellectual and supportive of monastic piety. Women were particularly important to the movement, and its greatest visual image is Surikov's painting of Morozova on a sledge going to her martyrdom. Eschatology figured prominently in their beliefs. For some, suicide seemed to be the only way to escape the antichrist. In the seventeenth-century alone more than 20,000 Old Believers died, many voluntarily committing themselves to the purgative flames that they believed preceded the Last Judgment. Although excommunicated and persecuted, the Old Believers remain a fragmented, minority movement to the present.

N. Lupinin, *Religious Revolt in the 17th Century: The Schism of the Russian Church* (1984); T. Robbins, "Apocalypse, Persecution, and Self-Immolation: Mass Suicides among the Old Believers in Late-17th-Century Russia," in *Millennialism, Persecution, and Violence: Historical Cases* (2000).

GREGORY J. MILLER

Old Church Slavonic

The term "Old Church Slavonic" (OCS), sometimes called "Old Slavic," refers to the earliest literary language of the Slavs. It was created by Constantine the Philosopher, better known by his monastic name, Cyril (see *Cyril and Methodius*), in preparation for the Byzantine mission to the Slavs of Moravia (863). Slavic dialects were not yet significantly differentiated in this period, and Old Church Slavonic was understandable to all Slavic speakers. Cyril devised the Glagolitic alphabet for the language, and he and his brother Methodius translated parts of the New Testament, the Psalter, and other theological and liturgical works from Greek into Old Church Slavonic. The translation work was continued by Methodius's disciples in Bulgaria, and the literary language came to be used throughout the Orthodox Slavic world, especially, though not exclusively, for texts connected with religious life. The complicated Glagolitic script was soon replaced by the Cyrillic alphabet, named in honor of Constantine-Cyril. Both Glagolitic and Cyrillic manuscripts of the tenth and eleventh centuries preserve this Slavic literary language.

Soon after the appearance of a written language, as Old Church Slavonic interacted with developing Slavic vernacular languages, local recensions gradually emerged, such as Russian Church Slavonic, Bulgarian Church Slavonic, and Serbian Church Slavonic. The broader term "Church Slavonic" is still used for the liturgical and literary language of the Orthodox and the Croatian Catholic Slavs.

R. Picchio, "Old Church Slavonic," in *The Slavic Literary Languages*, ed. A. M. Schenker and E. Stankiewicz (1980), 1–33.

ANDREA STERK

Olevianus, Caspar

(1536–1587), German-born student of John Calvin and important Calvinist theologian. Born to a Roman Catholic family in Trier, Olevianus studied law in France, where he converted to Protestantism (c. 1557) and joined the Huguenots. He then took up theology with Calvin in Geneva. After taking part in the failed Reformation of Trier (1559), Olevianus moved on to Heidelberg, where he took posts as professor of theology and as pastor, remaining until 1577. In these years he played a formative role in establishing Calvinist theology and church discipline in the Palatinate and made a minor contribution to the Heidelberg Catechism. Confessional politics forced Olevianus's departure from the Palatinate and led to a position as preacher to the court of Count

Ludwig of Sayn-Wittgenstein in Berleburg, allowing him to institute Calvinist church orders in further German territories and to complete his most significant theological work, *De substantia foederis gratuiti* (1585). With it, he laid the groundwork for the "covenant theology" of later Calvinism. During the last three years of his life, Olevianus taught at the Herborn Academy, which he had helped found.

L. D. Bierma, *German Calvinism in the Confessional Age: The Covenant Theology of Caspar Olevianus* (1996).

KENNETH G. APPOLD

Olivetan, Pierre Robert (c. 1506–1538),

French Protestant reformer and producer of an influential French translation of the Bible. A native of Noyon in Picardy and a close relative of John Calvin, Olivetan left France in 1529 to escape religious persecution and found refuge in Strasbourg, where he gained facility in both Greek and Hebrew. He served briefly as a tutor in the Swiss city of Neuchâtel before joining Guillaume Farel and the small circle of evangelicals working for evangelical reform in Geneva in 1532. Thereafter he divided his time between Geneva and the Piedmont Alps. While in the Alps he produced the work for which he is best known, a translation of the Bible that was to become the basis for French Protestant Bibles for the next two centuries. The first edition, published in Neuchâtel in 1535, included a preface by Calvin. Although Olivetan's Bible relied heavily on Jacques Lefèvre d'Etaples's Bible of 1530, he significantly revised Lefèvre's rendering of the Old Testament.

B. Bartélémy et al., *Olivétan, celui qui fit passer la Bible d'hébreu en français* (1986); B. T. Chambers, *Bibliography of French Bibles*, 2 vols. (1983, 1994).

CHRISTOPHER ELWOOD

Olivi, Peter John (1247/1248–1298), con-

troversial Franciscan teacher. Born John Olivi at Serignon, little is known of his early life. When he was twelve, Olivi joined the Franciscan order at Béziers, near his birthplace. By 1268, and perhaps as early as 1266, he was studying in the Franciscan school at Paris, where Bonaventure made a strong impression on him. He returned to southern France sometime before the late 1270s and served as lector in Franciscan schools. Sometime before 1283 he taught in convent schools at Montpellier and Narbonne. His teachings regarding the Virgin Mary, and perhaps other things, were investi-

gated in the 1270s by the Franciscan general Jerome of Ascoli, and his questions on the Virgin Mary were censured by the general (although we know little more about this episode than that it happened). His lectures on Holy Scripture—the bulk of his work—were well enough regarded that he was consulted when Pope Nicholas III's bull *Exiit qui seminat* (1279) was prepared (which was a milestone in controversies over Franciscan poverty). That same year, another Franciscan of uncertain identity sent a list of nineteen propositions drawn from Olivi's writings to the current Franciscan minister general (Bonagratia), who censured Olivi, then appointed a commission of seven Parisian masters to investigate his writings. In 1283, the commission published a condemnation and correction of Olivi's views that the minister-general ordered to be read out in all the Franciscan cloisters of Provence. Olivi was summoned to Avignon to assent to the commission's judgment. He did, while complaining of an unfair trial, and soon after he published a self-defense (1285). He was then allowed to answer the commission at Paris (he probably did) and was given a hearing before the general chapter of the entire order at Montpellier in 1287. His self-defense pleased the order. The current minister-general, Matthew of Aquasparta, appointed Olivi lector in the school of the Franciscan convent of Santa Croce in Florence. Two years later (1289), he was transferred to the convent of Montpellier, again as lector, at a time when Franciscan rigorists were arguing for an increasingly narrow interpretation of "poor use" (*usus pauper*), a doctrine attributable to Bonaventure, long defended by Olivi, supported by the bull *Exiit qui seminat*, and at the center of the growing controversy over religious poverty within the Franciscan order. Although investigated once again (1292, at the general chapter meeting in Paris), Olivi avoided censure for the rest of his life, completing a commentary on the Apocalypse of John a year before his death. Franciscan Spirituals favored this commentary, for which reason his teachings were condemned by the Franciscan general chapter of 1299. Olivi's views were posthumously investigated and censured by the Council of Vienne (1312), investigated and condemned by a commission appointed by John XXII (1318–1319), investigated by John XXII and submitted again to a theological commission, and condemned by the pope in 1326. The Dominican inquisitor Nicholas Eimerich (d. 1399) later claimed that Olivi's commentary on Matthew was condemned as well.

Numerous historians, Franciscans not least among them, have noted Olivi's debt to Bonaventure on questions of poverty and history, two points for which he was most conclusively censured, and they have pointed to continuities of his thought with earlier and contemporary scholasticism and biblical scholarship. This has undermined the judgment of Olivi's fourteenth-century detractors, who counted him as the source of Franciscan Spiritual heresies after he was dead and could no longer clarify his proximity to the likes of Angelo Clareno. Others have noted the date of the Apocalypse commentary, suggesting he developed in a radical direction late in life. The fairest historical judgment avoids condemnation and rehabilitation. Those of his teachings with the most radical potential were, at the least, foreshadowed in his commentaries on the Gospels, written ten to twenty years earlier than the Apocalypse commentary, while "the most vulnerable elements in Olivi's Apocalypse commentary were the ones that separated it from other commentaries and from Bonaventure" (Burr). In his description of the fifth and sixth periods of history, which adapted ideas found in Bonaventure and Joachim of Fiore, Olivi made one's position on poverty an indicator of one's position in an apocalyptic conflict, and he ranked the powers among Christ's adversaries. Although he did not name the pope, his apocalyptic view of the poverty controversy and his predictions of opposing powers played an important role in the antipapalism of Franciscan Spirituals. John XXII's theological advisors could therefore follow a track laid out by Olivi, from an apocalyptically conceived rebellion against authority to the Franciscan doctrine of poverty as such. This allowed them to condemn "poor use" in any form—the distinctive Franciscan version of religious poverty—even though many Franciscans were not guilty of the Spirituals' view of history and the papacy.

———

Pietro di Giovanni Olivi, opera edita et inedita (1999); *Bibliographia Franciscana*, supplement to the *Collectanea Franciscana* (includes Olivi), published periodically; D. Burr, *Olivi and Franciscan Poverty: The Origins of the Usus pauper Controversy* (1989); Burr, *Olivi's Peaceable Kingdom: A Reading of the Apocalypse Commentary* (1993); D. Flood, *Peter Olivi's Rule Commentary: Edition and Presentation* (1972); D. Flood and G. Gál, eds., *Peter of John Olivi on the Bible: Principia quinque in sacram scripturam, Postilla in Isaiam et in*
1 ad Corinthios (1997); K. Madigan, *Olivi and the Interpretation of Matthew in the High Middle Ages* (2003).

CHRISTOPHER OCKER

Olympias (c. 365–c. 410), wealthy deaconess, supporter of John Chrysostom. As the young widow of Nebridius, prefect of Constantinople, Olympias avoided remarriage and dedicated herself to the ascetic life. She founded a women's monastery next to the cathedral and used her considerable wealth to support the church and various charitable causes. Archbishop Nectarius ordained her deaconess when she was only thirty. Palladius reports that Olympias financially supported both Nectarius and his successor, John Chrysostom, and she seems to have had significant influence over both. A seventh-century source by Sergia describes the monastery's regimen and Chrysostom's frequent instructional visits. Palladius, Socrates, and Sozomen recount the events surrounding Chrysostom's exile in 404. Either his supporters or his enemies set fire to the church shortly after his departure. Olympias was implicated, questioned, and fined for refusing Communion from the new bishop, and she left the city. She remained a faithful supporter of Chrysostom in his exile, and his seventeen surviving letters to Olympias reveal their mutual concern for each other's health and well-being.

———

John Chrysostom, *Letters* 1–17; "Life of Olympias" and "Sergia's Narration Concerning St. Olympias," in *Jerome, Chrysostom, and Friends*, trans. E. A. Clark (1982), 107–57; Palladius, *Dialogue on the Life of St. John Chrysostom*, ed. Robert T. Meyer (1985); Palladius, *Lausiac History* 56, 61.3; Socrates, *Ecclesiastical History* 6.18; Sozomen, *Ecclesiastical History* 8.9, 22, 24, 27.

TERESA M. SHAW

Optatus of Milevis (fourth cent.), North African Catholic bishop and author. In response to the Donatist leader Parmenian, Optatus issued a treatise c. 365–367 commonly known as *On the Schism of the Donatists*, the ecclesiology of which was to influence Augustine greatly. Against the Donatists' exclusivist claims, Optatus argued for the catholicity and unity of the church. In his view, the true church extends throughout the known world. Those in communion with the Apostolic See in Rome and with the Eastern apostolic churches maintain that precious unity. Nor is the church holy because of its members (as the Donatists believed) but because it is founded on the Trinity, the sacraments, and the faith of believers. Optatus rejected Donatist sacramental theology: he insisted that the validity of the sacraments depends not on the moral status of the minister but on the Godhead itself. Optatus's volume includes an invaluable appendix of documents dating to the origins of the Donatist schism.

M. Edwards, trans. and ed., *Optatus: Against the Donatists* (1997); R. Eno, "The Work of Optatus as a Turning Point in the African Ecclesiology," *Thomist* 33 (1973): 668–85; J. E. Merdinger, *Rome and the African Church in the Time of Augustine* (2nd ed., 1999); C. Ziwsa, ed., CSEL 26 (1893).

JANE E. MERDINGER

Opus Caroli Regis Contra Synodum (*Libri Carolini*)

This late eighth-century theological treatise composed at the court of Charlemagne (768–814) challenged views ascribed to Byzantine theologians. *The Work of King Charles against the Synod*, to use its designation in the opening sentence (in place of *The Caroline Books*, a modern editor's title), responded to the decrees of the Second Council of Nicaea of 787. In the faulty translation received at the Carolingian court, the council seemed to endorse the worship of images, a position clearly hostile to Christian teaching. Theodulf, a Visigoth from Spain, court scholar, and bishop of Orléans led the effort to vindicate Christian orthodoxy. The *Opus Caroli regis* was some three years in the making. It presents a spirited defense of the Western view.

C. Chazelle, "Matter, Spirit, and Image in the *Libri Carolini*," *Recherches augustiniennes* 21 (1986): 163–84; *Opus Caroli regis contra synodum (Libri carolini)*, ed. A. Freeman and P. Meyvaert (1998).

JOHN J. CONTRENI

Orange, Councils of

Two synods attended by Gallic bishops and dignitaries, one convened in 441, the other in 529. The canons for both councils of Orange (Arausio in southern Gaul) survive. Their histories denote a change among Gallic ecclesiastics regarding their views on grace and predestination and also their recognition of papal authority. Gallic ecclesiastics gathered for a synod in 439 determined to meet every other year. Hence, the first council to convene at Orange did so in 441. Presiding over that session was Hilary, bishop of Arles, a partisan leader of the influential Lérins faction among Gaul's church leaders. This group, noted for its Semi-Pelagianism, also preferred Gallic ecclesiastical independence. Not surprisingly, certain of the canons pertain to the maintenance of Gallic episcopal solidarity. By the end of the fifth century, however, such uniformity had diminished greatly. In the next century, Caesarius of Arles was attempting to enhance his authority in Gaul with papal support. In 529 Caesarius presided over the Second Council of Orange. This synod dealt explicitly with doctrinal issues. Pope Felix IV had forwarded Caesarius a list of *capitula* ("articles") that expounded Augustinian views on grace and predestination. These formed the basis for the canons of Orange. The theological position set forth by the council can be described as an Augustinianism modified by the influence of those who rejected predestination and stressed the importance of human agency. Moreover, the council went beyond both positions by affirming the restored integrity of the will following baptism. Pope Boniface II in turn confirmed the acts of the council in 531.

J. P. Burns, ed. and trans., "The Synod of Orange, A.D. 529," in *Theological Anthropology* (1981); O. Pontal, *Die Synoden im Merowingerreich* (1986).

ALLEN E. JONES

Orant

The term, taken by art historians from the Latin *orans,* refers to a figure, common in early Christian art, shown in the posture of prayer. Usually female, the head is veiled, the eyes are upturned, and the hands are outstretched with raised palms (cf. 1 Tim. 2:8). The image is adapted from the Roman personification of piety (*pietas*), which often appears on coin reverses with the legend *pietas aug* or *pietas publica*, referring to the piety of the emperor toward his deceased predecessor or to the filial piety of the Roman people.

In Christian art the orant most commonly appears in funerary contexts and has been interpreted by some art historians as representing the (feminine) soul of the deceased rather than devotion to family or filial piety. Other scholars have argued that the praying figure represents the transference of loyalty of the baptized Christian to the new family of the church. Occasionally male figures from the Old Testament are represented in this posture, including Noah, Jonah, Daniel, and the three youths in the fiery furnace, which suggests the idea of deliverance from death or persecution. The orant very often appears adjacent to a representation of the Good Shepherd, perhaps representing the Savior with the individual who has been saved.

Some of the earliest examples of orants are shown with particular rather than standard features, suggesting that they were meant to be recognizable portraits of specific persons. Some surviving examples appear to have been left with blank faces, awaiting the sculptor's imposition of such a likeness. From the fifth century the personification of the church (*ecclesia*) was shown as an orant, and many portraits of the saints showed them in this posture.

R. Jensen, *Understanding Early Christian Art* (2000); G. Snyder, *Ante Pacem: Archaeological Evidence of Church Life before Constantine* (1985).

ROBIN M. JENSEN

Oratory of Divine Love Roman Catholic reforming brotherhood (confraternity) inspired by the life and work of Catherine of Genoa (1447–1510). Founded in 1497 by Ettore Vernazza (d. 1524), this highly distinguished group of aristocratic laymen, with the help of a few clergy, promoted moral reform of the church and the world through personal prayer, sacramental devotion, and deeds of charity, which program they called "the planting of divine love." Poverty and self-flagellation were strongly encouraged, although the movement was not monastic. Numbering at most fifty men, this brotherhood significantly influenced the Counter-Reformation of the Roman Catholic Church by promoting monastic reforms and by providing several of its major leaders, including Jacopo Sadoleto, who debated Calvin, and Gian Pietro Caraffa, who became Pope Paul IV (1555–1559). The Order of the Theatines grew out of this lay movement. Several other significant orders have historic ties to the Oratory: the Capuchins, the Oratorians, the Jesuits, the Ursulines, St. Camillus's Hospital Workers and St. Vincent de Paul's Daughters of Charity.

C. Black, *Italian Confraternities in the Sixteenth Century* (1989); J. C. Olin, ed., *The Catholic Reformation* (1992).

TIMOTHY MASCHKE

Ordinary Gloss This is a late medieval name for the medieval standard commentaries on the Bible and the authoritative legal collections. In the field of church law, the ordinary gloss on Gratian's *Decretum* was compiled by Johannes Teutonicus about 1216 and frequently printed since 1471 in a version revised by Bartholomaeus Brixiensis after 1245. The biblical *glossa ordinaria* was a work of the twelfth century compiled in the French cathedral schools as a tool for a new style of teaching the Bible. Its format on the pages of the manuscripts combined a window of Vulgate text written in large letters with marginal and interlinear glosses keyed to the appropriate biblical words by a system of marking devices. As a rule, interlinear glosses offered brief explanations of words and phrases; the majority of marginal glosses contained spiritual interpretations in the form of excerpts or summaries of passages from Western Fathers (Ambrose, Augustine, Jerome, Gregory the Great, Cassiodorus, Isidore of Seville, Bede), Carolingian authors (Alcuin, Hrabanus Maurus, Walahfrid Strabo, Paschasius, Haymo, and Remigius of Auxerre), and a few later writers (e.g., Lanfranc of Bec, Berengarius, Gilbert the Universal). Each biblical book was prefaced by prologues and short introductions (*argumenta* or *prothemata*), many of them attributed to Jerome. A set of an entire glossed Bible would have comprised more than twenty volumes. Most libraries possessed parts only.

It seems that the origins of the *glossa ordinaria* were connected with the cathedral school of Laon. Medieval sources credit Anselm of Laon (d. 1117) with the gloss on the Pauline Epistles, the Psalms, and the Gospel of John; his brother Ralph with that on Matthew and perhaps the Minor Prophets; and Gilbert the Universal with that on the Pentateuch, the Major Prophets, and Lamentations. The ascription of the entire gloss or its marginal parts to Walahfrid Strabo (d. 849) was an invention of the German humanist Abbot Johannes Trithemius (1462–1516). Parisian masters in the middle of the twelfth century, especially Gilbert of Poitiers, seem to have popularized the tool through their teaching and encouraged its completion and distribution. Peter Lombard is known to have revised the gloss on the Psalms and the Pauline Epistles (*magna glosatura*). Like him, the masters of the late twelfth century—Peter Comestor, Peter the Chanter, and Stephen Langton—based their biblical lectures on the standard gloss, a practice that continued throughout the following centuries. The text of the first printed edition (Adolph Rusch of Strasbourg, 1480/1481) served as a model for all subsequent printings until 1590. With the new approach to biblical interpretation in the Reformation era, the g*lossa ordinaria* lost its importance even in Roman Catholic circles.

————

C. F. R. De Hamel, *Glossed Books of the Bible and the Origins of the Paris Book Trade* (1984); M. Dove, ed., *Glossa ordinaria, Pars 22: In Canticum Canticorum*, in CCCM 170 (1996); K. Froehlich, M. T. Gibson, eds., *Biblia Latina cum Glossa Ordinaria: Facsimile Reprint*, 4 vols. (1992); B. Smalley, *The Study of the Bible in the Middle Ages* (3rd rev. ed., 1983).

KARLFRIED FROEHLICH

Origen (c. 185–c. 253), the first systematic theologian and arguably the most influential interpreter of the Bible in the Christian tradition. He is also a key figure in the history of Christian spirituality. In spite of his immense contributions, he has always been controversial.

As well as we can ascertain from historical data, Origen was reared in a well-to-do and devout Christian family in Alexandria. When he was fourteen, his father, who taught him to know the Bible almost by heart, died as a martyr. As an Alexandrian Christian, Origen had an extraordinarily rich cultural heritage. Alexandria, with its renowned library, had given birth to the discipline of textual and literary analysis (known as "grammar"), and it still flourished there, as did the study of philosophy, astronomy, and medicine. A thriving Jewish community had long related the Bible to this Greek high culture. Such cultural rapprochement also characterized Origen's Christian teacher, Clement of Alexandria, who relied heavily on his Jewish predecessor Philo. In this cultural climate Origen learned Hellenistic grammar and studied philosophy under Ammonius Saccas, a Platonist who also taught Plotinus. He sought out at least one Jewish teacher and made himself familiar with gnostic traditions. Origen himself became a Christian teacher at a young age, when persecution drove other teachers out of Alexandria. A wealthy layman, Ambrosius, a convert from Gnosticism, enabled him to become an astonishingly prolific author by paying for stenographers and copyists. Around 231 he left Alexandria because of conflicts with the city's bishop, Demetrius. He settled in Caesarea in Palestine, where he was ordained as a presbyter and spent his last two decades. He died after suffering torture in persecution under Emperor Decius.

Because of continuing controversies surrounding him, most of Origen's work was lost and much survives only in ancient translations.

The impressive body of work still left includes parts of his commentaries on John and Matthew in the original Greek and his commentaries on the Song of Songs, Matthew, and Romans in Latin translation. At Caesarea he preached homilies that have also come down to us mainly in Latin translation. *On First Principles* (*Peri Archon*), the treatise in which Origen set forth his system, survives in full only in Latin. We have original Greek texts of *Against Celsus* (often known by its title in Latin, *Contra Celsum*), a work in the apologetic tradition refuting a pagan attack on Christianity, and of two works that provide insights into his spirituality, *An Exhortation to Martyrdom* and *On Prayer*. We also have his treatise *On the Passover;* the *Dialogue with Heracleides*, the transcript of a theological investigation where Origen serves as a consultant; and two letters. His longest work, *The Hexapla*, a word-for-word comparison of Greek translations of the Old Testament with the Hebrew original, is lost.

In *On First Principles* Origen drew on Platonic philosophy to explain underlying connections between the fundamental doctrines of the church and to explore issues they did not clearly address. These were the doctrines that constituted a conventional list known in his time as the "rule of faith." In doing so he presented an open-ended and provisional theological system that explains how humanity, although alienated from God, nonetheless retains a kinship with God and how, through a gradual process of divinization, that alienation will eventually be overcome. In this system the grace and providence of a good God promote human transformation in a way that respects human freedom and retains human moral responsibility. Origen deals successively with God, the creation of the spiritual world, the fall of rational creatures from their original union with God, and God's provisions for the return of rational creatures to their original state. One such provision was the creation of our sensible world as a place of spiritual training. In the process Origen laid the foundations of future orthodox definitions of the Trinity (with his concept of the eternal generation of the Son) and of the union of divinity and full humanity in Christ (with his concept that they share each other's properties). He took seriously gnostic criticism of the Bible and the rule of faith—which he believed the gnostics understood simplistically—and offered a rational alternative. In doing so he opened himself to charges of heresy, beginning in his lifetime, because he denied that the Bible provides a consistently factual record of events and because he denied eternal damnation, finding it incompatible with God's goodness. He would later be anachronistically condemned as an Arian because he did not fully anticipate the doctrine of the Trinity.

Finding hidden meanings in Scripture—pointers to a higher reality—undergirds Origen's system. In *On First Principles* Origen argued that close attention, using techniques of Hellenistic grammar, reveals divinely planned flaws interwoven into the fabric of Scripture. Detecting them enables the spiritually advanced to perceive ever deeper meanings that explain God's saving plan and promote the soul's divinization. By such interpretation in his homilies and commentaries, Origen effectively transformed the Hebrew Scriptures from a quarry of isolated christological proof texts and moral maxims into a consistent testimony to Christ, expressing symbolically the same message the New Testament makes explicit. Nonetheless, for Origen the inherent limitations of human speech mean that the whole Bible is only an introduction to a spiritual reality in which the eschatological goal is unmediated communion with God.

———

G. W. Butterworth, trans., *On First Principles* (1936); H. Chadwick, trans. *Contra Celsum* (1965); H. Crouzel, *Origen*, trans. A. S. Worrall (1989); Crouzel, *Bibliographie critique d' Origène* (1971); Crouzel, *Bibliographie critique d'Origène, Suppléments* 1 and 2 (1971, 1982, 1996); J. W. Trigg, *Origen* (1998); Trigg, *Origen: The Bible and Philosophy in the 3rd-Century Church* (1985).

JOSEPH W. TRIGG

Orosius, Paulus (b. c. 380–385), Spanish presbyter, anti-Pelagian apologist, and Christian historian. Perhaps a native of Bracara (Braga) in northwestern Spain, Orosius opposed Priscillianism and Origenism. In 414 he departed for Hippo to escape the ravages of the barbarian invasion, to study Scripture, and to consult with Augustine on the errors of the Priscillians and Origenists. Augustine responded favorably to Orosius's memorandum (*Commonitorium*) on the two heresies by writing *To Orosius against the Priscillianists*.

At Augustine's request, Orosius sailed for Palestine to consult with Jerome. Bishop John summoned him to a synod in Jerusalem (415) to give an account of Caelestius's condemnation and Pelagian sympathies in North Africa. The synod dissolved without any official con-

demnation of Caelestius and Pelagius. Shortly thereafter, owing to a misunderstanding, John accused Orosius of heresy. Orosius defended himself in an apology addressed to the clergy in Jerusalem. He returned to Africa (416) with a letter from Jerome informing Augustine about the synod's results.

In Africa, at Augustine's request, Orosius composed his *Seven Books of History against the Pagans*, a universal history of events exonerating Christians of complicity in Rome's disasters. Orosius disappeared from history after 418.

———

CPL (1995), 571–74; R. J. Deferrari, trans., *Seven Books of History against the Pagans*, in FC 50 (1964); W. H. C. Frend, "Augustine and Orosius on the End of the Ancient World," *AugStud* 20 (1989): 1–38.

MARIANNE DJUTH

Orthodoxy The word "orthodox" carries two meanings derived from the Greek word *doxa*: correct belief and correct praise. In the Greek-speaking East, "catholic" was the term that characterized the church; "orthodox" was the term that characterized the right-believing and right-praising Christian individual. The use of the terms "Orthodox" and "Catholic" to distinguish distinct denominations began to appear in the Middle Ages.

The Orthodox Church is a communion of regional churches most of which are located in the territory that once constituted the eastern part of the Roman Empire or in territories whose Christianity came from Byzantine missionaries, such as the Slavic countries.

The term "Eastern Orthodox" identifies that communion of churches that recognize seven ecumenical councils, the last one being Nicaea II in 787 (e.g., the Greek Orthodox Church or the Russian Orthodox Church). "Oriental Orthodox" identifies those churches that did not accept the Council of Chalcedon (451) as ecumenical (e.g., the Coptic Orthodox Church or the Armenian Orthodox Church). These latter are also labeled Non-Chalcedonian churches or Monophysite churches. While "Orthodoxy" refers to a communion of regional churches, the designation preferred by the Orthodox is "Orthodox Church" in the singular.

The highest legislative and doctrinal authority in the Orthodox Church is the ecumenical synod that represents all the member churches. Within particular jurisdictions, the local synod is the highest authority. At the level of core belief, there is little that distinguishes Orthodoxy from Western Christianity. At the level of theology, there is much that distinguishes Orthodoxy. Augustine, whose influence is still pervasive in the West, had little influence on Orthodox theology; neither did scholasticism or the Reformation. The West, for example, has, since the Pelagian controversy, treated the question of grace and free will as a vexatious dogmatic issue. In the East, however, it is treated principally in discussions on spiritual development. While conciliar decrees and theological writings are important, the most important means for understanding Orthodox doctrine and Orthodox spirituality is the experience of the Orthodox liturgy, which is filled with theologically rich texts.

In its places of origin, Orthodoxy is organized territorially, generally following national borders. The patriarch of Constantinople holds a primacy of honor, but primacy in the Orthodox Church does not carry a significant right of jurisdiction. In places of Orthodox migration, multiple Orthodox jurisdictions exist together. In North America, for example, there are multiple national jurisdictions: Greek Orthodox, Russian Orthodox, Antiochian Orthodox, and so forth. While this situation presents some canonical anomalies, within Orthodox polity these jurisdictions have the status of a diaspora of their founding Orthodox jurisdictions.

By the time of the Council of Nicaea in 325, the Christian church was not simply a communion of local churches but a communion of local churches organized regionally. Most of the schisms within early Christianity followed those regional divisions. The schisms that followed the Councils of Ephesus (431) and Chalcedon (451) affected the regional churches of Antioch and Alexandria as well as the churches of Armenia and the Persian Empire. That left the church of Constantinople as the most significant church in the East that received the Council of Chalcedon. Eventually, all the Chalcedonian churches in the East were theologically and liturgically "Byzantinized," and non-Greek traditions were gradually marginalized. The religious heritage of Constantinople as it developed over several centuries is the common base for all Orthodoxy today.

Energetic Byzantine missionary initiatives in the eighth and ninth centuries accomplished the conversion of the Slavic peoples of the Balkan peninsula and of Kievan Russ to Christianity. Vladimir of Kiev was baptized in 988. Many of these initiatives were imperially financed and brought with them the Byzantine tradition of an attractive vernacular liturgy.

Eventually these churches became independent of their founding church. After the fall of Constantinople, the Russian Orthodox Church became the largest and most influential church in the Orthodox communion.

Although the mutual exchange of excommunications between Cardinal Umberto da Silva Candida and Patriarch Michael Caerularios in 1054 is symbolically important, there is no event that is definitive for the division of the Latin West and the Greek East. The collapse of Roman authority in the West and the subsequent rise of multiple nation-states in Western Europe put cultural and theological strains on what had been one church in one empire.

Theological disagreements over papal authority and the procession of the Holy Spirit and disciplinary differences such as clerical celibacy in the West and the use of leavened bread by the East were hotly debated in the Middle Ages. The behavior of crusading armies in the East further exacerbated a bad situation. The Councils of Lyon (1274) and Florence (1438) (see *Councils, Later Middle Ages*) negotiated reunions that were rejected by the majority of the Orthodox people. There have been no conciliar attempts at reunion since the Middle Ages, but on December 7, 1965, Patriarch Athenagoras of Constantinople and Pope Paul VI publicly abrogated the mutual excommunications of 1054.

The Byzantine Church has lived a large portion of its history in its home territory under hostile regimes. Beginning in the seventh century, Islamic conquests absorbed most of the homelands of Orthodoxy. The fall of Constantinople in 1453 inaugurated the era known in Greek as *Turkokratia*, which lasted until the fall of the Ottoman Empire. That reality has shaped and limited many aspects of its life, from scholarship to evangelization. The experience of a hostile government also shaped the life of the Russian Orthodox Church in the twentieth century. (*See also* Byzantine Rite; Cyril and Methodius; Church of the East, Middle Ages; Chalcedon, Definition of; Monophysitism)

J. Binns, *The Christian Orthodox Churches* (2002); D. Clendenin, ed., *Eastern Orthodox Theology: A Contemporary Reader* (2003); G. Maloney, *A History of Orthodox Theology since 1453* (1976); A. Papadakis and J. Meyendorff, *The Christian East and the Rise of the Papacy* (1994); D. Pospeilovsky, *The Orthodox Church in the History of Russia* (1998).

EUGENE M. LUDWIG, OFM CAP.

Osiander, Andreas (c. 1496–1552), German Lutheran reformer of the city of Nuremberg. Born near the city of Nuremberg, Osiander died in Königsberg. He is remembered as the reformer of Nuremberg and for his precipitation of a controversy on the doctrine of justification settled in Article III of the Lutheran Formula of Concord (1577). Osiander began his studies at the Univ. of Ingolstadt in 1515 and also studied at Leipzig. A gifted linguist, he learned Greek, Hebrew, and Aramaic and was particularly influenced by the humanism of Johannes Reuchlin, including his studies of the Jewish mysticism of the Cabbala. Ordained a priest in 1520, Osiander also taught Hebrew at the Augustinian monastery in Nuremberg; during these years he came under the influence of Luther. After becoming the pastor at Nuremberg's St. Lorenz church in 1522, Osiander used his position to lead Nuremberg into the Lutheran reformation. The mayor and council were among the seven original signers of the Augsburg Confession.

A noted and acerbic controversialist, Osiander participated in a number of key events of the Reformation as a colleague of the Wittenberg reformers. He was present at the Marburg Colloquy (1529), where he supported Luther in the sacramental controversy with Zwingli, he attended the Diet of Augsburg (1530), and he was one of the original signers of Luther's Schmalkald Articles (1537). Like Melanchthon, he was also interested in the developing science of astronomy. In 1543, Osiander published with an anonymous preface Copernicus's *Concerning the Heavenly Revolution of the Planets.*

Forced out of Nuremberg in 1548 as a result of Emperor Charles V's victory in the Schmalkald War, Osiander was appointed pastor and professor in Königsberg by Duke Albrecht of Prussia. From these positions, in 1550 he published two disputations, challenging Melanchthon's teaching of justification. He argued that Melanchthon inappropriately separated God's imputation of justification from the renewal that follows. Against his background in mysticism, Osiander proposed that justification and personal renewal come together as the divine nature of Christ dwells in the believer. Following his death, Osiander's son-in-law carried on the controversy.

In opposition to Osiander, the Formula of Concord made two primary arguments. It held that the divine and the human natures of Christ cannot be separated in justification and that while good works follow justification, they cannot be considered part of the doctrine itself. Though this marked the end of the controversy among Lutherans, Osiander's critique generated interest among the Ritschlians in the nineteenth century.

G. Seebass, *Das reformatorische Werk des Andreas Osiander* (1967).
                                                    JAMES ARNE NESTINGEN

Ossius of Cordova. See *Hosius of Cordova*

Otto I (912–973), German king and emperor. Otto I (the Great) built Germany into the strongest European state of the central Middle Ages, building on the achievements of his father, Henry I, founder of the Ottonian dynasty. Otto became king of Germany in 936, and although much of his first decade on the throne was spent subduing recalcitrant nobles, he soon moved on to an expansionist policy that united secular and religious goals in a highly effective manner. His importance rests especially in two areas: he won a series of important victories against the Slavs and Magyars that led to a great missionary period alongside expanding German territory, and his conquest of Lombardy led him in time to claim a revived imperial crown.

In the north and east, Otto's military victories (most decisively over a Magyar coalition at the battle of Lechfeld in 955 and over the Slavs in the same year) won Germany several tributary states, which he pacified especially with a vigorous missionary policy. Perhaps even more decisive for the history of Germany, his expansion of rule into northern Italy led to a long history of absentee German rulers and created a protectorship over the papacy that would lead to bitter conflict from the eleventh century.

K. Leyser, *Communications and Power in Medieval Europe* (1994); T. Reuter, *Germany in the Early Middle Ages, 800–1056* (1991).
                                                    PHYLLIS G. JESTICE

Otto of Freising (c. 1112–1158), German bishop, historian. Otto of Freising was the most important historian of the twelfth century. He was the son of Duke Leopold III of Austria, half-brother of Emperor Conrad III, and uncle of Frederick I Barbarossa. Dedicated to the church at a young age, Otto became a canon as a child. After study in Paris he became a Cistercian monk at Morimond, but family influence soon won him the bishopric of Freising (Bavaria).

Otto's two great historical works are a world chronicle, *The Two Cities*, and *The Deeds of Frederick Barbarossa*. In the chronicle, Otto enunciated a theory of world history based on Augustine's *City of God*, expressing his own love for monasticism as the best hope for the godly on earth. He also presented the history of *translatio imperii*, the transfer of universal power from the Greeks to its eventual culmination in the Germans. Otto had little hope for his own society, though: the final book of the chronicle describes the events of the last days. He was more hopeful in his biography of Frederick, of which only two books were complete when Otto died. He saw his nephew as a great ruler, well on the road to establishing an age of peace and glory.

Otto of Freising, *The Two Cities*, trans. C. Mierow (1928); Otto, *The Deeds of Frederick Barbarossa*, trans. C. Mierow (1953).

PHYLLIS G. JESTICE

Ottoman Empire   Although the origins of the Ottoman Empire are obscure, traditional historiography focuses on Turkish tribesmen from Central Asia who began arriving in Anatolia in the thirteenth century as *ghazis* ("raiders for the faith") along the Byzantine border in Anatolia.

The founder of the dynasty, Osman (d. 1324) was one of many Turkish military princes (emirs), but he was located directly adjacent to Byzantine territories and was able to expand his holdings at Byzantine expense both in Western Anatolia and into Europe. Under the leadership of Sultan Mehmed (Muhammad) II the Turks conquered Constantinople in 1453. Sultan Selim I expanded the empire to the east, conquering Palestine and Mamluk Egypt by 1517. The Ottoman sultan took the title of caliph and declared the two holy cities of Mecca and Medina to be under its protection. At the same time, the Ottomans developed a significant navy that controlled the eastern Mediterranean and patrolled the Indian Ocean.

In less than two hundred years the Ottomans had become a world superpower. Clearly the ability to unleash the power of jihad against the Byzantines was an important early factor in Ottoman success, but after the capture of Constantinople even more important was the development of a highly organized central bureaucracy centered on the person of the sultan. This elite bureaucracy and the most important branch of the Ottoman military, the superbly trained Janissaries, were drawn from a large pool of slaves who were recruited as children (often forcibly) from the Ottoman Balkan possessions. Ottoman military success was based on the Janissaries, the use of a feudally organized cavalry force, and the wide-scale use of gunpowder.

The Ottoman Empire is considered to have reached its height in internal development and expansion during the reign of Suleiman (r. 1520–1566). Under Suleiman's leadership the Ottomans pressed into Central Europe, besieging Vienna in 1529. Later sultans were generally more removed from direct leadership and in some cases thoroughly corrupted by the pleasures of the harem. The Treaty of Carlowitz in 1699 forced the Ottoman Empire to cede much of its Central European territory and opened up a period of the domination of the empire's trade by Western European powers. In the nineteenth century further relative decline of the empire made the Ottomans vulnerable to nationalist movements (as in Serbia, autonomous in 1829) that further eroded Turkish control in the Balkans. In 1914 the Ottoman Empire entered the Great War as an ally of Germany. In the postwar settlement, much of the empire was dismembered and divided among the victorious Allies under the mandate system. In 1923 modern Turkey was founded under the leadership of Mustafa Kemal (Ataturk) as a secular republic largely limited to Anatolia.

The Ottoman Empire has had a direct impact on the history of Christianity in several ways. After the capture of Constantinople, Greek scholars fled to Italy, carrying with them knowledge of the language and manuscripts that would be essential in the development of the Renaissance. Although the Ottomans continued to utilize and tolerate Orthodoxy in southeastern Europe, the political control over the appointment and activities of the patriarch of Constantinople encouraged the development of Moscow as a center of Orthodoxy and its self-identification as the "Third Rome." The advance of the Turks under Suleiman into Central Europe had a significant impact on the interconfessional conflict within Christianity. Ottoman pressure forced the Holy Roman Emperor Charles V to trade a limited toleration of Lutheranism at a crucial time in the early development of Protestantism in exchange for military support against the Turks. As the Ottoman Empire declined, Ottoman lands became important targets for Christian missions.

P. Coles, *The Ottoman Impact on Europe* (1968); D. Goffman, *The Ottoman Empire and Early Modern Europe* (2002); H. Inalcik, *The Ottoman Empire: The Classical Age, 1300–1600* (1973); D. Quataert, *The Ottoman Empire, 1700–1922* (2000).

GREGORY J. MILLER

Ottonian-Salian Imperial Church System

The Ottonian and Salian dynasties, whose members ruled Germany from 919 to 1125, relied so heavily on a close alliance with German bishoprics and monasteries that their government is often called an "imperial church system" (*Reichkirchensystem*). Rulers expanded the secular power of bishops and abbots, using them as local rulers instead of secular nobles. This theocratic style of rule made Germany Europe's strongest state in the tenth and eleventh centuries. But these rulers' very patronage of ecclesiastical authorities led to a strong reaction. Although they were usually quite conscientious in their appointments, reform circles in the late eleventh century began loudly to proclaim that any lay control of church goods and personnel was a sin, and the Investiture Controversy marked the effective end of this fruitful alliance of church and state.

The "system," if a system it was, can be said to have begun in the reign of Otto I (r. 936–973) who appointed his brother Bruno as both archbishop of Cologne and duke of Lorraine. It expanded in the long minority of Otto III (r. 983–1002), as the archbishop of Mainz preserved his throne and the women who acted as regents received more cooperation from churchmen than from secular magnates. It was the last of the Ottonians, Henry II (r. 1002–1024), who went furthest in using bishops and abbots as tools of regular government. It is unlikely, though, that even he thought in terms of a fully rationalized system.

T. Reuter, *Germany in the Early Middle Ages, 800–1056* (1991); Reuter, "The 'Imperial Church System' of the Ottonian and Salian Rulers: A Reconsideration," *JEH* 33 (1982): 347–74.

PHYLLIS G. JESTICE

Owen, John

(1616–1683), English congregationalist pastor and theologian. Theologically in the mainstream of English Calvinism, Owen championed Scripture as the sole ultimate authority in religious matters and emphasized absolute divine sovereignty over each individual's eternal fate. He endorsed covenant theology, teaching that God empowered and therefore required the elect to live piously, and he had a strong sense of divine providence and the immanence of the millennium that shaped his understanding of contemporary events. During the 1650s Owen served as a dean and vice-chancellor at his alma mater, Oxford, and was prominent in government circles. Following the Restoration and his fall from political influence he remained active as a pastor, writer, and advocate of congregationalism.

W. H. Goold, ed., *The Works of John Owen, D.D.*, 24 vols. (1850–1853); S. Griffiths, *Redeem the Time: The Problem of Sin in the Writings of John Owen* (2001); P. Toon, *God's Statesman: The Life and Work of John Owen* (1971).

DANIEL EPPLEY

Oxenstierna, Axel

(1583–1654), Swedish count and political figure. A member of the state council (from 1609) and chancellor (from 1612), he worked with Gustavus II Adolphus in making Sweden a leading power in Europe. The 1634 constitution was mainly his work. He played an important role in the king's endeavor to form a great evangelical alliance, and after the king's death (1632) he forced the evangelical princes in the alliance of Heilbronn (1633) to continue the war under Swedish command. He played an important role in the negotiations for the Peace of Westphalia (1648).

G. Wetterberg, *Kanslern: Axel Oxenstierna i sin tid* (2002).

INGUN MONTGOMERY

Pachomius

(c. 292–346), founder of cenobitic monasticism. Pachomius was born to a pagan family in southern Egypt. While stationed in Thebes, he and other newly drafted soldiers in Maximinus Daia's army were quartered in the local prison under such appalling circumstances that local Christians donated food to them. The charity inspired his conversion to Christianity. Pachomius became the disciple of the famous Egyptian anchorite Apa Palamon, who over seven years initiated him into the rigors of desert asceticism. Pachomius founded his first community of anchorites in a deserted village called Tabennesi. Within several years it had expanded to nearly a hundred monks. By the time of Pachomius's death, the original community had fostered at least seven monasteries for men and two for women along the Nile with reportedly over three thousand inhabitants. Much earlier, in 329, Athanasius, the bishop of Alexandria, traveled all the way up the Nile to seek his advice.

Pachomius has entered history as the founder of communal (or cenobitic) asceticism. Pachomian cenobitism emerged in Upper Egypt, in the Thebaid, while at the same time the deserts of Lower Egypt began increasingly to be populated by solitary anchorites, who were—at least according to legend—inspired by Anthony.

Reconstruction of the development of Pachomius's cenobitic model is not easy. Most of our sources (primarily his detailed biographies, actually hagiographies, in Coptic and Greek) date from the middle to late fourth century, the period during which his monastic communities were guided by two successors Theodore and Horsiesios. Although likely written within the monastic communities themselves, these texts (probably anachronistically) portray him as a model of late fourth-century orthodoxy. From Pachomius's lifetime we possess only two letters and two *Instructions*, though the Pachomian authorship of the latter remains debated. Regardless of the details of Pachomius's life, however, the impact of his legacy as one of the great names of monasticism is beyond dispute.

J. E. Goehring, "New Frontiers in Pachomian Studies," in *The Roots of Egyptian Christianity*, ed. A. Pearson and J. E. Goehring (1986), 236–57; P. Rousseau, *Pachomius: The Making of a Community in Fourth-Century Egypt* (1985).

SUSANNA ELM

Pacification of Ghent

A "peace alliance and union" that took place between the southern and northern provinces of the Netherlands in the aftermath of the massacre of thousands at Antwerp by Spanish troops sent by Philip II of Spain to suppress Calvinism. The Pacification (1576) called for expulsion of the Spanish, the end of the Inquisition, suspension of antiheresy edicts, and the guarantee of freedom of movement. Catholics were not to be attacked, and tacit approval was given to the existence of the Reformed Church. The Pacification failed to resolve religious and constitutional issues, and hostilities broke out again in 1579. With the failure of the alliance, Catholics in Hainault, Artois, and the city of Douai formed the Union of Arras, precursor to contemporary Belgium. The seven northern provinces signed the Union of Utrecht (1579) and declared independence from Spain (1581).

E. H. Kossman and A. F. Mellink, eds., *Texts concerning the Revolt of the Netherlands* (1574); H. Rowen, "The Dutch Revolt: What Kind of Revolution?" *Renaissance Quarterly* 43 (1990): 570–90.

JEANNINE E. OLSON

Pack Affair

The Pack Affair contributed to the political and religious instability in Germany during the sixteenth century. Otto von Pack (c. 1480–1537), a counselor of Duke George of Albertine Saxony and an ardent opponent of the Reformation, reported to Philip of Hesse in January 1528 that several Catholic bishops and princes had allied to eradicate heresy and partition evangelical territories. He even produced a forged copy of the agreement. Philip, eager to forge a Protestant military alliance, prevailed on Electoral Saxony to cooperate in a preventive strike. No fighting ensued because the Saxons, who were suspicious of Pack's assertion and wary of Philip's pugnaciousness, discovered that no Catholic alliance existed. Luther, Melanchthon, and Bugenhagen had also advised against any offensive military action. Philip did confiscate Franconian bishoprics to compensate for his military expenditures, and he compelled the archbishop of Mainz to renounce all spiritual jurisdiction in Hesse. The Pack Affair manifested Philip's brashness, confirmed an evangelical willingness to consider military action, and was cited by Emperor Charles V almost two decades later as a justification for the Schmalkald War.

K. Dülfer, *Die Packschen Händel* (1952); H. J. Hillerbrand, *Landgrave Philip of Hesse, 1504–1567* (1967).

KURT K. HENDEL

Paganism and Early Christianity

Paganism and Christianity were intertwined from the outset. The relationship between the two was simultaneously constructive, competitive, and inimical. Moreover, during the first six centuries CE, as the balance of social authority and political power between Christians and non-Christians shifted, so too did the particular features of exchange, interchange, and opposition.

Any attempt to understand this complex process must acknowledge several fundamental factors. First, Mediterranean polytheism was characterized by diverse practices and beliefs that may have expressed shared assumptions, but it never, with the exception perhaps of the imperial cult, embraced a centralized institutional framework or orthodoxy. "Paganism" was essentially a catchall category constructed by Christians to designate those who were neither Christians nor Jews. Second, although early Christians were driven toward unity by an ecumenical impulse, ancient Christianity also resists categorical reduction. It too was long characterized by variety and competition among claimants to the name. Because pagans and Christians formed neither discrete nor homogeneous social, religious, or cultural groups in the Roman world, the terms "paganism" and "Christianity," however convenient, are nevertheless problematic as descriptors of historical reality.

Paganism remained vital well into late antiquity and was only gradually eclipsed in the century or so after the conversion of Constantine. The political and social life of the cities and countryside of the Roman Mediterranean were inseparably bound to rituals and practices of sacrifice, processions, and prayer directed to and honoring a myriad of local and regional deities, such as Jupiter at Rome or Diana at Ephesus. These cults, whose maintenance was held to ensure security and prosperity, were often rooted, or believed rooted, in a primordial past. Furthermore, the great oracles, like those of Apollo at Delphi and Didyma, continued to speak, Asclepius continued to heal at his shrines, and ample evidence illustrates the popularity of such personal cults as those associated with Demeter, Mithras, and Isis. Thus, both civic and individual identity in the Roman Empire were linked to inherited or adopted practices and traditions largely seen as "successful" in the eyes of affiliates and practitioners. At the same time, intellectuals such as Celsus (late second cent.) and Porphyry (c. 232–305) developed ways of integrating local cults into a philosophical system that tended toward Platonic monotheism.

Christianity evolved within this multifaceted pagan world, and early Christians lived in intimate contact with their non-Christian fellows. Yet strife was a notable element of the relationship, most evident in the persecution of Christians at local and, by the mid-third century, at imperial levels. Violence was sporadic, however, and the pagan response was not universally hostile. Moreover, in reaction, Christians not only developed the characteristic literary forms of the apology and the acts of the martyrs but also refined the definitions of their own beliefs and practices. Similarly, pagan philosophical critiques encouraged Christian thinkers, such as Origen and Eusebius, to plumb ever more deeply the rich resources of Greek thought in order to grasp and express the meaning of Christian Scripture.

The fourth century was pivotal. The imperial support now offered to Christianity included legislation that gradually criminalized many non-Christian practices, such as sacrifice, and closed the temples to religious observances. Emboldened by such laws and benefiting from the increasing rate of conversion to Christianity, some Christians moved violently against local cults and their members. Saints' Lives, such as that of Martin of Tours, recount the campaigns against idolatry. Celebrated incidents mark the way. In the early 380s the emperor Gratian renounced the ancient title of Pontifex Maximus and withdrew imperial support for Rome's traditional priesthoods; in 391 a Christian crowd destroyed the Temple of Serapis in Alexandria and mocked the god's mysteries. Yet neither as practices nor as dispositions were traditional ways ever eradicated in late antiquity. While the worship of non-Christian deities is still documented in the sixth century, various pre-Christian practices, despite denunciation by some church leaders, maintained their appeal among Christians. Christians wore protective amulets inscribed with Christian names and signs and sought healing or made oracular consultations at the shrines of the saints. Throughout the centuries paganism was at once a reality and an image, dependent upon Christianity for its corporate existence and thereby empowered to play an ongoing role in the complex processes by which Christians defined themselves both before and after Constantine.

R. L. Fox, *Pagans and Christians* (1986); A. D. Lee, *Pagans and Christians in Late Antiquity: A Sourcebook* (2000); R. MacMullen, *Paganism in the Roman Empire* (1981); MacMullen, *Christianity and Paganism in the 4th to 8th Centuries* (1997); R. Wilken, *The Christians as the Romans Saw Them* (1984).

DENNIS E. TROUT

Palamas, Gregory   *see* Gregory Palamas

Palladius (c. 363–c. 431), a historian of early monasticism. Born in Galatia, Palladius moved to Egypt around 388, studying in Alexandria with Didymus the Blind. In 391 he settled first in Nitria, then in Kellia in Lower Egypt, where he apprenticed in the monastic life under Evagrius of Pontus. Around 400, as the Origenist controversy erupted, he went to Constantinople, where he befriended John Chrysostom, who ordained him bishop of Helenopolis in Bithynia. After John's deposition and exile, Palladius pleaded his case in Rome before Pope Innocent I. Arrested and exiled in 406 to Upper Egypt, he composed his *Dialogue on the Life of St. John Chrysostom*. Around 412 he returned to Galatia and was reportedly appointed bishop of Aspuna. In the 420s he composed his best-known work, the *Lausiac History*, a memoir of his years in Egypt. It contains some seventy brief portraits of holy figures. Its colorful anecdotes and brief morality tales are partially shaped by Evagrian theological perspectives. Originally written in Greek, the popular work was eventually translated into Latin, Coptic, Syriac, Armenian, and Ethiopic. The Coptic version seems to contain authentic additional material on Evagrius and other pioneers of Egyptian monasticism.

R. T. Meyer, trans., *Palladius: The Lausiac History*, ACW 34 (1965); J. Driscoll, "Evagrius, Paphnutius, and the Reasons for Abandonment by God," StudMon 39 (1998): 259–86.

WILLIAM HARMLESS, SJ

Palladius, Niels (1510–1560), Lutheran bishop at Lund and brother of Peder Palladius, the first Lutheran bishop of Zealand. Niels Palladius began studying at the Univ. of Wittenberg in 1534, receiving a master's degree in 1540. He was then called during 1544 to lecture at Maribo Convent in eastern Denmark. After another visit to Wittenberg, he was installed as priest at Our Lady's Church in Copenhagen during 1551. The following year he was ordained as bishop of Lund. Always concerned with the vitality of parish life, he published *Certain and Necessary Rules That Must Be Observed by Preachers* in 1556, the first book of theological instruction written for Reformed congregations in Denmark. A vigorous translator, Palladius was continuously preparing works by the German reformers for publication. Most notable was his translation of Veit Dietrich's *A Summary of Christian Doctrine*.

M. S. Lausten, *Biskop Niels Palladius: Et bidrag til den danske kirkes historie, 1550–1560* (1968).

DONAVON L. RILEY

Palladius, Peder (1503–1560), Danish Lutheran reformer, professor at the Univ. of Copenhagen, and first Lutheran bishop of Zealand. Peder Palladius was rector of the Latin school at Odense before beginning his studies in September 1531 at the Univ. of Wittenberg. He received a doctoral degree in 1537 and returned to Copenhagen the same year, accompanied by Johannes Bugenhagen, the parish pastor at Wittenberg. Bugenhagen had been called for the purpose of crowning Christian III and installing seven new bishops, thus fracturing the line of apostolic succession required in Roman Catholic ecclesiology. Palladius also worked with Bugenhagen to draft new church ordinances, the most significant being the *Visitatsbog*, written by Palladius during 1537. He intended it to provide direction for congregations in matters of doctrine, polity, and parish life. He also penned the *Alterbog* during 1556, an evangelical worship service in Danish, which became the standard liturgical manual until 1685. For the remainder of his life Palladius served as the king's advisor, overseeing church affairs in Denmark, Norway, Iceland, and the Faeroes.

J. Ertner, *Peder Palladius' lutherske teologi* (1988); O. P. Grell, ed., *The Scandinavian Reformation* (1995).

DONAVON L. RILEY

Pamphilus of Caesarea (d. 310), priest, martyr, and scholar. Pamphilus was a native of Berytus (Beirut) in Syria and studied in Alexandria. He then returned to Caesarea in Palestine, where he oversaw the care and expansion of Origen's library. He was arrested in 307, during the persecution under Diocletian. While in prison, Pamphilus wrote (with his disciple Eusebius, later bishop of Caesarea) a defense of Origen. He was beheaded on February 16, 310. Eusebius remained a devoted disciple and added his teacher's name to his own, calling himself *Eusebios Pamphilou*, "Eusebius, Disciple of Pamphilus." Eusebius also wrote a biography of Pamphilus, which is lost. The *Apology for Origen* is Pamphilus's only known work. It originally comprised six books. Eusebius was the joint author of the first five; the sixth was a collection of Pamphilus's letters on Origen that Eusebius added later. Only book 1 survives, in Rufinus's Latin translation. In this book, Pamphilus shows that Origen held orthodox doctrines in his work *On First Principles*. The book became part of the first phase of the Origenist controversy at the end of the fourth century: Jerome accused Rufinus of corrupting the text to make it orthodox, and claimed that Eusebius (whom Jerome considered an Arian), and not Pamphilus the martyr, was the author of the whole work.

Pamphilus, *Apologie pour Origène*, ed. R. Amacker and E. Junod (2002).

JOSEPH T. LIENHARD

Pamphlets After the European invention of the printing press in the mid-fifteenth century, the power of the new technology to effect social change became clear as the production of printed pamphlet literature exploded during the early years of the Protestant Reformation, particularly in German-speaking lands. Pamphlets (Ger. *Flugschriften*) provided a key medium through which the new religious ideas could be transmitted across great distances quickly, cheaply, and effectively. While the term is difficult to define precisely, pamphlets were generally small (most were eight pages or less), lightweight, easy to transport, and relatively inexpensive to produce. Their authors often addressed the laity, wrote in the vernacular rather than Latin, and took on topics of current concern. To reach the illiterate, printers often embellished their pamphlets with illustrations. During the sixteenth century pamphlet themes were predominantly, but not exclusively, religious. Production was enormous; some historians estimate one pamphlet per inhabitant of Germany in the 1520s. Pamphlet production was also widespread during this period in France and England, though German pamphlets have been more thoroughly researched. Pamphlets continued to play a role in religious and political controversies in Europe and North America into the nineteenth century. Pascal used them, as did the English Puritans of the seventeenth century. The eighteenth-century French and American revolutions gave rise to considerable pamphleteering. Thereafter their use was mostly political, and they were gradually superseded by newspapers.

M. U. Chrisman, *Conflicting Visions of Reform: German Lay Propaganda Pamphlets, 1519–1530* (1996); R. Hirsch, *Printing, Selling, and Reading: 1450–1550* (1974); H. J. Köhler, "Die Flugschriften der frühen Neuzeit: Ein Überblick," in *Die Erforschung der Buch- und Bibliotheksgeschichte in Deutschland*, ed. W. Arnold, W. Dietrich, and B. Zeller (1987), 307–45; R. W. Scribner, *For the Sake of Simple Folk: Popular Propaganda for the German Reformation* (1981, repr. 1994).

NATHAN BARUCH REIN

Papacy, Medieval In the course of the Middle Ages, the bishop of Rome became known as the pope (Lat. *papa*), indicating his position as father to all Christians in communion with him. This title did not give the Roman bishop any extraordinary powers in relation to his fellow bishops. These grew slowly over the course of the Middle Ages and especially after about 1050, during what might be called the first medieval reformation of the Christian church.

From the first centuries of Christianity, Rome maintained a special status because of the tradition that the apostle Peter there functioned as bishop. It was in Rome that Peter and Paul were said to have been martyred for their faith. All later bishops of Rome considered themselves to be the successors of Peter. The first medieval pope who had an impact on the entire church was Gregory I (590–604), later called "the Great." In the absence of secular authority in the city, he took over its defense and the feeding of its people. At the same time he sent out missionaries to convert the Anglo-Saxon people. As an able administrator and spiritual leader, Gregory became the ideal of medieval popes. They adopted the title he gave himself, *servus servorum Dei* ("servant of God's servants").

Medieval popes considered the see of Rome to be the first bishopric in Christendom, and they claimed the status of *primus inter pares*, or first among equals, among the bishops of the church. The bishops of Rome thus claimed a status superior to that of the patriarchs of the Eastern Mediterranean, including the patriarch of Constantinople.

In the 600s and 700s the bishops of Rome had great difficulty maintaining their position in the midst of an Italian peninsula where a Germanic tribe, the Lombards, threatened Rome. In calling upon Frankish kings to come to their assistance from about 750 onward, the popes forged an alliance with northern European kings of what after 800 became known as the HRE. The creation of this latter entity was fateful for the future of the papacy, which also asserted the right of temporal rule over central Italy. The territories that later became the Papal States were intended to provide the bishop of Rome with a zone of protection to keep secular rulers from interfering with his functions. In defending their lands, medieval popes, especially from the thirteenth century onward, became secular princes.

The early medieval popes sought the protection of the Eastern Roman emperor. In the sixth and seventh centuries, many of the bishops of Rome were in fact the emperor's appointees. The alliance with Charlemagne after his crowning as emperor in Rome in the year 800 was intended to create independence from Constantinople.

In 1054 centuries of tension between East and West ended with a schism between the Latin and the Greek churches. The pope excommunicated the patriarch of Constantinople, and the patriarch excommunicated the pope. For the rest of the Middle Ages there were many attempts to heal the schism. Doctrinally the two churches were separated only by an abstruse discussion about the procession of the Holy Spirit. In terms of authority, however, the patriarch refused to acknowledge the sovereign position of the pope as vicar of Christ in the church.

It was Gregory VII (1073–1085) who, inspired by the memory of Gregory the Great, made the papacy into the central authority within the Western church. In excommunicating the German king and Roman emperor Henry IV, Gregory claimed to have the power to create and depose kings and emperors. Thus began what the English medieval historian Colin Morris has called "the papal monarchy," the rule of the medieval church by the bishop of Rome and the reform party around him.

For these men and their successors, the words of Christ, "Thou art Peter, and upon this rock I will build my Church" (Matt. 16:18) conveyed to Peter and his successors the keys to the kingdom of heaven. In medieval art, Peter is shown with a key, and in wall paintings of Judgment Day it is he who leads the saved to the door of the heavenly Jerusalem, which he unlocks for them.

The papal monarchy was only possible because from the twelfth century the papal court and its chancery functioned as the best place in all of Western Christendom to resolve disputes over church lands and ecclesiastical privileges. The papal reformers were pragmatic idealists who from the eleventh century onward were able to create offices and courts to which institutions and individuals could have fruitful recourse.

Under Innocent III (1198–1216) papal power reached its zenith in medieval Europe. He saw to it that canon law became uniform for all of Western Christianity, and he held a successful meeting, the Fourth Lateran Council, which adopted standards that were to be in effect everywhere. From now on every Christian, male and female, was required to confess his or her sins once yearly and afterward, during Easter time, to take Communion in the parish church. In this manner every Christian was to have access to the sacraments, while at the same time every parish priest was to keep tabs on his parishioners.

After a series of confrontations between Pope Boniface VIII (1294–1303) and the French king Philip IV, medieval popes had to retreat from the high ground of power and no longer could claim sovereignty over both ecclesiastical and secular life. After Boniface's death, the papacy had to seek refuge from the political dangers and endless conflicts of the Italian peninsula and established itself in Avignon in what today is southern France. Soon after Pope Gregory XI's return to Rome in 1377 there occurred a schism within the Western church, with one pope in Rome and another in Avignon.

In 1417 the Council of Constance, after years of deliberation, elected a pope for the entire church. The council fathers intended to limit the powers of future popes, to ensure frequent councils, and to reform the church. These efforts continued until 1451, but the restored papacy did its best to resist them. By then the conciliar movement was moribund and the Renaissance papacy was in place, with popes who were more interested in art and mistresses than in spiritual life and church reform. The consequences, with the coming of the reformations of the sixteenth century, are still with us.

C. Morris, *The Papal Monarchy: The Western Church from 1050 to 1250* (1991); F. Oakley, *The Western Church in the Later Middle Ages* (1979); R. W. Southern, *Western Society and the Church in the Middle Ages* (1970).

BRIAN PATRICK MCGUIRE

Papacy, Renaissance and Reformation

Few social or religious institutions proved more adaptable or durable in the transition from the later Middle Ages to the early modern period than the papacy. It had been weakened considerably by a protracted struggle to establish the boundaries between spiritual and temporal authority within Christendom, by the Conciliarist controversy, and especially by the Western church's so-called Great Schism (1383–1449), which saw the emergence of two and sometimes three rival popes. By the turn of the seventeenth century, papal authority had been vastly strengthened, church teaching and practice had been reformed and regularized, and the popes found themselves at the head of a church vigorous enough and self-confident enough to launch the modern movement of Roman Catholic missions (with the leadership of the newly founded Society of Jesus and the other religious orders).

The Renaissance papacy, dating from the beginning of the reign of Nicholas V in 1447 to the end of Leo X's reign in 1521, has frequently been criticized, then and now, for its notorious worldliness. Nepotism was widespread as powerful Italian families struggled to control the church's wealth and influence. Faced with the challenge of developing their secular power in order to preserve their spiritual authority, moreover, the popes increasingly adopted the modus operandi of secular Renaissance princes. Positioning themselves in relation to the northern Italian city-states, the Habsburgs, the Valois, and the Ottoman Empire, they aggressively defended their interests, both temporal and spiritual, even when it required military force. The dangers were real; in 1527, furious over Clement VII's duplicity in dealings between the Habsburgs and the Valois, disaffected troops of the emperor Charles V attacked and brutally sacked Rome itself. Forced into hiding at the Castle Sant'Angelo, the pope was captured, held prisoner for six months, and released only after paying a large indemnity and promising neutrality. At the same time, the popes self-consciously styled themselves as patrons of learning and the arts, supporting the endeavors of the likes of Leonardo da Vinci and Michelangelo, and continuing a series of ambitious building projects in Rome. Thus, for example, Julius II, pope from 1503 to 1513, was later pilloried in Erasmus's *Julius Exclusus*. He was remembered both as a warrior who led his armies into battle and as a visionary who began construction on the new St. Peter's Cathedral in Rome.

At the same time, reforming impulses were never entirely absent, even within the Roman curia, as can be seen in the resolutions of the Fifth Lateran Council (1514). Only the crisis of Protestantism, however, eventually compelled reform in the Roman church. With this in mind, Catholic reform in the sixteenth century should be understood both as a reformation and as a counterreformation. Catholic reforming impulses finally began to bear lasting fruit in the papacy of Paul III (the former reform-minded Cardinal Alessandro Farnese, pope from 1534 to 1549), who summoned the council that eventually met at Trent in northern Italy from 1545 to 1563. Trent gave the Roman church a standardized confession of faith and a series of clear doctrinal alternatives to Protestantism, and

there soon followed a new catechism, a revised Vulgate Bible, and a new rite and breviary. Of almost equal importance, the implementation of the reforms agreed to at Trent depended first on the papal confirmation of the council (given by Pius IV in 1564) and then on the willingness of subsequent "reform popes" to implement its program. The founding of the Sacred Congregation of the Council by Pius IV in 1564 and its later strengthening under Gregory XIII and Sixtus V gave to the papacy itself the task of authoritatively interpreting the council's decrees. Thus, even in the midst of the changes forced by the Protestant movement and wrought by Trent, the reformed papacy stood in clear continuity with the papacy of the later Middle Ages and the Renaissance. The ecclesiological questions posed by the conciliar crisis and the Protestant Reformation had been resolved in a strongly hierarchical direction, and a papal absolutism had been confirmed that prepared the church for engagement with the emerging absolute monarchies of the early modern European states.

———

E. Duffy, *Saints and Sinners: A History of the Popes* (2nd ed., 2002); E. Garin, *Renaissance Characters* (1991); J. N. D. Kelly, *The Oxford Dictionary of Popes* (1989); W. Reinhard, "Papal Power and Family Strategy in the Sixteenth and Seventeenth Centuries," in *Princes, Patronage, and the Nobility: The Court at the Beginning of the Modern Age* (1991), 329–56.
MICKEY L. MATTOX

Papal Dispensations These suspended the application of canon law in particular cases. In the early church, dispensations were granted by bishops, and in the early Middle Ages also by church councils and popes. By the twelfth century some canonists limited the power of dispensation to papal authority, but others maintained that it still extended to bishops. In practice the papacy reserved this power in a growing number of cases (e.g., marriage) but increasingly delegated it, notably to the Penitentiary, the papal office of grace. In the later Middle Ages, most papal dispensations were sought by those wishing to pursue ecclesiastical careers but who were irregular, that is, unable to obtain or receive ecclesiastical office. Irregularity might arise from a "delict," a wrongdoing such as murder, or a "defect," notably illegitimacy. Clergy who disregarded excommunication or interdict also incurred irregularity. Papal dispensations were further required by couples who wished to marry contrary to canonical rules, notably the canon of 1215 prohibiting marriage between persons related within four degrees of consanguinity or affinity (i.e., relationship by blood or marriage). Dispensations might be obtained before or after the fact, though absolution was also required with retrospective ones.

A. van Hove, *De privilegiis et dispensationibus* (1939); K. Salonen, *The Penitentiary as a Well of Grace in the Late Middle Ages* (2001); M. A. Stiegler, *Dispensation, Dispensationswesen und Dispensationrecht im Kirchenrecht* (1901).

PETER D. CLARKE

Papal Election Decree   This decree
was a papal "declaration of independence" from lay control (1059). The reform element within the papal curia, led by Pope Nicholas II, took steps to perpetuate nascent church reform by limiting the right to choose a pope to members of the college of cardinals. The decree established that cardinal bishops would hold a preliminary election, to be confirmed by cardinal priests and deacons and the rest of the Roman clergy.

Nicholas II's document was revolutionary in two ways: it eliminated the German emperors completely from the election process and limited the Roman populace to acclaiming successful candidates. Emperors had appointed popes frequently since the ninth century and consistently since 1046. While the imperially named popes were capable men and indeed inaugurated the papal reform movement, by 1059 many reformers believed that no layperson of any rank should have such power. Change was possible in 1059, since the ruler of Germany, Henry IV, was a child and the papacy could also count on Norman support against possible imperial attack. Nicholas established the system of election that, with some later adjustments, is still in use today.

G. Tellenbach, *The Church in Western Europe from the Tenth to the Early Twelfth Century* (1993).

PHYLLIS G. JESTICE

Papal Reforms   *see* Reform Papacy

Papal States   Beginning in the early fourth
century with the conversion of Roman emperor Constantine to Christianity, the bishop of Rome began to acquire estates in the city of Rome and eventually throughout Italy and Europe, largely through pious bequests to the church. By the late sixth century, when Pope Gregory the Great ruled, the papacy controlled extensive lands in Italy, a fact we know from a document known as Gregory's Registers. The Registers reveal that the pope had large land holdings in Sicily, southern Italy, around the city of Rome, and in northern Italy near the city of Ravenna. These estates, together with hundreds of other farms scattered around Italy, made the papacy the largest landowner in Italy by the seventh century. Collectively these lands constituted the early medieval precedent of what eventually came to be known as the Papal States.

The next critical phase in the political recognition of the papacy's sovereignty over its estates in Italy occurred when ·Charlemagne, ruler of the Franks, officially codified the papacy's temporal rule over its Italian possessions in Carolingian legal codes in 781. The formal crowning of Charlemagne as Holy Roman Emperor by the pope on Christmas Day 800 established him and his successors as the new protectors of the papacy and military guarantor of the Papal States, a role the Western emperors played with varying levels of consistency and effectiveness throughout the medieval period.

By the twelfth century, the papacy had reached a new level of political sophistication marked by both the theoretical claims used to justify its secular power and the administrative structure used to govern its seven major provinces of Benevento, Bologna, Ancona, Campania e Marittima, the patrimony of St. Peter (Narni, Terni, and Sabina), Romagna, and the duchy of Spoleto.

On the level of theory, by the twelfth century the papacy was citing the document known as the "Donation of Constantine" to support its temporal claims, and it was also in this period, during the pontificate of Innocent III (1198–1216), that popes first began writing papal decrees claiming supreme princely power for the papacy in its lands. On the level of administration, this pope's reign also witnessed the consolidation of papal power in the form of increased uniformity in the imposition of papal taxes, courts of justice, and military captains in the Papal States. For both theoretical and administrative reasons, then, the reign of Innocent III is sometimes called the official birth of the Papal States.

These exalted claims and practical advances notwithstanding, the papacy in the later medieval period nonetheless constantly suffered from challenges to its rule by both internal and external competitors. Most noticeably, the Roman nobility constantly vied for power in the Papal States, controlled private armies, and frequently challenged papal claims. Similarly the German emperors, citing ancient privileges, frequently claimed temporal lordship in parts of the Papal States. Civil unrest and the competition for power in the Papal States, in short, undermined papal authority and even led to the removal of the papal court to the French city of Avignon for most of the fourteenth century.

By the early fifteenth century, when the papacy finally returned to Rome for good, papal power was much diminished, and various cities and regions of the Papal States had won a large measure of local autonomy. By the end of the century, however, and particularly during the reigns of the two powerful Renaissance popes, Alexander VI (1492–1503) and Julius II (1503–1513), papal power and control over the Papal States reached a new height, in large part because of direct use of large papal armies to subdue rebellious cities, nobles, or regions. The sixteenth century thus marked the most important phase of the political consolidation of the Papal States. It was also the period in which the theory of papal absolutism was most fully elaborated, especially by the papal theologians Robert Bellarmine and Cesare Baronius. This theory bolstered the papacy's claim to supreme temporal authority over its subjects in the Papal States.

On a practical military level, however, it was the new Constantine of the sixteenth and seventeenth centuries, the Spanish monarchy, that guaranteed papal control as the military protector of the Papal States. In this period, the Papal States largely became a client state of the Spanish Empire, a fact that led to the internal consolidation of papal power and one of its longest-lasting periods of political stability. It was also in this period that the papacy reincorporated the important duchies of Ferrara and Urbino back into the Papal States, further extending its territories in Italy.

———

R. Brentano, *Rome before Avignon: A Social History of Thirteenth-Century Rome* (1974); T. Dandelet, *Spanish Rome, 1500–1700* (2001); T. F. X. Noble, *The Republic of St. Peter: The Birth of the Papal State, 680–825* (1984); P. Partner, *The Lands of St. Peter* (1972); P. Prodi, *The Papal Prince: One Body and Two Souls: The Papal Monarchy in Early Modern Europe* (1987).

THOMAS DANDELET

Papebroch, Daniel (1628–1714), Jesuit historian. After studying theology at Louvain,

Papebroch collaborated with Jean Bolland on the *Acta Sanctorum*. He gathered material in Germany, Italy, and France for the eighteen volumes of this work, to which he contributed during almost fifty years. Papebroch did not hesitate to criticize on historical grounds existing prejudices. In 1695 his rejection of the belief that the Carmelite order originated with the prophet Elijah led to condemnation of the *Acta Sanctorum* by the Spanish Inquisition, a ban not lifted until after Papebroch's death. His study of medieval charters led him to deny the validity of documents from the Merovingian era and thus also of the founding charter of the Benedictine order. The resulting controversy between Jesuits and Benedictines inspired the Benedictine Jean Mabillon to publish his famous *De re diplomatica* in 1681, the conclusions of which Papebroch accepted. Papebroch ended his work on the *Acta Sanctorum* in 1709.

———

H. Delehaye, *L'oeuvre des Bollandistes à travers trois siècles, 1615–1915* (2nd ed., 1959); K. Hausberger, "Das kritische hagiographische Werk der Bollandisten," in *Historische Kritik in der Theologie*, ed. G. Schwaiger (1980), 210–44; D. Knowles, *Great Historical Enterprises: Problems in Monastic History* (1963).

JORIS VAN EIJNATTEN

Papias (c. 60–130), bishop of Hierapolis (Asia Minor) during the early second century. Papias appears to have been a contemporary of Polycarp of Smyrna. Little is known about him except that he authored a lengthy five-part treatise entitled *Expositions of the Sayings of the Lord* of which only fragments survive, mostly within the *Ecclesiastical History* of Eusebius. Brief comments about Papias himself are scattered throughout several later patristic sources, including the writings of Irenaeus and Jerome.

The loss of Papias's records about the traditions and theology of the nascent church is truly unfortunate. The fragments that remain provide glimpses into early Christian beliefs about the authorship of the NT Gospels and the early church's view of history. It was Papias who preserved the ancient tradition that Mark was the author of the Gospel of Mark and that the apostle Matthew stands behind the collection of Jesus' sayings that underlies the Gospel of Matthew (Eusebius, *Hist. eccl.* 3.39.15–16). He likewise recorded stories about events in the lives of the apostles, some of which served to complete Gospel episodes or to supplement popular, pious speculation.

W. R. Schoedel, "Papias: His Life and Work, Recent Studies," in *ANRW* 2.27.1 (1993), 235–70; Schoedel, *Polycarp, Martyrdom of Polycarp, Fragments of Papias* (1967); A. F. Walls, "Papias and Oral Tradition," *VC* 21 (1967): 135–40.

CLAYTON N. JEFFORD

Paracelsus (1493–1541), Swiss physician. Theophrastus Bombastus von Hohenheim, who named himself "Paracelsus," studied alchemy and chemistry at Basel. He was appointed city physician for Basel, a position he lost in 1528 due to his vociferous and flamboyant opposition to the prevailing Galenic medical philosophy of the day. Paracelsus proclaimed himself "the Luther of medicine," asserting that truth was to be discovered through experience, not through deference to authorities. He developed the revolutionary notions that chemicals are the basic building blocks of life and that disease derives not from an internal imbalance of the body's humors (as in Galenic medicine) but from some external attack on the body. He advanced a mystical cosmology, cosmogony, and anthropology. Paracelsus contended that to be a successful physician one must be a mystic. His tripartite description of human nature, which links the human microcosm to the cosmic macrocosm, influenced the German mystic Jacob Boehme and the Dutch physician Jean Baptista van Helmont. Finally, he attempted to make the most advanced medical treatments available to the poor.

A. G. Debus, *The Chemical Philosophy*, 2 vols. (1977); C. Webster, *From Paracelsus to Newton* (1982); A. Weeks, *Paracelsus* (1997).

RODERICK MARTIN

Paradise (in Churches) This term is used for the forecourt found in many Romanesque cathedrals and abbey churches, or for the monastic cloister, a large square yard surrounded by loggias and usually attached to the south flank of a church. In the first sense, the term originated at St. Peter's Basilica in Rome, due either to the striking view the forecourt offered of the facade mosaic of paradise (the Lamb of the Apocalypse), or, conversely, to the large bronze pinecone (*pigna*) fountain that was installed in the atrium in the late eighth century and popularly understood to be a symbol of the waters of paradise flowing from the tree of knowledge (in Middle Eastern tradition, a pine tree). Soon Benedictine monasteries such as Monte Cassino, St. Riquier, and Fulda began incorporating forecourts called paradises; such a structure is also labeled in the famous plan of the monastery of St. Gall (tenth cent.). Despite the popular association of the term "paradise" with "garden," there is no evidence that these paradises contained any plants; they were, rather, paved yards. Paradise as the name used for a monastic cloister first appears in Honorius Augustodunensis (fl. 1095–1135), who wrote about the symbolism of church architecture and furnishings. After that time, referring to the monastic cloister as a paradise became a commonplace in spiritual monastic writings.

E. R. Curtius, *European Literature and the Latin Middle Ages* (1953), 200; W. Dynes, "The Medieval Cloister as Portico of Solomon," *Gesta* 12 (1973): 61–69; M. Finch, "The Cantharus and Pigna at Old St. Peter's," *Gesta* 30, no. 1 (1991): 16–26; H. Augustodunensis, *Gemma Anima*, PL 172 (1854); J. Leclercq, "Le cloître est-il un paradis?" in *Le Message des moines à notre temps* (1958), 141–59; *The Marvels of Rome (Mirabilia urbis Romae)*, ed. F. M. Nichols (2nd ed., 1986); J. C. Picard, "Les origines du mot *Paradisus*-Parvis," *Mélanges de l'Ecole Française de Rome, Moyan-Age, Temps Modernes* 83 (1971), 159–86.

NANCY KATHERINE SPATZ LUCID

Pareus, David Waengler (1548–1622), German Reformed theologian, born in Silesia. When his Philippist teacher, Christoph Schilling, was ostracized for being a Calvinist, he accompanied him to the Palatinate, where he earned a doctorate from the Univ. of Heidelberg. From 1571 onward he became a vicar in various parishes, each of which he had to leave due to Catholic opposition. In 1574 he married Magdalena Stibels. In 1587/1588 he finished the first Calvinist translation of the Bible into German. From 1598 he was a professor at the Univ. of Heidelberg and in 1611 and 1619 its president. A prodigious writer, Pareus's most important work, *Irenicum sive de unione et synodo evangelicorum concillanda liber votivus paci ecclesiae et desideriis pacificorum dictatus*, appeared in 1614.

V. Press, *Calvinismus und Territorialstaat: Regierung und Zentralbehörden der Kurpfalz 1559–1619* (1970); K. Schurb, "Sixteenth-Century Lutheran-Calvinist Conflict on the 'Proto-evangelium,'" *CTQ* 54, no. 1 (1990): 25–47.

INGUN MONTGOMERY

Paris Foreign Mission Society

Roman Catholic mission organization, constituted in 1660–1661 as a result of efforts by Pope Alexander VII to undermine Portuguese dominance of East and Southeast Asian Catholic missions. The pope commissioned three apostolic vicars—François Pallu (1626–1684), Pierre Lambert de la Motte (1624–1679), and Ignatius Cotolendi—in what is now Vietnam, Laos, and southwestern China, to assume direction of the church's mission in the area. They founded the society and established a seminary for the training of European missionaries in Paris (1664). They particularly emphasized the importance of educating native clergy and in 1665 created a seminary in Thailand, the first of several in the area. The society has continued to play an important role in Roman Catholicism in southeastern Asia to the present.

———

G. M. Oury, *Mgr. François Pallu ou les Missions Etrangères en Asia au 17e siècle* (1985); J. Guennou, *Missions Etrangères de Paris* (1986).

ROBERT KOLB

Parmenian

Parmenian (early fourth cent.–391/392), Spanish or Gallic by birth, Donatist bishop of Carthage (362–391/392). His treatise *Against the Church of the Collaborators* (c. 362) contributed original insights into the nature of the church. Optatus of Milevis and, later, Augustine adopted some of his ideas while strongly rejecting others.

With imperial approval, Donatist bishops triumphantly returned from exile to Africa in 362. For the next thirty years as primate, Parmenian distinguished himself as a gifted tactician, orator, and spokesman for the Donatist cause. Under his guidance, Donatism reached its apex, becoming the dominant religion of the region and eclipsing the rival Catholic Church in popularity. Parmenian's *Against the Church of the Collaborators* specified that the true church alone possesses the gifts (*dotes*) ascribed to the bride in the Song of Songs. This concept helped mitigate Donatist insistence on the personal worthiness of ministers, emphasizing instead the stronger claim of the holiness of the institutional church.

Parmenian engineered the condemnation of the brilliant Donatist theologian Tyconius (c. 385), but Tyconius's concept of the two societies later would profoundly influence Augustine's masterpiece, *The City of God.*

———

Optatus of Milevis, *Against the Donatists,* trans. M. Edwards (1997), and in Augustine, *Against the Letter of Parmenian,* in *Works of Saint Augustine* 1/21 and in PL 43 (1844), 33–108; W. H. C. Frend, *The Donatist Church* (2nd ed., 1971); M. Tilley, "From Separatist Sect to Majority Church," StPatr 33 (1995), 260–65.

JANE E. MERDINGER

Parr, Katherine

Parr, Katherine (1513/1514–1548), sixth wife and widow of Henry VIII, first Protestant queen of England. She married Henry in 1543, having been married twice previously to older men. After the death of her second husband, she returned to court life, where she quickly caught the eye of Henry; the marriage would be propitious for the future of Protestantism in England. Though her past was entirely within the traditional church, she embraced Protestantism fully, being converted by Thomas Cranmer in 1544. She was stepmother to both Edward and Elizabeth and had close ties with Cranmer, Nicholas Ridley, and Hugh Latimer. Parr acted as queen and regent in 1544 during Henry's military campaign in France, with Cranmer acting as a close advisor; it was during this time that Cranmer's influence over her was at its greatest, committing her to the cause of a Protestant and reformed Church of England. Following Henry's death in 1547, she married Thomas Seymour, the younger brother of Lord Protector Somerset, uncle of Edward VI and brother of Queen Jane Seymour. She died in 1548 following the birth of her only child, Mary. Her funeral was the first Protestant funeral for royalty in England.

———

A. Martienssen, *Queen Katherine Parr* (1973).

ALDEN R. LUDLOW

Pascal, Blaise

Pascal, Blaise (1623–1662), French mathematician, scientist, and philosopher. Born in Clermont, he was taken to Paris in 1631, where he was educated privately by his father. He was exposed to a circle of scientists and philosophers during his formative years and developed a passion for mathematics. He wrote an important treatise on conic geometry at the age of sixteen, invented a calculating machine, and did innovative work in physics, statistics, and probability theory.

In 1646, while living in Rouen, he developed an intense interest in religion around the same time his family became committed to the Jansenist movement. On November 23, 1654, he experienced his "night of fire," a moment of spiritual illumination that caused him to redirect his life's interests. He entered into closer association with Port-Royal, the Jansenist convent where his sister lived as a nun. In 1656–1657, he published the *Provincial Letters* to defend the Augustinian theology of the Jansenists against the flexible moral theory and optimistic view of human nature taught by the Jesuits. He also began to sketch out a major defense of the Christian faith. It remained unfinished when he died at the age of thirty-nine, but the fragments were published in 1670 as Pascal's *Thoughts (Pensées)*. He attempted to persuade skeptics that humans can never be truly happy apart from God. For those who had lost confidence in traditional belief, he formulated his famous "Wager," which suggested that there was nothing to lose and much to gain in believing in God. Pascal thought that proofs would not convince nonbelievers of God's existence, but that "we know the truth not only through reason but also through the heart." His Wager is not a proof but rather a call to make a religious commitment and begin to walk the path that will lead to greater recognition of the truth of the Christian faith.

D. Adamson, *Blaise Pascal: Mathematician, Physicist, and Thinker about God* (1995); J. Cole, *Pascal: The Man and His Two Loves* (1995); B. Norman, *Portraits of Thought: Knowledge, Methods, and Styles in Pascal* (1988); M. O'Connell, *Blaise Pascal: Reasons of the Heart* (1997).

ERIC LUND

Pasch and the Paschal Controversy

The Christian celebration of Christ's resurrection occasioned extended debate in the early church over the day and dating of Easter and its correlation with the Jewish Passover. The original connection between Easter and Passover was established not only by Jesus' Last Supper but also by the image of Christ as the sacrificed paschal Lamb (1 Cor. 5:7–8). The early church ultimately merged two interpretive traditions: the Alexandrian, which derived *Pascha* from the Hebrew *pasach* and depicted it as the spiritual "Passover" of the faithful, and the Asiatic, which derived *Pascha* from the Greek *paschein* ("to suffer") and focused on Christ's redemptive passion. With Eusebius of Caesarea the merger of the two traditions appears in the East, and a thorough synthesis is evident later with Augustine in the West.

Controversy developed in the second century between churches in Asia Minor that celebrated the Pasch on the day of Jewish Passover, the fourteenth of the month of Nisan, for which they were dubbed Quartodecimans ("Fourteen-thers"), and the Roman church, which slated the Pasch in conjunction with Passover but delayed its actual observance until the Sunday after Passover (thereby enhancing the resurrection rather than the passion as the focal point of celebration). As Eusebius reports, Polycrates, bishop of Ephesus, defended the Quartodeciman usage on the authority of the apostles Philip and John, the martyr Polycarp of Smyrna, and other significant figures buried in Asia Minor. He also cited Melito of Sardis, whose recovered homily *On the Pascha* (c. 165) is a monument to the sophistication of Quartodeciman theology, with its meticulous application of Passover images to Christ. Nevertheless, Pope Victor I excommunicated the Quartodecimans. Irenaeus of Lyon, a native of Asia Minor who had relocated to episcopal ministry in Gaul, upheld the "Sunday only" custom but sympathized theologically with the Quartodecimans. His attempts to mediate failed.

Hippolytus of Rome mistakenly attacked the Quartodecimans for judaizing the paschal observance. As Melito demonstrates, the supplanting of the old Passover by the new paschal mystery of Christ was the reason for a Jewish dating for the festival. The momentum ultimately lay with those churches East and West seeking to divorce the paschal observance from the Jewish calendar.

New differences arose between Alexandria and Rome over the calculation of Easter according to the Julian (Roman) calendar. The Council of Nicaea ruled in favor of the Sunday-only usage and designated the Sunday following the full moon on or after the spring equinox (March 21) as Easter. In early medieval Britain, certain churches continued the Asiatic usage until conceding to the Roman custom at the Synod of Whitby (664). Later debates in the West involved complex calendar calculations and generated different datings of the Pasch in the Eastern Orthodox and Western churches.

R. Cantalamessa, *Easter in the Early Church: An Anthology of Jewish and Early Christian Texts* (1993); S. G. Hall, ed. and trans., *Melito of Sardis: "On Pascha" and Fragments* (1979); Hall, "The Origins of Easter," StPatr 15, no. 1 (1984): 554–67.

PAUL M. BLOWERS

Passion Plays

Attempts to portray the events of Christ's life leading up to the passion survive from the early Middle Ages, ranging from the ivories to the majestic mosaics of Ravenna. These remained the subject of several cyclical productions, such as Giotto's paintings in the Arena Chapel in Padua. But the most accessible genre for the portrayal of the events leading to the passion were the passions plays of late medieval northern Europe. These were urban events that required coordination between secular and religious institutions and in which the citizenry took an active part. While parishes maintained some elements of liturgical drama in Holy Week, such as the dramatization of Christ's empty sepulcher, passion plays such as that of Arras of the 1440s or the *Mystère de la Passion* of c. 1450 were extensive public plays (25,000 and 34,000 lines, respectively), beginning with the entry to Jerusalem and ending with the resurrection. Such plays fit into the devotional preoccupation with reliving and contemplating Christ's passion. They gave occasion for wide participation, as well as for exclusion: in German towns Jews were sometimes made to play the part of biblical Jews.

G. Frank, *The Medieval French Drama* (1954); K. Young, *The Drama of the Medieval Church*, vol. 1 (1933), 201–539.

MIRI RUBIN

Pastoral Care Pastoral care includes activities designed to instruct the laity in the norms and beliefs of Christian life and religion. It was a primary duty of the clergy and included baptizing, preaching, hearing confession, and granting absolution, in addition to performing blessings and offering less formal types of teaching. Expectations about the nature and availability of pastoral care differed at various times and places in the Middle Ages, as did the ecclesiastical personnel and structures involved.

In the early church a great deal of emphasis was placed on the figure of the bishop as the teacher of his flock and on the catechism of adult candidates for baptism. Baptism offered the complete remission of sins, and individuals might remain catechumens until a point in life when they were prepared to embrace an ascetic lifestyle in order to avoid future sin. The bishop likewise controlled admission to the state of penance for those who committed major sins after baptism; the rite of public penance was available only once and entailed the permanent adoption of a quasi-monastic life.

In the early Middle Ages the northern regions of Europe posed two problems: the conversion of the pagan peoples and the provision of pastoral care in the very large bishoprics typical of the newly converted lands, which were served by relatively few priests. Recent research from England and Ireland suggests that mother churches quite effectively provided ecclesiastical personnel to preach and perform the sacraments for the people of the diocese. Monks were heavily involved both in the conversion of the pagans and in serving the Christian population, for example, through preaching tours. Great monasteries founded in the newly converted lands became centers for the ongoing Christianization of the local population.

The reforms under the Carolingians (see *Carolingian Church*) showed a great deal of concern for delineating the respective roles of the secular clergy and the monks and for defining the religious duties of the laity. The influence of Irish monks led to the widespread adoption of repeatable, tariffed penances, while the liturgy was standardized and the norms of Christianity enforced by lay rulers' legislation (especially the baptism of children, the abolition of behaviors identified as pagan, and the compulsory payment of the tithe).

During the tenth to twelfth centuries, we know little of the interaction of priests with their local populations. Monks often served churches dependent on their monasteries and certainly provided the most convincing model of holiness for the period. Attention was focused on the development of Christian norms of aristocratic behavior, especially the control of violence through the Peace of God movement (see *Truce of God*) and the gradual invention of Christian knighthood. In addition, marriage became a sacrament. By the later twelfth century there were more local churches with the right to baptize as the rights of the old mother churches became less exclusive and chapels were elevated, in some places, to parish churches.

From the eleventh century onward, there were signs of a growing lay enthusiasm for religion that probably was based on somewhat higher levels of literacy and possibly on the growth of denser urban populations in this period. This "evangelical awakening," as it has been called, led to a new demand from the laity for religious instruction, along with new challenges for the institutional church in the form of proliferating experiments in modes of Christian life, exuberant preaching, and lay and clerical adherence to groups that were considered unorthodox for either their beliefs or their institutional structures.

Coupled with this enthusiasm, the greater centrality of canon law led the church to develop new definitions and clarify existing ones. In particular, the Fourth Lateran Council (see *Lateran Councils*) famously required that each Christian confess to his or her parish priest (*proprius sacerdos*) at least once a year at Easter. Although this requirement may seem minimal, it reflected a new concern with the actions of the lay individual and a new certainty that each Christian fit into the structural framework of the church in an organized and generalizable way. Confession was increasingly codified and discussed by the clergy as a powerful means of inculcating Christian values and controlling behavior.

Preaching, especially that done by members of the mendicant orders, was closely focused on the life of the laity, especially in the sermons *ad status* addressed to specific social groups, such as wives or knights, and in the use of *exempla*, vivid stories of the everyday world embedded in sermons to help make the preacher's point in a way that spoke to lay life. In addition, the first lay saints provided models for lay behavior. Although the laity themselves were not allowed to preach about dogma, they could exhort one another to lead more pious lives, a license that certain figures, such as Margery Kempe, used liberally to castigate their contemporaries and call for a reform of life and morals. In urban areas, the increase in the amount of preaching available, especially in those cities that had houses of all the major mendicant orders, gave a certain level of choice and the possibility of comparison for the lay audience.

A very important lay initiative that had bearing on pastoral care was the fraternity: a layman or laywoman might choose to join, help to commission sermons, and participate in prayers and ascetic practices. Although these activities were under the direction of a priest, the groups remained primarily focused on the needs of the laity who were their members.

Finally, vernacular literature often reflected ideas drawn from the clerical world of pastoral care, showing how they might become widespread in the population and come to belong, in some sense, to the laity as well as the clergy.

J. Blair et al., eds., *Pastoral Care before the Parish* (1992); J. Delumeau, ed., *Histoire vécue du peuple chrétien*, vol. 1 (1979); G. R. Evans, ed., *A History of Pastoral Care* (2000); Evans, *Faire croire: Modalités de la diffusion et de la réception des messages religieux du XIIe au XVe siècle* (1981); R. Rusconi, *L'ordine dei peccati: La confessione tra Medioevo ed età moderna* (2002); R. N. Swanson, *Religion and Devotion in Europe, c. 1215–c. 1515* (1995).

                                VICTORIA M. MORSE

Patriarchs The term appears as an honorific in the fourth century (Gregory of Nazianzus, *Oration* 42). Its first use in a precise legal context is found in the sixth century (Justinian, *Novella* 123.3; see *Corpus iuris civilis*) to designate the bishops of the sees of Rome, Constantinople, Alexandria, Antioch, and Jerusalem. In the church's first four centuries, its jurisdictional structures grew from strictly local governance to regional groupings that mirrored the civil divisions of the Roman Empire. By the time of the Council of Nicaea in 325, the sees of Rome, Alexandria, and Antioch were exercising some form of supervision beyond their own territories, an arrangement accepted at Nicaea as valid but exceptional. Supervision carried the right to ordain suffragan bishops but not the right of direct intervention. Subsequent conciliar legislation until the Council of Chalcedon (451) was concerned to define the areas of jurisdiction and regulate the mutual relations of the churches in the Eastern empire rather than relations with the church at Rome. The subsequent establishment of other sees with patriarchal rank came about as these areas gained political independence from Constantinople or simply because of their importance.

F. Dvornik, *Byzantium and the Roman Primacy* (1966); P. L'Huillier, *The Church of the Ancient Councils: The Disciplinary Work of the First Four Ecumenical Councils* (1995); J. Meyendorff, *Imperial Unity and Christian Divisions* (1989).

                    EUGENE M. LUDWIG, OFM CAP.

Patrick (c. 430–c. 493), missionary to Ireland and patron saint of parades on March 17. Patrick was born in Roman Britain, kidnapped at the age of fifteen by Irish pirates, and sold as a slave in Ireland. He escaped six years later, returned home, became ordained, and returned to Ireland as a missionary. He wrote two short works, a *Confession* and a *Letter to the Soldiers of Coroticus*, a British princeling. These are the only uncontested facts about his life.

No Irish source mentions him, except in passing, until the mid-seventh century. In the eighth century appeared thaumaturgic Lives of Patrick of little historical worth. Most complicating are the annals, chronological lists of events in Irish history, the earliest of which were begun in the eighth century. Some annals record Patrick's death in 461, others in 491 or 493. For generations scholars accepted the earlier date, partly motivated by Patrick's status as the Apostle of Ireland. The first bishop in Ireland was Palladius, a Roman deacon, who went there in 431. Anxious to get the national apostle to Ireland as soon as possible, scholars chose the earlier date and had Patrick there by 432. Recently scholars have begun to accept the later date, focusing on events in Irish secular and religious history that fit better with a mission for Patrick in the second half of the fifth century. Best known for expelling snakes and incinerating druids with celestial lightning, Patrick appears in his writings as a man of great faith, humility, courage, and determination, who relied upon God, not wonder-working, to convert the pagan Irish.

T. M. Charles-Edwards, *Early Christian Ireland* (2002); L. DePaor, *Saint Patrick's World* (1993); D. Dumville, ed., *Saint Patrick, A.D. 493–1993* (1993); R. P. C. Hanson, trans., *The Life and Writings of the Historical Saint Patrick* (1983).
JOSEPH F. KELLY

Patrick, Simon (1626–1707), bishop of Ely. A graduate of Queen's College, Cambridge, Patrick was named bishop of Chichester in 1689 and moved to Ely in 1691. He was an important figure in the revival of the Church of England, one of the founders of the Society for Promoting Christian Knowledge (SPCK), and a supporter of the Society for Propagation of the Gospel. Though he had received Presbyterian orders, he believed that Anglican ordination was important, and so Joseph Hall, bishop of Norwich, privately ordained him in 1654. As a supporter of the Church of England, he opposed the Roman Catholicism of James II and welcomed William and Mary. Despite his support of the church, he respected nonjurors and was instrumental in the genesis of later Anglican latitudinarianism and the Low Church tradition. His influence was deeply felt in revivals of the late seventeenth and early eighteenth centuries.

S. Patrick, *A Brief Account of the New Sect of Latitude-Men* (1662, repr. 1963).
ALDEN R. LUDLOW

Patristics, Reformation The Reformation was a particularly fruitful era for the development of interest in the church fathers and for what came to be known as patristic studies. The Renaissance stimulated interest in the Christian past for its own sake and in making the writings of the early church available in as accurate a form as possible. Complete treatises were preferred over collections of extracts, and there was a growing interest in the fathers' theology and their usefulness as biblical commentators and guarantors of doctrinal purity. Several patristic editions and especially Latin translations of Greek fathers were available before the Reformation. They were due largely to Greek scholars such as George of Trebizond (1396–1486) or John Bessarion (1403–1472), who translated works in the context of attempts at union with the Greek church during the Council of Florence (1438–1445). The same period also saw some eminent Western patristic editors and translators such as Ambrogio Traversari (c. 1386–1439), Leonardo Bruni (1370–1444), and Raffaele Maffei of Volterra (1451–1522). North of the Alps, editing the fathers became the special area of reform-minded humanists such as Beatus Rhenanus, famous for his editions of Tertullian and of the early *Ecclesiastical Histories*, and Erasmus, who was alone responsible for new or revised editions of Jerome, Augustine, John Chrysostom, Irenaeus, Ambrose, Athanasius, Hilary, Basil, and Origen. Although many of the earlier translations and editions continued to be published and used throughout the sixteenth century, Basel (where Rhenanus and Erasmus published their editions) became the publishing center for patristic texts. However, many more overtly confessional editions (with theologically slanted prefaces and notes) of fathers such as Irenaeus, Chrysostom, or Tertullian appeared later in the century in Paris, Geneva, and Rome. The Counter-Reformation gave rise to an improved level of patristic scholarship; editions by Catholics such as Jacques de Billy (Gregory of Nazianzus), François-Feu-ardent (Irenaeus), or Gentien Hervet (Chrysostom) are characterised by their high level of textual accuracy. It would be wrong to see the patristic editions of the later sixteenth century as theological controversy read into early documents; their main purpose for Protestants and Catholics alike was to help construct a confessional identity. The wish of both parties to give themselves a past also explains the appearance of new confessionally oriented histories of the early church: the Protestant *Centuries of Magdeburg* and the Catholic *Ecclesiastical Annals* by Caesar Baronius. Both were based on recent patristic editions and on unpublished material; each took historical scholarship to unprecedented heights.

The Reformation in its early years did not invent interest in the fathers but both profited from it and stimulated it. Martin Luther sharply distinguished between the authority of the Bible and that of the fathers, which he thought subject to correction in the light of scriptural evidence. This did not stop the Reformers from using the fathers' writings against the attacks of Catholic theologians or against one another (e.g., in the eucharistic quarrels of 1525–1536 between Zwinglians and Lutherans). Whereas Luther tried to divide sharply the fathers' authority from that of the Bible, Huldrych Zwingli and Martin Bucer adopted the "implicit normativity" approach. They tended to interpret the Bible through writings of the early church, which they interpreted in turn through the Bible. This made for a closer coexistence of biblical and patristic authority, but they were just as aware of the fathers' limitations as Luther and did not hesitate to criticize either their doctrine or their exegetical method. Catholics believed that the church as represented by the fathers was the only authoritative interpreter of Scripture, and they defended the notion of *consensus patrum*. John Calvin, aware of both the supremacy of Scripture and of its silence on certain points, used the fathers where he thought Scripture could not provide all the evidence (e.g., in relation to the doctrines of the Trinity and predestination). The later sixteenth and early seventeenth century witnessed the publication of a number of guides to patristic editions and literature. On the Protestant side theologians such as Andreas Hyperius, Abraham Scultetus, and André Rivet produced digests intended to ensure that pastors gave a Protestant interpretation of the fathers. Guides such Sixtus of Siena's *Bibliotheca sancta* or Possevino's *Apparatus sacer* fulfilled a similar function in the Catholic camp.

I. Backus, ed., *Reception of the Church Fathers in the West: From the Carolingians to the Maurists*, 2 vols. (1997); I. Backus, *Historical Method and Confessional Identity in the Era of the Reformation (1378–1615)* (2003).

IRENA BACKUS

Patron and Patronage Right

In church law, a patron is a lay or ecclesiastical person or corporation that holds a patronage right (*ius patronatus*) over a church office or property, called "advowson" in England. The definition of patronage right grew out of the criticism of lay dominion over churches in the second half of the eleventh century. Reforms denied laity the right to sell, give away, or use church property. Rather than sever all ties between donor and gift, canonists in the twelfth and thirteenth centuries attributed a *ius patronatus* to donors. According to it, a donor who established or supplied a

church, although relinquishing practical disposition of property given, retained certain rights in connection with it, the most important of which was the presentation of the candidate to an office associated with the donation (e.g., in the case of a parish church, the rector). The right was transferable by inheritance, gift, or fee. It was recognized in Europe through the early modern period, although it was challenged by the Calvinist claim that the choice of a pastor belongs to the congregation. The patron's right ended, declined, or was at least challenged in places where Calvinist influence was most strongly felt in the early modern period, for example, the Palatinate, the Dutch Republic, East Frisia, and Scotland. In Germany since the late Middle Ages, territorial princes increasingly dominated but seldom if ever monopolized the right. Although never formally abandoned by Lutheran territorial churches, the influence of lesser patrons was gradually supplanted by territorial administrations. Patronage survived the secularizations of the nineteenth century on the European continent but became increasingly obsolete in the twentieth century. It still exists in the Church of England.

P. Landau, "Patronat," *TRE* 26 (1996): 106–14; Landau, *Ius patronatus* (1975); J. Sieglerschmidt, *Territorialstaat und Kirchenregiment* (1987).

CHRISTOPHER OCKER

Paul III (1468–1549), curial careerist, patron of the arts, elected pope in 1534. Called "Cardinal Petticoat" because his sister was Alexander VI's mistress, Alessandro Farnese fathered three sons and a daughter before his ordination at age fifty-one. His election as Paul III did not bode well for reform. He made his teenaged grandsons cardinals, and lavish banquets, masked balls, and risqué plays were held in the Vatican, Rome reveled in bullfights and horse races funded by the papacy, and Lent began after a boisterous Carnival. Yet Paul's association with curial reformers and the naming of humanist cardinals signaled his understanding that change was needed. Multiple factors delayed the Council of Trent until 1545, but Paul's reform commission met within three years of his election to draft a litany of abuses, assigning the papacy blame for the existence of these abuses and responsibility for their elimination. Within the curia, some favored immediate institutional reform but ongoing dialogue with the Reformers on doctrinal issues. Others prevailed on Paul to take the doctrinal offensive, and he established the Holy Office of the Roman Inquisition with universal jurisdiction to apprehend heretics. Nevertheless, he also encouraged reform that linked institutional change with doctrinal purity. He approved Loyola's Jesuits and encouraged Philip Neri's street ministry and other reformist but loyally orthodox initiatives. Under his leadership Trent issued decrees on justification, the sacraments, Scripture, and tradition, while at the same time promulgating practical reforms to establish seminaries and regulate clerical life.

E. Duffy, *Saints and Sinners: A History of the Popes* (1997); R. P. McBrien, *Lives of the Popes* (1997).

PETER J. SCAGNELLI

Paul IV (1476–1559), papal diplomat and curialist, elected pope in 1555. His background included diplomatic missions to England, Flanders, and Spain, correspondence with Erasmus and familiarity with the aspirations of Catholic humanists, the pastoral administration of dioceses, and the founding of the Theatine community dedicated to evangelical renewal. However, by the time Giovanni Pietro Carafa was elected Paul IV, his vision of ecclesiastical reform had narrowed to zealous enforcement of doctrinal orthodoxy and an uncompromising determination to eliminate Protestantism. The Council of Trent was indefinitely suspended, while Paul promoted a vision of reform labeled the Counter-Reformation that operated through secret investigations, suppression of heresy, and imprisonment not only of offenders but also of suspected Protestant sympathizers. Paul directed the Holy Office of the Roman Inquisition to compile an Index of Forbidden Books banning not only suspect theological works but also humanist classics and even the works of Erasmus. Protestants were not the only object of his wrath. In Rome Jews were stripped of property and confined to ghettoes. He quarreled with the Catholic Queen Mary in England and joined battle against Catholic Spain. Rigorous toward others, he was blind to the corruption of his own family, upon whom he lavished wealth and favor. At his death the streets of Rome exploded in joyful riots as mobs toppled his statues, burned the offices of the Inquisition, and liberated its prisoners.

E. Duffy, *Saints and Sinners: A History of the Popes* (1997); R. P. McBrien, *Lives of the Popes* (1997).

PETER J. SCAGNELLI

Paul in Early Christianity   As Paul's own writings and the book of Acts make clear, Paul was a complex and controversial figure. As a zealous Jew, student of the Scriptures, and Pharisee who had been instrumental in the persecution of Christians (Phil. 3:4–6; Gal. 1:13–14), he had a life-changing encounter with the risen Christ (Acts 9:1–6; 22:1–16; 26:1–18; 1 Cor. 15:3–10) and came to believe that he had been made an apostle to the Gentiles. The literature by and about Paul creates its own problems, as it portrays Paul and his teaching in contradictory ways. These contradictions are both the result of and the cause of the radically differing views of Paul held by Christians in the first centuries.

There are seven letters in the New Testament that are generally recognized as having come from Paul himself: Romans, 1 and 2 Corinthians, Galatians, Philippians, 1 Thessalonians, and Philemon, all probably written in the 50s. Six other letters in the NT (Ephesians, Colossians, 2 Thessalonians, 1 and 2 Timothy, Titus) claim Paul's authorship. They were likely written by admirers of Paul who sought to adapt his message to the changing circumstances of the church. Among them, 2 Thessalonians warns against letters falsely attributed to Paul (2:2), despite its being likely in that number. Other writings that falsely claimed Paul's authorship (e.g., *3 Corinthians*) were not included in the canon.

A further source of confusion was that the Paul encountered in his undisputed letters differs significantly from the Paul of the Acts of the Apostles (probably written 80–85). For example, Acts 9:22–30 speaks of Paul, immediately after his conversion, making a trip to Jerusalem to meet the apostles (presumably for instruction and authorization of his mission), whereas Galatians 1:15–17 insists otherwise. Similarly, Acts 15 presents Peter and Paul in agreement over the mission to the Gentiles; Galatians 2:11–14 describes their disagreement. Acts 13:14–52 and 17:2–6 give the impression that Paul preached first to the Jews in a locality before he went to the Gentiles; yet Paul indicates that his work was with the pagans (1 Thess. 1:9–10 and 1 Cor. 12:2). By the second century the portrayal of Paul found in Acts trumped his self-description in his epistles.

The picture regarding Paul was further complicated by later documents that chose to emphasize particular elements of Paul's teaching to the neglect of his larger message. In one of these, *The Acts of Paul and Thecla* (late second cent.), Paul's ascetic teaching, especially on chastity, was presented as the focus of his preaching.

In the second century and beyond the figure of Paul to whom Christians appealed was a product of this literary mix. Both supporters and detractors could emphasize particular elements according to how they understood Paul. Marcion rejected the Old Testament with its law and its creator God. He believed that Paul, alone among the apostles, had understood Jesus' message of grace. In contrast, Ebionites insisted that observance of the OT law was binding on followers of Jesus; Paul, they believed, had distorted Jesus' message. Gnostics (especially Valentinus and his followers) sought to present themselves as comprehending the true message of Paul, which others had misunderstood. Nevertheless, many of those whose views would later be labeled as orthodox claimed Paul as their own. Irenaeus, for example, employed Paul not only against the gnostics but also in the statement of his own views regarding the unity of God, the incarnation, and the renewal of humanity.

In the centuries that followed, various elements from the large tradition associated with Paul were employed by a range of theologians in both East and West in the development of Christian theology, anthropology, and ethics.

Bart D. Ehrman, *Lost Scriptures* (2003); Ehrman, *Lost Christianities* (2003); W. S. Babcock, *Paul and the Legacies of Paul* (1990).

REBECCA H. WEAVER

Paul of Burgos (1351–1435), a converted rabbi and biblical exegete who was baptized Paul de Santa Maria (1390) and who became bishop of Cartagena on the Mediterranean coast (c. 1405), lord chancellor of Castile, and archbishop of Burgos (1415). Born Solomon-ha-Levi, he was thoroughly conversant in talmudic and rabbinical literature. King Henry of Castile appointed him keeper of the royal seal in 1406 and made him tutor of his son (John II of Castile). He obtained his doctorate in theology in Paris, where he became a proponent of the theology of Thomas Aquinas. A bitter enemy of his former coreligionists, he wrote the *Dialogus Pauli et Sauli contra Judaeos, sive Scrutinium scripturarum (Dialogue of Paul and Saul against the Jews, or Investigation of the Scriptures)*. He is most famous for his affirmations and criticisms of the *Literal Postill* of Nicholas of Lyra. The *Additiones (Additions)* were originally marginal notes (1,100 in all)

written in a volume of Lyra's *Postilla* that he sent to his son Alfonso. Many of them implied that Nicholas was not as competent in Hebrew as was thought and that Nicholas misinterpreted Thomas Aquinas when he quoted him. Paul had a more sophisticated understanding of Islam than did Nicholas.

S. Brant, ed., *Biblia Latina cum glossa ordinaria Walafridi Strabonis aliorumque et interlineari Anselmi Laudenensis et cum postillis ac moralitatibus Nicolai de Lyra et expositionibus Guillelmi Britonis in omnes prologos S. Hieronymi et additionibus Pauli Burgensis replicisque Mattiae Doering* (1498); *Dialogus Pauli et Sauli contra Judaeos, sive Scrutinium scripturarum* (1507); P. Krey, "Nicholas of Lyra and Paul of Burgos on Islam," in J. Tolan, ed., *Medieval Christian Perceptions of Islam* (1996).

PHILIP D. W. KREY

Paul of Samosata, bishop of Antioch, Syria (260–268). Because the authentic writings of condemned bishops are seldom extant, the main sources about Paul of Samosata are Eusebius's *Ecclesiastical History* (7.28–30) and heresiologies (Epiphanius, *Panarion* 65; Theodoret, *History of Heresies* 2.8). Paul of Samosata is depicted as a high-ranking royal official with bodyguards and secretaries, who inappropriately combined the worldly pomp with his ecclesiastical office. The bishop was opposed by local clergy years before the Synod of Antioch finally condemned him in 268. Nevertheless, it took an imperial decree to remove him from his office. The *Acts* of the council cannot be seen as mere later Apollinarian forgeries. Paul of Samosata's theological error was to teach an adoptionist Monarchian doctrine, which ultimately proved to be unorthodox, as certain Alexandrian Trinitarian views prevailed. He seems to have argued that the Logos was not a distinct divine *hypostasis* ("subsistence") but a divine enabling power operative in the man Jesus. The condemned bishop refused to confess that "the Son of God descended from heaven" (Eusebius, *Hist. eccl.* 7.30). Paul of Samosata affirmed the Logos as *homoousios* ("consubstantial") with the Father, but it is unclear what exactly he meant by that.

S. W. Coonrad, "Adoptionism: The History of a Doctrine" (PhD diss., 1999); U. M. Lang, "The Christological Controversy at the Synod of Antioch in 268/9," *JTS* 51, no. 1 (2000): 54–80.

TARMO TOOM

Paula (c. 346–404), Roman ascetic, monastic founder, friend of Jerome. A wealthy young widow with five children, Paula was among the prominent Roman women (including Marcella and others) who, beginning in the middle of the fourth century, practiced a kind of "home monasticism" that included physical asceticism and small group gatherings for scriptural study and prayer. When Jerome arrived in Rome (382) he was active in these circles, and Paula became his close friend and supporter. Along with her daughter, Eustochium, she traveled to Bethlehem after Jerome (385) and established monasteries for both men and women. The women were separated for meals and work according to social class and followed a strict regimen and discipline. In his letter to Eustochium after Paula's death, Jerome describes Paula's acts of piety in her pilgrimage through the Holy Land and to the monks in Egypt, her love of Scripture, her knowledge of Hebrew, her extreme physical renunciations (including fasting, weeping, and avoidance of baths), her grief at her daughter Blaesilla's death (which some attributed to severe fasting under the influence of Jerome), and her honorable death. Palladius implies that Paula was oppressed by Jerome's "envy."

Jerome, *Letters* 39, 45, 46, 108; Palladius, *Lausiac History* 36.6, 41.2; E. A. Clark, *Jerome, Chrysostom, and Friends* (1979), 35–106; J. N. D. Kelly, *Jerome* (1975), 91–103.

TERESA M. SHAW

Paulinus of Nola (c. 352–431), Roman aristocrat, poet, monk, and bishop. Meropius Pontius Paulinus was born in Aquitaine, raised in a Christian milieu, and educated at Bordeaux, where Ausonius was among his teachers. Family connections and Ausonius's support facilitated a senatorial career in Italy (c. 376–383), including the governorship of Campania. Renewed residency in Gaul and Spain (c. 383–395) was punctuated by marriage to Therasia, baptism, and a surprising declaration of secular renunciation. Ordained to the priesthood at Barcelona in 394, Paulinus returned to Italy in 395 to settle as a monk at the shrine of St. Felix outside Campanian Nola. There he lived, eventually as bishop, until his death.

The ascetic conversion from a noble background such as Paulinus's was controversial. A celebrated exchange of poems with Ausonius reveals Paulinus justifying himself before his mystified former teacher. Others, however, capitalized on the exemplary value of Paulinus's decision to give up his wealth, live simply, and serve God beside the tomb of a third-century confessor. Paulinus's story resists dichotomous reduction. He renounced his riches and secular authority amid the competitive tensions of a Christianizing society in which asceticism was a nascent ideology, monasticism was still in the formative stages, and the spiritual standing of the wealthy was rarely questioned. Paulinus transformed his preconversion social network into valuable epistolary and amicable relations with leading churchmen and Christian thinkers, including Sulpicius Severus, Jerome, Augustine, Rufinus of Aquileia, and the family of Melania the Elder. He used his wealth for almsgiving but also for lavishly rebuilding Felix's shrine. He redefined classical ideas of friendship and selfhood, while his poems achieved a new level of sophistication in the reconceptualization of Latin poetics. The prominent place held by the cult of Felix in his understanding of identity and piety is illustrated by his *Natalicia* composed annually for Felix's feast. In his final years Paulinus emerged as a leading Italian bishop.

C. Conybeare, *Paulinus Noster* (2000); Paulinus, *Epistulae and Carmina*, ed. G. Hartel (1894; rev. ed., 1999); Paulinus, *Letters*, trans. P. G. Walsh, 2 vols. (1966, 1967); Paulinus, *Poems*, trans. P. G. Walsh (1975); D. Trout, *Paulinus of Nola* (1999).

DENNIS E. TROUT

Peace and War in Christian Thought Roland Bainton presented three distinguishable Christian attitudes toward war and peace: the crusade, pacifism, and just war. These categories may be viewed as ideal types that allow one to sort through historical material and draw meaningful comparisons. Some data, of course, do not conform to these rubrics.

The crusade came to quintessential expression in the Middle Ages, though clear roots are present in the holy war tradition of the Old Testament (e.g., Deut. 7:2, 16; 20:16–18). The First Crusade, preached by Pope Urban II at Clermont in 1095, successfully captured Jerusalem in 1099. The Second Crusade, preached by Bernard of Clairvaux at Vézelay in 1146, was a demoralizing fiasco, though the loss of Jerusalem and nearly all of Palestine to Saladin in 1187 engendered renewed activity. It should be noted, however, that scholars now question the custom of numbering these campaigns and limiting them to the eleventh through thirteenth centuries. There were many, many expeditions. They were directed to the west as well as the east (e.g., Spain), and attacked internal enemies (e.g., the Albigensian Crusade in France) as well as external foes. The movement plausibly extended beyond the Spanish Armada of 1588. The spirit of the Crusades was institutionalized in part in military orders such as the Templars, but the influence of the Crusades was vastly larger. They played a decisive role in forming and differentiating the Christian West from Byzantine Christianity and from Islam.

An understanding of crusade that extends beyond its medieval roots suggests as a crucial ingredient the willingness to use lethal violence in the service of a loyalty that links indissolubly the cause of God with a temporal political goal. This loyalty promotes a Manichean dualism; thus, supporters of the good cause inalterably oppose others as an evil empire. It also yields optimism about pursuing the cause, a propensity to reduce political problems to military solutions, and a tendency to ignore moral restraints. This definition provides grounds for counting as crusaders sixteenth-century Anabaptist revolutionaries such as Melchior Hoffmann and Thomas Müntzer as well as Puritan revolutionaries in seventeenth-century England, but probably not Joan of Arc (d. 1431). Arguments continue today in the United States about whether to label various military campaigns as crusades, such as the Spanish-American War, World War I, and more recent engagements.

Christian pacifism is difficult to define with precision, though pacifists are clearly "against" war and "for" peace. But how extensive should opposition be to lethal violence? What is the relationship between responsibility to the state and peacemaking as protest? Is nonviolent resistance a strategy toward political goals, or a right-making characteristic of conduct? Different answers to these and other questions yield different stances. Almost every variant, however, is best comprehended as a set of practices that emanate from a way of life, not as conduct derived from moral principles. This way of life is anchored in the life and teachings of Jesus, perhaps especially the "hard sayings" of Matthew 5:38–48 and other parts of the Sermon on the Mount.

Pacifism appears in every age, though never dominantly after Constantine. Tertullian (d. 220) in the Latin West and Origen (d. 254) in the Greek East are early examples, and many monastic communities embodied pacifist tendencies up to and through the 1600s. The Czech Brethren and Waldenses were pacifist. Pacifism was institutionalized and expressed in a variety of sixteenth-century Anabaptist communions such as the Swiss Brethren including Michael Sattler (d. 1527), Dutch communities including Menno Simons (d. 1561), and Moravian or Hutterian groups including Peter Riedemann (d. 1556). It was also expressed in different forms by figures as diverse as Erasmus (d. 1536) on the Continent and by the Quakers and George Fox (c. 1691) in England.

Lisa Cahill suggests that Christian pacifism takes two forms. One sees discipleship as witnessing obedience to the example of the nonviolent and nonresistant Jesus; the other sees discipleship as love of neighbor embodied in compassion and service. In the United States, John Howard Yoder and Stanley Hauerwas express the former, while Dorothy Day, Thomas Merton, and certain representatives of the Social Gospel represent the latter.

Following the establishment of Constantinian Christianity in the fourth century, the church began to think in terms of the political responsibilities of the state. Augustine (d. 430), drawing on Ambrose and Stoic natural law, is credited with introducing just-war elements into Christianity. Thence developed an evolving and multifaceted tradition, in canon law by Gratian (d. 1160?) and successors, and by theologians including Thomas Aquinas (d. 1274), Victoria (d. 1546), Suarez (d. 1617), and Grotius (d. 1645). In various forms, this tradition found expression in the leaders or confessions of the established churches: Catholic, Lutheran, Reformed, and Anglican. In the United States, whose ethos often oscillates between crusading and pacifist sensibilities, just war thinking largely disappeared until its retrieval following the Vietnam conflict, perhaps most clearly symbolized by *The Challenge of Peace* (1983) issued by the National Conference of Catholic Bishops.

Just war theory assumes that some wars may be justified and some may not. Its purpose is to provide a principled basis for drawing distinctions between rejecting all wars and appealing (only) to military necessity. However, no consensus obtains about the exact meaning or the proper ordering of just war categories, though widespread agreement exists that questions of *jus ad bellum* (whether to go to war) include considerations of competent authority, just cause, right intention, last resort, relative justice, proportionality, and reasonable hope for success, and that questions of *jus in bello* (conduct in war) include considerations of discrimination and proportionality. These norms provide guidance, but they also seek to illumine, as they are answers to questions inevitably posed by violence. A noteworthy recent development exposited by Richard B. Miller is a tentative agreement between some just warriors and some pacifists that, despite genuine disagreements, the two traditions have enough in common to engage in genuine dialogue about mutual concerns. Meanwhile, debate continues whether wars of liberation are best conceived as just, as crusades, or as something entirely different.

R. Bainton, *Christian Attitudes toward War and Peace* (1960); L. S. Cahill, *Love Your Enemies* (1994); J. T. Johnson, *Morality and Contemporary Warfare* (1999); R. B. Miller, *Interpretations of Conflict* (1991); J. Riley-Smith, ed., *The Oxford History of the Crusades* (1999); L. B. Walters Jr., *Five Classic Just-War Theories* (1971).

CHARLES M. SWEZEY

Peace of Augsburg Having failed to impose a military end to the Reformation, Emperor Charles V agreed to terms with the political leadership of the Lutherans. The Peace of Augsburg (1555) effectively settled the religious question in Germany for the next half century. Its most important provision recognized a principle originally proposed by the Diet of Speyer (1526) that rulers had the right to determine their subjects' religion, a principle later expressed as *cuius regio, eius religion*, literally "his the rule, whose the religion." Though formally limited, the agreement effectively allowed for territorial determination of religion. Lutheranism had formal, legal standing in those sovereignties of the empire that had established it.

Two points in the agreement eventually proved its undoing. The ecclesiastical reservation settled property disputes with the papacy, specifying that in the case of future religious changes, the papacy would retain ownership of properties of bishops and abbots that turned Lutheran. Lutheran and Roman Catholic negotiators also agreed to exclude the other parties in the Reformation. The emergence of Calvinism as a powerful and aggressive alternative eventually made both provisions unworkable, a critical factor in the Thirty Years' War.

O. Christin, "Making Peace," in *A Companion to the Reformation World*, ed. R. Po-chia Hsia (2004).

JAMES ARNE NESTINGEN

Peace of God *see* Truce of God

Peasants' War Insurrection by German peasants in 1524–1526 due to economic, social, and political exploitation. Its first phase, from mid-1524 to early 1525, was similar to a general strike, as peasants refused to pay taxes and feudal dues. In March 1525 one of these unofficial alliances took a formal structure as the Christian Union of Upper Swabia and issued a manifesto, the *Twelve Articles*. The Christian Union swore to protect the historic rights of peasants and to defend the Word of God. By linking their demands for social and political reforms to defense of the Word of God, the peasants hoped to connect their movement to the reforms of Martin Luther. The *Twelve Articles* struck a popular nerve, and some 25,000 copies were distributed across southern and central Germany. Though Luther rejected the connection between his reforms and the peasants' grievances, he did believe that the peasants had many just demands and attempted to mediate between them and the princes. In mid-April 1525 Luther published two pamphlets in the attempt to find a solution to the crisis. The first, *An Admonition to Peace*, placed much of the responsibility for the crisis on the shoulders of unjust princes. The second, *The Weingarten Treaty*, republished a treaty made between a group of peasants and the Swabian League that Luther believed provided a model solution for the crisis. Luther's attempts to mediate, however, had little impact. Thomas Müntzer, an apocalyptic itinerant preacher and former follower of Luther, seized on the demands of the peasants and through his preaching emboldened their dissatisfactions. The peasants formed an army to achieve their demands and sacked monasteries, convents, castles, and villages as they marched. These attacks turned Luther against the peasants, and he published a blistering critique, *Against the Murdering Hordes of the Other Peasants*. On May 15, the princes attacked the peasant army at Frankenhausen, and thousands of peasants were horribly slaughtered by the better armed, trained, and equipped soldiers of the princes. Müntzer was captured and later executed in Mülhausen. The defeat in Frankenhausen spelled the end of the Peasants' War, though for more than a year small bands of peasants continued to fight in the Black Forest and the mountains of the Tirol.

M. G. Baylor, *The Radical Reformation* (1991); P. Blickle, *The Revolution of 1525* (1985);

T. Scott and R. W. Scribner Jr., eds., *The German Peasants' War: A History in Documents* (1991).

DAVID WHITFORD

Pecham, John (c. 1230–1291), Franciscan intellectual and church administrator who was born at Patcham (Sussex). In the 1240s, he may have been Roger Bacon's pupil at the arts faculty at Paris. During the 1250s, when he was at Oxford studying under Adam Marsh, he entered the Franciscan order. At that time, he may already have been a master of arts and in holy orders. Between 1257 and 1259, Pecham returned to Paris to start his study in theology, and he was a regent master in 1269–1270. Until about 1272, he remained lecturer at the Franciscan friary in Paris. He then became regent master in theology at Oxford, until his election as provincial in 1275. In 1277, Pecham became lecturer in theology at the papal university (*lector sacri palatii*). His nomination as archbishop of Canterbury occurred in 1279. During his academic years at Paris, Pecham became involved in several doctrinal controversies, such as the mendicant struggle and the debates about the unicity of substantial form and the world's eternity. The latter two brought him in contact with his Parisian contemporary Thomas Aquinas. The debate over the unicity of substantial form—that is, whether the powers of the soul are really distinct from one another and from the soul—was continued in 1286, when Pecham issued a condemnation against the Dominican Richard Knapwell. His treatises on optics became standard textbooks and were much quoted. In addition, he wrote quodlibetal questions, disputations, and treatises on Franciscan spirituality and poverty against the Dominicans (in particular his predecessor, Archbishop Robert Kilwardby).

D. L. Douie, *Archbishop Pecham* (1952); A. Boureau, *Théologie, science et censure au XIIIe siècele: Le cas de Jean Peckham* (1999).

J. M. M. H. THIJSSEN

Pelagius (c. 350–c. 425), Christian ascetic, moralist, and exegete from Great Britain, whose name is associated with Pelagianism. Pelagius arrived in Rome around 380. His purpose for migrating to Italy remains unknown. While in Rome, he acquired a reputation as a moral reformer along with the admiration of others for living an exemplary life. Often referred to as a monk, he rejected any formal affiliation with a religious community. During the 390s he encountered Caelestius and Rufinus the Syrian, both of whom were to exert an important influence on the Pelagian controversy. Sometime between 400 and 405, Pelagius voiced his dismay at Augustine's doctrine of grace when he overheard a bishop reciting the passage in the *Confessions*, "Give what you command, and command what you will." In Rome Pelagius began formulating his ideas on the Christian life in works such as *The Trinity*, *Excerpts from the Divine Scriptures*, and the *Expositions of Paul's Epistles*.

In 409 Pelagius and Caelestius escaped Rome before the Gothic invasion. They resided briefly in Sicily, then traveled to Africa after the sack of Rome. Within two years after his arrival, without ever seeing Augustine, Pelagius departed for Palestine. Caelestius remained in Carthage and began propagating antitraducianist (see *Traducianism*) ideas, perhaps inspired by Rufinus the Syrian's denial of original sin. When Caelestius refused to alter his views on human nature and the baptism of infants, Augustine and the African bishops condemned him. Shortly thereafter, Caelestius left for the East.

Pelagius aroused controversy in the East by attacking Jerome's writings. On the defensive, he was forced to extrapolate the anthropological basis of the ascetic practices he enjoined, as in his *Letter to Demetrias*. In his reply *On Nature*, he maintained that human beings not only possess the faculty of choice but also have instilled in their nature the strength needed to live a good life. He identified this natural capability, or possibility of sinlessness, with the grace of creation.

Pelagius's work came to Augustine's attention in 415 when Timasius and James, former followers of Pelagius, forwarded a copy of *On Nature* to Hippo. Augustine responded to Pelagius's errors in *On Nature and Grace* and dispatched the Spanish presbyter Orosius to Jerome to warn him about Pelagius's views. Pelagius avoided condemnation at the Synod of Diospolis, but Augustine, Jerome, and Orosius continued to attack his writings. Despite Pelagius's attempt to clarify his position in *The Defense of Free Will* (416), Innocent I upheld the decision of the councils of Milevis and Carthage that condemned both Caelestius and Pelagius. In 418 Innocent's successor, Zosimus, issued the *Epistola Tractoria* that effectively ended Pelagius's role in the controversy. From then on, the excommunicated bishop Julian of Eclanum took up the Pelagian cause, counterattacking

Augustine's doctrines of grace and original sin until the latter's death in 430.

In order to understand Pelagius's role as a moral reformer, it is important to distinguish Pelagianism as a descriptive term for a heresy from a Christian ascetic movement of the late fourth and fifth centuries. Pelagianism in the latter sense of the term encompasses a broad range of ideas and personalities that eventually came to be associated with Pelagius's name. Though at the epicenter of the controversy, Pelagius might not have gained the notoriety that he did if it were not for the contributions of others such as Rufinus the Syrian, Caelestius, and Julian of Eclanum. Nor is it fair to attribute all of their ideas to Pelagius, since each reacted differently to asceticism.

At its roots, Pelagianism was a lay movement composed of fervent Christians who deplored the laxness and indifference in the church. In Rome it attracted wealthy patrons who were eager to distribute their possessions to the poor and devote their lives to Christian practice. The theological storm that swirled around Pelagius and his followers emerged only after they attempted to provide a rational justification for the reforms they had initiated. It took an experienced pastor and bishop like Augustine to question the orthodoxy of a movement caught up in a form of Christian perfectionism that disputed the necessity of the redemption.

G. I. Bonner, *Augustine and Modern Research on Pelagius* (1972); T. de Bruyn, trans., *Pelagius' Commentary on St. Paul's Epistle to the Romans* (1993); CPL (1995), 728–59; G. de Plinval, *Pélage, ses écrits, sa vie, et son reforme* (1943); B. R. Rees, trans., *The Letters of Pelagius and His Followers* (1991); Rees, *Pelagius: A Reluctant Heretic* (1988); A. Souter, trans., *Pelagius's Expositions of the Thirteen Epistles of St. Paul*, 3 vols. (1922–1931).

MARIANNE DJUTH

Pellikan, Konrad (1478–1556), Swiss Reformed theologian and biblical scholar. A native of Alsace, Pellikan studied in Heidelberg, where he became a humanist. In 1502 he moved to Basel and collaborated on the publication of Luther's writings and several church fathers, notably Amerbach's edition of Augustine. In 1525 he was called to Zurich as professor of Greek and Hebrew. He had a considerable influence on the Zurich translation of the Bible and was an important biblical exegete. Pellikan was foremost a Hebrew scholar, and he completed the first Christian Hebrew grammar. Over time he gained a considerable knowledge of postbiblical Jewish literature, partly through study with rabbis. His attitude toward Judaism reflected none of the prejudice common to his time.

P. L. Nyhus, "Casper Schatzgeyer and Conrad Pellican: The Triumph of Dissension in the Early 16th Century," *ARG* 61 (1970): 179–204; C. Zürcher, *Konrad Pellikans Wirken in Zürich, 1526–1556* (1975).

GREGORY J. MILLER

Penance For Christians throughout the centuries Jesus Christ has been the source of reconciliation. The early church seemed to have difficulties in coming to terms with the gospel emphasis on compassion, forgiveness, and reconciliation, and the question of great or eternal sin. During the persecutions of the third and fourth centuries, the question culminated when Christians, who, to avoid further punishment during a persecution, had delivered holy things (Bibles, liturgical objects, etc.) to temporal authorities for destruction, asked to be reconciled with the Christian church. While Cyprian established the principle of lifelong penance, including the separation from Communion, Ambrose stressed penance as a healing process involving conversion of heart and life.

Influenced by Iro-Scottish and Anglo-Saxon monks, the tradition of tariff penance was established in Western Europe. The understanding of penance shifted from a merely public character to a more private one. A new emphasis on penance as satisfaction arose with attempts to make the punishment match the sin. Satisfaction became more punitive than medicinal.

Tariff penance being too rigorous and departing from its original purpose, the Fourth Lateran Council (1215; see *Lateran Councils*) established the sacramental understanding of penance with its decree that all members of the church should confess their sins to their priests at least once a year around Easter. The Fathers established the scholastic understanding that baptism removes the guilt of original sin but not its effect of making all humans prone to sin. When the grace from baptism is lost by "actual" mortal sin, the sacrament of penance is available to restore grace as many times as relapse into sin should make necessary. Early scholastic theologians distinguished between the external sacrament, confession and satisfaction, and the internal sacrament. While Peter Abelard and Peter Lombard claimed interior penance, as the result of the grace of perfect sorrow from the motive of pure love, to be the main element, Hugh of St. Victor and his followers insisted that the sinner was liable to eternal punishment unless he was first absolved by the priest. Finally, Thomas Aquinas taught that absolution is the "form" of the sacrament. Thus, late medieval scholasticism stressed more the ecclesiastical distribution of grace—the absolution of the priest—while the more spiritual understanding of penance in the eleventh and twelfth centuries became relevant for the reformation movement in the early sixteenth century.

The Wittenberg Reformation reacted against the corruption of the sacrament of penance through the practice of indulgences. Although evangelical theology still held three traditional elements of penance—contrition, confession, and absolution—and understood it as the third of the evangelical sacraments (along with baptism and the Eucharist), Luther and his followers weighed them differently than their predecessors. The purpose of the absolution is reduced to arousing in the sinner faith or confidence in God's mercy, since it is by such faith that the sinner becomes righteous in the eyes of God. Contrition is the first part of penance, but the contrition in question is not sorrow for sin but the terror of a stricken conscience when faced with God's threats of punishment through the law. The gospel promises the forgiveness of sin and the reconciliation with God through Christ, which yields faith or confidence in God's mercy.

The Swiss and southern German reformers, followed by Calvin, ultimately accepted Luther's reformulation of penance and justification but stressed the connection between repentance and the penitent, regenerate life. The Genevan Reformation especially stressed the lifelong practice of sobriety and taming of the flesh. Calvin still tried to eliminate false notions of human effort and emphasized internal contrition over external acts.

The Council of Trent rejected the Protestant critique entirely and made traditional scholastic definitions a rule of faith: penance is a virtue, a sacrament, and a work of satisfaction. Auricular confession to a priest is divinely ordained and necessary to salvation. The priest's absolution does more than declare that God has already forgiven a contrite sinner and more than confirm the promise contained in the gospel. It corresponds to the active contrition and satisfaction of the sinner, all of which synergistically yield salvation.

P. Anciaux, *Le Sacrament de la penitence* (1957); L. Braeckmans, *Confession et Communion au moyen âge et au concile de Trente* (1971); J. D. Crichton, *Christian Celebration* (1993); J. Dallen, *The Reconciling Community* (1986); J. Fitzsimons, ed., *Penance, Virtue, and Sacrament* (1969); J. T. A. Gunstone, *The Liturgy of Penance* (1966); M. Hebbelthwaite and K. Donovan, *The Theology of Penance* (1979); S. Hamilton, *The Practice of Penance, 900–1050* (2001); B. Poschmann, *Penance and the Anointing of the Sick* (1964); T. N. Tentler, *Sin and Confession on the Eve of the Reformation* (1977); C. Vogel, *Le Pécheur et la Pénitence dans l'Eglise ancienne* (1966); Vogel, *Le Pécheur et la Pénitence au moyen âge* (1969); O. Watkins, *A History of Penance* (1920).

MARKUS WRIEDT

Pepin III   *see* Carolingian church

Pérez de Pineda, Juan (c. 1500–1568), Spanish Reformed minister in Geneva and France, translator of the New Testament, and author. Before leaving Seville around 1549, Pérez de Pineda was rector of the Colegio de los Niños de la Doctrina, an orphanage that in the next decade became, along with the cathedral and the Hieronymite monastery of San Isidro, one of the institutional focuses for the diffusion of reformist ideas in Seville. From 1556 to his death in Paris, he served as a minister in Geneva (c. 1558–1561) and France (Blois, c. 1562–1563) and as chaplain to Renée of France (c. 1564–1568). He was responsible for a significant number of translations and original writings, including his Spanish translations of the New Testament (Geneva, 1556) and the book of Psalms (Geneva, 1557). He also edited Juan de Valdés's commentaries on Romans (Geneva, 1556) and 1 Corinthians (Geneva, 1557). These works were chiefly intended for Spain, especially Seville, where a growing movement of religious dissidents was already in gestation.

J. S. Herrero, "La Sevilla del Renacimiento (1474–1581)," in *Historia de las Diócesis Españolas*, vol. 10 (2002), 131–87; A. G. Kinder, "Juan Pérez de Pineda (Pierius): A Spanish Calvinist Minister of the Gospel in 16th-Century Geneva," *BHS* 53 (1976): 283–300; J. C. Nieto, *El Renacimiento y la otra España* (1997).

RADY ROLDÁN-FIGUEROA

Perfectionism Given varied expression in Christian history, perfectionism projects moral or religious perfection as a realizable goal of human beings either in this life or the life to come. Historically it has appeared both as a well-developed soteriological or eschatological principle and as a spiritual or ecclesial impulse resonant with the apocalyptic dimension of the gospel. The biblical language of "perfection," as in Jesus' dictum, "Be perfect, as your Father in heaven is perfect" (Matt. 5:8), or in Hebrews, which depicts the Savior as perfected through suffering (Heb. 2:10; 5:8–9), has proven conducive to diverse interpretations.

Patristic spiritual doctrine was an early and fertile ground for perfectionist notions. The Greek Fathers speculated that Adam and his posterity had fallen from an original paradisiacal perfection characterized by incorruptibility and impassibility. Clement of Alexandria, Origen, and later the Cappadocian Fathers envisioned the Christian life as a process of divine pedagogy wherein the Logos, even after his incarnation, was guiding fallen souls toward the recovery of that original perfection. Gregory of Nyssa envisioned this process as one of perpetual striving (*epektasis*) since the goal was the infinite perfection of God himself. In the West, Pelagian perfectionism stemmed from an understanding of grace as communicated through human moral freedom hampered but not fundamentally corrupted by original sin. Augustine acknowledged the conversion and perseverance of the fallen will by grace, but believed that ultimate perfection came only in the state of future beatitude. He applied a similar logic to the earthly perfectibility of the church itself.

Primitive ascetic groups such as the Montanists adhered to a rigorous perfectionism grounded in their claim of a fresh revelation of God's Spirit. The burgeoning ascetic and monastic movements of the fourth century and beyond responded to the gospel's eschatological message by establishing disciplines and forming communities that would pursue moral or spiritual perfection in advance of the coming kingdom of Christ. The projected "perfection" was not a state of sinlessness but a mature culmination of the interconnected virtues of humility, self-control, charity, and the like.

Medieval Western expressions of the spiritual ideal of perfection were quite varied. Twelfth-century followers of the visionary Joachim of Fiore, for example, imagined a quasi-utopian "third age" in which the church would receive direct revelation from the Holy Spirit and be led by a monastic elite who would preside over the spiritual perfecting of all the faithful. Thomas Aquinas, on the other hand, qualified the prospect of human perfection, taking Colossians 3:14 (charity as the "bond of perfection") as his starting point. Perfection was unattainable in this life relative to the totality of the loved object, God, and attainable in heaven only so far as the Christian's entire affection for God was concerned. Nevertheless, with respect to a believer's completely unobstructed affectionate movement toward God, perfection was possible in the earthly pilgrimage (*Summa theologiae* 2a, 2ae, q. 184).

By contrast the Protestant reformers, with their emphasis on human degradation before the gracious God, largely reiterated the Augustinian position. In the era of burgeoning Pietism and evangelicalism, however, a new stress on sanctification matched the reformers' preoccupation with justification. Quakers looked to the "inner light" of divine grace to bear fruit outwardly in the godly life. John Wesley found new inspiration from early Christian ascetics and envisioned perfection not as absolute sinlessness but as a dynamic relation of love and deliverance. Sanctificationist emphases prevailed among many later evangelicals. In the nineteenth century, Congregationalist Charles Finney and the leaders of the Wesleyan Holiness movement such as Phoebe Palmer espoused a state of "entire sanctification" as the full fruition of the cooperation of grace and free will and the presentation of a blameless believer before God (cf. 1 Thess. 3:13; 5:23). This view prompted a new round of skepticism from staunch Calvinists in the twentieth century such as B. B. Warfield, who branded such perfectionism as Neo-Pelagianism.

S. M. Burgess, ed., *Reaching Beyond: Chapters in the History of Perfectionism* (1986); R. N. Flew, *The Idea of Perfection in Christian Theology* (1934); J. K. Grider, *Entire Sanctification* (1980); B. B. Warfield, *Perfectionism*, 2 vols. (1931).

PAUL M. BLOWERS

Perkins, William (1558–1602), leading Puritan divine during the reign of Elizabeth I. Born in Warwickshire and educated at Christ's College, Cambridge, Perkins studied under Laurence Chaderton, graduating in 1581, and was to spend most of his adult life as a Fellow. A dramatic religious conversion in 1584 apparently transformed his life, and he started preaching to prisoners in the town jail and was then appointed lecturer at Great St. Andrew's Church, a post he held from 1584 to 1602. He was also a Fellow at Christ's from 1584 to 1595, when he married and thus had to resign. Perkins's connection to Puritanism is evident in his objections, from 1587 onward, to the practice of kneeling at Communion, and for his involvement in 1589 in an attempt to promote a Presbyterian book of discipline, an act that led to a summons before the Star Chamber (where the king's royal council met) in 1591, although he appears to have acted more as a witness for the prosecution than as a defendant in this case. Indeed, his writings show little interest in ecclesiological matters.

His major significance lies in his writings, which articulated a vigorous form of experimental piety rooted firmly in confessional Reformed orthodoxy, and his impact upon a generation of students at Cambridge that was to spearhead the theological and ecclesiastical tenets of Reformed theology with renewed vigor in the early seventeenth century.

D. K. McKim, *Ramism in William Perkins' Theology* (1987); R. A. Muller, *Christ and the Decree* (1986).

CARL TRUEMAN

Perpetua and Felicitas (d. 203), martyrs.
The poignant stories of Vibia Perpetua, a young Roman matron still nursing her newborn son when arrested, and of Felicitas, the pregnant (possibly) slave girl who gave birth to a daughter in prison shortly before both women were thrown to the beasts in the amphitheater at Carthage, are extant in the form of "passions" and "acts."

The original Latin *passio* contains Perpetua's own account of her house arrest, baptism, imprisonment, trial, condemnation, and dreamlike visions. The editor (perhaps, but probably not, Tertullian) relates the martyrs' ultimate fate, asserting the significance of new prophecies, visions, and "deeds of heroism." This has led to speculation that Perpetua and Felicitas were adherents of the "New Prophecy" (Montanism) or that, at least, the editor was. However, North African Christianity as a whole valued prophecies, visions, and martyrdoms highly. Regardless, there is no evidence that the martyrs belonged to a schismatic form of Montanism. Perpetua, Felicitas (with Saturnus, Saturninus, Revocatus, Secundulus), died as catholic martyrs, probably on March 7, 203, during birthday celebrations for Geta, son of Septimius Severus. That the martyrdoms

resulted from Septimius's edict forbidding conversion to Judaism and Christianity is doubtful, as the late evidence for this edict is suspect.

A substantially revised edition erroneously relegates the martyrdoms to the persecution of Valerian and Gallienus. It also deletes the original preface, eliminating the *passio*'s "Montanist-sounding" framework. Whether this revised edition is consciously anti-Montanist or primarily intended to reverse the untraditional role of women exhibited by the *passio* is debatable. The increasing tendency to downgrade the authority of Perpetua and Felicitas, however, is clearly evident in the *passio*'s manuscript tradition, Augustine's sermons, and the completely reshaped fourth-century Latin *acta*. The detail that Perpetua came from Thuburbo Minor is based on scribal errors.

The widespread popularity of the cult of Perpetua and Felicitas is attested by numerous inscriptions, mosaic medallions, murals, and a commemorative plaque from the Carthaginian basilica that was dedicated to their memory and contained their relics.

R. D. Butler, *The New Prophecy and "New Visions"* (2006); A. Jensen, *God's Self-Confident Daughters* (1996), 92–108; H. Musurillo, *The Acts of the Christian Martyrs* (1972), 104–31; W. Tabbernee, *Montanist Inscriptions and Testimonia* (1997), 54–59, 105–17; Tabbernee, "Perpetua, Montanism, and Christian Ministry in Carthage in c. 203 C.E.," *Perspectives in Religious Studies* 32 (2005): 421–41.

WILLIAM TABBERNEE

Persecution and Martyrdom in the Early Church
Christianity arose in a polytheistic culture that admitted a variety of religions. Why would this society persecute Christians? In antiquity it was believed that the welfare of a society depended on good relationships with the particular deities protecting that society. A population divided among a variety of cults was not a problem if in periods of stress it united to worship its patronal divinities. Christianity, however, required not the adhesion to one more god but conversion to the exclusive worship of one divinity. So the issue was not Christian's worship of their own god, but refusal to honor the divinities of the state. Jews escaped this onus because Romans considered their religion an ancient form of reverence for a national divinity, a status Christians could not share once non-Jews accepted the religion.

Persecution of Christians took several forms, both unofficial and government sponsored.

These included familial ostracism and social rejection of Jews who became Christians, such as Paul and Stephen in the New Testament and James in Eusebius (*Hist. eccl.* 2.1.2–6). There was also occasional mob violence.

State-sponsored repression was neither continuous nor uniform, but several significant periods stand out as formative of Christian memory. First, Nero's scapegoating of Christians for the fire in Rome in 64 CE produced stories of the martyrdoms of Peter and Paul and the use of Christians as human torches in imperial gardens. Imperial authorities probably rounded up Christians as putative political plotters as much as religious deviants. In the first two centuries Christianity was an underlying issue though Christians were charged with other crimes (e.g., Pliny, *Epistulae* 10.96; Justin, *Second Apology* 2; *Acts of Paul and Thecla* 16–21).

Between Nero and Septimus Severus persecution was sporadic and motivated by local governors attempting to appease civic interest groups (e.g., Polycarp in Smyrna c. 155). The first great persecution was that of Septimus Severus (r. 193–211), who forbade conversion to Christianity. Persecution was especially severe in Alexandria (Eusebius, *Hist. eccl.* 6.1–2, 4–5) and at Carthage (*Passion of Saints Perpetua and Felicity*). In the mid-third century two periods of persecution manifested the growth of Christianity and provided substantial contributions to martyrological literature. Decius and Valerian mandated universal calls to sacrifice in 249–250 and 256–260. They singled out bishops as heads of communities and upper-class Christians whose prosecution would serve as exemplary deterrents. The last major persecution in antiquity was during the reigns of Diocletian (303–305) and Galerius (303–311).

Christians were also persecuted and martyred outside the Roman Empire, especially in Persia. The prime reason was the suspicion that their religiosity made them allies of the Roman Empire with whom the Persians intermittently battled. Periods of peace alternated with periods of repression (256, 260, and 340–372) paralleling times of conflict with Rome.

The literature engendered by martyrdom is based on court accounts of trials and of patterns provided by the biblical stories of Daniel, the three youths in the furnace of Nebuchadnezzar, Susannah, and the Maccabee mother and brothers. With the exception of the martyrdom of Polycarp, the passion of Jesus is less important as a model. The apologetic speeches of martyrs find precedents in 4 Maccabees and the deaths of political prisoners and philosophers. The stories were not simply literary patterns for authors but were also models to which potential martyrs conformed their utterances and suffering.

Besides their individual stories, martyrs also inspired calendars and martyrologies. Calendars commemorated the martyrs' executions as their birthdays (*natalica*) into heaven. Carthage had a calendar by about 200 (Tertullian, *De corona* 3.3). Martyrologies were expansions of calendars that detailed the events without becoming full accounts of each death. Outstanding examples of the genre are *Martyrologium Hieronymianum* (fifth cent.) and that of Usuard (d. c. 875).

The cult of martyrs' relics is attested as early as Polycarp. It developed from annual commemorations of the dead at the sites of their burials. Eventually shrines (*martyria*) were erected on the site of the burials or at the locations of relics.

———

P. Brown, *The Cult of the Saints* (1981); A. J. Droge and J. D. Tabor, *A Noble Death: Suicide and Martyrdom among Christians and Jews in Antiquity* (1992); W. H. C. Frend, *Martyrdom and Persecution in the Early Church* (1965, 1981); J. W. van Henten and F. Avemarie, *Martyrdom and Noble Death: Selected Texts from Graeco-Roman, Jewish, and Christian Antiquity* (2002); H. Musurillo, ed. and trans., *The Acts of the Pagan Martyrs* (1954); Musurillo, *The Acts of the Christian Martyrs* (1972).

MAUREEN A. TILLEY

Peter Damian (c. 1007–1072), Italian monk, reformer, and theologian. Peter Damian, the greatest intellectual of the eleventh-century ecclesiastical reform movement, was a native of Ravenna. He worked as a teacher before becoming a monk at Fonte Avellana in 1035 and a prior in 1043, and he spent the rest of his life working to purify the church. Peter became an advisor to the reformed popes in the 1040s, and in 1057 he was named cardinal bishop of Ostia.

The large body of Peter Damian's extant works—letters, treatises, hagiography, and sermons—attests to his personal holiness and industry. He zealously advocated monastic reform, especially encouraging both monks and hermits to effect a true separation from secular society. Although he tried twice to resign his cardinalate, though, Peter was not allowed freedom to practice what he preached, both because of papal demands and his own sense of the needs of the church. While not a firebrand like Humbert or Hildebrand (Pope Gregory VII), Peter was still uncompromising in his reform efforts. The most influential of his works was the *Liber Gratissimus* (*Book of the Most Free Grace*), which compellingly laid out the principle that sacraments are gifts from God and therefore those who buy or sell them are guilty of sin—a central principle of the reform campaign. Peter Damian was declared a doctor of the church in 1828.

Peter Damian, *Letters*, trans. O. Blum (1989).
                                        PHYLLIS G. JESTICE

Peter Lombard (c. 1095–1160), scholastic theologian, bishop of Paris. Little is known about the life of this central figure of scholastic theology. Peter hailed from the region of Novara in Lombardy. Bernard of Clairvaux subsidized his studies at Reims and then recommended him (before 1136) to Gilduin, abbot of St. Victor near Paris. Peter's work shows him to have been fully conversant with the works of his contemporaries, especially Hugh of St. Victor's *De sacramentis*. By 1144 his reputation earned him mention in the *Metamorphosis Goliae,* and he participated in the Consistory of Reims (1148), which examined the writings of Gilbert of Poitiers for heresy. By 1145 he was a canon, and by 1156 archdeacon, of Notre Dame, a rare outsider in that close-knit group. He possibly spent a year and a half in Rome (1153–1154) as assistant to Bishop Theobald of Paris. Both his fame as a theologian and his tendency to find the solid middle ground surely contributed to his election in 1159 as bishop of Paris. He died a little less than a year later (July 21 or 22, 1160).

Though Peter lectured on most if not all of the books of the Bible, his written legacy is briefly told: the *Commentary* on the Psalms (before 1138; based on that of Gilbert of Poiters) and the *Collectanea* on the Pauline Epistles (the second redaction of which, c. 1158, reflects the influence of John of Damascus's *De fide orthodoxa,* which Peter may have acquired while in Rome in 1153–1154); these were later known collectively as the *glosa magnatura*. His greatest contribution to systematic theology is the *Four Books of Sentences*. He also left some fairly academic sermons.

I. C. Brady, ed., "Prolegomena," in *Sententiae in IV libris distinctae*, vol. 1, part 1 (1971); M. Colish, *Peter Lombard*, 2 vols. (1994); Peter Lombard, *Commentaria in Psalmos*, in PL 191 (1880); Peter, *Collectanea in omnes d. Pauli apostoli Epistolas* in PL 171–72 (1880); Peter, *Sententiae in IV libris distinctae*, ed. I. C. Brady, 2 vols. (3rd ed., 1971–1981); Peter, *Sermones*, in PL 171 (1893).
                                        THERESA GROSS-DIAZ

Peter of Alexandria, the seventeenth bishop of Alexandria, Egypt (300–311), head of the catechetical school, and martyr. He was imprisoned twice and finally beheaded during the persecution of Maximinus Daia. His martyrdom is described in a primarily hagiographical *Martyrdom of St. Peter*. The bishop is best known for his role in the Melitian schism and for his perhaps unconventional leniency toward readmitting the lapsed into the church, which is expressed in the fourteen canons of his Canonical Letter. His opponent, Melitus of Lycopolis, was a hard-liner, a man full of "his desire for preeminence" (Athanasius, *Ep. cler. Alex.*). Although in hiding, Peter managed to have his rival condemned and deposed by a local synod, before the Council of Nicaea finally reassured the Egyptians that Melitius indeed "deserved no mercy." Peter of Alexandria wrote several theological treatises, including *On the Resurrection*, *On the Godhead, On the Soul*, and *On Easter*, which have survived in small fragments in Greek, Latin, Syriac, and Armenian. These texts, which were later quoted in anti-Arian and anti-Origenist polemic, testify to the bishop's christological orthodoxy and to his dislike of certain themes and interpretations of Origen's theology.

Peter of Alexandria, *Works*, trans. J. B. H. Hawkins, *ANF*, vol. 6 (1957); T. Y. Malaty, *The Deans of the School of Alexandria: Pope Peter of Alexandria* (1994); T. Vivian, *St. Peter of Alexandria: Bishop and Martyr* (1988).
                                        TARMO TOOM

Peter the Fuller (d. 489), Monophysite bishop of Antioch (470–489). Peter is reported to have acquired the trade of a fuller while a monk in Constantinople, where his Monophysitism put him at odds with officials, who removed him from the monastery. Peter then traveled to Antioch, where he associated with the Apollinarians who were opposed to the bishop Martyrius. While the bishop was away seeking aid against the Monophysites, Peter claimed the see of Antioch with the support of Emperor Zeno in 470. Peter was exiled from Antioch on two occasions (472–475, 477–485) because of his Monophysitism. He was a signatory to Zeno's

Henotikon in 482, which enabled him to regain his office in Antioch. As bishop he made several changes to the liturgy in Antioch. He included reciting the Nicene Creed in the liturgy and began the blessing of the water on Epiphany, for example. His most important liturgical change was the addition of the phrase "who was crucified for us" to the Trisagion, leading to the accusation of Theopaschitism. The controversy over the addition continued into the sixth century, particularly in Syria. Peter's corpus contains primarily Syriac and Greek correspondence related to his defense of Monophysitism.

CSCO 83: 233-35, 87: 161–62; *ACO*, vol. 3, 6–25, 217–31; W. H. C. Frend, *The Rise of the Monophysite Movement* (1972); A. Grillmeier, *Christ in Christian Tradition*, vol. 2 (1995).

STEVEN A. MCKINION

Peter the Venerable (c. 1092–1156), French abbot. Peter the Venerable was the last great abbot of the Cluniac monastic confederation. He was a French noble who became a monk at Cluny in 1109 and abbot in 1122. Peter ended a decline that had set in under his predecessor, and he presided over Cluny's last period as the most influential monastery in Europe. During his long abbacy Peter reformed Cluny's finances and also improved the level of education at Cluniac houses. He was a significant theologian, best known today for his treatise against Islam (based on a translation of the Qur'an he had commissioned) and his opposition to the Petrobrusian heresy.

Due to his correspondence with the Cistercian Bernard of Clairvaux, Peter has unfairly gained a reputation as reactionary, advocating an old-fashioned Benedictine spirituality increasingly out of touch with twelfth-century values. Certainly he continued Cluny's exhausting liturgical practices, defended Cluny's aesthetic emphases, and maintained the personal control of Cluny's abbot over more than one thousand affiliated houses. But under Peter, Cluniac spirituality remained attractive to many people, and Peter's own moderation, including his shelter of Peter Abelard at the end of his tempestuous career, provided a necessary note of restraint in a volatile age.

G. Constable, *The Reformation of the Twelfth Century* (1996); J. Van Engen, "The 'Crisis of Cenobitism' Reconsidered," *Speculum* 61 (1986): 269–304.

PHYLLIS G. JESTICE

Peter's, St., Church of   see St. Peter's, Church of

Petrarch (Francesco Petrarca) (1304–1374), Italian lyric poet and humanist, commonly regarded as a founder of the Renaissance in the fields of literature and learning. Born in Arezzo, the son of an exiled Florentine notary, Petrarch lived in or near Avignon from 1311 until 1353, when he returned to Italy. In 1327, he first glimpsed Laura, the woman who inspired much of his poetry (she died of the plague in 1348). From 1330 to 1347 he served as diplomat for the Colonna family, visiting Flanders and the Rhineland. Petrarch discovered lost or neglected classical texts and made these available for scholars. He wrote treatises on the solitary life and the religious life, as well as a work on the world of antiquity. Petrarch's *Book without a Name* (*Liber sine nomine*) is a collection of nineteen letters lamenting the corruption and vice at the papal court of Avignon, which was published after his death for reasons of safety. This book presents a scathing picture of the immorality and greed common in the city Petrarch called the Babylon of the West.

G. Frasso, *Travels with Francesco Petrarca* (1974); W. J. Kennedy, *Authorizing Petrarch* (1994); N. Mann, *Petrarch* (1984); G. Mazzotta, *The Worlds of Petrarch* (1993).

PRISCILLA BAUMANN

Petri, Laurentius (1499–1573), archbishop of Sweden (1531–1573), younger brother of the reformer Olaus Petri. In 1527 he enrolled at the Univ. of Wittenberg, eventually returning to Sweden as a professor at the Univ. of Uppsala. In 1531 an assembly of the bishops in Uppsala with the support of the king ordained Petri as the first evangelical archbishop. The act of consecration was performed by the bishop of VästerÜs, Petrus Magni, who in 1524 had been installed by the pope in Rome; thus, the *succesio apostolica* was maintained in the Swedish Lutheran church.

Petri opposed the king's plan to establish a genuine state church, preferring an evangelical national church instead. His literary achievements include an exposition of Lutheran dogma (printed in Wittenberg in 1587), a 1542 hymn book including Luther's small catechism and a prayer book and a collection of his sermons published in 1555. He also had a key role in the 1541 Swedish translation of the Bible. His most important work was the Church Order adapted to the situation in Sweden, based on the 1553 Church Order of Wittenberg; the Order was approved in 1571.

———

E. E. Yelverton, *An Archbishop of the Reformation: Laurentius Petri Nericius Archbishop of Uppsala, 1531–1573* (1958); A. Andrén, *Réformationstid*, vol. 3 of *Sveriges Kyrkohistoria* (1999).

INGUN MONTGOMERY

Petri, Olaus (1493–1552), reformer of Sweden, elder brother of Laurentius Petri, who was the first evangelical archbishop of Sweden. Olaus studied in Uppsala, Leipzig, and Wittenberg; in Wittenberg (1516–1518) he heard Luther lecturing on Galatians and Hebrews. Upon returning to Sweden he was ordained a deacon and soon became the secretary of the bishop of Strängnäs and had care of the cathedral school. Complaints soon arose over his Lutheran preaching in the cathedral. In 1523 Gustavus Vasa was acclaimed king at Strängnäs, and in 1524 he summoned Olaus to Stockholm as the town clerk. In 1525 Olaus married (a few months before Luther). His first evangelical book in Swedish, *A Useful Instruction* (1526), inspired by Luther's *Prayerbook*, was soon followed by the Swedish translation of the New Testament. Many of his publications were translations of German works. His pamphlet *Why the Mass Ought to Be Held in Swedish* accompanied the publication of the Swedish Mass in 1531. Olaus also wrote tracts on the sacraments and on marriage and published a book of sermons.

———

C. Bergendoff, *Olavus Petri and the Ecclesiastical Reformation in Sweden* (1965).

INGUN MONTGOMERY

Peucer, Caspar (1525–1602), Lutheran physician and theologian. Peucer went to Wittenberg in 1540 and was taken into Melanchthon's home. After obtaining his MA in 1545, he became instructor in the faculty of arts in 1548 and then was professor of mathematics (1554) and medicine (1558). In 1550 he married Melanchthon's daughter, Magdelena, and assisted his father-in-law in his declining years. Peucer was appointed court physician to Elector August of Saxony and earned his confidence. This allowed him to promote Melanchthon's views, largely adopted by the Wittenberg faculty, on free will as a contributing factor in conversion and the Lord's Supper as a spiritual

rather than physical presence. He led the Philippists and later the Crypto-Calvinists and helped them formulate their opposition to the Gnesio-Lutherans. When Peucer was discovered by the Elector Augustus to be fostering the views of Calvin and not Luther, he was imprisoned (1574). He lived out his life as a physician and town counselor in Anhalt, whose prince had obtained his release in 1586. He collaborated with Melanchthon in writing *Chronicon Carionis* (1581) and wrote a history of his imprisonment, *Historia Carcerum* (1584).

———

W. Friedensburg, *Geschichte der Universität Wittenberg* (1917); R. Rosin, "Peucer, Caspar," in *The Oxford Encyclopedia of the Reformation*, vol. 3 (1995), 251–52.

DAVID P. SCAER

Pflug, Julius (1499–1564), German bishop and theologian, son of the chancellor of Duke George of Saxony. Trained in law in Bologna and Rome, he was influenced by humanism through Erasmus and Melanchthon and worked to reform the church from within. He attempted to reconcile Reformation-era differences and embraced such Lutheran teachings as the priority of grace, the centrality of Christ, and Scripture as the word of God but he held to the Catholic doctrines of merit, devotion to the saints, and purgatory. His church benefices and attachment to the Saxon court of Dresden and the archbishop of Mainz were factors preventing him from embracing the Reformation. He was present at Augsburg in 1530 and participated in the Regensburg Colloquy in 1541 that attempted to bring Lutherans and Catholics together, and he helped edit the Augsburg Interim, which imposed certain Catholic practices on Lutherans (1548). In 1554 he attended the Council of Trent, which defined post-Reformation Catholicism. Respected by Lutherans, with whom he desired reconciliation, he presided at the Colloquy of Worms in 1557. He was the last Catholic bishop of Naumburg-Zeitz (1541–1547).

———

J. Pflug, *Correspondence,* ed. J. V. Pollet, 6 vols. (1969–1982); B. Vogler, "Pflug, Julius," in *The Oxford Encyclopedia of the Reformation,* vol. 3 (1996), 252–53.

DAVID P. SCAER

Philadelphianism Influenced by the German mystic Jakob Böhme's notion of a coming spiritual church age, the English prophetess Jane Leade (1624–1704) formed the "Philadelphian

Society" in 1694 in London as a home for all God's children who had separated from the "Babel" of the established churches. Philadelphians sought to gather true believers from the scattered and divided churches and expected, probably by the year 1700, the prophesied millennial church of brotherly love, Philadelphia (Rev. 3:7–14). In the 1690s Böhmist circles in Holland and Germany began translating, publishing, and circulating the writings of English Philadelphians such as Jane Leade, John Pordage, and Thomas Bromley. These writings found ready acceptance in Germany among radical Pietists and among exiled French Huguenots. Noteworthy Pietist Philadelphians were Johann Wilhelm and Johanna Eleonora Petersen, Heinrich Horch, Johann Henrich Reitz, Konrad Bröske, and the notorious Eva von Buttlar. Von Buttlar claimed to be the second Eve, the helpmate of Jesus, the second Adam. In her society there was to be complete sharing of goods, including sexual relations among its members.

The most significant literary productions by German Philadelphians were Horch's *Mystical and Prophetical Bible* (1712) and J. F. Haug's eight-volume commentary known as the *Berleburg Bible* (1726–1742). Count Zinzendorf's Herrnhut was founded to promote Philadelphian ideals.

———

D. H. Shantz, "The Millennial Study Bible of Heinrich Horch," in *The Practical Calvinist*, ed. P. A. Lillback (2002), 391–414; N. Thune, *The Behmenists and the Philadelphians* (1948).

DOUGLAS H. SHANTZ

Philip II of Spain (1527–1598), Habsburg king of Spain and all of its European and overseas possessions. Philip inherited the throne from his father, Emperor Charles V in 1556; in 1580 he also became king of Portugal. Though nearly excommunicated for jurisdictional disagreements with various popes over control of the Spanish church, Philip was wholly committed to the Catholic cause. "I do not propose nor desire to be the ruler of heretics," he once wrote. Philip sank vast amounts of New World wealth into wars waged in the name of religion, the costliest of which was against his rebellious Calvinist Dutch subjects, who rejected the Catholic faith with iconoclastic fury. Philip also attacked England in 1588, but his fabled Great Armada—the largest fleet ever assembled— suffered a crushing defeat at the hands of English seamen and the weather. Famine and plague stalked the land as Philip died next to the main altar in his palace/monastery, the Escorial, but Spain remained at the summit of its power for nearly another century, and its missionaries continued to extend the reach of the Catholic Church ever further around the globe.

———

H. Kamen, *Philip of Spain* (1997); G. Parker, *Philip II* (1978); P. Williams, *Philip II* (2000).

CARLOS M. N. EIRE

Philip, Landgrave of Hesse (1504–1567), princely supporter of Luther's reformation. After a regency, Philip assumed rule of several Hessian principalities in 1518 and began immediately to strengthen his power at home and his influence on the wider German scene. His enthusiasm for Luther's reform led him to follow the Saxon model for church organization instead of that suggested by the Homberg Synod of 1526 within his own lands. He depended on the advice of Martin Bucer of Strasbourg and Adam Krafft, his court preacher, in institutionalizing reform. He founded the Univ. of Marburg in 1527 with Melanchthon's help. The Ziegenhain Constitution (1539), which reintroduced confirmation, consolidated his reform efforts. His desire for a united political front among evangelical reformers led him to several attempts at reconciling Luther and Zwingli, above all the Marburg Colloquy (1529). He played an important role in defending Lutheran reform at the diets of Speyer (1529) and Augsburg (1530) and stood among the seven princely subscribers of the Augsburg Confession. His efforts to form a league of Protestant princes succeeded with the organization of the Schmalkald League (1531) and included the development of a theory justifying armed resistance by "lesser magistrates" against a tyrannous emperor. His lifelong rivalry with the Habsburg family led him to free the duchy of Württemberg from its control and restore Duke Ulrich (1534). His bigamous marriage to Margarete von der Salle (1540) publicly embarrassed the reformers and led to imperial charges against him. Defeated by Charles V in the Schmalkald War (1547), he was imprisoned until 1552. He dedicated the last years of his life to rebuilding his lands and consolidating Protestant power within the German empire.

———

W. Heinemeyer, *Philipp der Grossmutige und die Reformation in Hessen* (1997); W. Wright, *Capitalism, the State, and the Lutheran Reformation: Sixteenth-Century Hesse* (1988).

ROBERT KOLB

Philippists In the latter half of the six-teenth century, this term, used especially by detractors, designated students and followers of Philip Melanchthon. After Martin Luther's death in 1546, tensions among his followers that had surfaced in the 1530s broke into the open. Disputes were sparked by the defeat of the Schmalkald League at the hands of the emperor and his allies, especially the Lutheran Maurice of Saxony, who thereby became elec-tor and gained control over the Univ. of Wit-tenberg. The 1548 imperial diet of Augsburg imposed a religious agreement upon the Protes-tants known as the Augsburg Interim. Some evangelical theologians counseled open resis-tance; others, including Melanchthon and pro-fessors at Wittenberg, rejected its theology but allowed imposition of liturgical adiaphora. Detractors (Gnesio ["genuine"]-Lutheran the-ologians) gathered in Magdeburg, including Nicholas von Amsdorf (1485–1565) and Matthias Flacius of Croatia (1520–1575), called this the "Leipzig" Interim. The proposal came before a provincial diet in Leipzig in December 1548 but was never approved. This sparked the adiaphoristic controversy (see *Adi-aphora and Adiaphoric Controversies*). Later Johann Pfeffinger (1493–1570) debated with Flacius over free will and original sin. Georg Major (1502–1574) crossed swords with von Amsdorf and others over the necessity of good works for salvation.

Finally, after Melanchthon's death in 1560, some members of the faculty at Wittenberg, including Melanchthon's son-in-law, Caspar Peucer (1525–1602), met secretly and agreed on a symbolic interpretation of Christ's pres-ence in the Lord's Supper somewhat similar to Melanchthon's understanding of Christ's actual presence. When their position became public in the 1570s, they were often called Crypto-Calvinists, but they were more accurately Crypto-Philippists. The Formula of Concord, published in *The Book of Concord* (1580), addressed these controversies for Lutherans.

L. D. Peterson, "The Philippist Theologians and the Interims of 1548" (PhD diss., Univ. of Wisconsin, 1974).

TIMOTHY J. WENGERT

Philips, Dirk (1504–1568), one of the most important leaders of early Dutch Anabaptism along with his brother Obbe and Menno Simons. The son of a priest, Dirk became an Observant Franciscan in Leeuwarden. In 1533 he was rebaptized by a follower of Jan Matthijs. In 1534, his brother Obbe ordained him an elder for the emergent Anabaptist community of Leeuwarden. His early leadership was con-sumed with the events at Münster, as mission-aries and writings were sent out from that place proclaiming it as the New Jerusalem and urg-ing Anabaptists to join the struggle. Both Dirk and Obbe opposed the revolutionary tenden-cies, and they gained the upper hand in the movement after Münster fell. Dirk ministered among the remnant Anabaptist communities and extended their reach throughout Frisia and northern Germany as far as Gdansk. He took a leading role in several of the controversies that plagued Dutch Anabaptism. Most importantly, he seems to have pushed for a rigorous appli-cation of the ban—excommunicating and avoiding unrepentant sinners—probably per-suading Menno Simons to take this position. Whether he always took a second role to the leading figure of Menno, it is clear that Dirk was of great importance for Dutch Anabaptism. Late in life he collected his various writings in *Enchiridion oft Hantboecxken van de chris-telijcke Leere* (1564). It saw four more editions, the last in 1627, and was translated into French (1626) and German (1715, 1802).

A. Friesen, "Menno and Münster: The Man and the Movement," in *Menno Simons, a Reap-praisal*, ed. G. R. Brunk (1992), 131–62; G. H. Williams, *The Radical Reformation* (3rd ed., 1992).

D. JONATHAN GRIESER

Philips, Obbe (c. 1500–1568), Dutch Anabaptist leader and older brother of the Anabaptist elder Dirk Philips. He was the son of a priest in Leeuwarden who became a sur-geon. During the 1520s, Obbe began reading reform tracts and probably joined a sacramen-tarian group. He was converted by Melchior Hoffman and struggled with the militant Jan Matthijs over the leadership of the Leeuwarden Anabaptist group. After an abortive revolt in Leeuwarden while Obbe was away on a preach-ing mission, Obbe went to Amsterdam, where he encountered Anabaptist revolutionaries who shared the tendencies of the ascendant apoca-lyptic Anabaptists in Münster. He consistently opposed the actions of radicals in Amsterdam, including their attempt to storm city hall. The tragedy of Münster led Obbe to reexamine his theology and his ordination. He had been ordained by Jan Matthijs, who had become a leader in Münster, but Obbe in turn had ordained other Anabaptist leaders, including David Joris and his brother Dirk Philips. By 1540 he had left the movement as it evolved under Dirk and Menno Simons. Nothing is known of his later life except his death date. His only surviving writing is the *Bekenntnisse*, which appeared after his death.

C. Livestro, "Obbe Philips and the Anabaptist Vision," *Mennonite Quarterly Review* 41 (1967): 99–115; G. H. Williams, *The Radical Reformation* (3rd ed., 1992).

D. JONATHAN GRIESER

Philo (c. 20 BCE–c. 50 CE), Hellenistic Jewish philosopher and author from the Egyptian city of Alexandria. According to Josephus, Philo's family was rich and politically influential. Philo's brother, Alexander, was a Roman tax official, and Philo's nephew, Tiberius Alexander, was procurator of Judea from 46 to 48 CE and later a prefect in Egypt (Josephus, *Jewish Antiquities* 18.159–60; 19.276–77; 20.100). Philo himself played a prominent role in the Jewish reaction to an attack on the Alexandrian Jews instigated by the Roman prefect Flaccus in 38 CE. Philo's treatise *The Embassy to Gaius* describes the mission of a delegation led by Philo that was sent to Emperor Gaius Caligula to plead for the rights of the Alexandrian Jews. Although deeply committed to Judaism, Philo appears to have visited the Jerusalem temple only once (*Providence* 2.64).

In addition to his training in Judaism, Philo received a thorough Hellenistic education, which would have included the study of literature, rhetoric, and philosophy. His family's wealth enabled Philo to devote much of his early life to philosophical contemplation and other intellectual pursuits, and, despite growing civic responsibilities, he was able to preserve sufficient time later in his life to reflect and comment on various religious matters, particularly the biblical writings attributed to Moses from the Septuagint.

Philo's interpretation of Scripture reflects both his commitment to his Jewish heritage and his devotion to Hellenistic philosophy, particularly to the views of Plato and the subsequent derivative philosophical movements, such as Middle Platonism. One of the most notable characteristics of Philo's exegesis is his use of allegory, an approach developed by Hellenistic scholars in Alexandria as they interpreted the works of Homer. For example, Philo interpreted Genesis 2:7 as God's physical and moral inspi-

ration of humans rather than God's actual breathing air into Adam (Leg. 1.36–39). The philosophical underpinnings and themes evident in Philo represent an important stream of thought present in the Jewish Diaspora and point to the variations present within Judaism at that time. It seems probable that the Hellenistic Jewish tradition that Philo's writings embody contributed to the philosophical foundation upon which the NT book of Hebrews was built.

Among the Hellenistic philosophical concepts that Philo introduces to the interpretation of Jewish texts is the term *Logos* ("word"). According to Philo, the Logos is a creative intellect or demiurge that is the extension of God, to whom Philo refers, in Platonic terms, as "the One." Although some earlier scholars argued that Philo's understanding of the Logos was an important precursor to the perspective portrayed in the Prologue to John's Gospel (John 1:1–18), many contemporary scholars suggest that the connection between Philo and John is much more tenuous.

Philo's Works, trans. William Heinemann, 12 vols., LCL (1929 to 1953); E. R. Goodenough, *An Introduction to Philo Judaeus* (1940); S. Sandmel, *Philo of Alexandria: An Introduction* (1979); D. Winston, *Logos and Mystical Theology in Philo of Alexandria* (1985).

J. DAVID CASSEL

Philoponus of Alexandria, John (c. 490–580), scientist, philosopher, theologian. Also known as "the Grammarian," John Philoponus has sometimes been confused with John the Grammarian of Caesarea. He was a pupil of the non-Christian Platonist Ammonius Hermeiou in Alexandria and was a scientific and philosophical author before becoming involved in the sixth-century christological controversies. His philosophical concern was to establish God's creation of the world against Aristotelian and Platonic assertions of the eternity and necessity of the material world. His scientific research was concerned with theories of motion. Later, Arab translators and William of Moerbeke transmitted some of his ideas to the medieval West.

Philoponus's Christology is adapted from Severus of Antioch and his favorite christological formula: "one synthetic *physis*." He equates the terms *physis* and *hypostatis* and is convinced that the Chalcedonian dyophysites (two *physeis*, or natures) are in fact Nestorians. While his Christology is generally unremarkable, his insistence upon the individuality of the incarnate hypostasis led him into Trinitarian positions that were condemned as tritheistic by the Sixth Ecumenical Council in 681.

CPG 3A (1979–), 366–70; T. Hainteller, "John Philoponus, Philosopher and Theologian in Alexandria," in Christ in Christian Tradition, vol. 2, part 4, ed. A. Grillmeier (1996); U. M. Lang, John Philoponus and the Controversies over Chalcedon in the Sixth Century (2001).
                                    EUGENE M. LUDWIG, OFM CAP.

Philosophy of Christ, an approach to Christian living often associated with Desiderius Erasmus, although the term and concept have roots in patristic writings (e.g., Clement of Alexandria, Chrysostom, and Augustine) and were used in monastic medieval literature and in humanist circles (Rudolf Agricola, Jacques Lefèvre d'Etaples, and Guillaume Budé). Erasmus defined the term in opposition to scholastic and monastic models for piety, rejecting dependence upon ceremony and form in favor of moral concern for others. He distinguished his program for piety from the *imitatio Christi* cultivated by the monks, instead propagating his philosophy of following Christ's example as the way of life of all Christians. Based upon Scripture and the wisdom found above all in Christ's words, but acknowledging the value of the moral instruction and example of ancient pagan philosophers as well, this philosophy of Christ embraced the upright life, continual learning, and pious devotion of those who obey God's commands in simplicity and dedication to God in everyday life. The expression or related expressions, with varying accents, are found in the works of some authors of the Protestant and Catholic Reformations.

John W. O'Malley, introduction to The Collected Works of Erasmus, vol. 66 (1988); J. McConica, Erasmus (1991).
                                    ROBERT KOLB

Philostorgius (c. 368–c. 440), early Byzantine church historian. He wrote an ecclesiastical history in twelve books, which continued that of Eusebius of Caesarea to 425. Born in Cappadocia, at age twenty Philostorgius moved to Constantinople and became a disciple of Eunomius. His history survives only in fragments, drawn especially from the epitome of the patriarch Photius and from the Passion of Artemius by John of Rhodes. The work is an apology for the cause of Eunomius and his teacher Aetius, and it attacks Athanasius and other orthodox Chris-

tians. Philostorgius's vivid descriptions of omens and portents suggest an apocalyptic cast of mind. In addition to theological concerns, the work provides extensive digressions on geographical, medical, scientific, and zoological subjects. His style is highly polished, and he draws on a wide range of sources. The fragments of his history are of particular interest to modern historians for the light they shed on nonorthodox Christianity of the period. He is also credited with a refutation of the work of Porphyry against the Christians and a panegyric of Eunomius, neither of which survives.

J. Bidez and F. Winkelmann, Philostorgius Kirchengeschichte (1981); R. Van Dam, Becoming Christian: The Conversion of Roman Cappadocia (2003); A. E. Nobbs, "Philostorgius' View of the Past," in Reading the Past in Late Antiquity, ed. G. Clarke et al. (1990).
                                    DAVID ROHRBACHER

Philoxenus of Mabbug (c. 440–523), spiritual and doctrinal writer, bishop, Monophysite. He was born in Tahel, Bēt Garmai, of Christian Persian parents. A severe persecution in 445–446 forced his family to migrate, reputedly to Tur 'Abdin. Attending the School of the Persians in Edessa, he was attracted to the Monophysite perspective and was eventually expelled for his views. Ordained bishop of Mabbug in 485, he adopted the Greek name Philoxenus ("lover of strangers/hospitable one"), perhaps as a variant of his Syriac name, Aksenāyā ("the stranger").

Along with Severus of Antioch, he was a vigorous leader of the Monophysite cause. When the emperor Anastasius, who was sympathetic to Monophysitism, died in 518, the Chalcedonian Justin proceeded at Easter the following year to expel Monophysite clergy, including Philoxenus.

Associated with the Philoxenian version of the Syriac New Testament, compiled by Polycarp in 507/508, Philoxenus wrote a number of commentaries on the Gospels, professions of faith, and letters on dogmatic, spiritual, and moral issues. His most widely read work was a collection of thirteen *mēmrē*, or discourses on the ascetical life, directed to monks in a monastery under his care.

E. A. W. Budge, ed., Discourses of Philoxenus, Bishop of Mabbogh, 2 vols. (1894); S. Brock, The Syriac Fathers on Prayer and the Spiritual Life (1987), 101–33.
                                    ROBERT A. KITCHEN

Phoebadius (d. after 392), bishop. All we know of Phoebadius is that he was bishop of Agen in Gaul in the late 350s and that in 392 Jerome spoke of his being alive but very old. He was the author of *Against the Arians*, a polemical work that responded to the pointedly anti-Nicene Formula of Sirmium (357). Phoebadius belonged to that generation of Latin bishops of the mid-fourth century who embraced the creed of Nicaea as normative and who defended it against an invigorated, imperially supported theology espousing a clear subordinationism. The Latin record of defending Nicaea was not at that time conspicuous: on the one hand, Serdica made no mention of Nicaea and Liberius of Rome broke while in exile, changed his position, and was allowed to return to his see; and, on the other, Hilary of Poitiers informs us that until he went into exile in the East he had never heard the creed of Nicaea. Phoebadius was the most balanced of the newly articulate co-Nicene Latin bishops, lacking the rashness of Lucifer of Cagliari and the muddleheadedness of Gregory of Elvira. His theology drew strongly on Tertullian but not slavishly, and he had a real sensitivity to the danger that formulae of divine unity can shelter modalism.

CCSL 64 (1985), 3–52; *DHGE*, vol. 16 (1967), 785–90; R. P. C. Hanson, *Search for the Christian Doctrine of God* (1988).

MICHEL RENE BARNES

Phos hilaron A hymn of praise to Jesus Christ. Already so ancient in the mid-fourth century that no one knew who wrote it (Basil, *On the Holy Spirit* 29.73), the "phos hilaron," or "cheerful light," of the Father is intoned by Christians as the light of day fades and evening lamps begin to shine. In greeting the true light at eventide, Christians may have taken over and sanctified an ancient pagan custom of welcoming an evening lamp with the words "Good Light." Few translators use the accurate adjective "cheerful," preferring a more traditional word such as "gracious" or "joyous." Eastern Christians have sung the hymn unchanged for at least sixteen hundred years; Western Christians rediscovered it in the seventeenth century, and many sing it at vespers. Steeped in biblical imagery, the lovely, simple, yet subtly profound hymn suggests, among other things, John the Evangelist's "true light which enlightens everyone" (John 1:9), the "radiance of [God's] glory" of Hebrews (1:3), and the seer John's lamb that alone will be a sufficient lamp to light

the celestial city (Rev. 21:23). The Greek text, the earliest extant manuscript of which dates only from the sixth or seventh century, is not metrical and thus is challenging both to poet-translators and tune writers.

M. E. Irwin, "Phos Hilaron: The Metamorphoses of a Greek Christian Hymn," *The Hymn* 40 (1989): 7–12.

MARY CATHERINE BERGLUND

Photian Schism Ninth-century controversy centered on the pope's claim to be the primal authority for all of Christendom, which the Greeks countered with their model of the five patriarchates of roughly equal status. Shortly after Photius (c. 820–c. 891) was all-too-rapidly made patriarch of Constantinople in 858, he became enmeshed in a dispute with Pope Nicholas I (858–867). Photius's predecessor, Ignatius, had been forced out of office by the emperor, which led Ignatius's supporters to contend that Photius was an unlawful usurper. Photius did not announce his accession to the pope until 860, giving Nicholas sufficient time to hear about the quarrel with the Ignatian party. In 861 Nicholas sent legates to Constantinople to investigate the situation. Photius called a council at Constantinople, with the legates presiding, to settle the claims between Ignatius and himself. The legates and the council agreed that Photius was the legitimate patriarch. Nicholas, however, declared that the legates had exceeded their authority, and he disowned their decision. In 863 the pope called a council at Rome, which then proclaimed Ignatius patriarch and Photius deposed.

The Byzantines, for their part, took no notice of the pope's action, and thus a significant break was created between Constantinople and Rome. The Byzantines were within their rights to take exception to the pope's action because he had exceeded his power as set by the Council of Sardica (343). The canon in question says that a bishop under sentence of condemnation may appeal to the pope who, if just cause warrants, can order a retrial. However, the retrial must be conducted by bishops local to the condemned bishop. The issue was further complicated by the active presence of Frankish missionaries in Bulgaria who were in direct conflict with Greek efforts in the area. Moreover, the Franks promoted a Latin version of the Creed that included the *filioque* clause. Photius considered the *filioque* to be deeply heretical and issued a condemnatory encyclical to the other Eastern patriarchs. The pope supported the *filioque* used by the Franks, even though it was not then used at Rome. In 867 the situation changed radically when the new emperor, in an attempt to placate the pope, deposed Photius and reestablished Ignatius. The emperor had Photius condemned and anathematized at the council of 869–870, which in turn called upon the emperor to resolve the missionary situation with the Bulgarian church. Khan Boris finally chose to side with the Greeks over Rome and had the Frankish missionaries expelled—and he rejected the use of the *filioque*. Photius and Ignatius were later reconciled, and Photius was reestablished as patriarch upon the death of Ignatius in 877. The Constantinopolitan council of 879 anathematized the council of 869–870, whereupon all condemnations of Photius were withdrawn. Although the external signs of the Photian Schism were thus smoothed over, the deeper issues of centralized papal authority and the *filioque* innovation were to prove much more divisive at a later date.

F. Dvornik, *The Photian Schism: History and Legend* (1948); J. A. Meijer, *A Successful Council of Union: A Theological Analysis of the Photian Synod of 879–880* (1975); A. Nichols, *Rome and the Eastern Churches* (1992).

MICHAEL D. PETERSON

Photinus (d. 376), bishop of Sirmium. A reputed disciple of Marcellus of Ancyra, he is associated with a Monarchian type of Trinitarianism, manifest in its view that the Son did not subsist until his incarnation and that his kingdom was not eternal. As none of Photinus's writings are extant, evidence for his views comes from his detractors. His theology was condemned by at least two small synods, in Milan and Rome, in the late 340s. A council in Sirmium (351) anathematized a series of views ascribed to him and installed a new bishop (Germinius). The condemnations indicate that Photinus claimed that the Son was born only a human being and did not exist prior to the incarnation.

Contemporary to Photinus are the doctrinal refutations by Marius Victorinus (*Adversus Arrium* 2.2), and the writer known as "Ambrosiaster." Both decried Photinus's denial of Christ's divinity. Slightly later, Zeno of Verona accused Photinus of teaching that "Jesus Christ assumed his beginning [*principium*] from the womb of the Virgin Mary and was made, not born, God on account of his righteousness" (*Tractate* 2.8).

That proponents of Photinian theology continued to endure persecution in the West is evident by the fact that Photinians, along with Donatists and Manicheans, were proscribed by law under emperors Valentinian I and Gratian (Socrates, *Hist. eccl.* 5.2; Sozomen, *Hist. eccl.* 7.1.3).

L. Speller, "New Light on the Photinians: The Evidence of Ambrosiaster," *JTS* 34 (1983): 99–113; D. Williams, "Monarchianism and Photinus as the Persistent Heretical Face of the Fourth Century," *Harvard Theological Review* 99 (2006): 187–206.

D. H. WILLIAMS

Pico della Mirandola, Giovanni

(1463–1494), Italian Renaissance philosopher and scholar. He studied at the universities of Bologna, Padua, and Paris. He became proficient in Latin, Greek, Hebrew, and Arabic. His interest in different philosophies convinced him that all philosophy held some common truth. In 1487 the pope condemned his ideas as heretical, and he fled to France. After returning to Florence he became influenced by the pietistic teaching of Girolamo Savonarola. He died mysteriously before entering a monastery. His greatest contribution, *Oration on the Dignity of Man* (1487), advocated free will and the ability of humankind to re-create itself and was condemned by most contemporary theologians.

K. S. Latourette, *A History of Christianity: Reformation to the Present*, vol. 2 (rev. ed., 1975); C. B. Schmitt, *Gianfrancesco Pico della Mirandola and the Fifth Lateran Council* (1970).

ELIZABETH GERHARDT

Pietà A popular theme in Western devotional art since the fourteenth century, the Pietà (also known as *Vesperbild*) depicts the Virgin Mary with the body of the dead Christ on her lap, with other figures occasionally added. The iconography of the Pietà was introduced to the West in the eleventh century through Byzantine icons featuring the Virgin's Lamentation, a scene described in the apocryphal *Gospel of Nicodemus*. The group was first adapted for Western patrons in Italian and German workshops, which produced paintings and sculptures for side altars and niches, for tomb decorations, and for private use. The freestanding sculpted version, which isolated Mary and Jesus by eliminating narrative references, first achieved popularity within the German Empire, especially among devout women whose mystical experiences influenced its iconography. By the fifteenth century, regional adaptations appeared throughout Europe.

Late medieval devotional interest in Christ's passion and in the sorrow of his mother, along with demand for emotionally vivid religious images, increased the Pietà's appeal. Scripture contains no direct reference to the episode, John's reference to Mary's vigil at the cross (19:2) notwithstanding, but a growing body of mystical and devotional writings, including the *Meditations on the Life of Christ* and the writings of Mechtild of Hackeborn and Angela da Foligno, along with the increasing popularity of passion plays and sermons, created a congenial environment for these images. The Pietà fell out of favor during the Protestant Reformation, and by the mid-sixteenth century the rate of production had declined. The best-known version, Michelangelo's Pietà at St. Peter's, is a heroic artistic achievement, but versions with less virtuosity draw attention to Mary's presentation of her son, a gesture consistent with medieval theologians' interest in the Virgin's contribution to the work of redemption.

H. Belting, *The Image and Its Public in the Middle Ages* (1981); W. Forsyth, *The Pietà in French Late Gothic Sculpture* (1995); E. Panofsky, "Imago Pietatis," in *Festschrift für Max J. Friedländer* (1927); J. Ziegler, *Sculpture of Compassion* (1992).

ADRIENNE NOCK AMBROSE

Pietism   The most important Protestant reform movement after the sixteenth-century Reformation, Pietism promoted renewal of piety and church life within Lutheran and Reformed churches in continental Europe. Pietists emphasized godly living over pure doctrine, piety over faith, sanctification over justification, and personal Bible reading over Sunday worship and sacraments. Pietism had diverse regional expressions, appealed to people in all levels of European society, and spread worldwide through extensive missionary endeavors. "Pietists" first appeared as a term of disdain in 1674 to describe the disciples of Spener. The usage took hold in 1689 in the context of disturbances in Leipzig surrounding the Collegium Philobiblicum, a student society under August Hermann Francke.

Areas of controversy among scholars of Pietism include its geographical and chrono-

logical extent and the proper methodology for research. A history of Pietism published in 1993 under the general editorship of Martin Brecht (*Geschichte des Pietismus*) casts the Pietist net widely enough to include English Puritanism, the Dutch second reformation, Methodism, and the eighteenth- and nineteenth-century awakenings in England and America. Johannes Wallmann, in contrast, defines Pietism "in a wider and narrower sense," the former including a variety of efforts to promote inward piety and the latter representing Pietism proper. Wallmann characterizes Pietism proper as a German phenomenon that began with Spener in terms of conventicles, chiliasm, and biblical devotion and was distinctive compared to the Puritans, orthodox Lutheranism, and even its forerunners such as Arndt.

Scholars find various cultural settings for the German Pietist movement, such as the seventeenth-century social crisis, the ongoing social-economic impact of the Thirty Years' War (1618–1648), the influx of religious refugees such as the French Huguenots, and a growing climate of individualism and secularism that undermined European Christendom. The increasing rationalization of religion under Protestant orthodoxy led to a crisis of piety in the third post-Reformation generation, with a loss of both the language and reality of religious experience. The most influential author who sought to address this deficit was Johann Arndt (1555–1621). Arndt's importance rests in his *Four Books of True Christianity* (1610), the most published book in German Protestant history. For Arndt, true Christianity consisted of the restoration of Christ's image in humanity through repentance, illumination, and union with Christ through love. Following Thomas à Kempis's *Imitation of Christ*, Arndt affirmed, "It is a thousand times better to love Christ than to be able to speak and dispute much about him (Eph. 3:19)." Arndt's work inspired a variety of seventeenth-century German Lutheran reformers, including Christian Hoburg, Friedrich Breckling, and most notably Spener.

There were three generations of Pietist reformers, represented by Spener (1635–1705), Francke (1663–1727), and Count Zinzendorf (1700–1760). Spener's efforts to renew church and society were marked by three innovations: formation of conventicle groups, an eschatology that hoped for better times, and encouragement of biblical devotion among the laity. In 1670 Spener began a twice-weekly devotional reading circle; by 1675 the number had grown to fifty and included men and women, nobles and craftsmen, educated and uneducated. This gathering is generally considered to mark the beginning of the Pietist movement. In 1675 Spener published his *Pia Desideria*, a classic statement of his reform program, including a diagnosis of the corrupt condition of the German church, a prognosis of the possibilities for future improvement, and a sixfold remedy to bring about this improved state. Spener found initial support among preachers in German imperial cities and in small territories whose sympathetic princes had ties to Spener.

Pietism changed in the 1680s and 1690s as some of Spener's younger followers turned the conventicles into separatist gatherings, disdaining the churches as "Babel." Under Francke the Pietist movement became more activist in bringing about reform of church and society. After building an orphanage in Halle in 1698, Francke went on to establish powerful educational, economic, and missionary organizations that proved both controversial and successful. His sale of books and medicines became profitable and a source of income for the orphanage and schools. Francke's aggressive spirituality has been tied to his emphases on conversion, the importance of experience for assurance of faith, and a strong work ethic. Frederick William I appointed Halle Pietists to positions of influence, bringing about a "cultural revolution" in Prussian church and society and the "restructuring of military, administrative, and economic life based on Pietist concepts of God, self, and vocation" (Gawthrop).

With Count Nikolaus Ludwig von Zinzendorf, new emphases appeared when in 1722 he turned his estate into a refuge for persecuted Moravians, Schwenkfelders, and Lutheran Pietists. The Herrnhut community became an ecumenical experiment that was in advance of its time in leveling class and gender distinctions and in promoting ecumenical cooperation in worldwide mission.

The Pietist legacy includes the impulse to modern individualism, evident in its literary genre of spiritual autobiography, the introduction of millenarianism into Protestant piety, the ecumenical impulse, and the beginning of world mission. Much research remains to be done, including the preparation of critical editions of the works of key figures such as Spener, Francke, and Zinzendorf, and social, economic, and cultural analyses of Pietist networks, means of communication, leadership, mobility and migration, and issues of women and gender.

M. Brecht et al., *Geschichte des Pietismus* (1993–); P. C. Erb, *Pietists: Selected Writings* (1983); R. L. Gawthrop, *Pietism and the Making of 18th-Century Prussia* (1993); C. Lindberg, ed., *The Pietist Theologians* (2005); J. Strom, "Problems and Promises of Pietism Research," *CH* 51 (2002): 536–54; J. Wallmann, *Der Pietismus* (1990).

DOUGLAS H. SHANTZ

Pighius, Albertus (c. 1490–1542), Dutch theologian and controversialist who helped shape the Roman Catholic Church's response to emerging Protestantism. Interested in nearly everything, he wrote on such topics as astrology, geography, the theological "errors" of the Christian East, and (negatively) the divorce of England's King Henry VIII. Serving during the papacies of Adrian VI, Clement VII, and Paul III, he staunchly defended papal authority, especially from any accusation of heresy against the pope himself. A similar position was adopted by many later Roman Catholic thinkers, including the influential Robert Bellarmine. As a participant in the Colloquy of Regensburg (1541), he endorsed, but did not originate, the controversial doctrine of double justification, on account of which he has sometimes been wrongly labeled a "semi-Lutheran." His defense of free will and doctrine of original sin earned the scorn of Protestants (who branded him a Pelagian), as well as some Roman Catholics, such as Johannes Eck.

J. Calvin, *The Bondage and Liberation of the Will: A Defence of the Orthodox Doctrine of Human Choice against Pighius* (2002); A. N. S. Lane, "Albert Pighius' Controversial Work on Original Sin," *Reformation and Renaissance Review* 4 (2000): 29–61.

MICKEY L. MATTOX

Pilgrimage Christian pilgrimage has always been primarily linked either with devotion to Christ and the desire to experience those places in Palestine associated with his life, death, and resurrection, or with a veneration for the martyrs and saints of the church and the need to visit the places where they have been buried. In both cases, the journey to the holy place has most often been undertaken with the hope of seeking God's aid or of asking for the intercession of the saint with God. Already a custom, pilgrimage to the Holy Land first became widely popular due to the visit to Palestine of the emperor Constantine's mother, St.

Helena, around 326. Further encouragement was provided by the crusading movement, inaugurated in 1095 by Pope Urban II. In the case of the martyrs and saints, pilgrimage from the beginning was connected with an intense devotion to relics, which were believed to guarantee more direct access to the saint's presence and healing power.

Christians could also view pilgrimage as a penitential exercise, a motive especially popular among early Celtic monks, and the frequency of pilgrimages definitely increased when the early medieval church in the West began assigning pilgrimage as a means of doing public penance for sin. Pilgrimage to particular saints' shrines could also be promoted by bishops or members of the secular nobility to increase their own political power and prestige. By supporting the veneration of certain saints, men and women could both cultivate an image of personal religious devotion and create the impression that the saint was his or her own favored protector and patron.

Popular pilgrimage sites in Western Europe included Rome, St. Iago de Compostella in Spain, Walsingham and Canterbury in England, and Chartres Cathedral in France. Apart from its relics, Chartres was a special place of pilgrimage due to the labyrinth on the floor of the nave, which pilgrims unable to travel to Rome or the Holy Land could walk as a substitute. The labyrinth itself was a complex symbol, representing not only a physical pilgrimage to a holy place but also the journey of the Christian life itself, beginning at baptism and culminating with entry into heaven.

More modern interpretations of pilgrimage also call attention to the fact that a person on pilgrimage steps outside the ordinary structures and practices of daily life and enters a world where these no longer apply. The sacred journey can thus give a new perspective on the life temporarily left behind. The frequency of pilgrimage declined somewhat due to criticism from both Catholic and Protestant reformers in the sixteenth century. It nevertheless remains a popular Christian activity, and sites such as Lourdes, France, and the shrine of Our Lady of Guadalupe in Mexico continue to draw pilgrims, as do the more ancient ones.

P. Brown, *The Cult of the Saints: Its Rise and Function in Latin Christianity* (1981); R. C. Finucane, *Miracles and Pilgrims: Popular Beliefs in Medieval England* (1977, 1995); J. Howard-Johnston and P. A. Hayward, eds., *The Cult of Saints in Late Antiquity and the Early Middle Ages: Essays on the Contribution of Peter Brown* (1999); V. Turner and E. Turner, *Image and Pilgrimage in Christian Culture* (1978).

DONNA SPIVEY ELLINGTON

Pilgrimage of Grace This series of uprisings in northern England between October 1536 and February 1537 showed popular resentment of Henry VIII's religious and social policies. Dissolution of monasteries, changes to the sacraments in the Ten Articles, increased taxation, erosion of the rights of landowners in the Statute of Uses, and hatred of Thomas Cromwell all contributed to spontaneous demonstrations in Lincolnshire, Yorkshire, and Cumberland. Robert Aske organized the Yorkshire protesters into an army some thirty thousand strong under the banner of St. Cuthbert but refused to move against the king unless negotiations failed. Henry sent north Thomas Howard, Duke of Norfolk, with a much smaller force. Norfolk accepted Aske's grievances and offered royal pardons if the protesters disbanded, but then used further demonstrations as an excuse for reprisals, executing several hundred, including religious and gentry. Aske himself was arrested and executed at York. The lasting outcome was Henry's much more thorough suppression of northern monasteries.

M. and R. Dodds, *The Pilgrimage of Grace, 1536–1537, and the Exeter Conspiracy, 1538*, 2 vols. (1915); S. Gunn, "Peers, Commons, and Gentry in the Lincolnshire Revolt," *Past and Present* 123 (1989): 52–79; S. Harrison, *The Pilgrimage of Grace in the Lake Counties* (1981).

DAVID A. LOPEZ

Pionius (d. c. 250), elder (presbyter) and martyr. He was put to death in Smyrna for his Christian faith during the Decian persecution. It is said that Pionius was arrested on the anniversary date of the martyrdom of Polycarp. His martyrdom is noted by Eusebius (*Hist. eccl.* 4.15.46–47) and is recorded at length in the *Martyrdom of Pionius*, an account written about 300 and presumed to be basically reliable. This account, reflecting the rhetorical style of its period, is important evidence for the Decian persecution and for life in Smyrna. It presents Pionius as both the typical Christian hero, who is innocent and blameless, and also as a model of and encouragement to faith. It contains major, moving speeches by Pionius, uses many scriptural citations, and reflects the anti-Semitism of the church at that time. Pionius is likely responsible for the preservation of the *Martyrdom of Polycarp* but is incorrectly claimed as the author of a *Life of Polycarp*, which was actually written about 400.

J. den Boeft and J. Bremmer, "Notiunculae Martyrologicae III: Some Observations on the Martyrologia of Polycarp and Pionius," *VC* 39 (1985): 110–30; R. L. Fox, *Pagans and Christians* (1986), 460–92; H. Musurillo, *The Acts of the Christian Martyrs* (1972, repr. 2000), xxviii–xxx, 136–67; L. Robert, *Le martyre de Pionius, prêtre de Smyrne* (1994).

DAVID M. SCHOLER

Pirckheimer, Caritas (1467–1532),

abbess of St. Clara convent in Reformation-era Nuremberg who was notable for her erudite defense of monastic life, and sister of Willibald Pirckheimer. Her patrician parents sent her to Nuremberg's St. Clara convent at the age of twelve to be educated in the humanist tradition. Her exceptional learning and mastery of Latin led to correspondence with many of the most prominent scholars and artists of early sixteenth-century Europe, including, via her brother's mediation, Erasmus of Rotterdam. As the early Reformation's hostility toward monastic life swept through Nuremberg and threatened her convent's safety, Pirckheimer took up her pen against the "heresy," provoking even more aggression toward her and her sisters. Tensions were eased when Philip Melanchthon visited the city in November 1525. After meeting with Pirckheimer in her convent, the reformer scolded the city's Protestants for their violent measures and advised them to proceed with greater respect for the convent's way of life and religious conviction. According to Pirckheimer's own account of her meeting with Melanchthon (recorded in her posthumously edited, autobiographical *Denkwürdigkeiten aus dem Reformationszeitalter*, 1852), the two humanist minds reached consensus on most points of discussion and parted in a spirit of friendship. Melanchthon's support was a considerable factor in keeping the Roman Catholic convent open until long after the death of its eloquent abbess. While Lutheran reformers rejected the validity of monastic vows, Pirckheimer's appeal to freedom of conscience proved an effective defense for convent life.

M. Jung, *Nonnen, Prophetinnen, Kirchenmütter* (2002).

KENNETH G. APPOLD

Pirckheimer, Willibald (1470–1530),

noted German humanist, brother of Caritas Pirckheimer, and intermittent supporter of the Lutheran Reformation. Born in Eichstätt to a wealthy Nuremburg patrician family, Pirckheimer studied law in Padua and Pavia (1489–1495), where he also immersed himself in Greek and Latin classics. In 1496, he was called back to Nuremberg to serve on the city council. Pirckheimer led an active public life both within and beyond the city, leading imperial troops against Switzerland in 1499 and later attending imperial diets as an official representative. While gout precipitated a retreat from public life after 1523, further controversies prevented Pirckeimer from devoting his remaining years as exclusively to scholarship as he would have liked. Nonetheless, his considerable lifelong literary production includes academic studies, poems, satires, translations, and correspondence with figures such as his friend Desiderius Erasmus.

Pirckheimer's relationship to the Reformation was complex. His humanist sympathies made him initially supportive and led to correspondence with Philip Melanchthon and to contact with Martin Luther, who stayed at Pirckheimer's Nuremberg house in 1518. Pirckheimer read Luther avidly and publicly satirized Luther's opponent Johannes Eck in 1520. In return, Pirckheimer was included in the bull that excommunicated Luther in 1521, although he was reinstated upon appeal. In subsequent years, Pirckheimer cooled to the Reformation, criticizing aspects of its theology and the excesses that threatened his sister Caritas and her convent, though he remained in contact with Melanchthon.

L. Spitz, *The Religious Renaissance of the German Humanists* (1963); M. Jung, *Nonnen, Prophetinnen, Kirchenmütter* (2002).

KENNETH G. APPOLD

Pius II (1405–1464), humanist and pope. Enea Silvio de' Piccolomini was born near Siena and studied at both Siena and Florence. In 1432 he attended the Council of Basel as secretary to Cardinal D. Capranic. Later he supported the opponents of Pope Eugenius IV and worked for the antipope, Felix V. While serving Felix, he became an advocate of conciliar theory. As imperial poet, he wrote the popular love story *Euryalas and Lucretia*. In 1445, he was reconciled to Eugenius and in 1446 received holy orders. After the fall of Constantinople (1453) he began to work for a crusade. He became cardinal in 1456 and pope in 1458. Pius II focused his attention on the war against the Turks, calling for a three-year crusade. In 1460 he promulgated the bull *Execrabilis*, which upheld papal authority and condemned the practice of appealing to a general council. In 1463 he retracted his earlier political views and published *In minoribus agentes*, a response to his critics in Bohemia and Germany. He died in Ancona soon after putting himself at the head of the crusaders.

E. Duffy, *Saints and Sinners: A History of the Popes* (1997); J. H. Lynch, *The Medieval Church: A Brief History* (1992); R. J. Mitchell, *The Laurels and the Tiara: Pope Pius II, 1458–1464* (1962).

ELIZABETH GERHARDT

Pius IV (1499–1565), pope. Born Gian Angelo Medici, he studied medicine and law at Pavia and went to Rome in 1527, where he held several offices. In 1545 he became archbishop of Ragusa, and in 1549 he was appointed cardinal. Under Julius III (1550–1555) he became papal legate in Romagna. He was elected pope in 1559 and appointed his nephew, Charles Borromeo, cardinal. Pius IV is best known for his reassembling of the Council of Trent in 1562–1563. He published a new Index of Prohibited Books in 1564, reformed the Sacred College, and worked on an edition of the Roman Catechism. In 1564 he allowed the laity to have the chalice in Germany and other surrounding countries, but the practice was rescinded by his successors. He survived an attempt on his life, but died the following year.

E. Duffy, *Saints and Sinners: A History of the Popes* (1997); K. S. Latourette, *A History of Christianity: Reformation to the Present* (rev. ed., 1975); J. H. Lynch, *The Medieval Church: A Brief History* (1992).

ELIZABETH GERHARDT

Plague An epidemic disease that is transmitted by fleas that feed on infected rodents. Outbreaks of plague occur cyclically, but the most virulent example, commonly called the bubonic plague or the Black Death, devastated Western Europe in the mid-fourteenth century, killing a third to half of the population. Effects of this plague were immediate and far-reaching, threatening communal stability, triggering persecution of Jews, and encouraging the growth of fanatical groups such as the Flagellants. Moreover, the resulting depopulation

weakened the church hierarchy, eroded the power of feudal structures, and contributed to violent uprisings such as that of the Jacquerie in France (1358) and the English Peasants' Rebellion (1381).

J. Aberth, *From the Brink of the Apocalypse: Confronting Famine, War, Plague, and Death in the Later Middle Ages* (2001); R. S. Gottfried, *The Black Death: Natural and Human Disaster in Medieval Europe* (1983); D. Herlihy, *The Black Death and the Transformation of the West* (1997).

PRISCILLA BAUMANN

Plethon, George Gemistus (1355–1452), Byzantine Platonic philosopher and courtier. His early education included the study of Plato. Hostile sources say that he spent time at the Turkish court at Bursa under the tutelage of Elisha the Jew. He taught in Constantinople until 1410, when Michael II exiled him to Mistra for heresy and paganism. There he became an advocate of the revival of classical Greek culture and religion.

In 1438, he was an advisor to the Greek delegation to the Council of Florence (see *Basel, Council of*). While in Florence, he made contact with many Italian Renaissance humanists who were interested in Plato. These contacts led him to write *On the Differences of Plato from Aristotle* in which he asserts the superiority of Plato. It was at this time that he adopted the name Plethon. Marsilio Ficino credits him with persuading Cosimo di Medici to found the Platonic Academy.

Plethon's final work, *Book of Laws*, is modeled on Plato's *Laws* and *Republic*. In it he expressly calls for a revival of classical Greek religion. Both Mark Eugenicus and Bessarion of Nicaea were among his Greek students. Plethon was highly regarded among the Italian Renaissance Platonists, and his body was brought from Mistra to Rimini and buried there.

PG 160 (1866); C. M. Woodhouse, *George Gemistus Plethon: The Last of the Hellenes* (1986).

EUGENE M. LUDWIG, OFM CAP.

Pliny the Younger (c. 61–112), Roman senator, orator, and writer. Son of an Italian landowner from Comum (Como), Pliny was adopted by his uncle, the polymath Pliny the Elder. He studied rhetoric under Quintilian and enjoyed a senatorial career that culminated in appointment by Emperor Trajan to the governorship of Bithynia-Pontus in Asia Minor (c. 110–12). His forensic and epideictic oratory won distinction and, along with wealth and ties of patronage, propelled his success. Pliny's poetry has not survived, but his *Panegyric* celebrating Trajan is the only extant Latin speech between Cicero and the panegyrics of the late empire. He is now best known for his ten books of *Letters*. These shed light not only upon Pliny's life but also upon early imperial society. The tenth book contains only correspondence between Pliny and Trajan. Letter 10.96, written from Pontus c. 112, provides the earliest external description of Christian worship and charts official misgivings. Amid ill-defined local troubles and because of their obstinacy in refusing to recant, Pliny executed some Christians as adherents of what he saw as a *superstitio* (an impious foreign cult). Other Christians he released after they sacrificed and reviled Christ. Trajan's reply (Letter 10.97) established Christianity's illegality, but cautioned against persecution, while sanctioning Pliny's sacrificial test for the future.

———

Pliny, *Letters and Panegyricus*, trans. B. Radice, 2 vols. (1969); R. Wilken, *The Christians as the Romans Saw Them* (1984); S. Hoffer, *The Anxieties of Pliny the Younger* (1999).

                                    DENNIS E. TROUT

Pneumatomachians

The term refers to several different groups who disputed the divinity of the Spirit in the latter half of the fourth century. Athanasius spoke of a group he termed the "Tropici" in his Letters to Serapion (c. 359). In the late 350s and early 360s some bishops in Asia Minor and in Egypt, many of whom were of the homoiousian party, argued that the Godhead encompassed the Father and the Son but not the Spirit (hence *pneumatomachoi*: "Spirit fighters"). In the 360s and 370s some of these subscribed to the Nicene Creed (still in its pre-381 form) while maintaining these beliefs. These groups in Egypt and Asia Minor appear to have been largely independent of each other. By the 380s those in Asia Minor were also called by their opponents "Macedonians," after Macedonius, the bishop of Constantinople who had been deposed in 360. There is, however, no evidence that they associated themselves with his name. After 372 Eustathius of Sebaste, formerly a friend and mentor of Basil of Caesarea, became prominent among them, renouncing a former allegiance to Nicaea. At the Council of Constantinople in 381 conciliatory attempts were made to entice

them back into the Nicene fold but without success. After Theodosius's antiheretical legislation of 383, they seem to have rapidly declined in number. Sozomen the historian presented them, in the third decade of the fifth century, as almost extinct. The more important polemics against "Macedonians" include Gregory of Nyssa's *To Eustathius against the Macedonians*, which is an important sermon against the same (GNO 3/1, 89–115), the fifth of Gregory of Nazianzus's *Theological Orations*, and the two anonymous *Macedonian Dialogues* (PG 28.1202–1250, 1291–1337).

———

R. P. C. Hanson, *The Search for the Christian Doctrine of God* (1988), 760–72; W.-D. Hauschild, "Die Pneumatomachen: Eine Untersuchung zur Dogmengeschichte des vierten Jahrhunderts" (PhD diss., Univ. of Hamburg, 1967); M. A. G. Haykin, *The Spirit of God: The Exegesis of 1 and 2 Corinthians in the Pneumatomachian Controversy of the Fourth Century* (1994).

                                    LEWIS AYRES

Poissy, Colloquy of

The Colloquy was a meeting held in 1561 west of Paris of Roman Catholic and Reformed clergy and theologians that was intended to reconcile Catholics and the growing group of Protestants in France. Initiated by the queen mother, Catherine de Médicis, regent for her son Charles IX, and her chancellor Michel de l'Hôpital, the colloquy met intermittently for a month. Debate was in French, in contrast to the Latin used at the international papal Council of Trent (1545–1563) that was unpopular in France. The spokesperson for the Catholics at Poissy was Charles de Guise, cardinal of Lorraine. His counterpart for the Reformed group was Theodore Beza, who was backed by Peter Martyr Vermigli, Nicolas Des Gallars, and others. John Calvin remained in Geneva. The colloquy broke down over the issue of the real presence of Christ in the Lord's Supper. Lorraine submitted for Reformed approval a Lutheran interpretation from the Augsburg Confession, perhaps as a compromise or perhaps to block proceedings. The Reformed group found it unacceptable. The crown granted toleration to the Reformed in January 1562, but a massacre of Protestants at Wassy in March of that year ignited religious warfare that continued intermittently until the Edict of Nantes (1598; revoked by Louis XIV in 1685).

———

D. Nugent, *Ecumenism in the Age of the Reformation: The Colloquy of Poissy* (1974);

N. M. Sutherland, "The Cardinal of Lorraine and the Colloque of Poissy, 1561: A Reassessment," *JEH* 28 (1977): 265–89; M. Turchetti, "Une question mal posée: La Confession d'Augsbourg, le Cardinal de Lorraine et les moyenneurs au Colloque de Poissy en 1561," *Zwingliana* 20 (1993): 53–101.

JEANNINE E. OLSON

Poland, Reformation in Never a unified movement, the Reformation in Poland consisted instead of a diverse group of Lutherans, Calvinists, Bohemian Brethren (who were exiled to Poland in 1548), and, later, the more radical Polish Brethren. Although the movement eventually attempted to define a universal Protestant stance (in its *Consensus Sendomiriensis* of 1570), it was weakened by internal divisions, which explains in large measure why it never gained a firmer foothold.

Lutheranism first entered Poland through ducal Prussia (the converted territory of the Knights of the Teutonic Order), which had recently become a vassal state of the Polish crown and was converted to Lutheranism in 1525. Königsberg, Krakow, and Lower Silesia became important entry points for the new teaching, through which it traveled further into Poland. Luther's ideas received a hearing in many Polish cities, but the movement remained predictably German. Of the 142 Lutheran churches in Great Poland at the end of the sixteenth century, for example, 110 were German and only 32 Polish.

Calvinism, on the other hand, had a wider appeal, particularly among the nobility in Minor Poland. Jan Laski (Jean à Lasco, 1499–1560), whose conversion to the Reformed faith in the late 1530s was followed by eighteen years of travel and work among Western European Protestants, provided the movement with leadership and theological guidance. Acquainted with many of the leading reformers, Laski worked for some years in Friesland and after the Interim made his way to London, where he pastored a congregation of foreign Protestants and influenced the course of the English Reformation. In 1556 he returned to Poland and served as a Protestant advisor to King Sigismund II Augustus (r. 1548–1572), who, faced with the conversion of many of his nobles, had extended the movement a measure of religious freedom. In 1559, Sigismund approved the adoption of the Augsburg Confession in ducal Prussia. Prominent reformers, including Philip Melanchthon and John Calvin, had appealed to him for support. By the 1560s a majority of the lay members of the Polish sen-

ate and nearly one-sixth of Polish parishes were Protestant, and it seemed as if the movement might even gain supremacy.

Confessional disunity, however, proved its undoing. Attempts to adopt a universal Polish Protestant confession, including Laski's introduction of a version of Melanchthon's Augsburg Confession, failed. By 1565, the Polish Reformed church had split into "major" and "minor" factions. The Minor Church, also known as the Polish Brethren, embraced more radical versions of reform. In the late sixteenth century, it was dominated by the Antitrinitarian Faustus Socinus (1539–1604). Nevertheless, with the formal adoption of a policy of toleration toward Protestants in the Warsaw Confederation of 1573, the movement in Poland reached its zenith. Thus, the country established itself as a haven for radicals who had been persecuted elsewhere, on account of which critics sometimes dubbed it a *paradisus hereticorum*. Even the eventual exile of the Polish Brethren (in 1660) resulted more from their radical social ideals than from any accusations of heresy, a measure of the success of the policy of toleration.

Meanwhile, however, efforts at Catholic reform were well under way, some having begun as early as the 1520s under the leadership of the archbishop Jan Laski (1455–1531), uncle of the Protestant reformer. Polish prelates, particularly Cardinal Stanislaus Hosius (1504–1579), were also active at the reforming Council of Trent and worked to see its decrees adopted in their native land. With a steady stream of Jesuit leaders arriving in Poland after 1565 at the initiative of Peter Canisius (1521–1597), the Roman church was strengthened. Schools were founded for the education of the sons of the Polish nobility, Jesuit preachers effectively undermined Protestant teaching, and traditional forms of Catholic piety were encouraged, particularly pilgrimages to holy sites and devotion to the Blessed Virgin Mary. Thus, the people were led back to the Catholic Church rather than being compelled to come in. Late in the sixteenth century the Jesuits were offered protection and support by King Sigismund III Vasa (r. 1587–1632), whose policies brought a de facto end to the policy of toleration. When in 1596 the Union of Brest achieved the voluntary reunification of the country's Orthodox bishops with Rome, the catholicization of Poland reached a new high.

N. Davies, *God's Playground: A History of Poland*, vol. 1, *The Origins to 1795* (1981); H. Jedin and J. Dolan, eds., *History of the Church*, vol. 5, *Reformation and Counter-*

Reformation (1990); J. Raitt, ed., *Shapers of Religious Traditions in Germany, Switzerland, and Poland, 1560–1600* (1981); G. H. Williams, *The Radical Reformation* (3rd ed., 1992).

MICKEY L. MATTOX

Pole, Reginald (1500–1558), cardinal, archbishop of Canterbury, papal legate. Pole was born in Staffordshire and educated at Oxford. He was the younger son of Sir Richard Pole by his wife Margaret, daughter of the Duke of Clarence, and enjoyed Henry VIII's favor. Beginning in 1521, he studied extensively in Padua, Rome, and Paris. Owing to his bloodline and his political connections in England and in Europe, Pole was both the beneficiary and the subject of intrigue in both church and state affairs. To Henry's great consternation, Pole was made cardinal in 1536 and served thereafter several times as papal legate to England and to the courts of Europe. Pole was the primary contributor to *De unitate*, written from 1535 to 1536. Following its publication, Pole fell out of favor with Henry and went into a twenty-year exile during which he depended upon papal protection to escape Henry's political and legal reach. In 1542 Pole was one of three legates who attempted to open the Council of Trent. After the death of Pope Paul III in 1549, he missed papal election by one vote in 1549. In 1553 he went as legate to Queen Mary and, in 1554, absolved England of the sin of schism. He became archbishop of Canterbury in 1556.

Pole's role in Marian persecutions and reforms has been the subject of serious debate. Recent scholarship has concentrated on Pole as a figure depicted in his own extensive writings.

———

D. Fenlon, *Heresy and Obedience in Tridentine Italy: Cardinal Pole and the Counter Reformation* (1972); T. F. Mayer, *Reginald Pole: Prince and Prophet* (2000).

JOHN E. GRISWOLD

Polish Brethren Collection of Antitrinitarian churches that originated in Poland after the 1530s. Initially they were a part of the Polish Reformed church. In 1565, however, they formally split and became known as the "Minor Reformed" church. Already in 1556, a certain Peter Gonesius had written in support of the ideas of the Spanish Antitrinitarian Michael Servetus (1511–1553), recently executed in Geneva. The Polish Antitrinitarian movement gradually gained adherents, but it was divided over doctrine and practice: some baptized infants, others adults; some held to scriptural

authority, others favored direct inspiration. They included tritheists, ditheists, and unitarians; some of the latter eventually became Jews. Protected by the nobleman Michal Sieniecki (1521–1582), they authored in 1574 a catechism that reflected unitarianism, pacifism, and socialism. This document was further refined in the Racovian Catechism of 1605, which taught that Jesus was a deified human being, emphasized the freedom of the will, and rejected predestination and the doctrine of original sin. After 1579 the group was influenced by Faustus Socinus (1539–1604), and Socinianism flourished into the seventeenth century and beyond.

———

S. Kot, *Socinianism in Poland* (1957); G. H. Williams, *The Radical Reformation* (3rd ed., 1992).

MICKEY L. MATTOX

Politiques Advocates of peace and temporary toleration, the Politiques considered tranquility and order as necessary preconditions for a lasting resolution of confessional differences. Originally coined by militant Catholics in the 1560s, the term "Politique" actually carried at the time pejorative connotations, as it purportedly described someone who put political interests above matters of faith. Some modern historians have mistakenly seen the Politiques as a cohesive movement that advanced secular arguments in favor of religious toleration. Neither position accurately reflects the views of leading proponents of moderation, such as Chancellor Michel de l'Hôpital (1505–1573), Henry, Duke of Montmorency-Damville (1534–1614), and the political theorist Jean Bodin (1530–1596). These and other like-minded men deeply valued religious uniformity as the bedrock of political and moral order in the kingdom encapsulated in the Gallican ideal of "One King, One Law, One Faith." The use of force to compel individual consciences struck them as highly dubious, however. For them, the eschewal of violence would allow meaningful dialogue and lasting reconciliation eventually to occur.

———

W. F. Church, *Constitutional Thought in Sixteenth-Century France* (1941); J. Franklin, *Jean Bodin and the Rise of Absolutist Theory* (1973); S.-H. Kim, *Michel de l'Hôpital: The Vision of a Reformist Chancellor during the French Wars of Religion* (1997).

MICHAEL WOLFE

Polycarp (d. c. 156), bishop of Smyrna (Asia Minor) during the late first through mid-second century. Polycarp was a contemporary of Papias of Hieropolis, Ignatius of Antioch, and Marcion of Sinope. His faith and reputation are evident in the letter to the Philippians that remains from his correspondence, as well as the account of his death preserved in the highly edited *Martyrdom of Polycarp*. Both of these writings are classified among the Apostolic Fathers.

Polycarp's *Epistle to the Philippians* is a careful reflection of common early Christian traditions and NT scriptures. It was written for two primary purposes: to call for trust in God and perseverance in righteousness (chaps. 1–12) and to serve as a cover letter for Polycarp's own collection of letters by Ignatius (chaps. 13–14). It is unclear whether our present text is a single letter or a combination of two separate works. The bishop argues on behalf of the need for order within the church, both as evidenced in traditional household codes and in terms of ecclesiastical hierarchy.

The *Martyrdom* is a secondary account of Polycarp's death in Smyrna. It preserves an eyewitness description of the event, edited in its details to reflect the crucifixion of Jesus. In its present form it has been structured into a letter for the church at Philomelium (Asia Minor). Names, situations, and details that are typical of the NT passion accounts permeate the narrative. The highly stylized death of the bishop became a standard genre by which later Christian martyrdoms were depicted well into the medieval period.

P. N. Harrison, *Polycarp's Two Epistles to the Philippians* (1936); W. R. Schoedel, "Polycarp of Smyrna and Ignatius of Antioch," *ANRW* 2.27.1 (1993): 272–358; W. R. Schoedel, *Polycarp, Martyrdom of Polycarp, Fragments of Papias* (1967).

CLAYTON N. JEFFORD

Pomerius, Julianus (later fifth–early sixth century), rhetorician, grammarian, priest, and author. Born in Mauretania (Morocco/ western Algeria), Pomerius emigrated to Gaul, perhaps in 484 at the start of persecution of Nicene Christians by the Arian Vandal king Huneric (r. 477–484). By the 490s Pomerius was living in Arles, where he taught grammar. Ordained a priest, he asssociated with leading aristrocrats and churchmen in Arles and elsewhere. Pomerius wrote *The Contemplative Life*, which survives complete, *The Nature of the Soul*, of which a few fragments survive, and *The Education of Virgins*, which is lost. His views were close to those of his fellow Africans

Tertullian and Augustine but were not identical. Advocating Augustine's reform idea that bishops should live an ascetic life in common with their clergy, Pomerius had a considerable impact on the pastoral practices of Caesarius of Arles and later on the Carolingian church.

R. A. Kaster, *Guardians of Language: The Grammarian and Society in Late Antiquity* (1988), 342–43; W. E. Klingshirn, *Caesarius of Arles* (1994), 73–82; M. L. W. Laistner, "The Influence during the Middle Ages of the Treatise 'De Vita Contemplativa' and Its Surviving Manuscripts," in *Miscellanea Giovanni Mercati* 2 (1946), 344–58; A. Solignac, "Les fragments du 'De Natura Animae' de Julien Pomère (fin Ve siècle)," *BLE* 74 (1974): 41–60.

WILLIAM E. KLINGSHIRN

Pomponazzi, Pietro (1462–1525), of Mantua, Aristotelian philosopher. He studied at the Univ. of Padua, where he received a doctorate in medicine in 1487 and lectured on Aristotle, achieving election to the chair of philosophy in 1499. He also taught at Ferrara and Bologna. In his controversial 1516 book *On the Immortality of the Soul*, he argued that the interpretation of the twelfth-century Arabic commentator Averroes positing a cosmic intellect in which individual humans participate was inconsistent with the teachings of Aristotle. He claimed instead that Aristotle grounded the human intellect in natural, bodily processes. A proponent of the doctrine of the double truth of philosophy and revealed religion, his professions of adherence to Christian teaching are considered by some to be insincere.

E. Cassirer et al., eds., *The Renaissance Philosophy of Man* (1948, 1956); M. L. Pine, *Pietro Pomponazzi: Radical Philosopher of the Renaissance* (1986).

J. LAUREL CARRINGTON

Ponce de la Fuente, Constantino (1502–1559), Spanish preacher and theologian. He studied at the Universidad Complutense de Alcalá and completed his doctorate in sacred theology at the Colegio de Santa María de Jesús (1534). In 1533, he was appointed as preacher at the Cathedral of Seville. During his first stay at Seville, he published two of his catechetical works: *Summa de doctrina christiana* (1544) and *Sermon de nuestro redentor en el monte* (1544). From 1548 to 1551 he joined the court of Charles V as chaplain and traveled with Philip II to the Low Countries and southern Germany. After his return to Seville he was elected in 1556 as honorary canon of the cathedral chapter of Seville. There he published *Confesión de un pecador* (1554), and *Cathecismo christiano* (1556). By 1558 his works were suspected of heresy, which led to his arrest and eventual death in prison. His remains were burned by the Inquisition in the Auto de Fe of 1560.

———

M. P. A. Ansa, *Constantino Ponce de la Fuente: El hombre y su language* (1975); J. C. Nieto, *El Renacimiento y la otra España* (1997).

RADY ROLDÁN-FIGUEROA

Ponet, John (1516?–1556), English theologian, political theorist, bishop of Rochester (1550–1551) and Winchester (1551–1553). Cambridge-educated Ponet's theological works include a Protestant catechism and defenses of clerical marriage and of Christ's spiritual (but not corporeal) presence in the Eucharist. Following Mary's ascension, Ponet went into exile at Strasbourg, where he published *A Short Treatise on Politic Power*, a discourse combining political theory and anti-Marian propaganda. In it he argued that while God ordained the institution of government to restrain sin, God left it to each community to determine the form of its government and to authorize rulers. Emphasizing that potentates were obligated to rule in accord with God's laws and the community's best interests, Ponet claimed that tyrants ought to be deposed by the nobility or restrained by the clergy, and he noted that occasionally even private individuals were authorized to commit tyrannicide by special divine commission. Finally, repentance and prayer for deliverance were always available to oppressed subjects. Against this highly suggestive background, Ponet denounced the Marian regime for undermining the eternal and temporal well-being of English subjects.

———

G. Bowman, "John Ponet: Political Theologian of the English Reformation" (PhD diss., Univ. of Minnesota, 1997); W. S. Hudson, *John Ponet: Advocate of Limited Monarchy* (1942).

DANIEL EPPLEY

Porphyry (c. 232–c. 308), Hellenistic Neoplatonic philosopher. Porphyry is best known for editing Plotinus's *Enneads*. He also wrote the *Life of Plotinus*, the *Eisagoge*, and *Sentences Leading to the Intelligible World*. Other writings exist only in fragments. His writings helped introduce the thought of Plotinus and Neoplatonism to Christian thinkers.

Porphyry abolished the barriers between the Plotinian *hypostases* ("subsistences"), telescoping the One, Mind, and Soul. He claimed the

human soul to be an intermediary between the intelligible and sensible worlds, asserted the union of soul and body, and argued against a substantial difference among classes of souls.

Porphyry was a staunch defender of Greek religion against the teachings of Christianity. In *Against the Christians* he attacked Christianity by applying historical and literary criticism to biblical texts.

———

A. H. Armstrong, *The Cambridge History of Later Greek and Early Medieval Philosophy* (1970); T. D. Barnes, "Porphyry *Against the Christians*: Date and Attribution of Fragments," JTS, NS 24 (1973): 424–42; R. M. Berchman, *Porphyry Against the Christians* (2005); R. M. Berchman, "Pagan Philosophical Views on Jews and Judaism," in *Approaches to Ancient Judaism*, vol. 12 (1997), 1–94; Berchman, "In the Shadow of Origen: Porphyry and the Patristic Origins of New Testament Criticism" *Origeniana Sexta* (1993): 657–63; P. Hadot, *Porphyre et Victorinus*, 2 vols. (1968); A. Smith, *Porphyry's Place in the Neoplatonic Tradition* (1974); Smith, "Porphyrian Studies since 1913," *ANRW* 2.36.2 (1988), 717–73; R. T. Wallis, *Neoplatonism* (1972).

ROBERT M. BERCHMAN

Porete, Marguerite see Marguerite Porete

Praemunire In English law the offense of promoting or recognizing papal authority to the derogation of royal authority. Enacted through several fourteenth-century statutes, praemunire was largely unenforced until the rise of the Tudors. In 1530–1531 Henry VIII employed the statutes in his pursuit of wealth, divorce, and the establishment of royal supremacy, using praemunire charges to wrest from the English clergy recognition as head of the English church and payments totaling about £120,000.

———

G. W. Bernard, "The Pardon of the Clergy Reconsidered," *JEH* 37, no. 2 (1986): 258–87; G. R. Elton, *England under the Tudors* (3rd ed., 1991).

DANIEL EPPLEY

Praetorius, Michael (1571–1621), German composer, theorist, and church musician. Praetorius held positions as cantor and kapellmeister in prominent cities and courts in his day. He was a prolific composer (over a thousand pieces of sacred music), especially of sacred vocal music based on Lutheran hymnody. His *Musae Sioniae* (1605–1610), a collection in nine parts, sets the

Lutheran hymn repertory in a variety of ways, from simple homophony to more complex polyphony. His *Syntagma musicum* (1614–1619), a three-volume work, treats systematically the theory and practice of music. This work provides scholars with invaluable information about the musical and religious practices of the early German baroque period and, in particular, the liturgical life of the Lutheran tradition at a critical point in its development. In his later work, an Italian influence can be detected as he became acquainted with musicians who worked in other European cities, towns, and the courts of the time.

Praetorius, in his prodigious output at the turn of the seventeenth century, summarized and codified the musical tradition of the early Reformation and provided his successors with a wealth of resources for the church and for the delight of musicians everywhere.

––––––

P. Bunjes, *The Praetorius Organ* (1966); S. Vogelsaenger, *Michael Praetorius beim Wort genommen: Zur Entstehungsgeschichte seiner Werke* (1987).

LINDA J. CLARK

Pragmatic Sanction of Bourges

Promulgated in 1438 by Charles VII upon advice from a council of French clergy, the Pragmatic Sanction reduced papal authority over the French church by ordering that cathedral chapters and monastic houses elect bishops and abbots without interference from Rome (although not from the king's influence). The edict also proscribed sending annates, the first-year's revenue from a benefice, to the Holy See. Since the papacy never recognized the edict's legitimacy, fifteenth-century French kings used it as a tool for negotiating with Rome. The Pragmatic Sanction of Bourges was canceled by the Concordat of Bologna (1516).

––––––

A. Black, *Monarchy and Community: Political Ideas in the Later Conciliar Controversy, 1430–1450* (1970).

SCOTT M. MARR

Praxeas (second–third cent.), described as a confessor from Asia Minor. This shadowy figure is known to us only through Tertullian's *Against Praxeas*, the anonymous *Against All Heresies* (8), and some comments by Hippolytus of Rome. It is agreed that Praxeas was a modalistic Monarchian, that is, one who maintained the unity of God by declaring the Trinity to be mere *personae* ("persons") as temporal modes of the one divine substance. Because of Praxeas's opposition to the Montanist emphasis on the separate hypostasis of the Holy Spirit, and his introducing modalism to Carthage, Tertullian devoted an entire polemical treatise against him. It seems that Praxeas's views had already found reception in Rome and that a patripassianist modalism may have already been shared by the Roman bishops Zephyrinus and Callistus. While some modern scholars have regarded Praxeas as a pseudonym, there is no substantial reason to think it was anything but the actual name for a historical figure.

––––––

E. Evans, *Tertullian's Treatise against Praxeas* (1948); R. Heine, "The Christology of Callistus," *JTS* 49 (1998): 56–91.

D. H. WILLIAMS

Preaching in the Early Church

Preaching developed out of Christians' commitment to proclaim the good news of Jesus both as a missionary act and for believers' edification. Little preaching material is extant prior to the third century, although some scholars have identified fragments in the New Testament (e.g., James and 1 Peter) in addition to the model speeches in Luke-Acts given by leaders such as Peter, Paul, and Stephen. "Homily" and "sermon," derived from Greek and Latin, respectively, referred originally to informal but serious philosophical conversations. In early Christian worship the "conversations," likely developed as prophecies (impromptu utterances), were discussed and tested by the assembly.

The Gospels' vocabulary for preaching emphasizes missionary activity. The Synoptics use *kēryssein* ("proclaim") and *euangelizesthai* ("proclaim good news") while John prefers *anangellein* ("report") and *martyrein* ("bear witness"). Itinerant apostles and prophets (as depicted in Acts, Luke 10, Matt. 10, and the *Didache*) preached in marketplaces, synagogues, and the newly established assemblies of Christians.

Second-century preaching to non-Christians shifted from proclamation to defense in response to sporadic persecution and public misinformation about Christianity. These works also hint at the place of preaching in worship. Justin Martyr (*1 Apol.* 67.3–5) related that the "president" of the assembly was in charge of "admonishing" and "exhorting" believers to imitate the message of the day's Scripture. Tertullian (*Apol.* 39) described the agape feast as a time for conversation, edification, and correction.

Homilies became the main vehicle for preaching within the church in conjunction with the growing homogenization of liturgy, the decline of the prophetic tradition, and the authority of the developing NT writings. Preaching was commonly limited to the bishop (or to presbyters with the bishop's authorization) and focused upon explaining and applying Scripture.

Christianity revived the art of rhetoric, which had ceased to be a tool in civic debate under the Roman Empire. Christian leaders equipped with classical educations employed their learning to teach and persuade their congregations on topics ranging from faith formation and moral edification to theological controversies, social crises, and natural disasters. The fourth and fifth centuries produced a golden age of preaching that addressed the challenges of applying Christian belief to everyday life, even to the point of offending the powerful.

Most leaders who were later revered as "fathers" of the church (e.g., Origen, Basil of Caesarea, Gregory of Nazianzus, John Chrysostom, Augustine of Hippo, Leo the Great, Gregory the Great) won their reputations by their preaching, and their homilies were preserved as models for later generations. They provide unique resources for examining the fathers' working theologies and historical contexts.

P. F. Bradshaw, *Early Christian Worship: A Basic Introduction to Ideas and Practice* (1996); M. B. Cunningham and P. Allen, eds., *Preacher and Audience: Studies in Early Christian and Byzantine Homiletics* (1998); D. G. Hunter, ed., *Preaching in the Patristic Age* (1989); A. Olivar, *La Predicación Cristiana Antigua* (1991); R. E. Osborn, *Folly of God: The Rise of Christian Preaching* (1999); A. Stewart-Sykes, *From Prophecy to Preaching: A Search for the Origins of the Christian Homily* (2001).

LISA D. MAUGANS DRIVER

Preaching, Medieval The shift from patristic to medieval preaching was occasioned by the collapse of classical Latin rhetorical education around the end of the Roman Empire in the West in 476. The effect of that collapse and recovery from it can be traced through representative preachers: Leo the Great (d. 461), Caesarius of Arles (470–542), Gregory the Great (540–604), and the Venerable Bede (673–735). Clergy lost faith in their ability to interpret the Bible as the church fathers had and, rather than writing their own, they collected fragments of patristic sermons into homiliaries used for devotional reading, aid in sermon preparation, and reading at the monastic night offices. Vernacular preaching undoubtedly flourished during this period, but almost none of it is preserved. Charlemagne (c. 742–814) established a literate clergy to catechize all the new Christians his military campaigns brought into the church. Anglo-Saxons such as Aelfric of Eynsham (c. 955–1020) also did catechetical preaching.

Gradually preaching revived, especially in the monasteries. In 1084 Guibert of Nogent wrote the first original book of homiletical instruction since Augustine's *De doctrina christiana*. A century later Alan of Lille wrote an *Art of Preaching* that anticipated the thematic sermon of the mendicant friars, but he did not subdivide the text as they would. Meanwhile abbots such as Bernard of Clairvaux (1090–1153) preached to form their monks spiritually. Abbesses also preached to their nuns; a few, such as Hildegard of Bingen (1098–1179), preached outside their convents as well.

Special clergy were needed for the new cities that were rising by the thirteenth century, clergy such as those in the orders of itinerant friars formed by Francis of Assisi (c. 1182–1226) and Dominic (1170–1221). Before the friars, most sermons had no outline other than that offered by the biblical passages they interpreted, but the friars created the first real sermon shape, that of the thematic sermon. These sermons were based on a single biblical verse "theme" with at least three components. A division of the sermon was devoted to each component, and these were broken into several subpoints. Textbooks began to appear, setting forth elaborate rules for constructing such sermons and all the ways that points could be "dilated." So that they could always be ready to preach, the friars developed many other preaching aids, including reference books containing supporting quotations or illustrations (exempla) and collections of sermon models or outlines.

Rhineland mystics in the thirteenth and fourteenth centuries such as Meister Eckhart and John Tauler were well known for their preaching. There were also dissident voices, such as those of John Wyclif (c. 1330–1384) and Girolamo Savonarola (1452–1498), although the extent to which either was "a Protestant before the Reformation" has been exaggerated. The medieval period was a rich one in the history of preaching.

D. L. d'Avray, *The Preaching of the Friars* (1985); O. C. Edwards Jr., *The History of*

Preaching, 2 vols. (2003); B. M. Kienzele, ed., *The Sermon* (2000); J. J. Murphy, *Rhetoric in the Middle Ages* (1974); R. H. Rouse and M. A. Rouse, *Preachers, Florilegia, and Sermons* (1979).

O. C. EDWARDS JR.

Preaching, Medieval Women's There is a little known tradition of women preaching with some regularity and with localized support in the high to late Middle Ages, especially within three spheres: within the monastic tradition, within the resurgence of lay piety starting in the twelfth century, and within the mendicant movements starting in the thirteenth century. Because women's preaching was performed either privately or spontaneously as street preaching, the actual sermons of these women rarely exist. Instead, their preaching is documented indirectly through its condemnation in episcopal and papal legislation and scholastic quodlibetal literature (where it was also sometimes supported), or through its celebration in hagiography, such as the *vitae* of Rose of Viterbo (d. 1251), the Italian adolescent street preacher, or of Angelina of Montegiove (d. 1435), the leader of Third Order Franciscans. There are, however, occasional extant sermon collections, such as those of Umiltà of Faenza (d. 1310), the Vallambrosan abbess, who preached to her sisters. Some women, such as Catherine of Siena (d. 1380), are believed to have preached in one form or another, but contemporary biographers rarely use the term "preach," probably to avoid a risk of scandal or accusation of wrongdoing. Just as lay preaching as a whole was closely monitored and legislated to be licit only by permission of local clerical authorities, preaching by women was closely monitored and usually became marginalized either as heretical or saintly so that the practice would not be widely imitated.

A. Blamires, "Woman Not to Preach: A Disputation in Brit. Lib. Ms. Harley 31," *Journal of Medieval Latin* 3 (1993): 34–63; "Women and Preaching in Medieval Orthodoxy, Heresy, and Saints' Lives," *Viator* 26 (1995): 135–52; R. McKelvie, *Retrieving a Living Tradition: Angelina of Montegiove, Franciscan, Tertiary, Beguine* (1997); B. Kienzle and P. Walker, eds., *Women Preachers and Prophets through Two Millennia of Christianity* (1998); K. Scott, "St. Catherine of Siena: 'Apostola,'" *CH* 61, no. 1 (1992): 34–46; P. Zama, *Santa Umiltà: La Vita e Sermones* (1974).

DARLEEN PRYDS

Preaching, Reformation Martin Luther's breakthrough to a new understanding of justification led to both a theological and a practical reform of preaching. Other Reformation-era movements also attached great importance to preaching.

For Luther, the preached word was a means of grace. Preaching was not merely the conveyance of information, the discussion of a theological topic, or moral admonition. The Holy Spirit used the preached word to create repentance and trust in God. Faith came from hearing this word (Rom. 10:17). Luther understood preaching to encompass both God's threats (law) and promises (gospel). The Holy Spirit was active in the preaching of the law to bring persons to awareness of their sin, and in the preaching of the gospel to proclaim the forgiveness of sin, and to raise listeners to faith and new life. In hearing the preached word, listeners experienced what Christ had done for them. Preaching also exposed false teaching and warned listeners to avoid it.

Preaching—whether on Sunday, weekdays, or other occasions (e.g., funerals)—became a focal point of Lutheran worship services. Lutherans preached in the vernacular and continued to use the lectionary inherited from the medieval church of Epistle and Gospel texts for each Sunday and feast day. Sermons on weekdays often preached *seriatim* ("serially") through biblical books. Luther and his fellow reformers energetically sought to improve parish preaching. Influenced by both patristic and humanistic models of preaching, Luther stressed simplicity and subordination of rhetorical style to content. His sermons generally followed a verse-by-verse method of explication, though sometimes he focused on one or two verses as the central message of the text. Luther generally rejected the medieval fourfold method of biblical interpretation and affirmed a literal reading of the text; however, he sometimes used allegorical interpretations. Luther and other Lutheran preachers (e.g., Johannes Brenz, Antonius Corvinus, and Johannes Spangenberg) published *Postils*, collections of model sermons for the Sundays and feast days of the church year, to aid the preaching of parish pastors. Some published collections of model wedding and funeral sermons. Lutherans also preached regularly on the catechism, using the texts of the Ten Commandments, Lord's Prayer, Apostles' Creed, and the words of institution of the sacraments, publishing sermons to aid this endeavor. While Luther never wrote a treatise on preaching, Philip Melanchthon wrote influential treatises on rhetoric. Adapting classical models for the preaching task, Melanchthon also recommended preaching by topics in the text. His homiletical methods dominated preaching in the latter half of the sixteenth century. The actual reception of Lutheran preaching is difficult to determine. Parish visitation committees inquired of both pastors and parishioners as to the doctrinal sufficiency and the effectiveness of preaching. As the sixteenth century progressed, the number of preaching treatises and model sermon collections multiplied. Pastors' libraries commonly contained several such works.

Preachers in the Reformed tradition shared the rejection of medieval fourfold exegesis but did not share the Lutheran understanding of preaching as a means of grace. Reformed sermons explained a biblical text and discussed basic doctrinal points related to the text, noting both arguments and counterarguments. Sermons condemned sin and exhorted listeners to ethical action. Reformed preachers emphasized simplicity and practicality. With few exceptions, Reformed preaching abandoned the lectionary, preferring to preach consecutively through a biblical book.

Late medieval Roman Catholic preaching generally expounded a topic or theme, using the biblical text as a point of departure or proof. In the fifteenth and sixteenth centuries, as humanistic emphases emerged, Roman preachers sought to exegete biblical texts. They celebrated God's grace and beneficence and sought to move the listener to admiration, praise, imitation of God's qualities, and deliberation about ethical behavior. Catholic preachers also published *Postils* to provide priests with proper models and to counteract the influence of Lutheran works. New religious orders arose that emphasized preaching. Catholics continued to base their preaching on traditional lectionary texts, with some changes made by the Council of Trent. The Council of Trent admonished clergy simply to preach the vices to avoid and the virtues to cultivate to obtain salvation. The council was concerned with improving parish preaching and stressed proper episcopal oversight to this end.

In the oral culture of Reformation Europe, preaching was a primary means of communication and was where theology met laity. For this reason the study of preaching is important for Reformation studies.

――――

F. W. Meuser, *Luther the Preacher* (1983); J. W. O'Malley, "Content and Rhetorical Forms in Sixteenth-Century Treatises on Preaching," in *Renaissance Eloquence: Studies in the Theory and Practice of Renaissance Rhetoric*, ed. J. J. Murphy (1983), 238–52; A. Pettegree, ed., *The Reformation of the Parishes: The Ministry and the Reformation in Town and Country* (1993); L. Taylor, ed., *Preachers and People in the Reformations and Early Modern Period* (2001).

MARY JANE HAEMIG

Prebends　In canon law, *praebenda* or *beneficium* means the right associated with a church office to receive a fixed income from church property or certain donations. From the ninth century, by the so-called division of goods, the initially unitary church assets developed into a chapter fund, of which the individual canons acquired the right to a portion. Rural churches developed differently, in that from the beginning they established separate funds from which the clergy were maintained. In the eleventh century, *canonicatus*, *praebenda*, and *beneficia* appear as synonyms in Italy.

Offices and prebends were closely linked, in that the former were classified according to the kinds of benefice and the prebend was granted together with the office; the institution of commendams allowed prebends to be granted without office. Incumbents could not be removed from office against their will, which guaranteed them independence and legal security. Well-endowed prebends gave their incumbents an income, a dwelling, freedom of action, and freedom of movement. Thus, the clergy became a much-used pool of personnel for tasks in the church and in secular rule (court, chancery, administration, justice, politics, diplomacy, etc.). Prebends also provided an income for university teachers. Thus, powerful social groups had various interests in how they were granted. In the late Middle Ages something like a market for prebends developed, and absentee pluralism (holding several prebends at once) seems to have been a widespread, or at least much deplored, problem.

――――

S. Lorenz and A. Meyer, eds., *Stift und Wirtschaft. Die Finanzierung geistlichen Lebens im Mittelalter* (2007); P. Moraw, "Stiftspfründen als Elemente des Bildungswesens im spätmittelalterlichen Reich," in *Studien zum weltlichen Kollegiatstift in Deutschland* (1995), 270–97; A. Pöschl, "Die Entstehung des geistlichen Benefiziums," *Archiv für katholisches Kirchenrecht* 106 (1926): 3–121, 363–471.

OLIVER AUGE

Precisionism   Applied to sixteenth- and seventeenth-century Puritans on account of their punctiliousness in observing external moral and religious rules and forms, this term was virtually synonymous with "Puritanism" in Elizabethan England. It applied to a rigorist strain within Dutch Calvinism hostile to humanist culture and more liberal forces within the church.

M. M. Knappen, *Tudor Puritanism: A Chapter in the History of Idealism* (1963).

JOHN TONKIN

Premonstratensian Order   An order of canons regular (also known as Norbertines or White Canons) organized in the early twelfth century by Hugh of Fosses (c. 1093–1161) out of the community of hermits who had gathered around Norbert of Xanten (c. 1080–1134) and out of filial communities founded by Norbert's group. Norbert was the founder, Hugh the co-organizer. A nobleman and a canon of the cathedral of Xanten, Norbert had resigned his benefices in 1115 to become a hermit. His sympathetic bishop, Bartholemew of Laon, provided him with a chapel dedicated to St. John at a place in the forest of Coucy called Prémontré. It became a base from which Norbert conducted tours as a preacher and to which he attracted men and women anxious to live the eremitical life associated with Christ and the apostles. He envisaged a community of activists who lived in evangelical poverty. In 1121, Norbert's group vowed to live according to the gospel and to follow the rule of St. Augustine. They adapted a habit of bleached wool. When Norbert accepted an appointment as archbishop of Magdeburg in 1126, exemplifying a reformer's virtues (he is said to have entered Magdeburg barefoot, and he immediately reformed local monasteries, attacked clerical concubinage, and fought to restore property that had been alienated from the church), the community at Prémontré elected Hugh of Fosses to succeed him as abbot. Hugh then wrote the first statutes for the order and won their approval at the general chapter held in Prémontré in 1134. Hugh's statutes were greatly influenced by Cistercian practices, including a requirement that each canon perform manual labor daily, an annual gathering of all abbots to a general chapter at Prémontré, the employment of lay brothers (*conversi*) to help farm and do other work, and the choice of remote places for abbeys. Meanwhile, Norbert converted the canons of Magdeburg's cathedral into a Premonstratensian chapter, which occurred in other German cathedrals, too, and early Premonstratensian cloisters also held parish churches. Prémontré became increasingly monastic, insisting on the complete claustration of women and phasing out double cloisters (beginning as early as the 1130s) but also requiring, in the statutes of 1154, both male and female houses to maintain a cloister school. The order grew very rapidly. By 1134, which was the year of the first statutes and also the year of Norbert's death, the order already counted sixty-eight foundations, most of which were located in northern France, along the lower Rhine, and scattered across northern Germany. When Hugh of Fosse died in 1161, there were over two hundred Premonstratensian foundations scattered across Europe, from England to southern Italy and central Spain (the number of Premonstratensian sites reached about five hundred by 1500).

I. Crusius and H. Flachenecker, eds., *Studien zum Prämonstratenserorden* (2003); K. Elm, ed., *Norbert von Xanten: Adliger, Ordensstifter, Kirchenfürst* (1984); J. A. Gribbin, *The Premonstratensian Order in Late Medieval England* (2001); C. H. Lawrence, *Medieval Monasticism* (2nd ed., 1989); P. F. Lefèvre and W. M. Grauwen, eds., *Les statuts de Prémontré au milieu du xiie siècle* (1978); F. Petit, *Norbert et l'lorigine des Prémontrés* (1981).

CHRISTOPHER OCKER

Presbyterianism   First devised in the sixteenth century, presbyterianism is a system of church government relying on an ascending series of representative church courts comprising clergy and lay elders or presbyters. Its origins may be found in the Genevan *Ecclesiastical Ordinances* (1541) and in the work of John Calvin who, following Martin Bucer, discerned in the New Testament four principal church offices—doctor, pastor or teaching presbyter, elder or ruling presbyter, and deacon—and a biblical pattern of ruling and maintaining discipline in the church through councils of elders. The term "bishop," in Calvin's estimation, was equivalent to "presbyter." Although he did not oppose the appointment of bishops, for example, in the English context, he believed a representative and collective system of church government had stronger biblical warrant than did episcopacy.

The first national synod of the French Reformed churches (1559) and its adoption of the *French Confession* and *Ecclesiastical Discipline* formed a model for a presbyterian polity to unify scattered congregations that would be adapted to other national contexts. The primary unit for maintaining discipline at the parish level was the *consistory* (in Scotland, "kirk session"; in Holland, *kerkeraad*) of pastors and lay elders. The *colloquy* (Scottish "presbytery," Dutch *classis*), comprising all local clergy and lay representatives, provided care and oversight of congregations in a city, town, or district. At the regional level the provincial synod, and at the national level the national synod (or, in Scotland, "general assembly") met at less frequent, regular intervals to oversee the whole church and establish its policies.

In England, Elizabeth I resisted efforts in the 1570s to introduce presbyterianism to the Church of England. In Scotland, James VI (James I of England after 1603) and his Stuart successors met considerable resistance to their efforts to strengthen the role of bishop, and bishops were finally abolished in the Church of Scotland in 1690. The Reformed churches of Hungary, on the other hand, adopted a reduced episcopacy.

Most presbyterian churches did not specify the precise powers of the respective assemblies. These came to be negotiated in ways appropriate to national and regional experience, although in some instances this process involved considerable conflict. For example, in the American colonies there was a clash between a Scottish model that stressed strong hierarchical oversight and the English Puritan and New England Congregational model that valued individual conscience and local discernment. While American Presbyterians managed a rough compromise, tensions between ecclesiastical uniformity and freedom of theological interpretation continue in Presbyterian church life.

P. Benedict, *Christ's Churches Purely Reformed* (2002); R. M. Kingdon, *Geneva and the Consolidation of the French Protestant Movement, 1564–1572* (1967); J. T. McNeill, *The History and Character of Calvinism* (1954).

CHRISTOPHER ELWOOD

Prierias, Sylvester (1456–1523), Dominican friar and vicar-general of his order's Lombardy province, early opponent of Luther. Prierias was born in Prierio, Piedmont, and died in Rome. At the age of fifteen he entered the Dominican order and later taught at Bologna and Padua from 1495 to 1508. His competence in Thomist theology and canon law was recog-

nized by the papacy, and in 1514 he was called to teach in Rome. In 1515 Pope Leo X appointed him master of the sacred palace, the pope's court theologian. Prierias's oft-reprinted writings cover a vast range of theological subjects. As papal theologian, he became involved in both the Reuchlin and Luther cases. In the former case, Prierias thwarted the majority of the papal commission, who were in favor of acquittal. In the latter case, he was entrusted with formulating the official papal dogmatic response to Luther's Ninety-five Theses, *De potestate papae dialogus* (1518), the basis for the citation of Luther to appear in Rome to answer charges of heresy. Although Rome decided Luther was guilty of heresy, he and Prierias continued their "dialogue" for the next two years. He is credited with being the first theologian to publicly attack Luther and to frame the Reformation debate in terms of the tension between the authority of the church and the authority of Scripture.

C. Lindberg, "Prierias and His Significance for Luther's Development," *SCJ* 3 (1972): 45–64; R. Saarinen, "Liberty and Dominion: Luther, Prierias, and Ringleben," *Neue Zeitschrift für systematische Theologie und Religionsphilosophie* 40 (1998): 171–81; M. Tavuzzi, *Prierias: The Life and Works of Silvestro Mazzolini da Prierio, 1456–1527* (1997).

FRANZ POSSET

Printing The technique of printing can produce an unlimited number of copies, on paper or a similar material, of a specified text or illustration. In the process as traditionally understood, ink is applied to a surface bearing a raised pattern of images or text; this surface is then forced mechanically against a sheet of paper, fabric, or other material, thus transferring the pattern. The basic technology of printing first emerged in China by the end of the second century CE. This earliest known form of printing relied on stone surfaces, carved with texts in relief and spread with ink, over which one laid sheets of paper. Movable type (a technique using individual carved characters that can be rearranged and reused, eliminating the need to carve each page separately) first appeared in eleventh-century China, where it was not developed further. It spread to Korea, where it was vigorously pursued in the succeeding centuries.

The European discovery of movable type is generally credited to Mainz goldsmith Johannes Gutenberg (c. 1399–1468), who printed his

Forty-two-line Bible by 1456. Little is known about Gutenberg himself, but he is thought to have developed two fundamental components of print technology that would remain basically unchanged until the twentieth century: the mechanical handpress and the materials and technique for casting type. These developments enabled the printer, operating with a small staff of assistants, to reproduce and disseminate texts rapidly and relatively cheaply.

By the end of the fifteenth century, most major cities in Europe had at least one print shop, and printing became an important commercial enterprise. The period of the Protestant Reformation saw an explosion of printed texts. Despite low levels of literacy, popular demand was high for printed religious tracts, pamphlets, broadsheets, and Bibles. Print was largely responsible for the unprecedented speed with which Protestant ideas were able to spread across a broad geographical area, while their Catholic opponents largely failed to capitalize on the new medium's potential. Luther called printing "God's highest and most extreme act of grace, by which the business of the Gospel is driven forward."

But its significance goes beyond its efficiency as a vehicle for the spread of information. In many cases it transformed knowledge itself. By making a single text infinitely reproducible, print contributed to a modern conception of knowledge as stable and fixed, rather than corruptible (as earlier, hand-copied manuscripts inevitably were). It thus became possible to focus attention on gaining new knowledge rather than simply preserving the old. In this way the discovery of print technology in the fifteenth century formed a cornerstone for the scientific revolution, the classical revival of the Renaissance, and the word- and Scripture-centered piety of the Protestant Reformation.

In the centuries that followed, the printing press continued to play an integral role in cultural and intellectual shifts. Devotional texts gained in popularity with the rise of Pietism in the seventeenth century. Beginning in the eighteenth century, both the French Revolution and the Enlightenment fostered a "public opinion" formed largely by means of printed texts. The introduction of steam power in the early nineteenth century enabled the mass production of printed matter, permitting, for example, the large-scale manufacture of inexpensive Bibles for missionary distribution around the world. This trend continued with the twentieth-century development of offset printing and automated typesetting techniques. The growth in computer and Internet technology in the late twentieth century has led some observers to forecast the replacement of print by electronic media, but this appears unlikely to happen in the immediate future.

R. Chartier, ed., *The Culture of Print: Power and the Uses of Print in Early Modern Europe* (1989); M. U. Chrisman, *Lay Culture, Learned Culture: Books and Social Change in Strasbourg, 1480–1599* (1982); E. Eisenstein, *The Printing Press as an Agent of Change: Communications and Cultural Transformations in Early-Modern Europe*, 2 vols. (1979); L. Febvre and H.-J. Martin, *The Coming of the Book: The Impact of Printing, 1450–1800* (1976); D. D. Hall, *Cultures of Print: Essays in the History of the Book* (1996); A. Johns, *The Nature of the Book: Print and Knowledge in the Making* (1998); M. McLuhan, *The Gutenberg Galaxy: The Making of Typographic Man* (1962); W. Ong, *Orality and Literacy: The Technologizing of the Word* (1982); S. H. Steinberg, *Five Hundred Years of Printing* (rev. ed. 1996).
NATHAN BARUCH REIN

Priscillian (340–386), a highborn Hispano-Roman holy man accused of heresy who led a controversial ascetic movement (Priscillianism) that spread across Iberia and into southern Gaul. Several bishops reacted negatively to the success of Priscillianism by accusing its adherents, who included men and women from the upper classes and some bishops, of all manner of heresy, especially Manicheism and Gnosticism. This led to an initial gathering of ten bishops at the First Council of Zaragoza (380) who adopted a cautious approach to the emerging movement. Once Priscillian was elected bishop of Avila by his followers, his detractors rejected the ordination as illegitimate, and a vigorous attack was led by bishops Hydatius of Mérida and Ithacius of Córdoba. Priscillian attempted, to no avail, to get the approval for his movement from Ambrose of Milan and Pope Damasus. In 383 the usurper Maximus led a revolt in Gaul that had grave consequences for Priscillian. Maximus was persuaded by Priscillian's enemies to convene a council in Bordeaux (384–385), where Instantius argued the cause for Priscillian, who was deposed as a heretic. Priscillian made the fatal mistake of appealing in person to Maximus, which resulted in his arrest, trial, and execution along with six of his followers at Trier. All of Priscillian's peninsular episcopal opponents were excommunicated by the pope, and they earned a condemnation from Ambrose. The movement, however, continued to flourish, especially in northwestern Iberia (in present-day Galicia and northern Portugal) well into the sixth century.

V. Burrus, *The Making of a Heretic: Gender, Authority, and the Priscillianist Controversy* (1995); H. Chadwick, *Priscillian of Avila: The Occult and the Charismatic in the Early Church* (1976); M. V. Escribano Paño, *Iglesia y Estado en el certamen priscilianista: "Causa ecclesiae et iudicium publicum"* (1988).

ALBERTO FERREIRO

Proba (fourth cent.), Latin poet. Author of the *Cento Vergilianus de laudibus Christi*, Proba was a woman of the Roman senatorial class, educated in classical literature. Most scholars associate the poem with Faltonia Betitia Proba, although some attribute it to her granddaughter, Anicia Faltonia Proba. The most likely date for a composition by the elder Proba is between 354 and 370.

Proba's poem takes the form of a *cento*, a composition created by piecing together lines and half-lines from a well-known poet, in this case Virgil. In 694 verses plus 15 lines of dedication, Proba tells the stories of the first eight chapters of Genesis, gives an overview of the exodus and law giving, and moves on to the life of Jesus, for which she draws upon Virgil's description of Aeneas's life and character.

Her *Cento* was a popular teaching tool into the Middle Ages because it provided access to the style of Virgil, Christian content, and some suitable quotations. By actively shaping her poem to conform to her vision of the Christian faith, Proba was engaging in the theological enterprise from which women were increasingly being excluded.

E. A. Clark and D. F. Hatch, *The Golden Bough, the Oaken Cross: The Virgilian Cento of Faltonia Betitia Proba* (1981); P. Wilson-Kastner et al., eds., *A Lost Tradition: Women Writers of the Early Church* (1981).

BARBARA J. MACHAFFIE

Proclus (c. 410–489), the greatest representative of Neoplatonism after Plotinus. Proclus's most elaborate works are the *Elements of Theology* and the *Platonic Theology*. He was a central figure for the transmission of Neoplatonic metaphysics into the medieval world through Pseudo-Dionysius the Areopagite.

Proclus saw his task as carrying through to logical conclusion the Neoplatonisms of Plotinus and Iamblichus. The result was an elaborate extension of the doctrine of *hypostases* ("subsistences"). In addition to the One, Proclus recognized within the One a series of three Unities (*Henads*). Since Unities constitute participated intermediaries, they function to establish a symmetry between the First Hypostasis and lower orders of reality by linking them to the One. Thus all reality is interrelated and imbued with divine Providence and cosmic sympathy.

Providence is the specific function of the Unities, and it is through theurgy that the human soul participates in Providence and its attributes, which include the virtues of faith, truth, love, and hope. Salvation depends upon a providential grace accessible only through theurgy.

R. M. Berchman, "Rationality and Ritual in Neoplatonism," in *Neoplatonism and Indian Thought* (2002), 229–68; E. R. Dodds, ed., *Proclus' Elements of Theology* (1963); A. C. Lloyd, *The Cambridge History of Later Greek and Early Medieval Philosophy* (1970); W. O'Neill, trans., *Alcibiades Commentary* (1965); L. J. Rosan, *The Philosophy of Proclus* (1949); R. T. Wallis, *Neoplatonism* (1972).

ROBERT M. BERCHMAN

Proclus of Constantinople (c. 390–446), patriarch of Constantinople, preacher, and theologian who influenced the development of Christology and Mariology. A native of Constantinople, Proclus was ordained deacon and presbyter by Patriarch Atticus (r. 406–425), through whom he gained access to the imperial family and supported the princess Pulcheria, then regent for her young brother Emperor Theodosius II, in her strong devotion to Mary. Ordained to be bishop of neighboring Cyzicus in 426, Proclus was never received by the clergy and people of that city, and he continued to live and preach in the capital, where his celebrated homily in praise of Mary as "God-bearer" (*Theotokos*) in the winter of 430–431 aroused the fierce opposition of Patriarch Nestorius. After the exile of Nestorius in 431 and the death of his successor Maximian, Proclus was elected patriarch in 434 and worked effectively to reconcile disputing and alienated groups until his death in 446. He restored the followers of John Chrysostom to communion with the church and collaborated in the reburial of Chrysostom's remains in the capital in 438. Proclus also intervened to maintain peace between the imperial church and the church in Armenia, which was troubled by growing criticism in the West of Antiochene Christology. Mainly remembered as an eloquent homilist, Proclus's moderate formulations of orthodox belief in Christ helped shape the language of the Chalcedonian formula.

J. H. Barkhuizen, *Hom. on Life of Christ* (2001); N. Constas, *Homily 1–5 on Mary* (2003); Constas, "Weaving the Body of God: Proclus of Constantinople, the Theotokos, and the Loom of the Flesh," *JECS* 3 (1995): 169–94; A. Grillmeier, *Christ in Christian Tradition*, vol. 1 (2nd ed., 1975), 520–23; F. J. Leroy, *L'homilétique de Proclus* (1967); M. Richard, "Proclus et le théopaschisme," *RHE* 38 (1942): 323–31.

BRIAN E. DALEY, SJ

Procopius of Caesarea (c. 500–565?), Byzantine historian. Procopius's writings are the best source for events in the age of Justinian. His books of secular history were written in a style reminiscent of Thucydides. They detail the deeds, especially military, of the great personalities of the era, many whom the author knew personally. Procopius was well placed to comment upon major historical events. He served for as many as fifteen years (from 527) as private secretary for the general Belisarius. His eight-volume *On the Wars* details Justinian's conflicts with the Persians, Vandals, and Goths. While providing exacting detail for the political maneuverings and military operations employed during the campaigns, this work (published by 557) also revealed the author's increasing disenchantment with the imperial administration. Procopius's *On Buildings*, conversely, praises Justinian for his patronage of many architectural splendors built in Constantinople and elsewhere. In contrast, Procopius's last book, the *Secret History*, completed in the 560s but unpublished, constitutes a scathing assault on four figures that dominated the Byzantine world. It harshly satirizes the imperial couple, Justinian and Theodora, while it depicts Belisarius as the dupe of his deceitful and malicious wife, Antonina. Procopius's death date is unknown. His promise to write an ecclesiastical history was apparently never fulfilled.

Procopius, *Works*, ed. and trans. H. B. Dewing, 7 vols., LCL (1961–93); A. Cameron, *Procopius and the Sixth Century* (1985).

ALLEN E. JONES

Procopius of Gaza (c. 460–c. 530), rhetorician. Not to be confused with his younger contemporary, Procopius of Caesarea, the Byzantine historian, Procopius held what seems to have been a municipal endowed chair of rhetoric at Gaza, making that town one of the principal schools of late antiquity. His student Choricus succeeded him and spoke of his life in his own *Oration* 8. He was among the last strong advocates of classical Attic usage, although he also advocated the use of rhetorical cadences that presupposed later development of the Greek language. His surviving rhetorical works include numerous orations and letters, a panegyric of Emperor Anastasius, a paraphrase of Homer, and two descriptions (*ekpraseis*): that of a clock and that of some paintings. The clock used the twelve labors of Heracles to tell the hours.

In addition to these rhetorical works, Procopius composed scriptural commentaries in a genre that he may have invented: the catena. These provide the verse-by-verse commentary through short excerpts from earlier commentators. Procopius favored Origen and commentators under his influence such as Didymus the Blind and Gregory of Nyssa. The catena thus resembles the typical Byzantine genre for a theological treatise, the florilegium, which constructs an argument by the judicious selection (or fabrication) of passages from earlier authorities.

N. G. Wilson, *Scholars of Byzantium* (rev. ed., 1996), 30–33.

JOSEPH W. TRIGG

Prophesyings The *Prophezei* (from 1 Cor. 14:26–33) was a method of theological instruction originated by Huldrych Zwingli in Zurich based on community study of Scripture in the original languages. They served as a combination preparatory course of study for the Reformed ministry and compulsory continuing education for clergy. Beginning in 1525, on every morning except Fridays and Sundays an exegesis of a chapter in the Hebrew Old Testament was presented in the Grossmünster, followed by an interpretation of the passage in Latin with reference to the Greek text of the Septuagint. The session concluded with a summary sermon in German for the entire Zurich community. Later the *Prophezei* was expanded to include an exegesis of the New Testament and additional lectures. Most of Zwingli's exegetical works, the Zurich Bible, and Bullinger's *Decades* first originated in the *Prophezei*. Similar institutions came into existence in Switzerland, the Rhineland, the Netherlands, England, and Scotland. For English Puritans, the Prophesyings were particularly important under James I, where they functioned as schools of practical divinity for ministers.

M. Brecht, "Die Reform des Wittenberger Hörengottesdienstes und die Entstehung der Zürcher Prophezei," *Zwingliana* 19 (1992): 49–62; F. Büsser, *Die Prophezeï: Humanismus und Reformation in Zürich* (1994).

GREGORY J. MILLER

Proprietary Churches and Monasteries

A proprietary church or monastery existed under a lordship, such that the lord had full disposition of its property and control of its spiritual administration, including an exclusive right to appoint the church's priest(s) or the monastery's abbot or abbess. Private foundations of churches were occasionally known in the late Roman Empire, and a distinction between public and private churches appears in Roman law as early as 388. But a donor's rights and powers expanded to involve complete disposition of the church, after the decline of Roman rule in the West, at the expense of the bishop's jurisdiction and in contrast to the episcopal protections provided by Byzantine law. Lay ownership of churches was an established (although not exclusive) practice in the Frankish kingdom by about 700 and in the Lombard kingdom in the eighth century (but not in Visigothic Spain). A lay owner's complete disposition of church property, including its heritability, were confirmed by Charlemage in 802. Carolingian churches could thus be categorized according to the variety of their owners: a king, a bishop, a monastery, or a free layman (Hincmar of Reims classed churches this way). Regulations for both the inheritance of churches and the uses of their property varied in different Carolingian regions, but the proprietary church became predominant among all manner of churches and monasteries in France until the twelfth century, and in Germany (excepting the cathedrals dominated by kings under different rules since the Saxon dynasty), Italy, Catalonia, Aragon, and Anglo-Saxon England. The proprietary church was not the first object of reform in the eleventh century, but after Pope Gregory VII the papacy attempted to impose increasing restrictions on lay disposition of church property and office and sharpened the distinction between temporal and spiritual (ecclesiastical) powers. Gratian restricted the powers of lay donors to a right of presentation of candidates for spiritual office and allowed lay use of church property only in times of emergency. Canon

lawyers subsequently defined lay powers over ecclesiastical property and appointments as *ius patronatus* ("patronage right").

P. Landau, "Eigenkirchenwesen," *TRE* 9 (1982): 399–404; Landau, *Ius patronatus* (1975).

CHRISTOPHER OCKER

Prosper of Aquitaine

(c. 390–c. 455), chronicler, poet, and theological writer. A native of Aquitaine, probably from the Gallo-Roman aristocracy, Tiro Prosper benefited from an excellent education. His literary output spans the genres of letters, verse, theological tractates, and historical chronicles. He first appears c. 426 on the fringes of the monastic milieu at Marseilles. As resistant, "Semi-Pelagian" responses to Augustine's doctrine of grace began to emerge from among the monks of southern Gaul, Prosper and his associate Hilary became ardent defenders of Augustine, who sent them *The Predestination of the Saints* and *The Gift of Perseverance* as ammunition in their polemical battle. As the controversy died down, Prosper moved to Rome, where he became an advisor to Leo I. Prosper used poetry as the vehicle for a robustly Augustinian theology of grace in his *Poem on the Ungrateful*, written c. 429–430 in response to Pelagian and "Semi-Pelagian" teaching. The *Poem on Divine Providence* seems also to have been from him, and he produced a number of prose theological works from the years 431–433. His time in Rome saw the production of a few other works, notably *The Call of All Nations*, which treated the universal call to salvation of the heathen, and the *Book of Sentences*, which was gleaned from Augustine's writings. Prosper's florilegia were important conduits for the transmission of Augustine's legacy to the Middle Ages, and his presentation also modified that legacy, softening Augustine's predestinarianism. Prosper's *Chronicle*, dependent on earlier church historians but adding the author's own material for the events of his lifetime, has been a valuable source for historians of the fifth-century West.

G. de Plinval, "Prosper d'Aquitaine interprète de saint Augustin," *REAug* 1 (1958): 339–55; R. Weaver, *Divine Grace and Human Agency* (1996).

THOMAS A. SMITH

Protestant Law

The Protestant Reformation was both a theological and a legal reform movement. The radical theological reforms inaugurated by Protestant theologians made possible fundamental legal reforms. The fundamental legal reforms instituted by Protestant jurists made permanent radical theological reforms. The Reformation produced new creeds and catechisms as well as new statutes and constitutions, each amply supported by a rich Protestant jurisprudence.   ·

Protestant theologians rejected the political rule of the medieval Catholic Church and its canon law. On that basis, Protestant magistrates engineered a massive shift of power and property from the church to the state. In Protestant lands, the state now assumed jurisdiction over numerous subjects previously governed by the Catholic Church: marriage and family life, inheritance and poor relief, moral and ideological crimes, and more. In Lutheran and Anglican lands, the state also came to exercise considerable control over the church's polity, property, and clergy.

Many of the new civil laws passed in these Protestant lands were shaped by the new Protestant theology. For example, Protestant theologians replaced the traditional sacramental understanding of marriage with a new idea of the marital household as a social estate or covenantal association of the earthly kingdom. On that basis, Protestant jurists developed a new civil law of marriage, featuring parental consent, state registration, church consecration, and peer presence for valid marital formation as well as absolute divorce on grounds of adultery, desertion, and other faults.

Protestant theologians replaced the traditional understanding of education as a teaching office of the church with a new understanding of the public school as a civic seminary for all persons to prepare for their vocations. On that basis, Protestant magistrates replaced clerics as the chief rulers of education, state law replaced church law as the principal law of education, and the general callings of all Christians replaced the special calling of the clergy as the raison d'etre of education.

Protestant theologians introduced a new theology of the three uses of the moral law, particularly as set out in the Ten Commandments. On that basis, Protestant jurists developed arresting new theories of natural law and equity, introduced sweeping changes in civil laws of social welfare and moral discipline, and developed an integrated theory of the retributive, deterrent, and rehabilitative functions of criminal law and ecclesiastical discipline.

Protestant theologians insisted that each person is called by God to be a prophet, priest, and king. Protestant jurists eventually cast this as the freedom of all to speech, worship, and rule in the community. Protestant theologians insisted that every person is sinful and in need of legal restraint. Protestant jurists eventually cast this into a theory of checks and balances to protect the offices of church and state from the sinful abuses of their officials.

J. Bohatec, *Calvins Lehre von Kirche und Staat* (1961); Q. Skinner, *The Foundations of Modern Political Thought*, 2 vols. (1978); L. Vallauri and G. Dilcher, eds., *Christentum: Sakularisation und modernes Recht*, 2 vols. (1981); J. Witte Jr., *Law and Protestantism: The Legal Teachings of the Lutheran Reformation* (2002).

JOHN WITTE JR.

Provinces, Ecclesiastical   The medieval church was a complex organism formed by ancient institutions and shaped by regional topography and traditions. In theory, metropolitan archbishops oversaw ecclesiastical provinces, in which subordinate (suffragan) bishops ruled their dioceses in person through episcopal visitations and synods, and at a distance through cathedral chapters, archdeaconries, rural deanships, and parish priests. At the heart of every province and diocese stood the cathedral, surrounded by a prelate's palace and canons' residences, the nexus of church administration. Bordering this priestly precinct was the cathedral city, the capital of the province or diocese shaped by a reigning prelate's economic, legal, and political lordship. Tithes, oblations, and benefices from province and diocese—the *spiritualia*—funded the ministry of the cathedral and the machinery of ecclesiastical administration. Income collected from manors, estates, markets, and tolls—the *temporalia*—supported the princely status and secular lordship of archbishops and bishops.

The actual development, structure, and functioning of an ecclesiastical province were much more intricate, cumbersome, and contentious. While the diocese or bishopric as an institution of regional rule took shape in early Christianity, the ecclesiastical province of a metropolitan archbishop did not receive its definitive form until the ninth century. Local landscape and traditions often helped to determine the extent and institutions of a province and diocese. Italian dioceses were far smaller and more numerous than their larger northern European counterparts. By the year 1000 there were over 180 bishoprics in Italy, Sardinia, and Corsica, as opposed to 17 in England and 30 in Germany. Episcopal administration varied across Europe. Some dioceses relied on a number of archdeacons, others sufficed with one or relied on the office of archpriest, as in Italy. Moreover, the secular domain of archbishop and bishop was not at all coterminous with an ecclesiastical province or diocese; the nature of a prelate's rule varied from place to place.

Within province and diocese, relations among the clergy became more difficult, especially by the end of the Middle Ages. Bishops defied the jurisdiction of their archiepiscopal superiors. Cathedral canons and archdeacons gained considerable independence and came to challenge archiepiscopal and episcopal sovereignty. Monasteries and ecclesiastical foundations often received the privilege of immunity from a prelate's oversight and discipline. Finally, lay magnates and city governments came to contest the church's claims to temporal lordship. Many cathedral cities in the HRE achieved independence from their ecclesiastical lords by the end of the Middle Ages, in some cases physically expelling or excluding archbishops and bishops. Such challenges to ecclesiastical jurisdiction foreshadowed the sixteenth century, when Protestant movements rejected episcopal and archiepiscopal authority over provinces and parishes, sees and souls. *See also* Metropolitan Bishops.

R. Brentano, *Two Churches: England and Italy in the 13th Century* (1968); E. U. Crosby, *Bishop and Chapter in 12th-Century England: A Study of the Mensa Episcopalis* (1994); J. H. Lynch, *The Medieval Church: A Brief History* (1992); A. S. Popek, *The Rights and Obligations of Metropolitans: A Historical Synopsis and Commentary* (1947); J. J. Tyler, *Lord of the Sacred City: The Episcopus Exclusus in Late Medieval and Early Modern Germany* (1999).
                                    J. JEFFERY TYLER

Prudentius, Aurelius Clemens

(348–c. 405), Latin poet. After serving in the imperial civil service, Prudentius, a native of Roman Spain, devoted himself to writing Christian poetry. He visited Rome, probably between 400 and 405, and in the latter year, at age fifty-seven, wrote the preface to an edition of his works that provides our limited biographical information. Like his contemporary Paulinus of Nola, Prudentius innovatively employed classical poetic forms to express Christian themes, working in a variety of meters and genres. Especially through his allegorical epic the *Psychomachia* (*Battle for the Soul*), famous for its personified Vices and Virtues, Prudentius had an abiding influence upon medieval art and literature. Other works include the *Cathemerinon* (*Daily Round*), a group of hymnlike poems dedicated to daily and seasonal occasions; the *Apotheosis* (*Divinity of Christ*), treating Christ's nature and errors regarding it; the *Hamartigenia* (*Origin of Sin*), emphasizing human moral responsibility over metaphysical dualism; the *Contra Symmachum*, a denunciation of paganism based upon the celebrated controversy surrounding the removal of the Altar of Victory from the Roman Senate House in 382; and the *Dittochaeon* (*Scenes from History*), a series of four-line poems presenting biblical scenes. The fourteen lyrical poems of Prudentius's *Peristephanon* (*The Martyrs' Crowns*), dedicated to tales of Roman and Spanish martyrs, are perhaps most studied today, in part because of their captivating blend of piety and graphic violence, in part because of their elaborate treatment of female martyrs. Prudentius's poetry embodies the Christian appropriation, not rejection, of Rome's pre-Christian literary legacy and espouses continued belief in Rome's imperial mission, tied now to the victory and propagation of Christianity.

M. P. Cunningham, ed., *Carmina* (1966); H. Thomson, trans., *Prudentius*, 2 vols. (1949–1953); C. Gnilka, *Prudentiana*, 2 vols. (2000, 2001); M. Roberts, *Poetry and the Cult of the Martyrs* (1993); M. Smith, *Prudentius' Psychomachia: A Reexamination* (1976).
                                    DENNIS E. TROUT

Psellus, Constantine

(1019–1078), Byzantine scholar, historian, courtier. He studied under John Mauropus, whose pupils included the future patriarch of Constantinople and the future emperor Constantine X. He served in various imperial posts throughout the eleventh century. When Constantine IX reorganized the Univ. of Constantinople in 1045, Psellus was given the chair of philosophy. Accusations of heresy led him and Xiphilinus to enter a monastery in 1054, where Psellus changed his name to Michael. His monastic stay was brief, and in 1059 Constantine X Ducas made him the tutor of his son. He was also the teacher of John Italos.

Psellus's best-known work is his *Chronographia*, which covers the years 976–1077 and which remains a valuable historical source. A man of broad learning, Psellus was instrumental in the revival of classical studies in Constantinople, especially of Homer and Plato, whom he regarded as anticipations of Christ. He claimed Gregory of Nazianzus especially as the model for using classical learning and syllogistic reasoning for a theological end. Some Byzantine ecclesiastical circles found Psellus's approach too secular, and his pupil John Italos was tried for heresy in 1082.

PG 112 (1864); E. R. A. Sewter, *Chronographia* (1953); G. N. Wilson, *Scholars of Byzantium* (1983).

EUGENE M. LUDWIG, OFM CAP.

Pseudepigraphy Derived from two Greek words that mean "false writing," pseudepigraphy refers to the phenomenon of writing documents under an assumed name. It is not to be confused with anonymity, where an author's identity is not revealed. Many early Jewish and Christian documents, including both canonical and noncanonical writings, claim to have been written by a notable figure in the tradition when in fact they were written by someone else. Most modern biblical scholars believe that much of the prophecy of Isaiah or the epistles of 1 and 2 Timothy and Titus in the New Testament, for example, were written by someone other than Isaiah of Jerusalem or the apostle Paul. Similarly, noncanonical works such as the apocalyptic document *I Enoch* or the *Letter of Peter to Philip* from the Nag Hammadi library claim to be revelations given to these heroes from the tradition when in fact they were written by someone else much later. Both the large number of pseudepigraphical writings and their widespread attestation in a variety of translations suggest that these documents were viewed by many Jews and Christians as authentic revelatory voices from the past.

Since authorship and historical veracity are linked with canonicity and views of the inspiration of Scripture, pseudepigraphy as understood in modern scholarship raises a theological problem for some. Scholars have offered various explanations for pseudepigraphy. Some have claimed that the concept of intellectual property was lacking in the ancient world, although this view has been refuted by others. Some argue that it was common for disciples to honor a revered teacher by writing in his name. Others have suggested that when Jews and Christians believed that the era of prophecy had ended it was necessary to write pseudonymously in order to get a hearing. Still others have emphasized that it was the one spirit of God working through different individuals whose personal identity is therefore not important. None of these explanations of pseudepigraphy have proven to be completely satisfactory.

Most scholars would agree that pseudepigraphical writings were not written with the intent to deceive others for personal gain. Instead, pseudonymous documents appear to have been motivated by a desire to perpetuate revered traditions and the appreciation of past heroes by retelling their stories for a new generation. Of necessity this process entailed reinterpretation and reformulation of the tradition in order to speak effectively to the new situation. Rather than a sign of deception, pseudepigraphy testifies to the adaptability and resilience of Jewish and Christian traditions in the hands of later representatives of these faith communities. By making use of the names of revered figures from the past, later authors were not primarily claiming literary authorship. They were attempting to provide authoritative tradition for the guidance of their faith community as it faced new challenges.

J. H. Charlesworth, *The Old Testament Pseudepigrapha and the New Testament* (1985); J. H. Charlesworth and C. A. Evans, eds., *The Pseudepigrapha and Early Biblical Interpretation* (1993); D. G. Meade, *Pseudonymity and Canon* (1986).

JAMES BRASHLER

Pseudo-Dionysius, an unknown figure (according to many scholars probably a Syrian monk) who near the end of the fifth century CE wrote under the pseudonym of Dionysius the Areopagite, the Athenian convert of Paul mentioned in Acts 17:34. The surviving works include four theological treatises: *Divine Names*, *Mystical Theology*, *Celestial Hierarchy*, and *Ecclesiastical Hierarchy*, as well as ten letters. The author lists other works that are either no longer extant or that are probably fictitious titles (e.g., *Symbolic Theology* and *Theological Outlines*). The apostolic authorship of the Dionysian corpus was generally accepted throughout the thousand or so years of its immense influence upon the theology of Eastern and Western Christendom.

Dionysius's works first appeared at the time of the Monophysite controversy of the early sixth century, and though their authenticity was suspect from the beginning, they were nevertheless embraced and rendered closer to orthodox doctrine by Maximus the Confessor. They made their way to the West through various translations beginning with Hilduin's in the eighth century. By the twelfth and thirteenth centuries many commentaries were composed on either select texts or the entire corpus by such authors as Johannes Scottus Eriugena, Hugh of St. Victor, Albertus Magnus, and Thomas Aquinas. The author had by now become the unrivaled authority on such issues as the proper method of interpreting names attributed to God in Scripture (*Divine Names*), the procession of divine illumination into and through creation by means of angelic triads (*Celestial Hierarchy*), and analogously triadic ecclesiastical and liturgical institutions (*Ecclesiastical Hierarchy*). Perhaps most importantly, the unknowability of God was conceived of with an intensified negativity (hence the term "negative theology") as a divine "darkness" in which the purified soul could achieve mystical union (*henosis*) with the divine (*Mystical Theology*).

The apostolic authorship was rejected by the sixteenth century, but it was only in the nineteenth century that scholars definitively proved the late fifth-century origin of the corpus and identified its fundamental structural elements as borrowed from the fifth-century Neoplatonism of Proclus (d. 489): for example, the dynamic structure of "remaining, procession, and return" characterizing the movement of God in the world as an overflowing of divine power, light, and love (*eros*); the triadic nature of the angelic ranks and their interaction in terms of "purification, illumination, and perfection"; the triad of "Being, Life, and Wisdom" used by Proclus to describe the first emanation from the One; the deification of the soul described as *henosis* with God; and the overwhelming emphasis on God's transcendence as "beyond all being." Since the sixteenth century, many have found it remarkable, and even repugnant, that so many elements of pagan Platonism were transmitted by the Dionysian corpus to the Latin West and were so casually assimilated into the heart of its theological traditions. While scholars have long disagreed as to whether Dionysius was a true Christian who strategically borrowed from Platonic doctrines, or a pagan Platonist masquerading as a Christian, most today agree that the pseudonymous author significantly changed his pagan sources in order to preserve a fundamentally creationist theology—God alone creates all things and is the agent of their return—and successfully adapted Platonism's dialectical ontology to a theology of divine immanence as omnipresent love, and of divine transcendence as a darkness transcending all being and all knowledge of beings. As yet there is no scholarly consensus as to the identity of the author beyond his Syrian monastic milieu at the turn of the sixth century.

H. U. von Balthasar, *The Glory of the Lord: A Theological Aesthetics*, 3 vols. (1982, 1984, 1986); S. Gersh, *From Iamblichus to Eriugena: An Investigation of the Prehistory and Evolution of the Pseudo-Dionysian Tradition* (1978); A. Louth, *Denys the Areopagite* (1989); C. Luibheid and P. Rorem, trans., *Pseudo-Dionysius: The Complete Works* (1987); B. McGinn, *The Foundations of Mysticism: Origins to the 5th Century* (1991); R. Roques, *L'univers dionysien: Structure hiearchique du monde selon le Pseudo-Denys* (2nd ed., 1983); P. Rorem, *Biblical and Liturgical Symbols within the Pseudo-Dionysian Synthesis* (1984).

MARK DAMIEN DELP

Pufendorf, Samuel von (1632–1694),

German jurist and historian, born in Meissen, Saxony, son of a strict Lutheran pastor. After studying at the universities of Leipzig and Jena, he taught law at the Univ. of Heidelberg (1661–1668) and the Univ. of Lund (1668–1676). He then served as court historian and privy councilor, first in Stockholm until 1688 and then in Berlin. He produced a thirty-three-volume history of Sweden, three volumes on the history and constitution of the HRE, and an influential treatise on church-state relations, *De habitu religionis christianae ad vitam civilem* (1687).

Pufendorf's greatest fame came from a series of works on natural law theory, particularly his massive eight-volume *De jure naturae et gentium* (1672) and a popular abridgement, *De officio hominis et civis* (1673). Drawing on Grotius, Hobbes, and Erhard Weigel, Pufendorf developed a detailed systematic account of natural law principles based on reason and mathematics alone. Pufendorf's natural law theory had great influence in early modern Scandinavia, Germany, Scotland, England, and America.

L. Krieger, *The Politics of Discretion* (1965).

JOHN WITTE JR.

Pulcheria (399–453), late Roman empress

(414–453). Pulcheria was the eldest daughter of Emperor Arcadius. After her father's death in 408, her younger brother Theodosius II became ruler of the eastern half of the empire. Theodosius and the Senate proclaimed Pulcheria *Augusta* (empress) in 414. She acted as regent and virtual co-ruler for several years.

Pulcheria and her two younger sisters took a vow of perpetual chastity. The imperial palace assumed a nearly tangible aura of piety.

Pulcheria's influence at the Constantinopolitan court was tremendous, although it decreased somewhat after Theodosius's marriage to Eudocia (421). Pulcheria, in league with Cyril of Alexandria, was effective in influencing Theodosius's decision to condemn Nestorianism after the Council of Ephesus (431); nevertheless, she was forced to abandon the imperial palace in 446. Three years later, however, she returned, and Eudocia, perhaps owing to Pulcheria's instigation, left for exile in Jerusalem. Upon her brother's death in 450, Pulcheria inherited the imperial rule. Having gained assurance that she would be able to maintain her virginity, she married the general Marcian, who shared her authority. With Pulcheria allied with Leo I, the imperial pair influenced the decisions pronounced at the (ecumenical) Council of Chalcedon in 451. Pulcheria died in 453 and was later recognized as a saint by the Roman and Eastern churches.

K. Holum, *Theodosian Empresses* (1982).

ALLEN E. JONES

Puritanism A diverse reform movement arose within the Church of England from c. 1550 to 1662, whose adherents were dissatisfied with the various religious settlements proposed by the governments of Edward VI, Elizabeth I, James I, and Charles I and who sought to bring the Church of England into conformity with the continental Reformation. While the term "Puritanism" is used to denote a very broad range of ideas, the issues in dispute related especially to the contents and application of the Book of Common Prayer. Two ideas were of particular importance to the Puritans: the regulative principle of worship, whereby all aspects of church practice were to be regulated by Scripture; and the notion that church discipline was to be carried out independent of the state (effectively the model for which Calvin struggled in Geneva). Over against these ideas, the Anglican church placed the Book of Common Prayer, which sanctioned elements excluded by the regulative principle, such as kneeling at Communion and clerical vestments, as well as Erastian church government, which effectively made the church an arm of the state.

John Knox had fought a vigorous campaign against the requirement of kneeling in the Communion service as required in the second Book of Common Prayer (1552), an action which led to the insertion of the so-called Black Rubric. Controversies continued during the reign of Elizabeth I (1558–1603) in campaigns against vestments, and then radical figures such as Thomas Cartwright launched campaigns against episcopacy itself, arguing for a specifically presbyterian form of polity. Archbishop John Whitgift crushed these campaigns in the 1580s and 1590s at the behest of Elizabeth, whose ecclesiastical policy had no place for sectarian disruption.

With the accession of James I (r. 1603–1625), the Puritans presented their demands in a Millennary Petition, a document that led to the abortive Hampton Court Conference of 1604. The Puritan notions of church discipline did not find a sympathetic hearing at court, especially because the Stuarts were committed to the divine right of kings, and their demands were rejected. Also troubling was the rise of separatist movements, including Congregationalist churches, which began to fracture the Puritan reform effort. The vigorous enforcement of Erastian and episcopalian church policy led numbers of Puritans to seek refuge in the Netherlands and in North America in the first three decades of the seventeenth century.

Under Charles I and his archbishop of Canterbury, William Laud, the Puritans suffered further persecution. However, during the 1640s a financial crisis precipitated by military problems in Ireland and Scotland led to an enhancement of parliamentary power and the convening of the Westminster Assembly. The Assembly offered a vision of church reform in contrast to that of the Prayer Book and in line with Puritan notions of worship and discipline. The downfall of Laud and the civil war that followed led to the execution of the king in 1649 and the establishment of a commonwealth under Oliver Cromwell. Although these events gave Puritanism its long-awaited opportunity, by this time the movement was fractured and Puritan attitudes toward the new regime were divided. Generally, Presbyterians regarded the execution of the king as a bad thing, while Independents, loyal to Cromwell, pushed for a more radical political realization of their goals. The collapse of the commonwealth after the death of Cromwell and the Restoration of 1660 signaled the end of Puritanism. The 1662 Act of Uniformity led to the departure from the church of almost two thousand ministers of Puritan sympathies. Puritanism ended and Nonconformity began.

Puritanism was never a unified movement, making it somewhat difficult to define with any degree of precision. Theologically, it generally combined a broad commitment to the Reformed confessional tradition with a strong experiential piety and, not infrequently, a vigorous Sabbatarianism. These traits are evident, for example, in the works of individuals such as William Perkins, William Ames, Richard Sibbes, and Richard Baxter, and find their confessional expression in the documents produced by the Westminster Assembly. Nevertheless, the categorization of a figure such as John Milton as a Puritan, which he undoubtedly was despite his essentially Arian views of the Godhead, indicates the problem of a purely theological definition. It is perhaps better, therefore, to see Puritanism as a descriptive term that refers to any number of critical tendencies relating to ceremonies and church discipline.

P. Collinson, *The Elizabethan Puritan Movement* (1967); C. Hill, *Society and Puritanism in Pre-Revolutionary England* (1964); P. Lake, *Moderate Puritans and the Elizabethan Church* (1982); A. Milton, *Catholic and Reformed: The Roman and Protestant Churches in English Protestant Thought, 1600–1640* (1995).

                                             CARL TRUEMAN

Puritanism in New England Puritanism began in England during the reign of Elizabeth I as a movement for further reform in the Protestant Church of England and flourished in both England and New England during the seventeenth century. Initially focused on the simplification of ritual and ceremony, English Puritans came to emphasize Calvinist theology and a piety of conversion, holiness of life, and congregational fellowship, all features reproduced in New England, where Puritans felt they could shape an ideal church and society.

Some Puritans immigrated to New England when their desired reforms seemed stymied by English monarchs and bishops, particularly by the promotion of anti-Calvinism and ceremonial innovations after 1625, when Charles I became king. The first emigrants, the "Pilgrims" who settled Plymouth in 1620, had a separatist background, stemming from a congregation formed in Scrooby, England, that had withdrawn from a Church of England deemed insufficiently reformed. Eventually fleeing to Holland, some then removed to Plymouth, where they soon elected William Bradford their governor (their pastor, John Robinson, died before he could join them). A much larger group, which repudiated separatism and regarded itself as an advance guard of reform

whose example would transform old England, founded the Massachusetts Bay Colony, and throughout the 1630s many English Puritans found refuge there. During the colony's formative years John Winthrop served as governor, and among its leading ministers were John Cotton, Thomas Shepard, and Richard Mather. Under the leadership of Thomas Hooker and John Davenport, some colonists moved into Connecticut, founding Hartford (1635) and New Haven (1637). In 1691 the Plymouth Colony was absorbed into Massachusetts.

These New England Puritans founded congregational churches, in which they sought to realize a membership entirely consisting of fully converted persons. The magistrates who governed the colony were responsible for providing places of worship and given authority to suppress heresy and blasphemy. Churches and magistrates together labored to create a "Bible commonwealth," a Christian society. Harvard College was authorized in 1636 (and opened in 1638) to train ministers. In 1646 and 1647 John Eliot and Thomas Mayhew began missions to Native Americans. New England Puritans thought of themselves as covenanted with God to be "a city on a hill," restoring primitive Christianity and fulfilling millennial prophecy.

New England Puritans, however, experienced disruption as a result of the tension between their ideal of a pure church and their determination that the church be a publicly supported institution caring for the whole population. Thus, the separatist and tolerationist Roger Williams and the antinomian Anne Hutchinson undermined the equilibrium of Puritan society by seeking a yet more purified church. The Cambridge Platform (1648) sought to restore balance by defining "the New England Way" of congregationalist polity; it was followed by movements to widen admission to baptism (the Half-Way Covenant, 1662) and the Lord's Supper and by the effort to create associations of congregations (the Saybrook Platform, 1708). During the later seventeenth century the New England colonies were disrupted by an Indian uprising (King Philip's War, 1675), the dissidence of Quakers and Baptists, and the Salem witch trials of 1692. By the end of that century many felt that the colony had failed in its mission, as evidenced in the reforming synod of 1679 and the nostalgic historical writings of Cotton Mather. The impact of Puritanism on American culture and religion has been pervasive, particularly manifest in biblicism, a focus on personal religious experience, and an impulse for reform.

F. J. Bremer, *The Puritan Experiment* (rev. ed., 1995); S. Foster, *The Long Argument: English Puritanism and the Shaping of New England Culture, 1570–1700* (1991); D. D. Hall, *The Faithful Shepherd: A History of the New England Ministry in the Seventeenth Century* (1972); P. Miller, *Orthodoxy in Massachusetts 1630–1650* (1933).

DEWEY D. WALLACE JR.

Purvey, John (c. 1353–c. 1428), English Wyclifite preacher. Ordained in 1377, Purvey was a close companion to John Wyclif during his last years at Lutterworth (1381–1384). Purvey probably translated and revised many of Wyclif's writings for popular circulation during these years and may also have revised Wyclif's English translation of the Bible. After 1384, Purvey lived among Lollard supporters in Bristol and continued to preach despite a 1387 ban from the bishop of Worchester. Purvey's writings were among the Lollard texts officially condemned in 1388 and 1389. Purvey was arrested in 1401 and tried, but he recanted and received a benefice in Kent. By 1403, he resigned this income and resumed Lollard preaching.

M. Deanesly, *Lollard Bible* (1920); H. Hargreaves, "The Latin Text of Purvey's Psalter," *Medium Aevum* 24 (1955): 73–90; A. Hudson, "John Purvey: A Reconsideration of the Evidence for His Life and Writings," *Viator* 12 (1981): 355–80.

DAVID A. LOPEZ

Pym, John (1584–1643), Puritan leader in Parliament. Pym was convinced Charles I was leaning toward reestablishing Catholicism in England and went so far as to believe the king was participating in a "popish plot." His fears, coupled with his confrontation with the king and general popular unrest, led to the English Civil War. Before he entered the House of Commons in 1614, he left Oxford without taking a degree and went on to study law. He was prominent in the Short Parliament of 1640 but came to the fore during the Long Parliament, in which he attacked many of Charles's ministers, including Thomas Wentworth, Earl of Strafford, who was impeached in November 1640 and executed as a traitor in May 1641. This opened up the idea that the king, too, could be tried for treason (as he was in 1649). Pym and Charles went head-to-head on many issues, the predominant one being the issue of the relationship between Parliament and the king. As Charles played the Catholic Irish against the Presbyterian Scots, Pym conceived his own role as that of savior of the kingdom. Realizing that a peaceful compromise between Parliament and the king was impossible, Pym saw the only possible outcome to be a use of force. He hoped to avoid outright confrontation and continued to seek accommodation with Charles. He drafted the Grand Remonstrance of 1641 for the king, attempting to appoint counselors chosen by Parliament. Confrontation finally came with parliamentary supporters rebelling, forcing the royal family to flee London on January 10, 1642. The next day London celebrated Pym and Parliament as heroes, and the city became a hotbed of demonstrations against Papists and Royalists. Charles retreated to York and made preparations for war. By July the bloodshed of the English Civil War was well under way. Pym was appointed lieutenant of the ordnance and eventually forged an alliance between England and Scotland. He died soon thereafter in 1643.

C. V. Wedgewood, *The King's Peace, 1637–1641* (1955); Wedgewood, *The King's War, 1641–1647* (1958).

ALDEN R. LUDLOW

Quakers   *see* Friends, Society of

Quartodecimans   This title, meaning "Fourteenthers," evolved in the second century to describe churches of Asia Minor that observed the Pasch, or Easter celebration, specifically on the date of the Jewish Passover, the fourteenth day of the month of Nisan. Rather than judaizing Easter, as they were accused, the Quartodecimans actually aspired to supersede the Jewish Passover tradition by exalting Christ as the true paschal lamb and by exploiting Hebrew Passover images to display the many dimensions of Christ's redemptive suffering. The Quartodeciman theologian Melito of Sardis outlined in his homily *On the Pascha* numerous correspondences between the Passover and the passion. These extended beyond typology to demonstrate that the God incarnate in Jesus was the one ubiquitously operative in Old Testament revelation in preparation for disclosure in Christ's passion.

The Roman church in the late second century accused the Quartodecimans of celebrating the Pasch on a day other than Sunday and thereby distracting worshipers from the resurrection itself. Irenaeus of Lyon and Polycrates of Ephesus defended the Quartodecimans, but Pope Victor I excommunicated them, triggering a backlash from numerous bishops who did not believe the issue should divide the church.

R. Cantalamessa, *Easter in the Early Church: An Anthology of Jewish and Early Christian Texts* (1993); S. G. Hall, ed. and trans., *Melito of Sardis: "On Pascha" and Fragments* (1979).
PAUL M. BLOWERS

Quenstedt, Johann Andreas
(1617–1688), German Lutheran dogmatician. He studied theology and philosophy at the universities of Helmstedt and Wittenberg and began to teach logic and metaphysics at Wittenberg in 1649. He received a doctorate in theology from the same institution in 1650 and served as professor of theology there after 1660. His most important book was *Theologica didactico-polemica*, published in 1685. It came to rank with the *Loci theologici* of his uncle, Johann Gerhard, as one of the most influential systematic theologies of the Age of Orthodoxy. Quenstedt was noted not so much for his creativity as for his mild disposition and his ability to create a comprehensive and clear summary of a century of Lutheran theological reflection.

L. Poellot, ed., *The Nature and Character of Theology: An Introduction to the Thought of J. A. Quenstedt from "Theologia Didactico-Polemica"* (1986); R. Preus, *The Theology of Post-Reformation Lutheranism*, 2 vols. (1970, 1972).
ERIC LUND

Quietism
Used loosely of any kind of spirituality minimizing human activity and responsibility, quietism refers properly to a spiritual ethos associated with Miguel de Molinos (1640–1697), Madame Guyon (1648–1717), and (less clearly) François Fénelon (1651–1715). Quietism rejects all human effort in favor of complete passivity and abandonment to God—a state of perfection achieved through mental prayer in which all acts of self-discipline, piety, or good works become pointless, sin impossible, and personal salvation a matter of indifference. Church authorities opposed the movement: Pope Innocent XI condemned sixty-eight propositions of Molinos in 1687, and an ecclesiastical commission at Issy condemned thirty-four articles of Guyon's works in 1695. Fénelon, who had signed the Issy condemnation while defending mystical spirituality, himself had twenty-three propositions condemned by the Holy See, but he quickly set aside his own opinions and and submitted to papal authority.

J.-R. Armogathe, *Le Quiétisme* (1973); R. H. Knox, *Enthusiasm* (1950), 231–87.
JOHN TONKIN

Quiñones, Francisco de los Ángeles
(1485?–1540), Spanish cardinal of the Roman Catholic Church. Quiñones joined the Franciscans in 1491 and steadily advanced within the ranks of his order. By 1521 he was elected provincial vicar, the next year he was made commissary general, and by 1523 he was general minister. Quiñones took an active role as mediator and diplomat throughout his career. He played a crucial role as mediator during the "Comuneros" uprising in Castile. He took advantage of his family ties with Charles V and served as intermediary between the emperor and the pope, Clement VII. After the sack of Rome, Quiñones played an important role in the negotiations that led to the deliverance of Clement VII, who then appointed Quiñones cardinal of the Holy Cross of Jerusalem. Quiñones's most enduring contribution was his reform of the *Breviarium Romanum* with the assistance of Diego de Meila, Gaspar de Castro, and Juan Ginés de Sepúlveda between the years 1529 and 1534. Although suppressed by the Council of Trent, the *Breviarium* became very popular, having over a hundred editions between 1535 and 1556. It had a marked influence on the Book of Common Prayer.

J. W. Legg, *The Second Recension of the Quignon Breviary* (1908–1912).
RADY ROLDÁN-FIGUEROA

Quodlibetal Disputations
Related to the "disputed questions" handled regularly by university professors, wherein a problem arising from the reading of some authoritative source(s) would be signaled and then resolved, quodlibetal disputations were more freewheeling discussions, in which questions about anything (*de quolibet*) could be raised by anyone who happened to be present (*a quolibet*). Whereas the former were private exercises, the latter, open to all, were public events. They developed first in theology at the Univ. of Paris during the thirteenth century and were held just twice a year (before Christmas and Easter). From here they spread to the other faculties (arts, medicine, and law), other universities, and other venues (e.g., religious *studia* and the curia). On opening day a master would entertain any and all questions from the floor, on some succeeding day he would provide a more

organized and detailed set of responses (the *determinatio*), and at some later date he might prepare a formal, fuller version for "publication." Invaluable sources for historians, not only are quodlibets revelatory of a particular master's theological and philosophical views, but they also provide, by the very variety of topics handled, an invaluable window onto the *mentalité* of the time.

B. C. Bazàn et al., *Les questions disputées et les questions quodlibétiques dans les facultés de théologie, de droit et de médicine* (1985).

STEVEN J. WILLIAMS

Quodvultdeus (late fourth cent.–c. 454), North African bishop of Carthage, exiled most of his reign. His writings were greatly influenced by Augustine. Quodvultdeus probably was the Carthaginian deacon of the same name who wrote two letters to Augustine (c. 427) requesting a handbook on heresies for the clergy at Carthage (see Letters 221–24 in Augustine's correspondence). Augustine complied by composing *On Heresies*, though it remained unfinished at his death. Around 437 Quodvultdeus succeeded Capreoleus as bishop of Carthage. Seven homilies usually attributed to Quodvultdeus attest to his vigorous defense of the faith in a city teeming with pagans, heretics, and Jews.

After a decade of marauding and pillaging across North Africa, the Vandals captured Carthage in 439. Their king Gaiseric confiscated Catholic churches there and banished Quodvultdeus and other clergy. (The Vandals were Arian Christians.) Quodvultdeus took refuge in Naples, where he actively campaigned against Arianism and wrote a treatise (*De promissionibus Dei*) on salvation history (long attributed to Prosper of Aquitaine). Most scholars now agree that five catechetical homilies usually ascribed to Augustine were written by Quodvultdeus. All of Quodvultdeus's works bear the unmistakable stamp of Augustine's genius.

CCSL 60 (1976); R. Eno, "Christian Reaction to the Barbarian Invasions and the Sermons of Quodvultdeus," in *Preaching in the Patristic Age*, ed. D. Hunter (1989), 139–61; T. Finn, "Quodvultdeus: The Preacher and the Audience," StPatr 31 (1995), 42–58.

JANE E. MERDINGER

Rabbula (d. 435), bishop of Edessa. According to an extant *Life*, Rabbula was born in Qenneshrin (Chalcis) to a Christian mother and a pagan father. He received a bilingual education (Syriac and Greek) in pursuit of an administrative career. As an adult he adopted the life of a Christian ascetic. He became bishop in 411/412.

During his episcopate, Rabbula worked to reform the Edessene church. He regulated the life of the clergy and the Sons and Daughters of the Covenant (groups of ascetics). He strove for social justice, devoting funds to the care of the poor and sick and restricting ecclesiastical luxury. His biographer claims he ended the gladiatorial games in Edessa. Three of his letters, two sermons, and some liturgical poetry are at least partially preserved; three collections of ecclesiastical canons survive.

In the christological controversies Rabbula sided with Cyril of Alexandria, some of whose works he translated into Syriac. In a sermon in Constantinople in 428 he rejected the teachings of Nestorius and defended the term *Theotokos* ("mother of God"). In Edessa he strove to suppress the writings of Theodore of Mopsuestia and the "School of the Persians."

G. G. Blum, *Rabbula von Edessa* (1969); G. W. Bowersock, "The Syriac Life of Rabbula and Syrian Hellenism," in *Greek Biography and Panegyric in Late Antiquity*, ed. T. Hägg (2000), 255–71; R. Doran, *Stewards of the Poor: The Man of God, Rabbula, and Hiba in Fifth-Century Edessa* (2006); H. J. W. Drijvers, "Rabbula, Bishop of Edessa: Spiritual Authority and Secular Power," in *Portraits of Spiritual Authority*, ed. Drijvers (1999), 139–54.

UTE POSSEKEL

Rabelais, François (c. 1483–1553), humanist, physician, and satirist. The son of a lawyer, Rabelais began his career as a Franciscan but found a more congenial environment for his classical studies in the Benedictine order. He corresponded extensively with Erasmus and Budé. Leaving the Benedictines in 1527 and assuming the role of a secular priest, he acquired a medical degree at Montpellier, practiced medicine in Lyon, and edited classical medical texts. For some time he enjoyed the ecclesiastical patronage of Cardinal Jean du Bellay, whom he accompanied to Rome, and of his brother Guillaume.

Rabelais' major writings, *Pantagruel* and *Gargantua*, popular tales with serious satirical intent, were condemned by the Sorbonne theologians for indecency and clerical satire. Virtually everything he wrote suffered the same condemnation and earned him a reputation as a hidden atheist. Though his orthodoxy remains under discussion, most see his critique of the church within the orbit of the movement of "Evangélisme" in the tradition of Jacques Lefèvre d'Etaples and Marguerite d'Angoulême—critical of particular aspects of church life while never rejecting the institution itself.

———

M. Bakhtin, *Rabelais and His World* (1984); L. Febvre, *The Problem of Unbelief in the Sixteenth Century: The Religion of Rabelais* (1982); D. M. Frame, ed., *Complete Works of François Rabelais* (1991).

                                                                                                                                             JOHN TONKIN

Racovian Catechism

This statement of faith was written for the Polish Brethren, a Reformation-era movement, and named for Rakow, the city where it was adopted. Divided into large and small catechisms, it was edited by Valentin Schmalz, Johannes Völkel, and Hieronymus Moskowski and incorporated the ideas of the Italian-born Fausto Sozzini (1539–1604), who defined Christ's work as providing an example of Christian life and not as atonement. Written in Polish in 1605, it appeared later in German (1608) and Latin (1609) and discussed Holy Scripture, the way of salvation, knowledge of God, the person of Christ, the offices of Christ as prophet, king, and priest, and the church. Excluded were discussions on the incarnation, the sacraments, and the Trinity. Christ was not God but was appointed as lord of heaven and earth. Resurrection took precedence over the crucifixion. The Racovian Catechism stood midway between Reformation understandings of Scripture and an awakening rationalism with its Arian and adoptionist Christology and its Pelagian understanding that humans cooperate in salvation. It was widely used by Antitrinitarians, especially in Poland, and was regarded as the classical expression of a burgeoning Unitarianism.

———

E. M. Wilbur, *A History of Unitarianism, Socinianism, and Its Antecedents* (1977).

                                                                                                                                             DAVID P. SCAER

Radegund

(c. 520–587), queen, ascetic, monastic founder. Of Thuringian royalty, Radegund was taken prisoner by the Merovingian king Chlothar (531) when he defeated her paternal uncle, who had himself murdered her father (Gregory of Tours, *Historia Francorum* 3.4, 7; George, *Venantius Fortunatus* [1995], Appendix 1, a poem she may have written). She became one of Chlothar's wives (c. 540) but left him (c. 550) when he had her brother killed (*Venantius Fortunatus Life* 1.12). Ordained a deaconness by Medard of Noyon, she founded a monastery at Poitiers in the early 550s on land granted by Chlothar, placed it under Caesarius's *Rule for Nuns*, and appointed Agnes as its first abbess (her letter in *Historia Francorum* 9.42). In 569 the emperor Justin II bestowed on the monastery a relic of the true cross (Baudonivia, *Life* 2.16), which the monastery (henceforth named "Holy Cross") still possesses. Fortunatus praised Radegund for her verse (George, *Venantius Fortunatus* [1995], Appendix 31; see also Appendix 3 for a poem she may have written).

———

B. Brennan, "Piety and Politics in 19th-Century Poitiers: The Cult of St. Radegund," *JEH* 47 (1996): 65–81; S. Coates, "Regendering Radegund? Fortunatus, Baudonivia, and the Problem of Female Sanctity in Merovingian Gaul," *SCH* 34 (1998): 37–50; J. George, *Venantius Fortunatus: Personal and Political Poems* (1995); J. A. McNamara and J. E. Halborg, trans., *Sainted Women of the Dark Ages* (1992).

                                                                                                                                             WILLIAM E. KLINGSHIRN

Radewijns, Florentius

(1350–1400), Dutch priest who was the disciple and "successor" of Geert Groote and first rector of the house of the Brothers and Sisters of the Common Life at Deventer. Born in Leyderdam, near Utrecht, Radewijns studied at the Univ. of Prague, where he received a master's degree in 1378, and then returned home to become canon of St. Peter's in Utrecht. Like his mentor Geert Groote, he pursued a clerical career until he experienced a "spiritual conversion." Following his conversion, inspired by a sermon from Groote, he relinquished his canonry, was ordained as a priest (1377), and accepted a benefice as a vicar for the altar of St. Paul at the church of St. Lebuinus in Deventer. Radewijns opened his vicarage to the Brothers and Sisters of the Common Life, a community of laymen and laywomen dedicated to observant religious practice based on apostolic ideals. After Groote's death in 1384, Radewijns worked to acquire his private house in Deventer and played a major role in the organization of a community of "Brethren" at Zwolle. Following Groote's wishes, he pushed for the formation of the Windesheim (south of Zwolle) congregation of canons regular (1387), a second branch of the Devotio Moderna. Most of Radewijns's writings served as instruction for communal living and spiritual exercises, including ascetic tracts.

J. P. Arthur, trans., *The Founders of the New Devotion: The Lives of Gerard Groote, Florentius Radewin, and Their Followers, by Thomas à Kempis* (1905); F. J. Legrand, ed., *Florent Radewijns: Petit manuel pour le dévot moderne* (1999); M. van Woerkum, *Florentius Radewijns: Schets van zijn leven, geschriften, persoonlijkheid en ideen* (1950).

TODD M. RICHARDSON

Radical Reformation   The radical movements, or the left wing of the sixteenth-century Protestant Reformation, were diverse, involving social and economic issues as well as religious ideas, practices, and actions. Their evangelical theologians, pastors, and lay leaders initially accepted the ideas of Luther and Zwingli but also desired more sweeping changes in church life and practices. Early dissenters from Luther include his Wittenberg colleague Andreas Karlstadt (1486–1451), who insisted that Scripture is the blueprint for church and social reforms, and Thomas Müntzer (c. 1489–1525), a leader of the Peasants' Revolt of 1525 who blended mysticism and fervent millennialism.

The largest group of radicals were the Anabaptists, who arose among followers of Zwingli in Zurich in January 1525, although there were early points of Anabaptist sentiment elsewhere. "Anabaptist" refers to those who practice believers' (adult) baptism (*Wiedertäufer*), but it also reflects an understanding of the church unlike anything Zwingli or Luther were prepared to accept. Rebaptism, a capital crime in most areas, symbolized an adult profession of faith, but it also threatened the unity of church and state. While it is not possible to speak of normative Anabaptist beliefs or practices, some outlines seem clear. Most Anabaptists insisted on believers' baptism, church life patterned after the early Christians, nonviolence, a withdrawal or at least a tension with society, and the use of church discipline. The Swiss Brethren typified Anabaptism in southern Germany, Austria, and Switzerland. Early leaders included the former Benedictine prior and weaver Michael Sattler (c. 1490–1527), author of the Schleitheim Confession of 1527, and Hans Denck (1500–1527), a teacher and editor.

A second center of Anabaptism developed in the Netherlands and northern Germany. Its origins may be traced to Melchior Hoffman (1495?–1543), an apocalyptic visionary and mystic who was convinced that Strasbourg was to be the site for the New Jerusalem and Christ's second coming, which was to take place in 1533. These ideas up were applied to Münster in Westphalia by John Matthijs (d. 1534) and John of Leiden (d. 1535). Matthijs gained control of the city and through forced rebaptisms and common ownership of goods sought to bring about God's millennial reign in 1534–1535. After his death and Leiden's brief leadership, during which polygamy was introduced, the city fell to combined Catholic and Lutheran forces. The Münster debacle confirmed the worst fears about the Anabaptists and gave the movement an unsavory reputation until the twentieth century. Menno Simons (c. 1496–1561), a priest who converted to Anabaptism in 1536, consolidated and encouraged the disheartened and scattered Melchiorite Anabaptists of northern Germany and Holland, shaping them into communities that rejected violence and political involvement. His leadership was so widely admired that the Anabaptism in this region gradually assumed the name "Mennonite."

A third center of Anabaptism developed in Moravia, initially led by Balthasar Hubmaier (c. 1480–1528) and Hans Hut (1470?–1527). After both were captured and executed, leadership of the Moravian settlements fell to Jacob Hutter (c. 1500–1536). He organized Hut's faction into tightly knit communities with a common ownership of goods (*Bruderhöfe*). Hutter's followers, known afterward as Hutterian Brethren or Hutterites, developed communal colonies in several areas of Eastern Europe, including the Ukraine. Three colonies, as well as some noncommunal Hutterites, immigrated to the United States in the 1870s.

A third category of radicals included the spiritualists and evangelical rationalists. Spiritualists rejected the outer or external forms of religious practice, such as the sacraments, emphasizing only an inner communion with God. The most prominent leader of this group was Caspar Schwenkfeld (1490–1561), a Silesian nobleman. A remnant of his once-numerous followers, the Schwenkfelder Church, has survived in eastern Pennsylvania, near Philadelphia. Evangelical rationalists, on the other hand, rejected such traditional doctrines as the Trinity and the deity of Christ. Among the former were the Polish and Transylvanian Socinians, forerunners of modern Unitarians, who were inspired by the works of Fausto Sozzini (Socinus) (1539–1604).

M. G. Baylor, ed. and trans., *The Radical Reformation* (1991); P. Blickle, *Communal Reformation* (1992); H.-J. Goertz, ed., *Profiles of Radical*

Reformers (1982); H. J. Hillerbrand, ed., *Radical Tendencies in the Reformation* (1987); C. A. Snyder, *Anabaptist History and Theology: An Introduction* (1995); G. H. Williams, *The Radical Reformation* (3rd ed., 1992).

DAVID B. ELLER

Ramban   *see* Moses ben Nachman

Ramus, Peter (1515–1572), French logician and philosopher. Ramus sought to reform the reigning Aristotelian logic so that academic subjects could be grasped in a less complicated manner. In the tradition of humanist philosophy, Ramus proposed a simplified dialectic for both logic and rhetoric. The logician's primary task was classification; the goal was to make subjects more easily understood and memorable. Method, the key feature, enabled a subject to be presented in an orderly way. This stood as a sharp contrast to Aristotelian reliance on syllogisms to derive truth. Ramus sought the inherent self-evidencing axiom in a subject. His method led to a series of divisions (often bifurcations) into components. When analyzing a subject this way, the result is a branching chart across a page as each part is opened up. A "visualized logic" where each part is immediately seen in relation to others, and to the whole, emerges.

Ramism spread throughout Europe. It particularly appealed to English Puritans, and a Ramist tradition emerged at Cambridge Univ. Leading Puritan Ramists were William Perkins and William Ames. Ramism functioned in numerous ways for the Puritans; as a tool for interpreting Scripture, they believed it helped uncover the mind of God.

D. K. McKim, *Ramism in William Perkins' Theology* (1987); P. Miller, *The New England Mind: The Seventeenth Century* (repr. 1970); W. J. Ong, *Ramus, Method, and the Decay of Dialogue* (repr., 1983).

DONALD K. MCKIM

Raphael (1483–1520), one of the most influential painters of the Italian Renaissance. Born in Urbino, Raphael worked in Florence from 1504 to 1508, absorbing influences from Leonardo da Vinci and Michelangelo. The balance and harmony of his early Madonnas are notable. He then moved to Rome, where he designed wall paintings for the papal apartments. The complex iconography of these paintings, a summation of contemporary theological and philosophical learning, includes the famous *School of Athens* (1509–1511). An eclectic painter who assimilated the best innovations from contemporary artists, Raphael was an excellent portraitist as well; his *Julius II* (1512) and *Baldassare Castiglione* (c. 1514) are remarkable character studies of probing intensity. Raphael died unexpectedly in 1520, leaving many commissions unfinished.

P. Joannides, *The Drawings of Raphael with a Complete Catalogue* (1983); R. Jones and N. Penny, *Raphael* (1987); J. Pope-Hennessy, *Raphael* (1970).

PRISCILLA BAUMANN

Ravenna, Churches of   Ravenna, on the northeastern coast of Italy, calls itself an "art city." The spectacular mosaics adorning its religious buildings and the distinctive sarcophagi manufactured there justify the name. As an imperial residence for the Western Roman emperor from 402, the capital of the Arian Ostrogothic kingdom of Theodoric from 493, and the seat of government for the Eastern Roman rule in Italy after 554, Ravenna benefited from royal munificence.

Ravenna may also be designated an "architecture city," for its Christian buildings exemplify the principal types of early Christian architecture. The so-called Mausoleum of Galla Placidia (empress, d. 450), which adjoined the Church of Santa Croce and at one time was an oratory, is in the shape of a Greek cross. Its impressive mosaics feature Christ as a shepherd, no longer the simple peasant depicted in the Roman catacombs but a seated royal shepherd holding a cross-shaped staff.

Splendid examples of early Christian basilicas include San Giovanni Evangelista (first half of the fifth century), San Apollinare Nuovo (built under Theodoric), and San Apollinare in Classe (dedicated in 549 at the port of Ravenna). San Apollinare Nuovo is noted for the two sequences of mosaics on the ministry and the passion of Jesus on the upper register of its side walls. Above the arches of the nave are mosaics depicting two processions: on the south wall martyrs approach the enthroned Christ flanked by archangels, and on the north wall virgins approach Mary and the infant Christ adored by the Three Wise Men. San Apollinare in Classe preserves an apse mosaic of Saint Apollinaris (first bishop of Ravenna) in prayer beneath a jewelled cross and flanked by sheep and the vegetation of paradise.

Two octagonal baptisteries reflect the religious history of Ravenna. The Baptistery of the Orthodox was built in the early fifth century and adorned with mosaics at mid-century. The mosiac in the dome directly above the restored octagonal font, restored but partially incorrect, depicts the baptism of Jesus by John the Baptist. The Baptistery of the Arians has much less elaborate decoration. Its dome mosaic, however, preserves the form of the baptism of Jesus copied from the original scene in the Baptistery of the Orthodox.

San Vitale (consecrated 547/548), the crown jewel of Ravenna's sparkling monuments, is an octagonal martyrion with an apse, dedicated to the martyr Vitalis. The altar area of the interior is covered with outstanding examples of mosaic art. Often reproduced are the court of Emperor Justinian on the north wall and the court of Empress Theodora on the south wall of the apse. The dome depicts Christ enthroned on the orb of the universe.

G. Bovini, *Ravenna Mosaics* (1956); G. Bustacchini, *Ravenna: Capital of Mosaic* (1988); F. W. Deichmann, *Ravenna: Hauptstadt des spätantiken Abendlandes*, 3 vols. (1969, 1974, 1989); S. K. Kostof, *The Orthodox Baptistery of Ravenna* (1965); O. G. von Simson, *Sacred Fortress: Byzantine Art and Statecraft in Ravenna* (1987); A. J. Wharton, *Refiguring the Post-Classical City: Dura Europus, Jerash, Jerusalem, and Ravenna* (1995).

EVERETT FERGUSON

Reccared (d. 601), Visigothic king who ruled Spain from 586 to 601. The barbarians who conquered Rome were usually small minorities governing large, Romanized populations. In the fifth century the Visigoths, or West Goths, occupied the Roman province of Hispania and established a kingdom. The barbarian kings were unable to win over the Hispano-Roman populace made up of Nicene, catholic Christians because the Visigoths were Arian Christians. King Leovigild (r. 568–586) copied Roman government, established a capital at Toledo, and issued gold coins to restore the economy, but his Arianism remained divisive. His son and successor Reccared realized that he could not unite the religiously divided kingdom and, at the encouragement of Bishop Leander of Seville, he converted to Nicene orthodoxy in 587, bringing his people with him. In 589 Reccared called the Third Council of Toledo, at which he and his people, including Visigothic Arian bishops, formally renounced Arianism and accepted the teachings of the early ecumenical councils. Resistance to the change was minor, and Reccared's

work initiated the concept of a united kingdom of Spain.

E. A. Thompson, *The Goths in Spain* (1969); P. D. King, *Law and Society in the Visigothic Kingdom* (1972); A. Ferreiro, *The Visigoths in Gaul and Spain* (1988).

JOSEPH F. KELLY

Reconquest Identifies in Iberian medieval history approximately seven hundred years of intermittent wars by Christians in the extreme north who had escaped permanent conquest by the Muslim invasions that began in 711. There a variety of independent Christian kingdoms emerged in Catalonia, Navarra, Aragón, Galicia, León, and Asturias. Asturias, with its seat of power in Oviedo, occupied the initial place of importance. Most historians date the "official" beginnings of the Reconquest with King Pelayo (c. 718–c. 733), who is alleged to have promised the salvation and restoration of a Catholic Spain. His victory in Covadonga in 718/719, although not significant in the short term, became a symbolic icon along with the restoration of the Regnum Gothorum—or Catholic Iberia under a single Christian monarchy—ruling once again in Toledo. The Reconquest also contributed significantly to the development of the holy war ideology in the medieval West. A factor that impeded the Reconquest was the lack of any real unity among the Christian kingdoms, who fought as much among themselves as with the Muslims. By the eleventh and twelfth centuries, however, the kingdom of León-Castilla emerged as the major contender for Christian hegemony under Alfonso VI (1065–1109). Moreover, in the wings was also Aragón, a small kingdom with a bright future. The major headway against the Muslims occurred in the eleventh century with the collapse of the Caliphate of Córdoba and the rise of the ta'ifa kingdoms that led to a deep fragmentation of the Muslim territories and many internal wars and that the Christians exploited in their favor. There was a temporary setback when the Almoravids, a Muslim sect of fundamentalists from North Africa that conquered the ta'ifa kingdoms, managed to check the Christian offensive. It was during this period that Rodrigo Díaz de Vivar (d. 1099), better known as "El Cid," flourished in the province of Valencia. With the collapse of the Almoravids, the Reconquest resumed in earnest and the papacy began to issue bulls that made the wars look more like crusades. At the battle of Las Navas de Tolosa in 1212 won by Alfonso VIII of Castilla (1158–1214) the Christians recaptured Toledo, and from then on the Muslim demise was secured. The Reconquest came to full fruition with the bloodless conquest of the last caliphate in Granada by Ferdinand and Isabela in 1492.

R. Collins, *Early Medieval Spain: Unity in Diversity, 400–1000* (1983); D. W. Lomax, *The Reconquest of Spain* (1978); J. F. O'Callaghan, *A History of Medieval Spain* (1975).

ALBERTO FERREIRO

Recusancy This term refers to Roman Catholic resistance to the English Reformation, principally the refusal to attend worship in the Church of England. Other crimes included refusing the oath acknowledging the sovereign's ecclesiastical supremacy, being or harboring a "Jesuit" or "seminary priest" from the exile College of Douai, maintaining the doctrine of transubstantiation, and sending children abroad for Catholic education. A vast complex of legislation called "penal laws" enacted between the Act of Uniformity (Elizabeth I, 1559) and the Catholic Relief Acts (George III, 1778 and 1791) specified punishments ranging from fines and ineligibility for civil office to confiscation of property and execution for high treason.

J. Bossy, *The English Catholic Community, 1570–1850* (1975); M. Hodgetts, *Secret Hiding Places* (1989); E. Norman, *Roman Catholicism in England* (1986).

PETER J. SCAGNELLI

Reform Papacy The tenth and eleventh centuries were a period of new religious consciousness in the Latin West that expressed itself in monastic reform and lay piety. With the backing of powerful nobles, several centers of reform developed, rather independent of one another: in Burgundy the monastery at Cluny was founded in 910, destined to become the most far-flung and influential of such movements; Lorraine also boasted important centers, such as Gorze (established in 935) and St. Maximin at Trier; Normandy saw similar developments at Bec and Fécamp. The focus of these various movements was the worldliness of contemporary religious life and the involvement of laymen in ecclesiastical affairs. It was against this background of widespread reform that the reform papacy took shape in the mid-eleventh century.

One of the many ironies of medieval history is the fact that the drive to liberate the church from lay interference was set in motion by that

very thing. In 1046 the German king, Henry III, went to Rome to receive the imperial crown from the pope, but what he found was a schismatic situation in which three rivals claimed the throne of St. Peter. Outraged, he summoned a council at Sutri, where he caused the three contenders to be deposed and a new pope of his choosing to be selected. In so acting, Henry III continued the tradition of Carolingian theocratic rulership, which traced back to the days of Charlemagne.

Two popes appointed by Henry III died quickly, but the third, Bishop Bruno of Toul who took the name Leo IX (1049–1054), proved to be a pivotal figure in the medieval papacy. Leo IX led a group of reformers whose views on the nature of the church became part of papal policy over the next several decades. Several of these reformers, men such as Humbert, Peter Damian, and Hildebrand (later Pope Gregory VII), were appointed as cardinals, and in the process Leo transformed this office from a primarily ceremonial one into a principal papal counselor and administrator.

Among the most pressing issues for this new papacy were those of simony and clerical marriage, or concubinage. Simony was the practice of purchasing church offices, and it was particularly condemned by Cardinal Humbert who, in uncompromising legal arguments, maintained that the bishop who had so acquired his office was in reality no bishop at all, and that those priests consecrated by him were not legitimate priests. While deploring simony with equal fervor, Damian defended the traditional view that the personal worthiness of the priest or bishop did not negate his sacerdotal power.

Unlike his immediate predecessors, who had not left Italy but relied solely on legates to represent them abroad, Leo IX traveled personally to France and Germany, where he convoked reform councils at Reims and Mainz in 1049, issuing anew his reform decrees and sitting in judgment over offending clerics. These actions had an impact of major significance, for they established the authority of Rome over cisalpine churches after a long period of neglect. Moreover, they demonstrated that the papacy, rather than being a mere spectator in the matter of ecclesiastical reform, as had been true during much of the tenth and early eleventh centuries, was now taking control of that movement. Papal reform, unlike the earlier monastic reform, which stressed withdrawal from the world, sought to transform the world.

Unfortunately, Leo IX died in 1054, and Emperor Henry III died in 1056. With their deaths the cooperation between the papacy and the empire came to an end. Under Leo's immediate successors the views of Cardinal Humbert came to dominate the reformers, including his radical notion that the underlying cause of all the ills in the church was the practice of lay investiture, which he regarded as a usurpation of sacral functions by an unqualified lay ruler. He argued that since the episcopal office was intrinsically superior to the royal one, bishops (and abbots) ought not to be subordinate to kings. At the Synod of Rome in 1059 the issue of lay investiture was added to the papal decrees against simony and immorality.

Showing also the influence of Humbert in papal actions are two other events of the year 1059, the first being the decree of papal elections that made this the preserve of the college of cardinals, and the second being the recognition of Robert Guisgard as both a papal vassal and the papal protector.

Little was done to press these issues during the pontificate of Alexander II (1061–1073) but with the accession of Gregory VII (1073–1085) enforcement became a reality. The youngest of the reforming cardinals whom Leo IX had recruited to Rome in 1049, Hildebrand was the only survivor of the original group by 1073, and he was clearly the dominant figure in the pope's inner circle of advisers. As Gregory VII, he reenacted the prohibition against lay investiture in 1075, thereby setting in motion the bitter struggle with Emperor Henry IV, son and successor to Henry III. At stake for Gregory was the proper ordering of the world; at stake for Henry was the very survival of his monarchy.

During the so-called Investiture Controversy, Gregory and Henry used every means of persuasion and force available to them to promote their position. Included among these is a remarkable collection of polemics in which the pope claimed the right to depose the emperor; the emperor in turn secured a condemnation and deposition of the pope. At times, the emperor and the German bishops were aligned against the pope and the German nobles; an antiemperor appeared alongside an antipope. Not until the Concordat of Worms (1122) was an accord reached between pope and emperor.

After Gregory's death in 1085 the controversy spread to France and England as well, but without the political consequences that adversely affected Germany. While the reformers argued that they were conservatives interested in restoring the ancient practices and liberties of the church, their policies and theories had a revolutionary effect upon the church

and upon the monarchies of the High Middle Ages. During the period of the Reform Papacy, the older Carolingian concept of theocratic kingship gave way to one that was subordinate to the papacy: the papacy of Leo IX, Gregory VII, and Urban II (1088–1099) helped propel the papacy to the leadership of Latin Christendom, preparing the way for the universal claims of Innocent III (1198–1216) and Boniface VIII (1294–1303).

———

G. Barraclough, *The Medieval Papacy* (1968); F. Eyck, *Religion and Politics in German History: From the Beginning to the French Revolution* (1998); K. A. Frech, *Reform an Haupt und Gliedern* (1986); B. Tierney, *The Crisis of Church and State 1050–1300* (1964); S. Weinfurter, *Herrschaft und Reich der Salier: Grundlinien einer Umbruchzeit* (1992).

PAUL B. PIXTON

Reformation Art   *see* Art, Reformation

Reformation Catechisms   Catechisms are manuals for instruction in the Christian faith. The *Didache* (c. 50–150) appears to be the earliest postapostolic catechism. Most Reformation catechisms took over the items found in Augustine's and in medieval catechisms: the Ten Commandments, the Lord's Prayer, and the Apostles' Creed. Catechisms were directed primarily to the youth, whose education contributed to an increasingly literate population. In 1520 Luther prepared discourses on the Ten Commandments, the Apostles' Creed, and the Lord's Prayer. His Small and Large Catechisms were written in response to the religious ignorance and indifference he found during his visitation of the churches in Saxony in 1528–1529. The Large Catechism was based on his catechetical sermons and published in April 1529 to help pastors with preaching. In addition to the three elements of earlier catechisms, Luther added sections on baptism and the Lord's Supper. His Small Catechism (May 1529) came to be used for instructing the youth, though it was first intended for pastors. Its order followed that of the Large Catechism, with the section on how to make a confession of sins placed between baptism and the Lord's Supper. While earlier catechisms began with the Creed, Luther began with the Commandments to confront learners with their sin. With a solution in the Creed, believers can approach God in the Lord's Prayer. An excess of catechisms, which Luther encouraged, allowed certain Lutheran factions

to advance their own causes. In response, Saxony required that only the Small Catechism be used. A further step in standardizing its use was its inclusion with the Large Catechism in the Book of Concord in 1580. In place of the section on how to make confession, Andreas Osiander substituted a section on the office of the keys. This version became popular and is still being translated into many languages, provides a link to Luther's theology, and has remained a bond among Lutherans for nearly five hundred years.

While Luther's Small Catechism was for those baptized as infants, Anabaptists generally used devotional literature to prepare older candidates for baptism. One exception was Balthasar Hubmeier's *Christian Catechism That Every Person Should Know before He Is Baptized in Water*. Set against Luther's debate with Erasmus on the freedom of the will, it assigns salvation to those who have engaged in acts of mercy. It lacked discussions of the Ten Commandments, the Apostles' Creed, and the Lord's Prayer, but it discussed baptism as the sign of humankind's relation to God. The Lord's Supper expressed the bonds among Christians.

Huldrych Zwingli produced *A Short Christian Introduction* in 1523 to assist ministers in preaching. In 1537 John Calvin prepared *Instruction and Confession of the Faith, Given for Use in the Church of Geneva*, in which he had sections on the Apostles' Creed, the Lord's Prayer, and the sacraments. This was followed by discussions on the purpose of life, the nature of man, free will, law, and predestination. Its complexity was more appropriate for the clergy rather than children. Calvin's French (1542) and Latin (1545) catechisms were written in question-and-answer form and were more accessible to children. As in pre-Reformation catechisms, Calvin's began with the Creed. Honoring God by the faith as outlined in the Creed was the first topic. Then the law shows how believers are to do God's will. Lastly, believers thank God by prayer.

The Heidelberg Catechism, commissioned by the Elector Frederick III of the Palatinate, remains the most widely used Reformed catechism. Written by Caspar Olevianus and Zacharius Ursinus and published in 1563, it offered a milder Calvinism in order to attract the Elector's Lutheran subjects. Its sections on human misery, redemption, and gratitude reflect Calvin's outline of creed, commandments, and prayer, but they lack his doctrine on predestination. Baptism is a sign of the

covenant to which children belong by virtue of their birth to Christian parents. Since Christ's human nature is confined to heaven, eating Christ's body means believing in him to receive the forgiveness of sins.

In England Henry VIII required priests to teach the Ten Commandments, the Apostles' Creed, and the Lord's Prayer. Justus Jonas's Latin translation of Andreas Osiander's German catechism was translated into English in 1548 by Thomas Cranmer. Another one appeared in the Book of Common Prayer in 1549. John Ponet wrote the moderately Reformed *A Short Catechisme* in 1553. The catechism included in the Book of Common Prayer of 1559 followed Calvin's order of creed, law, and prayer.

Roman Catholics responded to the Protestant challenge with their own catechisms. Even before the Reformation was under way Erasmus gave attention to catechetical reform, and in 1533 he wrote *A Lucid and Pious Explanation of the Creed, the Decalog, and the Lord's Prayer*. It was not addressed to the masses and encountered little success. More popular was Johann Dietenberger's *Catechismus*. Its order of creed, law, and prayer was used among the Reformed and included sections on the Hail Mary and the seven sacraments. George Witzel followed Dietenberger's outline and provided a narrative from creation to Christ's life and ended with the story of the church. Peter Canisius used the question and answer method in his three catechisms, which ranged from large to short (1554, 1556, 1558). He returned to Augustine's order of creed, prayer, and law and added sections on the sacraments and works. The Council of Trent commissioned a catechism so large that it was used by priests. In 1597 Roberto Bellarmino wrote *A Brief Christian Doctrine to Be Learned by Heart*. Its brevity contributed to its popularity.

By retaining Augustine's three parts of creed, prayer, and law, though in differing orders, Reformation-era catechisms built on an older theology and laid down a common foundation for the churches of that time. They also established boundaries among Christians that still exist.

C. P. Arand, *That I May Be His Own: An Overview of Luther's Catechisms* (2000); M. A. Noll, *Confessions and Catechisms of the Reformation* (1991); D. P. Scaer and R. D. Preus, eds., *Luther's Catechisms: 450 Years* (1979).

DAVID P. SCAER

Reformation Colloquies Formal public theological discussions held between Protestant and Catholic or among Protestant theologians to achieve doctrinal consensus but that often only highlighted significant differences. Imperial colloquies were held in 1540–1541 (Hagenau, Worms, and Regensburg), in 1546 (Regensburg) and in 1557 (Worms). In 1561 the queen of France organized a colloquy in Poissy. These colloquies provide insights into the theological and political issues in Europe as confessionalization and nationalization grew throughout the sixteenth century.

After the reading of the Lutheran Augsburg Confession at the Diet of Augsburg (1530), Philip Melanchthon and Johannes Eck continued conversations under the emperor's auspices. Agreement was found in several areas, but problematic for the Catholics were Lutheran proposals for communion in both kinds, priestly marriage, dissolution and disposal of monastic property, and especially the Lutheran rejection of the "doctrine of the Mass." The controverted issues were to be presented at a church council promised for the near future.

The Worms Colloquy (November 1540) was an official imperial colloquy between Eck and Melanchthon that was abandoned for the Regensburg Colloquy the following year. Calvin and several other Protestant reformers were also present.

The Regensburg Colloquy (April 27–May 22, 1541), under the aegis of Emperor Charles V who himself named the participants, was to discuss potential doctrinal reconciliation between Catholics (represented by Eck, Julius Pflug, Johann Gropper, and Cardinal Contarini) and Protestants (Melanchton, Martin Bucer, and Johannes Pistorius; Calvin attended some sessions). The participants agreed on original sin and the bondage of the will. The proposed compromise of "double justification" (*duplex iustitia*) whereby God both imputed and infused righteousness to sinners was subsequently rejected by both Catholics and the Protestants. Issues surrounding the Mass—sacrifice, transubstantiation, and the adoration of the host—were rejected by the Protestants. The Catholics conceded that the laity could receive the cup. The Protestants, particularly Bucer and Melanchthon, acquiesced to a verbal agreement on transubstantiation. Cardinal Contarini was somewhat tolerant of the evangelical ideas; however, Pope Paul III also sent Giovanni Morone as his nuncio and watchdog to the proceedings. At the close of the debate, the emperor promised to have the pope convene a general council soon.

The Regensburg Colloquy II (January 27–March 20, 1546), called by Emperor Charles to comply with his promise at the Diet of Worms (1545), was perhaps a move to cover his preparations for the Schmalkald War (1546–1547). The issue of justification was raised along with the questions on the real presence of Christ in the Lord's Supper. The colloquy ended when the Protestant leaders (Johannes Brenz, Bucer, Erhard Schnepf, and Georg Major) learned that the dialogue results were to be kept secret.

The Worms Colloquy (September 11–October 8, 1557) was the result of an agreement at the Diet of Augsburg (1555). The Catholic contingent (Peter Canisius, Gropper, and Michael Helding) met with Melanchthon, Brenz, and Schnepf (representing the Protestants) to discuss issues that had not yet been addressed. Canisius raised the relation between the Bible and tradition and then pointed to the disagreement among Protestants on original sin and justification. The meeting disbanded when they realized it had no political value.

The Colloquy of Poissy (September 1561), proposed by French Protestants and Catholics and supported by Queen Catherine de Médicis, mother of Charles IX, was a final attempt at reconciliation following the Council of Trent. The French Calvinists were headed by Theodore Beza (along with Peter Martyr Vermigli) and the Catholics by Cardinal de Lorraine. Beza immediately rejected the real presence of Christ in the Lord's Supper to the instant shouts of "Blasphemy!" After it was decided to convene fewer delegates, twelve men from each side met for discussion. When Beza attacked the primacy of the pope and apostolic succession, the Catholic participants refused further discussions.

The Colloquy of Montbéliard (1586) was a politically and theologically motivated debate between Lutherans (Laurentius Andreae and Andreas Osiander) and Calvinists (Beza, Anthony de la Fay, Abraham Musculus, Samuel Hubner, and Claude Albery) on the Lord's Supper, the person and nature of Christ, baptism, predestination, and election. The place of images, paintings, music, and ceremonies in worship was questioned by Andreae, and the discussion quickly became an open-ended debate. Although agreement was reached on images, deeper differences became evident. Most significant was whether baptism was a necessary means of regenerative grace (Andreae's position) or an outward sign of God's inward (and mysterious) action (Beza's position). Out of this meeting grew Andreae's *Epitome* (summary) of the Formula of Concord. The colloquies did not succeed in clarifying the religious divisions, let alone overcome them. However, these conversations did provide support for the Peace of Augsburg (1555) by demonstrating common commitments and acceptance of Protestants as dialogue partners.

G. R. Evans, *Problems of Authority in the Reformation Debates* (1992); G. Kretschmar, "The Imperial Diet of Regensburg and the 1541 Variata of the Augsburg Confession," in *Piety, Politics, and Ethics: Reformation Studies in Honor of George W. Forell*, ed. C. Lindberg (1984), 85–102; P. Matheson, *Cardinal Contarini at Regensburg* (1972); G. Müller, ed., *Die Religionsgespräche der Reformationszeit* (1980); D. Nugent, *Ecumenism in the Age of the Reformation* (1974); J. Raitt, *The Colloquy of Montbéliard* (1993); D. J. Ziegler, ed., *Great Debates of the Reformation* (1969).

TIMOTHY MASCHKE

Reformation Confessions The Protestant Reformation saw both a proliferation of creedal statements, or "confessions" (Ger. *Bekenntnisse*), and a heightening of their normative role in church life. The "confession of faith" in the modern sense developed around the time of the Reformation, as newly emerging religious groups felt the need to account for and defend their teachings comprehensively. The Protestants' particular concern for the "pure word of God" lent itself naturally to expression in written statements, and other churches, in responding to the Protestant challenge, tended to follow suit. The concept of confession is central in the thought of Martin Luther, who wrote that "confession is the chief task of faith" and "everything we do is a confession." Adherents of the nascent Protestant denominations, and others, used written statements of faith (1) to affirm their willingness to testify in the face of persecution, (2) to codify and communicate the fundamentals of their beliefs, and (3) to establish religious norms and boundaries for their communities by clearly distinguishing approved from rejected doctrine. These three functions parallel the meanings of the word "confession": the ritual act of avowing one's sinfulness before God, a formal statement of faith, or one of the four major

churches of the period (Anglican, Catholic, Lutheran, and Reformed).

The paradigmatic Reformation-era confession is the Lutheran Augsburg Confession. Philip Melanchthon penned the document, and nine Lutheran rulers, hoping to secure legal toleration for Lutheranism, affixed their signatures. It was presented to Emperor Charles V at the 1530 Diet of Augsburg. The text assumed several important functions. First, it provided a set of doctrinal norms that could guide the growing number of Protestant clergy in their preaching. Second, it provided the basis for political and military alliances between Lutheran groups. Finally, it drew a clear boundary between the Lutherans and other movements within Protestantism by demonstrating the inherent conservatism of Lutheran teachings over against the radicalism of the rejected groups. Accordingly, it emphasized points of agreement or similarity with Roman Catholicism—for example, laying particular stress on the doctrine of Christ's real presence in the sacrament of Communion, which Zwinglians and Anabaptists denied. This initial attempt to achieve legal toleration failed, however, and in 1540 Melanchthon wrote a new version (known as the *Confessio Augustana Variata*), this time emphasizing points of contact with the Reformed traditions. After bitter doctrinal struggles and factionalism through the 1550s and 1560s, Lutheranism assumed the theological identity it would keep up to the present day, codifying the resolution in the Formula of Concord, authored in 1577 by Jakob Andreae and Martin Chemnitz, which again stressed the distance between Lutheranism and the Reformed churches. *The Book of Concord*, first published in 1580, collects all the authoritative creedal statements for Lutheranism into a single volume.

The most significant among the period's Reformed confessions are the Helvetic Confessions, particularly the Second Helvetic Confession (1566), and the Heidelberg Catechism (1563). The most influential Reformed confessions, unlike their Lutheran counterparts, were generally adopted not by territorial rulers but by synods, and there is no single confession accorded universal authority by all Reformed Christians. Many confessions are identified with particular national churches, such as the Gallic Confession of 1559 (France) and the Belgic Confession of 1561 (the Low Countries). The Heidelberg Catechism, written by Zacharias Ursinus and Caspar Olevian in order to mediate between opposing theological factions in the German territory of the Palatinate, is accorded wide recognition in Reformed churches around the world. Other influential texts, such as Heinrich Bullinger's Second Helvetic Confession and Calvin and Bullinger's Zurich Consensus (or *Consensus Tigurinus*) of 1549, reflect the union of Zwinglian and Calvinistic branches of Reformed Christianity.

In the Anglican communion the Book of Common Prayer took on a parallel community-defining function. Its first version, authored by Thomas Cranmer, was published in 1549. Similar to the Augsburg Confession, it became the subject of acrimonious disputes between theologians of differing sensibilities, and it underwent repeated revisions. The Roman Catholic Church, as part of the Counter-Reformation efforts of the Council of Trent, produced the specifically anti-Protestant Tridentine Profession of Faith (*Professio Fidei Tridentina*, 1564), which was largely an affirmation of the authority of the traditional papal church.

———

A. C. Cochrane, ed., *Reformed Confessions of the 16th Century* (1966); R. Kolb, *Confessing the Faith: Reformers Define the Church* (1991); R. Kolb and T. J. Wengert, eds., *The Book of Concord* (2000); J. H. Leith, ed., *Creeds of the Churches* (3rd ed., 1983); J. Pelikan and V. Hotchkiss, eds., *Creeds and Confessions of Faith in the Christian Tradition* (2003); W. Reinhard, ed., *Bekenntnis und Geschichte: Die Confessio Augustana im historischen Zusammenhang* (1981); E. Sehling et al., eds., *Evangelische Kirchenordnungen des XVI. Jahrhunderts*, 16 vols. to date (1902–).

NATHAN BARUCH REIN

Reformation Contributions to Education

The Reformation was a complex set of interrelated and often contradictory proposals and counterproposals for the reform of church and society in and around sixteenth-century Europe. When these various proposals were coupled with movements meant to support them, a period of dramatic social upheaval ensued. Education was central to this mix, as the various affirmations and rejections of the era were intended to influence what people believed and how people lived. Indeed, the pedagogical plans of Roman Catholics (e.g., Erasmus of Rotterdam [1467?–1536], Ignatius Loyola [1491?–1556]) and Protestants (e.g., Martin Luther [1483–1546], John Calvin [1509–1564]) in many ways define the period and point to some of the distinctive, enduring contributions of the Reformation to education.

By the beginning of the fifteenth century there had been increasingly numerous, loud calls to expand educational opportunities for all people, clergy and laity alike. These calls originated from a plethora of sources: economic (the development of a middle class, trade, exploration, nascent capitalism), ecclesiastical (the establishment of universities and teaching orders), governmental (the rise of territorial states and cities), and ideological (renaissance humanism). To this end, Europeans began to found universities and local Latin schools. Simultaneously, they began replacing inherited scholastic pedagogical emphases on authorities with humanism's source-based emphases on the *philosophia Christi*.

In the sixteenth century, Roman Catholic and Protestant educators shared many of the same educational assumptions about method because, in many ways, they shared a common humanistic source, represented by the work of the Dutch humanist Erasmus. His books, original-language editions of biblical texts and writings on pedagogy, greatly influenced Reformation educators. He advocated training children with praise and games, even tailoring methods to the readiness of particular learners (i.e., age-appropriate classes). His goal was to produce Christian citizens capable of ethical reflection and moral responsibility, informed by classical intellectual traditions (particularly Greek and Latin). This program can be seen as a transalpine adaptation of Italian Renaissance emphases on original texts (*ad fontes*) and classical learning. This program, with its basic commitment to the educational formation of students, was to influence Western pedagogy for centuries.

Protestants, then, set out to reform the educational ministry of the church by focusing on their interpretations of the basics of Christian doctrine, both in terms of content (doctrine) and sources (the Bible). Therefore, the Reformers translated the Scriptures and other important ancient Christian texts into the vernacular. They also wrote catechisms, pamphlets, and doctrinal works, all of which were designed to advance educational reform. Furthermore, they also preached, lectured, debated, and disputed in order to educate their constituents.

Luther is representative here. His vision of a literate populace, both young and old, able to understand the basics of the Word of God, led him to write his famous Small Catechism, along with its accompanying Large Catechism of 1529. This work made use of a long-standing tradition of churchly education—catechesis—while simultaneously reforming it.

By structure and content, this initiative underscored distinctively Lutheran doctrinal themes (law and gospel, word and sacrament, prayer and vocation). The catechism has played an unparalleled role in the context of Lutheran theological education, as it quickly became, and has remained, a standard introduction to Lutheran piety and doctrine used in homes, parishes, and theological seminaries.

Other Protestants followed Luther's educational lead, even as they moved in directions different from his. Notable here is Calvin's work in Geneva and John Sturm's (1507–1589) in Strasbourg. These reformers' interpretation of humanistic character-formation within the context of a Christian community of learning produced educational systems oriented around biblically based ethical doctrines. This humanistic heritage, which served as the basis for most pedagogical strategies of the period, transcended confessional differences. Even followers of the Roman Catholic reformer Ignatius Loyola were deeply influenced by it. The Jesuits organized their schools to teach their students to be "soldiers of Christ" and defenders of the church. Particularly within the order, the Society of Jesus emphasized full obedience to God's will, embodied in the commands of one's superiors.

M. Alexander, *The Growth of English Education, 1348 to 1648: A Social and Cultural History* (1990); M. Edwards, *Printing, Propaganda, and Martin Luther* (1994); A. Farrell, *The Jesuit Code of Liberal Education: Development and Scope of the* Ratio Studiorum (1938); P. Grendler, *Books and Schools in the Italian Renaissance* (2002); J. Kittelson and P. Transue, eds., *Reform and Resilience: Universities in Transition, 1300–1700* (1984); J. N. H. Lawrence, "The Spread of Lay Literacy in Late Medieval Castile," *Bulletin of Hispanic Studies* 62 (1985); L. Spitz and B. S. Tinsley, *The Reformation and Humanist Learning: Johann Sturm on Education* (1994); G. Strauss, *Luther's House of Learning: Indoctrination of the Young in the German Reformation* (1978); W. Woodward, *Desiderius Erasmus concerning the Aim and Method of Education* (1904).

WILLIAM R. RUSSELL

Reformation Eucharistic Controversies

see Eucharistic Controversies in the Reformation

Reformation Liturgies

The variety and complexity of the reform of the medieval Catholic liturgy by the Reformers illustrates the centrality of worship to the accomplishment of their aims. The Reformers' understanding that salvation is received, not achieved, and that God justifies a person through grace by faith alone led to the mostly gradual but sometimes abrupt dismantling of much of the liturgical practices and piety of the medieval Catholic Church. In these reforms the word of God became central to worship, and praise, proclamation, and education became the central aims of the worshiping community, now understood as "the priesthood of all believers." Bibles, tracts, the Mass itself, and texts of musical compositions were revised and translated into the vernacular. Congregational singing was encouraged. Hymns, metrical paraphrases of the psalms and translations of the Ordinary of the Mass were produced and collected in hymnals and songbooks. The Lord's Supper was celebrated with both bread and wine.

Luther revised and then translated the Mass into German (*Formula Missae*, 1523; *Deutsche Messe*, 1526). To replace daily Communion, he created morning and evening prayer services from the Latin breviary. These services focused on the reading of Scripture and the sermon. His reforms were more revisions than replacements of the liturgy of the medieval church; thus, to that extent, he brought the music and aspects of the ceremonial over into the churches under his sway, albeit in "purified" form. The one exception was the canon of the Mass. His insight that the Eucharist was God's gift to people and not the people's sacrifice to God led to his radically altering the eucharistic prayer, excising and rearranging parts.

John Calvin and his followers created a liturgy based on Scripture and the customs of the "ancient church." Calvin elevated the sermon to the central place in worship and revised the Mass, translating it into the vernacular. Calvin himself was an advocate for weekly Communion; however, the Genevan Council preferred quarterly celebrations. Calvin, too, recognized the importance of congregational participation, and he worked with poets and musicians to translate and set the entire book of Psalms in metrical verse.

Huldrych Zwingli, residing in Zurich, wrote *An Attack on the Canon of the Mass* in August 1523. There he criticized the piety of the medieval Mass, saying that the Mass itself is not a sacrifice but a *memorial* of Christ's sacrifice, the bread and wine being reminders of grace rather than grace itself. He sought a replacement for the Mass guided solely by Scripture. Simplicity and silence were its hallmarks. True to these principles, he and his colleagues "cleansed" the churches of all accretions of the medieval church, including statues, paintings, murals, service books, choir music, and organs.

In England under the direction of Thomas Cranmer, archbishop of Canterbury, reform of the Mass was also accomplished. Although not averse to much traditional piety, Cranmer did work with continental scholars and church leaders from both Lutheran and Reformed circles, as well as with the rising "Puritan" dissidents. The result of these collaborations was the Book of Common Prayer (first issued in 1549). Although it retained the structure of the Latin Rite, it included many of the changes of the other reformers. It centered in Scripture, advocated the use of English rather than Latin, and drastically reduced the number of rules (rubrics) governing the practice of worship. It was oriented toward use by the congregation as a whole and ruled by the English Bible. In it, too, one can see the beginnings of the theological diversity that characterized the Anglican *via media* tradition. One's faith is measured by one's conscience alone. To others' beliefs, one exercises "charity." To the extent that this charity was practiced, the book managed to gain support among a broad sector of worshipers holding a wide variety of beliefs. However, Puritans and a growing number of other dissenters found that the revisions did not go far enough. They wished to follow more closely the direction of Calvin. This led in the direction of greater simplicity and focus on Scripture as the only guide to liturgical practice. The Puritans published the Middleburg Liturgy in 1586.

Y. Brilioth, *Eucharistic Faith and Practice* (1956); H. Davies, *Worship and Theology in England* (1970); C. Eire, *War against the Idols: The Reformation of Worship from Erasmus to Calvin* (1986); R. Leaver, "Theological Consistency, Liturgical Integrity, and Musical Hermeneutic in Luther's Liturgical Reforms," *LQ* 9 (1995): 117–38; D. MacCulloch, *Thomas Cranmer: A Life* (1996); B. Spinks, *Luther's Liturgical Criteria and His Reform of the Canon of the Mass* (1982); B. Thompson, *Liturgies of the Western Church* (1961).

LINDA J. CLARK

Reformation Marriage Courts

The Protestant Reformation established a variety of tribunals to address legal questions of sex, marriage, and family life. Sometimes these were specialty marriage courts, built on late medieval prototypes. More typically, they were civil courts or consistory courts of wider competence with new jurisdiction over questions of marriage, family life, and sexual crime. Sometimes these courts were empowered to dispose fully of the cases before them, but more often they shared power with other civil tribunals and depended on the latter to compel their witnesses and to implement their decrees. Occasionally these courts both promulgated laws and adjudicated cases on sex, marriage, and the family, but mostly they implemented the new civil statutes on sex, marriage, and family life promulgated by civil legislators.

Whatever their form and function, these Protestant marriage courts replaced the Catholic church courts that had traditionally governed marriage and family disputes. The medieval Catholic Church had regarded marriage as a sacrament of the church that was subject to ecclesiastical jurisdiction. The church's canon law governed questions of marital formation, maintenance, and dissolution; parental roles, rights, and responsibilities; child control, custody and care; and sexual deviance, fornication, prostitution, and more.

Lutherans, Calvinists, Anabaptists, and Anglicans alike rejected the sacramental nature of marriage. Marriage was for them primarily a social estate or covenantal association of the earthly kingdom. Marriage required no prerequisite faith or purity and conferred no sanctifying grace as did the true sacraments of baptism and the Eucharist. Accordingly, marriage and family life were not subject to the church and its canon law but to the state and its civil law. Early in the Reformation, Protestant magistrates issued comprehensive new civil laws of marriage and the family, either as freestanding acts or as lengthy provisions within more general church orders or civil ordinances.

These new civil laws set out the requirements of betrothal and marriage, banns and weddings, parental consent and peer witness, and church consecration and civil registration. They defined the parent or guardian's duties of baptism and catechesis, education and inheritance, support and emancipation. They also set out rules with respect to spousal abuse and neglect, annulment and separation, divorce and remarriage.

Implementation of these new laws lay with the Reformation marriage courts. In Zurich, Bern, and other Swiss cities, influenced by Huldrych Zwingli and Heinrich Bullinger, special marriage courts were established to administer the new civil laws of marriage. These were specialty courts, staffed by ministers and magistrates, under the general supervision of the city councils.

Some Lutheran polities had special marriage courts, but most had consistory courts that held jurisdiction over several subjects, including marriage and the family. These courts usually disposed fully of the cases before them, with appeal allowed to the city or territorial council. Judges on these courts, who were often theology and law professors, also issued learned opinions (*consilia*) that became important sources of marriage law within and beyond the local polity.

In Calvin's Geneva, a consistory court comprising a civil and a clerical bench had primary jurisdiction over sex crimes and over marriage and family disputes. This court disposed of most of the cases before it using spiritual admonitions, including the ban and excommunication in extreme cases. Cases of divorce, marital property disputes, and criminal punishment for serious sexual crimes, however, were automatically removed or remanded to the city council for proper legal disposal.

In Anabaptist communities, marriage and family questions were usually resolved informally by elders of the community. Few sixteenth-century Anabaptist communities maintained detailed marriage laws or formal tribunals for marriage disputes. They preferred methods of mediation and punishments of shunning—ostracism, if necessary. Anabaptists generally prohibited their members from litigating marriage and family cases in state courts. Many also refused to register their marriage certificates or marital properties with the civil authorities—a perennial source of tension and sometimes reprisal.

In sixteenth-century Anglican England, traditional church courts continued to exercise jurisdiction over marriage and family questions. These courts implemented the new parliamentary laws on marriage and family life but followed medieval canon law procedures—written pleadings, representation by counsel, preparation of court records, with occasional episcopal intervention. Only in extreme cases could English parties appeal to the royal courts or equity courts for relief, or press for an annulment or divorce by a private act of Parliament.

E. J. Carlson, *Marriage and the English Reformation* (1994); R. H. Helmholz, *Marriage Litigation in Medieval England* (1974); R. M. Kingdon, *Adultery and Divorce in Calvin's Geneva* (1995); W. Koehler, *Zurcher Ehegericht und Genfer Konsistorium*, 2 vols. (1942); S. Ozment, *When Fathers Ruled: Family Life in Reformation Europe* (1983); G. H. Williams, *The Radical Reformation* (3rd ed., 1992); J. Witte Jr., *From Sacrament to Contract: Marriage, Religion, and Law in the Western Tradition* (1997); J. Witte Jr. and R. M. Kingdon, *Sex, Marriage, and Family in John Calvin's Geneva*, 3 vols. (2004).

JOHN WITTE JR.

Reformation Music The Protestant Reformation produced a tremendous outpouring of musical activity. Centered in various regions, cities, and towns, this activity had as its primary focus the congregation at worship; however, subsidiary efforts resulted in the use of vernacular religious texts as the inspiration for ballads and part music sung in homes, courts, and city squares. Innumerable publications were made of Psalters, hymnals, and choral collections, with texts both in the vernacular and in Latin. Twentieth-century theologian and hymnist Eric Routley described this outpouring as an expression of the "moral ecstasy" that inspired the religious ideas of the Reformation. Composers, theorists, and musicians codified and, in many instances, created the great musical forms now commonly used in Christian worship: anthems, motets, cantatas, psalm settings, hymns and spiritual songs, oratorios, and organ music.

Martin Luther was one of the most important figures in this musical outpouring. Building on a nascent vernacular tradition, he himself wrote many hymns and psalm paraphrases and set some of them to music, "A Mighty Fortress Is Our God" being the most famous. He considered music to have a theological dimension. For him music exerted extraordinary power for good in the life of a believer, a power surpassed only by the word of God. Music is an instrument through which faith is strengthened and growth in the knowledge of Christ is accomplished. According to Luther, music in worship had three central functions: to offer praise to God, to edify the faithful, and to aid in devotion. A liturgical conservative in comparison to others in the movement, he brought forward most of the medieval musical tradition into his reforms of worship, including its forms and the use of choirs and instruments. Luther sought musicians to help in the liturgical renewal that he was generating—composers such as Johann Walter and the music publisher Georg Rhau—and brought them to Wittenberg. Together they developed and published music for congregations to sing: metrical psalm paraphrases; the sung parts of the Mass, such as the Gloria and the Sanctus, translated into German; and hymns. This musical activity spread the ideas of the Reformers throughout Central and Western Europe.

John Calvin followed many of the same paths that Luther forged. He and Luther were in agreement about the nature of music and its appropriateness for worship. Under his guidance, poets and musicians created the Genevan Psalter (1539–1562), translating, over a period of years, all of the psalms into metrical, vernacular verse and setting them to melodies. Calvin, however, differed with Luther on what should be sung. He brought a more judicious use of music into worship. He believed that musical expression characteristic of medieval Catholicism obscured rather than illumined the all-important biblical text. He also thought that music in worship must not be frivolous but have "weight" and "majesty." It should consist only of the psalms and only sung in unaccompanied unison. He agreed that music had great power, but he maintained that that power could easily pervert the sense of the singing and distract from prayer. These strictures did not apply outside of worship; composers set psalm texts for the musical delight and edification of the faithful in musical activities outside the church's worship. The composer Claude Goudimel (c. 1514–1572) wrote both homophonic and polyphonic settings of the texts of the Genevan Psalter that were widely sought after.

The Puritans in England followed Calvin's lead. When Elizabeth I ascended the throne, the Marian exiles returned to England, bringing with them an English version of Calvin's Psalter—the Anglo-Genevan Psalter (1556). By 1564, another English version—the Sternhold and Hopkins Psalter—was complete. Thus, the practice of congregational singing was firmly established among the English by the middle of the sixteenth century. However, psalm singing did not eradicate other forms of musical activity in English worship. Particularly in the cathedral establishments and in the Chapel Royal, elaborate choral and instrumental music was still performed with contrapuntal settings of texts both in English and in Latin. Thus, during Elizabeth's reign, the English choral tradition thrived in many places. The great choral composers also provided settings of the metrical psalms for the Psalters bound in the backs of their Bibles. Unaccompanied unison psalm singing may have held sway in worship in local parish churches, but choral singing also thrived at this time, both inside and outside the churches.

C. Garside, "Some Attitudes of the Major Reformers toward the Role of Music in the Liturgy," *McCormick Quarterly* 21 (1967): 151–74; M. Jenny, *Luther, Zwingli, Calvin in ihren Liedern* (1983); P. LeHuray, *Music and the Reformation in England, 1549–1660* (1967); J. L. Mays, *Psalms* (1994); N. Temperley, *The Music of the English Parish Church* (1979); P. Westermeyer, *TeDeum: The Church and Its Music* (1998).

LINDA J. CLARK

Reformation, Second   This term refers to the conversion of a number of prominent territories in the Holy Roman Empire from Lutheranism to Calvinism, or more properly, Reformed Protestantism, in the period 1555–1618. In religious life the movement advocated a Reformed view of the Eucharist and Christology and the impulse to further discipline the lives of Christian believers. In the political realm the adherents tended to pursue an activist foreign policy that often led to military assistance to coreligionists in the Netherlands and France.

The South German Reformation had long possessed tendencies similar to the Zwinglian Reformation in Zurich, though the provisions of the Peace of Augsburg (1555), which only recognized Lutheranism and Catholicism as legal confessions, seemed to preclude the espousal of a wholesale Reformed outlook in the empire. The conversion of the Electoral Palatinate to the Reformed faith with the publication of the Heidelberg Catechism in 1563 under the sponsorship of Frederick III the Pious (r. 1559–1576) challenged the status quo. Reformed territories such as the Palatinate claimed their Reformed stance was in line with Philip Melanchthon's altered version (*Variata*) of the Augsburg Confession. Lutheran princes objected to this apparent violation of the Peace of Augsburg but balked at Emperor Maximilian II's effort to exclude Frederick from the religious peace at the 1566 Diet of Augsburg. A number of smaller territories joined the movement, such as Bremen and Emden and the county of Nassau. The University of Heidelberg and later the Herborn Academy served as the movement's flagship institutions. A strong Crypto-Calvinist faction even flourished in Saxony in the late sixteenth century. Elector Johann Sigismund introduced Calvinism into Brandenburg in 1613, though the territory's inhabitants largely remained Lutheran. Under the direction of Christian of Anhalt, Calvinist princes organized together in the Protestant Union (1608). The denouement of the movement's activist foreign policy came with the Palatine elector Frederick V's gamble to claim the Bohemian crown in the wake of the Bohemian Revolt (1618). Military defeat spelled the end of Palatine adventurism. While the Second Reformation was never a broadly popular movement, Calvinism survived the early modern period as a vibrant wing of German Protestantism.

Scholars have debated the appropriateness of the expression "Second Reformation" in light of the continuity between the Second Reformation and the earlier Bucerian and Philippist streams within German Protestantism. Similarly dubbing the movement the Second Reformation perhaps overstates the importance of what was in reality a Reformed manifestation of the larger process of confessionalization. Nevertheless, the expression possesses a basic utility in denoting the confessional shift from Lutheranism to Calvinism. The Second Reformation should not be confused with the closely related Dutch movement *Nadere Reformatie* ("further Reformation"), later German Pietism, or subsequent efforts to revitalize Protestantism such as the Holiness and Charismatic movements.

H. J. Cohn, "The Territorial Princes in Germany's Second Reformation, 1559–1622," in *International Calvinism 1541–1715*, ed. M. Preswich (1985); B. Nischan, *Prince, People, and Confession: The Second Reformation in Brandenburg* (1994); V. Press, *Calvinismus und Territorialstaat* (1970); H. Schilling, ed., *Die reformierte Konfessionalisierung in Deutschland* (1986).

CHARLES D. GUNNOE JR.

Reformation Social Welfare In his 1520 *Address to the German Nobility*, Luther declared that "nobody ought to go begging among Christians," and he quickly put the thesis into practice, drafting a new poor relief ordinance for the Wittenberg city council.

The adoption of a new ordinance for poor relief was often the vanguard of the Reformation in German towns, anticipating liturgical reforms by several years. The reform of social welfare nonetheless had profound theological motives and implications. Medieval theologians regarded poverty, at least in its voluntary, religious form (as with the mendicant orders), as meritorious. Almsgiving was motivated by the spiritual benefit accruing to the almsgiver.

The poor thus had a fixed, necessary role in medieval society as the means by which the rich might save themselves.

The new Protestant orders put into legal and institutional form Luther's theological description of good works as directed not toward God as a means of salvation but to the service of the neighbor. The new orders included the prohibition of begging and private almsgiving, establishment of a common chest often supported by taxes rather than by voluntary contributions, and regulations for support of the local poor, both the destitute and the "house poor"—wandering paupers were aided briefly and then sent on their way. Andreas Karlstadt explicitly contrasted the old worship of graven images with evangelical service to the poor, and with considerable success reformers appropriated the income of medieval religious endowments to poor relief and education.

Luther's poor ordinances for Wittenberg and Leisnig (1523) were the model for a growing body of similar laws in Nuremberg (1522), Strasbourg (1522), and Altenburg (1527) which became influential in their own right. In northern Germany and Denmark, Luther's proposals for poor relief were given form by the church orders prepared by Johann Bugenhagen, who further separated the poor chest from the funds supporting the church and its ministers. Lutherans regarded poor relief as a community responsibility; the precise institutional division of responsibilities between church and secular government was a matter of indifference.

In addition to direct relief, these orders made provision for rudimentary medical care for the poor. Lutherans gave special status to midwives, who were sworn to attend the poor in childbirth free of charge, to supply scriptural consolation and, in an emergency, to administer baptism. Bugenhagen regarded such midwives as "ministers" (*Kirchendienerinnen*) of the church.

The most influential Roman Catholic treatise on the reformation of poor relief, Juan Luis Vives's *De subventione pauperum* (1526), was written after the first Lutheran reforms and likely influenced by them. When Roman Catholic governments did adopt new orders for poor relief, as in Ypres (1525), Bruges (1556), and, with Charles V's efforts, in the empire (1531) and Spain (1540), they were accused of crypto-Lutheranism. To their Catholic critics, any regulation of the religious mendicants was unacceptable, as was secular, tax-supported poor relief. Almsgiving must be voluntary in order to benefit the giver, and it belonged under the institutional purview of the church, not the secular government.

John Calvin, familiar with the system of relief in Strasbourg as it had further developed under Martin Bucer, included poor relief in the Genevan ecclesiastical ordinance of 1541. Calvin identified the diaconate as one of the four offices in the NT church, further distinguishing—on the basis both of his exegesis and of the already existing situation in the Genevan *hôpital*—between deacons who collected funds for the poor and those who distributed them. To avoid overstraining the Genevan relief system under the influx of religious exiles to Geneva, a separate fund and administration were established for them.

Calvin's model was influential on Reformed churches elsewhere, especially in Scotland. In the Netherlands, church and civic systems of relief often operated in parallel; in France the Huguenot consistories came to administer poor relief. Calvin had defended the propriety of a female diaconate from Scripture, and in a few places, as in Amsterdam, female deacons saw to the relief of poor women. In England under the Elizabethan Poor Law of 1601, churchwardens in each parish had charge of poor relief, funded by both taxation and voluntary contributions.

C. Lindberg, *Beyond Charity: Reformation Initiatives for the Poor* (1993); E. A. McKee, *John Calvin on the Diaconate and Liturgical Almsgiving* (1984); J. Olson, *One Ministry, Many Roles: Deacons and Deaconesses through the Centuries* (rev. ed., 2006); C. H. Parker Jr., *The Reformation of Community: Social Welfare and Calvinist Charity in Holland, 1572–1620* (1998); J. Pound, *Poverty and Vagrancy in Tudor England* (1986).

CHRISTOPHER B. BROWN

Reformation, Women and the

The Protestant teaching of the holiness of all vocations and the home as the cradle of faith gave women's domestic roles as spouses and mothers positive religious meaning. However, despite the principles of justification by faith and the priesthood of all believers espoused by the Reformers, as well as efforts to provide basic education for girls (to enable them to read the Bible), the Reformation reinforced patriarchal family and societal structures.

As the monastic way of life was deemed futile and convents were closed or transformed in Reformation cities, women lost significant opportunities for education, religious practices, and self-expression in an all-female environment. Women could express their religious callings outside the monastery but preferably in domestic vocations within marriage. A self-supporting single woman was a rare exception.

The Reformation's effect on women's lives was ambiguous. Women were central as the recipients and implementers of the new faith in their environments, often behind the scenes. Even if the Reformers addressed women as a group, women were affected by and contributed to the Reformation as individuals, with their choices depending much on their station in life.

Because convents had fostered women's spirituality and provided an alternative to domestic life, it is not surprising that some vehement opposition to the Reformation came from convents. Katherine Rem wrote to her family in 1523 defending her decision to stay in her convent in Augsburg, as did Caritas Pirckheimer. Some nuns aspired to combine their old and new faith: Anna Sophia of Quedlinburg, an abbess of an imperial canoness house, after becoming a Protestant, made monks and priests in her "jurisdiction" adhere to the Augsburg Confession and converted her monastery into an elementary school. Women who responded to Protestant preaching by leaving the safety of their convent broke the order, and their stories—such as in the letter of Ursula of Münsterberg from Saxony (1528)—were used as Protestant propaganda.

Ex-nuns often married the new Protestant pastors. The most famous of them, Katharina (Katie) von Bora, married Martin Luther himself, who had helped her to escape from her convent. In many ways Katie exemplifies the promises and the losses the Reformation presented to women. She ruled the domestic realm, raised children, and implemented Protestant faith through the home. Pioneering the model of the Protestant pastor's wife, she supported her husband's public ministry of teaching, without writing theological treatises herself.

The Luthers' marriage exemplified the Protestants' positive view of marital relations and love, sexuality, and parental duties. In spite of recognized spiritual equality, spousal duties were divided into public and private realms. The continued exclusion of women from public ministry and teaching suggests an assumption of a degree of inferiority in the female gender.

Noble ladies in positions of influence were exceptionally able to promote the Reformation in public ways. For instance, Queen Dorothea and her spouse King Christian III made Denmark a Lutheran state, and Elizabeth I of England as the head of the church in her country navigated a unique "middle way" for the Anglican Church.

Queen Marguerite of Navarre, a humanist writer familiar with both Calvin's and Luther's ideas prepared the way for the Reformation in Navarre. Her daughter Jeanne d'Albret espoused Huguenot beliefs and protected Calvinist leaders, striving for religious freedom in her land. Their kindred spirit, Renee of Ferrara, also an associate of Calvin, likewise lent protection to Huguenot refugees while navigating family ties to the Catholic side and the effects of the religious war in France, an environment in which aristocratic ladies were used for political alliances via marriages regardless of their religious affiliation.

Aristocratic women were also central in the reform within the Catholic Church and were similarly vulnerable to persecution. The Renaissance poet Vittoria Colonna from Italy was suspected of heresy because of her association with unorthodox reforming voices (Capuchins and Valdensians). Teresa of Avila, who reformed the Carmelite order and modeled the spiritual life of prayer, also encountered persecution in the form of the Inquisition.

Within the Radical Reformation, prophets such as Ursula Jost and Barbara Rebstock from Strasbourg could assume spiritually authoritative roles among the different branches of the Anabaptists, but as a result, they faced suspicion and the serious threat of being drowned as heretics. Women did not need to be radicals, though, to suffer the death of a martyr, as revealed in the heresy trials of Anne Askew and others in England during the reign of the Catholic Queen Mary.

Compared to medieval visionary women, Reformation women wrote little, and those who did—typically noble women or nuns—encountered opposition. Argula von Grumbach, a Bavarian woman who defended a student accused of Lutheran heresy; Katherine Zell, the active wife of an ecumenical pastor in Alsace; and Marie Dentiere, an ex-abbess chronicling the Genevan reformation were all criticized, even though they wrote with sound biblical knowledge and authority assumed from the principle of the priesthood of all believers. Women's roles in the Reformation went unrecognized for a long time due to a lack of written sources and biases regarding the importance of women's roles.

R. Bainton, *Women of the Reformation in Germany and Italy* (1971); Bainton, *Women of the Reformation in England and France* (1974); S. Marshall, ed., *Women in Reformation and Counter-Reformation Europe: Public and Private Worlds* (1989); L. Roper, *The Holy Household: Women and Morals in Reformation Augsburg* (1989); C. A. Snyder and L. H. Hecht, eds., *Profiles of Anabaptist Women: Sixteenth Century Reforming Pioneers* (1996); M. Wiesner-Hanks, *Convents Confronting Reformation: Catholic and Protestant Nuns in Germany* (1999); Wiesner-Hanks, *Reformation Texts with Translation (1350–1650): Women of the Reformation* (1996).

KIRSI STJERNA

Reformed Church   The Reformed Church emerged at the same time as the Lutheran Church, but it developed its own distinctive trajectory that brought it into increasing conflict with the Lutheran and Anabaptist traditions. The Reformed Church was initially shaped by the pastors and theologians of the Swiss territories, especially Huldrych Zwingli and Heinrich Bullinger in Zurich, Johannes Oecolampadius in Basel, and John Calvin and Theodore Beza in Geneva. However, the Reformed Church grew rapidly throughout Europe—in France, England, Scotland, the Palatinate, the Netherlands, Poland, and Hungary.

Many of the early leaders of the Reformed Church were initially shaped by their commitment to the recovery of classical literature begun by philologists such as Guillaume Bude and Desiderius Erasmus. Like their predecessors, Reformed pastors sought the genuine meaning of Scripture on the basis of the most reliable Hebrew and Greek manuscripts. They also read Scripture in the context of the Greek and Latin church fathers and Greek and Latin classical authors. The Reformed pastors shared with Erasmus a suspicion that elaborate ceremonies in worship concealed hypocrisy, whereas God should be worshiped in spirit and truth.

The Reformed agreed with Martin Luther that the Church of Rome had replaced the word of God with human teachings. However, they departed from Luther and his colleagues in Wittenberg by emphasizing different themes in the word of God, and these differences eventually brought them into conflict with Wittenberg. Luther had opposed the Roman teaching of penitential satisfactions, and in its place he affirmed the word of absolution offered in baptism, private confession, the sermon, and the Lord's Supper. Pastors such as Zwingli and Oecolampadius opposed the combination of the Roman worship of creatures with the worship of the

Creator. Since God is spirit, God cannot be represented by images, pictures, or statues. Since God is the Creator, only God can choose a self-revelation by sending the Holy Spirit to those whom God freely elects. Since God sent the Son to die on the cross to save humanity from sin, no one should turn to water, bread, and wine for pledges of God's grace. Since Christ has ascended to heaven, his body and blood cannot be sought under bread and wine.

John Calvin attempted to heal the rift between Wittenberg and Zurich by insisting that sacraments are pledges of God's mercy that truly offer to us the reality they represent, even though they can only do so by the power of the Holy Spirit. Calvin was able to bring Zurich into agreement with him in 1549, but this consensus was rejected by Lutheran theologians as being a more dangerous form of Zwingli's teaching. However, the teaching of Calvin and the Zurich Consensus fundamentally shaped the teaching on the sacraments in subsequent Reformed confessions, such as the French Confession (1559), the Scots Confession (1560), the Second Helvetic Confession (1566), the Heidelberg Catechism (1563), and the Thirty-nine Articles (1571).

The Reformed pastors were also shaped by their defense of infant baptism over against the advocates of believers' baptism. They defended infant baptism by drawing a strong analogy between circumcision under the law and baptism under the gospel. To make this analogy credible, they also denied that the law of Moses was essentially different from or opposed to the gospel of Jesus Christ (as both the Lutheran and Anabaptist pastors seemed to claim), since both are rooted in the covenant made with Abraham. This led subsequent Reformed pastors and theologians to draw analogies between the whole form of worship instituted by God in Israel—from sacrifices and priesthood to the temple and the kings—with the form of worship instituted by Christ in the gospel, and to make the covenant central to the relationship between God and humanity.

The Reformed pastors were also deeply troubled by the tyrannical exercise of ecclesiastical power by the bishops and priests of Rome. To counter this tyranny, they insisted that elected lay elders work with pastors and/or bishops in their exercise of ecclesiastical discipline. The suspicion of episcopal authority without accountability led some in the Reformed Church to reject the office of bishop altogether in favor of the polity of the church in Geneva, made up of teachers, pastors, elders,

and deacons. This divergence regarding the office of bishop led to long-lasting ecclesiastical conflicts within the Reformed churches of England and Scotland.

———

A. C. Cochrane, *Reformed Confessions of the Sixteenth Century* (1966, 2003); J. T. McNeill, *The History and Character of Calvinism* (1954); A. Pettegree, *Calvinism in Europe, 1540–1620* (1994); M. Prestwich, *International Calvinism, 1541–1715* (1994); J. Rohls, *Reformed Confessions* (1998).

RANDALL C. ZACHMAN

Refugee and Stranger Churches

The vicissitudes of religious policy in the sixteenth century, combined with the changing economic structure of Europe, created a significant mobile population of refugees. This resulted in the establishment in many cities of churches that were effectively organized and managed by refugee populations themselves, that were subject to their own discipline, and that enjoyed considerable independence from the ecclesiastical policies of the indigenous authorities. This facilitated the development of ecclesiastical and liturgical practices that were attuned to the particular linguistic and cultural demands of refugee populations. Such churches also impacted the wider culture of the cities in which they existed by offering alternative models of church life that could create both political and religious tensions. Thus, for example, the cities of Strasbourg, Frankfurt am Main, and London all, at various times, permitted the organization by foreign Protestants of church congregations along disciplinary lines laid down by the refugees themselves. In so doing, the potential problems of forcing significant minority populations to conform to the aesthetics of an alien culture church were somewhat circumvented.

In Strasbourg, the existence of a significant population of French-speaking refugees gave Calvin, also an exile, an early opportunity for church leadership where, under the influence of Martin Bucer, he headed the French church from 1538 to 1541. He also formulated a distinctive French liturgy and attempted to put into place a church discipline that emphasized the independence of the church in spiritual matters.

In London, the establishment of a Stranger Church under the pastoral oversight of the Polish reformer Jean à Lasco proved significant not simply for the refugees but also for the more radical English reformers. The fact that the Anglican authorities allowed dispensations on crucial areas of Anglican ceremonial proved an incentive to individuals such as John Hooper and John Knox in their own quest for more rigorous reformation of the church as well as a concern to the Catholic-dominated Parliament which was worried about how far Cranmer was willing to push his reforms. As a result, the existence of the refugee church almost certainly influenced the decision publicly to face down the radical challenge posed by Hooper with regard to clerical vestments.

During the Marian exile, an English congregation was established at Frankfurt am Main. Led by William Whittaker, the congregation called John Knox to serve as pastor. What followed was a profound struggle over church order that focused on the use of the Book of Common Prayer. Knox's party pushed for a thoroughly new liturgy, purged of unacceptable rites, while another party, led by Richard Cox, fought for the use of the Book of Common Prayer, arguing that the church in exile needed "an English face." The conflict, and the triumph of the Coxian party, was suggestive of the Puritan conflicts of the Elizabethan church, particularly as key players, such as Cox and Whittaker, returned to England with the accession of Elizabeth.

A. Pettegree, *Foreign Protestant Communities in 16th-Century London* (1986).

CARL TRUEMAN

Regensburg Colloquy

A meeting organized in 1541 by Emperor Charles V, who sought to unite German territories politically by reconciling theological differences that divided the German churches. He invited leaders of all German estates and cities and their clergy to attend the colloquy and to discuss their differences. The curia viewed the emperor's move with suspicion, noting that Charles was in effect convening an imperial diet to discuss spiritual matters, but Charles countered that the colloquy was intended only for his German territories.

In 1540–1541 preliminary meetings held at Hagenau and Worms set terms for the colloquy. At Regensburg discussions would focus on the *Regensburg Book*, which was drafted primarily by Johannes Gropper and Martin Bucer. An imperial representative convened the colloquy, and each side had three representatives. Philip Melanchthon, Bucer, and Johann Pistorius represented the Lutherans. Johannes Eck, Gropper, and Julius Pflug spoke for Roman Catholics. Rome sent Cardinal Gasparo Contarini as papal legate.

Following heated discussion, representatives tentatively agreed that justification is by faith alone but that such faith must be increased by acts of faith and efficacious love. Melanchthon responded to the emperor that the words "efficacious love" should be rewritten or removed or fresh disputes would arise. Tentative agreement on justification notwithstanding, deep differences remained concerning transubstantiation, clerical celibacy, church reform, and authority to discern and interpret Scripture.

When an overall agreement became impossible, the emperor sought a partial agreement that might lead to more productive discussions at a later time, but attempts to reach even partial agreement broke down. Charles V's final attempt to reunite the German churches failed.

C. Augustijn, "The Quest of Reformatio: The Diet of Regensburg 1541 as a Turning-Point," in *The Reformation in Germany and Europe: Interpretations and Issues*, special vol. of *ARG* (1993): 64–80; K. Ganzer and K.-H. zur Mühlen, eds., *Akten der deutschen Reichsreligionsgespräche im 16. Jahrhundert* (2000); A. Lexutt, *Rechtfertigung im Gespräch: Das Rechtfertigungsverständnis von Hagenau, Worms und Regensburg 1540/41* (1996); P. Matheson, *Cardinal Contarini at Regenburg* (1972); G. Pfeilschifter, ed., *Acta Reformationis Catholicae Ecclesiam Germaniae Concernentia Saeculi XVI*, vol. 6 (1974).

SUZANNE S. HEQUET

Regular Clergy

The term "regular" comes from the Latin *regula*, meaning "rule." "Regulars" (often "religious" in modern usage) were the monks, nuns, regular canons, and friars who had taken vows to live according to a rule, whether in communities or as hermits associated with communities. Female regulars were by definition laypeople, because women could not be ordained, while male regulars could either be laymen or ordained members of the clergy. From the eleventh century, it was increasingly common for monks to be ordained priests because of the growing importance of the liturgy in the monasteries. Regular canons were all priests, because their mission was pastoral care; similarly, in the thirteenth century, the mendicant friars quickly took on prominent roles in pastoral care and were therefore almost all ordained after the first generation. The term "regular clergy" thus indicates those men who, in addition to being bound by vows to observe the rule of a given community of monks, canons, or friars, had also received from a bishop the sacrament of holy orders. The term is sometimes used more generally as a synonym for "regulars." (See *Gerhoch of Reichersberg*.)

C. H. Lawrence, *Medieval Monasticism: Forms of Religious Life in Western Europe in the Middle Ages* (2nd ed., 1989).

VICTORIA M. MORSE

Reina, Casiodoro de (c. 1520–1594),
Spanish Protestant reformer, translator of the Bible into Castilian. A member of the religious community of the convent of San Isidro in Seville, Reina fled Spain in 1557 after the Inquisition learned of the book-trafficking activities of Julián Hernández, who smuggled Protestant literature to dissidents in Seville. After a short stay in Geneva, Reina settled in London as pastor of an incipient Spanish Protestant congregation. There he authored the *Spanish Confession of Faith* (1560). In 1563, Reina fled London under charges of heresy and sodomy, finding temporary refuge in Antwerp. By 1569, Reina had completed his translation of the Bible and managed to have it published in Basel. He also wrote a commentary on the Gospel of John (1573). He was finally cleared of the charges of sodomy and heresy in 1579. That same year, Reina began his ministry at the French-speaking Evangelical Church of the Augsburg Confession in Antwerp. In 1585, following Spanish attacks on Antwerp, Reina led this congregation to Frankfurt, where he died in 1594.

A. G. Kinder, *Casiodoro de Reina: Spanish Reformer of the Sixteenth Century* (1975); Kinder, "Casiodoro de Reina," in *Bibliotheca Dissidentium*, vol. 4 (1984), 99–153.

RADY ROLDÁN-FIGUEROA

Relics
A relic consists of the body of a saint, some portion of the body, or items such as clothing that have come into contact with a saint's body or with the body of Christ himself. Already appearing in the New Testament (Acts 19:11–12), relics first began to be important for Christianity during the second century in connection with devotion to the martyrs. Accounts of the martyrdom of Polycarp (c. 156) testify to the importance for early Christians of recovering his body so that they could hold worship services near it and thus in his presence. Relics emerged as one aspect of the "communion of the saints" eventually enshrined in the Apostles' Creed. Early Christians celebrated the

Eucharist in the catacombs near the bodies of the martyrs or "friends of God," because this best ensured the unity of the worshiping community on earth with those who surrounded the throne of God in heaven. This understanding eventually led to the burial of relics within the altars of churches, a custom reaffirmed in the eighth century by the Second Council of Nicaea (787) and by Charlemagne, who also required relics to secure the validity of sworn oaths.

Relics also were linked to the Christian concept of pilgrimage. Those seeking healing or exorcism traveled to a saint's shrine to make their request for intercession in person. Politically, bishops in the early church viewed relics as signs of a saint's personal patronage for their office and therefore as guarantees of episcopal power. The translation of relics from one person to another could be used to create networks of episcopal patronage and friendship.

The growing importance of relics in the Western church led to the plundering of the Roman catacombs and martyrs' shrines in the early Middle Ages by men who hoped to sell the relics elsewhere in Europe. Indeed, the successful theft of a relic could be viewed as a sign that the saint wished to dwell elsewhere. The Crusades, beginning in 1096, further increased the search for authentic relics, possession of which could secure prominence for a church or monastery by creating lucrative pilgrim traffic. The manufacture and sale of spurious relics was likewise a result of these same developments. Such abuses led to increasing criticism of relics by Catholic reformers, and measures adopted at the Council of Trent (1545–1563) sought to curb excesses associated with relics, insisting on the authentication of all relics. At the same time the council upheld the traditional theological significance of relics along lines already laid down by the early church.

S. Boiron, *La controverse née de la querelle de reliques à l'époque du concile de Trente (1500–1640)* (1989); P. Brown, *The Cult of the Saints: Its Rise and Function in Latin Christianity* (1981); P. J. Geary, *Furta Sacra: Thefts of Relics in the Central Middle Ages* (1978); J. Howard-Johnston and P. A. Hayward, eds., *The Cult of Saints in Late Antiquity and the Early Middle Ages: Essays on the Contribution of Peter Brown* (1999).

DONNA SPIVEY ELLINGTON

Remonstrance of 1610
A petition drawn up by the party in the Reformed Church of the Netherlands that opposed the predesti-

narian teachings represented in the Belgic Confession. The document, from which the Remonstrants derived their name, was the product of a meeting in Gouda of over forty Arminian partisans under the leadership of Johannes Uitenbogaert. The meeting came shortly after the death of Jacob Arminius, whose doctrine they espoused.

Uitenbogaert presented the petition to a sympathetic advocate of Holland, Jan van Oldenbarnevelt, implying that the state, rather than church confessions or synods, should have ultimate jurisdiction in ecclesiastical affairs. The document detailed the Arminian position on five disputed articles of doctrine. The first defined election as God's foreknowledge of a person's faith and perseverance. The second affirmed the universal intent and extent of Christ's atonement, limited only by a person's free acceptance of Christ. The third point affirmed the necessity of divine regeneration as a prerequisite for faith among fallen persons, but Remonstrant theologians also held that this regenerative grace was universally available and downplayed the effects of original sin on human faculties. The fourth point declared that this grace could be resisted by the human will. Finally, the Remonstrants considered unresolved the question of whether persons persevere in faith partly through their own efforts or wholly by God's grace.

This document caused a heated controversy with the Dutch Reformed Church and resulted in the condemnation of the Remonstrants at the Synod of Dort.

A. W. Harrison, *The Beginnings of Arminianism to the Synod of Dort* (1926); R. A. Muller, *God, Creation, and Providence in the Thought of Jacob Arminius* (1991).

RAYMOND A. BLACKETER

Renaissance A French word meaning "rebirth," used by historians to designate either a historical period (broadly speaking, from 1370 to 1620) or specific cultural developments and mindsets found during that period. Many people of that time, beginning with the poet Petrarch (1304–1374), used metaphors of renewal and rebirth to speak of their own age and their self-awareness. Many since then have followed their usage.

The "rebirth" referred at first to a rediscovery of ancient Greek and Latin literature, prized not merely as a model for literary style but chiefly for its educational value in a changing world. Above all, the ancients provided moral models

for politicians, clergy, educators, and new kinds of social leaders. The humanist movement epitomized the new cultural ideal, establishing new kinds of education that came to rival, and sometimes even displace, the scholasticism that had come to dominate the universities. However, the modern imagination of the Renaissance takes a narrower focus that is limited to the dramatic transformation in the arts of painting, architecture, sculpture, literature, and music throughout Europe after 1400, much of it influenced by ancient classical models.

These educational, literary, and artistic changes received powerful political and financial patronage across Europe, from Italy all the way to Britain, Poland, and Scandinavia. The reason for this support was the widely shared conviction that the revival of antiquity stirred up energies of governmental and church reform. The classical inspired the modern. Ancient tradition enabled innovation to occur.

Over the centuries, the term "Renaissance" has broadened to refer not simply to the rebirth of antiquity but the birth of independent new trends. Today, whether one uses "Renaissance" or the neutral term "early modern Europe," certain specific features distinguish this epoch from previous and subsequent periods. These features include, in politics and economy, a transition from feudal regimes with agricultural economies to networks of monarchies and states based increasingly on banking, commerce, and concepts of state or personal sovereignty. All these developments were bolstered by discoveries across the globe and the rich resources they yielded after 1492. In diplomacy, the age saw the establishment of permanent embassies for political and commercial affairs. Mercenary armies became broadly used. Widespread religious restlessness yielded new forms of piety and religious organization. The papacy handed over much practical control of national churches to Catholic princes. Most importantly, the advent of movable print after the 1450s intensified all these and other changes.

After 1520, many features attributed to the Renaissance overlapped with those of the Reformation. In fact, the Reformers' desire for "rebirth" of the ancient church, as well as their intention to break with decadence and return to purity of belief and practice, followed a mindset established by earlier Renaissance thinkers and religious figures such as Lorenzo Valla. This interplay of features that we classify as "Renaissance" and "Reformation" typifies personalities such as Erasmus and Philip

Melanchthon, or groups such as the Jesuits, or cultures such as those of Elizabethan England and the Calvinist Netherlands.

By 1600, all these developments had made it common in religious, educational, and social circles to think of a threefold historical division. This comprised, first, a pristine pagan and Christian antiquity, then a lengthy and decadent "Middle Ages," and finally the current period of renewal. In the 1700s, Enlightenment thinkers also saw themselves in continuity with the movement that had broken away from an assumed medieval corruption and ignorance, although they played down religious features of the period since 1400.

The 1800s revived fascination with the Renaissance, thanks chiefly to Jacob Burckhardt's evocative book, *The Civilization of the Renaissance in Italy* (1860). He argued that the Renaissance gave birth to the modern world, a view sympathetic to his contemporaries' liberalism, nationalism, and individualism. His success also built on a popular nineteenth-century notion that a distinctive spirit marked each specific historical period (*Zeitgeist*) and people (*Volksgeist*). Despite revision and even rejection, Burckhardt's views have influenced historians into the present.

Church historians have struggled to interpret the relationship of Renaissance and Reformation. One tradition, typified by Wilhelm Dilthey (1833–1911), saw Renaissance and Reformation as parallel, harmonious movements in the general European march toward the liberation of the human spirit. In this version, the Renaissance was an Italian accomplishment matched by the Reformation as its German complement. Theologian Ernst Troeltsch (1865–1923) gave this a twist: he acknowledged the Renaissance as modern but rejected the Protestantism of the period up to about 1800 as a continuation of irrational, authoritarian medieval religiosity. Only with liberal, rational Protestantism taking shape since about 1800 did he see Christian faith enter the modern age. Protestant reactions against Troeltsch and Dilthey (led by such figures as Karl Barth [1886–1968] and Reinhold Niebuhr [1892–1971]) contrasted what they considered Renaissance secularism with a supposed Reformation orthodoxy and godliness.

Roman Catholic views of the Renaissance have been traditionally ambivalent, because of Catholic tendencies to regard both the earlier medieval age and the later Catholic reform (after 1550) as pinnacles of Catholic culture. Luminaries such as Francis of Assisi and Thomas Aquinas, on the earlier side, or Teresa of Avila and Francis de Sales, on the later one, left traditional Catholics suspicious of the Renaissance, even if it did produce Michelangelo and Thomas More.

Since the 1960s, Catholic, Protestant, and secular scholars such as John O'Malley, William Bouwsma, Charles Trinkaus, and their students have demonstrated the deep religious dynamics within Renaissance thinkers and cultures. They have also discovered the great receptivity to "Renaissance" influences among leading Catholics and Protestants of the Reformation. Accordingly, current scholars emphasize greater continuity between Renaissance and Reformation, whether Protestant or Catholic.

W. Ferguson, *The Renaissance in Historical Thought: Five Centuries of Interpretation* (1948); W. Kerrigan and G. Braden, *The Idea of the Renaissance* (1989); C. Nauert, *Humanism and the Culture of Renaissance Europe* (1995); E. Rice and A. Grafton, *The Foundations of Early Modern Europe, 1460–1559* (2nd ed., 1994); D. Wilcox, *In Search of God and Self: Renaissance and Reformation Thought* (2nd ed., 1987); Z. Schiffman, ed., *Humanism and the Renaissance* (2002).

JAMES MICHAEL WEISS

Renaissance Platonism Most frequently associated with the philosopher Marsilio Ficino (1433–1499), the resurgence of interest in Plato in Italy during the fifteenth and sixteenth centuries owes its origins to a number of factors. The Council of Ferrara and Florence (1438–1439) brought Greek scholars to Italy at a time when there was growing resistance on the part of humanists to the dominance of Aristotle in the universities. Already in the fourteenth century Petrarch, based on his readings of Augustine and of Cicero, had proclaimed Plato to be Aristotle's superior as a source of wisdom. The Florentine humanists Coluccio Salutati and Leonardo Bruni likewise favored Plato, the latter of whom translated seven of Plato's dialogues. Cosimo de Medici, the leading citizen of Florence, was inspired upon hearing the lectures of the Greek émigré Gemistos Pletho to sponsor the establishment of the Platonic Academy. Under his patronage Marsilio Ficino set about translating a complete set of Plato's dialogues and writing detailed commentaries. Ficino's colleagues and disciples included Pico della Mirandola, Christoforo Landino, and Cosimo's grandson Lorenzo, who continued Medici patronage and wrote poetry inspired by Platonic theories of love. The papal curia in

Rome was equally important as a center of the Platonic revival, a noteworthy figure being the Greek churchman John Bessarion, who became a Roman cardinal in 1439.

The attraction of Plato for many lay in an appreciation of his literary qualities combined with the strong belief that Platonic philosophy was more in harmony with Christianity than Aristotle. Renaissance Platonists engaged in a vitriolic debate with those who preferred Aristotle and believed Plato to be explicitly pagan and of questionable moral value, especially in his seeming endorsement of homoeroticism. Into this camp fell the Greek émigré George of Trebizond and the Florentine political reformer Savonarola. Platonists such as Bessarion and Ficino responded by drawing on the ancient Neoplatonists, particularly Proclus, in stressing Plato's belief in the immortality of the soul and in deemphasizing indications of polytheism by focusing on Plato's belief in an underlying unity.

In the early sixteenth century treatises on Platonic love became popular, notable examples being Pietro Bembo's *Asolani* and Baldassare Castiglione's discussions of love in *The Book of the Courtier*. Poetry, music theory, and the visual arts all were deeply indebted to the Platonic revival. Theories of magic embraced by Paracelsus and Giordano Bruno took their inspiration from it as well.

B. P. Copenhaver and C. B. Schmitt, *Renaissance Philosophy* (1992); K. Eisenbichler and O. Z. Pugliese, ed., *Ficino and Renaissance Neoplatonism* (1986); J. Hankins, *Plato in the Italian Renaissance* (1991); P. O. Kristeller, *The Philosophy of Marsilio Ficino* (1964); N. A. Robb, *Neoplatonism of the Italian Renaissance* (1935, 1968); C. Trinkaus, *Renaissance Transformations of Late Medieval Thought* (1999).

J. LAUREL CARRINGTON

Renato, Camillo (c. 1500–c. 1575), Italian Anabaptist reformer. Born Paul Ricci, in Sicily, he became an eloquent exponent of Anabaptism (e.g., believers' baptism, soul sleep, Antitrinitarianism). His peripatetic tendencies—and the need to avoid persecution, from Roman Catholics and Magisterial Protestants alike—connected him with many facets of Italian reformist activity. It also made him change his name and opinions rather opportunistically. In his twenties, he became a Franciscan, took the name Lisia Phileno, and was ordained a priest. In 1540, he was arrested in Modena, Italy, tried by the Inquisition, and saved from the fire by

his recantation (he received life imprisonment). In 1541, he escaped prison, changed his name to Camillo Renato, and moved to northern Italy. However, the Reformed powers of Raetia excommunicated him until he recanted. In 1552, he was arrested in Bergamo, abjured all heresies, and returned to Raetia. Active until his death, Renato wrote against Calvin's burning of Servetus and dramatically influenced Lelio Sozzini and, through him, Socianism.

J. Tedeschi, ed., *Italian Reformation Studies in Honor of Laelius Socinus* (1965); G. Williams, "Camillus Renatus and Individual Immortality," in *Harry Wolfson Jubilee Volume*, vol. 2 (1965).

WILLIAM R. RUSSELL

Renée of France (1510–1575), French princess, duchess of Ferrara by marriage, protector of reformers. Renée was the second daughter of the king of France, Louis XII, and Anne of Brittany. She was raised at the Valois court of Francis I, her brother-in-law, where the influence of his sister, Marguerite of Angoulême, and of humanist reformers was strong. When Francis sought allies against Charles V, Holy Roman Emperor, Renée was married to Hercule d'Este of Ferrara in 1528. Accompanied to Ferrara by her reform-minded governess, Madame de Soubisse, Renée allowed Reformed worship and protected reformers such as Clément Marot. John Calvin visited Ferrara in 1536 and subsequently corresponded with Renée, hoping to win her to a more explicit espousal of the Reformed faith. Her husband forced her to abjure her beliefs in 1554, threatening loss of contact with her two daughters. After his death in 1559 she returned to France and her château of Montargis, where she professed loyalty to the crown but maintained a Reformed household, protecting Calvinists such as Nicolas Des Gallars. Her burial without ostentation indicated that her convictions were Reformed.

C. Blaisdell, "Renée de France between Reform and Counter-Reform," *ARG* 63 (1972): 196–226.

JEANNINE E. OLSON

Resistance Theory Theories of political and military resistance to government enforcement of religious conformity that blossomed in the hothouse of religious diversity during the Reformation. Resistance took many forms. Initially, passive disobedience dominated. Later, more active aspects of resistance arose, ranging from riots or uprisings to full-blown military campaigns. Resisters were confronted with a two-pronged problem, however. On the one hand, Paul had admonished Christians to be obedient to authority (Rom. 13). On the other hand, Peter had affirmed that Christians must serve God and not human authorities (Acts 5:29). The attempt to reconcile these conflicting obligations drove the development of resistance theory.

The earliest theories were developed in response to the Diet of Augsburg (1530) in which Emperor Charles V pledged to eradicate Lutheran heresy. Lawyers developed the earliest theories in the two most prominent Protestant territories—Hesse and Electoral Saxony. The Hessian jurists argued the empire was not a monarchy but a confederation of princes in which each pledged fidelity not only to the emperor but also to the empire itself. Thus, princes served to check the power of the emperor. The Hessian theory became a central tenet of all later resistance theory—that is, the right of lesser magistrates to resist the actions of a tyrannous superior. The Saxon jurists next proposed a way to discern when a superior magistrate became a tyrant. Based on legal theory, the Saxon jurists argued that when a superior committed an illegal act of notorious injury (such as a judge attempting to settle a legal matter in his own favor contrary to law, evidence, or precedent), then the individual ceased to have sovereignty over that particular matter. This theory accomplished two important points: it provided a solution to the problem of resisting a tyrannous superior and it prevented general disorder and chaos. A superior might be resisted in his attempt to enforce religious beliefs, but he remained sovereign in all other matters. For rulers concerned with justifying their own resistance but loath to encourage rebellion in their own lands, the Saxon jurists had delivered a workable legal and practical solution. The Hessian and Saxon theories convinced Protestant theologians who issued a short tract (the Torgau Declaration) and a longer pamphlet (*Dr. Martin Luther's Warning to His Dear Germans*) in support of resistance.

These early theories were not immediately put to the test, because the emperor was prevented from moving against the Protestant princes until the Schmalkald War (1546–1547). Following the emperor's stunning defeat of the Protestant princes, he put into place a religious decree (the Augsburg Interim) that demanded the reinstitution of Catholicism across the empire. Resistance to the Interim was swift and centered in the city of Magdeburg. There Nicholas Gallus and the pastors of Magdeburg issued a pamphlet, *Confession, Instruction, and Warning* (1550), that represents a significant step forward in resistance theory. It combined the Hessian and Saxon theories of resistance together with a complete reinterpretation of Romans 13. The Magdeburg Confession shifted the focus from divinely ordained obedience to government to the statement that government is "not a terror to good works but to bad." Thus, when government terrorizes the good, it is not ordained by God and may therefore be fought with impunity.

The combination of the Hessian and Saxon theories with the theological reinterpretation of Romans 13 provided a theologically grounded resistance theory on fire. This hybrid theory was picked up and expanded upon by Calvinist theorists. Theodore Beza's *Du Droit des Magistrates* was originally published as a revision of the *Magdeburg Confession*. Peter Martyr Vermigli and François Hotman both continued the development of the theory of inferior magistrates. In England and Scotland John Knox, John Ponet, and Christopher Goodman all continued the development of resistance theory by expanding its application to monarchies. Reformation-era resistance theory, with its combination of legal and theological rationales, persisted for centuries. Its influence can be seen in the work of John Milton and John Locke. Aspects of the theory helped support and justify the American and French revolutions, the resistance of the Confessing Church in Nazi Germany, and the anti-apartheid movement in South Africa.

J. S. Klan, "Luther's Resistance Teaching and the German Church under Hitler," *JRH* 14 (1987–1988): 432–44; H. Scheible, ed., *Das Widerstandsrecht als Problem der deutsche Protestanten, 1523–1546* (1969); D. M. Whitford, "The Duty to Resist Tyranny: The *Magdeburg Confession* and the Reframing of Romans 13," in *Caritas et Reformatio: Essays on Church and Society in Honor of Carter Lindberg*, ed. D. M. Whitford (2002); E. Wolgast, *Die Religionsfrage als Problem des Widerstandsrechts im 16. Jahrhundert* (1980).

DAVID WHITFORD

Restoration Acts Upon the death of Oliver Cromwell in 1658, it was clear to the English people that the commonwealth and protectorate had failed. General Monck recalled the Long Parliament, which then restored the Stuart monarchy, and Charles II ascended the throne in May 1660. The Restoration was a reaction against Puritanism and all that it had wrought upon England since the execution of Charles I in 1649. Parliament's goal was to restore not only the monarchy but the Church of England as well. Bishops were restored to their positions, and Dissenters were expelled. The Clarendon Code established the guidelines for the church and its ministers, particularly in the 1661 Corporation Act, which excluded Puritans from political office, and the 1662 Act of Uniformity, which reestablished the Book of Common Prayer as the only official form of worship in the kingdom. The restoration of the throne, coupled with the series of acts in the Clarendon Code, effectively thwarted Puritanism as a political force in England.

———

A. Whiteman, "The Re-Establishment of the Church of England 1660–1663," in *Transactions of the Royal Historical Society* (1995), 111–31; G. R. Cragg, *The Church and the Age of Reason, 1648–1789* (1990).

ALDEN R. LUDLOW

Reuchlin, Johannes (1455–1522), German humanist and great uncle of Philip Melanchthon. He studied in Paris and Basel, where he wrote a popular Latin lexicon, *Vocabularius Breviloquus* (1475). Reuchlin received his master of arts in 1477, studied law, and was licensed in 1481. He became proficient in Hebrew and wrote on Jewish texts in *De verbo mirifico* (1494). He also wrote the Latin comedies *Serius* and *Henno*. In 1502 he became one of three justices in the Swabian League. His most important work, *De rudimentis Hebraicis* (1506), renewed interest in the study of the Hebrew language and spurred new studies of the Old Testament in its original language. Late in life he was embroiled in controversy with Johann Pfefferkorn and the Dominicans involving the destruction of Jewish books, which Reuchlin opposed. He was accused of heresy, and Leo X ruled against him in 1520. Nevertheless, he remained a loyal Catholic, encouraging his grand-nephew, Melanchthon, to sever his friendship with Luther.

———

K. S. Latourette, *A History of Christianity: Reformation to the Present* (rev. ed., 1975); H. Oberman, *Luther: Man between God and the Devil* (1989); P. Wortsman, trans. and ed., *Recommendation whether to Confiscate, Destroy, and Burn All Jewish Books* (2000).

ELIZABETH GERHARDT

Rhegius, Urbanus (1489–1541), Lutheran reformer in southern and northern Germany. Rhegius was born in Langenargen on Lake Constance, most likely the son of the priest, Conrad Rieger. Humanistically and theologically trained and a student of the biblical languages, he was ordained in 1519 and appointed cathedral preacher in Augsburg in 1520. He soon criticized indulgences and began to proclaim the Reformation. Dismissed in 1521, he spent 1522–1523 in Hall, Tirol, where he continued his evangelical preaching. Expelled again, he returned to Augsburg and became preacher at St. Ann. He married Anna Weissbrucker in June 1525, and the couple had seven daughters and four sons. On Christmas Day, 1525, Rhegius celebrated the first evangelical Mass in Augsburg. He was present at the Diet of Augsburg in 1530, was consulted as Philip Melanchthon produced the Augsburg Confession, and met Duke Ernst of Lüneburg. The latter invited Rhegius to lead the Reformation in his territories and appointed him superintendent. Rhegius shaped the organization and character of the church in Lower Saxony, paying particular attention to the training of pastors. He also produced church orders for Lüneburg (1531) and Hannover (1536). His writings stressed the orthodox character of the evangelical faith, defended the Lutheran understanding of the gospel, and affirmed the necessity of repentance and good works for faithful living.

———

M. Liebmann, *Urbanus Rhegius und die Anfänge der Reformation* (1980); H. Zschoch, *Reformatorische Existenz und konfessionelle Identität: Urbanus Rhegius als evangelischer Theologe in den Jahren 1520 bis 1530* (1995).

KURT K. HENDEL

Ricci, Matteo (1552–1610), pioneer Jesuit missionary in China. Born in Italy, Ricci entered the Jesuits and dreamed of becoming a missionary in Asia. He studied theology in Goa, India, and then Chinese in Macao. Ricci and Michele Ruggieri, a Jesuit who had earlier visited China, donned the robes of Buddhist monks and entered China; in 1585 they set up a small church. Ricci's knowledge of mathematics and science opened doors among the Chinese elite, for whom he wrote books in Chinese on Western science, philosophy, and religion. He emphasized commonalities of Christianity and Confucianism in order to convince intellectuals and government officials to permit evangelization. Ricci then abandoned his Buddhist habit and donned the silk robes of a Confucian scholar. In 1601 the emperor allowed Ricci and a Jesuit companion to live in Beijing and granted them a subsidy for scientific research. During Ricci's lifetime Chinese converts numbered only about a thousand, but thanks to Ricci the Jesuits gained a niche in both the imperial court and the Chinese intellectual elite that would endure for two centuries.

J. Spence, *The Memory Palace of Matteo Ricci* (1984); V. Cronin, *The Wise Man from the West* (1955).

JOHN PATRICK DONNELLY, SJ

Richard of St. Victor (d. 1173), prior and encyclopedic author. Richard is thought to have been a Scot. The dates of his birth and entry into the monastery of St. Victor are unknown, but he became subprior there in 1159 and prior in 1162. Richard's works reflect a theology based on Scripture and an encyclopedic view of the sciences. His *Liber exceptionum* (*Book of Exceptions*) serves as an introduction to the liberal arts as well as to Scripture; the *De Emmanuele* (*On Emmanuel*), however, treats hermeneutical problems common to twelfth-century exegesis. Richard's most famous work is *De trinitate*, which is a theology of divine love. He rejects the Boethian definition of "person." Instead he insists on the rational character of human beings and on the incommunicability of divine persons. In spiritual doctrine Richard distinguishes between people who know God only by knowledge and those who know God also by experience.

R. Berndt, "The School of St. Victor in Paris," in *Hebrew Bible/Old Testament: The History of Its Interpretation*, ed. M. Saeboe (2000), 475–79; *LTK³* 8 (1999), 1174–75; H. Nakamura, "Cognitio sui bei Richard von Sankt Viktor," in *Scientia und Disciplina: Wissenschaftpraxis und Wissenstheorie im 12. und 13. Jahrhundert*, ed. R. Berndt (2002), 127–56; A. Orazzo, "Caritá e Trinitá in Riccardo di S. Vittore," *Rassegna di Teologia* 40 (1999): 615–26; PL 196 (1855); *TRE* 29 (1998): 191–94.

RAINER BERNDT

Richelieu, Armand Jean du Plessis, Duke of (1585–1642), French cardinal and statesman. After initially training for a military career, he was ordained and appointed bishop of Luçon (1607), an ecclesiastical office controlled by his noble family. He was elected to represent the clergy in the Estates-General of 1614 and served as a secretary of state during the regency of Marie de Medici. His diplomatic skills helped avert civil war in France, and for

those efforts he was made a cardinal in 1622. From 1624 until 1642, he commanded great influence over French politics as chief minister for King Louis XIII. He contributed to the growth of absolutism by establishing mercantilist economic policies and diminishing some of the privileges of the nobility. He suppressed numerous uprisings and conspiracies by noble factions, including the 1627 rebellion by militant Huguenots in La Rochelle. During the Thirty Years' War, he supported an alliance with Swedish Protestant forces against the Catholic Holy Roman Emperor in order to advance French dominance over the rival Habsburg dynasty, which ruled Germany and Spain. He favored the Jesuits in their conflict with the Jansenist movement.

J. Bergin. *The Rise of Richelieu* (1991); G. R. R. Treasure, *Cardinal Richelieu and the Development of Absolutism* (1972).

ERIC LUND

Ridley, Nicholas (c. 1502–1555), English reformer. Ridley was deeply influenced by the eucharistic theology of Thomas Cranmer, which denied corporeal presence yet asserted a "real" spiritual presence. Young and prominent, he was converted to Protestant doctrines in the 1530s but had previously been a supporter of Reformed views; as early as 1525 he was censured for refusing to attack Lutheran doctrines. Ridley's influence was widespread, for he was one of only twelve preachers licensed by Cambridge Univ. who was enabled to preach anywhere in the country. He served as chaplain to Cranmer beginning in 1537, after which his career blossomed quickly. He was made master at Pembroke in 1541, chaplain to Henry VIII in 1541, bishop of Rochester in 1547, and bishop of London in 1550, replacing Bishop Bonner. He was deprived of his bishopric in 1553, under Mary Tudor, due to his Protestant eucharistic views; this, coupled with his support of Lady Jane Grey would eventually lead to his burning at the stake. Following a sermon at St. Paul's Cross in which he preached a coup, denounced Mary and Elizabeth as illegitimate, and voiced support of Grey, he was imprisoned. Following a disputation at Oxford in 1554, he was, with Cranmer and Latimer, pronounced a heretic. He was burned at the stake with Latimer soon thereafter.

J. G. Ridley, *Nicholas Ridley: A Biography* (1957); D. M. Loades, *The Oxford Martyrs* (1970).

ALDEN R. LUDLOW

Riedemann, Peter (1506–1556), early Hutterite leader. Born in Silesia and trained as a shoemaker, Riedemann was apparently rebaptized and ordained a leader by 1529, when he first appeared in official records after his imprisonment in Gmunden. During that imprisonment, Riedemann wrote his remarkable *Account of Our Faith*. In 1532, he escaped from prison and made his way to the Hutterite community in Moravia. In 1533, he was sent on the first of his missions to spread the Hutterite message in the German-speaking lands. After a prison term in Nuremberg from 1533 to 1537, he continued working among Anabaptists both in Moravia and in Germany, including missionary trips to Hesse and Württemberg. He was arrested again, this time in Hesse. During his imprisonment (1540–1542), he worked on another *Account of Our Faith*, intended as an explanation of Hutterite doctrine to Landgrave Philip of Hesse. It would become the definitive statement of Hutterite theology and was one of the few books the group had printed. In February 1542 he returned to Moravia and remained there, for the most part, for the rest of his life. In addition to his doctrinal works, Riedemann wrote a number of hymns and at least thirty-five surviving letters, including six to his wife and many to the far-flung remnant Anabaptist communities. After Jacob Hutter, from whom the Hutterites take their name, Riedemann was the most important early leader of the group.

R. Friedmann, "Peter Riedemann: Early Anabaptist Leader," *Mennonite Quarterly Review* 44 (1970): 5–44; H. J. Hillerbrand, ed., *Anabaptist Bibliography, 1520–1630* (2nd ed., 1991).

D. JONATHAN GRIESER

Riemenschneider, Tilman (1460–1531), renowned German sculptor of the late Gothic style whose prolific workshop in Würzburg produced sculptural objects of consistently high quality for almost forty years. Working usually in wood but also in alabaster and sandstone, Riemenschneider simplified sculptural techniques, broke with the tradition of polychromed finishes, and experimented with unadorned surfaces thinly glazed, leaving the texture of the wood visible. Reimenschneider's work is characterized by the quietly expressive faces and spiritual focus of his figures, as well as for its sensual forms and dynamic drapery. Some of his important carved altarpieces still exist, such as the *Altarpiece of the Holy Blood* (1499–1505) in Rothenburg.

Numerous smaller sculptures include subjects such as the Lamentation, Adam and Eve, the Virgin and Child on the Crescent Moon, and popular saints. Having sided with the peasants during the revolt of 1524–1525, Riemenschneider was imprisoned and perhaps tortured. Presumably he produced no more art during the remaining five years of his life.

M. Baxandall, *The Limewood Sculptors of Renaissance Germany* (1980); J. Bier, *Tilman Riemenschneider: His Life and Work* (1982); J. Chapuis et al., *Tilman Riemenschneider: Master Sculptor of the Late Middle Ages* (1999).

PRISCILLA BAUMANN

Rimini, Council of *see* Ariminum, Council of

Rinck, Melchior (c. 1493–1553?), Anabaptist leader in Hesse. Educated at the universities of Leipzig and Erfurt, where he excelled in Greek, Rinck was an early convert to Lutheranism and served as a chaplain in Hersfeld (1523) and later as a pastor in Thuringia. He apparently became a close associate of Thomas Müntzer (1489–1525) and participated in the Peasants' War of 1525. He next appeared in Landau in 1527. Here he met and was baptized by the southern German Anabaptist leader Hans Denck (c. 1500–1527). Rinck accompanied Denck to Worms, where he helped formulate a doctrinal statement of seven articles, but both were soon expelled. Rinck reappeared in mid-1528 in Hersfeld as an Anabaptist evangelist. An audience with the Landgrave Philip of Hesse (1509–1567) led to a debate with theologians at the Univ. of Marburg, which resulted in his banishment from Hessian territory in 1528. However, Rinck would not abandon his congregation in Hesse; he was captured and jailed in 1529. Except for a few months in 1531, he spent the remainder of his life in prison.

C. A. Snyder, *Anabaptist History and Theology: An Introduction* (1995); G. H. Williams, *The Radical Reformation* (3rd ed., 1992).

DAVID B. ELLER

Ritual Murder The first written account of this accusation against Jews was composed by the monk Thomas of Monmouth, of the cathedral priory at Norwich. Although similar stories may have been circulating in continental Europe before this date, Thomas's hagiographical account was to be highly influential. It gave significance to the finding in 1144 of a boy's body in Thorpe Wood outside Norwich by attributing the boy's killing to the Jews of Norwich. The narrative account attributed to contemporary Jews the desire to reenact the crucifixion upon an innocent child (usually male) with metal instruments and ritualized humiliation. The story also formed the core of accusations against many Jewish communities mainly in England, France (Blois, 1171), the HRE (Boppard, 1180; Speyer, 1196), and elsewhere in Europe in the later medieval centuries, and in Catholic lands up until the twentieth century. The accusation was never officially endorsed by the papacy and was rejected in the later twentieth century, but it was one of the most deeply imagined and animating representations of Jewish evil, attached as it was to the death of children, although cases are even known of accusations of ritual murder before a corpse had even been found. This tale existed in parallel with, although it is not the same as, the blood libel.

————

R. P. Hsia, *The Myth of Ritual Murder: Jews and Magic in Reformation Germany* (1988); J. M. McCulloh, "Jewish Ritual Murder: William of Norwich, Thomas of Monmouth, and the Early Dissemination of the Myth," *Speculum* 72 (1997): 698–740.

MIRI RUBIN

Rochelle, Synod of Held in 1571, this first national gathering of representatives of the French Reformed churches to meet with royal authorization consolidated many of the theological and polity developments of the movement's early stages. With Theodore Beza as moderator, the synod confirmed in slightly revised and definitive forms the church's founding documents: the French Confession and Ecclesiastical Discipline (both first adopted in 1559). Several actions affirmed distinctive positions taken by Calvin and the Genevan church: the ecclesiastical use of excommunication, rejection of Erastianism, and condemnation of opponents of the claim that the Eucharist conveys the *substance* of Christ's body and blood.

The synod also demonstrated the great political gains the Reformed had made. Present at the synod were all the prominent Huguenot nobles, including their nominal leader Henry of Navarre (later Henry IV). This show of strength, together with the role played by Beza, a representative of Geneva, heightened fears among France's Catholics that Protestant "outsiders" were on the verge of a takeover and fed anxieties that would eventually break out in

the frenzy of violence known as the St. Bartholomew's Day Massacre in 1572.

————

R. M. Kingdon, *Geneva and the Consolidation of French Protestantism, 1564–1572* (1967).

CHRISTOPHER ELWOOD

Rogers, John (c. 1500–1555), English Bible publisher and reformer. While serving as a priest to English Catholics living in Antwerp, Belgium, Rogers was converted to Reformed doctrines by the English Bible translator William Tyndale. When Tyndale was imprisoned in 1535, Rogers used Tyndale's translation of the New Testament, completed with Coverdale's translations of the Hebrew Scriptures, to publish the pseudonymous "Matthew's Bible." This edition was in many respects the foundation for the later Authorized (King James) Version of 1611. Following the death of Henry VIII, and under the safety of Edward VI's Protestant rule, Rogers returned to England in 1548. In 1551 he was named prebendary of St. Paul's; he preached openly against papal authority, which led to his arrest and execution in 1555. Rogers was the first Protestant executed by Mary Tudor's regime.

————

A. McGrath, *In the Beginning* (2001).

ALDEN R. LUDLOW

Roman Empire Historians conventionally date the beginning of the empire as 27 BCE, when Julius Caesar's grand-nephew Octavian, who four years earlier had defeated Mark Antony and gained possession of the entire Roman world, was given the title of "Augustus" by the Roman Senate. Octavian adopted it as his name, and this title was used by all later Roman emperors. Augustus purported to have restored the Roman republic and claimed only to be *Princeps* (first man of the Senate), hence the name for the first phase of the empire, the principate. But Augustus's control of the military and of the law-making process meant that Rome now had a monarchy. Augustus dealt with several problems that the republic had ignored. He created a professional army that defended strategically organized frontiers. He allowed the provincial populations to become Roman citizens. He attempted to unify the disparate populations of the empire by creating a cult of "Rome and Augustus" in which all could share.

Chronologically, Roman imperial history is subdivided into dynasties of Roman emperors. Those related to Augustus comprise the Julio-

Claudian dynasty (27 BCE–68 CE), during which time Roman emperors consolidated power at the expense of the Senate. In the reign of Augustus's successor Tiberius (14–37) Christ was crucified in Judea, and under Nero (54–68) Christians were blamed for a fire that destroyed much of Rome.

Augustus failed to provide for a constitutional means of choosing the next emperor. When Nero died in 68 without naming a successor, civil wars broke out as various armies named candidates. Vespasian, who had been suppressing a Jewish revolt, was the ultimate victor and established the Flavian dynasty (69–96).

The Antonine dynasty (96–192) also is known as the *pax Romana* ("Roman peace"), the period when the Roman Empire was at its most peaceful, most prosperous, and most effectively governed. Even so, a Jewish revolt under Bar Kochba (131–133) was savagely repressed, and many Jews were expelled from Palestine. Christianity increasingly attracted the attention of the government, as when Emperor Trajan (98–117) advised Pliny, governor of Asia, not to give credence to anonymous denunciations of supposed Christians.

Emperor Marcus Aurelius (161–180) spent much of his reign dealing with barbarian attacks on the northern frontier. Another period of civil wars followed the death of his son Commodus (180–192). The ultimate victor, Severus (193–211), inaugurated a period of increasing favor to the army. Extravagant military pay raises instituted by Severus and his son Caracalla (211–217) led to the debasement of the silver coinage and rampant inflation. Soon thereafter, the army got completely out of control during a period known as the "Military Anarchy" or "Imperial Crisis" (235–284).

Beginning in 284, Emperor Diocletian (284–305) introduced reforms intended to bring peace and stability back to the empire. He lessened the possibilities of revolts by fragmenting the sources of authority: civilian and military careers were separated, the army was divided into the border army and field army, and the existing fifty provinces were subdivided into over a hundred. Diocletian also named three co-emperors, based on ability. In doing so he created a tetrarchy, or rule by four. Acknowledging the failure of the money economy, he introduced the *annona*, in which taxes were collected and expenditures made in kind. His reign marks the beginning of the later Roman Empire.

Diocletian's retirement in 305 led to another round of civil wars in which Constantine (306–337) emerged victorious. Constantine returned to a dynastic form of succession, which was maintained by all subsequent emperors. He stabilized the economy by changing to the gold standard and established a second capital at Constantinople. His most lasting legacy results from the great favor he showed to the Christian church. Subsequent years brought the rise of what has been dubbed the Christian empire.

The late fourth century saw the beginning of the so-called barbarian invasions. By the end of the fifth century, the entire western half of the empire had been incorporated into barbarian kingdoms. The eastern half of the Empire, known to modern historians as the Byzantine Empire, survived until 1453, when it was overcome by the Turks.

Christian historians saw it as no accident that the rise of Christianity coincided with the rise of the Roman Empire, which, as attested by Christ's "render unto Caesar" and Paul's pride in his Roman citizenship, was an implicit part of the Christian world. Whereas some Christians condemned equally the Roman Empire and classical culture, most, like the African Augustine, recognized the value of both in God's plan.

———

A. Cameron, *The Later Roman Empire* (1993); H. H Scullard, *A History of Rome* (3rd ed., 1975); R. MacMullen, *Christianizing the Roman Empire* (1984).

RALPH W. MATHISEN

Romanos the Melodist (c. 485–c. 555), Greek religious poet and hymn writer. Born in Emesa, Syria, in a bilingual environment (Greek and Syriac), Romanos was educated as a deacon in Berytus (Beirut) before he moved to Constantinople. He reputedly composed over a thousand hymns and was called the "Christian Pindar."

Romanos is best known for a new genre of hymn, the *kontakion*, a sung, metrical sermon normally treating biblical themes. It is considered the pinnacle of Byzantine poetry. The *kontakion* introduced new metrical and structural patterns into Greek poetry to replace those of classical Greek. Its use of dialogue between biblical characters created dynamic drama that engaged the attention of listeners.

Many have recognized the strong influence of the Syriac hymns of Ephrem (d. 373) upon Romanos in developing the *kontakion*. Also influential was the Syriac *Diatessaron*, a harmony of the Gospels used in the Syriac church until the fifth century, on which Ephrem had written an important commentary.

W. L. Petersen, "The Dependence of Romanos the Melodist upon the Syriac Ephrem: Its Importance for the Origin of the Kontakion," *VC* 39 (1985): 171–87; Petersen, *The "Diatessaron" and Ephrem the Syrian as Sources of Romanos the Melodist* (1985); Romanos the Melodist, *The Kontakion*, trans. E. Lash (1995).

ROBERT A. KITCHEN

Rome, Sack of Occupation and destruction of the city of Rome by Emperor Charles V's army in 1527–1528. Charles V ordered the invasion of Italy in 1526 because Pope Clement VII had allied with France and Venice (the League of Cognac) against him. Charles had insufficient funds to support the invasion and therefore encouraged plunder as the army invaded. In March 1527 the army attempted to sack Florence, but when the city's reinforcement troops arrived, the army moved south to the largely undefended Rome. Rome quickly fell, and Pope Clement VII retreated to the Castel Sant'Angelo. During the seven months of Clement's confinement, the emperor's forces ravaged the city. While all the soldiers plundered for profit, some followers of Martin Luther believed their destructive work served a higher religious mission and was a sign of God's punishment for the sins of the church. Across Europe many saw it simply as a tragedy. The sack ended when Clement ransomed himself and fled to Orvieto in early December. The consequences for Clement and Charles did not last long; in 1529 they entered into an alliance of their own through the Treaty of Barcelona.

E. R. Chamberlain, *The Sack of Rome* (1979); L. Guicciardin, *The Sack of Rome* (1993).

DAVID WHITFORD

Root and Branch Petition Introduced by London Puritan factions at the beginning of the Long Parliament (1640), the petition refers to Malachi 4:1, a passage in which the arrogant and evil are destroyed by fire, leaving them "neither root nor branch." Presenting a long series of grievances, the petition, which was attended with nearly 15,000 signatures, sought to sweep out the Anglican High Church episcopacy; it was organized into the Root and Branch Bill of 1641. The petition and subsequent bill floundered due to a lack of consensus: some factions desired a state church, while others sought a presbyterian or congregationalist model. The bill was accepted by the House of Commons but rejected by the House of

Lords. One suggestion was implemented: Charles I was compelled to exclude bishops from the House of Lords. Though the petition failed, it was effectively implemented with the advent of the Civil War and the resultant commonwealth and protectorate.

H. Gee and W. J. Hardy, eds., *Documents Illustrative of English Church History* (1896).

ALDEN R. LUDLOW

Rosary Derived from the Latin *rosarium* (a garland of roses) and German *Rosenkranz*, the term "rosary" emerged amid the proliferation of floral garden imagery in fourteenth-century literature. This late medieval trend, prominent in German and Dutch secular and devotional literature, produced allegorical works that used botanical language to describe religious experience; it reflects the dissemination of mystical motifs outside the cloister, as well as the importance of the Song of Songs in contemporary religiosity.

The Ave Maria, a prayer combining the Vulgate translations of the salutation of the angel Gabriel to Mary (Luke 1:28) with Elizabeth's greeting of the expectant virgin (Luke 1:42), had been recited as a lay alternative to the Psalter since at least the twelfth century, in imitation of the monastic practice of chanting 150 psalms. Devotees used chains of prayer beads for counting and often saw their prayers as having an almost creative force. In the thirteenth century, for example, the recitation of fifty repetitions of the Ave prayer among a community of Beguines was likened to the creation of a spiritual *corona* or *Rosenkranz* for Mary. In the fourteenth century legends of devotees whose Aves miraculously transformed into roses became widespread. The practice attracted the interest of fifteenth-century members of the observant reform movement, including the Carthusian Dominic of Prussia, who added meditations on the life of Christ to the end of each Ave. Dominic's meditations circulated widely and inspired Alanus de Rupe, who developed an extended version and established the first confraternity dedicated to the prayer.

In 1475 Dominican Jakob Sprenger (coauthor of the *Malleus Maleficarum*) established the first papally sanctioned confraternity in Cologne. Lenient membership policies, generous indulgences, and aggressive promotion attracted members by the thousands, with Emperor Frederick III among the first. The newly invented printing press facilitated distribution of handbooks and broadsheets to potential members, and painted altarpieces, often sponsored by confraternities, also helped circulate and standardize the practice. Soon similar confraternities were being established across Europe, with women joining in unusually large numbers. The contributions of the Dominican order to the devotion's success fueled the misconception that the order's founder, St. Dominic, established the practice in the thirteenth century.

Martin Luther's forceful rejection of the devotion was reiterated by later Protestant reformers. Meanwhile, the practice became a tool in the Counter-Reformation, where it was promoted, especially by Jesuits, for its ability to reinforce essential doctrine. In 1569, the pope designated an official form of the prayer, and in 1572 Pius V attributed the Christian victory over the Turks at Lepanto to the intercession of Mary invoked by praying the Rosary. Today the prayer remains the most popular private devotion among Roman Catholics.

———

S. Beissel, *Geschichte der Verehrung Marias in Deutschland* (1909); J. Hamburger, *Nuns as Artists* (1997); S. Ringbom, "Maria in Sole and the Virgin of the Rosary," *Journal of the Warburg and Courtauld Institutes* 25 (1962): 326–30; A. Winston-Allen, *Stories of the Rose* (1997).

ADRIENNE NOCK AMBROSE

Rothmann, Bernard (c. 1495–1535),

Anabaptist theologian. Born in Westphalia, he earned a master's degree at the Univ. of Mainz. Ordained a priest, he became a chaplain in Münster but soon thereafter briefly studied at Cologne, visited Wittenberg, and embraced Lutheran reforms. In 1531 he introduced the Reformation to the bishopric of Münster. In 1534 he accepted rebaptism. These events led to a power struggle within Münster among Catholics loyal to the bishop, Lutherans supported by the town council, and the Anabaptist followers of Rothmann. In February of that year, city council elections went to the Anabaptist faction.

Rothmann embraced the radical apocalyptic views of John Matthijs of Haarlem (d. 1534) and John Brockels of Leiden (d. 1535), who arrived in 1534 with visions of setting up the messianic New Jerusalem. Matthijs, Brockels, and Rothmann were strongly influenced by the fiery blend of apocalyptic speculation and spiritualism expounded by the Strasbourg Anabaptist Melchior Hoffman (1495?–1543). Under the reign of Matthijs and Brockels the "Münster kingdom" experienced forced rebaptisms, communal sharing, and polygamy. Rothmann's writings, including *Restitution* and *Concerning Wrath*, called for the return of NT Christianity and God's divine judgment. He probably died when Catholic and Lutheran forces took the city in June 1535.

———

W. J. De Bakker, "Bernard Rothmann: Civic Reformer in Anabaptist Muenster," in *The Dutch Dissenters: A Critical Companion to Their History and Ideas,* ed. I. B. Horst (1986); C. A. Snyder, *Anabaptist History and Theology: An Introduction* (1992); G. H. Williams, *The Radical Reformation* (3rd ed., 1992).

DAVID B. ELLER

Roussel, Gérard (c. 1480–1555), Christian humanist reformer, preacher, and bishop of Oloron. Born in Picardy, Gérard Roussel was a founding member Lefèvre d'Étaples' Cenacle of Meaux, which promoted an evangelical form of Christianity strongly influenced by Luther's views on faith and grace. Roussel translated the Pentateuch in the 1520s. While resisting calls to break with the Roman Church, he demanded an immediate end to the most glaring abuses in the church. Fearing persecution, Roussel took refuge in Strasbourg in 1525 before returning to France under the protection of Francis I's sister, Marguerite de Navarre. Roussel delivered the 1533 Lenten sermons at the Louvre that drew such large crowds that the site had to be changed three times. In reaction, the Sorbonne theologians sponsored their own series of Lenten sermons that leveled charges of heresy and Lutheranism against Roussel. After Easter, the Sorbonne sent a delegation of theologians, including its archconservative syndic Noël Béda, that enjoined the king to press charges of heresy against Roussel. Francis I instead banished the Sorbonne delegation. Later that year, however, the king agreed to imprison Roussel and other reformers if the pope supported his plans to invade Italy. Upon his release the next year, Roussel sought safety at Marguerite's court in Pau. With her support, Roussel was made a canon of Meaux, then by papal appointment abbot of Clairac in 1530, and eventually bishop of Oloron in Béarn in 1536. He collaborated on a new confession of faith for Marguerite known as the Mass of Seven Points.

———

P. J. Landa, *The Reformed Theology of Gérard Roussel, Bishop of Oloron (1536–1555)* (1976).

MICHAEL WOLFE

Rufinus of Aquileia (345–410), ascetic and translator. Born in northern Italy, he studied at Rome, where he began a lifelong relationship with Jerome. After living in an ascetic community in Aquileia (368–373), he went to Egypt (373–380), where he visited some famous monks, studied in Alexandria with Didymus the Blind, and became acquainted with the works of Origen. In 380 he moved to the Holy Land with the wealthy Roman noblewoman Melania the Elder, for whom he served as spiritual advisor. On the Mount of Olives they founded a double monastery, for women and for men. Rufinus favored the works of Origen, but in 393 Jerome, now in Bethlehem, questioned Origen's orthodoxy along with Rufinus's support of him. After reconciling with Jerome in 397, Rufinus returned to Italy.

In Aquileia in 399 Rufinus began his fruitful literary career. He translated into Latin Origen's difficult *On First Principles* with a preface suggesting that Jerome admired the great Alexandrian. He also deleted some of Origen's more debatable views. Infuriated, Jerome wrote directly to Rufinus, but Jerome's allies in Rome publicized the conflict. Jerome attacked with several works. Rufinus wrote one very able reply, showing Jerome to be a hypocrite, but when his friend, Bishop Chromatius of Aquileia, recommended a dignified silence, Rufinus agreed and withdrew from the controversy. Jerome continued to assail Rufinus, even after the latter's death.

In 407 Rufinus fled Italy ahead of a Gothic invasion. He died in Sicily in 410. Although he composed some original works, his contribution to Christian intellectual life was his translation of the Greek fathers, especially Origen, into Latin.

E. Clark, *The Origenist Controversy* (1992); A. di Berardino, *Patrology*, vol. 4 (1986), 247–54; Rufinus, *On the Apostles' Creed*, ACW 20 (1955); Rufinus, *Church History* (1997).

JOSEPH F. KELLY

Rule of Faith As a brief summary of belief used by the early church as a guideline for interpreting Scripture, the *regula fidei* had vital significance as the means to distill thematic unity from the diverse Scriptures in the narrative of God's providential care for humanity from creation to the culmination of history. Irenaeus (*Haer.* 1.8–10) and Tertullian (*Praescr.* 7, 16–17) held that Scripture could not be regarded as self-interpreting but must be appropriated through the publicly attested apostolic tradition synthesized in the rule. They argued that the rule provided a universal and consistent witness to Christian preaching in opposition to the multiplicity of gnostic biblical interpretation. The rule was institutionalized through its application in catechetical instruction and narration in baptismal liturgy (Hippolytus, *Tradi. ap.* 21). In contrast to later creeds, the rule had no fixed verbal form and could vary in scope. Elements of the rule adduced by Irenaeus and Tertullian include the identity of God the Father as the creator of the universe, a narrative of the saving work of Jesus Christ, and affirmation of the return of Christ for a final judgment. In this way, the *regula fidei* explicitly grounds the doctrine of salvation on the mutual work of God the Father and Christ, but the role of the Holy Spirit remains only loosely defined.

P. S. Grech, "The *Regula Fidei* as a Hermeneutical Principle in Patristic Exegesis," in *International Symposium on the Interpretation of the Bible* (1998), 589–601; E. Osborn, "Reason and the Rule of Faith in the Second Century AD," in *The Making of Orthodoxy: Essays in Honour of Henry Chadwick*, ed. R. Williams (1989), 40–61; F. Young, *The Art of Performance: Towards a Theology of the Holy Scripture* (1990).

RICHARD A. LAYTON

Rule of the Master Medievalists long accorded to the *Rule* of Benedict originality and dominance in Western monasticism. Other rules were known to have existed contemporaneously with it or to have appeared later, but Benedict was considered the original, insightful monastic founder. Since most scholars of medieval monasticism were Benedictine monks, Benedict had more than scholarly importance. In the 1930s, however, some Benedictine scholars suggested that the founder had drawn upon an anonymous and little-known text called the *Rule of the Master*. Thus began a scholarly debate that lasted until the 1960s and is well recounted by David Knowles. Scholars now accept that the *Rule of the Master* was composed early in the sixth century in central Italy, close in both space and time to Benedict. The Master, an Italian abbot, drew upon Eastern monastic sources for his rule. His rule presents the abbot as an autocrat with little concern for the views of other monks. He even designated his successor. The rule itself is harsh, verbose, and obsessed with petty points. There is little evidence of its having been used outside of one monastery. Indeed, if not for Benedict's use of it, the *Rule of the Master* would have remained obscure.

D. Knowles, *Great Historical Enterprises* (1963); C. H. Lawrence, *Medieval Monasticism* (1997); L. Eberle, trans., *The Rule of the Master* (1977).

JOSEPH F. KELLY

Rupert of Deutz (c. 1076–1129), mystic and monastic theologian. Born near Liège, Rupert made his monastic profession in 1091 and received ordination in 1108. He had mystical visions between 1100 and 1108, by which time he was encouraged to write. Many of his works employ a symbolic interpretation of Scripture. His exposition of the Divine Office is in fact a theological commentary on the liturgical year and its rites. He published the first theology of history since Augustine, and his commentary on John is a kind of general introduction into theology. From 1113 to 1118 he took part in contentious discussions about the Eucharist and predestination. From 1119 on he lived at Siegburg, whose Abbot Kuno, along with Archbishop Frederic I of Cologne, proved to be among Rupert's most convinced supporters. At the end of 1120 he was named abbot of Deutz, where he wrote a kind of drama of history as well as works on Matthew, the Song of Songs, and an apologetical work on the Old Testament, *Dialogus inter Christianum et Judaeum* (*Dialogue between a Christian and a Jew*). Rupert is one of the most prominent figures of what used to be called "monastic theology." As a theologian, he employed a threefold periodization of time. In the field of Christology, he taught the unconditional incarnation, along with a coherent mariological interpretation of the Song of Songs.

M. Aliotta, "La teologia mistica di Ruperto di Deutz; Il simbolismo erotico," *Synaxis* 12 (1994): 17–46; *LTK³* 8 (1999): 1366–67; *TRE* 29 (1998), 474–83.

RAINER BERNDT

Ruusbroec, Jan van (1293–1381), considered the foremost of the Flemish Mystics. Born at Ruusbroec, a small commune between Brussels and Hal, he was raised by his uncle, canon of St. Gudule's, in the city of Brussels. Ordained as a priest in 1317, he served as vicar of the collegiate church of St. Gudule for twenty-five years. In 1343, desiring more solitude, he and two friends left Brussels for a small hermitage at Groenendael, which had been given to them by John III, Duke of Brabant. Soon so many disciples joined them that they decided it was necessary to organize a monastic community. In 1349, Groenendael was formally established as a monastery of Canons Regular of St. Augustine. Ruusbroec remained there until his death in 1381, becoming well known for his doctrine of complete detachment from the world, his intense personal love for God, and his capable direction of the devout. His writings were distributed beyond Flanders and Brabant, especially in Holland, Germany, and France. Ruusbroec had a deep impact on the many individuals who sought his counsel, especially Geert Groote. His friendship with and influence on Groote helped to define the spiritual direction of the *Devotio Moderna*. Some doctrines of Ruusbroec, especially as expounded in the third book of *Spiritual Marriage*, were attacked by Jean Gerson as pantheistic but were then defended by John of Schoonhoven and Denis the Carthusian, among others. Ruusbroec died at Groenendael in 1381.

G. de Baere, *Jan van Ruusbroec: Opera Omnia* (2002); A. Dirkens, B. B. de Ryke, eds., *Maître Eckhart et Jan van Ruusbroec: Études sur la mystique rhéno-flamande, xiiie–xive siècle* (2004); R. van Nieuwenhove, *Jan van Ruusbroec: Mystical Theologian of the Trinity* (2003); P. Verdeyen, *Ruusbroec and His Mysticism* (1994); G. Warnar, *Ruusbroec: Literatuur en mystiek in de veertiende eeuw* (2003); J. A. Wiseman, trans., *John Ruusbroec: The Spiritual Espousals and Other Works* (1985)

TODD M. RICHARDSON

Sabas (439–532), Palestinian monk. He led the second generation, following Euthymius, into the Judean desert. His hagiography (by Cyril of Scythopolis) presents Sabas as a great founder of monasteries but not as a theologian or teacher. After years spent first in a communal monastery (457–473) and then as an anchorite (469–483), Sabas established the Great Laura (483), a type of monastic settlement characterized by groups of cells in close proximity and loose association with each other. This arrangement allowed both solitary and communal activity. The Great Laura (which still stands, although it is inactive) served as the basis for further monastic settlements of both the Laura and more traditional communal type, all of which were headed by disciples of Sabas. This expansion resulted in part from overcrowding in the Great Laura and in part as a strategy for moving rebellious monks. Sabas is credited with increasing the number of Judean monasteries and with establishing a written rule for the confederation of settlements. Cyril also presents Sabas as providing spiritual authority to the patriarch in Jerusalem and as promoting the cause of Chalcedon, thus making the Judean monasteries vital to the Palestinian church.

————

J. Binns, *Ascetics and Ambassadors of Christ: The Monasteries of Palestine, 314–631* (1994); Cyril of Scythopolis, *Lives of the Monks of Palestine*, trans. R. M. Price (1991); J. Patrich, *Sabas, Leader of Palestinian Monasticism* (1995).

REBECCA KRAWIEC

Sabbatarianism A movement that insists on observance of the seventh day of the week as a religious day of rest (Exod. 20:8–11). By the sixteenth century, Christians had long since spiritualized this command and observed instead the first day, Sunday, as the day of Christ's resurrection, a symbolic "eighth day" of divine re-creation pointing to the eventual fulfillment of the church's hope. The literal command was interpreted as an element of Jewish ceremonial law that had been superseded. In their zeal to return Christianity to its pristine origins, some radical sixteenth-century reformers turned their attention to Sabbath observance. Their attempts to reinstitute it were generally seen—sometimes correctly—as efforts to "judaize" Christianity. In Silesia and Moravia, Oswald Glaidt and Andreas Fischer led a small group of Sabbatarians who initially expected the immediate return of Christ to judge the world (*chiliasm*) but later developed a principled and less eschatological Sabbatarianism. Other reformers explicitly rejected their ideas; Martin Luther, for example, wrote against them in *Wider die Sabbater* (1538). In Transylvania after 1588, a second and explicitly Judaized form of Sabbatarianism arose among Unitarians. Rejecting the adoration of Jesus and reinstituting Jewish rites, this group moved beyond acceptable Unitarian boundaries. Adherents were forced to practice secretly. Persisting against all odds, they were allowed to practice their faith legally, as "pros-elyte" Jews, only after the Austro-Hungarian emancipation of the Jews in 1867.

————

D. Liechty, *Andreas Fischer and the Sabbatarian Anabaptists* (1988); Liechty, *Sabbatarianism in the Sixteenth Century* (1993).

MICKEY L. MATTOX

Sabellius (third cent.), heretical theologian, said to have come from Libya but active in Rome. Sabellius's theology is not known through any extant works. (Pseudo-)Hippolytus's heresiology does not discuss his views, and Eusebius refers only to Sabellius's "infidelity" to the Son and "irreverence" to the Holy Spirit (*Hist. eccl.* 7.6). Novatian refutes the Sabellian exegesis (*Trin.* 26–28). Epiphanius, in his *Panarion*, adds that Sabellius taught "similarly to Noetians" and presents him as saying that Father, Son, and Spirit were "three names in one entity." Sabellius was a representative of modalistic Monarchianism, which tried to conciliate Jesus' divinity with the categorical statement in Isaiah 44:6, "Besides me there is no God." The Sabellian designation "Son-Father" meant that the Son was an economical mode of the Father. Sabellius's heretical views proved damaging to the reputation of Callistus, bishop of Rome (217–222), and Callistus had him expelled from the church (Hippolytus, *Haer.* 9.7). In time, Sabellianism became a standard heresy and had to be refuted even if it was no longer relevant. Sabellius's Trinitarian views were also attributed to other perceived heretics, such as Marcellus of Ancyra.

————

W. Bienert, "Sabellius und Sabellianismus als historisches Problem," in *Logos: Festschrift für Luise Abramowski*, ed. H. C. Brennecke et al. (1993), 124–39; P. L. Gavrilyuk, *The Suffering of the Impassible God* (2004).

TARMO TOOM

Sabina (second cent.), Roman matron whose home on the Aventine Hill was a place of Christian meeting. According to later legend, she was converted by a slave girl and followed her in martyrdom under Emperor Hadrian (117–138).

A house of the second or third century lies beneath the Church of Santa Sabina, consecrated shortly after 432. In the sixth century the name changed from *titulus Sabinae* to *titulus S. Sabinae*, reflecting the elevation of Sabina to the status of martyr and saint. The name indicates that the church is a "title church," named for the patron in whose house the church had met. Santa Sabina is an outstanding example of the early Christian basilicas in Rome and remains almost intact as a model of them. The building exemplifies classical proportions, and the interior columns may have been taken from earlier buildings. One treasure of the church is the carved cypress doors at the entrance, a rare survival of wood carving from antiquity. Eighteen of the original twenty-eight panels of biblical scenes survive, including one of the earliest depictions of the crucifixion.

F. Darsy, *Santa Sabina* (1961); R. Delbrück, "Notes on the Wooden Doors of S. Sabina," *Art Bulletin* 34 (1952): 139–45; R. Krautheimer, *Corpus basilicarum christianarum Romae*, vol. 4 (1976), 69–94.

EVERETT FERGUSON

Sachs, Hans (1494–1576), popular German vernacular writer and proponent of the Reformation. Born in Nuremberg, Sachs attended a city school from 1501 to 1509, apprenticed as a shoemaker at age fifteen, trained as a master singer, and eventually earned his living as a master shoemaker. His literary activity was remarkable. More than six thousand of his works have been identified, and they include mastersongs, poems, dramas, carnival plays, fables, humorous tales, and prose dialogues. Their primary purpose was not to entertain but to identify societal abuses, foster civic morality, and promote the common good. Influenced by Martin Luther, Sachs used his gifts on behalf of the Reformation after 1520. In 1523 he published his famous *Wittenberg Nightingale*, a long didactic poem and popular summary of Reformation ideas. His four prose dialogues of 1524 gave voice to the laity in matters of faith. Although silenced for a time by the Nuremberg city council, he remained a loyal supporter of the Reformation and continued to promote Reformation themes in biblical dramas and in poetic renderings of Scripture based on Luther's translation.

B. Balzer, *Bürgerliche Reformationspropaganda: Die Flugschriften des Hans Sachs in den Jahren 1523–1525* (1973); B. Könneker, *Hans Sachs* (1971).

KURT K. HENDEL

Sacrament, Medieval Definition
The diverse ceremonies observed by early Christian communities in commemoration of Christ's life and death received their first conceptualization by Augustine. Sacraments were

channels of grace and a promise of salvation. They were ineffable acts, which were nonetheless experienced through visible and tangible signs: the water of baptism, the bread of the Eucharist, the oil of extreme unction. Augustine also emphasized that as long as they were administered by a priest, sacraments were efficacious by virtue of their enactment and did not depend on the priest's virtue. Yet Christian life abounded with many varying rituals, and only in the twelfth century was a list of seven sacraments formulated in the authoritative theological textbook of Peter Lombard (d. 1160). Thomas Aquinas (d. 1274) extended the discussion of the sacraments to include issues of necessity and to clarify God's role in their operation. This included baptism, confirmation, ordination, marriage, confession, Eucharist, and extreme unction. An understanding of these sacraments was in turn disseminated to the laity through pastoral handbooks, sermons, visual images, and tales. Above all loomed the sacrament of the Eucharist, which conveyed grace through a unique experience of communion— the reception of Christ's body in the form of consecrated bread. Whereas other sacraments could be administered in dire necessity by a cleric in lower orders or even by a layperson, the Eucharist was a sacrament apart, which epitomized priestly status and the dependence of laypeople upon sacerdotal mediation of the sacraments. Debate about the nature of the sacraments continued among scholars throughout the remaining medieval centuries, but pastoral teaching continued to ground Christian life in the sacraments, which were to be received by parishioners in their local churches. The nature of sacramental action also provided some of the issues for fierce polemical discussion in the sixteenth century.

G. Macy, *The Theologies of the Eucharist in the Early Scholastic Period: A Study of the Salvific Function of the Sacrament according to the Theologians c. 1080–c. 1220* (1984); M. Rubin, *Corpus Christi: the Eucharist in Late Medieval Culture* (1991).

MIRI RUBIN

Sacramentarianism In the broadest sense this refers to the denial of salvific significance of any of the sacraments of the church. The term came to be commonly used for those who denied the doctrine of the real presence of Christ in the Eucharist during the Reformation, such as Johannes Oecolampadius, Andreas Karlstadt, and most importantly Huldrych

Zwingli. Sacramentalist teaching had several sources, most notably Erasmus, and was drawn in part from iconoclasm against perceived medieval superstitious practices. According to Zwingli, a sacrament does not communicate grace but commemorates it. For Zwingli the sacramental signs serve only to aid the believer's spiritual exercise of recalling God's grace and as opportunities for the community to confess its faith. As at the Colloquy of Marburg (1529), the sacramentalists often supported their interpretation of the Lord's Supper by referring to John 6:63: "the Spirit gives life; the flesh is of no avail." Some later radical reformers, such as Caspar von Ossig Schwenkfeld (d. 1561), rejected the need for sacraments at all. Martin Luther was adamantly opposed to these formulations as embodying grievous errors concerning the nature of God, the church, and salvation. For Luther, sacramentalism made salvation dependent upon personal piety. He wrote fiercely against it in tracts such as *Against the Heavenly Prophets in the Matter of Images and Sacraments* (1525). Sacramentarianism remained a focal issue in the divisions within Protestantism for centuries.

R. H. Bainton, *Studies on the Reformation* (1963); G. H. Williams, *The Radical Reformation* (3rd ed., 1992).

GREGORY J. MILLER

Sacraments Sacraments are sign-acts that convey the reality of Christ in the church. The number of these actions, and their ritual components and theological interpretations, are all matters of historic differences among the churches. Orthodox churches retain the term "mystery" (Grk. *mysterion*) for these sign-acts. The Roman Catholic Church and Protestant churches use the term "sacrament" (Lat. *sacramentum*), although some traditions employ the term "ordinance" to emphasize biblical authority for a practice.

The *sacramentum* in classical Latin was a sum of money to accompany a contract or case at law, which was forfeit if the case were lost or the contract unfulfilled. The word could mean promise, pledge, or oath and could refer to the act of making a promise or pledge. Latin-speaking North African Christians (e.g., Tertullian) were the main source for the term. In contrast, the Greek *mysterion* (1 Cor. 4:1; 15:51; Rom. 16:25–27; Col. 1:26–27; Eph. 3:4; 6:19, etc.) evokes a sense of transcendence, revelation, and personal encounter. Renewal in sacramental theology and practice draws on the

meanings of both terms, but particularly the New Testament and patristic sense of mystery as participation in Christ through symbol or sign-act.

The number of sacraments is a matter of relatively late debate. Early and classical-era sermons and other writings use "sacrament" for a variety of practices, which include liturgical feasts, objects used in meaningful ways (e.g., palms and ashes), and core texts such as the Lord's Prayer and the Creed. As late as Hugh of St. Victor (d. 1142) a broad use of the term is evident. Pseudo-Dionysius distinguished three rites as primary (baptism, the Eucharist, unction) and added three more (ordination of the priest, monastic consecration, and the funeral). Similar classifications of primary rites and of other practices, and discussions of six sacraments, are found in Orthodox sources through the medieval period. In general, the Orthodox churches never officially adopted a single list of sacraments, but Western terminology influenced Orthodox theology from the Middle Ages.

The Western church from the twelfth century on began to limit the number of sacraments, primarily through the requirement of explicit institution by Christ. Hugh of St. Victor identified some thirty sacraments, in three groups. Peter Lombard was probably the first to discuss what became the traditional list of seven: baptism, confirmation, the Eucharist, penance, unction, ordination, and matrimony. These same seven are summarized in the "Decree to the Armenians" of the Council of Florence (1439) and were affirmed by the Council of Trent (1545–1563). Lutherans, Calvinists, and other Protestants limited the sacraments to just baptism and the Eucharist (or Lord's Supper), primarily by insistence on explicit institution in words by Christ. Anglican tradition famously distinguished the "two sacraments ordained of Christ our Lord in the Gospel" from another "five commonly called sacraments" (article 25, the Thirty-nine Articles of the Church of England). For most Protestants, the other five became parts of the ministries of pastoral care and order in the congregation.

Christian thinking about sacraments has been influenced significantly by Augustine of Hippo (354–430). The distinction between sign (*signum*) and the reality of the thing signified (*res*) became basic sacramental vocabulary. Commenting on John 15:3, Augustine said, "The Word is joined to the element and the result is a sacrament, itself becoming, in a sense, a visible word as well" (*Johannis evangelium tractatus*, 80.3). According to Augustine, the sacraments or visible signs are necessary for the existence of the community of faith and are the visible form of God's invisible grace. Sacraments convey what they say, and the holiness of the sign depends on the grace of God and not upon the character of the minister or the recipient. Sacraments are God's communication and convey God's grace in the church.

Thomas Aquinas (1225–1274) and medieval scholasticism developed the thought of Augustine within the context of the recovery of Aristotelian metaphysics. The causation and efficacy of the sacraments became central issues. The validity of a sacrament was understood to require appropriate matter (bread, wine, water, etc.) and the correct form (words spoken, e.g., "I baptize you in the name of the Father and the Son and the Holy Spirit"), with the intention to do what the church does. God was believed to communicate grace by these means (or instrumental causes), when faith and repentance were present on the part of the recipient (i.e., no impediments were raised). Sacramental efficacy was said to be *ex opere operato*, that is, reliable when the valid sacrament was received with faith (as a right disposition). The institution of a sacrament was seen as either explicit in Scripture or implicit in the words and acts of Christ. A full system of pastoral management developed around the seven sacraments by which one is made part of the church and is guided from birth through death.

The Reformation of the sixteenth century was in large part a reformation of worship and therefore of sacrament. It was a conservative reform in some ways. Two sacraments having explicit origin or institution in Scripture (baptism and the Lord's Supper) were retained. Baptism of infants was given its own liturgical ceremonies for the first time, with a strongly Augustinian theology of grace. The other five sacraments became, in effect, pastoral rites of care for persons and of order in the church. Those Protestants called "Anabaptists" (rebaptizers) by their opponents insisted on profession of faith by candidates for baptism, and some Protestants criticized the term "sacrament" itself as unbiblical. In general, however, reformation in this period meant to recover the biblical origin, celebration, and theology of sacramental worship. The proclamation of the word of God was considered central. Sacramental rites were greatly simplified according to form and matter among the Calvinists or Reformed, but with more retention of ceremonies by Lutherans and in the Church of England.

The norms of weekly Lord's Supper and the unity of preaching and sacrament in the congregation were established in the memories of most Protestant traditions, though practice never fulfilled these norms. Twentieth-century sacramental renewal among both Protestants and Roman Catholics has drawn on fresh interest in patristic and NT theology, with the goals of recovery of preaching in Roman Catholic liturgy and of sacraments in Protestant worship. The study of symbol and ritual in the human sciences and in philosophy, and philosophical interest in language and sign, has contributed to critical rethinking of sacramental theology and practice.

A. Chupungco, ed., *Sacraments and Sacramentals*, vol. 4 of *Handbook for Liturgical Studies* (2000); J. Martos, *Doors to the Sacred: A Historical Introduction to Sacraments in the Catholic Church* (2001); D. McKim, ed., *The Westminster Handbook to Reformed Theology* (2001); A. Schmemann, *For the Life of the World: Sacraments and Orthodoxy* (2002); J. White, *The Sacraments in Protestant Practice and Faith* (1999).

STANLEY R. HALL†

Sacraments, Orthodox The proper term for the sacraments in Orthodox theology is "the holy mysteries," which is to say the great things accomplished by God in Christ through the Holy Spirit. Orthodox sacramental doctrine is both pneumatological and ecclesiological. The starting point of Orthodox treatment of sacraments is how the church celebrates these mysteries and how the Orthodox believer enters into them. Bishop Nicholas Cabasilas's work of the fourteenth century, *Life in Christ*, is a good example of Orthodox sacramental theology. This approach does not lend itself well to a formal definition of sacraments generally or of the essential character of any particular sacrament.

The Orthodox Church was not involved in the sacramental discussions that took place in the West in the Middle Ages and at the time of the Reformation. As a consequence, issues of their number or of their "matter" and "form" are less evident in historical practice or theological discussions. The septenary number of the mysteries is received by the Orthodox Church but has never been rigorously defined. There are theologians, especially prior to the thirteenth century, who accept the number seven as a symbolic rather than a restrictive number and speak of monastic tonsure, royal coronation, or the funeral of the dead in sacramental terms. The pneumatological character of Orthodox sacramental practice is especially evident in the prominent placing of the epiclesis, or invocation of the Holy Spirit, not only over the bread and wine of the Eucharist but also over the water of baptism and the oil for the anointing of the sick.

———

A. Coniaris, *These Are the Sacraments: The Life-giving Mysteries of the Orthodox Church* (1975); A. Schmemann, *For the Life of the World: Sacraments and Orthodoxy* (1973); Schmemann, *Of Water and the Spirit: A Liturgical Study of Baptism* (1974); J. D. Ziziolas, *Eucharist, Bishop, Church: The Unity of the Church in the Divine Eucharist and the Bishop during the First Three Centuries* (2001).

EUGENE M. LUDWIG, OFM CAP.

Sacred College From the mid-eighth century the seven bishops of the bishoprics neighboring Rome performed liturgical functions at the basilica of St. John Lateran in Rome, and about the same time priests who presided over the twenty-eight title churches of Rome performed similar duties in each of the four patriarchal basilicas of the city (i.e., St. Peter's, St. Paul's, St. Lawrence, and St. Mary Major). The bishops were designated by the term *cardinalis* (principal, chief) because they officiated outside their own personal churches. By the eleventh century the priests of the title churches also employed the term, the meaning of which had changed to reflect the growing importance of those clergy who had become closely associated with the pope: *cardinalis* now had its derivation in *cardo, cardinis* (head, axis, or hinge). The liturgical functions of the cardinals retreated in importance before their growing institutional significance, as expressed in the papal election decree of Nicholas II (1059), which gave them the primary function of electing the pope.

From the late eleventh century the cardinals also added their signatures to important papal documents. Members of the sacred college (or college of cardinals) headed the great departments of state in the twelfth century, and the consistory eventually replaced the old Roman synod as the principal advisory body to the pope. Cardinal bishops and cardinal priests often acted as papal legates, representing the papacy throughout the far reaches of the Roman church; oftentimes they ran into conflict with local archbishops and bishops who regarded them as intruders in the historical machinery of

church government. In 1274 Gregory X's constitution *Ubi periculum* gave canonical definition to the conclave, the practice of locking up the cardinals until they came to agreement over the next pope. During the upheavals of the fourteenth century some cardinals claimed a share in church governance, but this was never officially recognized. A dispute between the sacred college and the recently elected Pope Urban VI in 1378 ultimately resulted in the schism and the conciliar period (see *Conciliarism*).

———

K. Jordan, *Die Entstehung der römischen Kurie* (1962); E. Kartusch, "Die Mitglieder des Kardinalskollegiums in der Zeit von 1181–1227" (diss., Vienna, 1948); S. Kuttner, "Cardinalis: The History of a Canonical Concept," *Traditio* 3 (1945): 129–98; E. Schilenz, *Studien zur Geschichte des Kardinalats im 13. und 14. Jahrhundert* (1913); B. Tierney, *Foundations of the Conciliar Theory* (1955).

PAUL B. PIXTON

Sacred Heart of Jesus, Devotion to the Catholic devotion pictures the wounded heart of Jesus as the living token and symbol of a redemptive love both human and divine. Glimpsed in medieval mysticism and theology (Bernard, Gertrude, Mechtild, Bonaventure, Henry Suso) as well as in lay piety (Mass of the Five Wounds, the Devotio Moderna), an explicit devotion to the Sacred Heart was popularized in the seventeenth century as the Jesuits, along with Francis de Sales, Jane de Chantal, Marie d'Incarnation, and others, countered the austerity of Jansenism and cultural secularization with the devotion's warm, affective love for Christ and encouragement of more frequent Communion. The Sacred Heart devotion emphasizes two themes: thanksgiving for the inexhaustible riches of Christ (Eph. 3:8) and reparation for the wounding of Christ's heart by our sinfulness and indifference to his love (John 19:34).

———

J. Bovenmars, *A Biblical Spirituality of the Heart* (1991); K. Rahner, "Some Theses for a Theology of Devotion to the Sacred Heart," in *Theological Investigations*, vol. 3 (1967), 338–40; J. Weber, "Devotion to the Sacred Heart: History, Theology, and Liturgical Celebration," *Worship* 72 (1998): 236–54.

PETER J. SCAGNELLI

Sadoleto, Jacopo (1477–1547), humanist scholar and reform cardinal. Born in Modena into a family of jurists, Sadoleto was drawn to the study of letters, and he made his mark with his poem on the Laocoon. Leo X appointed him to the Apostolic Secretariat in 1513. In 1517, while secretary to Pope Leo X, he received the benefice of the bishopric of Carpentras to which he withdrew in 1527 upon giving up his position in the papal secretariat. There he produced his widely read book on the instruction of youth (1530) and his commentary on Romans (1535). The latter alarmed Erasmus because of its strongly Pelagian position; it was also condemned by the theology faculty of Paris and was later banned by Rome. Sadoleto was called back to Rome in 1536 by Paul III to work on the commission on reform headed by Gasparo Contarini. Their confidential report claimed that the moral and financial corruption of the papacy had led to the Reformation conflict. Sadoleto sought to engage more moderate Protestants such as Philip Melanchthon and Johann Sturm, but to no avail. Sadoleto also wrote the people of Geneva in 1539, inviting them to return to the Roman church on the basis of the historical continuity of the living Catholic tradition. From 1545 until his death, Sadoleto worked with Paul III to prepare for the Council of Trent, urging the restoration of the church's moral authority as well as its orthodoxy.

R. M. Douglas, *Jacopo Sadoleto* (1959); J. C. Olin, *The Catholic Reformation* (1969); J. Sadoleto and J. Calvin, *A Reformation Debate* (1966).

RANDALL C. ZACHMAN

Sahdona Martyrius (seventh cent.),

bishop, spiritual writer of the Church of the East. Born in Halmon in Bēt Nūhādrā, Sahdona was greatly influenced toward the monastic vocation by his mother and a local holy woman, Shirin, to whom his mother had taken him during his youth. He entered the renowned monastery of Bet 'Abē (forty miles northeast of Mosul, Iraq) and was eventually appointed bishop of Bēt Garmai (near Kirkuk, Iraq) sometime between 635 and 640.

Sahdona's Christology owed more to Chalcedon than to the Church of the East: he advocated one, not two, *hypostases* (Syriac, *qnōmē*) in the incarnate Christ. As a result, he was removed twice from his position. Consequently, his writings were transmitted only in Chalcedonian circles.

His major work is *The Book of Perfection*, a long book on the moral and monastic ("perfect") life. The book is notable for an extraordinarily large number of biblical citations. He

also wrote a few letters to solitary monks and maxims on wisdom which are extant.

Sahdona Martyrius, *Oeuvres spirituelles: Livre de la Perfection, Lettres à des amis solitaires, Maximes sapientiales*, ed. A. de Halleux (1960–1965); S. P. Brock, *Syriac Fathers on Prayer and the Spiritual Life* (1987), 197–239.

ROBERT A. KITCHEN

St. Bartholomew's Day Massacre

On August 24, 1572, the feast day of St. Bartholomew, a paroxysm of violence by Catholic mobs against Huguenots broke out in Paris and spread to the provinces. Many contemporary observers believed Queen Catherine de Mèdicis (1519–1589) and her son, Charles IX (1550–1574), plotted the massacre. However, there is no evidence to substantiate this theory. The massacre occurred just as hopes for peace crested following the Treaty of St. Germain in August 1570 that ended the third civil war. Catherine hoped to end the religious strife by the marriage of her daughter, Marguerite de Valois (1553–1615), to the Huguenot prince Henri de Navarre (1553–1610). The pope vehemently opposed the marriage, as did powerful Catholics at the Valois court because they feared it would render permanent the concessions granted to the Huguenots two years before. Rumors that Gaspard de Coligny (1519–1572), a leading Huguenot, hoped to persuade the impressionable king to invade the Low Countries to assist Dutch rebels in their struggle against Habsburg Spain, many of them fellow Calvinists, further alarmed Catholics. The Guise family fanned these fears, since the proposed dynastic alliance would displace their influence with the king. The St. Bartholomew's Day Massacre largely grew out of the desire of resentful Catholics to foment an open break between the crown and the Huguenots in the context of widespread Catholic dismay at the spread of heresy. A failed assassination attempt against Coligny on August 22 by Guise henchmen precipitated the mass murders that came two days later. The killings continued into October and reached the towns of Rouen, Lyon, Bourges, Orléans, and Bordeaux. An estimated 3,000 persons were killed in Paris, 30,000 in all of France. Pope Gregory XIII and King Philip II of Spain welcomed the news of the massacres. The Huguenots, however, were horrified, and the killings rekindled confessional hatred and civil war.

B. Diefendorf, *Beneath the Cross: Catholics and Protestants in Sixteenth-Century Paris*

(1991); R. M. Kingdon, *Myths about the St. Bartholomew's Day Massacres, 1572–1576* (1988); N. M. Sutherland, *The Massacre of St. Bartholomew and the European Conflict, 1559–1572* (1973).

MICHAEL WOLFE

St. Nicholas   *see* Nicholas, St.

St. Thomas, Church of   *see* Mar Thoma (St. Thomas) Church

St.   Catherine,   Monastery   of

According to legend, Catherine of Alexandria was a learned virgin and martyr of the early fourth century. Her connection with Mount Sinai began when her body was found nearby about 800. Although her story has no historical basis, she became a popular saint in the Middle Ages.

From the fourth century there was a monastery near Mount Sinai to commemorate Moses' call at the burning bush, and pilgrim churches commemorated Moses' receiving the law and Elijah's hearing the still, small voice. Emperor Justinian rebuilt the monastic complex in the sixth century, building a new church (between 548 and 565) and enclosing the monastery with protective walls.

Although the monastic community of St. Catherine's is the smallest of the autocephalous (self-governing) churches in the Orthodox family, it possesses intellectual and artistic treasures valuable to the larger Christian world. The library contains manuscripts in many languages. The church is one of the earliest to retain the original woodwork of the ceiling. The well-preserved apse mosaic gives dramatic expression to the transfiguration of Jesus. From the perspective of art history the most notable feature of the monastery is its collection of icons, which includes some of the earliest known (painted in the sixth and seventh centuries). Among the sixth-century icons are the Virgin and Child between saints Theodore and George, St. Peter, and in encaustic a bust of Christ with a book in his left hand and giving a blessing with his right.

M. S. El-Din, *Sinai: The Site and the History* (1998); G. H. Forsyth and K. Weitzmann, *The Monastery of St. Catherine on Mount Sinai: The Church and the Fortress of Justinian* (1973); G. Galey, *Sinai and the Monastery of St. Catherine* (1986); K. Weitzmann, *The Monastery of St. Catherine on Mount Sinai: The Icons* (1976).

EVERETT FERGUSON

St. Peter, Church of   Constantine

ordered the construction of a memorial church on the Vatican hill at the site revered since the second century as the place of Peter's martyrdom or burial. Excavations under the present St. Peter's found a memorial (*tropaion*) that had been set up in the late second century. The original St. Peter's was built between about 321 and 333. This largest of the Constantinian basilicas combined the functions of a funeral hall for congregational meeting with a martyr's shrine.

Bronze railings and a canopy supported by four spiral columns identified the sacred spot in front of the apse at the intersection of the transept (crossing hall) and the nave. The altar was located in front of the shrine and under the triumphal arch. Two aisles on each side of the nave were marked by double rows of twenty-two columns. The taller nave formed a clerestory; a roof was made of timber. The lay of the land around the memorial dictated that the entrance to the church be on the east. Steps led to a vestibule that gave entrance to a large atrium, surrounded by porticoes and containing in its center a fountain for ritual ablutions. Five doors led into the five-aisled basilica.

The present Church of St. Peter, built between 1506 and 1626, replaced the Constantinian basilica. A succession of great architects worked on it, including Bramante, Raphael, and Sangallo; the dome was designed by Michelangelo. In the shape of a Latin cross, it is the largest church in Christendom, extending 619 feet in length. St. Peter's is not a cathedral; the cathedral church of Rome is the Lateran basilica.

G. T. Armstrong, "Constantine's Churches: Symbol and Structure," *Journal of the Society of Architectural Historians* 33 (1974): 5–16; R. Krautheimer, S. Corbett, and A. K. Frazer, *Corpus basilicarum christianarum Romae*, vol. 5 (1977), 165–279; D. W. O'Connor, *Peter in Rome: The Literary, Liturgical, and Archaeological Evidence* (1969); J. M. C. Toynbee and J. B. Ward-Perkins, *The Shrine of St. Peter and the Vatican Excavations* (1956).

EVERETT FERGUSON

Sainthood   In the early church the term

"saint" applied to a baptized person who thereby became blessed and received eternal life. Gradually it was applied more exclusively to those second- and third-century martyrs such as Perpetua (d. 202) and Polycarp (d. 155) who died in defense of the faith, and whose burial places became shrines where they were honored and commemorated by believers.

Christian saints are regarded as mediators or channels of divine grace between heaven and earth whose sacrificial imitation of Christ, either through martyrdom or fulfillment of the gospel, guarantees them eternal life. This endows them with the ability to protect their disciples, console them in their hour of need— including the performance of miracles with God's aid—and intercede for God's favor in the court of heaven.

The ascetic life became a prerequisite for those leading the perfect Christian life. Such early desert monks as Anthony of Egypt whose lives are described in the *Vitae patrum* attracted pilgrims due to their miracle-working skills and became the prototypical saints. The miracles performed by the saints (which reflect the miracles attributed to Moses, Elijah, and Jesus) may include (1) the cure of disease or other disability; (2) visions, revelations, clairvoyance, or precognition; (3) exorcism; (4) military victory; (5) rescue from prison or execution; (6) the calming of storms, rain making, or the stanching of fires; (6) the transformation of water into wine; and (7) the revival of the dead. The relics of the saints—that is, both their bodily remains and physical objects (such as the cross) with which they had been in contact— represented the agencies through which the Spirit had acted in this world.

Saints may be divided in several hagiographical categories, which adhere to a tradition of ancient stereotypes (or *topoi*) and endow the saint with particular heroic virtues that appeal to different constituencies and serve the church by responding to new challenges. The founders of religious orders (e.g., Benedict of Nursia and Basil of Caesarea) and monastic saints represent living exemplars of the monastic rule. While they often ministered to lay audiences, they were largely venerated within their monastic orders. The mendicant saints (e.g., Francis of Assisi and Dominic Guzmán [see *Dominic*]) often established institutions such as hospices, hospitals, schools, and orphanages in order to minister to the needy and face the intellectual challenges of the church's foes. The dynastic saints (e.g., King Louis IX of France and King Wenceslas of Bohemia), drawn from the nobility, assisted the spread of the faith through a militant battle against infidels or through uniting the tribe or nation under the banner of Christianity. The episcopal saints (e.g., Nicholas of Myra [or Bari] and Thomas Becket of Canterbury), often served as de facto heads of a city-state, served as intermediaries with the central government, and concerned themselves with the welfare of

the citizens. The missionary saints (e.g., Martin of Tours and Patrick of Ireland) did battle against an enemy faith and brought new souls to the church through preaching and personal example. Lay saints, more prevalent after the twelfth century, integrated the religious life with the demands of secular society (e.g., Elizabeth of Thuringia or Joan of Arc).

Statistically, about a quarter of the Catholic saints are female, and the clergy and upper classes are more represented; geographically, Italy and the Mediterranean have provided more saints than other regions. Nevertheless, the cults appeal to all social classes and have served as a means of cementing the allegiance of believers to the church.

The notion of Christian sainthood was a subject of considerable controversy in the Middle Ages. Heretics rejected the cult of the saints; some observers, such as Guibert of Nogent and Erasmus, criticized the proliferation of false relics and the gullibility of the laity. Attempts were therefore made by the ecclesiastical hierarchy to channel religious enthusiasm into authorized directions, limiting those objects, persons, and times regarded as sacred. The reburial of saints (*translatio*), and the discovery (*inventio*) and display (*ostensio*) of relics were occasions for public rejoicing and the attracting of pilgrims, since the consecration of a church required the presence of holy relics. The experience of early Christianity had taught that unrestrained sectarianism could result from the enthusiastic veneration of persons to whom the charismatic power to perform miracles was attributed. The proliferation of saints' cults both as a result of popular enthusiasm or episcopal encouragement therefore led to growing papal intervention.

The first clear evidence of papal involvement in the confirmation of a cult is the bull of canonization of Ulrich of Augsburg. Following the presentation of a book containing Ulrich's life and miracles by Liutolf, bishop of Augsburg, at a Lateran council in 993, a letter from Pope John XV authorized a cult in Ulrich's honor. Shortly after the death of the hermit Simeon of Padolirone (d. 1016), whose body was interred at Mantua, Pope Benedict XV used the term *canonizare* for the first time to indicate the permission granted by the pope to venerate sacred relics and to include a saint in the liturgical calendar.

In the eleventh and twelfth centuries the popes continued to issue such bulls of canonization, many of which imply the existence of some kind of quasi-judicial inquiry under episcopal auspices into the putative saint's life and miracles. The first indication of a claim to the exclusive papal right of canonization and control over sacred relics is Alexander III's 1171 letter *Audivimus*, sent to the king of Sweden, chastising the attribution of miracles to a man who had died in a state of drunkenness. Alexander added that a holy life, miracles, and papal authorization are necessary prerequisites for the establishment of a cult. In 1234 this letter was inserted into the *Decretals* of Gregory IX, a standard collection of canon law, and became the locus classicus for the creation of a cult (although popular and episcopal initiatives continued unabated). The procedure for the appointment of a papal commission of inquiry (an *inquisitio*) into the life and miracles of a putative saint appears to have been established during Alexander's pontificate. Commissions composed of high ecclesiastics schooled in theology and canon law were sent a list of questions to be posed to the hundreds of witnesses who often testified in a court proceeding. The aim was to ensure that veneration was only accorded to persons who had lived an orthodox Christian life and who, during their lifetimes or posthumously, had performed miracles through divine intervention.

While the church sought to stress the centrality of the heroic virtues of potential saints, the public was often more impressed by their miracles. The official aim of a saint's ministry was to strengthen the faith of believers, spread the faith, and combat the claims of heretics, Jews, and other nonbelievers. The evidence was summarized for consideration by the papal curia, which then recommended the establishment of a cult or asked for further evidence. The papal bull typically summarized (1) why and by whom the canonization had been initiated, (2) the sacred life of the saint, and (3) the miracles he or she had performed. In addition, it fixed the feast date of the new cult and granted indulgences to pilgrims visiting the tomb. The dossier of the saint became the foundation of the sacred liturgy, icons, art, sermons, and other aspects of a cult, while the enthusiasm generated by the cult was often generated by local pride or patriotism as each state, profession, noble family, religious order, or movement sought official recognition of its saints.

―――――

M. Goodich, Vita Perfecta: *The Ideal of Sainthood in the Thirteenth Century* (1982); R. Grégoire, *Manuale di agiologia: Introduzione alla letteratura agiografica* (1987); T. Head, ed., *Medieval Hagiography: An Anthology* (2000); E. W. Kemp, *Canonisation and Authority in the Western Church* (1948); R. Kieckhefer,

Unquiet Souls: Fourteenth-Century Saints and Their Religious Milieu (1984); A. Vauchez, *Sainthood in the Later Middle Ages*, trans. J. Birrell (1997); D. Weinstein and R. M. Bell, *Saints and Society: The Two Worlds of Western Christendom, 1000–1700* (1982); S. Wilson, ed., *Saints and Their Cults: Studies in Religious Sociology, Folklore, and History* (1984).

MICHAEL GOODICH†

Saints' Lives, Medieval   *see* Medieval Saints' Lives

Salazar, Domingo de (1512–1594),

Spanish missionary, first bishop of Manila. Salazar attended the Univ. of Salamanca, where he was a student of Francisco de Vitoria, the great theological defender of Amerindian rights, and also heard Bartolomé de las Casas, champion of the Indians, whose disciple he later proclaimed himself. Becoming a Dominican in 1545, he spent twenty-three years in Mexico, which included a disastrous mission to Florida. His defense of the Indians in 1575 in Spain was bitterly opposed, but it led Philip II to make him bishop of Manila.

Arriving in 1581, he summoned a synod to deal with the injustices to Filipinos. The synod demanded Spaniards make restitution for every injustice committed in the conquest and denied absolution to the recalcitrant. When a new governor rejected Salazar's norms on *encomenderos*' (Spanish settlers) collection of tribute by forced labor, the bishop began to question radically Spain's right to the Philippines without the free consent of Filipinos. At the age of seventy-nine, he left for Spain with fellow Dominican Miguel de Benavides to argue before the king. Defeated in the debate, he died shortly afterward, leaving it to future bishop Benavides to win a favorable decision before Philip's death in 1598.

―――――

L. Gutiérrez, OP, *Domingo de Salazar, OP: First Bishop of the Philippines, 1512–1594* (2001).

JOHN N. SCHUMACHER, SJ

Salem Witch Trials   The fear and persecution of witches, widespread in Europe from the later Middle Ages onward, reached to Salem Village in Massachusetts, where it burst forth into panic in 1692 at a time of general discouragement in the colony. Beginning with the claim of young girls that they had been bewitched, and abetted by the alarm of the local minister, persons who were chiefly socially

marginal and isolated women were accused, and nineteen, including one minister, were hanged. Another man was executed for refusal to plead guilty. The trials came to an end when accusations were made against prominent citizens and neighboring ministers registered disapproval of the court's proceedings, especially its reliance on "spectral evidence," evidence supplied by those possessed by demons. Many colonists, including Samuel Sewall, who had been a judge in the case, soon came to the realization that innocent persons had been executed. After 1692 such executions ceased.

C. Hansen, *Witchcraft at Salem* (1969); P. Boyer and S. Nissenbaum, *Salem Possessed: The Social Origins of Witchcraft* (1974); M. B. Norton, *In the Devil's Snare: The Salem Witchcraft Crisis of 1692* (2002); B. Rosenthal, *Salem Story* (1993).

DEWEY D. WALLACE JR.

Salmerón, Alfonso (1515–1585), Spanish preacher, biblical scholar, and theologian. Salmerón was one of the first companions of Ignatius Loyola (1491–1556), and he took part in the foundation of the Society of Jesus on September 27, 1540. Born in Toledo, Salmerón enrolled at the Colegio Trilingüe of the Univ. of Alcalá in 1528. In 1533, he left Alcalá with Laínez in order to join Ignatius in Paris. In 1536, Salmerón obtained his master of arts degree under the guidance of Francis Xavier, who was the regent at Collège de Beauvais, Univ. of Paris. He was ordained as priest in Venice the following year. In 1549, Salmerón obtained his doctorate in theology at the Univ. of Bologna. He briefly taught at the Univ. of Ingolstadt (November 1549–August 1550). He introduced the Society of Jesus to Naples, where he became its first provincial, a post he held with brief interruptions from 1558 until 1576. Salmerón participated as a papal theologian in the three periods of the Council of Trent (1545–1547, 1551–1552; 1561–1563). He made a lasting impression in the council for his rhetorical skills, but there is no agreement about his influence on the outcomes of Trent. Salmerón's most important literary contributions were his biblical commentaries, published posthumously by his assistant Bartolomé Pérez de Nueros y Maynar between 1597 and 1602.

W. Bangert, *Claude Jay and Alfonso Salmerón: Two Early Jesuits* (1985); J. W. O'Malley, *The First Jesuits* (1993).

RADY ROLDÁN-FIGUEROA

Salvian of Marseilles (c. 400–c. 480), presbyter and writer. Born to a noble family in the vicinity of either Cologne or Trier, Salvian with his wife Palladia adopted the ascetic life after the birth of a daughter. In the mid-420s he came to the island monastery of Lérins in southern Gaul. He moved to Marseilles in the 430s and probably remained there for the rest of his life. He was a presbyter by 431, though we have no knowledge of his pastoral ministry. Gennadius, writing c. 470, speaks of Salvian as still alive, in a "good old age" (*De viris illustribus* 68). He was the author of several works, though his extant writings consist of only the treatise *To the Church*, nine letters, and his most famous work, the long treatise *On the Governance of God*. This last work, valuable as a historical source for the barbarian raids in Gaul, addresses Christians who harbored doubts about divine providence in the face of collapsing Roman hegemony. It compares the virtues of Romans unfavorably with those of the barbarians, paralleling Roman Christians with the children of Israel in the exodus who tried God's patience and were chastised.

A. Hamman, "L'actualité de Salvian de Marseilles," *Aug* 17 (1977): 378–93; D. Lambert, "The Uses of Decay: History in Salvian's *De gubernatione Dei*," *AugStud* 30 (1999): 115–30.

THOMAS A. SMITH

Samuel von Pufendorf   *see* Pufendorf, Samuel von

Sarpi, Paolo (1552–1623), antipapal historian, Venetian theologian and statesman. He entered the Servite order in 1565, taking the name Paolo. He taught theology and canon law in Mantua and was ordained in 1574. He served as his order's provincial in 1579 and then as procurator-general in Rome (1585–1588). Disenchanted by the Roman curia and the new and powerful order of the Jesuits, he returned to Venice, where he vented his papal animosity, although he served his order as vicar-general from 1599 to 1604. His friendship with Protestants emboldened Venetian inquisitors. As a result, Rome blocked several attractive ecclesiastical appointments. This drove Sarpi to serve the senators of the Venetian Republic as their official counselor. When Paul V overstepped his papal rights by imposing the interdict against Venice in 1606, Sarpi encouraged the Senate to ignore the pope. After Rome mended relationships, he lost senatorial favor. Sarpi published original medical research on the human eye, but his most important work, *Istoria del Concilio Tridentino di Pietro Soave Polano* (*History of the Council of Trent*), published pseudonymously in London (1619), was a vicious attack on Trent as a papal attempt to thwart reform.

J. Lievsay, *Venetian Phoenix: Paolo Sarpi and Some of His English Friends* (1973); D. Wootton, *Paolo Sarpi: Between Renaissance and Enlightenment* (1983).

TIMOTHY MASCHKE

Sattler, Michael (c. 1490–1527), southern German Anabaptist leader and martyr. Born near Freiburg, in Breisgau, Sattler entered the Benedictine monastery of St. Peter and rose to the position of prior. Protestant ideas, however, caused him to abandon the monastic life. He married Margaretta, a Beguine sister, and the couple made their way to Zurich in early 1525. He joined the emerging Anabaptist movement there probably under the influence of William Reublin (1480?–c. 1559). He was expelled from Zurich that November.

Sattler made his way to Strasbourg, where he was initially welcomed by Wolfgang Capito (1478?–1541) and Martin Bucer (1491–1551), the leading reformers there. He also met the Anabaptist leader Hans Denck (c. 1500–1527), but differences in their views soon became apparent. He presented to Capito and Bucer a detailed summary of Anabaptist beliefs, and although these points were discussed with an open spirit, Sattler realized his position in Strasbourg was untenable. He followed Reublin to the Hohenbern area of Württemberg, making his home at Horb and leading an Anabaptist community there.

The Schleitheim Confession of 1527 was undoubtedly penned by Sattler. It called for a sectarian and pacifist church withdrawn from the world. Upon his return home from the Schleithem conference, Sattler and several others were arrested. He was tried at Rottenburg on the Neckar River, cruelly tortured, and then burned at the stake.

C. A. Snyder, *The Life and Thought of Michael Sattler* (1984); J. H. Yoder, *The Legacy of Michael Sattler* (1973).

DAVID B. ELLER

Saturninus   (second cent.) Christian gnostic. The sect named for Saturninus is known in the work of Irenaeus (*Haer.* 1.24.1–2). Followers of Saturninus supposed seven archon (ruler) angels created by the unknown Father. These angels in turn created the world and humanity. At least some, if not all, human beings have the "spark of life" within them from the unknown Father and believe in the Savior. The body, because it was created by inferior angels, is necessarily a corrupt shell for the "spark." The Savior is a formless entity who came in the semblance of a human being to destroy the God of the Jews, who is understood to be an archon bent on destroying the unknown Father. The Savior also came to rescue those who believe in him and to return the "spark of life" that they possess to its original source.

R. Grant, *Gnosticism: A Source Book of Heretical Writings from the Early Christian Period* (1961); W. Foerster, *Patristic Evidence*, vol. 1 of *Gnosis: A Selection of Gnostic Texts* (1972); K. Rudolf, *Gnosis: The Nature and History of Gnosticism* (1983).

RODNEY S. SADLER JR.

Sava of Serbia (c. 1175–c. 1236), youngest son of Stefan Nemanja, grand župan of Serbia, and the first archbishop of an independent Serbian church. Born Rastko, as a youth Sava secretly left his homeland to become a monk on Mount Athos. Despite pressure from his royal family he remained on the Holy Mountain, took the monastic name Sava, and eventually influenced his father to abdicate his throne and become a monk himself. Together father and son established Hilandar monastery, the Serbian monastery on Mount Athos, which would play an incomparable role in the religious and cultural history of medieval Serbia.

Sava was eventually ordained a priest. He then returned to his homeland in 1208 and became abbot of Studenica monastery. He founded monasteries, trained native clergy, and sent missionaries to still largely pagan areas of Serbia. On a diplomatic mission to Nicaea in 1219 Sava was ordained archbishop by the Byzantine patriarch, and the Serbian church was granted independent status. Sava established around ten suffragan bishops in Serbia and continued to build up monastic and liturgical life. Among his writings is a Life of his father, canonized as St. Symeon. His *Nomocanon*, a Slavonic compilation of Byzantine civil and canon law, became the basic constitution of the Serbian, Russian, and Bulgarian churches. After a pilgrimage to Palestine, Sava died in Bulgaria.

D. Obolensky, *Six Byzantine Portraits* (1988), 115–72.

ANDREA STERK

Savonarola, Girolamo (1452–1498), Dominican friar, prophetic preacher, religious and political reformer. A native of Ferrara, Savonarola studied medicine and liberal arts there but entered a Dominican convent in Bologna, becoming a friar in 1476 and being ordained priest in 1477. Biblical exposition occupied him for the next thirteen years as he moved from Ferrara to San Marco, Florence, in 1482, to Bologna in 1487, and back to Florence at the invitation of Lorenzo de Medici in 1490. Elected prior of San Marco in 1491, by 1493 he had established a reformed observant congregation there while at the same time mixing in Florence's elite humanist and religious circles.

A powerful preacher, his fame grew and his message became increasingly apocalyptic in character. When his prophecy of the invasion of a king to bring vengeance upon Italy for her sins appeared to be fulfilled in the invasion of French king Charles VIII in 1494, his popularity grew immensely.

When the unpopular Piero de Medici was expelled from the city, Savonarola took a direct role in Florentine politics and assisted in the 1494 political revolution that saw Florence adopt a structure based on the Venetian pattern. For the next three years he pursued an agenda of religious, social, and political reform. Though he was successful in establishing a system of public welfare, his campaigns against secular festivals and his puritanical measures culminating in the "bonfires of vanities" generated popular opposition, while his pro-French foreign policy alienated Pope Alexander VI and led to a summons to Rome (which he refused), excommunication, and a threat of interdict. Having lost both government and popular support, he was arrested, tortured, and executed on May 23, 1498. His influence endured for some time after his death, however, in the political structure of Florence, in biblical and patristic studies within humanist circles, and in the religious reform movement of "evangelism" that stressed personal spiritual renewal.

L. Polizzotto, *The Elect Nation: The Savonarolan Movement in Florence, 1494–1545* (1994); R. Ridolfi, *The Life of Girolamo Savonarola* (1976); D. Weinstein, *Savonarola and Florence: Prophecy and Patriotism during the Renaissance* (1970).

JOHN TONKIN

Scandinavia, Reformation in Evangelical ideas first reached Scandinavia around 1520. Theologically, the reformation of the Nordic countries was a direct consequence of Luther's reformation in Germany. Politically, the reformation in Scandinavia helped to accelerate the dissolution of the Scandinavian Union, created in 1397, into two territorial or national states, with Denmark and Norway on one side and Sweden and Finland on the other side. The struggle for sovereignty also led the state to try to bring the international Catholic Church under local control, a policy for which evangelical theology provided a justification.

Denmark and Norway. The brutal attempts of the Danish king, Christian II, to expand his control antagonized the lay and ecclesiastical nobility in his realms. In Sweden he had more than eighty members of the Swedish lay and ecclesiastical aristocracy executed in Stockholm in November 1520. The "Stockholm bloodbath" started a revolt led by Gustav Vasa, who in 1523 became king of Sweden. The same year, Christian was forced to leave Denmark and his uncle Duke Frederik of Schleswig became king. Both Vasa and Frederik were positively inclined toward the new evangelical ideas emanating from Wittenberg and wanted to establish a national church under royal control. However, their ideas of a national church were quite different, and thus the early reformation in the two countries developed differently and largely independently. Economic problems as well as dynastic tensions in both countries promoted the support of the evangelical movement. Popular support for Protestantism was at that time stronger in Denmark than in Sweden. In Denmark, the king provided royal protection to the evangelical preacher Hans Tausen in 1526, and Tausen then ordained Jørgen Jensen Sadolin as a minister. Denmark was the first Scandinavian country to establish legally the evangelical movement by a Protestant Church Order, signed by King Christian III in September 1537. The Church Order was written with the assistance of Johannes Bugenhagen, Luther's Wittenberg colleague who had been sent to aid the reformation in Denmark. The Church Order was modeled after the one in Wittenberg and placed the church under the control of the crown. At the same event, Bugenhagen ordained seven new superintendents, who became servants of the government, swearing allegiance to the king.

In Norway the Reformation was rather different, being primarily an act of government. The clergy remained Catholic throughout the Reformation period, and no Lutheran reformer appeared in Norway. The government's policy was determined by the wish to avoid all controversy in religious matters, and government officials were instructed to act cautiously. The first Lutheran superintendent (bishop) of Bergen, Geble Pederssøn, who was ordained in 1537, had been appointed already in 1525 as the Catholic bishop. As it proved impossible to find a Lutheran candidate for the see of Oslo, the Catholic bishop Hans Reff was reappointed as superintendent of Oslo and Hamar in 1541. The archbishopric of Trondheim remained vacant for nine years until Torbjørn Oavssøn Bratt was appointed superintendent in 1546. Apart from Hans Reff, the first generation of Lutheran superintendents in Norway were all Norwegians, as opposed to later in the century when almost all the bishops were Danes. In 1609 Norway got a Church Order of its own, not very different from the Danish one.

Sweden and Finland. Evangelical ideas had reached Stockholm in 1522, where they appear to have been spread by visiting merchants. The German population in Stockholm was soon won over to the evangelical faith and in 1524 recruited an evangelical minister, Nicholaus Stecker, who had studied in Wittenberg. Stockholm and a few towns at the Swedish and Finnish coasts gradually developed some popular support for the Reformation. But the peasantry tried to defend the old church through several rebellions. From the very beginning the struggle for national freedom became linked with the effort to diminish the power of the Catholic Church in Sweden. The king's chancellor, Laurentius Andreae, outlined a new church policy. In 1524 he wrote his well-known letter to the monks in Vadstena in which he declared that the church was the community of believers.

The evangelical movement in Sweden needed a vernacular, evangelical literature; thus, in 1526, on the initiative of Laurentius Andreae, a translation of the New Testament into Swedish was published. The translation was done by a team of scholars, and Laurentius Andreae and Olaus Petri played a central role in organizing the project and writing the preface.

The Diet of Västerås in June 1527, summoned to find a solution to the financial problems of the government, resulted in a statute of Västerås that permitted the crown to confiscate superfluous church property. The king avoided making any important changes in religion, but the parliament decided that the word of God should be purely preached in Sweden. But it was not until 1544, during the Succession Parliament, which also met in Västerås, that the king and the representatives of the estates promised never to deviate from "the teachings that have become accepted" and to take action against "those who argue against such Christian teachings or try to suppress them." At this occasion the clergy debated ecclesiastical ceremonies and agreed to remove some ancient rites, such as the adoration of saints, the use of holy water and incense, requiem Masses, and a number of Catholic holidays. In Sweden the apostolic succession was preserved because the Catholic bishops were allowed to stay in office, but they had to approve changes in ceremonies. In 1531 a new archbishop of Uppsala was appointed: Laurentius Petri, a member of the evangelical party and a brother of Olaus. It was the marriage of the king that made it important to show that the church was well-organized. The church of Sweden gradually developed in a Lutheran direction, but more Catholic elements remained in it than in any other Lutheran churches.

In Finland the Reformation followed to a great extent the developments in Sweden. Young Finnish theologians who had studied at German universities brought Reformation ideas home with them. The first evangelical bishop of Åbo was Martin Skytte (1528–1550). Michael Agricola (1510–1557), the main reformer of Finland, studied in Wittenberg from 1536 to 1539. The principle that the word of God had to be preached in the mother language of the people forced the creation of a written Finnish language. In 1548 the Finnish New Testament, revised by Agricola, was published.

There is no doubt about Luther's great significance for the first generation of Swedish and Finnish reformers. All the leading Swedish and Finnish reformers, with the exception of Laurentius Andreae, had studied in Wittenberg and had met Luther.

The translation of Luther's works also shows his influence in Scandinavia. In Denmark nineteen titles with twenty-eight editions appeared. In Sweden and Finland the only translation that appeared during Luther's lifetime was of his Small Catechism.

L. Grane and K. Hørby, eds., *The Danish Reformation against Its International Background* (1990); O. P. Grell, ed., *The Scandinavian Reformation: From Evangelical Movement to Institutionalisation of Reform* (1995); Grell, "Scandinavia," in *The Reformation World*, ed. A. Pettegree (2000), 257–76.

INGUN MONTGOMERY

Schleitheim Confession An early Swiss Brethren (Anabaptist) doctrinal statement, the Confession was named after an area in the canton of Schaffhausen where an early Anabaptist congregation emerged. The first Anabaptist synod convened at Schleitheim in early 1527 and adopted seven brief articles known as the "Brotherly Union" (*Brüderlich Vereinigung*), undoubtedly written by the former Benedictine prior Michael Sattler (c. 1490–1527), who had joined the Anabaptists in 1525. The articles discussed the importance of believers' (adult) baptism, excommunication (the ban), observance of the Lord's Supper as a memorial, separation from the world, the role of shepherds (pastors or teachers), loving pacifism (nonresistance), and the nonswearing of oaths.

The articles reflect the centrality of Scripture for Sattler and others at the synod but were not a comprehensive statement of Christian beliefs, nor were they adopted by Anabaptist groups that emerged in northern Germany and the Netherlands, or in Moravia. The importance of the Brotherly Union is that it set forth a unique set of beliefs and practices that helped give a clearer definition to subsequent Swiss Brethren development in Switzerland and southern Germany.

The Confession clearly distinguishes between citizenship and participation in Christ's kingdom and avoiding an evil kingdom—the world—ruled by Satan. There is no connection between these realms, and faithful Christians must isolate themselves from everything that is "outside the perfection of Christ." The Schleitheim articles thus offered a vision of a true church where obedience to Christ is normative. They called for a church without power or protection, defenseless before the world, a church withdrawn and separated from the wider society.

C. A. Snyder, "The Influence of the Schleitheim Articles on the Anabaptist Movement: An Historical Evaluation," *Mennonite Quarterly Review* 63 (1989): 323–44; Snyder, *Anabaptist History and Theology: An Introduction* (1995).

DAVID B. ELLER

Schmalkald League This was a defensive alliance of significant Protestant estates of the HRE established as a result of the 1530 Diet of Augsburg and lasting until 1547. Among the founding members, along with the Electors Saxony and Hesse, were three mid-German princes, the two counts of Mansfeld, and eleven cities from Strasbourg to Bremen. By 1535 six further cities, two princes of Anhalt, two dukes of Pomerania, and Duke Ulrich of Württemberg joined the league. In 1537 Duke Heinrich of Saxony and his son Moritz joined.

The league was the most significant power in the empire opposed to imperial plans for a central monarchy. With this orientation the league had the sympathies of the Catholic princes. The league was for purely defensive purposes. Its members were to protect one another in case any one of them should be attacked "on account of the pure Word of God." Luther, who originally rejected such an alliance on theological grounds, allowed himself to be convinced by the jurists that the legal position of the imperial princes and imperial cities legitimated the alliance.

A high point of the league was the restoration of territory to Duke Ulrich of Württemberg and thus its assignment to the Protestant faith. Without the power of the league, the expulsion of King Ferdinand of Bohemia, brother of the German emperor, would not have been achieved.

After 1541 the league stagnated because of opposing interests among the major Imperial princes and the southern German cities. At the same time there were tensions between the major leaders in Electoral Saxony and Hesse. Although the league had been founded without confessional definition, further potential members from imperial legal and Calvinist territories such as Denmark and Prussia were not accepted for confessional reasons.

T. A. Brady, *Protestant Politics: Jacob Sturm (1489–1553) and the German Reformation* (1993); H. Scheible, *Das Widerstandsrecht als Problem der deutschen Protestanten, 1523–1546* (1969).

MARTIN TREU

Schmalkald War (1546–1547) To stem the advance of the Reformation in the HRE and to strengthen his own monarchical position, Emperor Charles V decided to confront the Schmalkald League with military force. The temporary respite from war with France and the Turks, and the collapse of all the religious colloquies in the empire, provided Charles with the opportunity to act on this decision. Protestant refusal to attend a council called by Pope Paul III provided Charles with a further excuse. According to his statements, Charles did not treat his action as a religious war but as the enforcement of the imperial ban against Electoral Saxony and Hesse who, in a preventive war against Braunschweig, had taken Duke Heinrich the Younger of Braunschweig-Wolfenbüttel prisoner.

The war played out in two phases. After the Schmalkald League proved ineffective in containing the weaker powers of the emperor in

Regensburg and in hindering their union with papal troops, there was an indecisive battle at Ingolstadt. League troops then withdrew to northern Germany.

In the spring of 1547, King Ferdinand, together with Duke Moritz invaded Electoral Saxony. Moritz, a member of the Schmalkald League, went over to the imperial side with the promise he would receive the title of elector of Saxony. In the battle at Mühlberg on April 24, 1547, Elector Johann Friedrich was taken prisoner by Charles V's Spanish troops, and the war ended. Johann Friedrich and Philip of Hesse were placed in imperial custody.

The emperor inflicted harsh punishment, especially in the southern German cities. Protestant pastors had to leave the country, but the restoration of Catholicism proved to be impossible. In the Saxon and Hessian territories the resistance to the reimposition of Catholicism was even stronger. At the same time, the Catholic princes took a stand against the expansion of the central power of the emperor in the empire.

W. Held, *Die Schlacht bei Mühlberg an der Elbe* (1997); E. Wolgast, *Die Wittenberger Theologie und die Politik der evangelischen Stände* (1977).

MARTIN TREU

Scholasticism Scholasticism is an approach to the historiography of medieval philosophy which is motivated by the idea that it is possible to single out certain basic features that differentiate medieval philosophy from ancient and modern philosophy. It emphasizes the unity and homogenity of medieval thought over and against its pluralism. Starting from the middle of the nineteenth century, various scholars have attempted to characterize this unity, but no one has succeeded in clearly defining what scholasticism is. Most of these attempts have taken a doctrinal perspective and present the second half of the thirteenth century as the pinnacle of medieval scholasticism.

The dominant model of scholasticism up until a few decades ago assumed that medieval thinkers were basically interested in the same spheres of inquiry as philosophers today—logic, epistemology, philosophy of science, ethics, metaphysics, psychology, and natural theology—that their main shared concern was the reconciliation of faith and reason, and that Thomas Aquinas was its focal point. Etienne Gilson even claimed that scholastic philosophy was *Christian* philosophy. According to Gilson,

Christianity expanded the horizon of the patrimony of ancient philosophy. On account of their Christianity, scholastic thinkers were provided with new philosophical themes, which they embedded within their theology.

In contrast to this view, most modern historians of medieval philosophy have discarded a doctrinal model of scholasticism. For one thing, they believe that it unduly focuses on one single topic, namely, that of the relation between reason and faith. Although the theme is an important one, it certainly was not the only one that worried medieval thinkers. Moreover, the concept of Christian philosophy can also be attached, and perhaps with more reason, to the seventeenth century, when philosophers made a concerted effort to establish a *philosophia christiana*. In addition, it overlooks important elements of Jewish and Arabic philosophy in medieval Latin philosophy.

Precisely because of all these unwarranted connotations, and also because of the wealth of new texts that reveal the sheer variety and heterogenity of medieval philosophy, contemporary scholars employ the term "scholasticism" with caution. Instead, they prefer to refer to *medieval* philosophy in the sense of philosophy that was practiced during the Middle Ages and to reserve the term "scholasticism" as the characterization of a *method*. Two essential features of this method were (1) the acceptance of authoritative literature in several domains of learning, and (2) the way in which this literature was handled. Medieval thinkers generally developed their own thought in relation to that of their predecessors, rather than stressing their own originality. They believed that texts from past traditions played an instrumental role in their search for truth. They invested these texts with *auctoritas*, or authority. In the field of theology, the Bible was the most authoritative text. It contained a concealed truth, which had to be discovered by means of clever exegesis, supported by the writings of the church fathers and the councils.

Discrepancies among the "authorities" were the focus of works such as Peter Abelard's *Sic et Non* and Peter Lombard's theological textbook the *Sentences* (see *Four Books of Sentences*). Both works were collections of thematically organized opinions of authoritative authors that were tackled with various tools of interpretation and analysis. In the fields of philosophy, medicine, or law the attitude toward authorities was slightly different, though the method of approach was the same. There, authorities such as Aristotle, Galen,

Gratian, or Justinian were considered important representatives of a living tradition who had to be treated with respect but whose views were not necessarily true. The authoritative sources of reflection could and did contain errors, which had to be exposed and discussed.

The interpretation and critical questioning of the authoritative sources—in other words, hermeneutics—relied on an array of technical tools that were derived from medieval logic and semantics. Examples of such tools are (1) the making of distinctions, such as between simply true and true from a certain perspective (*simpliciter* and *secundum quid*) and (2) the analysis of the literal meaning of a text and its authorial intention or of the use of terms within the context of a proposition, and the effects this has on its meaning.

The introduction of scholasticism as a method is associated with the availability of Greek and Arabic texts in Latin and the role they played at the nascent universities, and it is chronologically situated at the beginning of the thirteenth century. The philosophical material that was translated mainly consisted of texts by Aristotle and of ancient commentaries on them. This ancient legacy was disseminated in the Latin West through university teaching. By the middle of the thirteenth century almost all known works by Aristotle were compulsory reading and teaching in the curricula of all universities. Teaching practice was characterized by reading the set texts, commenting on them, and disputing about them. The *quaestio*, or question, was the most widely used format and came to be the icon of the scholastic method. It was not a genuinely open question but a question induced by a source text (e.g. Aristotle's *Ethics*), which allowed the commentator to present his own views with respect to a certain issue.

Not all philosophical works that were produced during the Middle Ages were the fruit of the scholastic method, though the majority were, due to the dominant role of academic, that is, university-related, philosophy. This institutional factor also explains the continuity of scholasticism in certain parts of Europe up until the seventeenth century.

During the Renaissance and the early modern period the technical nature of scholasticism came to be increasingly perceived as an obstacle to the advancement of learning and became the object of ridicule and hostile attacks. This reaction toward scholasticism, however, went hand in hand with a doctrinal indebtedness and a shared interest in many of the same topics. During the nineteenth century, under the aegis

of Pope Leo XIII, a revival of scholasticism took place that is generally known as neoscholasticism. It had a profound impact upon the official Roman Catholic view of the harmony between reason and faith. The movement found its inspiration in the thought of Thomas Aquinas and played a crucial role in rekindling the interest in and study of medieval philosophy. (See *Aristotle and Medieval Theology*; *Aristotle, Translations of; Universities, the Rise of; Mendicant Schools*)

———

J. A. Aertsen and A. Speer, eds., *Was ist Philosophie im Mittelalter?* (1998); R. Ariew, *Descartes and the Last Scholastics* (1999); L. M. De Rijk, *La philosophie au moyen âge* (1985); R. French, *Canonical Medicine: Gentile da Foligno and Scholasticism* (2001); J. Inglis, *Spheres of Philosophical Inquiry and the Historiography of Medieval Philosophy* (1998); J. Marenbon, *Later Medieval Philosophy (1150–1350)* (1991); R. Schönberger, *Was ist Scholastik?* (1991).

J. M. M. H. THIJSSEN

Schütz Zell, Katharina (1498–1562), Protestant lay reformer of Strasbourg. She received a good vernacular education but never learned Latin. Devout from childhood, she was unable to feel assured of her salvation until she was converted to freedom from fear by the Lutheran teaching of Matthew Zell, to become a "fisher of people." She married Zell in 1523 and defended her action (she was one of the first women to break canon law by marrying a priest) with an *Apologia* (*Entschuldigung*) in 1524. The two established a remarkable partnership in ministry. Besides active pastoral service, Schütz Zell also wrote a letter to *The Women of Kentzingen* (1524) to encourage them in their biblical witness; an exposition of the Lord's Prayer for two women of Speyer seeking to know how to please God (1532); a hymnbook (*Lobgsäng*; 1534–1536) to help laity teach their households; a sermon-lament at Zell's burial (*Klag red*; 1548); personal meditations on the Psalms; a long letter to Caspar von Ossig Schwenkfeld (1553) affirming friendship but refusing to be identified as his disciple (unpublished until 1999; Schütz Zell has long been considered a Schwenkfelder, but that view must be now revised); a defense of her faith (*Ein Brieff*, a remarkable source for the early Reformation in Strasbourg; 1557) to Ludwig Rabus, who accused her of heresy; and a final devotional booklet (*Den Psalmen Miserere*; 1558).

E. A. McKee, *Katharina Schütz Zell*, vol. 1, *The Life and Thought of a Sixteenth-Century Reformer* (1999); vol. 2, *The Writings, a Critical Edition* (1999); McKee, *Popular Piety in Sixteenth-Century Strasbourg: Katharina Schütz Zell and Her Hymnbook* (1994); McKee, *Church Mother: The Writings of a Protestant Reformer in Sixteenth-Century Germany* (2006).

ELSIE MCKEE

Schwenckfeld, Caspar von Ossig

(1489–1561), Silesian nobleman and lay theologian. An early adherent of the Lutheran Reformation, he helped institute Protestant reforms in Silesia in 1522. However, developing a more mystical view of the Christian life, Schwenckfeld began to question Luther's ideas about a saving faith. By 1525 he had rejected the Lutheran concept of real presence (the body and blood of Jesus present in the elements of the bread and wine) for an inward and spiritualist understanding of the Lord's Supper. The following year he called for a suspension of the Eucharist until, through God's will, all could agree in love and unity. The Marburg Colloquy (1529) among Luther, Zwingli, and others on the Lord's Supper dismissed Schwenckfeld's views.

He went into self-imposed exile in 1529, finding refuge for a few years in Strasbourg. Here he was in conversation with the city's leading reformers, Martin Bucer (1491–1551) and Wolfgang Capito (1478?–1541). He also met with various Anabaptists, including Pilgram Marpeck (c. 1495–1556) and Melchior Hoffman (1495?–1543). Forced to leave Strasbourg in 1534, he traveled to Ulm but was soon on the move again. He spent his remaining years in the Ulm-Augsburg area, writing extensively and guiding various conventicles of believers who shared his ideas.

Schwenckfeld considered spiritual rebirth and inner experience of Christ to be essential but outward rituals and creeds to be unnecessary because they are not a means to salvation. Although Schwenckfeld held that no new church should be organized, a handful of his followers from Silesia immigrated to eastern Pennsylvania, near Philadelphia, in the 1730s, where the Schwenckfelder Church was organized in 1782.

P. C. Erb, *Schwenkfeld and Early Schwenkfelders* (1986); E. R. McLaughlin, *Caspar Schwenkfeld, Reluctant Radical: His Life to 1540* (1986); A. Séguenny, "Caspar von Schwenkfeld," in *The Reformation Theologians,* ed. C. Lindberg (2002).

DAVID B. ELLER

Scillitan Martyrs

North Africa's first-known martyrs are twelve Christians who were beheaded at Carthage on July 17, 180. Their story, extant in three Latin "acts" and a Greek one, consists almost exclusively of the official transcript of the final session of a trial conducted by P. Vigellius Saturninus, governor of Africa Proconsularis 180/181, in the *secretarium* at Carthage.

Saturninus's questioning of six of the martyrs (Speratus, Nartzalus, Cittinus, Donata, Secunda, and Vestia), reveals that they had with them "books and the letters of Paul, a just man," providing unique evidence for second-century (Old Latin?) biblical codexes, including a collection of Paul's epistles. The abrupt beginning of the proconsul's interrogation indicates that this was not the first time that Speratus and his five companions had appeared before him (or before some other official). Saturninus's judgment applies also to six other, but not yet mentioned, Christians (Veturius, Felix, Aquilinus, Laetantius, Januaria, and Generosa). These six, according to the governor, had, like the rest, refused to conform to his demands. Consequently, they must have been interrogated at an earlier session not recorded by the *acta*. Whether, like the others, they also came from the still-to-be-located North African town called "Scilli" (or, more likely, "Scillium"), as implied by the title of these *acta*, is probable but not certain.

H. Musurillo, *The Acts of the Christian Martyrs* (1972), 86–89.

WILLIAM TABBERNEE

Scots Confession

The first confession of faith of the Reformed Church of Scotland. The confession was drafted by six ministers, including John Knox, and was endorsed by the Scottish Parliament in 1560 and 1567 and officially approved by King James VI in 1581. Written in twenty-five articles, the confession is broadly Calvinist. Scripture is recognized as the sole authoritative standard of religious truth. Justification by grace through faith, excluding merit but entailing sanctification through the power of the Holy Spirit, is affirmed. The true "catholic" church is identified as the multitude of persons chosen by God for salvation, known to God alone, of which Christ is the only head. True "particular" churches are characterized by right preaching of God's word, right administration of the sacraments (baptism and Communion), and maintenance of ecclesiastical discipline to promote virtue. Infant baptism is approved, as is the teaching that through the sacraments suitable partakers are united with Christ. Transubstantiation and belief that the sacraments are "bare signs" are rejected. Magistrates are identified as lieutenants of God, obligated to use their authority to promote true religion. The Scots Confession retained its official status in the Church of Scotland until the Westminster Confession of Faith was adopted in 1647.

J. H. S. Burleigh, *A Church History of Scotland* (1960); J. Pelikan and V. Hotchkiss, eds., *Creeds and Confessions of Faith in the Christian Tradition* (2003).

DANIEL EPPLEY

Scotus, John Duns (c. 1266–1308), Franciscan theologian. He was ordained as a priest on March 7, 1291, at St. Andrews Priory, Northampton, in the diocese of Lincoln. He studied at Oxford and commented on the *Sentences* of Peter Lombard there c. 1299 and at Cambridge (date unknown). From 1302 to 1303 he lectured in Paris, to which he returned in 1304 after a brief spell of exile, due to a dispute between the French king Philip the Fair and Pope Boniface VIII over church taxation. In 1305 he became the Franciscan regent master of theology at Paris, from which he was transferred in 1307 to the Franciscan studium in Cologne.

Scotus's major work is his *Commentary on the Sentences*, which has a complex textual tradition. Its first version in two books, known as the *Lectura*, was begun at Oxford. This version was revised and expanded into the *Ordinatio* (in earlier editions known as the *Opus Oxoniense*). Yet another version originated in the form of student notes at Paris, the *Reportationes Parisienses*. The relationship between the second and third versions is controversial and further complicated by the inclusion of additions from students and secretaries who attempted to complete Scotus's work. Other important works are his *Quodlibetal Questions* and his commentaries on Aristotle's *Categories, De interpretatione, Sophisticis Elenchis, Metaphysics*, and *De anima*.

Scotus is mainly known as a theologian who employed a highly theoretical method of analyzing theological and philosophical problems (hence his nickname "the Subtle Doctor"). The best known among the "tools" he used is the formal distinction, created by the mind, but having some kind of being in the extramental world (*res*). He was an advocate of the theory of consubstantiation, according to which Christ's body is present in the Eucharist because it comes to exist in the same place as the substance of bread, rather than converting the substance of bread (transubstantiation). He also laid the foundation of the dogma of the immaculate conception of Mary. In philosophy, he is credited with creating a new theory of modalities, an analysis of the notion of possibility, and works of innovative metaphysics. He broke with the tradition of applying analogically the concepts of "being" to God, creation, substance, and accidents and instead advanced a theory of the univocity of being. The issue in this controversy was whether "being" can be applied to, for instance, creatures just in the same sense as to God. Thinkers such as Thomas Aquinas and Henry of Ghent believed that "being" was used in a different, though related, sense for God and creatures. According to them, "being" was an analogous term. Scotus, however, argued that "being" was a univocal term, which was applied in the same sense to creatures and to God.

R. Cross, *Duns Scotus* (1999); Duns Scotus, *Opera Omnia, studio et cura Commissionis Scotisticae ad fidem codicum edita* (1950–); L. Honnefelder, R. Wood, M. Dreyer, eds., *John Duns Scotus, Metaphysics and Ethics* (1996); T. Williams, ed., *The Cambridge Companion to Duns Scotus* (2003); A. B. Wolter, OFM, *The Philosophical Theology of John Duns Scotus* (1990).

J. M. M. H. THIJSSEN

Scythian Monks In 518, a group of monks in Scythia became involved in a dispute with the Scythian bishops. The monks accused the bishops of heresy because they opposed a theopaschite formula, "one of the Trinity was crucified," which the monks were proposing as a necessary addition to the christological formula of the Council of Chalcedon (451) to remove any suspicion of Nestorianism. Bishop Paternus of Tomi and four monks led by John Maxentius brought the dispute to Constantinople. When the imperial court was unable to reconcile the monks and their bishop, the monks decided to go to Rome to appeal directly to Pope Hormisdas. He rejected their appeal and ordered them to disband and leave Rome.

Justinian initially opposed the theopaschite formula as an innovation. By 520, when the monks returned to Constantinople, its introduction as a means for the Chalcedonian party to express its belief in the personal unity of Christ had become imperial policy. The Scythian monks continued as a small but vocal group in Constantinople with imperial protection. They maintained a rivalry with the more popular Acoemetae (sleepless) monks and were instrumental in their condemnation in 534 as Nestorians. The greatest significance of the Scythian monks is their attempt to turn a theopaschite formula to the defense rather than the attack of Chalcedon.

Works of John Maxentius, in PG 85 (1860).

EUGENE M. LUDWIG, OFM CAP.

Sebaste, Forty Martyrs of (d. c. 320)

Roman soldiers who refused to recant their faith during the reign of Licinius in the city of Sebaste in Armenia (Sivas in present-day Turkey). Although no contemporaneous records document this martyrdom, Basil of Caesarea, Gregory of Nyssa, and others describe the event. Earlier scholars accepted the purported eyewitness account of the *Testament of the Forty Martyrs of Christ* as authentic. Although this work is still used devotionally, it is a later composition.

According to the sources, Licinius decreed Christianity illegal and the governor of Cappadocia ordered all Christian soldiers to renounce their faith. Forty refused and the governor ordered them stripped and taken to a frozen lake to lie on the ice until they either died or recanted. Every soldier remained steadfast, except one. The bravery of the thirty-nine so moved one guard that he confessed his faith and joined the others. By morning all were dead. The bodies were burned and the ashes thrown into the river. Local Christians collected the ashes, distributed them, and within fifty years the Forty Martyrs were venerated throughout the Roman world.

Basil, *In Sanctos Quadraginta Martyres*, in PG 31 (1857), 507–26; Gregory of Nyssa, *In Laudem SS. Quadraginta Martyrum*, in PG 46 (1858), 49–788; H. Musurillo, ed., *The Acts of the Christian Martyrs* (1972).

WILLIAM B. SWEETSER JR.

Sebeos

Since the mid-nineteenth century this name has been employed to designate the author of an Armenian history of the Near East extending from the end of the fifth through the mid-seventh centuries CE, although affinities between the work and Sebeos, bishop and signatory of the acts of the Synod of Duin in 645, are rather tenuous. Extant manuscripts all derive from a codex of 1672 from the Amirdolu Monastery near Bitlis, a well-known scriptorium of historical works. The received text evinces several problematic readings and is transmitted together with accounts of the Armenian ethnogenesis and origin of the Mamikonian house, which are really independent. This narrative of the transition from late antiquity to Islamic rule in the region is of considerable significance as one of the few contemporary non-Muslim sources. Its account is divided into three phases: the first two trace the background and course of the penultimate (572–591) and final (603–630) Perso-Roman wars, the latter focusing on the reign of Khusro II and the campaigns of the emperor Heraclius, while the third documents the overturning of this binary geopolitical polarity through Muslim conquests from Syria/Palestine through Mesopotamia and Persia into Anatolia.

Approaching the latter from the apocalyptic tradition of the book of Daniel that is characteristic of one strand of early Armenian historiography, the work views it ominously as divine punishment visited on the sins of the Christian community. The book exerted an important influence on Armenian historians from the tenth century onward.

R. Thomson, trans., *Armenian History Attributed to Sebeos* (2000).

S. PETER COWE

Second Reformation see *Reformation, Second*

Secular Clergy

The secular clergy were responsible for the administration of the sacraments to the laity. The term "secular" means that these men lived "in the world" (*saeculum*) rather than in communities that followed a rule (*regula*) (see *Regular Clergy*). The secular clergy were the subordinates of a bishop, from whom they received holy orders. During the Middle Ages, the boundaries were sharpened between the lay and clerical state: although secular clerics were allowed to own property, they could be judged only in ecclesiastical courts, and those in major orders were increasingly expected to be celibate. Clerics wore the tonsure as a distinguishing mark of their status.

Due to the prestige of the monastic life, the secular clergy had to struggle against a sense of inferiority to the regulars. In the later Middle Ages, the prestige of the secular clergy increased because the eucharist and masses for the dead were increasingly central to lay spirituality, because the seculars controlled the universities, and because the rights and duties of parish priests were more sharply defined. The controversy with the mendicant orders over pastoral care highlighted ongoing tensions between the regular and secular modes of life.

R. Brentano, *The Two Churches: Italy and England in the Thirteenth Century* (2nd ed., 1988); R. N. Swanson, *Religion and Devotion in Europe, c. 1215–c. 1515* (1995); J. Shinners and W. J. Dohar, eds., *Pastors and the Care of Souls in Medieval England* (1998).

VICTORIA M. MORSE

Sedulius (fl. 425–450), Latin poet. Sedulius's life is poorly documented, but he apparently lived in Italy and Greece and wrote in the second quarter of the fifth century. His major work is the *Carmen Paschale*, a gospel epic in five books. Book one recounts select OT miracles; the remainder presents Christ's life from infancy through ascension. Sedulius knew Juvencus's gospel epic and creatively engaged the classical poetry of Virgil, Ovid, and Lucan. His didactic aims are evident, first, in his selection of OT episodes that could be understood to prefigure Christ and NT scenes that highlighted Christ's power and, second, in his insistence upon Nicene orthodoxy and a fully divine Christ. Sedulius was no less alert to the theological debates crystallized by Arius and Nestorius than to the pagan literary traditions he inherited. Sedulius also wrote a prose version of the *Carmen*, the *Opus Paschale*, and two hymns on salvation history and Christ's life. Venantius Fortunatus considered Sedulius as an influence, and the *Carmen*, known to Bede, Aldhelm, and Alcuin, was very influential through the Middle Ages.

J. Huemer, ed., *Sedulii opera omnia* (1885); C. Springer, *The Gospel as Epic in Late Antiquity: The "Paschale Carmen" of Sedulius* (1988); P. Van der Laan, "Le *Carmen Paschale* de Sédulius," in *Early Christian Poetry*, ed. J. den Boeft and A. Hilhorst (1993).

DENNIS E. TROUT

Sedulius Scottus (fl. 840s–870s), poet, grammarian, and exegete, one of the most brilliant scholars of the mid-ninth century. He arrived on the Continent about 845 and joined an Irish colony at Liège in the Carolingian middle kingdom. His major work on ethics, *De rectoribus christianis*, has recently been identified as having been written about 868–869 for Charles the Bald, when the western Frankish prince gained the kingship of the middle kingdom; Sedulius thus appears during the years 868–875 as the "propagandist" (Staubach) of the new king and future emperor. Among his commentaries on classical grammarians, his works on Donatus, Priscianus, and Eutyches are known, as well as a commentary on Porphyry's *Isagoge*, which is an introduction to the logic of Aristotle. Manuscript 8407 of the Bibliotheque de l'Arsenal at Paris contains a Greek Psalter written by Sedulius. His broad range of interests is clear in his excerpts from classical, biblical, and patristic texts; that the only complete manuscript, the *Collectanea*, was part of Nicholas of Cues's library, suggests its ongoing influence. His poems dedicated to members of the royal family, to bishops, and to others show his many relationships and reveal his skill in the liberal arts. His biblical commentaries on Matthew and Paul are comparatively short, but they are far more than simple abbreviations of commentaries of the type written by Hrabanus Maurus and others. Sedulius had no remarkable career and never became abbot of a monastery. Traces of his teaching and education are also found in northern Italy, and he may have worked toward the end of his life as a teacher there.

S. Scottus, *On Christian Rulers, "De Rectoribus Christianis," and the Poems*, trans. E. G. Doyle (1983); CCCM 40B–C (1977); D. Simpson, ed., *Collectaneum miscellaneum*, in CCCM 67 (1988–1990); Simpson, ed., *Kommentar zum Evangelium nach Matthaus*, in *VL*, supplements 14, 19 (1989–1991); H. J. Frede, ed., *Collectaneum in Apostolum* in *VL*, supplements 31–32 (1996–1997). R. Düchting, *Sedulius Scottus: Seine Dichtungen* (1968); M. Lapidge and R. Sharpe, *A Bibliography of Celtic-Latin Literature* (1985), 177–80; J. Meyers, *Le classicisme lexical dans la poésie de Sedulius Scottus* (1994); D. Shanzer, "A New Edition of Sedulius Scottus' Carmina," *Medium aevum* 63 (1994): 104–17; N. Staubach, *Rex christianus: Hofkultur und Herrschaftspropaganda im Reich Karls des Kahlen* (1993), 105–221.

JOHANNES HEIL

Seekers An essentially mystical and anarchic orientation emerging in the context of seventeenth-century Puritanism. Seekers were mainly drawn from the unlearned, which included alienated individuals who withdrew from various forms of institutional religion. Seekers withdrew from church structures in the apparent belief that the true church was defunct and its rituals and ordinances invalid. Charismatic and nonrevolutionary in orientation, Seekers waited patiently for a new dispensation that God would establish in his own time. Some Seekers eventually merged with the Friends (Quakers).

W. C. Braithwaite, *The Beginnings of Quakerism* (1912); J. F. McGregor and B. Reay, *Radical Religion in the English Revolution* (1984).
                                                        JOHN TONKIN

Semi-Pelagianism The term was coined in the seventeenth century to describe a theological perspective on grace, predestination, and free will that flourished in the fifth century, especially in Gaul. From 418 it found expression among persons who had difficulty accepting either Pelagius's defense of absolute free will or Augustine of Hippo's views on predestination. An early spokesman for this position was John Cassian, whose *Conference* 13 is his attempt to find a moderate position between the extremes of Pelagianism and predestination. Although he affirms the necessity of grace for salvation, Cassian argues that in some cases the good will precedes the work of grace. This position, shared by the monks of the nearby island monastery of Lérins, became widespread in Gaul, as the partisans of Lérins became a prominent ecclesiastical faction. The most well-developed expression of these views came from Faustus of Riez. Gallic bishops assembled for the synods of Arles (473) and Lyons (474), both of which condemned as heretical the views of an overtly predestinarian priest named Lucidus, and selected Faustus to write a tract that presented the bishops' position. The result was Faustus's *On Grace*.

Not all Gauls were Semi-Pelagians, and at the turn of the next century, one prominent figure, Avitus of Vienne, voiced stern opposition to the doctrine. The long conflict was resolved in 529 at the Second Council of Orange, over which Caesarius of Arles, an Augustinian trained at Lérins, presided. The council adopted a form of Augustinianism that had been modified by prolonged engagement with its Gallic opponents.

R. A. Markus, "The Legacy of Pelagius: Orthodoxy, Heresy, and Conciliation," in *The Making of Orthodoxy: Essays in Honour of Henry Chadwick*, ed. R. D. Williams (1989), 214–34; R. H. Weaver, *Divine Grace and Human Agency: A Study of the Semi-Pelagian Controversy* (1996).
                                                ALLEN E. JONES

Seneca the Younger (c. 4 BCE–65 CE), philosopher and statesman. During the reign of Claudius he was exiled to Corsica on the basis of an adultery charge. Empress Agrippina recalled him to Rome to tutor her son Nero, whom he subsequently served as political advisor. Implicated in the Piso conspiracy (the plot of Gaius Calpurnius Piso to have Nero assassinated) Seneca was forced to commit suicide. He wrote extensive treatises on natural history, geography, and ethics as well as nine tragedies adapted from Greek plays. Indeed, his ethical writings greatly contributed to the popularity of Stoicism in ancient Rome. He firmly believed in divine providence and insisted that the virtuous man could never be unhappy. Seneca looked upon anger as the greatest vice, considering it temporary insanity. Death is not an evil and may even be a good. A collection of Latin apocryphal letters between Paul and Seneca, known to both Jerome and Augustine, were forged in the fourth century apparently for the purpose of linking Christianity to the classical literary tradition. During the sixth century, Martin, bishop of Braga, used Seneca's works extensively in writing his own *On Anger*. Martin also wrote the widely circulated *Rules for an Honest Life*, which was published as a work by Seneca.

Seneca, *Works*, trans. J. W. Basore et al., 10 vols., LCL (1968–79); G. G. Strem, *The Life and Teaching of Lucius Annaeus Seneca* (1981).
                                        KENNETH B. STEINHAUSER

Septuagint The letter attributed to Aristeas recounts the Septuagint's legendary origin: in the third century BCE at the request of the Egyptian ruler Ptolemy II, the Pentateuch was rendered into Greek by seventy-two Jewish translators. Some traditions give the number of translators as seventy, which led to the designation "Septuagint" (from the Latin for "seventy") and the abbreviation "LXX." Gradually the term "Septuagint" came to refer to the Greek translation of the entire Hebrew Bible.

Moreover, the Septuagint also contains books originally written in Greek (e.g., 2 Maccabees), others translated from a no-longer-extant Hebrew version (e.g., 1 Maccabees, Judith), and "Greek additions" to books in the Hebrew Bible (e.g., Susanna, Bel and the Dragon). Although Aristeas's letter asserts that the Septuagint was produced to fulfill Ptolemy's desire to add the Pentateuch to the holdings of the renowned library in Alexandria, it was surely created to meet the needs of Greek-speaking Jews in Egypt.

The Septuagint is significant not only for textual study of the Hebrew Bible but also for NT and patristic studies because it is the earliest Christian Old Testament. Its importance for the early church (not least in debates with Jews when the Septuagint differed in critical ways from the Hebrew) led some to expand upon Aristeas's account, thereby bolstering the Septuagint's authority even more. Thus, for example, Irenaeus (*Haer.* 3.21.2) claimed that the seventy translators, although physically isolated from one another, each produced exactly the same text, thereby confirming the Septuagint's divine inspiration.

––––––

M. Hadas, ed., *Aristeas to Philocrates* (1951); S. Jellicoe, *The Septuagint and Modern Study* (1968); S. M. Paul et al., *Emanuel: Studies in Hebrew Bible, Septuagint, and Dead Sea Scrolls in Honor of Emanuel Tov* (2003); A. Pelletier, *Lettre d'Aristée à Philocrate* (1962); *Septuaginta: Vetus Testamentum Graecum* (1931–); B. A. Taylor, *X Congress of the International Organization for Septuagint and Cognate Studies* (2001).

ANGELA RUSSELL CHRISTMAN

Sepúlveda, Juan Ginés de (1490–1573), Spanish theologian, philosopher, and jurist. He studied at the Univ. of Alcalá (1510–1513), the Colegio de San Antonio de Sigüenza (1513–1514), and the Spanish College at Bologna (1515–1523), where he completed his doctorate in theology. His translations of Aristotle's works include *De mundo* (1523), *Meteorum libri IV* (1532), and *Politica* (1548). A skilled polemicist, he also wrote works against Luther (*De fato et libero arbitrio contra Luterum*, 1526), Erasmus (*Antapología pro Alberto Pío in Erasmum*, 1532), and Henry VIII (*De ritu nuptiarum*, 1531). In the service of Charles V as chronicler and chaplain (1536), Sepúlveda took on the cause of the emperor and, eventually, of the Spanish crown. Accordingly, he defended the right of conquest over the indigenous population of the New World. As a consequence, an intense and prolonged debate ensued between Sepúlveda and Bartolomé de las Casas (1474–1566), climaxing in the inconclusive council of Valladolid of 1550 called by Charles V.

––––––

L. Hanke, *All Mankind Is One: A Study of the Disputation between Bartolomé de las Casas and Juan Ginés de Sepúlveda in 1550* (1994); L. R. Pagán, *Violent Evangelism: The Political and Religious Conquest of the Americas* (1992).

RADY ROLDÁN-FIGUEROA

Serapion of Thmuis (d. after 362), a fourth-century Egyptian bishop and ally of Athanasius. He had served as abbot of a monastic community before being named bishop of Thmuis in the Nile Delta. He was a disciple and friend of Antony, and a source for certain stories in Athanasius's *Life of Antony*. According to Jerome's *On Illustrious Men*, Serapion was well respected for his learning. In 353 Athanasius tapped Serapion for a delicate diplomatic mission to Emperor Constantius.

Serapion is best known as a recipient of Athanasius's treatises. Around 360 Serapion asked Athanasius how to counter arguments posed by those who denied the divinity of the Holy Spirit. Athanasius answered with four landmark treatises: *Letters on the Holy Spirit.* Serapion had also received from Athanasius the Festal Letter of 339 and an account of the death of Arius. Several texts attributed to Serapion have come down to us: a treatise, *Against the Manichees*; a handful of letters, including one preserved only in Syriac and Armenian, written to console two monks on the occasion of Antony's death; and a collection of thirty prayers, the so-called *Sacramentary of Serapion.* The *Sacramentary* offers rare glimpses into the liturgical life of mid-fourth-century Egypt, but Serapion's contribution remains a matter of dispute.

––––––

D. Brakke, *Athanasius and Asceticism* (1998); M. E. Johnson, *The Prayers of Sarapion of Thmuis* (1995).

WILLIAM HARMLESS, SJ

Serbian Orthodox Church see Sava of Serbia

Serdica, Council of Convoked in 342 or 343 as an ecumenical council in Serdica (modern Sofia), it split into two councils that anathematized each other. When the Eastern bishops

discovered that the Westerners meant to overturn the previous condemnations of Athanasius of Alexandria, Marcellus of Ancyra, and Paul of Constantinople, they departed to the nearby city of Philoppopolis. There they issued a lengthy recrimination of Julius of Rome, Ossius of Cordova, and the bishops with them for communing with heretics and favoring Monarchianism. The so-called fourth creed of Antioch (341) was appended to their letter. Meanwhile, the Western bishops, under the leadership of Protagenes of Serdica and Ossius of Cordova, exonerated Athanasius and the others and proceeded to condemn those at Philoppopolis.

The Greek and Latin versions of the Westerners' encyclical letter are found in Athanasius (*Apol. sec.* 44–49) and Hilary of Poitiers (*Adversus Valentem et Ursacium*), respectively. It is noteworthy, however, that the "creed" of Serdica is found only in two later versions of the encyclical, as preserved in Theodoret (*Hist. eccl.* 8.1–52) and *Codex Verona* LX (58), fols. 81^r–88^r (*EOMIA* I. 645–53). The insinuation is that the primary concern of the council was about ecclesiastical politics and only indirectly about doctrine.

R. P. C. Hanson, *The Search for the Christian Doctrine of God* (1988); S. G. Hall, "The Creed of Sardica," StPatr 19 (1989), 173–84.

                              D. H. WILLIAMS

Sergius of Radonezh (c. 1314–1320),

Russian monastic reformer, contemplative, and saint. Born in Rostov with the name Bartholomew, his father was the boyar Cyril, who was forced to move his family to Radonezh, a village twenty-five miles northwest of Moscow. After the death of his parents, Sergius and his brother Stephen removed to the forests near Radonezh, where they established a chapel dedicated to the Holy Trinity. There they lived the solitary life until Stephen, unable to endure the solitude, left for Moscow. At age twenty-three, Bartholomew was tonsured Sergius by Abbot Metrophanes. He continued to live the eremitic life for several years until a loosely organized community, called a skete, developed around him. He was persuaded to adopt the Stoudite monastic rule that established cenobitic (community) life at Holy Trinity Monastery. He also adopted Athonite hesychasm (mystical quietness). Holy Trinity became the model for a Russian monastic resurgence that had been suppressed during Tartar invasions. He had great influence over all levels of society, stopped four civil wars, and sup-

ported Grand Prince Dmitri of Moscow in his successful resistance to the Tartars in 1380. In 1378 he was offered and refused the metropolitan see. During his lifetime he established forty monasteries throughout Russia but left no writings. Canonized sometime before 1449, he is generally considered the greatest Russian saint.

G. P. Fedotov, "St. Sergius of Radonezh," in *The Russian Religious Mind*, vol. 2, *The Middle Ages: The 13th to the 15th Centuries* (1966); "St. Sergius: The First Hermit and Mystic," in *A Treasury of Russian Spirituality*, ed. G. P. Fedotov (1965); S. Hackel, "Late Medieval Russia: The Possessor and the Non-Possessors," in *Christian Spirituality* (1987); P. Kovalevksy, *Saint Sergius and Russian Spirituality* (1976).

                              MICHAEL D. PETERSON

Servetus, Michael (1511–1553), physi-

cian, condemned heretic, a native of Navarre. Servetus's biblical studies led him to reject Trinitarian dogma. He published his views in a treatise, *De Trinitatis erroribus libri VII* (1531). The book outraged both Catholics and fellow Protestant theologians, who condemned it. In 1532, Servetus responded with his *Two Dialogues on the Trinity*, which asserts that the church had turned from Jesus during subsequent years of doctrinal development.

Servetus moved to Paris to study medicine. His discovery of the pulmonary circulation of the blood was his greatest scientific achievement. While in Paris, he began an anonymous correspondence with John Calvin, who recognized Servetus from his writings and condemned his Antitrinitarian views. Servetus sent Calvin his major work, *Christianismi restitutio* (1553) that fully explained his theology. In addition to rejecting the Trinity, Servetus claimed that Christ's humanity was made up of three elements: the Logos, conceived as the model of all created things, and not divine; the soul; and the human body. When Calvin responded by sending him a copy of his *Institutes*, Servetus replied with insults. Calvin then indirectly notified the Inquisition at Lyon, and Servetus was captured and imprisoned but escaped to Geneva. In Geneva, he disguised himself and attended Calvin's church, but he was recognized and arrested. He was burned at Champel on October 27, 1553.

R. H. Bainton, *Hunted Heretic: The Life and Death of Michael Servetus (1511–1553)* (1953); J. Friedman, *Michael Servetus: A Case*

Study in Total Heresy (1978); A. G. Kinder, *Michael Servetus* (1989).

ELIZABETH GERHARDT

Sethians Like the Cainites, the Sethians took the name of a son of Adam whom they identified as demonstrating exemplary characteristics. For them, Seth was the epitome of virtue, demonstrating what it meant to be a righteous and just human being, and the father of an elect race of people from whom the Sethians were descended. Seth was not just an early biblical figure. He was Jesus the Christ himself and continues to be a persistent salvific presence among human beings. Sethians believed that the world was created through the interaction of three sentient principal elements in hierarchical relationship: light above, pneuma (spirit) between, and darkness below. The resulting heavens and earth are shaped like a womb, which gives birth to the hosts of living creatures. There are two competing deities for Sethians: the perfect father, who gave the mind to human beings so that they can overcome darkness and human bodies, and the Father below, who is the God known in the Hebrew Scriptures. Salvation consists of being cleansed by drinking a pure spring water, of refusing to serve the Father below who is the God of Scripture and a violent and ferocious wind, and of putting on heavenly clothes. The sacred writings of this group include *The Secret Book (Apocryphon) of John*, *The Reality of the Rulers*, *The Revelation of Adam*, and *Three Forms of First Thought*.

W. Barnstone, ed., *The Other Bible: Ancient Alternative Scriptures* (1984); W. Barnstone and M. Meyer, eds., *The Gnostic Bible* (2003); B. D. Ehrman, *Lost Scriptures: Books That Did Not Make It into the New Testament* (2003); J. M. Robinson, *The Nag Hammadi Library in English*, (4th ed., 1996); K. Rudolf, *Gnosis: The Nature and History of Gnosticism* (1983).

RODNEY S. SADLER JR.

Seuse, Heinrich (c. 1295–1366), Dominican mystic. Seuse, declared blessed in 1831, is known for his poetic, sensitive mysticism and theology of *Gelassenheit*, or "yieldedness to God." From a wealthy, religious family, Seuse (or Suso) was educated by the Dominicans. After his conversion at eighteen, he practiced extreme asceticism, eventually pursuing reduced self-mortification in his search for enlightenment. After ordination he studied in Cologne (1324–1327) with Meister Eckhart and

was accused for defending his "heresies." A traveling preacher and writer in southern Germany, the Rhineland, and the Netherlands, Seuse provided pastoral care for the Dominican sisters in the area. Suspected of heresy, he moved to Ulm in 1348 and finished his popular *The Little Book of Truth* and *The Little Book of Wisdom*.

J. M. Clark, *The Great German Mystics: Eckhart, Tauler, and Suso* (1969); E. M. Filthaut, *Heinrich Seuse: Studien zum 600 Todestag, 1366–1966* (1966); J. Hardin, "Heinrich Seuse," in *German Writers of the Renaissance and Reformation, 1280–1580* (1997).

KIRSI STJERNA

Severinus (c. 410–c. 480), patron of Austria. Although circumstantial evidence indicates he may have been African or Roman, the Life of Severinus relates only that he came from the east (perhaps Egypt) to evangelize Noricum (present-day Austria) at the time of the death of Attila the Hun (453). Despite his repeated attempts to live as a hermit, he attracted so many followers that he founded a number of monasteries.

Although tradition holds that Severinus healed the sick, ransomed captives, and was an advisor to local kings, his Life stresses his efforts on behalf of the poor and his ability to foretell the future. He is said to have preached a sermon that caused a rich woman to distribute her wealth to the poor during a famine and to have predicted, during a series of invasions, the fall of several towns after the inhabitants refused to follow his command to pray for deliverance. His prediction of his own death and the subsequent removal of all Romans from Noricum was fulfilled when Odovacer occupied the province six years after Severinus's death and expelled the Roman inhabitants. The refugees took his body with them to Italy, and ultimately to Naples in 910, where the Abbey of San Severino was built as his shrine.

L. Bieler, trans., *Life of Saint Severin by Eugippius* (1965).

WILLIAM B. SWEETSER JR.

Severus of Antioch (c. 465–538), Monophysite bishop of Antioch (512–528). Severus studied in Alexandria and Berytus (Beirut). Soon after his baptism in 488 he became a monk. He was influenced by the Monophysitism of Peter the Iberian, and in 508 he traveled to Constantinople to seek support for Monophysite monks there. When Flavian was deposed as bishop of Antioch in 512, Severus ascended to the see. He rejected the Council of Chalcedon (451) and spent most of his time producing anti-Chalcedonian polemic; however, Severus also confronted the radical Monophysitism represented by Julian of Halicarnassus and Sergius the Grammarian. He claimed to represent the Christology of Cyril of Alexandria, as did Leontius of Jerusalem. The rise of the orthodox emperor Justin I resulted in Severus's removal from office. He traveled first to Egypt, where he lived under the protection of the Monophysite Timothy of Alexandria, and then to Constantinople, where he joined in Justinian's failed attempt to reconcile Chalcedonians and Monophysites. Afterward, Severus was sent back into exile in Egypt, where he died. Because of his excommunication his works survive only in Syriac translations.

CSCO (1903–), 93–94 (1929), 101–2 (1933), 112–13 (1938), 119–20 (1949), 133–34 (1952), 244–45 (1964), 295–96 (1968), 301–2 (1969), and 318–19 (1971); R. Chesnut, *Three Monophysite Christologies* (1976); W. H. C. Frend, *The Rise of the Monophysite Movement* (1972); J. Lebon, *Le Monophysisme sévérien* (1909); I. R. Torrance, *Christology after Chalcedon* (1988).

STEVEN A. MCKINION

Sexuality, Early Christian Sexuality was a contentious topic among early Christians. This situation was due partly to ambivalent attitudes in Greco-Roman society and partly to conflicting tendencies within early Judaism. From Judaism Christians inherited a belief in the essential goodness of creation and the human body. Jewish tradition also emphasized, however, the centrality of procreation and, therefore, strongly condemned homosexual activity and adultery. Moreover, apocalypticism, which greatly influenced the first Christians, stressed the imminence of a "new creation" and thus subordinated all sexual activity to the future life. Such a view is reflected in this saying of Jesus: "Those who belong to this age marry and are given in marriage; but those who are considered worthy of a place in that age and in the resurrection of the dead neither marry nor are given in marriage" (Luke 20:34–35).

From Greco-Roman culture Christians inherited ambivalent attitudes toward sexuality. . Stoic moralists tended to be strict, forbidding extramarital relations and restricting sex to procreation (e.g., Musonius Rufus). Some medical writers believed that celibacy made the body stronger and healthier, whereas the emission of seed caused the loss of life-giving spirit (e.g., Soranus, Galen). Differences of gender and social status also were crucial in determining the morality of sexual acts in the Greco-Roman world. For a male head of the household to make sexual use of male or female slaves was widely regarded as unproblematic. The same acts by a Roman matron, however, were considered reprehensible. Legal custom enshrined this double standard, which Christians had difficulty changing.

Christianity extended and intensified the ambivalence about sex in Judaism and the Greco-Roman world. Sexual purity played a significant role in establishing and maintaining social boundaries between Christians and non-Christians. The apostle Paul, for example, traced the origin of homosexual activity to the practice of idolatry (Rom. 1:24–27). There were reports that some early Christians engaged in sexually promiscuous rituals, but for the most part Christians were distinguished by their sexual restraint. In the second century the pagan physician and philosopher Galen noted that many Christians lived exemplary lives of perpetual celibacy.

Sexual asceticism continued to hold a significant place throughout the early Christian period. Celibacy was often given theoretical justification by means of interpretations of Genesis. Thinkers such as Origen, borrowing from Philo and Middle Platonic philosophy, argued for a two-stage creation. Originally God made humankind spiritual; human bodies (and hence sexual differentiation) emerged only after the fall. While Origen did not reject the body as evil, he tended to view sexuality as a distraction from spiritual existence. This approach to human origins influenced subsequent Christian thought, both orthodox and heretical. More radical Christians, such as the Encratites, took this connection between sexuality and sin as a reason for rejecting sexual behavior altogether.

There were, however, more moderate currents in early Christian thought. In the early fourth century the distinguished orator Lactantius discussed the origins and purpose of human sexuality. For Lactantius the making of the human body and its procreation through sexual relations were part of God's original providential design of creation. The very intensity of sexual desire was a sign that God wished human beings to "increase and multiply" (*Divine Institutions* 6.23.2). It is the devil, Lactantius argued, who distorts natural desire and directs it toward illicit and unnatural sexual activity.

In the early years of the fifth century, Augustine developed an interpretation of human sexuality that combined different features of these earlier traditions. Against the Origenist view, Augustine argued that humans were originally created to be physical, even sexual, persons. God intended sexual intercourse to be the normal means of propagating the human race (*Literal Commentary on Genesis* 9.9.14; *City of God* 14.23). On the other hand, Augustine held that the sin of Adam and Eve had profoundly damaged human nature. Human beings now experience in their bodies an "animal instinct" (*bestiale motum*) that was not present in the original creation. This "concupiscence" or "lust of the flesh" works against the conscious, rational desires of the human mind. Thus, postlapsarian sexuality became, for Augustine, a symptom of the more fundamental dislocation or alienation of humanity from God that resulted from the fall.

B. Brooten, *Love between Women: Early Christian Responses to Female Homoeroticism* (1996); E. Clark, *St. Augustine on Marriage and Sexuality* (1996); P. Brown, *The Body and Society: Men, Women, and Sexual Renunciation in Early Christianity* (1988); M. Foucault, *The Care of the Self,* vol. 3 of *The History of Sexuality* (1986); A. Rouselle, *Porneia: On Desire and the Body in Antiquity* (1988).

DAVID G. HUNTER

Shenoute of Atripe (c. 348–465), monk, prolific author. The leader of the White Monastery (a modern appellation) in Upper Egypt, near Sohag, for nearly eight decades (385–465) after having joined about 371, Shenoute produced voluminous writings which survive in fragmentary form. There is as yet no critical edition of either his public sermons and correspondence (the *Discourses*) or his monastic literature (the *Canons*). Both the monastery and Shenoute's leadership were interconnected with their surrounding environs. His writings are an abundant source of information about the relationship between monasticism, orthodox Christianity, and both pagan and heretical religion in this remote region. Shenoute was an active and sometimes violent crusader against what he saw as wrongful religious practices. He served as a voice for Alexandrian theology in Upper Egypt and even traveled to the Council of Ephesus in 431. Nevertheless, he thought of himself primarily as a monk. He united three geographically disparate monastic communities (two male and one female, totaling several thousand cenobites), as well as local hermits, under his strong and authoritarian leadership. Shenoute remains an important saint in the Coptic Orthodox Church. His feast day is July 14.

Besa, *Life of Shenoute,* trans. D. Bell (1983); R. Krawiec, *Shenoute and the Women of the White Monastery* (2002); S. Emmel, "Shenoute the Monk," in *Monasticism between the Inheritance and the Future,* Fiftieth Anniversary Symposium of the Monastic Institute, Pontificio A. S. Anselmo, Rome (2002), 151–74.

REBECCA KRAWIEC

Shroud of Turin The shroud is a linen cloth with bloodlike stains and front and back images of a naked man, beaten, pierced many times in the head, once in the side, and punctured through hands and feet. The cloth appeared around 1357 in the collegiate church of Lirey, France, but is unreported before that date. It attracted pilgrims and gifts because it conformed to Gospel accounts of the execution and burial of Jesus. Its veneration aroused immediate alarm because no authenticating documents accompanied it. It was judged inauthentic and its display was prohibited; the resulting furor elicited papal intervention, and the cloth was again exhibited with the caveat that it was a representation of Jesus' shroud, not the true shroud. The canons of Lirey entrusted the shroud to the De Charny family, who never returned it. In 1453 it was given to the House of Savoy. The shroud became an object of intense private devotion at Chambéry until 1506, when Julius II authorized an official cult. In 1578 it was transferred to Turin. Photographs made in 1898 showed the impressions on the cloth were like photographic negatives, thought impossible for medieval artists to render. Examiners concluded the image was that of a man subjected to treatment consistent with accounts of Jesus' execution, but authenticity was not established. Although analysis has been hindered by inaccessibility, carbon 14 tests were permitted in 1988; three independent laboratories dated the cloth between 1260 and 1390.

I. Wilson, *The Shroud of Turin* (1978); H. Kersten and E. R. Gruber, *Das Jesus Kommplott* (1992).

LORNA SHOEMAKER

Sickingen, Franz von (1481–1523), German knight and political agitator. Born into a wealthy Palatinate noble family, Sickingen served his Elector as a soldier and government official until 1515. For the next two years he carried out several military campaigns for personal territorial or financial gain. After 1518 he was a field commander for the emperor but became a supporter of the Reformation, largely to further his own dynastic and economic agendas. He did promote reform of the church in his lands and offered the Ebernburg castle as a refuge to Luther and other reformers. Luther declined the offer. In 1522 Sickingen began a military campaign against the archbishop of Trier, ostensibly for the sake of the gospel. His true objectives were likely the creation of his own principality and his social elevation to princely status. His efforts failed when he was besieged by Hesse, the Palatinate, and Trier in 1523. Seriously wounded, he succumbed to his wounds on May 7, the day of his surrender. Sickingen was a bold political figure whose ideals were clouded by personal ambition.

K. H. Rendenbach, *Die Fehde Franz von Sickingens gegen Trier* (2nd ed., 1965); H. Ulmann, *Franz von Sickingen* (1872).

KURT K. HENDEL

Sidonius Apollinaris (c. 430–485), Gallo-Roman aristocrat, man of letters, and bishop of Clermont. Born at Lyon into a well-connected family when Gaul was divided between German kings and Roman emperors, with Emperor Eparchius Avitus (455–456) as an eventual father-in-law, Sidonius attained the Urban Prefecture at Rome (468) under Emperor Anthemius. His poetry, collected in 469, reveals creative adaptation of such traditional occasional genres as the panegyric and the wedding poem (*epithalamium*). In his youth he was already influenced by the monastic ideals emanating from Lérins. During a period of retirement in the 460s he was baptized by Faustus of Riez and studied theology under Claudianus Mamertus. Consecrated bishop of Clermont in 470, he organized resistance to the Gothic advance, although the city was eventually ceded to the Goths and Sidonius temporarily confined by King Euric. His letters, modeled on those of Pliny and published between 477 and 481, and his poems illustrate the dynamic tensions of political and social life in late-Roman Gaul. As German kings effectively replaced Roman emperors, other Gallo-Roman aristocrats found similar outlets for their aspirations at German courts and in the church.

W. B. Anderson, ed. and trans., *Sidonius: Poems and Letters*, 2 vols. (1936); A. Loyen,

ed. and trans., *Sidoine Apollinaire: Poèmes, Lettres*, 3 vols. (1960, 1970); J. Harries, *Sidonius Apollinaris and the Fall of Rome* (1994).

DENNIS E. TROUT

Siger of Brabant (c. 1240–c. 1284), Flemish member of the faculty of arts at the Univ. of Paris (c. 1266–1276), portrayed by nineteenth- and early twentieth-century scholarship as an Averroist and the leader of a radical minority of the arts faculty. The thirteen articles condemned on December 10 by the bishop of Paris, Étienne Tempier, allegedly directed at Siger and his associates, were summarized by Mandonnet (1911) as: the negation of providence, the affirmation of the eternity of the world and the unity of the human intellect, and the suppression of moral liberty. More recently, Van Stehenbergen (1977), Gauthier (1983 and 1984), and Putallaz and Imbach (1997) have, on the basis of closer examination of Siger's work itself, recast his persona as an early advocate of the freedom of philosophers in the arts faculty to teach the pure doctrine of Aristotle, as opposed to altering controversial points to agree with the truths of the Catholic faith. The radical adherence to the letter of Aristotle's physical writings resulted in Siger's teaching the Averroist doctrine that Aristotle posited one universal, separate intellect by which every individual human being derives the ability to form universal concepts. While he was to change his view in his later commentary on the *Liber de causis* (*Book of Causes*), most likely influenced by Thomas Aquinas's polemical *On the Unity of the Intellect* as well as by the condemnations of 1270, Siger nonetheless came under censure by the more far-reaching and important condemnations of March 7, 1277, of Bishop Tempier.

Scholars are divided as to whether, confronting imminent arrest, Siger returned to Liege near his home, only later coming to the court of Pope Nicholas IV in Orvieto, or whether he went immediately in 1276 to Orvieto to put his case directly before Pope John XXI. Siger is reported to have been stabbed to death by his mentally deranged secretary.

R.-A. Gauthie, "Notes sur Siger de Brabant, I. Siger en 1265," *Revue des sciences philosophiques et théologiques* 67 (1983): 201–32; F.-X. Putallaz and R. Imbach, *Profession: Philosophe. Siger de Brabant* (1997); J.-P. Torrell, *The Person and His Work*, vol. 1 of *Saint Thomas Aquinas* (1996); F. Van Steenbergen, *Maitre Siger de Brabant* (1977).

MARK DAMIEN DELP

Sigibert I and Brunichilde

Sigibert I and Brunichilde Merovingian king and queen of Austrasia. Sigibert (d. 575) received a fourth of his father Clothar I's lands (561). His reign was marked by constant battles with his brother Chilperic, king of Neustria. A Visigothic princess, Brunichilde (d. 613) converted from Arianism to Catholicism upon their marriage. Her sister wed Chilperic but was soon found strangled, a death blamed upon Fredegund, one of Chilperic's wives. This led to continuous bad blood between the queens. In 575, after winning a decisive battle against Chilperic, Sigibert was killed with poisoned knives by Fredegund's soldiers.

Sigibert's stepmother, Radegunde, had him get part of the true cross for her monastery at Poitiers (569). Brunichilde was also profoundly religious, corresponding with Gregory the Great, aiding Columbanus and Augustine of Canterbury, and founding many monasteries.

After Sigibert's assassination, Brunichilde saved her son Childebert, who became king of Austrasia, but she was imprisoned. Upon beholding the prisoner, Merovech, Chilperic's son, fell in love and married her. However, Chilperic separated them and put Merovech under house arrest. Merovech fled and later had himself killed in order to escape his father (578). Brunichilde returned to Austrasia and, after the death of Childebert, governed for her grandsons. Upon their deaths she attempted to govern for her great-grandson but was forced into exile. Fredegund's son, Lothar II, had her tortured for three days, then forced her to ride naked on a camel, then had her tied to a horse and dragged to her death.

G. Bordonove, *Les Rois qui ont fait la France: Clovis* (1988); R.-X. Lanteri, *Brunehilde: La Première Reine de France* (1995).

MARIANNE M. DELAPORTE

Simon Magus

Simon Magus (first cent.), magician. In the New Testament, Acts 8:9–24 records the conversion of Simon by Phillip and Simon's subsequent encounter with Peter and John. Simon had acquired a considerable following in Samaria because of his impressive magical powers. Therefore, later Christian writers gave him the designation *Magus* ("magician"). In the ancient world, a magician did not simply perform deceptive tricks, but was considered to be a healer, a fortune teller, and a transmitter of spiritual knowledge and power. Impressed by the outpouring of the Holy Spirit when Peter and John met with the Samaritan converts, Simon wanted to buy the capability to confer the Holy Spirit. Peter and John rebuffed his misguided attempt to purchase spiritual power and urged Simon to repent. The term "simony," referring to the practice of buying or selling spiritual power, derives from this incident.

The church fathers Justin Martyr, Irenaeus, and Hippolytus link Simon with heretical groups, while other early Christian writings report confrontations between Simon and the apostle Peter. The apologist Justin Martyr wrote that Simon came to Rome accompanied by his wife, a former prostitute named Helen. He attracted a following in Rome with his magic and by claiming to be a "great power." The second-century *Acts of Peter* describes a contest between Peter and Simon in which Peter overcomes the Samaritan magician by praying to God. Later the Pseudo-Clementine literature has Peter confronting Simon in Antioch. Some scholars believe that the third-century heresiologist Hippolytus used extracts from a work by Simon himself to link Simon with primitive gnostic speculation. Others question this connection.

T. Adamik, "The Image of Simon Magus in the Christian Tradition," in *The Apocryphal Acts of Peter*, ed. J. Bremmer (1998), 52–64; W. A. Meeks, "Simon Magus in Recent Research," in *RelSRev* 3 (1977): 137–42.

JAMES BRASHLER

Simon, Richard

Simon, Richard (1638–1712), French Catholic pioneer of historical-critical study of the Bible. After completing studies in theology and Oriental languages at the Sorbonne in 1662, he joined the Oratory and began teaching philosophy at the order's college in Juilly. From 1663 until 1678, he worked as a librarian for the Oratorians in Paris, during which time he was also ordained as a priest. The *Critical History of the Old Testament*, which he completed in 1678, stirred up controversy among Catholics because it questioned the reliability of the Latin Vulgate translation. It also cast doubts on the reliability of the chronology of parts of the Old Testament and claimed that a group of public scribes, rather than Moses, authored most of the Pentateuch. Bishop Bossuet had the book confiscated and burned. Simon was ousted from his religious order. He returned to Dieppe, the city of his birth, where he worked on another book, his *Critical History of the Text of the New Testament*, which was published in Rotterdam in 1689. Protestants also criticized his books because they cast doubts on traditional theories of biblical inspiration.

S. L. Greenslade, ed., *The Cambridge History of the Bible* (1963); R. Steinmann, *Richard Simon et les origines de l'exégèse biblique* (1960).

ERIC LUND

Simons, Menno (1496–1561), leader of the Dutch Anabaptists. Simons, while not the founder of the Anabaptist movement in the Netherlands, gathered the remnants of the Anabaptists after the fall of Münster (1535) and united them into what became known as the Mennonite church. Born the son of a farmer in the province of Friesland in 1496, Menno was ordained a priest in Utrecht. Little is known of his early education, but from his writings it appears that he knew Latin, had some familiarity with Greek, and had read some of the fathers of the early church. In his later writings, Menno indicates that he had some doubts about his role as a priest and had come into contact with Sacramentarians in nearby Emden who denied the doctrine of transubstantiation. Over the next decade, Menno remained a priest, but he also followed the great religious debates of the day. He read Erasmus, Luther, Zwingli, and the defenders of the Roman Catholic Church. As he explained later, his method was to compare their writings with Scripture. By the end of the 1520s, Menno had decided that Scripture alone was the authority for the church and that both the Catholics and the Protestants had failed to remain true to the Scriptures.

In the early 1530s, Menno, still a parish priest, was exposed to the work of Melchior Hoffman, the furrier and lay preacher who brought the practice of adult baptism to the Netherlands. Hoffman's preaching was popular in Friesland and Emden, regions which had already seen the spread of Sacramentarian ideas. Hoffman also preached the imminent return of Christ and the end of the world. After Hoffman was imprisoned in 1533, many of his followers fell under the leadership of Jan Matthiis and Jan of Leyden, who called Christians to gather in Münster to await the second coming of Christ. These Anabaptists took over and ruled the city from 1534 to 1535, when they were defeated by the combined forces of the bishop of Münster and Philip of Hesse.

The remnants of Hoffman's followers, the peaceful "Melchiorites," influenced Menno, and in early 1536 he left his position as priest and began long years of travel through the Low Countries and the HRE. Shortly after leaving the priesthood, although the exact date is uncertain, Menno came into contact with Dirk and Obbe Philips, peaceful Melchiorites who convinced Menno to be baptized as an adult. Menno quickly became a respected leader for the remnants of the Dutch Anabaptists and spent the rest of his life establishing new Anabaptist congregations and revitalizing old ones.

He was also called upon to settle disputes among the Anabaptists. Under his guidance, the violent and chiliastic Anabaptists were gradually banned from congregations, leaving behind a more moderate form of Anabaptism. In the middle of the sixteenth century, Anabaptist congregations began to recover from the Münster disaster and to unite under Menno's leadership. The churches under Menno's guidance practiced a Christian discipleship based on a strict interpretation of the New Testament. Those who could not live according to the standards of the community were banned from church. Menno also espoused Hoffman's Christology, that Christ was more divine than human and that he passed through Mary's body like light passes through water. Later Mennonites would abandon this Christology.

Little is known of Menno's family, but he did marry sometime after his second baptism. He and his wife had at least three children. Menno died in 1561 after twenty-five years of almost constant traveling and preaching.

C. J. Dyck, ed., *A Legacy of Faith: The Legacy of Menno Simons* (1962); A. Friesen, *Erasmus, the Anabaptists, and the Great Commission* (1998); C. Krahn, *Dutch Anabaptism: Origin, Life, and Thought, 1450–1600* (1968); L. Verduin and J. C. Wenger, eds., *The Complete Writings of Menno Simons, c. 1496–1561* (1956); S. Voolstra, "Menno Simons (1496–1561)," in *The Reformation Theologians*, ed. C. Lindberg (2002), 363–77.

AMY R. CALDWELL

Simplicianus of Milan (d. c. 400), priest, Ambrose's successor as bishop of Milan, and friend of Augustine. He was an important participant in intellectual and religious circles in the second half of the fourth century, first in Rome where he knew the philosopher Marius Victorinus and had some influence on his conversion to Christianity (Augustine, *Conf.* 8.2–5) and then in Milan where he certainly knew Ambrose well and may have had a part in his baptism (since Augustine calls him Ambrose's father "in the receiving of grace"; *Conf.* 8.2). He is best known for his role in spurring Augustine's conversion by telling of Victorinus's example (*Conf.* 8.2–5) and for his correspondence with others on matters of theology and especially biblical interpretation (Ambrose, *Letters* 37, 38, 65, 67; Augustine, *Letter* 37 and *Ad Simpl.*), although none of his own letters survive. He succeeded Ambrose as bishop of Milan in 397, perhaps as Ambrose's handpicked successor. Eighty years after his death, however, he was remembered especially for having urged Augustine to devote his talent and time to expounding Scripture (Gennadius of Marseilles, *Vir. ill.* 36).

P. Courcelle, *Recherches sur les 'Confessions' de saint Augustin* (1950); Paulinus of Milan, *Life of Ambrose*, in *The Western Fathers*, ed. F. R. Hoare (1954).

WILLIAM S. BABCOCK

Siricius (d. 399), bishop of Rome from 384. After succeeding Pope Damasus, Siricius continued his predecessor's policy of promoting the authority of the see of Rome. Siricius's letters are the earliest surviving examples of papal decretals (*decretalia*), directives written in the style of imperial edicts. He spoke of the apostle Peter acting through the ministry of the bishops of Rome (*Epistula* 1.1) and claimed to exercise "care over all the churches" (*Epistula* 6.1). In practice, Siricius's decrees were directed only to bishops in the western provinces of Gaul, Spain, and Africa, and to Bishop Anisius of Thessalonica.

Siricius was especially concerned with the discipline of the clergy. He attempted to enforce a regular sequence of clerical promotion and to require celibacy of deacons, presbyters, and bishops. Siricius also tried to limit the entry of monks into the episcopacy by insisting that they spend time in the lower ranks of the clergy. In 385 Siricius presided over the trial and expulsion of Jerome from Rome, earning his abiding contempt (Jerome, *Epistula* 45.2, 127.9). Siricius also condemned Jerome's opponent, the monk Jovinian, for equating marriage and celibacy. Siricius was buried in the cemetery of Priscilla on the Via Salaria.

P. Coustant, ed., *Epistulae Romanorum Pontificum* (1721), 623–700; Coustant, *Epistolae et decreta*, PL 13 (1845), 1131–78; Coustant, *Liber Pontificalis*, 40; C. Pietri, *Roma Christiana* (1976); J. T. Shotwell and L. R. Loomis, *The See of Peter* (1927, repr. 1965).

DAVID G. HUNTER

Sirmium, Synods of These fourth-century synods dealt with the question of the divinity of Christ. Sirmium was a residence of emperors in ancient Pannonia (modern Serbia). The synod of 351 condemned an allegedly Sabellian bishop, Photinus of Sirmium, "whose insanity was by no means mild" (Epiphanius, *Pan.* 71). The First Creed of Sirmium was fostered by the condemnation of twenty-seven heretical theses, the first of which declared that those who said the Son was "from another substance and not from God, and that there was a time or age when He was not, the holy Catholic Church regards as aliens" (Hilary, *De synodis* 38). In 357, another synod rejected the key Nicene word "consubstantial" (*homoousios*). The synod's designation "blasphemy of Sirmium" comes from Hilary's assessment of Ossius of Cordova's signing of this subordinationist creed (*De synodis*, 11). The synod in 358 marked the temporary triumph of the Homoian party (so called because it held that that the Son was "like" [*homoios*] the Father). The Dated Creed of May 22, 359, attempted reconciliation by suggesting to drop the problematic talk about God's essence (*ousia*) altogether. In 378, there was probably another synod in Sirmium, which championed the Nicene cause again and pledged allegiance to the troublesome term "consubstantial."

R. P. C. Hanson, *The Search for the Christian Doctrine of God* (1988); J. N. D. Kelly, *Early Christian Creeds* (3rd ed., 1981).

TARMO TOOM

Sixtus II, bishop of Rome (257–258), probably of Greek origin, martyr. Sixtus II was martyred together with his deacons while celebrating liturgy. His "baptism by blood" took place during the persecution of Valerian, which was directed specifically against the insubordinate Christian clergy. Although he is venerated as a martyr, Sixtus's significance lies in his reestablishment of the relationship between Rome and North Africa, which had deteriorated because of the uncompromising stance of his predecessor, Pope Stephen I. The controversial issue was the necessity of rebaptism. Sixtus, in principle, affirmed the validity of baptisms administered by heretics, as long as these were properly performed in the name of the Trinity. Perhaps by allowing a peaceful coexistence of different practices, Sixtus managed to promote a spirit of reconciliation between the more liberal Rome and the less tolerant African and Anatolian sees. Pontius, Cyprian's biographer, called Sixtus "a good, peace-making priest" (*Life of Cyprian* 14).

Nothing has survived from Sixtus's literary heritage, except an Armenian fragment of his letter to Dionysius of Alexandria. Rufinus of Aquileia mistakenly considered him to be the author of the *Sentences of Sextus*, a second-century collection of maxims. Eusebius mentions Sixtus in various lists (*Hist. eccl.* 5.6, 7.5) and Cyprian announced Sixtus's martyrdom to African churches (Letter 80).

R. Davis, ed., *The Book of Pontiffs (Liber Pontificales)* (2nd ed., 2000).

TARMO TOOM

Sixtus IV (1414–1484), Franciscan theologian and preacher, patron of the arts, elected pope in 1471. The anomaly of a Franciscan whose coronation tiara cost more than a third of the Holy See's annual income epitomizes the paradox of Sixtus IV, whose pontificate highlighted the progressive secularization of the papacy and its unabashed embrace of the Renaissance. A heavily funded but failed crusade inaugurated his reign, portending its violent excesses. Overtures toward reunion with the Russian church proved fruitless, the reforming Council of Constance was annulled, and appeals to general councils were banned. The Spanish Inquisition, which he helped inaugurate, and Tomás de Torquemada, whom he promoted, are infamous, and the nepotism that saw six nephews become cardinals (one later Julius II) spawned a homicidal conspiracy. Nevertheless, a beautified Rome, the Sistine Chapel, and the Vatican archives are likewise the legacy of this Franciscan friar turned Renaissance prince.

E. Duffy, *Saints and Sinners: A History of the Popes* (1997); E. Lee, *Sixtus IV and Men of Letters* (1978); R. P. McBrien, *Lives of the Popes* (1997).

PETER J. SCAGNELLI

Sleidan, Johannes (1505–1556), first historian of the Protestant Reformation. After studying law in Liège, Cologne, and Louvain, Sleidan became secretary of the du Bellay brothers, French diplomats, and in their service worked for an alliance of German Protestant governments with the French crown. Among other literary works, he produced a Latin translation of Martin Bucer's catechism (1544). From 1544 he served as a diplomat for Strasbourg, traveling extensively in its behalf and representing it in preparations for Protestant participation at the second session of the Council of Trent (1551). Bucer and Jakob Sturm urged him to write a chronicle of the Schmalkald League; the product of those efforts was his *On the State of Religion and State under Emperor Charles V* (1555), a chronological account of the events of 1517–1555 based on archival sources from Protestant courts and municipalities. Not a history of Reformation dogma but rather of the events that carried the Reformation to its establishment, Sleidan's work wove together analyses of political, constitutional, social, and religious factors so skillfully that it influenced historiography for more than three centuries. He also composed a history of the world, *On the Four Greatest Empires* (1556).

I. Vogelstein, *Johann Sleidan's Commentaries* (1986).

ROBERT KOLB

Society of Friends *see* Friends, Society of

Society of Jesus Traditionally, the origins of the Society of Jesus (the Jesuits) are traced back to a group of students at the Univ. of Paris who gathered on Montmartre in 1534 to devote themselves to divine service. Its formal beginnings date from September 27, 1540, with Pope Paul III's bull *Regimini militantis ecclesiae*. The Formula of the Institute of 1539 (subsequently incorporated directly into the papal bull) sketched a fellowship devoted to "work for the advancement of souls in Christian life and doctrine, and for the propagation of the faith by public preaching and the ministry of God's word, by spiritual exercises and works of charity, more particularly by grounding in Christianity boys and unlettered persons, and by hearing the confessions of the faithful, aiming in all things at their spiritual consolation." It further proposed an elected superior general with a life term and, in addition to vows of poverty, chastity, and obedience, a special vow to be at the pope's disposal for "the advancement of souls and the spreading of the faith."

The Jesuits were clerks regular rather than monks: they undertook ministry rather than contemplation, exchanged the habit and cowl for less prescriptive clerical dress, eschewed chanting the hours in choir, moderated monastic austerities, instituted no second order for women, and stood firm in their refusal to become bishops or take other posts in the church hierarchy. In spite of the fourth vow, the polemical trope that the Jesuits were the "shock troops" of the pope or of the Counter-Reformation cannot be sustained. The vow did put them at the service of the pope for missions, but the Society always had its own imperatives that sometimes coincided with those of the papacy and sometimes did not. While some Jesuits did play noteworthy roles in opposing Protestantism, many more occupied themselves in "helping the souls" of those among whom they lived.

From Francisco Xavier's departure for the Indies in 1541, the missions stamped the character of the Society. The spiritual fellowship engendered by the *Spiritual Exercises*, the bonds of organization and support linking the missionaries to Rome, and the flexibility allowed in practice resulted in remarkable accomplishments in Mughal India, in Japan, in China, in the Americas, and elsewhere. The Society also organized internal missions in Catholic Europe itself in accordance with the wider phenomenon of rural Christianization.

Yet the Society's greatest impact derived from its network of schools. The Formula had mandated colleges to train novices, but in 1547 the magistrates of Messina asked Ignatius to establish the first formal Jesuit school there. It was a success, and Jesuit schools spread rapidly. Practices and curricula were codified in 1599 in the *Ratio studiorum*, and at its height, this Jesuit educational empire included more than eight hundred schools spanning the globe. It was often via these schools that the Jesuits introduced all the other ministries of their "way of proceeding."

The Society attracted numerous members (some 13,000 by 1615) and enemies. Protestant princes railed against Jesuit spies and Catholic courtiers resented the power of Jesuit confessors. In 1554, the Sorbonne censured the Society; the Jesuits were accused of casuistry by their own Catholic rivals, who bridled at some of their penitential practices. Their defense of orthodoxy against Jansenism earned the Society a century and a half of wasting conflict and many open and hidden enemies, and their evangelism threatened non-Catholic religious and secular authorities alike and produced Jesuit martyrs in England, in the Low Countries, in Japan, and elsewhere. In 1773, the Catholic Bourbons bullied Pope Clement XIV into suppressing the order as the opening salvo on ecclesiastical privileges and papal authority. Although the Society was restored everywhere in 1814, the suppression of the order responsible for so many of its characteristics and accomplishments presaged the passing of early modern Catholicism itself.

W. V. Bangert, *A History of the Society of Jesus* (1972); J. Broderick, *The Progress of the Jesuits (1556–1579)* (1940); J. C. Olin, ed., *The Catholic Reformation: Savonarola to Ignatius Loyola* (1992); J. W. O'Malley, *The First Jesuits* (1993); O'Malley, ed., *The Jesuits: Cultures, Sciences, and the Arts, 1540–1773* (1999); A. Ravier, *Ignatius of Loyola and the Founding of the Society of Jesus* (1987).

BENJAMIN W. WESTERVELT

Socinianism   An Antitrinitarian movement that arose within the Polish Minor Church in the sixteenth century. The group is named for Faustus Socinus (1539–1604), who became the leading architect of its theology after he arrived in Poland from Siena in 1579. Following his lead, the Socinians offered a rationalized account of Christian faith similar but not identical to the emerging unitarian one. God is one and indivisible; hence, there can be no trinity of divine persons. Jesus Christ is an exalted man (*purus homo*), not the preexistent Son; the Word *was*, not *became*, flesh (cf. John 1:14). Mary is therefore not the "mother of God." However, Jesus was miraculously conceived and made the Word in the sense of becoming God's spokesman. As a perfect man whom God has raised from the dead, he is to be adored (a point denied by "nonadorantist" unitarians). There is no hell; the godless will be annihilated. They also accepted the authority of Scripture but rejected original sin and predestination. These views were summarized in the Racovian Catechism of 1605. Sheltered by the tolerance mandated by the Warsaw Confederation of 1573, Socinians avoided the severe consequences faced by heterodox groups elsewhere in sixteenth-century Europe. Thus, their influence was considerable, even on such distant figures as John Locke, largely because of successful publication efforts. In 1660, they were banished from Poland and dispersed widely in Germany and Hungary.

E. M. Wilbur, *A History of Unitarianism* (1946); G. H. Williams, *The Radical Reformation* (3rd ed., 1992).

MICKEY L. MATTOX

Socrates   (470/469–399 BCE), Greek philosopher who proposed that the "unexamined life is not worth living." Socrates left no written record. It is principally Plato in the early "Socratic" *Dialogues* who presents us with substantive material on his character and teachings. A man of intellectual genius, moral integrity, personal charisma, and physical courage, he challenged the intellectual, moral, political, and religious views of his contemporaries. He also assailed the relativist theories of the Sophists, who claimed, in Protagoras's words, "Man is the measure of all things."

A distinguishing feature of his teaching method is dialectic or dialogue. Socrates poses a question, such as "What is virtue?" and draws his dialogue partner into attempts at definition. *Elenchus*, a form of refutation that exposes the flawed outcome of the other person's premises or beliefs, is often intensified by irony. Although Socrates praises the other for superior wisdom, as the conversation proceeds it becomes clear that the person is ignorant and the praise insincere. Deepening the irony, Socrates maintains a distance from answers and dogmatic assertions, even to the point of claiming ignorance. He seldom offers a positive view on matters but shows how shaky the views of those who claim to know really are.

Socrates focused almost exclusively on moral and political philosophy. Virtue is an intellectual matter that involves knowing what is good for humanity and the state. Mastery of knowledge leads to appropriate action. Since he equates knowledge with virtue, he often draws analogies between being virtuous and having mastered knowledge in areas ranging from shoe making to statecraft. To achieve virtue and knowledge, he argues, it is necessary to discipline emotional and appetitive drives by reason. Thus, moral goodness or virtue lies exclusively with the implication that if one knows what is good, one cannot fail to be a good person and act in a morally upright way. This leads to his famous dictum in the *Protagoras* that evil is due to ignorance. Finally, Socrates did not claim the soul immortal. He says in the *Apology* that such is at best a plausible hope.

J. Barnes, *The Presocratic Philosophers* (1996); T. C. Brickhouse and N. D. Smith, *The Trial and Execution of Socrates: Sources and Controversies* (2002); W. K. C. Guthrie, *Socrates* (1971); G. N. A. Hanfmann, "Socrates and Christ," *Harvard Studies in Classical Philology* 60 (1951): 205–33; M. J. McPherran, *The Religion of Socrates* (1996); G. Vlastos, *Socrates: Ironist and Moral Philosopher* (1991).

ROBERT M. BERCHMAN

Socrates of Constantinople (c. 380– after 439), early Byzantine church historian. He wrote an ecclesiastical history in seven books which continued that of Eusebius of Caesarea to 439. He narrated the fourth-century struggle over Arianism, with particular emphasis on the role of Athanasius, and he also discussed the tribulations of the bishop John Chrysostom, whom he admired but not uncritically. Although church affairs dominate the history, Socrates treated secular events as well. His theory of "cosmic sympathy" suggests that disturbances in secular affairs often reflected or caused disturbances in ecclesiastical affairs. He was an enemy of division in the church and felt that a strong and pious emperor was needed for unity. His work concludes with a celebration of the peace and harmony brought to the church by Emperor Theodosius II. Socrates wrote in an uncomplicated style to differentiate his work from heavily rhetorical pagan histories and to make it accessible to ordinary Christians. He wrote favorably of the value of the Greek classics for Christians and was in general a humane and nonpartisan writer for his time. His judicious use of many sources, both written and oral, ensures the value of his work for historians.

D. Rohrbacher, *The Historians of Late Antiquity* (2002); G. W. Trompf, *Early Christian Historiography* (2000); T. Urbaincyzk, *Socrates of Constantinople* (1997).

DAVID ROHRBACHER

Solemn League and Covenant This 1643 agreement stated that Scottish forces would support Parliament in the English Civil War. Its signatories were to maintain the Presbyterian system in Scotland, reform the church in England and Ireland "according to the Word of God, and the example of the best reformed churches," and eliminate all Catholic vestiges in doctrine, liturgy, and church polity.

King Charles I of England rejected the covenant. A more serious threat to the Scottish alliance was Oliver Cromwell's hostility to Presbyterianism and the execution of Charles I (1649), which led Scottish Covenanters to embrace Charles's son (the future Charles II), who subscribed to the covenant (1650) and was crowned king of Scotland (1651). The defeat of Scottish forces in 1651 under his nominal leadership effectively ended Scottish dreams of imposing Presbyterian uniformity on the three kingdoms.

I. B. Cowan, *The Scottish Covenanters, 1660–1688* (1976); W. Makey, *The Church of the Covenant* (1979).

CHRISTOPHER ELWOOD

Somaschi This was a popular name given to the Clerks Regular of St. Majolus, founded in 1532 at Somasca near Venice by St. Jerome Emiliani (1486–1537). Like the Theatines, Barnabites, Ursulines, and others, the Somaschi were part of a broad reform movement, distinct from traditional monastic and mendicant orders, incorporating both clergy and laity, and integrating personal spiritual renewal with communal service of diverse social needs. Today's international Somaschi Order retains the original community's dedication to the care of orphans, a vision that early expanded to include parochial and educational work. During the seventeenth century the Somaschi directed seminaries established in response to the decrees of the Council of Trent. The community came under fire during the Enlightenment, and difficulties recurred during successive waves of political turmoil, first under Napoleon when the community almost ceased to exist, and again during the anticlericalism that accompanied the unification of Italy. The modern revival of the Somaschi dates from the early twentieth-century missions to Central America, augmented by the affiliation of several modern communities that share the order's spirit by incorporating modern drug rehabilitation and therapy programs into services offered by the community.

L. Mascilli Migliorini, *I Somaschi* (1992); C. Pelligrini, *Saint Jerome Emiliani* (1994).

PETER J. SCAGNELLI

Sophia The Greek term means "wisdom." Christian perspectives regarding *sophia* emerge from the Hebrew sapiential tradition, which urges people to seek wisdom and suggests that the beginning of wisdom is fear of God (Prov. 1:7; 15:33). This tradition holds that wisdom is a great legacy that lights up the face and is more powerful than brute force (Eccl. 8:1; 9:16). Wisdom is personified as a woman who points to her existence before creation and her partnership with God in creation (Prov. 8:22–36).

The Jewish philosopher Philo of Alexandria interprets the sapiential tradition by identifying wisdom, "the beginning," "the image," and "the sight of God" as the guiding force in creation. He also equates wisdom with "the word of God" (*Leg.* 1.43.3–5; 1.65.3–6).

Although the New Testament does not systematically deal with the concept of wisdom, several passages seem to link divine wisdom with Christ. First Corinthians 1:24 says Jesus is the "power" and "wisdom" of God, and Ephesians states that God's plan was to reveal the hidden mystery of God, namely, God's wisdom, to the world through the church (Eph. 3:9–10). In the mid-second century, Irenaeus distinguished between Wisdom, which he identified as the Spirit, and the Word, which he identified as the Son (*Haer.* 3.20.1–3), but his contemporary Justin Martyr suggested that Christ is Wisdom (*Dial.* 61–62, 100, 126). In the late second and early third centuries, Clement of Alexandria equated Wisdom and the Word (*Protr.* 1; *Paed.* 1.2), and Origen declared that one of Christ's names is Wisdom (*Princ.* 1.3.1).

Patristic interpreters soon began to emphasize the parallel between Proverbs 9:1, which says, "Wisdom built herself a house," and the Prologue of the Gospel of John (1:14), which states, "the Word became flesh" (e.g., Hippolytus, *Fr. Prov.* 9.1; Cyprian, *Letter* 63.5.1–2). In the fourth century, the implications of the wording of Proverbs 8–9 became pivotal in the Arian Controversy. The Arians argued that Proverbs 8.22 indicates that Jesus had not existed forever but had been created prior to all else and was thus subordinate to the Father. Athanasius, in his *Discourses against the Arians*, attempted to refute this argument by declaring that the Word is neither a work nor a creature; the Word, rather, is a coworker and cocreator with the Father and reveals the Father first by his works and then by the incarnation (*C. Ar.* 2.16.22).

Gnostic tradition viewed Sophia differently. Gnostics believed that Sophia, one of the divine emanations, fell from the spiritual realm (*pleroma*) and was responsible for the disastrous creation of the material world (Irenaeus, *Haer.* 1.1–7). Contemporary feminist theologians have revived the concept of Sophia as key to understanding feminine elements of Christology.

M. Hengel, "Jesus als messianischer Lehrer der Weisheit und die Anfänge der Christologie," *Sagesse et Religion* (1976): 147–88; K. Rudolph, *Gnosis* (1984); E. Schüssler Fiorenza, *Jesus: Miriam's Child, Sophia's Prophet: Critical Issues in Feminist Christology* (1995); R. Wilken, ed., *Aspects of Wisdom in Judaism and Early Christianity* (1975).

J. DAVID CASSEL

Sophronius (c. 560–638), bishop of Jerusalem. Sophronius, known as "the Sophist," was born in Damascus and became a teacher of rhetoric. He later became a monk and lived in both Egypt and Palestine before finally settling at the Theodosius monastery in Jerusalem. He traveled extensively with his friend John Moschus, who dedicated his *Pratum spirituale* to him. Sophronius was a vigorous opponent of Monotheletism and while still a monk argued unsuccessfully before the bishops of Alexandria and Constantinople against the imperially promoted heresy. He became bishop of Jerusalem in 634, and his synodal letter after his election is a strong rejection of Monotheletism. He helped to negotiate the surrender of Jerusalem to the Muslims shortly before his death in 638. Sophronius is best known among Eastern Christians for his composition of the prayer for the great blessing of water on the feast of the Theophany (Epiphany) that occurs on January 6. Its rhetorical beauty and theological depth are a testament to his learning.

H. Chadwick, "John Moschus and His Friend Sophronius the Sophist," *JTS* 25 (1974): 41–74; J. Duffy, "Observations on Sophronius' 'Miracles of Cyrus and John,'" *JTS* 35 (1984): 71–90; PG, vol. 87, part 3 (1860).

EUGENE M. LUDWIG, OFM CAP.

Sorsky, Nil *see* Nil Sorsky

Soto, Domingo de (1495–1560), Spanish Dominican theologian, confessor to Emperor Charles V, participant at the Council of Trent, and luminary of the School of Salamanca. Soto embodied the spirit of renewal in Catholicism and did much to enhance it. Educated at Alcalá and Paris, Soto joined his fellow Dominicans Francisco de Vitoria and Melchior Cano in promoting a positive, or fundamental, theology that stressed natural law and ethics and downplayed the abstract philosophical questions of medieval scholasticism. At Trent, Soto ardently defended tradition on a number of key issues, such as free will, justification, the canon of Scripture, and the authority of the Vulgate. In 1552 he succeeded Melchior Cano in the principal chair of theology at Salamanca. Soto authored a number of influential texts, including a manual of logic, the *Summulae* (1529); a defense of Catholic soteriology, *De natura et gratia* (1547); a digest of political and legal theory, *De iustitia et iure* (1553); and a pioneering study of poverty, *Deliberatio in causa pauperum* (1545). Renowned for piety as well as learning, Soto campaigned for the education of the poor and defended the rights of the American natives.

J. B. Plans, *La escuela de Salamanca y la renovación de la teología en el siglo XVI* (2000); J. S. Di Liso, *Domingo De Soto: Dalla logica alla scienza* (2000); A. Pagden, *The Fall of Natural Man* (1987).

CARLOS M. N. EIRE

Sozomen (c. 380–c. 449), early Byzantine church historian. He wrote an ecclesiastical history in nine books which continued that of Eusebius of Caesarea. The preface to the history states that it will continue up to 439, but the work as we have it trails off around 425 in the unfinished ninth book. Sozomen was born near Gaza and spent time with Palestinian monks in his youth. His title *scholasticus* suggests that he went to law school, probably in Beirut. The major, though unacknowledged, source for his work was the history of Socrates of Constantinople. Sozomen's work was more artfully written and organized than that of Socrates. The superiority of deeds to reason was an important theme, which he illustrated particularly in lengthy profiles of monastic figures whom Socrates had omitted. He also provided more material about the spread of Christianity beyond the Roman Empire than Socrates had. While Sozomen shared Socrates' concerns about strife in the church, he did not agree with his doctrine of imperial supremacy and championed the superior claims of bishops. Sozomen's work remains valuable to modern historians primarily for the digressive additions he made to Socrates' history.

B. Grillet, G. Sabbah, and A.-J. Festugière, *Sozomène: Histoire ecclésiastique, livres I–II* (1983); D. Rohrbacher, *The Historians of Late Antiquity* (2002); G. W. Trompf, *Early Christian Historiography* (2000).

DAVID ROHRBACHER

Sozzini, Fausto (1539–1604), Italian religious teacher and nephew of Lelio Sozzini (1525–1562). In 1562 Sozzini published a book on John's Gospel in which he denied the divinity of Christ. During his studies in theology at Basel he wrote *De Jesu Christo servatore* (1578), which opposed the evangelical teaching of the Reformers. The following year he moved to Poland, where he promoted unitarian doctrines. He was forced to leave Cracow in 1598 after his authorship of several anonymous writings became public. Following his death at Luclarvice, his Antitrinitarian and Anabaptist views in Poland became known as Socinianism. These religious ideas expanded into Hungary, Moravia, and Transylvania, but public pressure by the Jesuits led to the 1658 banishment of the Socinians.

F. C. Church, *The Italian Reformers, 1534–1564* (1932); J. Riatt, ed., *Shapers of Religious Traditions in Germany, Switzerland, and Poland, 1560–1600* (1981); G. H. Williams, *The Radical Reformation* (3rd ed., 1992).

ELIZABETH GERHARDT

Sozzini, Lelio (1525–1562), Italian humanist and teacher. Born in 1525 of a distinguished family of jurists, Sozzini studied law at Padua and then became interested in the Scriptures and the reform movement. He moved to Venice, the center of Protestantism in Italy, and visited several reformers in France, Switzerland, and Germany. In Germany he was a guest of Philip Melanchthon in Wittenberg. In 1552 he went to Italy to persuade his nephew, Fausto Sozzini, of his beliefs. Two years later he moved to Switzerland and had contacts with Calvin. He was critical of the burning of Michael Servetus, and his views came under suspicion. He had a deep interest in the role of reason in matters of faith and published *A Confession of Faith* (1555) and *De sacramentis dissertatio* (1560).

S. Caponetto, *The Protestant Reformation in Sixteenth-Century Italy* (1999); F. C. Church, *The Italian Reformers, 1534–1564* (1932); S. Lubieniecki, *History of the Polish Reformation* (1995).

ELIZABETH GERHARDT

Spain, Reformation in Catholic to the core, home to the most vigilant inquisition of all, Spain not only proved inhospitable to Protestants but led the way in combating them and in reforming and reinvigorating Catholicism.

By the time Martin Luther challenged the papacy, Spain had already begun to experience a reformation of its own led by Francisco Ximenez de Cisneros (1436–1517), a dynamic Franciscan reformer. Ximenez held many high offices, sometimes simultaneously, and he used them all to improve the church. As confessor to Queen Isabella and provincial of the Franciscans in Castile, Ximenez first reformed his own order, ridding it of abuses and corruption. As archbishop of Toledo and primate of Spain, he extended his reforming efforts to the clergy as a whole, ridding the Spanish church of a good deal of corruption. He also established the Univ. of Alcalá in 1508 for the express purpose of improving the education of the clergy and stimulating intellectual and spiritual revival; in addition, he sponsored the translation and publication of devotional texts, planting the seeds for an unprecedented mystical flowering. As inquisitor general and regent of Castile, he strengthened the Inquisition, pursuing dissenters and heretics, imposing religious uniformity, and tightening the church's grip on everyone.

All currents of reform that flowed into Spain or arose from within had to contend with the ubiquitous Inquisition. This made it nearly impossible for Protestantism to make inroads. In the 1520s and 1530s, two movements suspected of Protestant leanings were snuffed out. One was the mystical heresy of the so-called *Alumbrados*, or "Illumined Ones," who downplayed the role of free will and the external signs of the church. The other group consisted of the followers of Erasmus, who in addition to stressing interior faith, also criticized corruption and hypocrisy in the church. Though Erasmus found his greatest following at the Univ. of Alcalá, ironically, the Inquisition clamped down on suspected Erasmians. In some cases, such as that of the humanist Juan de Vergara, one could be accused of Lutheranism, Erasmianism, and Illuminism simultaneously. Or one could be suspected of simply leaning toward heresy, as happened to Alonso Ruiz de Virúes, preacher at the court of Charles V. Though many were cleared, like Ruiz de Virúes, or lightly sentenced, like Vergara, Erasmianism withered quickly in Spain—especially after a gathering of theologians at Valladolid (1527) found much to censure in Erasmus.

"Lutheranism" did not openly surface in Spain until 1556–1559, by which time the land was awash with reformers, mystics, and saints-to-be who not only embodied Catholicism but were busy opposing Protestantism and strengthening the Catholic Church from within. The two cells of suspected "Lutherans" suddenly discovered in Seville and Valladolid were very small and consisted of few prominent people, save for Constantino Ponce de la Fuente and Agustín Cazalla, courtiers to Charles V and Philip II. Quickly rounded up by the Inquisition, many of the accused confessed to being *luteranos*. In 1559, twenty-six of these men and women were burned as heretics. At roughly the same time, charges of Lutheranism were also leveled against the archbishop of Toledo, Bartolomé de Carranza, but the accusations were hard to prove. Imprisoned by the Inquisition, he appealed to Rome and languished in prison until 1576. Though he died a few weeks after being freed, with an inconclusive verdict shadowing his reputation, he was proven innocent by twentieth-century scholars.

The Inquisition tried individual Protestants over the course of its subsequent history, but after 1559 there was no trace left of an organized Protestant movement anywhere in Spain. Only in exile could one survive as a Protestant. Among those who chose exile, the most notable are Juan Pérez de Pineda, who translated the New Testament into Spanish and served as a Calvinist pastor in Geneva and France; Casiodoro de la Reina, who translated the Bible into Spanish (1569) while living in England, Germany, and Switzerland; Cipriano de Valera, who lectured at Oxford, translated Calvin's *Institutes* into Spanish, and improved upon Reina's translation of the Bible (1602); and Michael Servetus, who authored a number of radical theological treatises while working as a physician in France. Exile did not guarantee freedom from persecution, however, as Michael Servetus discovered in Calvin's Geneva, where he was burned alive in 1552 for denying the Trinity.

Within Spain itself, the renewal of Catholicism begun in the early 1500s continued to flourish for another two centuries, its vibrancy manifested not only by its global missionary effort but also by its saints and mystics, art and architecture, literature, and, most importantly, adherents, who seemed to have taken their religion quite seriously, creating new lay confraternities, endowing Masses for the dead, establishing new processions and pilgrimages, buying devotional texts, giving to charity, entering monasteries and seminaries, and bequeathing to the church as much as one quarter to one half of Spain's real estate.

———

M. Bataillon, *Erasme et l'Espagne,* 3 vols. (2nd ed., 1991); J. A. Burgos, *Luteranismo en Castilla durante el siglo XVI* (1983); C. M. N. Eire, *From Madrid to Purgatory* (1995); L. A. Homza, *Religious Authority in the Spanish Renaissance* (2000); A. G. Kinder, *Spanish Protestants and Reformers in the Sixteenth Century: A Bibliography* (1983; supplement, 1994).

CARLOS M. N. EIRE

Spalatin, Georg (1484–1545), secretary to Elector Frederick the Wise and friend of Luther. Spalatin studied in Erfurt beginning in the summer semester of 1498 and was a member of the circle of students of the well-known humanist Nikolaus Marschalk. In 1508 he took priestly vows. In November of that year, Elector Frederick III of Saxony called him to Torgau as tutor to the princes. In 1516 he was appointed secretary for church and university affairs by the prince, becoming Frederick's confessor in 1518, and in 1522, the court chaplain.

During this time, from around 1514 onward, Spalatin developed an increasingly close friendship with Luther. Contacts between Frederick and Luther were entirely through Spalatin. After Frederick's death in 1525, he took a pastoral position in Altenburg, where he married and after 1528 served as superintendent. He died in Altenburg.

Without Spalatin's mediation neither the reform of Wittenberg Univ. nor the protection of Luther by the Elector would have been conceivable. Spalatin propagated the ideas of Luther and Melanchthon, most importantly as the translator of their Latin writings.

———

I. Höss, *Georg Spalatin, 1484–1545, ein Leben in der Zeit des Humanismus und der Reformation* (2nd ed., 1989); M. Treu, "Die deutsche Übersetzung der 'Querela pacis' des Erasmus von Rotterdam," in *"Der Buchstab tödt—der Geist macht lebendig": Festschrift für Hans-Gert Roloff,* ed. J. Hardin and J. Jungmayr (1992).

MARTIN TREU

Spencer, John (1601–1671), English Catholic controversialist. He was converted to Catholicism while studying at the Univ. of Cambridge and became a Jesuit in 1627. He went on to study moral theology in Liège and returned to England, where he participated in an important dispute with two Anglican theologians, Peter Gunning and John Pearson, the future bishops of Ely and Chester. He wrote polemical books against Protestantism, such as *Questions Propounded to the Doctors of the Reformed Religion* (1657), *Schisme Unmask't* (1658) and *Scripture Mistaken* (1660). In later life, he served as chaplain to the Earl of Shrewsbury.

———

G. Stroumsa, "John Spenser and the Roots of Idolatry," *History of Religions* 41 (2001): 1–23.

ERIC LUND

Spener, Philipp Jakob (1635–1705), father of German Pietism, and the leading Lutheran author and churchman of his century. Born in Rappoltsweiler in upper Alsace, as a child Spener was influenced by English devotional writers and by Johann Arndt's *Wahres Christentum*, his favorite reading next to the Bible. The court preacher Joachim Stoll exercised significant influence upon the young Spener with his Arndtian piety and biblical preaching, and he also served as Spener's tutor. During his theology studies in Strasbourg, Spener came under the influence of the Orthodox theologian Johann Conrad Dannhauer, whose systematic theology *Hodosophia* *christiana* (1649, 1662) Spener practically memorized.

From 1659 to 1662 Spener made academic journeys that took him to Basel, where he continued his study of Hebrew and rabbinics, and to Geneva, where he was influenced by the preaching and mystical devotion of Jean de Labadie. In 1664 Spener received his doctorate from Strasbourg Univ. for his dissertation on Revelation 9:13–21. He canvassed some fifty biblical commentaries, many of them Reformed chiliastic interpretations, and became less certain of the orthodox Lutheran eschatology of the soon-coming last judgment.

In 1666 Spener became senior Lutheran minister in Frankfurt, an imperial city with about fifteen thousand people, twelve Lutheran ministers, Catholic and Reformed minorities, and over one thousand Jews. Spener remained in Frankfurt until 1686; these years were decisive for Spener's Pietist reform program. Spener came to see that church reform by way of new practices and ordinances achieved no more than outward change, not the inward renewal of which Arndt had spoken. When a group of men approached Spener in 1670 with the idea of meeting in homes for spiritual edification, Spener agreed, and he was joined by Johann Jakob Schütz and Johannes Anton Tieffenbach. In 1674 Spener changed the format from a devotional reading circle to a Bible study, which met on Monday and Wednesday afternoons. By 1675 the number had grown to fifty and included men and women, nobles and craftsmen, educated and uneducated; by 1680 over a hundred attended. This was the beginning of the Pietist movement.

In spring 1675 a new edition of Johann Arndt's sermons appeared with Spener's introduction; that fall the introduction was published on its own, entitled *Pia Desideria*. The work was a classic statement of Spener's reform, including a diagnosis of the corrupt condition of the German church, a prognosis of the possibilities for future improvement, and a sixfold remedy that would bring about this improved state. First, there must be greater attention to Bible reading, privately and in small groups, the "foremost means for improvement." Second, the priesthood of all believers must be taken seriously through mutual encouragement and edification. Third, practical Christianity must be expressed in love of neighbor and accountability to a confessor. Fourth, the truth should be promoted by love and an exemplary life rather than theological disputation. Fifth, the education of pastors

should include the praxis of Christian living and reading the German mystics. Sixth, preaching should nurture the fruit of the Spirit according to the model of Arndt's sermons.

Spener's reform was a real innovation in its promotion of home gatherings for Bible study (*collegia pietatis*) and in its hope for better times for the church, marked by the conversion of the Jews (Rom. 11:25–26) and the fall of the papacy (Rev. 18–19). Within two years *Pia Desideria* was being discussed in churches all over Germany. Spener found initial support among preachers in imperial cities in German lands that had ties to Spener and the Frankfurt *collegia*. The movement spread to small territories whose princes had ties to Spener, notably the counties of Hessen-Darmstadt, Solms-Laubach, Stolberg-Gedern, and Waldeck. Spener's views also found a warm reception in Scandinavian lands and in the Baltic.

In the late 1670s and early 1680s the Pietist movement entered a second phase as separatist conventicles began to proliferate and become a subject of gossip and criticism focused on the prominence of women preachers and prophets and on claims to perfection in keeping God's law. Students in Leipzig, such as August Hermann Francke, as well as in Tübingen, Hamburg, and Halle, became the radical vanguard of the growing reform movement. Spener moved away from conventicle practice in the 1680s. His prolific publications included volumes of sermons, tracts, devotions, catechisms and, in the 1690s, polemics in defense of his movement, making him the most widely read German Protestant author of his day.

———

P. J. Spener, *Pia Desideria*, trans. T. G. Tappert (1964); K. J. Stein, *Philipp Jakob Spener, Pietist Patriarch* (1986); J. Wallmann, *Philipp Jakob Spener und die Anfänge des Pietismus* (2nd ed., 1986).

DOUGLAS H. SHANTZ

Spengler, Lazarus

Spengler, Lazarus (1479–1534), influential politician, hymnist, and leading advocate of the Reformation at Nuremberg. As both a civil and religious leader, Lazarus Spengler occupies a particular place of importance in the history of the Reformation. He was a civil servant and servant of the Reformation, policy maker and confessor, advisor to the governing authorities and influential lay theologian. After listening to the sermons of Johann von Staupitz during 1516–1517, Spengler began working for the reform of the church in Nuremberg. During 1518, after meeting Martin Luther, he published *Defense and Christian Reply of an Honorable Lover of Divine Truth*, defending the Wittenberger's teachings. The influence of Luther's message of justification by faith alone can also be heard in Spengler's hymn "Through Adam's Fall All Men Fell." During the next decade, he published several treatises for congregations struggling with the reform of church polity and congregational order. Thus, the *Main Articles through Which Christendom Has Been Misled*, the *Schwabach Articles of Visitation*, and the *Brandenburg-Nuremberg Church Order of 1533* witness to Spengler's skill as an apologist and advocate inspired by a restless devotion to the freeing message of the gospel.

H. J. Grimm, *Lazarus Spengler: A Lay Leader of the Reformation* (1978).

DONAVON L. RILEY

Speyer, Protestation of (1529), Reformation confession. The first Diet of Speyer (1526) suspended the Edict of Worms (1521) and allowed each estate of the Holy Roman Empire to deal in religious matters as it deemed justifiable before God and the emperor. The majority present at the second Diet of Speyer (1529) proposed to put the Edict of Worms back into force until a council convened. The evangelical rulers and some imperial cities protested against several parts of the proposal, including the proposition that the majority can rule the minority in questions of faith. The protesting estates said they would render to the emperor required obedience but that in matters of faith God must be obeyed above all. They declared they would hold to the first Diet of Speyer. The protestation received legal status when they appealed to a general council and the emperor. The protestation, both a religious act of confession and a political protest, provided the evangelical movement with a new unity and identity.

J. Ney, ed., *Die Appellation und Protestation der evangelischen Staende auf dem Reichstage zu Speier 1529* (1906, repr. 1967); W. Steglich, "Die Stellung der evangelischen Reichsstaende und Reichsstaedte zu Karl V. zwischen Protestation und Konfession, 1529/30," *ARG* 62 (1971): 161–92.

MARY JANE HAEMIG

Spinoza, Baruch (1632–1677), Dutch rationalist philosopher. Growing up in Amsterdam in a Portuguese Jewish family, his early education consisted primarily of the study of the Torah and Talmud. Later, while working in his father's import business, he studied secular subjects at a school administered by an ex-Jesuit who introduced him to the philosophy of Descartes. At the age of twenty-four he was excommunicated by a council of rabbis because of his unorthodox religious beliefs. To support himself, he took up the trade of polishing optical lenses. After 1660 he increasingly devoted his life to philosophical reflection, but few of his writings were published before his death. He is recognized as one of the founders of higher criticism of the Bible because, in his anonymously issued *Theological-Political Treatise* (1670), he presented novel theories about the authorship of various biblical books. In his *Ethics* (1677) he argued for a pantheistic understanding of God. He proposed the existence of one infinite divine substance, identifiable with nature as a whole.

R. Mason, *The God of Spinoza* (1997); S. Nadler, *Spinoza: A Life* (1999); J. S. Preus, *Spinoza and the Irrelevance of Biblical Authority* (2001).

ERIC LUND

Spiritual Exercises A congeries of explanations, directives, contemplations, rules, and notes by Ignatius Loyola, the *Spiritual Exercises* is a manual for generating a mystical experience. By 1522, Ignatius had recorded aspects of his own spiritual transformation and used the resulting text to guide others to "make an election" (decision) by overcoming the self, ordering one's life, and freeing the election from disordered affections. Addressed to a spiritual director leading an exercitant through the process, the text strikes a balance between an attentive but neutral director and a submissive and obedient exercitant who is nonetheless encouraged to linger wherever "thought, relish, and consolation" emerge. Over a scripted yet flexible four-week retreat, the *Exercises* move the exercitant from personal sinfulness to the kingdom of Christ, the passion and the resurrection. At every stage, the exercitant uses experience and the senses to imagine, for example, the anguish of the damned, the arrayed hosts of Christ and Satan, and the road to Jerusalem.

The early Jesuits used the *Exercises* for shaping novices for ministry. Almost as early, offering retreats based on the *Exercises* became one of those ministries. Thus, those outside the order experienced Ignatian spirituality too, often in simplified form. This shifted the *Exercises* from its original goal of facilitating a singular election, but it bore fruit for spiritual instruction, won admirers, and became a familiar part of the Jesuit ethos.

Ignatius Loyola, *Spiritual Exercises and Selected Works*, ed. G. E. Ganss (1991).
                    BENJAMIN W. WESTERVELT

Spiritual Franciscans   *see* Franciscan Spirituals

Spottiswoode, John (1565–1639), archbishop and Scottish church historian. Spottiswoode entered the ministry as a proponent of strict Presbyterianism but moderated his views to support the royal prerogative in religious matters. When James VI succeeded to the English throne in 1603 (as James I), Spottiswoode was appointed archbishop of Glasgow (1603) and archbishop of St. Andrews (1615). As moderator of the General Assembly of 1618, he persuaded a reluctant Church of Scotland to adopt Anglican liturgical practices favored by the king in the Five Articles of Perth. King Charles I appointed him chancellor of Scotland in 1635. The Scottish revolt against the imposition of the unpopular English prayer book in 1637 forced him from office, and he died shortly afterward in London. He is best known for *The History of the Church of Scotland*, composed at the behest of James and published posthumously in 1655.

J. Kirk, *Archbishop Spottiswoode and the See of Glasgow* (1988).
                    CHRISTOPHER ELWOOD

Stapleton, Thomas (1535–1598), English Catholic theologian. He studied at Oxford, earning a master's degree in 1556; in 1558 he was ordained a priest, but the accession of Elizabeth I later that year forced him to flee to Paris, where he studied biblical languages. He returned briefly to England in 1563 but refused to take the Oath of Royal Supremacy and went into exile. He played a key role in founding a seminary for Englishmen at Douai and served there as professor of theology (1569–1585). He was Regius Professor of Scripture at Louvain from 1590 until his death. He entered a Jesuit novitiate in 1585 but soon discovered that his temperament was unsuited to Jesuit life.

Stapleton was a brilliant controversialist, attacking John Calvin, Theodore Beza, and John Jewel in his major work, *Antidota apostolica contra nostri temporis haereses* (3 vols., 1595–1598). He also wrote a biography of

Thomas More, several short controversial works in English, a catechism, and a guide for sermons on the Sunday Gospels. He translated Bede's *Ecclesiastical History of the English People*.

M. O'Connell, *Thomas Stapleton and the Counter Reformation* (1964).
                    JOHN PATRICK DONNELLY, SJ

Staupitz, Johann von (c. 1468–1524), Augustinian Hermit and Luther's fatherly friend. Staupitz entered the Order of Augustinian Hermits around 1490. After studies in Cologne and Leipzig, he received his doctorate in theology in 1500 at Tübingen. From 1502 he served the prince of Electoral Saxony as the first dean of the theology faculty of the new Univ. of Wittenberg; from 1503 to 1520 he was also the general vicar of more than thirty German cloisters of the Observant Augustinian Hermits. As vicar he sought to unite observant and conventual cloisters—that is, those who observed monastic vows of poverty more strictly, and those who were less observant. The resistance of the observants to such unity was the occasion for Luther's 1510 journey to Rome.

In 1512 Staupitz called Luther as his successor as professor of Bible at Wittenberg Univ. He himself worked as a preacher and spiritual writer mainly in southern Germany. Under the impact of the Reformation he resigned from his offices in 1520, and in 1522 he entered the Benedictine Order. He died as the abbot of St. Peter's in Salzburg. Luther viewed him as his spiritual father, but Staupitz's mindset remained caught between the late Middle Ages and the Reformation.

B. Hamm, "Johann von Staupitz (c. 1468–1524), spätmittelalterlicher Reformer und 'Vater' der Reformation," *ARG* 92 (2001); R. Markwald and F. Posset, *125 Years of Staupitz Research* (1995).
                    MARTIN TREU

Stephen I (d. 258), bishop of Rome (254–258) and advocate of Roman primacy. He is most noted for his confrontations with Cyprian, bishop of Carthage, over Roman claims to jurisdiction both in the deposition of bishops in Spain and Gaul and in the question of rebaptism of Christians initially baptized by heretics and schismatics. In the latter dispute, Cyprian argued for respecting the traditions of local churches in such matters. Stephen, for the first time, asserted the authority of the Roman church on the basis of an appeal to the inherent

authority of Peter and Paul (traditionally thought to have been martyred in Rome). Stephen appeared ready to excommunicate Cyprian, the African churches, and churches in the East that agreed with Cyprian's position. Stephen was apparently martyred in 258 in the persecution of Valerian, and the threats died with him. The episcopate of Stephen is a turning point in the increasing claims of Roman jurisdiction, especially over churches in the Roman West.

The controversies between Stephen and Cyprian are recorded in the letters of Cyprian (*Letters* 65–77) and described briefly in Eusebius (*Hist. eccl.* 7.2–9).

J. P. Burns, *Cyprian the Bishop* (2002); G. W. Clarke, *The Letters of St. Cyprian of Carthage*, vol. 4 (1989); H. L. Lawlor and J. L. Oulton, *Eusebius* (1927); J. J. Sebastian, *"Baptisma Unum in Sancta Ecclesia": A Theological Appraisal of the Baptismal Controversy in the Work and Writings of Cyprian of Carthage* (1997).

CHARLES A. BOBERTZ

Stephen Bar Sudayli (480–550), mystical writer. Our knowledge of Stephen's life comes largely from secondary sources. He was born in Edessa and probably belonged to the same Anti-Chalcedonian party as did Jacob of Serug and Philoxenus of Mabbug. Both of these men mention him as a person who holds a doctrine that the punishment of evil is not eternal. Conflict with Jacob may have motivated his migration to Egypt. He fared no better there, and Philoxenus wrote condemning his opinions about universal salvation. He relocated to Palestine in the 340s and no more is known of him after that.

Stephen's only surviving work is the *Book of Hierotheos*, which claims to be a source mentioned in Pseudo-Dionysius. Some have proposed him as the actual author of the works of Pseudo-Dionysius. The Origenism of Evagrius was clearly an influence on Stephen, and some have found in him the moving force of the Origenistic revival in Palestine in the sixth century. He moves beyond Origen and Evagrius in a radically monist direction. Philoxenus says that on the wall of his cell he had written, "Every ousia is homoousios with the divine ousia."

A. L. Frothingham, *Stephen bar Sudaili, the Syrian Mystic, and the Book of Heirotheos* (1886);

F. S. Marsh, ed. and trans., *The Book Which Is Called the Book of the Holy Hierotheos* (1969).

EUGENE M. LUDWIG, OFM CAP.

Stillingfleet, Edward (1635–1699), English theologian and bishop. An influential latitudinarian church leader, Stillingfleet strove for a middle way between confessional dogmatism and freethinking. His *Irenicum* (1659) urged an end to England's ecclesiastical factionalism, arguing that any system of church polity imposed by the magistrate was acceptable, as long as it accorded with natural law and apostolic practice and furthered the peace and unity of the church. His *Origines Sacrae* (1662) defended the historical reliability of the Bible, and his *A Rational Account of the Grounds of the Protestant Religion* (1664) typified the rationalist defense of Protestant orthodoxy against the claims of both Catholic and freethinking critics. Stillingfleet was appointed bishop of Worcester in 1689, and late in his career he devoted himself to defending Trinitarian doctrine.

J. Marshall, "The Ecclesiology of the Latitude Men, 1660–1689: Stillingfleet, Tillotson, and 'Hobbism,'" *JEH* 36 (1985): 407–27.

CHRISTOPHER ELWOOD

Stockholm Bloodbath On November 8–10, 1520, ninety-four Swedish nobles, clergy, and peasants were executed by the Danish king, Christian II. In 1520, as Sten Sture the Younger continued fighting in support of Swedish emancipation from the Kalmar Union and Danish rule, King Christian II of Denmark invaded Sweden to enforce a papal interdict. By the first day of November, Christian had successfully besieged Stockholm and a truce had been drafted recognizing him as king in return for the promise of pardon and a constitutional government. At the coronation banquet on November 4, the archbishop of Uppsala, Gustav Trolle, himself a Dane, declared Christian hereditary king of Sweden before a gathering of Swedish nobles and clergy. Three days later Trolle pronounced them guilty of treason and heresy. On the evening of November 9 and during the following day more than eighty nobles and two bishops, Matthias of Strengnas and Vincent of Skara, were brought into the Great Market Square of Stockholm and beheaded; others were drowned. Within two years, Gustav Vasa, supported by the peasants of the Dalarna region and the Hanseatic League, drove the Danes out of Sweden permanently.

G. Z. Nordstrom, *Stockholms blodbad: Ett drama fran 1520 i bild ach text* (1979).

DONAVON L. RILEY

Stoicism The most important and influential among the Hellenistic schools of philosophy, Stoicism had three phases: the Early Stoa (312–204 BCE), which included its founders Zeno, Cleanthes, and Chrysippus; the Middle Stoa (155–100 BCE), which included Panaetius and Posidonius; and the Later, or Roman, Stoa (94 BCE–180 CE), which included Seneca, Musonius Rufus, Epictetus, and Marcus Aurelius.

The Stoics offered a coherent philosophy in three parts: physics, ethics, and logic. Stoic theology and physics is pantheistic and materialistic. The Stoic universe is a perfect organism with all of its parts interacting for the good of the whole. The cosmos has an active principle, God, and a passive principle, matter. Only bodies exist and interact. Body is infinitely divisible and contains no void. The universe is imbued with divine reason (*Logos*), and its development is providentially determined by God; the cosmos is identically repeated from one world cycle to the next in endless generation and conflagration.

Stoics argued that human persons essentially are part of the world. Human nature belongs to Nature, and human reason (*logos*) is akin to the divine reason. Thus, human actions and cosmic events are not of two different orders. Moreover, since God orders and sustains the universe, there is no possibility for randomness. To the contrary, everything in the universe is determined.

If persons fully recognize the implications of this relationship, they will act rationally in accordance with Nature (God). They will see that everything that happens is the result of predetermined order and that happiness is gained by resignation to one's fated place in the cosmos. Such knowledge the Stoics called wisdom or divine excellence. Wisdom results in happiness, and happiness teaches that only virtue is good and only vice bad. Thus, through bravery the wise person knows what to fear and what not to fear; through justice how to give what is deserved; and through self-control what emotions to extinguish. To be wise is to accept one's lot in life without emotional disturbance.

Finally, no early Stoic postulated the immortality of the soul. Some middle Stoics probably held that the soul survives for a limited time after death.

M. L. Colish, *The Stoic Tradition from Antiquity to the Early Middle Ages* (1985); B. Inwood and L. Gerson, trans., *Hellenistic Philosophy: Introductory Readings* (1998); A. A. Long, *Hellenistic Philosophy* (1986); J. M. Rist, *Stoic Philosophy* (1978); F. H. Sandbach, *The Stoics* (1975); R. W. Sharples, *Stoics, Epicureans, and Sceptics* (1996).

ROBERT M. BERCHMAN

Strauss, Jakob (c. 1480–after 1527), German evangelical theologian and reformer. Born in Basel, Strauss became a Dominican shortly before 1500 and completed a theological doctorate at Freiburg im Breisgau. He appeared as an evangelical preacher in 1521 in Hall near Innsbruck; expelled in 1522, he then enrolled at the Univ. of Wittenberg. On Luther's recommendation he was appointed preacher to Count Georg von Wertheim but was dismissed because his attempts at reform were regarded as too aggressive. His zeal for reform continued in his preaching at Eisenach (1523), where his advocacy for the poor led to a controversy over usury that required Luther's and Melanchthon's intervention. During the Peasants' War (1525) the peasants listed him, along with Luther and Melanchthon, as trustworthy judges of their demands. Strauss cautioned restraint but held both the peasants and the authorities responsible for the violence. Arrested after the war but not prosecuted, he left Eisenach for Nuremberg and Schwäbisch-Hall, finally coming to Baden-Baden in 1526. No record of his life after 1527 is extant.

H. Barge, *Jakob Strauss: Ein Kämpfer für das Evangelium in Tirol, Thüringen und Süddeutschland* (1937); J. Rogge, *Der Beitrag des Predigers Jakob Strauss zur frühen Reformationsgeschichte* (1957).

KEN SUNDET JONES

Sturm, Jakob (1489–1553), Strasbourg nobleman and stettmeister (chief magistrate). Born in Strasbourg, Sturm pursued a clerical career under Jakob Wimpfeling in Heidelberg. From 1504 to 1508 Sturm studied theology at Freiburg. After returning to Strasbourg he was influenced by Erasmus, whom he met in 1514. In 1517 Sturm became secretary to Count Palatine Henry, but in 1523 he gave up his clerical status and became evangelical. He married a daughter of Alsatian nobility. When she died a few years later, he did not remarry.

In 1524 Sturm entered the large senate council of Strasbourg, becoming stettmeister in 1526. During the Peasants' War in 1525, he investigated claims between rebels and the Swabian League. At Speyer in 1529 he signed a mutual defense pact with Protestant cities and estates. In Marburg he joined Philipp of Hesse to mediate differences between Lutherans and Zwinglians on Communion, but their efforts failed. At Augsburg in 1530 he sponsored the Tetrapolitan Confession. He later played a central role in the formation of the Schmalkald League.

Sturm, with fellow Scholarchs, supported academic reforms, including the appointment of Johann Sturm (no relation) as rector. Following the defeat of the Schmalkald League in 1547, although guildsmen and clergy opposed reconciliation with Charles V, Sturm negotiated a settlement. When Sturm died in 1553, Johannes Marbach preached his funeral sermon.

_____

T. A. Brady Jr., *Protestant Politics: Jacob Sturm (1489–1553) and the German Reformation* (1995); J. M. Kittelson, *Toward an Established Church: Strasbourg from 1500 to the Dawn of the Seventeenth Century* (2000).

SUZANNE S. HEQUET

Sturm, Johann (1507–1589), German evangelical, humanist, and educator.

Born in Schleiden near Aachen, Sturm was schooled with the count's son at Manderscheid castle. In 1521 Sturm studied at the College of St. Jerome in Liege, entering the College of Three Languages in Louvain three years later. In 1528 he visited Strasbourg, where lectures by Martin Bucer influenced him to become evangelical. In 1529 Sturm joined a printing firm, moved to Paris, and married Jeanne Pison. From 1531 to 1534 he lectured on Cicero at the Collège de France. By 1534, Sturm had the support of an elite group of benefactors who sought to balance the power of Charles V against Francis I and Reformed German princes. When these efforts failed, Sturm traveled to Strasbourg in 1537, accepting an invitation to reorganize the city's schools.

Sturm's proposed model for education in Strasbourg incorporated methods from the school he had attended in Liege. He established a course of liberal studies that included philosophy, ancient languages, history, mathematics and theology. Strasbourg Scholarchs (a board that controlled education in the city) appointed Sturm rector of their academy, where he served for forty-three years.

In 1562–1566 during the Huguenot wars, Sturm supported the Huguenots, losing much of his wealth when they were defeated. Toward the end of his life, doctrinal disputes compelled city magistrates to relieve Sturm of his position in 1581. He retired to Northeim, where he died in 1589.

_____

J. M. Kittelson and P. J. Transue, *Rebirth, Reform, and Resilience: Universities in Transition 1300–1700* (1984); L. W. Spitz and B. S. Tinsley, *Johann Sturm on Education* (1995).

SUZANNE S. HEQUET

Suárez, Francisco (1547–1617), theologian, philosopher, political theorist.

Born in Granada, Spain, he studied at the Univ. of Salamanca before entering the Jesuits in 1564. After completing his Jesuit training and teaching at several Jesuit colleges in Spain, he was assigned to the Roman College (1580–1585), then in Spain at the universities of Alcalá (1585–1593) and Salamanca (1593–1597). His last twenty years were at the Univ. of Coimbra in Portugal.

His *Disputationes metaphysicae* (1597), largely based on Aristotle, long remained influential in both Catholic and Protestant countries. He wrote extensive commentaries on Thomas Aquinas's *Summa theologiae*. The most important was his tract *De legibus* (1612), a major contribution to the development of international law. His *Opuscula sex* (1599) dealt with divine grace and human freedom, then a subject of bitter dispute between Jesuits and Dominicans. His four-volume *De virtute et statu religionis* (1608–1625) explained and defended religious orders, especially the Jesuits. At the urging of Paul V, he wrote his *De defensione fidei* (1613), which defended English Catholics against James I, who demanded that they take an oath affirming royal supremacy over religious matters in England. The king had copies burned and encouraged Anglican theologians to write refutations. Suárez was the most important and prolific theologian of the scholastic revival in the Counter-Reformation. The Paris 1857 edition of his works ran to twenty-eight volumes.

_____

J. Fichter, *Man of Spain: Francis Suárez* (1940); R. Wilenius, *The Social and Political Theory of Francisco Suárez* (1963).

JOHN PATRICK DONNELLY, SJ

Subintroductae The term is a fifth- or sixth-century translation of the Greek *syneisaktoi*: "people brought into [the house] together" or, more pejoratively, "illegitimately introduced." It denotes a form of ascetic life popular in late antiquity and afterward: a spiritual marriage in which a man and one or several women who had vowed sexual continence shared a house, even a bed. Perhaps inspired by scriptural passages such as Galatians 3.28, the praxis may have been motivated by the understanding that ascetic discipline requires the presence of desire. Practical reasons such as shared household duties are equally likely. Eusebius first mentioned it in the third century (*Hist. eccl.* 7.30.2).

Modern scholars have had difficulty finding an adequate terminology for this arrangement. "Marriage" implies legalization, which was not the case, and "chaste marriage" does not require a vow of abstinence. Medievalists have coined the term "spiritual marriage." The Latin *subintroductae*, or "females brought in surreptitiously," implies a social arrangement not borne out by the sources, namely, that men owned the houses into which women were "introduced." Frequently the women held the superior (financial) status. Since sexual relations were often suspected, the practice was opposed from the early fourth century. However, the symbioses of male and female religious persons continued to enjoy popularity.

H. Achelis, *Virgines Subintroductae* (1902); S. Elm, *Virgins of God* (1994); B. Leyerle, *Theatrical Shows and Ascetic Lives* (2001).

SUSANNA ELM

Suetonius, Gaius Tranquillus (c. 70–130), equestrian official, scholar, and biographer. The son of a military tribune, Suetonius attracted the patronage and friendship of Pliny the Younger (see, e.g., Pliny, Letters 1.18, 3.8, 10.94), with whom he may have traveled to Bithynia-Pontus (c. 110–112). Under Trajan and Hadrian, Suetonius administered three imperial secretariats before the latter dismissed him for unknown reasons (c. 122). Much of his diverse literary output, which included works in Greek and Latin on such topics as famous courtesans and the Roman year, is lost. His *On Illustrious Men*, a collection of short biographies of Roman men of letters, survives incompletely but informs such works as Donatus's *Life of Virgil* and Jerome's *Chronicle*. Suetonius's fame now rests on his *Caesars*, twelve imperial biographies from Julius Caesar (d. 44 BCE) to Domitian (d. 96 CE). Suetonius highlighted anecdotes believed to shed light on the emperors' personalities, but he also utilized important documentary evidence. Like his contemporaries Tacitus and Pliny, he is a crucial witness to the early history of Christianity. *Claudius* 25.4 tantalizingly records that Claudius expelled the Jews from Rome following disturbances provoked by a certain "Chrestus." *Nero* 16.2 explicitly reports Nero's persecution of Rome's Christians, though only implicitly linked to the fire of 64, and designates Christianity a *superstitio* (impious foreign cult).

B. Baldwin, *Suetonius* (1983); J. C. Rolf, trans., *Suetonius*, 2 vols. (1913–1914); A. Wallace-Hadrill, *Suetonius: The Scholar and His Caesars* (1983).

DENNIS E. TROUT

Sulpicius Severus (c. 360–420), Gallo-Roman aristocrat, ascetic spokesman, and writer. A native of Aquitaine, Severus was presumably educated at Bordeaux. After his wife's death, and influenced by the example of the monastic bishop and wonder-worker Martin of Tours, he abandoned a promising secular career for ascetic retreat on his property at Primuliacum in the vicinity of Toulouse (c. 390–394). Severus's secular renunciation paralleled that of his Bordelais friend Paulinus of Nola, from whom thirteen letters to him survive. Although a layman, Severus built a basilica complex, assembled relics, and established himself as an accomplished Christian writer. His influential *Life of St. Martin* (c. 397), *Letters*, and *Dialogues* promoted and defended ascetic values when Western monasticism was still nascent. His innovative *Chronicle* of sacred history to the year 400, indebted in style and manner to Sallust, is an important source for Priscillianism and Arianism in Gaul. Gennadius (*Vir. Ill.* 19) later held, perhaps wrongly, that Severus became a priest and temporarily championed ideas associated with Pelagius. Paulinus of Périgueux and Venantius Fortunatus based their verse lives of Martin upon Severus's *Life*.

J. Fontaine, ed. and trans., *Sulpice Sévère: Vie de Saint Martin*, 3 vols. (1967–1969); B. M. Peebles, trans., *Sulpicius Severus: The Writings* (1949); G. de Senneville-Grave, ed. and trans., *Sulpice Sévère: Chroniques* (1999); C. Stancliffe, *St. Martin and His Hagiographer* (1983).

DENNIS E. TROUT

Swabian League In the late medieval period cities and territories in the southwestern region of Germany known as Swabia joined together for safety and commercial benefits. In 1488 these territories and cities formed a more comprehensive federation at Esslingen that united bishops, princes, knights, and twenty-two imperial cities. To govern the league, an assembly or council convened on an ad hoc basis, often in Ulm, to resolve differences and settle disputes. Initially the council had two houses, representing respectively the nobles and cities. Later a third house, for princes, was included.

The league established a vigorous judicial system. Its three-judge panels often peacefully resolved disputes and disagreements among member parties. League members also supported a strong army. If members failed to comply with decisions of the council or its courts, military action could result. In 1499 the league supported Emperor Maximilian I in the Swabian War against the Swiss Confederacy. Later, following several peasant insurrections, the league's army crushed the Peasants' Rebellion in 1525. In the following years, ducal rivalries weakened support for the league, which disbanded in 1534.

E. Bock, *Der schwäbische Bund und seine Verfassungen: 1488–1534* (1927); H. Hesslinger, *Die Anfänge des schwäbischen Bundes und seine verfassungspolitische Bedeutung bis 1492* (1969); T. F. Sea, "The Swabian League and Government in the Holy Roman Empire of the Early Sixteenth Century," in *Aspects of Late Medieval Government and Society*, ed. J. G. Rowe (1986), 247–76.

SUZANNE S. HEQUET

Swabian Syngramma A publication issued to counter the polemic of the Swiss reformer Johannes Oecolampadius (1482–1531) against Luther's doctrine of the real presence of Christ in the Lord's Supper. Drafted at the end of 1525 by Johannes Brenz (1499–1570), the Lutheran reformer of Schwäbisch-Hall, it sought to repel the Zwinglian opinion that found the doctrine of real presence "not only uncultivated, but wicked and frivolous." The Syngramma emphasized the real presence of Jesus Christ in the sacrament through the promise proclaimed in the words of institution.

J. M. Estes, *Christian Magistrate and State Church: The Reforming Career of Johannes Brenz* (1982); H. Ehmer, "Johannes Brenz (1499–1570)," in *The Reformation Theologians*, ed. C. Lindberg (2002).

DONAVON L. RILEY

Swiss Brethren Among the first of the sixteenth-century Anabaptist groups. The Brethren originated in Zollikon, now a part of Zurich, in early 1525 when a former priest by the name of Georg Blaurock (d. 1529) requested adult (believers') baptism from Felix Manz (c. 1500–1527) in the home of Conrad Grebel (c. 1498–1526). By consenting, Grebel and Manz broke with Zwingli, the city's reformer. They felt that he had compromised their hopes for a truly reformed church patterned after the New Testament. The city council took swift action against these Anabaptists, whom they considered a threat to the unity of church and state. In spite of severe persecution the Swiss Brethren spread rapidly to other Swiss cantons, southern Germany, and Austrian territories.

Although never normative, the Schleitheim Confession, written in 1527 by Michael Sattler (c. 1490–1527), was affirmed by many of the Swiss Brethren. The Schleitheim Confession called for a sectarian church obedient to the New Testament, pacifist in orientation, and withdrawn from the larger society. Several congregations of Swiss Brethren are now part of the Mennonite Church.

G. H. Williams, *The Radical Reformation* (3rd ed., 1992).

DAVID B. ELLER

Switzerland, Reformation in The late medieval development of the Swiss Confederation is crucial to understanding the course of the Swiss Reformation. By the start of the sixteenth century the Confederation was an unequal mixture of wealthy urban members (Zurich, Bern, Basel, Schaffhausen, Lucerne, Freiburg, and Solothurn) and poorer, largely rural states (Uri, Schwyz, Unterwalden, Zug, Appenzell, and Glarus).

Huldrych Zwingli's work in Zurich was the beginning point of the reform movement. From his arrival in 1519 as stipendiary priest in the Grossmünster, Zwingli began a program of *lecto continua* preaching—sermons on whole books of the Bible and not simply selected passages. These sermons were the catalyst for reform, and from the pulpit Zwingli attacked the venality of the hierarchical church and the profiteering of the mercenary service, and he inveighed against idolatrous worship and moral turpitude. God who is spirit must be worshiped in spirit, and true religion, therefore, must be purged of all attempts to reduce the divine to material representations (i.e., the Mass and religious images). Zwingli's preaching brought him notoriety and infamy. His denunciation of established religion and mercenary service jarred with influential elements of Zurich society, and there were protests from other parts of the Confederation. The influence of Luther's teachings, particularly in the cities of Bern and Basel, was creating unrest along the lines found in Germany. For his part, Zwingli saw little difference between what he was preaching and what he read by Luther.

The crucial year was 1523, when two disputations were held in Zurich resulting in the de facto establishment of the new faith. The result of Zwingli's alliance with sympathetic magistrates was a new polity that envisaged a central role for the political rulers. This position stimulated the dissent led by Konrad Grebel. By the middle of the 1520s the evangelical movement was present in both urban and rural areas, and the Swiss found themselves caught up in the vicissitudes of the Peasants' War. The war made the magistrates extremely nervous about the effects of evangelical preaching, and in Bern and Basel there were attempts to control what was taught from the pulpits. In Zurich also, opposition remained considerable, and the Reformation Mandate of spring 1525 was only narrowly passed by the council at a poorly attended session. The first reforms pertained to worship, and a new order for celebration of the Lord's Supper was introduced on Maundy Thursday, 1525. Other key institutional reforms included morals mandates, a new marriage court, and the *Prophezei*, the foundation of higher education.

The nature of reform in Zurich was fairly conservative: the parochial system was retained and virtually all of the urban and rural clergy remained. In Bern and Basel evangelical movements were struggling, and these movements lacked a person with the authority and charisma of Zwingli, although the crucial role of Johannes Oecolampadius in Basel in formulating the theological character of the Swiss Reformation has been recently recognized. Nevertheless, in contrast to Zurich the laity played a much more significant role in the implementation of the Reformation in Bern and Basel. The guilds gave decisive weight to the movement, forcing the hesitant councils in the cities to act. In Bern, however, Niklaus Manuel, the painter and politician, played a pivotal role.

The Disputation of Bern in 1528, which led to the implementation of the Reformation in the city, was the most important gathering of Swiss reformers and a decisive stage in the formation of Swiss Reformed theology. In Basel revolutionary activity among the lower guilds succeeded in strengthening the council's hand to introduce the new faith in early 1529.

By the end of 1529, Zurich, Bern, Basel, and Schaffhausen had adopted the Reformation. Further, the movement had made stunning gains in the eastern part of the Confederation in St. Gall, Appenzell, and Glarus. The focus for hostilities between Catholics and Reformed was the Mandated Territories (lands jointly governed by the Confederates). The First Kappel War of 1529 saw virtually no military conflict, but it stirred bad memories of Zurich's previous attempts at domination of the Confederation. Particularism in Confederation overrode confessional solidarity, and Zwingli was dismayed by the lack of support from the other Reformed states. Relations between Zurich, Bern, and Basel were fragile, and the failure to find common purpose led to the rash attempt by Zurich to force the matter in 1531, when an army was sent out and defeated at a surprise battle at Kappel in the night of October 11. The result was the fragmentation of the Swiss Reformation.

It was the work of Zwingli's successor, Heinrich Bullinger, that eventually succeeded in restoring unity to the Swiss Reformed churches. Bullinger, in his forty years as head of the Zurich church, established a new relationship with the political authorities, gave the Swiss Reformation a clearer theological profile through his leadership, international influence, and writings (in particular the Second Helvetic Confession of 1566), and became a father figure to reform movements across Europe, from Hungary to England. Although the two men were not especially close, Bullinger was a key ally of John Calvin, and their agreement on the Lord's Supper (*Consensus Tigurinus*) in 1549 marked an important stage in the development of Reformed thought. In both Bern and Basel the Reformed tradition of Zwingli and Oecolampadius was locked in a struggle with Lutheran influences, and during the 1530s and 1540s both saw rancorous theological struggles that led the magistrates to clamp down on the churches. Although Bullinger's status as the leading churchman was recognized, neither Bern nor Basel saw itself as subordinate to Zurich. Basel had extensive contacts with the empire and was involved in the network of southern German cities, while Bern was preoccupied with the conquest of the Pays du Vaud and the expansion toward Geneva after 1536. Until the end of the end of the sixteenth century Basel retained a distinct theological character and refused to sign the Second Helvetic Confession of 1566, which was the key theological document of the Swiss Reformation.

E. Campi and B. Gordon, eds., *Heinrich Bullinger and the Formation of the Reformed Tradition* (2004); B. Gordon, *The Swiss Reformation* (2002); H. Guggisberg, *Sebastian Castellio, 1515–1563: Humanist and Defender of Religious Toleration in a Confessional Age* (2003); G. R. Potter, *Zwingli* (1976); J. M. Stayer, *Anabaptists and the Sword* (1976); L. P. Wandel, *Voracious Idols and Violent Hands: Iconoclasm in Reformation Zurich, Strasbourg, and Basel* (1995).

BRUCE GORDON

Symeon Stylites (Symeon the Elder)

(386–459), the first stylite. Symeon ascended a pillar (*stylos* in Greek) as part of his ascetic practice, a move that led to widespread fame, frequent visits from pilgrims, and years of imitation throughout Byzantium after his death. (Symeon the Younger was also a stylite, living about a century after the first Symeon.) Symeon's third and final pillar stood sixty feet high and had a platform six feet square on which Symeon stood in continual prayer. The three versions of his hagiography share a basic narrative structure: Symeon's conversion upon his suddenly understanding the gospel; his inability to fit his (extreme) ascetic tendencies within communal monasticism; his expulsion from two monasteries; and his eventual success as an ascetic working within the ecclesiastical structure of the Syrian church. The three versions differ in their view of Symeon's ascetic practice. Theodoret of Cyrrhus's version naturalizes Syriac asceticism into Greek culture by presenting Symeon's actions as ideal philosophy, which allowed the human Symeon to conquer his body. The Syriac version presents the soul and body as united in the expression of God's purpose. The later Greek life emphasizes the need for extreme penance to atone for the overwhelming burden of sin.

R. Doran, trans., *The Lives of Symeon Stylites* (1992); S. A. Harvey, "The Sense of a Stylite: Perspectives on Simeon the Elder," *VC* 42 (1988): 376–94; Harvey, "The Stylite's

Legacy: Ritual and Religious Identity in Late Antiquity," *JECS* 6 (1998): 523–39.

REBECCA KRAWIEC

Symmachus (d. 514), Roman deacon, pope. Born in Sardinia, Symmachus was baptized in Rome. On the day that he was elected bishop (498), a powerful rival faction elected the archpresbyter Laurentius to the same see. Theological disagreement over the *Henoticon* of Zeno, which Laurentius supported and Symmachus did not, along with conflicts in Rome over control of ecclesiastical wealth and patronage toward the poor, contributed to the schism. Laurentius initially stepped aside at the behest of King Theoderic and became bishop of Nuceria. His claims were revived when charges were brought against Symmachus (500/501). Councils were held (501, 502), and Laurentius took control of the papal administration in the Lateran palace. Symmachus set up a parallel administration at St. Peter's. The dispute generated a large dossier of partisan documents, including the fictional letters and church councils sometimes called the Symmachian forgeries. Theoderic forced Laurentius into exile (506/507), but remnants of the schism persisted to the end of Symmachus's pontificate.

J. D. Alchermes, "Petrine Politics: Pope Symmachus and the Rotunda of St. Andrew at Old St. Peter's," *CHR* 81 (1995): 1–40; R. Davis, trans., *The Book of Pontiffs* (2nd ed., 2000); E. Wirbelauer, *Zwei Päpste in Rom: Der Konflikt zwischen Laurentius und Symmachus (498–514)—Studien und Texte* (1993).

WILLIAM E. KLINGSHIRN

Synesius of Cyrene (c. 370–413), bishop and author. Synesius combines seamlessly the ideals of a Neoplatonist philosopher with those of a Christian. His family traced its descent to the Hieracleidae, the mythical founders of Cyrene. He studied at Alexandria, where he became a devout disciple of the famous philosopher Hypatia, to whom several of his letters are addressed. About 397 he went to Constantinople as an ambassador of Cyrene and remained until 400. While there he wrote *On Government* and *On Providence*, valuable sources for contemporary imperial politics. Besides these works, nine hymns, 156 letters, and several oratory discourses survive. Of the latter, the *Dion* defends a more philosophical and involved life like Synesius's own against a too-rigorous Christian asceticism. He shared the Neoplatonists' interest in the occult (e.g., the Chaldean oracles) and wrote a treatise on divination by dreams (*De insomniis*). Elected bishop of Ptolemais (410), he devoted himself to the multiform duties of this office, without, however, concealing his desire for retreat from the daily bustle. His final years were embittered by the death of his three sons and the ruin of his country through invasions. His last letter was to Hypatia, his "mother, sister, and teacher."

A. J. Bregman, *Synesius of Cyrene, Philosopher-Bishop* (1982); A. Cameron and J. Long, *Barbarians and Politics at the Court of Arcadius* (1993).

SUSANNA ELM

Taborites This radical Hussite group, which gained prominence in 1419, rejected ecclesiastical practices not commanded by the Bible and the existing feudal order. They formed brotherhoods, "warriors of God," comprising largely the urban and rural poor and a few yeomen. After councilors of the Prague "New Town" were thrown from the windows of their city hall in July 1419, Nicholas of Husinec led one of these groups to a settlement near Usti. They renamed the town "Tabor" after the biblical Mount Tabor, where the armies of Deborah and Barak faced a Canaanite army that threatened Israelite tribes (Judg. 4).

The Taborites recognized only two sacraments: baptism and Holy Communion. The laity received bread and wine from celibate priests. Worship was simple, conducted in everyday dress, and in Czech. Jan Žižka (c. 1360–1424), leader of the Orebites, who had forced the acceptance of the Four Articles of Prague, joined forces with the Taborites in 1420. He became one of the four captains of Tabor and its leading military strategist. He suppressed the "communistic" Adamites and defeated both Catholic and Utraquist (moderate Hussite) armies. After his death in 1424, Žižka's troops were known as the "Orphans," while Prokop the Bald led the Taborites' forces. They raided Austria, Germany, Poland, and Hungary and defeated an imperial army in 1531 but shortly thereafter were defeated in Hungary. A combined Roman Catholic–Utraquist army annihilated the Taborites and killed Prokop at Lipany in May 1434.

F. M. Bartoš, *The Hussite Revolution, 1424–1437*, trans. J. M. Klassen (1986); F. G. Heymann, *John Žižka and the Hussite Revolu-*

tion (1955); R. Žížan, *The History of the Unity of Brethren* (1992).

DAVID P. DANIEL

Tacitus, Cornelius (c. 56–120), Roman senator, orator, and Latin historian. Born in Cisalpine or Narbonese Gaul and married to a daughter of Gnaeus Iulius Agricola, senator and governor of Britain, Tacitus made his career at Rome under the Flavians. Promoted to the senate by Emperor Vespasian (69–79), Tacitus served as praetor under Domitian (81–96), who probably designated him for his consulship of 97. Finally, under Trajan, Tacitus governed Roman Asia (112–113). The selection of Tacitus in 97 to eulogize L. Verginius Rufus attests to his reputation as a speaker (see Pliny, Letter 2.1).

His writings include a biography of his father-in-law, the *Agricola*, the ethnographic *Germania*, and the *Dialogus*, on the decline of oratory. Tacitus's reputation rests on his historical masterpieces: the *Histories*, covering the years 69–96 (though only Tacitus's narrative for 69 and 70 survives), and the *Annals*, largely preserved, treating the emperors from Tiberius to Nero. Tacitus, holder of a state priesthood (*quindecemvir*), commented unflatteringly on Judaism and Christianity. *Histories* 5.4–5 passes harsh but ill-informed judgment on practices that Tacitus identified as demonstrative of Jewish depravity and misanthropy. *Annals* 15.44 (cf. Suetonius, *Nero* 16.2) cynically presents Nero's scapegoating of Rome's Christians after the fire of 64, though Tacitus himself had no sympathy for a religion characterized by "hatred of the human race."

R. Mellor, *Tacitus* (1993); R. Syme, *Tacitus*, 2 vols. (1958).

DENNIS E. TROUT

Tall Brothers (late fourth–early fifth cent.), named for their stature, leaders among the monks of Nitria and Kellia. Three were ordained by the Alexandrian bishop Theophilus: Dioscorus as bishop of Hermopolis, and Eusebius and Euthymius as priests who served in Alexandria. A fourth, Ammonius, avoided ordination by cutting off his left ear. Coming to abhor Theophilus's acquisitiveness, Eusebius and Euthymius eventually returned to Nitria.

In 399 the Brothers became embroiled in the Anthropomorphite Controversy, a bitter debate over whether biblical anthropomorphisms used to describe God are to be understood literally or figuratively. The debate was especially important among monks influenced by Evagrius of Pontus.

Initially, Theophilus sided with proponents of a figurative reading. Faced with hostile opposition, however, he quickly reversed himself, thereby acquiring fierce loyalists and creating a pretext for expelling the Tall Brothers from Nitria. Accusing them of Origenism, Theophilus led a mob that ransacked Nitria in a fruitless search for the Brothers, who then fled Egypt with roughly three hundred fellow monks.

Hounded by Theophilus's long reach, only about fifty of the Brothers' companions arrived in Constantinople. John Chrysostom cautiously received the monks but did not restore them to communion, for he knew that Theophilus would regard such an action as an attempt to elevate Constantinople over Alexandria. The Brothers appealed to Empress Eudoxia, who together with her husband summoned Theophilus to Constantinople to stand trial. Ironically, this summons proved to be John's undoing, for Theophilus used his journey to Constantinople as an opportunity to rally support against John and ultimately depose him at the Synod of the Oak. Seeing John as the larger prize, Theophilus reconciled with the battle-weary monks as a necessary political move in preparation for the synod.

———

D. J. Chitty, *The Desert a City* (1966); J. N. D. Kelly, *Golden Mouth: The Story of John Chrysostom* (1998).

STEVEN D. DRIVER

Tallis, Thomas (c. 1505–1585), English church musician and composer. Tallis's life spans the extraordinary changes in the religious lives of people in sixteenth-century England, including Henry VIII's establishment of the Anglican church, the reign of Edward VI and the publishing of the first editions of the Book of Common Prayer (1549 and 1552), the brief return to Catholicism under Mary, and finally the emergence of relative stability during the reign of Elizabeth I.

The move of Henry VIII to rid England of papal supremacy had extraordinary consequences for musicians. When the monasteries were dissolved, the elaborate choirs and musical establishments housed and supported by them were also dissolved. Reformers attacked the complex polyphonic music associated with the Catholic Mass and demanded clarity of text and simplicity of melody. Tallis was among the first musicians to compose music for the new liturgy, setting texts in the clear, syllabic manner sought by Thomas Cranmer and others. He also wrote choral music for the liturgies of the court and cathedral, moving deftly among the various forms and genres demanded of musicians in a turbulent time. With his friend William Byrd, he is the primary representative of an enduring English polyphonic style characterized by lovely melodic line, contrapuntal texture, and an expressive treatment of texts in Latin and in English.

———

D. Wulstan, *English Choral Practice, c. 1400–c. 1650* (1995).

LINDA J. CLARK

Tatian (2nd cent.), Syrian apologist and educator. What is known of Tatian's life comes primarily from autobiographical sections in *Oration against the Greeks*. After a pagan upbringing and training in Syria, he was converted to Christianity in Rome and became a pupil of Justin's. Returning to Syria after 165, he founded an influential school and wrote many works, several of which are noteworthy. *The Diatessaron*, a harmony of the church's Gospels written in Greek or Syriac, was the standard Gospel text for Syriac churches until the fifth century, when the four canonical Gospels replaced it. It can only be reconstructed from its many witnesses. The *Oration against the Greeks* is a highly polemical work against Greek culture. Tatian argues that the fulfillment of OT prophecies in Jesus reveals that supreme truth is found in Christianity. Irenaeus, Clement of Alexandria, Origen, and Eusebius wrote against the Gnosticism evident both in Tatian's writings and in his strong affiliation with the Encratites.

———

E. Hunt, *Christianity in the 2nd Century: The Case of Tatian* (2003); W. L. Petersen, *Tatian's "Diatessaron": Its Creation, Dissemination, Significance, and History in Scholarship* (1994); Tatian, "The *Diatessaron* of Tatian," trans. H. W. Hogg, in *ANF*, vol. 10 (1986), 35–131; Tatian, *Tatiani oratio ad Graecos: Theophili Antiocheni ad autolycum*, ed. M. Marcovich (1995); "Tatian's Address against the Greeks," trans. J. W. Ryland, in *ANF*, vol. 2 (1986), 65–83.

D. JEFFREY BINGHAM

Tauler, Johannes (c. 1300–1361), German theologian, preacher, and mystic. Born in Strasbourg, Tauler entered the Dominican order as a young man. He was active in this city as a preacher and spiritual adviser, concerned mainly with the pastoral care of nuns, until 1338–1339, when the political conflict between the emperor and the church forced him to leave and move to Basel. From there he returned c. 1346. In Basel, and after his return in Strasbourg as well, he was in close touch with the movement of the "Friends of God," a group of laypeople turned toward a life of spirituality with an emphasis on ethical renewal. In his German sermons, Tauler shows the strong influence of Meister Eckhart, especially his teachings on the union between the soul and God and on paths of ethical perfection. However, many of his works follow a more pedagogical pattern than Eckhart's speculative mysticism, and Tauler is seen as a thinker in his own right who is engaged in philosophical discussions with his contemporaries, quoting the major theological authors as well as the "pagan masters" Plato, Aristotle, and Proclus. Tauler's sermons and several inauthentic works associated with his name (e.g., the *Theologia Germanica*) had a very strong influence upon others, including his devoted readers Martin Luther, Peter Canisius, and the Spanish mystics of the sixteenth century. His works first appeared in print in 1498, and they were translated into Latin by the Carthusian Laurentius Surius in 1548.

J. Tauler, *Sermons* (1985).

NIKLAUS LARGIER

Tausen, Hans (1494–1561), Danish reformer. Educated in Erasmian humanism at the universities of Rostock and Copenhagen, Tausen studied at Wittenberg in 1523–1524 and became dedicated to Martin Luther's doctrine of justification by faith alone. Upon his return to Denmark, Tausen was summarily expelled from his cloister for preaching a message critical of Roman Catholic tenets and polity. In 1526 he was retained by King Frederick I to serve as royal preacher. During the summer of 1529 Tausen, assisted by other Danish reformers, drafted the *Confessio Hafniensis*, a confession of forty-three articles intended to further encourage and sustain church reform in Denmark. Following Frederick's death in 1533, a short-lived civil war erupted, out of which Christian III was crowned and Lutheranism was introduced as the religion of Denmark. Thereafter Tausen taught Hebrew at the Univ. of Copenhagen. He translated the Pentateuch into Danish and published a book of sermons intended for use by preachers throughout the church year. In 1541 he was appointed bishop of the Ribe, where he remained until his death.

M. S. Lausten, *A Church History of Denmark* (2002); Lausten, "Hans Tausen," in *Oxford Encyclopedia of the Reformation*, ed. H. Hillerbrand, vol. 4 (1996), 145–46.

DONAVON L. RILEY

Te Deum The venerable *Te Deum* is an ancient Latin hymn of praise and thanksgiving sung continually by the church since at least the sixth century. Early Christian literature, including Benedict's rule, which prescribes the hymn for Sunday matins, employs its longer title, *Te Deum laudamus* ("We praise you, God"). A charming but highly improbable legend traces the hymn to a spontaneous antiphonal song of Ambrose and Augustine on the occasion of Augustine's baptism at the hands of the hymn-writing bishop. Some scholars attribute the hymn to the ecclesiastical writer and missionary bishop Nicetas of Remesiana (d. c. 414) in whose work ancient writers found a simple and direct elegance similar to that of the *Te Deum*. The fact that the hymn does not conform to the strophic and metric character of Latin hymnody contemporary to Nicetas is an argument in favor of earlier composition. The hymn divides into three segments, possibly of separate provenance: verses praising God the Father, verses comprising a creedal-like profession of faith in Christ, and a set of primarily psalm-based intercessions (often omitted). Anglican Morning Prayer includes the *Te Deum* among its canticles; the Catholic Office of Readings prays the hymn on Sundays, solemnities, and feasts. The *Te Deum* underlies the well-known "Holy God, We Praise Thy Name."

A. E. Burn, *The Hymn* Te Deum *and Its Author* (1926).

MARY CATHERINE BERGLUND

Teellinck, Willem (1579–1629), founder of Dutch Reformed Protestantism, was born into a strong Calvinist governor's family. After a stay with Puritans in England, Teellinck abandoned a political career as a doctor of law in order to introduce their kind of piety into the church and society of the Netherlands. He studied theology in Leiden before serving as a pastor in the province of Zeeland (Haamstede, 1607–1613, then Middelburg until his death). His ministry emphasized intense preaching, catechesis, discipline, and Sabbath sanctification. His writings influenced Dutch Pietism for many generations up to today's evangelical audience. He translated several English Puritan writings, and himself wrote dozens of devotional treatises, culminating in a complete program for "further reformation." Beside the practice of piety in congregational and public life, and mission among Jews and Asian colonial peoples, he emphasized personal faith experience in congeniality with late medieval mystical writers. Gisbertus Voetus called him "a second Thomas à Kempis, but Reformed."

W. Teellinck, *North Star*, trans. A. Godbehere (2002); W. J. op 't Hof, *The Dutch Reception of English Puritanism* (2003).

FRED VAN LIEBURG

Tempier, Étienne (d. 1279), theologian and bishop. Tempier was born in Orléans and is mainly known for the condemnations that he issued in 1270 and 1277. However, he started his ecclesiastical career as a theologian in Paris, where he became chancellor of the university in 1263. Apart from three sermons, little else has survived from his theological writings. On October 7, 1268, he was ordained bishop of Paris and in this capacity exercised ecclesiastical jurisdiction over the university. Around that same time, various theologians, among them Bonaventure, expressed concern over philosophical views that were being taught at the university with no attention paid to their implications for Christian faith. On December 6, 1270, Bishop Tempier condemned 13 theses (*articuli*), mainly drawn from Greek and Arabic authors who had been translated into Latin (see *Aristotle, Translations of*; *Avicenna*; *Averroes*; *Siger of Brabant*). On March 7, 1277, he issued a far more wide-ranging condemnation of 219 (or 220) propositions touching on various aspects of medieval theology and philosophy, such as the notion of philosophy, the world's eternity, the unicity of the intellect, human freedom, and ethics. Those scholars who would still teach or support any of these propositions would be excommunicated. Scholars still debate the historical background, the juridical ramifications, and the impact of Tempier's actions on medieval intellectual life.

J. Aertsen, K. Emery, and A. Speer, eds., *Nach der Verurteilung von 1277. Philosophie und Theologie an der Universität von Paris im letzten Viertel des 13. Jahrhunderts* (2000); J. M. M. H. Thijssen, *Censure and Heresy at the University of Paris, 1200–1400* (1998); J. F. Wippel, "The Condemnations of 1270 and 1277 at Paris," *Journal of Medieval and Renaissance Studies* 7 (1977): 169–201.

J. M. M. H. THIJSSEN

Templars (Poor Knights of the Temple of Solomon) The Order of the Temple was a military order founded between 1119 and 1129 and suppressed in 1312. Generally considered to be the first military order, it rose out of the concerns of the period, including pressures for church reform, the need for the defense of pilgrims and others, and changing attitudes toward warfare. Its creation was supported by the Cistercian Bernard of Clairvaux in his tract *In Praise of the New Knighthood*. Templars took monastic vows and lived by a variant of the Cistercian rule. They were not technically monks, however; nor were they crusaders. They were answerable only to the pope. The Templars were soon drafted to serve as defenders of the manpower-starved Latin East, where they distinguished themselves repeatedly. By the thirteenth century they were viewed as the custodians of the Holy Land.

Not everyone admired them. A few theologians disliked their combination of the military and religious vocations. They developed a reputation for hoarding money (largely untrue) and pursuing their own agenda (sometimes true). In 1307 Philip IV of France, for reasons that remain unclear, arrested the Templars throughout France and charged them (probably unjustly) with blasphemy, heresy, witchcraft, homosexuality, and other offenses. In 1312 Pope Clement V suppressed them, preserving papal control of the military orders but destroying the Templars forever.

Since the fourteenth century, a complicated mythology has grown up claiming that the Templars were a gnostic organization that somehow survived 1312. These claims are rejected by historians.

M. Barber, *In Praise of the New Knighthood: A History of the Order of the Temple* (1994); M. Barber and K. Bate, *The Templars: Selected Sources* (2002); H. Nicholson, *The Knights Templar: A New History* (2001); J. Upton-Ward, *The Rule of the Templars* (1992).

PAUL CRAWFORD

Teresa of Avila (1515–1582), Spanish mystic and reformer of the Carmelite order. Teresa de Ahumada y Cepeda presented a model for a mystical process of purification and prayer. She was canonized in 1622 and declared a doctor of the church in 1970. The daughter of the aristocratic Catholic Alonso Sanchez de Cepeda (who also had Jewish ancestry) and his second wife Dona Beatriz de Ahumada, the extroverted and attractive Teresa was sent to a convent to guard her from vanity and romantic flirtations. Then she experienced health problems but also a desire to join a religious order. At the age of twenty, with her father's reluctant approval and financial support, Dona Teresa joined the Carmelite Monastery of the Incarnation at Avila. Serious physical afflictions forced her to leave her convent temporarily to seek treatment. The illness almost killed her, leaving her paralyzed for years.

Upon recovery and after years of convent life, Teresa experienced a spiritual conversion at the age of thirty-nine and a spiritual betrothal to Christ two years later. Her frequent mystical experiences made Teresa a topic of conversation in town. She sought assurance from Peter of Alcantara, among others, that it was God who was behind her tribulations and revelations. Teresa's visions caused not only her personal transformation but also evoked an institutional response: following the Franciscan ideal, the now Discalced Carmelites would live an austere life, supported by their own labor, with common property only, and with new religious names.

The new order, independent since 1594, dictated enforced enclosure. The oath of obedience proved to be a difficult balancing act for the charismatic Teresa, who was striving for reform in the church. A gifted administrator, she endured persecution in 1575–1579 while at the same time managing to establish seventeen monasteries (beginning in 1567) in collaboration with a priest known as John of the Cross.

Teresa's eloquent style, rhetorical skill, and intense theology are manifested in her Life, *Spiritual Testimonies, Soliloquies,* and *The Way of Perfection.* Her central treatise, *The Interior Castle,* illustrates her mystical journey of intentional prayer and purification through "seven mansions" toward union with God.

G. T. W. Ahlgren, *Teresa of Avila and the Politics of Sanctity* (1996); C. Slade, *St Teresa of Avila: Author of a Heroic Life* (1995); A. Weber, *Teresa of Avila and the Rhetoric of Femininity* (1990); R. Williams, *Teresa of Avila* (1991).

KIRSI STJERNA

Terminism, a Pietistic view of repentance. Building on concerns of Johann Conrad Dannhauer and Philip Jakob Spener regarding abuses of piety through hopes of deathbed repentance, Johann George Böse (1662–1700) taught that God limits the time in which people may repent, after which repentance is not possible. Most orthodox Lutherans opposed this view, but in Leipzig's theological faculty he won support. Adam Rechenberg developed a moderate view of terminism.

ROBERT KOLB

Tertullian of Carthage (c. 155–c. 225), brilliant and highly eccentric Christian apologist, polemicist, and biblical expositor. Erroneously identified by Jerome (*Vir. ill.* 53) as a priest, Tertullian was a layman, certainly married, who probably lived in Carthage all his life. Insinuations from his writings indicate that he converted to Christianity in adulthood after initially being captivated by the conviction and courage of Christian martyrs he had witnessed. He had an extensive education and expressed himself in a convoluted style of Latin imbued with satire and irony that occasionally rendered his statements obscure and yet perfectly suited him as he engaged Roman pagans, Jews, Christian heretics, and catholics. The scope of his thirty-one extant writings, produced over a twenty-five-year period (c. 196–220), are mainly polemical: against pagans, Marcionites, Christian gnostics, and catholics who opposed the disciplinary authority of Montanism. There are also devotional essays on prayer, baptism, penitence, and martyrdom, as well as small treatises, many from his pro-Montanist period, on what constitutes appropriate Christian practice (monogamy, chastity, veiling of unmarried women, etc.). The authorship of *The Pallium* and part of *Against the Jews* is still debated.

Though he never provides a comprehensive view of Christian theology, his writings are pervasively theological, providing Christianity with a fundamental grammar and construction of Trinitarian doctrine, Christology, anthropology, and Christian devotional practices. As many as forty neologisms pertaining to theological vocabulary have been attributed to him (e.g., *trinitas*) as well as the employment of familiar terms for Christian usages, such as *substantia, persona,* and *sacramentum.* While he was not the first Christian writer in Latin, Tertullian may be credited as the creator of Christian Latin.

What made Tertullian such a formidable writer was the depth in which he translated his learning in social and political philosophy, classical literature (Latin and Greek), Roman history, and rhetoric into the Christian structures he had adopted. No better examples of this can be found than in his works *Apology* and *To the Heathen*, which defend Christian customs and rationality in light of his extensive formation in classical rhetoric and his practical grasp of Roman jurisprudence. There is no need, as one finds in older scholarship, to identify the Christian Tertullian with the jurist Tertullianus from the same era.

There was a certain restlessness in Tertullian's brilliance. Just as he was led to embrace Christianity as the fulfillment of a dissatisfied life, so he continued to seek an ever fuller knowledge and a more authentic Christian ethic, driven in part by the more stringent religious ethos of North African Christianity. Tertullian particularly sought the vivid realization of God's revelation in his time, that is, the certitude of divine authority. He wanted to ascertain beyond all doubt what were the norms for preserving the apostolic faith and where one looks for the establishment of those norms. It is for this reason that Tertullian found the Montanist claims of prophetic immediacy so attractive. Later in life, he associated himself with this puritanical movement, which called itself the "New Prophecy," then sweeping through the western parts of the Roman Empire. The Montanists' message was not antiorthodox in a strict doctrinal sense, but the very nature of their self-professed prophetic authority, by which they advocated a world-denying ethic, meant a challenge to episcopal forms of authority in the church was inevitable.

There is a growing consensus among scholars that Tertullian did not convert to Montanism in that he abandoned catholicism or ceased from attending catholic church services. Indeed, a more consistent Trinitarian theology (*Prax.* 2) and a greater elaboration of the church's rule of faith (*The Veiling of Virgins* 1) came out of the context of Tertullian's devotion to the revelations of the New Prophecy. Nevertheless, his association with a condemned Christian movement has always denied him canonization, and although his writings were used extensively by later patristic and medieval authors, they were officially condemned in the sixth-century *Decretum gelasianum*.

———

T. D. Barnes, *Tertullian: A Historical and Literary Study* (1971, 1985); E. F. Osborne, *Tertullian: First Theologian of the West* (1997); C. Trevett, "Tertullian and the Church," *JTS* 47 (1996): 668–71; Trevett, "The Status of Women and Gnosticism in Irenaeus and Tertullian," *JTS* 47 (1996): 282–84; J. H. Waszink, "Tertullian's Principles and Methods of Exegesis," in *Early Christian Literature and the Classical Intellectual Tradition*, ed. W. R. Schoedel and R. L. Wilken (1979), 17–31.

D. H. WILLIAMS

Tetrapolitan Confession In 1530 the cities of Strasbourg, Constance, Memmingen, and Lindau presented the Tetrapolitan Confession to Charles V at the Diet of Augsburg. This confession, written by Martin Bucer and Wolfgang Capito, followed much of Philip Melanchthon's Augsburg Confession but disagreed with it on Christ's bodily presence in the Lord's Supper.

In the late 1520s and 1530s the evangelicals divided on the nature of Christ's physical presence in the Lord's Supper. Martin Luther and his followers insisted Christ was corporeally present in the sacramental bread and wine, while southern German cities and territories and the Swiss held that Christ's body was spiritually or symbolically present in the elements. The Tetrapolitan Confession stated that Christ is truly in the elements, "but especially to the spirit, through faith." Melanchthon and other Lutherans at the diet rejected this, feeling it diminished the teaching that—without respect to one's faith—Christ was physically present in the Lord's Supper. Strasbourg's delegates, Jakob Sturm and Matthis Pfarrer, insisted on revisions to make the Tetrapolitan less offensive. Revisions were made, but about one year later Strasbourg adopted the Augsburg Confession to join the Protestant alliance formed at Schmalkald. Notwithstanding, Strasbourg did not refute the Tetrapolitan Confession until 1598.

———

M. Bucer, *Martin Bucers Deutsche Schriften*, ed. R. Stupperich, vol. 3 (1969), 13–185; "The Tetrapolitan Confession of 1530," in *Reformed Confessions of the 16th Century*, ed. A. C. Cochrane (1966), 51–88; J. M. Kittelson, *Wolfgang Capito: From Humanist to Reformer* (1975).

SUZANNE S. HEQUET

Tetzel, Johann (c. 1465–1519), indulgence preacher. Tetzel's entrance into the Dominican cloister in Leipzig cannot be exactly dated, though he studied theology in the university there beginning in 1482. For a time he was the prior at Glogau (Poland), from 1504 to 1510 he worked for the German Order in Livonia, and in 1509 he was made inquisitor for Poland and Saxony.

In 1516 he began to serve Cardinal Albert of Mainz by marketing the St. Peter's indulgence in the archbishopric of Mainz. In 1517 his aggressive selling of indulgences called forth Luther's criticism in the Ninety-five Theses. In 1518, by means of special papal permission, he was promoted to doctor of theology through a disputation against Luther's criticism of indulgences that was held at the Univ. of Frankfurt (Oder). He died in the cloister in Leipzig at the same time Luther was there during the Leipzig Disputation. Tetzel's image as the archetypal representative of the debased old church was fostered in Luther's tract *Against Hans Wurst* (1541) and was still found in caricatures in the following century.

P. Fabisch and E. Iserloh, eds., *Dokumente zur Causa Lutheri*, part 1 (1988); C. V. N. Bagchi, *Luther's Earliest Opponents* (1991).

MARTIN TREU

Teutonic Order   A military order. Pope Honorius III (1216–1227) officially put the brothers of the hospital of Holy Mary of the Germans in Acre (i.e., the Teutonic Order) on an equal footing with the Templars and Hospitallers in a bull dated 1221. Holy Roman Emperor Frederick II (1215–1250) made the master a "prince of the empire," sent him to Prussia in 1226, and granted the order numerous properties in his empire. Grand Master Hermann von Salza (1210–1239) led the order into many areas outside of the Holy Land and absorbed the Livonian Swordbrothers (1237). In the thirteenth century, the order had about two dozen provinces located throughout Europe and the Mediterranean.

The organization originally was a hospital for German speakers, established by crusaders from Lübeck and Bremen at the siege of Acre during the Third Crusade. It transitioned to a military-religious order in 1198. Brothers took monastic vows and wore white mantels with a black cross.

After 1291, the headquarters of the order moved from Acre to Prussia via Venice. The order campaigned against pagans in the Baltic and dominated the region until the Polish-Lithuanian army defeated it at Tannenberg on July 15, 1410. The order "secularized" when, under the influence of Martin Luther, Grand Master Albrecht of Brandenburg (1510–1525) became a "prince of Poland." The weakened papal military order moved its headquarters to Germany. Today it exists as a hospital order.

———

U. Arnold, "Eight Hundred Years of the Teutonic Order," in *The Military Orders: Fighting for the Faith and Caring for the Sick*, ed. M. Barber (1994), 222–35; A. Forey, *The Military Orders from the 12th to the Early 14th Centuries* (1992); M. Tumler, *Der Deutsche Orden im Werden, Wachsen und Wirken bis 1400* (1955); W. Urban, *The Teutonic Knights: A Military History* (2003).

ERHARD "ERIK" P. OPSAHL

Thaumaturgus, Gregory   *see* Gregory Thaumaturgus

Theatines   This Roman Catholic religious order was founded by Gaetano of Thiene and other members of the Oratory of Divine Love in 1524; it followed a very strict form of the Augustinian rule. The name is derived from the town of Theate (Chieti) in central Italy where Bishop Gian Pietro Caraffa (later Pope Paul IV) presided, perhaps indicating Caraffa's significance as cofounder. Approved by Pope Clement VII in June 1524, a month after its founding, the congregation endeavored to reform the religious and moral life of the clergy and laity through strong preaching, devotional piety, and works of charity (particularly hospital care). The congregation developed rapidly in spite of its strict rule of poverty (begging was even prohibited) and austere lifestyle. The Theatines strove to elevate the moral character of the clergy as well as to eradicate the perceived heresies of Luther's teachings as they spread throughout Europe, particularly in the persons of Peter Martyr Vermigli and Bernardo Ochino. Two sisterhoods organized by Ursula Benincasa, the Sisters of the Immaculate Conception of the Virgin Mary and the Hermitesses, emphasized adoration of the sacrament. They continue to promote mission activities.

———

H. O. Evenett, "The New Orders," in *The Reformation, 1520–1559*, vol. 2 of *The New Cambridge Modern History*, ed. G. R. Elton (1990), 313–38; L. Scupoli, *Spiritual Combat* (1960).

TIMOTHY MASCHKE

Theban Legion   (d. c. 285), martyrs. According to legend, a legion made up of Christians from the area around Thebes was recruited to serve on the Egyptian frontier. Emperor Maximian sent this legion to Gaul in 285 to quell a rebellion. The commander, Maurice, and his troops were devout and refused an order to sacrifice to the emperor. Upon hearing of their disobedience, the emperor ordered their massacre. While the *passio* (written between 443 and 450) is clearly a later invention, Christian soldiers from Egypt were employed against a revolt in Gaul in 285/286.

According to legend, the location of the massacre was revealed in 385 to a local bishop in a dream, and he unearthed the bones of Maurice. The bishop then established a small monastery near the spot on September 22, 396. It was renovated by the Burgundian king Sigismund in 515 as a sign of his catholic conversion and became an important royal monastery in Merovingian Gaul.

Veneration of the Theban Legion was important in medieval piety, and the cult spread throughout Germany. From the beginning, Maurice was consistently portrayed as an African, and the monastery was an important pilgrimage site on the road between Paris and Rome; it remains active today in the town of St. Maurice, Switzerland.

———

S. F. Girgis, *The Coptic Origin of the Theban Legion* (1980).

WILLIAM B. SWEETSER JR.

Thecla (first cent.?), virgin and martyr. Knowledge of Thecla comes from the apocryphal *Acts of Paul and Thecla*, written near the end of the second century. According to the account, Thecla, a wealthy, betrothed virgin of Iconium, overhears Paul preaching a gospel of chastity. Captivated by the apostle's passion for the virgin life, she ends her engagement and dedicates herself to perpetual virginity. Her action evokes the wrath of her family and local Roman authorities, and Thecla is condemned to death by fire. Saved by a miraculous storm, she sets out to find Paul. In her travels she is again condemned to death and miraculously rescued. After she has baptized herself, Paul commissions her to teach.

Scholars have traditionally regarded the story of Thecla as largely legendary. Some recent scholarship has suggested that communities of women may have preserved it in oral form in order to maintain a record of apostolic practice that supported the teaching and sacerdotal ministries of women. A related claim is that Thecla's story was circulated by celibate women who needed encouragement in the face of parental rejection and societal hostility.

In the fourth century, Hagia Thecla outside of Seleucia became an important pilgrimage center, promoted in part by the writings of church fathers who saw Thecla as a model of the ascetic life. Because of her willingness to die, she has also been honored in Christian history as a martyr.

———

L. C. Boughton, "From Pious Legend to Feminist Fantasy: Distinguishing Hagiographical License from Apostolic Practice in the Acts of Paul/Acts of Thecla," *JR* 71 (1991): 362–83; V. Burrus, *Chastity as Autonomy: Women in the Stories of the Apocryphal Acts* (1987); S. J. Davis, *The Cult of St. Thecla: A Tradition of Women's Piety in Late Antiquity* (2001); D. R. MacDonald, *The Legend and the Apostle: The Battle for Paul in Story and Canon* (1983).

BARBARA J. MACHAFFIE

Theoderic I (c. 454–526), "the Great," Ostrogothic king. Theoderic was born in Pannonia (Hungary), the son of the Arian Ostrogothic king Theodemer and a Nicene Goth, Erelieva. After spending ten years as an honored hostage in Constantinople, he succeeded (c. 474) to the Ostrogothic throne. In 488, Zeno, the Byzantine emperor, dispatched Theoderic to Italy, where five years later he defeated and killed the barbarian king Odovacar.

The resultant Ostrogothic kingdom of Italy looked very Roman, with its capital at the imperial city of Ravenna and an administration full of Roman senators. Despite his Arianism, Theoderic allowed Nicenes full freedom of religion and even became involved in Nicene church controversies, intervening in 502 in a disputed episcopal election at Rome between Symmachus and Laurentius. Theoderic was related by marriage to the kings of the Vandals, Burgundians, Franks, and Visigoths. In 507, he became titular king of Visigothic Spain, and it appeared that an Ostrogothic empire was in the making.

Toward the end of Theoderic's reign problems arose. In 522 the influential senators Symmachus and Boethius were accused of treason and executed. Theoderic died in 526, and the dream of an Ostrogothic empire died with the Byzantine invasion of Italy ten years later.

———

A. H. M. Jones, "The Constitutional Position of Odoacer and Theoderic," *Journal of Roman Studies* 52 (1962): 126–30; J. Moorhead, *Theoderic in Italy* (1992).

RALPH W. MATHISEN

Theodora I (c. 500–547), empress consort of Justinian I, emperor of the East. She was raised to the rank of patrician by Justinian, married him in 523, and was made Augusta when he succeeded to the throne in 527. Although never coregent, she exercised a profound influence over Justinian. Some contemporary sources, especially the scandalous accounts in the *Secret History* (*Anecdota*) of Procopius of Caesarea, cast sordid aspersion on Theodora's character. It was reported that her father was a bear keeper at Constantinople's Hippodrome circus, that she was an actress in her youth, had been a wool spinner, and had had a child out of wedlock. However, there is general consensus that she was a person of outstanding intellect and accomplishment who, during Justinian's reign, made great strides as a moral reformer. Her strength of character is well demonstrated in her courageous support of Justinian during the January 532 Nika insurrection, where Justinian was precariously close to being overthrown. In theology she was supportive of the Monophysite party and, during the controversy of the Three Chapters, most likely influenced Justinian in his unsuccessful attempt to reconcile the Monophysites—in disregard of the doctrinal definition made at the Council of Chalcedon in 451.

R. Browning, *Justinian and Theodora* (rev. ed., 1987); J. A. S. Evans, *The Empress Theodora: Partner of Justinian* (2002); W. G. Holmes, *The Age of Justinian and Theodora*, 2 vols. (1905); W. Schubart, *Justinian and Theodora* (1943).

MICHAEL D. PETERSON

Theodore of Mopsuestia (c. 350–428),

bishop, exegete. Theodore studied under the pagan orator Libanius in Antioch, then together with fellow student John Chrysostom he went to study Scripture under Diodore of Tarsus. Consecrated bishop of Mopsuestia in 392/393, Theodore supported Nicene Christianity and opposed the Pneumatomachians, who denied the full divinity of the Holy Spirit.

Theodore gave maturity to the Antiochene exegesis and Christology that Diodore had initiated. The outcome was both fame and infamy. Theodore was linked to the Nestorian heresy, which was condemned at the Council of Ephesus (431). In the sixth century Emperor Justinian condemned Theodore and his writings in the Three Chapters edict. Within the "Nestorian" church, which extended from Syria into the Persian Empire and exists today as Assyrian Christianity, Theodore is a revered theologian. Most of Theodore's extant works and fragments are in Syriac.

The grammatical/historical method of the rhetorical schools played a key role in

Theodore's Antiochene exegesis. "History" in premodern culture did not mean the science of reconstructing events on the basis of material evidence. Instead, *historia* referred both to a narrative genre and to analysis of the basic sense of narrative units. Study of the Bible followed methods that grammar schools applied to classical literature: determine the purpose, the hypothesis, and the narrative integrity. This approach was in contrast to the philosophical methods adapted by Alexandrians.

Theodore believed this method enabled the interpreter to discern the one true meaning of a passage or entire book of Scripture. He dismissed the exegesis from the school of Alexandria (Egypt) for presuming that the Bible has multiple layers of meaning and blamed their theological mistakes on poor foundational methodology—that is, Alexandrians failed to do proper background work that would have limited and focused their interpretations. The Alexandrians, whose methodology owed more to philosophical analysis, sought a text's meaning (often moral) that is at times clothed in misleading wording. Theodore emphasized that certain things in the Bible did in fact happen, whereas he thought with the less disciplined Alexandrian exegesis that events and their interpretation became obscured by spiritualized meanings detached from what actually happened and from a given narrative's more obvious purpose.

Adherence to a grammatical/historical method led Theodore to limit how much a Christian could read Christ into Old Testament narratives. If, for instance, the context of the psalms is David and the kingdom of Israel, then the basic purpose and meaning of the psalms cannot jump out of that narrative context and into the New Testament context. Only rarely would Theodore allow that a messianic passage in the OT might refer to Christ. The extent to which Theodore limited a Christian reading of the OT verged on making the OT irrelevant for Christians.

In the realm of Christology the distance that Theodore put between the OT and the NT mirrored that which he strove to maintain between the human creature and the Word's impassible divinity in Christ. Theodore described Christ's humanity as the "assumed man" and his divinity as the Word. Both he and Diodore attacked Apollinarianism for its diminishment of Christ's humanity, purporting that Christ had a divine, not human, mind (*nous*). Instead, Theodore defended a formula that protected the full humanity of Christ, joining the divine and human in a harmony of wills through God's grace. Christ is the indwelling of the Word in the "assumed man" by God's pleasure.

A sixth-century commentator, Leontius of Byzantium, saw that the danger of Theodore's thought was not merely the foundation he lay for Nestorian Christology but the diminishment of the Old Testament as Christian Scripture.

R. A. Greer, *Theodore of Mopsuestia: Exegete and Theologian* (1961); F. G. McLeod, *The Roles of Christ's Humanity in Salvation: Insights from Theodore of Mopsuestia* (2005); J. McWilliam-Dewart, *The Theology of Grace of Theodore of Mopsuestia* (1971); R. A. Norris, *Manhood and Christ: A Study in the Christology of Theodore of Mopsuestia* (1963); J. J. O'Keefe, "'A Letter That Killeth': Toward a Reassessment of Antiochene Exegesis, or Diodore, Theodore, and Theodoret on the Psalms," *JECS* 8, no. 1 (2000): 93–104; R. C. Hill, ed. and trans., *Theodore of Mopsuestia Commentary on the Twelve Prophets* (2004); D. Z. Zaharopoulos, *Theodore of Mopsuestia on the Bible: A Study of His Old Testament Exegesis* (1989).

LISA D. MAUGANS DRIVER

Theodore the Studite (759–826), Byzantine monastic reformer, abbot, iconodule (supporter of religious images), and theologian. Born in Constantinople, he was much influenced by his uncle St. Plato, abbot of the Saccudium Monastery. About 780 he became a monk at Saccudium and in 787 was ordained monk-priest by Patriarch Tarasius. In 787 he succeeded his uncle as abbot. In 797 he was banished to Thessalonica by Tarasius for his opposition to the adulterous marriage of Emperor Constantine VI. However, he was recalled to Saccudium in the following year when Constantine was deposed by his mother, Irene. In 799 Theodore and the majority of his monks relocated to the failing monastery at Studios in Constantinople to avoid the constant Saracen raids at Saccudium. Under the genius of Theodore's direction, Studios became the center of monasticism in the Christian East. In 809 he was once again banished from Constantinople over the controversy surrounding the adulterous marriage of Constantine VI, this time when he objected to emperor Nicephorus I's restoration of Joseph of Kathara, a priest who had performed the wedding ceremony. Theodore returned to Studios after Nicephorus's death in 811. In 815 Theodore, a staunch iconodule, was exiled when he opposed the

iconoclastic policy of Emperor Leo V. He was allowed to return after Leo's assassination in 820; however, the new emperor, Michael, banned image worship in Constantinople, and Theodore was constrained to spend the end of his days on the Tryphon peninsula. His works include two catechetical treatises, a commentary on the Presanctified Liturgy (a eucharistic service attributed to Gregory the Great), sermons, tracts against the iconoclasts, letters, and poetry. Theodore is greatly honored in the Orthodox Church for his contribution to the flowering of monasticism, for his support of the independence of the church in the face of official repression, and for his unwavering support of icons.

R. Cholij, *Theodore the Stoudite: The Ordering of Holiness* (2002); A. Gardner, *Theodore of Studium: His Life and Times* (1905); Theodore the Studite, *On the Holy Icons*, ed. and trans. C. P. Roth (1981).

MICHAEL D. PETERSON

Theodoret of Cyrrhus (c. 393–c. 460), exegete, historian, apologist, bishop. In 416 this native of Antioch took vows and completed his education in philosophy and the Bible among Syriac monks and later was appointed bishop of Cyrrhus near Antioch (423). By 431, Theodoret was recruited to defend the Christology of Nestorius, former bishop of Antioch. Nestorius, as bishop of Constantinople, provoked many by discouraging the use of *Theotokos* ("Godbearer") as a title for Mary out of his concern that believers were confusing the divine and human in Christ. Following Nestorius's condemnation at Ephesus in 431, Theodoret likely helped compose the Formula of Union, which was accepted by the principal opponents, Cyril of Alexandria and John of Antioch (433). The conflict reignited when the monk Eutyches preached Cyril's extreme Christology, declaring Christ to be "one nature" (monophysis). For his opposition to Monophysitism, Theodoret was deposed at the "Robber Council" of Ephesus in 449. The Council of Chalcedon (451) restored Theodoret to his see when he agreed to the condemnation of Nestorius that took into account Antiochene concerns. Little is known of the remainder of his life.

Theodoret was an active writer whose letters illuminate pastoral issues of his time. He engaged in apologetics and antiheretical works against Apollinarians and Arians, as well as Monophysites. His *Ecclesiastical History* continues Eusebius's work, and his *Religious His-*

tory describes holy men and women in Syria. Theodoret stood at the end of a distinct Antiochene tradition of exegesis that developed under Diodore of Tarsus and Theodore of Mopsuestia. Theodoret found the strict Antiochene interpretation, which limited reading the Old Testament in light of the New Testament, to be inadequate since he believed, for instance, that the Psalms must be meaningful for Christians, not just for ancient Israelites.

G. W. Ashby, *Theodoret of Cyrrhus as Exegete of the Old Testament* (1972); J.-N. Guinot, "Theodoret of Cyrus: Bishop and Exegete," in *The Bible in Greek Christian Antiquity*, ed. and trans. P. M. Blowers (1997), 163–93; T. E. Urbainczyk, *Theodoret of Cyrrhus: The Bishop and the Holy Man* (2002).

LISA D. MAUGANS DRIVER

Theodosius I (c. 346–395), Roman

emperor (379–395). Theodosius, a member of a distinguished military family from Spain, was living in retirement in 378 when the eastern Roman emperor Valens died at the hands of rebellious Visigoths in the battle of Adrianople. Gratian, one of two emperors ruling in the West, arranged Theodosius's elevation as ruler in the East. Theodosius pacified the Visigothic soldiers and established an important precedent by settling them in Thrace as *foederati* (federates serving the Romans). In 383 a usurper in the West, Magnus Maximus, killed Gratian. Theodosius had to recognize Maximus's legitimacy, but when the latter moved against the Italian emperor Valentinian II, Theodosius marched westward and defeated and killed the usurper (388).

Theodosius and his court were staunch proponents of Nicene Christianity. The emperor issued an edict of 380 that forbade heresy. He replaced an Arian bishop of Constantinople with the Nicene Gregory of Nazianzus. In 381 Theodosius presided over the Council of Constantinople, which permanently established the Nicene interpretation of Christ's essential relationship with God the Father. Arianism thenceforth was on the wane in the empire.

In 391 Bishop Ambrose of Milan issued a famous rebuke of the emperor. He caused Theodosius to perform extended penance for having ordered the massacre of seven thousand persons who had rioted in Thessalonica. In 392, Theodosius issued an edict making Christianity the only legal religion in the realm. The emperor's officials were noted for their heavy-handedness in the destruction of pagan temples

in the East, most notably the Serapeum in Alexandria. Upon Valentinian II's demise in 392, Theodosius became sole ruler of the whole empire. It was to be the last such instance. Upon his death, Theodosius's sons Arcadius and Honorius separated the empire into what would become permanent eastern and western halves.

J. F. Matthews, *Western Aristocracies and Imperial Court, AD 364–425* (1975).

ALLEN E. JONES

Theodosius II (401–450), eastern Roman

emperor (408–450). Theodosius became ruler of the eastern half of the empire at age seven. He benefited from good advisors, including his sister Pulcheria, who acted as regent during his minority and continued to exercise influence throughout her brother's long reign. As much a scholar as ruler, Theodosius presided over a restructuring of the school at Constantinople, thereby making the capital as important a center for Christian studies as Alexandria. In 438 Theodosius issued the first official codification of Roman law, the Theodosian Code, which was valid in the eastern and western halves of the empire. It was during Theodosius's long tenure that Huns north of the Danube began to pose a formidable threat to Roman interests. The emperor responded to the menace by offering (increasingly larger) gifts of tribute to Hun leaders, most notably Attila, so as to dissuade them from making forays into the realm. Additionally, Theodosius ordered a stout circuit wall constructed about Constantinople (completed 413), thus making the city virtually impregnable.

A second problem that beset Theodosius was the tumultuous debate over the person of Christ. In 431 the emperor summoned the Council of Ephesus, which condemned the view of Nestorius, patriarch of Constantinople, that Jesus has two independent natures and that Mary gave birth to the human nature only. In 448 the archimandrite Eutyches, who postulated a single, presumably divine, nature for the incarnate Word, was deposed at a synod called by Flavian, the patriarch of Constantinople. At the urging of Dioscorus, the patriarch of Alexandria, Theodosius called another synod, the so-called Robber Council of Ephesus (449), which restored Eutyches and made Monophysite doctrine orthodox. Theodosius died the next year, leaving the threat posed by the Huns and the theological turmoil caused by the christological debates unresolved.

J. B. Bury, *History of the Later Roman Empire*, 2 vols. (repr. 1958); K. Holum, *Theodosian Empresses* (1982).

ALLEN E. JONES

Theodulf of Orléans (c. 760–821), theologian, poet, bishop. Theodulf was of Visigothic origin. He is first mentioned as being at Charlemagne's court in 785, and he became with Alcuin of York one of the two most important royal counselors. He directed the redaction of the *Libri Carolini* (the Caroline Books), which present the Western position on images, though their restrictive attitude toward the veneration of images was soon abandoned. The most important among his many contributions to the Carolingian reform is the revision of the text of the Latin Bible, in which he even drew on the Hebrew text of the Old Testament and which differed from Alcuin's more influential revision. Sometime before 798 he was appointed bishop of Orléans and abbot of the nearby monastery of Fleury, which became one of the leading centers of learning in the Carolingian empire. The content and form of his diocesan statutes helped to establish a genre of *capitula episcoporum* ("chapters of bishops"). Some of his hymns, such as *Gloria, laus et honor* ("Glory, Praise, and Honor") for Palm Sunday, are still in use. He was a witness of Charlemagne's imperial coronation at Rome in 800; on this occasion he received the pallium.

His breadth as a theologian is documented by his treatises on sensitive theological problems such as the debate with Byzantium over the *filioque* clause (809) and the theology of baptism (811/812). He played a leading role at the reform synod of 813, but he was not able to maintain his position when Louis the Pious rose to power. After 819 he was accused of having supported the revolt of Bernhard of Italy (Charlemagne's grandson), then deposed and imprisoned. It is hard to determine to what degree the accusations against him were true, yet his fall should be seen in context of the general measures taken against members of the "Spanish" party under Louis the Pious.

Opera Omnia, in PL 78 (1849), 353–79, and PL 105 (1851), 187–380; E. Dümmler, ed., *Carmina*, vol. 1 of MGH Poetae Latini aevi Carolini (1881), 437–581; A. Freeman, ed., *Opus Caroli regis contra synodum (Libri Carolini)*, supplement vol. 1 of MGH Concilia (1998); P. Brommer, ed., *Capitularia*, vol. 1 of MGH Capitula Episcoporum (1984), 73–184; H.

Sauer, ed., *Theodulfi Capitula in England: Die altenglischen Übersetzungen, zusammen mit dem lateinischen Text* (1978); E. Dahlhaus-Berg, *Nova antiquitas et antiqua novitas: Typologische Exegese und isidorianisches Geschichtsbild bei Theodulf von Orléans* (1975); A. Freeman, "Carolingian Orthodoxy and the Fate of the *Libri Carolini*," *Viator* 16 (1985): 65–108; Freeman, "Scripture and Images in the *Libri Carolini*," *Texte e imagine nell' alto medioevo*, *Settimane di Studio* 41 no. 1 (1994): 163–94.

JOHANNES HEIL

Theologia Germanica Edited by Martin Luther in 1516, then again in a longer version in 1518, the anonymous fourteenth-century text called *Theologia Germanica* (*Eyn deutsch Theologia* in the 1518 edition) has often been compared to the writings of Johannes Tauler. It is indeed one of the most significant examples of late medieval spirituality, written in German and testifying to the strong influence of Tauler and Eckhart on the one hand, and to the importance of the connection between the mystical tradition and the Reformation on the other. The *Theologia Germanica* inherits from Eckhart the emphasis on union with God and detachment, while it focuses more intensely on the imitation and love of Christ, as well as the function of grace and obedience. A key aspect is to be seen in the distinction between true love and freedom and the "false" ideas of love and freedom that can be found in the so-called heresy of the Free Spirit. Thus, the text reflects on issues that have been raised in the context of and after the condemnation of Eckhart. While Luther praised the text, mentioning it together with the Bible and the works of Augustine, Calvin and many Catholic theologians dismissed its significance. Since Luther's 1518 edition, the *Theologia Germanica* became one of the most popular mystical treatises, published in many languages in at least 190 editions.

B. Hoffman, trans., *The "Theologia Germanica" of Martin Luther* (1980).

NIKLAUS LARGIER

Theopaschite Formula The designation refers to the controversial statement that "God suffered" in the flesh. Although the formula was essentially orthodox, the Monophysites employed it to advance their Christology. Around 520 a group of Scythian monks led by John Maxentius traveled to Rome and Constantinople lobbying for acceptance of the phrase "One of the Trinity suffered in the flesh" in order to make a clearer statement against both Nestorianism and Apollinarianism. The bishop of Rome, Hormisdas, opposed the formula, as he feared it could too easily be interpreted as Monophysite. The Monophysites did employ the formula.

Emperor Justinian I supported the phrase in order to satisfy the Monophysites at the Council of Constantinople (533). The bishop of Rome at the time, John II, approved of the formula at the council.

L. D. Davis, SJ, *The First Seven Ecumenical Councils (325–797)* (1983); J. A. McGuckin, "The Theopaschite Confession (Text and Historical Context): A Study in the Cyrilline Reinterpretation of Chalcedon," *JEH* 35 (1984): 239–55.

STEVEN A. MCKINION

Theophilus of Alexandria (d. 412),

bishop (385–412). Theophilus greatly endeavored to retain and even elevate the authority of Alexandria within Egypt and abroad. Long the principal bishopric of the eastern Roman Empire, Alexandria's prominence was threatened by the rising stature of the bishop of Constantinople.

In his early years he worked to establish monuments to the see of Alexandria and to himself. Most famously, in 391 he seized the Serapeum and converted it into a church. His mania for building led to accusations of pharaonic delusions and misappropriation of funds.

In 399, the Anthropomorphite Controversy arose when Theophilus first sided with many monks in Nitria and Kellia, among them the Tall Brothers, and then suddenly reversed his course. Labeling them Origenists, Theophilus excommunicated the Tall Brothers and violently drove hundreds of monks from their communities. The Tall Brothers and around fifty fellow monks eventually appealed to John Chrysostom, the bishop of Constantinople, whom Theophilus regarded as a bitter rival. Perceiving this as an attempt by Constantinople to exercise jurisdiction over Alexandria, Theophilus engineered the deposition of John at the Synod of the Oak in 403.

E. A. Clark, *The Origenist Controversy: The Cultural Construction of an Early Christian Debate* (1992); J. N. D. Kelly, *Golden Mouth: The Story of John Chrysostom—Ascetic, Preacher, Bishop* (1998).

STEVEN D. DRIVER

Theophilus of Antioch (second cent.),

apologist and sixth bishop of (Syrian) Antioch. A work on history is attributed to Theophilus, and Eusebius (*Hist. eccl.* 4.20, 24) and Jerome (*Lives of Illustrious Men* 25, Letter 121.6) credit him with works opposing Hemogenes and Marcion and with some catechetical writings. Theophilus's only extant work, *To Autolycus* (c. 180), reflects early interreligious dialogue, the use of the *logos* doctrine, and the original use of "Triad" to denote the Godhead. The first book, a response to Autolycus's hostile stand against the name "Christian," reveals the inadequacies in Autolycus's religious system (such as idolatry and emperor worship) and explains and defends the essential aspects of Christianity (such as faith, a transcendent God, and the resurrection). The second book, which includes appeals to the Sibylline Oracles, is largely an exposition of Genesis. It argues that the prophets present a consistent doctrine of God and cosmology, superior to pagan writings, which advocate man-made religion. The third book intends to prove the antiquity, consistency, and trustworthiness of Scripture in contrast to the contradictory writings of the pagan poets and philosophers, which contain inferior ethics and histories. The Prophets and Gospels are accurate and truly ethical.

R. Rogers, *Theophilus of Antioch: The Life and Thought of a 2nd-Century Bishop* (2000); Theophilus, *Tatiani oratio ad graecos: Theophili Antiocheni ad Autolycum*, ed. M. Marcovich (1995); *Theophilus of Antioch: Ad Autolycum*, ed. and trans. R. M. Grant (1970).

D. JEFFREY BINGHAM

Theophylact (1050–1125), Byzantine arch-

bishop and scholar. Theophylact was born on the island of Euboea. In Constantinople he was a pupil of Michael Psellus (see *Constantine Psellus*) and became the first teacher of rhetoric in the patriarchal school. He was the tutor of Constantine Doukas, the future Constantine VII Porphyrogenitus. He served as a deacon in the Great Church in Constantinople, and around 1080 he was named archbishop of Ochrida in Bulgaria. His correspondence reveals that he found Bulgaria uncivilized and looked upon the appointment as an exile. He ultimately resigned from his see and died in Salonica.

Theophylact's writings include a *Life* of Clement of Ochrida, but he is best known for his extensive scriptural commentaries. He wrote commentaries on the entire New Testament and the Prophets and produced a compendium of John Chrysostom's commentaries on Luke. He adopted a literal approach and focused on practical moral application. He was used and admired by Erasmus. While Clement firmly held to the Greek position in the disputes with the Latins, Theophylact's approach is generally irenic. He argues that some Latin practices, such as the use of unleavened bread, had no theological significance and ought not divide the church.

PG 123–26 (1864); P. Gautier, *Theophylactus, of Ochrida, Archbishop of Ochrida, ca. 1050–ca. 1108*, 2 vols. (1980–1986); M. Mullet, *Theophylact of Ochrid: Reading the Letters of a Byzantine Archbishop* (1997).

EUGENE M. LUDWIG, OFM CAP.

Theotokos This Greek devotional and theological title for Mary the mother of Jesus means "God-bearer" or, more often, connotes "Mother of God." Originating in third-century Egypt, *Theotokos* was used by Christians across the eastern Roman Empire in the fourth century. Only toward the end of the fourth century did Christians examine and develop the title's theological implications, especially regarding Christology and Mary's role in the incarnation. By the fifth century the rival theologians of Antioch and Alexandria engaged in a struggle over the use of *Theotokos* for Mary. Bishop Nestorius of Constantinople, an Antiochene, feared that popular devotion to Mary as Theotokos perpetuated a dangerous Christology by confusing or melding the human and divine in Christ. According to Nestorius, Mary could be mother of Christ's humanity but not of his divinity. Riding the popular outrage at Nestorius's perceived attack on Mary, the Alexandrians, led by Bishop Cyril of Alexandria, insisted that the two natures are so joined in the one person of Christ as to allow, and even require, the title *Theotokos*. In 431 at the Ecumenical Council of Ephesus, the Alexandrian view prevailed in Greek Orthodoxy, though not without alienating the Syriac and other Eastern Christians of the "Nestorian" church.

L. Gambero, ed., T. Buffer, trans., *Mary and the Fathers of the Church* (1999); H. Graef, *Mary: A History of Doctrine and Devotion* (1963); M. O'Carroll, *Theotokos: A Theological Encyclopedia of the Blessed Virgin Mary* (1983); M. Starowieyski, "Le titre θεοτόκος avant le concile d'Ephèse," StPatr (1989): 236–42.

LISA D. MAUGANS DRIVER

Thirty-nine Articles Elizabeth I and the Convocation issued these moderate doctrinal statements in 1563 (English version, 1571) to define Elizabeth's position on significant ecclesiastical issues against both Catholic conservatism and Puritan radicalism. They parallel Archbishop Cranmer's more radical Forty-two Articles (1553) and like those do not constitute a comprehensive creed.

Articles 1 to 8 summarize the traditional Chalcedonian reception of the Nicene Creed, and the authority of Scripture. Articles 9 to 16 cover sin, grace, and good works, moderately holding both justification by faith alone and the necessity of repentance and public forgiveness. Articles 17 to 21 define the predestined elect in England, against Rome and fallible ecumenical councils. Articles 22 to 37 cover organization: ministry, ceremonies, sacraments, authority, and relation to civil powers. Articles 38 and 39 cover almsgiving and oathtaking. Article 29, that those who receive the Eucharist not in a state of grace do not truly receive Christ, was suppressed shortly after initial publication to court alliance with German Lutheran princes, but it was reinstated in 1571.

Adherence to the Articles was required for all clergy and graduates of Cambridge and Oxford until 1865; since then, clergy need only acknowledge that the Articles are consistent with Scripture and faith. They are significant for their moderate formulation of England's Reformation at a crucial period and for their cooperative relationship between church and state.

E. Bicknell, *Theological Introduction to the Thirty-nine Articles* (1919, 1955); E. Gibson, *Thirty-nine Articles*, 2 vols. (1896, 1897); J. Newman, *Tract 90* (1841).

DAVID A. LOPEZ

Thirty Years' War A series of religious and political conflicts in Central Europe flowing from continuing religious unrest following the Peace of Augsburg (1555) and conflicting dynastic aspirations among the ruling houses of Europe. The war was fought in four phases: Bohemian-Palatinate (1618–1625), Danish (1625–1629), Swedish (1630–1635), and French (1635–1648).

The war began in Bohemia when Protestants revolted against the Roman Catholic emperor, Ferdinand, and threw two of his representatives out a palace window (the Defenestration of Prague). The revolt quickly spread to the Rhineland Palatinate. In September 1619 the Bohemian Diet elected Frederick V of the Rhineland Palatinate their king. The Bohemians were defeated at White Mountain (1620) by the Catholic League, led by General Tilly and Duke Maximillian of Bavaria. The war then moved to the Palatinate, which fell when Heidelberg was occupied (1622).

The second phase broke out when the Danish, Dutch, and English all sought to curb the power of the Habsburg emperor. In 1625 Christian IV of Denmark invaded Saxony. In 1626, the defeat of Christian's army by imperial forces under Tilly and Albrecht Wallenstein led to the Treaty of Lübeck (1629). In the same year the emperor issued the Edict of Restitution, which called for the return of ecclesiastical property appropriated by Protestants since 1555.

The next phase began when King Gustavus Adolphus of Sweden landed troops in Pomerania. Gustavus had both religious (Lutheran) and territorial (threat of Ferdinand's power) reasons for joining the war. The French under Cardinal Richelieu aided Gustavus's attempt to curb imperial Habsburg power. In 1631 Gustavus defeated Tilly at Breitenfeld and then defeated Wallenstein at Lützen, but Gustavus was mortally wounded in the last battle. In 1634 imperial forces won a major victory at Nördlingen. Germany was exhausted by war, and the majority of Protestant princes agreed to peace with the emperor in the Treaty of Prague (1635).

The final phase of the war was a battle for political hegemony in Europe between France and the Habsburgs. The Swedes, unwilling to relinquish territory seized earlier, aided France. Much of Europe erupted into devastating war, and the calls for peace grew louder with each passing year. Negotiations for a settlement began in 1640 between the French, the HRE, the Swedes, and the German princes. The Peace of Westphalia was concluded in 1648.

G. Parker, ed., *Thirty Years War* (1997); C. V. Wedgwood, *The Thirty Years War* (1969).

DAVID WHITFORD

Thomas à Kempis (c. 1380–1471), Dutch

priest and author of the *Imitation of Christ*. Born at Kempen (northern Netherlands), Thomas was thirteen when he entered schools associated with the Brothers and Sisters of the Common Life in Deventer. Florentius Radewijns, superior of the "Brethren" during that time, not only provided financially for Thomas's care and education but also played a major role in his spiri-

tual growth and development. Chief among the influences on Thomas during his early years with the Brethren was their ambition to, above all, emulate the life and virtues of the first Christians, especially in the love of God and neighbor, focusing on simplicity, humility, devotion, and charity. After completing his studies at Deventer (1399), Thomas was admitted to the Canons Regular of Windesheim (see *Windesheim Congregation*) at Mount St. Agnes, near Zwolle, where his brother John was the first prior. He was ordained a priest in 1413 and spent most of his life in this convent, where he served as procurator (treasurer), subprior twice, novice-master, chronicler, and copyist.

In 1441, Thomas completed and signed his name to a codex containing the four books of the *Imitation of Christ* (now housed in the Royal Library in Brussels). Though some dispute his authorship of the highly popular book, most agree he was at the very least its final redactor. In this work, Thomas defines the imitation of Christ as the way of the cross, denying oneself and bringing one's life into total conformity with the pattern exhibited in the life of Christ. By meditating on Christ's sacred humanity, the Christian arrives at contemplation of his divinity and a union with God that liberates the soul. Thomas wrote about three dozen works, the bulk of which was dedicated to offering instructions for novices and junior canons and for writing spiritual treatises. His writing is either ascetical, such as the *Imitation of Christ* and *Soliloquy of the Soul*, or historical in scope, such as the biographies of Geert Groote and St. Lydwina of Schiedam. In 1471 he died from "dropsy" and was buried at Mount St. Agnes.

K. M. Becker, *From the Treasure House of Scripture: An Analysis of Scriptual Sources in "De Imitatione Christi"* (2002); P. van Geest, *Thomas à Kempis* (1996); J. E. G. de Montmorency, *Thomas a Kempis: His Age and Book* (1906); V. Scully, trans., *Thomas à Kempis: Meditations and Sermons on the Incarnation, Life, and Passion of Our Lord* (1906).

TODD M. RICHARDSON

Thomas Aquinas (1224/1225–1274),

Dominican theologian. Thomas was born at Roccasecca to lower aristocracy in the service of Emperor Frederick II. He was an oblate at the neighboring abbey of Monte Cassino (c. 1230–1239), where he was educated in the humane religiosity of the Benedictine rule in preparation for a widely expected promotion to abbot. From 1239, at the imperial university in Naples, he was introduced to a more comprehensive corpus of Aristotelian writings than was studied at the time in universities to the north. Here Thomas developed his central and abiding conviction about the compatibility of the animal foundations and the spiritual capacities of human beings and thus also of Aristotelian and Christian anthropologies. In April 1244, he received the habit of the papally fostered Dominican order, for which he was taken by his family into forced detention until Frederick's deposition in mid-1245. Thomas continued his philosophical studies and began his theological formation at Paris from 1246 on, the year after Albert the Great began teaching there in theology.

Thomas accompanied Albert to Cologne for the establishment of the *studium generale* there (1248–1252). As academic assistant (*baccalaureus*) to Albert, Thomas transcribed his commentaries on the recently translated *Nicomachean Ethics* and on parts of the *Corpus Dionysiacum*. The first of Thomas's own courses on the Old Testament date from this time, as does his ordination to the priesthood.

In 1252, Thomas returned to Paris to comment on Peter Lombard's *Sentences*. Amid violent protests associated with the mendicant controversy, Thomas received his master of theology degree in 1256 and was accepted soon after as a regent master. His first magisterial disputation, *De veritate* (1257), displays a programmatic affirmation of the epistemological and anthropological implications of Aristotle's stress on the finite spontaneity (*intellectus agens*) of human knowledge.

In 1259 Thomas returned to Italy, where, along with biblical commentaries, systematic disputations, and homiletic addresses, he authored his first extracurricular overview of theological systematics, the *Summa contra Gentiles*. This *Summa* develops a plausible, argumentative, and narrative account of Christianity in the face of Islamic challenges. Thomas's tenure as conventual lector at Orvieto (1261–1265) provided contact with the papal court there, resulting in the beginnings of the *Catena aurea*, Thomas's new patristic gloss on the Gospels drawn from Western (especially Augustine) and Eastern (notably Chrysostom) fathers. This work inaugurated a lasting shift toward a more salvific-historical dimension in his theology.

From 1265 to 1268, while serving as regent master of a new Dominican *studium* of his province in Rome, Thomas conceived and began his second, largely extracurricular, *Summa theologiae*, designing it in particular for beginning students of theology and completing its first part while in Rome. Although Thomas never completed the work, it would soon become the best known of all his works and ultimately the chief work of Roman Catholic theology to modern times. Toward the end of his tenure in Rome, Thomas began another extracurricular project, his literal commentaries on Aristotle. The commentaries attempt to develop a less heterodox potential within Aristotle than many of his defenders and detractors at the time were suggesting. In Thomas's view, the former propagated a view of humanity that was too animalistic, the latter one that was too spiritualistic.

The engagement of these two opposed movements demanded much of Thomas's attention during the second Parisian regency (1268–1272). Thomas defined his own position in relation to them in, for example, *De unitate intellectus* and *De aeternitate mundi*. The anthropological implications were articulated in the second part of the *Summa theologiae*, where Thomas's keen sense of human passions is inscribed into moral theology as a program of impassioned reason, expressing Thomas's basic anthropological thesis of the intellectual soul as the unique substantial form of the body: genuinely and actively intellective in the midst of its sensuality (*pace* Averroes), yet by the soul's very need for and reliance upon its corporeal coprinciple, limited in the range of its transcendence and self-sufficiency by the soul's need for and reliance upon its corporeal coprinciple (*pace* Neo-Augustinianism). The composition of the *Summa* was aided by numerous classroom disputations. Thomas's second regency in Paris experienced a flare-up of the mendicant controversy that had inaugurated his first regency there. While Thomas's interpretation of Aristotle, supported by pre-Arabic commentaries, mitigated the heterodox Aristotelianism perceptible in the arts faculty, the criticism of his theology by the Neo-Augustinian revival would intensify, although his teaching from this period shows an increased appropriation of Augustine.

Returning to his alma mater, Thomas became the founding lector of the Dominican *studium generale* at the Univ. of Naples. His exegesis of the letters of Paul in the New Testament and his treatment of the *mysteria vitae Christi* and of Christian and pre-Christian sacraments (*Summa theologiae* III) showed an increasingly Christocentric (and Augustinian) sense of the need for grace. With the exception of one letter on providence and freedom, Thomas ceased writing three months prior to his death at Fossanova, when he was on the way to the Second Council of Lyon.

Two censures of the arts faculty by the bishop of Paris (1270, 1277) and the theology faculty's censure of Aegidius Romanus (Giles of Rome), a selectively "Thomistic" student of Thomas, came as challenges to Thomas's thought. His positions, which grew from the key thesis of the unity of the substantial form, were directly criticized in 1277 by a preparatory investigation at Paris and by the censure of Archbishop Robert Kilwardby at Oxford. Kilwardby and William de la Mare, both adherents of Bonaventure, unpacked these brief legal censures in longer critiques of Thomas. In 1278 Robert's open letter to Peter of Conflans and William's *Correctorium fratris Thomae* triggered reactions from those who defended Thomas's thought ("correctories dispute"), helping to shape the reception and the view of Thomism well beyond his canonization in 1323.

———

Opera omnia (Leonina, 32 vols. sqq., 1882 sqq.; Parma, 25 vols., 1852/1948 sqq.; Vivès, 34 vols., 1871 sqq.; Busa, 7 vols., 1980); M.-D. Chenu, *Toward Understanding St. Thomas* (1964); M. Dauphinais and M. Levering, eds., *Reading John with St. Thomas Aquinas* (2005); G. Emery, *Trinity in Aquinas* (2004); E. Gilson et al., *Thomas Aquinas, 1274–1974: Commemorative Essays* (1974); P. Glorieux, ed., *Le premières polémiques thomistes*, 2 vols. (Correctoria Quare/Sciendum, 1927, 1956); P. M. Hall, *Narrative and Natural Law* (1994); T. Hibbs, *Dialectic and Narrative in Aquinas* (1995); J.-P. Müller, ed., *Le Correctorium Corruptorii*, 3 vols. (Circa/Quaestione 1941, 1954); F. J. Roensch, *Early Thomistic School* (1964); R. Schenk, *Die Gnade vollendeter Endlichkeit* (1989); T. Schneider, *Die Einheit des Menschen* (1973); J.-P. Torrell, *St. Thomas Aquinas*, 2 vols. (1996, 2003); R. Van Nieuwenhove and J. Wawrykow, eds., *The Theology of Thomas Aquinas* (2005); F. Van Steenberghen, *Thomas Aquinas and Radical Aristotelianism* (1980); J. Wawrykow, *God's Grace and Human Action* (1995); T. G. Weinandy et al., eds., *Aquinas on Doctrine* (2004); J. A. Weisheipl, *Friar Thomas d'Aquino* (1974, 1983); http://www.corpusthomisticum .org (July 2007).

RICHARD SCHENK, OP

Thomas of Marga (ninth cent.), Syriac bishop, historian of the Church of the East. Thomas was a native of Salakh who entered the renowned monastery of Bēt 'Abē (forty miles northeast of Mosul, Iraq) in 832. He became secretary to the patriarch, Abraham (837–850) by whom he was consecrated bishop of Margā. Later he was appointed metropolitan of Bēt Garmai (near Kirkuk, Iraq). Around 840 he wrote the *Book of Governors*, primarily a history of Bēt 'Abē. It also included biographies of a number of other Mesopotamian monks. The book is one of the major sources for the monastic history of the Church of the East. Book six of the *Book of Governors* is a history of the Rabban Cyprian monastery in Birtha.

———

E. A. W. Budge, ed. and trans., *The Book of Governors: The Historia Monastica of Thomas, Bishop of Margā* (1893); C. F. Robinson, *Empires and Elites after the Muslim Conquest: The Transformation of Northern Mesopotamia* (2001); C. Villagomez, "The Fields, Flocks, and Finances of Monks: Economic Life in Nestorian Monasteries, 500–850" (PhD diss., UCLA, 1999).

ROBERT A. KITCHEN

Thomism The comprehensive identification of predominant themes and programmatic emphases throughout the works of Thomas Aquinas was first undertaken by his Neo-Augustinian critics; to a large degree, they were the first authors of "Thomism." Their need to contrast Thomism with the Augustinian tradition, their neglect of Thomas's exegetical work on Scripture, and the unpublished state of the third part of the *Summa theologiae* at the time of William de la Mare's first redaction of his *Correctorium fratris Thomae* meant that the "Augustinian" themes of justification, prevenient grace, and sacraments that would mark Thomism vis-à-vis the Reformation and Molinism were still missing in the early formation of Thomism. As was clear already in Robert Kilwardby's prohibition of Thomistic positions at the Univ. of Oxford (March 18, 1277) and in his open letter to Peter of Conflans defending his decree, the identification of Thomism first crystallized around the anthropological implications of Thomas's insistence upon the rational soul as the *unica forma corporis* ("sole form of the body"): Thomas's stress on the limitations of human knowledge (the importance of the senses), of liberty (the importance of the passions), and of death (the importance of the body). The Dominican General Chapter held in

1278 in Milan saw the initial critique of Thomas's basic thought by the Dominican supporters of Kilwardby (the "Cantuarienses") as scandalous, *in scandalum ordinis*, and called for the defense of Thomas's *doctrina*. This was the beginning of progressively favorable endorsements within the Dominican order itself. Lasting through the fifteenth century, this "first Thomism" is characterized by the *Defensiones* ("defenses"). In England, especially under the provincialate of William Hothum, early Thomists included Richard Knapwell, Robert Orford, William of Macclesfeld, and Thomas Sutton. The latter interpreted Thomistic epistemology in a realist, nearly empiricist manner that contrasted both with much of the work of Thomas himself and with early continental Thomists such as Bernard of Trilia, John of Paris (notably in his political works, going well beyond Thomas), Peter of Palude, John of Naples, and especially Herveus Natalis. First Thomism continued to develop beyond the immediate horizon of Thomas in response to criticism not only from Dominicans such as James of Metz, Durandus, and the German Albert school but also from thinkers such as Henry of Ghent, John Duns Scotus and his school, and the increasingly nominalist atmosphere of the universities. From Giles of Rome and Peter of Tarantaise on, students of Thomas's thought, in only partial agreement with their master (not just "Thomists"), also made an important contribution to the origin and development of "Thomism."

While many of the earliest Thomists were sensitive to the development within the thought of Thomas himself (producing both lists of "places where Thomas seemed to speak better in the *Summa* than in the *Sentences*" and the genus of *Concordantia textuum discordantium*, that is, concordances of textual disagreements among Thomas's statements), the tendency was toward a more systematic, less developmental view of his thought. The work of John Capreolus (1380–1444), celebrated as the *Princeps Thomistarum* ("foremost of Thomists"), marks the transition from the period of the first Thomism to that of the "second Thomism" (roughly fifteenth and sixteenth centuries), characterized by the comprehensive, often article-by-article commentaries of the pre-Tridentine and Tridentine era, both Dominican and non-Dominican (notably the Carmelite Thomas-commentators at Salamanca, the *Salmanticenses*). This period saw the extension of Thomism to answer issues raised for international law by the conquest of the Americas

and the clash of civilizations (cf. the work of Francisco de Vitoria, c. 1485–1546, on just war and institutional law). Thomism also answered questions of Christian existence raised by the beginnings of the Reformation. Thomists of this period included Thomas de Vio Cajetan (d. 1534), Domingo de Soto (d. 1560), and Melchior Cano (d. 1569). Marked by new attention to many of the properly theological contributions previously latent in Thomas's thought, this "second Thomism" is also generally distinguished from the period of the intra-Catholic "Disputations" that shaped the "third Thomism" in the first decades after the Council of Trent (especially by what became known as the Thomist-Molinist debates, 1581–1611), showing that, despite the post-Tridentine replacement of Peter Lombard's *Sentences* by Thomas's *Summa theologiae* as the leading handbook of Catholic systematics, Thomism remained one—paradigmatic—school within Roman Catholic thought. John of St. Thomas (John Poinsot, d. 1644) developed a hermeneutics of the limits and potential of Thomas's writings for understanding problems that became explicit only after Thomas's death.

————

A. Michelitsch, *Kommentatoren zur Summa Theologiae des hl. Thomas von Aquin* (1924, repr. 1981); M. Grabmann, *Mittelalterliches Geistesleben* I–III (1956, repr. 1981); F. J. Roensch, *Early Thomistic School* (1964); L. A. Kennedy, *A Catalogue of Thomists, 1270–1900* (1987); R. Cessario, *A Short History of Thomism* (2005); D. Berger and J. Vijgen, eds., *Thomistenlexikon* (2006).

RICHARD SCHENK, OP

Three Chapters The christological controversies of the fifth century, which pitted the approach of Antioch against that of Alexandria, were not entirely resolved by the Council of Chalcedon (451). The emperor Justinian hoped to convince the Monophysites that the Chaldeconian formula affirming two complete natures (divine and human) in the one person (*prosopon, hypostasis*) of Christ was not a return to heretical Nestorianism. In 544 he promulgated anathemas (the "Three Chapters") against the sources of Nestorian Christology, condemning the person and writings of Theodore of Mopsuestia, Theodoret of Cyrus's attack on Cyril's Twelve Anathemas, and Ibas of Edessa's letter to Maris. Many, including Vigilius of Rome, resisted posthumous condemnations. Vigilius eventually was convinced to support the Three Chapters' anathemas, which had been adopted by the Second Council of Constantinople (553). Nevertheless, Justinian did not convince the Monophysites, and his pressure on Vigilius further alienated Western bishops from the emperor.

J. Meyendorff, "Chalcedonians and Monophysites after Chalcedon," *GOTR* 10, no. 2 (1964–1965): 16–36; A. C. Outler, "'The Three Chapters': A Comment on the Survival of Antiochene Christology," in *Tribute to Arthur Vööbus: Studies in Early Christian Literature and Its Environment, Primarily in the Syrian East*, ed. R. H. Fischer (1977), 357–64; N. P. Tanner, ed., *Decrees of the Ecumenical Councils: From Nicea I to Vatican II* (1990).

LISA D. MAUGANS DRIVER

Tillotson, John (1630–1694), English theologian and archbishop of Canterbury. Reared in a Puritan family, by his ordination in 1661 Tillotson had turned his back on Calvinism and embraced the moderate rationalist position of the Latitudinarians, of which he became a principal exponent. One of the most famous and popular preachers of his day, Tillotson rose quickly through the ranks of the Church of England, becoming archbishop of Canterbury in 1691.

His theological writings posit a harmony between reason and revelation. Reason is the foundation and criterion of revealed religion. Revelation supplements, but does not contradict, what reason discerns. Tillotson's distrust of religious enthusiasm, his rationalist account of faith, and his description of miracles as evidence of the divine origin of religious doctrine broadly influenced English theology in the early Enlightenment.

J. Marshall, "The Ecclesiology of the Latitude-men, 1660–1689: Stillingfleet, Tillotson and 'Hobbism,'" *JEH* 36 (1985): 407–27; I. Rivers, *Grace, Sentiment, and Reason* (1991).

CHRISTOPHER ELWOOD

Toledo, Councils of Between 400 and 702, eighteen episcopal councils were held to deal with problems facing the church in Spain. Scholars consider the first three to be the most important. The initial council occurred when Toledo was part of the Roman province of Hispania. Eighteen bishops attended, and it dealt with issues such as clerical celibacy, the spotty acceptance of the decrees of the Ecumenical Council of Nicaea (325), marriage regulations, and the condemnation of Priscillianism, an ascetic movement founded by a Spanish layman named Priscillian who was executed for sorcery in 386 by a pretender to the imperial throne. Toledo's condemnation repeated a similar act of another Spanish council in 380, but Priscillianism survived till the seventh century.

The Second Council of Toledo met in 527, when the Iberian peninsula was ruled by several barbarian tribes including the powerful Visigoths, in whose kingdom Toledo lay. Since bishops who did not attend the council still signed its documents, it is uncertain how many actually attended. The council produced five decrees, three dealing with clerical life, one with church lands, and the last with decrees of consanguinity in marriage, no small matter since marriage regulations in barbarian societies differed from those of the Roman Empire in which Christianity had been formed.

The third and most significant council of Toledo met in 589 after the Visigoths had consolidated their rule over Spain. The Visigoths had been Arian Christians who rejected the doctrine of the Trinity proclaimed at the ecumenical councils of Nicaea (325) and Constantinople I (381). Because the large Hispano-Roman populace adhered to Nicene orthodoxy, unity in Spain had not been possible. In 587 the Visigothic king Reccared (r. 586–601) converted to Nicene Christianity and won over many of his people and nobility. To regularize matters, the king called a council to meet at Toledo under the leadership of Bishop Leander of Seville, who had converted Reccared. This heavily attended council officially rejected Arianism, and the eight Visigothic Arian bishops publicly accepted Nicene orthodoxy. The council also passed disciplinary decrees. The fifteen subsequent councils of Toledo served to increase royal and episcopal authority. They also dealt with the stubborn survival of pagan customs, especially among the rural peasantry.

J. Hillgarth, *Visigothic Spain* (1985); P. D. King, *Law and Society in the Visigothic Kingdom* (1972); P. Linehan, *History and Historians of Medieval Spain* (1993), chaps. 1–3.

JOSEPH F. KELLY

Toleration Act This 1689 act by the English Parliament exempted Protestant dissenters from statutes requiring religious conformity, granting them freedom of worship. Dissenters were required to swear an oath of loyalty to William III and Mary II and subscribe to essential components of the Thirty-nine Articles. The act thus effectively defined toleration in narrow terms. It rewarded dissenters for their support of the Glorious Revolution (1688) while maintaining Anglican dominance by rejecting proposals for a more inclusive established church and avoiding an extension of protection to Unitarians, Deists, atheists, or Jews.

J. Coffey, *Persecution and Toleration in Protestant England, 1558–1689* (2000).

CHRISTOPHER ELWOOD

Toleration in the Reformation

The modern concept of toleration must be differentiated from the idea of toleration in the Reformation, which was premised mainly on religious belief and its implied political consequences, and occasionally in relation to cultural or ethnic differences. To a lesser degree toleration ensured the limited freedom of worship, yet freedom of religion never implied freedom from religion. Most Reformation writings on toleration focused exclusively on freedom of conscience, as championed by Luther at the Diet of Worms and by other humanist reformers influenced by Erasmus. However, many reformers predisposed toward some form of religious tolerance argued strongly against it for political reasons. When Luther published his classic statement on religious toleration, *On Secular Authority* (1523), he was adamant that civil authorities should under no circumstances try to fight heresy with the sword. Within only two years, however, Luther amended his original stance in response to the radical demands of Thomas Müntzer and Andreas Karlstadt and the outbreak of the German Peasants' War. Luther realized that his rigid separation of secular and spiritual authority into two kingdoms was no longer tenable, and he reinvoked the right of civil authorities to use force to prevent blasphemy and insurrection. Brutal persecution of the Anabaptists was justified on the assumption that heretics were by definition revolutionaries, thus dealing a serious blow to the practice of religious toleration.

Toward the middle of the sixteenth century Sebastion Castellio and other radical reformers espousing toleration were inspired by Erasmus's writings and Luther's earlier, more tolerant views. In direct rebuttal to Calvin's justification of executing heretics like Michael Servetus, Castellio published his seminal essay on toleration, *On Heretics*, in both Latin and French editions, which included a substantial part of Luther's tract. Castellio argued that to persecute anyone for the sake of religion is irre-

ligious, since God desires the salvation of all humanity and has created no one for damnation—a pointed attack on Calvin's doctrine of predestination. Belief in universal salvation or universalism, integral to the spread of religious toleration, was forged by the radical reformers Hans Denck and Sebastian Franck. They believed God was available to every spiritual person "without any mediation." Franck even stated, "I have my brothers among the Turks, Papists, Jews, and all peoples." Despite his marked influence on toleration, Luther also epitomized the worst of religious intolerance by adding his anti-Jewish vitriol to the renewed upsurge of anti-Semitism during the sixteenth century. In Janus-like contrast to Franck's precursory ecumenism, Luther envisaged Satan's final, apocalyptic assault on the church led by the devil's legion of Jews, Romans, heretics, and Turks.

O. P. Grell and B. Scribner, eds., *Tolerance and Intolerance in the European Reformation* (1996); H. R. Guggisberg and B. Gordon, *Sebastian Castellio, 1515–1563: Humanist and Defender of Religious Toleration in a Confessional Age* (2003); J. Lecler, *Toleration and the Reformation*, 2 vols. (1960); C. J. Nederman and J. C. Laursen, eds., *Difference and Dissent: Theories of Tolerance in Medieval and Early Modern Europe* (1996); H. A. Oberman, *The Roots of Anti-Semitism: In the Age of Renaissance and Reformation* (1984).

MARVIN L. ANDERSON

Tomás de Torquemada

(1420–1498), first general inquisitor of Spain. Born in Valladolid, he was a nephew of Cardinal Juan de Torquemada (1388–1468). Tomás was prior of the friary of Santa Cruz in Segovia for twenty-two years. In 1482 he was appointed by Pope Sixtus IV (1471–1484) as one of seven new Dominican inquisitors for the crown of Castile. In 1483, the pope appointed him, first as inquisitor general of Castile and later as inquisitor general of Aragon, Valencia, and Catalonia. In 1488, a new council charged with authority over the operations of the inquisition in the territories of the Catholic monarchs, that is, Isabella and Ferdinand, was created. This body was named *Consejo de la Suprema y General Inquisicion*, and de Torquemada became the presiding figure of this council, with the title of inquisitor general.

H. Kamen, *The Spanish Inquisition: A Historical Revision* (1998).

RADY ROLDÁN-FIGUEROA

Torquemada, Juan de *see* Juan de
Torquemada

Traducianism This view holds that the
propagation of the human soul is analogous to
the propagation of the human body from the
parents at conception. The opposing belief is
creationism.

Both positions maintain that the soul is a created entity distinct from God, that it is rational,
and that it does not exist prior to the body. They
differ in regard to the immediateness of the
soul's origin. The traducianist maintains that
each post-Adamic soul originates through the
mediation of a previous soul, which in turn is
generated from a soul antecedent to it, with
Adam's soul as the ultimate source. The creationist claims that God creates each individual
soul *ex nihilo* without any element derived
from Adam through human generation.

Tertullian, advocating a form of material traducianism, argued that the soul is a corporeal
reality akin to an airy substance such as breath.
Augustine of Hippo dismissed traducianism on
the grounds of the soul's incorporeality. The
disputed issues of original sin and baptism of
infants during the Pelagian controversy
exposed the logical tensions within creationism. Augustine concluded in *The Literal Meaning of Genesis 10* that there is insufficient
evidence in Scripture to warrant the adoption
of either position.

E. Hill, trans., *The Literal Meaning of Genesis*,
in *Works of St. Augustine*, part 1, vol. 13 (2002);
M. Mendelson, "'The Business of Those
Absent': The Origin of the Soul in Augustine's
'De Genesi ad Litteram' 10.6–16," *AugStud* 29
(1998): 25–81; E. A. Quinn, trans., *On the Soul*,
in FC 10 (1950); J. Rist, *Ancient Thought Baptized* (1994).

MARIANNE DJUTH

Transubstantiation A verb "to be tran-
substantiated" existed by 1140, but the noun
"transubstantiation" gained its prominence in
Christian faith and worship early in the following century, and above all in the canons of
the Fourth Lateran Council of 1215. The council enjoined Christians the duty of annual confession and Communion following sincere
penance, and faith in the Communion as reception of Christ's body in the eucharistic wafer.
From early Christian times the Eucharist, the
ritual reenactment of Christ's Last Supper, was
a central part of Christian worship. It was only
from the eleventh century that discussion of its

nature became sustained within the schools of
Christendom, above all in those of Paris. There
the meaning of the ritual was theologically and
philosophically refined. In preceding centuries
it was believed that Christ was present in the
sacrament, but the nature of this presence was
discussed from the ninth century along with the
divergent understanding of a spiritual-symbolic
presence as opposed to a real-physical one.
Since a physical interpretation prevailed, theologians sought to explain the presence of
Christ's body under the appearance of bread
and wine. Aristotelian terminology, which distinguished between the substance of a thing
and its external attributes ("accidents"),
opened a way for understanding eucharistic
presence. Transubstantiation meant that a
change of substances, from bread and wine to
flesh and blood, occurred at the moment of the
priestly consecration in Christ's own scriptural
words "Take, eat, this is my body" (Matt.
26:26). Much effort was invested in refining
this understanding and teaching it to the laity.
Yet transubstantiation remained a challenging doctrine, one that perplexed medieval folk
and was ultimately rejected and derided by
Protestants.

J. Goering, "The Invention of Transubstantia-
tion," *Traditio* 46 (1991): 147–70; G. Macy, "A
Re-evaluation of the Contribution of Thomas
Aquinas to the 13th-century Theology of the
Eucharist," in *The Climate of the Early Uni-
versity: Essays in Honor of Otto Grundler*, ed.
N. Van Deusen (1997).

MIRI RUBIN

Travers, Walter (c. 1548–1635), Puritan
theologian of Elizabethan England. Born in
Nottingham and educated at Cambridge,
Travers showed an early commitment to church
reform in England, which deepened during a
six-year stay in Geneva (1570–1576), where he
befriended the Calvinist reformer Theodore
Beza. In Geneva Travers wrote his most significant work, *Ecclesiastical Discipline* (1574),
spelling out a presbyterian system of church
polity. After refusing to sign Elizabeth I's moderately reformist Thirty-nine Articles, Travers
left England to be ordained in Antwerp in 1578,
returning later to teach privately under the auspices of Lord-Treasurer Burghley. Burghley's
protection led to a lectureship at London's
Temple Church, where Travers engaged in a
celebrated rivalry and ecclesiological debate
with his Anglican colleague Richard Hooker.
Travers was dismissed in 1586 but had, along

with Thomas Cartwright, become one of the leading minds of English Puritanism. Both collaborated on the *Book of Discipline*, a defining work of English presbyterian church order drafted mostly by Travers. After a number of years as provost of Trinity College in Dublin, Travers withdrew for health reasons and spent the last decades of his life in poverty and relative obscurity.

P. Collinson, *The Elizabethan Puritan Movement* (1967).

KENNETH G. APPOLD

Trent, Council of   Assembled in response to calls for institutional and theological reform, the council spanned eighteen years, although it conducted business only during three brief periods (1545–1546, 1551–1552, and 1562–1563). Disparate elements in the church had hoped that a general council would resolve the growing crisis posed by dissent, as the Council of Constance (1414–1417) had resolved the Great Schism. Luther himself appealed to a future council in 1518 to arbitrate his quarrel with the pope, and Charles V hoped a council would provide the reform that would restore the religious unanimity of his empire.

The coded slogan advanced at the Diet of Nuremburg (1522–1524) captured the minimum conditions: a "free [independent of the papacy], Christian [open to all and guided by Scripture] Council in German lands [out of Italy and responsive to German concerns]." Although the papacy had dominated the last council (Lateran V, 1512–1517), it sought to avoid a new council beyond papal control, hence the aphorism of Pope Clement VII: "Never call for a council, never refuse one directly." After delays, postponements, and a decade of imperial pressure, however, Pope Paul III finally summoned the Catholic world to meet in Trent—German speaking and barely in Italy—in 1543. Even so, a handful of prelates appeared there only in December 1545 to inaugurate the council that papal legate Marcello Cervini remarked was scarcely larger than a diocesan synod.

Its goals were to state Catholic dogma, to reform the church, and to bring peace to warring Catholic powers. The assembled prelates themselves immediately fought over its agenda. The emperor's allies promoted immediate consideration of the reforms he believed were at the heart of the Protestant challenge. A faction of theological hardliners, however, sought to come directly to the doctrinal matters polarizing Christian Europe. A compromise saved the

council: reform and doctrine would be treated in tandem. Although the final decrees promulgated by the council support the misconception that it merely endorsed Catholic doctrine and practice, the record of debate establishes that each issue was aired extensively, and both candid criticism and some remarkably radical proposals surfaced before the prelates settled on more conservative positions.

The popes who reigned during the council never controlled its activities or agenda. No pope ever visited Trent or Bologna (where the council was briefly transferred in 1547) during the council or addressed it, although they vigorously participated in its deliberations through their legates and secretaries of state. Nonetheless, the council remained independent. Indeed, it was so episcopal an enterprise that other constituencies, such as the religious orders, sometimes feared they would lose their autonomy.

Many opportunities were missed at Trent. Protestant delegates attended the second phase of the council, but their insistence on revisiting the work of the first phase (understandable, since such important doctrines as justification had been decided during it) led to an impasse and precluded their participation. Conflicts between the Catholic powers interfered with the attendance of bishops at different times, and a hoped-for "reformation of the princes" was entertained but never took place. The reassessment of the role of the papacy in the church was left for Vatican I. Some of the most important results of the council were not immediately apparent or immediately realized. The single most important decree probably emerged from the twenty-third session, requiring a seminary in every diocese. Although implementation was a long time coming in many places, it signaled a fundamental shift for Catholic clerical culture.

More broadly, the council transformed Catholicism by empowering bishops to become reformers, leading, as Hubert Jedin observed, to the transformation of bishops "from feudatories to pastors." Reformers like Carlo Borromeo in Milan gained the authority and the tools needed to transform and revitalize their dioceses. A focus on "Tridentinism" left untouched important dimensions of Catholic experience—for example, the missions—but its very narrowness permitted its greatest contribution. It enabled reform of a church still so local that the reforms could only be guaranteed by the local bishop.

H. Jedin, *Geschichte des Konzils von Trient*, 4 vols. (1948–1975; ET, 2 vols., 1957, 1960);

J. W. O'Malley, *Trent and All That: Renaming Catholicism in the Early Modern Era* (2000); H. J. Schroeder, *The Canons and Decrees of the Council of Trent* (1978); R. Trisco, "Carlo Borromeo and the Council of Trent," and J. B. Tomaro, "San Carlo Borromeo and the Implementation of the Council of Trent," in *San Carlo Borromeo: Catholic Reform and Ecclesiastical Politics in the Second Half of the Sixteenth Century* (1988).

BENJAMIN W. WESTERVELT

Tridentine Profession of Faith   A brief confessional statement of the most important dogmatic affirmations of the Council of Trent, also sometimes referred to as "Pius IV's Creed." In response to the petition from the prelates of the council, Pius IV confirmed the canons and decrees of the council in the bull *Benedictus Deus* in January 1564. The council had lasted eighteen years, and the process of implementing it was only beginning. Notwithstanding suspicions on both sides, the bishops relinquished implementation to the papacy. As part of a wider initiative including the preparation of the new breviary, a new missal, a new version of the Index, a catechism, and a new curial committee to oversee implementation (the Congregation of the Council), Pius IV promulgated the profession in the papal bull *Injunctum nobis* in November 1564.

The terse profession, only about six hundred words in its Latin form, is both an affirmation of doctrine and an oath of obedience. It begins with the creed of Constantinople and then commands assent to the following: the church's authority to interpret Scripture; the seven sacraments; the Mass as a sacrifice; transubstantiation; purgatory; invocation of the saints; relics; indulgences; obedience to the papacy; and acceptance of the canons of the Council of Trent and the other ecumenical councils. Although there is no reason why the *Professio* could not be demanded of any Catholic, it is intended to ensure the orthodoxy and reliability of those with responsibility for other "subjects," concluding "I shall see to it that my subjects or those entrusted to me by virtue of my office hold it [the *Professio*], teach it, and preach it." In 1877 affirmations of papal infallibility and the decrees of Vatican I were added, and in 1910 further language repudiating modernism was added. The *Professio* remains in effect to this day. While in a narrow sense the *Professio* accurately captures the dogmatic conservatism of the Council of Trent, it creates a false impression of the work of the council.

For one thing, it gives no evidence of the massive reforms of ecclesiastical structure that played such a major role in the council, especially in its final phase, and it provides no indication of the deep and passionate debates over dogma that took place before the prelates at the council confirmed Catholic teaching. Thus, the *Professio* breathes less the spirit of Trent than the imperatives of confessionalism, which were simultaneously driving Protestant communities to distinguish their doctrinal integrity via creeds, confessions, and catechisms.

J. H. Leith, ed., *Creeds of the Churches: A Reader in Christian Doctrine from the Bible to the Present* (1963).

BENJAMIN W. WESTERVELT

Trinity in Early Christian Controversy   The doctrine of the Trinity represents a uniquely Christian concept of God. The Latin word *trinitas* ("tri-unity") was Tertullian's neologism, and it combined the notions of God's oneness and threeness. Inheriting the concept of one true God from Judaism, Christians affirmed the triune nature of God on the basis of their conviction that God was experienced in Jesus Christ and in the Holy Spirit. God's economic activity "distributed the Unity into a Trinity" (Tertullian, *Prax.* 2). Although both the NT and the Apostolic Fathers mention triadic formulas (e.g., Matt. 28:19; *1 Clement* 46:6), the mere early existence of formulas does not explain the emergence of Trinitarian theology. Christians who "set forward God the Father and God the Son and the Holy Spirit and proclaim both their power in unity and their diversity in rank" (Athenagoras, *Leg.* 10.5) had to make a case for the uniplurality of God. The emerging Trinitarian theology worked out the implications of the Christian faith given in scriptural witness and worship.

Developing these implications proved to be a long and difficult process that entailed many controversies, condemnations, creeds, and councils. Although the Trinitarian phase of the argument cannot be severed from the christological one, prior to the Council of Constantinople (381) it was the relationship among Father, Son, and Holy Spirit that received more attention. Most of the inadequate understandings of the Trinity in that period can be reduced either to tritheism (hardly taught by any theologians, although some were accused of it), subordinationism, or modalism. It became evident that Father, Son, and Holy Spirit could not be distinguished by nature, by temporal priority, as parts of God, as members of a genus, as three names or successive modes of the same entity, or as three activities. Father, Son, and Holy Spirit could only be distinguished as "persons" (*hypostaseis*). Distinguishing among the persons is possible by considering their modes of origination or relation. Father is "unbegottenness," Son is "begottenness," and the Holy Spirit is "procession," although all three are the triune God. "The three are the single God" (Gregory of Nazianzus, *Or. Bas.* 39.11).

Presuming the indivisible oneness of God, Origen distinguished among the three divine "persons" (*hypostaseis*) (*Fr. Jo.* 2.75), argued for the doctrine of the monarchy of the Father (*Princ.* 4.4.1), and assigned the three hypostases their "special actions" (*Princ.* 1.3.7–8). The Alexandrian balanced all this with the doctrine of the eternal generation of the Son (*Princ.* 1.2.4). Thus, Origen's alleged "subordinationism" was not temporal but causal or logical. The Son is "second" because he is caused, not because he is ontologically less divine.

The fourth century was the culmination of the Trinitarian debates. One of the notable figures, Arius, interpreted the doctrine of the monarchy of the Father in a subordinationist-temporal sense ("the Father is greater than I" [John 14:28]). On the other hand, a major controversialist, Athanasius, insisted on the eternal generation of the consubstantial Son ("The Father and I are one" [John 10:30]). Arius taught that the Son was a "perfect creature" (G. Opitz, *Urkunden zur Geschichte des Ariantschen Streites*, 6; cf. Prov. 8:22; Acts 2:36), and Athanasius, presuming that "created" was opposed to "begotten," countered that a "created" Son could neither redeem nor deify the creatures (*Syn.* 51). He championed the belief that the Son was "begotten" from the essence of the Father (*C. Ar.* 1.9). Arius's views were condemned at the Council of Nicaea (325), which called the Son "consubstantial" (*homoousios*) with the Father. What followed was a troubled period, in which theologians attempted to figure out what exactly the term "consubstantial" meant and whether to use this "unbiblical" designation at all. Eventually, all kinds of Arians, semi- or neo-, were refuted by the Cappadocians and by the edicts of Theodosius. The pro-Nicene Basil, Gregory of Nyssa, and Gregory of Nazianzus rejected the "modalism" of Marcellus of Ancyra, refuted the subordinationism of the Anomoeans and Pneumatomachians and also the "soft" subordinationism of some late Origenists/Eusebians and Homoians. The Cappadocians did not allow any "unlikeness" to be postulated among the three persons of the Trinity on the level of the divine nature (*ousia*). Neither did they tolerate the identification of "unbegottenness" (*agennesia*) as the nature of God. Basil sorted out the semantic ambiguity of the confusing condemnation of Nicaea (i.e., *hypostasis* or *ousia*) by distinguishing between "person" and "nature" (*Ep.* 236.6). This distinction enabled him to affirm both hypostatic distinctness and essential unity within the Trinity. The *Theological Orations* (27, 29–31) of Gregory of Nazianzus offer perhaps the best presentation of the classical doctrine of the the Trinity, including the affirmation of the consubstantiality of the Holy Spirit (31.10). The Council of Constantinople "concluded" the development of the classical doctrine of Trinity in the sense that afterward the discussion shifted to Christology, to the unity of the two natures in one person of Christ.

Western theologians mostly echoed rather than determined the course of the classical Trinitarian theology. Augustine's original contribution became evident as the problem of the *filioque* arose. His reasoning caused Western theologians to focus primarily on the "economical sending" of the Holy Spirit (Gal. 4:4–5; John 20:28) rather than on the Spirit's "theological proceeding" (John 15:26). Despite refining the terms, "exhausting" exegesis, and trying to get the metaphysics straight, the majority of the participants of the Trinitarian controversy realized, nevertheless, that "to know you [i.e., God] as you are in an absolute sense is for you alone" (Augustine, *Conf.* 13.16.19).

L. Ayres, *Nicea and Its Legacy* (2004); J. Behr, *The Way to Nicaea* (2001); Behr, *The Nicene Faith*, 2 vols. (2004); B. Bobrinskoy, *Mystery of the Trinity* (1999); F. Courth, *Trinität in der Schrift und Patristik* (1988); R. P. C. Hanson, *The Search for the Christian Doctrine of God* (1988); T. Marsh, *The Triune God* (1994); K.-H. Ohlig, *One or Three?* (2002); E. Osborn, *The Emergence of Christian Theology* (1993); W. G. Rusch, *The Trinitarian Controversy* (1980); C. Stead, *Philosophy in Christian Antiquity* (1994); B. Studer, *Trinity and Incarnation* (1993); R. Williams, *Arius* (2nd ed., 2001).

TARMO TOOM

Trisagion From the Greek for "thrice holy," the Trisagion is a doxology used in both Eastern and Western worship. It remains in the Eastern liturgy and made its way into the Roman Good Friday service via the Gallican liturgy. Probably derived from the language of Isaiah 6:3, it states, "Holy God, Holy Almighty One, Holy Everlasting One, have mercy on us." It dates from the middle of the fifth century, when reference to it is found in the *Acts* of the Council of Chalcedon (451). Generally, Western churches considered it to be addressed to the Trinity, while Eastern churches regarded it as addressed to Christ. A controversy emerged in the late fifth century, when the Monophysite bishop of Antioch Peter the Fuller added the phrase "who was crucified for us" to the doxology. Use of the addition fueled the Theopaschite controversy, as its inclusion in the Trisagion implied either that the Trinity suffered or that Christ suffered in his divinity, a standard accusation against the Monophysites.

———

S. P. Brock, "The Thrice-holy Hymn in the Liturgy," *Sobornost* 7 (1985): 24–34; J. Quasten, "Oriental Influence in the Gallican Liturgy," *Traditio* 1 (1943): 55–78.

STEVEN A. MCKINION

Truce of God   The Truce of God and the Peace of God represented attempts to curtail violence among Christians. Where the late tenth-century peace movements aimed to protect noncombatants (clergy, peasants, merchants) and church property, the truce attempted to place temporal limits on fighting. The Council of Elne-Toulouges in the county of Roussillon (France) in 1027 prohibited fighting from the ninth hour on Saturday to the first hour on Monday in observance of the Lord's Day. Subsequent councils extended this local effort both temporally and geographically. In a letter to the clergy of Italy, Archbishop Reginald of Arles (1035–1041) and other French churchmen added Thursday, Friday, and Saturday, the traditional days of Christ's ascension, passion, and entombment, to the list. The weeks-long liturgical seasons of Lent and Advent were also eventually designated as violence-free days under pain of secular punishment and excommunication. The Lateran Council of 1179 applied the prohibitions to all of Christendom. The extension of the truce was driven by church and secular leaders and lacked the popular impulse of the Peace of God. Secular leaders appreciated the justification the truce gave them to manage violence for legitimate ends, ostensibly to protect the church and the Christian people from miscreants. As it became more difficult in the eleventh century to justify violence against Christians, church leaders pointed out that violence could legiti-

mately be used to defend Christians from pagans and infidels. The Council of Clermont in 1095 encouraged the European warrior aristocracy to train their fighting skills on Muslims in the Holy Land (see *Crusades*).

———

T. Head and R. Landes, eds., *The Peace of God: Social Violence and Religious Response in France around the Year 1000* (1992); H. Hoffmann, *Gottesfriede und Treuga Dei* (1964).

JOHN J. CONTRENI

Tudor, Mary   *see* Mary Tudor

Tunstall, Cuthbert   (1474–1559), archbishop of Durham. Tunstall was a student at Oxford, Cambridge, and Padua. He met with, among other noted scholars, Thomas More and Erasmus. Henry VIII sent him on several political missions and, in 1522, made him bishop of London. One of the earliest and strongest critics of the popular availability of Scripture in English, Tunstall declined to support William Tyndale's efforts. Failing to receive Tunstall's support, Tyndale left England for Wittenberg and Antwerp, never to return. Tunstall became bishop of Durham in 1530. Although he initially opposed royal supremacy, Tunstall eventually came to support it. While he supported royal leadership of the church, however, he remained Catholic in doctrine. He opposed the Act of Uniformity in Parliament but enforced it within his own diocese. He opposed several acts of reform legislation, including the act permitting priests to marry. He was thereafter imprisoned in his home in 1551 and removed from his bishopric in 1552. Mary Tudor restored him to office in 1554; although he enjoyed her support, he did not participate in the Marian persecutions. Following Elizabeth's accession, Tunstall refused to take the Oath of Supremacy. He was, again, deprived of his bishopric and held in custody at Lambeth Palace for the final months of his life.

———

C. Sturge, *Cuthbert Tunstall: Churchman, Scholar, Statesman, Administrator* (1938).

JOHN E. GRISWOLD

Twelve Articles of the Peasants

The manifesto of the Peasants' War issued in 1525 by the Christian Union of Upper Swabia with this initial title: "The basic and just articles of the whole peasantry, concerning the difficulties with ecclesiastical and secular authorities by whom they feel themselves burdened." The articles presented the grievances of the peasants in economic, political, and religious terms and sought to connect their demands to the reforms of Martin Luther. More than 25,000 copies of this popular pamphlet were printed in March 1525. The Twelve Articles demanded: (1) the right to elect and dismiss their own pastors, (2) the abolishment of the "lesser" tithe (on fruits and vegetables) and local administration of the "greater" tithe (on grain), (3) the end of serfdom, (4) freedom to hunt in the forests and fish in the streams, (5) freedom to gather wood in the forest, (6) reduction in the obligations owed to feudal lords, (7) that peasants be paid for their work on behalf of their lords and their lords honor their agreements, (8) that tax levies on property be reevaluated and judged fairly, (9) that criminal punishments fit the crime, (10) that community property be administered by the community, (11) that the death tax be abolished, and (12) that if one or more of their articles were contrary to Scripture they would revoke it.

After their demands were not met through peaceful means, the peasants resorted to violence and were soundly defeated by imperial forces in May 1525.

M. Baylor, ed., *The Radical Reformation* (1991); P. Blickle, *The Revolution of 1525* (1985).

DAVID WHITFORD

Tyconius (d. c. 400), Donatist lay theologian and biblical interpreter in Roman North Africa. He is best known for his surviving writings—*The Book of Rules*, on the interpretation of Scripture, and *On the Apocalypse*, a commentary surviving only in fragments—and for his influence on Augustine of Hippo. Tyconius's theology led him to break with the Donatists, but he never joined the catholic church. He held that the church is a mixed body, containing both the good and the evil, and that the body of Satan is similarly mixed. Neither church nor world, then, can presently be seen as unambiguously good or evil. This view undercut the Donatists' theological perfectionism, which held that the church must safeguard its religious purity in the present by rigorous separation from the world. In contrast, Tyconius located the separation of the good and the evil at the end of time in the final judgment. This position was rooted in Tyconius's interpretation of Scripture for which, in *The Book of Rules*, he established seven rules to guide biblical exegesis, rules which Augustine applauded—despite some cautionary revisions—in *On Christian Doctrine* (3.42–56). Tyconius's chief

influence on Augustine, however, lay in his Pauline insistence that the law does not justify but rather evokes faith and that it is faith that receives grace. Augustine would ultimately conclude that even faith is a gift of grace, but his reading of Tyconius in the early 390s was one of the chief factors that sparked this development in his theology. Here, then, Tyconius lies at the fountainhead of the interpretation of Paul on law and grace that, through Augustine, was to dominate the Western theological tradition.

W. S. Babcock, ed., *The Book of Rules of Tyconius* (1989); P. Bright, *The Book of Rules of Tyconius: Its Purpose and Inner Logic* (1988); P. Fredriksen, "Apocalypse and Redemption in Early Christianity," *VC* 45 (1991): 151–83; K. Steinhauser, *The Apocalypse Commentary of Tyconius: A History of Its Reception and Influence* (1987).

WILLIAM S. BABCOCK

Tyndale, William (c. 1494–1536), English Bible translator and Protestant reformer. Details of Tyndale's life prior to his graduation from Oxford with an MA in 1506 remain largely unknown. Probably born in the Cotswolds of Gloucestershire, he devoted his Protestant efforts primarily to the translation of the Bible into English. When Tyndale's efforts to produce an English Bible met serious opposition, first and most notably from Cuthbert Tunstall, bishop of London, Tyndale left England, never to return. He traveled to Wittenberg, Cologne, Worms, and then to Antwerp. While in Cologne he published his first New Testament—heavily dependent upon Erasmus's critical edition in Greek—in 1526. Although he found support, especially among English merchants, his journeys were plagued with shipwreck, intrigue, and betrayal. Arrested in May 1535, Tyndale spent most of the year in prison in the Low Country town of Vilvorde. Eventually he was judged a heretic and degraded from the priesthood. Early in October, Tyndale was strangled, and his body was burned.

While scholars continue to debate Tyndale's relative political and religious importance, none challenge his peerless work as a Bible translator. Tyndale's political and theological works included *The Parable of the Wicked Mammon* (1528), his most explicit contribution favoring justification by faith alone, and *The Obedience of a Christian Man* (1528), a treatise on theology, law, and government, and a response to speculations on the afterlife and the Anabaptist doctrine of soul-sleep. Tyndale's interpreters have cast much of his theological and political corpus as responses to criticism, chiefly but not exclusively from Thomas More.

The most recent treatment of Tyndale's biography highlights a tension in his choices and selections between word-for-word translations on the one hand and the desire for a fluid, uniquely English rendering of the Bible on the other. In the midst of this tension Tyndale developed phrases and pace that have characterized and shaped the English language. Scholars charged with the production of what became known as the King James or the Authorized Version of the Bible began from Tyndale's efforts. England embraced the language of William Tyndale's translation, whose circulation exceeded that of Shakespeare's works.

D. Daniel, *William Tyndale: A Biography* (1994); A. Richardson and J. A. R. Dick, eds., *William Tyndale and the Law* (1994).

JOHN E. GRISWOLD

Ubertino da Casale (1259–c. 1341), controversial Franciscan.

Ubertino entered the Franciscan order in 1273, probably at Genoa, and visited Portiuncula and Greccio in the 1280s. He studied under Peter John Olivi in the monastery of Santa Croce in Florence (1287–1289) and at the University of Paris (c. 1274–1283 or c. 1289–1298) but disliked scholasticism. Ubertino returned to central Italy, where he became acquainted with several renowned mystics, including Angela of Foligno, and became a principal defender of Franciscan Spirituals, promoting their cause at the Council of Vienne and at Avignon (1309–1312). His *Arbor vitae* (*Tree of Life,* 1309) and polemical writings of c. 1310–1312 exemplify Franciscan Spiritual viewpoints. Participating in the great debates over poverty at the papal court in Avignon in 1312, he helped instigate Pope Clement V's bull *Exivi de paradiso,* which provided an authoritative interpretation of the Franciscan rule's stipulations on poverty but did not end the controversy in the order nor prevent Clement's successor, John XXII, from condemning the strictest interpretation of religious poverty and persecuting its adherents. Ubertino was permitted to transfer to the Benedictine order in 1317, and his views became more moderate. His *Tractatus de altissima paupertate Christi et apostolorum eius et virorum apostolicorum* (*Tractate Concerning the Most High Poverty of Christ, His Apostles, and Apostolic Men,* 1322) expressed a less radical interpretation of Peter John Olivi's teachings on poverty than the prevailing Spiritual opinion he had earlier helped to form. Ubertino now argued that Christ and the apostles lacked personal property but did use property to tend to necessities. In 1325 Ubertino was nonetheless accused of adhering to heretical teachings ascribed to Peter John Olivi, and he fled to Avignon. In 1328 he was in Rome, at the the time of the coronation of Ludwig of Bavaria, to which the Franciscan minister-general, Michael of Cesena, and his companions (Bonagratia of Bergamo and William of Ockham, investigated at Avignon in late 1327 and 1328) had fled. Nothing is known of his subsequent life, except that he preached against John XXII, to some extent itinerantly, until he died in obscurity sometime before 1341.

Arbor vitae crucifixae Jesu (1485, repr. 1961); D. Burr, *The Spiritual Franciscans* (2001); C. Davis, *Ubertino da Casale and His Conception of "Altissima Pauperta"* (1984).

CHRISTOPHER OCKER

Udall, John (c. 1560–1592), Puritan writer.

He is best known as a Puritan contributor to the Marprelate Tracts, which appeared as a series of books beginning in 1588. Though the tracts appeared pseudonymously under the name "Martin Marprelate," scholars generally concur that several people, including Udall, authored the tracts. Throughout the late 1580s he was central in the overall dispute between the Church of England, with its Anglican Rite, and the Puritan theology to which he was devoted. In 1590 he was convicted of producing and distributing Puritan propaganda. He did not deny authorship, and he was charged with sedition and libel. Released from prison in 1592, he died soon thereafter.

P. Collinson, *The Elizabethan Puritan Movement* (1990).

ALDEN R. LUDLOW

Ulfila (fourth cent.), missionary to, and bishop of, the Goths.

Ulfila was of Cappadocian origin, born among Goths, and a key figure in converting the "barbarians." After Ulfila came to Byzantium, he was ordained by Eusebius of Nicomedia. In 360, the bishop of the Goths participated in the Synod of Constantinople, which issued a homoian creed (Socrates, *Hist. eccl.* 2.41). Ulfila's confession (a fragment) together with his formal statement of faith, which defends the superior divinity of the Father with many traditional adjectives, is among the main evidence for reconstructing his theology. Because of Ulfila's subordinationism,

Theodoret complained, "The result is that up to this day the Goths assert that the Father is greater than the Son, but they refuse to describe the Son as a creature, although they are in communion with those who do so" (Theodoret, *Hist. eccl.* 4.33) Ulfila is reported to have composed tracts in Gothic, Latin, and Greek, but none survives. He is also credited with creating the Gothic script and translating some parts of the Bible from Greek to Gothic. Only Gospels (in the order of Matthew, John, Luke, Mark), Pauline letters, and fragments of Ezra and Nehemiah are extant.

———

T. D. Barnes, "The Consecration of Ulfila," *JTS* 41 (1990): 541–45; H. Sivan, "Ulfila's Own Conversion," *HTR* 89, no. 4 (1996): 373–86.

TARMO TOOM

Ulrich von Hutten   *see* Hutten, Ulrich von

Umayyad Caliphate

A line of thirteen caliphs during the years 661–750 brought a period of political instability and dispute over succession among Muslims to an end. The Ummayah family was descended from the Quraysh but not direct relatives of the Prophet. The family was able to change the caliphate from an elective into a virtually hereditary institution. Damascus remained their capital until their overthrow by the Abbasids. The wealth of the Umayyad caliphate was adequate to finance the Great Mosque of Damascus and the Dome of the Rock in Jerusalem.

Among many Muslim historians, the Umayyads have a reputation for corruption and tyrannical administration. Their attitudes toward the peoples of newly conquered lands, forcing them to seek the patronage of established Arab families, helped contribute to their overthrow by the Abbasids.

One Umayyad, al-Rahman, known later as ad-Dakhil ("the immigrant") escaped execution in Syria and founded an Umayyad kingdom in Spain. This Umayyad line lasted until the dissolution of the Moorish kingdom in 1073. The learning and prosperity of this kingdom, especially in philosophy, rivaled that of Baghdad. It was a significant conduit of Arab learning to the West.

———

F. Robinson, ed., *The Cambridge Illustrated History of the Islamic World* (1998); N. Shaban, *Islamic History: A New Interpretation*, vol. 1 (1976); T. Sonn, *A Brief History of Islam* (2004).

EUGENE M. LUDWIG, OFM CAP.

Uniate Churches

Uniate Churches, also called Eastern Rites, are Eastern Christian jurisdictions canonically in communion with the Catholic Church. The term is considered pejorative by Eastern Catholics, who prefer the term Eastern Catholic Churches. These churches retain their own liturgical usage and canon law under the jurisdiction of their own hierarchy. They relate to the Roman Church through the Congregation for the Oriental Churches.

It is difficult to generalize about this group of about fifteen million people. The majority derive from Orthodox jurisdictions that entered into Catholic communion sometime after the sixteenth century. The Italo-Greeks of southern Italy and Sicily and the Maronites of Lebanon are exceptions. Most follow Byzantine usage, but East and West Syrian, Coptic, Ethiopian, Armenian, and "Thomas Christian" liturgical traditions are also represented.

Many Orthodox consider the Eastern Catholic Churches as ecumenical obstacles and see in them a Roman attempt to establish competing structures in Orthodox lands. Self-perceptions among Eastern Catholics vary. Those who emphasize their identity as "Orthodox in communion with Rome" see their own future in the reintegration of their respective Eastern churches (e.g., the Patriarchate of Antioch, the Church of Ukraine). Others are inclined to emphasize their Catholic uniqueness.

———

J. D. Faris, *Eastern Catholic Churches: Constitution and Governance* (1992); R. G. Roberson, *The Eastern Christian Churches* (1995); Vatican Council II, *Decree on the Eastern Catholic Churches* (1964).

EUGENE M. LUDWIG, OFM CAP.

Uniformity Acts

This series of four acts spanned over one hundred years and sought to bring uniformity to all aspects of worship and prayer within the Church of England. The acts date from 1549, 1552, 1559, and 1662. The 1549 Act, passed by Edward VI and supported by Thomas Cranmer, firmly established the Book of Common Prayer as the only form of worship in England. It sought to do away with "diverse and sundry forms and fashions" in the English churches. The 1552 Act introduced the second prayer book and asserted Protestant doctrine more forcefully than the prior act; it compelled worship attendance "upon every Sunday, and other days ordained and used." These two acts were repealed in 1553 when Mary I ascended the throne and reasserted

Catholicism. When Elizabeth took the throne, the acts of 1549 and 1552 were used for the 1559 Act, often incorporated verbatim. Called the *via media*, the new act sought to find a "middle way" between Catholic and Protestant sympathies. It remained in force until 1640. The final 1662 Uniformity Act was drafted upon the restoration of the monarchy following the Civil War. Though it sought to find a middle way between Puritanism and the Anglican Rite, it effectively expelled Puritans from the Church of England, giving birth to the Free Church and Dissent movements.

G. Bray, *Documents of the English Reformation* (1994).

ALDEN R. LUDLOW

Universals   The problem of universals was widely discussed in medieval philosophy. It was motivated by the linguistic phenomenon that some terms are predicated of many things. For instance, the term "man" can be predicated of Socrates and Plato. To what can one ascribe this universality? What does the universal signify, if the things, or better, the singulars, of which it can be predicated are obviously unique and numerically different? Historically, the problem was introduced into the Middle Ages through Boethius's translations and comments in Latin on Aristotle's *De interpretatione* and *Categories*, and Porphyry's *Isagoge*. In particular the latter text, initially written as an introduction to Aristotle's *Categories*, proved to be crucial. Porphyry formulated several questions concerning universals, without, however, discussing them.

In the medieval debate, two options were offered: either the universality inheres in the things themselves (i.e., in extramental reality), or the universality lies in the language and at the corresponding mental or conceptual level. Put differently, the categorization of singular things into genus and species is either founded on metaphysical entities such as essences or common natures that are somehow constitutive of those things, or it is solely based upon our way of thinking and speaking about those things. The former position is labeled realism. The latter position, which claims that only the words and the corresponding concepts to which these words refer are universal, is called nominalism or conceptualism. The best-known medieval nominalists are Peter Abelard (1079–1142) and William of Ockham (c. 1285–1347). Both set out to refute the realist positions of their contemporaries William of Champeaux and Duns Scotus, respectively, as being incoherent, and then concluded that since things (*res*) cannot be universal, only (mental) words can be universal. But how can these universal concepts signify singular things? Both Abelard and Ockham believed that the resemblance between singular things provides the basis for the signification (*significatio*) of a single universal term to many things. Realists had less difficulty in explaining the signification of universal terms, since they believed in the existence of real universals that could be discovered in the singular things. Their problem, however, was in explaining how things that share the same common nature are individuated.

P. V. Spade, *Five Texts on the Mediaeval Problem of Universals* (1994); M. M. Tweedale, *Abailard on Universals* (1976); Tweedale, *Scotus vs. Ockham: A Medieval Dispute over Universals*, 2 vols. (1999).

J. M. M. H. THIJSSEN

Universities, Rise of   Unknown in antiquity, these specialized schools of higher education developed in high medieval Europe out of a unique confluence of religious, social, political, and economic conditions. The two earliest universities were located in Paris and Bologna. Originally under the control of the local bishop and subject to all sorts of secular pressures as well, both were able to win a large measure of independence for themselves by appealing to the church in Rome; a succession of pontiffs gladly answered these appeals not only because it suited their larger plans of centralization but also because the two institutions could be used as training centers and authoritative mouthpieces in the crucial domains of theology and canon law, respectively. The unintended result was to foster an intellectual revolution of far-reaching consequences. Not only did theology and law become professionalized, but so did medicine and philosophy. As each discipline advanced, each eventually outdistanced not only the "authorities" that made up its core texts but also the traditional ideas of contemporary religious and political leaders. Moreover, with an undergraduate formation grounded in Aristotle's logic, filled with Aristotle's empirical science, and characterized by a style of inquiry that insisted on hearing arguments *pro* and *contra*, the graduates produced by the universities came to see thinking, learning, and questioning as natural human activities to be exercised in complete freedom.

Through the early fourteenth century the papacy sponsored or assisted a number of university foundations across Europe. But by this time the university movement was beginning to escape from church control. By the end of the Middle Ages universities were well on their way to becoming organs of, if not instruments of, the state; while it was the popes who had done so much to help the universities realize their potential, it was the princes in the end who inherited their power.

A. B. Cobban, *The Medieval Universities* (1975); H. Rashdall, *The Universities of Europe in the Middle Ages*, rev. and ed. F. M. Powicke and A. B. Emden (1936); H. de Ridder-Symoens, ed., *Universities in the Middle Ages* (1992); J. Verger, *Les universités au moyen âge* (1973).

STEVEN J. WILLIAMS

Ursinus (Beer), Zacharias (1534–1584),

Silesian Reformed theologian and chief author of the Heidelberg Catechism. A native of the German city of Breslau (Wroclaw) in modern Poland, Ursinus studied in Wittenberg under Philip Melanchthon, who exercised a profound and enduring influence upon him. Later study in Zurich and Geneva brought Ursinus closer to a Reformed theological position. Ursinus became a theology professor at the Univ. of Heidelberg and rector of the Palatine seminary in 1561 and took an active role in the conversion of the Palatinate to the Reformed faith. Ursinus is regarded as the primary author of the Heidelberg Catechism (1563). After Lutheran critics decried the Heidelberg Catechism's deviance from the Augsburg Confession, Ursinus became its chief defender and interpreter. Ursinus's commentary on the catechism became one of the most significant theological textbooks in the Reformed communion, and his *Admonitio Christiana* (1581) was an influential rebuttal of *The Book of Concord*.

C. J. Burchill, "On the Consolation of a Christian Scholar: Zacharias Ursinus (1534–83) and the Reformation in Heidelberg," *JEH* 37 (1986): 565–83; E. Sturm, *Der junge Zacharias Ursin: Sein Weg vom Philippismus zum Calvinismus (1534–1562)* (1972); D. Visser, *Zacharias Ursinus: The Reluctant Reformer* (1983).

CHARLES D. GUNNOE JR.

Ursula (fourth cent.), legendary virgin and

martyr for whom the Ursulines, the oldest and largest teaching order of women in the Roman Catholic Church, are named. With no historical evidence for Ursula's existence, her legend rests on a ten-line inscription from the second half of the fourth century in Cologne. It states that a senator named Clematius renovated an old basilica on the site where some virgins had been martyred under Maximian. Ursula was first associated with these martyrs in the ninth century; her legend grew in subsequent centuries, and the unearthing of supposed relics in Cologne in 1155 secured her place in popular piety.

According to the *Golden Legend*, Ursula was the daughter of a Christian British king. He promised her to the son of another king. She consented to the marriage only after the prince agreed to be baptized and to wait three years for her to complete a pilgrimage, accompanied by eleven or 11,000 virgins. She and her companions then went to Rome and were martyred on their return home by the Huns in Cologne.

M. Thiebaux and P. Shengorn, trans., *The Passion of Ursula and the 11,000 Virgins* (1996); P. M. Waters, *The Ursuline Achievement: A Philosophy of Education for Women* (1994).

WILLIAM B. SWEETSER JR.

Ursulines   A Roman Catholic order for

women, the Order of St. Ursula was founded in 1535 at Brescia, Italy, by Angela Merici (1474–1540). By naming themselves after Ursula, believed to have been a virgin princess from Britain, martyred while on pilgrimage to Rome in the fourth century, the sisters emphasized their commitment to lives of chastity (abstinence from sex), piety (they emphasized prayer, confession, and attendance at Mass), and service (works of charity, Christian education especially for girls, and the care of sick women).

Pope Paul III approved the order in 1544. In 1572, Pope Gregory XIII permitted adherents to make simple vows and pronounced the Ursulines a religious order. In 1612 under Pope Paul V the Paris house introduced solemn vows, a form of the Rule of St. Augustine, and cloistered living. The order became well-known for its educational work and expanded through Europe, the Americas, and the Far East. Each house operated with relative autonomy from the others until 1900, when a world congress of Ursulines met in Rome and formed the "Roman Union." This union allows for several expressions: the Order of St. Ursula, with its solemn vows and cloisters; the congregations of Ursulines without solemn vows; and the *Societas sanctae Ursulae*, whose members live separately from one another.

T. Ledóchowska, *Angela Merici and the Company of St. Ursula, according to the Historical Documents* (1969); R. Ruether and E. McLaughlin, eds., *Women of Spirit: Female Leadership in the Jewish and Christian Traditions* (1979).

WILLIAM R. RUSSELL

Ussher, James (1581–1656), archbishop of Armagh, scholar, and historian. From a well-established Anglo-Irish family, Ussher studied at Trinity College (Dublin). In 1615 he drafted the Lambeth Articles for the Irish Church (based on the Thirty-nine Articles of the Church of England) and in 1624 was appointed archbishop of Armagh (the chief prelate of Ireland). He was a strong supporter of the Stuart monarchy. His main interest was in scholarship, especially church history. He wanted to demonstrate that Anglicanism agreed with the teaching of the early church, although his diverse convictions are not easily harmonized. He was erudite, irenic, and strongly Calvinist in theology. His famous chronology of the Bible was included in the margin of the Authorized Version and was printed in some English Bibles into the twentieth century. He resided in England after the Irish rebellion of 1641.

R. B. Knox, *James Ussher, Archbishop of Armagh* (1967).

GREGORY J. MILLER

Utraquists   A group of moderate Czech Hussites, also known as Calixtines. They insisted that Holy Communion be received in both kinds (*sub utraque specie*), that the laity and not just the priests receive wine from the chalice (*calix*). Socially conservative, they used the Czech language in worship and rejected the jurisdiction of the Roman pontiff, while retaining apostolic succession and the seven sacraments. The Compacts of Prague and the Basel Council (1433, 1437) and the peace of Kutná Hora (1485) were the legal bases for their existence. Jan Rokycana (c. 1390–1471) was elected archbishop but was never confirmed; real authority was in the hands of a synod, an administrator, the Prague Utraquist consistory, and lay defenders elected by the Utraquist estates. During the administration of Václav Koranda (1471–1479) the Utraquists began to split into two groups: conservatives ready to reunite with Rome and "neo-Utraquists." Václav Mitmánek (1510–1553) sought in vain to unite the "neo-Utraquists," Bohemian Brethren, and Lutherans. Following the unsuccessful revolt of the non-Catholic estates in 1547 and the adoption of the Bohemian Confession of 1562, the "old Utraquist" consistory annulled the compacts in 1567. In 1591 they accepted the jurisdiction of the Roman hierarchy. The "neo-Utraquists," Lutherans, and Bohemian Brethren negotiated a common Bohemian Confession in 1575 but received only an oral promise of toleration from Maximilian II. Not until 1609 (Letter of Majesty) was a Czech Protestant church order recognized. But the influence of Helvetic Reformed views had divided the nominal Czech Protestant union that disappeared with the Habsburg victory at White Mountain (1620).

K. J. Dillon, *King and Estates in the Bohemian Lands, 1526–1564* (1976); W. Eberhard, *Konfessionsbildung und Stände in Böhmen, 1478–1530* (1981); F. G. Heymann, "The Hussite-Utraquist Church in the Fifteenth and Sixteenth Centuries," *ARG* 52 (1961): 1–26.

DAVID P. DANIEL

Uvedale, John   *see* Udall, John

Vadian (1484–1551), humanist scholar, poet, physician, and reformer. Born Joachim von Watt in St. Gall, Switzerland, into a respected, civic-minded family, Vadim was educated at Vienna, where his scholarly interests ranged from poetry to geography and botany. Appointed poet laureate (1514), professor of poetry and university rector (1516), and doctor of medicine (1517), he seemed destined for an influential career in Vienna but in 1518 returned to St. Gall. A council member from 1521, Bürgermeister in 1525, and a major office holder thereafter, he was drawn into the Reformation orbit, influenced initially by Erasmus and later by Zwingli, Luther, and Melanchthon. He studied the church fathers and lectured on the creeds and the book of Acts.

The Reformation in St. Gall was legislated in 1526, and the abbey was secularized in 1529 (only to revert to Catholic control in 1531). Vadian saved numerous manuscripts from the destruction of the abbey and exercised a moderating influence on the Reformation. His last two decades were devoted to historical research and writing. His work was based on abbey manuscripts, including chronicles of the abbey, the city and Lake Constance, and histories of monasticism, Roman emperors and Frankish kings. He bequeathed his library and manuscripts to the town.

C. Bonorand, *Vadians weg vom Humanismus zur Reformation und seine Vorträge über die Apostelgeschichte 1523*, vol. 7 of *Vadian-Studien* (1962); W. Näf, *Vadian und seine Stadt St Gallen* (1957); E. G. Rupp, *Patterns of Reformation* (1969).

JOHN TONKIN

Valdes, founder of the Waldensians. Valdes was a rich merchant of Lyon who, after a conversion experience (c. 1173), commissioned vernacular translations of books of Scripture and excerpts from the Fathers, gave away his wealth, and undertook a life of poverty and preaching in accordance with Christ's commission at the Sending of the Seventy. Alexander III commended his zeal for poverty in 1179, but a request for a general permission to preach was diplomatically declined, as decisions on the right to preach were left to the local clergy. Valdes remained a layman and so fell foul of the tradition that preaching should be the reserve of the priesthood. He assented to an orthodox profession of faith at a diocesan council in 1180, but two years later anxieties over preaching and the behavior of some followers led to excommunication by the archbishop of Lyon and, in 1184, to condemnation of the Waldensians at the Council of Verona. Valdes and his companions believed that they had a divine call to preach and insisted on doing so. Reconciliation with the church, desired by Valdes, never occurred. A strong personality, his decisions on preaching, literal adherence to the commission to the Seventy, and translating Scripture were of lasting importance.

E. Cameron, *The Waldenses* (2000); M. Lambert, *Medieval Heresy* (3rd ed., 2002); W. L. Wakefield and A. P. Evans, eds., *Heresies of the High Middle Ages* (1969).

MALCOLM D. LAMBERT

Valdés, Alfonso de (c. 1490–1533), Spanish humanist, imperial secretary, preeminent Latinist, and brother of Juan de Valdés. Attached to the imperial court of Charles V in the early 1520s, Valdés attended the Diet of Worms and learned firsthand about Martin Luther. Valdés also corresponded with Erasmus of Rotterdam and became one of his most ardent advocates at court. Valdés published an account of the sack of Rome (1527) by Charles V's troops, entitled *Diálogo de las cosas ocurridas en Roma*, in which he defended the emperor's aggression against Pope Clement VII. Around 1528, an Erasmian piece written by Valdés began to circulate, entitled *Diálogo de Mercurio y Carón*, in which he seemed to express some sympathy with Protestant ideas. Though this piece earned him the scrutiny of the Inquisition, he remained at court. At the Diet of Augsburg (1530), Valdés met Philip Melanchthon, translated the Augsburg Confession into Spanish, and made efforts to mediate between Protestants and Catholics. All of Valdés's conciliatory efforts came to an abrupt end when he fell victim to the plague in Vienna.

D. Donald and E. Lázaro, *Alfonso de Valdés y su época* (1983); J. C. Nieto, *Juan de Valdés and the Origins of the Spanish and Italian Reformation* (1979).

CARLOS M. N. EIRE

Valdés, Juan de (c. 1490–1541), Spanish humanist, promoter of the Protestant Reformation in Italy, brother of Alfonso de Valdés. Educated at the Univ. of Alcalá, Valdés rubbed shoulders with some Alumbrados early in his career—"Illumined Ones," condemned by the Inquisition for their mystical teachings and apparent disdain for rituals and symbols. Like his brother Alfonso, Juan became an ardent disciple of Erasmus of Rotterdam. In 1529 he published the *Diálogo de doctrina cristiana*, a treatise laced with sympathy for Protestant teachings, which eventually made it into the *Index of Forbidden Books*. In 1531 he moved to Rome and in 1534 to Naples, where he established a circle of like-minded reformers that included prominent figures such as Giulia Gonzaga and Vittoria Colonna. Two other members of this group, Peter Martyr Vermigli and Bernardino Ochino, eventually converted to Protestantism. In 1536, Valdés published the *Alphabeto christiano*, a treatise that pleased many in Protestant circles. Though he never openly broke with the Catholic Church, Valdés espoused a faith that was deeply influenced by Erasmian piety and Protestant theology, especially on issues such as justification, biblical authority, and the intercession of the saints. Protestants have long revered him as one of their own.

M. Bataillon, *Erasme et l'Espagne*, 3 vols. (2nd ed., 1991); M. Firpo, *Tra alumbrados e "spirituali": Studi su Juan de Valdes* (1990); J. C. Nieto, *Juan de Valdés and the Origins of the Spanish and Italian Reformation* (1979); W. Otto, *Juan de Valdés und die Reformation in Spanien im 16. Jahrhundert* (1989).

CARLOS M. N. EIRE

Valentine, St. (d. c. 270), martyr. Confusion exists as to whether a person named Valentine ever existed or whether the late, unreliable legends of two martyrs actually describe an earlier martyrdom of one man. Early martyrologies mention two Valentines martyred in Rome on February 14. One Valentine is said to have been a priest who, after refusing to renounce his faith, was executed by Emperor Claudius and his relics translated to the church of St. Praxedes in Rome. The second Valentine was reportedly the bishop of Interamna (Terni), who refused to renounce his faith during the same persecution under Claudius, was martyred, and his relics returned to Terni. There is no other historical evidence for either individual.

There is no reason to associate the martyrdom of Valentine with courtship and love. Although Valentine (the priest) was said to have defied an imperial edict by performing marriages between Roman soldiers and their fiancées, this legend is clearly a later invention. Most scholars contend that the pagan festival of Lupercalia, observed in mid-February, is the basis for Valentine's Day. Others cite the medieval tradition, popularized by Chaucer, that birds pair off on February 14.

R. Krautheimer, ed., *Corpus Basilicarum Christianarum Romae*, vol. 4 (ET, 1970); H. A. Kelly, *Chaucer and the Cult of Saint Valentine*, vol. 5 of *Davis Medieval Texts and Studies* (1986).

WILLIAM B. SWEETSER JR.

Valentinus (second cent.), Egyptian Christian teacher. Valentinus was educated at Alexandria and was active as an educator in Rome in the mid-second century. A respected Christian leader in his pre-gnostic life, he was for a time a candidate for bishop of Rome. The most significant text that many scholars attribute to him is *The Gospel of Truth*, a brief book that established the essential core of his belief system. It included some themes found in other gnostic systems, such as pleroma (fullness), wisdom (though not personified), and the significance of wisdom and *gnosis* ("knowledge") for attaining salvation. However, in this early Gospel Valentinus did not yet demonstrate a complete break with traditional Christian thought. Later Valentinians espoused a version of Valentinus's system that was distinctly gnostic, with three Christs—one spiritual, one psychic, and one physical—each with unique responsibilities. Texts by disciples of Valentinus such as Ptolemaeus evidence personified wisdom (Sophia and Achamoth) and an ignorant demiurge (creator) who is inferior to the perfect Father. Valentinians held to the belief that Jesus, though psychically the son of the Creator, was endowed with special power from the Savior that descended upon him as a dove during his baptism.

W. Barnstone, ed., *The Other Bible: Ancient Alternative Scriptures* (1984); W. Barnstone and M. Meyer, eds., *The Gnostic Bible* (2003); B. D. Ehrman, *Lost Scriptures: Books That Did Not Make It into the New Testament* (2003); W. Foerster, *Patristic Evidence*, vol. 1 of *Gnosis: A Selection of Gnostic Texts* (1972); J. M. Robinson, *The Nag Hammadi Library in English* (4th rev. ed., 1996).

RODNEY S. SADLER JR.

Valerian (d. after 450), bishop of Cemele (Cimiez) in southern Gaul. Little is known of his life. He probably was a monk of the island monastery of Lérins prior to his accession to the episcopate sometime before 439. He may be the Valerian to whom Eucherius of Lyon addressed the ascetical treatise *De contemptu mundi*. His name appears on the register of subscribers at the councils of Riez (439) and Vaison (442), which supported—against Pope Leo I—the claims of the see of Arles to metropolitan status over the churches of Gaul. Two extant homilies are attributed to him, as well as an *Epistola ad monachos de virtutibus et ordinae doctrinae apostolicae*. His doctrinal positions, where explicit, are unexceptional, but he surely imbibed the teachings on divine grace and human agency that were current in the monastic milieu of southern Gaul and that have been (somewhat misleadingly) labeled "Semi-Pelagian."

R. W. Mathisen, "Petronius, Hilarius, and Valerianus: Prosopographical Notes on the Conversion of the Roman Aristocracy," *Historia* 30 (1981): 106–12; C. Tibiletti, "Valeriano di Cimiez e la teologia dei Maestri Provenzali," *Aug* 22 (1982): 513–32.

THOMAS A. SMITH

Valerian (c. 190–c. 260), Roman emperor (253–260). A member of a Roman senatorial family, Valerian ascended the throne during the mid-third-century imperial crisis. In addition to usurpations, the empire also was suffering from external assaults by Alamanni and Goths on the Danube and Persians from the east. Upon his arrival at Rome, Valerian elevated his son Gallienus as co-emperor. While Gallienus tended to the west, Valerian moved eastward (c. 256) to confront the Persian emperor Shapur, who had invaded Syria. In 257 he initiated an imperial persecution of Christians, reportedly at the instigation of the Egyptian general Macrian. A first edict forbade Christians from worshiping publicly and ordered that all clerics sacrifice to the Roman gods. A harsher, second edict ordered execution of those high clergy who refused to sacrifice, plus punishment and confiscation of property of socially prominent laymen. The fourth-century historian Eusebius of Caesarea detailed Valerian's persecution in his *Ecclesiastical History*. Notable among the martyrs were Pope Sixtus II and Cyprian of Carthage. In 260 Valerian marched his plague-ridden army beyond the empire's boundaries into Mesopotamia. At Edessa, Shapur tricked and captured him. Persian rock carvings depict Valerian prostrating himself before the Persian monarch. Valerian died in captivity. Gallienus immediately ended his father's persecution.

R. Selinger, *The Mid-Third-Century Persecutions of Decius and Valerian* (2002).
ALLEN E. JONES

Valla, Lorenzo (1407–1457), Italian humanist, philologist, and biblical scholar. He was born in Rome to a family that for several generations had served in the papal curia. In 1530 he went to northern Italy, where he spent some years traveling as a private tutor in addition to teaching rhetoric at the Univ. of Pavia. In 1535 he migrated south as secretary to King Alfonso of Naples. He remained there until 1447, when he returned to Rome as a papal scribe. No stranger to controversy, Valla drew criticism for his preference for Quintilian over Cicero and for his support for Epicureanism and denunciation of Stoicism in *On the True and the False Good*. His most provocative work was his *Oration on the Donation of Constantine* (1440), using his philological expertise to prove that the papacy's claim that Constantine had granted the western empire to the church was based on a later forgery. Other works include the *Elegancies of the Latin Language*, *Annotations* on the New Testament, and *Dialectical Disputations*.

E. Cassirer et al., eds., *The Renaissance Philosophy of Man* (1956); J. Monfasani, *Language and Learning in Renaissance Italy: Selected Articles* (1994); C. Trinkaus, *Renaissance Transformations of Late Medieval Thought* (1999).
J. LAUREL CARRINGTON

Vasa, Gustavus (1496–1560), king of Sweden (1523–1560). He led the resistance against the Danish supremacy and its king, Christian II, who, in the so-called Stockholm Bloodbath (1520), had slaughtered a number of nobles, including Vasa's father. In 1521 Vasa was chosen as regent, and with the defeat of the Danes (summer 1523) a parliamentary session elected him king of Sweden on June 6 (which later became the national day).

Developments during Vasa's reign led to the rise of Protestantism in Sweden. The Catholic archbishop of Sweden, Gustaf Trolle, followed King Christian to Denmark, and since the pope hesitated to appoint a successor, most of the sees became vacant, severely weakening the church. At the same time, the ideas of the Reformation reached Sweden and some of its leading figures, such as Ölaus Petri and Laurentius Andreae, became members of the king's staff. They provided him with an understanding of the church as a communion of believers that facilitated the king's pressure on monastic finances and the introduction of the Reformation.

The Diet of Västerås, June 16, 1527, was the Reformation breakthrough in Sweden. It proclaimed freedom of religion for Protestants and Catholics alike as long as they based their beliefs on the pure and simple word of God. This positive recognition of evangelical doctrine made the diet a revolution in religion as well as in church politics.

In 1531 Vasa himself appointed a new archbishop, the evangelical reformer Laurentius Petri. In the 1544 Diet of Västerås it was finally decided that Sweden should be a hereditary kingdom with an evangelical monarch.

O. P. Grell, ed., *The Scandinavian Reformation* (1995); M. Roberts, *The Early Vasas: A History of Sweden, 1523–1611* (1968).
INGUN MONTGOMERY

Venantius Fortunatus (c. 540–600), poet, hagiographer, and bishop. A native of northern Italy educated at Ravenna, Fortunatus relocated to Gaul in 566. His wedding poem for the Frankish king Sigibert brought him the attention of Merovingian and Gallo-Roman notables desirous of connections to fading Roman literary and rhetorical traditions. He traveled widely in Gaul but was resident primarily at Poitiers, of which he became bishop late in life. His patrons included Gregory of Tours and the royal nun Radegund of Poitiers. His poetry testifies to extensive connections in Merovingian lay and ecclesiastical society. Fortunatus's occasional verse displays considerable generic variety, including panegyrics, epitaphs, consolations, and two famous hymns, *Vexilla regis* and *Pange lingua*, written to celebrate the reception of relics of the cross at Poitiers. In the mid-570s Fortunatus composed a verse life of Martin of Tours based upon the prose account of Sulpicius Severus. His corpus also includes hagiographic prose lives of saints and bishops, including Hilary of Poitiers, Germanus of Paris, and Radegund. Fortunatus was Merovingian Gaul's major poet, controlling and passing on a rich tradition of Latin poetry, classical and Christian.

S. Quesnel, ed. and trans., *Venance Fortunat: Vie de Saint Martin* (1996); M. Reydellet, ed. and trans., *Venance Fortunat: Poèmes*, 2 vols. (1994, 1998); J. W. George, trans., *Venantius Fortunatus: Personal and Political Poems* (1995); J. W. George, *Venantius Fortunatus* (1992).

DENNIS E. TROUT

Vergerio, Pier Paolo (1498–1565), Italian

lawyer, papal nuncio, first bishop to become "Lutheran." Born in Capodistria to an aristocratic family, he earned his law degree (Padua, 1524) and adjudicated in Venice, where his bride, Diana, died within the year (1526). Turning to ecclesiastical service, he attended the Diet of Augsburg (1530), was appointed curial papal secretary in Vienna (1532) and papal nuncio to Ferdinand (1533) and was elected bishop of Modruz (Croatia) and then Capodistria (1536), where he investigated "Lutheran" heresies. In 1535, Vergerio met Luther in Wittenberg but characterized him as "a beast." As unofficial envoy at the Worms-Regensburg Colloquy (1540–1541), he studied the Augsburg Confession and Apology and was accused of being too conciliatory toward evangelicals. Returning home, he began a diocesan reform following the new "Evangelism." Inquisitorial investigations (1545–1549) resulted in his departure from Italy and, more significantly, from the Catholic Church.

He briefly served as pastor in Vicosoprano and then as legal advisor to the Lutheran Duke Christoph of Würtemberg. He collaborated on publishing evangelical books in Slovenia and Croatia (Luther's Small Catechism and Primus Trubar's Slovenian Bible translation). Vergerio untiringly promoted reform in Italy until he died in Tübingen.

A. J. Schutte, *Pier Paolo Vergerio: The Making of an Italian Reformer* (1977)

TIMOTHY MASCHKE

Vermigli, Peter Martyr (1499–1562), Flo-

rentine humanist and internationally influential Reformed theologian. Born in Florence, Vermigli joined the Augustinian order in his teens and went on to study scholastic philosophy in Padua, earning a doctorate. Ordained a priest in 1525, he began a career of teaching and religious leadership that soon led to prominent positions in Augustinian houses throughout Italy. Vermigli belonged to the reform-minded Catholics in Italy and was friends with the Spanish reformer Juan de Valdés, active in humanist circles, and in close contact with agents of church reform such as the noted Cardinal Gasparo Contarini. Vermigli's own reformist teaching and practice drew sharp criticism from conservatives, and he fled Italy in 1542 rather than submit to the newly instated Inquisition.

Vermigli devoted the rest of his life to the Protestant Reformation and became one of its most powerful exponents. Much of his influence came through his academic teaching and writing, which focused heavily upon biblical commentary. After barely a month in exile, he joined Martin Bucer in Strasbourg to teach Old Testament in 1542. Invited to England by Archbishop Thomas Cranmer, Vermigli took a regius professorship at Oxford in 1548. Here his lectures on the Bible and teachings on the Eucharist, as well as his contributions to the Book of Common Prayer, left a powerful mark on the English Reformation. Having married the former nun Catherine Dammartin in 1545, his personal life as a married cleric drew attention, too. After the death of Edward VI and the ascendancy of Queen Mary, Vermigli returned to Strasbourg in 1553, where his conflict with prevailing Lutheran views of the Eucharist prompted a further move to Zurich three years later. In Switzerland, he remained as productive as ever, teaching and publishing actively and frequently substituting for Calvin in the Geneva Academy. Throughout the later years of his life, he maintained close contact to the English reform movement, both through its exiles in continental Europe and its proponents at home. He dedicated his lectures on Romans to Queen Elizabeth I (1558). Vermigli died shortly after returning from the Colloquy of Poissy (1561), where he had accompanied his colleague Theodore Beza. Vermigli wrote prolifically and published numerous biblical commentaries, controversialist writings, and theological *Loci communes*.

F. James III, "Peter Martyr Vermigli," in *The Reformation Theologians*, ed. C. Lindberg

(2002); Pietro Martire Vermigli, *Peter Martyr Library* (1994–).

KENNETH G. APPOLD

Vestiarian Controversy This English dispute over the use of vestments persisted throughout the reigns of Edward VI and Elizabeth I and was·one of the founding issues of Puritanism. Radical reformers objected to vestments as merely Roman, not biblical, and they resented attempts by moderate, royalist bishops to enforce conformity. The bishops, supporting Elizabeth, tended to view lack of conformity as promoting dangerous dissent. The issue erupted in 1550, when John Hooper refused to be consecrated bishop of Gloucester in the prescribed garments (surplice and rochet). Although Hooper later compromised in using traditional vestments, his public refusal had struck a radical chord; by 1563 opposition to vestments of any kind had significant support in the Convocation. In 1566 Matthew Parker, archbishop of Canterbury, with Elizabeth's full support, countered this movement by promulgating the *Advertisements*, listing detailed requirements for use of vestments throughout England. In London, thirty-seven priests were deprived of their offices for failure to comply, which caused significant disturbances in the city. Elsewhere, enforcement of the *Advertisements* was inconsistent, since some bishops sympathized with the Puritans. Vigorous pamphlet campaigns were waged on both sides throughout Elizabeth's reign; the issue was notably raised in the Marprelate Tracts (1588–1589). By the end of the sixteenth century, this controversy lost much of its immediacy, being submerged in larger issues of church governance.

———

W. Haugaard, *Elizabeth and the English Reformation* (1968); J. Primus, *The Vestments Controversy* (1960).

DAVID A. LOPEZ

Victor of Vita (mid to late fifth cent.), North African bishop and historian. Victor was from the city of Vita and later served as bishop there or at an unknown locale.

During the reign of the Vandal king Huneric (477–484), Victor was a priest at Carthage. He witnessed firsthand the cruelty and contempt with which the Arian Vandals treated Catholics during their occupation of North Africa. Victor wrote the *History of the Vandal Persecution* c. 484. Book 1 describes the invasion and conquest of North Africa by King Gaiseric and his Vandal hordes up to Gaiseric's death in 477. Book 2 relates events during the rule of Huneric (Gaiseric's son) and includes information on the abortive council of 484, convoked by Huneric to convince African Catholic bishops of Arianism's superiority. Book 3 narrates events from the council until June 484, the period when Huneric unleashed his wrath against the intransigent bishops by confiscating churches, banishing over five hundred clergy from Carthage, and levying severe penalties on Catholics who refused to embrace Arianism. Though biased and naive, Victor's history provides a wealth of details not found elsewhere. His work includes a valuable list of Catholic bishops in Vandal Africa.

———

CSEL 7 (1881); C. Courtois, *Victor de Vite et son oeuvre* (1954); W. H. C. Frend, *The Rise of Christianity* (1984); J. Moorhead, trans., *Victor of Vita: History of the Vandal Persecution* (1992).

JANE E. MERDINGER

Victorinus, Caius Marius (fourth cent.), rhetorician and theologian. Marius Victorinus is most widely known through Augustine's description of his conversion (*Conf.* 8.2.3– 8.5.10). Victorinus was a well-established rhetor and Neoplatonic philosopher in Rome who late in life converted to Christianity. His previous literary accomplishments included translations, from Greek into Latin, of works by Plotinus, Porphyry, and important Neoplatonic commentators. These translations probably were the Neoplatonic books that influenced Augustine. Victorinus's Christian writings are significant: he was a staunch defender of the Nicene formula of the consubstantial Trinity at the very time that anti-Nicene theology was at its ascendency. He was the first to employ a "noetic triad"—a psychological model—to support a theology of "three in one." But his most influential writings may be his series of commentaries on Paul's epistles that mark the beginning of that explosion of late fourth-century Latin interest in Paul associated with Ambrosiaster, Pelagius, Rufinus, Tyconius, and Augustine. Victorinus's polemically developed Trinitarian theology is argued in technical and frequently obscure Neoplatonic concepts; however, he begins *Against Arius* from scriptural exegesis, and his Pauline commentaries are direct and follow the grammatical style typical of rhetorical exegesis. The extent of his influence on later Latin Trinitarian theology (e.g., Augustine) is a matter of scholarly controversy.

R. Markus, "Marius Victorinus and Augustine," in *The Cambridge History of Later Greek and Early Medieval Philosophy*, ed. A. H. Armstrong (1970), 331–40.

MICHEL RENE BARNES

Victorinus of Poetovio (late third cent.), bishop, martyr, and writer. Victorinus authored the earliest biblical commentaries composed in Latin. Jerome (*Vir. ill.* 74) ascribed nine commentaries to him, including *On the Apocalypse,* along with the treatise *Against All Heresies* and "many other works." *On the Apocalypse* survives, along with a chronological fragment on the life of Jesus and a short treatise *On the Fabrication of the World.* Jerome states that Victorinus was bishop of Poetovio (present-day Ptuj or Pettau) and that he died a martyr. Internal evidence seems to indicate that *On the Apocalypse* was composed during the reign of Gallienus (258–260). Although written in an unpolished style, his works exhibit a wide familiarity with Christian culture, both eastern and western. *On the Fabrication of the World* revels in number symbolism. *On the Apocalypse* interprets the book more as a summary of the Christian faith, with emphasis on the unity of the two testaments, than as a revelation of the future. Significantly, the book sealed with the seven seals of Revelation 5:1 is the Old Testament. Christ's passion opens it and reveals its true meaning.

M. Dulaey, *Victorin de Poetovio. Premier exégète latin*, 2 vols. (1993); V. de Poetovio, *Sur l'Apocalypse et autres écrits*, ed. M. Dulaey, SC 423 (1997).

JOSEPH W. TRIGG

Vienne, Council of (1311–1312) Pope Clement V called the Fifteenth Ecumenical Council in 1308 to consider various reforms. Most famously, the council, pressured by King Philip IV of France, disbanded the Templars (*Vox clamantis* or *Vox in excelso*, March 22, 1312). Philip unsuccessfully pressured the council to condemn posthumously Pope Boniface VIII, who had embarrassed Philip by dying (1303) after one of Philip's knights beat him. Vienne's extant decrees (reissued as Pope John XXII's *Clementinae*, 1327) include defining mendicants' pastoral responsibilities, condemning Beguines and Beghards, creating *studia* for eastern languages (Greek, Hebrew, Arabic) at major universities, considering financial reform for papal revenues, restricting the power of inquisitors, and condemning usury. The doctrinal decrees of the council eventually helped reconcile Spiritual and Conventual Franciscans.

J. Lecler, *Vienne*, in *Histoire des conciles oecuméniques*, vol. 8 (1964); G. Mollat, *Popes at Avignon*, trans. J. Love (1963); N. Tanner, *Decrees* (1990), 333–401.

DAVID A. LOPEZ

Vigilius (d. 555), bishop of Rome (537–555). Vigilius's notoriety stems from his involvement in the Three Chapters controversy. In 543 Emperor Justinian I issued a condemnation of Theodore of Mopsuestia, Theodoret of Cyrus, and Ibas of Edessa, all proponents of Antiochene Christology. The emperor hoped to placate Monophysites by this condemnation.

Justinian summoned Vigilius to Constantinople and demanded the Roman bishop's assent to the edict. The bishop initially consented to the Three Chapters, but after a massive protest in the West, he rescinded his agreement. A council was called to meet in Constantinople in 553 to address the controversy. Due to underrepresentation from the West Vigilius boycotted the council and was placed under house arrest in Constantinople. Six months later he reluctantly consented to the Council of Constantinople's decision and was released. Vigilius died in Syracuse while traveling back to Rome from Constantinople. All of his extant literature is related to the Three Chapters controversy.

F. Carcione, "Vigilius nelle controversie christologiche," *Studi e ricerche sull'Oriente cristiano* 10 (1987); G. Every, "Was Vigilius a Victim or an Ally of Justinian?" *Heythrop Journal* 20 (1979): 257–66; PL 69 (1848), 12–328.

STEVEN A. MCKINION

Vincent de Paul (1581–1660), French priest and apostle of charity, canonized in 1737. Endowed with an aptitude for scholarship and personal charisma, "Monsieur Vincent," as he was known, was ordained at the extraordinarily young age of twenty. De Paul abandoned a profitable chaplaincy to preach spiritual renewal for clergy and laity and to advocate tirelessly on behalf of the poor, for whose physical and spiritual needs he provided by the astute organization and management of a vast network of charitable services. He founded the Congregation of the Mission ("Lazarists" or "Vincentians") for popular preaching and priestly formation. Influenced by Francis de Sales's collaboration with Jane de Chantal, de Paul helped Louise de Marillac found the Daughters of Charity, an innovative community of noncloistered women serving the rural and urban poor, orphans, prostitutes, galley slaves, and battlefield wounded. The work of these communities continues to this day, while the lay-founded and directed Saint Vincent de Paul Society, in countless parishes worldwide, continues his legacy of immediate practical charity to those in need.

————

B. Pujo, *Vincent de Paul, the Trailblazer* (2003); M. Purcell, *The World of Monsieur Vincent: The Life of St. Vincent de Paul* (1989); J. Roman, *Saint Vincent de Paul: A Biography* (1999).

PETER J. SCAGNELLI

Vincent of Lérins (d. before 450), Gallo-Roman monk and writer. Writing under the pseudonym Peregrinus ("the pilgrim," probably denoting his status as a monk), Vincent produced a work entitled *Peregrinus against Heretics*, now commonly known as the *Commonitorium* (*Aid to Memory*), described by Gennadius (*Vir. ill.* 65) as a "powerful disputation" against heresy. In this, Vincent's best-known and most influential work, he developed criteria for distinguishing between authentic Christian teaching and heretical teaching. In a famous formula (the so-called Vincentian canon), he asserts that belief in the true Catholic faith entails holding to "what has been believed everywhere, always, and by all [*quod semper, quod ubique, quod ab omnibus*]." Where universality is wanting, one should appeal to the antiquity of a doctrine. Two other works have been attributed to Vincent. The authenticity of the *Objections of Vincent*, referred to in a work by Prosper of Aquitaine, is disputed. These presumably articulated hesitations about some teachings of Augustine. The *Excerpts*, a patchwork of anti-Nestorian texts taken from Augustine's writings, seems likely to be authentic. Though some controversialists have regarded him as suspect due to a "Semi-Pelagian" doctrine of grace, Vincent was widely admired from the sixteenth through the nineteenth centuries among Protestants and Catholics seeking criteria for normative doctrine.

————

W. O'Connor, "Saint Vincent of Lérins and Saint Augustine," *Doctor Communis* 16 (1963): 123–257.

THOMAS A. SMITH

Viret, Pierre (1511–1571), accomplished author and preacher, early leader of the Reformation in France and French-speaking Switzerland, where he was born. Educated in Paris, he embraced the Reformation. Returning to his home in Orbe (1530), he promoted reform. Joining Guillaume Farel in Geneva (1534), he preached and participated in public disputations with Catholics. By May 1536 the Reformation triumphed in Geneva. John Calvin arrived, and Viret became intimate friends with Farel and Calvin. Viret moved to Lausanne in 1536 and, with Farel and Calvin, helped establish the Reformation. He served as pastor and teacher there with interludes in Geneva. Viret attempted to establish Geneva-style discipline and ran afoul of the leaders in Bern, who controlled Lausanne and no longer appreciated him as pastor and professor in the Lausanne academy. He joined Calvin in Geneva as a pastor and teacher in 1559. He left in 1561, giving ill health as the reason. Some scholars attribute his departure to the preeminent role that Theodore Beza had taken in Geneva. Viret went to southern France. There he preached to crowds of thousands, was active in the national synods of the French Reformed Church, advocated more lay participation in church government than most Reformed colleagues, and aided the queen of Navarre, Jeanne d'Albret, in the Reformation in her domains.

————

B. Roussel, ed., "Conference on Pierre Viret," *Bulletin de la Société de l'Histoire du Protestantisme Français* 144 (1998): 757–893; R. Linder, *The Political Ideas of Pierre Viret* (1964).

JEANNINE E. OLSON

Virgil (70–19 BCE), premier Latin poet. Born near Mantua, Virgil experienced the political and social turmoil of the disintegrating Roman Republic and emerging Augustan Principate. In uncertain times and eventually with imperial patronage, he composed three masterpieces of Latin poetry: the pastoral *Eclogues* (c. 39–38); the *Georgics* (c. 29), a didactic poem on farming; and the *Aeneid*, the story of Trojan Aeneas's journey to Italy and an epic of Roman origins. While Virgil's poetry engaged contemporary issues, its ideological complexity and metaphorical richness ensured timeless appeal. Virgil's works, central to Roman education and identity, profoundly influenced early Christian poetry and thought. The language and style of Juvencus's seminal *Poem on the Gospels* (c. 330) are indebted to Virgil, and Augustine conducted a life-long dialogue with Virgil's texts. The messianic fourth *Eclogue* was read as a prophecy of Christ's birth, and Virgil himself is sometimes construed as proto-Christian. As such, he eventually guided Dante through the *Inferno* and *Purgatory*. Often allegorized or modernized, Virgil's works exercised abiding influence through the Renaissance and modern eras. Milton and T. S. Eliot, among others, were close readers.

D. Comparetti, *Vergil in the Middle Ages* (1885; rev. ed., 1997); S. MacCormack, *The Shadows of Poetry: Vergil in the Mind of Augustine* (1998); C. Martindale, ed., *The Cambridge Companion to Virgil* (1997); T. Ziolkowski, *Virgil and the Moderns* (1993).

DENNIS E. TROUT

Virgin Mary in Medieval Art Whether depicted as a stately queen, simple maiden, or grieving mother, the Virgin Mary in the Middle Ages was perhaps the most visible reminder of Christian faith. Following her official recognition as Theotokos ("God-bearer") at the Council of Ephesus in 431, Mary's image gained prominence in churches throughout the Christian world, as attested by apse mosaics of the enthroned Virgin and Child, widespread beginning in the fifth century. The influence of pre-Christian art on Marian iconography is traceable in these early examples, which often resemble the Egyptian goddess Isis and her son Horus.

In the ninth and tenth centuries, Carolingian and Ottonian illuminators commemorated Marian feasts, including the Purification, Annunciation, Assumption, and Nativity, with scenes in lectionaries and other liturgical books. These painted miniatures, influenced by Byzantine prototypes, later influenced the sculpture, stone relief, and stained glass that decorated twelfth- and thirteenth-century cathedrals. Cathedrals such as Chartres, built as a shrine for Mary's sacred tunic, presented arriving pilgrims with an impressive visualization of salvation history.

The Gothic cathedrals dedicated to Mary, Queen of Heaven, were but one manifestation of the increase in Marian devotion apparent beginning in the twelfth century. Reinvigorated veneration of the Virgin Mary as the source of Christ's humanity, and her perceived intercessory efficacy, propelled institutional patronage of Marian images to new heights. In this context, scholastic theologian Thomas Aquinas asserted that only images of the Virgin deserved to be venerated with "hyperdulia," a greater reverence than was owed to other saints but less than was due God.

Influential written sources for medieval Marian imagery included widely available adaptations of the apocryphal account of Mary's early life known as the *Proto-Evangelium of James*, and descriptions of visions experienced by two mystics, Elisabeth of Schönau and Brigitte of Sweden. Despite the dearth of direct references to Mary in the Bible, allegorical and typological methods favored by medieval interpreters uncovered relevant passages. Mary was associated with the woman described in Revelation 12, as well as with the bride of the Song of Songs. The "black but comely" bride (Song 1:5) was cited in connection with the Black Madonna images found in shrines throughout Europe. Patristic writings were also influential, as well as illustrated representions of Mary as a type of the church (Ambrose of Milan), and as "the new Eve" (Justin Martyr).

During the fourteenth and fifteenth centuries, the trend toward realism and accessibility in Marian representation accelerated. The practice of private viewing encouraged more intimate, emotionally intense images, including the Madonna of Humility and the Pietà. New iconographical themes, including the Madonna of Mercy, the Virgin with St. Anne and the Christ child, and Mary in a Wheat Dress, emerged as the use of religious images found wider acceptance. Their popularity was enhanced by the papal indulgences offered to those who prayed before them, and by increased availability due to new printing techniques. In the sixteenth century the scriptural emphasis of the Protestant Reformers and the caution of the Roman Catholic Church created a more restrictive climate for Marian images, which increasingly became a vehicle for artistic prowess or doctrinal instruction.

I. Forsyth, *Throne of Wisdom* (1972); M. R. Katz, ed. *Divine Mirrors: The Virgin Mary in the Visual Arts* (2001); D. Norman, *Siena and the Virgin* (1999); J. Pelikan, *Mary through the Centuries* (1996); M. Warner, *Alone of All Her Sex* (1983).

ADRIENNE NOCK AMBROSE

Visigothic Hispano-Roman Councils Regional and national episcopal assemblies that convened in Iberia from c. 300 to 694. The *acta* ("acts") of the councils in Iberia are an abundant resource for our understanding of the internal life of church and society. They are a unique window into matters of doctrine, sacraments, liturgy, the development of holy orders, relations with the monarchy, canon law, and morals. Since the see of Toledo came to hold both the ecclesial primacy within Iberia and the seat of the Visigothic kings, it comes as no surprise that at least eighteen councils met there. Most of these Toledan councils were national assemblies reflecting concerns pertinent to the entire Iberian Peninsula. Only the decrees of the Eighteenth Council of Toledo have not survived.

The first two councils of Toledo were provincial and met before Toledo was a metropolitan see. The first truly national assembly was the Third Council of Toledo of 589, which was convened to celebrate the official conversion from Arianism to the Catholic Nicene confession by Reccared, the first Visigothic Catholic king. Two other provincial councils of Toledo were the ninth (655) and eleventh (675), while the fourteenth (684) lies somewhere between a provincial and a national assembly. In all, twelve councils of Toledo were national assemblies: councils 3 (589), 4 (633), 5 (636), 6 (638), 7 (646), 8 (653), 10 (656), 12 (681), 13 (683), 15 (688), 16 (693), and 17 (694). Some councils distinguish themselves more than others in terms of their agendas and decisions. For example, the First Council of Toledo (400) condemned in detail the heresy of Priscillian, while the Third Council of Toledo (589) brought to an end Arianism and introduced the *filioque* clause into the Nicene Creed. The Fourth Council of Toledo (633) made the liturgy in Iberia uniform, later known as the Mozarab Rite, and it also established the protocols and rules of deliberation for all future councils. The rest of the councils in general established a close relationship, for better or worse, between the bishops and the Visigothic monarchy. Moreover, of great importance were the deep fraternal ties developed with the Roman see. Finally, the councils of Toledo made significant contributions to canon law that found their way into the *Liber iudiciorum*. This legal code became part of the canon law collection known as the *Hispana*, which subsequently shaped Carolingian codes of canon law and ultimately the highly influential medieval *Decretum* of Gratian.

In addition to the councils of Toledo, there convened across Iberia numerous regional councils that enhance our knowledge significantly and complement the Toledan councils. The earliest of these met in Elvira (present-day Granada) in c. 300–306, followed by Zaragoza

I (380) and Toledo I (c. 397–400), all predating the Suevic and Visigothic kingdoms in Iberia. Prior to the assimilation of the Suevic Kingdom in northwestern Iberia in 585 by the Visigoths, two significant councils met in the metropolitan see of Braga in 561 and 572 under the watch of Martin of Braga. The remainder of the councils are: Tarragona (516), Gerona (517), Barcelona I and II (540 and 599), Lérida (546), Valencia (549), Narbonne (589), Seville I and II (590 and 619), Zaragoza II and III (592 and 691), Huesca (598), Egara (614), Mérida (666), and Braga III (675). Together all of the councils testify to a vibrant, growing church that proved to be more stable than the Visigothic monarchy that did not survive the Muslim invasion and conquest of 711.

A. Ferreiro, *The Visigoths in Gaul and Spain A.D. 418–711: A Bibliography* (1988); J. Orlandis and D. Ramos-Lissón, *Historia de los Concilios de la España Romana y Visigoda* (1986); R. L Stocking, *Bishops, Councils, and Consensus in the Visigothic Kingdom, 589–633* (2000); J. Vives, *Concilios Visigóticos e Hispano-Romanos* (1963).

ALBERTO FERREIRO

Visitations, Church Conducted periodically as early as the sixth century, church visitations involved on-site observations of churches and other ecclesiastical institutions by church leaders who inspected, examined, and, if necessary, corrected practices. During the Middle Ages, bishops ideally were to visit each church in their diocese every three years. Ecclesiastical laws, including a system for appeals, were established to correct offenders.

In the sixteenth century evangelical German estates and cities sought methods to improve organization of their new churches. Churches and schools were in dire need of trained clergy and teachers. They also needed financial support, as they no longer received income from church property and monasteries. Martin Luther and fellow reformers were concerned and called for visitations to assess the actual conditions in local parishes. Each territory was divided into regions, with representatives from both church and state assigned to examine the economic and religious affairs of parishes. When lack of specific directions hampered the progress of the visitations, Philip Melanchthon drafted more specific instructions in 1528 for use in Saxony. Visitation reports formed the basis for seeking both financial and ministerial support from local governments. Continued visitations helped ensure that in local parishes pastors and teachers had adequate financial support and a solid understanding of evangelical doctrines.

C. Harline, E. Put, and A. Rijksarchief, "A Bishop in the Cloisters: The Visitations of Mathias Hovius (Malines, 1596–1620)," *SCJ* 22, no. 4 (1991): 611–39; E. M. Kern, "The 'Universal' and 'Local' in Episcopal Visitations," in *Infinite Boundaries: Order, Disorder, and Reorder in Early Modern German Culture*, ed. M. Reinhart (1998), 35–54; P. Melanchthon, "Instructions for the Visitors of Parish Pastors in Electoral Saxony, 1528," in *Luther's Works*, vol. 40, ed. C. Bergendoff and H. T. Lehmann (1958), 263–320.

SUZANNE S. HEQUET

Vitoria, Francisco de (1483/1486–1546),

Spanish Dominican theologian, father of the School of Salamanca, political philosopher, and defender of aboriginal Americans. Educated in Paris, Vitoria returned to Spain in 1523 to teach at Valladolid. In 1526 he was elected to the principal chair of theology at the Univ. of Salamanca, where he revolutionized theological education by lecturing on the works of Thomas Aquinas rather than on Peter Lombard's *Sentences*. Though he did not publish while teaching, Vitoria's well-prepared lectures—totally rewritten each year—provided his students with much material to edit and publish after his death; his *Relecciones theologicae* (1557) went through several editions in various countries during the sixteenth and seventeenth centuries. Vitoria shifted the focus of theology onto ethical questions and relied heavily on the concept of natural law, drawing upon Aquinas and Aristotle. Vitoria proved most influential when dealing with political issues, especially questions of human rights, authority, international relations, warfare, and revolution. His treatises on the Spanish conquest of the New World, *De Indis* and *De iure belli*, in which he championed the rights of the natives, set the tone for all subsequent discussions and helped to bring about protective legislation. Still widely studied in the twentieth century, Vitoria has been dubbed the "Father of International Law."

F. C. Urbano, *Pensamiento de Francisco de Vitoria* (1992); R. Hernandez, *Francisco de Vitoria* (1995); A. Pagden, *The Fall of Natural Man* (1987); M. R. Molinero, *Doctrina colonial de Francisco de Vitoria* (1998).

CARLOS M. N. EIRE

Vives, Juan Luis (1492–1540), Spanish

philosopher, educator, pacifist, and humanist. Born in Valencia to Jewish converts condemned by the Inquisition, Vives spent most of his life in exile. He studied in Paris (1509–1512), where he embraced humanistic learning, then moved to the Low Countries, where he became a disciple of Erasmus of Rotterdam and began to gain renown with a scathing critique of medieval scholasticism, *Adversus pseudodialecticos* (1519). In 1522, Vives published a commentary on Augustine's *City of God*, which earned him an appointment at the court of Henry VIII of England as preceptor to the future queen, Princess Mary. He also lectured at Oxford until 1527, when he was briefly imprisoned for objecting to the annulment of King Henry's marriage to Catherine of Aragon.

Upon returning to the Netherlands, Vives devoted himself to teaching and writing, always with revisionism and reform in mind. In addition to publishing one of the most popular Latin textbooks of his age, *Exercitatio linguae Latinae* (1538), Vives tackled the subject of educational reform in *De tradendis disciplinis* (1531), where, among other things, he recommended that students be taught in their vernacular languages and that women receive more schooling. Earlier, in his *De ratione studii puerilis* (1523), he had proposed that children should study nature directly and discover truth through induction. Vives also suggested ways of improving poor relief in *De subventione pauperum* (1526). An advocate of peace and European unity, Vives linked personal and social ethics in *De anima et vita* (1538), proposing individual self-control as the key to harmony and that all humans could be taught to better understand and tame their emotions. In his final opus, *De veritate fidei* (1543), Vives defended the truth claims of Christianity while skirting the theological controversies that were splintering the faith and tearing Europe apart. The legacy of Vives is as complex as his age. Though read by Catholics and Protestants alike, he was also distrusted: Protestants winced at his emphasis on the freedom of the will; Catholics listed his works in the *Index of Prohibited Books*. In various ways, Vives was a pioneer who calls to mind some of the great thinkers of the following two centuries.

P. C. Dust, *Three Renaissance Pacifists* (1987); F. J. Fernandez Nieto, A. Melero, and A. Mestre, eds., *Luis Vives y el humanismo europeo* (1998); J. A. Fernández, *Juan Luis Vives* (1990); C. G.

Noreña, *Juan Luis Vives* (1970); Fernández, *Juan Luis Vives and the Emotions* (1989).

CARLOS M. N. EIRE

Vladimir (972–1015), prince, saint, and apostle of Kievan Rus'. Born at Kiev, he was the son of Svyatosolav I, ruler of a fragmented Russia. At the death of his father he was forced into exile in Scandinavia. There he secretly built an army and, in 980, captured Kiev by defeating his older brother. Many other military successes followed. Vladimir, a pagan, converted to Christianity in 988 under the influence of his Christian grandmother, Princess Olga, and because of his political relations with the Byzantine court of Emperor Basil II. At his baptism he received the Christian name Basil and soon married the emperor's sister Anna. Subsequently, all the souls of Kievan Rus' were strictly compelled to be baptized in the Dnieper River, but without the advantage of catechesis. For centuries thereafter the popular religion of Kievan Rus' was a syncretistic form of Christianity and paganism. Despite his inattentiveness to the salvation of the common people, Vladimir built many churches and monasteries and pursued charitable works. He was canonized as an apostle to the Slavs in the twelfth century.

J. Korpela, *Prince, Saint, and Apostle: Prince Vladimir Svjatoslavic of Kiev: His Posthumous Life, and the Religious Legitimization of the Russian Great Power* (2001); A. Poppe, "St Vladimir as a Christian," in *The Legacy of St Vladimir: Byzantium, Russia, America* (1990), 41–46; V. Volkoff, *Vladimir the Russian Viking* (1985).

MICHAEL D. PETERSON

Vulgate Latin version of the Old and New Testaments compiled in the fourth and fifth centuries. Beginning in the late second century, the Bible was translated into Latin piecemeal; the translations varied in quality, and the collection was never unified. Jerome wrote of the confused Latin text, "there were as many versions as codices" (Prefaces to Joshua and to the Gospel). In the late fourth century, Jerome set out to correct and improve the Latin translation of the Bible. In what is now called the Vulgate, the books of the Hebrew canon are Jerome's new translation from the Hebrew, except for the Psalms, where Jerome's translation of the Gallican Psalter from the Septuagint was rejected. Wisdom, Ecclesiasticus, Baruch, and 1 and 2 Maccabees are Old Latin versions. All of the New Testament is a revision of the Old Latin.

The Vulgate (a name applied to this text only since the thirteenth century and first used officially by the Council of Trent) was not thought of as one "Bible" until all the books were bound in one codex, called a "pandect." Cassiodorus is the first to mention such a codex (*Institutes* 1.12.3); the oldest extant copy is from the seventh century (Codex Amiatinus). The Vulgate replaced the Old Latin only gradually, and copies of the Vulgate and the Old Latin were mutually contaminated in the editorial process. Efforts to standardize the text of the Vulgate were common: the most notable were by Alcuin or his associates in the ninth century, by the faculty of the Univ. of Paris in the thirteenth century, and by Popes Sixtus V and Clement VIII in 1590 and 1592 (the Sixto-Clementine Vulgate).

The Vulgate was the first book printed using movable type (the Gutenberg Bible of 1456). Robert Stephanus produced the first critical edition (Paris, 1528). John Wordsworth and others published a critical edition of the Vulgate New Testament (1889–1954). In 1908, Pope Pius X commissioned a community of Benedictine monks in Rome to produce a complete critical edition; the work is still in progress. In 1969 Robert Weber and others published a two-volume interim edition. In 1979 the Holy See published the *Nova Vulgata*, a revision of the Vulgate text in light of the Hebrew, Aramaic, and Greek originals for use in Latin liturgies.

The Vulgate canon follows the list of canonical books that has been standard in the West since Augustine (including the Apocrypha and additions to Esther and Daniel). The Stuttgart edition includes, in an appendix, the Prayer of Manasseh, 3 and 4 Esdras, Psalm 151, and the Epistle to the Laodicenes.

R. Loewe, "The Medieval History of the Latin Vulgate," in *Cambridge History of the Bible*, vol. 2 (1970), 102–54; H. F. D. Sparks, "Jerome as Biblical Scholar," in *The Cambridge History of the Bible*, vol. 1 (1970), 510–41; E. F. Sutcliffe, "Jerome," in *Cambridge History of the Bible*, vol. 2 (1970), 80–101; R. Weber et al., eds., *Biblia Sacra iuxta vulgatam versionem*, 2 vols. (1969).

JOSEPH T. LIENHARD

Waldensianism Condemned as heresy in 1184, Waldensianism was a movement of repentance and reform initiated by Valdes of Lyon, who sought a life of poverty and preaching aided by vernacular translations of Scripture but fell foul of the unwillingness of ecclesiastical authority to allow laymen to preach. The movement was held together by the class of male celibate preachers, also called masters, who traveled two by two on the pattern of Christ's commission to the Seventy, visiting the faithful and sustained by translations of Scripture, works of exhortation, and catechetical material in the vernacular. Schools inculcated literacy and rote learning of Scripture, sometimes in astonishing bulk, and Waldensian women also preached sporadically at various times in their history. A literal fidelity to the text of Scripture led them to reject oaths, judgments of blood, and the doctrine of purgatory. Masters and followers maintained high ethical standards but as persecution increased were forced to accept an underground existence in which beliefs were concealed in outward conformity to Catholicism but kept alive in families as an inheritance; they were visited by their preachers in secrecy and at night to instruct, exhort, and above all hear their confessions. A split between Valdes's followers, the Poor of Lyon, who did not abandon hope of reconciliation to the church, and the Poor Lombards, a more radical Italian group who rejected the validity of the sacraments administered by unworthy priests, was never healed. A legendary history developed that traced Waldensianism back to churchmen who rejected the Donation of Constantine and transmuted Valdes into a priest called Peter. The Hussite movement encouraged Waldensians, some of whom joined its most radical elements but also stimulated persecution, as churchmen feared them as possible underground allies to the Hussites. Persecution had in any case over centuries reduced their numbers, although they retained mountain redoubts in Haut-Dauphine and certain high valleys in Piedmont. Waldensians generally were absorbed into the Calvinist Reformation, but those in Piedmont, although accepting Calvinist tenets at the Synod of Chanforan in 1532, retained their ancient name and came to play a significant part in Protestant polemics in the sixteenth and seventeenth centuries as examples of the long continuity of protest against the Catholic Church. Oliver Cromwell waged a diplomatic campaign to defend the Waldensians against a persecuting duke of Savoy, Milton's poetry commemorated their sufferings, and the Glorious Return, a campaign of Genevan exiles in 1689–1690 to reconquer their homeland, stirred popular imagination. Modern Waldensians form a small Protestant church with pastorates in Italy and South America.

G. Audisio, *The Waldensian Dissent* (1999); P. Biller, *The Waldenses, 1170–1530* (2001); E. Cameron, *Waldenses* (2000); M. Lambert, *Medieval Heresy* (3rd ed., 2002); P. Stephens, *The Waldensian Story* (1998); S. K. Treesh, "Europe's Peasant Heretics: The Waldensians, 1375–1530" (PhD diss., Rutgers Univ., 1988).
MALCOLM D. LAMBERT

Wars of Religion in France The controversies occasioned by the rise of Calvinism coupled with aristocratic factionalism and the desultory rule of Henry II's (1519–1559) sons plunged France into protracted war. Religion mixed with political ambition contributed to the unrest, as the Guise, Bourbon, and Montmorency families, each of them associated with different religious positions, vied for ascendancy at the royal court. The Guises promoted militant Catholicism, while the Bourbons allied with the French Calvinists, or Huguenots. The Montmorencys eventually became involved with Catholics, known as the Malcontents, who favored moderation. Different regions in the realm came under the control of these factions as royal authority and confessional unity disintegrated.

The Guises dominated during Henry II's brutal campaigns of persecution and the ensuing brief reign of Francis II (1544–1560), especially after the Conspiracy of Amboise in 1560 when Huguenots plotted a coup at court. Their influence waned, however, under Charles IX (1550–1574) whose mother, Queen Catherine de Mèdicis (1519–1589), held sway. She and Chancellor Michel de l'Hôpital (1505–1573) pursued reconciliation at the Colloquy of Poissy (1561) and with the Edict of Toleration (1562). However, a massacre of Huguenots at Vassy in March instigated by the Guises plunged the country into the first civil war, which ended in the Edict of Amboise (1563). The royal tour in 1564–1566 to pacify the country proved a failure as Huguenot forces, led by Louis, Prince of Condé (1530–1569), seized several fortified towns across the kingdom in 1567. No sooner did the Edict of Longjumeau end the second civil war in March 1568 than hostilities broke out again in the autumn. Huguenot defeats at the battles of Jarnac, where Condé perished, and Moncontour in 1569 raised Catherine's fears that the Guises might again exert excessive influence at court. She therefore granted the Huguenots' new leader, Gaspard de Coligny (1519–1572), favorable conditions in the Edict of St. Germain in August 1570.

Catherine's hopes to cement the peace by marrying her daughter, Marguerite of Valois (1553–1615), to Henry of Navarre (1553–1610), the titular head of the Huguenots, were dashed by a resumption of violence with the St. Bartholomew's Day Massacre (in August 1572). A fourth civil war ended poorly for the king. Charles IX's death in May 1574 brought to the throne his brother, Henry III (1551–1589). A fifth religious war in 1575, which saw an alliance between Catholic Malcontents and the Huguenots, ended in May 1576 in the Edict of Beaulieu. Catholics strongly criticized Henry III at the Estates-General that November, which further enhanced the standing of Henry, Duke of Guise (1550–1588), as a Catholic League was formed. Two more civil wars over the next four years further disrupted the country, as peasant revolts erupted across many regions as a result of the accumulated social and economic distress brought on by twenty years of intermittent conflict.

Matters worsened after the death of Francis, Duke of Anjou (1554–1584), because the Huguenot Henry of Navarre now became the presumptive heir according to the laws of succession. An eighth war, known as the War of the Three Henrys, broke out as the Catholic League attracted support from Philip II of Spain in the Treaty of Joinville (December 1584) and from Henry III in the Treaty of Nemours (July 1585). A Paris uprising in May 1588 instigated by the Guises, known as the Day of the Barricades, chased the king out of the capital. Henry III tried to reclaim his authority at the Estates-General in Blois in December by ordering the assassination of the Duke of Guise and the Cardinal of Guise. His plan failed miserably as Catholics across the realm joined the League in open revolt. In desperation, the king allied with Henry of Navarre, only to fall victim to an assassin on August 1, 1589, on the outskirts of Paris.

The regicide ushered Henry IV to the throne, though his legitimacy remained suspect for many Catholics until he converted to Catholicism on July 25, 1593. His coronation in 1594 and subsequent absolution by Pope Clement VIII in 1595 paved the way for the reunification of the realm, as did the open war that Henry IV declared against Spain and Savoy in 1595. Hostilities both inside the country and abroad came to an end in 1598 when Henry IV issued the Edict of Nantes to placate the Huguenots and signed the Treaty of Vervins with Spain and Savoy. Louis XIV revoked the Edict of Nantes in 1685.

———

B. Diefendorf, *Beneath the Cross: Catholics and Protestants in Sixteenth-Century Paris* (1991); M. Holt, *The French Wars of Religion, 1562–1629* (1995); R. J. Knecht, *The French Wars of Religion, 1559–1598* (1996).

MICHAEL WOLFE

Wealth and Charity
In its Christian theological formulation, charity constitutes heartfelt love for God and genuine compassion for others, which results from a joyful response to unmerited divine love. Throughout church history, the concept has manifested itself most tangibly in the practice of providing for those in need from one's own financial means. As both a concept and a practice, charity has been central to Christianity from its earliest days to the present.

Theologians have recognized that Jesus' teaching on charity was a central theme of his ministry, as he declared that love of God and neighbor encapsulates all the law and prophets. A central passage for the medieval church was Matthew 25, in which Jesus identified the righteous as those who feed the hungry, give drink to the thirsty, take in the stranger, clothe the naked, and visit the sick and imprisoned; these acts formed the basis of the seven works of charity. Most mainline denominations have not understood the New Testament to condemn wealth per se but rather that Jesus and the apostles admonished all to give liberally to the needy and warned against the presumptions that wealth can spawn. Though individuals and communities in the early church demonstrated a conspicuous commitment to benevolent activity, no systematic theological treatment of charity appeared until Augustine. He held up charity as the essence of devotion to God and the substance of moral responsibility in all human interactions. Thomas Aquinas built upon and significantly expanded Augustine's conception without altering his fundamental conclusions.

The actual exercise of individual charity became encased within the sacramental system of the Roman Catholic Church in the Middle Ages. Giving to the poor was regularly prescribed as penance, particularly for those with means, to demonstrate contrition in an economy of salvation. This requirement brought rich and poor into a mutually interdependent relationship, as the well-to-do distributed wealth to the poor in return for spiritual benefits. All poverty, from this perspective, was sacred, entitling the poor to alms from the rich. In the sixteenth century, critics argued that this understanding led to indiscriminate giving to the "undeserving poor" and promoted begging. Despite changes in practice, munificence to the needy has nevertheless remained a meritorious work in the Catholic Church into the present day.

The salvific implications in medieval charity were also a powerful motivation in the development of institutions dedicated to charitable service. Despite some differences across Europe, the primary institutional means of social provision were monasteries and various parish agencies, most notably almshouses and hospitals. Monasteries, the earliest charitable institutions in Europe, supplied food to the poor in the local vicinity and offered hospitality to travelers from outside the surrounding area. Within the parish, almshouses and hospitals housed widows, orphans, the sick, and the disabled poor, while "outdoor" relief efforts provided food for the domiciled poor. Parish officials, such as churchwardens or Holy Spirit Masters, managed both "indoor" and "outdoor" efforts from tithes, contributions, private endowments, and parish properties.

The social upheavals of the late Middle Ages and the changing structure of the economy in the sixteenth century brought most parish institutions into crisis, just as humanists and Protestants challenged the basic premises of medieval charity. Protestants severed the notion of religious merit from charitable activity, though all Protestant reformers maintained that relief of the needy was a central obligation of any true Christian community. Reform-minded Catholics, influenced by Christian humanism, also sharply criticized contemporary charitable institutions without altering the church's traditional concept of charity. Economic turmoil and widespread dissatisfaction with existing institutions led Protestant and Catholic reformers to undertake a major reorganization of charitable agencies in cities and towns throughout Europe. The primary components of the new program included: prohibiting begging, centralizing all parish institutions under lay control, establishing a common chest to fund poor relief, and creating public work projects. Some Protestant groups, such as Calvinists and Mennonites, instituted church deacons who worked either alongside or in conjunction with the reorganized municipal program. Likewise, in Catholic countries a number of religious orders and confraternities emerged that performed a variety of services, especially to orphans and young single women. At the end of the sixteenth century, work projects began to give way to workhouses that became increasingly punitive in nature.

The basic structure of provision remained in place until the late nineteenth and early twentieth centuries, though poor relief legislation made significant modifications and placed greater restrictions on the needy. Problems caused by urbanization and industrialization ultimately led to the creation of the welfare state, whose future at the start of the twenty-first century is somewhat fragile. The emergence of public assistance did not by any means displace the significance of private charity in the twentieth century, secular or religious. Charitable organizations continue to form an important source of social provision, an enduring legacy to the Judeo-Christian tradition.

D. T. Critchlow and C. H. Parker eds., *With Us Always: A History of Private Charity and Public Welfare* (1998); G. Gilleman, SJ, *The Primacy of Charity in Moral Theology* (1961); C. Lindberg, *Beyond Charity: Reformation Initiatives for the Poor* (1993); M. Mollat, *The Poor in the Middle Ages: An Essay in Social History*, trans. A. Goldhammer (1978).

CHARLES H. PARKER

Wearmouth and Jarrow These twin Northumbrian Benedictine monasteries were founded by Benedict Biscop (c. 628–690). Wearmouth, overlooking the mouth of the Wear, was founded in 674 and dedicated to St. Peter; Jarrow, overlooking the Tyne a few miles away, was founded in 682 and dedicated to St. Paul. Benedict was a Northumbrian gentleman who served King Oswy before becoming a monk. King Egfrith provided the land for the monasteries that were built by Frankish stonemasons and glaziers, introducing these arts to the Anglo-Saxons. Benedict also brought the Abbot John, archcantor at St. Peter's in Rome, to teach liturgy and chants. Benedict based his monastic rule on that of St. Benedict and on observations made at seventeen monasteries he visited. The abbeys became a chief center for learning in Western Christendom. The library at Jarrow was the largest north of the Alps, thanks in part to Benedict's journeys to Rome. Jarrow is best known as the abbey where Bede spent his life, writing, among other books, the *Lives of the Abbots of Wearmouth and Jarrow*. The abbeys housed over six hundred monks and, while Benedict remained the abbot-founder, he chose two abbots to run them. Upon his death Coelfrid, abbot of Jarrow, replaced him. Under his rule the *Codex Amiatinus*, the oldest surviving complete Latin Bible in one volume, was produced. The abbeys were destroyed by the Viking raids of 867–870 but were restored c. 1074.

P. Wormald, *The Times of Bede: Studies in Early English Christian Society and Its Historian* (2006); G. Bonner, ed., *Famulus Christi: Essays in Commemoration of the Thirteenth Centenary of the Birth of the Venerable Bede* (1976).

MARIANNE M. DELAPORTE

Weigel, Valentin (1533–1588), dissenting Lutheran pastor. Born in Saxony, he was a student at Leipzig and Wittenberg during the years of inter-Lutheran disputes. In 1567 he became pastor at Zschopau (Saxony), where he remained until his death. Weigel wanted harmony among Christians and held that the "letter" and the "external" were less important than inner authority in discerning truth. In 1572 he defended his orthodoxy in a pamplet (*A Little Book on the True and Saving Faith*), and in 1577 and under pressure signed the Formula of Concord. *Dialog on the Nature of Christianity* (1584) criticized clerical tyranny over the conscience and argued for toleration. Influenced by the medieval mystical traditions, including the *Theologia Deutsch*, Weigel stood in the spiritualist tradition of Schwenckfeld and Böhme and is also considered to have influenced Pietism. In later centuries many dissenting views were labeled "Weigelism," but care should be given to distinguish his beliefs from those of others.

R. Hvolbek, "Being and Knowing: Spiritualist Epistemology and Anthropology from Schwenckfeld to Böhme," *SCJ* 22 (1991): 97–110; S. Ozment, *Mysticism and Dissent: Religious Ideology and Social Protest in the Sixteenth Century* (1973); A. Weeks, *Valentin Weigel (1533–1588): German Religious Dissenter, Speculative Theorist, and Advocate of Tolerance* (2000).

MARY JANE HAEMIG

Wenceslas (c. 903–929/935), Přemyslid duke and patron saint of Bohemia. The life of Wenceslas (Václav) is shrouded in legend. Born near Prague to Duke Vratislav, a Christian, and Drahomira, who may have been a pagan, Wenceslas received a Christian education under the direction of his paternal grandmother, Ludmila. When his father died,

Drahomira became regent for the boy and allegedly had his grandmother murdered in 921. The young Wenceslas soon took the reins of government, banished his mother, and had his grandmother's relics translated to Prague.

As a ruler Wenceslas pursued a pro-Saxon policy, even naming the Prague cathedral after St. Vitus, patron saint of Saxony. His submission to the Saxon king, Henry I, may have particularly provoked the animosity of his younger brother Boleslav, who favored Bavaria. Boleslav mounted a coup and had Wenceslas murdered in 929 or 935, but he soon repented and had his brother's relics interred in St. Vitus's cathedral.

Though his assassination was largely political, Wenceslas was considered a martyr. Already in the tenth century the Bohemian church recognized him as a saint. The Lives present Wenceslas as deeply pious, irreproachable in character, an ascetic, and a model of Christian charity. The cult of saints played an important role in maintaining the sociopolitical order, and Wenceslas was quickly adopted as patron of the state and the ruling dynasty in Bohemia.

R. Folz, *Les saints rois du moyen âge en occident (VIe–XIIIe siècles)* (1984), 23–57; M. Kantor, *The Origins of Christianity in Bohemia: Sources and Commentary* (1990).

ANDREA STERK

Western Church and the Jews The major challenge presented by Jews to the church was a theological one: how was it that despite their refusal to acknowledge Christ, Judaism survived as a viable religion? There is much evidence of an Augustinian ambivalence in the medieval church: Jews are both siblings of Christians and guilty of deicide; they should be treated with love but are inferior and debased; they should be protected, but their condition must give evidence of the consequences of unbelief. Of bishops, the Carolingian bishop Agobard of Lyon ranks among the least hospitable, having fulminated against Jews active in the Carolingian court. Bishop Rudiger Huozmann of Speyer ranks among the most tolerant. In 1084, he granted Jews protection and economic privileges and allowed them to employ Christian nurses and servants as well as sell nonkosher meat to Christians.

The papacy stood between exclusion and indulgence. From the early Middle Ages on, it promoted a consistent policy. Pope Gregory the Great, informed by Roman legal traditions, notably the code of Theodosius, established, in Kenneth Stow's words, "enduring principles regarding Jewish relations" (Stow 1992). These principles were basically two: the superiority of Christianity over Judaism and Christian tolerance of Jews in the expectation of their ultimate conversion to Christianity. In Gregory I's words (596), "Even as it is not allowed to the Jews in their assemblies presumptuously to undertake for themselves more than that which is permitted them by law, even so they ought not to suffer any disadvantage in those [privileges] which have been granted them."

Jews were to be a protected minority, but held in contempt, within ever clearer boundaries pronounced in conciliar and papal legislation. Numerous church councils tried to limit social interaction between Christians and Jews, in order to protect the former from the latter's alleged contaminating influence. Conciliar statutes protested against the use of Jewish testimony against Christians at court, applied papal warnings against Jewish ownership of slaves (Gregory the Great; Fourth Council of Toledo, 633), campaigned, often at papal instigation, against "immodest" Jewish usury (the Councils of Narbonne [1227] and Beziers [1246] are two of many examples), and supported more generous borrowing privileges for crusaders from Jewish moneylenders (moratoria on the principal and remission of the interest paid before joining a crusade). The Fourth Lateran Council decreed, among other things, that Jews were to wear distinctive marks on their dress and refrain from appearing in public three days before Easter and especially on Good Friday, since some were alleged to show contempt for Christ on these holy days. Although Innocent III (1198–1216), Innocent IV (1243–1254), and Gregory X (1271–1276) opposed popular violence against Jews, instigated by accusations of ritual murder, blood libel, and desecration of Christian ritual objects, Jewish historians have often noted that by the thirteenth century, traditional ambivalence had been stretched to a breaking point. The papacy seems to have embraced a more aggressive attitude toward the conversion of Jews in that century, which continued into the following century. Popes did not protest the expulsions of Jews from England (1290), France (1306, 1322, 1394), Spain (1492), numerous German cities (early fifteenth century), or Sicily and southern Italy (by 1541). The expulsions helped bring about, after all, a more integrally Christian polity (Stow 1992).

Opinion on the role of the hierarchical church and theology in popular anti-Judaism varies. While historians such as Stow (Stow 1992) have stressed the nonreligious sources of European enmity toward Jews, focusing on the urban, "protobourgeois" Jews who increasingly became identified by a populace living in miserable conditions with the ruling classes and social inequities, Jeremy Cohen has noted that "while one ought not blindly to postulate a direct cause-and-effect relationship between Christian theology and anti-Jewish violence in the Middle Ages, one cannot deny that Christian antisemitism took its toll on the medieval Jewish experience" (Cohen in Sapir Abulafia 2002). In his turn, Gavin Langmuir distinguished between Christian anti-Semitism, which he defined as irrational beliefs about Jews, and Christian anti-Judaism, arguing that anti-Semitism emerged in the twelfth and thirteenth centuries because of rising doubts among Christians over central church teachings. The prevailing Christian discourses on Jews and Judaism were overwhelmingly inimical, but exactly whether and how they contributed to the worsening conditions of Jewish life in late medieval Europe remains a matter of debate. It was also increasingly clear that the church's position of ambivalent tolerance, ensconced in canon law, offered much less than safety to Jews.

J. Cohen, ed., *Essential Papers on Judaism and Christianity in Conflict: From Late Antiquity to the Reformation* (1991); G. Langmuir, *History, Religion, and Antisemitism* (1990); S. Grayzel, *The Church and the Jews in the Thirteenth Century*, ed. K. R. Stow (1989); J. R. Marcus, ed., *The Jew in the Medieval World* (1938); U. Hubert, *Les signes d'infamie au moyen âge: Juifs, sarrazins, hérétiques, lépreux et filles publiques* (1891); A. Sapir Abulafia, ed., *Religious Violence between Christians and Jews: Medieval Roots, Modern Perspectives* (2002); S. Simonsohn, *The Apostolic See and the Jews*, 8 vols. (1988); K. R. Stow, *Alienated Minority: The Jews of Medieval Europe* (1992); Stow, *Popes, Church, and Jews in the Middle Ages: Confrontation and Response* (2007).

VARDA KOCH OCKER

Western Schism *see* Great Western Schism

Westminster Assembly This assembly of theologians and lay leaders was called by England's "Long Parliament" to reform the English church. Against a background of deep religious division and social unrest that culminated in civil war, Parliament suspended the episcopacy and called an assembly of divines to Westminster Abbey in 1643 to propose measures of church reform. The assembly opened on July 1, 1643, and was attended by 121 leading clergymen and 30 lay delegates. Since most Episcopalians remained away out of loyalty to the king, who opposed the assembly, the largest group of participants was Presbyterian, the rest Erastians and congregationalist Independents backed by Oliver Cromwell. After England's "Solemn League and Covenant" with Scotland in September 1643, Scottish Presbyterian influence on the assembly grew and shows in the major documents it drafted: the Westminster Confession, Directory of Public Worship, and two Westminster Catechisms. The model of church government proposed was presbyterian-synodal but contained Erastian and Independent compromises. England's Parliament approved most of the results in 1648, and while they were overturned in the Restoration (1660), they remained influential in Scotland and New England. The assembly was never dissolved officially.

———

J. L. Carson and D. W. Hall, *To Glorify and Enjoy God* (1994); A. F. Mitchell, *The Westminster Assembly* (1883).

KENNETH G. APPOLD

Westminster Confession This document is a doctrinal statement drafted by the Westminster Assembly and is a definitive confession of English-speaking Presbyterianism. As the most significant theological product of the assembly's intent to reform the Church of England, the Westminster Confession of Faith was completed in December 1646 and ratified by Parliament in June 1648; the Church of Scotland had accepted it in August 1647. The Confession consists of thirty-three articles spanning the basic doctrines of the Christian faith. Its theological positions largely reflect Reformed orthodoxy and in most cases resemble those of continental Reformed confessions. Especially noteworthy are its strong assertion of scriptural authority (1), an affirmation of double predestination that leaves room for both infralapsarian and supralapsarian viewpoints (3), and its distinction between the visible and invisible church (25). Puritan influences appear particularly in the doctrines of assurance (18) and the Sabbath (21); Presbyterian compromises with Independents and Erastians condition the articles on civil magistrates (23) and church censure (30). While its importance for

the Church of England ended with the Restoration, the Confession remains valid for Presbyterians worldwide and has also been adopted by many Baptists and Congregationalists.

———

L. Duncan, ed., *The Westminster Confession into the 21st Century* (2003); W. G. Crampton, *Study Guide to the Westminster Confession* (1996).

KENNETH G. APPOLD

Westphal, Joachim (1510–1574), Lutheran pastor and controversialist. Born in Hamburg and educated in Wittenberg, he was appointed pastor in Hamburg in 1541. Elected superintendent in 1571, he served until his death. A student of Melanchthon's, he came to oppose his teacher on several issues. Westphal, a "Gnesio-Lutheran," was involved in the confessional controversies after Luther's death. He published critiques of the Augsburg and Leipzig Interims and opposed the crucial assumption that doctrine and ceremony could be separated. Westphal was known for his role in keeping Reformed refugees from England out of Hamburg in the 1550s. Beginning in 1552 he published attacks on the Reformed teaching on the Lord's Supper and traded polemical treatises with Calvin until 1558. Westphal confessed the real presence of the body and blood of Christ in the bread and wine against Calvin's doctrine of "spiritual" presence. Westphal disputed with Major on the role of good works in salvation and Flacius on original sin.

———

R. Kolb, *Confessing the Faith: Reformers Define the Church, 1530–1580* (1991); A. Pettegree, "The London Exile Community and the Second Sacramentarian Controversy, 1553–1560," *ARG* 78 (1987): 223–51; J. Tylenda, "The Calvin Westphal Exchange," *Calvin Theological Journal* 9 (1974): 182–209.

MARY JANE HAEMIG

Westphalia, Peace of This treaty, signed on October 24, 1648, in Münster and Osnabrück in the German territory of Westphalia, ended the Thirty Years' War. The treaty was struck between Sweden and France and their opponents Spain and the HRE. The treaty dramatically revised the nature of the HRE by recognizing the sovereignty and independence of its states. This effectively brought to an end the empire in all but name and drastically undercut Habsburg power in Central Europe. The treaty also brought to an end religious war in Europe. It confirmed the Peace of Augsburg (1555), mandating that each territorial ruler in Germany determined the religious affiliation of his land. If he changed religion, however, he would relinquish his land. Calvinism was given legal standing, and religious persecutions and forced migrations were largely abandoned. From this point forward, war in Europe was mainly fought for political rather than religious ends.

D. Croxton, *Peacemaking in Early Modern Europe: Cardinal Mazarin and the Congress of Westphalia, 1643–1648* (1999); G. Parker, ed., *Thirty Years War* (1997).

DAVID WHITFORD

Weyer, Johann (c. 1515–1588), German Protestant physician. Born in Brabant, probably schooled in the Devotio Moderna tradition and influenced by the irenic musings of Erasmus, Weyer studied from around 1530 under Heinrich Cornelius Agrippa of Nettesheim (1486–1535), whose skepticism about the alleged powers of witches he imbibed. Weyer's *De praestigiis daemonum* was published first in Latin in 1563 and then repeatedly and in various translations over the ensuing decades, during the height of Europe's persecution of witches. It was one of the most controversial works of the sixteenth century. In it, on the bases of legal, medical, philological, and theological reasons, Weyer argued that witchcraft is impossible. Both witches and their persecutors were deluded. Noting the presence of witches in the Bible and in Roman law, Weyer observed that it was only in his own age that any widespread persecution of witches had been justified on the basis of these texts.

C. Baxter, "Johann Weyer's *De prestigiis daemonum*; Unsystematic Psychopathology," in *The Damned Art*, ed. S. Anglo (1977); H. C. E. Midelfort, "Johann Weyer and the Transformation of the Insanity Defense," in *The German People and the Reformation*, ed. R. Po-chia Hsia (1988); G. Zilboorg, *The Medical Man and the Witch during the Renaissance* (1935).

RODERICK MARTIN

Whitby, Synod of   The synod was called in 664 by King Oswy of Northumbria (d. 670) at the double monastery of Whitby in Yorkshire, ruled by the Abbess Hilda, in order to establish unity of practice in the realm concerning the date of Easter and the style of monastic tonsure. Oswy was from Northern

Ireland and followed Celtic practice. His wife, Eanflecda, grew up in Kent. She followed Roman practice, as did his son, Alfrith, who was persuaded to do so by Wilfrid, the abbot of Ripon, who although educated at Lindisfarne was influenced by travel on the Continent. The issue of dating Easter had been resolved by the Council of Nicaea (325), but the Celtic church celebrated Easter according to the method of dating of Anatolius, bishop of Laeodicea, whose work preceded the council. At the synod, Colman, bishop of Lindisfarne, and Chad, bishop of the Mercians, defended the Celtic position, while Wilfrid and Agilbert, bishop among the West Saxons, defended the Roman. Colman argued that the Celtic dating of Easter was the method used by John the apostle as well as Anatolius and Columba. King Oswy settled the matter by siding with Rome, at which point Colman and other Irish monks of Lindisfarne left Northumbria. Northumbria accepted the Roman custom, and in 669 Archbishop Theodore of Canterbury imposed it on all of England.

Bede, *A History of the English Church and People*; H. Mayr-Harting, *The Coming of Christianity to Anglo-Saxon England* (1991).

MARIANNE M. DELAPORTE

Whitgift, John (1530–1604), archbishop of Canterbury from 1583 to 1604. The son of a wealthy merchant of Grimsby, Whitgift was educated in London and Cambridge. As professor, master of Trinity College, and vice chancellor, Whitgift served Cambridge until 1577, when he became bishop of Worcester. Six years later he was raised to the see of Canterbury, becoming the third and last archbishop to serve in that position during the reign of Queen Elizabeth I. Whitgift was known for both incorruptibility and compassion. His tenure as archbishop was characterized by remarkable peacefulness and distinguished by formidable growth in Anglican reform. Recent scholarship has concentrated on Whitgift's political work as a skilled propagandist and an advantaged archbishop of Canterbury (the only one to serve on Queen Elizabeth's Privy Council and the only one to enjoy, generally, the queen's favor throughout his service). It has also emphasized Whitgift's theological and political sophistication in his defense of Anglican ecclesiology and Elizabethan hierarchy against Presbyterian reform efforts. Professor Thomas Cartwright spearheaded these reform efforts in his 1570 Cambridge lectures, which asserted that Presbyterian church government was divinely ordered in Scripture. In 1572, an *Admonition for the Parliament* called for a change to Presbyterian order in the Church of England. Whitgift responded on behalf of church and crown in 1572 and 1573.

Unlike Cartwright, Whitgift separated soteriology from ecclesiology, accepting several tenets of Calvinist Presbyterian theology but rejecting popular election of church leaders and most features of Genevan theocracy. Whitgift's particularly popular emphases on peace and order were grounds for preferring an episcopalian hierarchical church order to a Presbyterian one. Some scholars have seen in the Whitgift-Cartwright controversy a microcosm of the larger Anglican-Puritan dispute, a contest between competing worldviews and sharply contrasting theological assumptions.

P. Collinson, *The Elizabethan Puritan Movement* (1990); P. Lake, *Anglicans and Puritans? Presbyterianism and English Conformist Thought from Whitgift to Hooker* (1988).

JOHN E. GRISWOLD

William of Auvergne (c. 1190–1249), French academic and bishop. William was born in Aurillac, became a canon of Notre Dame and then master at Paris in arts (after 1215) and subsequently theology (1225). In 1228 William was elected bishop of Paris at papal initiative and in this role fostered mendicant involvement in the university. Alongside some twenty publications on the immortality of the soul, good and evil, freedom and grace, and other topics, seven of William's treatises (on the Trinity, creation, the soul, the incarnation, faith and law, sacraments, and virtues and morals) were collected into the *Magisterium divinale et sapientiale*. As the title suggests, *The Teaching of God in the Mode of Wisdom* (R. Teske's translation) combines theology and philosophy, theory and praxis, and God-talk and reflection on human affairs, and it displays an independent, critical use of ancient (Aristotle), Arabic (Avicenna), and Jewish (Avicebron, Maimonides) sources. As Bonaventure emphasizes (*In librum sententiarum* 3.40.3), William's application of Maimonides' analysis of the older cult to the younger one prepared the covenantal (noninstrumental) interpretation of sacramental causality. Sensitive to the voluntary dimensions of the soul, William's analysis of the older covenant was generally an actualizing call for the reformation of those appealing to the newer one. William's novel reception and critique of

Aristotle (e.g., on truth) inaugurated the ambivalent discussions of the later thirteenth century.

Opera omnia (1674, repr. 1963); William of Auvergne, *De anima* (1998, ET 2000); William, *De gratia* (1966); William, *De immortalitate animae* (ET 1991); William, *De trinitate* (1976, ET 1989); William, *De universo creaturarum* (ET 1998); S. P. Marrone, *William of Auvergne and Robert Grosseteste: New Ideas of Truth* (1983).

RICHARD SCHENK, OP

William of Auxerre (1140/1150–1231), French scholastic theologian. Although William was one of the most famous theologians of the thirteenth century, his early years are shrouded in darkness. He appears to have received all his advanced education at the Univ. of Paris, after which he joined its theology faculty. How long he taught there is unclear, though it probably covered the last several decades of his life. His writings include the liturgical work *Summa de officiis ecclesiasticis* (*Summa of Ecclesiastical Offices*), which much influenced William Durand's classic *Rationale divinorum officiorum* (*The Rationale of Divine Offices*), and the *Summa aurea* (*Golden Summa*, 1215–1229), which was based on his university teaching and exerted a large impact on later scholastic thought.

William's work marks a monumental change in theological mentality and method that was taking place at the time. Specifically, William was the first writer to state explicitly that theology might meet the requirements of being a "science" in the Aristotelian sense of the term; the articles of faith, he said, constituted its first principles. Also, at a time when Aristotle's logic had become widely accepted for the practice of theological speculation but the *libri naturales* (Aristotle's natural philosophy) had not, William gave the latter a kind of stamp of approval by citing Aristotle's *De anima* (*On the Soul*) several times. Instrumental in helping to reconcile the church to Aristotle, he thus paved the way for the great scholastic syntheses of the next one hundred years.

J. Ribailler, ed., *Magistri Guillelmi Altissiodorensis Summa aurea* (1980–1987).

STEVEN J. WILLIAMS

William of Moerbeke (fl. 1260–1286), Flemish Dominican translator of Greek manuscripts into Latin, especially known for his extensive translation of Aristotle. He probably learned Greek while living first in Nicaea and then at Thebes in 1260. He is attested to have been at the papal court in Viterbo from the years 1268 to 1271, and in 1272 at the papal court in Orvieto as "penitentiary and chaplain to the pope." He was archbishop of Corinth from April 1278 until his death during a mission at the papal court at Perugia. Until recently William has been portrayed as having collaborated with Thomas Aquinas at Orvieto, at the request of Pope Urban IV, to lay "the foundations of a Christian Arisotelianism." While it is certain that Aquinas relied on William's translations and received them as soon as they were completed, recent scholarship has dispelled the notion that William served as Thomas's personal translator. In addition to translating works of Aristotle such as *On the Soul*, *Politics*, *On the Heavens*, *Metaphysics*, *Meteorology*, and the works of seminal commentators such as Themistius, Alexander of Aphrodesius, and John Philoponus, William translated late ancient authors such as Archimedes, Ptolemy, and Galen. His translation of Proclus's *Elements of Theology* proved instrumental in Thomas's recognition that the famous *Liber de causis* (*Book of Causes*), universally believed to be Aristotle's final word on theology, was actually an anonymous Arabic paraphrase of Proclus's text. Furthermore, by examining subsequent versions of certain translations, such as William's translation of Aristotle's *Politics*, scholars have been able to trace the growth of William's knowledge of Greek as well as his understanding of the texts. Such work has broadened our knowledge of the methods of medieval translation and of the state of the manuscripts used.

J. Brams and W. Vanhamel, *Guillaume de Moerbeke: Recueil d'Études à L'occasion du 700ᵉ Anniversaire de sa mort* (1989); M. Grabmann, *Guglielmo di Moerbeke, O.P., il traduttore delle opere di Aristotele* (1946); J.-P. Torrell, *Saint Thomas Aquinas*, vol. 1, *The Person and His Work* (1996).

MARK DAMIEN DELP

William of Ockham (c. 1288–1347), Franciscan theologian.

Ockham has long been recognized as one of the major thinkers of the late Middle Ages. He began his philosophical training at the London convent of the Franciscans, c. 1305–1306. The convent was an important intellectual center and a place through which leading Franciscan academics from Oxford and Paris passed. By 1310, Ockham moved to the study of theology, either at London or Oxford. There is no evidence that Ockham ever studied at Paris. In the years 1317–1319, Ockham delivered his lectures on Peter Lombard's *Sentences*. Only his lectures on book 1, known as the *Scriptum*, survive in an authorized version. Books 2–4 are a *reportatio*, that is, a transcript made from his oral presentation. Around 1321 Ockham became a lecturer, possibly at the Franciscan convent in London. Among his fellow Franciscans there were Walter Chatton and Adam Wodeham. It was the beginning of a very productive period that saw the appearence of Ockham's commentary on the *Physics*, his commentary on several logical works by Aristotle, his famous *Sum of Logic* (*Summa logicae*), and several controversial treatises on the Eucharist. This phase of intensive work in philosophy and theology ended in 1324 when Ockham was summoned to the papal court at Avignon on the charge of disseminating false and even heretical views in his commentary on the *Sentences*. For the next four years, Ockham resided at the Franciscan convent there, his theological studies unfinished. The Oxford theologian John Lutterell played an important role in the Avignon investigation, since he drew up a preliminary list of allegedly erroneous propositions that were culled from Ockham's commentary. The list was reviewed and later revised by a papal committee of theologians. Ockham did not await the outcome of the process but fled Avignon in the night of May 26, 1328. He settled in Munich, at the court of Emperor Ludwig of Bavaria. This phase of Ockham's life, which lasted until his death, was marked by a profusion of political writings, which include *The Work of Ninety Days* (*Opus nonaginta dierum*) and the *Dialogus*. Pope John XXII and his successor Benedict XII were his favorite targets. At the basis of Ockham's polemics against these popes were Franciscan theories of evangelical poverty and the ownership of property as distinct from its use. His belief that the church was run by heretical popes made Ockham develop new theories about papal and secular powers to define the Christian faith. Ockham is often characterized as a nominalist, but this label is ambiguous and hence not very useful. In metaphysics, Ockham is known for his principle of parsimony, or "Ockham's razor"—the principle that a plurality of entities is not to be posited without necessity. Although it is a matter of debate whether Ockham himself faithfully followed this principle, he invoked it in his rejection of the existence of universal natures or essences, his reduction of Aristotle's ten categories to substance and quality, his rejection of sensible species as the causal intermediaries between perceiver and perceived object, and his view that motion is no thing beyond the moving object. Another notorious doctrine is that of intuitive and abstractive cognition. Intuitive cognitive acts are capable of causing evident assent to empirical propositions. Abstractive cognitive acts (e.g., memory or imagination) do not have such effect. Ockham held an elaborate semantic theory about the relation between mental language, its extramental referents, and conventional (spoken and written) discourse.

William Ockham, *Opera philosophica et theologica*, ed. G. Gàl et al., 17 vols. (1967–1988); *Opera politica*, ed. H. S. Offler et al., 4 vols. (1967–1988); M. McCord Adams, *William Ockham*, 2 vols. (1987); J. Miethke, *Ockhams Weg zur Sozialphilosophie* (1969); P. V. Spade, ed., *The Cambridge Companion to Ockham* (1999).

J. M. M. H. THIJSSEN

William of Orange (1533–1584),

German nobleman and leader of the Dutch Revolt against Spain. Son of the count of Nassau-Dillenburg and nephew of René of Châlon, William inherited extensive properties in the Netherlands and Burgundy, in addition to the princedom of Orange. Favored by Emperor Charles V, he held high positions within the Habsburg administration of the Netherlands. William, raised in a Lutheran environment, later pledged loyalty to the Roman Catholic faith. Committed to a policy of religious moderation and opposed to the Spanish encroachment on local prerogatives (his initial silence on these issues earned him his nickname, William the Silent), William resigned from office when the Spanish king Philip II sent the duke of Alva to pacify the Low Countries. William then became the leader of the Dutch revolt against Spain. In 1572 exiles who pirated off the Dutch coast captured the town of Brielle in Zeeland, allowing William to fight successfully on Dutch soil. William, a so-called *politique*, preferred the formal coexistence of two or three confessions within the state to persecution in the name of religious unity. Having converted to Calvinism in 1573, he was on the verge of realizing his religious ideals in the 1570s. However, the Union of Utrecht (1579) created the northern Netherlands as a separate state that then outlawed Roman Catholicism. William was assassinated by Balthasar Gerards, a French Catholic working for the Spanish.

K. W. Swart, *William the Silent and the Revolt of the Netherlands* (1978); C. V. Wedgwood, *William the Silent: William of Nassau, Prince of Orange, 1533–1584* (2nd ed., 1989).

JORIS VAN EIJNATTEN

William of St. Amour (c. 1200/1210–

1272), subdeacon, canon, Bible scholar, and controversialist. Born at St. Amour, William became a master of arts and law at Paris in 1238, and before 1250, a regent master of theology. In 1250, tensions between mendicant and secular (that is, nonmonastic) masters of theology, which had first erupted at the university between 1229 and 1231, began to escalate again, culminating in 1253 with an expulsion of Dominican and Franciscan masters and prompting papal intervention on their behalf. The restoration of mendicant masters guaranteed controversy at the university, which continued to 1257. William was the most important member of the antimendicant party. Argument centered on the nature and legtimacy of the mendicant orders, the friars' encroachment on parish ministry, the perfection claimed for their particular forms of religious life, and the radical Joachimism of a Franciscan named Gerard of Borgo San Donnino. William, who opposed all these things, articulated the secular masters' complaint to the court of Pope Innocent IV in 1254 as a case of heresy, and Innocent, who had previously supported the friars, now endorsed university statutes to their disadvantage and restricted their pastoral activity in parishes. The pope died just weeks after doing this, and his successor, Alexander IV, in that same year (1254), reversed these decisions. Alexander restored the right of friars to work in parishes, and he weakened the university statutes against them. William argued against the friars in three academic disputations of October to December 1255 (one of which was his response to Bonaventure's *De mendicitate*, or *On Beggary*), in some seven polemical sermons preached in 1255–1256, in a polemical treatise known as *De periculis novissimorum temporum* (*On the Perils of the Most Recent Times*), and in his own defense before the cardinals when investigated at the papal court in October 1256. The 1256 investigation concluded with the condemnation of *De periculis*; Pope Alexander IV had already ordered that William be deprived of his benefices in June of that year. William left Italy and returned to the place of his birth, where he remained for the rest of his life. At St. Amour, he completed, in 1266, another polemical work known as the *Collectiones catholice et canon-ice scripturae* (*Conclusions from Catholic and Canonical Scripture*).

The controversy over the friars, however, did not end with William's own misfortune, in part due to the wide distribution of the writings just mentioned. His polemic against the friars was taken up by the French vernacular poets Rutebeuf and Jean de Meung (in the *Roman de la Rose*), and his influence can be traced through Richard FitzRalph to English vernacular writers, including Chaucer and Piers Plowman, and to John Wyclif.

M.-M. Dufeil, *Guillaume de Saint-Amour et la polémique universitaire Parisienne, 1250–1259* (1972); William of St. Amour, *De periculis novissimorum temporum/On the dangers of the last times,* G. Geltner, ed. and trans. (2008); P. R. Szittya, *The Antifraternal Tradition in Medieval Literature* (1986); B. Roest, *A History of Franciscan Education (c. 1210–1517)* (2000); A. Traver, *The Opuscula of William of Saint-Amour: the Minor Works of 1255–1256* (2003).

CHRISTOPHER OCKER

William of St. Thierry *see* Abelard, Peter; Mysticism, Medieval

Willibrord

(c. 658–739), Anglo-Saxon missionary. Northumbrian by birth, Willibrord was educated at the monastery of Ripon under the supervision of Wilfrid of York. In his early twenties he joined the English community at the monastery of Rath-Melsigi in Ireland, from which he was sent by Egbert to convert the pagans of Frisia. Willibrord and his band of twelve companions reached Frisia about 690 and from the very beginning received strong support from the Austrasian *major domus* (mayor of the palace), Pippin II. At a fairly early stage of his mission, Willibrord traveled to Rome to seek the pope's approval for his mission, and encouraged by Pippin, he visited Rome again in 695, where he was consecrated by the pope as "the archbishop of the Frisians." On his return, Willibrord received the castle of Trajectum (modern Utrecht) from Pippin, where he established the center of his new ecclesiastical province. In 698 Willibrord founded the monastery of Echternach on a villa donated to him by Irmina of Oeren, mother-in-law of Pippin II. Willibrord's missionary activity was concentrated in the region of Frisia, although he also reached Thuringia, Denmark, and Heligoland (an island between the coasts of Frisia and Denmark). Despite many difficulties, Willibrord continued his mission with some success. He died at the age of eighty in Utrecht, and in accordance with his will, his body was transferred to the basilica of Echternach.

W. Levison, *England and the Continent in the Eighth Century* (1946); G. Kiesel and J. Schroeder, eds., *Willibrord* (1989); I. N. Wood, *The Missionary Life* (2001).

YITZHAK HEN

Windesheim Congregation

The name of a union, or "congregation," of regular canons and canonesses that originated in the Netherlands and spread to Germany and northern France. The congregation was formed in 1394 or 1395 between four monasteries heavily influenced by followers of Geert Groote: Eemstein (1382), Windesheim (1387), Marienborn (in Arnheim, 1392), and Nieuwlicht (near Hoorn, 1392). Many ancient houses of Augustinian canons soon joined the congregation, and the congregation established a few new foundations. It became the most rapidly organized wing of the Modern Devotion. All but 4 of its 102 monasteries (16 of which were for canonesses) were founded or "incorporated" (transferred) to the congregation before 1500. Outside of Protestant areas, the congregation survived to the beginning of the nineteenth century.

R. R. Post, *The Modern Devotion* (1968); J. van Engen, *Devotio Moderna: Basic Writings* (1988); A. J. Hendrikman, ed., *Windesheim 1395–1995* (1996); A. J. Hendrikman, P. Bange, R. Th. M. van Dijk, A. J. Jelsma, G. E. P. Wrielink, eds., *Kloosters, Teksten, Invloeden* (1996); W. Kohl, E. Persoons, A. G. Weiler, eds. *Monasticon Windeshemense*, 4 vols. (1976–1984).

CHRISTOPHER OCKER

Wishart, George

(c. 1513–1546), Scottish reformer and the second great Protestant martyr in Scotland after Patrick Hamilton (c. 1504–1528). A major influence upon John Knox, Wishart was celebrated in both Knox's *History of the Reformation in Scotland* and John Foxe's famous *Book of Martyrs*. Little is known of his youth until his education on the Continent, where he received an arts degree at Louvain in 1532. An ordained priest, he was back in Scotland by 1535, where King James V and Cardinal David Beaton, archbishop of St. Andrews, were defending the Roman Catholic Church against Protestant challenges. Wishart's troubles began when he was summoned to answer to the bishop of Brechin in 1538 for teaching the New Testament in Greek. He then fled to Bristol, England, where his preaching created controversy, so he moved on to Germany and Switzerland before returning to England and then Scotland in 1543. Wishart's theology may be described as broadly Zwinglian, and he translated from Latin into English the First Helvetic Confession (1536), the first statement uniting the Swiss Reformed cantons. Wishart's translation was published posthumously (1548?) with the probable intent to unify Protestants during the reign of Edward VI. Wishart's dynamic itinerant preaching that attacked Catholic orthodoxy stirred the wrath of Cardinal Beaton, who also suspected that Wishart was involved in plots against him. Wishart was arrested, brought to St. Andrews Castle, and tried and burned at the stake. Soon afterward, Protestant leaders murdered Beaton.

John Foxe, *Book of Martyrs* (1563, repr. 2004); M. Graham, "Scotland," in A. Pettegree, ed., *The Reformation World* (2000), 410–30; J. Kirk, "The Religion of Early Scottish Protestants," in *Humanism and Reform: The Church in Europe, England, and Scotland, 1400–1643*, ed. J. Kirk (1991), 361–411; John Knox, *History of the Reformation in Scotland*, 2 vols., ed. W. C. Dickinson (1949); C. Rogers, *Life of George Wishart* (1876); http://www.wishart.org/books (Wishart Society).

CARTER LINDBERG

Witchcraft The belief that certain people, often women, may possess magical or supernatural power, sometimes because of a personal pact with the devil or a malignant spirit. The existence and implicitly malevolent quality of witchcraft were acknowledged in both Roman law and in the Bible. Nonetheless, for most of its history, the church has had an attitude of uncertainty toward witchcraft. Some church fathers, notably Tertullian and Augustine, believed witchcraft a potential threat, while others, such as Chrysostom, denied its existence.

While often associated with the so-called dark ages, witchcraft and its persecution were hardly prevalent features in Christendom until the late fifteenth century. The zenith of witchcraft persecution in Europe seems to have occurred between 1470 and 1620. In the High Middle Ages, by contrast, there was far more personal danger in being, or in being looked upon by authorities as, a heretic, Jew, or leper.

The publication of the Dominican *Malleus maleficarum* (*The Hammer of Witches*) in 1486 was both a response to a growing sense of the need for a systematic account of witchcraft and fuel to fire the increasing persecution of witches. This work shifted the focus of authorities from the view of witchcraft as a species of heresy, to the notion of the witch's personal pact with the devil. It is arguable that much of the energy that had formerly been devoted to the persecution of marginal groups generally was transferred to the persecution of witches in particular in the wake of the Reformation. Protestantism, moreover, lacked the established Roman Catholic tradition of assimilating popular religion.

Protestant emphasis on the power and activity of the devil may also have helped foster the persecution of witches. But Catholics, too, were heavily invested in witchcraft persecution. Indeed, the most sophisticated advocate of witchcraft persecution in early modern Europe was the Catholic political theorist Jean Bodin, while its staunchest opponent was the Protestant physician Johann Weyer. The decline of witchcraft persecution has often been attributed to the benevolent influence of the Enlightenment, but the persecution of witches was declining well before the eighteenth century. Whether the persecution of witches was stimulated more by intellectuals or authorities, or by simmering discontent from the lower orders of society, remains subject to debate. There is more consensus that the end of persecution was caused less by intellectual rejections of its alleged power or existence than by what one scholar has termed a "crisis of confidence" in those most involved in actually carrying it out—that is, both people in positions of power and regular folk who came to recognize persecution as a kind of self-destructive frenzy more dangerous than witchcraft itself.

S. Anglo, ed., *The Damned Art* (1977); W. Behringer, *Shaman of Oberstdorf* (1998); R. Briggs, *Witches and Neighbors* (1996); S. Clark, *Thinking with Demons* (1997); N. Cohn, *Europe's Inner Demons* (1975); H. C. E. Midelfort, *Witch Hunting in Southwestern Germany* (1972); W. Monter, ed., *European Witchcraft* (1969); E. Peters, *The Magician, the Witch, and the Law* (1978).

RODERICK MARTIN

Wittenberg Concord Attempts to form a military-political alliance for protection against Emperor Charles V and papal forces before the 1530 Diet of Augsburg were stymied by controversy between Luther and Zwingli on the nature of Christ's presence in the sacrament of the Lord's Supper. Through the early 1530s, the Strasbourg reformer, Martin Bucer, negotiated extensively with Luther and the southern German and Swiss reformers, seeking a common formula. Though never fully accepted, it was achieved in the Wittenberg Concord of 1536 with the statement that with the bread and the wine, the body of Christ is essentially and truly received. But another issue remained, that of whether the ungodly, those who participate in the sacrament unworthily, actually receive the body of Christ.

Bucer, Wolfgang Capito, Philip Melanchthon, and others met with Luther in Wittenberg to work out the terms of agreement, Melanchthon taking final responsibility for the text. They retained the earlier formulation and agreed that by eating and drinking, the unworthy bring judgment on themselves. Luther and the Lutherans accepted the agreement, despite some continued evidence of hesitation among their critics. The Wittenberg Concord effectively ended the sacramental controversy among the evangelical parties of Germany, thereby allowing broader expansion of the Schmalkald League. Despite their best efforts, Bucer and Capito had less success in Switzerland. Opposition was especially strong in Constance and then in Zurich. In the end, the Swiss reformers went their own way.

_____

J. Kittelson and K. Schurb, "The Curious Histories of the Wittenberg Concord," *CTQ* 50, no. 2 (1986): 119–37; W. Russell, *Luther's Theological Testament: The Schmalkald Articles* (1994).

JAMES ARNE NESTINGEN

Witzel, Georg (1501–1573), theologian and advocate of conciliation. Born in Vacha, near Fulda, Witzel attended the Univ. of Erfurt. Attracted by Luther's ideas, he studied Scripture and the church fathers in Wittenberg, was ordained a priest, and was married. Turning soon against Luther, he was thenceforth loyal to Rome, but he remained married and devoted his life to the cause of religious reunion, tirelessly promoting a middle way between papal and Lutheran extremes.

His career took him to the court of Duke George of Saxony in 1538, and subsequently to Fulda as advisor to the abbot. In 1539 he collaborated closely with Bucer at a Leipzig colloquy. Holding the apostolic church of antiquity as his ideal, he criticized the blindness and indifference of church leaders, scholastic doctrinal definitions, and superstitious practices surrounding the Mass. He favored a broad renewal of communal liturgical life, a vernacular Bible, the use of both German and Latin in worship, Communion in both kinds, and preaching for edification. Many of his conciliatory ideas found their way into the 1547 Interim. Hoping for a national council convened by the emperor to effect reunion, he was faced instead with the Council of Trent, which he regarded as intransigent and preoccupied with nonessentials. Given the militant activities of the Jesuits, his conciliatory approach lost favor, and he suffered the fate common to many moderates who recognize merit and faults on both sides, regarded by both with suspicion and criticized as a vacillator and relativist.

_____

J. P. Dolan, *History of the Reformation* (1965).

JOHN TONKIN

Wodeham, Adam (d. 1358), philosopher and theologian. Wodeham taught at several Franciscan *studia* before moving to Oxford. Three sets of lectures on Peter Lombard's *Sentences* are known, which he delivered at *studia* in London and Norwich (1329–1332) and at the Univ. of Oxford (around 1332), respectively. Only the Norwich lectures, known as the *lectura secunda*, have been edited.

Often perceived as a defender of William of Ockham, Wodeham shows familiarity with the works of Franciscan and secular contemporaries and near-contemporaries, such as Duns Scotus, Walter Burley, William Crathorn, Robert Holcot, and Peter Auriol. Wodeham recognized and elaborated the skeptical consequences of the debate between Ockham and Auriol over sensory illusions. He also seems to be the first known advocate of the theory of the *complexe significabile*, that is, the theory that a proposition signifies a state of affairs. For instance, the significate of the proposition "A human is a living being" (*homo est animal*) is "that a human is a living being." At the Univ. of Paris, this theory was defended by Gregory of Rimini. Wodeham also wrote a treatise on infinity and continuity (*Tractatus de indivisibilibus*). There he refutes atomism and defends the uncommon position that not all infinites are equal but one infinity can be larger than another. He was well-versed in the prevailing semantic theories about the properties of terms and of how they can affect the meaning of propositions, and he applied these logical skills to propositions that concern theology and philosophy.

W. Courtenay, *Adam Wodeham* (1978); E. Karger, "William of Ockham, Walter Chatton, and Adam Wodeham and the Objects of Knowledge and Belief," *Vivarium* 33 (1995): 171–96; A. Wodeham, *Tractatus de indivisibilibus,* ed. R. Wood (1988); Wodeham, *Lectura secunda,* ed. R. Wood and G. Gàl (1990).

                              J. M. M. H. THIJSSEN

Wolsey, Thomas Cardinal (c. 1472/.

1473–1530), important and successful administrative and political genius during the reigns of Henry VII and VIII in England. Educated at Oxford, Wolsey graduated young, receiving his BA in 1488, followed by an MA in 1491. He was made a full fellow at Magdalen College in 1497 and ordained a priest the following year. He held many benefices, the most important as chaplain to the archbishop of Canterbury, Henry Deane. Upon Deane's death, he served Sir Richard Nanfan, who was also governor of Calais. It was in Calais that Wolsey showed his strengths in foreign politics and policy, as well as domestic administration. He made such an impression upon Nanfan that he was presented to Henry VII. When Nanfan died in 1507, Wolsey joined the royal court as chaplain, where Henry VII used him for numerous foreign and diplomatic missions.

Wolsey's political career was well on the way to prominence when Henry VIII ascended the throne in 1509. Henry kept Wolsey, bestowing on him many positions of power, including Royal Almoner, Registrar of the Order of the Garter, and Canon of Windsor. Siding with Pope Julius II, Wolsey urged Henry to war against the French. His power, wealth, and prestige continued to grow as he was appointed bishop of London in 1514, archbishop and then cardinal of York (1515), and lord chancellor of England at the end of 1515.

Though popular with Henry, many in both government and church despised Wolsey. The first of his problems was an indictment of *praemunire* (serving a foreign dignitary) in 1514, for many felt Wolsey too close to the pope. Henry pardoned Wolsey; ironically, after the pardon the pope appointed Wolsey legate *a latere,* making him the most powerful church official in England and, effectively, the head of the Church in England. Upon the death of Leo X in 1521 he was a legitimate contender for the papacy, but a lack of support from Charles V put him out of the running.

When Henry brought the "great matter" of his divorce from Catherine of Aragon to Wolsey's attention, Wolsey became entangled in the king's personal affairs. This matter was the beginning of his downfall, for he found himself torn between the power allotted him by the pope and that allotted him by the king. He had the marriage invalidated and tried to get a papal annulment. He failed to obtain an immediate solution, which quickly made him an enemy of Anne Boleyn, who pushed her Protestant agenda until Henry turned against him. Wolsey's power and wealth were so great he was a threat even to Henry, his revenues close to being one-third that of the king's. He was once again indicted for *praemunire* in 1529, facing forty-four charges; Wolsey's fall was swift, and he was forced to cede his possessions to Henry, including his residences Whitehall and Hampton Court. Henry allowed him to remain archbishop of York. Rather than quietly passing his later years in the north of England, however, Wolsey set out to work with Pope Clement VII in preventing Henry from being with Anne. This led to a charge of treason in 1530. He died on his way from York to London to face trial, and was buried at the abbey at Leicester. His influence continued through his protégé and successor, Thomas Cromwell.

G. Cavendish, *Thomas Wolsey, Late Cardinal, His Life and Death Written by George Cavendish, His Gentleman-Usher* (2000); C. Ferguson, *Naked to Mine Enemies: The Life of Cardinal Wolsey* (1958).

                              ALDEN R. LUDLOW

Women and the Reformation *see* Reformation, Women and the

Wonderyear The twelve months between

April 1566 and April 1567 symbolize the beginning of the Dutch Revolt. Preceded by steadily increasing Catholic Habsburg control over the Netherlands, Philip II attempted to curb the power of the Dutch Estates by imposing taxes, and he supported the pope's plans to impose a new episcopate on the Low Countries. On April 5, 1566, some two hundred Dutch noblemen petitioned the Spanish authorities to suspend the Inquisition, but the persecution of heretics continued. Field sermons began near Antwerp in June, while in August and September an "iconoclastic storm" broke out, beginning in the Flemish south and rapidly spreading northward. This public expression of deeply rooted religious, political, and social dissatisfaction led to the wholesale destruction of religious images by Calvinist mobs. In the short run, the Wonderyear led to greater Spanish repression under the duke of Alva, sent to impose order in 1567. Ultimately, it proved to be a lasting watershed in the religious history of the Netherlands.

G. Marnef, "The Dynamics of Reformed Militancy in the Low Countries: The Wonderyear," in *The Education of a Christian Society: Humanism and the Reformation in Britain and the Netherlands*, ed. N. S. Amos, A. Pettegree, and H. van Nierop (1999), 193–210; A. Pettegree, *Emden and the Dutch Revolt: Exile and Development of Reformed Protestantism* (1992).

JORIS VAN EIJNATTEN

Worms, Concordat of

This imperial-papal agreement formally ended the investiture controversy. On September 23, 1122, near Worms, Emperor Henry V and representatives of Pope Calixtus II (1119–1124) exchanged documents that brought to an end the bitter struggle between the papacy and the empire over the issue of lay investiture, which had raged since the days of Gregory VII and Henry IV. Henry V solemnly promised to renounce in perpetuity the traditional right to invest bishops and abbots with ring and staff, the symbols of their ecclesiastical office, and to permit canonical elections and unhampered consecration of all prelates in the empire. The pope conceded to Henry personally that in Germany bishops and abbots would be elected in his presence and that he could decide between the two candidates in disputed elections. He could invest those elected with the temporalities (*regalia*) of their office by means of a scepter before consecration, thereby allowing him opportunity to confirm or reject the candidate. In Burgundy and Italy election was to be entirely in the hands of the local chapter, and prelates were to be invested automatically with their temporalities within six months of their elections.

These documents (which have come to be known as the Concordat of Worms) constituted a compromise between the claims of the emperor and the pope: while the emperor retained considerable influence over elections in Germany, he effectively lost control over the Burgundian and Italian churches. Nevertheless, Calixtus had difficulty getting the fathers attending the First Lateran Council (1123) to approve the agreement. Although Henry V died in 1125 and the papal concession to him expired, the Concordat came to be viewed as a general accord without temporal limits, and it thereby became the framework of relations between church (*sacerdotium*) and state (*imperium*) for the twelfth and thirteenth centuries. Emperor Frederick Barbarossa's attempts to reinstitute control over the elections of prelates was short-lived, and by 1200 consecration, rather than investiture, had come to be regarded as the point from which the exercise of episcopal authority commenced.

R. L. Benson, *The Bishop Elect: A Study in Medieval Ecclesiastical Office* (1968); P. Classen, "Das Wormser Konkordat in der deutschen Verfassungsgeschichte," in *Investiturstreit und Reichsverfassung*, ed. J. Fleckenstein (1973), 411–60; K. Ganzer, *Papsttum und Bistumsbesetzungen in der Zeit von Gregor IX bis Bonifaz VIII* (1968); H. Rudorff, *Zur Erklärung des Wormser Konkordats* (1906); G. Tellenbach, *The Church in Western Europe from the Tenth to the Thirteenth Century*, trans. T. Reuter (1993).

PAUL B. PIXTON

Worms, Diet of

Remembered as the occasion of Luther's legendary protest, "Here I stand, I can do no other," the Diet of Worms originally had a less poetic purpose. A formal assembly of the sovereigns who ruled the patchwork of cities, bishoprics, and territories of the HRE (basically Germany and its environs), it was called in 1521 at the city of Worms to resolve the controversy sparked by Luther's indulgences protest. Having failed in its own attempts to quell the conflict, the papacy formally excommunicated Luther in January 1521. But a coalition of disparate interests—political, social, and economic—had sprung up behind him, threatening both the unity of the church and the peace of the empire. Charles V, a young Habsburg recently elected Holy Roman Emperor, recognized that the reforming movement had to be addressed. Negotiating with Fredrick the Wise, Luther's head of state and one of the electors who had put him in office, Charles gave Luther a safe conduct to attend the diet in April 1521. Through a legal ploy, Luther obtained the opportunity to speak. When the drama ended, he was outlawed and the movement behind him proscribed. He escaped by night, on horseback.

M. Brecht, *Martin Luther: His Road to Reformation, 1483–1521* (1985).

JAMES ARNE NESTINGEN

Worms, Edict of

In 1521 the annual imperial diet convened in Worms, from January

27 to May 25. Although Emperor Charles V was concerned with administrative and military matters, he allowed the enemies of the excommunicated Martin Luther to present their case. Although Charles's advisors still refused to approve an imperial mandate against Luther, the controversial monk was nevertheless summoned to defend himself before the diet, which he did quite eloquently on April 17 and 18. The subsequent edict placing Luther and his followers under imperial ban was largely drafted by the papal legate, Girolamo Aleandro, and announced by Charles at the conclusion of the diet. Many powerful princes challenged the edict's legality and led an energetic campaign to have it rescinded; few actually used it to suppress Luther's supporters. Charles acceded to the Luther party's demands at the 1526 diet in Speyer, largely because he needed their support in the current campaign against the Turks. Once the military threat had passed, however, the emperor reissued the edict at the 1529 diet. The five princes and fourteen imperial cities who protested reinstatement of the edict became known as "Protestants."

D. Jensen, *Confrontation at Worms: Martin Luther and the Diet of Worms* (1973).

JOEL F. HARRINGTON

Wyclif, John (c. 1330–1384), English theologian and church reformer. Wyclif was a systematic and thorough critic of the church, whose criticism bore upon all aspects of late medieval ecclesiastical authority, practice, and devotion. In England he was the academic founder of the heretical movement known as Lollardy, and abroad his works fundamentally influenced the Prague reformer Jan Hus (d. 1415). His reliance on Scripture in matters of church polity and doctrine anticipated Protestant teachings.

Wyclif's career seemed destined for prominence. By 1356 he was a junior fellow of Merton College, Oxford. He served briefly as the master of Balliol College in 1360–1361, until he obtained a number of benefices that disqualified him from that position but enabled him financially to pursue an academic vocation at the prestigious university. In 1365 he was appointed as the master of the new Canterbury College; a rival successfully challenged Wyclif's candidacy, despite the latter's expensive attempts to keep the position. About 1372 Wyclif obtained his doctorate and may have entertained hopes of promotion to the episcopacy. Major advancement eluded him, never to materialize again, for

shortly Wyclif was teaching questionable doctrines to audiences outside academia.

While previously Wyclif had spurned nominalist principles on the basis of his strict views of philosophical realism, his first concerted attack on conventional norms regarding clerical ownership of property and authority came in his *On Civil Lordship* (1375–1376). Wyclif argued that God grants ownership and authority only to the righteous; the unjust have rights to nothing except retribution. He further concluded that property enticed the clergy away from their rightful duty to preach; therefore, the secular authority was obligated to relieve the clergy of this temptation. As Wyclif relied increasingly on biblical authentication for all matters of doctrine and practice, he came to reject canon law.

In 1377, Pope Gregory XI (1370–1378) condemned Wyclif and his recent writings as he warned King Edward III of the danger Wyclif posed to the state as well as the church. Wyclif's principal accuser, however, died, and his successor, Urban VI (1378–1389), was too embroiled in conflict with the college of cardinals to divert attention to a university professor. In the meantime, Wyclif wrote a series of treatises that clearly negated clerical authority, rejected conventional religiosity, and denounced mendicant religion. As the schism solidified, Wyclif grew ever more convinced of corruption in the established church, infecting even the papal see.

In Wyclif's *The Truth of the Holy Scriptures* (1377–1378), he posited the absolute inerrancy and sufficiency of Scripture in all matters of doctrine, for Scripture represented the immutable will of God. In *The Power of the Pope* (1379), Wyclif decried papal abuses; he intimated that the pope, if he opposes the "law of Christ," is possibly the antichrist. By 1380, Wyclif irreparably alienated the mendicants in his work *On Apostasy*. He denied the doctrine of transubstantiation and castigated those who adhered to it as confederates of Satan. By 1381, Wyclif was forced to leave Oxford, but he continued to write, finding more parallels between a decadent clerical hierarchy and Christ's final enemy.

Wyclif's critique of ecclesiastical structure and practice needs to be seen in the context of heightened tensions and expectations in the late Middle Ages. Demographic changes and economic hardships brought on by the Black Death and compounded by increased taxation to fund the war with France exacerbated social tensions. Rancor bred rebellion in the Peasant Revolt of 1381, which clerical contemporaries blamed on

Wyclif; he denied any association, and modern historians have exonerated him. Resentment mounted against the privileged status of wealthy bishops and friars, yet one finds clear evidence of deepening religious fervor, evidenced in the growth of lay fraternities, eucharistic devotion, and a vibrant appetite for religious instruction for clerics and laity. Wyclif's theology and philosophy (the two are inextricably intertwined) were paradoxically in tune with and antithetical to prevailing trends in the late fourteenth century. He disdained nominalistic speculation, as he secured knowledge and truth in biblical sources. He contended that the established church had abandoned its pastoral mission; only fiscal chastisement would truly restore the clergy to their proper role as preachers and models of holy comportment, to be administered by the only genuine authority—the crown. Individuals should amend their lives by conforming to biblical instruction about piety, rather than intensifying ritualistic devotions. His followers, the Lollards, conveyed his ideas beyond university walls to the halls of Parliament; a disendowment bill was presented probably in 1410. Clerical and secular authorities were determined to eradicate Lollardy, a radical movement that hoped to empower the laity and revolutionize the church.

J. H. Dahmus, *The Prosecution of John Wyclif* (1952); H. Kaminsky, "Wycliffism as Ideology of Revolution," *CH* 32 (1963): 57–74; A. Kenny, ed., *Wyclif in His Times* (1986); K. B. McFarlane, *John Wycliffe and the Beginnings of English Nonconformity* (1953); H. B. Workman, *John Wyclif: A Study of the English Medieval Church*, 2 vols. (1926).

CURTIS BOSTICK

Wynfrith   *see* Boniface

Xavier, Francis (1506–1552), Spanish

Jesuit and missionary. Born of a noble family in Navarre, Xavier studied at Paris, where he met Ignatius Loyola and joined the early companions that became the Jesuits. After the group professed vows in Paris in 1534 they set out for Venice. When warfare in the Mediterranean precluded a pilgrimage to Jerusalem, they went to Rome and placed themselves at the service of Pope Paul III, who verbally approved them as an order in 1539. Xavier participated in the discussions with Ignatius that helped to form the Constitutions of the Jesuits. Originally, Ignatius intended to keep Xavier with him in Rome as secretary of the Jesuits, but the illness of another Jesuit who had been assigned to a mission in India led to Xavier's assignment there. He left Rome in 1540 and arrived in Goa in 1542. His work included preaching on the Fishery Coast, voyages to investigate missionary possibilities in Malacca, Java, and the Moluccas, and the translation of Christian prayers into indigenous languages. In 1549 he arrived in Japan, where he was the first to preach Christianity. It was his intention to go to China, but he died on the island of Sancian before reaching it. Xavier was canonized in 1622.

W. V. Bangert, *A History of the Society of Jesus* (1972); J. W. O'Malley, *The First Jesuits* (1993); G. Schurhammer, *Francis Xavier: His Life, His Times*, 4 vols. (1973–1982); F. Xavier, *The Letters and Instructions of Francis Xavier* (1992).

PAUL V. MURPHY

Xiphilinus, John   *see* Psellus, Constantine

Zanchi, Girolamo (1516–1590), Italian

Protestant refugee and Calvinist theologian. The son of a lawyer, Zanchi joined the Augustinians in 1531. In 1541 he studied the writings of the Reformers under the direction of Peter Martyr Vermigli. Although he had only fifteen months of contact with Vermigli, it was the defining experience of his life. He became a convinced Protestant yet remained in Italy until forced to flee the Inquisition in 1552. Zanchi spent time in Geneva, where he had close contact with Calvin before being called to Strasbourg in 1553 as professor of Old Testament. A controversy with the Lutheran pastor Johannes Marbach over the Lord's Supper and predestination, however, forced him to leave. He became professor of theology in Heidelberg in 1568. Along with Vermigli, Zanchi has been called one of the fathers of Protestant scholasticism for his strong ties to the theological method of Aquinas. His theology was officially sanctioned at the Synod of Dort (1619) and remained highly influential throughout Reformed circles.

C. J. Burchill, "Girolamo Zanchi: Portrait of a Reformed Theologian and His Work," *SCJ* 15 (1984): 185–207; J. P. Donnelly, "Italian Influences on the Development of Calvinist Scholasticism," *SCJ* 7 (1986): 81–101.

GREGORY J. MILLER

Zell, Katharina   *see* Schütz Zell, Katharina

Zell, Matthew (1477–1548), popular preacher, Protestant reformer of Strasbourg. Born in Kaysersberg, Alsace, and educated at Erfurt, Ingolstadt, and Freiburg im Breisgau, he came to Strasbourg in 1518 as priest of the cathedral parish and was preaching Luther's ideas by 1521. There were a significant number of converts but also episcopal opposition, to which he responded in 1523 with *The Christian Apologia (Christeliche verantwortung)*, which includes sermon summaries, affirmations of justification by faith and the authority of Scripture, and polemic against traditional sacramental and theological teaching. Zell put his new biblical faith into action by marrying Katharina Schütz in December 1523; the couple modeled new roles of married pastor and pastor's wife, a rather remarkable partnership of pastoral care, and undogmatic teaching. Primarily a practical man, Zell left fine theological definitions to Bucer, Capito, and Hedio and focused on preaching simple (Protestant) biblical truth. He produced two catechisms—1535 (Lord's Prayer and the Decalogue) and 1536 (Apostles' Creed)—and preached with fiery soul and great popularity until a few days before his death.

M. Weyer, "L'Apologie Chretienne du réformateur strasbourgeois Matthieu Zell" (PhD diss., Strasbourg, 1981); M. Zell, *Christeliche verantwortung* (1523).

ELSIE MCKEE

Zeno (c. 440–491), eastern Roman emperor (474–491). Born in Isauria (in Asia Minor) where he was raised a soldier, Zeno became a general under Emperor Leo I, whose daughter he married. He became co-emperor with his own son Leo II (474) and then sole emperor upon the latter's demise. Zeno's empire faced pressing problems, including Germanic threats, usurpations, and Christian doctrinal disputes. After defeating the usurper Basiliscus in 475/476, Zeno next addressed the ambitions of his general Theoderic, king of the Ostrogoths. In 489 Zeno sent Theoderic with his Goths to Italy to engage the barbarian general, Odovacer, who had deposed the last legitimate Western emperor. Although Theoderic would eventually establish his own independent kingdom in Italy, Zeno nevertheless had rid his Eastern realm of that menace.

Another disruption for Zeno was Monophysitism. This christological doctrine had been disallowed at the Council of Chalcedon in 451. In an attempt to pacify the Monophysites and thereby to secure Eastern (especially Egyptian) loyalties, Zeno published in 482 the *Henoticon (Unifier)*. This statement, although it did not violate the teaching of Chalcedon, called for adherence to the councils of Nicaea (325), Constantinople (381), and Ephesus (431) only. Moreover, it did not address the basic issue of the relation of the natures of Christ. Zeno's compromise effort failed to quell dissent.

A. Cameron, *The Mediterranean World in Late Antiquity, AD 395–600* (1993).

ALLEN E. JONES

Zeno of Verona (d. c. 371), saint and bishop. Although his writings indicate he may have been from Africa, little is known of Zeno. His Life, written four centuries after his death by Coronatus Notarius, has no historical value. Ambrose of Milan, his contemporary, mentions him, and Gregory I incorrectly identifies him as a martyr. An authentic episcopal list from the tenth century lists Zeno as the eighth bishop of Verona, consecrated in 362. All other information about him comes by inference from his ninety-three extant sermons (sixty complete, the rest in summary form).

Zeno was a popular preacher, orthodox theologian, church builder, advocate of monasticism, and a strong pastoral presence. He founded one of the first convents so that consecrated women could leave their homes in service for the wider community. He tried to ensure that the priests in his diocese were trained and competent. He lived a life of poverty and praised his congregation for their generosity to the poor and strangers. He seems to have baptized adults by total immersion, prohibited wailing at funerals, and stopped abuses in the *agape* meal.

G. P. Jeanes, ed., *The Day Has Come! Easter and Baptism in Zeno of Verona* (1995).

WILLIAM B. SWEETSER JR.

Ziegenbalg, Bartholomäus (1682–1719), first Protestant missionary to India. Born in Pulsnitz, Germany and educated in Goerlitz and Berlin, he arrived 1703 in the Lutheran pietist center of Halle. In 1705 Danish king Frederick IV decided to send missionaries overseas. Through his German Pietist friends he selected Zeigenbalg and Heinrich Plutschau. The two arrived in Tranquebar (Tarangambadi) in south India in July 1706. Ziegenbalg immediately began learning Portuguese and Tamil and soon started a school and worship services.

First converts were baptized in 1707. Despite intermittent opposition from local Danish authorities he continued his work in India until his death, returning to Europe only once (1715–1716). A student of Hinduism, Ziegenbalg collected Tamil manuscripts and engaged in discussions with Hindus of all ranks. His *Genealogie der malabarischen Götter*, written in 1713 but not published until 1867, demonstrates his knowledge of Hinduism. Respected by the Indians, he was known as a critic of Hinduism who nevertheless praised the virtuous life of Hindus. While preaching Christianity he never sought to replace indigenous traditions and customs with those imported from Europe. Ziegenbalg compiled two Tamil dictionaries and a grammar. He translated the New Testament and part of the Old Testament into Tamil. The SPCK, of which he was a corresponding member, sent a printing press in 1712 on which he printed Portuguese, German, and Tamil books.

Daniel Jeyaraj, *Inkulturation in Tranquebar: Der Beitrag der frühen dänisch-halleschen Mission zum Werden einer indisch-einheimischen Kirche (1706–1730)* (1996); Brijraj Singh, *The First Protestant Missionary to India: Bartholomaeus Ziegenbalg 1683–1719* (1999).

MARY JANE HAEMIG

Zosimus (417–418), bishop of Rome.

Upon the death of Innocent I (417), Zosimus became bishop of Rome. Though pope for less than two years, Zosimus played a pivotal role in the Pelagian controversy.

His Greek name suggests that he may have been of Eastern extraction. This origin may account for his initial sympathy for Pelagius and Caelestius. Shortly after he became pontiff, Zosimus convened a synod in the Basilica of St. Clement and reopened the case against Pelagius and Caelestius. When both professed their allegiance to the Christian faith, Zosimus, impressed by their sincerity and orthodoxy, acquitted them of any wrongdoing. He sent a letter to Africa that severely chastised the African churches for their condemnation of such devout Christians. The African bishops reaffirmed the condemnation of Innocent I. After an exchange of letters with the African bishops, the intervention of Emperor Honorius to prevent civil unrest, and possibly his own reading of Pelagius's *Expositions of Paul's Epistles*, Zosimus relented. He issued the *Epistola Tractoria* in which he condemned Pelagius and Caelestius. The enforcement of this document by imperial decree in Italy resulted in the excommunication of eighteen bishops, along with Julian of Eclanum.

———

G. Bonner, *St. Augustine of Hippo: Life and Controversies* (1963); CPL (1995), 1644–47; R. Davis, trans., *The Book of Pontiffs* (2nd ed., 2000).

MARIANNE DJUTH

Zwick, Johannes (c. 1496–1542),

Swabian reformer and writer. Zwick studied in Constance, Basel, Freiburg, and Padua. In 1518 he was ordained to the priesthood, and in 1521 he began to teach law in Basel. His conversion to the Reformation came during his tenure as priest in the village of Riedlingen after 1522. In 1525 he moved to Constance, where he worked with Thomas and Ambrosius Blarer for the Reformation in the city. Together with the Blarer brothers he campaigned for the Reformation in Constance, Swabia, and the Thurgau. After the departure of Ambrosius Blarer, Zwick was the principal leader of the Reformation in Constance. Theologically he was deeply influenced by the thought of Huldrych Zwingli. In the negotiations leading to the Wittenberg Accord of 1536, Zwick supported the Zwinglian position against the Lutherans. His theology was largely pastoral in character, and he was a writer of devotional literature. In addition to his prayer books, catechisms, and school ordinances, Zwick was a prolific and talented author of hymns. He died in Bischofszell in Thurgau during the plague epidemic of 1542.

———

B. Moeller, *Johannes Zwick und die Reformation in Konstanz* (1961).

BRUCE GORDON

Zwickau Prophets

Sixteenth-century enthusiasts or spiritualists. Weaver Nikolaus Storch, blacksmith Thomas Drechsel, and former Wittenberg student Markus Thomae Stübner taught and preached in Zwickau, Germany, in the early 1520s. They were influenced by Thomas Müntzer, pastor in Zwickau from August 1520 until April 1521. They believed God is revealed directly and inwardly to the individual and that outward mediation of God's Word by preaching or Scripture was unnecessary. They rejected infant baptism and claimed they could foretell the future. Advised by new Lutheran pastor Nicolaus Hausmann, the Zwickau City Council cited several people for heretical teaching in December 1521. As a result, Storch, Drechsel, and Stübner fled to

Wittenberg, where they met with Melanchthon but left soon afterward. Contrary to some accounts, they were not the cause of the Wittenberg disturbances that caused Luther to leave the Wartburg and return to Wittenberg. In 1522 Luther interviewed each and rejected their views. Their subsequent histories are largely unknown. They are generally not regarded as founders of Anabaptism.

S. C. Karent-Nunn, *Zwickau in Transition, 1500–1547: The Reformation as an Agent of Change* (1987); O. Kuhr, "The Zwickau Prophets, the Wittenberg Disturbances, and Polemic," *Mennonite Quarterly Review* 70 (1996): 203–14.

MARY JANE HAEMIG

Zwingli, Huldrych (1484–1531), Swiss humanist, theologian, reformer of Zurich, and founder of Reformed Protestantism. Zwingli studied first at the Univ. of Vienna and then at the Univ. of Basel, where he received his BA and MA degrees in 1504 and 1506. Ordained as a priest in September 1506, he became pastor at Glarus, where he taught himself Greek, corresponded with his humanist friends, and read voraciously in the works of the ancient classics and the church fathers. During this period the writings of the great humanist Desiderius Erasmus had an enormous impact on Zwingli. In 1516 he accepted a position as pastor at the Benedictine Abbey at Einsiedeln in Schwyz, where he continued his humanistic endeavors, studying the Greek New Testament and learning Hebrew.

On January 1, 1519, Zwingli preached his first sermon as common preacher (*Leutpriester*) at the Great Minster (Grossmünster) at Zurich, a position he held until his death. Although he claimed to develop an evangelical understanding of the Christian message in 1516, it appears that he did not break with Erasmus on the matter of free will until late 1520, when he came to a Pauline position on human nature and the necessity of divine grace.

Zwingli's first reforming activity was a sermon defending several people who had broken the Lenten fast in 1522; in the same year, he petitioned the bishop of Constance to abolish celibacy. In both of these attacks on ecclesiastical regulations, Zwingli appealed to Scripture. Then in September he published *On the Clarity and Certainty of the Word of God*, in which he maintained that the Bible is the exclusive authority in matters of faith and the Christian life.

In late January 1523 at the First Zurich Disputation, Zwingli defended himself against the accusation of heresy with his Sixty-seven Articles, a summary of his theology. Consequently, the city council authorized Zwingli to continue his preaching from the Bible. In July, Zwingli published a comprehensive defense of his Sixty-seven Articles in which he developed three doctrines that became hallmarks of Reformed Protestantism: that salvation comes through faith in Christ, by divine grace; that the Eucharist is a memorial of Christ; and that the moral law, as the revelation of God's will, has never been abrogated. Zwingli also stated his doctrine of the single sphere: the civil government is sovereign over the Christian community, or the local church, which includes everyone, even infants. By the end of 1525 Zurich was a reformed city and canton; the city council had replaced the Mass with the Reformed Lord's Supper and had created a new Marriage (or Morals) Court in the place of the Bishop's Court in Constance.

Some of Zwingli's more radical followers rejected his doctrine of the single sphere. They insisted that the church should be free of governmental control and that it should consist only of committed Christians. They also contended that there was no biblical support for infant baptism. When they baptized each other as adults and formed their own self-disciplining congregation, Zwingli denounced them as Anabaptists, or rebaptizers. In his writings against them, he stressed the doctrine of the single sphere and defended infant baptism. Zwingli taught that infant baptism was the sacrament of the new covenant, which had replaced circumcision, the sacrament of the old covenant.

Zwingli always insisted that he came to his evangelical understanding of the gospel independently, through his own study of the New Testament, with no influence from Martin Luther. Although Zwingli and Luther were in general agreement, they disagreed on the doctrines of the Eucharist and the moral law. After more than three years of public controversy over the Eucharist, Zwingli and Luther met in October 1529, at the Marburg Colloquy, where they tried to come to an agreement. They could not resolve their differences. Zwingli defended his position that the bread and the wine signify the body and blood of Christ; Luther would not budge from his view of the real presence. Their disagreement on gospel and law was less public but not less important. Rather than opposing gospel and law, as Luther did, Zwingli included the law within the gospel; he tied faith and works together and taught that the law continues to inform the Christian of the duty to live according to God's will. This doctrine demonstrates that Erasmus had a permanent influence on Zwingli's thought.

But Zwingli did not teach freedom of the will and salvation by good works, as he made clear in his 1530 treatise, *On the Providence of God*, in which he closely connected predestination with God's providence. He asserted that without God's election, faith is impossible. However, because children of Christians have been baptized into the covenant, they are considered to be elect persons until they show that they lack faith. Zwingli did not develop a doctrine of double predestination; he spoke only of the decree of election to salvation, not of a decree of reprobation.

On October 9, 1531, the Catholic Swiss states declared war on Zurich, and on October 11 the Catholic forces attacked at Kappel, south of Zurich. In less than an hour, five hundred Zurich-ers, including Zwingli, were killed on the battlefield. Zwinglianism, the fount of the Protestant Reformed tradition, did not die with Zwingli but continued to flourish under the leadership of Heinrich Bullinger. Zwingli's distinctive doctrines of the single sphere and single predestination later distinguished Zwinglianism from Calvinism within Reformed Protestantism. However, his doctrines of the Eucharist (following the *Consensus Tigurinus* of 1549 between Bullinger and Calvin) and the moral law became an integral part of the theology of Reformed Protestantism.

O. Farner, *Zwingli the Reformer: His Life and Work* (1968); U. Gäbler, *Huldrych Zwingli: His Life and Work* (1986); C. Garside, *Zwingli and the Arts* (1966); B. Gordon, *The Swiss Reformation* (2002); G. W. Locher, *Zwingli's Thought: New Perspectives* (1981); G. R. Potter, *Zwingli* (1976); W. P. Stevens, *The Theology of Huldrych Zwingli* (1986); R. C. Walton, *Zwingli's Theocracy* (1967).

J. WAYNE BAKER